Premier's Message

It is with great pleasure that I acknowledge the second publication of the Manitoba Geographical Names Program. ***A Place of Honour:*** *Manitoba's War Dead Commemorated in its Geography* is the companion volume to the highly successful ***Geographical Names of Manitoba*** published last year. The new book commemorates the sacrifices of more than 4,000 Manitoba casualties of the Second World War and serves to witness the impact of those losses on families, friends, and our society – both then and now.

Last February, I had the opportunity to visit a Commonwealth War Graves Cemetery in Durnbach, Germany and saw the graves of several young men from towns close to where I grew up. Their familiar names brought the tragedy of war closer to home for I believe some of them may have danced with my mother in Neepawa.

This year marks the 60th anniversary of the invasion of Dieppe. 913 Canadians lost their lives in that operation – 80 of them Manitobans. Last August, a small contingent of Dieppe veterans returned to that small community and were surprised to find the streets of the village thronged with people shouting "Bravo!" and "Merci!" Some villagers held up babies to be kissed by the passing men, the youngest among them aged 78. Clearly, the French people have not forgotten the Canadians and their effort to free their nation; it is even more incumbent upon us as Manitobans to do the same.

I know the people of Manitoba are proud of their heritage. The dawning of a new millennium and the gradual passing of the Veterans' generation seems an appropriate time for such a retrospective. I congratulate the staff of the Manitoba Geographical Names Program for their foresight and diligence in bringing this project to completion. I also recognize that the impetus for this work came from the families themselves and I thank them for their valued contribution. I would expect this publication to be widely read for general interest as well as for research and educational purposes for generations to come.

On behalf of the Government of Manitoba, I trust you will enjoy this publication and will take a moment to reflect upon the sacrifices of our fellow Manitobans and Canadians in preserving the freedom we enjoy today.

The Honourable Gary Doer
Premier of Manitoba
Winnipeg, 2002

Minister's Message

Manitoba, with its wealth of lakes, islands, bays, and other natural geographical features, is proud of its efforts to commemorate its fatal casualties of the Second World War, the Korean War and, more recently, a soldier killed in 1996 while serving with NATO Peacekeeping Forces in Bosnia – Herzegovina.

During the last thirty years, the Province has provided more than 2,950 families with attractive commemorative name certificates identifying the geographical feature named after their loved ones. As a result of this communication and the research of volunteers and staff, we have received hundreds of letters, photos and biographical sketches submitted in solemn remembrance by families to keep memories alive.

Some of the most valuable information extracted from original handwritten letters home, diaries and log books, was compiled with photos and stories into this publication, ***A Place of Honour.*** They give readers a unique and personal perspective of life during war and personal experiences of those directly affected by it. Some readers may be shocked to learn how young many of them were – never having an opportunity to reach beyond their hopes and dreams, to start careers, to raise families and to enjoy retirement. Instead, they gave up all they had for what we enjoy today.

I take this opportunity to thank the families for their support in providing the material to share with current and future generations. Manitoba is committed to the stewardship of all the documentation received and will continue to acknowledge such further contributions to the geographical names records.

I congratulate the Manitoba Geographical Names Program staff for their expertise and dedication to this publication initiative and the completion of this first edition of a living and lasting memorial to those who lost their lives in war for the sake of our peace and liberty.

Steve Ashton

The Honourable Steve Ashton
Minister of Manitoba Conservation
Winnipeg, 2002

Table of Contents

Acknowledgement
of
Financial Contributions
to
A Place of Honour Trust Fund

We at Manitoba Conservation take this opportunity to express our gratitude to those who have made financial contributions to help defray some of the costs associated with this publication. A total of almost five thousand dollars was raised by donations from one hundred and six individuals.

Foreword

This publication is dedicated to the families of those Manitobans who lost a loved one as a casualty of war. Our Province has recognized their sacrifice in the commemorative naming of more than 4,200 lakes, islands, bays and other geographical features after them.

'We will remember them' is a promise too often taken for granted. This book has been compiled in an effort to help current and future generations understand the determination and at times, the plight of the soldiers, as well as offer an insight into the impact of their loss on families and communities. We are opening a window on their lives to show readers that these war casualties were real persons and not just war statistics.

After the end of the Second World War, the Geographic Board of Canada, now known as the Geographical Names Board of Canada, established a policy of using the names of decorated casualties for any unnamed geographical features for mapping and resource development purposes. When initiated in the late 1940s, this commemorative naming program included advising the next-of-kin of the naming of a feature after their relative. The Board used the addresses given by the service personnel on the date of enlistment, but this practice had to be discontinued as these addresses became more and more out of date over the years. The resumption of peace time mapping programs by the Federal government soon resulted in the depletion of the decorated casualty list. In 1955, the Board adopted the policy of using any of the casualty names whether

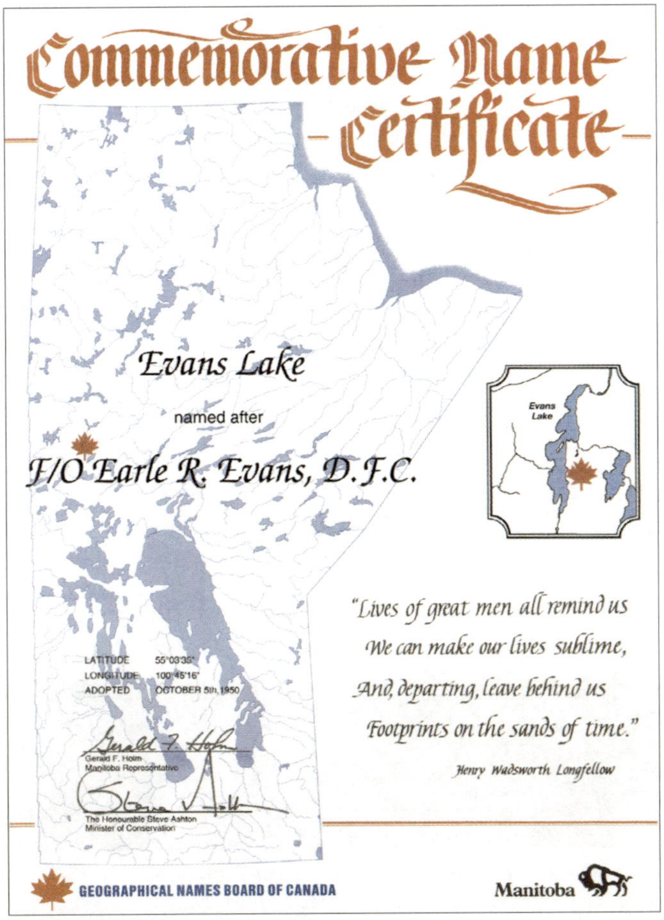

Certificate sample reduced from 28 x 38 cm.

decorated or not. When Manitoba's member of the Board received the copy of the casualty list in 1955, 36 decorated and 32 undecorated casualty names of the 3,714 service personnel had been applied.

In 1972, Manitoba began issuing a full-colour Commemorative Name Certificate to next-of-kin on request as tangible evidence of the official naming of a feature after their loved ones. This was often the first contact with the family of a casualty.

By 1992, only about half the World War II casualty names had been applied to geographical features. To treat all those on the list fairly, it was decided in 1994 to complete the naming of geographical features after the rest of them. During this project, over 400 additional Manitoba casualties were identified – those who had enlisted in other provinces or with the Royal Air Force. Subsequently, the project continued to grow to include nearly 2,000 additional names applied during 1994-95, the naming of features after the 37 Korean War casualties in 1998, 17 Merchant Mariners in 2001 in addition to the seven Victoria Cross winners from World War I.

Since the last commemorative initiative began in 1994, a corps of staff and volunteers have made a special effort to contact as many of the families as possible and more than 1,000 families were contacted during the first year. To date, 2,889 of the 4,246 families have been located and provided with Commemorative Name Certificates. The initial certificate continues to be provided free of charge to the eldest next-of-kin, while duplicates for other members of the family or friends are available at a nominal charge.

As the number of family contacts increased, so did the submission of photographs, hand-written stories and biographical details of soldiers to our office. At first, I wasn't entirely sure what we might do with them, beyond committing to the families that when the time was right, we would share their stories with fellow Manitobans and Canadians for public interest, educational purposes and most importantly, to remind readers of the price of war.

With the success of the publication *Geographical Names of Manitoba*, the availability of a qualified editor, the growing collection of photos and documentation, together with the support of the Department Executive, the time was now most certainly right. Staff, volunteers and family contacts agreed. This project was destined to be completed during the lifetime of the remaining families and friends who still remember the last goodbyes, who still love and grieve.

This is a much overdue work, an awesome work. Everyone that is more than 50 years old has had the privilege to live in and amongst a generation of heroes. Most of us are now realizing, unfortunately in many cases too late, that it's important to recognize our relative, neighbour, family friend or fellow employee who, in some way, participated in one of the most violent episodes in the history of civilization.

I grew up on a farm near the town of Erickson and as a child, stood at attention at the Cenotaph on a cold Remembrance Day service in 1956. Like most of my fellow classmates, I found it difficult to understand why so many people were in tears. I understand now that it was because that small town and its surrounding district lost 19 sons to the Second World War. Many veterans returned home to establish farms, other businesses and to raise families. Some were scarred for life – seldom talking about the war even to family and friends. Yet they were determined more than ever to forge ahead on behalf of their fallen comrades. I consider myself very fortunate to have known them – as community leaders, neighbours and family – for two of them were my uncles, John and Leslie Nylen. I now regret not asking them more questions about their experiences so I could be more cognizant of the role they played during the war and to thank them for the wonderful life we all cherish today.

This book will help put faces to those who, until now, were just names on a community cenotaph. It causes you, the reader, to witness first hand the tragedy of war in the words of the soldiers, brothers and sisters and the commanding officers. Your heart will feel for the families – just imagine putting yourself in the shoes of a father whose son was, in 1942, studying medicine at the University of Manitoba and you are so proud. He goes to war and you later receive a letter from his Commanding Officer saying "... a finer death in battle has never taken place." Your son was already a Lieutenant when he was killed – he was just 20 years old. What would he have been today if he had survived?

These young men and women have been commemorated by the naming of lakes, islands, bays, and other geographical features. To some families, it has been a source of comfort in providing a form of closure to those still grieving. This becomes evident each time we receive a call or letter from a family member saying: "It makes me happy to know there is some geographical feature named for him, thus honouring his life which he gave to his country." Most of them were so young, still in their teens – I quote one brother's insight:

> ... young men and women grew up fast and had to, some with no teenage life and some with no opportunity to have or raise children. Perhaps this generation will take heed of the past and take heart in the future as freedom is not a right, but a privilege that from time to time may have to be defended.

This message has been brought home to us in the last weeks and months, first with the horrific events of September 11, 2001 and now as I write this message, Canadians are laying to rest 'four of our own,' killed in the war against terrorism in Afghanistan.

Now, with this generation we renew our pledge to remember them.

Acknowledgements

I acknowledge the dedicated work of Dr. A. P. (Tony) Buchner, the editor, my other colleagues, Assistant Toponymist Des Kappel, and our special assistants Dale Stevenson, Ron Palka, Victor Bergen and Elaine Deonarine. Thanks must also be extended to my former colleagues Jack Schreuder, Jack Mercredi and John Hemmerling.

The early project assistance of Barbara MacIntosh, Executive Secretary of the Geographical Names Board of Canada and her staff is gratefully acknowledged. I must also thank the former Executive Secretaries of the Board, Helen Kerfoot and Alan Rayburn, both of whom were my mentors in the field of toponymic sciences and in the management of these unique heritage resources.

This publication exists today for many reasons, but mostly because of special people who instilled in us the value of remembering our war heroes. These included veterans of the Second World War with whom I worked – Allen Roberts, John Klaponski, Richard Bagot and John Pople to mention a few. There were many volunteers working diligently on the Commemorative Names Project – members of the project's Co-ordinating Committee: Les Allison, Albert Chartrand, Bert Cheffins, Norman Clark, Stanley Fulham and George MacDonald; the local community co-ordinators: Richard Cleaver, Irene Clark, Jim Coyne, Bill Edge, Shirley Foot, Alex Godkin, Cecil Pittman, Herman Rempel, Agatha Shelest, Ronald Schmidt, Eric Smith and Morley Young. We acknowledge the assistance of researchers/writers Doug Chisholm and Floyd Williston. Sincere appreciation also goes to members of my family – to my mother-in-law Neilona Robinson and my father Walter, for proof-reading; to my wife Jean, son Ryan and daughter Shawna for working with me several evenings and weekends on various aspects of the Commemorative Names Project and for their continued understanding and support.

Over the years there have been many other staff and volunteers involved in the Commemorative Names Project – their contribution of time and talent is recognized. I apologize to any individuals that I may have overlooked.

We have taken all the information recorded on file over the past 55 years, edited it where necessary and presented it to the best of our ability considering the limited resources available for such a project. In October 2001, we wrote to nearly 2,900 families and received more than 2,000 responses. Unfortunately, many of those we tried to contact were already deceased and this too identified the urgency of completing this project as quickly as possible.

To those relatives of casualties for whom a photo, biographical sketch, letters home or other suitable stories are not found in this edition, we invite you to contact us at the address shown below. It is never too late.

We will remember them.

Gerald F. Holm
Provincial Toponymist,
Manitoba Member, Geographical Names Board of Canada (GNBC)

To provide additional information, please contact:

Manitoba Geographical Names Program
Manitoba Conservation
1007 Century Street
Winnipeg, Manitoba, R3H 0W4
Telephone: (204) 945-1798
gholm@gov.mb.ca

Fax: (204) 945-1365

Manitoba Geographical Names Program Staff.
L-R Tony Buchner, Gerry Holm, Des Kappel, Dale Stevenson.

Introduction

This is not a military history. Innumerable histories have been published since the end of the Second World War focusing upon Canadian casualties, specific branches of the service and various military campaigns. Some of these appear in the bibliography. The source of information on these men and women is not primarily historical, archival or military. It is the families and friends of these people, and in some cases, the words of the casualties themselves as expressed in their letters and diaries. In describing these times and events on a personal or familial level, it becomes apparent that the loss of these men and women continues to be felt throughout our province and indeed, throughout the world.

In connection with various Millennium events in recent years, numerous discussions have centred upon the most important or influential historical events and people of the last 100 or 1000 years. The World Wars seemed conspicuously absent. Yet there is no denying the magnitude of the human drama they represented, whether it be measured in the toll in human life or the lasting geopolitical consequences.

Immediately after the war, people returned to their former lives and many seemed eager to forget about it. Despite his earlier popularity, Winston Churchill was elected out of office only months after the cessation of hostilities in Europe. More than five decades later, it is difficult for many to comprehend what drove so many men and women to enlist. Pre-war Canada was suffering the effects of the Great Depression and men like Gladstone's Harvey Bounting and Morden's James Lewis travelled far and wide in search of employment, "riding the rails" and helping at neighbouring farms at harvest time. Stonewall's Franklin Murray even rode his bicycle to Geraldton, Ontario to find work in the mines. One particularly Canadian theme is that of young, unemployed men making their way to England before the war to enlist in the RAF. In Canada, it was necessary to have a university education or a private pilot's license to become an air force pilot – qualifications beyond the financial means of most. The RAF had no such restrictions, and a Canadian candidate's status as a British subject meant that they could learn a useful skill at no charge.

> The Canadians in the RAF were indeed a sort of "lost legion" whose exploits were seldom communicated to their homeland. Yet when Canadian forces were only beginning to mobilize, the "Can-RAF Boys" were carrying this country's name into the earliest battles of the Second World War. In the Battle of France, 1940, they served in scores. Few Canadians remember them today (Halliday 1970).

But it would be a grave disservice to suggest that enlistment was viewed largely as an economic opportunity. John Bissett of Winnipeg and Ross Fahrni of Gladstone were practising lawyers when they enlisted. Sammy Sheps was celebrating the receipt of his fee for his first legal case, but enlisted two days after Canada declared war. Dr. Arthur Hay was a practising physician in Winnipeg and had recently been awarded the Gold Medal in Surgery while Dr. Wendell Kippen had just begun his medical internship at Winnipeg General Hospital. Henry Fargey of La Rivière was a recent civil engineering graduate employed in the mines at Sherridon. Winnipeg's Thomas Cook played for the Winnipeg Blue Bombers for a year before enlisting and was expected to be "one of the future Bomber greats." Ralph Webb re-enlisted after having distinguished himself during the First World War and serving two terms as Mayor of the City of Winnipeg.

Not only careers were left behind; families were as well. One would expect that a married person might be less inclined to hazard the dangers of active service. Charles Doyle of Winnipeg felt that it was precisely because he had a wife and family that he had all the more reason to fight. His daughter later learned that every time he trained new troops to go overseas, he would ask to go as well – he hated to send such young men overseas while he remained behind.

Men and women showed a remarkable determination to enlist for active service. Winnipeg's Edward Wright managed to join the RCAF at age 15; he was already a veteran of the Army and Merchant Navy. With his death on active service a year later, he is believed to be the youngest Commonwealth airman to lose his life in the Second World War. So eager was Shoal Lake's Ellis McLeod to join the Air Force that at the age of 16, he ordered several copies of his birth certificate to practise altering it. Ernest Alexander of Winnipeg, on the other hand, was a veteran of the First World War. The only way he could qualify for active service was by claiming that he was ten years younger than he really was. The position of Observer on an air crew demanded almost perfect vision. Lloyd Webster from Roland managed to become a navigator/observer despite being nearly totally blind in one eye; he memorized the eye chart and thus passed the vision test.

This enthusiasm and determination is at least partially rooted in the origins of the people themselves. Many enlistees had been born in countries currently overrun or threatened by invading armies. Many others were born to parents from those places and also felt something of a patriotic duty to defend their ancestral homelands. Aileen Small, a school teacher at Lac du Bonnet wrote a regular newsletter to troops overseas from her area. One included the following:

> Hello Soldier: The big day came, D-Day, June 6, a date we will all remember. I felt close to tears that day, yet thrilled too, at the thought that this is the beginning of the end. At school we had two minutes silence and prayers. We listened to the King's message broadcast from London. The little ones didn't quite know what to make of it all but the older children seemed properly impressed. We sang: "There'll Always be an England" (13 June 1944).

Joseph Gertel was also motivated by very personal reasons: "You know damn well that the Jews have a great stake in the outcome of this war and I don't think that any of us should be hesitant in doing his share to the best of [his] capacity."

Most Canadians are familiar with the names of some of the major battles in northwestern Europe and Italy, but Canadians – and Manitobans in particular – were engaged in happenings world-wide from Alaska to the Caribbean and from South Africa to the Orient. Furthermore, they distinguished themselves in some of the most pivotal events of both World Wars. McCreary's Allan Angus, and MacGregor's Mark Brown became Canada's first two "aces" during the Second World War. Together with ten other young Manitobans, they took part in the Battle of France and the subsequent Battle of Britain during which the threat of an invasion of Britain was at least temporarily averted. Vernon Byers from Flin Flon and Harvey Glinz from Winnipeg's Rathgar Avenue were two of the airmen who had been hand picked from all over the Commonwealth and America to join No. 617 Squadron (the Dam Busters) for the raid on the Ruhr dams. This squadron became the most heavily decorated in RAF history. At the age of 18,

Stonewall's Alan McLeod became the world's youngest winner of the Victoria Cross when it was awarded to him in 1918. That same year, Billy Barker from Dauphin and Winnipeg became the most heavily decorated serviceman of the First World War. The now-legendary secret agent Frank Pickersgill from Winnipeg (formerly of Ashern) actively collaborated with the French Resistance and Winnipeg's Jimmy Wernham was one of the 76 airmen who escaped from Stalag Luft 3 – the incident better known as The Great Escape.

If Canada "came of age as a nation" during the First World War, it joined a community of nations on a more equal footing during the Second World War. I believe most Manitobans would be surprised to know the extent to which the people of northwestern Europe feel indebted to Canada. In France and Holland, local people have in many cases "adopted" graves of Manitoba war casualties and continue to tend them over 50 years later. Throughout the German occupation of France, a local lady living in La Baule dedicated all her time and energy to maintaining the graves. With money collected secretly from the generous local people she provided a cross for the grave of every fallen Allied serviceman, had hedges planted and employed a permanent gardener to tend the cemetery. Her devotion to this work was honoured by the award of the King's Medal for Service in the Cause of Freedom.

Many others continue to contact Canadian relatives of local casualties to provide them with photographs and information on their missing relatives. The parents of Michael Wiwsianski (a.k.a. Wish) received a letter from Mme. Yve Fortier:

> For three years I have unceasingly searched to locate the person who has the numbers (identification) from the Halifax plane which crashed at Moncé-en-Belin the 23 May, 1944. My most ardent desire was to contact the eight families so as to let them know there would be a mother over here that does not forget them (1947).

The letter was accompanied by a snapshot of the writer placing flowers at the site of the crash and another photo showing her 17 year-old son, in the uniform of the French air force, standing at attention on the spot. Thirty years later, Michael Wiwsianski's family received a letter from the Moncé-en-Belin Town Council requesting their permission to use their son's name for a street in their village.

Fifty-four years after the death of Winnipeg's 16 year-old Edward Wright, the people of Sandon, Staffordshire erected a monument on the site where his Lancaster aircraft crashed. The ceremony involved a fly-past by a Lancaster and a Spitfire. Fifty-one years after his death, the former wife of John Keith Crossing was contacted by a man from Holland who offered her plane tickets to Holland so she could pick up a photograph his father had taken of the Wellington's crash site in 1942. MacGregor's William Younie crashed near Ecquetot, France in 1944. On the 50th anniversary of the event, his Welsh wife and other family members were invited to the village for a commemorative ceremony. Arrangements were subsequently made for the formal "twinning" of Ecquetot and her Welsh village. Since that time, residents and school groups from both villages have visited one another.

More than 50 years after the end of the war, the commemoration of these men and women through the naming of geographical features is more than a polite gesture to their families. Flying Officer John Collyer's son wrote:

> I have no memories of my Dad as he left for overseas when I was a very small baby. All I have of him is three letters, some pictures and stories told me by my Mother and Grandparents. I am very proud of him and what he and others like him did for this country. These young servicemen must be remembered for what they did. Too many of today's youth think it could never happen to them. As recent events have shown, and as we older ones know, it can and does happen, all too often.

Frank Foord's sister wrote that:

> With no known grave he has always just been 'Missing in Hong Kong.' Now with a spot at last in Canada in his name, he will finally have a resting place.

John Glover's sister said:

> ... there's a lake named for him in northwestern Manitoba since 1974. I'm so sorry that his mother wasn't told of this; she always said she thought that she would feel better if she knew he had a resting place. All we know is that he's in the North Sea.

David Henderson's widow reflected that:

> The Commemorative Names Project ... is a very apt recognition of the sacrifice David made. I've been thinking for a long time that some individual memorial should be made for him, as he was one of the many airmen who were shot down and his body never recovered. [It's like] a proper burial.

Edward Jones's niece phrased it most eloquently:

> His death meant that there was no one to carry on the family name and it ended with his death. And so, it is important and comforting to know there is a place in Manitoba called Jones Point. The family name did not die after all.

Families of at least 22 World War II casualties have visited the geographical features named after their deceased relatives and erected some sort of permanent marker there. When Mr. Charles Shiaro died in 2001, his final request was that his ashes be spread on Shiaro Lake, named after his brother Private Arthur P. Shiaro who was killed in France in 1944.

A. P. Buchner
Toponymic Projects Officer
Manitoba Geographical Names Program
Manitoba Conservation
1007 Century Street
Winnipeg, Manitoba, R3H 0W4

Gordon McQueen (centre) and friends at McQueen Lake, 1988. The plaque is dedicated to his brother, Lieutenant Lewis J. McQueen who was killed in France on his 24th birthday.

Using this Volume

Surname

Verification of the spelling of a casualty's surname is not always straightforward. Occasionally, a serviceman would enlist under a name spelled differently from his/her parents and it is not unknown for brothers to spell their names differently from one another. In such cases, the variations are acknowledged by the inclusion of the notation "(sp.)" after the name. In instances in which a serviceman enlisted under an alias, this is also indicated. In extremely problematical cases, the spelling used was based upon the signature on the enlistment documents or attestation papers.

Rank

The surname is followed by the casualty's rank. If he/she died while serving in an Acting status, he/she is afforded the benefit of the full rank. If a casualty's position was more commonly known by a description rather than a rank (e.g., Regimental Sergeant Major as opposed to Warrant Officer 1), then both are listed.

Given Names

The forenames are usually listed as a full first name with initials. If a casualty more commonly used a middle name, then that is spelled in full also. Nicknames are also listed unless they are extremely common such as Bill for William or Jim for James.

Place of Residence

As may be expected, there is some variation in the grounds used by servicemen to specify their place of residence. Some used the name of the place where they were born and raised; others used a more current but temporary address while a few used the mailing address of their next-of-kin. Once again, the place of origin used here is generally that indicated in the enlistment documentation.

Regimental Number

The regimental number is the most reliable method of identifying a casualty. In some cases, a number could change throughout one's service career, as in the case of a promotion to the officer's ranks. Many senior ranks, particularly in the land forces, did not use such numbers.

Military Affiliation

For the Air Force, the squadron number is listed. Many Manitobans served at the training centres operated by the Commonwealth Air Training Plan and these are so identified. The military affiliation of Navy casualties is listed as the name of the ship on which they served or the shore installation where they were posted. Details of the sinking of the ship are listed only when they are relevant to the casualty's death.

Decoration

Military decoration immediately follows regimental affiliation. These range from "Mentioned in Dispatches" to the Victoria Cross. If a decoration was awarded twice it is customarily presented as a bar to be worn with the original medal (e.g., Military Cross and Bar).

Date of Death

There are discrepancies between various documents concerning the precise date of death of many casualties. The sinking of a ship might result in numerous casualties over a period of a few days. Similarly, many aircraft were reported missing and no documentation exists on the fate of the crew. Even official documents include presumptions of the precise date of death and a discrepancy of a day is not considered significant for current purposes.

Age at Death

During the late 1940s and early 1950s, a "Final Verification" form would be sent to the last known address of a casualty's next-of-kin in order to confirm various details for commemorative purposes. This involved the replacement of temporary wooden crosses with permanent stone markers. The age of the casualty at date of death was one of the questions asked. There are more discrepancies between various sources regarding the age of the casualty than with any other vital statistic. The Commonwealth War Graves Commission for example, seems to have often simply subtracted the year of birth from the year of death, which of course will result in an "error" of one year 50% of the time. Additionally, it was not uncommon for young men to add a year or two to their ages so that they could enlist. In more than one case, this involved "doctoring" their birth certificates.

Place of Commemoration

The remains of barely more than half of the Commonwealth casualties of the two World Wars were ever recovered and identified. The Commonwealth War Graves Commission was established in 1917 to ensure that all of the dead are commemorated in a permanent way with no distinctions of rank, race or creed. The term "commemoration" in the present context thus includes place of burial as well as location of a commemorative monumental inscription.

Family Members

The "Final Verification" form (see *Age at Death* above), sent to the last known address of the next-of-kin would be signed by surviving family members – generally parents and spouses. Thus, these need not constitute a complete list of relatives. In many cases the listed next-of-kin would themselves have passed away or changed residences since the casualty identified them on his/her attestation papers. The family members listed here emphasize lineal relations (e.g., parents, spouses and children) as opposed to collateral kin (e.g., brothers, sisters, cousins, nephews and nieces).

Geographical Feature Named in the Casualty's Honour

At the close of the Second World War, the federal government named a number of features across Canada after decorated Canadian casualties. This was often done without regard for the casualty's place of origin. Thus Manitoba has a number of features named after casualties who originated in other provinces and several Manitoba casualties are commemorated by a geographical feature outside Manitoba. In the interest of inclusiveness and wherever possible, all Manitoban casualties are included in the present volume. The lake, river or other feature named after these men and women is followed by an alphanumeric code throughout the body of the text (e.g., 64 G/15). This is the map reference in the National Topographic System (1:50,000 scale) on which this feature can be found. Reference to the map on page vi will give some indication of where the lake, hill, bay, etc. can be found.

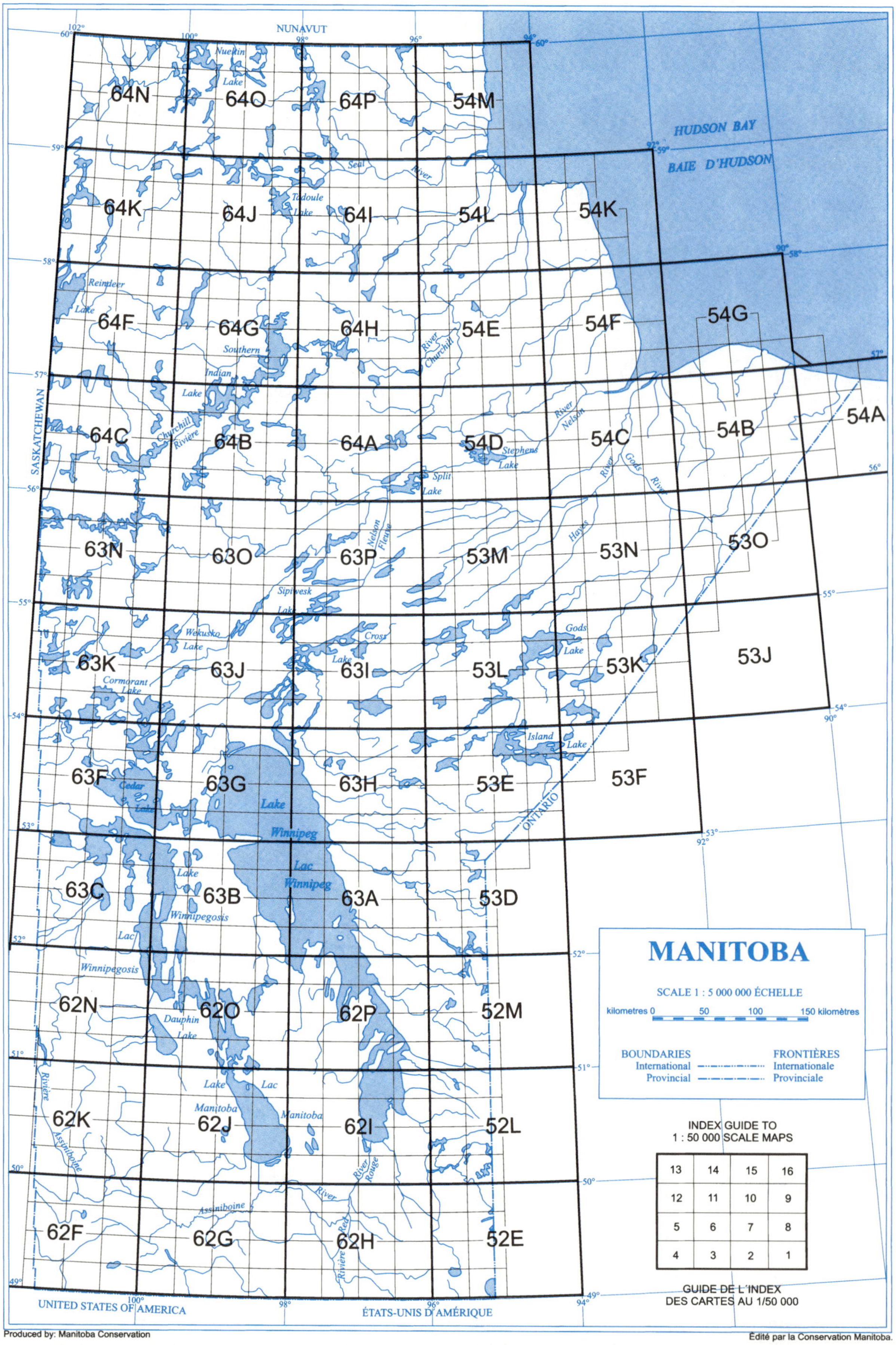

Produced by: Manitoba Conservation

Édité par la Conservation Manitoba.

Index of NTS 1:50,000 maps of Manitoba

A PLACE OF HONOUR

Manitoba's War Dead Commemorated in its Geography

A

Aandal, Private **Ralph B.** of Winnipeg (H 18844). Calgary Highlanders. He died 16 December 1944 at the age of 19 and is commemorated at the Groesbeek Canadian War Cemetery in Holland. He was the son of the Reverend Martin and Clara S. Aandal of St. Vital. These are some excerpts from a few of his letters home:

I had a nice trip out here. We rode on the train for quite a ways. Then we got off and rode on camel for miles and miles. The sand is about 40 feet deep. In other words, I am at Shilo (18 April 1944).

Well, I am in Debert, for how long I don't know. Talk about rain and fog – you've got to blow a whistle when you walk around so you don't bump into someone. The training is tough here but I don't know if we will take any of it or not. One of the two pips got killed Friday. A mortar bomb fell short; he was in the way. It makes a neat job. Say hello to pop and all the kids. Tell pop to brush up on his cribbage. So long, Ralph (17 September 1944).

I really froze this morning. The Governor General of Canada came to camp to inspect us. He *would* come on a day like this, it's the coldest day yet. We stood at attention for three hours; my hands were a deep blue. His wife was with him too. She talked to a few of us. When she spoke to me I nearly asked her to get me a discharge. At 12 o'clock it was all over and we got the greatest surprise of our lives. The Governor ordered our Brigadier to dismiss the troops for the day to catch up on our sleep. We really cheered the old boy. I ran in the hut and held my blankets by the stove until they nearly caught on fire. Then I went to bed and slept until 5, had supper and did a job I really love – I washed all my dirty clothes. Both my feet have gone to sleep. I am sitting on the flooring writing on my Bren box. I carry the Bren in our section. My address is still the same except I am in D Coy. Good Night. Love Ralph (2 October 1944).

Well, I am overseas at last. I had a nice trip and saw a lot of things which I can't write and tell you about. We are reinforcements over here, so we don't know when we will be going in action. I lost that little diary Vernon gave me. I felt bad about that, but tell him I will try to get another one and if I can't, I will remember everything that happens and tell him all about it. [Vernon, his little brother, had given him a diary for him to keep a journal of everything that happened so he could read it when he came back]. Well that's about all I can think of writing that wouldn't be censored. By the way, tell Lil to say hello to Mai Page and tell her I still love her like the seven year itch. Well, So Long for Now. Ralph (24 October 1944).

Well, I've left England and am now in Belgium. I had quite a bit of fun in England. I saw all the big art galleries and the wax museum. It really was worthwhile seeing. By the way, how about sending me some cigarettes? I am not broke but I hate the cigs they hand us. Make it Players Mild if you can. The meals are lovely – hard tack mutton or Bully beef – lovely! So long. Love Ralph. I am in a new place now. A. Coy. Calgary Highlanders (13 November 1944).

This last letter was postmarked the day he died:

I got a letter from Ruby. She told me Art's brother had been killed over here. I was sorry to hear that as I was hoping I would meet him someplace, but I guess that's out now. I just hope Art keeps his head down. I know mine is always pretty close to the ground. It's pretty grim here at times. We catch all the counter attacks. We have had 18 so far. We have been resting a few miles behind the lines for a couple of days. We are going in again in a couple of days. Right now I am sitting in a nice warm kitchen. We are living in their barn, but I got in good with the old lady, even if she can't speak English. We are still on the German border. How does the war look from a distance? When do you think it will crack? I haven't been sick at all out here. It's funny we all haven't gone to the hospital. We are laying in water day and night. I've seen me dive in up to my chest. Say hello to the rest of the family. By the way Pop, don't let them chase you around too much. Give a woman an inch and she'll take a mile. Love Ralph (14 December 1944).

Aandal Lake (64 K/5), northeast of Reindeer Lake was named after him in 1972. His sister adds (9 March 1995): "Since we have not a gravesite here in Manitoba [Aandal Lake] is so very meaningful to us, his family."

Abbott, Sergeant **William G.** of Winnipeg (R 100271). No. 408 Squadron. He died 23 May 1943 at the age of 21 and is commemorated at Bournemouth North Cemetery, England. He was the son of William G. and Emily A. Abbott of Winnipeg. ***Abbott Lake*** (64 P/11), east of Nejanilini Lake was named after him in 1974.

Abel, Sergeant **Frederick J.** of Portage la Prairie (H 6154). Winnipeg Grenadiers. He died a prisoner of war 28 November 1942 and is commemorated at the Sai Wan War Cemetery in Hong Kong. He was survived by his wife Eva Abel of Portage la Prairie. Veteran Richard Trick recalled his experience in the internment camps and afterwards:

It was a "second hand" soldier uniform Richard Trick put on in 1939. "They were uniforms from the First World War," says Richard Trick, who at the age of 23 joined up and was shortly sent to Jamaica. Trick's role during his early days of service was to guard the German prisoners of war who had been captured when their battleship sank off the coast of South America. But within 17 months, the young Lance Corporal was on his way to Hong Kong. "We left for China on October 25, 1941," he said. "I was home from Jamaica in Stonewall just long enough to get married."

Anxious days awaited his young bride Helen, as the dark days of Pearl Harbour came and went, and she knew her new husband was now somewhere in the hills of the Orient fighting the Japanese. What she didn't learn until quite some time after the fact was that Richard had been taken prisoner of war. "We were taken prisoners on December 22, 1941 and we were prisoners of war for 44 months," says Trick. While a PoW, Trick was forced to work in the mines and shipyards, to survive on a meagre diet. He has many recollections of those dark days. "I was 95 lbs. when we came out when the war was finished," said Trick.

After the war ended, Trick was to spend days in hospital, his health badly compromised by the camp experience. More days after that and a long, arduous journey home in poor health were to pass before he was home on October 25, 1945. Trick joined the Royal Canadian Legion #52 in February 1946, the same month he received his discharge and so became a veteran. He said he joined the Legion because he recalled the injustices faced by WWI veterans who had had, at first, no Legion to help them with family needs and personal needs. "I saw the merit of being a member," he said. "There were pensions to fight for. People had lost husbands, sons, fathers. The fight had not ended" (The *Argus* 6 November 1995).

Abel Lake (64 K/15), northeast of Lac Brochet was named after Sergeant Frederick Abel in 1972.

Abey, Pilot Officer **Mitchell G.** of Winnipeg (J 9511). No. 418 Squadron. He died 31 July 1942 at the age of 26 and is commemorated at Bergen-op-Zoom Canadian War Cemetery in Holland. He was an observer on Boston III W8326 on evening Intruder operations to Leeuwarden. The pilot and wireless air gunner were also killed. ***Abey Lake*** (64 P/6), southeast of Nejanilini Lake was named after him in 1974.

Abgrall, Private **Hervé** of St. Boniface (H 6960). Winnipeg Grenadiers. He died 19 December 1941 and is commemorated at the Sai Wan War Cemetery in Hong Kong. ***Abgrall Lake*** (64 K/14), northeast of Reindeer Lake was named after him in 1972.

Abigail, Lance Sergeant **Leonard D.** of Benito (H 70611). Queen's Own Cameron Highlanders. He died 18 September 1945 at the age of 30 and is commemorated at the Groesbeek Canadian War Cemetery in Holland. He was the son of Fredrick M. and Elizabeth J. Abigail of Benito and was survived by his wife Gladys I. Abigail of Benito and their unborn daughter. ***Abigail Lake*** (64 H/15), north of Etawney Lake was named after him in 1963.

Abram, Private **Albert J.** of The Pas (L 86912). South Saskatchewan Regiment. He died 20 July 1944 and is commemorated at Bretteville-sur-Laize Canadian War Cemetery in Calvados, France. ***Abram Lake*** (64 F/14), east of Reindeer Lake was named after him in 1961.

Ackerman, Rifleman **Harold A.** of Portage la Prairie (H 18706). Royal Winnipeg Rifles. He died 12 April 1945 at the age of 19 and is commemorated at the Groesbeek Canadian War Cemetery in Holland. He was one of the two sons of Harold and Violet Edith Ackerman (née Joyce) of Portage la Prairie. ***Ackerman Lake*** (64 N/12), southwest of Nueltin Lake was named after him in 1972.

Ackland, Lieutenant **Clifford N.** of Winnipeg. Lake Superior Regiment. He died 1 March 1945 and is commemorated at the Groesbeek Canadian War Cemetery in Holland. ***Ackland Lake*** (64 K/13), north of Lac Brochet was named after him in 1972.

Adair, Flying Officer **David Kenneth** of Winnipeg (J 29705). No. 100 Squadron. He died 17 June 1944 at the age of 26 and is commemorated at the Groesbeek Canadian War Cemetery in Holland. He was one of the four children of David N. and Mildred Adair of Winnipeg. Born in London, England, he had come to Canada with his parents in 1919. He was later awarded a scholarship to study Theology at St. John's College and was a bible class teacher and young people's sport educator. ***Adair Lake*** (64 O/1), north of Tadoule Lake was named after him in 1961.

Adam, Sergeant **Robert N.** of Oberon (H 40755). Royal Winnipeg Rifles. He died 14 April 1945 at the age of 37 and is commemorated at the Holten Canadian War Cemetery in Holland. He was the son of Robert N. and Margaret Adam and was survived by his wife Catherine Adam of Winnipeg. ***Adam Creek*** (64 P/10) which flows southeast into Caribou River was named after him in 1974.

Adams, Flying Officer **Douglas A.** of Newdale (J 23329). No. 172 Squadron. He died 14 August 1944 at the age of 21 and is commemorated at the Runnymede Memorial in Surrey, England. He was the son of William L. and Margaret Adams and the brother of Flying Officer Gavin R. Adams (see entry). ***Adams Bay*** (64 O/8) on the southwest shore of Baird Lake was named after him in 1988.

Adams, Private **Frederick W.** of Winnipeg (H 19188). Queen's Own Cameron Highlanders. He died 20 August 1942 and is commemorated at Brookwood Military Cemetery in Surrey, England. ***Adams Rapids*** (64 O/4), in the North Seal River was named after him in 1995.

Adams, Flying Officer **Gavin R.** of Newdale (J 9176). No. 87 Squadron. He died 24 November 1943 at the age of 23 and is commemorated at the Alamein Memorial in Egypt. He was the son of William L. and Margaret Adams of Newdale and the brother of Flying Officer Douglas A. Adams (see entry). ***Adams Peninsula*** (64 O/8) on the west shore of Baird Lake was named after him in 1988.

Adams, Flight Sergeant **Harry W.** of Ninette (R 106018). No. 7 Operational Training Unit, RCAF. He died 28 September 1942 at the age of 22 and is commemorated at the Runnymede Memorial in Surrey, England. He was the son of Walter H. and Ellen E. H. Adams of Ninette. ***Harry Adams Island*** (63 P/5) in Wintering Lake was named after him in 1995.

Adams, Private **John H.** of Winnipeg (H 6294). Winnipeg Grenadiers, Mentioned in Dispatches. He died a prisoner of war 26 August 1942 at the age of 27 and is commemorated at the Sai Wan War Cemetery in Hong Kong. His death and that of three other Grenadiers sparked a war crimes investigation after the war. It was determined that he had been executed after trying to escape. Nine of the ten Japanese military personnel involved were found guilty. See **Payne,** Sergeant **John O.** for additional details. He was the son of Alfred and Irma M. Adams and was survived by his wife Rose C. Adams of Winnipeg. Prior to enlisting he had been employed as a printer. ***Adams Lake*** (64 G/11), east of Big Sand Lake was named after him in 1994.

Adams, Lieutenant **Lloyd H.** of Winnipeg. 1st Canadian Parachute Battalion. He died 6 June 1944 and is commemorated at Ranville War Cemetery at Calvados, France. ***Adams Hill*** (64 O/7), southeast of Sandhill Lake was named after him in 1995.

Adams, Lieutenant **Sidney A. Armstrong** of Winnipeg. Royal Canadian Engineers. He received his Bachelor of Architecture degree from the University of Manitoba in May, 1942 and was appointed Lieutenant with the RCE three weeks later. He was killed by mortar fire 17 June 1944 at the age of 25 and is commemorated at Beny-sur-Mer Canadian War Cemetery at Calvados, France. He was the son of Earl V. A. and Mildred Adams of The Pas. ***Sidney Adams Bay*** (63 P/9) in Dafoe Lake was named after him in 1995.

Adams, Rifleman **William C.** of Selkirk (H 41531). Royal Winnipeg Rifles. Rifleman Adams took part in the Normandy invasion and was captured and executed while a prisoner of war 8 June 1944 at the age of 20. He had managed to enlist while still only 17 years of age and is commemorated at Beny-sur-Mer Canadian War Cemetery at Calvados, France. He was the son of Percival A. and Marion Adams of Petersfield. ***Adams Creek*** (63 N/7) which flows northeast into Burntwood Lake was named after him in 1995.

Addison, Corporal **Willis K. "Addie"** of Winnipeg (H 42254). Loyal Edmonton Regiment. He died 12 December 1943 at the age of 29 and is commemorated at the Moro River Canadian War Cemetery in Italy. He was the son of Willis C. and Clara Addison and was survived by his wife Madge M. Addison (née Sisson) of Truro, Nova Scotia. His sister-in-law relates that in his last letter home he wrote "I'm looking down at the Adriatic, hoping for a ship to take me home." He was killed in action at Ortona. ***Addison Lake*** (64 K/11), northeast of Reindeer Lake was named after him in 1972.

Adie, Leading Supply Assistant **William C.** of Winnipeg (V 9681). HMCS *Avalon*, the Royal Canadian Navy shore establishment in St. John's, Newfoundland. He died 12 December 1942 at the age of 28 and is commemorated at Mount Pleasant Cemetery in St. John's, Newfoundland. He was the son of William A. and Minnie A. Adie of Winnipeg. His brother recalls (11 December 1996):

> Bill was born in Tamworth, Staffordshire, England in 1914. He attended Queen Elizabeth's Grammar School in Tamworth until the family left for Canada in 1926. Our mother was a widow, our father having been killed in 1918 in France. He and I attended Beacon Hill School in Victoria before moving to Winnipeg. He went to Kelvin High and was a member of the Sea Cadets in Winnipeg. He was always interested in the sea and shipping. After high school, he trained as a commercial artist. My wife and I have quite a few of his works hanging on our walls.

Adie Creek (54 B/5), which flows northeast into Machichi River was named after him in 1964.

Adlard, Pilot Officer **William R.** of Winnipeg (J 88714). No. 429 Squadron. He died 23 April 1944 at the age of 19 and is commemorated at the Reichswald Forest War Cemetery in Germany. He was the son of Alfred C. and Alice J. G. Adlard (née Laing) of Winnipeg. ***Adlard Lake*** (64 J/10), west of Tadoule Lake was named after him in 1975.

Affleck, Private **Allen S.** of Crystal City (H 20714). Queen's Own Cameron Highlanders. He died 19 August 1942 at the age of 37 and is commemorated at Dieppe Canadian War Cemetery in Seine-Maritime, France. He was the son of John E. and Maria Affleck of Winnipeg. ***Affleck Lake*** (64 N/6), southwest of Nueltin Lake was named after him in 1972.

Agerbak, Corporal **Tage G.** of Pilot Mound (H 6293). Winnipeg Grenadiers. He died 20 December 1941 and is commemorated at the Sai Wan Memorial in Hong Kong. He was the son of Anton C. and Cammilla C. Agerbak and was survived by his wife Rose Agerbak of Pilot Mound. His brother Borge was in the same action.

> Not far away that same morning [24 December 1941], Corporal Borge "Buster" Agerbak a 27 year-old member of the Winnipeg Grenadiers, found shelter with 15 other men in a lantern-lit concrete pillbox loaded with crates of ammunition and rifles. Over a fire, the soldiers were roasting pilfered chicken. Corporal Agerbak had left Pilot Mound, Manitoba, and his wife of eight days, and, with his brother Tage, headed off on the train west, hoping to see the world. Inside the bunker, the men talked of Christmas. Outside there was an ominous hush. "This is probably the silence before the storm," a voice in the darkness said.
>
> Corporal Agerbak heard the whistling sound of an incoming shell from a Japanese cruiser offshore. The pillbox took a direct hit. The blast filled Corporal Agerbak's left side with scores of tiny shrapnel fragments and hurled him to the floor. The lantern crashed down onto the ammunition boxes. The living screamed in pain and fought in the darkness to escape. The impact, however, had jammed the door. Fire broke out. Smoke filled the chamber. The ammunition began exploding, killing men as they tried to get out. They clawed at each other as they tried to squeeze through a 30-centimetre observation slit.
>
> A second shell hit and the front wall collapsed inward, burying men in rubble. The concussion punctured both of Corporal Agerbak's eardrums and temporarily blinded him. Everywhere men screamed or moaned. The survivors stumbled over the bodies of their dead friends.
>
> Borge "Buster" Agerbak, now 76 and living in Sanford, Manitoba, still has operations to remove the shrapnel from his body. He has returned three times to Hong Kong trying to find out what happened to his brother Tage, one of the many Canadian soldiers whose bodies have never been found. The last time Mr. Agerbak went looking for his brother on hills now dotted with white condominiums was 1990 (Wood 1991).

(Borge made three more trips to Hong Kong between 1991 and 2000). ***Agerbak Lake*** (64 N/3), southwest of Nueltin Lake was named after Corporal Tage Agerbak in 1972.

Aikenhead, Flight Sergeant **Lloyd L.** of Cartwright (R 91917). No. 427 Squadron. He died 21 June 1942 at the age of 25 and is commemorated at Delfzijl General Cemetery, Holland. He was the eldest of the three sons of Frank and Iva J. Aikenhead and was survived by his wife Muriel Aikenhead (née Bell) R. N. of Baldur and their unborn son. In 1982, his widow was invited to visit the cemetery by the people of Delfzijl. ***Aikenhead Bay*** (63 N/3) in Kississing Lake was named after Flight Sergeant Aikenhead in 1972.

Aitken, Sergeant **John** of Winnipeg (1110660). No. 50 Squadron, RAF. This native of Grenock, Scotland died 13 June 1943 at the age of 21 and is commemorated at the Reichswald Forest War Cemetery in Kleve, Germany. ***John Aitken Lake*** (53 K/11), south of Edmund Lake was named after him in 1995.

Aitken, Private **John A.** of Winnipeg (H 6576). Winnipeg Grenadiers. He died 19 December 1941 at the age of 34 and is commemorated at the Sai Wan Memorial in Hong Kong. He was the son of William and Elizabeth Aitken and was survived by his wife Jessie P. Aitken of St. James and their young son. When war was declared, John was a member of the staff at Stony Mountain Penitentiary. He enlisted 21 September 1939. ***Aitken Lake*** (64 I/11), west of Reindeer Lake was named after him in 1974.

Aitken, Private **Victor W.** of Roland (H 19856). Queen's Own Cameron Highlanders. He died 3 March 1945 at the age of 23 and is commemorated at Brookwood Memorial in Surrey, England. He was the son of William and Isabella Aitken of Bayton, Manitoba. ***Aitken Island*** (63 I/7) in Lawford Lake was named after him in 1995.

Aitkens, Sergeant **William R.** of Winnipeg (H 35579). Royal Canadian Artillery. He died 31 August 1941 at the age of 31 and is commemorated at Brookwood Military Cemetery in Surrey, England. He was the son of William R. and Harriet Aitkens and was survived by his wife Christina T. Aitkens of Winnipeg and their two daughters. His brother writes (20 November 2001):

> William's interest in the army showed itself early and he joined the 11th Medium Battery as soon as he was eligible. He was the pride of us all.

He had been working at the Sherridon Mines in northern Manitoba. He was one of the fortunate few holding down a good job during the depression. He was a loyal family man who along with his wife and daughters supported his mother and younger brother.

Aitkens Lake (64 F/3), north of Vandekerckhove Lake was named after him in 1994.

Akeroyd, Private **Robert K.** of St. Vital (H 204630). Calgary Highlanders. He died 29 August 1944 at the age of 26 and is commemorated at Bretteville-sur-Laize Canadian War Cemetery in Calvados, France. He was the son of Frank and Rebecca Akeroyd and was survived by his uncle Thomas M. Crow of Sturgeon Creek. ***Akeroyd Lake*** (52 L/3), southeast of Lac du Bonnet was named after him in 1973.

Albert, Flight Sergeant **John A.** of Emerson (R 134836). No. 427 Squadron. He died 31 August 1943 at the age of 22 and is commemorated at the Reichswald Forest War Cemetery in Germany. He was the son of Thomas and Olivine Albert of Sandy Lake, Manitoba and was survived by his wife Norma T. Albert. ***Albert Lake*** (64 J/9), east of Tadoule Lake was named after him in 1975.

Alcock, Sergeant **Arthur F.** of Souris (R 101979). No. 24 Operational Training Unit, RCAF. He died 17 June 1942 at the age of 22 and is commemorated at Evesham Cemetery in Worcestershire, England. He was the son of Arthur F. and Isabella Alcock of Souris. ***Alcock Lake*** (64 J/16), north of Tadoule Lake was named after him in 1975.

Aldridge, Sergeant **Thomas** of Winnipeg (R 177535). No. 158 Squadron. He died 25 July 1943 at the age of 21 and is commemorated at the Kiel War Cemetery in Germany. He was the eldest of the three children of John Thomas R. and Martha A. S. Aldridge of Winnipeg. His sister recalls (6 November 2001):

Thomas was born [in] 1922 ... at 621 Garwood Avenue. He attended Earl Grey and Kelvin schools where he was active in all sports especially soccer of which he was chosen team captain. He was very interested in horses and racing and spent many happy hours with his Dad at Whittier Park Race Track, learning to be a trainer. He owned a lovely thoroughbred called Papau who continued to race successfully after Tommy joined the Air Force in April, 1942. Tom was trained at Edmonton, Saskatoon and Macdonald, Manitoba where he graduated in April, 1943. He was sent overseas in May, 1943 and was reported missing in action over Hamburg, Germany July 24/25, 1943. He was survived by his parents and two sisters, Patricia and Doreen.

Aldridge Lake (64 I/14), north of North Knife Lake was named after him in 1974.

Alexander, Company Quarter Master Sergeant **Ernest J.** of Winnipeg (H 59030). Royal Winnipeg Rifles. He died 18 October 1943 at the age of 55 and is commemorated at Moosomin South Cemetery, Saskatchewan. He was survived by his wife Jessie E. Alexander of Winnipeg and by their daughter B. Isabel Rumble. His grandchildren write (9 January 2002):

Although our grandfather died long before we were born, our grandmother and mother often spoke to us of him. He was born in Edinburgh, Scotland and came to Canada as a young man where he served in Saskatchewan with the Royal Canadian Mounted Police. In World War I, he enlisted with the 1st Canadian Mounted Rifles and served from 1916 to 1918. Following his return from the First World War, he continued in police work, first in Saskatchewan and then in Winnipeg. Perhaps our favourite story is how he enlisted for World War II with the Royal Winnipeg Rifles in 1940 by saying he was 10 years younger than he really was. He spent a year in camp with the Royal Winnipeg Rifles and then went on staff at Fort Osborne Barracks where he died on the third anniversary of his joining up.

Alexander Lake (63 P/3), east of Sipiwesk Lake was named after him in 1995.

Alexander, Rifleman **George** of East Kildonan (H 40950). Royal Winnipeg Rifles. He died 16 July 1944 at the age of 21 and is commemorated at Beny-sur-Mer Canadian War Cemetery in Calvados, France. He was the son of William H. and Mary Alexander of Winnipeg and was survived by his wife Kathleen L. Alexander of Winnipeg. ***Alexander Creek*** (64 I/16), which flows south into Lavallée Channel on the Seal River was named after him in 1974.

Alexander, Signalman **Robert K.** of Winnipeg (V 53604). HMCS *Chippawa*. He died 30 August 1945 at the age of 21 and is commemorated at Elmwood Cemetery in Winnipeg. He was the son of Robert M. and Joan Alexander of Winnipeg. ***Alexander Bay*** (53 F/13) in Angling Lake was named after him in 1996.

Alexander, Private **Selena P.** of Winnipeg (W 22255). Canadian Women's Army Corps. She died 9 October 1944 at the age of 26 and is commemorated at Brookside Cemetery in Winnipeg. She was the daughter of John and Wilhelmina Alexander of Winnipeg. ***Alexander Island*** (53 E/15) in Island Lake was named after her in 1995.

Allan, Private **Andrew A.** of Stonewall (V 53604). South Saskatchewan Regiment. He died 19 August 1942 at the age of 29 and is commemorated at Dieppe Canadian War Cemetery in Seine-Maritime, France. He was the son of Alexander and Hannah Allan. His niece recalls (16 November 2001):

Andrew was born at Brithdir, Saskatchewan just south of Humboldt on August 30, 1912. He attended Pilot Grove School, completing Grade 9 before leaving to work with his father on the farm. As the eldest son, he worked with his father until the 'dirty thirties,' then he 'rode the rails' looking for work like many other young men of his day. He found work in the bush at a lumber camp, at a fox ranch, and worked for awhile for a Mr. Pierce on a farm near Reston, Manitoba.

Andrew enlisted in the army at Stonewall, Manitoba on June 20, 1940. He did his basic training at Shilo. While at Shilo, he was able to visit his family at the farm at Fairlight, Saskatchewan before going overseas. He went overseas with the South Saskatchewan Regiment on December 16th, 1940. While stationed in England, he managed to visit his relatives in Scotland. He met his brother, Munro, who had also enlisted, on a visit there when their leaves matched.

On August 18th, 1942, Andrew's regiment shipped out for France. He was listed as missing in action at the battle of Dieppe, and was later confirmed as killed in action on August 19, 1942, just 11 days before his thirtieth birthday. The last letter received by his sister Elizabeth Widger was dated August 7, 1942 from England. In it he wrote, "I'm going to be back fur ranching next year if we get to Hitler's back yard this fall. Tell Lennie (Elizabeth's husband) that he'd like breaking [bush] with one of our tanks. It would not upset as easy as a Rumley. Munro won't be needing a car after the war because he will bring home a jeep."

Mrs. Kay Thompson is the daughter of Elizabeth and Leonard Widger. She writes:

> My mother rarely mentioned her brother. War memories were painful to her because many of the young men of the community had signed up for the war. As she once said sadly to me: " So many of them never came back." My dad was Andrew's close friend and they all used to go dances together. In fact, that's how my mum and dad met. My dad died on October 6, 1988. My mum will celebrate her 85th birthday on November 8, 2001.
>
> Since I wasn't born until after the war, I never had the chance to know my Uncle Andrew, but I named one of my sons Robert Andrew in his memory. I have since wondered how our family might have been different if he had returned from the war. I had the chance to read part of one of Andrew's diaries and I felt he must have been a lonely person. He had met a girl that he had mentioned to my mother and he had asked her to let this girl know if anything happened to him. But when mother wrote her, she knew because the casualty list had already been published. But his last letter to mom shows the eternal optimism of a farm boy – things were sure to be better 'next year.'

Allan Bay (63 I/16) in Kapechekamasic Lake was named after him in 1995.

Allan, Trooper **Hugh R.** of Winnipeg (M 26927). Calgary Tank Regiment. He died 8 August 1944 at the age of 38 and is commemorated at Bretteville-sur-Laize Canadian War Cemetery in Calvados, France. ***Allan Peninsula*** (64 N/5) in Snyder Lake was named after him in 1995.

Allan, Sergeant **J. A. Lawrence** "Laurie" of Winnipeg (R 80235). No. 419 Squadron. He died 28 April 1943 at the age of 20 and is commemorated at the Runnymede Memorial in Surrey, England. He was the son of James A. and Marion E. Allan of St. James. Prior to the war, he had been a Cadet Sergeant Major with the Queen's Own Cameron Highlanders. ***Allan Island*** (64 F/3) in Vandekerckhove Lake was named after him in 1994.

Allan, Private **James A.** of Winnipeg (H 9467). Queen's Own Cameron Highlanders. He died 8 August 1944 at the age of 38 and is commemorated at Bretteville-sur-Laize Canadian War Cemetery in Calvados, France. He was the son of James C. and Joan Allan and was survived by his wife Jean Allan of Winnipeg. ***Allan Point*** (64 I/13) in Shethanei Lake was named after him in 1995.

Allan, Master **John** of Winnipeg. SS *George L. Torian*, Canadian Merchant Navy. The *George L. Torian* was torpedoed and sunk by U-129 off British Guyana in the Caribbean. Master Allan died 22 February 1942 at the age of 38 and is commemorated at the Halifax Memorial. He was survived by his wife Margaret Allan of St. Catharines, Ontario. ***John Allan Lake*** (63 P/2), east of Cotton Lake was named after him in 2001.

Allan, Able Seaman **John M.** of Winnipeg (V 24900). HMCS *Alberni*. The *Alberni* was torpedoed and sunk by U-480, southeast of the Isle of Wight; 59 of her ship's company were lost. Able Seaman Allan died 21 August 1944 at the age of 24 and is commemorated at the Halifax Memorial. He was the son of David M. and Mary M. Allan of St. Vital. ***Allan Lake*** (64 I/2), east of North Knife Lake was named after him in 1957.

Allan, Pilot Officer **Ralph G.** of Winnipeg (J 16754). No. 432 Squadron. He died 28 May 1943 at the age of 21 and is commemorated at the Runnymede Memorial in Surrey, England. He was the son of George and Alice W. Allan and was survived by his wife Audrey C. Allan of Dunston-on-Tyne, Durham, England. ***Allan Hill*** (54 D/14), southeast of Whitecap Lake was named after him in 1995.

Allard, Private **Paul** of St. Boniface (H 18433). Queen's Own Cameron Highlanders. He died 29 July 1944 at the age of 19 and is commemorated at Bretteville-sur-Laize Canadian War Cemetery in Calvados, France. He was the sixth of the 12 children of Albert J. and Denise Allard (née Lavack) of St. Boniface. ***Allard Lake*** (64 H/10), northeast of Southern Indian Lake was named after him in 1963.

Allardyce, Private **Lancelot M.** of Langruth (H 10877). Calgary Highlanders. He died 10 October 1940 at the age of 41 and is commemorated at Brookwood Military Cemetery in Surrey, England. He was the son of John M. and Edith Marion Allardyce of Winnipeg. His niece writes (1 November 2001):

> "Laddie" was born in Peking, China where his parents were missionaries, his mother coming from Australia and his father from Scotland. In 1903, he came to Canada with his parents where they homesteaded in the Burnside district of Portage la Prairie. Laddie attended school in Burnside and went with his parents to the Burnside Church. He farmed with his father until he enlisted in World War I at the age of 16. However, just as his Regiment was to be shipped overseas, the war ended. After being demobilized in 1919, he went to Langruth, Manitoba and settled on a farm which he worked for many years. Happening to be in Calgary in September, 1939 when World War II broke out, he enlisted in the Calgary Highlanders. He was sent to England in the summer of 1940 with the 2nd Canadian Division. Laddie was killed in an air raid in October of 1940 at Aldershot where he was stationed. His younger brother Bill was overseas with the Princess Patricia's Canadian Light Infantry at this time and was able to attend his funeral. I remember my grandmother getting a letter from an officer after he died saying that he was such a great help to the younger men in his unit as he had some experience from the First World War and was like a "fatherly figure" to them.
>
> Uncle Laddie was a very fun loving man, and my sister and I have many happy memories of visiting him and other family members at Langruth during the summer holidays. We are happy to know that there is a small place in Manitoba bearing his name when he is buried so far away.

Allardyce Creek (64 N/13), which flows north and west into Tanuck Lake was named after him in 1972.

Allen, Flying Officer **Ernest J.** of Winnipeg (J 20587). No. 439 Squadron. He died 12 August 1944 at the age of 23 and is commemorated at Bretteville-sur-Laize Canadian War Cemetery in Calvados, France. He was the son of Ernest and Mary A. Allen and was survived by his wife Zella M. Allen of St. James. ***Allen Hill*** (64 P/12), west of Nejanilini Lake was named after him in 1995.

Allen, Pilot Officer **John F.** of Winnipeg (J 86516). No. 61 Squadron. He died 20 February 1944 at the age of 29 and is commemorated at Rheinberg War Cemetery in Germany. He was the son of John W. and Mary F. Allen of Winnipeg. ***Allen Lake*** (63 B/6), northeast of Waterhen Lake was named after him in 1969.

Allen, Lance Corporal **Sidney A.** of Russell (H 20242). Queen's Own Cameron Highlanders. Lance Corporal Allen enlisted at the beginning of the war and took part in the Dieppe Landing on his twenty-third birthday. He died 21 July 1944 at the age of 25 and is commemorated at Bretteville-sur-Laize Canadian War cemetery, Calvados, France. He was the son of George A. and Jessie Allen of Russell, Manitoba. His sister recalls (19 January 1994):

When my mother received the notice that Sid was missing, the first thing she said was "I hope he didn't drown," as he had never learned to swim. Sid curled, played goalie in hockey and skied. He was a true nature lover. He enjoyed his time in the Whiteshell.

Allen Creek (64 I/16), which flows south into Seal River was named after him in 1995.

Allery, Lieutenant **Frank Q.** of Winnipeg. Royal Winnipeg Rifles. He died 24 August 1943 at the age of 29 and is commemorated at Brixham (St. Mary) Churchyard in Devon, England. He was the fourth of the five children of Frank H. G. and Florence S. Allery of Winnipeg. ***Allery Lake*** (64 K/13), northeast of Reindeer Lake was named after him in 1972.

Alleyn, Pilot Officer **Foster R.** of Winnipeg (J 85507). No. 426 Squadron. He died 20 February 1944 at the age of 22 and is commemorated at Woensel General Cemetery in Eindhoven, Holland. One hundred twenty-nine aircraft took part on this raid on Leipzig. One hundred and twelve thousand pounds of high explosives and four hundred and twenty-two thousand pounds of incendiaries were released. Eighteen crews (128 men) failed to return. ***Alleyn Lake*** (63 K/13), east of Embury Lake was named after Pilot Officer Alleyn in 1984.

Allison, Signalman **Charles E.** of Winnipeg (H 38590). Royal Canadian Corps of Signals. He died 17 September 1944 at the age of 23 and is commemorated at the Calais Canadian War Cemetery in France. He was the son of Robert W. and Adeline Allison of The Pas. ***Allison Lake*** (64 K/6), northeast of Reindeer Lake was named after him in 1972.

Allison, Private **Lyle M.** of Swan River (H 8760). Royal Regiment of Canada. He died 12 August 1944 at the age of 20 and is commemorated at Bretteville-sur-Laize Canadian War Cemetery in Calvados, France. He was the son of Thomas and Florence Allison of Vancouver. ***Allison Island*** (64 F/1) in Barrington Lake was named after him in 1995.

Allnutt, Lieutenant **Alasdair M.** of Winnipeg. Fort Garry Horse. He died 18 June 1944 at the age of 28 and is commemorated at Beny-sur-Mer Canadian War Cemetery in Calvados, France. He was the son of Alexander J. and Agnes M. Allnutt and was survived by his wife Elsie J. Allnutt of Edmonton, Alberta. ***Allnutt Lake*** (64 K/13), northeast of Reindeer Lake on the Manitoba - Saskatchewan boundary was named after him in 1972.

Alloway, Flight Lieutenant **Alexander H. F.** of Winnipeg (C 831). No. 110 Squadron. He died 22 January 1941 at the age of 23 and is commemorated at Brookwood Military Cemetery in Surrey, England. He was the son of Mr. and Mrs. C. V. Alloway of Winnipeg. ***Alloway Lake*** (63 J/3), east of North Moose Lake was named after him in 1973.

Allum, Rifleman **Harold E.** of Oak Lake (H 41620). Royal Winnipeg Rifles. He died 9 June 1944 and is commemorated at Beny-sur-Mer Canadian War Cemetery in Calvados, France. He was the son of Thomas H. and Alice M. Allum (née Forward) of Oak Lake and was survived by his wife Rose Allum of Winnipeg and their son.

Better known as "Ted" by his family and friends, he was born on the family farm in the Oak Lake district. He received his education at Runnymede School and continued working on his father's farm until he enlisted at Souris in March, 1941. Prior to his overseas posting, he married and had a son – Wayne Stanley. Harold landed with C Company of the Royal Winnipeg Rifles on Juno Beach on D-Day, June 6, 1944. He lost his life three days later a short distance inland during the intense fighting (Pittman n.d.).

Allum Island (52 E/14) in Frances Lake southeast of Brereton Lake was named after him in 1976.

Alyward, Private **Frances E.** of The Pas (H 42114). Royal Canadian Ordnance Corps. He died 25 November 1944 at the age of 29 and is commemorated at Schoonselhof Cemetery in Antwerp, Belgium. He was the son of Nick and Emma Alyward and was survived by his wife Pauline Alyward of Roblin, Manitoba. ***Alyward Lake*** (64 O/5), south of Nueltin Lake was named after him in 1975.

Amos, Lance Corporal **George** of Winnipeg (H 2957). Princess Patricia's Canadian Light Infantry. He died 23 May 1944 at the age of 31 and is commemorated at the Cassino War Cemetery in Italy. He was the son of Frederick and Elizabeth B. Amos and was survived by his wife Winifred P. Amos of Carnduff, Saskatchewan. ***Amos Lake*** (64 K/7), northeast of Reindeer Lake was named after him in 1972.

Andersen, Pilot Officer **Nels P. H.** of Gladstone (C 95210). No. 408 Squadron. He died 21 February 1945 at the age of 21 and is commemorated at Rheinberg War Cemetery in Germany. He was the youngest son of Hans P. and Hulda C. Anderson (née Helin) of Woodside, Manitoba.

Nels was born at Tyndall, Manitoba March 20, 1923. He moved with his family to the Woodside district in 1932. Nels joined the Royal Canadian Air Force in 1943 and served as an air gunner, being promoted to Pilot Officer on February 20, 1945. Nels was flying in a Halifax aircraft when it was shot down over the target during a night trip to Worms, Germany. All members of the crew were killed (Pittman n.d.).

Andersen Lake (64 F/3), north of Vandekerckhove Lake was named after him in 1994.

Andersen, Flight Sergeant **Paul** of Winnipeg (R 208718). No. 44 Squadron. He died 16 July 1944 at the age of 20 and is commemorated at the Runnymede Memorial in Surrey, England. He was the son of Octavius and Ingeborg Andersen of Winnipeg. ***Andersen Narrows*** (64 O/15) in Dyker Lake was named after him in 1995.

Anderson, Sergeant **A. Willard.** of Selkirk (R 84116). No. 120 Squadron. He died 23 August 1942 at the age of 28 and is commemorated at the Ottawa Memorial. ***Willard Anderson Lake*** (64 B/3), south of Mynarski Lakes was named after him in 1995.

Anderson, Gunner **Albert E.** of Woodlands (H 59768). Royal Canadian Artillery. He died 8 May 1942 at the age of 19 and is commemorated at Brookwood Military Cemetery in Surrey, England. He was the son of Thomas and Edith Anderson of Woodlands. ***Anderson Esker*** (64 I/2), east of North Knife Lake was named after him in 1992.

Anderson, Pilot Officer **Alexander J.** of Minnedosa (J 90357). No. 61 Squadron. He died 26 August 1944 at the age of 22 and is commemorated at the Runnymede Memorial in Surrey, England. He was the son of William and the late Jessie Anderson of Minnedosa. ***Anderson Peninsula*** (53 M/5) in Silsby Lake was named after him in 1985.

Anderson, Rifleman **Birger G.** (H 8718). Royal Winnipeg Rifles. He died 1 August 1944 and is commemorated at Bretteville-sur-Laize Canadian War Cemetery in Calvados, France. ***Birger Anderson Lake*** (64 I/3), west of Blyth Lake was named after him in 1995.

Anderson, Private **Carl I.** of Lac du Bonnet (H 5922). Royal Canadian Army Service Corps. He died 27 October 1944 at the age of 26 and is commemorated at the Adegem Canadian War Cemetery, Maldegem, Belgium. He was the son of Mr. and Mrs. Ivor E. Anderson and was survived by his wife Betty Anderson of Lac du Bonnet. ***Carl Anderson Island*** (53 M/4) in Bear Lake was named after him in 1995.

Anderson, Flying Officer **Charles E.** of Winnipeg (J 13450). No. 298 Squadron. He died 5 August 1944 at the age of 21 and is commemorated at Essoyes Communal Cemetery in Aube, France. ***Anderson Creek*** (64 P/2), which flows southwest into Big Spruce River was named after him in 1974.

Anderson, Private **Edward L.** of Brandon (H 59858). Queen's Own Cameron Highlanders. He died 14 September 1944 and is commemorated at the Adegem Canadian War Cemetery in Maldegem, Belgium. ***Edward Anderson Lake*** (64 H/1), south of Billard Lake was named after him in 1995.

Anderson, Pilot Officer **Edward W.** of Winnipeg (J 28498). No. 3 Personnel Reception Centre, RCAF, Bournemouth, England. He died 10 September 1943 at the age of 29 and is commemorated at Bournemouth North Cemetery in Hampshire, England. The cause of death was listed as due to "a fall from a third floor window of a hotel" (Allison 1991). He was the son of O. T. and Gertrude Anderson of East Kildonan and was survived by his wife Edith Anderson of Winnipeg and their daughter. ***Edward Anderson Point*** (54 D/14) on Whitecap Lake was named after him in 1995.

Anderson, Trooper **Eric A.** of St. James (H 102248). Calgary Regiment. He died 13 December 1943 at the age of 30 and is commemorated at the Moro River Canadian War Cemetery in Italy. He was the son of Oscar and Hilda Anderson of St. James. ***Eric Anderson Lake*** (53 N/14), north of Whitefish Lake was named after him in 1995.

Anderson, Flight Lieutenant **F. Cameron** of Winnipeg (DC 3409). No. 221 Squadron. He died 2 February 1943 at the age of 25 and is commemorated at the Malta Memorial. He was the son of Frederick T. and Ethel M. Anderson of Winnipeg. ***Anderson River*** (64 O/7), which flows southeast into Munroe Lake was named after him in 1989.

Anderson, Pilot Officer **Frank E.** of Winnipeg (J 9568). No. 459 Squadron. He died 24 July 1942 at the age of 21 and is commemorated at the Alamein Memorial in Egypt. He was the son of Francis H. and Rhea E. Anderson of Kildonan. ***Frank Anderson Lake*** (63 P/8), west of Thom Lake was named after him in 1995.

Anderson, Pilot Officer **Frederick** of Winnipeg (J 86041). No. 138 Squadron. He died 30 March 1944 at the age of 21 and is commemorated at the Runnymede Memorial in Surrey, England. The names of 20,456 Commonwealth airmen including 3000 Canadians are commemorated at this memorial alone. ***Frederick Anderson Lake*** (64 P/2), northwest of Meades Lake was named after Pilot Officer Anderson in 1995.

Anderson, Warrant Officer 1 **Harold G. "Hal"** of Pine Falls (R 86274). No. 14 Squadron. He died 1 April 1943 at the age of 22 and is commemorated at Fort Richardson Post Cemetery, Alaska. He was the eldest son of Alexander and Frances M. Anderson (née Linklater) of Pine Falls. His sister recalls (7 February 1997):

> The family ... moved to Pine Falls, Manitoba in 1927. Harold attended school in Pine Falls. He was known to his family as Hal and to his friends as Andy. While growing up he was active in hockey and ball, was a loving son and brother. He helped his father in the bakery when needed and went to work for the Manitoba Paper Company in Pine Falls when he left school.

Harold Anderson Lake (53 M/1), south of Swampy Lake was named after him in 1995.

Anderson, Flight Lieutenant **Henry T.** of Winnipeg (R 39021). No. 253 Squadron. He died 19 May 1940 at the age of 20 and is commemorated at Lille Southern Cemetery in Nord, France. ***Henry Anderson Peninsula*** (53 K/10) on Little Stull Lake was named after him in 1995.

Anderson, Sergeant **Herbert L.** of Matlock (R 197565). No. 34 Operational Training Unit, RCAF. He died 19 December 1943 at the age of 20 and is commemorated at Burnaby (Forest Lawn) Memorial Park, British Columbia. He was the son of Herbert J. and Ethel L. Anderson of Vancouver. ***Herbert Anderson Lake*** (54 E/9), northeast of Fly Lake was named after him in 1995.

Anderson, Private **John** of Selkirk (H 7144). Queen's Own Cameron Highlanders. He died 21 July 1944 at the age of 24 and is commemorated at Bretteville-sur-Laize Canadian War Cemetery in Calvados, France. He was the son of Joseph T. and Mary E. Anderson of Selkirk and the brother of Private Vernon Anderson (see entry). ***John Anderson Lake*** (64 J/4), northwest of Morand Lake was named after him in 1995.

Anderson, Flight Sergeant **Leonard R.** of Minnedosa (R 91822). No. 101 Squadron. He died 7 December 1942 at the age of 24 and is commemorated at the Runnymede Memorial in Surrey, England. He was the son of Otto and Anna Anderson and was survived by his wife Louise Anderson of Winnipeg. ***Anderson Hill*** (64 N/8), southwest of Shannon Lake was named after him in 1989.

Anderson, Leading Aircraftman **Marino Harold** of Winnipeg (R 215787). Royal Canadian Air Force. He died 26 May 1945 at the age of 21 and is commemorated at Brookside Cemetery in Winnipeg. He was the son of Olafur T. and Gertrude Anderson of Winnipeg. ***Anderson Rapids*** (64 C/11), south of Lake Winnipeg was named after him in 1995.

Anderson, Flight Lieutenant **Peter Murray** of Union Point (J 16379). No. 207 Squadron, Distinguished Flying Cross (1943), Mentioned in Dispatches (1944).

> This officer has completed numerous sorties including several attacks on targets in Italy. He has always displayed great courage and skill. One night in February, 1943 he completed a successful attack on Lorient in difficult circumstances. Three nights later he flew with distinction in an attack on the same target (DFC Citation 1948).

He died 11 April 1945 at the age of 23 and is commemorated at Brussels Town Cemetery in Belgium. His sister-in-law reports that (9 May 1995):

While attending the University of Manitoba in 1941, he joined the RCAF and graduated as a pilot. After his first tour of operations, he received the DFC from King George VI at Buckingham Palace. While returning from a bombing mission on his second tour with a badly shot-up plane, his crew bailed out to safety; Murray did not make it out of the plane.

Anderson Island (64 J/9) in Tadoule Lake was named after him in 1974. He is also honoured on NTS map 105 H, Yukon.

Anderson, Private **Peter T. G.** of Morris (H 200067). Queen's Own Cameron Highlanders. He died 20 July 1944 at the age of 28 and is commemorated at Bretteville-sur-Laize Canadian War Cemetery in Calvados, France. He was the son of Peter and Lydia O. M. Anderson (née Ducharme) and was survived by his wife Gladys F. B. Anderson (née Tanner) and their son Peter Jr. ***Peter Anderson Lake*** (64 O/12), north of Shannon Lake was named after him in 1995.

Anderson, Private **Ralph G.** of Winnipeg (H 62962). Toronto Scottish Regiment. He died 18 September 1944 at the age of 19 and is commemorated at the Calais Canadian War Cemetery in France. He was the son of Clarence E. and Olga O. Anderson of Toronto. ***Ralph Anderson Lake*** (53 L/5), north of Bolton Lake was named after him in 1995.

Anderson, Trooper **Stewart L.** of Bagot (H 77432). 12th Manitoba Dragoons. He died 19 April 1945 at the age of 25 and is commemorated at the Holten Canadian War Cemetery in Holland. He was the son of William M. and Isabella Anderson of Bagot. ***Stewart Anderson Lake*** (53 L/6), southeast of Joint Lake was named after him in 1995.

Anderson, Private **Vernon** of Selkirk (H 17897). Princess Patricia's Canadian Light Infantry. He died 14 December 1943 at the age of 19 and is commemorated at the Moro River Canadian War Cemetery in Italy. He was the son of Joseph T. and Mary E. Anderson of Selkirk and the brother of Private John Anderson (see entry). ***Vernon Anderson Lake*** (64 C/9), northeast of Eden Lake was named after him in 1995.

Anderson, Squadron Leader **William A.** of Winnipeg (AC 1099). No. 407 Squadron, Distinguished Flying Cross.

This officer has always shown the greatest keenness and enthusiasm for operational flying. On one occasion, he carried out a successful low level attack on a well defended convoy off Ameland, obtaining a hit on the largest vessel of some 10,000 tons. On another occasion, he attacked convoys at night, always at a low level, and in the face of intense anti-aircraft fire, obtaining a hit on a 2500 ton vessel from fifty feet. He also attacked the vessel with machine gun fire. On another sortie Squadron Leader Anderson was detailed to illuminate, with flares, the position of a convoy to direct a bombing force to the attack. He skilfully accomplished his mission in the face of fire from the ship. He assumed command of a flight in November, 1941. This officer has at all times shown great courage (DFC Citation 1944).

He died 12 February 1942 at the age of 23 and is commemorated at the Runnymede Memorial in Surrey, England. He was the son of David W. and Anne W. Anderson of Winnipeg and was survived by his wife Joyce H. Anderson (née Morkhill) of Winnipeg. He had been flying missions against enemy shipping in the North Sea and developed a characteristic method of attack:

He dive-bombed the ship, pulled out at the height of the mast and dropped delayed action bombs. A brilliant flash followed and immediately afterwards a large cloud of steam and black smoke obscured the superstructure (*Winnipeg Free Press* 19 February 1942).

His niece writes (5 November 2001):

Bill, as family and friends knew him, attended St. James Collegiate and United College and spent two years at the University of Manitoba. He loved all sports, participating in hockey, rugby, football, swimming and skiing and was especially active in track and soccer meets. He also loved to draw cartoons and his Flight Book as well as college books contain some very entertaining drawings.

Bill joined the Royal Canadian Air Force in August of 1939, one month before war broke out. Offered the choice of dropping out of the Air Force, he elected to stay. He received his training at the Winnipeg Flying Club, in Borden, Ontario and finally in North Sydney, Nova Scotia.

While stationed in Nova Scotia, Bill married Joyce Morkhill in 1940. Joyce was also from Winnipeg and they were dating before he joined the RCAF. I remember watching a home movie of their wedding after my Uncle Billy had been sent overseas, and Joyce was so excited at seeing it, she had my grandfather show it to us several times. They both looked so very happy.

One of the silly things I remember was the time Uncle Billy tried to teach me how to blow my nose. Like all kids at age four or five, I kept sniffing up instead of blowing down. Uncle Billy knelt down beside me, in his uniform, and kept at it until I finally did.

A more serious incident occurred a few months later. We were having Sunday dinner with my grandparents and Bill and Joyce when he got the call to report for duty. We all clambered into my grandfather's car to go to Stevenson Field to see him off. My younger sister and I knew it was serious and for once, kept very quiet. We certainly didn't realize that we would never see him again. Bill was killed in action over the English Channel the day before his 24th birthday.

Bill's brother, David, also joined the RCAF, was stationed in England, but never saw active duty as Bill had done. David was always a bit upset about not participating in the same way as Bill. David died in Calgary in 1999. Bill was awarded the Distinguished Flying Cross in 1943. It was awarded to his wife, Joyce, posthumously at an investiture ceremony in the Manitoba Legislative Building on March 20, 1944.

William Anderson Lake (64 F/2), east of Wells Lake was named after him in 1994.

Andre, Lieutenant **John** of Winnipeg. Royal Canadian Artillery. He died 18 February 1943 at the age of 30 and is commemorated at Brookwood Military Cemetery in Surrey, England. He was the son of Nate and Sara Andre and was survived by his aunt Mrs. E. L. Casey of Minneapolis, Minnesota. ***Andre Lake*** (64 K/13), northeast of Reindeer Lake was named after him in 1972.

Andres, Trooper **David** of Winnipegosis (B 144317). Sherbrooke Fusiliers. He died 13 August 1944 at the age of 24 and is commemorated at Bretteville-sur-Laize Canadian War Cemetery in Calvados, France. He was the son of John and Mary Andres and was survived by his wife Fern A. Andres (née Delaney) of St. Catharines, Ontario. ***Andres Lake*** (64 N/9), west of Turner Lake was named after him in 1995.

Andrew, Bombardier **Alfred E.** of Glencairn (H 59628). Royal Canadian Artillery. He died 16 October 1944 at the age of 27 and is commemorated at Bergen-op-Zoom Canadian War Cemetery in Holland. He was the eldest of the seven children of Edwin A. and Blanche Andrew. His sister recalls (23 January 1997):

His schooling was at a one-room schoolhouse which continued in Parry, Saskatchewan where the family moved in 1925. Due to several years of drought, the family moved back to Manitoba in 1932 and settled in the Glencairn district. The move to Manitoba was made in two horse-drawn wagons driven by Alf and his father while his younger brother Wilf herded the cattle behind on horseback. In 1933 he set out to find work which included riding boxcars to the west coast looking for employment. He returned to Manitoba and worked cutting cord wood and for farmers which earned him five dollars a month. Coming from a musical family, Alf played the violin and along with other members of his family, could often be found providing the music for house parties and local school functions. In 1940, Alf volunteered to join the Royal Canadian Artillery.

His sisters and brother add (17 October 2001):

Alfred was born August 28th, 1917 on a homestead at Agardsley, Manitoba. In 1940, he took six weeks basic training and in 1941 joined the Armed Forces. He had one weekend at home and in March, 1941, left for overseas. Known as "Big Andy" by his comrades and Sergeant, he liked the army life and planned on making it his career at war's end.

Andrew River (64 O/16), which flows east into Baralzon Lake was named after him in 1987.

Andrews, Flying Officer **Edward J.** of Winnipeg (J 20403). No. 420 Squadron. He died 28 May 1944 at the age of 21 and is commemorated at Heverlee War Cemetery, Leuven, Vlaams-Brabant, Belgium. ***Andrews Lake*** (53 M/7), north of Knee Lake was named after him in 1995.

Andrews, Pilot Officer **James W.** of Blackdale (J 18204). No. 35 Squadron. He died 22 June 1943 at the age of 23 and is commemorated at the Runnymede Memorial in Surrey, England. He was the son of Thomas W. and Mary I. Andrews of Winnipeg. He had enlisted in 1940 while enrolled at the University of Manitoba. ***Andrews Island*** (63 I/10) in Walker Lake was named after him in 1988.

Andrews, Pilot Officer **John F.** of Transcona (41648). No. 144 Squadron, RAF. He died 13 June 1940 at the age of 24 and is commemorated at Harpswell (St. Chad) Churchyard in Lincolnshire, England. He was the son of Harold M. and Primrose Andrews of Vancouver. ***Andrews Bay*** (64 K/16) in Apeecheekamow Lake was named after him in 1995.

Andronyk, Lance Corporal **Stephen** of Roblin (H 1341). Argyle and Sutherland Highlanders. He died 9 August 1944 and is commemorated at Beny-sur-Mer Canadian War Cemetery in Calvados, France. ***Andronyk Lake*** (63 I/9), southeast of Walker Lake was named after him in 1982.

Angus, Flying Officer **Allan B.** of McCreary (40281). No. 85 Squadron, RAF, Distinguished Flying Cross. He enlisted in August, 1937 and was shot down 16 May 1940. He was 22 years of age and is commemorated at Fretin Communal Cemetery, Nord, France. He was the son of Benjamin and Daisy Angus and was survived by his wife Catherine J. Angus of Kennington, Kent and their young daughter. According to his brother (8 February 1988):

Alan … moved with his parents to McCreary [in 1919]. He took his schooling at Rosamond School in McCreary, following which he clerked in Kliman's General Store for several months. Allan always had a strong desire to become a pilot and I recall when the government was doing an aerial survey of Clear Lake in the Riding Mountains they landed their plane each evening on a farm just out of McCreary and my brother would go out to the plane every day after school and the pilots (Shields and Walker) encouraged his interest.

Due to the depression in 1936, my parents were unable to afford the fees for pilot training so Allan wrote to the Royal Air Force in England and they replied he would have to apply in person and pass an examination. On his 18th birthday, Allan got a ride into Winnipeg with a salesman and secured transportation to Montreal accompanying a load of cattle. This transportation was arranged by the veterinarian in McCreary who also gave Allan a letter of introduction to a veterinarian in Montreal who, in turn, obtained passage on a grain boat to England at a cost of $25.00. Upon arrival in England, he was advised by the Royal Air Force that examinations and enrolment were only considered in the fall. Meantime, Allan secured work with Rolls Royce Motors and in the fall made application with the Royal Air Force and was accepted. He enrolled for a three year term. It was his plan to obtain his pilot's license and return to Canada and become a commercial pilot. However, by the end of the three year term, Allan had become a Flying Officer, married an English girl and had a daughter. In 1938 he decided to continue with the Royal Air Force for another three year period.

The *Winnipeg Free Press* offered this retrospective in 1970:

On May 10, 1940, German Forces opened an offensive against Holland, Belgium and France. Within six weeks these three countries had been over-run and the British Expeditionary Force, an army of more than 350,000 men, had been driven from the continent, though it had escaped capture through the Dunkirk evacuation which lasted from May 27 to June 4.

A little-known fact is that in those six weeks of heroic disasters, more than 125 Canadians saw action, though no units of this country's armed forces had as yet been committed to battle. They were the pioneers of Canada's wartime effort, for they had enlisted in the Royal Air Force by the hundreds in the immediate pre-war years. When the war broke out there were more Canadian pilots in the RAF than in the RCAF.

The definition of an "ace" is any pilot who destroys five or more enemy aircraft. The first two Canadian aces of the war were Manitobans flying in France – Flying Officer Allan B. Angus of McCreary and Flight Lieutenant Mark H. "Hilly" Brown [see entry] of Portage la Prairie.

Flying Officer Angus had a short, spectacular career with No. 85 Squadron, [a] Hurricane unit attached to the British Expeditionary Force. He shot down his first enemy machine, a JU.88 bomber, over Armentieres early in the morning of May 10, 1940. On this occasion the German gunner put several bullets into his oil system and Angus had to crash-land in a wood. On May 14 he shot down two HE111 bombers. Two days later, however, he and another pilot ran into a force of 75 German aircraft. In a savage dogfight, Angus managed to destroy two enemy bombers, but he himself was shot down and killed (Halliday 1970).

Angus Island (64 J/14) in Bain Lake was named after him in 1989.

Angus, Private **Benjamin N.** of Angusville (H 75191). Queen's Own Cameron Highlanders. He died 24 July 1944 at the age of 30 and is commemorated at Bretteville-sur-Laize Canadian War Cemetery in Calvados, France. He was the son of William J. and Martha E. Angus of Angusville. ***Angus Lake*** (62 N/15), southeast of Swan River was named after him in 1973.

Antoniak, Private **Frank E.** of Volga (B 83672). Royal Canadian Army Supply Corps. He died 27 July 1944 at the age of 29 and is commemorated at Beny-sur-Mer Canadian War Cemetery in Calvados, France. He was the son of Fred and Mary Antoniak of Volga, Manitoba. ***Antoniak Lake*** (64 O/6), south of Corbett Lake was named after him in 1995.

Antonyszyn, Gunner **Elie** of Rorketon (H 614971). Royal Canadian Artillery. He died 15 July 1945 at the age of 22 and is commemorated at the Holten Canadian War Cemetery in Holland. He was the son of Michael and Lena Antonyszyn of Rorketon. ***Antonyszyn Lake*** (64 P/1), southeast of Nejanilini Lake was named after him in 1974.

Arbour, Company Sergeant Major (Warrant Officer 2) **Abram** of Winnipeg (H 19489). Queen's Own Cameron Highlanders, Military Cross.

During the night 7th - 8th August, 1944, the QOCH of Canada attacked and captured the town of Fontenay de Marmion. On consolidation, "B" Company was allotted the defence of the northern section of the town in the vicinity of Battalion Headquarters. During the early hours of the morning on August 8th, the enemy shelled and mortared the town very heavily. The Company Commander was wounded and CSM Arbour immediately took over command of the Company and completed reorganization of the defensive position.

At approximately 0800 hours, an enemy counter attack in some strength moved against "B" Company's position. This attack was pinned down by small arms fire and CSM Arbour personally formed and led a counter attack force to mop up the enemy with utter disregard for personal danger and with absolute confidence he formed a complete force of Company Headquarters and No. 10 Platoon and under covering fire from No. 11 and 12 Platoons assaulted and killed or captured the enemy force which threatened his Company's position. CSM Arbour, by his speed in handling a difficult position and superb courage, was directly responsible for the Battalion holding and consolidating its objective (MC Citation 1944).

Born in Bender Hamlet near Narcisse, this veteran of Dieppe died 23 August 1944 at the age of 25 and is commemorated at Bretteville-sur-Laize Canadian War Cemetery in Calvados, France. He was the son of Nathan and Etta Arbour and was survived by his wife Clarice M. Arbour (née Horton) of Newhaven, Sussex, England and their daughter. ***Arbour Lake*** (64 C/15), east of Reindeer Lake was named after him in 1949 and four decades later, his daughter brought her children to Manitoba from their home in Texas to visit the lake named after her father.

Archer, Leading Seaman **Arthur E.** of Winnipeg (2560). HMCS *Fraser*. The *Fraser* was lost in a collision with the British cruiser HMS *Calcutta* during the evacuation of France in 1940. Leading Seaman Archer died 25 June 1940 at the age of 31 and is commemorated at the Halifax Memorial. He was the son of George and Sarah Ann Archer of Winnipeg and was survived by his wife Neva G. Archer of Vancouver and their two children. His daughter writes (28 November 2001):

My dad was a loving husband and father to his wife Neva and his two children Norma (six years) and Art (two years). We moved to Halifax from Victoria so as to be nearer to him when he came home on leave. It wasn't easy for my mom to move to a strange city during war time with two little ones, but this showed their love for each other. I treasure a birthday card my dad sent me on my third birthday while away at sea. The Navy was my dad's life. He and his brother Fred served several years in peace time so were well trained when the war broke out. My uncle Fred survived the war. The one thing I regret is not knowing where his body lies, although the sea would have most likely been his choice. Dad's mom and he never knew of each other's death as there was only a day in between. Besides his brother Fred, he left to mourn his father and many sisters and brothers. Most of them lived in Winnipeg at this time.

Archer Creek (64 I/7), which flows north into North Knife River was named after him in 1957.

Argo, Sergeant **William** of Rapid City (R 106448). No. 23 Operational Training Unit, RCAF. He died 29 January 1943 at the age of 20 and is commemorated at Honington (All Saints) Churchyard in Suffolk, England. He was the son of William and Isobel Argo of Rapid City. ***Argo Lake*** (64 O/15), east of Nueltin Lake was named after him in 1975.

Argue, Lance Corporal **Reginald G.** of Moore Dale (H 17103). Princess Patricia's Canadian Light Infantry. He died 23 May 1944 at the age of 24 and is commemorated at the Cassino War Cemetery in Italy. He was the son of Robert H. and Ethel M. Argue of Brandon. ***Argue Lake*** (52 E/14), southeast of Lac du Bonnet was named after him in 1974.

Arksey, Pilot Officer **Walter L.** of Langruth (J 89952). No. 460 Squadron. He died 11 June 1944 only two days after he received his commission. He was 21 years of age and is commemorated at Viroflay New Communal Cemetery, Yvelines, France. His nephew and namesake Walter Arksey of Kanata, Ontario has visited the site. Pilot Officer Arksey was the third of the nine sons of John and Maude Arksey of Langruth. According to his brother (11 November 2001):

Walter Lynwood Arksey was born March 14, 1923. He enlisted in the Royal Canadian Air Force in the fall of 1942 and completed one year of training in Canada before leaving for overseas in the fall of 1943. A Pilot Officer with the 460 (RAAF) Squadron, he went into action in May, 1944 and was reported missing June 11 that year.

Walter's aunt Lucy (Lou) Senton of Winnipeg remembers seeing him off on the train on October 27, 1943. She says he was a kind-hearted young man with a good sense of humour, typical of the many bright young farm boys who saw the armed forces as a way out of life on the prairies during the depression. In a letter home written just weeks before his death, Walter spoke of the sights and people of England: "It really isn't too bad over here," he wrote, "but the sooner I can set foot on Canadian soil the better" (n.d.).

Arksey Lake (64 P/15), northeast of Nejanilini Lake was named after him in 1974.

Armitage, Gunner **George Archibald** of Elva (H 92484). Royal Canadian Artillery. He died 2 June 1943 at the age of 35 and is commemorated at Melita Cemetery, Manitoba. He was the son of William and Alma I. Armitage of Elva. ***Armitage Lake*** (54 D/15), northeast of Myre Lake was named after him in 1996.

Armstrong, Sergeant **Arthur Ronald** of Brandon (R 291562). No. 1659 Conversion Unit, RCAF. He died 17 May 1945 at the age of 20 and is commemorated at the Runnymede Memorial in Surrey, England. According to his sister (8 November 1985):

My brother ... died in a plane crash over Fife, Scotland in May, 1945 and his and the rest of the crew's bodies (except three of the tail crew) were never recovered. As it happened right after VE-Day, my Mom and Dad felt their only son would be coming home. Mom never got over the shock and wouldn't talk about Ron after that.

Armstrong Island (64 F/3) in Vandekerckhove Lake was named after him in 1988.

Armstrong, Private **George** of Winnipeg (H 6239). Winnipeg Grenadiers. He died a prisoner of war 5 October 1942 at the age of 54 and is commemorated at the Sai Wan War Cemetery in Hong Kong. He was the son of Creighton and Elizabeth G. Armstrong of Fivemiletown, Northern Ireland. ***Armstrong Rapids*** (64 P/10) in Cameron River was named after him in 1995.

Armstrong, Flight Sergeant **George P.** of Portage la Prairie (R 157239). No. 142 Squadron. He died 25 November 1943 at the age of 19 and is commemorated at Florence War Cemetery, Italy. He was the only son of Dr. George P. (MC, ED, MD, FACS) and Ulieta M. Armstrong of Portage la Prairie. ***George Armstrong Lake*** (53 K/14), west of Edmund Lake was named after him in 1995.

Armstrong, Flying Officer **John K.** of Boissevain (J 28574). No. 433 Squadron. He died 29 July 1944 at the age of 24 and is commemorated at the Kiel War Cemetery in Germany. He was the second of the six children of Roy H. and Myrtle L. Armstrong of Boissevain. He had completed Grade 12 at Boissevain Collegiate and was enrolled in the Faculty of Agriculture at the University of Manitoba when he enlisted. His younger sister recalls (26 November 2001):

He was someone we looked up to as he helped his father on the farm and I remember him and his brother Laverne both away at the war. It was a strange day when my parents heard of him "missing in action." The next day, my other brother (two years younger than John) was also reported missing. Fortunately, Laverne was rescued in Burma, so you can see we knew what war was, even as young people.

Armstrong Esker (64 N/11), north of Kasmere Lake was named after Flying Officer Armstrong in 1989.

Armstrong, Flying Officer **Oswald W.** of Rossburn (J 40427). No. 44 Squadron. He was shot down over Germany 3 February 1945 at the age of 22 and is commemorated at Durnbach War Cemetery in Bavaria, Germany. He was the third of the seven children of Walter and Mabel Armstrong (née Fisher) of Rossburn. His brother recalls (6 December 2001):

Oswald attended elementary schools at Ekford and Perth, Manitoba – schools no longer in existence. He graduated from Grade 12 in 1939, writing his final exams on Friday and going to work in the Rossburn Branch of the Bank of Toronto on Monday. He remained in their employ until his enlistment in the RCAF in 1942. He took navigator training at No. 7 Air Observer School in Portage la Prairie, going overseas in January, 1943. Oswald arrived in England in February, 1943, approximately the same day I arrived in Algiers. He attempted to see me in Devon where I was stationed on his first leave. Since I was already out of the country, we never did meet in uniform.

His sister adds (19 January 1995):

From the many letters we received from my brother, we gathered he was very lonely, like so many other young people who had never dreamed that they would ever be so far away from home. He travelled to Scotland to discover his roots and when he bought a bike, he explored his neighbourhood.

He flew quite a few missions over Germany and on the night of February 2/3, his plane was shot down. No word was received of Oswald's whereabouts until some time in 1946 when four of the seven crew members' bodies were discovered in a cemetery near Karlsruhe.

And again (6 December 2001):

I was close to him as a quiet, but determined, gentle person with many friends. His bank manager spoke glowingly of his work - both as to his accuracy and devotion to job and relations with their customers. Oswald was a constant reader and a loyal friend, a skier, hockey player, member of the United Church and an active correspondent, writing home weekly.

His last latter home was addressed to his sister and was dated 2 February 1945, the day before he went missing. He told her that he had sore knees but would not report sick because he wanted to be home in time for her graduation from St. Boniface Hospital. His sister adds (19 January 1995):

I was home on holidays (from Nurse's training at St. Boniface Hospital) just after VE-Day and witnessed my parents and all our family having a trying time. Each Prisoner of War Camp liberated raised our hopes that Oswald would be located and then have our hopes dashed.

Armstrong Hill (64 I/12), east of Tadoule Lake was named after him in 1995.

Armstrong, Pilot Officer **Robert H.** of Winnipeg (J 92624). No. 625 Squadron. He died 23 October 1944 at the age of 21 and is commemorated at Harrogate (Stonefall) Cemetery in Yorkshire, England. He was the son of Robert W. and Elizabeth Armstrong of Winnipeg. ***Armstrong Bay*** (64 B/13), in the west end of Southern Indian Lake was named after him in 1979.

Armstrong, Leading Aircraftman **Ross A.** "Sandy" of Winnipeg (R 59102). No. 1 Service Flying Training School. He died 30 October 1940 at the age of 25 and is commemorated at Elmwood Cemetery in Winnipeg. He was the ninth son of William S. and Carlotta J. Armstrong of Winnipeg. He volunteered immediately after Britain declared war, "hoping to compensate for the sacrifice his oldest brother endured with the loss of a leg at age 15 during World War I." According to his sister (14 April 1998):

Sandy's school years were spent at Riverview and Lord Roberts elementary schools and Kelvin High School. He was an all-round sports enthusiast whose *forte* was track and field. His inter-high school record in the half-mile stood for many years and he was chosen to participate in Hamilton, Ontario prior to the schoolboy games in Australia. Sandy loved soccer and hockey and was an ardent curler at Fort Rouge Curling Club from 1929 - 1933, once winning the Junior Championship during that period. They were presented with the Calhoun Trophy and also, to their amusement, with a "Calhoun" fedora. He also loved horse racing, not so much to wager as to just watch the horses run.

Sandy found work at the Hudson's Bay Company driving and delivering. Then he was accepted as an apprentice electrician at City Hydro. Before volunteering for the RCAF in 1939, one of his last jobs was on a crew laying landing lights at Stevenson Field, later integrated into Winnipeg Airport. Sandy was sent to Manning Pool in early 1940, then back to Winnipeg where he and seven other young men began training on what was familiar ground to Sandy – Stevenson Field. After preliminary training he was assigned to Camp Borden. In the evening of October 30, 1940, Sandy was flying solo during a violent storm when his aircraft went down. He was to have received his wings the following day.

Sandy was returned to Winnipeg by the Padre of Camp Borden and two of his brothers. He was interred in the Armstrong family plot in Elmwood Cemetery. He was the first casualty of many among the young men who volunteered from the Fort Rouge area of Winnipeg. Tragically, all of those who trained at Stevenson Field perished within one year. Sandy, the youngest son, and the last one home with his mother was cherished by his family and hosts of friends.

Armstrong Point (64 J/12) in Descôteaux Lake was named after him in 1995.

Arnason, Corporal **Olafur B.** of Winnipegosis (L 1141). Saskatoon Light Infantry. He died 15 December 1943 at the age of 25 and is commemorated at the Moro River Canadian War Cemetery in Italy. He was the son of Kris and Mary Arnason and was survived by his wife Frances J. Arnason of Vancouver. ***Arnason Lake*** (64 F/2), southeast of Wells Lake was named after him in 1994.

Arnold, Flying Officer **William B.** of Winnipeg (J 27477). No. 357 Squadron. He died 20 May 1945 at the age of 32 and is commemorated at the Sai Wan War Cemetery in Hong Kong. He was the son of Florent G. and Edna G. Arnold of Kingston, Ontario and was survived by his wife Catherine M. Arnold of Kingston, Ontario. ***Arnold Island*** (63 I/7) in Molson Lake was named after him in 1995.

Arnold, Pilot Officer **William H.** of Winnipeg (J 4708). No. 10 Operational Training Unit, RCAF. He died 27 July 1941 at the age of 21 and is commemorated at Brookwood Military Cemetery in Surrey, England. He was the son of William E. and Alice M. Arnold of Winnipeg. ***Arnold Bay*** (64 B/16) in Chapman Lake was named after him in 1995.

Arthur, Able Seaman **Charles H.** of Winnipeg (V 24520). HMCS *Stadacona*. He died 1 October 1943 at the age of 39 and is commemorated at Brookside Cemetery in Winnipeg. He was survived by his wife Leona Arthur of Winnipeg. ***Arthur Lake*** (64 K/1), east of Chartrand Lake was named after him in 1997.

Arthurs, Pilot Officer **John W.** of Sifton (J 6148). No. 62 Squadron. He was reported missing over Burma during a reconnaissance tour 29 April 1942. He was 22 years of age and is commemorated at the Singapore Memorial. He was the son of William F. and Olga V. Arthurs of Sifton. This student of Brandon and Wesley colleges enlisted in 1940, hoping to continue his education upon his return. ***Arthurs Lake*** (63 K/13), northeast of Embury Lake was named after him in 1988.

Ash, Private **William Kenneth** (A 109161). Essex Scottish Regiment. He died 19 February 1945 at the age of 27 and is commemorated at Groesbeek Canadian War Cemetery in Holland. He was the son of Edward J. and Alice A. Ash (née May). His sister recalls (7 November 2001):

> In the early years, his parents farmed in Saskatchewan and Alberta. He was born in Percival, Saskatchewan and moved to Winnipeg in 1926 and would have been nine years old. They lived in central Winnipeg and he liked fishing and baseball and was a lot of fun. There were five boys and two girls in the family. He was the youngest boy.
>
> He enlisted in Winnipeg and had two older brothers in the Forces, Leo Edmund and Walter Raymond, both Engineers and at one point in the war they were coming from Italy to Holland and just missed their brother Ken by a couple of weeks. Had they met up with him, he may have survived the war.

In a letter from Holland to his sister he wrote:

> Dear Ruth: I have received two letters from you, but I haven't had [time] to answer them for we have moved to a place and were told that we would be here for some time. No fighting or even looking for a Jerry, so I got to work and made me a home. It took me a week to do the most important part of it, but I have the best place of them all now, and most comfortable too. The first day there was only myself and another fellow in it. Now there is five of us. If I had of made it bigger, there would be more in it, but the more the merrier. At least I can sit down and write a letter in comfort. That's more than a lot of them can do.
>
> I'm glad to hear you're feeling good and I hope it is all over by the time you get this letter, that you are back home in the best of health. It better be a girl too, and give her a good name, one like her mother. But you more than likely had it named six months ago, boy or girl.
>
> Well I'm not going to say much more tonight for I have a lot of letters to write. This is the first letter that I have wrote in two weeks. Some of the letters that I have to answer are a month old. So I will close for now. Wish the best of luck to you. Yours truly, Ken (30 January 1945).

His last letter was written only eight days before his death:

> Dear Ruth: I received the telegram today, but I'm not showing [illegible]. But nevertheless, I'm glad to hear all's well. And I'm hoping that you will be home by the time this letter gets there and feeling fine. I don't mean that you should rush things. Do what is best for you, even if it does take a little longer.
>
> We are doing good over here. Sometimes we have a tough break. Other times we get it easy. Not too bad. You will be reading some big news shortly. I hope that it will be better than I think it will. But I give Jerry a short time, then it will be all over. So until later, I will close for now. Yours truly, Ken (11 February 1945).

Ash Lake (53 M/11), southwest of Ransom Lake was named after him in 1996.

Asham, Private **Gilbert G.** of Crane River (H 204651). Calgary Highlanders. He died 7 September 1944 at the age of 26 and is commemorated at the Calais Canadian War Cemetery in France. He was the son of John and Ida Asham of Crane River, Manitoba. ***Asham Lake*** (64 H/6), northeast of Northern Indian Lake was named after him in 1995.

Ashbery, Warrant Officer 2 **Hedley W. H.** of Winnipeg (C 97656). Canadian Postal Corps. He died 8 February 1946 at the age of 35 and is commemorated at Beechwood Cemetery in Ottawa. He was survived by his brother Ernest J. H. Ashbery of Basingstoke, England. ***Ashbery Lake*** (64 N/6), southwest of Nueltin Lake was named after him in 1972.

Ashley, Able Seaman **Robert P.** of Winnipeg (V 9615). HMCS *Ottawa*. The *Ottawa* was escorting Convoy ON.127 in the North Atlantic when it was struck by two torpedoes from U-91; 114 of her ship's company were lost. Able Seaman Ashley died 13 September 1942 at the age of 21 and is commemorated at the Halifax Memorial. He was survived by his sister Molly Ashley of Winnipeg. ***Ashley Lake*** (64 I/4), west of North Knife Lake was named after him in 1957.

Ashley-Pryce, Private **John** of Virden (L 27026). Royal Canadian Army Service Corps. He died 22 July 1943 and is commemorated at Agira Canadian War Cemetery, Sicily. ***Ashley-Pryce Lake*** (64 I/3), west of North Knife Lake was named after him in 1974.

Ashmall, Telegraphist **Royden G.** of Winnipeg (V 24241). HMCS *Racoon*. The *Racoon* was torpedoed and sunk by U-165 while escorting Convoy QS.33 in the St. Lawrence River; there were no survivors. Telegraphist Ashmall died 7 September 1942 at the age of 25 and is commemorated at the Halifax Memorial. He was the only son of George J. and Eliza Ashmall of Winnipeg. According to a childhood friend (4 May 1995):

> Royden was born … in Coventry, England. He came to Canada with his parents … when he was six years old. They settled in Winnipeg. Royden had a paper route on Wellington Crescent. He then worked as a "soda jerk" at Snell's Drugstore on Academy Road. From Snell's, he went to Gutta-Percha Rubber and like many during the Depression, worked many hours of overtime with no pay and had to fight to get supper money. After promising his mother he would *not* enlist, he applied to the army and air force and was turned down because of a childhood accident to his leg. He was then accepted by the Royal Canadian Navy Volunteer Reserve. I first met Royden in 1937 and my eldest son is named after him.

Ashmall Point (63 B/10), on the west shore of Lake Winnipeg was named after him in 1970.

Ashton, Pilot Officer **John B.** of Winnipeg (42552). No. 607 Squadron, RAF. He enlisted in June, 1939 and died 17 July 1940, early in the Battle of Britain. He was 26 years of age and is commemorated at Hawarden (St. Deiniol) Churchyard in Flintshire, Wales. He was the son of Harry W. and Frances W. Ashton of East Kildonan. ***Ashton Lake*** (64 N/16), north of Nahili Lake was named after him in 1995.

Askew, Flight Sergeant **George W.** of Cartwright (R 134348). No. 419 Squadron. He died 26 July 1943 at the age of 22 and is commemorated at the Reichswald Forest War Cemetery in Germany. He was the son of William R. E. and Josephine Askew of Cartwright and the brother of Flight Sergeant John R. Askew (next entry). ***Askew Lake*** (64 I/7), northeast of North Knife Lake was named after him in 1974.

Askew, Flight Sergeant **John R.** of Cartwright (R 134417). No. 1659 Conversion Unit, RCAF. He died 28 January 1943 at the age of 23 and is commemorated at Ripon Cemetery in Yorkshire, England. He was the son of William R. E. and Josephine Askew of Cartwright and the brother of Flight Sergeant George W. Askew (previous entry). ***Askew Island*** (53 L/8) in Webber Lake was named after him in 1995.

Askey, Pilot Officer **Michael W.** of Winnipeg (J 19049). No. 92 Squadron. He died 28 October 1943 at the age of 21 and is commemorated at the Alamein Memorial in Egypt. A newspaper article six months before his death indicated that:

> Sergeant Michael Askey, RCAF, born in Saskatoon and son of the Reverend William Askey, former rector of Christ Church, now a chaplain overseas is credited with shooting down three enemy aircraft in one day, April 20 over Tunisia. Sergeant Askey, 20 years old, left Saskatoon when a small boy and received his education in Winnipeg where his father went to become rector of All Saints Church. Mr. Askey was also a chaplain in the First Great War. His son was an insurance statistician before joining up, and volunteered for service in Tunisia last December.
>
> As the young RCAF fighter pilot's score became known, news [was] received that two other Canadians were credited with two enemy planes destroyed and one probably destroyed in earlier air battles. Askey got the first triple off Cape Bon, a Macchi-202. He fired one burst, then saw the plane crash on a beach. That kill came in the morning. In the afternoon he attacked two Macchis off Pantelleria Island. The pilot of the first plane bailed out when Askey's bullets sprayed the cockpit and as the second turned for an attack, Askey scored hits on the enemy's wing and cockpit and saw the machine dive into the sea. "I don't think the first pilot's chute opened," said Askey. "I never saw him after he jumped." The kills brought Askey's score to four. His first victim was a Messerschmitt-109 last month (*Star Phoenix* 27 April 1943).

Askey Lake (64 O/10), southeast of Nueltin Lake was named after him in 1961.

Aspholm, Signalman **Rueben L.** of Flin Flon (H 38928). Royal Canadian Corps of Signals. He died 13 February 1945 at the age of 23 and is commemorated at Brookwood Military Cemetery in Surrey, England. He was the son of Albert and Esther Aspholm and was survived by his wife Dorothy V. Aspholm of Elmwood. ***Aspholm Lake*** (53 M/5), south of Hackland Lake was named after him in 1996.

Astbury, Flying Officer **John W. "Jack"** of Portage la Prairie (J 21524). No. 405 Squadron. He died 14 January 1944 at the age of 21 and is commemorated at the Hanover War Cemetery in Germany. He was the only child of Alderman Charles B. and Catherine Astbury of Portage la Prairie. His was the first Canadian built Lancaster which was dubbed the "Ruhr Express." ***Astbury Lake*** (52 E/14), southeast of Lac du Bonnet was named after him in 1974.

Astle, Lieutenant **Sidney W.** of Winnipeg. Lord Strathcona's Horse. He died 6 September 1943 at the age of 28 and is commemorated at Brookside Cemetery in Winnipeg. He was survived by his wife Elizabeth Astle of Barrie, Ontario. ***Astle Lake*** (64 K/12), northeast of Reindeer Lake was named after him in 1972.

Atchison, Pilot Officer **John M.** of Brandon (J 95411). No. 424 Squadron. He died 5 March 1945 at the age of 23 and is commemorated at the Berlin 1939 - 1945 War Cemetery in Brandenburg, Germany. ***Atchison Lake*** (64 O/13), east of Nueltin Lake was named after him in 1975.

Atkins, Flight Sergeant **Milton W.** of Winnipeg (R 101589). No. 207 Squadron. He died 11 August 1942 at the age of 22 and is commemorated at the Runnymede Memorial in Surrey, England. He was the son of Ernest J. and May P. Atkins of St. James. ***Atkins Lake*** (63 J/13), east of Wekusko Lake was named after him in 1972.

Atkinson, Sergeant **Albert E.** of Minnedosa (R 134035). No. 429 Squadron. He died 14 May 1943 at the age of 19 and is commemorated at Rheinberg War Cemetery in Germany. He was the son of John and Hazel H. Atkinson of Wellington, British Columbia. His younger sister recalls (29 November 1996):

> As a teenager I remember going with him (I was 6 - 8) while he practised archery on the local rabbits. He got parts for the bow and arrow in a kit and made them himself. He also had a .22 rifle and shot crows and rabbits under a bounty plan to make some money. He sang bass in the church choir and played bass horn in the town band. He was very popular at school and was good at sports.
>
> Before he joined the air force, he was learning to run the projector at the local movie theatre. One night the film caught fire; he held the projector room door shut until all the patrons were out causing him to have singed eyebrows and hair. One member of his aircrew was a prisoner of war and after the war came to visit my mother. He said Al stayed in the plane until everyone else was out.

Atkinson Bay (64 P/1) in Nykolaishen Lake was named after him in 1995.

Atkinson, Flying Officer **Merle W.** of Hartney (J 8359). No. 76 Squadron. He died 1 October 1942 at the age of 20 and is commemorated at the Kiel War Cemetery in Germany. He was the son of John B. and Elizabeth J. Atkinson of Hartney, Manitoba. On one of his first combat missions, he was ordered to bail out, thus becoming a member of the "Caterpillar Club" – those who's lives had been saved by the use of a Caterpillar Parachute. His sister recalls (10 April 1995):

> He was educated at Melgund rural school and Hartney High School. He enjoyed playing softball and was a catcher for his Air Force buddies' team while training in Regina in 1941. He was also an avid NHL fan of Foster Hewitt's Hockey Night in Canada. He regularly kept the stats for all six National Hockey League teams, but the Toronto Maple Leafs were his favourites. Even after being stationed in England, he wanted us to send him the hockey stats.

He kept a diary of his thoughts after his first few flights. One entry written after one of his first combat flights reads "Now I know what it is like to be really scared." ***Merle Atkinson Island*** (64 N/16) in Nueltin Lake was named after him in 1995.

Atkinson, Lance Corporal **Ronald E.** of West Kildonan (H 6905). Winnipeg Grenadiers, Military Medal. He died 8 October 1943 at the age of 32 and is commemorated at the Sai Wan War Cemetery in Hong Kong. He was one of the four children of William H. and Eva G. Atkinson (née Ingrain) and was survived by his wife Dolores M. Atkinson (née Perch) of Winnipeg and their three children. His son writes (October 16, 2001):

Lance Corporal Atkinson was born December 23, 1911 in Selkirk, Manitoba. He played defence with the Selkirk Rambler Hockey Club, champions of the Selkirk and District Hockey League 1929-30.

There are a few letters to his wife and children, written from the prison camp in Hong Kong in which he maintained that things were going well and looked forward to the war ending and returning home. His last letter was to Mr. Ralph Cappell, a member of the Home Guard in Hong Kong, asking Ralph to write to his wife and leaving his possessions to Ralph. Mrs. Delores Atkinson eventually married Ralph Cappell in Hong Kong and resided there for many years.

The *Globe and Mail* (Wood 1991) reported that:

Harold Atkinson and his older brother Ronald said good-bye to their family in Winnipeg ... and climbed aboard a train heading west. They had no idea where they were going. Several recruits fled the train. About 40 tried to mutiny on the Vancouver docks.

On October 27, almost the entire contingent left Canada, still unaware of its destination. They stopped in Pearl Harbor to refuel. Many of the soldiers' first and only rifle practice involved shooting at gasoline cans tossed from the fantail of the converted troopship, *Awatea*. The number of rounds fired in practice by members of the Royal Rifles averaged just 35. When they arrived in Hong Kong on November 16, 30 per cent had never fired a single shot. Worse, the battalion's supply ship – carrying 212 vehicles – never reached Hong Kong island. The Canadians had no trucks, no motorcycles and virtually no artillery.

After the fall of Hong Kong, Lance Corporal Atkinson was taken prisoner of war. ***Ronald Atkinson Lake*** (64 H/12), north of Wood Lake was named after him in 1995.

Attridge, Private **James S.** of Flin Flon (L 51063). Royal Canadian Infantry Corps. He died 2 February 1942 at the age of 23 and is commemorated at the Regina Cemetery in Saskatchewan. He was the son of Mr. and Mrs. Sidney N. Attridge of Flin Flon. ***Attridge Lake*** (64 F/15), west of Big Sand Lake was named after him in 1961.

Attwood, Corporal **Walter G.** of Brooklands (H 37718). Royal Canadian Army Service Corps. He died 14 November 1942 at the age of 33 and is commemorated at Brookwood Military Cemetery in Surrey, England. He was the son of George and Ruth Attwood and was survived by his wife Frances W. B. Attwood of Pontiac, Michigan. ***Attwood Lake*** (64 N/16), west of Nueltin Lake was named after him in 1972.

Aubin, Flight Sergeant **J. G. Marcel** of Carman (R 152693). No. 156 Squadron. He died 22 September 1943 at the age of 25 and is commemorated at the Hanover War Cemetery in Germany. ***Aubin Lake*** (52 L/6), east of Lac du Bonnet was named after him in 1973.

The 12th Manitoba Dragoons crossing the Seine River in Staghound armoured cars 28 August 1944. Courtesy of the National Archives of Canada (PA-144143).

B

Badams, Private **Robert Fredrick.** of Winnipeg (H 10317). Lincoln and Welland Regiment. He died 21 April 1945 at the age of 27 and is commemorated at the Holten Canadian War Cemetery in Holland. He was the son of Henry P. and Victoria Badams of Winnipeg. He had been employed by Macleod's Limited at the time of his enlistment and their internal newsletter recalled his years of service there:

> The cause of freedom is well served when four brothers in one family respond to their county's call. This thought came readily to mind when word reached Macleod's Limited, Winnipeg office, that Fred Badams, for many years assistant shipper at Winnipeg, has been killed on active service. Fred's place as third in a family of four boys may somehow have influenced him to join the army, though his three brothers preferred service in the navy.
>
> First employed by the firm in 1932 as a temporary helper in the binder canvas factory, it was not until December, 1934 that Fred became a "regular." Office and warehouse associates alike admired the "calm, even tenor of his ways;" it seemed that Fred went out of his way to be courteous and obliging; he was a favourite of everyone.
>
> "Taps" sounded for Robert Fred Badams on April 21st last. There had been heavy fighting in Holland, but the fighting now was on German soil. During an attack, Fred was up in front with the signal corps. The job of laying wire had been completed when the enemy laid down a heavy screen of mortar fire. Fred was killed instantly. We who knew Fred well can say with certainty: "It is by men like these that Freedom stands" (*The Friendly Tiger* June 1945).

Badams Lake (64 K/13), northeast of Lac Brochet was named after him in 1972.

Badre, Aircraftman 2 **Michael J. M.** of Winnipeg (R 119530). Photographer, RCAF. He died 24 January 1942 at the age of 23 and is commemorated at Assumption Gardens in Winnipeg. He was the son of Philip and Najibeh Badre of Winnipeg. Prior to the war, he had been an accomplished writer, photographer and the editor of St. Mary's College newsletter in Brockville, Ontario. ***Badre Lake*** (63 K/16), northwest of Wekusko Lake was named after him in 1973.

Bagg, Flight Sergeant **Arthur J.** of The Pas (R 106054). No. 15 Squadron. He died 8 March 1943 at the age of 22 and is commemorated at Verdun-sur-Meuse (Faubourg Pave) French National Cemetery, Meuse, France. He was the son of Charles and Sarah G. Bagg of The Pas. His sister recalls (3 December 2001):

> Sergeant Arthur James Bagg enlisted in the RCAF in 1941 or 1942. It was probably 1941 as he visited some of his parents' relatives in England after arriving there. He was killed ... during a bombing raid, presumably over Germany. He had told us in one of his letters that his aircraft was connected to the "Bay Line" which we took to mean a Hudson bomber as the "Bay Line" was and still is the railway from The Pas to Churchill. He also mentioned Robin Hood at one time which we gathered meant Nottingham.
>
> In a letter [which arrived] after his death, he told me that our mother was feeling very sorry for her neighbour who had lost her son, Art's good chum. He told me to tell her that he didn't have a charmed life either. I don't believe I showed her that letter.
>
> After the war, my sister who had been in the Air Force (Women's Division) visited a chap in a Winnipeg hospital with TB. He had been a prisoner of war for over two years. He had been a member of the crew in which our brother had been tail gunner. He told her that Art had seen "something" coming and told them to "get the hell out," which they did. But he didn't. He was the only one who didn't. After the war our Mother received a ... Cross and a picture of his grave near Verdun.

Bagg Lake (64 N/16), west of Nueltin Lake was named after him in 1961.

Bailey, Gunner **Henry E.** of Winnipeg (H 67408). Royal Canadian Artillery. He died 5 July 1944 at the age of 23 and is commemorated at Beny-sur-Mer Canadian War Cemetery in Calvados, France. He was the son of Ernest L. and Maud E. Bailey of Winnipeg. ***Bailey Bay*** (64 B/9) in Uhlman Lake was named after him in 1995.

Bailey, Flight Sergeant **Martin** of Stockton (R 119568). No. 75 Squadron. He died 28 August 1943 at the age of 26 and is commemorated at Durnbach War Cemetery in Bavaria, Germany. He was the son of Reuben and Elizabeth Bailey of Stockton, Manitoba. After attending the University of Manitoba and obtaining his Teaching Certificate from the Normal School there, he taught Grades 1 to 8 in a one-room school near Wawanesa for four years. He enlisted in 1941 and was reported "missing presumed dead" on his third mission. ***Bailey Point*** (64 I/4) on the south shore of Ashley Lake was named after him in 1989.

Bailey, Able Seaman **Norris B.** of Pointe du Bois (V 31265). HMCS *St. Croix*. The *St. Croix* was torpedoed and sunk by U-305 south of Iceland while escorting Convoy ON.202. Five officers and 76 men were rescued by HMS *Itchen*, but only one of these survived the loss of the *Itchen* two days later. See VanSickle, Ordinary Seaman Harold A. for additional information. Able Seaman Bailey died 20 September 1943 at the age of 25 and is commemorated at the Halifax Memorial. He was survived by his mother Maria J. Taitinger of Claresholm, Alberta. ***Bailey Peninsula*** (53 M/5) in Utik Lake was named after him in 1996.

Bailey, Pilot Officer **Russell Norman** of Winnipeg (J 9880). No. 3 Personnel Reception Centre, RCAF. He died 6 June 1942 at the age of 23 and is commemorated at Bournemouth North Cemetery in Hampshire, England. He was the son of George and Lillian Bailey of Winnipeg. ***Bailey Island*** (64 F/3) in Goldsand Lake was named after him in 1988.

Bailie, Private **Thomas F.** of Winnipeg (H 103063). 48th Highlanders of Canada. He died 4 September 1944 at the age of 21 and is commemorated at Montecchio War Cemetery in Italy. He was the son of Thomas and Olive M. Bailie of Winnipeg. ***Bailie Lake*** (64 H/4), northeast of Gauer Lake was named after him in 1995.

Baillie, Flight Sergeant **John R.** of Winnipeg (R 74696). No. 405 Squadron. He died 9 September 1942 at the age of 20 and is commemorated at the Runnymede Memorial in Surrey, England. ***Baillie Peninsula*** (54 E/2) in Long Lake was named after him in 1995.

Bain, Lieutenant **Douglas M.** of Winnipeg (O 3670). Steamship *Empire Wave*. He died 1 October 1941 at the age of 29 and is commemorated at the Halifax Memorial. He was the son of Archibald D. and Lillie F. Bain of Winnipeg. ***Bain Lake*** (64 J/14), northwest of Tadoule Lake was named after him in 1957.

Bain, Corporal **Grigor E.** of Winnipeg (H 36944). Queen's Own Cameron Highlanders. He died 23 July 1944 at the age of 20 and is commemorated at the Bayeux War Cemetery in Calvados, France. He was the son of Major Grigor E. (ED) and Barbara D. J. A. Bain of Winnipeg. A native of Portage la Prairie, he had represented that city for many years at the Manitoba junior golf championships. ***Bain Bay*** (64 P/15) in Rankmore Lake was named after him in 1995.

Baird, Flight Sergeant **Gordon D. R.** of Shoal Lake (R 95331). No. 111 Squadron. He died 16 July 1942 at the age of 22 and is commemorated at the Ottawa Memorial. He was the brother of Warrant Officer Nelson Baird (see entry) and the son of James H. and Sarah A. Baird of Winnipeg. He was survived by his wife of nine months Mona Baird (née Dott) of Norwood. ***Baird Bay*** (64 C/8) in Granville Lake was named after him in 1995.

Baird, Flying Officer **Jack D.** of Winnipeg (J 44950). No. 6 Operational Training Unit, RCAF. He died 6 December 1944 at the age of 20 and is commemorated at Blacon Cemetery in Cheshire, England. He was the son of Samuel G. and Elsie K. Baird of Winnipeg. ***Baird Lake*** (64 O/8), southeast of Nueltin Lake was named after him in 1961.

Baird, Warrant Officer 2 **Nelson G.** of Shoal Lake (R 191011). No. 408 Squadron. He died 7 March 1945 at the age of 21 and is commemorated at the Kiel War Cemetery in Germany. He was the son of James H. and Sarah A. Baird of Winnipeg and the brother of Flight Sergeant Gordon Baird (see entry). Previously shot down over France, he had managed to bail out safely and return to England. At the time of his death, he was attempting to log as many missions as possible so that he could get a leave back to Winnipeg to marry his fiancée Peggy Warren. ***Baird Island*** (64 C/8) in Granville Lake was named after him in 1995.

Baker, Flying Officer **Henry D.** of Neepawa (J 15823). No. 418 Squadron. He died 9 April 1943 at the age of 24 and is commemorated at St. Andre-de-L'Eure Communal Cemetery, Eure, France. He was the son of George A. and Mary R. Baker of Neepawa and was survived by his wife Julia Baker.

> Henry was born March 5, 1919 in the Springhill district. He attended school there, completing his Grade 11 at the Neepawa Collegiate. In his last ten years at home, he participated in a Diesel Engineering correspondence course, completing his practical training at Chicago, Illinois. He also farmed in the area until he joined the Royal Canadian Air Force at Calgary in July, 1940. He trained in Toronto and Camp Borden, returning to Calgary to complete a Wireless Operator course. He graduated from the Bombing and Gunnery School at Macdonald in August, 1941. Henry received his Pilot Officer's commission in August, 1942. Henry served in Great Britain and over continental Europe. He married Julie Wilkinson from Surrey, England on March 23, 1943. She was serving in the MT Section of the Royal Air Force in England. Henry was flying on Boston aircraft No. 8325 during an intruder operation over the Melun/Bretigny area of France and was never heard from again (Pittman n.d.).

Baker Peninsula (64 P/2) on the north shore of Thuykay Lake was named after him in 1985.

Baker, Flying Officer **Herbert Allan** of Carman (J 25280). No. 12 Operational Training Unit, RCAF. He died 29 January 1944 at the age of 27 and is commemorated at Botley Cemetery in Oxfordshire, England. His sister visited the grave in 1968 and again in 1981. He was the seventh of the nine children of Mr. and Mrs. William Baker of Graysville. According to his sister (19 February 1996):

> Allan was very interested in farming, which he was doing with his aged father and brother seven years younger. All letters home inquired of his pigs, what was happening with the sheep, the colour of the new colt and to sell or fatten the bull.

In some of the many letters home from various parts of England and Scotland he wrote:

- The blackouts make it difficult to find your way in a strange place, with approximately the light of a match. It's certainly a black looking world at night when up in the air.
- Recently took a course on finding, flying and landing on a beam. It is certainly marvellous! You find an airport, come in and land without seeing ground, lights or anything else. Night flying here is a cinch, so many aids to navigation, almost impossible to lose yourself.
- A wonderful sight to see the big formations of bombers going and coming from their raids.
- Officers lack for nothing, however, in the ranks it could be different. Better food than at a restaurant. The food is really good and plentiful. Nice fresh vegetables and fruit which you can practically pick and eat. The bread is quite dark.
- Dinners are late, so not much time to take in a dance or show as transportation stops at 10:30 PM.

Baker Island (53 L/5) in Bolton Lake was named after him in 1995.

Baldock, Private **John L.** of Balmoral (H 103599). Seaforth Highlanders of Canada. He died 10 December 1943 at the age of 20 and is commemorated at the Moro River Canadian War Cemetery in Italy. He was the third of the 10 children of George P. and Lottie E. Baldock of Balmoral. ***Baldock Island*** (64 H/11) in Hibbert Lake was named after him in 1995.

Ballantyne, Trooper **Lochart** of East St. Paul (H 63987). Fort Garry Horse. He died 11 June 1944 at the age of 27 and is commemorated at Beny-sur-Mer Canadian War Cemetery in Calvados, France. He was the son of John and Eleanor Ballantyne and was survived by his wife Agnes Ballantyne of Ayr, Scotland. ***Ballantyne Lake*** (64 N/15), west of Nueltin Lake was named after him in 1972.

Baller, Lieutenant **Christopher F.** of Winnipeg. Royal Montreal Regiment. He died 5 July 1943 at the age of 36 and is commemorated at Brookwood Military Cemetery in Surrey, England. He was the son of Christopher J. and Mary E. Baller of Winnipeg. ***Baller Lake*** (53 F/13), southeast of Angling Lake was named after him in 1996.

Balloch, Flying Officer **James H.** of Winnipeg (J 23131). No. 427 Squadron. His aircraft was shot down over Düsseldorf on the return flight from a bombing raid over Kassel, Germany. He died 22 October 1943 at the age of 25 and is commemorated at the Runnymede Memorial in Surrey, England. He was the son of Mrs. Matthew Balloch of Vancouver. This native of Manchester, England immigrated to Canada with his family shortly after the First World War. ***Balloch Lake*** (63 K/16), west of Wekusko Lake was named after him in 1973.

Bambridge, Flight Sergeant **James H.** of Coulter (R 147187). No. 619 Squadron. He died 9 June 1943 at the age of 26 and is commemorated at the Runnymede Memorial in Surrey, England. He was the son of George H. J. and Alice B. Bambridge of Coulter, Manitoba. ***Bambridge Lake*** (64 O/7), southeast of Nueltin Lake was named after him in 1975.

Bangle, Lance Corporal **Clarence F.** of Walkerburn (H 17778). Princess Patricia's Canadian Light Infantry. He died 23 May 1944 at the age of 21 and is commemorated at the Cassino War Cemetery in Italy. He was the fourth of the 10 children of Rexford E. and Mary J. Bangle (née Laroque) of Walkerburn. His younger brother recalls that (10 May 1999):

> He was a typical farm boy enjoying animals, especially horses and playing with his siblings climbing trees, drowning gophers, looking for duck eggs etc. Clarence got his education in a one-room schoolhouse [at] Grand Narrows. For the most part, he walked the two and a half miles to school. His early teen years were spent helping his father on the farm or in a bush camp in winter. He was particularly close to his brother Leo, next in line on the family tree. Clarence and Leo enlisted in the Princess Patricia's Canadian Light Infantry. Shortly after his father's death in 1942, Clarence was sent overseas.

Bangle Lake (64 O/10), northwest of Nejanilini Lake was named after him in 1975.

Barakovich, Sapper **Stephen** of Woodridge (H 36456). Royal Canadian Engineers. He died 8 August 1944 at the age of 24 and is commemorated at Bretteville-sur-Laize Canadian War Cemetery in Calvados, France. He was the son of Joseph and Agatha Barakovich of Montreal. ***Barakovich Lake*** (64 N/2), southwest of Nueltin Lake was named after him in 1972.

Baraskewich, Lance Corporal **Mike** of Foxwarren (H 41707). Royal Winnipeg Rifles. He died 5 July 1944 at the age of 23 and is commemorated at Beny-sur-Mer Canadian War Cemetery in Calvados, France. He was the son of Wasyl and Eva Baraskewick (sp.) of Foxwarren. ***Baraskewich Lake*** (64 I/6), northwest of North Knife Lake was named after him in 1974.

Barbe, Flight Sergeant **Maurice J.** of Flin Flon (R 110597). No. 50 Squadron. He died 27 January 1943 at the age of 20 and is commemorated at Lincoln (Newport) Cemetery in Lincolnshire, England. ***Barbe Lake*** (63 K/6), south of Egg Lake was named after him in 1983.

Barber, Flying Officer **Herbert B.** of Carberry (J 5686). No. 83 Squadron. He died 26 July 1942 at the age of 24 and is commemorated at the Runnymede Memorial in Surrey, England. He was one of the two children of Boyd E. and Adelaide V. Barber (née Dingle), the stepson of Isabel MacKay and the husband of Margaret Barber (née Miller) of Toronto. His sister recalls (16 January 1998):

> Herb was raised by his paternal grandmother (who was the sister of M. K. Boyd, deputy during some years of a large Manitoba constituency to the Federal Parliament in Ottawa and sister also of W. J. Boyd, industrialist, who built one of the first "sky-scrapers" on Portage Avenue. It is still there and named now (I believe) the Boyd Medical Centre.
>
> Despite these more prosperous situations, our small family, which moved to Winnipeg when Herb was 10 years old with our father and step-mother (born Isabel MacKay of Kenton, Manitoba), suffered difficulties during the depression. But we both had the advantage of well-staffed, well-disciplined Winnipeg schools and High Schools (Daniel McIntyre).
>
> Herb completed first year at the University of Manitoba, then went alone to Toronto where he found employment with Ford, before enlisting in the Air Force (I think in 1940; I do not know the date). Prior to going overseas, he married Margaret Miller of Toronto (who much later married M. E. Gostlin of Blenheim, Ontario).
>
> We saw Herb for the last time at his departure; I was in Montreal at McGill University. Margaret accompanied him to Halifax. He had no time to return on leave; he was announced "missing" on July 15, 1942. He remained and still remains very present to those close to him.

Barber Island (53 E/13) in Stevenson Lake was named after him in 1995.

Barbour, Private **Victor** of Poplar Point (H 65062). Royal Canadian Army Service Corps. He died 20 October 1944 at the age of 25 and is commemorated at the Groesbeek Memorial in Holland. He was the son of Andrew and Anna Barbour of Poplar Point. ***Barbour Lake*** (52 E/14), southeast of Lac du Bonnet was named after him in 1974.

Barclay, Flying Officer **Arnold S.** of Tyndall (J 24738). No. 640 Operational Training Unit, RCAF. He died 20 February 1944 at the age of 21 and is commemorated at the Berlin 1939 - 1945 War Cemetery in Brandenburg, Germany. He was survived by a son, Ian. ***Barclay Lake*** (52 L/6), east of Lac du Bonnet was named after him in 1973.

Barclay, Flight Sergeant **Philip G.** of Winnipeg (R 80160). No. 22 Operational Training Unit, RCAF. He died 31 May 1942 at the age of 21 and is commemorated at Rheinberg War Cemetery in Germany. He was the only child of Philip G. and Mary H. Barclay of Winnipeg. ***Barclay Island*** (64 C/5) in Kamuchawie Lake was named after him in 1995.

Baril, Flight Sergeant **Joseph A.** Roger of St. Boniface (R 287567). No. 354 Squadron. He died 22 April 1945 at the age of 19 and is commemorated at the Singapore Memorial. He was the son of Joseph T. and Anna E. Baril (née Gendreau) of Norwood. According to his sister (21 July 1992):

> Roger was born and lived in St. Boniface until he enlisted in the Air Force. He was educated at Provencher School and grew up during the depression. He is remembered as a happy, calm, easy-going boy. The family had a big, mongrel dog named Buster. It soon became apparent that he was Roger's dog. He would hitch the dog to a child's wagon in summer or a sled in winter and in this manner, he delivered newspapers and groceries for a local grocery store.
>
> As a teenager, he became a great swimmer. He loved to swim from Provencher Bridge to Norwood Bridge and back. Yet he died by drowning. He worked at MacDonald Aircraft along with his sister Lucille. Without telling anyone, he left during lunch hour one day, and when he returned he had enlisted. He trained at Macdonald near Portage. He was sent to England and on to India.
>
> The plane in which he flew, a Liberator, was hit by anti-aircraft fire and came down in the Bay of Bengal. It broke in two and went down rapidly. Five crew members escaped and five died. Roger, a rear gunner, did not make it out of the plane. Flight Sergeant Roger Baril died at sea on April 22nd, 1945. He would have been 20 years old that coming September. So young to die!

Baril Lake (63 J/3), east of South Moose Lake was named after him in 1973.

Barker, Flying Officer **Gerald L.** of The Pas (J 20378). No. 458 Squadron. He died 22 July 1943 at the age of 26 and is commemorated at the Malta Memorial. He was the son of Henry E. and Mary Barker and was survived by his wife Shirley O. Barker of Niagara Falls, New York. ***Barker Lake*** (63 B/6), northeast of Waterhen Lake was named after him in 1969.

Barker, Warrant Officer 2 **James M.** of Holland, Manitoba (R 253004). No. 406 Squadron. He died 9 August 1945 at the age of 21 and is commemorated at Brookwood Military Cemetery in Surrey, England. He was one of the seven children of James N. and Margaret E. Barker of Glenboro and was survived by his wife Mary Barker (née Elchuk) of Toronto and their son whom he never saw. ***Barker Island*** (63 N/13) in Sisipuk Lake was named after him in 1995.

Barker, Lieutenant **Reginald D.** of Winnipeg. Royal Canadian Artillery. He died 8 June 1944 at the age of 36 and is commemorated at the Beny-sur-Mer Canadian War Cemetery in Calvados, France. He was the son of George W. and Eva Barker of Toronto. ***Barker Bay*** (64 H/6) in Northern Indian Lake was named after him in 1995.

Barker, Lieutenant Colonel **William G. "Billy"** of Winnipeg. No. 201 Squadron, Royal Air Force, Mentioned in Dispatches, Distinguished Service Order and Bar, Military Cross and Two Bars, Croix de Guerre (France), Silver Medal for Military Valour (Italy), Victoria Cross.

For conspicuous gallantry in action. He flew at a height of 500 feet over the enemy's lines and brought back most valuable information. On another occasion, after driving off two hostile machines, he carried out an excellent photographic reconnaissance (Military Cross Citation 1917).

For conspicuous gallantry and devotion to duty. He has done continuous good work in co-operation with the artillery and has carried out successful reconnaissances under most difficult and dangerous conditions (Bar to Military Cross 1917).

For conspicuous gallantry and devotion to duty. When on scouting and patrol work, he has on five different occasions brought down and destroyed five enemy aeroplanes and two balloons, though on two of these occasions he was attacked by superior numbers. On each occasion, the hostile machines were observed to crash to earth, the wreckage bursting into flames. His splendid example of fearlessness and magnificent leadership have been of inestimable value to his squadron (Distinguished Service Order 1918).

For conspicuous gallantry and devotion to duty. When leading patrols, he on one occasion attacked eight hostile machines, himself shooting down two, and on another occasion seven, one of which he shot down. In two months he himself destroyed four enemy machines and drove down one and burned two balloons (Second Bar to Military Cross 1918).

A highly distinguished patrol leader whose courage, resource and determination has set a fine example to those around him. Up to the 20th July, 1918, he had destroyed thirty-three enemy aircraft – twenty-one of these since the date of the last award (Second Bar to the Military Cross) was conferred on him. Major Barker has frequently led the formation against greatly superior numbers of the enemy with conspicuous success (Bar to the Distinguished Service Order 1918).

On the morning of the 27th October, 1918, this officer observed an enemy two-seater over the Foret de Mormal. He attacked this machine and after a short burst, it broke up in the air. At the same time a Fokker biplane attacked him, and he was wounded in the right thigh, but managed, despite this, to shoot down the enemy aeroplane in flames.

He then found himself in the middle of a large formation of Fokkers who attacked him from all directions, and was again severely wounded in the left thigh, but succeeded in driving down two of the enemy in a spin.

He lost consciousness after that and his machine fell out of control. On recovery, he found himself being again attacked heavily by a large formation, and singling out one machine he deliberately charged and drove it down in flames.

During this fight, his left elbow was shattered and he again fainted and on regaining consciousness he found himself still being attacked, but notwithstanding that he was now severely wounded in both legs and his left arm shattered, he dived on the nearest machine and shot it down in flames.

Being greatly exhausted, he dived out of the fight to regain our lines, but was met by another formation which attacked and endeavoured to cut him off, but after a hard fight he succeeded in breaking up this formation and reached our lines where he crashed on landing.

This combat, in which Major Barker destroyed four enemy machines (three of them in flames), brought his total successes to fifty enemy machines destroyed and is a notable example of the exceptional bravery and disregard of danger which this very gallant officer has always displayed throughout his distinguished career (Victoria Cross Citation 1918).

He is recognized as the most decorated serviceman of the First World War anywhere in the world. Barker survived the war and together with Billy Bishop, formed the Bishop and Barker Company. He was the first president of the Toronto Maple Leafs, installed in 1924 and was also the first acting director of the Royal Canadian Air Force at its founding in 1924. He was killed in a flying accident in 1930 at the age of 35 and is commemorated at the Mount Pleasant Cemetery in Toronto. Billy Bishop once characterized him as "the greatest fighter pilot the world has ever known." ***Billy Barker Lake*** (63 P/9), north of Cauchon Lake was named after him in 2001.

Barkman, Private **George R.** of Steinbach (H 42309). Canadian Provost Corps. He died 23 February 1944 at the age of 24 and is commemorated at Brookwood Military Cemetery in Surrey, England. He was the son of J. E. and Anna Barkman of Hochstadt, Manitoba. ***Barkman Lake*** (63 P/12), southeast of Thompson was named after him in 1961.

Barlow, Trooper **Charles Elmer** of Fisher Branch (H 77670). 12th Manitoba Dragoons. He died 5 March 1945 at the age of 23 and is commemorated at the Groesbeek Canadian War Cemetery in Holland. He was the son of Charles A. and Grace Barlow of Fisher Branch and was survived by his wife Alice A. Barlow (née Withoff) and their three week-old daughter. He was killed the day before he was to return to England on leave to see his daughter for the first time. ***Barlow Island*** (64 N/1) in Egenolf Lake was named after him in 1995.

Barlow, Flying Officer **Percy** of Souris (J 39368). No. 61 Squadron. He died 17 December 1944 at the age of 35 and is commemorated at Durnbach War Cemetery in Bavaria, Germany. He was the son of Thomas J. and Mary A. Barlow of Souris. ***Barlow Bay*** (53 M/12) on the southwest side of High Hill Lake was named after him in 1995.

Barlow, Warrant Officer 1 **Thomas** of Winnipeg (R 91649). No. 152 Operational Training Unit, RCAF. He died 17 February 1944 at the age of 33 and is commemorated at Rawalpindi War Cemetery, Pakistan. He was the son of James and Sarah Barlow and was survived by his wife Kathleen H. Barlow. ***Barlow Lake*** (64 B/13), west of Southern Indian Lake was named after him in 1958.

Barnes, Warrant Officer 2 **Arthur J. G.** of Winnipeg (R 157147). No. 138 Squadron. He died 28 April 1944 at the age of 22 and is commemorated at the Runnymede Memorial in Surrey, England. He was the son of Walter George and Bessie Barnes of Victoria, British Columbia. His sister recalls (7 November 2001):

> Arthur and his sisters, Evelyn and Doris, enjoyed a happy childhood growing up in St. James, a suburb of Winnipeg surrounded by prairies, woods, dairy farms and goat farms. Arthur's parents emigrated from the English counties of Devon and Surrey in the early 1900s. They settled in Winnipeg along with accompanying brothers and sisters and formed a happy, close knit family in their newly-adopted country.
>
> Arthur received his early and high school education at Britannia Elementary School and Linwood Collegiate in St. James. He was fun loving, quiet, sociable and enjoyed various sports with his close boyhood friends. The Barnes family had a cross-border collie named Buster. During the winter months, Arthur would hitch Buster to a small sleigh and race up and down frozen, snow-covered Roseberry Street in St. James. The picture of this excited teenage boy, the eager, barking Buster and the flying snow was a sight to behold! While growing up, Arthur attended St. James Anglican Church and enjoyed various activities in the church, Wolf Cubs, Scouts and Venturers.
>
> After graduating from high school and technical school, Arthur was employed by the T. Eaton Company, the largest retail department store in Winnipeg. He enjoyed working there until his enlistment in the Royal Canadian Air Force on 20 February 1942. Sister Evelyn also heeded the call to enlist in the RCAF, Women's Division. Sister Doris was employed as a stenographer at RCAF No. 8 Service and Repair Depot in Winnipeg. Father George who served as a member of the local Home Guard was a World War I veteran of the Battle of the Somme and Vimy Ridge.
>
> In Canada, Arthur trained at various Bombing and Gunnery schools in Manitoba and Alberta before graduating as a bomb aimer from No. 5 AOS Station at Winnipeg. He departed from Halifax 18 April 1943 and continued Advanced Operational Training in the United Kingdom. Subsequently, Arthur joined up with an aircrew whose members were of British, Australian and Canadian origin – a truly Commonwealth crew.
>
> Arthur was taken on strength No. 138 RAF Squadron on 8 February 1944. Squadrons 138 and 161 operated out of Tempsford, Bedfordshire. These were designated SOE (Special Operations Executive) Squadrons or "Ghost Squadrons." Special duties involved dropping SOE or SIS agents by parachute as well as arms containers to the Underground fighters in France, the Low Countries and Belgium. The two squadrons engaged in night bombing when not on Special Duties. The seven-member crew Halifax II was the principal heavy aircraft flown by No. 138 Squadron during 1944.
>
> Arthur flew 12 operational flights as a bomb aimer with this squadron. On 27 April 1944, his final mission before being "spelled," Arthur's crew took off flying RAF Halifax LL356. The crew joined three other Halifaxes on Operation Code OSRIC 59 to perform supply drops over Belgium. Heavy flak was encountered over German-occupied Belgium and only three aircraft (two damaged by flak) returned to base. Arthur's aircraft went missing over the North Sea. The body of his pilot, Flight Sergeant George Williamson (RAAF) was recovered after two months, washed up on North Beach of Terschelling Island off the Netherlands coast. The bodies of the remaining crew were never recovered.

Barnes Bay (64 C/3) in McKnight Lake was named after him in 1993.

Barnes, Private **Earl R.** of Medora (H 65994). Princess Patricia's Canadian Light Infantry. He died 13 October 1943 at the age of 23 and is commemorated at the Moro River Canadian War Cemetery in Italy. He was the son of Horace H. and Helena M. Barnes of Medora. ***Barnes Island*** (64 N/15) in Goose Lake was named after him in 1989.

Barnett, Trooper **Alfred Thomas** of Winnipeg (H 100160). Lord Strathcona's Horse. He died 23 September 1944 at the age of 21 and is commemorated at Cesena War Cemetery in Italy. He was the son of Alfred and Kathleen Barnett of Winnipeg. He had been employed as an office boy at the time of his enlistment. ***Barnett Lake*** (63 N/12), south of Sisipuk Lake was named after him in 1972.

Barnett, Flight Sergeant **Joseph Roy** of Winnipeg (R 101691). No. 1 Air Observers School. He died 14 January 1943 at the age of 21 and is commemorated at the Ottawa Memorial. He was the son of Arthur J. and Myra C. Barnett of St. James. He enlisted in the RCAF 17 May 1941 and was posted to No. 1 Air Observers School at Malton, Ontario the following year. It was during a navigational training exercise that his Anson aircraft failed to return to base. Roy and three other members of the crew were killed (Pittman n.d.). ***Barnett Island*** (64 J/12) in Jamie Lake was named after him in 1995.

Barnson, Leading Aircraftman **Arthur T.** of Selkirk (R 91572). No. 1691 Meteorological Flight. He died 3 December 1943 at the age of 21 and is commemorated at Harrow Cemetery in Middlesex, England. He was the son of Paul and Elizabeth Barnson of Selkirk. His brother recalls (16 December 1994):

> He resided in Selkirk, Manitoba, attending the Selkirk schools, completing his Grade 12. During his growing-up years he enjoyed hockey, horse back riding, hunting and attended the Rangers at Selkirk United Church. His main goal after graduation was to join the RCMP, however his chest measurements were not quite sufficient and he was turned down. This was December 27, 1940. Arthur joined the RCAF in January of 1941. While in Canada, he served at Brandon Manning Depot, Mossbank, Saskatchewan [and] Paulson Bombing and Gunnery School, Manitoba. Arthur was then sent overseas in March of 1943. He was reported missing an was later reclassified as killed December 3, 1943.

Barnson Lake (64 G/14), east of Big Sand Lake was named after him in 1994.

Baroni, Sergeant **Raymond J.** of Neepawa (R 196074). No. 9 Squadron. He died 16 December 1943 at the age of 21 and is commemorated at the Berlin 1939 - 1945 War Cemetery in Brandenburg, Germany. He was the youngest of the eight children of Michael and Marie Baroni of Glendale, California. His sister recalls him as a "grand chap, badly missed by many. [His] mother visited his grave in East Germany" (18 October 2001).

> He was born at Winnipeg, Manitoba, December 6, 1922. Raymond's family moved to Neepawa in 1928. He attended school there until he returned to Winnipeg to continue his education at St. Paul's College. Raymond enlisted in the Royal Canadian Air Force in 1942, training as an Air Gunner. He was sent overseas in June, 1943 (Pittman n.d.).

Baroni Lake (64 P/14), northeast of Nejanilini Lake was named after him in 1974.

Barr, Sergeant **Henry C. "Ray"** of Winnipeg (R 291559). No. 5 Operational Training Unit, RCAF. He died 10 January 1945 at the age of 20 and is commemorated at Brookside Cemetery in Winnipeg. He was the son of Henry and Caroline Barr of Winnipeg. Barr Lake (64 P/3), southeast of ***Nejanilini Lake*** was named after him in 1974.

Barre, Rifleman **Aurele E.** of McCreary (H 102948). Royal Winnipeg Rifles. He died 27 September 1944 at the age of 20 and is commemorated at the Calais Canadian War Cemetery in France. He was the son of Henri and Amanda Barre of McCreary. According to his niece (11 June 1987):

> Aurele was born … in Hearst, Ontario. The family moved to Rosetown, Saskatchewan when he was a year old where his father worked for a farmer. From there, when Aurele was six years old, they moved to McCreary, Manitoba. He completed Grade 9 and because jobs were scarce he worked with his father doing various jobs such as cutting cordwood and harvesting for farmers. In 1942 he joined the army.

His sister adds:

> Aurele was employed mainly as a farm labourer and for a short period of time he delivered mail. He was well known for his quiet personality and his consideration of others. Aurele trained in Canada prior to his posting to England in May, 1943. He transferred to the Royal Winnipeg Rifles, landing with "C" Company of that regiment on Juno Beach, D-Day, June 6, 1944. It was during the advanced battles in France that Aurele lost his life. He had a sister Bernice serving with the Women's Auxiliary Air Force and a brother Maurice serving overseas (Pittman n.d.).

Barre Creek (62 P/1), which flows west into Lake Winnipeg was named after him in 1982.

Barré, Private **Leonard M. "Peter"** of Belleview (H 87641). Royal Canadian Army Service Corps. He died 9 May 1945 at the age of 30 and is commemorated at the Holten Canadian War Cemetery in Holland. ***Barré Lake*** (64 H/2), east of Fidler Lake was named after him in 1995.

Barrett, Rifleman **Arthur E.** of Portage la Prairie (H 17445). Regina Rifle Regiment. He died 9 June 1944 at the age of 21 and is commemorated at Beny-sur-Mer Canadian War Cemetery in Calvados, France. He was one of the 12 children of Reginald B. and Edith E. Barrett of Portage la Prairie. A newspaper account (n.d.) indicated that:

> Mrs. Reg Barrett received word Saturday that her son, Rifleman Arthur E. Barrett, had been killed in action June 9 in France. Born in Portage 21 years ago, Arthur Barrett received his education in the public schools and collegiate here. Enlisting in Winnipeg in 1940, he went overseas the following year. He was attached to the Regina Rifles. Previous to his enlistment, he was employed with his father the late Reg Barrett in the shoe-repair business.

Barrett Lake (64 K/11), northeast of Reindeer Lake was named after him in 1972.

Barrett, Flight Sergeant **Martin** of Winnipeg (R 135579). No. 49 Squadron. He died 9 July 1943 at the age of 19 and is commemorated at Schoonselhof Cemetery, Antwerp, Belgium. He was the son of Michael J. and Anna Barrett of Winnipeg. ***Barrett Island*** (64 F/2) in Thomsen Lake was named after him in 1994.

Barrett, Private **Wilfred P.** of Brandon (H 6463). Winnipeg Grenadiers. He died 25 December 1941 at the age of 24 and is commemorated at the Sai Wan Memorial in Hong Kong. Shortly thereafter, the *London Times* (n.d.) reported that:

> ... [t]he heroic defence of Hong Kong was not only beyond price as an inspiring example of valour and devotion; it also gained a footing in precious time, and, whether or not it may prove to have rivalled in that respect the decisive achievement of our forces in Crete, the invader would have gained vital days if it had been decided to yield the colony without a struggle.

According to his brother (24 April 1994):

> Wilfred Barrett was born … in the Village of Lenore, Manitoba. Commencing his schooling at the age of six years in the Village of Rapid City, Manitoba and graduating from Grade 11 from Miniota, the family having moved to Miniota as his father had taken a job as section foreman on the CPR railway. During the years between leaving school and joining the services, he worked on farms in the area and in 1939 went to work on the CNR. Wilfred was an excellent hockey player and baseball pitcher for the Village of Miniota.
>
> In September of 1939, Wilfred enlisted in the Canadian Army, joining the Winnipeg Grenadiers. In February, 1940 they were sent to Jamaica for garrison duty and some training. He returned home for a short leave prior to his being sent to Hong Kong where he was killed in action on Christmas Day, 1941. There is no record of his body being recovered for burial but his name appears on the memorial in Hong Kong.

He was survived by his wife Marie Barrett (née McPherson) of Winnipeg. ***Barrett Bay*** (63 N/3) in Kississing Lake was named after him in 1972.

Barron, Private **Oliver A.** of Winnipeg (H 20873). Winnipeg Grenadiers. He died 19 December 1941 and is commemorated at the Sai Wan Memorial in Hong Kong. ***Barron Lake*** (63 K/16), west of Wekusko Lake was named after him in 1973.

Barron, Flight Sergeant **Percival E.** of Mafeking (R 107770). No. 420 Squadron. He died 29 March 1943 at the age of 28 and is commemorated at the Groesbeek Canadian War Cemetery in Holland. He was the son of Oliver and Mary R. Barron (née Thorne) of Mafeking, Manitoba. According to his brother (20 March 1996), before the war he:

> … worked as a guide at a resort near Flin Flon where he met interesting people and especially one gentleman who was soon to make an impact on his life. Percy's dad – Oliver Barron who could not read or write, joined the army during World War I and was decorated in France for "Bravery on the Battle Field" by King George V. Four brothers joined the Service during World War II. Alex Baron to the Army, Dave to the Navy, Percy to the Air Force and Phil to the Navy.
>
> Percy was determined to be part of an aircrew in the RCAF, but was rejected because of his Grade 6 education, but this desirous man would not be beaten. He referred his problem to his friend he had met while guiding at Beaver Lake, who was a teacher at the University of Saskatchewan, and soon received some sort of credentials also advising him to go to a recruiting depot in Regina, where he was accepted. From then on he worked diligently for his qualification as an air gunner.
>
> My brother spent his final leave in Canada with me in late August of 1942. We spent several days in Mafeking with our folks. We also hiked the Porcupine Mountains, the Steep Rock River, Red Deer River, the Blue Berry Plains and Dawson Bay where we worked together for Glen Burrel's fishing and logging operations. On the last day of our leave Percy brought down a beautiful five point white-tailed deer; that rack is still proudly displayed in my home.
>
> I always remember the pledge we made before we last parted, he for Britain, and me back to the west coast: "Bear in mind that if anything should happen to either of us, we are not to grieve but the remainder of us is to have a celebration." When I received the news in the form of a telegram, I contacted brother Phil who was in Esquimalt, BC on HMCS *Naden I* and celebrate we did. Percy's wish was fulfilled and I pray with confidence that the Great Spirit will watch and guide my special Métis brother in a new world.

Barron Island (63 I/4) in the Nelson River was named after him in 1995.

Barske, Flight Sergeant **Paul J.** of Whitemouth (R 157138). No. 428 Squadron. He died 26 November 1943 at the age of 20 and is commemorated at Durnbach War Cemetery in Bavaria, Germany. ***Barske Lake*** (52 L/5), southeast of Lac du Bonnet was named after him in 1973.

Barthelette, Gunner **George** of Marchand (H 100346). Royal Canadian Artillery. He died 1 October 1943 at the age of 36 and is commemorated at Bari War Cemetery in Italy. He was the son of Frank and Lucie Barthelette and was survived by his wife Rose Barthelette of Fort Garry. ***Barthelette Lake*** (64 N/1), southwest of Nueltin Lake was named after him in 1972.

Bartko, Private **Peter** of Winnipeg (H 20387). 1st Canadian Parachute Battalion. He died 2 August 1944 and is commemorated at Ranville War Cemetery, Calvados, France. ***Bartko Creek*** (64 N/7), which flows northeast into MacMillan Lake southwest of Nueltin Lake was named after him in 1972.

Bartlett, Gunner **Joseph** of Winnipeg (H 5001). Royal Canadian Artillery. He died 30 November 1939 at the age of 31 and is commemorated at St. Mary's Cemetery in Winnipeg. He was the son of Mr. and Mrs. Peter Bartlett of Carrick, Manitoba. ***Bartlett Island*** (64 C/8) in Granville Lake was named after him in 1995.

Baskerville, Rifleman **Ernest C.** of Mayfield (H 1797). Royal Winnipeg Rifles. He died 8 June 1944 at the age of 21 and is commemorated at Beny-sur-Mer Canadian War Cemetery in Calvados, France. He was the son of Adrian E. and Delia A. Baskerville of Gladstone. It was later discovered that he had been one of 34 Manitoba soldiers who had been executed while a prisoner of war. A newspaper account (n.d.) written during the subsequent trial indicated that:

> Eight members of the North Nova Scotia Highlanders of Amherst and Truro were mowed down in cold blood by German guards with automatic weapons after their capture at Authie, France, June 7, 1944, a Canadian eye-witness told the military court trying SS Major-General Kurt Meyer Wednesday on war crimes charges. The witness called by the prosecution was Sergeant William McKay of Toney River, Nova Scotia who gave details of the mass shooting.
>
> McKay was wounded twice in the Authie Battle which occurred while the Canadians were fighting toward Caen, Normandy. He was taken to the village by a German guard and was left unguarded in a doorway for five minutes. A short distance down the street he saw Corporal Thomas R. Davidson and seven North Novas who were prisoners. "The first thing, I heard firing and saw our boys tipping over in the road," McKay said. "I could see the guns of two German guards firing."
>
> As the trial completed its third day, Private George P. Talbot of Truro, Nova Scotia described how a stretcher-bearer who had been attending wounded men was forced to join the marching prisoners. At one moment, the stretcher-bearer's shadow moved along the road behind his, Talbot said. Then there was a burst of gun fire and it was gone.
>
> An affidavit by Captain J. A. Trainor of Truro, second in command of A Company of the North Novas who was another Canadian captured at Authie, described how "I saw a number of Germans going around the area shooting our wounded lying on the ground." Sergeant Dudka of Stellaston, Nova Scotia described to the Canadian military court the slaying of Private J. Metcalfe of Buron, where the Canadians' captors searched them, then stood them with their faces to the wall. "I heard a commotion and as I turned around I saw a guard pulling on Metcalfe's pocket," Sergeant Dudka said. "He then let go of the pocket and Metcalfe stumbled forward and the guard fired approximately four shots at him. Metcalfe dropped ten feet away from the guard. He had been hit twice in the right side. The guard let him lie there for 20 minutes. Metcalfe moved. The guard then emptied the remainder of the magazine of his machine-gun – about 15 rounds – into Metcalfe."

His brother recalls (5 November 2001):

> Ernie, as he was affectionately called, was born in Hazlet, Saskatchewan. In the early thirties, his family farm became part of the big dustbowl. Crops dried up and with no feed for the cattle, the family moved to Mayfield, Manitoba in hopes of a better life. Ernie loved farming and even if the work was hard, especially during seeding and harvesting, he always found time to repair the automobile used in summer months. He also liked to fix any machinery that had broken down.
>
> Arnie had a trapline in winter and earned a few extra dollars to spend, as money was scarce in the thirties. Hunting deer in the fall was not just a sport but also a necessity. Ernie was an excellent shot and always got his deer to add to the family larder for the long winter months. Ernie was a happy person with a contagious smile. He was always a popular part of any group. He is sadly missed by his loving family and friends.

Baskerville Lake (64 P/10), east of Nejanilini Lake was named after him in 1974.

Baskerville, Flight Lieutenant **John E.** of Winnipeg (37537). No. 51 Squadron, RAF. Enlisting in November, 1935, he participated on the first RAF attack on a land target – Hornum on Sylt Island (Allison 1978). He died 19 March 1940 at the age of 25 and is commemorated at the Kiel War Cemetery in Germany. He was the son of William F. and Minnie M. Baskerville of Winnipeg and was survived by his wife Jane B. Baskerville of Winnipeg. ***Baskerville Island*** (53 K/6) in Sharpe Lake was named after him in 1995.

Bassett, Lance Corporal **Richard** of Badger (H 102368). Queen's Own Cameron Highlanders. He died 23 October 1944 at the age of 23 and is commemorated at Bergen-op-Zoom Canadian War Cemetery in Holland. He was the son of Edward and Lillian M. Bassett of Badger, Manitoba. ***Bassett Lake*** 64 N/14), west of Nueltin Lake was named after him in 1972.

Bastable, Sergeant **Gerald** of St. James (H 16547). 12th Manitoba Dragoons. He died 14 August 1944 at the age of 20 and is commemorated at Bretteville-sur-Laize Canadian War Cemetery in Calvados, France. He was the son of Dennis and Elizabeth Bastable and was survived by his wife Myrtle Bastable of Aldershot, Hampshire, England. ***Bastable Lake*** (54 C/6), southwest of York Factory was named after him in 1964.

Bate, Flying Officer **Arthur J.** of Transcona (J 36280). No. 101 Squadron. He died 6 November 1944 at the age of 21 and is commemorated at the Reichswald Forest War Cemetery in Germany. He was the son of Arthur T. and Eva M. Bate of Transcona. ***Bate Lake*** (52 L/6), east of Lac du Bonnet was named after him in 1973.

Bate, Leading Aircraftman **Thomas C.** of Oakville (R 56779). No. 8 Repair Depot, RCAF. He died 26 January 1942 at the age of 41 and is commemorated at Brookside Cemetery in Winnipeg. He was the son of Thomas and Ruth E. Bate of Oakville and was survived by his wife Mable Bate of Winnipeg. ***Bate Island*** (64 O/1) in Glass Lake was named after him in 1995.

Bateman, Warrant Officer 2 **John H.** of Baldur (R 103889). No. 32 Operational Training Unit, RCAF. He died 19 September 1943 at the age of 20 and is commemorated at the Ottawa Memorial. He was the son of Sydney and Margaret Bateman of Innisfail, Alberta. ***Bateman Island*** (53 K/11) in Edmund Lake was named after him in 1996.

Bateman, Sergeant **John T.** of Winnipeg (H 37667). Royal Canadian Army Service Corps. He died 8 February 1945 at the age of 28 and is commemorated at the Groesbeek Canadian War Cemetery in Holland. He was the son of William and Eileen Bateman and was survived by his wife Olive P. Bateman of New Westminster, British Columbia. ***Bateman Lake*** (64 I/11), northwest of North Knife Lake was named after him in 1974.

Batters, Flight Sergeant **Harold Mark** of Portage la Prairie (R 95487). No. 401 Squadron. He died 4 December 1942 at the age of 24 and is commemorated at Longuenesse (St. Omer) Souvenir Cemetery, Pas de Calais, France. He was the son of Harold E. and Rowena Batters of Portage la Prairie. Before enlisting, he was keenly interested in raising pure-bred cattle. He took an active part in the Boys' Cattle Club of Portage as well as the Seed Grain Club. He won first prize in judging competitions at Portage, Carman and Brandon exhibitions. ***Batters Lake*** (63 K/13), southwest of Wabishkok Lake was named after him in 1988.

Baumann, Rifleman **Jacob L.** of St. Boniface (H 16033). Regina Rifle Regiment. He died 13 August 1944 at the age of 25 and is commemorated at Bretteville-sur-Laize Canadian War Cemetery in Calvados, France. His sister visited his grave in 1945. He was the son of Jacob and Helen Baumann and was survived by his wife Florence L. Baumann (née Blair) of Prince Rupert, British Columbia and their two young children. His sister writes (7 July 1999):

> Jacob was born in Plum Coulee. He attended school there and when we moved to Winnipeg he attended high school at Provencher School, St. Boniface. He joined the PPCLI and married Florence Blair. They had two children Elizabeth and Jacob. He was posted overseas and was injured by an exploding "field stove." After hospitalization he was posted to [the] Regina Rifles as a medical assistant.
>
> We received a letter from Padre Jamieson who was present when Jacob was killed. He said Jacob had accompanied him on a trip to "No Man's Land" to care and administer to wounded men. They waited for an ambulance when another shell hit them and Jacob apparently was hit in the abdomen. He died on the way to hospital. The Padre said Jacob had always been ready to help, he was gentle and patient with the wounded, he had courage and always put himself out for others. He appeared to be ready to meet his Maker.

Baumann Lake (64 K/14), northeast of Reindeer Lake was named after him in 1972.

Baumgarten, Flying Officer **Raymond L.** of Portage la Prairie (J 14523). No. 428 Squadron. He died 13 May 1943 at the age of 23 and is commemorated at Weerselo (Deurningen) Roman Catholic Cemetery, Holland. He was the youngest of the four children of William and Maria Baumgarten (née Lamport) of Portage la Prairie. His cousin writes (26 November 2001):

> Raymond was ... born November 29, 1919 at Melita, Manitoba. His family and he moved to Portage la Prairie in 1934 where he continued to farm (about 11 miles north) with his father. He signed up with the RCAF during World War II. Enthusiasm and adventure called this tall, handsome prairie boy to fight for his country. His plane and crew were shot down over Holland. No remains were ever recovered.

Baumgarten Lake (64 O/14), east of Nueltin Lake was named after him in 1975.

Baxter, Rifleman **Clifford H.** of Winnipeg (H 40802). Royal Winnipeg Rifles. He died 12 October 1944 at the age of 28 and is commemorated at the Adegem Canadian War Cemetery in Belgium. He was the son of William H. and Ethel M. Baxter of Winnipeg. ***Baxter Lake*** (63 J/16), east of Setting Lake was named after him in 1972.

Baxter, Private **Donald** of Winnipeg (H 40770). Lake Superior Regiment. He died 6 August 1944 at the age of 24 and is commemorated at Beny-sur-Mer Canadian War Cemetery in Calvados, France. He was the son of William H. and Ethel M. Baxter. ***Baxter Island*** (664 O/2) in Brownstone Lake was named after him in 1995.

Bayer, Flying Officer **Edward G. "Jerry"** of St. Andrews (J 27270). No. 1667 Conversion Unit, RCAF. He died 7 March 1944 at the age of 20 and is commemorated at Harrogate (Stonefall) Cemetery in Yorkshire, England. He was the son of Granville L. and Anne F. Bayer. His sister recalls her impressions of his brief military career (17 January 1997):

> As the War changed lives and plans in every household, "Jer" decided that money to supplement the family income and forward my education was more important for him than college, so he tabled his dreams for later. After passing his Grade 11 exams, he bought six shirts which he would wash and iron for each day, and acquired [a] position as messenger with the Dominion bank in Winnipeg at a salary of $400.00 per annum.
>
> Following Mother's precedent, Jer boarded in town during the week, coming home to help with chores most week-ends. He joined the Young People's Association at St. Mark's Church in St. Vital and began to have his own life, which might have been a thousand miles away as far as his bereft sister was concerned.
>
> For his mother, this time was infinitely precious. She was boarding then at Mrs. Nixon's, right at Portage and Main, where the old Queen's Hotel used to be. They could take the bus back to town late Sunday afternoon, and spend an evening together. During the week they could go to a show, have coffee at Child's just downstairs from Mrs. Nixon's or go to Moore's or Picardy's. They could not afford luxuries, but those brief interludes with her grown and gorgeous son gave my mother her happiest hours in all the bleak years she endured.
>
> The bells of hell were ringing now, and heard throughout the world. Inevitably, this even-tempered, peaceable, good-humoured lad reached eighteen and, with legions of his contemporaries, enlisted. He was dashing in the uniform of the Royal Canadian Air Force. He loved to fly, and his whole face shone with the joy of adventure.
>
> With a sense of the righteousness of their cause, and with decisions all made for them, these bright young heroes lived intensely, many of them still thinking of war as hand-to-hand battle with the traditional enemies of their fathers rather than the impending annihilation, devastation unimagined. As the truth began to dawn, they tried to tell us about it, but words were thin and weak. His final letter said again how he hated bombing missions. And then there were no more words.
>
> The war in the air had turned in favour of the Allies by spring of 1944 and the skies were thick with fighters and bombers on the dark night of March the seventh. Returning from a raid over Berlin, Flying Officer Bayer's hulking Lancaster was in collision with another plane over the English Channel; both aircraft were demolished and all aboard were killed.
>
> There were no answers to the anguished questions, only pathetic souvenirs – a packet of letters, a blood-stiff glove, two halves of a pipe. Perhaps in precognition I had written some lines of poetry, and when the same "they" who wired messages of death let us have fifty letters incised on the gravestone in the Military Cemetery at Harrogate in Yorkshire, we sent: "He has flown as only the young can fly, who have Homecoming in their eyes."

In a letter home which he never mailed he said " I loathe bombing cities. In Dresden last night I knew there were people praying in the cathedral." ***Bayer Lake*** (64 H/4), north of Gauer Lake was named after him in 1995.

Bayne, Private **George** of Winnipeg (H 19553). Queen's Own Cameron Highlanders. He died 19 August 1942 at the age of 35 and is commemorated at Dieppe Canadian War Cemetery in Seine-Maritime, France. He was the son of George P. and Katherine Bayne and was survived by his wife Natalie "Nell" Bayne of Winnipeg. ***Bayne Lake*** (52 L/6), southeast of Bird Lake was named after him in 1982.

Bazinet, Private **Henry J. P.** of Deerhorn (H 6878). Winnipeg Grenadiers. He died a prisoner of war 12 June 1945 and is commemorated at the Yokohama War Cemetery in Japan. ***Bazinet Lake*** (63 K/12), southeast of Manistikwan Lake was named after him in 1984.

Bazzlo, Private Mike of Winnipeg (H 16621). Princess Patricia's Canadian Light Infantry. He died 8 December 1943 and is commemorated at the Moro River Canadian War Cemetery in Italy. ***Bazzlo Lake*** (63 J/13), northeast of Wekusko Lake was named after him in 1972.

Beach, Warrant Officer 1 **Roy B.** of Winnipeg (R 162352). No. 427 Squadron. He died 31 March 1944 at the age of 29 and is commemorated at the Hanover War Cemetery in Germany. He was the son of Nathaniel B. and Florence M. Beach of Toronto. ***Beach Island*** (63 P/4) in Sipiwesk Lake was named after him in 1995.

Beardy, Gunner **Rose** of Cross Lake (H 101785). Royal Canadian Artillery. He died 30 July 1944 at the age of 26 and is commemorated at Beny-sur-Mer Canadian War Cemetery in Calvados, France. He was the son of Abraham and Madeline Beardy (née Ross) of Cross Lake. ***Beardy Creek*** (62 O/9), which flows northwest into Lake St. Martin was named after him in 1972.

Beaton, Flying Officer **Alexander F.** of Hartney (J 13842). No. 428 Squadron. He died 28 May 1943 at the age of 24 and is commemorated at the Runnymede Memorial in Surrey, England. He had partially completed his third tour of duty. He was the son of Norman and Mary Beaton of Brandon. ***Beaton Lake*** (64 O/6), southeast of Nueltin Lake was named after him in 1975.

Beaton, Flying Officer **Herbert J.** of Shoal Lake (J 42250). No. 431 Squadron. He died 5 March 1945 at the age of 22 and is commemorated at the Hanover War Cemetery in Germany. He was the son of Alex and Ada M. Beaton of Shoal Lake. Having no known living relatives, a commemorative certificate was issued to the Town of Shoal Lake and was placed alongside a plaque and clock which had been donated to the town by Flying Officer Beaton's mother. ***Beaton Island*** (64 C/16) in Barrington Lake was named after him in 1995.

Beattie, Flying Officer **Hugh Donald** of Winnipeg (J 10119). No. 405 Squadron. He was presumed dead 14 May 1943 at the age of 21 and is commemorated at Oud Avereest General Cemetery in Holland. He was the son of Hugh D. and Margaret J. Beattie of Winnipeg. Prior to enlisting, he had been employed by the Sovereign Life Assurance Company. A newspaper obituary (n.d.) added that:

> Flying Officer Beattie was born in Elmwood 21 years ago, and attended Lord Selkirk and St. John's technical high schools. He was a member of King Memorial church and the Boys' Brigade. He was an enthusiastic curler and a member of the Elmwood Junior Curling Club.

His sister-in-law recalls (20 February 1995):

> Don was very close to his family and they were very proud of him. He was very articulate and his log book and diary – which I have – are very clear and concise in all his phases of his training and sorties up till the day before he died. He was a good looking, pleasant, kind, thoughtful young man with a wonderful smile.

Beattie Lake (64 F/6), north of Wells Lake was named after him in 1994.

Beatty, Warrant Officer 2 **Donald Lyall "Terry"** of Souris (R 124012). No. 426 Squadron. He died 26 May 1943 at the age of 24 and is commemorated at Brussels Town Cemetery in Belgium. He was the youngest of the four sons of John W. and Sarah Beatty of Souris. His cousin recalls (23 April 1995):

> Terry's family moved [from Carlyle, Saskatchewan] to Souris where his father farmed and also was employed by the CPR. Had Terry survived I'm sure he would have entered the Ministry because that was one of his main interests.

Beatty Island (63 I/7) in Molson Lake was named after him in 1995.

Beatty, Flight Sergeant **James M.** of Winnipeg (R 152879). No. 1663 Conversion Unit, RCAF. He died 2 December 1943 at the age of 20 and is commemorated at Harrogate (Stonefall) Cemetery in Yorkshire, England. He was the son of Walter M. and Verna E. Beatty of Winnipeg. Beatty Bay (53 L/6) in Joint Lake was named after him in 1995.

Beauchamp, Sapper **Aime** of Winnipeg (H 2949). Royal Canadian Engineers. He died 23 February 1943 at the age of 21 and is commemorated at Brookwood Military Cemetery in Surrey, England. He was the son of Joseph and Philomene Beauchamp of Fort Garry. ***Beauchamp Creek*** (64 I/1), which flows north into South Knife Lake was named after him in 1974.

Beaudry, Corporal **Henry J.** of Ashern (H 46176). Lake Superior Regiment. He died 15 April 1945 at the age of 28 and is commemorated at the Holten Canadian War Cemetery in Holland. He was the son of W. C. and Annie Beaudry of Ashern. ***Beaudry Lake*** (63 N/4), southwest of Kississing Lake was named after him in 1982.

Beaulieu, Private **Laurent T. J.** of St. Leon (H 10902). Queen's Own Cameron Highlanders. He died 23 November 1944 at the age of 22 and is commemorated at the Groesbeek Canadian War Cemetery in Holland. He was the son of Aurele and Malvina Beaulieu of St. Leon. ***Beaulieu Lake*** (64 N/6), southwest of Nueltin Lake was named after him in 1972.

Bebee, Rifleman **Charles Wesley** of Winnipeg (H 7173). Regina Rifle Regiment. He died 9 June 1944 at the age of 26 and is commemorated at Beny-sur-Mer Canadian War Cemetery in Calvados, France. He was the son of Charles W. and Elizabeth Bebee of Winnipeg. His brother recalls (26 November 2001):

> He was my older brother by seven years. My memories of Wesley consist of those you would expect to have of an older brother. I recall he liked to hunt, deer mostly, and I remember he played the violin. Then there were the cars – there

always seemed to be a lot of old cars around the house on Martin Avenue in Elmwood. I also have the letters he wrote my mother to remember him by. The letters, torn, tattered, yellowing with age, some with pages missing, were written while Wesley was overseas, mostly dated in the last few months of 1943. These letters reflect his hopes, his needs, his fears.

He hoped that he would see his family again and asks endless questions about those at home. He was constantly reassuring "Ma" that he was fine and "not to worry about me," he wrote, "because I am OK." He wrote on October 30, 1943: "Well it will soon be Christmas. I sure wish I could be home for it but I can't. So I'll have to do my best over here."

He often wrote a note of thanks for the goods he would receive – shoes, candy, chocolates, and ah yes, the cigarettes. Small pleasures sent by loved ones – Ma, our sisters Lil, Bella, Bessie, our brother Andy and our Uncle Willie. Then there was the fear – not for himself – but for his younger brother. He wrote in one letter: "so Dib (my nickname) went and joined the army, well all I can say is he is a darn fool" – a fear expressed as only an older brother could!

Bebee Lake (64 K/7), northeast of Reindeer Lake was named after him in 1972.

Becker, Craftsman **Albert C.** of East Kildonan (H 2622). Royal Canadian Corps of Electrical and Mechanical Engineers. He died 18 June 1944 at the age of 25 and is commemorated at Chingford Mount Cemetery in Essex, England. He was the son of Walter K. A. and Mary C. Becker of East Kildonan. ***Becker Lake*** (64 I/4), west of North Knife Lake was named after him in 1974.

Beech, Pilot Officer **Gerard M.** of Baldur (J 9160). No. 9 Squadron. He died 29 July 1942 at the age of 24 and is commemorated at Becklingen War Cemetery in Germany. He was the brother of Pilot Officer William L. Beech (see next entry). ***Beech Lake*** (64 N/4), east of Quasso Lake was named after him in 1995.

Beech, Pilot Officer **William L.** of Baldur (87448). No. 234 Squadron, RAF. He enlisted in September, 1939 and died 16 January 1941. He was 20 years of age and is commemorated at St. Eval Churchyard in Cornwall, England. He was the brother of Pilot Officer Gerard M. Beech (see previous entry) and was survived by his wife of 16 days. ***Beech Point*** (64 I/14) in the Wolverine River was named after him in 1995.

Beitz, Private **Fredrich** (H 204105). Princess Patricia's Canadian Light Infantry. He died 24 May 1944 at the age of 22 and is commemorated at the Cassino War Cemetery in Italy. He was the son of Reinhardt and Susan Beitz of Winnipeg. ***Beitz Lake*** (64 I/9), northeast of North Knife Lake was named after him in 1974.

Bélanger, Private **Alphonse G. "Googie"** of Selkirk (H 20283). Queen's Own Cameron Highlanders. He died 19 August 1942 at the age of 22 and is commemorated at St. Sever Cemetery Extension, Rouen, Seine-Maritime, France. He was the fourth of the nine children of Alphonse and Valerie Bélanger (née Bedard) of Selkirk. Participating in the Dieppe Raid in 1942, his parents were notified of his death three months later. ***Bélanger Lake*** (52 E/14), southeast of Lac du Bonnet was named after him in 1974.

Bélanger, Private **Charles J.** of Selkirk (H 22977). Lake Superior Regiment. He died 26 April 1945 at the age of 21 and is commemorated at the Holten Canadian War Cemetery in Holland. He was the son of George and Constance Bélanger of Selkirk. His sister recalls (29 November 2001):

Charlie was born in Selkirk, the sixth child in a family of eleven. After graduating from high school, he was employed by the Manitoba Steel Foundries. He was recruited by the Canadian Army and went overseas

to serve his country. Upon returning to Canada, it was his intention to enter the holy priesthood, but he lost his life in a crossfire at the Kusten Canal in Holland just six days before the end of the war. His older brother Noel served with the Royal Canadian Navy while his younger brother Edward served with the Royal Canadian Air Force. Two of Charlie's sisters, Margaret and Georgiana, visited his grave in Holland and returned with memorial pictures.

The family continues to hold memorial services for him on April 26. ***Bélanger Bay*** (64 I/7) in Prosnyck Lake was named after him in 1995.

Belanger, Sergeant **Joseph** of Transcona (H 17835). 1st Canadian Special Services Battalion. He died 16 September 1944 at the age of 25 and is commemorated at Mazargues War Cemetery, Marseilles, Bouches-du-Rhone, France. He was the son of Joseph E. and of Angelina Belanger of Transcona. Prior to enlisting, he had been the principal of La Fortune School at Woodridge, Manitoba. ***Belanger Island*** (64 O/9) in Connolly Lake was named after him in 1995.

Belfie, Sergeant **Frank C.** of Winnipeg (H 19803). West Nova Scotia Highlanders. He died 17 December 1943 at the age of 24 and is commemorated at the Moro River Canadian War Cemetery in Italy. He was the son of Arthur M. and Lydia Belfie and was survived by his wife Margaret K. Belfie of Sutton, Surrey, England. ***Belfie Lake*** (64 K/13), northeast of Reindeer Lake was named after him in 1972.

Bell, Trooper **Adam Stewart** of Oak Lake (H 246). Royal Canadian Armoured Corps. He died 6 September 1944 at the age of 39 and is commemorated at Oak Lake Cemetery, Manitoba. He was the son of Catherine Bell of Oak Lake. ***Bell Bay*** (64 F/6) in Wells Lake was named after him in 1994.

Bell, Sergeant **Alvin** of Gilbert Plains (M 45527). South Alberta Tank Regiment. He died 21 August 1944 at the age of 32 and is commemorated at Bretteville-sur-Laize Canadian War Cemetery in Calvados, France. He was the son of William A. and Rose A. Bell and was survived by his wife of two months Lilian Bell of Leeds, Yorkshire, England and their unborn son. Near the end of the war, Mrs. Bell immigrated to Canada and settled at Gilbert Plains. ***Alvin Bell Lake*** (53 M/11), south of Ransom Lake was named after Sergeant Bell in 1996.

Bell, Flying Officer **David** of Winnipeg (J 35329). No. 429 Squadron, Distinguished Flying Cross.

In October, 1944, Flying Officer Bell was the captain and pilot of an aircraft detailed to attack Cologne. It was his first mission as captain. In the bombing run, considerable anti-aircraft fire was encountered and the aircraft was hit. The flight engineer was wounded. Flying Officer Bell promptly directed another member of the crew to render first aid to his injured comrade. Almost as the bombs were released, the aircraft was again hit. The port aileron was broken in half and it became exceedingly difficult to keep the aircraft on an even keel, but displaying the greatest determination, Flying Officer Bell flew the badly damaged aircraft to the nearest available airfield in this country where he effected a masterly landing. This officer displayed great tenacity and devotion to duty in trying circumstances (DFC Citation 1946).

He died 30 November 1944 at the age of 28 and is commemorated at Runnymede Memorial in Surrey, England. He was the son of William and Annie Bell of Winnipeg and was survived by his wife Barbara Bell. ***Bell Island*** (64 G/12) in Denison Lake was named after him in 1986.

Bell, Private **Everett** of Winnipeg (H 56362). Canadian Forestry Corps. He died 27 January 1942 and is commemorated at Brookwood Military Cemetery in Surrey, England. ***Bell Rapids*** (64 I/12) in the Stanley River was named after him in 1995.

Bell, Private **Gordon** of Winnipeg (H 6298). Winnipeg Grenadiers. He died 6 June 1945 at the age of 25 and is commemorated at the Yokohama War Cemetery in Japan. He was the son of William and Rachel F. Bell of Winnipeg. His sister recalls that (6 February 1995): "Dufferin School on Logan Avenue was the school he went to; his special interests were church plays [at] St. Andrew's Church, music [and] entertaining people." ***Bell Peninsula*** (53 M/1) in Semmens Lake was named after him in 1995.

Bell, Lieutenant Colonel **John K.** of Winnipeg. Royal Winnipeg Rifles. He died 17 September 1942 at the age of 56 and is commemorated at Elmwood Cemetery in Winnipeg. He was survived by his wife Georgina Bell of Winnipeg. ***John Bell Lake*** (63 N/15), east of Highrock Lake was named after him in 1996.

Bell, Private **Tom F.** of Inglis (H 10112). Queen's Own Cameron Highlanders. He died 21 July 1944 at the age of 19 and is commemorated at Bretteville-sur-Laize Canadian War Cemetery in Calvados, France. He was the son of Michael and Emma T. Bell of Inglis. ***Bell Hill*** (63 N/4), west of Kississing Lake was named after him in 1995.

Bellamy, Pilot Officer **John A.** of Winnipeg (J 95238). No. 424 Squadron. He died 7 March 1945 at the age of 31 and is commemorated at Rheinberg War Cemetery in Germany. He was the son of George O. and Catherine R. Bellamy and was survived by his wife Verne E. Bellamy of Vancouver. ***Bellamy Lake*** (64 P/4), south of Nejanilini Lake was named after him in 1978.

Bellingham, Flying Officer **Adam S.** of Winnipeg (J 8657). No. 420 Squadron. He died 24 July 1943 at the age of 28 and is commemorated at the Malta Memorial. He was the son of Adam S. and Margaret P. Bellingham and was survived by his wife Jona I. Bellingham of Fairbury, Nebraska. ***Bellingham Lake*** (64 N/9), southwest of Nueltin Lake was named after him in 1972.

Belsham, Gunner **Douglas J.** of Winnipeg (H 35232). Royal Canadian Artillery. He died 6 October 1940 at the age of 22 and is commemorated at St. John's Cemetery in Winnipeg. He was the son of Mr. and Mrs. Frederick O. Belsham of Winnipeg. ***Belsham Lake*** (64 J/14), northwest of Tadoule Lake was named after him in 1972.

Beltz, Corporal **Charles M.** of Winnipeg (H 20648). Winnipeg Grenadiers. He died 19 December 1941 during the final days of the defence of Hong Kong and is commemorated at the Sai Wan Memorial in Hong Kong. ***Beltz Lake*** (63 K/16), northwest of Wekusko Lake was named after him in 1973.

Belyea, Pilot Officer **Alan C.** of Winnipeg (J 86414). No. 103 Squadron. He died 31 March 1944 at the age of 21 and is commemorated at the Hanover War Cemetery in Germany. He was the son of Daniel A. and of Gladys E. Belyea of Vancouver. ***Belyea Lake*** (64 H/3), west of Settee Lake was named after him in 1995.

Belyea, Corporal **Graham S.** of Winnipeg (H 2832). Canadian Army Corps of Military Staff Clerks. He died 1 May 1941 at the age of 20 and is commemorated at the Halifax Memorial. He was the son of Daniel A. and Gladys Belyea of Winnipeg and was survived by his wife Helen Belyea of Ste. Anne, Manitoba. ***Belyea Island*** (63 N/3) in Kississing Lake was named after him in 1972.

Benedictson, Private **Allan F. I.** of Riverton (H 23504). Queen's Own Cameron Highlanders. He died 1 May 1945 at the age of 20 and is commemorated at the Holten Canadian War Cemetery in Holland. He was the son of F. Valdimar and Kristin S. Benedictson of Riverton, Manitoba. His high school teacher (Bend 1982) recalls:

> I had just started as a member of a four person staff at Teulon Collegiate. The day was over and as I was preparing to leave, a clean cut, light-haired boy appeared at the class room door. "Sir, my name is Allan Benedictson. I came from Riverton. Is it possible to take Grades 9, 10 and 11 French in one year?" he asked. "Possible but not probable. Why would you want to do that?" I replied. "I want to go to University and I have to get French before I can be admitted. Will you teach me?" "Yes," I said. "How much?" "Twenty-five dollars at Christmas and twenty-five at Easter; if you don't pass you get your money back," I said. "When do I start?" "Tomorrow night at 8 o'clock at my house."
>
> For two nights a week the boy turned up never late once. Actually, our gate made a slight noise when it opened. If you looked at the clock when you heard the gate, the hands would show within one minute of eight. One Friday night a few weeks later, the late Mr. Walter Griffin Sr. showed up at the house. "I've just finished digging up some potatoes and they're lying on the ground. Do you think you could get some boys to come with you to pick them tomorrow?" he asked.
>
> I rounded up Allan and three other boys and we reported for work. Mr. Griffin's "some potatoes" was the understatement of the year. They seemed to be everywhere. We started to pick but three of the boys quit at noon leaving only Allan and myself. Never before or since have I seen his equal as a potato picker. He fastened the pail to his belt and appeared to be on all fours as he went down the rows. Working as fast as I could, there was no way I could keep up. All afternoon he picked a row and a half to my one. I know one thing; when we finished the job that night I didn't care if I ever saw another potato as long as I lived!
>
> The last French lesson before Christmas, Allan handed me a check for $25. "Is this money put up by your parents because the cost of sending you here to school is considerable," I asked. "No sir, this is my own money. In the summer I mend nets. It is piece work and I am the only boy. The rest are all women. I can make pretty good money because I can mend net as fast as any woman there and faster than most of them," he replied. I immediately remembered the potato patch and I knew he was telling the truth. "You can keep your money. I stated a fee because I wanted to make sure you were serious and would not be a waste of my time," I said. "No, a deal is a deal," he said. "If that is the way you feel we will split the difference and you have now paid in full," I answered.
>
> It can be truly said that I have never worked with a finer one than Allan Benedictson, late of Riverton. He was one of many of that generation who gave everything they had for those they left behind.

Benedictson Lake (63 K/16), northwest of Wekusko Lake was named after him in 1973.

Benham, Lieutenant **John W.** of Winnipeg. Royal Winnipeg Rifles. He died 8 June 1944 at the age of 31 and is commemorated at Bretteville-sur-Laize Canadian War Cemetery in Calvados, France. He was the son of Alfred W. and Grace M. Benham of Winnipeg and was survived by his wife Millicent Benham. ***Benham Lake*** (64 N/12), southwest of Nueltin Lake was named after him in 1972.

Benn, Rifleman **Stanley C.** of Isabella (H 41972). Queen's Own Cameron Highlanders. He died 22 August 1942 at the age of 23 and is commemorated at Brookwood Military Cemetery in Surrey, England. Born at Uno, Manitoba 9 December 1918, he was survived by his parents Thomas H. and Unice Benn (née McKay) of Isabella, Manitoba. His sister recalls (8 December 2001):

> I was five months old when he went to war. Then when I was two, he came back for Christmas – he'd bought me a doll and doll clothes. That was his last visit. He always liked riding horses and went with dad to cut and saw wood. Dad told me that he always carried me around; he looked after me when I was outside. He really favoured me a lot. When my brother left after Christmas, I cried and cried and Mom and Dad had a hard time stopping me. Dad gave me all of Stanley's things after that. He wasn't feeling well and told [me] to take over. My favourite big brother.

Benn Lake (63 K/13), east of Embury Lake was named after him in 1984.

Bennett, Lieutenant **Dennis B.** of Winnipeg. Royal Winnipeg Rifles. He died 14 September 1944 at the age of 23 and is commemorated at the Calais Canadian War Cemetery in France. He was survived by his step-mother Edith M. Bennett and by his aunt Mrs. W. A. Hutchings of Worthing, Sussex, England. ***Bennett Bay*** (64 I/10) in Lovat Lake was named after him in 1995.

Bennett, Flying Officer **Donald E.** of Dunrea (J 12978). No. 420 Squadron. He died 5 March 1943 at the age of 28 and is commemorated at the Reichswald Forest War Cemetery in Germany. He was the son of George S. and Sadie E. Bennett of Evansburg, Alberta. His sister recalls (21 November 2001):

> During the early 1930s, Donald was one of the many unemployed who rode the freights looking for work. One of his letters, written November 5, 1934 describes this adventure. It is most interesting, humorous and revealing of those times. He obtained harvest work for $20.00 per month followed by winter employment on a farm. He had room and board ($5.00 per month) from the farmer and $5.00 per month from the government. Don later farmed rented land at Stoughton, Saskatchewan and Dunrea, Manitoba. He took time off one winter to attend Agricultural College at Vermilion, Alberta. He completed two years in one as well as being editor of their 1938 Year Book. His letters from overseas consisted mostly of the interesting things he saw in his travels around England and Scotland whenever he had leave.

Bennett Island (64 H/4) in Gauer Lake was named after him in 1995.

Bennett, Flying Officer **Donald H.** of Stony Mountain (J 37881). No. 166 Squadron. He died 31 December 1944 at the age of 24 and is commemorated at Nederweert War Cemetery in Holland. He was the only son of George Howard and Eileen Bennett of Stony Mountain. His nephew writes (13 November 2001):

> Don flew 33 missions into the heart of Germany beginning September 30, 1944. A superb, all-round athlete who represented Stony Mountain in many athletic events (track, hockey, baseball), Don was close to his sister Gwen, also a gifted athlete (he addressed some of his letters to her to "Fleet Foot") and he wrote her frequently.
>
> Awaiting assignments in England in February, 1944, Don frequently flashed his sense of humour and wrote: "It's tough being an officer, though. We are stuck away in a room all by ourselves and I've been having quite a conversation with the light bulbs and arguments with the doorknobs. The last statement is true, anyway, for the doors stick."
>
> In early October, 1944, Don revealed his prairie hockey roots, writing: "One can't do much around here for we are on duty all the time, liable to be called out at any time. However, I have taken chances and toured into Grimsby a couple of times. They have a rink in town and I believe we shall be getting some hockey hours in, but I haven't had a skate as yet."
>
> In late October, 1944, Don wrote reassuringly of his bombing assignments: "Yeah, we're on another 'do' tonight. This will be number seven, the number is getting higher, eh? Hope I can or we can keep it up. Since I wrote last we've done a couple on Duisberg, on Willemshaven and Essen. I really can't say much about them, everything happens so darned fast but they don't seem bad anyway. The only excitement is around the target and we don't stay there any longer than we have to."
>
> In December, 1944, Don wrote, fatefully: "Well Sis, twenty-two trips in now so your finger-crossing must be helping us. Only eight more and that isn't very long to keep 'em crossed is it? Keep 'em crossed."

Bennett Peninsula (64 P/7) in Wallbridge Lake was named after him in 1995.

Bennett, Squadron Leader **Gordon E.** of St. Boniface (J 15248). No. 405 Squadron, Distinguished Flying Cross and the Distinguished Service Order.

> As captain of aircraft, Squadron Leader Bennett has taken part in a very large number of sorties during which he has successfully attacked such targets as Berlin, Mannheim and Munich. He has displayed skill of a high order whilst his unconquerable spirit of determination and contempt for danger have been a notable feature of his efforts throughout. Squadron Leader Bennett has rendered valuable service (DSO Citation 1949).

The actual mission for which he was awarded the DFC was described in a newspaper article (n.d.):

> The four-motored bomber, previously damaged by flak, was struck by eight incendiaries from another Allied aircraft flying at a higher altitude, just as the bombs were dropped. The blaze took 15 minutes to extinguish. The bomber then flew through dense, freezing clouds. Limping home with holes in the aircraft large enough to fall through, minus lights, petrol gauges, electric system, heat or hydraulics, Bennett set the Halifax down on an aerodrome in southern England.

He died 25 May 1944 at the age of 24 and is commemorated at Bergen-op-Zoom Canadian War Cemetery in Holland. He was the son of George V. and Clara Bennett (née Whyman) of Winnipeg and was survived by his wife Nancy F. Bennett (née Ferguson) of Winnipeg. In a letter home to his sister he wrote:

> Dear Ida: Just a few lines to thank you for the parcel. It sure was good of you to send it. How do you like married life? I am glad to hear that you finally got him. Poor Bill … it was a long, hard fight. He did his best, but I guess that he was no match against you. Well being a married man myself I can of course sympathise with Bill. But all kidding aside, I know that you will be very happy. My only wish is that I was home and we could all get together; it sure would be some size of a family.
>
> The razor blades you sent me are very important. Tell my friends that when they write me to put one razor blade in each envelope. I am going to remind the Mrs. to do so. It has been a very bad day today. I just got my fire going and my room is starting to warm up. I just came back from leave. The fellow that is supposed to clean up after me has neglected to do so and my joint was in a mess. I am finally getting settled down.
>
> I am going on to a new type of plane. She looks like a honey. I don't think I will be leaving this station though. Give my regards to all the gang at work. Also tell old man Macken. Tell Bill that I will drop him a "hair raising" letter one of these days. I'll title it *A Canuck in the RAF*. I am keeping a diary. She sure is going to be kept right to the facts. I met all our aunties and cousins, so I guess that is all the news for now. Love and kisses, Gordon (6 December 1941).

His brother recalls (21 November 2001):

As a pre-schooler, Gordon enjoyed one of the early cowboy movie stars, Ken Maynard. At Christmas, he was given a grey-coloured toy horse (the same colour as Ken Maynard's horse) which was mounted on four wheels and he would tow the thing around the house for hours. As he grew up, he would play football with others, using frozen cabbage heads, turnips etc., as in those days no one had the money to buy things like a football. He had a good circle of friends and they would get together and cycle out to the open fields to pick crocuses in the spring, tiger lilies and other flowers in the summer. They would lay on their backs in the grass and watch the clouds gather and dissipate and guess what some clouds would represent such as elephants, horses, airplanes etc.

He went to some of the air shows at Stevenson airfield where he got a bang out of a number of small aircraft attempting to break released balloons with the tips of their propellers. He also thought it was really something to see an all-metal Ford tri-motor cabin aircraft do a loop. As he lived close to the Red River, he watched the airport from the foot of Brandon Avenue and the aircraft coming and going. There were the single pusher engine flying boats used to patrol the northern areas and single engine and tri-motor Fokker aircraft on floats.

For several years in a row, Gordon and I received a hockey stick and puck for Christmas. For a number of weeks before Christmas, we would cut kindling and hide it so we could start a fire in the kitchen cook stove to keep warm while we opened the few gifts we received. However, with the hockey sticks we would be out on the street at 2 AM Christmas morning playing hockey under the street lamps.

Gordon had a black cocker spaniel which he named Trixie. They would go to the Norwood Golf Course and Trixie would hide in some of the small bushes and when a golf ball came her way she would run out and retrieve it. Gordon would wait a week or two and then sell the balls to the golfers. When Gordon was overseas during the war, Trixie was ill from old age but Mother would not put her down, as she was apprehensive that it might affect Gordon. Soon after Gordon was killed on active duty, Trixie passed away.

Gordon Bennett Lake (53 N/4), east of Fish Lake was named after him in 1995.

Bennett, Private **Ruben R.** of McCreary (H 8957). Princess Patricia's Canadian Light Infantry. He died 23 May 1944 and is commemorated at the Cassino War Cemetery in Italy. He was the son of Chester and Martha Bennett of McCreary. ***Bennett Point*** (64 N/7) in Watkins Lake was named after him in 1995.

Bennett, Flying Officer **Stanley A.** of Winnipeg (164183). Royal Air Force. He died 2 August 1945 at the age of 24 and is commemorated at Ramleh War Cemetery, Israel. ***Bennett Rapids*** (64 I/16) in the Lavallée Channel was named after him in 1995.

Bennett, Pilot Officer **William J. B.** of Holland, Manitoba (R 137695). No. 22 Operational Training Unit, RCAF. He died 6 October 1942 at the age of 23 and is commemorated at Birmingham (Witton) Cemetery, Warwickshire, England. ***Bennett Hill*** (64 O/13), east of Nueltin Lake was named after him in 1996.

Benoit, Private **Daniel N.** of Winnipeg (H 20737). Queen's Own Cameron Highlanders. He died 19 August 1942 at the age of 20 and is commemorated at Dieppe Canadian War Cemetery in Seine-Maritime, France. He was the son of David W. and Maria Benoit of Winnipeg. ***Benoit Lake*** (64 J/1), south of Tadoule Lake was named after him in 1975.

Benson, Flight Lieutenant **Ivor B. "Benny"** of La Rivière (J 27009). No. 429 Squadron. He died 25 February 1945 at the age of 27 and is commemorated at the Runnymede Memorial in Surrey, England. He was the eldest of the six children of Swan D. and Elinor Benson and was survived by his wife Anne Benson (née MacDonald) of Winnipeg. He was reported missing in action on his second last mission before coming home on furlough. ***Benson Island*** (63 P/2) in Cotton Lake was named after him in 1995.

Benson, Sergeant **Johann A.** of Stonewall (R 106241). No. 8 Air Observer School. He died 11 August 1943 at the age of 23 and is commemorated at Brookside Cemetery in Winnipeg. He was the son of Johann and Minnie H. L. Benson of Norwood. ***Benson Point*** (64 F/8) in Cline Lake was named after him in 1995.

Benton, Private **Roger A.** of Minnedosa (436215). "A" Company, 4th Battalion, Canadian Infantry (Central Ontario Regiment.). He died 13 June 1916 at the age of 28 and is commemorated at Ypres (Menin Gate) Memorial, Ieper, West-Vlaanderen, Belgium. He was the son of James A. and Hannah Benton (née Debnam) of Innisfail, Alberta. He had been employed as a grain dealer at the time of his enlistment in Edmonton in January, 1915. ***Benton Lake*** (53 M/12), south of Split Lake was named after this World War I casualty in 1985.

Benville, Flying Officer **Lawrence J.** of Winnipeg (J 40216). No. 408 Squadron. He died 5 January 1945 at the age of 21 and is commemorated at the Sage War Cemetery in Germany. He was the son of John and Violet Benville and was survived by his wife Margaret D. Benville. ***Benville Lake*** (64 P/2), southeast of Nejanilini Lake was named after him in 1974.

Benzie, Pilot Officer **John** of Winnipeg (42185). No. 242 Squadron, RAF. Pilot Officer Benzie died 7 September 1940 at the age of 25 and is commemorated at the Runnymede Memorial in Surrey, England. He was the son of John and Agnes Benzie of Winnipeg. After the war, his mother learned of the plan to use the names of decorated servicemen for geographical features in Canada. She wrote a letter to the Geographic Board of Canada which read in part (12 January 1953):

I just want to draw your attention to my son, the late Pilot Officer Jack Benzie of the 242 fighter squadron – all Canadians of the RAF. The reason he joined the RAF: When he left school there was no work, so he joined the PPCLI. After he was through there, there still was no work. He thought if he could be a flier, he could come back and fly north to the mines, but the war came and he had to fight in the Old Country. He had to pay all his own expenses going to England and [it] was not an easy matter to get into the RAF those days. He was a Manitoba Marksman and he put eight months in the Camerons and five years in the Camerons Cadets. He is remembered in Westminster Abbey and his name is on the Honour Roll there. And if he is worth remembering there, he is worth remembering in his native land, as I say:

He is a lad without a grave,
and was blown to pieces
That the world might be saved.

I will give you one little incident that he came through. Coming from France, he was all alone and three planes attacked him. He shot one Messerschmitt down but the other two shot him. His plane went on fire and he was shot in the leg, but he came down in his parachute – he was 800 feet up at the time. When he landed, the Frenchmen kicked him and clubbed him, but a "Civilian" came along and told them that he was a British Officer, so after that, they could not do enough for him. He came back with the bunch from Dunkirk. I am his Mother, and as I say he has no Grave. Gentlemen, think it over. All his history is in Ottawa. The Canadian government recognizes him although he was in the Royal Air Force. Yours sincerely, Agnes Benzie. PS. He was two months in Southport Hospital with his leg. Then he went back fighting and was killed in the Battle of Britain.

As recently as 25 years after the war, it was lamented that "few Canadians remember the CAN-RAF boys today" (Halliday 1970), but they have not been forgotten overseas. A woman in England wrote a letter to the editor of the *Winnipeg Free Press*:

This year [1990] sees the 50th anniversary of the Battle of Britain and various museums all over Britain are organizing displays to commemorate this event and these displays are being organized by people who are dedicated and giving their spare time voluntarily.

I am enclosing some photos of a young pilot who fought in the Battle of Britain and was killed on active service. He was Pilot Officer John Benzie, a Canadian. One of the photos is of him standing with his mates taking a breather after the battle had begun. They are all Canadians of 242 Squadron based at Cottishall, Norfolk, England and these brave lads were led by the famous legless ace pilot Sir Douglas Bader.

Pilot Officer Benzie came from Winnipeg. His parents originally emigrated from Scotland to Canada. When John was young, his ambition was to learn to fly and become a bush pilot. However, three years after leaving school, he joined the Princess Patricia's Canadian Light Infantry. Then in February, 1939 he worked his way to England where he joined the RAF and got his wings in July, 1939.

At the outbreak of war, he was sent to France and on May 23, 1940 he shot down a German Messerschmitt 109 fighter plane. Later that same day, he too was unfortunately shot down. He managed to bail out despite being injured in both legs and when he landed, he was nearly killed by the French who took him to be German because of the short haircut. Indeed they took all flyers to be the enemy. He had landed just south of Dunkirk and hitched a lift on a lorry to that town where the British were evacuating their troops from the beaches. Back in Britain, he was sent to a hospital in Torquay, Devon to recover from his wounds before returning to his squadron.

The 7th of September 1940 was the fateful day that John Benzie flew with Douglas Bader to fight the enemy and never returned. Thirty-six years later to the day, on September 7, 1976 his remains were found in his partly buried Hurricane aircraft where it had crashed and his remains are now buried in a military cemetery in England.

My friends and I will never forget those brave men who fought against such odds. We owe them so much, which is why we are giving our services to the [British] museums voluntarily as a tribute to them. We are trying to gather together photos of pilots and aircrew who took part in the Battle of Britain to be put on display for creation of a national archive (Miss W. English, Slough, Berkshire 1990).

It has been estimated that over 2000 Canadians joined the RAF at the beginning of the war and between 1943 and 1945 "colonials" comprised as much as one-third of that force (Allison 1978). ***Benzie Lake*** (64 C/3), southwest of Granville Lake was named after Pilot Officer Benzie in 1953.

Bergquist, Flight Sergeant **Edwin R.** of MacGregor (R 95456). No. 83 Squadron. He died 13 October 1942 at the age of 20 and is commemorated at the Runnymede Memorial in Surrey, England. ***Bergquist Lake*** (64 J/15), northwest of Tadoule Lake was named after him in 1975.

Berlin, Sergeant **Yale** of Winnipeg (H 13114). Royal Canadian Engineers. He died 21 August 1944 at the age of 29 and is commemorated at Ancona War Cemetery in Italy. He was the son of Meyer M. and Lily Berlin of Winnipeg. ***Berlin Lake*** (64 K/11), northeast of Reindeer Lake was named after him in 1972.

Bernard, Private **Emile Y.** of Ste. Rose du Lac (H 1534). Argyle and Sutherland Highlanders. He died 2 August 1944 at the age of 21 and is commemorated at Bretteville-sur-Laize Canadian War Cemetery in Calvados, France. He was the son of Jules and Marie Bernard (née Dumas), and was survived by his wife Sarah M. Bernard (née Spence) of Ste. Rose du Lac and their two daughters. ***Bernard Island*** (64 C/12) in Laurie Lake was named after him in 1995.

Bernath, Private **Frank** (H 9616). Princess Patricia's Canadian Light Infantry. He died 29 March 1944 at the age of 23 and is commemorated at the Moro River Canadian War Cemetery in Italy. He was the son of John and Mary Bernath of Stratton, Ontario. ***Bernath Lake*** (64 O/5), northwest of Blackfish Lake was named after him in 1995.

Berrisford, Ordinary Seaman **Gordon H.** of Selkirk (V 42923). HMCS *St. Croix*. The *St. Croix* was torpedoed and sunk by U-305 south of Iceland while escorting Convoy ON.202. Five officers and 76 men were rescued by HMS *Itchen*, but only one of these survived the loss of the *Itchen* two days later. See **VanSickle,** Ordinary Seaman **Harold A.** for additional information. Ordinary Seaman Berrisford died 20 September 1943 at the age of 19 and is commemorated at the Halifax Memorial. He was the son of William and Gladys Berrisford of Selkirk. ***Berrisford Lake*** (64 F/6), northwest of Wells Lake was named after him in 1994.

Berry, Pilot Officer **John L.** of Roland (J 90142). No. 424 Squadron. He died 31 March 1944 at the age of 21 and is commemorated at Durnbach War Cemetery in Bavaria, Germany. His sister and nephew visited the grave in 1975. It was his third operational mission. He was the son of John A. and Ellen I. Berry of Carman, Manitoba. ***Berry Rapids*** (64 P/11) in the Cameron River were named after him in 1995.

Berry, Sergeant **Wallace Llewellyn** of Virden (R 59127). No. 35 Squadron. He died 15 August 1941 at the age of 25 and is commemorated at Reichswald Forest War Cemetery, Germany. He was the youngest son of Lewis D. and Philipena L. Berry (née Brill) of Virden. Prior to enlistment, he enjoyed hunting, boxing and hockey. He took considerable pleasure in writing poetry, composing the following while *en route* to Toronto where he hoped to become a pilot:

An Airman's Hymn

When the last long flight is over
And the happy landing's past
When my altimeter tells me
That the crack-up's come at last
I'll swing her nose for the ceiling
And I'll give my crate the gun
I'll open her up and let her zoom
For the airport of the sun.
Then the great God of flying men
Will smile on me – sort of slow
As I stow my crate in the hangar
On the field where flyers go.
Then I'll look upon His face
The Almighty Flying Boss
Whose wing spread fills the heavens
From Orion to the Cross.

Berry Peninsula (63 I/2) in Mishepowistik Lake was named after him in 1995.

Berzenski, Lance Corporal **George** of Russell (H 6700). Winnipeg Grenadiers, Mentioned in Dispatches. He died a prisoner of war 26 August 1942 at the age of 26 and is commemorated at the Sai Wan War Cemetery in Hong Kong. His death and that of three other Grenadiers sparked a war crimes investigation after the war. It was determined that he had been executed after trying to escape. Nine of the ten Japanese military personnel involved were found guilty. See Payne, Sergeant John O. for additional details. He was the son of Mr. and Mrs. John Berzenski and was survived by his wife Louise M. Berzenski of Fort St. John, British Columbia and their two children. At the time of his enlistment, he had been employed as a mechanic. ***Berzenski Lake*** (64 F/3), north of Vandekerckhove Lake was named after him in 1994.

Best, Flight Lieutenant **John D.** of Winnipeg (J 11043). No. 1666 Operational Training Unit, RCAF. He died 11 July 1944 and is commemorated at Harrogate (Stonefall) Cemetery in Yorkshire, England. ***Best Island*** (64 O/1) in Munroe Lake was named after him in 1995.

Bestick, Sergeant **Frank F.** of Selkirk (580598). No. 38 Squadron, RAF. He enlisted in January, 1939 and died 12 April 1940. He was 21 years of age and is commemorated at the Runnymede Memorial in Surrey, England. ***Bestick Lake*** (64 F/16), northwest of Kustra Lake was named after him in 1995.

Bettess, Able Seaman **Edward** of Winnipeg (V 24438). HMCS *Louisburg*. The *Louisburg* was attacked by Italian aircraft and sank east of Oran while escorting a convoy from Gibraltar to Bone, Algeria; 38 of her ship's company were lost. Able Seaman Bettess died 6 February 1943 at the age of 21 and is commemorated at the Halifax Memorial. He was the son of George B. and Selena M. Bettess of Winnipeg. ***Bettess Lake*** (64 N/13), west of Nueltin Lake was named after him in 1972.

Betts, Flight Sergeant **Norman Garnett** of Winnipeg (R 134551). No. 434 Squadron. He died 23 August 1943 at the age of 27 and is commemorated at Heverlee War Cemetery, Leuven, Vlaams-Brabant, Belgium. It was his first operational mission. He was the son of George H. and Kathleen M. Betts of Winnipeg. Prior to enlisting in 1941, he was employed by the Canadian Pacific Express Company. He was well known in amateur hockey circles with the local junior teams, the Fort William seniors, and playing professionally for Kansas City in the American Association Hockey league. Fifty-two years after his death, his sister received a letter from a man in Belgium:

> Dear Mrs. Elliot: Firstly I must apologize for writing out of the blue like this, I hope you do not mind too much. I was given your address by your friend … from whom I received a letter yesterday. I read in her letter that you also would like to take part in helping me collect the information for my research. In the spring of this year, I had placed a message in a local newspaper of the town Winnipeg via the mayor, with the hope to get in touch with the next-of-kin of the late Flight Sergeant Norman Garnett Betts, your brother who sadly was killed in action in my country during the Second World War.
>
> About one year ago, I started with my research on the fate of Royal Air Force bombers' crews, shot down over the Limburg area, a province in the northeast part of Belgium, during the five years of German occupation. I believe the casualties were heavy as the path of the bombers was directly in the line of the Ruhr area and consequently very heavily defended. Almost three hundred bombers of the Royal Air Force crashed in our province and many young airmen died in atrocious circumstances during the dangerous operational sorties.
>
> Today, at least four War Cemeteries of the British Commonwealth are the last sleeping witnesses of the hard air-strikes which took place every night in the dark sky of the province of Limburg. So many books were written about the actions of the ground forces and last year we celebrated here in Belgium the fiftieth anniversary of the liberation by the Allied ground troops. It seems that the nocturnal air war between the Royal Air Force nightbombers and the German nightfighters is nearly forgotten here in Belgium. A lot of families in the Commonwealth countries lost their sons, brothers, fathers, husbands, cousins and other relatives in their fight against Nazism in Europe. Perhaps the only cold comfort that many descendants ever had was to know that their beloved member of the family was buried in friendly ground where they still rest today!
>
> As you probably know, the intention of my research is to write a book who gives a detailed view on each bomber and crew that was brought down in the province of Limburg. Every crash is another story with different young men – mostly volunteers – in the leading parts. These brave young people, who mostly did not possess a driving license but were qualified to fly a twin- or four-engined bomber, took great risks every night to liberate us from the German occupation. I think that it is the obligation for my generation to remember the sacrifices of all that young airmen who took off during the war and came never back home. They gave their lives for the peace and freedom that we have today (29 November 1995).

Betts Island (64 P/13) in Baralzon Lake was named after Flight Sergeant Betts in 1987.

Betts, Leading Seaman **Roy H.** of Pine Falls (V 704). HMCS *Haida.* He died 6 August 1944 at the age of 30 and is commemorated at Plymouth (Weston Mill) Cemetery in Devon, England. He was the son of Thomas and Maria Betts. ***Betts Lake*** (64 I/13), northwest of North Knife Lake was named after him in 1974.

Beverley, Sergeant **George** of Winnipeg (R 116049). No. 113 Squadron. He died 26 February 1943 at the age of 26 and is commemorated at Elmwood Cemetery in Winnipeg. He was the son of George G. and Christina Beverley of Winnipeg and was survived by his wife Pearl E. Beverley of Winnipeg. ***Beverley Lake*** (53 L/11), west of Gods Lake was named after him in 1983.

Beyak, Flying Officer **Alexander E.** of Winnipegosis (J 14791). No. 429 Squadron. He died 22 October 1943 at the age of 20 and is commemorated at Schoonselhof Cemetery, Antwerp, Belgium. He was the son of Mrs. Nellie Beyak. ***Beyak Lake*** (52 E/14), southeast of Lac du Bonnet was named after him in 1974.

Beyak, Private **John D.** of Winnipegosis (H 510513). Royal Canadian Artillery. He died 19 September 1945 at the age of 28 and is commemorated at Winnipegosis Greek Catholic Cemetery. He was the son of Dmetro and Pauline Beyak of Winnipegosis. ***Beyak Island*** (64 O/12) in Shannon Lake was named after him in 1995.

Bialoskorski, Private **Henry** of St. Vital (H 43637). Lake Superior Motor Regiment. He died 22 April 1945 at the age of 21 and is commemorated at the Holten Canadian War Cemetery in Holland. He was the son of Stanley and Helen Bialoskorski of Winnipeg. ***Bialoskorski Lake*** (64 I/2), east of North Knife Lake was named after him in 1974.

Bickford, Rifleman **Cyril E.** of Sydney (H 1478). Regina Rifle Regiment. He died 11 November 1944 at the age of 22 and is commemorated at Brookwood Military Cemetery in Surrey, England. He was the son of Samuel N. and Lottie G. Bickford of Sydney, Manitoba. ***Bickford Lake*** (64 I/5), southeast of Tadoule Lake was named after him in 1974.

Bidochka, Gunner **Frederick** of Rossburn (H 67083). Royal Canadian Artillery. He died 20 July 1944 at the age of 22 and is commemorated at Bretteville-sur-Laize Canadian War Cemetery in Calvados, France. He was the son of Nick and Kate Bidochka and was survived by his wife Jessie Bidochka (née Robertson) of Paisley, Scotland. He was the brother of Lance Corporal Michael Bidochka (next entry). ***Bidochka Island*** (63 N/7) in Guthrie Lake was named after him in 1995.

Bidochka, Lance Corporal **Michael** of Rossburn (H 41516). Royal Winnipeg Rifles. He died 11 October 1944 and is commemorated at the Adegem Canadian War Cemetery in Belgium. He was the son of Nick and Kate Bidochka and the brother of Gunner Frederick Bidochka (previous entry). ***Bidochka Lake*** (62 N/15), southeast of Swan River was named after him in 1973.

Bieber, Stores Petty Officer **Edgar E.** of Winnipeg (V 9844). HMCS *Athabaskan*. The *Athabaskan* was sunk by a torpedo from a German destroyer while operating in the English Channel. Her captain and 128 men were lost, 83 taken prisoner and 44 men rescued by HMCS *Haida*. Petty Officer Bieber died 29 April 1944 at the age of 27 and is commemorated at the Halifax Memorial. He was the son of Andrew P. and Caroline Bieber of Winnipeg. ***Bieber River*** (64 A/16), which flows southeast into Assaikwatamo River was named after him in 1963.

Bieber, Flying Officer **Wilbert J. "Bert"** of Miniota (J 21271). No. 4 Wireless School, RCAF. He died 7 August 1943 at the age of 22 and is commemorated at Miniota Cemetery in Manitoba. He was the son of Phillip and Suzanne Bieber of Rosetown, Saskatchewan. His obituary (n.d.) read:

> The tragedy of war occurred on the Saturday previous whilst on flying duties from No. 4 Wireless School at Brantford, Ontario, and the Yale training plane piloted by F/O Bert Bieber was scheduled to go on a flight with the Burch flying squadron failed to show up and fears were entertained that something had happened. Later the report came in that there had been a plane crash four miles south of Burford village. This was the missing plane. The pilot and his mechanic were badly smashed up.
>
> The body arrived by train on Wednesday afternoon and was escorted by Flying Officer Gagnon of the same squadron and one of Bert's friends, and he spoke very highly of that boy we knew so well and thought so much of. His brother officers will miss Bert very much. His devotion to duty, his congenial company and consideration for the safety of all those he came in contact with in the course of duty, will always remain in their thoughts.

Bieber Lake (53 E/3), southwest of Island Lake was named after him in 1978.

Biebrick, Private **Clarence D.** of Whitemouth (H 1689). North Shore (New Brunswick) Regiment. He died 17 September 1944 at the age of 19 and is commemorated at Bretteville-sur-Laize Canadian War Cemetery in Calvados, France. He was the son of William and Emily Biebrick of Winnipeg. ***Biebrick Island*** (63 K/16) in Woosey Lake was named after him in 1973.

Biehl, Sergeant **William M.** of Morden (622666). No. 78 Squadron, RAF. He died 13 June 1944 at the age of 26 and is commemorated at Poix-de-Picardie Churchyard, Somme, France. He had:

> ... enlisted in July, 1938 as groundcrew ... and remustered to aircrew as a wireless operator-air gunner in 1942. During an air raid in London, he was commended for his action in rescuing people who were buried in the rubble. He completed 28 operations [and] on the next mission to support the D-Day landings, they were shot down over Amiens (Allison 1978).

Biehl Lake (64 J/5), northwest of Sprott Lake was named after him in 1995.

Biggerstaff, Pilot Officer **Richard A.** of Brandon (J 95425). No. 426 Squadron. He died 5 March 1945 at the age of 19 and is commemorated at Harrogate (Stonefall) Cemetery in Yorkshire, England. He was the son of Richard W. and Helen A. Biggerstaff (née Redman) of Brandon. He had tried to enlist in 1942, but was turned away because he was too young. ***Biggerstaff Lake*** (64 P/5), south of Nejanilini Lake was named after him in 1974.

Bignell, Private **Peter** of The Pas (H 102853). Seaforth Highlanders of Canada. He died 9 December 1944 and is commemorated at Ravenna War Cemetery in Italy. ***Bignell Island*** (64 O/5) in Shannon Lake was named after him in 1975.

Bigurski, Rifleman **Walter J.** of St. Germain (H 42175). Royal Winnipeg Rifles. He died 3 January 1944 at the age of 20 and is commemorated at Brookwood Military Cemetery in Surrey, England. He was the son of John and Mary Bigurski of St. Germain, Manitoba. ***Bigurski Lake*** (52 E/14), southeast of Lac du Bonnet was named after him in 1974.

Bill, Flying Officer **Victor E.** of Winnipeg (J 6683). No. 10 Squadron. He died 4 September 1943 at the age of 22 and is commemorated at the Ottawa Memorial. He was the son of Thomas and Isabelle Bill and the husband of Winnifred Bill. ***Bill Lake*** (64 H/10), west of Buckland Lake was named after him in 1995.

Billing, Flight Sergeant **James W.** of Winnipeg (R 110092). No. 427 Squadron. He died 2 March 1943 at the age of 22 and is commemorated at Feltwell (St. Nicholas) Churchyard in Norfolk, England. He was the son of Ernest A. and Gertrude Billing of Vancouver. ***Billing Lake*** (64 O/5), west of Booth Lake was named after him in 1995.

Bilodeau, Gunner **Robert J.** of Winnipeg (H 16308). Royal Canadian Artillery. He died 21 February 1945 at the age of 21 and is commemorated at the Groesbeek Canadian War Cemetery in Holland. He was shipped overseas in 1940 and landed in France on D-Day, later fighting in Belgium and Germany. In a letter home he wrote:

> Dear Mrs. Benjamin: Well it's been a long time before I have wrote to you which I am very sorry for not doing, but there really isn't very much to talk about, but we shall try and give you a bit of news.
>
> When we arrived over here we had our landing leave. Some of us went to England and some went to Scotland. Four of us boys went to Edinburgh, Scotland and we had a wail of a time. We went to dances and met some very nice girls who took us to some very nice places. The people in Scotland are very friendly to the boys. We had a very nice house to stay at but I don't think you can beat good old Canada.
>
> We have had a little snow over here but not much to talk about. We had a very nice Christmas, that is, as good as you can expect, but the New Year was pretty quiet. We have a very good camp but there [aren't] very many places to go. Say Mrs. Benjamin, there is a fellow over here that asked me to say hello to your husband. His name is Bombardier Harris. He says he knows Captain Benjamin. Well I don't think there is much more to talk about. You know I'm not very good at writing letters and I do hope that the family is feeling fine and in good health, so guess that will be all for now. Maybe we will have more to say next time. Goodbye and good luck. Yours truly, Bob Bilodeau (23 January 1942).

Bilodeau Lake (54 C/2), southwest of York Factory was named after him in 1964.

Bingham, Flying Officer **Clifford M.** of Winnipeg (J 22033). No. 10 Operational Training Unit, RCAF. He died 20 June 1943 at the age of 22 and is commemorated at the Runnymede Memorial in Surrey, England. He was the son of Lieutenant Colonel William J. and Olive Bingham of Winnipeg, and was survived by a younger brother Bill and sister, Jean. His sister recalls (n.d.):

> Clifford's father, Colonel Bingham of the Royal Winnipeg Rifles, left for overseas in 1941. Clifford, like all his young Winnipeg friends, volunteered as war broke out. He was just 19. He flew in No. 10 Operational Training Unit (OTU) as part of Coastal Command squadron stationed in St. Eval, Cornwall where he took part in the Battle of the Atlantic, fighting the deadly German U-boats that sank so many allied ships, killing so many thousands, and threatening to starve England into defeat.
>
> Coastal Command's theatre of operations stretched over an immense area, from far out in the Atlantic, over to the Norwegian coast, and south to the Bay of Biscay off the coast of Spain. Clifford had been in England barely two months when he was killed. He was shot down by anti-aircraft fire while attacking a U-boat in the Bay of Biscay on June 20, 1943 at the very peak of the battle to defeat the U-boat menace. He was piloting an Armstrong Whitworth Whitley bomber, flying with a crew of five other brave young men. Their names, to be read forever alongside Clifford's in the St. Eval Parish Church Book of Remembrance, are Flying Officer Archibald B. C. Durnell, Pilot Officer Frederick W. Tomlins, Flight Sergeant Harry Martin, Sergeant Walter Ettle and Sergeant Robert W. Warhurst.
>
> Clifford had arrived safely in April, 1943, and father and son were able to meet in Kew in lilac time where they shared a few precious days together. Two months later Colonel Bingham received news from Clifford's Wing Commander that Clifford's crew had been lost in the sea. He is as missed today as that day.

Bingham Lake (64 N/9), southwest of Nueltin Lake was named after him in 1972.

Birch, Lance Corporal **W. J. Thomas** of Franklin (H 41463). Royal Winnipeg Rifles. He died 6 June 1944 at the age of 25 and is commemorated at Beny-sur-Mer Canadian War Cemetery in Calvados, France. He was the son of Joseph and Miriam Birch of Neepawa. He had been born in the Rural Municipality of Rosedale 14 September 1918, receiving his education at Eden and enlisting in 1942. He worked on farms prior to joining the Royal Winnipeg Rifles at Winnipeg in October, 1940, training at Winnipeg, Shilo and Debert, Nova Scotia. He was killed in the D-Day landings in Normandy (Pittman n.d.). ***Birch Peninsula*** (53 L/6) in Joint Lake was named after him in 1995.

Bird, Company Sergeant Major **William E.** of East Kildonan (H 40503). Royal Winnipeg Rifles. He died 25 September 1944 and is commemorated at the Calais Canadian War Cemetery in France. He was survived by his wife Catherine Bird of Winnipeg. ***Bird Island*** (64 H/6) in Northern Indian Lake was named after him in 1995.

Birkett, Lieutenant **George A.** of Winnipeg. Winnipeg Grenadiers. He died 19 December 1941 at the age of 34 and is commemorated at the Sai Wan Memorial in Hong Kong. He was the eldest son of Mr. and Mrs. Allan Birkett of St. Vital. He was survived by his wife and two daughters in Vancouver. When the surviving Grenadiers returned to Winnipeg several years later, his family learned of his fate through a newspaper account (14 September 1945):

> Captain G. A. Birkett, Winnipeg, died alone on a pillbox on Jardine's Hill, December 19, 1941, in a successful effort to allow the remnants of his platoon to escape to safety. Though severely wounded in the leg, the Winnipeg officer refused treatment and grabbing two Bren guns took his stand in an evacuated Japanese position to fight off the attack while his men made their way back to the main company located in a different area in the Jardines sector.
>
> Leonard Mulvaney of 79 Morley Avenue, Winnipeg, a member of Birkett's platoon, told of Birkett's death yesterday, shortly after his arrival from Niigata camp in northern Japan, with two other Manitobans, Joseph Campbell of Mafeking and James Downie of 443 Banning Street, Winnipeg. Mulvaney termed Captain Birkett "one of the bravest men I have ever seen. He was always right in the lead and saved all our lives."
>
> On December 19, Birkett's platoon was scheduled for a special raid on Lami Island. "But," said Mulvaney, "the Japanese saved us the trouble and came over to us instead. From early that morning we fought without a break, defending the Jardines while the Japanese crept around our flanks and poured sniper fire into our ranks." In an effort to discover the position of the flank, Birkett's platoon was ordered to investigate the shallow hills nearby. Taking one section at a time, Birkett led the men over exposed ground, then returned for the next group. Finally, all sections commenced an advance [to] where the Japanese were believed to be. A volley of rifle and machine gun fire cut the ranks and Captain Birkett ordered the men to take refuge in a pillbox.
>
> "He stood beside me and I could see the blood running down his legs. I asked him to let me treat him, but he told me not to bother, to look after the other men first." A blast from a mortar shell knocked Mulvaney out of the pillbox and when he got back Birkett ordered the men to retire while he remained to cover the retreat. "The last we saw of him," Mulvaney tells, "he was standing on top of the pillbox firing a Bren gun at the approaching Japanese." Mulvaney declared that Birkett was one of the strict disciplinarians of the regiment and because of that was not as popular as some of the others. "But after what he did, we know just how great a man he was."
>
> Mulvaney learned Japanese during his stay at the camp at Niigata, which made his life slightly easier for him, but though he looks tanned and well he is still very weak. He is wondering also as to the fate of his twin brother Tom whom he last saw in Hong Kong. "I carried him into the hospital," said Mulvaney, " and have never seen him since. I asked the Red Cross and the camp officials but though they have him on the nominal roll they don't appear to know where he is."
>
> The treatment at Niigata camp was on a par with the others. The Japanese stole the Red Cross rations and beat and cursed the prisoners. "They had two prisoners, one a Canadian, the other a US marine out in a blizzard." Mulvaney related. "They had nothing on but shorts and were forced to stand with their hands behind their backs from early morning. When released, the marine was unable to make his hut and collapsed. They smashed his head in with a rifle butt." The Canadian got as far as Mulvaney's hut but dropped to the floor exhausted and died in a few hours.

Upon his return to Canada, Captain Njall O. Bardal recommended both Lieutenant Birkett and Sergeant Major John Osborn for decorations and Birkett for a posthumous promotion. Osborn received the Victoria Cross; why Birkett received neither the promotion to captain nor an award is unknown. ***Birkett Lake*** (64 H/13), northeast of Southern Indian Lake was named after him in 1963.

Birkinshaw, Flying Officer **Leonard W.** of Rapid City (J 8038). No. 407 Squadron. He died 20 January 1943 at the age of 29 and is commemorated at the Runnymede Memorial in Surrey, England. He was the son of William E. and Ann R. Birkinshaw of Rapid City and was survived by his wife Dorothy B. Birkinshaw (née McQuinn) of Rapid City. ***Birkinshaw Lake*** (53 E/7), south of Island Lake was named after him in 1973.

Birnie, Trooper **William M.** of Reston (H 103477). Fort Garry Horse. He died 8 August 1944 at the age of 29 and is commemorated at Bretteville-sur-Laize Canadian War Cemetery in Calvados, France. He was the eldest child of William and Mary Birnie of Ewart, Manitoba. A brother recalls (13 November 2001):

"Gregor" grew up very involved in those social activities that typified the life style of our local community; and in local team sports – especially softball. Some may remember him as a Bridge player of some ability. He was a cheerful, versatile worker, proud of a job well done, a competent farmer, a good neighbour, respected and remembered. Sorely missed, his siblings each and together have many fond memories of the time shared with him.

Birnie Lake (64 H/16), southwest of Condie Lake was named after him in 1995.

Birston, Rifleman **Hilliard J. H.** of Selkirk (H 10721). Royal Winnipeg Rifles. He died 8 June 1944 and is commemorated at Beny-sur-Mer Canadian War Cemetery in Calvados, France. He was survived by his wife Mary Birston of Selkirk. ***Birston Lake*** (64 P/9), east of Nejanilini Lake was named after him in 1974.

Bishoff, Rifleman **Emanuel** of West Kildonan (H 1463). Royal Winnipeg Rifles. He died 8 June 1944 at the age of 18 and is commemorated at Beny-sur-Mer Canadian War Cemetery in Calvados, France. He was the son of Emanuel and Katherine Bishoff of Arborg, Manitoba. His sister recalls (9 November 2001):

Emanuel joined the army in the fall of 1943 at the age of 17; our parents didn't know where he was. He wanted to go overseas to help his two older brothers who were over there from the beginning.

Emanuel was up to pranks in grade school – crawling out of the classroom on his stomach or calling his teacher by her nickname "Muzzy." He came home for Easter in 1944. We had a great time. He loved to sing and his favourite was *Put Your Arms Around Me Honey*. He turned 18 on May 31 and was sent over to Normandy where he was taken prisoner with 18 other soldiers and put in front of a firing squad.

Bishoff Lake (52 E/14), southeast of Lac du Bonnet was named after him in 1974.

Bishop, Colonel **Clarence V.** of Winnipeg. Royal Canadian Artillery. He died 1 December 1945 at the age of 55 and is commemorated at Royal Oak Burial Park in Victoria, British Columbia. He was survived by his wife Lilian H. Bishop of Victoria. ***Bishop Bay*** (53 L/5) in Bolton Lake was named after him in 1995.

Bishop, Pilot Officer **Denis C. "Dinty"** of Winnipeg (J 25805). No. 15 Elementary Flying Training School. He died 27 October 1943 at the age of 27 and is commemorated at St. John's Cemetery in Winnipeg. He was the son of Jack and Molly Bishop of Winnipeg and was survived by his wife Bernice N. Bishop (née Sherk) of Regina and their two year-old daughter Judy. He attended Machray School and St. John's Technical School. Previous to enlistment with the RCAF in 1942, he worked as an apprentice in the composing room of the *Winnipeg Free Press*. His sister recalls (26 October 2001):

He was a great brother, although seven years older, we got along very well. He was always busy and on-the-go. He loved the piano and played for his own pleasure. He loved photography and was interested in every facet. He took pictures of everything and everyone. Then he would develop, print and enlarge his pictures – always striving to do better. He loved flying most of all and was so proud to be a pilot. We still miss him.

Bishop Island (64 J/16) in Overby Lake was named after him in 1989.

Bissett, Squadron Leader **Jack M.** of St. Vital (J 16991). No. 427 Squadron, Distinguished Flying Medal.

[He] has displayed great courage and determination to accomplish his tasks successfully. He has taken part in many sorties including attacks on various targets in the well defended Ruhr area. A fearless captain, his fine example has proved inspiring. [He is] one of the keenest captains in the squadron and has always shown the greatest courage and determination throughout his tour, in the course of which he has attacked some of the most heavily defended areas in Germany. He has always set an example to those who worked with him, and is a real asset to the squadron (DFM Citation 1943).

He died 31 March 1944 at the age of 23 and is commemorated at Rheinberg War Cemetery in Germany. He was the son of Norman and Caroline Bissett (née Montgomery) of St. Vital. ***Bissett Lake*** (64 A/9), north of Waskaiowaka Lake was named after him in 1950.

Bissett, Lieutenant Commander **John E.** of Winnipeg (O 6680). HMCS *Athabaskan*. He died 18 March 1944 at the age of 53 and is commemorated at Mount Royal Cemetery in Montreal. He was survived by his sister Florence A. Bissett of Winnipeg, who, like her brother, practised law in Manitoba. Upon her death in 1987 she bequeathed her estate to the Winnipeg Foundation to create a fund in memory of her brother. She directed that 50% of the fund was to be used to provide assistance to law students.

The late John Edwin Bissett was born in Montreal in 1890, the son of Mr. and Mrs. E. H. Bissett, who moved thereafter to Winnipeg, where he attended Winnipeg public schools and Winnipeg Collegiate. After receiving a degree in Arts and Science from McGill University, Mr. Bissett commenced the study of law in Manitoba, articling with S. E. Richards, later Mr. Justice Richards. From 1917 to 1919, he served as a sub-lieutenant in the Royal Navy on minesweepers operating out of southern British ports. He then returned to Winnipeg and completed his law course and was called to the Bar.

For some years, he practised with the firm of McWilliams, Gunn, Honeyman, Allan and Bissett and later conducted his own practice until 1941, when he enlisted in the Royal Canadian Navy as a Lieutenant Commander and was attached to Naval Headquarters in Ottawa where he died in 1944 (Headnotes and Footnotes 1988).

Bissett Island (64 C/8) in Granville Lake was named after him in 1979.

Bissonnette, Sergeant **Guy A. R.** of Lorette (R 91666). No. 78 Squadron. He died 26 July 1942 at the age of 21 and is commemorated at the Runnymede Memorial in Surrey, England. He was survived by his mother Rosa Bissonnette of Norwood Grove. The RCAF Padre, Squadron Leader Ernest Stanston wrote to his mother shortly afterwards:

I am sure you will be glad to know I visited him a few days before he took off. He was in good spirits, brave, hardworking and happy to have a place in the defence of those ideals dear to the heart of us all. His life was lived on a high plane and was a credit to those who loved him. He was a grand lad and I always enjoyed visiting him with his comrades (30 July 1942).

Bissonnette Lake (64 F/9) on the Katimiwi River, northeast of Jordan Lake was named after him in 1986.

Bjarnason, Warrant Officer 2 **Albert Lloyd** of Langruth (R 100110). No. 424 Squadron. He died 29 July 1943 at the age of 22 and is commemorated at Enfidaville War Cemetery in Tunisia. He was the son of Eyjolfur and Margaret Bjarnason of Portage la Prairie. According to his brother (8 March 1995):

> Lloyd grew up on a farm, first of all near Froude, Saskatchewan and later moving to another farm at Griffin, Saskatchewan. He took his schooling at St. Elmo School, a one-room country school and finished his Grade 11. In 1937, he moved with his parents to a farm at Langruth, Manitoba where he worked on the farm and did commercial fishing on Lake Manitoba during the winter.
>
> In April, 1941 he joined the RCAF [and] went overseas in the winter of 1942. His squadron made 23 bombing trips over Germany. In May, 1943 the unit was sent to Libya, North Africa. On July 23, 1943 his plane crashed into a hangar as they were taking off and all the crew were killed.

Bjarnason Lake (64 H/16), southwest of Condie Lake was named after him in 1995.

Bjornson, Lance Corporal **Baldur H.** of Winnipeg (H 7026). Queen's Own Cameron Highlanders. He died 1 October 1944 at the age of 32 and is commemorated at Bergen-op-Zoom Canadian War Cemetery in Holland. He was one of the six children of Brunjolfur and Maria Bjornson of Gimli. ***Bjornson Lake*** (63 I/15), east of Cross Lake was named after him in 1972.

Bjornson, Private **Joel T.** of Winnipeg (K 85316). Princess Patricia's Canadian Light Infantry. He died 18 September 1944 at the age of 25 and is commemorated at Coriano Ridge War Cemetery in Italy. He was the son of Herman and Freda Bjornson of Winnipeg. ***Bjornson Island*** (53 L/13) in Oxford Lake was named after him in 1995.

Black, Flying Officer **Angus J.** of Carman (J 24704). No. 57 Squadron. He died 22 June 1944 at the age of 22 and is commemorated at Bergen-op-Zoom War Cemetery, Holland. ***Black Bay*** (64 F/1) on the northwest shore of Melvin Lake was named after him in 1989.

Black, Private **Douglas A.** of Brandon (H 17223). Princess Patricia's Canadian Light Infantry. He died 8 August 1944 at the age of 32 and is commemorated at Florence War Cemetery, Italy. He was the son of Hugh A. and Agnes M. Black of Vancouver. ***Black Esker*** (63 I/1), north of Little Bolton Lake was named after him in 1995.

Black, Private **Gervase E.** of Winnipeg (H 63909). Loyal Edmonton Regiment. He died 20 September 1944 at the age of 25 and is commemorated at Coriano Ridge War Cemetery in Italy. He was the son of William A. and Frances W. Black and was survived by his wife Dorothy I. Black of Burnaby, British Columbia and their son. ***Black Hill*** (64 A/4), northwest of Rock Lake was named after him in 1995.

Black, Second Lieutenant **Gilford N.** of High Bluff (O 670709). No. 551 Bomber Squadron. He died 26 September 1943. He had come to Manitoba from Iowa with his family when he was two years old. Upon the outbreak of war, he returned and became a navigator with the U. S. Army Corps. He was survived by his mother Mrs. May Black. ***Gilford Black Lake*** (63 N/4), west of Kississing Lake was named after him in 1996.

Black, Lieutenant **James W.** of Winnipeg. Lord Strathcona's Horse. He died 30 May 1944 at the age of 24 and was commemorated at the Cassino War Cemetery in Italy. He was the son of James W. and Annie M. Black and was survived by his wife Dorothy M. Black of Winnipeg. ***Black Rapids*** (64 I/15) in the Seal River was named after him in 1995.

Black, Warrant Officer 2 **Roland E.** of Winnipeg (R 123878). No. 103 Squadron. He died 2 December 1943 at the age of 20 and is commemorated at the Berlin 1939 - 1945 War Cemetery in Brandenburg, Germany. He was the son of John and Georgina Black of Vancouver. ***Black Peninsula*** (64 O/10) in Kapusta Lake was named after him in 1995.

Black, Lieutenant **Thomas Stewart** of Winnipeg. Royal Winnipeg Rifles. He died 7 April 1945 at the age of 27 and is commemorated at the Holten Canadian War Cemetery in Holland. He was the son of William S. and Ida E. Black and was survived by his wife Elsie O. Black of Winnipeg. ***Stewart Black Peninsula*** (53 E/16) in McGowan Lake was named after him in 1995.

Black, Corporal **Walter A.** of Russell (SH 800223). Princess Patricia's Canadian Light Infantry. He died 14 November 1951 at the age of 25 and is commemorated at the United Nations Cemetery in Pusan, South Korea. ***Walter Black Lake*** (53 M/10), southwest of Stupart Lake was named after this Korean War casualty in 1998.

Blackford, Lieutenant **James E.** of Winnipeg. Winnipeg Grenadiers. He died 1 September 1944 and the age of 39 and is commemorated at Brookside Cemetery in Winnipeg. He was survived by his wife Agnes Blackford of Winnipeg. ***Blackford Lake*** (53 K/11), southeast of Edmund Lake was named after him in 1996.

Blacklock, Private **Archibald A.** (H 22342). Rocky Mountain Rangers. He died 15 March 1945 at the age of 36 and is commemorated at Brookwood Military Cemetery in Surrey, England. He was the son of George and Emma Blacklock and was survived by his wife Mary Blacklock of Fort William, Ontario. ***Blacklock Lake*** (53 M/14), south of Hubley Lake was named after him in 1996.

Blackstock, Lance Sergeant **Ernest David** of Brooklands (H 3650). Royal Canadian Artillery. He died 25 August 1944 at the age of 25 and is commemorated at Bretteville-sur-Laize Canadian War Cemetery in Calvados, France. He was the son of William and Helen Blackstock of Brooklands and was survived by his wife Doris I. Blackstock. ***Blackstock Lake*** (64 H/7), northeast of Gauer Lake was named after him in 1963.

Blackwell, Sergeant **Henry W.** of Neepawa (R 80013). No. 19 Operational Training Unit, RCAF. He died 26 November 1941 at the age of 28 and is commemorated at Kinloss Abbey Burial Ground, Moray, Scotland. According to his brother (26 January 1998):

> Unfortunately, his duty in the forces was terminated on a return flight over Europe from a bombing sortie. His airplane was shot down as he

was nearing Scotland. His crew escaped by parachuting. Henry tried to bring his bomber down, but was unable to make it. Evidence of burning was found on some of his effects. He was buried at Kinloss Abbey Military Cemetery where his body remains. This is a beautiful but sad place. His name and data have been inscribed on the Blackwell family plot grave stone in the Neepawa Cemetery. Thank you again for naming a lake in northern Manitoba in his name – a permanent memorial for a promising life taken far too soon. We are proud of his endeavours to bring peace to a troubled world.

Blackwell Lake (64 H/9), northwest of Freeman Lake was named after him in 1995.

Blackwood, Leading Aircraftman **James R.** of Basswood (R 116449). No. 14 Elementary Flying Training School. He died 25 September 1941 at the age of 19 and is commemorated at Basswood Cemetery. He was the only son of Robert R. and Nellie Blackwood of Basswood, Manitoba. His cousin recalls (28 November 2001):

Jimmie received his education at Basswood Consolidated School. He joined the RCAF on July 14, 1941 in Winnipeg and trained at Brandon, Regina and Portage la Prairie. Jimmie and LAC Leslie J. Kane from Oakland, California were both killed in a flying accident while undergoing training at No. 14 EFTS at Portage la Prairie. They were both on routine solo flights when the accident occurred. The two Tiger Moths they were piloting were in mid-air collision before they crashed one mile east of Newton, Manitoba. Jimmie was the first fatality of the Basswood area during World War II. A military funeral was held at Basswood with the guard of honour from Rivers.

Blackwood Lake (53 M/9), northeast of Oxford Lake was named after him in 1985.

Blair, Rifleman **Fred W.** of Winnipeg (H 40969). Royal Winnipeg Rifles. He died 23 August 1943 at the age of 24 and is commemorated at Rochdale Cemetery in Lancashire, England. He was the son of Arthur J. and Priscilla A. Blair and was survived by his wife of ten months Margaret E. Blair (née Martin) of Rochdale, Lancashire, England. Their daughter was born the following spring. According to his widow (31 March 1998):

I am not aware of the exact area in England or Scotland my first husband was in when he was killed; all I know is that they were using live ammunition on manoeuvres resulting in his death. He is buried in my home town of Rochdale. My daughter and I left Southampton, England on January 13, 1947 on the *Aquitania* and arrived in Halifax, Nova Scotia on January 21, 1947. I was receiving [a] War Widows Pension until I [re]married.

Blair Island (63 K/16), in Loonhead Lake was named after him in 1973.

Blair, Private **Reginald R.** of Winnipeg (H 16196). Princess Patricia's Canadian Light Infantry. He died 20 December 1944 at the age of 20 and is commemorated at Ravenna War Cemetery in Italy. He was the son of James J. and Flora Blair of Georgetown, Ontario and was survived by his wife Nancy F. Blair of Lancing, Sussex and their 20 month-old son. His wife writes (8 November 2001):

He was born in Georgetown, Ontario on 17 March 1924. He joined the PPCLI in 1939 under the care of a Captain Leach. He trained in Manitoba and was posted to England early in 1940. We met in Brighton later that year. Soon, he was sent elsewhere in England, but was posted back to Brighton where we met again at the end of 1941. We married late in 1942 and our son was born in April, 1943, two months prematurely. He was given embarkation leave at that time. If our son had not been premature, he would never have seen his son, as my husband was killed just over a year and a half later. My son and I were in Canada at the time of his death, living with my husband's parents. I returned to England at the end of the war with my son.

Blair Bay (64 P/3) in Hoguycho Lake was named after him in 1996.

Blair, Warrant Officer 2 **William** of Meadows (R 119545). No. 1659 Conversion Unit, RCAF. He died 28 May 1944 at the age of 30 and is commemorated at Stoneykirk Cemetery, Wigtownshire, Scotland. He was the son of Robert and Mary Blair of Meadows, Manitoba. ***Blair Lake*** (53 M/6), north of Oxford Lake was named after him in 1985.

Blakely, Private **Albert E. "Bert"** of Grandview (151543). 43rd Battalion, Canadian Infantry (Manitoba Regiment). He died 21 September 1916 at the age of 19 and is commemorated at the Vimy Memorial, Pas de Calais, France. He was the son of Robert and Matilda Blakely of Grandview. ***Blakely Lake*** (64 G/5), southeast of Hurst Lake was named after him in 2001.

Blamey, Warrant Officer 2 **Claude C.** of Winnipeg (R 97675). No. 200 Squadron. He died 6 January 1943 at the age of 20 and is commemorated at Fajara War Cemetery, Gambia. He was the son of Urban C. and Kathrine M. Blamey of Vancouver. ***Blamey Lake*** (53 K/4), west of Red Sucker Lake was named after him in 1995.

Blanchard, Private **Robert** of Winnipeg (H 77586). Winnipeg Grenadiers. He died 23 December 1941 and is commemorated at the Sai Wan War Cemetery in Hong Kong. ***Blanchard Lake*** (64 O/1), east of Munroe Lake was named after him in 1975.

Blank, Rifleman **Elmer W.** of Lac du Bonnet (E 30291). Royal Rifles of Canada. He died 28 January 1945 at the age of 22 and is commemorated at the Yokohama War Cemetery in Japan. He was the son of Herbert and Martha Blank of Winnipeg. Rifleman Blank died a prisoner of war after the fall of Hong Kong. Prisoners at the Niigata Camp north of Tokyo were greeted by the camp commander whom the inmates nicknamed "Bluebeard:"

You are my slaves. You are descendants of the Anglo-Saxon piracy that we are fighting today. You are here to work, and you shall work until you die and be glad to. If you prove to be willing workers we will send you home when the war comes to an end. That will be when the Americans on their hands and knees are begging for mercy. It will be the year 1950. Though you are sick in body and mind, your hands belong to me (*The Winnipeg Tribune* 14 September 1945).

Blank Island (62 O/13) in the Waterhen River was named after him in 1981.

Blatt, Private **Louis** of Winnipeg (H 36824). North Shore (New Brunswick) Regiment. He died 8 August 1944 and is commemorated at Bretteville-sur-Laize Canadian War Cemetery in Calvados, France. His brother writes (26 August 1997):

I am told that a new museum has been built in Winnipeg … and that a part of the museum will have memorabilia of the Jewish Orphanage. My

brother Louis and myself and two other[s] were there also. I feel that the museum should have the original [commemorative] certificate you sent to be hung up there.

Blatt Lake (64 K/5), northeast of Reindeer Lake was named after him in 1972.

Blaydes, Pilot Officer **Herbert I.** of Winnipeg (J 88416). No. 9 Squadron. He died 25 June 1944 at the age of 28 and is commemorated at Coulonvillers Communal Cemetery, Somme, France. He was the only child of Herbert I. and Claudia Blaydes (née Jenkins) and was survived by his wife Marguerite M. Blaydes (née Thompson) of St. James and their four month-old daughter. His daughter (6 April 1998) describes him as an:

> ... honours student who graduated from Kelvin Collegiate in Winnipeg [and] worked in [an] office at Winnipeg Electric. After completing a business course, he enlisted in the RCAF and trained as a navigator in Edmonton, Alberta.

Blaydes Lake (64 J/10), west of Tadoule Lake was named after him in 1975.

Blenkhorn, Sergeant **Charles R. S.** of St. Vital (R 123873). No. 22 Operational Training Unit, RCAF. He died 4 May 1943 at the age of 22 and is commemorated at Stratford-upon-Avon Cemetery in Warwickshire, England. He was the son of Clifford S. and Eva M. Blenkhorn of St. Vital. ***Blenkhorn Lake*** (64 J/13), northwest of Tadoule Lake was named after him in 1975.

Blevins, Flight Lieutenant **Kenneth J.** of Winnipeg (J 11762). No. 436 Squadron. He died 11 October 1945 at the age of 31 and is commemorated at Brookwood Military Cemetery in Surrey, England. He was the son of James A. and Beulah B. Blevins and was survived by his wife Asta M. Blevins of Winnipeg. ***Blevins Lake*** (64 O/15), east of Nueltin Lake was named after him in 1961.

Blue, Rifleman **Norman** of Winnipeg (H 10934). Royal Winnipeg Rifles. He died 5 July 1944 at the age of 18 and is commemorated at Beny-sur-Mer Canadian War Cemetery in Calvados, France. He was the son of Peter W. and Marguerite M. Blue of Fort Garry. ***Blue Island*** (63 N/13) in Sisipuk Lake was named after him in 1995.

Blueman, Corporal **Henry K.** of Flin Flon (H 6379). Winnipeg Grenadiers. He died a prisoner of war 19 January 1945 at the age of 28 and is commemorated at the Yokohama War Cemetery in Japan. He was the son of William and Mary Blueman and was survived by his wife Martha B. Blueman of Flin Flon. ***Blueman Lake*** (64 C/5), southeast of Reindeer Lake was named after him in 1973.

Blyth, Pilot Officer **Colin J.** of Winnipeg (J 89962). No. 405 Squadron. He died 29 July 1944 at the age of 22 and is commemorated at Norre Havrvig Churchyard in Denmark. He was the son of Frederick and Emily Blyth of Winnipeg. According to his brother (23 January 1997):

> [The] family immigrated to Winnipeg from Norwich, England in 1924. He was educated at La Vérendrye, Earl Grey and Kelvin High Schools. He was a member of All Saints Church Choir as a soprano and later as a tenor.

Blyth Island (64 C/4) in McCallum Lake was named after him in 1995.

Blyth, Ordinary Seaman **John M.** of Winnipeg (V 9799). HMCS *Otter*. The *Otter* was destroyed by an accidental explosion and fire off Halifax. Two officers and 17 men were lost. Ordinary Seaman Blyth died 26 March 1941 at the age of 18 and is commemorated at Brookside Cemetery in Winnipeg. He was the son of Mr. and Mrs. John S. Blyth of Winnipeg. According to his brother (13 February 1996):

> Jack attended Centennial School in West Kildonan from Grade 1 to Grade 9. He was a good speed skater and went into a lot of competitions and won a few awards for his school. He was also a great model airplane builder; there were planes hanging from the ceiling in our bedroom so you could see nothing but planes. These were planes with gas motors in them and some of the planes had a wing span of six feet or better. Then he would take them out and fly them and crash them and go back and make another. This was his hobby.
>
> He joined the RCNVR in 1940. He served some time in Winnipeg and then was sent to Halifax that same year. This was pretty much Jack's life – school and building airplanes. He never worked at a job for anyone. He came right out of school into the Navy. Jack never had much of a chance to see life as an adult. He was taken away of the age [of] 18.

Blyth Lake (64 I/3), west of North Knife Lake was named after him in 1957.

Boak, Private **William** of Portage la Prairie (H 17810). Princess Patricia's Canadian Light Infantry. He died 20 July 1942 at the age of 23 and is commemorated at Brookwood Military Cemetery in Surrey, England. He was the son of Mike and Mary Boak of Portage la Prairie. ***Boak Lake*** (64 K/14), northeast of Lac Brochet was named after him in 1972.

Boal, Private **Hugh** (H 19475). Queen's Own Cameron Highlanders. He died 19 August 1942 and is commemorated at Dieppe Canadian War Cemetery in Seine-Maritime, France. He was survived by his sister Bella Boal of Ballymena, Antrim, Northern Ireland. ***Boal Lake*** (64 N/16), west of Nueltin Lake was named after him in 1972.

Boatfield, Trooper **Jack** of Winnipeg (H 77433). 12th Manitoba Dragoons. He died 10 October 1944 at the age of 25 and is commemorated at the Adegem Canadian War Cemetery in Belgium. He was the son of William and Edith Boatfield of Napinka, Manitoba. ***Boatfield Lake*** (52 L/6), southeast of Lac du Bonnet was named after him in 1973.

Bocking, Warrant Officer 2 **Stanley** of Winnipeg (R 71058). No. 87 Squadron. He died 30 July 1942 at the age of 22 and is commemorated at Colerne (St. John The Baptist) Churchyard in Wiltshire, England. He was the son of Alfred L. and Agnes Bocking of Winnipeg and was survived by his wife Nettie Bocking of Calgary. According to his brother (6 January 1995):

> Stan was my only and younger sibling. He was born in Winnipeg and attended public schools in Winnipeg – the old Tache School in Norwood and Norwood Collegiate. In 1938-39 he was attending United College. On the outbreak of war he joined the RCAF as a pilot (I believe he trained at Summerside, PEI). At the time, I was commanding an RAF squadron in the Middle East. At the time of his death Stan was serving with 87 (United Provinces) Squadron, RAF based in central England (Middle Wallop) [flying] Hurricane 2c's.
>
> Just after Stan's death I spoke with his wingman on his final operation. He advised me that he and Stan were returning to base after a night sweep (train busting) over Europe. Nearing their home base, he advised Stan that his (Stan's) aircraft appeared to be on fire. The fire increased and his wing man urgently told Stan to use his parachute. But they were too low and Stan's aircraft crashed in flames killing him instantly.

Bocking Lake (64 I/14), north of North Knife Lake was named after him in 1974.

Bodkin, Pilot Officer **Alvin G.** of Napinka (J 45826). Royal Canadian Air Force. He died 7 October 1944 at the age of 35 and is commemorated at Napinka Cemetery. He was the son of Frank G. and Henrietta Bodkin and was survived by his wife Hilda Bodkin (née Ward) of Toronto and their unborn daughter. According to a cousin (28 April 1995), he was born in:

> ... Harriston, Ontario. [His] mother died in 1909. His grandmother Margaret Bodkin of Napinka raised Alvin from two months of age until he finished school. After finishing school, he went to Regina, Saskatchewan where his father was, got a job with the Bank of Commerce, worked there, then transferred to Winnipeg where he lived with his wife Hilda (Ward). He joined the RCAF in Winnipeg, I think around 1941 or 42. Was stationed in Abbottsford, BC at the time of his death. Alvin died of a heart attack due to very high altitude while on a training exercise. Alvin loved music from a very early age, was an excellent pianist, also played other instruments.

Bodkin Lake (53 M/11), southeast of Ransom Lake was named after him in 1996.

Bodley, Flight Sergeant **William** of Winnipeg (R 92475). No. 100 Squadron. He died 11 April 1943 at the age of 23 and is commemorated at Rheinberg War Cemetery in Germany. He was the son of George and Ada Bodley of Vancouver. ***Bodley Lake*** (64 O/2), southwest of Munroe Lake was named after him in 1995.

Boehmer, Private **Roy D.** of Winnipeg (H 20102). Queen's Own Cameron Highlanders. He died 19 August 1941 at the age of 25 and is commemorated at Brookside Cemetery in Winnipeg. He was survived by his wife Phyllis Boehmer of St. Boniface. Just prior to the war, he had gained something of a reputation as a boxer, having entered the Saskatchewan amateur championships in the heavyweight division. ***Boehmer Lake*** (63 P/2), west of Cotton Lake was named after him in 1996.

Bohémier, Pilot Officer **Joseph Eloi** of Ste. Anne (J 93491). No. 441 Squadron. He was reported missing 23 January 1945 while in action near Iceland and was presumed dead two years later. He was 26 years of age and is commemorated at the Runnymede Memorial in Surrey, England. He was the son of Jean M. and Florida Bohémier (née Leclair) and was survived by his wife Gilberte Bohémier (née Gagnon) of Montreal. His sister recalls that (10 February 1997):

> He graduated from Ste. Anne Collegiate, [was] called to do military training in the army and when this was completed [he] joined the air force and trained as a pilot. He completed his operations over Germany and was due back in Canada. Instead, his wife received the sad message he was missing in action.
>
> Hobbies included playing the clarinet, guitar and piano accordion. He was also a member of the school orchestra with his two brothers. He enjoyed art, especially doing water colour paintings. In sports he was keen on playing hockey, softball, swimming and even horseback riding. His family felt they had been blessed by his presence as [he was] loveable, courageous and very popular with all who knew him.
>
> He loved animals around the farm. His favourite was his dog "Buster," a German Shepherd that was raised from a pup. Buster helped Eloi round up the cows. Told to get the cows, Buster would do just that. Told that one was missing, Buster rounded that one up too. Buster knew when Eloi was coming home on leave; all of a sudden he was scratching at the door begging to be let out. He knew Eloi was at the highway a good distance from the farm. Buster was also eager to carry home Eloi's schoolbooks but he had to rest a few times for the books were heavy and it was a long way to the farm.
>
> His life was not measured by the years he lived, but by the cheer and love he radiated. He therefore accomplished his noble task with courage and bravery. We loved him dearly. No life is truly great that is not useful to mankind.

Bohémier Lake (63 K/16), west of Wekusko Lake was named after him in 1973.

Boisvert, Warrant Officer 2 **J. G. Louis** of Pine Falls (R 101506). No. 1 Operational Training Unit, RCAF. He died 19 September 1943 at the age of 34 and is commemorated at Thornaby-on-Tees Cemetery in Yorkshire, England. He and Flight Sergeant F. J. V. McGrath, RAAF were killed when their aircraft crashed near Topcliffe in Yorkshire. He was survived by his wife Annette Boisvert. ***Boisvert Lake*** (64 F/2), northeast of Dunsheath Lake was named after him in 1980.

Boisvert, Gunner **Maurice** (H 24135). Royal Canadian Artillery. He died 1 August 1944 and is commemorated at Brookwood Military Cemetery in Surrey, England. ***Boisvert Island*** (54 D/6) in Stephens Lake was named after him in 1996.

Bojarski, Rifleman **Charles R.** of Brandon (H 14413). Royal Winnipeg Rifles. He died 15 August 1944 at the age of 20 and is commemorated at Bretteville-sur-Laize Canadian War Cemetery in Calvados, France. He was the son of John and Antonia Bojarski of Brandon. ***Bojarski Lake*** (64 J/6), southwest of Tadoule Lake was named after him in 1975.

Boles, Pilot Officer **William Harold** of Deloraine (J 18781). No. 426 Squadron. He died 27 November 1943 at the age of 30 and is commemorated at the Runnymede Memorial in Surrey, England. He was the son of Mr. and Mrs. H. G. Boles and was survived by his wife Margaret A. Boles (née Gage) of Medora, Manitoba and their two daughters Barbara and Sandra. His sister recalls (27 November 2001):

> Harold played hockey, sang in the choir, loved music and was an excellent pianist. Prior to joining the RCAF in 1941, he worked for the Municipality and was the pianist in an orchestra which played at the local dances. When he was stationed "somewhere in England," he and some of his crew saw a field of corn. They asked the farmer if they could have some as they really wanted a "corn feed." The farmer told them it was feed for his animals but that they could have some of it if they really wanted to. They decided to take some and cook it and even though it tasted terrible, it reminded them of home.

In a letter to his sisters, he refers to his brothers-in-law who were avid duck hunters: "Glad to hear the shooting was so good," he wrote. "As far as I am concerned, I wouldn't mind helping with the eating but there is altogether too much shooting going on over here to enjoy it too much" (9 November 1943). In his last letter home to his mother he wrote:

> The mail hasn't been too bad lately, but I can never have too many letters. It's nearly a year since I last was in Deloraine and it seems longer. Sometimes I wonder if it's all a dream or not. Often I'm afraid that Barbara will be grown up before I see her again and I sure would like to see Baby Sandy before she gets too big (1 August 1943).

Boles Lake (64 O/15), east of Nueltin Lake was named after him in 1975.

Bollert, Aircraftman 1 **Frank D.** of Winnipeg (R 134422). No. 120 Recce Squadron. He died 20 June 1942 at the age of 21 and is commemorated at Brookside Cemetery in Winnipeg. He was the son of Ernest B. and Elsie Bollert of Winnipeg. ***Bollert Lake*** (64 P/11), east of Nejanilini Lake was named after him in 1974.

Bondoluk, Private **Alexander** of Oak Point (H 65409). 4th Canadian Armoured Division. He died 19 November 1944 at the age of 29 and is commemorated at Bergen-op-Zoom Canadian War Cemetery in Holland. He was the son of Alexander and Maria Bondoluk of Winnipeg. ***Bondoluk Lake*** (64 J/5), southwest of Tadoule Lake was named after him in 1975.

Bonner, Flying Officer **Murray W.** of Miniota (J 21902). No. 1663 Conversion Unit, RCAF. He died 19 August 1943 at the age of 23 and is commemorated at Harrogate (Stonefall) Cemetery in Yorkshire, England. He was the son of James W. and Janet Eliza Bonner of Miniota. His sister recalls (21 November 2001):

> He was born in a farm home in Miniota, Manitoba, the second of five children, three boys and two girls. He completed Grade 12 at Miniota and worked on the home farm before joining the air force. He trained at High River, Alberta and graduated as a pilot at Dauphin, Manitoba.
>
> He did really well at school and school sports, mainly softball (pitcher) and hockey. He had a great love of farming and his ponies, spending many happy hours riding. His plan was to attend University after the war and study Agriculture. A commemorative plaque is in the family plot in the Miniota Cemetery overlooking the Assiniboine Valley.

Bonner Lake (64 F/3), northeast of Goldsand Lake was named after him in 1994.

Book, Flying Officer **Archibald N.** of Winnipeg (J 23434). No. 304 Operational Training Unit, RCAF. He died 1 January 1944 at the age of 24 and is commemorated at Kilarrow New Parish Churchyard, Isle Of Islay, Argyllshire, Scotland. He was the son of Archibald B. and Gertrude N. Book and was survived by his wife Fleur-ange Book (née Gauthier) of Montreal. He was flying a bomber over the Hebrides when the engines failed. He ordered the crew to bail out, but stayed on board to ensure that the aircraft would not hit any populated places. According to his brother (17 June 1997):

> Archibald Neville Book was born in Winnipeg on March 16th, 1919. Growing up in Winnipeg, he took part in various sports, particularly tennis, hockey and canoeing. He was active in Scouting, from Cubs through Rovers and as an assistant Cub Master. In Rovers, his interest in canoe-building was whetted. Eventually, he was taking weekend and longer trips, both in the St. Alban's Rover Crew's canoes which he had helped build, and in his own home-made kayak.
>
> At that point, having gone through Riverview Elementary, Lord Roberts Junior High and Kelvin High Schools and having taken a successful year at United College in the University of Manitoba, he decided business was more to his interest and enrolled at Success Business College. From there he got a job with Canadian Industries Limited, whose offices were in northwest Winnipeg. While with CIL, he took flying lessons with the Winnipeg Flying Club, gaining his commercial licence in 1941. In the same year, he put in his stint in the Army camp at Portage la Prairie. This decided him to join the air force, which he did in January, 1942.
>
> While training at Summerside, PEI, he met and married Fleur-ange Gauthier who was in the Women's Division of the air force. Shortly after the wedding he was sent to Britain, but his wife was not; there were no children.

Book Lake (64 O/8), southwest of Nejanilini Lake was named after him in 1975.

Boon, Bombardier **Richard** of Winnipeg (P 9869). Royal Canadian Artillery. He died 23 January 1944 at the age of 45 and is commemorated at Harrowsmith Cemetery in Ontario. He was the son of Mr. and Mrs. Abram Boon of Oldham, Lancashire and was survived by his wife Sarah C. Boon of Hartington. ***Boon Lake*** (52 L/3), southeast of Lac du Bonnet was named after him in 1973.

Booth, Flying Officer **James R.** of Winnipeg (J 22097). No. 115 Squadron. He died 28 January 1944 at the age of 20 and is commemorated at the Runnymede Memorial in Surrey, England. He was the son of James A. W. and Sadie K. Booth of Winnipeg. ***Booth Bay*** (64 I/2) in Halldorson Lake was named after him in 1995.

Booth, Pilot Officer **Robert A.** of Winnipeg (C 19795). No. 405 Squadron, Croix de Guerre avec Palme (Belgium). He died 28 April 1944 at the age of 26 and is commemorated at Webbekom Churchyard, Diest, Vlaams-Brabant, Belgium. He was the son of Frederick R. and Emma Booth of Winnipeg. ***Booth Lake*** (64 O/5), south of Nueltin Lake was named after him in 1961.

Borkowsky, Flight Sergeant **Edward** of Russell (R 189482). No. 78 Squadron. He died 6 October 1944 at the age of 22 and is commemorated at the Reichswald Forest War Cemetery in Germany. He was the son of Louis and Mary Borkofsky (sp.) of Russell. ***Borkowsky Lake*** (64 C/3), east of Russell Lake was named after him in 1993.

Borne, Rifleman **Cecil M.** of Oak Lake (H 42243). Regina Rifle Regiment. He died 9 June 1944 at the age of 20 and is commemorated at Beny-sur-Mer Canadian War Cemetery in Calvados, France. He was the son of Lorenzo A. and Laura R. Borne of Oak Lake, Manitoba. His chaplain wrote to Mrs. Borne shortly after his death:

> Dear Mrs. Borne: I am your son's padre. I am writing to confirm the report which you have already received of his death and to express my sincere sympathy. I deeply regret that I am not personally acquainted with you. An expression of sympathy from a stranger is always so cold. However, I knew "Cec" so well that I am certain that he has mentioned me in his letters. I share with you a great personal loss in his death, though I am at a loss to know what to say to you.
>
> I think that you would prefer that I should tell you exactly how he met his death. It happened on the night of 8 – 9 June, when our position was attacked by a Panzer Division, and we were subjected to the full force of the fire from enemy tanks. "Cec" was on the outer defences guarding the road to our Headquarters. The tanks over-ran his position and although he and his pals fought it out to the last, it was a hopeless struggle and Cec was among the ones that lost their lives. Small comfort though it be, Cec could not have suffered, for his death was instantaneous. I attended to his burial myself and he lies in the courtyard of a French house, with a number of his comrades. Later on, all the Canadians who fall on active service in France will be buried in a central cemetery and you will be informed of its location.
>
> I was very well acquainted with Cec and his platoon. Many a time I have ridden with them on their carriers, chatted with them in their billets and talked over a cup of tea and a cigarette seated around a fire when we have been out on schemes. There is so little that I can say. Letters are most inadequate to convey our feelings on occasions such as this. I do hope that the kindly help of bosom friends may ease the burden for you, the way in which the comradeship which has grown up amongst us here holds us all in its firm grip these days. And we are finding, and I know that you do too, that our simple Christian faith brings comfort and strength as nothing else can.
>
> I do hope that you will feel free to write to me if there is anything at all which I can do to help you out. There may be many questions that you would like to ask, things which I have overlooked in our present

rush. If you will let me know, I shall be only too glad to answer. With kindest regards, Very sincerely, Graham M. Jamieson (26 June 1944).

Borne Lake (63 K/12), southwest of Manistikwan Lake was named after him in 1984.

Boroski, Sergeant **Frank** of Rockwood (R 67510). No. 139 Squadron. He died 2 June 1941 at the age of 21 and is commemorated at the Runnymede Memorial in Surrey, England. ***Boroski Lake*** (64 I/8), northeast of North Knife Lake was named after him in 1974.

Bostrom, Lance Corporal **George** of Winnipeg (H 19511). Queen's Own Cameron Highlanders. He died 4 August 1944 at the age of 27 and is commemorated at Beny-sur-Mer Canadian War Cemetery in Calvados, France. He was the son of Mr. and Mrs. Frank O. Bostrom of Winnipeg and was survived by his wife Emilie Bostrom of Winnipeg. ***Bostrom Island*** (52 L/3) in Crowduck Lake was named after him in 1973.

Boswell, Private **Ernest A.** of Roblin (H 6063). Winnipeg Grenadiers. He died a prisoner of war 29 November 1943 at the age of 30 and is commemorated at the Sai Wan War Cemetery in Hong Kong. He was survived by his wife Agnes Boswell of Roblin, Manitoba and their two children. Born in London, England, he lost his father in World War I and when his mother remarried, he was sent to an orphanage in Canada at the age of 12. He enlisted in September, 1939 and served in the West Indies for 16 months before going to the Orient. ***Boswell Lake*** (63 I/16), northeast of Cross Lake was named after him in 1973.

Botterill, Flight Sergeant **Harold W.** of Winnipeg (R 196196). No. 424 Squadron. He died 1 November 1944 at the age of 21 and is commemorated at Nederweert War Cemetery in Holland. He was the son of George F. and Sarah H. Botterill of Los Angeles, California. ***Botterill Lake*** (63 P/15), southeast of Witchai Lake was named after him in 1996.

Botting, Pilot Officer **Ross M.** of Stonewall (J 92204). No. 355 Squadron. He died 19 March 1945 at the age of 22 and is commemorated at the Singapore Memorial. He was the son of Ross and Ellen Botting of Winnipeg. ***Botting Lake*** (64 N/9), southwest of Nueltin Lake was named after him in 1972.

Bouchard, Corporal **Louis J.** of Vassar, Manitoba (H 26762). Fort Garry Horse. He died 15 August 1944 and is commemorated at Bretteville-sur-Laize Canadian War Cemetery in Calvados, France. He was the brother of Rifleman Zepherin Bouchard (next entry). ***Bouchard Lake*** (54 B/7), northeast of Shamattawa was named after him in 1964.

Bouchard, Rifleman **Zepherin H.** of Vassar (H 103483). Royal Winnipeg Rifles. He died 4 July 1944 and is commemorated at Beny-sur-Mer Canadian War Cemetery in Calvados, France. He was the brother of Corporal Louis Bouchard (previous entry). ***Bouchard Island*** (53 E/16), west of Grand Island in Island Lake was named after him in 1983.

Boulton, Flying Officer **Clive A.** of Russell (J 85059). No. 405 Squadron. He died 15 March 1945 at the age of 21 and is commemorated at the Hanover War Cemetery in Germany. He was the son of Laurence C. and Jennie D. Boulton of Vancouver. ***Boulton Island*** (63 N/5) in Kipahigan Lake was named after him in 1995.

Boulton, Private **Wilbert R.** of Morden (H 95593). Princess Patricia's Canadian Light Infantry. He died 23 July 1943 at the age of 24 and is commemorated at Agira Canadian War Cemetery, Sicily. He was the son of Albert and Harriet C. Boulton of Morden. ***Boulton Lake*** (52 L/11), northwest of Black Lake was named after him in 1982.

Bounting, Private **Harvey F.** of Gladstone (H 10279). Queen's Own Cameron Highlanders. He died 11 November 1944 at the age of 27 and is commemorated at the Groesbeek Canadian War Cemetery in Holland. He was the second of the seven children of Jay S. and Annie C. Bounting of Senlac, Saskatchewan. According to his sister-in-law (28 December 1997):

> ... he grew up on the family farm and took his schooling at Penile – a country school. He quit school at an early age, taking work where he could find it, as a farm hand on neighbouring farms and as far away as it was necessary to go. He was a good-natured fellow who liked to dance and took a lot of enjoyment in fixing the old cars of the time. Getting an old car or a stalled one to run again was his pride and joy. His travelling, looking for work, took him eventually to Manitoba where he joined the army at Camp Shilo in 1941. After his training, he was sent overseas and very soon to the front lines. He was wounded once and returned to England to recover. While there, he had a brief reunion with his brother Lawrence, also serving in the army. After a short recovery period, he again returned to the front lines in Holland and was killed in action.

Bounting Lake (64 P/9), east of Nejanilini Lake was named after him in 1974.

Boutilier, Bombardier **Robert C.** of St. Boniface (H 3657). Royal Canadian Artillery. He died 31 August 1944 and is commemorated at Brookwood Military Cemetery in Surrey, England. ***Boutilier Lake*** (63 O/4), north of Wekusko Lake was named after him in 1970.

Bower, Flying Officer **William Richardson "Richard"** of Union Point (J 8763). No. 14 Squadron. He died 23 November 1942 at the age of 31 and is commemorated at the Suez War Memorial Cemetery, Egypt. He was the son of William E. and Viola A. Bower of Union Point. His brother recalls (20 December 2001):

> William Richardson (Richard) Bower enlisted in the RCAF in May, 1941. He trained as a pilot in Canada and was graduated with a commission as a Pilot Officer. On completion of operational training in the United Kingdom, he was posted to North Africa. He, with his crew, flew a Blenheim aircraft to North Africa in July, 1942 and was posted to RAF No. 14 Squadron equipped with Marauder B26 aircraft. After several bombing operations, Flying Officer Bower lost his life on November 23 while on low level bombing practice due to the malfunctioning of the flying controls on the tail section. Richard and his crew were killed.
>
> Richard was survived by his father and Mother, sister Beth and brother Donald. In 1983, I was pleasantly surprised to learn that a creek in northern Manitoba had been named after Flying Officer William R. Bower. This does seem a suitable marker for Richard as his home at Union Point was on the Red River and he spent time along the banks of that river.

Bower Creek (64 I/7), which flows southeast into North Knife River was named after him in 1974.

Bowes, Private **David W.** of Winnipeg (H 6752). Winnipeg Grenadiers. He died 27 February 1944 at the age of 24 and is commemorated at the Yokohama War Cemetery in Japan. He was taken prisoner of war after the fall of Hong Kong. He was survived by his mother Mary Bowes of Winnipeg. According to his sister (29 October 2001):

Private David William Bowes was the second son of John and Mary Ann Bowes. He arrived with our parents from England in 1925 and settled near Balmoral, Manitoba. He worked on the farm and was a great help to my mother who had seven other children to look after. When the war came along, he joined the Winnipeg Grenadiers, was captured and interned. From all reports, he was very ill and had little or no food. He died in 1944.

Bowes Lake (64 N/16), west of Nueltin Lake was named after him in 1972.

Bowes, Flying Officer **Donald S.** of Winnipeg (J 37559). No. 419 Squadron. He died 31 March 1945 at the age of 21 and is commemorated at Becklingen War Cemetery in Germany. He was the son of Victor A. and Elizabeth S. M. Bowes of Winnipeg. ***Bowes Creek*** (64 G/11), which flows south into Sanderson Lake was named after him in 1986.

Bowles, Private **Irvine H.** of Treherne (K 59182). Perth Regiment. He died 26 May 1944 at the age of 31 and is commemorated at the Cassino War Cemetery in Italy. He was the son of Arthur and Jennie Bowles, and was survived by his wife Deborah M. Bowles (née Hamilton) of Port Alberni, British Columbia and their three children aged 11, 9 and 6. His son writes (30 October 2001):

When Dad was growing up, things were pretty rough; money was scarce. Pinkerton District was an active community – dances, picnics, curling and hockey. Dad and Mom were married in 1932. We moved to Port Alberni on Vancouver Island in 1937 where Dad worked in a sawmill. We moved to Vancouver in 1940 where Dad worked at Dominion Bridge. In 1942, Dad volunteered for the Army. This was part of the last letter we had from Dad:

Dear Ken, Jean and Bill: And how are my little darlings getting along? Ken, are you helping Mother to do her work? Jeanie, are you washing the dishes for Mother? And Billie, wild man, are [you] bringing in the wood? How is our dog getting along, Billie? Well kids, I was out to see Uncle Howard today and he wants to know if you are all going to school. So I told him that you would all be going. Well, be good kids and help Mother, and I will soon be home again. Lots of love, Dad (n.d.).

Bowles Lake (64 G/5), southwest of Hurst Lake was named after him in 1996.

Bowman, Captain **Allan S.** of Winnipeg. Winnipeg Grenadiers. He died 19 December 1941 at the age of 35 and is commemorated at the Sai Wan Memorial in Hong Kong. He was the son of Edward A. and Lily S. Bowman and was survived by his wife Margaret A. Bowman of Winnipeg. ***Bowman Island*** (64 O/4) in Blackfish Lake was named after him in 1995.

Bowman, Trooper **George** of Winnipeg (H 55). Lord Strathcona's Horse. He died 15 April 1945 at the age of 26 and is commemorated at the Groesbeek Canadian War Cemetery in Holland. He was the son of William and Marjorie A. Bowman of Winnipeg. ***Bowman Creek*** (53 M/6), which flows northeast into Gowan River was named after him in 1985.

Boyd, Ordinary Seaman **Barney W.** of Winnipeg (V 34758). HMCS *St. Hyacinthe*. He died 3 March 1943 at the age of 18 and is commemorated at Elmwood Cemetery in Winnipeg. He was survived by his mother Ethel M. Boyd of Winnipeg. According to his sister (12 April 1995):

My brother lived all his short life at 363 Ainslie Street, Sturgeon Creek. He joined the Navy on his 18th birthday (April 14, 1942) and died March 3, 1943.

He went east with his group in August, 1942 and was training in Saint-Hyacinthe, Quebec when an outbreak of scarlet fever hit the barracks in December and he died from complications resulting from the disease in March. He was buried with Navy honours from Holy Trinity Church in Winnipeg (then the "Navy" church) and rests in the military plot in Elmwood Cemetery. A short, happy life – always loved and remembered by me.

Boyd Bay (63 N/2) in Batty Lake was named after him in 1995.

Boyd, Lance Corporal **David V.** of Winnipeg (6056). Winnipeg Grenadiers. He died during the final days of the defence of Hong Kong – 22 December 1941 - and is commemorated at the Sai Wan Memorial in Hong Kong. ***Boyd Creek*** (64 G/15), which flows northeast into South Seal River was named after him in 1986.

Boyd, Leading Stores Assistant **Harold K.** of Winnipeg (V 37248). HMCS *Mahone*. He died 9 October 1945 at the age of 34 and is commemorated at Brookside Cemetery in Winnipeg. Prior to enlisting, he had been employed by the *Winnipeg Tribune* in the advertising department for 16 years. He was survived by two sisters Mrs. Ralph "Babe" Morrison of Winnipeg and Mrs. Edith Kelly of Giroux and a brother, Gordon, of Winnipeg. He wrote several letters home to his sister:

Dear Babe and Ralph: Many thanks for the parcel; I'm sure sorry to put you to all that trouble. So you are getting all wet these days, eh? You should come to a good part of the world where they have all the sunshine your heart desires. We sure have had nice weather here. Surprised that you were worried about me getting the parcel as I thought from the amount of postage on it, they sent a man down to deliver it personally. I haven't much news as we are doing nothing apart from study. It sure is a lot of work – not so hard, but an awful lot of detail.

Had a letter from Alice. She enclosed $1 for cigarettes. I thought that was very nice of her, though she didn't mention Gordon at all. I wonder if he knows? What was wrong with Donnie [his nephew]? Is he OK again? Can't figure out what is wrong with Edith. I wrote her just as soon as I arrived, but haven't had any word from her. Guess she will write in time.

Well, just finished supper and guess it is time to get down to study again. Hope all is going well with all. I haven't heard or had time to see George Gibson, but no doubt will in time. Still lots of talk of us going East after our exams, but only talk, so I'm not getting excited yet. Hope you find time to write again soon – and lots. Best love to Donnie, Bernice and Jean and everything that is good for you two. Best Love, Harold, HMCS *Naden*, Esquimalt (n.d.).

In a later letter from Halifax he wrote in part:

Dear Babe and Ralph: Well, here is your young brother in the far away City of Halifax and I sure as hell wish it were far, far away from me. The Navy life is OK, but the City of Halifax is nothing but a dirty hole. It's so bad I'm afraid to go out at nights and that must be bad. In fact, there doesn't seem to be anything to go out for. I had a hard time finding a room, but have a rather clean one now. It costs $40 without meals and would be worth about $10 in Winnipeg. Anyway, I'm glad to have the chance to see it and I'm ready to leave any time I can get a ship. I don't know when though, maybe soon. There is plenty for me to learn, it is just a question whether I could learn it on board or have to know it all before. I think I know enough now to get along, but maybe the Navy doesn't (n.d.).

Soon afterwards, his body was found floating in Halifax Harbour. ***Boyd Point*** (63 I/7) in Molson Lake was named after him in 1995.

Boyd, Flight Sergeant **Jack M.** of Fairfax (R 59286). No. 77 Squadron. He died 31 October 1941 at the age of 25 and is commemorated at the Kiel War Cemetery in Germany. He was the son of Irvine W. and Isabel M. Boyd of Fairfax. ***Boyd Island*** (53 E/16), southwest of Loonfoot Island in Island Lake was named after him in 1984.

Boyer, Private **Alvin B. E.** of Winnipeg (H 195217). Royal Canadian Regiment. He died 5 January 1945 at the age of 23 and is commemorated at Argenta Gap War Cemetery, Italy. He was the son of Joseph and Lenna Boyer and was survived by his wife H. A. Caroline Boyer of Winnipeg. She recalls (2 April 1998):

> He was six feet, four inches tall and so very proud of his uniform and all it meant. He was a very active, hard-working person, always ready to reach out with a helping hand and he had a smile for one and all – very caring and thoughtful.

Boyer Lake (64 N/7), east of Topp Lake was named after him in 1995.

Boyle, Private **Arthur W.** of Winnipeg (H 71089). Royal Canadian Infantry Corps. He died 1 January 1943 at the age of 30 and is commemorated at St. James Cemetery in Winnipeg. He was the son of Henry R. and Martha Boyle and was survived by his wife Edna Boyle of Winnipeg. ***Boyle Lake*** (64 F/3), northeast of Goldsand Lake was named after him in 1994.

Boyle, Sergeant **James A.** of Winnipeg (H 19966). Queen's Own Cameron Highlanders. He died 5 October 1944 at the age of 25 and is commemorated at Bergen-op-Zoom Canadian War Cemetery in Holland. He was the son of Reginald C. and Helga C. Hughes of Vancouver. ***Boyle Bay*** (63 N/6) in Girouard Lake was named after him in 1995.

Boyle, Corporal **Peter M.** (H 20075). Queen's Own Cameron Highlanders. He died 7 December 1941 and is commemorated at Brookwood Military Cemetery in Surrey, England. ***Boyle Island*** (64 P/12) in Nejanilini Lake was named after him in 1995.

Bozak, Private **Harry G.** of Winnipeg (H 18546). Queen's Own Cameron Highlanders. He died 30 March 1945 at the age of 20 and is commemorated at the Groesbeek Canadian War Cemetery in Holland. He was the son of John and Anne Bozak of Winnipeg. His niece writes (22 December 2001):

> The family was as close as any family in those days; they worked hard to put food on the table. My Mom and Harry, being the youngest, were always in trouble. He, from what I understand, was a very caring and helpful son who loved life. He would have done anything for his family. He loved children and knew my sister (Mary's first-born) only a short time before he was killed. He had a great laugh and was so kind. Mom said he laughed, joked and had a great time at family functions such as Christmas time.
>
> He also had a girlfriend named Lilly. I only learned about her from reading his letters. As I read the letters though, I felt his loneliness at times when he'd say to Mary (his sister) to kiss Snooksie (a nickname for my sister Marilyn) goodnight for him and that he wishes he was home to play with her. He said "I hope she doesn't forget me."
>
> His Mum ... worked in a drug store on Selkirk Avenue and her job was reading tea leaves. But then she read her own one day and saw that Death would come to her own son overseas. She never read again.

In one of his last letters home to his sister he wrote in part:

> Dear Mary: This is your little brother Harry writing you a few lines, letting you know that everything is fine. I guess you're wondering why I didn't write you a letter letting you know that I have been wounded. I wrote a letter to Olga telling her all about it, and was to tell Dad and you not to mention anything about it to Mom because you know what will happen if she found out. She'll cry and worry her head off and I know that she won't sleep at night. So please don't say a word to her. I'm doing fine now and I'm starting to walk. I'm still weak in the knees; that is because I have been laying in bed for 16 days – anybody laying that long is bound to have stiff legs. Mary, I wouldn't worry if I were you because everything will be ok. If you want to know where I got hit, well it was somewhere in Belgium if it makes you feel better.
>
> Well anyway, how is everything by you and Snooksie, how is she getting along? I really miss her. She was a lot of fun to play with. Dad is going to feel pretty bad when he hears about me, but don't worry, I'll be back home all in one piece. Well anyway, I'll be good as new in a week's time. If I had a letter from you, I would write more in my letters, but I guess I'll get my letters pretty soon. So long for now. Love, Harry (26 September 1944).

Bozak Lake (64 I/10), northeast of North Knife Lake was named after him in 1974.

Brad, Pilot Officer **Harold A.** of Isabella (J 88650). No. 106 Squadron. He died 27 April 1944 at the age of 20 and is commemorated at Durnbach War Cemetery in Bavaria, Germany. He was the son of Alva E. and Marion M. Brad of Isabella. ***Brad Lake*** (52 M/12), northeast of Sasaginnigak Lake was named after him in 1980.

Braden, Sergeant **Alvin J.** of Portage la Prairie (H 70239). 12th Manitoba Dragoons. He died 19 May 1944 at the age of 26 and is commemorated at Brookwood Military Cemetery in Surrey, England. He was the son of John A. and Kathleen A. Braden of Portage la Prairie and was survived by his wife Ethel Irene Braden (née Hannah) of Portage la Prairie and their two year-old son. According to a contemporary newspaper account: "The first word received of his illness was a telegram advising Mrs. Braden her husband was seriously injured with a fractured skull. The second message arrived a short time later advising her of his death (n.d.)." ***Braden Lake*** (54 E/14), east of North Knife Lake was named after him in 1964.

Bradley, Flight Sergeant **Frederick** of Winnipeg (R 86295). No. 418 Squadron. He died 10 July 1942 at the age of 20 and is commemorated at the Runnymede Memorial in Surrey, England. His sister recalls (5 November 2001):

> My brother Fred was born and raised in Winnipeg and even at a very early age, he was an avid sportsman. He was skating and playing hockey well before he reached his teens. Hockey, snowshoeing and skiing were his winter sports. In the summer, cricket and soccer were his choices. He played cricket for the Winnipeg Wanderers up till he joined the Air Force. However, his main all year hobby was photography. He built his own dark room, enlarger and all the other equipment he required, and spent many hours taking pictures from still life to portraits and printed all his own photographs. To this day, 2001, I have many fine photographs he took of family picnics, fishing trips and other family activities from the 1930s that never fail to bring back many happy memories.
>
> Fred joined the Royal Canadian Air Force in 1941 and after completing his training was sent overseas and attached to No. 418 City of Edmonton Squadron flying Boston aircraft. He had completed one tour of 30 missions and was on his second tour when his aircraft was shot down near Flushing, Holland during operations over enemy-held territory.

Bradley Bay (63 I/8) in Robinson Lake was named after him in 1995.

Bradley, Warrant Officer 1 **Gordon C.** of Brandon (R 80038). No. 103 Squadron. He died 3 August 1943 at the age of 21 and is commemorated at Hamburg Cemetery in Germany. ***Bradley Point*** (64 J/12) in McDennon Lake was named after him in 1995.

Bradley, Pilot Officer **Irvine C.** of Portage la Prairie (J 93970). No. 464 Squadron. He died 1 January 1945 at the age of 22 and is commemorated at Heverlee War Cemetery, Leuven, Vlaams-Brabant, Belgium. He was the son of William C. and Margaret Jessie Bradley (née Brown) of Portage la Prairie. In a letter to his sister, he wrote:

Dear Marg: Hi Sis, how goes the big battle of living? Hope you have been keeping in good health but I guess your spirits would be a little dampened when Lorne's leave was cancelled around the 20th of May. I'll bet you will both be cursing the air force. Mom and Dad told me about it in a letter but they could not give me a reason for it. Anyway, I hope he can get it soon so that you will be able to be with your Hubby again. How's the job and how is the boss treating you? Making lots of money I suppose. Have not got any letters from you yet and you owe me one too. I wrote to you in Halifax just before I left Canada so let's hear all the news and soon. So far, I've had three letters from home, two of this type and one ordinary, also one from Freddy bawling me out for not writing to her but my letter to her must have got to her a day or so after that. I hope so anyway.

I think Mom and Dad were relieved when they got my telegram stating my safe arrival here. We had a very lovely and quiet trip and I was not sick at all. There were only a very few of us on the boat so everything was the best and the food was super. My own crew came with me but not Austy and my other pals. They came later and are here with me now. Austy and I went out for a bit of celebration the day after he got here. There is plenty of beer and whiskey over here. The beer is not bad either. The place where we are stationed now is a summer resort and it is really beautiful at this time of year. This is the only place I have been stationed so far. Right now we are mucking about doing a bit of ground school and not much of that – just hanging about waiting posting to different courses which myself and my crew have yet to complete. On the whole, I believe it will be some months before we will get into operations.

No doubt you will have heard from home that I spent seven days leave with Roy and Emma and little Jane. Emma is a very nice person and Roy has not changed appreciably. They are quite happy and settled into married life. The countryside around the farm is marvellous. I thoroughly enjoyed my leave with them. I also spent one night in London on my way up there and really had a time staggering from pub to pub on Piccadilly Circus. Oh yes, while I was at Roy's, he took me to the city of York and showed me about there. It is a very old place and we saw the historical Yorkminster Cathedral. Roy is quite busy all the time, but he took a half day off to show me around. He works very hard and has a lot of responsibility being a farm manager. They certainly have a lovely baby. Think I will go up to Scotland next time I get leave and visit Mrs. Woodrow or Aunty Jenny. I guess poor Grandma's health is failing, Marg or Dad told me about her having a slight stroke on Easter. I got a very good snap of her in a recent letter from home.

Got my first taste of bombing the other day but I was lucky and did not happen to be any nearer than a block away from the nearer ones but that's plenty close. A lot of people got it though. They can certainly make a terrible mess in a very short time. The AA [anti-aircraft] boys and fighters got some of them so it was not one-sided at all. None of my buddies got killed or injured.

I've had several English girls out since coming over and find them quite nice although a bit possessive. They sure seem to like Canadians too. The latest girl I've been seeing is Irish and a real cute number, bags of fun too and a splendid dancer.

Started to write this in school today but am finishing it over in the "Y" tonight. Facilities for service men and women are really organized over here. We get excellent food – better and more of it than you can buy in restaurants. So am not having too bad a time. Sure glad I brought civvies as the old "blues" get kind of hot in this lovely weather. Drop me a line real soon. Your loving brother, Irv (1 June 1943).

Bradley Lake (63 F/10), west of Driftwood Lake was named after him in 1981.

Bradley, Pilot Officer **Lloyd L.** of Winnipeg (J 24703). Royal Canadian Air Force. He was lost at sea when Danish troop transport ship the MV *Amerika* was torpedoed. He died 22 April 1943 at the age of 22 and is commemorated at the Ottawa Memorial. He was the son of Joseph A. and Annie J. Bradley of Winnipeg and was survived by his wife of one month Florence S. Bradley (née Davis) of Pipestone. She recalls (22 November 2001): "He attended Kelvin High School and was employed in Winnipeg prior to enlisting in the RCAF. His dream was to attended University and to study medicine." ***Bradley Island*** (63 N/10) in the Churchill River was named after him in 1995.

Bradshaw, Lieutenant Colonel **Charles G.** of Winnipeg. Veterans Guard of Canada. He died 18 February 1946 at the age of 54 and is commemorated at Elmwood Cemetery in Winnipeg. He was survived by his wife Dorothy M. Bradshaw of Wainwright, Alberta. ***Bradshaw Lake*** (54 E/11), southeast of North Knife Lake was named after him in 1995.

Bradshaw, Sergeant **James** of Winnipeg (R 59582). No. 114 Squadron. He died 27 October 1941 at the age of 23 and is commemorated at the Runnymede Memorial in Surrey, England. He was the son of Leonard and Jessie Bradshaw. When he left Canada, his sister requested that he keep a diary of day-to-day happenings. These are a few of the last entries:

- Have started operations over France (Rotterdam, Cologne, Friesian Islands). Attacked convoy and lost first plane: P/O Jones, F/S Davies, P/O Cholman. Lost two planes at Rott: P/O Alexander, F/S Tweedale, P/O Edwards, F/S Briggs (27 August 1941).
- My pilot, S/L Harris asked me how I would like to go to another squadron. Bud and I just looked at one another and I said "No!" He said he would try to fix it so I wouldn't have to go but doubted it very much. Do hope he can. Bugger it (31 August 1941).
- Have been posted to 114 Squadron all by myself. Have to leave Bud, Paton and Barley. Have gone to the CO but he cannot let me stay so I'll be on my way tomorrow (7 September 1941).
- Am leaving tomorrow for 114 Squadron at West Raynham near Kings Lynn. It is just about 20 miles from Swanton Morley so I will be able to get back once in a while to see all my pals there (8 September 1941).
- Arrived here OK at 12:30 noon and was told I was flying at 2 o'clock so they sure don't waste much time here. The fellows seem to be OK and very friendly but nothing like the old gang at #88. I will feel more at home in a few days though (n.d.).
- Was on an operation this morning at 7:30 and was back by 15 to 9. We are having the day off today also tomorrow so I am going to Norwich and then to Weston and then to Lenwade to see Mrs. Lock and Edna and Iris and Reg and Jack. Also going to pick up my bike (11 September 1941).
- Bud has been shot down on attacking a convoy. Have hopes of him being a prisoner of war. I wish I could have stayed at 88 with him. S/L Harris was the only one to get back. I used to fly with him and would have been with Bud on that attack. Today is my birthday, such luck (18 September 1941).

- Lost crew on practice bombing on old ship. P/O Brown – Canadian Observer killed, also rest of crew P/O Fielding Australian pilot and Sgt. Collier, Air Gunner (24 September 1941).
- Aunt Stella and Fred Lottie George came down to see me. Had a very nice afternoon. Went to Thakeham, had a picnic near Draine. They left about 5 o'clock. Sure wished I could go back with them (27 September 1941).
- Met Norm Paton and Bob in Norwich. Heard all details on Bud's hard luck. Went to cinema with Howard Davidson, a Canadian pilot in this squadron. Took 2 girls home in blackout – had to run for 2 miles to catch bus at 12 o'clock – Bad (28 September 1941).

Bradshaw Island (63 N/10) in Burntwood Lake was named after him in 1979.

Brady, Private **James** of North Kildonan (H 6574). Winnipeg Grenadiers. He died 19 December 1941 at the age of 21 and is commemorated at the Sai Wan Memorial in Hong Kong. He was one of the three children of John and Mary Brady and was survived by his wife Eleanor Brady of Winnipeg. His service record indicates that he had been "Killed outright" at Mount Butler after having been taken prisoner at 10:00 AM. His sister recalls (26 October 2001):

> James received all of his education in Winnipeg, attending Lord Selkirk High School in Elmwood. He was a very good student. He enjoyed all sports – I will always remember him listening to Hockey Night in Canada on the radio every Saturday night. He was very well liked as a boy and very good to his sisters. After completing high school, he worked in a grocery store briefly, but joined the army almost immediately upon Canada's declaration of war. He lost a few close friends in the war. It was a sad day when my mother received the telegram. He was so young when he was taken from us.

Brady Lake (54 F/11), northeast of Split Lake was named after him in 1964.

Brain, Major **Donald.** Princess Patricia's Canadian Light Infantry. He died 10 December 1943 and is commemorated at the Moro River Canadian War Cemetery in Italy. ***Brain Lake*** (64 O/7), northwest of Sandhill Lake was named after him in 1995.

Branch, Lance Corporal **James D.** of Winnipeg (H 8597). Royal Winnipeg Rifles. He died 25 September 1944 at the age of 21 and is commemorated at the Calais Canadian War Cemetery in France. He was the son of the Reverend C. Theodore and Isabel Branch of Goliad, Texas. ***Branch Lake*** (64 A/11), east of Campbell Lake was named after him in 1996.

Brander, Pilot Officer **Huntley D. "Spike"** of Winnipeg (J 1447). No. 7 Squadron. He died 30 June 1941 at the age of 25 and is commemorated at Becklingen War Cemetery in Germany. He was the son of Edith Brander of Wolfville, Nova Scotia and was survived by his sister Mrs. H. B. Jodrey. In 1934, he gradated in Mathematics from Acadia University and then spent two years in Post Graduate work at the University of Toronto. Upon completion of his education, he moved to Winnipeg and worked in the actuarial department at Great West Life until enlisting in 1940 (Great West Life Bulletin 1941). ***Brander Lake*** (64 J/11), west of Tadoule Lake was named after him in 1975.

Brandon, Flight Sergeant **Melvyn H.** of Reston (R 91867). No. 418 Squadron. He died 1 April 1942 at the age of 21 and is commemorated at Saffron Walden Cemetery in Essex, England. In a letter to Flight Sergeant Brandon's parents, Sergeant G. R. Holm wrote:

> Dear Mrs. Brandon: Today I saw and talked with Bill Reeves and he told me about Mel's death. I, as was Bill, one of Mel's best friends. We have gone through our course together ever since we joined up and it was a very great shock to me to hear that he had passed on. For myself and for his many friends who are here with me, may I extend my sincerest sympathy to you and your family at the loss of such as he. He was one of the most popular fellows in our "gang" and I'm sure we will never find another man to replace him (19 April 1942).

A friend he had met in England also sent her condolences:

> Dear Mrs. Brandon: I expect you are wondering who I am. Lilian is my name and I was a great friend of Mel's. We met when Mel first arrived in Bournemouth in November last. A few weeks ago, I had a letter from a friend of Mel's, Fred Bradley who informed me of the tragic news. I wanted to write this short letter to you to tell you how sorry my parents and I are; he was the grandest person we'd ever known. I do know Mel was always happy when on leave as he always came to us. I thought perhaps this may help you to know this. The news was a great shock to us and I'm sure it must have been to both you and Mr. Brandon. I've heard such a lot about you from Mel but still this letter seems difficult to write. I will close now, hoping you will pardon me in taking the liberty in writing to you (Lilian Suddrey 24 April 1942).

His sister recalls (8 July 1995):

> Mel hated to leave Dad on the farm but didn't want to be conscripted. He had hoped to be a pilot but they needed navigators at the time and he qualified so… He wrote home regularly and had money forwarded. He often mentioned the beautiful scenery and how peaceful it was flying above the clouds at night. Only once did he mention their bombing raid being successful.

Brandon Lake (64 H/16), southwest of Condie Lake was named after him in 1995.

Brandow, Sergeant **Roy L.** of Selkirk (R 134525). No. 420 Squadron. He died 29 March 1943 at the age of 21 and is commemorated at the Reichswald Forest War Cemetery in Germany. ***Brandow Lake*** (64 P/8), east of Nejanilini Lake was named after him in 1974.

Brandson, Paymaster Lieutenant **Thomas L.** of Winnipeg (O 8360). HMCS *Athabaskan*. The *Athabaskan* was sunk by a torpedo from a German destroyer while operating in the English Channel. Her captain and 128 men were lost, 83 taken prisoner and 44 men rescued by HMCS *Haida*. Lieutenant Brandson died 29 April 1944 at the age of 28 and is commemorated at the Halifax Memorial. He was the youngest child and only son of Dr. Brandur J. and Adalbjorg Brandson and was survived by his wife Shirley Brandson of Winnipeg. His nephew writes (24 December 1998):

> I remember Tommy well, even though I was only about ten when I last saw him. Indeed, he was a favourite uncle, always pleasant and considerate. He was the sole surviving son of the legendary Dr. Brandur Brandson, a leader in the Icelandic community and Professor of Surgery at the University of Manitoba and Chief at the Winnipeg General Hospital. Tommy did not choose to follow in his father's footsteps as I am told that he could not stand to see people suffering. Instead he chose training in commerce, and I suspect his outgoing personality is why he was elected Senior Stick at the University of Manitoba by his peers.
>
> After the first torpedo struck, he was seen safely on deck. However, it was his duty to throw the lead-covered code book overboard and he was down below when the second torpedo struck.

Brandson Lake (64 N/13), west of Nueltin Lake was named after him in 1972.

Brandt, Rifleman **James R.** of Justice (H 103033). Royal Winnipeg Rifles. He died 24 June 1944 at the age of 20 and is commemorated at Brookwood Military Cemetery in Surrey, England. He was the son of Charles A. and Margaret E. Brandt of Justice, Manitoba. ***Brandt Lake*** (64 O/4), northeast of Egenolf Lake was named after him in 1975.

Braun, Lance Corporal **Bernard** of Swan River (H 70515). South Saskatchewan Regiment. He died 20 July 1944 and is commemorated at Bretteville-sur-Laize Canadian War Cemetery in Calvados, France. ***Braun Lake*** (64 N/4), southwest of Nueltin Lake was named after him in 1972.

Bray, Flying Officer **Reginald S.** of Alexander (J 21420). No. 11 Advanced Flying Unit, RCAF. He died 26 July 1944 at the age of 25 and is commemorated at Blacon Cemetery in Cheshire, England. He was the son of Louis J. and Constance M. V. Bray (née Shore) of Alexander. ***Bray Island*** (53 L/9) in Gods Lake was named after him in 1995.

Braybrook, Private **Frederick G.** of Hargrave (L 27190). 1st Canadian Special Services Battalion. He died 23 May 1944 at the age of 22 and is commemorated at Beach Head War Cemetery, Anzio, Italy. He was the son of William and Violet Braybrook. ***Braybrook Lake*** (52 M/12), southwest of Family Lake was named after him in 1980.

Breen, Sergeant **William J.** of Winnipeg (R 58998). No. 427 Squadron. He died 31 August 1943 at the age of 22 and is commemorated at Schoonselhof Cemetery in Antwerp, Belgium. ***Breen Island*** (63 N/7) in Burntwood Lake was named after him in 1995.

Brezden, Private **Walter** of Fishing River (H 615227). Canadian Army. He died 21 June 1945 at the age of 23 and is commemorated at Holy Ghost Cemetery in Fishing River, Manitoba. He was the son of Nat and Annie Brezden of Fork River. ***Brezden Lake*** (64 C/4), east of McCallum Lake was named after him in 1981.

Brezino, Private **Joe** of Spring Well (B 64985). Royal Hamilton Light Infantry. He died 21 February 1945 at the age of 23 and is commemorated at the Groesbeek Canadian War Cemetery in Holland. He was the son of Anton and Dora Brezino of Spring Well, Manitoba. ***Brezino Creek*** (54 F/5), which flows north into Silcox Creek was named after him in 1964.

Bridal, Rifleman **Jack W.** of Crystal City (H 42139). Royal Winnipeg Rifles. He died 29 March 1945 at the age of 19 and is commemorated at the Groesbeek Canadian War Cemetery in Holland. He was the third of the ten children of Clifford and Lulu Bridal of Clearwater, Manitoba. He had enlisted previously, but was discharged when it was discovered that he was under-age. He re-enlisted the day after his 18th birthday. His sister recalls that (1 August 1995):

> Jack was out working on a farm at age 15 for Norris Stone of Clearwater. When Jack finished that job, Stone gave Jack a bonus of a beautiful dapple-grey horse named Daisy which he treasured and loved. Later he worked for Bernie and Vera Stewart of Clearwater while waiting to join his two older brothers in the service. Jack landed in England on December 25, 1944 and from there went to Belgium and Germany. The night Jack was killed … he was cleaning his buddy's gun in a shack when a German sniper got him in the back and through his heart so he died instantly. Jack's buddies kept in touch with my parents for quite some time after his death as they thought highly of him.

Bridal Lake (64 C/8), north of Granville Lake was named after him in 1970.

Brigden, Flying Officer **Donald A.** of Carman (J 24901). No. 442 Squadron. He died 1 January 1945 at the age of 21 and is commemorated at the Groesbeek Canadian War Cemetery in Holland. He wrote a letter to his brother and his family a few days before his death:

> Dear Clayt, Urla and Helen: Well, here it is time to write another letter – after the celebrations are all over and we have settled down to a more or less normal life – at least till New Years. First of all, I want to thank you for the lovely parcel for Xmas. Everything in it was very much appreciated as you guessed, and just what I needed. You sure did a swell job at packing it, as it arrived here in perfect condition. I also received the chocolate bars which you bundled up for me – all in all, thanks for everything.
>
> We spent quite a nice Xmas considering everything. Our Wing had the party and dinner Xmas Eve – and what a party – everything from beer to champagne – you should have been there. We had turkey for dinner and our mess hall was all decorated up to make it look like Xmas. We got up early the next morning and flew, just to wish them a Merry Xmas in our own way, but I don't think they appreciated it very much.
>
> Your mail is coming through very good lately and hope you are receiving mine all right. The post office must have been very busy over here and they did a very good job at getting our parcels all here before Xmas. Received the picture that you sent me – thanks a lot. You and Urla look the same as ever, but Helen sure is growing isn't she? Well, must close now as it is getting late and us pilots have to get our sleep. Thanks again for the swell Xmas parcel folks. Don (27 December 1944).

Brigden Lake (64 K/6), south of Lac Brochet was named after him in 1966.

Brisebois, Private **Paul E.** of South Junction (H 19128). Royal Canadian Ordnance Corps. He died 15 May 1942 at the age of 27 and is commemorated at Brookwood Military Cemetery in Surrey, England. He was the son of Louis and Marie L. Brisebois of South Junction, Manitoba. ***Brisebois Lake*** (64 F/7), east of Reindeer Lake was named after him in 1961.

Brissette, Trooper **George J.** of South Junction (H 63513). Fort Garry Horse. He died 6 June 1944 and is commemorated at Beny-sur-Mer Canadian War Cemetery in Calvados, France. ***Brissette Lake*** (64 N/14), west of Nueltin Lake was named after him in 1972.

Broadfoot, Pilot Officer **Clifford M.** of Winnipeg (J 24702). No. 434 Squadron. He died 20 February 1944 at the age of 21 and is commemorated at the Berlin 1939 - 1945 War Cemetery in Brandenburg, Germany. ***Broadfoot Lake*** (64 J/10), west of Tadoule Lake was named after him in 1975.

Broder, Flight Lieutenant **John G.** of Winnipeg (J 5048). No. 1664 Conversion Unit, RCAF. He died 24 February 1944 at the age of 28 and is commemorated at Harrogate (Stonefall) Cemetery in Yorkshire, England. He was the son of Merritt G. and Effie F. Broder and was survived by his wife Lorna L. Broder of Winnipeg. ***Broder Lake*** (64 O/12), south of Nueltin Lake was named after him in 1975.

Brodie, Signalman **Stanley F.** of Winnipeg (H 20284). Royal Canadian Corps of Signals. He died 21 July 1944 at the age of 26 and is commemorated at Beny-sur-Mer Canadian War Cemetery in Calvados, France. He was the son of Benjamin J. and Clara A. Brodie and was survived by his wife Agnes W. S. Brodie of Winnipeg. ***Brodie Lake*** (63 I/7), north of Molson Lake was named after him in 1973.

Brogden, Private **Robert R.** of Cartwright (H 16600). Princess Patricia's Canadian Light Infantry. He died 25 April 1943 and is commemorated at Brookwood Military Cemetery in Surrey, England. According to his sister (18 April 1995):

> [He] joined that Battalion in 1940 and went overseas in March that year. He was killed when a dud explosive burst during a training manoeuvre in Sussex, England in April, 1943 and is buried there in Brookwood Cemetery. A number of our family has visited his grave in past years.
>
> [He] was born, raised and educated at Cartwright. As a teenager, he went to work at Darlingford, Manitoba and when he joined the PPCLI from there he gave his address as Darlingford. Therefore his name is commemorated on their cenotaph as well as at Cartwright. Robert was a runner and I have in my possession a plaque he won in England for 2nd place at their Battalion sports in 1941 (for running). He was a happy-go-lucky chap and loved life but didn't have a chance to grow old.

Brogden Lake (63 I/16), east of Cross Lake was named after him in 1973.

Brooks, Private **Earl D.** of Hamiota (H 20036). Queen's Own Cameron Highlanders. He died 13 September 1944 at the age of 26 and is commemorated at the Adegem Canadian War Cemetery in Belgium. He was the son of Ben F. and Gene M. Brooks of Hamiota. ***Brooks Point*** (53 L/12) on the southwest shore of Laidlaw Lake was named after him in 1983.

Brooks, Flight Sergeant **Lucien D.** of Kelwood (R 74800). No. 229 Squadron. He died 25 April 1942 at the age of 21 and is commemorated at the Capuccini Naval Cemetery on Malta. He was the son of Frederick T. and Marie A. Brooks of Powell River, British Columbia. ***Brooks Hill*** (64 P/3), northwest of Meades Lake was named after him in 1995.

Brooks, Lance Corporal **Melvin Ronald** of Pilot Mound (H 1260). Royal Winnipeg Rifles. He died 16 February 1945 at the age of 22 and is commemorated at the Groesbeek Canadian War Cemetery in Holland. He was the son of William and Mary Brooks of Winnipeg. His brother received the following letter from one of Lance Corporal Brooks' friends, a Corporal Boyle:

> Dear Alex: I received your most welcome letter last night but had a counter attack and I was busy; I haven't had my boots off for 96 hours, but I had better answer your letter now before I go to sleep. On the day Ron was killed, our platoon had its orders to go and take out a group of farm buildings; but our section was the only one to get action, and we took the house out and 86 prisoners and we sure dug into it. About 15 minutes later, they started to mortar fire and a mortar landed on the edge of Ron's trench.
>
> He never knew what hit him Alex; he died instantly. But he had a flesh wound in the leg before and I bandaged it and ordered him to go back, but he wouldn't go as there was only four of us left out of ten. Ron wasn't cut or bruised by the mortar, Alex and I will say he had guts and I shall never forget him. Together we had one of the best sections in the Company and now I am again with only three men and myself left. So Alex, we buried Ron in Germany; but he was to be lifted and taken back to Holland and I think by this time he has been.
>
> Well Alex, I come from Orillia, Ontario, but I hope to travel out west when I get home and if I do, I will drop in and see you, as I would like to meet you. Ron used to tell me all the time about your Discharge and managing the store. I will close for now, hoping to hear from you soon. Frank (31 March 1945).

Brooks Rapids (64 P/15) in the Caribou River was named after him in 1995.

Brooks, Trooper **Raymond A.** of Emerson (H 26532). Fort Garry Horse. He died 9 August 1942 at the age of 20 and is commemorated at Brookwood Military Cemetery in Surrey, England. He was the son of Arthur and Rose Brooks. ***Brooks Lake*** (52 L/13), south of Happy Lake was named after him in 1982.

Brooks, Private **Robert** of St. Charles (H 35253). Lanark and Renfrew Scottish Regiment. He died 13 December 1944 and is commemorated at Villanova Canadian War Cemetery, Italy. ***Brooks Peninsula*** (64 A/5) in Baldock Lake was named after him in 1995.

Brophy, Captain **John P.** of Winnipeg. Princess Patricia's Canadian Light Infantry. He died 13 June 1944 at the age of 36 and is commemorated at Beach Head War Cemetery, Anzio, Italy. He was the son of Arthur and Agnes Brophy and was survived by his wife Vivien Brophy of Toronto and their two daughters. ***Brophy Lake*** (64 N/12), southwest of Nueltin Lake was named after him in 1972.

Bross, Private **Carl J.** of St. Boniface (H 6372). Winnipeg Grenadiers. He died a prisoner of war 23 February 1944 at the age of 22 and is commemorated at the Yokohama War Cemetery in Japan. He was the son of Michael and Barbara Bross of St. Boniface. ***Bross Lake*** (64 K/14), northeast of Reindeer Lake was named after him in 1972.

Broten, Sergeant **Kenneth O.** of Starbuck (H 1845). Royal Winnipeg Rifles. He died 16 February 1945 at the age of 22 and is commemorated at the Groesbeek Canadian War Cemetery in Holland. He was the son of Henry and Florence Broten of Starbuck, Manitoba. ***Broten Lake*** (54 C/13), southwest of York Factory was named after him in 1964.

Broughton, Ordinary Signalman **Arthur W.** of Winnipeg (V 24224). HMCS *Levis*. The *Levis* was torpedoed by U-74 120 miles off Cape Farewell, Greenland resulting in 18 lives lost. Ordinary Signalman Broughton died 19 September 1941 at the age of 23 and is commemorated at the Halifax Memorial. He was the son of Joseph W. A. and Clara J. Broughton of Winnipeg. His sister recalls (6 December 1995):

> Arthur was born and raised in Winnipeg. He attended Earl Grey School. Arthur was a member of St. Luke's Church and sang in the choir there from age 12 – 14. In his early teens he worked for Brookings Drug Store which was located on Grosvenor Avenue and Stafford Street. Before joining the Navy in 1940, Arthur worked for the CPR.
>
> Arthur was known for his outgoing and friendly personality. All who knew him loved him, for he was a dear son, brother and friend who was always there for everyone. He loved to tease his family and friends, especially his Mom. His zest for life was his most endearing quality.
>
> Like all the young men and women who gave their lives for freedom during the war, he had high hopes and dreams for the future; these were taken away at far too young an age. Arthur's name lies alongside his grandmother's at Chapel Lawn Cemetery. His resting place is in the Atlantic Ocean.

Broughton Lake (64 B/9), south of Southern Indian Lake was named after him in 1962.

Brown, Flying Officer **Alan F.** of Winnipeg (J 25827). No. 429 Squadron. He died 23 May 1944 at the age of 23 and is commemorated at Harrogate (Stonefall) Cemetery in Yorkshire, England. He was the only child of Francis H. and Willa W. Brown of Winnipeg and the godfather of Alan F. Deacon of Winnipeg. A reporter for the *Winnipeg Free Press* was at Bomber Command in England during Flying Officer Brown's second last mission. His aircraft was late returning from its target.

> In a matter of minutes, all but two of the planes were back. In one squadron, *N for Nuts* was still unreported and in another *U for Uncle* was the blank spot. This staff was a veteran one. It had gone through all the grief that can befall a bomber squadron. They might have shrugged their shoulders and said: "Not bad tonight – only two lost." Not so. The lines in their faces were drawn more deeply. Without realizing it they were trying to bring these two planes back by sheer force of will power. The young lady had lost her cheerfulness. She kept looking at the loudspeaker.
>
> Suddenly, *N for Nuts* came in. The chalk boy bounded across to the blackboard to enter him up. Everyone stirred, relaxed muscles. Conversation which had lagged, picked up. This was indeed a good night. Only *U for Uncle* was unreported. Yet this relief was only momentary and tension returned, broken only by the conversation between the circling aircraft and the young lady. Perhaps five minutes passed. The mechanical superintendent had his watch out. He knew how long *U for Uncle* could stay in flight. He had taken note of the time of the take off, made a calculation. There was still a margin of minutes. Not many perhaps, but enough. And then eight minutes after the leader, *U for Uncle* spoke. The young lady beamed. "All safe home tonight," she said. The mechanical superintendent clicked his watch shut.
>
> What nobody had mentioned during those endless minutes was that *U for Uncle* was almost entirely a Winnipeg crew. The voice of *U for Uncle* was that of Flying Officer Alan Brown, formerly of Scott and Bathgate and one time a carrier for the *Free Press*. This night he had carried upwards of five tons of high explosive to a target which meant much for the second front. The navigator was Flying Officer W. G. "Curly" Hunter, formerly the manager of Liggett's drug store on Vaughan and Portage and the son of George Hunter of Fontana apartments, Stradbrook Avenue. The bomb aimer was Sergeant Jack Leach of East Kildonan and the mid-upper gunner was Sergeant Larry Morris of St. Boniface.
>
> Later on they told me why they were late. They had reached the last leg of the course eight minutes too early. That would never do, so Hunter had plotted a side trip out of harm's way which had brought them back into the bomber stream right on time. Entering the stream is always a very dangerous manoeuvre, but while they had seen many planes close at hand, they had got in safely. When they reached the target, there were no flares to sight on. Apparently the first set of flares had been put out by a great explosion, caused by earlier flights. So *U for Uncle* did a wide circle while the pathfinders had put down new flares. Again they had to come back into the stream, but the turn had been made without accident and the bombs cleared. *U for Uncle* was now late and on the return flight saw two bombers shot down. But she came safely through, slowed her speed to reduce gasoline consumption and to avoid circling over the home field.
>
> So ended one night's operation. The story told by the official communiqué the following day was brief and to the point: "Last night the RAF bombed the rail yards at Louvain" (Dexter 1944).

Brown Esker (53 M/1), south of Swampy Lake was named after Flying Officer Brown in 1995.

Brown, Private **Albert** of Balmoral (H 101378). Princess Patricia's Canadian Light Infantry. He died 23 July 1943 at the age of 27 and is commemorated at Agira Canadian War Cemetery in Italy. He was the son of Paul and Anne Brown of Balmoral, Manitoba. His niece recalls (3 February 1995):

> Albert enjoyed playing and watching all sports. He spent much of his free time enjoying his family and his friends. His brother Ernie, who resides in Winnipeg, comments that so much of Albert's youth and early adulthood was spent working very hard on his parents' farm in Balmoral.

Brown Island (64 J/1), in the South Seal River was named after him in 1975.

Brown, Lieutenant **Albert H.** of Brandon. Royal Canadian Artillery. He died 8 August 1944 at the age of 26 and is commemorated at Bretteville-sur-Laize Canadian War Cemetery in Calvados, France. He was the son of Patrick G. and Georgetta A. Brown and was survived by his wife Norma D. Brown of Brandon. ***Albert Brown Lake*** (53 M/4), north of Bear Lake was named after him in 1995.

Brown, Private **Alexander** of Renwer (H 6931). Winnipeg Grenadiers. He died a prisoner of war 26 May 1943 at the age of 24 and is commemorated at the Sai Wan War Cemetery in Hong Kong. He was the son of Thomas T. and Mary Brown of Renwer, Manitoba. ***Brown Hill*** (62 N/14), southeast of Sarah Lake was named after him in 1991.

Brown, Captain **Basil F.** of Winnipeg. Royal Winnipeg Rifles. He died 8 June 1944 at the age of 33 and is commemorated at Beny-sur-Mer Canadian War Cemetery in Calvados, France. He was the son of William J. and Susie E. Brown and was survived by his wife Irene Brown of St. James. ***Basil Brown Lake*** (64 N/1), west of Minuhik Lake was named after him in 1995.

Brown, Flight Sergeant **Cecil A.** of Gilbert Plains (R 106507). No. 434 Squadron. He died 18 August 1943 at the age of 32 and is commemorated at the Kiel War Cemetery in Germany. He was the son of Bruce E. and Sarah L. Brown of New Westminster, British Columbia. According to his brother (8 November 1996):

> Following graduation from High School, he worked in the printing business for the *Gilbert Plains Maple Leaf*. In 1934, he left Gilbert Plains and settled in New Westminster, BC where he worked for the Scott Paper Company until he enlisted in 1939.

Brown Point (54 D/6) on the north shore of Stephens Lake was named after him in 1982.

Brown, Pilot Officer **Duncan S.** of Headingley (J 94612). No. 158 Squadron. He died 18 December 1944 at the age of 20 and is commemorated at Brussels Town Cemetery in Belgium. His Halifax aircraft crashed near Brabant, Belgium during a trip to Duisberg, Germany (Allison and Hayward 1991). He was the eldest of the four children of Harry D. and Martha Della Brown of Headingley. He had been a student at United College in Winnipeg prior to enlisting in 1942. ***Brown Peninsula*** (64 O/14) in Nueltin Lake was named after him in 1985 and a memorial stone was laid in his memory at The Commonwealth Garden of Memorials in St. James in 2001.

Brown, Private **Edward H.** of Petersfield (H 60603). Princess Patricia's Canadian Light Infantry. He died 22 April 1945 at the age of 22 and is commemorated at the Holten Canadian War Cemetery in Holland. He was the son of William E. and Alice M. Brown of Petersfield, Manitoba. ***Edward Brown Lake*** (64 C/14), south of Vandekerckhove Lake was named after him in 1995.

Brown, Pilot Officer **Francis Norman** of Rathwell (J 94898). No. 429 Squadron. He died 5 January 1945 at the age of 19 and is commemorated at the Sage War Cemetery in Germany. He was the son of Francis and Winnifred Brown of Rathwell, Manitoba. ***Norman Brown Lake*** (64 P/6), northeast of MacLeod Lake was named after him in 1995.

Brown, Private **George D.** of Winnipeg (H 16583). Princess Patricia's Canadian Light Infantry. He died 25 July 1943 at the age of 31 and is commemorated at Agira Canadian War Cemetery in Italy. He was the second of the four children of Donald and Ida Brown. ***Brown River*** (64 I/3), which flows northeast into North Knife Lake was named after him in 1995.

Brown, Sapper **George R.** of Bowsman (H 37768). Royal Canadian Engineers. He died 23 September 1942 at the age of 25 and is commemorated at Brookwood Military Cemetery in Surrey, England. He was the son of Alexander J. and Rose Brown of Bowsman, Manitoba. ***George Brown Lake*** (64 O/2), southwest of Munroe Lake was named after him in 1995. His sister writes (12 July 1996):

> The naming of a lake in our beloved Manitoba is a truly fitting memorial that will be forever there. It fills us with many varied emotions, not the least of which is the comfort and peace it would have afforded our parents also. George's two nieces and two nephews, who are now approaching middle age, were pleased to read it and will always treasure the memorial given to the uncle they never knew.

Brown, Aircraftman 2 **Gordon F. C.** of Winnipeg (R 101665). No. 1 Initial Training School. He died 15 August 1941 at the age of 20 and is commemorated at Elmwood Cemetery in Winnipeg. He was the son of Cyril E. and Kathleen V. M. Brown of Winnipeg. ***Gordon Brown Island*** (53 K/11) in Edmund Lake was named after him in 1995.

Brown, Sergeant **Gordon W. E.** of Winnipeg (H 16733). Algonquin Regiment. He died 18 September 1944 at the age of 28 and is commemorated at the Adegem Canadian War Cemetery in Belgium. He was the son of Wesley and Ethel Brown and was survived by his wife Jessie B. Brown of St. James and their two sons. ***Gordon Brown Lake*** (63 P/5), west of Wintering Lake was named after him in 1995.

Brown, Flying Officer **Harold A.** of Ste. Rose du Lac (J 18028). Royal Canadian Air Force. He died 11 July 1945 at the age of 23 and is commemorated at Regina Cemetery, Saskatchewan. He was the son of George and Sarah J. Brown of Ste. Rose du Lac, Manitoba. ***Harold Brown Island*** (53 M/14) in the Dafoe River was named after him in 1995.

Brown, Flight Lieutenant **Harold E.** of Winnipeg (J 8965). No. 627 Squadron. He died 28 September 1944 at the age of 29 and is commemorated at the Rheinberg War Cemetery in Germany. He was survived by his wife Jessie M. Brown of Rolla, North Dakota. ***Harold Brown Bay*** (63 P/7) in the Nelson River was named after him in 1995.

Brown, Flight Sergeant **Ian S.** of Winnipeg (R 124176). No. 100 Squadron. He died 17 April 1943 at the age of 20 and is commemorated at Rheinberg War Cemetery in Germany. He was the son of N. D. and Minnie Brown of Winnipeg. ***Ian Brown Lake*** (53 L/2), north of Island Lake was named after him in 1995.

Brown, Trooper **John C.** of Sturgeon Creek (H 26536). Fort Garry Horse. He died 8 August 1944 at the age of 39 and is commemorated at Bretteville-sur-Laize Canadian War Cemetery in Calvados, France. He was the son of Peter and Emma Brown and was survived by his wife Irene M. Brown of Sturgeon Creek, Manitoba. ***John Brown Lake*** (54 D/1), southeast of Stephens Lake was named after him in 1992.

Brown, Sapper **Magnus** of Headingley (H 19880). Royal Canadian Engineers. He died 3 June 1944 at the age of 47 and is commemorated at Brookwood Military Cemetery in Surrey, England. He was the son of William and Margaret Brown and was survived by his wife Edith A. Brown of Headingley. ***Brown Falls*** (63 N/6) in the Kississing River was named after him in 1995.

Brown, Wing Commander **Mark H.** of MacGregor (37904). No. 249 Squadron, RAF, Distinguished Flying Cross and Bar, Croix de Guerre, Military Medal, Czechoslovak Military Cross. Wing Commander Brown joined the RAF prior to the outbreak of war (1936) and along with Flying Officer Allan B. Angus of McCreary (see entry) became one of the two first Canadian "aces" of the war.

> Of the two, Brown was the first to see combat. He had gone to France in the fall of 1939 with No. 1 Squadron, flying Hurricane fighters and as early as November 23, 1939 he had shared in the destruction of a German DO.17 bomber. On May 10, 1940 he and another pilot shot down a DO215 bomber and by the end of the French campaign, Brown's score stood at six enemy machines destroyed, six probably destroyed and two damaged. For his work he was awarded the Distinguished Flying Cross.
>
> One of Brown's most notable combats was on May 19 when 12 Hurricanes intercepted a large force of German bombers and escorting fighters over northern France. In a fierce dogfight, he crippled one bomber, then forced another to land in a ploughed field where the enemy crew were taken prisoner by French infantry (Halliday 1970).

A contemporary newspaper account added:

> A versatile pilot as well as a fighter, Brown was reputed to be the first man to fly a German Messerschmitt 109 back to England for research inspection. He'd fly any machine to attack any enemy, once ploughing with another British fighter into 16 Junker 87s which they drove back from a British target. Easy going and good natured, he accepted his part in the war as strictly business. To his men he was known as Hilly, a contraction for Hildebrande. How he got that nickname, none of his men could explain.
>
> Born at Portage la Prairie, he was educated mainly in MacGregor, where he was formerly employed in the Bank of Montreal. Later he worked for the bank in Russell and at several Saskatchewan points, learning to fly at the Brandon Flying Club in his spare time. He was so keen on flying that he could hardly wait after he received his pilot's license at Brandon to go to England.
>
> Just before he left home, a little fellow he knew came to him and pleaded with him to take a button which had been worn by the boy's father, a veteran pilot of the last war. The little fellow insisted that it would bring him luck, so Brown took the button and it became one of his most prized possessions. He wore it at the top of his tunic throughout his dazzling career in the Battle of Britain, the Battle of France and the Middle East. Brown passed his pilot officer's examination for the RAF in three months.

> One of the first pilots to meet the black hordes of Messerschmitt 109s ... he and his comrades often were on duty as long as 20 hours a day. Two of the four British squadrons in France at that time shot down as many as 300 enemy planes. A typical gay, good humoured Canadian flier, he had many adventures in his Hurricane on the frontier patrol on the western front. Once when his plane was shot down in flames, he said that the thing that annoyed him most was that his moustache, which he had raised so carefully, had been burned off.
>
> He left France on the last boat, having had a spot of airplane trouble in the north, two days before the French accepted Germany's armistice terms, just nicely catching the last transport in each case. He came out with only his old uniform. He was one of the gallant few to whom so many owed so much during the Battle of Britain, flying in the Royal Air Force in days when the odds were nine British planes to 150 German machines. In those days, the Nazis made heavy raids on British air stations, dropping 2000 bombs on one of the main airdromes in a single afternoon, and the roads were clogged with crashed Messerschmitts (*Canadian Press* 15 January 1942).

Confirmation of his death came in an unusual manner:

> From the Mediterranean has come word that Wing Commander Mark Henry Brown of Glenboro, Manitoba, holder of the Distinguished Flying Cross and Bar, and who was credited with destruction of more than 20 Axis planes, had died in an air battle. Wing Commander Brown had been reported missing following air operations by the air ministry on November 12 last.
>
> A brief message which came fluttering down from an enemy plane over an isolated desert airdrome reported that the 30 year-old ace had been killed in a crash while fighting. The note added that he had been buried with full military honours. The plane which dropped the message was not identified, but it was believed to be Italian. The Italians had been suffering a heavy toll at the hands of Brown's outfit which they had come to fear and respect (*Winnipeg Free Press* 15 January 1942).

He died 12 November 1941 at the age of 29 and is commemorated at Catania War Cemetery, Italy. He was the youngest of the five children of Mr. and Mrs. S. T. Brown of Glenboro. ***Brown Rapids*** (53 M/15), in the Bigstone River was named after him in 1989.

Brown, Sergeant **Norman C.** of Portage la Prairie (R 146053). No. 22 Operational Training Unit, RCAF. He died 26 August 1943 at the age of 20 and is commemorated at the Calais Canadian War Cemetery in France. He was the son of William H. and Thelma Brown. ***Brown Narrows*** (64 O/10) in Bangle Lake was named after him in 1995.

Brown, Pilot Officer **Raymond C.** of Winnipeg (J 95211). No. 415 Squadron. He died 24 February 1945 at the age of 20 and is commemorated at the Reichswald Forest War Cemetery in Germany. He was survived by his wife Helen Brown. ***Raymond Brown Lake*** (53 N/9), east of Whitefish Lake was named after him in 1995.

Brown, Private **Robert M.** of Arden (B 116705). Black Watch (Royal Highland Regiment) of Canada. He died 8 August 1944 at the age of 29 and is commemorated at Bretteville-sur-Laize Canadian War Cemetery in Calvados, France. He was the son of John A. and Lillian Brown of Arden, Manitoba and the husband of Renée A. Brown of Kapuskasing, Ontario. ***Brown Lake*** (42 J/4) in central Ontario was named after him in 1971.

Brown, Trooper **Ross M.** of Neepawa (B 142165). 14th Canadian Hussars. He died 6 January 1945 and is commemorated at the Groesbeek Canadian War Cemetery in Holland. ***Ross Brown Lake*** (64 N/8), southeast of MacMillan Lake was named after him in 1996.

Brown, Warrant Officer 1 **Wilfred D.** of Virden (R 86267). No. 112 Squadron. He was awarded the Purple Heart while serving with the American Armed Forces. He died 19 September 1943 at the age of 21 and is commemorated at the Alamein Memorial in Egypt. ***Brown Lake*** (54 K/5), southeast of Churchill was named after him in 1948.

Brown, Able Seaman **William H.** of Winnipeg (V 9807). HMCS *Stadacona*. He died 21 June 1945 at the age of 29 and is commemorated at Elmwood Cemetery in Winnipeg. He was survived by his mother Sarah Brown of Winnipeg. ***William Brown Lake*** (64 A/6), east of White Stone Lake was named after him in 1995.

Browne, Sergeant **James S.** of Sturgeon Creek (B 64303). Queen's Own Rifles of Canada. He died 14 August 1944 at the age of 29 and is commemorated at Bretteville-sur-Laize Canadian War Cemetery in Calvados, France. He was the son of Ernest W. and Cathrine Browne of Sturgeon Creek, Manitoba. ***James Browne Lake*** (54 E/2), east of Long Lake was named after him in 1995.

Brownfield, Flying Officer **Thomas R.** of Winnipeg (C 7176). No. 219 Squadron. He died 17 November 1942 at the age of 22 and is commemorated at Catterick Cemetery in Yorkshire, England. He was the son of Charles D. and Rachel Brownfield of Calgary. ***Brownfield Lake*** (64 O/16), north of Nejanilini Lake was named after him in 1975.

Brownie, Warrant Officer 2 **James M.** of Winnipeg (R 91773). Royal Canadian Air Force. He died 2 July 1943 at the age of 26 and is commemorated at Elmwood Cemetery in Winnipeg. He was the son of William H. and Elizabeth Brownie of East Kildonan and was survived by his wife Margaret P. Brownie of Winnipeg Beach. ***Brownie Bay*** (63 K/12) on the northeast shore of Athapapuskow Lake was named after him in 1973.

Brownlee, Flight Sergeant **David E.** of Sinclair (R 86420). No. 14 Operational Training Unit, RCAF. He died 28 August 1942 at the age of 21 and is commemorated at Cottesmore (St. Nicholas) Churchyard Extension, Rutland, England. He was the youngest of the seven children of David J. and Eveline M. Brownlee of Reston, Manitoba. According to his brother (18 April 1995), he was: "Born and educated at Sinclair, he was popular among the younger set and took an active part in sports. He enlisted in the air force January 7, 1941 and arrived overseas January, 1942." ***Brownlee Lake*** (64 H/15) in the Kississing River was named after him in 1995.

Brownstone, Rifleman **Yude** of Winnipeg (H 10710). Royal Winnipeg Rifles. He died 4 July 1944 at the age of 20 and is commemorated at Beny-sur-Mer Canadian War Cemetery in Calvados, France. He was the son of H. William and Clara Brownstone of Winnipeg. One of the prime objectives immediately following the D-Day invasion was the capture of Caen and the nearby Carpiquet airfield. More than three-quarters of a million men and over 100,000 vehicles had landed at Normandy, but were unable to move inland because of heavy enemy fortifications. In spite of the advantage of naval artillery support, control of the skies, and numerically superior tanks and personnel, the Allies were unable to capture Caen for 33 days mainly due to the 12th SS Panzer Hitlerjugend

(Hitler Youth) Division. Canadian and British troops spearheaded the July 4 assault on Caen. Canadian losses were even higher than they had been on D-Day; approximately 250 of the Royal Winnipeg Rifles were lost. Rifleman Brownstone's older brother recalls:

> Yude had a job in a fur factory before he enlisted. He was always the kind of person who threw himself completely into what he was doing. I can picture him on the road to Caen, eager to get the job done and to come back home. I was in the Air Force during the war and I remember the last time I saw him. I was stationed at Brandon at the time and he and a friend came up from Shilo to visit. Soon after, I went home to my parents' place in Winnipeg on leave. I went in the front door and my mother had had her head shaved she was in so much grief. That was how I found out what had happened to him (12 October 2001).

Brownstone Lake (64 O/2), northwest of Tadoule Lake was named after him in 1975.

Bruce, Private **Edward** of Bluff Creek (H 100733). North Nova Scotia Highlanders. He died 25 July 1944 at the age of 30 and is commemorated at the Bayeux Memorial in Calvados, France. He was the son of Samuel and Ann M. Bruce of Bluff Creek, Manitoba. ***Bruce Island*** (64 C/5) in Boulder Lake was named after him in 1995.

Bruce, Pilot Officer **George R.** of Winnipeg (67580). No. 133 Squadron, RAF. He enlisted early in 1939 and is presumed to have died 23 October 1941 while on a flight to Ireland. He was 27 years of age and is commemorated at Faughanvale Presbyterian Churchyard, Londonderry, Northern Ireland. He was the son of George A. and E. Bruce of Winnipeg. ***Bruce Bay*** (64 P/5) in Lidster Lake was named after him in 1995.

Bruce, Private **William E.** of Gladstone (SH 4831). Royal Canadian Regiment. He died 23 October 1952 at the age of 25 and is commemorated at the United Nations Cemetery in Pusan, South Korea. ***Bruce Peninsula*** (53 E/13) in Stevenson Lake was named after this Korean War casualty in 1998.

Bruce, Sergeant **William I.** of Winnipeg (R 186736). No. 1 Air Observers School. He died 7 August 1944 at the age of 20 and is commemorated at Brookside Cemetery in Winnipeg. He was the son of William N. and Cora E. Bruce and was survived by his wife Helen D. Bruce of Winnipeg. ***Bruce Lake*** (64 P/14), northeast of Nejanilini Lake was named after him in 1975.

Brumwell, Rifleman **John Roy** of Roblin (H 19561). Royal Winnipeg Rifles. He died 6 September 1944 at the age of 25 and is commemorated at the Calais Canadian War Cemetery in France. He was the son of Chester and Velma G. Brumwell of Roblin, Manitoba. ***Brumwell Lake*** (64 G/16), southeast of Chipewyan Lake was named after him in 1995.

Bruneau, Private **Donat** of St-Pierre-Jolys (B 126729). 4th Princess Louise Dragoon Guards. He died 3 December 1944 at the age of 23 and is commemorated at Cesena War Cemetery in Italy. He was the son of Raymond and Emilia Bruneau of St-Pierre-Jolys. According to his brother (13 February 1998):

> The National Archives provided his family with copies of his service files. We discovered a man of slight build, 5'7 1/2", fair complexion, blue eyes, brown hair, unmarried, who was working as a bush worker for Spruce Falls Paper Company, Kapuskasing, Ontario at the time he joined the Canadian Army. Donat enlisted in Toronto on April 9, 1943 ... just a few weeks short of his 22nd birthday.

Bruneau Island (64 P/5) in Nejanilini Lake was named after him in 1995.

Bryans, Pilot Officer **William S.** of Winnipeg (J 89271). No. 97 Squadron. He died 27 August 1944 at the age of 25 and is commemorated at the Runnymede Memorial in Surrey, England. He was the son of James E. and Blanche Bryans of Winnipeg. ***Bryans Island*** (53 L/12) in Rat Lake was named after him in 1996.

Brydon, Private **Harry B.** of Roblin (H 800191). Princess Patricia's Canadian Light Infantry. He died 8 October 1951 at the age of 24 and is commemorated at the United Nations Cemetery in Pusan, South Korea. According to his sister (29 August 1998), he was "... born in Roblin [in] 1929, received his Grade 12 in Roblin and then worked in Roblin Creamery." ***Brydon Island*** (53 M/5) in Utik Lake was named after this Korean War casualty in 1998.

Brydon, Private **Ralph** of Roblin (H 103952). Canadian Scottish Regiment. He died 10 June 1944 at the age of 23 and is commemorated at the Bayeux Memorial in Calvados, France. He was the step-son of Charles and Emma Brydon of White Rock, British Columbia. According to his sister (10 November 1996), he was:

> ... born May 14, 1921 in Edson, Alberta to Sidney and Elena Paine. Two days later, Elena died and Ralph and two of his sisters were adopted by Elena's sister and her husband, Charles and Emma Brydon. They were brought to Roblin where Charles had a General Store. Ralph attended school in Roblin and then went farming on land that Charles owned. He lived there until he enlisted in 1941 or 1942. His hobbies were wood-working, fishing and helping his neighbours with farm-related projects. A man well-liked and deeply missed by all friends, neighbours and family.

Brydon Lake (64 H/3), east of Thorsteinson Lake was named after him in 1995.

Bryson, Warrant Officer 2 **George** of Deloraine (R 166147). No. 106 Squadron. He died 27 April 1944 at the age of 20 and is commemorated at Durnbach War Cemetery in Bavaria, Germany. He was the son of Mr. and Mrs. James Bryson and brother of Christina Bryson of Deloraine. Just prior to enlisting, he had been working in the mines at Sherridon, Manitoba. ***Bryson Lake*** (64 N/11), southwest of Nueltin Lake was named after him in 1972.

Buchanan, Flight Lieutenant **David** of Winnipeg (J 11854). No. 45 Atlantic Transport Group, Ferry Command. He was reported missing on a flight from London to Canada via the Azores on 26 March 1945. He was 29 years of age and is commemorated at the Ottawa Memorial. He was the son of Dugald and Marjorie Buchanan and was survived by his wife Sylvia M. Buchanan of Winnipeg. Flight Lieutenant Buchanan had formerly been the goalie of the Trail Smokeeaters who won the World Hockey Championship Title in 1939 with a score of 42 to 1. ***Buchanan Island*** (64 B/3) in Mynarski Lakes was named after him in 1995.

Buchanan, Rifleman **Norman** of Miami, Manitoba (H 75052). Royal Winnipeg Rifles. He died 16 February 1945 at the age of 31 and is commemorated at the Groesbeek Canadian War Cemetery in Holland. He was the son of Norman and Elisabeth Buchanan and was survived by his wife Lillian Buchanan of St. Claude, Manitoba. ***Buchanan Bay*** (64 J/12) in McDennon Lake was named after him in 1995.

Buckels, Engine Room Artificer 1 **William** of Winnipeg (V 67942). HMCS *Scotian*. He died 25 August 1945 at the age of 48 and is commemorated at Brookside Cemetery in Winnipeg. He was survived by his mother Louise Cubie of Winnipeg. ***Buckels Lake*** (64 N/13), west of Nueltin Lake was named after him in 1972.

Buckham, Aircraftman 2 **John A.** of Brandon (R 96233). No. 1 Initial Training School, Toronto. He died 26 August 1941 at the age of 19 and is commemorated at Brandon Cemetery. He was the son of James M. and Winnie Buckham of Brandon. ***Buckham Lake*** (64 H/1), southwest of Billard Lake was named after him in 1995.

Buckingham, Sergeant **George E.** of Crystal City (R 59263). Royal Canadian Air Force. He died 7 July 1941 at the age of 22 and is commemorated at Brookwood Military Cemetery in Surrey, England. He was the son of James and Edith Buckingham (née Hayward) of Aylesbury, Saskatchewan and the grandson of Mrs. Howe of Crystal City. ***Buckingham Island*** (63 N/4) in Kipahigan Lake was named after him in 1995.

Buckley, Flight Lieutenant **Kenneth A.** of MacGregor (J 6237). No. 257 Squadron. He died 1 March 1944 at the age of 24 and is commemorated at Brookwood Military Cemetery in Surrey, England. He was the son of Francis R. and Doris Buckley and was survived by his wife Katherine M. Buckley of MacGregor, Manitoba. ***Buckley Lake*** (64 J/15), west of Stony Lake was named after him in 1989.

Buckoski, Lance Corporal **William** of Winnipeg (H 35800). Royal Canadian Army Medical Corps. He died 26 June 1943 and is commemorated at Brookwood Military Cemetery in Surrey, England. ***Buckoski Lake*** (64 I/12), northwest of North Knife Lake was named after him in 1974.

Bugg, Private **Orville G.** of Portage la Prairie (H 102519). Queen's Own Cameron Highlanders. He died 8 April 1945 at the age of 24 and is commemorated at the Groesbeek Canadian War Cemetery in Holland. He was the son of George and Sophia Bugg of Portage la Prairie. ***Bugg Lake*** (64 K/14), northeast of Reindeer Lake was named after him in 1972.

Buick, Warrant Officer 2 **John A.** of Waskada (R 87708). No. 12 Squadron. He died 9 January 1943 at the age of 28 and is commemorated at the Runnymede Memorial in Surrey, England. He was the son of Sam and Isabella Buick (née Reeki) of Pierson, Manitoba. According to his sister (n.d.):

> John was a very particular person in everything he did, from pressing his own clothes to making any required alterations even though his mother was a trained seamstress. The extremely dry conditions in the Waskada area during the thirties forced many people to move to new areas to find employment. In 1939, John worked his way to British Columbia and before reaching there was able to save enough money to purchase a car and rent a house. He made his house available to the youth from his hometown area that were also looking for employment there, providing they adhered to his strict rules. He enlisted in the RCAF at No. 1 Manning Depot, Brandon in 1941. John trained at Dauphin and Rivers, completing his training at Regina where he received his wings. I was nursing at Dauphin during John's time there and recall John showing me the airplanes he flew in. Being the perfectionist he was, rather than going to dances or other functions, he would rather check the aircraft from back to front making sure everything was perfect. I was nursing at the King George and King Edward hospitals in Winnipeg when John passed through on his way to his overseas posting. I was the only member of the family present to bid him farewell. The troop ship John was on had to divert to another course when it came under attack by enemy ships and was able to continue its voyage without any further problems. John was attached to No. 2 Group, Royal Air Force stationed in Lincolnshire, England and was a crewmember on a Lancaster bomber that went missing during a mine-sewing operation near Heligoland. It was believed their plane was downed by enemy action over their target. Two other Canadians also lost their lives and another four crewmembers, not Canadian, were reported missing and presumed killed.

Buick River (64 N/11), which flows southeast into Jonasson Lake was named after him in 1972.

Bujarski, Sapper **Cazmer "Charlie"** of Hadashville (A 20326). Royal Canadian Engineers. He died 2 December 1940 at the age of 21 and is commemorated at Brookwood Military Cemetery in Surrey, England. He was the son of Michael and Eva Bujarski of Hadashville. ***Bujarski Lake*** (63 K/16), west of Wekusko Lake was named after him in 1973.

Bulachowski, Signalman **Michael** of Portage la Prairie (H 100509). Royal Canadian Corps of Signals. He died 12 August 1944 at the age of 31 and is commemorated at Bretteville-sur-Laize Canadian War Cemetery in Calvados, France. He was the son of Joseph and Ann Bulachowski and was survived by his wife Kathleen C. Bulachowski of Ituna, Saskatchewan. ***Bulachowski Lake*** (64 K/11), northeast of Reindeer Lake was named after him in 1972.

Bulkley, Able Seaman **Cecil E.** of Winnipeg. SS *Elmdale*, Canadian Merchant Navy. The *Elmdale* was lost 1 November 1942 and Able Seaman Bulkley is commemorated at the Halifax Memorial. ***Bulkley Lake*** (63 P/2), northwest of Cotton Lake was named after him in 2001.

Bullion, Pilot Officer **George Roy** of Baldur (J 92177). No. 273 Squadron. He died 11 December 1944 at the age of 21 and is commemorated at the Singapore Memorial. He was the son of Edward and Margaret E. Bullion of Baldur, Manitoba. ***Bullion Lake*** (64 N/11), southwest of Nueltin Lake was named after him in 1972.

Bulloch, Flight Sergeant **Earl K.** of Reston (R 162158). No. 467 Squadron. He died 12 September 1944 at the age of 28 and is commemorated at Durnbach War Cemetery in Bavaria, Germany. He was the son of James I. and Nellie M. Bulloch of Reston, Manitoba. His sister recalls (13 September 1995):

> Earl was born at Reston May 5, 1916. He has three surviving sisters, I being the eldest. Earl went to school in Reston, then took teacher training in Winnipeg in 1935, taught school at four different schools in Manitoba and was teaching at Moore Park in 1942 when he enlisted. He went overseas in September, 1943 and the bombing mission that killed him and the Australian boys was their first. He hadn't married.

His nephew adds (14 November 2001):

> Flight Sergeant Bulloch was my uncle and I have the same initials as he had. Even though I was born in November, 1943 and he was killed in 1944, I never got to meet him. He was an accomplished violinist and pianist. Family meant a lot to him as he wrote home frequently, not only to his parents, but to his sisters, always asking about his nieces and nephews.

Bulloch Lake (64 P/13), north of Nejanilini Lake was named after him in 1974.

Bunt, Chief Officer **Gordon D.** SS *Vancouver Island*, Canadian Merchant Navy. The *Vancouver Island* was torpedoed by U-558 in the North Atlantic while *en route* from Montreal to Cardiff; all 65 crew, eight gunners and 32 passengers were lost. Chief Officer Bunt died 15 October 1941 at the age of 48 and is commemorated at the Halifax Memorial. ***Bunt Lake*** (63 P/7), north of Cauchon Lake was named after him in 2001.

Burch, Sapper **Morris** of Cypress River (K 40960). Royal Canadian Engineers. He died 21 September 1944 at the age of 39 and is commemorated at Beny-sur-Mer Canadian War Cemetery in Calvados, France. He was the son of Mr. and Mrs. Alfred Burch. ***Burch Lake*** (64 N/6), southwest of Nueltin Lake was named after him in 1972.

Burch, Pilot Officer **Roy V.** of Selkirk (J 85620). No. 578 Squadron. He died 24 March 1944 at the age of 28 and is commemorated at the Berlin 1939 - 1945 War Cemetery in Brandenburg, Germany. He was the son of Lancelot C. and Amy M. Burch of Winnipeg. ***Burch Rapids*** (54 M/5) in the Caribou River west of Long Lake was named after him in 1984.

Burgess, Able Seaman **George A.** of Winnipeg (V 9320). SS *Holystone*. He died 15 February 1941 at the age of 29 and is commemorated at the Halifax Memorial. He was the son of George and Edith Burgess of Winnipeg. ***Burgess Lake*** (54 B/3), northeast of Shamattawa was named after him in 1964.

Burgess, Gunner **Lawrence W.** of Winnipeg (H 16244). Royal Canadian Artillery. He died 12 October 1944 at the age of 22 and is commemorated at Cesena War Cemetery in Italy. He was the son of Dan and Lillian Burgess of Winnipeg. ***Burgess Island*** (64 N/4) in Spencer Lake was named after him in 1995.

Burke, Warrant Officer 2 **Laurie F.** of Keyes (R 116385). No. 45 Atlantic Transport. He died 22 November 1943 at the age of 20 and is commemorated at Port-of-Spain (St. James) Military Cemetery, Trinidad and Tobago. He was the son of Aliston and Gertrude Burke of Keyes, Manitoba. ***Burke Island*** (64 H/6) in Northern Indian Lake was named after him in 1995.

Burkitt, Flight Lieutenant **John A.** of Brandon (J 6712). No. 58 Squadron. He died 26 April 1945 at the age of 26 and is commemorated at Mandal Churchyard in Norway. He was the son of Frederick and Ethel Burkitt of Brandon. His sister recalls (10 November 2001):

> Jack was stationed in the Hebrides and was on his last mission when his plane was shot down somewhere near Norway. The bodies of him and one other crew member washed ashore and were buried at Mandal. When the Silver Broom was held in Winnipeg around 1976, a letter was sent to the *Winnipeg Tribune* by a couple from Norway who attended the affair. They said they had visited a beautiful churchyard in the little village of Mandal, Norway and had seen graves of Canadian airmen. They listed four names and one was my brother's. They hoped relatives would see the names and know their loved one was buried in a beautifully cared for churchyard. They enclosed their address and I wrote to say one grave was my brother's. Then they wrote back and sent pictures of the churchyard and Jack's grave.
>
> In winter, a sheaf of wheat or oats is tied to each tombstone and the air is filled with the song of birds. On Christmas Eve, each grave is cleared of snow and a lighted candle is set on the tombstone. What a lovely picture and how very thoughtful of this kind couple to give information and pictures of our loved one's resting place in Norway.

Burkitt Lake (53 N/7), east of Patch Lake was named after him in 1995.

Burlingam, Flying Officer **David Garrett "Garry"** of Petersfield (J 8347). No. 400 Mustang Squadron. He died 19 August 1942 at the age of 25 and is commemorated at Coxyde Military Cemetery, Koksijde, West-Vlaanderen, Belgium. He was the son of Reginald T. and Reita M. Burlingam of St. Andrews, Manitoba. ***Burlingam Lake*** (64 H/2), east of Holmes Lake was named after him in 1995.

Burnett, Pilot Officer **Leslie G. E.** of Winnipeg (J 18329). No. 426 Squadron. He died 24 August 1943 at the age of 21 and is commemorated at the Berlin 1939 - 1945 War Cemetery in Brandenburg, Germany. ***Burnett Lake*** (64 N/15), west of Nueltin Lake was named after him in 1972.

Burney, Private **Doris** of Brandon (W 10290). Canadian Women's Army Corps. She died 23 December 1943 at the age of 23 and is commemorated at Boissevain Cemetery, Manitoba. She was the daughter of Gerald and Mildred Burney of Boissevain. ***Burney Lake*** (64 F/6), north of Wells Lake was named after her in 1994.

Burnie, Flying Officer **Glenn D. W.** of Winnipeg (J 36277). No. 1652 Conversion Unit, RCAF. He died 24 August 1944 at the age of 22 and is commemorated at Harrogate (Stonefall) Cemetery in Yorkshire, England. He was the son of David W. and Mary Burnie of Winnipeg. ***Burnie Lake*** (64 K/16), northeast of Reindeer Lake was named after him in 1962.

Burns, Lieutenant **Ralph H.** of Winnipeg. Essex Scottish Regiment. He died 19 February 1945 at the age of 31 and is commemorated at the Groesbeek Canadian War Cemetery in Holland. He was the son of Walter and Maude A. Burns and was survived by his wife Margaret W. Burns of Wadena, Saskatchewan. ***Burns Island*** (64 C/9) in Eden Lake was named after him in 1995. His niece writes (21 February 1997): "Ralph, like so many young men of his generation, died before having the opportunity to start families, so it is particularly appropriate to give their names to something permanent."

Burns, Flight Sergeant **William** of Makaroff (R 140724). No. 431 Squadron. He died 22 October 1943 at the age of 19 and is commemorated at the Runnymede Memorial in Surrey, England. He was the son of Sergeant William C. D. and Annie Burns of Roblin, Manitoba. According to his sister (7 June 1995):

> William Burns was born in Denny, Scotland. [He] came to Canada with his parents in 1927 and took up residency at Makaroff, Manitoba. William was known to family and friends as Willie. He spent his school years at Makaroff and loved sports (hockey being his favourite) and boxing. Willie was a healthy, happy and ambitious fellow and above the love for sports, he loved his family very much. Early 1942, he enlisted with the RCAF where he took his training at Macdonald Aerodrome and then to Halifax and for overseas ... where he was stationed at Pokes Down, Bournemouth, England. On October 22, 1943, according to word received from the Royal Canadian Air Force overseas: "The crew had a sortie over Kassel, Germany and did not return from their mission."

Burns Bay (64 O/9) in Sokalski Lake was named after him in 1995.

Burnside, Sergeant **David George D.** of Brandon (R 166252). No. 30 Operational Training Unit, RCAF. He died 3 September 1943 and is commemorated at St. Patrick Churchyard in Jurby on the Isle of Man, United Kingdom. He was attempting to make an emergency landing on the Isle of Man. The son of David and Marion F. Burnside, he was survived by his wife Dorothy E. Burnside of Winnipeg. ***Burnside Lake*** (54 E/1), northeast of Split Lake was named after him in 1985.

Burr, Private **Leonard G.** of Dauphin (H 41329). Lake Superior Regiment. He died 14 August 1944 at the age of 23 and is commemorated at Bretteville-sur-Laize Canadian War Cemetery, Calvados, France. He was the son of Hiram D. and Alice I. Burr of Dauphin. According to his brother (12 October 2001):

He had a great concern for others, particularly for his Mother; in every letter he closes with "love and please don't worry." His Mother did worry of course, and lived into her 101st year worrying all the time about her three sons in the army, but particularly about Len. I don't think that a day went by that she didn't think about her son beneath the soil of France.

She came to Canada in 1912 from England. His paternal ancestors have been traced back to the 1600s when they first arrived in North America. Len was born in England while his Mother was visiting her ill Mother. He went to school at a young age in Killarney, Manitoba and later in Dauphin. Len had many friends. He was a very quiet, unassuming person, slow to anger, physically very strong and a good athlete. He excelled in swimming, baseball, hockey and boxing. I remember the autumns in the late 1930s when he would be excused from school to "go harvesting." He loved to field pitch or spike pitch which required extra strength and stamina. Top wages, $1.00 per day!

I also remember as a 14 year-old, when he and his older brother joined the Army in 1940 and the early morning troop train that left Dauphin with the flower of Canadian youth. Particularly, the festive mood, laughter and fun everyone seemed to be having with the exception of the very old (I thought) who were more quiet perhaps because of their insight that the young were unaware of. Also, the two or three Army Sergeants who tried in vain to control these boisterous and undisciplined young men, attempting to have them line up on the Station platform for roll call or other military procedures that were so foreign to them. It was a comical riot. The Sergeants finally gave up and hollered "Okay, forget it, get on the train." Our little town was then emptied of young men.

Len was mustered into the Winnipeg Rifles but missed the overseas draft because of an illness. He then joined the Winnipeg Grenadiers but also missed the draft to Hong Kong because of a broken leg which occurred a day before the departure. His letters home indicated how devastated he was. Consequently, he wrote his brother asking him to "claim" him, which he did. Len finally got overseas, joining his brother in the Lake Superior Regiment. He had the opportunity to stay in Canada and instruct in Signals, but that was too tame for him.

In Len's time, young men and women grew up fast and had to, some with no teenage life and some with no opportunity to have or raise their children. Perhaps this generation will take heed of the past and take heart in the future as freedom is not a right, but a privilege that from time to time may have to be defended.

These are some excepts from a few of his letters home:

- I'm in training for boxing now. We have a boxing school and we will train until January 15 and then we will go into the ring if we are good enough. We will get a chance to go to Vancouver. That will be for the whole Pacific Command. I'm classed in the lightweight. Tonight was our first practice and we were given a few pointers. I had the gloves on with our Regimental Sergeant Major who weighs about 210 pounds. He seems to think he can make boxers out of us. So tell Melvin he better practise because he is going to box with the champ of the Pacific Command when I get home ... I hope (8 December 1942).
- I was out in the country today and I picked up a poppy for you. I hope it's all together when you get this letter. It sure looks nice to see them out in the fields (6 June 1943).
- I got engaged, Mum. She's a swell girl and I think the world of her. Her name is Joyce Webster and I gave her your address and Lorraine's. She said she would write right away. It will be some time before we get married. Don't know just when yet. I'll send you a picture of her (1 December 1943).
- The first time I've had Christmas without snow and they are just playing *When the Lights go on Again, All Over the World* over the wireless and it sounds pretty good. They are playing *White Christmas* now. It's sure hard to write when you get music like that (14 December 1943).
- No Mum, I don't intend to get married for a while yet. There's a little score to settle first and then if everything is okay, I'll make up for lost time. But I do want to get in on the big stuff first. I hope it won't be long now. We had a little excitement the other night. I saw planes being shot down. It sure looked nice to see all the search lights and guns going off (23 January 1944).
- Say, can you imagine, I had a real orange the other day. It's the first one I've had since I was last at home. Boy, was it ever good. We had quite a little noise this morning – another air raid. My knife and fork were on the shelf and I thought they were going to walk away. It sure shook the hut (February 1944).
- Joyce was supposed to come down last Saturday, but I received a telegram with some bad news. They were bombed last Saturday, that was why she couldn't make it. Thank Heavens there was no one hurt. I don't know yet just how bad it was (21 February 1944).
- Did Joyce tell you about the mess they made of their place, also Alice's and they just got through fixing it up from the last one. It cracked the walls, knocked the ceiling down and knocked doors off their hinges. It was quite a mess. The bombs landed just about a block away. One in front and two at the back, so there was quite a terrific blast (5 March 1944).
- I was at Joyce's in London when the warning went off. We were out front watching it when all of a sudden, a big flash and dust and smoke and everything seemed to go up. Another bomb landed about five blocks away, but it didn't do any damage this time. It didn't take long to get in the dugout. We were in them about four nights. It was only for an hour or so. I was just wondering how they were last night as there was quite a raid on (25 March 1944).
- Well, it's near the end of the paper, isn't it? I wish you folks wouldn't worry because old E. J. [his older brother] and I are keeping our heads down. I mean down. So please don't worry. That's all for now; I'll drop a line again soon. Cheerio for now, lots of love, Len(30 June 1944).

This was the last letter received from him. His older brother later wrote to a younger brother from the Canadian Field Hospital:

They are going to give me a reboard. I don't think I will be in the fight again. It sure is no joke. I had a letter from Mum today; she sure is taking it hard. We might as well look on the bright side of things. As Len and I said, if either one of us got it first, we would want it quick and I am going to tell you how Len got his. His head was shot away, he never knew what hit him. That's a lot better than lying in hospital suffering then kick the bucket. His pal in the same carrier got the same. But don't tell the folks at home, because I think they have suffered enough.

I will say I'm very fortunate to be here in one piece, but I know how you felt at the time. I've seen it all and all I want to see now is Canada where I can have my own home and not bother anybody. Those paratroopers are a tough outfit. That is one outfit I sure wouldn't want to be in, but you are your own boss now (28 December 1944).

Burr Lake (62 N/14), southeast of Swan River was named after Private Burr in 1966 and Burr Island (63 N/2) in Hutchinson Lake was named after him in 1995.

Burt-Gerrans, Pilot Officer **Harold F.** of Winnipeg (J 16744). No. 422 Squadron. He died 19 December 1942 at the age of 26 and is commemorated at the Runnymede Memorial in Surrey, England. He was the son of James T. and Nellie C. Burt-Gerrans and was survived by his wife Magdalene Burt-Gerrans of Winnipeg. ***Burt-Gerrans Lake*** (53 M/11), northeast of Ransom Lake was named after him in 1996.

Burton, Private **Arthur W.** of Napinka (H 18162). Royal Hamilton Light Infantry. He died 20 February 1945 at the age of 20 and is commemorated at the Groesbeek Canadian War Cemetery in Holland. He was the son of Charles and Mary Burton of Napinka. ***Burton Point*** (64 N/16) in Goose Lake was named after him in 1995.

Burton Aircraftman 1 **Frank E.** of Eden (R 165509). Royal Canadian Air Force. He died 12 December 1942 at the age of 19 and is commemorated at Gander Cemetery in Newfoundland. A survivor of the ill-fated SS *Caribou*, he was killed in the fire that later swept through the Knights of Columbus hostel in St. John's, Newfoundland. He was the son of James and Clara L. Burton of Eden. His sister recalls (18 October 2001):

> After completing his education at Glenholm District school, he worked on his father's farm, later going on the harvesting trips in various places and lastly, in the bush camps in Ontario in winter. He enlisted in the RCAF at Toronto, having trained at Galt and St. Thomas, Ontario. One of his sisters visited his gravesite in August, 1995 and saw his name on the monument which was dedicated to the memory of the 99 servicemen and women who lost their lives in that fire.

Burton Peninsula (64 O/16) in the Townsend River was named after him in 1987.

Burton, Captain **Lloyd G.** of Portage la Prairie. Princess Patricia's Canadian Light Infantry. He died 17 September 1944 at the age of 24 and is commemorated at Coriano Ridge War Cemetery in Italy. He was the eldest son of Frank and Eugenie V. Burton of Portage la Prairie and was survived by his wife Avril M. Burton (née Black) of London, England. According to a contemporary newspaper account (n.d.):

> On leaving Royal Military College, he joined the Princess Patricia's Canadian Light Infantry and proceeded overseas in October, 1940. He was through the Sicilian campaign and has served throughout the Italian campaign. Captain Burton was an active member of St. Mary's Anglican church and took a leading part in Scouts. He was married on November 15, 1941 to Miss Avril Marie Black … who survives him and is at present in New York City.

Burton Bay (63 P/15) in Goose Hunting Lake was named after him in 1995.

Burton, Flight Sergeant **William H.** of Winnipeg (R 162245). No. 434 Squadron. He died 22 October 1943 at the age of 21 and is commemorated at the Hanover War Cemetery in Germany. He was the son of George and Eleanor Burton and was survived by his wife Dorothy B. Burton of Stratford-upon-Avon. ***Burton Rapids*** (64 P/14) in the Roberts River was named after him in 1995.

Busch, Rifleman **Christian** of Brandon (H 41411). Royal Winnipeg Rifles. He died 7 September 1945 at the age of 36 and is commemorated at Brandon Cemetery. He was survived by his wife Annie Busch of Brandon and their children. ***Busch Lake*** (54 D/15), south of Myre Lake was named after him in 1996.

Bushell, Lieutenant **Andrew F.** of Portage la Prairie (CDN 134). Royal Norfolk Regiment. He died 8 August 1944 at the age of 20 and is commemorated at the Bayeux War Cemetery, Calvados, France. He was the son of Harold L. V. and Annie M. Bushell of Portage la Prairie and was survived by his fiancée Eleanor Osborne of Portage la Prairie. Believed to have been the youngest lieutenant in the British army at the time, he had been studying medicine at the University of Manitoba when he enlisted in 1942. In a letter to his father, Lieutenant Colonel I. H. Freeland wrote (n.d.):

> It is with great regret that I write to you to tell you about the death in action of your son. The battalion fought a very fierce battle on 7th and 8th August, and it was during the heaviest of the German counter-attacks about 9:30 AM on the 8th, that your son was killed. He was commanding the leading platoon in his company, which took the brunt of the attack by infantry and tanks, and for a brief period the enemy penetrated the position. It was during this dangerous moment that your son was killed encouraging his men to the last. If your son's company had not stood firm, the battalion might well have been over-run. A finer death in battle has never taken place.
>
> During the few months that your son had been with me he had made himself both a first class officer and one of the most popular officers in the battalion. His men loved him and will speak of his qualities for a long time to come. We have all lost a personal friend and the regiment a fine officer.

A year later, Lieutenant Bushell's father received a letter from his son's "batman:"

> Dear Sir: I am writing to you in regards to Lt. Andrew Frazer Bushell. I wrote the War Department there requesting information of the whereabouts of the Lieutenant's family. I received your address in reply. I am in the US Army; at the time I am in the O'Reilly General Hospital here at home. I have some pictures and the Lieutenant's billfold that I [had] taken from a German Officer. I hate to destroy these pictures as I thought maybe you would want them. I would have wrote sooner, but I have been laid up with a wound and just didn't take time to do so. I am enclosing a picture of a girl that I take to be the Lieutenant's wife. I have several more and will send them to you or his wife if you are the right people. I understand that the Lieutenant was killed while serving his country. I want to express my sympathy. I guess I was one of the more fortunate ones. I nearly lost an arm, but it is turning out in nice shape thanks to our wonderful doctors. My home address is Corporal Edward L. Chadick, 1310 Boonville Avenue, Springfield, Missouri. I do hope to hear from you in the near future (29 June 1946).

Mr. Bushell confirmed that his was the right family and sent Corporal Chadick a money order for his trouble. The letter drew this response:

> Dear Friend: I guess you think I forgot you. I haven't. I have been on the road ever since I received your letter. I am awfully sorry about the delay in sending the things that I wrote you about. But I am sending them today. Also I am sending you the money order back. I couldn't live with myself if I accepted it and used it for this purpose. You don't know just how happy it makes me to be able to do this. I am sorry that I did not get the watch and other things. I would have sent them too. I believe that you wanted to know how I came to have these things. I had a German Lieutenant and nine of his men cornered in a farm house. I killed the Lieutenant and two of his men. When it was over, I picked up the Lieutenant's map case and belt and put it in the tank. I found all this stuff in the map case. I sent it home and when I arrived here, I decided to try and find you so that I could send Andy's things to you. It isn't much, but I know that you will treasure them highly.
>
> You asked if I thought that this war would end wars. Frankly, I don't. In fact, this one isn't over yet. I hate to think that we will have to go to war again, but it looks like we will. You spoke about my arm. It is really nothing when you see so many that are worse than yourself. I feel that I am the luckiest fellow on earth to get back in as good a shape as I have. I was wounded on October 27, 1944 by enemy shell fire. I received a

shrapnel wound in the upper part of my left arm. It shattered the bone and cut all the nerves and muscles. I lost about two inches of bone and it went back together in pretty bad shape. Also the nerves failed to respond after they were put back together. I have had three operations. The last was a tendon transplant. The doctors say that in about 15 years, the arm will be about one-quarter as strong as it ever was. But I still feel like I am real lucky. Once again I want to say how sorry I am that I am so late in sending the things. I do hope you will forgive me. I would really love to meet you and your family and Miss Eleanor. Maybe someday I can. I know by your letter that I could not meet a finer family of people. Well I will close for now. Hoping to hear from you soon. Tell your family "hello" for me and also Eleanor. I do hope the things get through OK. I am enclosing a picture of myself. It isn't a recent one. It is one that was taken just before I left for overseas duty. I haven't any recent ones as I have no camera now and can't buy one here. I lost mine on the invasion of France. Well, so long for now; please answer when you can. Very sincerely, Eddie (29 July 1946).

Bushell Lake (64 K/13), northeast of Reindeer Lake was named after Lieutenant Bushell in 1972.

Buss, Trooper **Herman** of Morris (H 100845). Lord Strathcona's Horse. He died 24 May 1944 at the age of 21 and is commemorated at the Cassino War Cemetery in Italy. He was the son of Mr. and Mrs. E. Buss of St. Vital. His brother was only three miles away at the time, serving with the 3rd Field Regiment, 1st Division. He composed a poem (1982) which reads in part:

In memory to our Brothers all,
Who paid a price beyond recall;
We bow our heads, in peace we pray,
While crosses guard where comrades lay.

Buss Lake (52 L/11), west of Black Lake was named after him in 1982.

Butcher, Private **Frederick J.** of Ninette (H 65074). Royal Canadian Army Service Corps. He died 3 December 1943 at the age of 20 and is commemorated at Agira Canadian War Cemetery in Italy. He was the son of Thomas and Cora A. Butcher of Ninette and was survived by his fiancée Betty Smith of London, England. According to his niece (3 February 1995):

My Dad remembers his brother Fred as being quite the character, a person who had a good sense of humour, was outgoing and always ready to lend a hand. Growing up on the farm meant there was a lot of hard work, but it was not all work and no play. One of the things they used to do was to race over the prairies on two horses each, one foot on each horse and away they'd go. Although Fred has been gone these fifty years, he is not forgotten. It makes us happy to know that there's a lake named in his honour, to honour his life which he gave to his country.

Butcher Lake (64 N/6), southwest of Nueltin Lake was named after him in 1972.

Butcher, Pilot Officer **Frederick Lloyd** of Birtle (J 44112). No. 5 Bombing and Gunnery School, RCAF. He died 24 May 1944 at the age of 24 and is commemorated at Birtle Cemetery. He was the son of Frederick and Elsie M. Butcher of Solsgirth and was survived by his wife Helen Butcher of Solsgirth, Manitoba. ***Butcher Island*** (63 H/9) in Gunisao Lake was named after him in 1989.

Butcher, Sergeant **Joseph G.** of Carman (R 59269). Royal Canadian Air Force. He died 25 February 1941 at the age of 25 and is commemorated at Greenwood Cemetery in Carman. He was the son of Francis J. and Frederica I. Butcher of Carman. ***Butcher Bay*** (64 O/8) in Nejanilini Lake was named after him in 1995.

Butler, Sergeant **Earl N.** of Dauphin (H 200099). 1st Canadian Special Services Battalion. He died 9 February 1944 at the age of 29 and is commemorated at Beach Head War Cemetery, Anzio, Italy. He was the son of Thomas C. and Minie M. Butler of Kamsack, Saskatchewan. ***Butler Lake*** (63 K/16), west of Wekusko Lake was named after him in 1973.

Butler, Flight Lieutenant **George E. C.** of Winnipeg (J 13114). No. 4 Squadron. He died 14 November 1944 at the age of 28 and is commemorated at the Ottawa Memorial. He was the son of Charles E. and Vera Butler and was survived by his wife Dorothy T. Butler of Winnipeg. ***Butler Island*** (64 F/7) in Wells Lake was named after him in 1995.

Butt, Private **Konrad** of Winnipeg (H 18559). Cape Breton Highlanders. He died 1 May 1945 at the age of 20 and is commemorated at the Holten Canadian War Cemetery in Holland. He was the son of Konrad and Anna Butt of Winnipeg. ***Butt Lake*** (64 I/15), northeast of North Knife Lake was named after him in 1974.

Butterworth, Trooper **Fred** of Winnipeg (H 9540). Fort Garry Horse. He died 13 April 1945 at the age of 23 and is commemorated at the Holten Canadian War Cemetery in Holland. He was the son of Fred and Doris Butterworth of Winnipeg. ***Butterworth Lake*** (64 N/12), southwest of Nueltin Lake was named after him in 1972.

Button, Stoker 1 **Edmund A.** of West Kildonan (V 46458). Motor Torpedo Boat 460. He died 3 July 1944 at the age of 20 and is commemorated at the Halifax Memorial. He was the son of Edward J. and Lillian Button of Winnipeg. ***Button Lake*** (52 M/13), north of Vickers Lake was named after him in 1979.

Byers, Flight Sergeant **Charles Ross** of Winnipeg (R 127557). No. 547 Squadron. He died 18 August 1943 at the age of 21 and is commemorated at the Runnymede Memorial in Surrey, England. He was the son of Charles W. and Winifred B. Byers of Weston, Ontario.

"He was a first-class navigator, enthusiastic about his work, and full of the right offensive spirit," said the young man's commanding officer in a letter to his parents. "We all liked him immensely, and we can ill afford his loss." Sergeant-Observer Byers graduated from Weston Collegiate Institute, later being employed in the Aircraft Division, National Steel Car Company, Malton (*The Globe and Mail* 22 September 1943).

Byers Bay (64 P/3) in Naelin Lake was named after him in 1995.

Byers, Flight Lieutenant **Harold N.** of Souris (J 13485). No. 440 Squadron. He died 23 January 1945 at the age of 25 and is commemorated at Nederweert War Cemetery in Holland. He was survived by his wife Frances M. Byers of Vancouver. In an account of the action which resulted in his death, Pilot Officer N. Hughes wrote:

I was flying Red 4 on a dive-bombing mission on the village of Dremmen. A considerable amount of flak was encountered over the target. Red 3 (Flight Lieutenant H. N. Byers) was first in on target. At 6000 feet during the dive his aircraft was enveloped in black smoke. I believe his bombs were away before this happened. His aircraft came out of the dive and began to climb straight ahead. All this time his aircraft

> was on fire. Between 8000-9000 feet the tail fell off and the remainder cartwheeled into the ground behind German lines. No parachute was seen. I completed my bombing and returned to base (n.d.).

Flight Lieutenant Byers' Commanding Officer, Squadron Leader H. O. Gooding offered the following (n.d.):

> Despite the short space of time Flight Lieutenant Byers was with my squadron, he became admired and respected by both his fellow pilots and our groundcrew and he made many friends.

Byers Lake (64 J/16), north of Tadoule Lake was named after him in 1975.

Byers, Pilot Officer **Vernon W.** of Flin Flon (J 17474). No. 617 (Dam Buster) Squadron. His target was the Sorpe Dam; the Squadron lost 53 men on this mission. See **Glinz,** Flying Officer **Harvey S.** for additional information on the sole mission for which this squadron was created. He died 17 May 1943 at the age of 32 and is commemorated at the Runnymede Memorial in Surrey, England. He was the son of Frank and Ruby J. Byers of Codette, Saskatchewan. ***Byers Bay*** (73 P/11) in Trout Lake, Saskatchewan was named after him in 1968.

Bynski, Private **Charles** of Molson (H 82143). Lake Superior Regiment. He died 27 April 1945 and is commemorated at the Holten Canadian War Cemetery in Holland. ***Bynski Lake*** (64 F/6), northwest of Wells Lake was named after him in 1994.

Entry of the 2nd Canadian Infantry Division into Dieppe 3 September 1944. Courtesy of the National Archives of Canada (PA-131233).

C

Cadzow, Private **James** of Winnipeg (H 9676). Algonquin Regiment.. He died 3 March 1945 at the age of 31 and is commemorated at the Groesbeek Canadian War Cemetery in Holland. He was one of the four sons of Catherine Cadzow of Winnipeg. ***Cadzow Island*** (63 K/16) in Loonhead Lake was named after him in 1973.

Calder, Private **Clifford A.** of Treherne (H 65991). Princess Patricia's Canadian Light Infantry. He died 9 October 1943 at the age of 23 and is commemorated at Bari War Cemetery in Italy. He was the son of William and Blanche Calder of Portage la Prairie and was survived by his wife Myrtle Calder of Winnipeg. ***Calder Island*** (64 C/8) in Granville Lake was named after him in 1995.

Calder, Lance Corporal **George John** of Swan Lake (H 37865). Royal Canadian Army Service Corps. He died 30 July 1942 at the age of 27 and is commemorated at Brookwood Military Cemetery in Surrey, England. He was the son of George and Elspeth Calder of Swan Lake and was survived by his wife Germaine Calder. ***Calder Creek*** (64 I/9), which flows east into North Knife River was named after him in 1974.

Calder, Pilot Officer **Robert G.** of Winnipeg (J 19340). No. 1666 Heavy Conversion Unit, RCAF. He died 3 March 1944 at the age of 26 and is commemorated at Morningside Cemetery in Edinburgh, Scotland. He was the son of George H. and Nora P. Calder and was survived by his wife Elizabeth M. F. Calder of Edinburgh. ***Calder Lake*** (64 O/6), south of Nueltin Lake was named after him in 1961.

Caldwell, Flight Sergeant **Andrew Glenn** of Reston (R 281867). No. 429 Squadron. He died 6 March 1945 at the age of 20 and is commemorated at Brookwood Military Cemetery in Surrey, England. He was the son of Alexander C. and Sarah A. Caldwell of Reston, Manitoba. ***Caldwell Bay*** (64 I/3) in North Knife Lake was named after him in 1995.

Caldwell, Flight Lieutenant **Ian M.** of Winnipeg (J 4888). No. 41 Operational Training Unit, RCAF. He died 31 July 1944 at the age of 28 and is commemorated at Blacon Cemetery in Cheshire, England. He was the son of Colin and Ethel Caldwell of Winnipeg. ***Caldwell Lake*** (64 A/10), north of Waskaiowaka Lake was named after him in 1950.

Caldwell, Flight Sergeant **Wilson G.** of Carberry (R 8575). No. 102 Squadron. He died 16 December 1941 at the age of 26 and is commemorated at the Runnymede Memorial in Surrey, England. He was the son of Benjamin W. and Mary I. Caldwell of Carberry. ***Caldwell Island*** (53 K/13) in Gods Lake was named after him in 1995.

Callan, Flight Sergeant **Morris K.** of Winnipeg (R 90563). No. 102 Squadron. He died 10 November 1942 at the age of 24 and is commemorated at Texel (Den Burg) Cemetery, Holland. A local resident wrote (30 May 1995):

> On 10-11 '42 is crashed close to my village. The Halifax DT539 DY_A with a crew of 8 man. The following day, I was a boy of 4 years old, witness of the wreckage and I've never forgot this. I'm retired now and after 43 years fishing I can spend more time to the research of this crash and other details of the air war 1939 - 1945. On the Commonwealth Cemetery on Texel are buried 168 mostly airmen. I've found 28 Commonwealth, four US and four German crash locations on and near our island in the sea. So washed ashore many times airmen on the beaches. I try to recover the stories of these airmen before she crashed and collect a lot of information.

Callan Island (54 D/6) in Stephens Lake was named after him in 1982.

Callan, Lieutenant **William Edward** of Winnipeg (O 11250). HMCS *Shawinigan*. The *Shawinigan* was torpedoed and sunk by U-1228 while on independent anti-submarine patrol in the Cabot Strait; all hands were lost. Lieutenant Callan died 24 November 1944 at the age of 30 and is commemorated at the Halifax Memorial. He was the son of William and Minnie A. Callan of Winnipeg. A local newspaper reported that:

> Lieutenant Callan has been on active service on the Pacific and Atlantic for the last four and a half years. He was born in Winnipeg and attended Lord Roberts and Kelvin schools, also Success Business College and the Angus School of Commerce. Prior to enlistment, he was employed as a bookkeeper by Neaman's Fur Company. Besides his mother, he has a sister, Reta, at home (*The Winnipeg Tribune* 7 December 1944).

Callan Lake (54 B/2), northeast of Shamattawa was named after him in 1964.

Calmain, Sergeant **William H.** of Winnipeg (H 42206). Royal Winnipeg Rifles. He died 16 August 1944 at the age of 25 and is commemorated at Bretteville-sur-Laize Canadian War Cemetery, France. He was the son of William K. and Ida M. Calmain of Winnipeg. ***Calmain Lake*** (63 J/13), north of Wekusko Lake was named after him in 1972.

Camelon, Private **Wilmer** of Winnipeg (H 16455). Princess Patricia's Canadian Light Infantry. He died 22 July 1943 and is commemorated at Agira Canadian War Cemetery in Italy. ***Camelon Lake*** (64 N/5), southwest of Nueltin Lake was named after him in 1972.

Cameron, Flying Officer **Clare R.** of Roland (J 29338). No. 550 Squadron. He died 30 August 1944 at the age of 30 and is commemorated at the Runnymede Memorial in Surrey, England. He was the son of Arthur and Anne Cameron and was survived by his wife Doris E. Cameron. ***Cameron Rapids*** (64 N/6) in the Thlewiaza River was named after him in 1995.

Cameron, Sergeant **Donald A.** of Winnipeg (R 119790). No. 7 Air Observer School. He died 9 October 1942 at the age of 20 and is commemorated at Elmwood Cemetery in Winnipeg. He was the son of Howard S. and Bessie Cameron of Winnipeg. ***Cameron Island*** (64 H/4) in Gauer Lake was named after him in 1995.

Cameron, Flying Officer **Douglas N.** of Winnipeg (J 26595). No. 640 Squadron. He died 17 June 1944 at the age of 21 and is commemorated at Herwen-en-Aerdt (Tolkamer) General Cemetery, Holland. He was the son of Mr. and Mrs. W. N. Cameron and was survived by his wife Denise M. Cameron of Whitton, Middlesex. His friend Murray Peden, DFC writes of hearing the news of his death:

> I lost another good friend a day or two after we got back, the night of June 16-17. Doug Cameron … had been the pilot of a Halifax of 640 Squadron which took off from Leconfield the night of June 16th to carry out a bombing attack on the oil plant at Sterkrade, a suburb of Essen. On the return journey his Halifax was shot down at Spijk, near Lobith, Holland, and the entire crew killed. Doug had been a friend and classmate of mine at Gordon Bell, and had chummed around with me and Rod Dunphy. It had been Doug who had urged me to look up his attractive former date, Joyce Wright when I left McLeod to go to Edmonton ITS; and when, on my embarkation leave, I had gone to visit

the family in Portage la Prairie, Doug Cameron had been the last man to shake my hand as I was leaving town (Peden 1988).

Cameron Hill (64 I/11), north of Quinn Lake was named after him in 1995.

Cameron, Pilot Officer **Jack B.** of Waskada (J 19735). No. 408 Squadron. He died 14 January 1944 on his second mission. He was 27 years of age and is commemorated at the Hanover War Cemetery in Germany. He was the third of the four children of Wesley T. and Jennie A. Cameron (née Hunter) of Waskada. His brother's daughter-in-law writes (24 November 1996):

> Jack grew up on a farm in the Addington district, five miles east of Waskada at Cranmer Siding. Jack was raised in the Presbyterian faith and attended school at Addington School. During the depression years, he and his older brother Keith "rode the rails" to Vancouver Island where they found employment in the logging industry. Jack was reputed to be a handsome young man who had yet to marry.

Jack Cameron Lake (54 E/5), northeast of Embleton Lake was named after him in 1995.

Cameron, Sergeant **Laurence H.** of Shoal Lake (R 59243). Royal Canadian Air Force. He died 20 July 1945 at the age of 48 and is commemorated at Shoal Lake Cemetery, Manitoba. He was the son of George and Margaret Cameron of Regina and was survived by his wife Anne B. Cameron of Shoal Lake. ***Cameron Creek*** (64 A/6), southeast of White Stone Lake was named after him in 1995.

Cameron, Private **Robert** of Winnipeg (H 3814). Queen's Own Cameron Highlanders. He died 20 December 1944 at the age of 34 and is commemorated at Groesbeek Canadian War Cemetery in Holland. He was the son of Duncan and Jessie Cameron. ***Cameron Peninsula*** (53 L/2) in Island Lake was named after him in 1995.

Cameron, Flying Officer **William P.** of Winnipeg (J 21453). No. 625 Squadron. He died 20 October 1943 at the age of 20 and is commemorated at the Runnymede Memorial in Surrey, England. He was the son of Henry and May Cameron of Winnipeg. His brother writes (14 November 2001):

> Bill worked hard and played hard. He loved life and did his best to support our needy family as long as he lived – which was only 20 years. "Willy," as he signed his letters, loved flying and couldn't wait to get into action. He spoke highly of all his crew and they apparently were a closely knit group. For example, at a meeting of the crew, they all agreed to volunteer for the Pathfinders, knowing that after 45 missions they could come home.

Cameron River (64 P/10), which flows east into Caribou River was named after him in 1974.

Campbell, Leading Aircraftman **Allan R.** of Winnipeg (R 59932). No. 11 Service Flying Training School. He died 10 January 1943 at the age of 19 and is commemorated at Brookside Cemetery in Winnipeg. He was survived by his mother Pearl B. McLean of Winnipeg. ***Campbell Point*** (64 H/4) in Gauer Lake was named after him in 1995.

Campbell, Corporal **Duncan** of Winnipeg (H 20481). Queen's Own Cameron Highlanders. He died 20 July 1944 at the age of 22 and is commemorated at Bretteville-sur-Laize Canadian War Cemetery, France. He was the son of Murdo and Dolina Campbell

of Winnipeg. His brother recalls (24 January 2002):

> The last time I saw Duncan was when we went on leave together to Scotland in 1943. We travelled to the Isle of Lewis where our parents were born. We were greeted by our relatives and had a wonderful holiday. I was serving in Italy when I received my father's letter, informing me that Duncan had been killed in action on July 20, 1944. He wrote: "I guess we have to try and take this terrible loss the best we can. It's going to be hard."

Campbell Esker (64 G/15) which starts south of Sandberg Lake and runs northeast to the southwest shore of Chipewyan Lake was named after him in 1989.

Campbell, Flight Sergeant **Frederick A.** of Gilbert Plains (R 123725). No. 100 Squadron, King's Commendation for Valuable Services in the Air. He died 31 August 1943 at the age of 23 and is commemorated at Rheinberg War Cemetery in Germany. He was the son of John R. and Dorothy M. Campbell of Victoria, British Columbia and the brother of Private Glen R. Campbell (next entry). ***Campbell Rapids*** (64 O/15) on an unnamed river which flows southwest into Kapusta Lake was named after him in 1995.

Campbell, Private **Glen R.** of Gilbert Plains (B 143536). Hastings and Prince Edward Regiment. He died 15 September 1944 and is commemorated at Coriano Ridge War Cemetery in Italy. He was the son of John R. and Dorothy M. Campbell of Victoria, British Columbia and the brother of Flight Sergeant Frederick A. Campbell (previous entry). ***Glen Campbell Hill*** (64 O/15), north of Blevins Lake was named after him in 1996.

Campbell, Private **Howard K.** of Winnipeg (L 1403). Royal Canadian Army Service Corps. He died 17 February 1945 and is commemorated at Salerno War Cemetery, Italy. ***Howard Campbell Lake*** (64 C/12), northwest of Craig Lake was named after him in 1995.

Campbell, Engine Room Artificer 4 **James** of Winnipeg (V 50107). HMCS *Shawinigan*. The *Shawinigan* was torpedoed and sunk by U-1228 while on independent anti-submarine patrol in the Cabot Strait; all hands were lost. ERA Campbell died 24 November 1944 at the age of 23 and is commemorated at the Halifax Memorial. He was the son of Robert and Catherine Campbell and was survived by his wife Eileen E. Campbell (née Todd) of Winnipeg. A local newspaper reported that:

> ERA Campbell enlisted in February, 1942, and served 15 months as instructor at Royal Canadian Naval College, Victoria, BC. After serving three months in Ottawa under the director of naval engineering, he was later transferred to the *Shawinigan*. Artificer Campbell was educated at Principal Sparling and Daniel McIntyre schools and prior to his enlistment was employed as a draftsman for the Dominion Bridge Company. His wife is the former Eileen Elizabeth Todd. A brother, LAC Donald, is an instructor with the RCAF at St. Thomas. His parents ... and two sisters, Rosalind and Ethel, reside at 1568 Erin Street. Two other sisters, Mrs. W. Simmons and Mrs. George Owens, are both of Winnipeg (*The Winnipeg Tribune* 7 December 1944).

Two months before his death, he wrote a letter to his sister Mrs. Ruby Owens and her husband George:

> Hello Ruby, George and "Nippers:" It's nice and quiet down in the mess tonight – only another fellow and myself – the others are all ashore. I've been writing letters all day, so I thought it would be a good time to drop

you a few lines. First of all, I had better ask how you are. Seems from the last few letters I received from home, misfortune has been dogging your footsteps. Gee, I hope by the time this letter reaches you that things are cleared up somewhat. What were you trying to do George, play Superman? It's a bird, it's a plane – it's Owens. Getting kinda old to go throwing yourself around that way aren't you?

All kidding aside though, I hope by the time that this letter reaches you, it finds you all in better shape. How's the sciatica Rube? I guess if it's not one thing it's another. How are the kiddies keeping? I guess Heather and Donnie are quite a size by now. Heather should be just about ready for school in a little while shouldn't she? What a relief, eh? Free from mischief from 9 to 4 – Gee, if I'm not careful, I'll be getting a blast from you, won't I?

I guess Mom told you we were down in Bermuda a while back. Give me Canada any time. Cold in winter, warm in summer. Course, can't kick, had a trip into New York a while back, though never got the chance to get around and see much of it. If we get back there again, I'm going to try and get a good look at it – but there's not many bars I missed on Staten Island. If you want to see God's forsaken country though, you have to go to Newfoundland. That's the best place yet that I ever laid eyes upon that could murder the King's English so much and still get away [with] it. I could scarcely credit my ears, but you'll get used to it.

Have you seen anything of Eileen lately? She said she was going up to see how George was. By Golly, it's certainly a long time since you last received a letter from me. I forgot your address so you'll receive this letter c/o Mr. and Mrs. R. Campbell. I haven't a heck of a lot of news to tell you Ruby. Had a little excitement to break the monotony, but there again I'm censored. No use giving the censor an overtime job with his scissors. How's Flo keeping? Going to drop her a line tonight too. So long for now all, keep well will you, look after yourself too. Give my best to Heather, DJ and what the little tykes name. So long for now, Jim (24 September 1944).

His brother adds (16 November 2001): "His parents and siblings were devastated by the horror of the war so close to our shores and never really came to terms with such a devastating family tragedy. Rest in Peace, Jimmy." ***Campbell Hill*** (64 N/1), northwest of Minuhik Lake was named after him in 1989.

Campbell, Private **James A.** of Teulon (M 17345). Seaforth Highlanders of Canada. He died 16 September 1944 and is commemorated at Coriano Ridge War Cemetery in Italy. He was one of the two children of William and Alice Campbell of Teulon and was survived by his wife Helene Campbell. According to his brother (8 December 1995):

Jim was born in Teulon, Manitoba, then our parents moved to Saskatchewan. He went to school there and eventually became a teacher. After a few months of teaching, he found it wasn't to his liking. He took further education and became a chemist. He did some work in England with the army as a chemist, but went overseas as a fighting man with his unit. He was very athletic and enjoyed working in gymnastics. He joined the service in Alberta and went overseas from there.

James Campbell Bay (54 D/15) in Strobus Lake was named after him in 1996.

Campbell, Pilot Officer **James D.** of Winnipeg (J 94333). No. 426 Squadron. He died 9 February 1945 at the age of 20 and is commemorated at Harrogate (Stonefall) Cemetery Yorkshire, England. He was the son of Norman L. and M. Goldie Campbell of Winnipeg. ***James Campbell Lake*** (53 M/8), west of Swampy Lake was named after him in 1995.

Campbell, Pilot Officer **James D.** of Austin (J 95169). No. 199 Squadron. He died 16 September 1944 at the age of 22 and is commemorated at the Runnymede Memorial in Surrey, England. He was the son of Lorne D. and Mary E. Campbell (née Johnson) of Austin, Manitoba. ***Campbell Peninsula*** (64 K/10) in Maria Lake was named after him in 1986.

Campbell, Private **John** of Plumas (H 98137). Essex Scottish Regiment. He died 29 October 1943 at the age of 48 and is commemorated at Plumas Cemetery in Manitoba. He was survived by his sister Mrs. Isabelle Brown. ***John Campbell Lake*** (64 P/8), east of Caribou Lake was named after him in 1995.

Campbell, Sergeant **John G.** of Winnipeg (R/95404). No. 22 Operational Training Unit, RCAF. He died 13 February 1943 at the age of 23 and is commemorated at Stratford-upon-Avon Cemetery in Warwickshire, England. He was the son of Gilbert and Mary Campbell and was survived by his wife Helen Campbell of Winnipeg. ***Campbell Narrows*** (63 I/6) in Butterfly Lake was named after him in 1995.

Campbell, Private **John L.** of Winnipeg (H 4051). Royal Canadian Army Service Corps. He died 4 September 1940 and is commemorated at Brookwood Military Cemetery in Surrey, England. ***John Campbell Island*** (64 J/5) in Sprott Lake was named after him in 1995.

Campbell, Pilot Officer **John T.** of The Pas (J 15888). No. 405 Squadron. He died 1 October 1942 at the age of 22 and is commemorated at the Kiel War Cemetery in Germany. He was the son of John A. and Elsie M. Campbell of The Pas. ***John Campbell Bay*** (53 F/13) in Angling Lake was named after him in 1995.

Campbell, Private **Joseph W.** of Holland, Manitoba (H 1418). Argyle and Sutherland Highlanders. He died 24 October 1944 at the age of 21 and is commemorated at Bergen-op-Zoom Canadian War Cemetery in Holland. He was the son of Lloyd J. and Ada L. Campbell. According to his brother (21 March 1996):

Joseph Wilfred Campbell was born and educated in the Town of Holland. He was raised on the family farm and one of his favourite things was working and playing with the horses. His favourite sport was curling. He had two older brothers Robert and Glen and one younger brother Raymond and one younger sister Winnifred. He had a great personality and was a joy to be with.

His step-brother adds (31 December 2001):

He enlisted with the PPCLI in 1942, trained at Fort Garry and Shilo and was later attached to the Argyle and Sutherland Highlanders, going overseas with that unit. He was part of the Normandy invasion and was wounded early in the fall. You might say: Born in Holland (Canada), died in Holland (Netherlands).

Due to my mother dying at an early age, I was taken in and raised by Joe's mother and dad and family at age three. They say I took his place at the dinner table – Joe had enlisted by that time. Joe was a happy person, always smiling or laughing. He was a farm boy, loved horses and enjoyed curling in winter time. He was a favourite of the girls at dances.

Joseph Campbell Lake (53 N/15), northeast of Whitefish Lake was named after him in 1995.

Campbell, Pilot Officer **Ronald B.** of Winnipeg (J 3746). Royal Canadian Air Force. He died 15 June 1941 at the age of 21 and is commemorated at Bone War Cemetery in Algeria. He was the son of Neil and Doris Campbell of Toronto. ***Campbell River*** (64 O/2), which flows southeast into Brownstone Lake was named after him in 1995.

Campbell, Lance Corporal **Samuel** of St. Vital (H 35434). South Saskatchewan Regiment. He died 19 August 1942 and is commemorated at Dieppe Canadian War Cemetery, France. He was survived by his wife Martha Campbell. ***Campbell Falls*** (64 B/8) on an unnamed river which drains Pakwaw Lake was named after him in 1995.

Campbell, Flight Lieutenant **William G.** of Strathclair. No. 428 Squadron, Commendation for Valuable Service.

> This officer is employed as a Staff Pilot in No. 6 (O) AFU which appointment he has held since June 1943. He is a most reliable pilot and an excellent officer. His energy and dogged persistence in his flying duties are an inspiration to other pilots; he is a pillar of strength to his Commanding Officer (1 January 1945).

He died 30 April 1945 at the age of 23 and is commemorated at Blacon Cemetery in Cheshire, England. He had been with the Air Force for five years and flown a great number of missions. He and his crew were killed on what was to be their last mission, a week before the war in Europe ended. He was survived by his parents John M. and Katherine E. Campbell of Strathclair and by his sister Louise, also of Strathclair. After his last leave at home, his mother wrote in her diary:

> This was Billie's last day with us. His leave was so short this time. He and Don spent the morning going around town talking to old friends. It's turned very cold – 40 below. Dad took us to the train in the cutter in the afternoon. Billie looked so handsome and grown up in his uniform. He shook hands with Don and Dad. I held my boy and we said goodbye again. His eyes. My little boy. My darling boy (10 January 1943).

Fifty-four years later, his nephew received a request for information from a Sandon, Staffordshire resident who explained (n.d.):

> When we moved into Sandon House (wife Kathy, daughters Sarah and Kate and son James) some 21 years ago, I found whilst clearing out the stables a tube with a bright orange box kite inside which thank goodness I kept through curiosity. Some years later, the previous occupant of the house called by who explained that it was from the Lancaster that had crashed in the village. He was Doctor Bocking, one of the first on the scene and did his best to help the men, but sadly to no avail. I spoke to people in the village and most were surprised that very little was known of these chaps who had laid down their lives for us so close to the end of the war.
>
> I approached RAF Stafford who were very helpful and supplied me with copies of photographs of the crashed plane. These had never been seen by any non Air Force people before. I quietly went to the field, and from still existing features located the exact place of the crash. Of course nothing can be seen now but for the grassy field, but it was a moving experience.
>
> After many stop/start efforts at getting information together, I handed my file over to our local branch of the British Legion whose members (mostly retired now!) had the time and contacts to take the search forward. In our local church there are many memorials to local people lost in wars and conflicts, but none to these chaps who actually died in our midst. We have decided that the memorial stone and inscription will be erected close to the crash site, on the roadside of the hedge, so that it can be seen by all who pass. The site will be kept mown and tidy by village volunteers. Would it be possible please if it is not too much trouble to send the information and copies of photographs that you have. We would treasure anything you send and will collate it with all the other information that we have to make a lasting book of history. Yours Sincerely, Donald Mitchell.

A memorial to Flight Lieutenant Campbell and his crew was dedicated at the site of the crash (Sandon, Staffordshire) in 1999. The ceremony included a flypast of a Lancaster and Hurricane. ***Campbell Lake*** (64 A/11), west of Waskaiowaka Lake was named after him in 1950.

Campbell, Flight Sergeant **William W.** of Winnipeg (568247). No. 230 Squadron, RAF. He enlisted in August, 1935 as a Tradesman and later remustered to aircrew becoming a navigator (Allison 1978). He died 13 April 1944 at the age of 32 and is commemorated at Roye New British Cemetery, France. ***William Campbell Point*** (64 B/9) on Baldock Lake was named after him in 1995.

Camsell, Flight Sergeant **Philip S.** of East Kildonan (R 134429). No. 61 Squadron. He died 2 October 1943 at the age of 29 and is commemorated at Durnbach War Cemetery, Germany. He was the son of Philip S. and Mabel Camsell and was survived by his wife Gladys Camsell of Winnipeg. ***Camsell Lake*** (52 L/6), east of Lac du Bonnet was named after him in 1978.

Candline, Flight Sergeant **Albert E.** of Winnipeg (R 100359). No. 408 Squadron. He died 29 July 1944 at the age of 21 and is commemorated at the Runnymede Memorial in Surrey, England. ***Candline Lake*** (63 H/1), northeast of Weaver Lake was named after him in 1974.

Canfield, Flying Officer **Glen R.** of Winnipeg (J 10623). No. 525 Squadron. He died 6 March 1944 at the age of 22 and is commemorated at Lisbon (St. George) British Churchyard, Portugal. He was the son of Joseph W. and Carmen Canfield. ***Canfield Lake*** (64 O/3), south of Nueltin Lake was named after him in 1961.

Cann, Private **Leslie F.** of Winnipeg (H 10735). Royal Canadian Regiment. He died 16 September 1944 at the age of 19 and is commemorated at Coriano Ridge War Cemetery in Italy. He was the son of Joseph and Sarah Cann. ***Cann Lake*** (64 K/6), northeast of Reindeer Lake was named after him in 1972.

Cann, Flying Officer **Robert L.** of Winnipeg (J 36389). No. 432 Squadron. He died 18 December 1944 at the age of 22 and is commemorated at Dieppe Canadian War Cemetery, Hautot-sur-Mer, France. He was the son of Leslie and Margaret Cann. A family friend writes (3 September 1997):

> … I met Robert who at the time was on leave from overseas duty. He seemed a happy young man – blond, blue eyes, reserved and handsome in his uniform. My husband's aunt loved him dearly and shed many a tear for Robert. By chance, I was at Eaton's one day when I saw her by an escalator weeping so uncontrollably; she had just received [the] news, dear Bobby had been killed over Dieppe. It was a few weeks before Christmas – his first outing.

Cann Island (64 N/9) in Nahili Lake was named after him in 1995.

Cant, Stoker 1 **Daniel** of Winnipeg (V 56590). HMCS *Valleyfield*. The *Valleyfield* was torpedoed and sunk by U-548 50 miles south of Cape Race, Newfoundland; 125 of her ship's company were lost.

> About thirty minutes before midnight on May 6 (1944) the Canadian frigate *Valleyfield* was approaching Newfoundland with a mid-ocean group which included two other Canadian frigates and two corvettes. The ships had completed their portion of a run with a convoy from the United Kingdom. Escort duties had been turned over to a local group some hours before, and the men of the mid-ocean ships were already making plans for a first night in St. John's.
>
> There were small icebergs scattered about the area, and radar contacts were many and confused. None of any apparent significance had been obtained, however, as it came time for the watches to change in *Valleyfield*, which was a little astern of the other ships. The officer on the bridge had just sent down word for his relief to be wakened when the instruments gave sudden warning of the presence of a submarine. As the

buzz of the Action Stations signal ran through the lower decks, there came the crash of a torpedo ripping into the port side; and then a tremendous explosion. Great chunks of metal lifted skyward, filling the air with flying splinters; there was the roar of escaping steam, the grind of tearing metal and the crash of falling superstructure. The mainmast swung in drunken circles as the wallowing ship, broken nearly in half, staggered and began to settle.

The bow sloped off to starboard and dipped steeply. Within a minute or so the forecastle was lying almost on its side. Men simply stepped off into the water, whose temperature, taken a few minutes before, had registered 32 degrees. As the ship, for a last moment, held precariously together, the settling stern lifted the bow from the sea. It rose threateningly above swimmers choking [them] with thick, nauseous oil which filled their eyes, mouths and noses. Then it leaned away, broke off with a rending crash and sank. The after part tilted forward, upended vertically in its turn and remained for a long moment silhouetted in the moonlight, rudder and screws to the sky.

It went under slowly with a vast moan of escaping air and steam, and then a freezing silence fell over the dark sea. The voices which had made a brave effort to farewell the ship with *For She's a Jolly Good Fellow* were no longer heard; the shouts of encouragement grew rarer as the icy water tightened its grip on numbing limbs. Other ships of *Valleyfield's* group had been several miles ahead of her at the moment of the torpedoing and had no knowledge of it until some time later. *Giffard* was the first to return to the position but, as always, search for the enemy had to take precedence over rescue work. As the sister frigate passed and merged into the darkness, to be gone perhaps for hours more, some of *Valleyfield's* men gave up, let go their hold on Carley floats or wreckage and sank from sight. When *Giffard* returned from an unavailing hunt, 115 officers and ratings had been lost. The Atlantic was secure for the passage of invasion supplies, but men still had to die to keep it so (Schull 1987).

Stoker Cant died 7 May 1944 at the age of 19 and is commemorated at the Halifax Memorial. He was the son of Robert and Janet Cant of Winnipeg. ***Cant Lake*** (64 N/13), west of Nueltin Lake was named after him in 1972.

Cantin, Flying Officer **Clément F. A.** of McCreary (J 7452). No. 213 Squadron. He died 9 October 1942 at the age of 23 and is commemorated at the Alamein Memorial in Egypt. He was the son of Amedee and Julienne Cantin and the brother of Flying Officer Maurice R. Cantin and Battery Sergeant Major Wilfred R. Cantin (next two entries). His brother recalls (26 October 2001):

F/O Cantin had completed high school at McCreary prior to the outbreak of war in 1939 and was working in a local garage. He joined the RCAF in 1940 and completed his elementary flying at Portage la Prairie and service flying on Harvards at Yorkton, Saskatchewan. [He] arrived in the UK in November of 1941 and completed his training on Hurricanes and Spitfires. In April of 1942, his squadron was transferred to North Africa. Clement was looking forward to his return after the war and to attending the University of Manitoba.

Cantin Creek (64 P/15), which flows southwest into Round Sand Lake was named after him in 1974. Cantin Lake (53 E/6), southwest of Island Lake was named after his mother, Mrs. Julienne Cantin. She had ten children, all of whom served in World War II. This is believed to be a record. She was also very involved with the Red Cross and the Free French Movement in Canada. She was presented with the French Legion of Honour by Count Jean de Hautecloque, former French Ambassador to Canada as the representative of all Canadian mothers in the liberation of France. She was also chosen as the Silver Cross Mother in 1960 and laid the wreath at the Cenotaph in Ottawa on Remembrance Day.

Cantin, Flying Officer **Maurice R.** of McCreary (J 20214). No. 514 Squadron. He died 26 November 1943 at the age of 21 and is commemorated at the Berlin 1939 - 1945 War Cemetery in Brandenburg, Germany. He was the son of Amedee and Julienne Cantin and the brother of Flying Officer Clement F. A. Cantin and Battery Sergeant Major Wilfred R. Cantin (previous and next entry). His brother recalls (26 October 2001):

F/O Cantin completed high school at McCreary, Manitoba and joined the RCAF in 1941. He took his elementary flying training at Portage la Prairie and service flying at No. 10 in Dauphin on Cessna Cranes. [He] completed his training in July, 1942 and immediately went overseas. Advanced training was on Airspeed Oxfords, Wellington and Lancaster bombers. His operational aircraft was a Lancaster designated "M for Mother." He made several operational flights, but he and his crew were shot down on a major Berlin raid. We have visited his grave in the Berlin War Cemetery. Maurice looked forward to his weekends and furloughs when he could visit with his sister who was a nurse at No. 10 CGH in London and with his brothers stationed at Aldershot.

Cantin Island (64 J/14) in Belsham Lake was named after him in 1989.

Cantin, Battery Sergeant Major **Wilfrid R.** of McCreary (H 26329). Fort Garry Horse. He died 4 November 1940 at the age of 26 and is commemorated at McCreary Roman Catholic Cemetery, Manitoba. He was the son of Amedee and Julienne Cantin of McCreary and was survived by his wife Evyline Marie Cantin (née Craig) of Barrie, Ontario. He was the brother of Flying Officer Clement F. A. Cantin and Flying Officer Maurice R. Cantin (previous two entries). BSM Cantin had been in the Manitoba Horse Militia prior to the war and operated an International Harvester Agency in McCreary. He was killed in a motorcycle accident while at Camp Borden. His wife later joined the CWAC. ***Cantin Bay*** (64 J/14) on the north shore of Belsham Lake was named after him in 1989.

Cantlon, Private **George C.** of Hartney (H 14806). Royal Regiment of Canada. He died 14 August 1944 and is commemorated at the Bayeux Memorial in France. ***Cantlon Lake*** (64 K/9), northeast of Reindeer Lake was named after him in 1972.

Canty, Rifleman **Alfred W.** of East Kildonan (H 40744). Royal Winnipeg Rifles. He died 8 June 1944 at the age of 29 and is commemorated at Beny-sur-Mer Canadian War Cemetery, France. He was the son of John and Lillian Canty. ***Canty Lake*** (52 E/14), southeast of Brereton Lake was named after him in 1974.

Carberry, Lance Corporal **Samuel R.** of Winnipeg (H 17006). Winnipeg Grenadiers. He died 19 December 1941 at the age of 20 and is commemorated at the Sai Wan War Cemetery in Hong Kong. He was the son of Samuel and Margaret Carberry. According to his cousin (6 January 2000):

He attended Luxton School as well as St. John's High. He also attended St. John's Cathedral Anglican Church. He was active in sports, particularly football, hockey and running. At 16, he joined the non-permanent armed forces and once war broke out, enlisted with the Princess Patricia's Canadian Light Infantry. He apparently also instructed in Portage la Prairie. One week prior to departure, he transferred to the Winnipeg Grenadiers as he heard they were deploying to Hong Kong.

Carberry Lake (52 L/4), southeast of Lac du Bonnet was named after him in 1973.

Carcary, Flight Sergeant **Albert A.** of Carman (R 86290). No. 73 Squadron. He died 22 July 1942 at the age of 22 and is commemorated at the Alamein Memorial in Egypt. He was the brother of Private William T. Carcary (next entry). Their cousin recalls (31 October 2001):

"Ab" was fun loving, mischievous, adventurous and a "prankster first class." Bill was a good natured, quiet young man with a charming smile. He loved sports – fishing, hunting and riding his horse. There was a beautiful Memorial Service held in Carman in May of 1942 to pay tribute to these young men. I remember the flowers, the singing, the church crowded with our extended family and the entire community. Their parents, Jean and Alex Carcary were devastated. They had lost their two sons to the war in a period of under six months. Their mother struggled with her grief for months and I strongly suspect that the love and help of neighbours, friends and family were her saving grace.

Carcary Island (64 O/3) in Canfield Lake was named after him in 1995.

Carcary, Private **William T.** of Carman (H 6350). Winnipeg Grenadiers. He died 24 December 1941 at the age of 21 and is commemorated at the Sai Wan Memorial in Hong Kong. He was the son of Alexander and Jean Carcary. He was the brother of Flight Sergeant Albert A. Carcary (previous entry). ***Carcary Lake*** (64 N/12), southwest of Nueltin Lake was named after him in 1972.

Carefoot, Private **Spence R.** of Virden (L 27788). Regina Rifle Regiment. He died 12 July 1943 at the age of 19 and is commemorated at Bone War Cemetery in Algeria. He was the son of Thornton and Florence Carefoot. According to his sister he (20 March 1995):

… was born in Virden, Manitoba [and] received his primary education in a rural school known as Pacific School before taking his elementary schooling at Hargrave, Manitoba. Spence joined the Regina Rifle Regiment on June 23rd, 1940, trained at Dundurn, Saskatchewan, then at Debert. He left Debert August 25, 1941 and landed in England September 1, 1941 where he trained until June 28, 1943 when he embarked for North Africa arriving July 11, 1943. While on a bathing parade the next day, July 12, 1943 he died of a heart attack.

Carefoot Lake (64 I/3), west of North Knife Lake was named after him in 1974.

Carey, Private **Clarence A.** of Brandon (H 77735). Essex Scottish Regiment. He died 6 September 1944 at the age of 20 and is commemorated at Beny-sur-Mer Canadian War Cemetery, France. He was survived by his mother Margaret J. Lyons. ***Carey Island*** (64 C/12) in Tod Lake was named after him in 1995.

Carey, Flight Lieutenant **Douglas M.** of Brandon (J 16480). No. 12 Squadron, Distinguished Flying Cross.

This officer is an excellent operational pilot and captain of aircraft, whose gallantry in the face of enemy action has been outstanding. On the majority of the sorties in which he has participated the primary target has been bombed successfully. Flight Lieutenant Carey has completed missions to most of the major German objectives and undeterred by opposition, has pressed home his attacks regardless of the hazards encountered (DFC Citation 1948).

He died 31 March 1944 at the age of 22 and is commemorated at the Hanover War Cemetery in Germany. He was the son of William and Myrtle Carey of Brandon. According to his nephew (27 January 1997):

He was raised and educated in Brandon, being an avid hockey player in winter and worked on the farm in summer. His father Bill was a fireman in [the] Brandon Fire Department for 47 years. Apparently, [Flight Lieutenant Carey] was awarded the DFC because he flew 36 sorties over Germany when most airmen were only allowed to fly 30 missions before they were taken out of combat service. His medals and photographs of his aircrew are in the Commonwealth Air Training Museum [at] the Brandon Airport. At the British Cemetery, his entire aircrew of the Lancaster bomber are buried together in the same row.

Carey Lake (54 K/6), southeast of Churchill was named after him in 1948.

Carey, Flight Sergeant **John J.** of Winnipeg (R 53908). No. 103 Squadron. He died 29 August 1942 at the age of 22 and is commemorated at the Runnymede Memorial in Surrey, England. He was the son of Leo and Janet Carey of Ottawa. ***Carey Bay*** (64 P/2) in Spruce Lake was named after him in 1995.

Carley, Able Seaman **Douglas** of Winnipeg. He served aboard the SS *Cortona*. The *Cortona* was *en route* from Liverpool to Montevideo when it was torpedoed off the west coast of Scotland 11 July 1942. All crew seem to have escaped in two lifeboats despite the rough water. They stayed together for three days, but at dawn on the fourth day, there was no sign of the second lifeboat. Able Seaman Carley was presumed dead on 14 July 1942 and he is commemorated at the Halifax Memorial. He was the brother of AC2 Edward C. Carley (next entry) and was survived by his mother Florence Carley. ***Carley Island*** (63 P/2) in Cotton Lake was named after him in 1996.

Carley, Aircraftman 2 **Edward C.** of Winnipeg (R 80290). No. 9 Advanced Flying Unit. He died 13 January 1942 at the age of 36 and is commemorated at Kirkinner Cemetery in Wigtownshire, Scotland. He was the brother of Able Seaman Douglas Carley (previous entry) and was survived by his mother Florence Carley of Winnipeg. ***Carley Lake*** (64 I/8), northeast of North Knife Lake was named after him in 1974.

Carlisle, Pilot Officer **Elden F.** of Flin Flon (J 94462). No. 298 Squadron. He died 3 April 1945 at the age of 27 and is commemorated at Vanse Churchyard, Norway. He was the son of Martin and Frances Carlisle. ***Carlisle Lake*** (63 K/12) at Flin Flon on the Manitoba - Saskatchewan boundary was named after him in 1940.

Carlson, Pilot Officer **Alfred** of Winnipeg (J 90059). No. 426 Squadron. He died 27 January 1944 at the age of 20 and is commemorated at the Runnymede Memorial in Surrey, England. He was the son of John and Esther Carlson. ***Carlson Island*** (64 J/16) in Overby Lake was named after him in 1989.

Carlson, Private **Clifford E.** of Benito (H 87461). Royal Canadian Army Service Corps. He died 20 October 1944 at the age of 23 and is commemorated at the Adegem Canadian War Cemetery in Belgium. He was the son of Mr. and Mrs. Charles E. Carlson and was survived by his wife Elsie Carlson of Emsworth, Hampshire, England, sister Dorothy and younger brother Herb. According to his aunt Rhoda Carlson of Benito (24 November 2001):

Clifford left home at 15 years and worked on various farms in the Alpine district of Manitoba. When he was older, Clifford worked in logging camps in the winter. In October of 1940, Clifford visited his aunt and uncle in Benito. They understood that he was going to Flin Flon to seek work in the mine. However, he met some other young men in Swan River and decided to go to Winnipeg where he joined the Army. Clifford sailed for England on his 21st birthday in April of 1941.

Clifford loved to dance but was very conscious of his feet which he thought were too small (size 9) for his size (six-foot-four, 200 pounds). To remedy this, he purchased a pair of black Oxfords (very popular at the time) which made his feet appear larger. Clifford also enjoyed movies, picnics and family gatherings.

Carlson Lake (64 F/6), east of Reindeer Lake was named after him in 1961.

Carlson, Rifleman **Gordon L.** of Erickson (H 43255). Royal Winnipeg Rifles. He died 25 September 1944 at the age of 26 and is commemorated at the Calais Canadian War Cemetery in France. He was the third child of Henry and Emma Carlson. His sister recalls (14 January 2002):

His was the childhood of any farm boy, mainly home-made play and through school years to Grade 9 in the rural school – a two and a half mile walk from home. With no interest in continuing high school, he spent the next years working at home and at times for some of the neighbours. When he was drafted into compulsory military training, he had his own quarter section farm which he was developing.

For about two years, the various training programs moved him from camp to camp, from Prince Albert across Alberta as far as Nanaimo and Courtenay, BC and back to the BC interior. His heart was at home on the farm and he applied for leave for the busy seasons but these were never granted. In early summer of 1944, he enlisted in the regular army and was glad to be posted with the Winnipeg Rifles as that was where the home boys were. He was home on furlough in July, then sent east and on to England.

He was impressed with the beauty of the English and French countryside and wrote of the grand welcome given them as they moved through the French villages. People lined the streets throwing flowers, offering drinks and cheering them on. His last letter was written on September 18, only one letter from his mother had caught up to him. A week later, on September 25, he was dead, a scant two months since he left home, still making plans for the future.

Carlson Bay (64 F/16) in Kustra Lake was named after him in 1984.

Carlstrom, Corporal **Roy S.** of Winnipeg (H 1154). Argyle and Sutherland Highlanders of Canada. He died 9 September 1944 at the age of 19 and is commemorated at the Adegem Canadian War Cemetery in Belgium. He was the son of Emanuel and Olga Carlstrom. In a letter to his parents he wrote:

Dear Mom, Pop: I am sorry I never wrote sooner, I have been busy up till lately, and now that I am on my leave I find time to do a lot of things. I told you last time that I was going to Scotland. And this time it happened same as last time, I never got there. I got as far as London, that's all. Isn't it disgusting? Boy it sure takes a lot more money to go on leave than it does back home. And there's lots of places and things to see anyway. Well, I have a lot more things to cram in this letter, but there's no room. So give my love to John and everybody, Roy (10 January 1944).

Carlstrom Lake (64 I/11), northwest of North Knife Lake was named after him in 1978.

Carnegie, Pilot Officer **Robert C.** of Arrow River (J 94257). No. 424 Squadron. He died 12 January 1945 at the age of 21 and is commemorated at Aabenraa Cemetery in Denmark. His aircraft was shot down over Killund Bay, Denmark while on a night bombing mission to Flensburg, Germany. He was the third of the six children of Mr. and Mrs. E. Carnegie of Arrow River. His sister recalls (13 December 2001):

Bob grew up on a farm and attended school in Beulah, Manitoba. He was a good student and enjoyed sports – hockey, baseball, curling. When about 10 years old, he won a prize at a local talent show when he danced the sailor's hornpipe and played the bagpipes. He was not keen on dancing, but did become an excellent piper under his father's tutelage. He left school and went to Union Bay, British Columbia where he worked with his brother in a garage and drove a school bus.

He was interested in the RCMP and upon return to Manitoba, completed the tests and personnel interviews required for admission. However, the Service Call came and he joined the RCAF. In Britain, apart from training, he enjoyed visits with brother Bill of the Army Signals Corps and they visited relatives in Scotland at every opportunity. Bob was a rear gunner and part of a good crew – a crew of veterans with 17 to 28 trips to their credit. Only the pilot of their crew survived. Bob was well liked and a fine person.

His sister-in-law adds (9 May 1995): "Several family members have visited his grave on various occasions and are very appreciative of the care given to his grave and all other grave sites in the cemetery." ***Carnegie Lake*** (53 E/2), south of Island Lake was named after him in 1978.

Carnegie, Flying Officer **Thomas S.** of Winnipeg (J 28217). No. 138 Squadron. He died 1 June 1944 at the age of 21 and is commemorated at the Runnymede Memorial in Surrey, England. He was the son of John E. and Mary Carnegie of Winnipeg. According to his nephew (n.d.):

We don't know much about Uncle Tom as both parents and his brother Corporal Jack Carnegie are now dead. He lived with his parents at 312 Queen Street in St. James and was good friends with Walter Morris and Irwin Montgomery. He was educated in St. James, attending Assiniboine School and Linwood College. He enlisted in August, 1941 and received training at Pennfield Ridge, St. Thomas, Rivers and Regina, graduating from No. 2 AOS Edmonton on July 9, 1943.

It was said that he was a quiet man, not given to excess and was well liked. He was certainly serious when photographed. He worked for the T. Eaton Company in Winnipeg and wore a gold ring issued to servicemen which he left behind (since lost). He was engaged to 'Grace' of St James when he left for overseas and we still have his RCAF ID tag with her name and the date 14.7.43 inscribed on the back.

He was an excellent golfer and won the Crow Flight Championship for western Canada (sometime prior to enlisting in August, 1941). We have Uncle Tom's photo scrap book with about 150 photos which was passed on by his mother. He kept this book throughout his training at Pennfield Ridge and Edmonton until his departure from Halifax. Included are many photos of his family and fellow servicemen/women, especially Walter Morris, Miller Bell, friends at the "Do Fly Inn" in La Pointe, their Anson Bomber No. 6687 at Pennfield and a photo of Tom in front of his hut with a service sweater and tie. Inscribed on the back: "somebody pinched that sweater."

We don't know exactly how Tommy went down, whether it was over land or sea, but our father, Jack, thought that it was probably over the English Channel after picking up fire from the continent. According to our mother Agnes, Dad never really got over losing his only sibling and said repeatedly that he wished it were himself instead. Dad received news of Tommy's death while on duty in Paris.

Possibly the last time Jack and Tommy saw each other was in London. Dad had been overseas for some time already and came from Brighton so they spent a day together before going to visit relatives in Bury (Uncle Percy and Aunt Addie, Mary's sister). Tommy was not much of a spender, apparently and being new to England he would constantly be holding out a handful of coins and asking dad, "How many bobs have I got in there, Jack?" As with all loss, it is immeasurable and irretrievable. The loss of Tommy at age 21 was no less for his family. He remains an example of honour and grace to this day.

Carnegie Island (64 C/8) in Granville Lake was named after him in 1995.

Caron, Pilot Officer **Gérald Antoine A. A.** of Winnipeg (J 88406). No. 500 Squadron. He died 7 March 1944 at the age of 22 and is commemorated at the Malta Memorial. He was the son of Allan and Georgie Caron of Winnipeg. ***Caron Lake*** (64 K/16), southwest of Nueltin Lake was named after him in 1962.

Carpenter, Lieutenant **Frank B.** of Winnipeg. Royal Canadian Artillery. He died 19 August 1942 and is commemorated at Dieppe Canadian War Cemetery, France. He was the son of Frank and E. S. Carpenter. ***Carpenter Lake*** (53 N/10), northeast of Whitefish Lake was named after him in 1995.

Carrier, Private **Frank** of Elm Creek (H 41524). Lake Superior Regiment. He died 2 March 1945 and is commemorated at the Groesbeek Canadian War Cemetery in Holland. He was survived by his mother Emma Carriere (sp.). ***Carrier Creek*** (63 J/13), which flows west into Grass River was named after him in 1972.

Carriere, Trooper **Florio** of St-Pierre-Jolys (H 63772). British Columbia Dragoons. He died 29 May 1944 at the age of 23 and is commemorated at the Cassino War Cemetery in Italy. He was the son of Daniel A. and Laura Carriere of St. Pierre, Manitoba. ***Carriere Point*** (64 K/16) in Stevens Lake was named after him in 1995.

Carrière, Private **Frédéric** of St. Eustache (H 18003). Essex Scottish Regiment. He died 26 October 1944 and is commemorated at Bergen-op-Zoom Canadian War Cemetery in Holland. He was survived by his wife Georgia S. Carrière of St. Eustache. ***Carrière Island*** (64 C/9) in Eden Lake was named after him in 1995.

Carrière, Private **Victor V. "Shorty"** of The Pas (H 14906). Royal Regiment of Canada. He died 24 October 1944 at the age of 25 and is commemorated at Schoonselhof Cemetery in Antwerp, Belgium – the birthplace of his father-in-law. He was survived by his wife, a son, a daughter, four brothers, six sisters and numerous other relatives. He was the eldest of 12 children. His daughter recalls (22 November 2001):

My father was originally from Cumberland House, Saskatchewan, but was living at The Pas where my mother was when he enlisted. They had been married in 1942. I was five and a half months old when my father died. My brother was almost two at the time. His last leave was spent with his family at The Pas. My mother tells me he was a very proud father. Prior to enlisting in the army, he was a trapper and was farming with his father-in-law out of The Pas. My mother says that my father's plans for the future when he returned from the war were to continue farming. He loved the outdoors.

Carrière Lake (64 F/5), east of Reindeer Lake was named after him in 1961.

Carrière, Rifleman **William J.** of Elm Creek (H 17729). Royal Winnipeg Rifles. He died 8 June 1944 and is commemorated at Bretteville-sur-Laize Canadian War Cemetery, France. He was survived by his mother Emma Carrière. ***Carrière Bay*** (64 H/5) in Wood Lake was named after him in 1995.

Carruthers, Sergeant **Donald P.** of Winnipeg (R 100418). No. 53 Operational Training Unit, RCAF. He died 23 May 1942 at the age of 20 and is commemorated at Llantwit Major Cemetery, Glamorganshire, Wales. He was the only son of Perry D. and Stella B. A. Carruthers. A versatile athlete, he was the winner of many university trophies in sport, receiving faculty crests for hockey, rugby, track, basketball and swimming. He also won the 1941 trophy for high aggregate points at the faculty's annual track and field event. He had completed two years of study in the Faculty of Agriculture at the University of Manitoba when he enlisted in 1941. He was one of the five World War II casualties from Rathgar Avenue in Winnipeg. ***Carruthers Lake*** (64 P/11), east of Nejanilini Lake was named after him in 1974.

Carruthers, Pilot Officer **George W.** of Dauphin (J 92333). No. 419 Squadron. He died 13 June 1944 at the age of 20 and is commemorated at Vieux-Berquin Communal Cemetery, France. He was the son of Walter E. and Florence E. Carruthers of Dauphin and was survived by his wife Hazel Carruthers (née Thompson) of Dauphin and four brothers and four sisters. According to his brother (15 December 1994):

[His] Lancaster aircraft KB731 [was declared] missing during a night attack against the marshalling yards at Cambrai, France. Flying Officers William Lacey and E. R. Lowe, Pilot Officers D. J. Applin and M. R. Larkin were killed. One Canadian, Ray Forbes of Portage la Prairie and RAF Flight Engineer Barrie Wilson-Law bailed out to safety.

He adds (22 November 2001):

George was born and raised on the family farm nine miles southwest of Dauphin. When he was a teenager, two airports were established near Dauphin. When George was of age to enlist, it was an easy choice as the skies around Dauphin were full of planes. He trained in eastern Canada, but his love of the farm and horses never faltered; he spent many of his leaves on farms in that area. Ironically, at the same time, young trainees from the Dauphin stations spent their spare time working at the Carruthers and other farms in the area.

Carruthers Bay (64 F/2) in Thomsen Lake was named after him in 1994.

Carscadden, Private **Lorne E.** of Virden (5067). 27th Battalion (Manitoba Regiment). He died 21 August 1917 at the age of 26 and is commemorated at the Vimy Memorial, Pas de Calais, France. He was survived by his mother Annie Birch (formerly Carscadden) of Virden. He described himself as a "General Merchant" when he enlisted in Winnipeg in October, 1916. ***Carscadden Lake*** (54 D/5), east of Split Lake was named after this World War I casualty in 1978.

Carson, Corporal **John J.** of Dauphin (H 8057). Perth Regiment. He died 14 September 1944 and is commemorated at Coriano Ridge War Cemetery in Italy. ***Carson Bay*** (64 P/13) in Spratt Lake was named after him in 1995.

Carson, Flight Sergeant **Rodney A.** of Winnipeg (A 4161). No. 3 Repair Depot. He died 2 March 1945 at the age of 31 and is commemorated at Brookside Cemetery in Winnipeg. He was the son of Austin and Mary Carson of Winnipeg and was survived by his wife Lois K. Carson of Ottawa. ***Carson Island*** (63 N/10) in Flatrock Lake was named after him in 1995.

Carswell, Private **Richard** of Domain (H 19940). Queen's Own Cameron Highlanders. He died 19 August 1942 during the Dieppe raid. His brother indicates that his body later washed ashore in Holland. Private Carswell was 32 years of age and is commemorated at Ameland (Nes) General Cemetery, Holland. He was the son of Robert and Katherine Carswell and was survived by his wife Isabella (Ella) Carswell (née Rae) of Edinburgh, Scotland and their daughter. His niece writes (12 November 2001):

> Dick was born on December 15, 1909, one of the eight children of Katherine and Robert Carswell of Osborne, Manitoba. He attended school and worked in the Osborne area and enjoyed country dances and playing baseball on local teams with his brothers. He moved to Fort Garry with some of the family in the 1930s and joined the Camerons in January, 1940. After training at Shilo and Quebec City, he went overseas in December of the same year and arrived in Scotland on Christmas Day. In 1941, he married Isabella Rae of Edinburgh and the following year his daughter Ellen was born. In 1946, his widow and daughter immigrated to Canada and resided in Winnipeg.

Carswell Lake (64 F/4), east of Reindeer Lake was named after him in 1961.

Carter, Leading Aircraftman **George A.** of Winnipeg (747780). No. 229 Squadron, RAF. He died 24 February 1940 at the age of 27 and is commemorated at Nottingham Southern Cemetery, Nottinghamshire, England. He was the son of George and Mary Carter and was survived by his wife May Carter of Nottingham. ***Carter Island*** (53 L/4) in Bolton Lake was named after him in 1995.

Carter, Pilot Officer **Robert G.** of Elm Creek (J 85344). No. 431 Squadron. He died 26 July 1944 at the age of 21 and is commemorated at Durnbach War Cemetery, Germany. He was the son of William and Janet Carter. ***Carter Lake*** (63 K/15), northwest of Elbow Lake was named after him in 1993. Family members had a commemorative plaque placed there in 1995.

Cartwright, Able Seaman **Gordon D.** of Winnipeg (V 24087). HMCS *Sackville*. He died 14 October 1942 at the age of 20 and is commemorated at the Halifax Memorial. He was the son of Charles and Elizabeth Cartwright. ***Cartwright Island*** (64 N/3) in Keehn Lake was named after him in 1995.

Carufell, Rifleman **George J.** of Winnipeg (H 41550). Royal Winnipeg Rifles. He died 6 June 1944 at the age of 36 and is commemorated at Beny-sur-Mer Canadian War Cemetery, France. He was survived by his mother Julia Matheson of Vancouver. ***Carufell Lake*** (64 I/13), northwest of North Knife Lake was named after him in 1974.

Caruso, Private **Frank T.** of Winnipeg (H 6445). Winnipeg Grenadiers. He died a prisoner of war 13 January 1944 and is commemorated at the Yokohama War Cemetery in Japan. The official cause of death was listed as beriberi. He was the husband of Mrs. K. Caruso of Winnipeg. ***Caruso Lake*** (54 C/7), southwest of York Factory was named after him in 1964.

Carver, Private **Hugh A.** of Beaconia (H 20770). Queen's Own Cameron Highlanders. He died 19 August 1942 at the age of 25 and is commemorated at Dieppe Canadian War Cemetery, Hautot-sur-Mer, France. He was the son of William and Maggie Carver. ***Carver Lake*** (64 K/10), northeast of Reindeer Lake was named after him in 1972.

Casey, Sergeant **Murray G.** of Brandon (R 275076). No. 22 Operational Training Unit, RCAF. He died 31 August 1944 at the age of 19 and is commemorated at the Runnymede Memorial in Surrey, England. He was the only child of Henry N. and Aileen Casey of Brandon. According to his cousin (22 March 1996): "... [he] attended Alexander and Earl Haigh Schools and prior to his enlistment was employed with Fleet Aircraft at Fort Erie, Ontario for five months. He enlisted in November of 1944 and was only overseas two months." ***Casey Lake*** (63 C/14), south of Vandekerckhove Lake was named after him in 1982.

Casey, Flight Sergeant **Theodore E. J.** of Winnipeg (R 91856). No. 57 Squadron. He died 11 February 1943 at the age of 20 and is commemorated at the Runnymede Memorial in Surrey, England. He was the son of Edgar and Mary Casey. ***Casey Island*** (64 O/15) in Boles Lake was named after him in 1995.

Caskey, Flying Officer **Irvine N.** of Portage la Prairie (J 18411). No. 620 Squadron. He died 6 June 1944 at the age of 24 and is commemorated at La Délivrande War Cemetery, France. He was the son of Will A. and Mabel Caskey of Macdonald, Manitoba. ***Caskey Lake*** (52 E/14), east of Brereton Lake was named after him in 1974.

Cassells, Private **James A.** of Shoal Lake (H 103870). Princess Patricia's Canadian Light Infantry. He died 15 December 1943 at the age of 21 and is commemorated at the Moro River Canadian War Cemetery in Italy. He was the seventh of the 14 children of William and Frances Cassells of Shoal Lake. According to his sister-in-law (22 April 1995):

> He was born on the family farm in Shoal Lake, Manitoba on July 26, 1922. He was a quiet boy and an excellent student. He excelled at soft ball and loved to play his harmonica and sing Country and Western songs. He joined the PPCLI in December, 1942 and was killed in action in Italy.

Cassells Lake (64 J/8), south of Tadoule Lake was named after him in 1975.

Cassidy, Flight Sergeant **Fredrick W.** of Winnipeg (R 74701). No. 419 Squadron. He died 3 September 1942 at the age of 25 and is commemorated at Warnant Communal Cemetery, Belgium. He was the son of Caswell and Dorothy Cassidy of Vancouver. ***Cassidy Lake*** (53 N/14), north of Whitefish Lake was named after him in 1995.

Caswill, Private **Gabriel J. "Jack"** of Winnipeg (H 6130). Winnipeg Grenadiers. He died 25 December 1941 at the age of 42 and is commemorated at the Sai Wan Memorial in Hong Kong. He was the son of Gabriel J. and Emma Caswill (née Brooks) and was survived by his wife Marjorie N. Caswill of Winnipeg. ***Caswill Lake*** (64 I/1), northeast of South Knife Lake was named after him in 1974.

Catte, Private **Newton W.** of Swan Lake (H 101199). Princess Louise Dragoon Guards. He died 1 September 1944 at the age of 22 and is commemorated at Montecchio War Cemetery in Italy. He was the son of Walter and Dora Catte and was survived by two siblings, Gladys and William of Treherne. His sister writes (20 November 1995):

> He attended the school of Norquay, a few miles north of Swan Lake, Manitoba. He was a quiet man and farmed with his father until joining up. [H]e also enjoyed hunting. He was stationed in Winnipeg, Dundurn, England, North Africa and finally Italy where he lost his life.

Catte Lake (64 N/6), southwest of Nueltin Lake was named after him in 1972.

Caumartin, Lance Corporal **Armand** of McCreary (H 102912). Royal Winnipeg Rifles. He died 4 July 1944 at the age of 26 and is commemorated at Beny-sur-Mer Canadian War Cemetery, Reviers, France. He was one of the five children of Urgel and Lydia Caumartin. According to his sister-in-law (n.d.):

> He was born October 15, 1918 and received his education at a small country school, completing his Grade 6. His friends and family knew him as a very quiet person blessed with a witty yet dry sense of humour. Armand discontinued his schooling to help his father on the farm, working there until he enlisted in the army in 1941. He trained at Camp Shilo prior to his posting overseas in 1942. Armand landed on Juno Beach on D-Day June 6, 1944 with C Company of the Royal Winnipeg Rifles.

Caumartin Lake (64 I/5), southeast of Tadoule Lake was named after him in 1974.

Cavaghan, Pilot Officer **Eric G.** of Winnipeg (J 6167). No. 419 Squadron. He died 30 May 1942 at the age of 22 and is commemorated at Viroflay New Communal Cemetery, France. He was the son of Stanley and Alice Cavaghan. His nephew writes (5 December 2001):

> Eric was born in Winnipeg in 1919. He was raised in St. James and lived at the corner of Ferry Road and Ness Avenue. This was the rear of the family grocery store. Eric graduated from St. James Collegiate in June, 1935. On graduation, Eric joined the Hudson's Bay Company and was posted at Norway House. Upon returning to Winnipeg, Eric was employed by the Toronto Dominion Bank on north Main Street until entering the Air Force. He qualified for his wings in December, 1941. My aunt was very bitter about losing Eric and when my two brothers and myself returned from overseas, the subject was taboo.

Cavaghan Lake (64 P/2), southeast of Nejanilini Lake was named after him in 1974.

Caverly, Leading Aircraftman **Robert J.** of Winnipeg (R 116313). Repair and Supply, Royal Canadian Air Force. He died 27 October 1944 and is commemorated at Schoonselhof Cemetery in Belgium. ***Caverly Lake*** (62 N/15), southeast of Swan River was named after him in 1973.

Cawker, Flight Lieutenant **Douglas E.** of Winnipeg (J 8759). No. 432 Squadron. He died 22 March 1944 at the age of 24 and is commemorated at the Hanover War Cemetery in Germany. He was the son of Harold and Alice Cawker. His obituary read in part:

> He was born in Winnipeg in 1920, attended Assiniboine, Laura Secord and Gordon Bell schools. He was a member of the Gordon Bell inter-high rugby championship team in 1937. An active member of the Westminster Actimist Club and a teacher in Westminster Sunday School, he was employed by the Searle Grain Company at the time of his enlistment (*Winnipeg Tribune* 29 November 1944).

His brother writes (15 October 2001):

> This story truly has several beginnings. The first was March 22, 1944, wartime England. The second was the September 1988 Commonwealth Aircrew Reunion, Winnipeg. The next was April 2, 1990, Philipstein-Braunfels, West Germany and the latest was June 2 and 3, 1990 Sutton-on-the-Forest, Yorkshire.
>
> I decided in early 1988 that I would, for the first time, attend the Wartime Aircrew Reunion in Winnipeg in September of that year. Before doing so, I wrote to RCAF Headquarters in Ottawa requesting my wartime and peacetime air force career information from the Archives. At the same time, I also asked for the archives of my late brother, Douglas, who was killed March 22, 1944 piloting a MK III Halifax on a bombing raid to Frankfurt. My purpose in obtaining the latter was to find out what squadron he had been with so that I might find some of Doug's cohorts at the Winnipeg Reunion.
>
> I was at EFTS when he went missing and I knew next to nothing of his whereabouts except for "RCAF Overseas" which had been his address since December 1941. His archives told me more than I had ever expected. He was with 432 Leaside Squadron based at Eastmoor (eight miles north of York). His aircraft was shot down by a night fighter at 10:00 PM and crashed two kilometres northeast of Philipstein (80 kilometres north of Frankfurt). The crew was buried in uniform in separate graves in the northwest corner of the Philipstein Cemetery by a Lutheran pastor with several villagers in attendance. The graves were well looked after with flowers in the summer and pine bough coverings in the winter.
>
> All I had known prior to this information was that he had gone missing, then months later presumed dead and then by the time I finished SFTS, confirmed killed in action. And in 1946, our family received information that he was buried in the Allied War Graves Cemetery near Hanover. I don't know why, but until I received the archive information, the idea had not previously occurred to me that he and his crew had to have been buried somewhere else for approximately two years before being moved to the Hanover cemetery.
>
> Upon receipt of the Reunion package from Winnipeg, I discovered that 432 Squadron was planning a Squadron Dinner and Bash, so armed with the archive information, I contacted a Flight Lieutenant Len Hossie of Mississauga who was in charge of the 432 Reunion Committee. I presented them with a picture of Doug and the details of his last flight which they previously did not have. They made me an Honorary Member of the Squadron and Jody and I attended the Winnipeg dinner where we met some obviously wonderful people, a couple of whom had known Doug briefly.
>
> While in Winnipeg, we stayed with my sister, Ruth, who was a twin of Doug's, and she gave me a diary he had written for a few months during 1943. As a result, we were able to meet a Jim Vann whom Doug mentioned in the diary; they had been together overseas as Flight Lieutenants for 20 months instructing at various stations – Grantham, Ossington, Fraserborough. Jim and Doug had been the best of friends. Jim was posted to 432 after Doug, but he had gone missing before Jim arrived on squadron. Jim ended up as a Squadron Leader with two tours and a DFC and Bar. It was nice to talk to someone who had known my brother for such a long wartime period (I was but 16 when he left home and I only remembered him as a role model who had gone to become a pilot in the RCAF). Subsequently, two other brothers joined the RCAF, Ed becoming a pilot and Hugh an Observer.
>
> That pretty well takes care of September 1988. What of April 1990? Well we decided to go and visit the original gravesite and perhaps find someone who had tended the graves. Having an extremely limited knowledge of the German language, I sent a copy of that part of the archives which described the crash and burial to a Canadian-German friend, Fred Gottgetrue. Fred was an ex-Luftwaffe ME 109, FW 190 and JU 88 pilot. Anyway, Fred translated the archive information and a covering letter to Whom It May Concern, explaining what I wished to accomplish at Philipstein.

So in April, 1990, Jody and I flew to Frankfurt, drove up to Philipstein to learn that Braunfels – a larger town five kilometres away, was the "county seat" and we took the translation to a lady in the tourist office. Soon she had the Town Manager (the Bürgermeister was away) come to see us and he went away on a search for information, having made an appointment to meet us after lunch. He subsequently took us to the original gravesite (Germany recycles its graves every 25 years unless one wishes to fund its very costly perpetuity), and he gave us a tour of the towns of Philipstein and Braunfels. Both are very picturesque towns, the latter surrounded by outer and inner walls with a superb schloss high on a central hill. The whole countryside north of Frankfurt east of the Rhine is pretty, rolling hills with well forested areas and plenty of rich farm land and fruit trees. It looks quite prosperous today. Then after coffee and cake in his well appointed office, he took us to the office of the President of the local Historical Society. A man of 57 who was only 11 years old in 1944, he showed us the town records where no entry had been made between the 19th and 25th of March 1944 with respect to births, deaths, burials etc.

However, he remembered hearing the air battle going on and seeing a crash on the nearby hillside. His mother would not let him go to see it as it was late at night. He told us he'd been a "Hitler Youth" at the time (as was every able-bodied boy ages 10 and older) and he'd been taught how evil all of Germany's enemies were. The next day, he went to the crash site which was now under guard by the Wehrmacht and he remembered (explaining through interpretation by the Town Manager, both men with tears in their eyes) seeing the bodies under tarpaulins.

One had a foot sticking out with a hole in the sock. As a young boy, he had thought about having holes in his own socks and how perhaps the "enemy" was not as evil as he'd been told. It was a lasting impression which had obviously affected him greatly and still moved him 46 years later. We subsequently checked the local church records to no avail so it turned out that was as near as I could get to any first-hand information, but it was satisfying. (Perhaps I'll go back again on a further search some day).

Since then, on June 2 and 3, Jody and I attended the unveiling of a beautiful memorial sundial in the 'village pound' at Sutton-on-the-Forest, Yorkshire, placed there in memory of all who served at Eastmoor RAF airbase with the three Canadian squadrons: 415, 429 and Doug's 432. Ex-squadron members and friends and families raised the funds and the people of Sutton put on a great two days. They had a flower festival in their "All Hallows" church with a Canadian and wartime theme to some of the displays. For example, the pews were decorated by the Sunday School children, each with a replica of our provincial flags and flowers with lovely, live floral displays. I am sure that when they are grown up years from now, those children will remember the Canadian invasion of 1990.

We held a quick march-past after the unveiling with the town Mayoress and other dignitaries taking the salute. One of our 'types' was quite slow in marching due to age and a cane, and the parade ended up as a single rank flight going by to the cheers of the townsfolk and we parade members of the first flight who had already marched-past, broken-off and come back to town centre to cheer him on. Needless to say, there was a great deal of reminiscing in the Rose and Crown with considerable overflow quaffing of the "juice of the barley" outside on the High Street. The next day, they served punch on the church lawn after a Sunday morning memorial service which was attended by 150 Canadians and almost as many townspeople. My brother Bob from Vancouver and his wife, and Doug's twin, my sister Ruth from Winnipeg were with us at Sutton and it really was a Sentimental Journey for all of us.

Cawker Lake (63 B/6), northeast of Waterhen Lake was named after him in 1969.

Cederlund, Trooper **Hans W.** of Lac du Bonnet (H 103607). 14th Canadian Hussars. He died 6 October 1944 and is commemorated at Bergen-op-Zoom Canadian War Cemetery in Holland. In 1943, Aileen Oder of Lac du Bonnet began writing "newsletters" to local men overseas which always began "Hello Soldier" (Oder 1975). This reply is from Trooper Cederlund who had formerly been a Grade 8 pupil of hers:

Dear Miss Small: I sure was surprised to get the copy of that paper you sent. It also gave me a bit of pleasure to hear all about the Lac du Bonnet and district news. I really don't know what to say to you. I'm hoping we're still friends as we used to be. (Oh yeah). Seriously though, I may have been a devil when I went to school but I have changed a lot since. You probably would be surprised if you were to meet me now. I even surprise myself sometimes.

You know I almost feel sorry for the guys who get a copy of your paper and don't know you. I'm glad I do, and if you were to say that we were good friends, I would be still happier. Well I'll quit now. I should like to hear from you in person, not just through a newspaper. Cheerio for now. Your sincere friend, Hans Cederlund.

Cederlund Lake (64 G/16), east of Big Sand Lake was named after him in 1963.

Chabluk, Rifleman **Michael Meron "Chab"** of Oakbank (H 20671). Regina Rifle Regiment. He died 18 February 1945 at the age of 25, along with one of his comrades when, while engaged in an attack, their personnel carrier hit a land mine. Rifleman Chabluk is commemorated at the Groesbeek Canadian War Cemetery in Holland. He was the eldest of the 13 children of Steve and Annie Chabluk of Oakbank and was survived by his wife Vivienne B. Chabluk of the Isle of Wight and their son Meron. He writes (22 November 2001):

"Chab," as he was known to his comrades, was born December 4, 1919 at Cooks Creek, Manitoba. He left home at the age of 16 and went to work for a local farmer where he worked for room and board and a wage of $5.00 a month.

Rifleman Chabluk's sister Sophie recalls (22 November 2001):

I remember that first Christmas after he left home; he came back at Christmas with presents for everyone in the family. I got a new dress and one of the brothers, Elmer, got a mouth organ. Meron enlisted in Winnipeg with the Cameron Highlanders in 1940. He later transferred to the Regina Rifles and went overseas in September of 1941. I was very saddened because he wouldn't be here for my wedding.

Chab was a very generous and fun-loving person without a mean bone in his body. He was also quite handsome and had many different girlfriends. Each time he had a new girlfriend he would write to me that he was REALLY in love this time and he was going to marry her. His letters always ended with "Sis, can you send me some cigs? I love you all."

Meron finally did marry a young girl in England. At the end of December, 1944, Chab's leave was ending and he was to return to his regiment. He came back three times to say goodbye to his wife Vivienne, his infant son and his mother-in-law. Then he left. That was the last time they saw one another.

Chabluk Lake (64 K/9), northeast of Reindeer Lake was named after him in 1972.

Chaboyer, Private **David J.** of St. Laurent (H 41688). Winnipeg Grenadiers. He died 13 March 1945 at the age of 21 and is commemorated at the Yokohama War Cemetery in Japan. He was the son of Mr. and Mrs. Vital Chaboyer. ***Chaboyer Island*** (63 N/7) in Guthrie Lake was named after him in 1995.

Chaboyer, Private **Marcel** of St Laurent (H 63696). Winnipeg Grenadiers. He had been reported missing presumed dead 19 December 1941 during the final defence of Hong Kong and this is the date provided by most sources. Repatriation documents, however, indicate that he had been taken prisoner of war. In January, 1943 he was sentenced to two years' hard labour for an unspecified offence. This sentence may have been extended as the *Questionnaire of Fatal Casualties "C" Force* indicates that he:

> Died while serving hard labour in July, 1945 and his ashes were sent to his Commander at No. 8 Camp, Fukuoka District. The ashes are to be brought back to Canada by ... Sergeant Major ... Bert Caldwell (6 October 1945).

He would have been 25 years of age and is commemorated at the Sai Wan Memorial in Hong Kong. He was survived by his wife Rose Chaboyer of St. Laurent. His brother recalls that he (24 October 2001):

> ... was a fisherman on Lake Manitoba helping his Dad. We walked to the bus when he left; it was the last time we saw him. He liked to play ball with his friends. [He didn't have] much time – he seemed to work all the time on the lake.

Chaboyer Lake (63 K/16), west of Wekusko Lake was named after him in 1973.

Chalcroft, Aircraftman 1 **Walter James G.** of West Kildonan (R 59826). Royal Canadian Air Force. He died 7 June 1941 at the age of 30 and is commemorated at Brookside Cemetery in Winnipeg. He was the son of Walter and Lillian Chalcroft of Winnipeg and was survived by his wife Phoebe Cathleen Chalcroft of Petersfield and their two daughters. ***Chalcroft Lake*** (64 P/8), southeast of Nejanilini Lake was named after him in 1974.

Chalmers, Flight Sergeant **Alfred R.** of Brandon (R 95021). No. 101 Squadron. He died 30 August 1944 at the age of 21 and is commemorated at Dejbjerg Churchyard in Denmark. ***Chalmers Lake*** (64 H/16), southwest of Condie Lake was named after him in 1995.

Chalmers, Sergeant **David R.** of Lorette (R 71447). No. 3 Personnel Reception Centre, RCAF. He died 23 May 1943 at the age of 38 and is commemorated at Bournemouth North Cemetery, Hampshire, England. He was one of 21 airmen killed during an enemy bombing attack on the Metropole Hotel in Landsdowne Square, Bournemouth. He was the son of Samuel and Rose Chalmers and was survived by his wife Barbara Chalmers of Osoyoos, British Columbia and their four children. ***Chalmers Island*** (64 F/5) in Reindeer Lake was named after him in 1995.

Chambers, Pilot Officer **George W.** of Winnipeg (J 86747). No. 640 Squadron. He died 3 June 1944 at the age of 20 and is commemorated at Bretigny-sur-Orge Communal Cemetery, France. He was the son of David and Elizabeth Chambers. His sister recalls that he was very interested in aeroplanes and aviation at a very early age. ***Chambers Island*** (64 N/9) in Shannon Lake was named after him in 1972.

Chambers, Flight Sergeant **Henry** of Winnipeg (R 124142). No. 149 Squadron. He died 26 October 1943 at the age of 20 and is commemorated at Regina Cemetery. He was the son of John and Paraska Chambers. ***Chambers Lake*** (64 H/2), north of Holmes Lake was named after him in 1995.

Chambers, Flying Officer **Stanley V.** of Dauphin (J 88244). No. 619 Squadron. He died 4 December 1944 at the age of 21 and is commemorated at Durnbach War Cemetery, Germany. He was the son of Samuel and Marian Chambers. ***Chambers Bay*** (53 L/3) in Sakkink Lake was named after him in 1995.

Champagne, Pilot Officer **Roland M. J.** of St. Norbert (J 95080). No. 626 Squadron. He died 15 October 1944 at the age of 24 and is commemorated at the Reichswald Forest War Cemetery in Germany. He was the fifth of the 12 children of Alphonse and Francesca Champagne (née Baril). According to his sister (21 September 1992), he "... enlisted in August, 1941 as an aero-engine mechanic, remustering in April, 1943 to aircrew. [H]e was a *Free Press* carrier for eight years." ***Champagne Creek*** (63 N/1), which flows northwest into Limestone Point Lake was named after him in 1972.

Chapman, Flight Sergeant **Edward Drummond** of Brandon (R 57927). No. 23 Squadron. He died 7 November 1941 at the age of 19 and is commemorated at the Runnymede Memorial in Surrey, England. He was the only son of Edward and Isabel Chapman (née Drummond). His brother-in-law writes (29 November 2001) that he was:

> ... born in Brandon on April 21st, 1922 and spent his boyhood on the farm homesteaded by his paternal grandfather in 1882. He attended school in the Harrow District. The farm, being situated on the side of the Minnedosa River Valley made an ideal spot for a boy to grow up, with lots of open space and wooded areas and the whole river valley to explore. Growing up in the "dirty thirties," boys had to make their own entertainment and being so near the river, Drummond and his friends became good swimmers, keen skaters and hockey players. While leading an active outdoor life, he was also an avid reader. He built his own crystal set and spent many hours listening to the "Northern Messenger" and the hockey games on Saturday nights. Always interested in aircraft, he built models, most of which made one glorious flight from the barn roof.
>
> In 1938, the family moved to Vancouver, where, with his bike, he soon became better acquainted with the city than most born and bred Vancouverites. He worked for a time at Woodward's Department Store and then moved to S. K. F. Bearings, where he stayed until his enlistment. On the outbreak of war, he applied to join the RCAF, but was rejected as being underage, but as soon as he reached the required age, he reapplied and was accepted as aircrew. Sent to Camp Borden, he took his pilot's training on Tiger Moths and on winning his wings, trained on Ansons at Egmont. As Sergeant Pilot, he was then posted as Staff Pilot to the Rivers, Manitoba Navigational School, where he daily and nightly flew over his old home.
>
> He applied for an overseas posting, was accepted, and arrived in England at a critical stage when Britain was just beginning to strike back at Germany. At the time, he was considered to be the youngest Canadian pilot in active service overseas, and was promoted to Flight Sergeant.
>
> In one of his letters home, he told of being with some friends looking over some ruins and wondering if they were ancient or new ruins, when they were met by a lady and her two daughters whom they at once recognized as Queen Elizabeth and the Princesses. The Royal party told them the history of the place and also how happy they were to see them over with them.
>
> On November 7, 1941, on the day after the first heavy raid on Berlin, he was on check flight with his crew when they were seen to disappear over the Channel and no further information has ever been discovered. Of the

class with which he first trained, with something over twenty, only three or so survived the war. Besides his parents, he left two sisters in Vancouver. He was reunited with his mother in 1962 and his father in 1976.

Chapman Bay (63 H/16) on the northwest shore of Stevenson Lake was named after him in 1985.

Chapman, Private **George S.** of Flin Flon (H 22499). Queen's Own Cameron Highlanders. He died 26 February 1945 and is commemorated at the Groesbeek Canadian War Cemetery in Holland. ***Chapman Lake*** (64 B/16), east of Southern Indian Lake was named after him in 1949.

Chapman, Private **James E.** of Morris (H 6271). Winnipeg Grenadiers. He died a prisoner of war 15 August 1942 at the age of 41 and is commemorated at the Sai Wan War Cemetery in Hong Kong. He was survived by his wife Vida Chapman of Belmont and their son Jim and three daughters Margaret, Beulah and Shirly Ann. His son writes (7 January 2002) that he was:

> ... a Station Agent for the CNR and went to serve his country with the Winnipeg Grenadiers. He left behind a young family. Their memories recall a cheerful happy Dad – always there with a helping hand. During his career with the CNR he did relief agent work around Manitoba and Saskatchewan. Information from survivors have told the family that Jim worked hard at trying to help keep the morale up in the prison camp.

Chapman Rapids (64 J/4) in the Mistay River was named after him in 1975.

Chapman, Second Radio Officer **Norman E.** of Winnipeg. SS *Coimbra*, Canadian Merchant Navy. The *Coimbra* was lost 14 January 1942 and Officer Chapman is commemorated at the Halifax Memorial. He was the son of Mrs. V. E. D. Chapman of Terrace, British Columbia. ***Chapman Island*** (63 P/7) in Prud'homme Lake was named after him in 2001.

Charles, Private **Henry W.** of Winnipeg (H 16697). Lincoln and Welland Regiment. He died 24 October 1944 at the age of 24 and is commemorated at Bergen-op-Zoom Canadian War Cemetery in Holland. He was the eldest of the five children of Edgar and Phyllis Charles. According to his sister (25 November 1999), he:

> ... lived most of [his] life in west-end Winnipeg (Beverley Street). Henry loved to skate and in summer play baseball and fish. He loved the outdoors. Dad was a ... delivery man and we didn't have a great deal of money. We made do and didn't have any assistance. Henry loved school but was a slow learner, but kept plugging. We loved our brother and missed him when he went to war. Mother was a war bride from the first world war and came over to marry Dad and got married in Russell, Manitoba. Henry's Aunt Mary and Aunt Ann lived in Tottenham and Henry spent most of his leaves with them. They loved him dearly. Henry had a good life with love and caring. We still miss him. He was killed by a German sniper in the forest.

Charles Point (64 O/15) on Blevins Lake was named after him in 1995.

Charles, Rifleman **James F.** of Gilbert Plains (H 101172). Regina Rifle Regiment. He died 28 July 1944 at the age of 28 and is commemorated at Beny-sur-Mer Canadian War Cemetery, France. He was the only son of Robert and Annie Charles of Gilbert Plains. His obituary read in part:

> [He] joined the Canadian Armed Forces in the year 1940. He enlisted into the Winnipeg Light Infantry where he began his training and later at Camp Shilo, Manitoba. While there, he joined the Regina Rifle Regiment. Later on, he volunteered as a reinforcement in the Queen's Own Cameron Highlanders of Canada and training in England. June 6, 1944: he was one of the Canadians who took part on D-Day. July 28, 1944: he died on active duty in Caen, France – his 28th birthday (n.d.).

Charles Bay (63 P/10) in the Nelson River was named after him in 1995.

Charles, Flight Sergeant **John H.** of Winnipeg (R 59571). No. 61 Squadron. He died 31 May 1942 at the age of 22 and is commemorated at Rheinberg War Cemetery in Germany. He was the son of Major John L. and Elene Charles. Major John Charles was the CNR's Regional Chief Engineer and as a consequence, the CNR proposed naming a railway point after him. The ***community of Charles*** (63 N/11), north of Sherridon was named after the railway point in 1954.

Charlet, Rifleman **Ernest** of Winnipeg (H 69954). Queen's Own Rifles of Canada. He died 20 October 1944 at the age of 21 and is commemorated at the Adegem Canadian War Cemetery in Belgium. He was the son of Karl and Fanny Charlet. According to his sister (14 April 1997), he:

> ... was born in White Russia [in] 1923 and at the age of seven, our family, consisting of my mother, father, Ernest and myself came to Winnipeg [in] 1930. He attended Aberdeen and St. John's Technical High School. Shortly after graduating from high school, [he] enlisted in the army, serving in Kiska, England, France and Belgium. While in Belgium, he was wounded and ... died of these wounds.

Charlet Lake (64 O/1), north of Tadoule Lake was named after him in 1975.

Charney, Private **Peter "Buck"** of St. Boniface (H 16285). Princess Patricia's Canadian Light Infantry. He died 23 May 1944 at the age of 27 and is commemorated at the Cassino War Cemetery in Italy. He was the son of Peter and Magda Charney and was survived by his wife Winnifred Charney of Croydon, Surrey and their son. He writes (23 November 2001):

> The last letter my mother received from my father was just after he had landed in Italy, somewhere south of Rome, and contained these words: "Then, on landing here we saw that famous Mount Vesuvius with the smoke coming out. I was just thinking of making a trip up there to warm up a bit. It's been so cold around here since we arrived. On the road we saw tanks just as they were knocked out of action scattered here and there through the country. And now and again, we passed little cemeteries of the Allied soldiers and also of the German soldiers. Yes, it does make a fella think."
>
> In July, 2001, his grandson and namesake Peter W. Charney visited his grandfather's grave site while travelling in Europe and was overwhelmed with the beauty of it and the care that had been given to the Cassino Military Cemetery.

Charney Lake (64 K/11), northeast of Reindeer Lake was named after him in 1972.

Chartier, Private **Raymond L.** of Dauphin (H 3911). Royal Canadian Army Service Corps. He died 29 September 1944 at the age of 23 and is commemorated at Riverside Cemetery in Dauphin. He was the son of Mr. and Mrs. William Chartier of Dauphin and was survived by his wife Amelia Chartier of Winnipegosis. ***Chartier Lake*** (63 O/4), north of Wekusko Lake was named after him in 1970.

Chartrand, Private **Adelard J.** of Camperville (H 46044). Lake Superior Regiment. He died 9 March 1945 and is commemorated at the Groesbeek Canadian War Cemetery in Holland. ***Chartrand Peninsula*** (64 P/4) in Duffin Lakes was named after him in 1995.

Chartrand, Corporal **Harry L.** of Inwood (H 40960). Royal Winnipeg Rifles. He died 19 August 1944 at the age of 26 and is commemorated at Bayeux War Cemetery, France. He was the son of Gaspard L. and Josephine Chartrand of Inwood. He had attended the Allen School at Inwood and prior to enlisting he worked at the Inwood Creamery. ***Chartrand Rapids*** (64 P/5) in the Wolverine River was named after him in 1995.

Chartrand, Lance Sergeant **Lawrence** of Camperville (H 41247). Royal Winnipeg Rifles. He died 8 June 1944 and is commemorated at Beny-sur-Mer Canadian War Cemetery, France. He was the son of Cyprien and Veronique Chartrand of Camperville, Manitoba and the brother of Rifleman Louis Chartrand (next entry). ***Chartrand Lake*** (64 K/1), northwest of Big Sand Lake was named after him in 1961.

Chartrand, Rifleman **Louis** of Camperville (H 41294). Royal Winnipeg Rifles. He died 8 June 1944 at the age of 26 and is commemorated at Beny-sur-Mer Canadian War Cemetery, France. He was the son of Cyprien and Veronique Chartrand and the brother of Lance Sergeant Lawrence Chartrand (previous entry). ***Chartrand Point*** (63 I/1) in Slippery Rock Lake was named after him in 1995.

Charuk, Lance Corporal **Nicholas J.** of Oak Bluff (H 6557). Winnipeg Grenadiers. He died 30 November 1943 and is commemorated at the Yokohama War Cemetery in Japan. ***Charuk Lake*** (52 E/11), southeast of Brereton Lake was named after him in 1974.

Chaske, Rifleman **Tom** of Edwin (H 8778). Royal Winnipeg Rifles. He died 12 December 1944 at the age of 24 and is commemorated at the Groesbeek Canadian War Cemetery in Holland. He was the son of Tom and Nyjookwah Chaske of Edwin, Manitoba and was survived by his wife Marjorie Chaske. ***Chaske Lake*** (64 O/3), northeast of Egenolf Lake was named after him in 1975.

Chatwin, Captain **George T.** of Winnipeg. Royal Canadian Army Pay Corps. He was aboard the SS *Nerissa*, the only ship torpedoed while carrying Canadian troops to the United Kingdom. Captain Chatwin died 1 May 1941 at the age of 44 and is commemorated at the Halifax Memorial. He was the son of Thomas and Adeline Chatwin of Winnipeg and was survived by his wife Lilly Alma Chatwin (née Downie) of Winnipeg and their two daughters. He wrote letters home to his wife on nearly a daily basis:

> Dear Alma: We arrived in Montreal this morning and were glad to be able to stretch our legs after being cramped up in a train for two and a half days. It was quite a crowd that saw me off at Winnipeg; it gives you that "delightful sorrow" feeling – and they sang *For He's a Jolly Good Fellow*. In a way, I was glad you were not at the station, though you were certainly in my mind. Later, I went in to dinner with Captain Townshend, certainly not because I wanted anything to eat, but for the sake of something to do.
>
> It rained all day, next day and the view from the window might have been anywhere – Saskatchewan, Manitoba or Ontario. I got up at seven o'clock. At lunch, seated next to me was an English lord. Had I not known it, he might have been just an ordinary salesman. Later, I had quite an interesting conversation with his secretary (male). He said the social barrier in England was rapidly disappearing and that now Canadians were even more reserved than the English people.
>
> Passing through Quebec, the towns are much closer together and you are hardly out of sight of a few houses between stations. Montreal is a large city but you feel rather cramped. The main street is only half the width of our Main Street. The buildings are taller, the traffic wilder and the policemen do not know where anyplace is; half of them are French as are a lot of the civilian population. Captain McQuilty gave me a cigarette lighter before I left – with my initials on – it is very nice and it works. Flo gave me a couple of books which fortunately, I had not read.
>
> I am enclosing a key for the suite which I inadvertently took away with me, also a key to my desk at the barracks. You might phone George Mull to pick it up sometime. I am going to try to look up Harry Wiffe this afternoon as we will be here until dinner time this evening. It is lunch time now, but I am going to take a long walk – I need some exercise. Best wishes to all my friends and Love and Kisses to Paddy and Joanie and yourself. I am, Your loving husband, George (19 April 1941).
>
> Dear Alma: Arrived here [Halifax] late today. Was very glad to get off the train and stretch again. I met Dave Dickie in Montreal yesterday; he is stationed there temporarily. He and Mrs. Dickie came down to the station to see me off and brought me a magazine and a tin of cigarettes. Mrs. Dickie looks much the same – they have three children now.
>
> The trip from Montreal to Halifax was quite uneventful, the weather was warm and it rained a little. Halifax, from what I have seen of it, is a gloomy place with narrow streets, but I have only been here an hour. I do not know just how long I will be here, but not very long I think. I am going to try and see Mrs. Goodeve for a few minutes if I can. I have to go now to check for pay documents etc., so I may not have another opportunity to write before I leave. Remember me to my friends and Love to Paddy and Joanie and to yourself. Your loving husband, George (20 April 1941).
>
> Dear Alma: We are still on the way. It seems a long way and a long time since I saw you all. I visited Mrs. Goodeve when in Halifax. She is living with Anne her daughter and she sees her son for a few days every month. She wishes to be remembered to you.
>
> The boat trip so far has been pleasant enough – missed a couple of meals on the first day out – but have picked them up since. I watched Halifax recede in the distance, the sea gulls following us, a cruiser, some destroyers then fog for the rest of the day. There is one family aboard: mother, father and three little children, going home to England. Another lady and her husband, a number of civilians (male) and some soldiers, sailors and airmen, the latter includes some Norwegians. Love to Pat and Joan. Your loving husband, George (22 April 1941).

This veteran of the First World War had participated in the famous charge of B Squadron of the Fort Garry Horse at Cambrai in 1917. ***Chatwin Lake*** (64 K/15), southwest of Nueltin Lake was named after him in 1961.

Chawanski, Flight Sergeant **Adam P.** of Winnipeg (R 196076). No. 419 Squadron. He died 23 May 1944 at the age of 22 and is commemorated at Rheinberg War Cemetery in Germany. He was the only son of Joseph and Katherine Chawanski of Winnipeg. ***Chawanski Lake*** (64 P/14), northeast of Nejanilini Lake was named after him in 1974.

Chemin, Gunner **Henri** of Notre Dame de Lourdes (H 16956). Royal Canadian Artillery. He died 16 January 1943 at the age of 35 and is commemorated at Assumption Gardens in Winnipeg. He was survived by his mother Marie Chemin, by his wife Yvonne Chemin of Winnipeg and their two children. ***Chemin Island*** (64 I/3) in North Knife Lake was named after him in 1974.

Chepil, Warrant Officer 2 **Mack** of Edwin (R 117497). No. 428 Squadron, DFM.

This airman captained an aircraft detailed to attack a target at Le Creusot one night in June, 1943. Soon after crossing the enemy coast, the hydraulic system in the bomber became unserviceable but Sergeant Chepil continued his flight. Later, one engine caught fire and became unserviceable. In spite of this, the target was bombed after the bomb doors had been opened by an emergency method. Sergeant Chepil afterwards flew the damaged aircraft to base. This airman displayed outstanding determination and devotion to duty, setting an inspiring example (DFM Citation 19 July 1943).

He died 3 August 1943 at the age of 27 and is commemorated at the Runnymede Memorial in Surrey, England. He was the son of Steve and Pearl Chepil (née Staryski) of Edwin. According to his family:

His short and heroic career ended … when British and Canadian bombers in great strength fought through fierce electrical storms, heavy icing and violent winds to attack Hamburg. His and 29 other bombers failed to return to base (n.d.).

Chepil Lake (64 C/15), southwest of Barrington Lake was named after him in 1949.

Cherry, Private **William H.** of Wellwood (H 101104). Princess Patricia's Canadian Light Infantry. He died 10 December 1944 at the age of 20 and is commemorated at Ravenna War Cemetery in Italy. He was the son of William and Sarah Cherry (née Aston). Born in County Armagh, Northern Ireland, he came to Canada with his parents and sister in 1929. According to his sister (21 September 1998), he:

… lived on a farm in the [Wellwood] area [and] attended Wellwood Consolidated School. He was a rural boy of his time. He was interested in nature, hunting and trapping and was the proud owner of a .22 rifle. He spent a lot of time tramping through the bush and pasture land in the district. He learned to skate and played hockey with his friends. He was a talented artist who did pencil sketches – mostly of animals and birds. He was a radio fan who liked Hockey Night in Canada and the Lone Ranger. He liked music, singing and could even yodel. His favourite song was *The Wabash Cannonball*. While in training in England, he was able to spend two furloughs with his relatives in Northern Ireland.

Cherry Lake (64 J/6), west of Tadoule Lake was named after him in 1975.

Chess, Pilot Officer **James B.** of Winnipeg (J 86590). No. 419 Squadron. He died 21 January 1944 at the age of 21 and is commemorated at the Berlin 1939 - 1945 War Cemetery. ***Chess Island*** (64 N/9) in Shannon Lake was named after him in 1972.

Chewter, Private **George W.** of Winnipeg (H 6510). Winnipeg Grenadiers. He died 12 November 1942 at the age of 42 and is commemorated at the Sai Wan War Cemetery in Hong Kong. He was the son of George W. and Alice Chewter (née Hole) of St. Boniface. ***Chewter Lake*** (64 N/12), southwest of Nueltin Lake was named after him in 1972.

Cheyne, Private **Harold F.** of Melita (H 95328). Royal Canadian Ordnance Corps. He died 26 February 1942 at the age of 19 and is commemorated at Melita Cemetery, Manitoba. He was the son of Mr. and Mrs. George Cheyne. ***Cheyne Lakes*** (64 J/6), southwest of Tadoule Lake was named after him in 1957.

Chiesche, Sergeant **Frederick J.** "Tiny" of Alexander (H 29141). Royal Canadian Artillery. He died 24 January 1945 and is commemorated at Gradara War Cemetery in Italy. A friend of his wrote (26 March 1997):

"Tiny" Chiesche was the hero of the teenagers in the town of Alexander during the middle 1930s. Boys and girls liked him equally well. He chewed Copenhagen, was physically big and tough, but had a gentle heart. He was a baseball umpire of unchallenged authority and an avid supporter of girls and boys teams which added to our heroic aura. Tiny worked for Messrs. Jack and Archie Teitch who were bachelor farmers living north of Alexander. He was a very knowledgeable horseman and took great pride in the condition of the animals on the farm.

A few of us teenagers were in a restaurant in Brandon one occasion and were thrilled to have Tiny with us. Across the aisle at another table, a young man and woman were engaged in a heated argument which attracted our considerable attention. The argument exploded and the man threw a glass of water in the woman's face. Tiny eased himself, went over and tapped the man on the shoulder and advised him that where Tiny came from, men didn't do that and he had better watch it.

We argued his umpiring decisions sometimes, but he just looked down at us and said nothing. On occasion he might have ridded himself of Copenhagen which told us the argument was over. To us, he was a great young man. After all these years, it is sad to realize his loss. These few remarks about Tiny will help repay the memories he left with me and the others who formed the circle of his young friends.

Chiesche Lake (52 E/14), southeast of Brereton Lake was named after him in 1974.

Chislett, Flight Sergeant **Herbert A.** of Minnedosa (R 101535). No. 50 Squadron. He died 16 August 1942 at the age of 23 and is commemorated at the Reichswald Forest War Cemetery in Germany. He was the son of Alfred and Laura Chislett of New Westminster, British Columbia.

He was born in Winnipeg and moved to a farm at Bethany where he was educated and later farmed with his father. He moved to the west coast for a while and on his return to Manitoba he joined the RCAF. "Herby" was well liked by all who knew him and was an active pupil in the school or any organization he entered. Although conservative in nature, he possessed a personality that won and kept for him friends wherever he went (Pittman n.d.).

Chislett Lake (53 E/3), southwest of Island Lake was named after him in 1978.

Chisnell, Trooper **Norman W.** of St. Vital (H 63984). Royal Canadian Hussars. He died 15 August 1944 at the age of 22 and is commemorated at Bayeux War Cemetery, France. He was the son of William and Elizabeth Chisnell and the brother of Sergeant Robert H. Chisnell (next entry). ***Chisnell Lake*** (52 L/4), southeast of Lac du Bonnet was named after him in 1973.

Chisnell, Sergeant **Robert H.** of St. Vital (R 186823). No. 23 Operational Training Unit, RCAF. He died 18 August 1943 at the age of 19 and is commemorated at Oxford (Botley) Cemetery Oxfordshire, England. He was the son of Flight Lieutenant W. G. H. and Elizabeth Chisnell and the brother of Trooper Norman W. Chisnell (previous entry). ***Chisnell Bay*** (64 P/12) on the west shore of Nejanilini Lake was named after him in 1974.

Chmielowiec, Flying Officer **Theodore** of Winnipeg (J 27442). No. 180 Mitchell Squadron. He died 23 April 1944 at the age of 24 and is commemorated at Brookwood Military Cemetery in Surrey, England. He was the son of Theodore and Antonina Chmielowiec of Winnipeg. According to his nephew (16 April 1997), he was:

… born [in] Winnipeg [and] attended St. John's Technical High School, completing Grade 12. [He] attended United College for one year, but [was] forced to withdraw … for financial reasons. [He] worked for the Dominion of Canada Department of Revenue from 1938 – 1942 [and] enlisted in 1942 in the Air Force. [His] special interest … was photography.

Chmielowiec Lake (64 O/7), southeast of Nueltin Lake was named after him in 1975.

Chopp, Lieutenant **Stanley A.** of Winnipeg. Queen's Own Cameron Highlanders. He died 24 July 1944 at the age of 28 and is commemorated at Bretteville-sur-Laize Canadian War Cemetery, France. He was the son of Steve and Helen Chopp and was survived by his wife Betty Chopp of Winnipeg and their son. ***Chopp Lake*** (64 K/12), northeast of Reindeer Lake was named after him in 1972.

Choquette, Rifleman **Edmond J.** of Glenora (H 20691). Royal Winnipeg Rifles. He died 28 October 1944 at the age of 26 and is commemorated at the Adegem Canadian War Cemetery in Belgium. He was the son of Wilfred and Delina Choquette and the brother of Private Lawrence Choquette (next entry). ***Choquette Lake*** (64 N/6), southwest of Nueltin Lake was named after them in 1972.

Choquette, Private **Lawrence Thaddie** of Glenora (H 20805). Queen's Own Cameron Highlanders. He died 8 August 1944 and is commemorated at Beny-sur-Mer Canadian War Cemetery, France. He was the son of Wilfred and Delina Choquette and the brother of Rifleman Edmond Choquette (previous entry). ***Choquette Lake*** (64 N/6), southwest of Nueltin Lake was named after them in 1972.

Choquette, Rifleman **Morris J.** of Oakville (H 16015). Royal Winnipeg Rifles. He died 8 June 1944 at the age of 24 and is commemorated at Beny-sur-Mer Canadian War Cemetery, France. He was the son of David and Mary Choquette and was survived by his wife Nora Choquette of Brixham, Devon, England. ***Choquette Bay*** (64 P/4) in Oolduywas Lake was named after him in 1989.

Choquette, Rifleman **Roland J.** of St. Boniface (H 18201). Royal Winnipeg Rifles. He died 15 August 1944 at the age of 22 and is commemorated at Bretteville-sur-Laize Canadian War Cemetery, France. He was the son of George and Aurora Choquette. ***Choquette Point*** (64 I/13) on Shethanei Lake was named after him in 1989.

Chornous, Flight Sergeant **William** of Winnipeg (R 191275). No. 153 Squadron. He died 29 November 1944 at the age of 20 and is commemorated at the Reichswald Forest War Cemetery in Germany. He was the son of Daniel and Mary Chornous. According to his brother (12 November 2001):

> He was born June 28, 1924 in the village of Sologne in the western Ukraine and immigrated to Canada with his Mother in 1927. Our Father had arrived the year before. He attended Strathcona, Lord Nelson and Isaac Newton schools and was employed by Braid Builders Supplies at the time of his enlistment. He trained in Winnipeg as a Navigator. His Lancaster aircraft was shot down over Dortmund, Germany.

Chornous Lake (64 J/12), west of Tadoule Lake was named after him in 1978.

Chown, Flight Lieutenant **Douglas G. C.** of Winnipeg (C 1614). Royal Air Force Ferry Command. He died 9 December 1942 at the age of 23 and is commemorated at Gander Cemetery, Newfoundland. He was the son of Dr. Gordon and Penelope Chown. His sister recalls (29 November 2001):

> Douglas Gordon Cameron Chown was born in Hindhead, Surrey, England on February 4, 1919. Later that year, he came with his parents to Winnipeg. His early years were spent in the family home with his brother and two sisters at 588 Broadway Avenue. He attended Mulvey Elementary School and Gordon Bell High School where he was elected Class President. He was a member of All Saint's Church where he was a faithful and conscientious member of the 14th Winnipeg Boy Scout Group of which he became a King's Scout in 1934. There is a stained glass window in his Loving Memory on the north wall of the entrance to the church. His name is also listed on the RCAF plaque at the church along with all the other All Saint's young men who lost their lives in the RCAF during World War II.
>
> He joined the Air Force on September 9, 1939 and spent three years instructing flying at many Air Force stations across Canada. He received his wings at Trenton, Ontario, achieving the rank of Pilot Officer. He was highly respected by his senior officers as an instructor of keen, energetic LACs. As a result, he was promoted to the rank of Flying Officer and Flight Lieutenant and his service was confined to Canada, 1939 – 1942.
>
> However, in December of 1942, he was assigned to do overseas duty. On December 9, he took off from Montreal's Dorval Airport, piloting a small Boston bomber along with a co-pilot and a navigator. Suddenly, the weather became totally inclement for flying. A heavy snowfall occurred, like a blizzard, and the visibility to fly became almost impossible. As a result, the plane crashed in the hinterland of Gander and burst into flames. The co-pilot did not survive the crash, the navigator was not injured and the pilot, Douglas, suffered major internal injuries and a broken leg.
>
> In the frigid weather, the navigator set up flares for five days and cared for Douglas in an attempt to alert planes to the area of the emergency landing. To no avail; Flight Lieutenant Douglas Gordon Cameron Chown died of injuries and exposure. He is buried in a lovely, peaceful cemetery in Gander.

Chown Lake (64 P/10), east of Nejanilini Lake was named after him in 1974.

Christensen, Trooper **James W.** of McCreary (H 14438). Royal Canadian Armoured Corps. He died 19 December 1943 at the age of 18 and is commemorated at McGillivray Cemetery in McCreary. He was the fifth of the seven children of Danish immigrants Carl and Anna Christensen of McCreary. According to his sister (16 January 1997):

> A High School drop-out, he worked for MacDonald Brothers Aircraft Limited in Winnipeg prior to enlisting in the army (Tank Corps) in 1943 – a few months before his eighteenth birthday. [He] was posted to Brampton, Ontario. On December 18th, while walking back to camp with two comrades, he was accidentally struck down by an automobile and died on December 19th from injuries sustained. He was released on the 20th and shipped home to McCreary. Funeral service was held in Knox United Church on December 25th, 1943.

Christensen Lake (64 G/16), southeast of Chipewyan Lake was named after him in 1995.

Christie, Lieutenant **James H.** of Winnipeg. North Nova Scotia Highlanders. He died 12 August 1944 and is commemorated at Bretteville-sur-Laize Canadian War Cemetery, France. ***Christie Island*** (53 L/13) in Oxford Lake was named after him in 1995.

Christie, Gunner **Ronald J.** of Rapid City (H 66682). Royal Canadian Artillery. He died 5 June 1942 at the age of 21 and is commemorated at Brookwood Military Cemetery in Surrey, England. He was the son of Ben and Mary Christie. ***Christie Bay*** (64 O/16) in Baralzon Lake was named after him in 1987.

Christmas, Lieutenant **Richard E.** of Winnipeg. Royal Winnipeg Rifles, Mentioned in Dispatches. He died 6 June 1944 at the age of 27 and is commemorated at Beny-sur-Mer Canadian War Cemetery, France. He was the son of Herbert and Mabel Christmas. According to his nephew (18 April 1997):

> He was educated at Lord Roberts school and St. John's College. He was very active in Boy Scouts and was an active member of St. Alban's

Anglican Church. Before joining the army, he was employed with the British North America Insurance company. Had he survived the war, he contemplated a career in the church or the insurance industry. He joined the Royal Winnipeg Rifles in 1940. My uncle received his commission of 2nd Lieutenant on August 12, 1940. He went overseas with the battalion in July, 1942 and for one year acted as instructor in a battle course. On March 22, 1945 Lieutenant R. E. Christmas of the Canadian Infantry Corps was mentioned in a dispatch for distinguished service. He was wounded in action on the Normandy Beach on June 6, 1944 and died later from his wounds.

Christmas Lake (54 K/12), east of Churchill was named after him in 1948.

Christofferson, Private **Edmond A.** of Middlebro (H 20844). Queen's Own Cameron Highlanders. He died 5 October 1942 at the age of 20 and is commemorated at Brookwood Military Cemetery in Surrey, England. He was the eldest son of William and Catherine Christofferson and was survived by four brothers and three sisters. His sister recalls (22 November 2001):

> Edmond was a fun person to be around. He loved to go hunting and trapping. He wrote letters to me on a regular basis from the army. He died of a gunshot wound to the right shoulder. When the army was going to send home all of his personal belongings, we never received them. Later we found out the ship had sunk.

Christofferson Lake (64 N/1), southwest of Nueltin Lake was named after him in 1972.

Chrupalo, Lance Corporal **John** of Winnipegosis (H 46042). Lake Superior Regiment. He died 18 August 1944 and is commemorated at Bretteville-sur-Laize Canadian War Cemetery, France. He was the son of Andrew and Rosie Chrupalo. ***Chrupalo Lake*** (64 I/16), northeast of North Knife Lake was named after him in 1974.

Chudzik, Pilot Officer **Stanley F.** of Winnipeg (J 18248). No. 218 Squadron. He died 18 August 1943 at the age of 23 and is commemorated at Lyon (La Doua) French National Cemetery, France. He was the son of Frank and Lena Chudzik and was survived by his wife Brenda K. Chudzik of Downham Market, Norfolk. His widow writes (3 June 1998):

> He came to England in 1942 to train younger men to fly warplanes. I believe he was at a place called Trenton before this. He served in Coastal Command for a while in 1943, then was moved to Downham Market to fly bombing missions to the European continent. He was shot down returning from Turin, Italy on the night of 17th – 18th August 1943. Two of his crew survived – the rear gunner and navigator. I understand he managed to keep the plane airborne long enough for these two men to bail out. He was aged 23 years when we were married and 23 years when he died. We never celebrated his birthday, so I am unable to tell you his date of birth.

Chudzik Lake (64 O/2), southwest of Munroe Lake was named after him in 1995.

Chudzik, Pilot Officer **William J.** of Winnipeg (J 89953). No. 420 Squadron. He died 11 June 1944 at the age of 21 and is commemorated at Theuville Communal Cemetery, France. He failed to return from a bombing mission over Versailles, France. Pilot Officer Chudzik was survived by his mother Sophie Chudzik of Winnipeg. ***Chudzik Island*** (53 E/15) in Island Lake was named after him in 1995.

Chura, Private **Philip** of Winnipeg (H 20141). Queen's Own Cameron Highlanders. He died 12 July 1943 at the age of 41 and is commemorated at Cracow Rakowicki Cemetery in Poland. He was the son of Demko and Nettie Chura and was survived by his wife Jean Chura of Cobourg, Ontario. ***Chura Lake*** (54 C/3), southwest of York Factory was named after him in 1964.

Claridge, Warrant Officer 1 **William T.** of Sinclair (R 11959). No. 419 Squadron. He died 28 April 1944 at the age of 21 and is commemorated at Maastricht General Cemetery, Holland. He was the son of Joseph and Hannah Claridge of Ashington, Northumberland, England. ***Claridge Lake*** (64 H/7), northwest of Solmundsson Lake was named after him in 1995.

Clark, Private **Albert G.** "Abbie" of Carman (H 3524). Princess Patricia's Canadian Light Infantry. He died 23 May 1944 at the age of 34 and is commemorated at the Cassino War Cemetery in Italy. He was the son of George C. and Mary Clark of Carman and was survived by his wife Joan Clark of Hounslow, Middlesex. He was the brother of Trooper Cecil S. Clark and Private Arlie Clark (see entries). His niece writes (17 November 2001):

> Albert George Clark was born June 3, 1909 in Carman. Prior to his enlistment in September, 1940 he had been employed as a clerk at the Ryall Hotel in Carman. After training for four months at Fort Osborne Barracks, he went overseas early in 1941. Abbie lost his life fighting for Rome at age 34 on May 23, 1944. Albert was survived by his parents, five sisters and four brothers. Two of the brothers were with the Canadian forces overseas: Cecil with the Lord Strathcona Horse in Italy and Arlie with the Winnipeg Grenadiers in a prison camp after being at Hong Kong.
>
> On a post card dated July 31, 1943 to his Mother, Albert wrote he hoped his sister Laura was getting on OK but Laura died in September, 1943. In a Christmas card, Albert wrote "stay with hope to see you all soon."
>
> Although I never knew my uncle, my mother said Albert was quiet and had a kind and caring nature. The large family grew up on a farm and attended Boyne School. Albert did very well at school and his father wanted him to further his education but he chose to work on the farm. He made games and puppets out of wood and he enjoyed playing the violin at house dances which was the local entertainment at the time.

Clark Falls (64 C/3) on the unnamed river which connects Abrey Lake and McKnight Lake was named after him in 1995.

Clark, Sergeant **Alexander "Sandy"** of Glenboro (K 57599). 1st Canadian Scottish Regiment. He died 27 October 1944 at the age of 28 and is commemorated at the Adegem Canadian War Cemetery in Belgium. He was one of the three sons of John and Annie Clark of Oakner, Manitoba. His obituary read in part: "He enlisted in June, 1940 with the Canadian Scottish Regiment, going overseas in 1941. Sergeant Clark was previously wounded in England when the train he was travelling on was bombed. Two other brothers are overseas" (n.d.). ***Clark Point*** (64 N/3) on Harrison Lake was named after him in 1979.

Clark, Pilot Officer **Ari B.** of Amaranth (J 91164). No. 76 Squadron. He died 26 December 1944 at the age of 21 and is commemorated at the Runnymede Memorial in Surrey, England. ***Clark Peninsula*** (64 P/15) on the north shore of Falloon Lake was named after him in 1985.

Clark, Private **Angus Arlie** of Carman (H 6873). Winnipeg Grenadiers. He died 15 August 1947 at the age of 28 and is commemorated at Greenwood Cemetery in Carman, Manitoba. He was the son of George C. and Mary Clark of Carman and the brother of Trooper Cecil S. Clark and Private Albert G. Clark (see entries). His niece writes (17 November 2001):

Angus Arlie Clark was born May 9, 1919 in Carman. He was raised on the family farm and went to Boyne School. As a boy, he enjoyed playing baseball and swimming. Arlie was on the quiet side and had a kind and caring nature.

He joined the Winnipeg Grenadiers on April 15, 1941 and served in Jamaica. In October, 1941 he went to Hong Kong where he was among those taken prisoner by the Japanese on Christmas Day. He was held prisoner until October, 1945 and then returned to Canada. Arlie was very ill with tuberculosis and weighed 87 or 78 pounds when he returned. He was never well enough to go home and died at the King Edward Hospital in Winnipeg.

Arlie Clark Lake (53 M/14), southeast of Hubley Lake was named after him in 2002.

Clark, Trooper **Cecil S.** of Carman (H 363). Lord Strathcona's Horse. He died 21 January 1945 at the age of 33 and is commemorated at Argenta Gap War Cemetery, Italy. He was the son of George C. and Mary Clark of Carman and was survived by his wife Nettie Clark (née Martin) of Carman and their son Richard. He was the brother of Private Albert G. Clark and Private Arlie Clark (see entries). His niece writes (17 November 2001):

Cecil Scott Clark was born May 11, 1911 in Carman. He enlisted in June, 1942 and went overseas the following November. He served with the Fifth Army in Italy and had seen service from the beginning of the Mediterranean campaign. Cecil drowned on active service in Italy. One of his brothers, Arlie, was with the Winnipeg Grenadiers and was a prisoner of war in Japan after being at Hong Kong. Another brother, Albert, was killed on active service overseas a few months earlier. He grew up on the family farm near Carman and attended Boyne School. Cecil was quiet and had a kind and caring nature.

His daughter-in-law adds (20 April 1998):

He was quite involved in sports, especially baseball and enjoyed working with, and riding horses. He worked for a local farmer who had several heavy horses. He left for overseas shortly after his only son was born and was killed a couple of months before he was to return home.

Cecil Clark Lake (64 O/1), southeast of Munroe Lake was named after him in 1995.

Clark, Flying Officer **Clarence T.** of Isabella (J 20627). No. 405 Squadron. He died 24 November 1943 at the age of 25 and is commemorated at the Runnymede Memorial in Surrey, England. He was the son of Samuel G. and Katherine M. Clark of Isabella and the cousin of Flying Officer James Clark (see entry). His nephew writes (7 December 2001):

He was the captain of a Lancaster bomber which failed to return to its base after a bombing raid over Berlin on the night of November 23rd and the early morning of November 24th, 1943. His training was at Virden, Saskatoon and Halifax before going to England. His letters home tell us he flew as captain to an RAF crew of six. Quoting from his second last letter home:

"There is of course a great deal I could write about normally which I must omit now. I have been in the majority of larger English cities, seen their colleges, churches and many famous old pubs. Not that I ever do a lot of drinking, not from any moral point of view, but it doesn't mix with operational flying – as we say, there is not future in it. The lives of seven men depend on my ability as an efficient captain and that, if nothing else, would be enough to keep me up to scratch" (7 October 1943). Our family is justly proud of Uncle Clarence, and regret that we only know of him through his letters and family stories.

Clark Hill (64 J/5), west of Sprott Lake was named after him in 1989.

Clark, Corporal **David A.** of Kississing (B 46847). Hastings and Prince Edward Regiment. He died 30 January 1944 at the age of 25 and is commemorated at the Moro River Canadian War Cemetery in Italy. He was the son of Arthur and Bess Clark and was survived by his wife Madeleine Clark. ***David Clark Lake*** (53 K/10), southwest of Kistigan Lake was named after him in 1995.

Clark, Flying Officer **James H.** of Isabella (J 20955). No. 299 Squadron. He died 7 June 1944 at the age of 24 and is commemorated at Hermanville War Cemetery, France. Flying Officer Clark's aircraft was shot down following a raid to southern France. He was the son of Robert T. and Laura M. Clark of Isabella, Manitoba and the cousin of Flying Officer Clarence Clark (see entry). His nephew writes (4 December 2001):

I never had the opportunity to meet my Uncle Jim, but fortunately, from reading his numerous letters home, I was able to gain insight into the type of individual he was. Jim had a very special relationship with his parents and siblings. Upon departure for flight training and the subsequent posting overseas, he promised that he would write home twice a week – a promise he kept. As a consequence of his outgoing nature, his sense of humour and his open view on life in general, he had a good number of friends. Jim was an adventurous sort and took great delight in exploring different areas on leave. As much as he enjoyed these adventures, it was always his desire to return home to take over the family farm.

Clark Esker (64 J/1), northeast of Chipewyan Lake was named after him in 1989.

Clark, Trooper **John F.** of Carberry (L 155867). Royal Canadian Armoured Corps. He died 25 November 1945 at the age of 37 and is commemorated at Khedive Cemetery, Saskatchewan. He was the son of James and Margaret Clark of Prince Albert. ***Clark Lake*** (64 L/9), north of Reindeer Lake on the Manitoba - Saskatchewan boundary was named after him in 1962.

Clark, Leading Bombardier **Robert A.** of Boissevain (H 92362). Royal Canadian Artillery. He died 31 August 1944 at the age of 25 and is commemorated at Montecchio War Cemetery in Italy. ***Robert Clark Lake*** (53 M/6), south of Schwatka Lake was named after him in 1995.

Clark, Flight Sergeant **Vernon E.** of Grandview (R 205305). No. 1664 Heavy Conversion Unit, RCAF. He died 7 August 1944 at the age of 23 and is commemorated at the Runnymede Memorial in Surrey, England. He was the son of Rutledge and Grace Clark. His brother writes (11 February 1997):

He received his Public School Grade 8 at the Mount Gap School in the district. He remained on the family farm until he joined the armed forces. He arrived overseas in October, 1943. Vern had a great personality – always determined to better himself in life. He could not tolerate high altitudes due to sinus problems, so was moved to several crews which was a setback during his training. The family received a letter from the Royal Canadian

Casualties Officer Overseas stating that the entire crew of his aircraft had fallen into the North Sea off Scarborough, Yorkshire at 3:00 PM, Monday, August 7th, 1944 during air bombing exercises.

Vernon Clark Lake (64 F/9), east of Jordan Lake was named after him in 1995.

Clarke, Flight Sergeant **Gerald F.** of Winnipeg (R 71424). No. 401 Squadron. He died 28 February 1942 at the age of 22 and is commemorated at the Runnymede Memorial in Surrey, England. He was the son of William J. and Ernestine Clarke and was survived by his wife Gratia A. Clarke and their unborn daughter. His wife recalls (31 October 2001):

> Gerry was counting the days off to the birth of his child. He died doing what he loved, flying the famous Spitfires. His squadron was escorting our bombers back over France when they encountered some ME 109s. Gerry radioed that he had been hit but thought he could make it back to base. He never made it over the English Channel. The Squadron's dead are all commemorated on a plaque in St. George's Chapel of Remembrance at Biggin Hill, Kent. I loved him dearly.

Clarke Narrows (63 I/16) in Kapechekamasic Lake was named after him in 1995.

Clarke, Pilot Officer **Harold W.** of Winnipeg (J 5703). No. 408 Squadron. He died 21 January 1942 at the age of 20 and is commemorated at the Runnymede Memorial in Surrey, England. He was the son of George H. and Georgina M. Clarke of Winnipeg. ***Clarke Island*** (64 J/11) in Clifton Lake was named after him in 1975.

Clarke, Flying Officer **James W.** (J 12829). No. 422 Squadron. He died 25 May 1943 at the age of 21 and is commemorated at Irvinestown Church Of Ireland Churchyard, County Fermanagh, United Kingdom. He was the son of James W. and Maria Clarke of Princeton, New Jersey. ***James Clarke Lake*** (63 N/2), southwest of Batty Lake was named after him in 2000.

Clarke, Private **John G.** of Scandinavia, Manitoba (H 203121). Calgary Highlanders. He died 28 February 1945 at the age of 21 and is commemorated at the Groesbeek Canadian War Cemetery in Holland. He was the son of Mr. and Mrs. Tom Clarke of Minnedosa and was survived by his wife Katherine Clarke of St. Catharines, Ontario. ***Clarke River*** (54 M/2), which flows east into Little Seal River was named after him in 1984.

Clarke, Sergeant **Leo** of Winnipeg (72132). 2nd Battalion, Canadian Infantry (Eastern Ontario Regiment), Victoria Cross.

> For most conspicuous bravery. He was detailed with his section of bombers to clear the continuation of a newly-captured trench and cover the construction of a "block." After most of his party had become casualties, he was building a block when about twenty of the enemy with two officers counter-attacked. He boldly advanced against them, emptied his revolver into them and afterwards two enemy rifles which he picked up in the trench. One of the officers then attacked him with the bayonet, wounding him in the leg, but he shot him dead. The enemy then ran away, pursued by Acting Corporal Clarke, who shot four more and captured a fifth (*London Gazette* 24 October 1916).

He died 19 October 1916 at the age of 24. He was the son of Henry T. and Rossetta C. N. Clarke of 785 Pine Street, Winnipeg. ***Leo Clarke Lake*** (63 P/8), southwest of Goulet Lake was named after him in 2001.

Clarke, Warrant Officer 1 **Robert E.** of Winnipeg (R 69558). No. 226 Mitchell Squadron. He died 19 August 1944 at the age of 37 and is commemorated at Bretteville-sur-Laize Canadian War Cemetery in Calvados, France. He was survived by his mother Helen Clarke and by his wife Vera J. Clarke of Putney, London, England. ***Robert Clarke Bay*** (53 L/12) in Rat Lake was named after him in 1996.

Clarke, Pilot Officer **Robert E.** of Matlock (J 11210). No. 7 Squadron. He died 17 September 1942 at the age of 20 and is commemorated at Amsterdam New Eastern Cemetery, Holland. According to his nephew (10 October 2001):

> Robert Edward Clark Jr. was born in Winnipeg on the 14th September 1922 to R. E. Clark Sr. and Myrtle Lorena Clark (née Bowler). In his youth, he helped his father as a homesteader and farmer. He was a very good student (often winning awards), an excellent swimmer and had a mischievous sense of humour.
>
> He enlisted in the RCAF on the 25th of June 1941 using the old family name "Clarke" and received his King's Commission on the 15th of July 1942. Volunteering for No. 7 (RAF) Squadron Pathfinder Force, he was assigned to fly a Short Stirling four-engine bomber. The Pathfinder Force was designated to fly in front of the main bomber stream into Germany to mark targets – very dangerous duty.
>
> At age 20, in the first month of the creation of No. 7 Squadron, Robert and his international air crew were shot down over the English Channel. Six of the crew were lost, but Robert's body was recovered from the sea by the occupying forces near Lemmer, Holland.

Clarke Rapids (64 O/9) on the unnamed creek which drains Arthur Thompson Lake was named after him in 1995.

Clarke, Pilot Officer **Wilfred V.** of Winnipeg (J 15667). No. 9 Squadron. He died 1 August 1942 at the age of 30 and is commemorated at Heverlee War Cemetery, Belgium. He was survived by his wife Anna Clarke. ***Clarke Bay*** (64 F/3) on the northwest shore of Vandekerckhove Lake was named after him in 1989.

Clarke, Private **William A. "Alfie"** of Selkirk (H 1831). South Saskatchewan Regiment. He died 4 February 1945 at the age of 20 and is commemorated at the Groesbeek Canadian War Cemetery in Holland. He was the son of Mr. and Mrs. C. A. Clarke of Winnipeg. ***William Clarke Lake*** (64 C/10), east of Finch Lake was named after him in 1995.

Clasper, Flight Lieutenant **Robert** of Winnipeg (J 15920). No. 412 Squadron. This native of Sculcoates, Yorkshire died 27 September 1944 at the age of 22 and is commemorated at the Runnymede Memorial in Surrey, England. He was the son of Robert and Mary Clasper of Winnipeg. His brother writes (26 June 1995):

> From his childhood days, flying, planes and aviation were a prime interest in his life. His chief hobby was building model planes. Upon graduating from high school, he enlisted in the RCAF in February, 1941 and became a pilot under the

Commonwealth Air Training Plan. He trained at Brandon, Regina, Calgary, Lethbridge and High River. In 1942, he served in England and Scotland with 421 Squadron. In February, 1943, he served with 93 Squadron (RAF) in North Africa, Malta and Sicily. In October, 1943 [he] returned to Canada as an instructor. Upon the European invasion, [he] returned to combat service with 412 Squadron. [On] September 27, 1944 [he was] reported missing on operations in [the] vicinity of Nijmegen and presumed dead as of that date. No trace of his body or plane was ever found.

Clasper Lake (64 N/10), southwest of Nueltin Lake was named after him in 1972.

Claydon, Flight Lieutenant **David A.** of St. Vital (J 16564). No. 622 Squadron. He died 20 January 1944 at the age of 22 and is commemorated at the Berlin 1939 - 1945 War Cemetery, Germany. He was the fourth child of Ebenezer and Lillian Claydon of Winnipeg. He was in college prior to enlisting and intended to join the family business, Claydon Brothers Construction. ***Claydon Lake*** (64 P/12), west of Nejanilini Lake was named after him in 1974.

Cleaver, Trooper **James E.** of Oak River (B 58532). Royal Canadian Armoured Corps. He died 9 March 1944 at the age of 27 and is commemorated at Brookwood Military Cemetery in Surrey, England. He was the son of Thomas and Frances J. Cleaver of Oak River. ***Cleaver Bay*** (53 M/5) in Hackland Lake was named after him in 1996.

Cleaver, Lance Corporal **William G.** of Moore Park (H 59098). Canadian Provost Corps. He died 25 September 1943 at the age of 23 and is commemorated at Brookwood Military Cemetery Surrey, England. He was the son of Ernest J. and Mabel Cleaver of Moore Park. According to his brother (n.d.): "He worked on the farm and enjoyed all sports. He enlisted in the Provost Corps [in] 1942 and went overseas in August of 1942. Bill died … at South Shields, England." ***Cleaver Island*** (64 P/5) in the Wolverine River was named after him in 1995.

Clegg, Flying Officer **Alan B.** of Winnipeg (J 16173). No. 415 Squadron. He died 14 June 1943 at the age of 23 and is commemorated at the Runnymede Memorial in Surrey, England. He was the son of Arthur Benjamin and Margaret E. Clegg of Winnipeg. His sister recalls (15 December 2001):

Alan was an only son survived by his parents Ben and Maggie and two sisters, Violet and Margaret. He enlisted in the RCAF in August, 1940. He did his wireless Operator training and Bombing and Gunnery School in Montreal and Fingal, Ontario. In July, 1941, he had ten days embarkation leave before going to England. He and the same crew put in two tours of operations – ordinarily one tour of "ops" allowed you to return to Canada for 28 days' leave. The year of 1943 was when the German submarines were creating the worst havoc and Coastal Command was very much in demand. Alan's crew were awaiting their leave home when a call went out for "volunteers." Their crew answered the call at 1:30 PM, June 13, 1943 and went searching for German U-boats in the Bay of Biscay area – some of the roughest waters in the world. Alan's crew were never heard from again; they were "Reported Missing" and six months later "Presumed Dead."

In September, 1984, we visited the Runnymede Memorial and saw Alan's name carved into concrete pillar #172, enshrined there along with 20,454 other airmen. This beautiful shrine is on the grounds where King John signed the Magna Carta in 1215, "the most famous document in the history of government."

In June, 1983, we were pleased to learn that a lake in northwestern Manitoba had been named after Flying Officer Alan B. Clegg in April, 1972. We were interviewed by CBC prior to Remembrance Day, 1983 re our thoughts about this as a suitable memorial. We assured them Mother and Dad would have been as proud as we were. Very suitable indeed in that Alan was a lover of the great outdoors!

Clegg Lake (64 N/9), southwest of Nueltin Lake was named after him in 1972.

Clegg, Leading WREN **Olive I.** of Binscarth (W 1396). HMCS *Protector*. She died 17 June 1944 at the age of 24 and is commemorated at Binscarth Cemetery, Manitoba. She was the daughter of Morley E. and Louise Clegg (née Beard) of Binscarth. According to her sister (1 March 1997):

She received her education in Jellicoe and Binscarth schools and took Grade 12 at Russell High School. Later she took a Home Economics Short Course at Minnedosa. For a time she did housework at Birtle until she obtained employment with the Manitoba Telephone System as a telephone operator.

In the spring of 1943 she enlisted in the Navy and was stationed at Galt, Ontario for basic training as a telegrapher and then to the Naval Base at Sydney, Nova Scotia where she contracted military tuberculosis (galloping consumption) and died in June, 1944. At Knox United Church she had a funeral with full military honours with the Chaplain and naval pall bearers from HMCS *Chippawa* in Winnipeg.

Clegg Island (54 D/6) in Stephens Lake was named after her in 1996.

Cleunion, Private **Lucien J.** of Winnipeg (H 18177). Princess Patricia's Canadian Light Infantry. He died 4 January 1945 at the age of 20 and is commemorated at Ravenna War Cemetery in Italy. He was survived by his mother Marie Cleunion of Winnipeg. His sister's recollections (9 April 1998) of their childhood together is a postcard of Canadian life at that time:

Born and raised in Winnipeg, Lucien was the only son of Marie Cleunion, widow, who was the sole support of Lucien and his younger sister Margaret. At an early age, Lucien undertook a share in the finances of the family; he secured an ice-delivery route, hauling blocks of ice regularly to households in his neighbourhood and supplying the means of refrigeration in those days. Lucien had nine customers, netting five cents per block, half of which he gave to his mother. When he joined the army, he continued to send money home to his mother and sister.

Lucien had good scholastic and sports records in the three levels of school that he attended. Somerset Elementary saw him helping out on the School Patrol Team that was initiated by the Winnipeg Board of Trade to guard busy street crossings and ensure safe passage for younger students on their way to school in the mornings, at noon hours and at school closing times. In 1938, Lucien's school won the Championship Award for Efficiency of School Patrols. In addition to this community service, Lucien played soccer at Hugh John Macdonald Junior High, where his team won the Senior A title in the city league in 1940. At Daniel McIntyre High, he was a member of the championship team in Senior B Soccer. Later, Lucien coached Somerset in the Junior A Soccer Tournament, where the team won second place, and managed the team later when it again won second place. As well, in the North Winnipeg Junior Hockey Tournament, Lucien was mentioned as an outstanding goalie. And somehow, he found time to pitch baseball.

Lucien had little time for hobbies. Nevertheless, he collected pictures of National Hockey League players, mainly of the Toronto Maple Leafs, such as Syl Apps, Gordie Drillon and Gump Worseley. The pictures were offered by Beehive Corn Syrup in exchange for labels from their cans. Saturday evenings found Lucien and Margaret glued to the radio, listening to Foster Hewitt's famous hockey broadcasts. A secondary hobby was the trading of comic books with his school-mates.

Lucien completed high school at the age of 17 1/2 years. His first, and only employment (aside from his childhood job of delivering ice) was in the CPR Shops in Winnipeg where he hoped to establish himself in a career. However, as soon as he attained to 18 years of age, he offered himself to his country, enlisting with the Princess Pats at the beginning of January 1942. Almost immediately, he was posted overseas into the battles raging in Italy. His brief life was over at the age of 20.

Cleunion Lake (63 N/3), south of Kississing Lake was named after him in 1972.

Clifford, Flying Officer **Lewis B.** of Winnipeg (J 21295). No. 77 Squadron. He died 7 September 1943 at the age of 22 and is commemorated at Durnbach War Cemetery, Germany. He was the son of Lewis T. C. and Hettie Clifford and was survived by his wife Jane T. Clifford of Winnipeg. *Clifford Lake* (53 M/6), north of Oxford Lake was named after him in 1985.

Clifton, Private **Arthur** of Winnipeg (H 16360). Princess Patricia's Canadian Light Infantry. He died 15 December 1943 and is commemorated at the Moro River Canadian War Cemetery in Italy. *Clifton Lake* (64 J/11), west of Tadoule Lake was named after him in 1972.

Climo, Gunner **George Edward "Ted"** of McAuley (H 1054). Royal Canadian Artillery. He died 25 April 1945 at the age of 20 and is commemorated at the Holten Canadian War Cemetery in Holland. He was the youngest of the four children of George and Freda Climo. According to his sister (15 January 2002):

Details of "Ted" are not too clear anymore. We had a very uneventful life as children, raised on a farm in Manitoba during the dry years in the thirties. Ted was a good-natured lad. As soon as he became 18 years of age he joined up. His first base was Camp Shilo as far as I remember. While growing up, Ted attended Rutherglen School. His hobbies were riding his bicycle and playing ball in summer. Winter he would enjoy skating and hockey.

She adds (7 August 1995):

When Ted was 11, the family moved in to the village of McAuley where his father ran the hardware store. Ted's mother was active in the local Women's Institute. Ted was very dear to her and his death came as a great blow, especially as it came in the last few weeks of the war. In 1981, mother and I went to Holland and visited the grave site in Holten. The Dutch people take pride in keeping the sites neat and children place flowers regularly. We have a plaque in his remembrance on my father's and mother's grave in McAuley. Teddy was a very gentle young man. His older brother Ralph also served overseas, but he was able to return home. Greater love hath no man than this, that a man lay down his life for his friend. John 15:13.

Climo Lake (64 I/6), north of North Knife Lake was named after him in 1974.

Cline, Warrant Officer 2 **Gordon A.** of Glenboro (R 106223). No. 415 Squadron. He died 10 April 1943 at the age of 22 and is commemorated at the Runnymede Memorial in Surrey, England. He was the son of Andrew R. and Elizabeth Cline. According to his nephew (n.d.):

On the night of April 10, 1945, a convoy of five ships was intercepted – a 8000-ton merchant vessel heavily guarded by a destroyer and three escort ships – in the face of intense and accurate flak fire from all five vessels, the five Hampdens carried out their torpedo attacks. All were considerably shot up. One piloted by F/S G. A. Cline was seen to go down near the blockade runner.

Cline Lake (64 F/8), southeast of Jordan Lake was named after him in 1986.

Clisby, Rifleman **Melvin O.** of Ninette (H 41383). Royal Winnipeg Rifles. He died 7 June 1944 at the age of 22 and is commemorated at Beny-sur-Mer Canadian War Cemetery, France. He was the son of Charles and Petra Clisby of Ninette and was survived by his wife Margery E. Clisby of Ninette. *Clisby Lake* (64 J/12), west of Tadoule Lake was named after him in 1957.

Clougher, Bombardier **John J.** of Brandon (H 66730). Royal Canadian Artillery. He died 2 August 1941 at the age of 41 and is commemorated at Brandon Cemetery. He was survived by his wife Alexandra Clougher of Staffordshire, England. *Clougher Lake* (64 I/2), southwest of South Knife Lake was named after him in 1974.

Clueit, Trooper **Christopher V.** of Winnipeg (H 157). Lord Strathcona's Horse. He died 12 December 1944 and is commemorated at Ravenna War Cemetery in Italy. *Clueit Lake* (62 P/16), west of Family Lake was named after him in 1978.

Cluff, Sapper **William J. "Chuck"** of Binscarth (H 105084). Royal Canadian Engineers. He died 28 April 1945 at the age of 27 and is commemorated at the Holten Canadian War Cemetery in Holland. He was the son of William and Jessie Cluff. His niece and nephews write (28 November 2001):

Chuck was a quiet, wonderful man, loved by all his stepbrothers, stepsisters, nieces and nephews. He visited all his family on his leaves. He was killed in Germany with three other soldiers when driving over an underground mine.

Cluff Lake (62 N/15), southeast of Wellman Lake was named after him in 1973.

Coaffee, Private **Cyril H.** of Winnipeg (H 33034). Royal Canadian Army Medical Corps. He died 2 July 1945 at the age of 48 and is commemorated at Elmwood Cemetery in Winnipeg. He was survived by his mother Harriott Coaffee. *Coaffee Lake* (63 P/2), northeast of Cotton Lake was named after him in 1996.

Coates, Private **James D.** of Melita (H 87735). Royal Canadian Army Service Corps. He died 11 June 1942 at the age of 29 and is commemorated at Melita Cemetery, Manitoba. He was the son of Robert and Mary Coates. *Coates Island* (63 I/1), in Holenchuk Lake was named after him in 1995.

Coates, Private **Roy H.** of Morris (H 65199). Royal Canadian Army Service Corps. He died 2 May 1945 and is commemorated at the Holten Canadian War Cemetery in Holland. *Coates Lake* (64 N/4), southwest of Nueltin Lake was named after him in 1972.

Cochrane, Rifleman **George A.** of Matheson Island (H 100773). Royal Winnipeg Rifles. He died 15 August 1944 at the age of 25 and is commemorated at Bretteville-sur-Laize Canadian War Cemetery, France. He was the son of William and Gertrude Cochrane of Matheson Island, Manitoba. *Cochrane Point* (53 L/16) on Gods Lake was named after him in 1995.

Cohen, Lieutenant **Lawrence** of Winnipeg (CDN 423). Warwickshire Regiment. He died 8 July 1944 at the age of 22 and is commemorated at Bretteville-sur-Laize Canadian War Cemetery, France. He was the son of Isaac and Anne Cohen (née Shore). His brother recalls (10 October 2001):

Lawrence Cohen was born in Winnipeg on November 30, 1921. The family lived in Winkler,

Manitoba until his father died in 1924 during an epidemic of Western Equine Encephalitis. His mother and a young brother then moved to Winnipeg.

Lieutenant Cohen attended Winnipeg schools, Machray, St. John's High School and the University of Manitoba in the Arts and Science Faculty where he majored in Economics. He enrolled in the COTC. In 1943, he enlisted and took further officer training in Gordon Head, British Columbia, Camp Shilo in Manitoba and Camp Borden, Ontario. He then went overseas, joining the British Army, 2nd Royal Warwickshire Regiment where there was a shortage of officers, through the CanLoan Program. His regiment was shipped from England to Normandy shortly after D-Day. He died in battle in early July, 1944 and was ultimately interred in the Canadian Cemetery near Caen, France.

Cohen Lake (64 I/9), northeast of North Knife Lake was named after him in 1974.

Cohen, Warrant Officer 2 **Syd** of Winnipeg (R 95142). No. 7 Bombing and Gunnery School, RCAF. He died 15 March 1943 at the age of 20 and is commemorated at Middlechurch (Independent Bnay Abraham) Cemetery, Manitoba. He was the son of Ben and Bertha Cohen. ***Cohen Island*** (64 C/6) in Kaykayk Lake was named after him in 1995.

Coker, Pilot Officer **Charles Kenneth** of Brandon (J 17259). No. 115 Squadron. He died 30 May 1943 at the age of 21 and is commemorated at Heverlee War Cemetery, Belgium. He was the son of Henry and Daisy Coker of Brandon. His sister recalls (18 November 2001):

Ken was the oldest son in the family and loved to read. If you wanted to know about anything, you could ask him and he would find out. He was a quiet, reserved person and always ready to help; we all missed him so much when he left to go overseas. My younger brother has been over to Belgium to see his grave.

Coker Lake (64 P/5), south of Nejanilini Lake was named after him in 1974.

Colbeck, Sub-Lieutenant **Arthur W.** of Crandall (O 14690). HMCS *Clayquot*. The *Clayquot* was torpedoed by U-806 and sunk while taking station on Convoy XB.139 in the approaches to Halifax Harbour; eight of her crew were lost. Sub-Lieutenant Colbeck died 24 December 1944 at the age of 22 and is commemorated at the Halifax Memorial. He was the son of John and Jeannie Colbeck of Crandall, Manitoba. ***Colbeck Lake*** (64 N/3), north of Lac Brochet was named after him in 1961.

Cole, Private **Allan B.** of Flin Flon (L 104753). Lake Superior Regiment. He died 14 December 1944 and is commemorated at Bergen-op-Zoom Canadian War Cemetery in Holland. He was the son of Mr. and Mrs. Bert Cole. ***Cole Peninsula*** (64 O/13) in Nueltin Lake was named after him in 1996.

Cole, Gunner **Benjamin H.** (F 56426). Royal Canadian Artillery. He died 7 November 1945 at the age of 25 and is commemorated at Canso (Fourth Hill) Cemetery in Nova Scotia. He was the son of Howard and Melinda Cole of Canso, Nova Scotia and was survived by his wife Evelyn Cole. ***Cole Island*** (54 D/15) in Cygnet Lake was named after him in 1996.

Cole, Flight Sergeant **Robert J. L.** of Portage la Prairie (R 106214). No. 142 Squadron. He died 16 October 1942 at the age of 20 and is commemorated at Grimsby (Scartho Road) Cemetery Lincolnshire, England. He was the eldest son of Robert and Lila Cole and was survived by his wife of nine months Kathleen Cole (née Dymond). She recalls (16 October 2001):

Bob Cole was born in Portage la Prairie, Manitoba in March, 1920 and attended school there, graduating from Portage Collegiate in 1938. He was keenly interested in sports and took part in many provincial meets as a 100-yard runner. He also coached the basketball team and took the lead in many of the school's operettas.

He was stationed in Virden and Saskatoon. There he played on the winning basketball team at Air Force Training Base No. 4. He left for overseas in March of 1942 and was killed in October of that year. We were married at Portage la Prairie on January 24, 1942.

Cole Bay (64 G/4) in Grandmother Lake was named after him in 1994.

Coll, Lieutenant **William J.** of Winnipeg (CDN 545). Royal Canadian Infantry Corps, on loan to the Dorsetshire Regiment. He died 17 July 1944 at the age of 28 and is commemorated at Hottot-les-Bagues War Cemetery, France. He was the son of William P. and Caroline W. Coll of Winnipeg and was survived by two sisters and a younger brother who served overseas during the war. His brother writes (22 January 2002):

CanLoan Officer Lieutenant William J. Coll enlisted in the Queen's Cameron Highlanders of Canada at Winnipeg, Manitoba after graduating from Daniel McIntyre Collegiate Institute in September, 1939 and proceeded overseas to England with his regiment in December of the same year. In August, 1942 Lieutenant Coll participated in the raid on Dieppe, France and returned safely to England. He was selected for Officer training soon after the raid and was returned to Canada.

He received his commission and was appointed Lieutenant (Infantry) November, 1943. He returned to England in March, 1944 whereupon he volunteered for service with the British Army CanLoan Program and became a platoon commander with the 1st Dorsetshire Regiment just prior to the D-Day invasion of France.

Coll Lake (64 I/10), northeast of North Knife Lake was named after him in 1978.

Collett, Gunner **Stanley H. "Kelly"** of Portage la Prairie (H 54906). Royal Canadian Artillery. He died 23 October 1940 at the age of 33 and is commemorated at Hillside Cemetery, Portage la Prairie. He was survived by his mother Ada Collett. ***Collett Lake*** (64 K/13), northeast of Reindeer Lake was named after him in 1972.

Collier, Flying Officer **Clarence M.** of Souris (J 23592). No. 405 Squadron. He died 16 December 1943 at the age of 27 and is commemorated at Cambridge City Cemetery in Cambridgeshire, England. He was the son of Mr. and Mrs. A. E. L. E. Collier. ***Collier Lake*** (64 O/16), west of Baralzon Lake was named after him in 1987.

Collins, Private **Albert C.** of Brandon (H 64824). Princess Patricia's Canadian Light Infantry. He died 18 September 1944 at the age of 21 and is commemorated at Coriano Ridge War Cemetery in Italy. He was the son of Albert and Margaret Collins. ***Albert Collins Lake*** (53 K/13), northeast of Gods Lake was named after him in 1995.

Collins, Private **Avery B.** (H 46398). Lake Superior Regiment. He died 30 April 1945 and is commemorated at Brookwood Military Cemetery in Surrey, England. ***Avery Collins Lake*** (64 P/2), northwest of Meades Lake was named after him in 1996.

Collins, Trooper **Donald James** of Winnipeg (H 103127). Fort Garry Horse. He died 8 August 1944 at the age of 22 and is commemorated at Beny-sur-Mer Canadian War Cemetery, France. He was the son of James and Sarah Collins. According to his sister (8 December 1994):

> My brother … was born … in the Winnipeg General Hospital. Our home at that time was Springfield, Manitoba, just east of Transcona. He went to Brooklands School from Grade 1 to 8, then to Cecil Rhodes for Grade 9. He left in mid-term to take a job with Gillis and Warren on Fort Street; he worked as a shipper in the Parts [Department]. It was an automobile firm. He left to go to Trans Canada [Airlines] in the shipping department and then to the army. He was at Fort Osborne for a time and at Fort Garry, University of Manitoba where the troops were stationed. He later went to Camp Borden with the Armoured Regiment then England and France as a … dispatch rider in the Fort Garry Horse.

Collins Lake (63 K/14), northeast of Athapapuskow Lake was named after him in 1951 and Collins Hill (64 A/5), south of Baldock Lake was named after him in 1995.

Collins, Flying Officer **James T.** of Winnipeg (J 39957). No. 12 Squadron. He died 7 February 1945 at the age of 21 and is commemorated at the Groesbeek Canadian War Cemetery in Holland. He was the son of Frederick W. and Mary Collins and was survived by his wife Gladys M. Collins of Dorset, England. ***Collins Peninsula*** (63 O/8) on Paint Lake was named after him in 1995.

Collins, Private **Keith G.** of Darlingford (K 50752). Seaforth Highlanders of Canada. He died 23 May 1944 at the age of 37 and is commemorated at the Cassino War Cemetery in Italy. He was the son of William W. and Julia A. Collins. He was working in the mines in British Columbia when war was declared, so he enlisted there. ***Collins Esker*** (64 I/3), south of Blyth Lake was named after him in 1995.

Collins, Private **Norman A.** of Rossendale (H 67225). South Saskatchewan Regiment. He died 20 July 1944 and is commemorated at the Bayeux Memorial in France. ***Collins Rapids*** (64 C/16) in the Hughes River was named after him in 1995.

Collins, Pilot Officer **Russell T. F.** of Winnipeg (J 45008). No. 62 Operational Training Unit, RCAF. He died 6 October 1944 at the age of 26 and is commemorated at Stonefall Cemetery in Yorkshire, England. He was the son of Mr. and Mrs. H. W. Collins of Elmwood and was survived by his wife Irene Collins of Elmwood and their young son. ***Collins Narrows*** (53 E/16) in Island Lake was named after him in 1995.

Collins, Corporal **Wesley** of Point Douglas (H 17827). Royal Winnipeg Rifles. He died 5 July 1944 at the age of 24 and is commemorated at Beny-sur-Mer Canadian War Cemetery, France. He was the son of Walter and Jean Collins of Winnipeg and was survived by his wife Alison Collins of Winnipeg and their 18 month-old daughter Elizabeth. His wife recalls (20 November 2001):

> Wesley was at the lake with his family when war was declared. The family proceeded to pack up camp and head back to Winnipeg so the boys could enlist. After taking officer training courses, he was an instructor at Fort Garry for two years before going overseas. While overseas, Wesley and I exchanged letters weekly and I remember him expressing a desire to see his "little princess" again, how much he missed everyone and wanting to come home soon. I have many fond memories and was lucky enough to be blessed with a close, loving family.

Collins Creek (63 O/7), which flows northeast into Wuskwatim Brook was named after him in 1995.

Collister, Pilot Officer **John W.** of Brandon (J 90351). No. 12 Squadron. He died 29 July 1944 at the age of 20 and is commemorated at Durnbach War Cemetery, Germany. He was the son of Thomas and Stella Collister. ***Collister Lake*** (64 J/14), northwest of Tadoule Lake was named after him in 1975.

Collyer, Flying Officer **John W.** of Winnipeg (J 23976). No. 640 Squadron. He died 17 June 1944 at the age of 31 and is commemorated at Herwen-en-Aerdt (Tolkamer) General Cemetery, Holland. He was the son of James and Ethel M. Collyer and was survived by his wife Agnes A. Collyer of Winnipeg. His son writes (6 November 2001):

> I have no memories of my Dad as he left for overseas when I was a very small baby. All I have of him is three letters, some pictures and stories told me by my Mother and Grandparents. I am enclosing a copy of his last letter, written to me just two months before his death. I am very proud of him and what he and others like him did for this country:
>
> Dear Son: How are you fella, fine I hope. I want to thank you for all the parcels and the valentine, pretty good boy to your Dad, hope you are a good boy for your mother, because if you are not, I will be right over there after you. Don't forget son, that though your Dad is a long way away, I am always thinking of you and mother and am only waiting for the day that I can get home to you both. Meanwhile son, be a good soldier – look after your mummy and granny, do what they say, because they know best, and always be a man.
>
> Well son, we are licking Jerry and hope soon to have him where he can't do any more damage, so be a good fella, give Mum and Granny a kiss for me, and tell Mummy I love you both. Be seeing you son. All my love always, Your Dad (15 April 1944).

Collyer Lake (63 K/16), west of Wekusko Lake was named after him in 1973.

Colter, Flight Sergeant **James C.** of Crystal City (R 95411). No. 418 Squadron. He died 27 August 1942 at the age of 21 and is commemorated at the Runnymede Memorial in Surrey, England. He was the youngest of the four children of Herbert and Barbara Colter of Crystal City, Manitoba. His sister writes (29 May 1995):

> He was educated in Crystal City schools and during those years he was deeply interested in team sports and excelled in his playing of hockey. After graduation from school, he secured employment with the Royal Bank and from 1937 until 1941 he was with the Bank in Crystal City, Deloraine and Melita respectively.
>
> In March, 1941 he enlisted with the RCAF and took his training at High River, Alberta and at Fort McLeod, Alberta where he received his wings October 24th, 1941. He was posted overseas in November, 1941 and was on active duty at Bradwell Bay with Squadron No. 418. While on a mission August 27, 1942 he went missing and was never found. He was the youngest of the Colter family, blessed with a quick and ready wit. He was much loved and deeply mourned by his parents, his brothers Orville and Karl and sisters Erma, Marguerite and Olive.

Colter Lake (64 O/15), east of Nueltin Lake was named after him in 1975.

Colvin, Private **Frederick J.** of Carman (H 6848). Winnipeg Grenadiers. He died a prisoner of war 1 January 1944 at the age of 23 and is commemorated at the Yokohama War Cemetery in Japan. He was the son of Andrew and Ethel Colvin of Carman. ***Colvin Lake*** (64 N/11), southwest of Nueltin Lake was named after him in 1972.

Colwell, Trooper **Dexter** of Winnipeg (H 95371). South Alberta Tank Regiment. He died 21 August 1944 and is commemorated at Bretteville-sur-Laize Canadian War Cemetery, France. ***Colwell Lake*** (64 H/1), west of Hogg Lake was named after him in 1995.

Comba, Warrant Officer 1 **William M.** of Killarney, Manitoba (R 59670). No. 220 Fortress Squadron. He died 14 June 1943 at the age of 21 and is commemorated at the Runnymede Memorial in Surrey, England. ***Comba Lake*** (63 K/16), west of Wekusko Lake was named after him in 1973.

Combaz, Flying Officer **Alfred J.** of Norwood (J 29388). No. 478 Squadron. He died 21 February 1945 at the age of 24 and is commemorated at the Runnymede Memorial in Surrey, England. He was the son of Alfred and Augustine Combaz of Norwood. ***Combaz Lake*** (64 O/6), southeast of Nueltin Lake was named after him in 1975.

Comeau, Private **Joseph Gaston** of St. Boniface (H 616843). Maisonneuve Regiment. He died 30 July 1945 and is commemorated at the Groesbeek Canadian War Cemetery in Holland. ***Comeau Lake*** (54 E/12), southeast of North Knife Lake was named after him in 1964.

Comeault, Lieutenant **Jules A.** of Letellier. Royal 22nd Regiment. He died 2 December 1944 at the age of 22 and is commemorated at Ravenna War Cemetery in Italy. He was the son of Edmond and Rose Comeault of Letellier. A former teacher at Saint Boniface College wrote (Bernier 1999):

> This very bright lad arrived on the scene of Saint Boniface College in 1935. Almost immediately he exhibited his true aptitudes by becoming a formidable opponent for his fellow citizen of Letellier, Jacques Bruyere, who was head of his class. Jules Comeault had been well prepared by a classical education by the Letellier parish priest, Father J.-P. Gagnon, who had sensed in this young boy a brilliant mind and had coached him in the elements of Latin.
>
> For some time thereafter, we lost sight of him until he emerged in Italy with the noted Canadian "Van Doos" Regiment. With his comrades in arms, Jules attended an audience with Pope Pius XII, a momentous occasion which led him to report to his parents the thrill of this unique encounter that left him more deeply steeped in his true Catholic faith. The letter he wrote them was couched in such expressive terms and revealing such sincere feelings of faith and hope that the parish priest at Letellier saw fit to read it as his address to the congregation one Sunday morning in the very church where Jules himself had been baptized.
>
> This was the most moving missive that the young officer had hoped to deliver himself when, very young, he had aspired to the priesthood. Later, it would also become the most eloquent parliamentary discourse that this future Catholic deputy would deliver. This precious document is now in the hands of his family, who have proudly and generously shared it with his parish and his College.

His father received a letter from the Chaplain of the "Van Doos:"

> Dear Mr. Comeault: You have surely by now been officially advised of the painful news of the death of your son, Lieutenant Jules-Armand Comeault, felled on the field of honour. As Chaplain of the Royal "Van Doos," I offer you my sincere condolences.
>
> Mortally wounded while leading his men to an eventually victorious advance on the night of December 2nd, Lt. Comeault was removed to the Field First Aid Station some 200 yards back from where he had been stricken by enemy fire. I was there with the medical officers at the time and I can assure you that every resource was put to use to save your son's life. He had already by then become very weak and was immediately given a blood transfusion with some slight hope of saving him. He recognized me and kept communicating verbally with me until he lost consciousness. I had recently been inducted into his regiment and had several times seen your son attending Mass and receiving the Sacraments. As a matter of fact, on the eve of this fateful attack, he had encouraged the men in his detachment to receive the Sacraments as he was doing. He was well prepared for this eventuality and he died as a good Christian and a brave soldier.
>
> "If I die," he said to me as I held him during the blood transfusion, "say a Mass for me and please write home on my behalf." He also spoke of a nun, one of his sisters I believe, and requested that I tell her he had died "a good Catholic soldier." Subsequently, I proceeded to administer the Last Rites of the Church. He prayed devoutly with me as the field doctors treated him continuously with all the resources at their command. Your son became unconscious and at 1 AM, passed away peacefully as I cradled his head between my hands.
>
> As I had promised, I said a Mass for him in the combat zone. In writing to you to express my deepest sympathy, I want to offer you the comfort of knowing that Jules' memory is real and vivid amongst us. Young and full of energy as he was, he had friends in the entire Regiment, particularly with the soldiers under his command. These men really loved him and would have followed wherever he led. Now they miss him keenly. To this I was witness when the shock of the news of his death reached them; they truly bemoaned the loss of their "good little Lieutenant Comeault." These men join me, Mr. Comeault, to offer you and you family our heartfelt condolences. Devotedly yours, Captain A. Tessier, OMI (31 December 1944).
>
> Lieutenant Jules Comeault spoke Italian and was aware of the military situation in Italy. After the liberation of Rome and before resuming the attack toward Bologna, his Regiment visited the Vatican and Pope Pius XII. After his visit, Jules commented, "It was worthwhile to cross Hitler's line to witness such an event." In the group were Band members of the Infantry Corps who played their own music. Soldier Billy Oryschik of Emerson, Manitoba said he never played his clarinet better. "I must have played like an angel to maintain the atmosphere of this grand demonstration," he said (*Southeast Journal* 10 November 1999).

Comeault Creek (54 B/16), which flows northeast into Kaskattama River was named after him in 1964.

Compton, Pilot Officer **Orville F.** of Winnipeg (J 88175). No. 429 Squadron. He was presumed dead 13 August 1944 at the age of 22 and is commemorated at the Hanover War Cemetery in Germany. He had been "officially" missing for two years after his 33rd mission. He was the son of Francis R. and Honor C. Compton of Winnipeg. According to his niece (28 July 1997):

> Orville attended Elim Chapel Sunday School, Winnipeg from three years to fifteen years. There is a plaque on the wall in the church with other members who were killed in the Second World War. Orville worked in drugstore delivery etc. Orville was an instructor in the Winnipeg Roller Rink till he signed up for service. I understand that they had a plaque after the war in the Roller Rink. Orville had a boat-tail Roadster Essex – he drove it everywhere.

Compton Lake (63 N/1), southeast of Sherridon was named after him in 1970.

Comstock, Private **William D.** of Winnipeg (H 1413). Seaforth Highlanders of Canada. He died 2 September 1944 and is commemorated at Gradara War Cemetery in Italy. ***Comstock Lake*** (52 L/6), east of Lac du Bonnet was named after him in 1973.

Condie, Signalman **James R.** of Winnipeg (V 9836). HMCS *Spikenard*. The *Spikenard* was torpedoed and sunk by U-136 south of Iceland, while escorting Convoy SC.67; there were only eight survivors. Signalman Condie died 10 February 1942 at the age of 20 and is commemorated at the Halifax Memorial. He was the son of John and Ruth Condie of Winnipeg. ***Condie Lake*** (64 I/1), east of North Knife Lake was named after him in 1957.

Condie, Pilot Officer **Robert C. "Bert"** of Crystal City (J 2929). No. 7 Service Flying Training School. He died 2 April 1941 at the age of 24 and is commemorated at Crystal City Cemetery, Manitoba. He was the son of Robert and Helen Condie and was survived by his wife Erma Condie of Crystal City and their unborn son. A contemporary newspaper reported that:

> Constable R. Condie received the shocking news on April 2 that his son, Pilot Officer Bert Condie, had been killed in a plane crash which also took the life of a brother officer. Mr. Condie and Mrs. H. C. Colter, mother of Mrs. Bert Condie, took the train at Brandon that night for MacLeod, where also Mr. and Mrs. Chas. McLaren of Golden Prairie, Saskatchewan, Mr. and Mrs. Earl G. McKitrick of Lethbridge and Physical Instructor Harold Gilbert, RCAF of Calgary were gathered, the latter arriving by plane soon after the accident.
>
> Mr. Condie returned on Saturday via Brandon while the body of his son was given military escort via Winnipeg over CPR lines. A few minutes before the arrival of the train here, on the day of burial, a telegram was received from the hospital at McLeod, announcing the birth of a son to Mrs. Condie and the late Pilot Officer R. C. Condie, RCAF (*Crystal City Courier* 10 April 1941).

Condie Island (63 I/7) in Lawford Lake was named after him in 1995.

Conley, Pilot Officer **Walter F.** of Norwood (J 95141). No. 429 Squadron. He died 5 November 1945 at the age of 25 and is commemorated at Harrogate (Stonefall) Cemetery Yorkshire, England. He was the son of Mr. and Mrs. Walter Conley and was survived by his wife of 11 months Megan Conley of Brynteg, Denbighshire, Wales. She still lives in Wales and writes (28 March 1998):

> … I have remarried (to an ex-RAF aircrew member) and both belong to the Croydon and Sutton Branch (UK) of the Canadian Veterans Association, so [we] keep in touch with current happenings in Canada. My late husband and members of his crew are buried at Stonefall Commonwealth Cemetery. We are able to visit regularly to pay our respects to some 600 RCAF aircrew who are buried there in beautifully tended grounds, overlooked by Canadian maples that were planted some 50 years ago.

Conley Lake (64 G/5), south of Big Sand Lake was named after him in 1994.

Connolly, Company Sergeant Major **Bert** of Winnipeg (H 19261). Queen's Own Cameron Highlanders. He died 19 August 1942 and is commemorated at Dieppe Canadian War Cemetery, France. ***Connolly Lake*** (64 O/9), north of Nejanilini Lake was named after him in 1975.

Conrad, Regimental Sergeant Major (Warrant Officer 1) **George A.** of Winnipeg (P 10257). Royal Canadian Engineers. A veteran of the First World War, he died 7 July 1942 at the age of 48 and is commemorated at Brookside Cemetery in Winnipeg. He was survived by his wife Mary E. Conrad of St. James. ***Conrad Lake*** (64 C/9), northeast of Eden Lake was named after him in 1995.

Conway, Lance Corporal **Victor G. H.** of Winnipeg (H 26732). Fort Garry Horse. He died 6 June 1944 at the age of 29 and is commemorated at Beny-sur-Mer Canadian War Cemetery, France. He was survived by his mother Elizabeth Hawkins of Winnipeg. ***Conway Lake*** (63 I/7), east of Molson Lake was named after him in 1973.

Cook, Flight Sergeant **Alexander** of Winnipeg (R 157058). No. 103 Squadron. He died 12 June 1943 at the age of 20 and is commemorated at Raalte General Cemetery, Holland. ***Cook Rapids*** (64 B/8) in the Pecheponakun River was named after him in 1995.

Cook, Flight Lieutenant **Benjamin T.** of Glenella (19826/J 16158). No. 413 Squadron, Distinguished Flying Medal.

> This airman has participated in numerous operational sorties against enemy targets, including nearly all the most heavily defended centres in Germany and Italy. He also took part in the daylight raid on Le Creusot. Throughout, Flight Sergeant Cook has set and maintained a high standard of courage and navigational skill which has been a fine example to others (DFM Citation 1944).

He was awarded the DFM while serving with No. 97 Squadron, RAF. He died 18 October 1947 while on a photographic survey flight from Penticton to Calgary. The wreckage was found five years later and the federal government erected a cairn at the site. He was 27 years of age and is commemorated at the Ottawa Memorial. He was the son of William Jeff and Edith Cook of Arden and was survived by his wife Gladys M. Cook of Penticton, British Columbia. ***Benjamin Cook Lake*** (64 P/1), south of Caribou Lake was named after him in 1996.

Cook, Flying Officer **Lorne F.** of Kenton (J 24619). No. 23 Operational Training Unit, RCAF. He died 24 November 1943 at the age of 22 and is commemorated at Pershore Cemetery, Worcestershire, England. He was the son of Fred and Naomi Cook of Kenton, Manitoba. ***Cook Peninsula*** (64 O/8) on Martin Moore Lake was named after him in 1995.

Cook, Ordinary Seaman **Thomas A.** of Winnipeg (V 24177). HMCS *Barrie*. He died 26 June 1941 at the age of 25 and is commemorated at St. Mary's Cemetery in Winnipeg. He was the son of Ernest E. and Mary A. Cook of Winnipeg. He was described as "a star Winnipeg rugby player" and was expected to be "one of the future Bomber greats." A newspaper account indicated that:

> ... [he] served but one year with the team after graduating from Greg Kabat's St. Paul's College Crusaders. Tommy gave up a good position to join the Royal Canadian Navy. In [June] of this year he gave his life for his country in a naval accident off Halifax. May he rest in peace (n.d.).

Cook Creek (64 N/7), which flows northwest into Tatowaycho Lake was named after him in 1995.

Cook, Flying Officer **Thomas J.** of Winnipeg (C 3010). No. 3 Wireless School, RCAF. He died 8 July 1941 at the age of 45 and is commemorated at Brookside Cemetery in Winnipeg. He was the youngest of the nine children of John W. and Mary Cook of Marmora, Ontario and was survived by his wife Cassie Cook (née Passco) of Winnipeg and their three daughters. He attended the University of Ottawa from 1913 to 1915, intending to enter the priesthood, but joined the Royal Flying Corps (later Royal Air Force) in Toronto in 1917. According to his daughter (2 April 1995):

Following his discharge, Dad moved to Moose Jaw, Saskatchewan where a brother was living and he and Mother were married there on August 2, 1923. Three daughters were raised in a warm and loving home. We learned to ice skate on a rink Dad built in our back yard as we pushed Mother's kitchen chairs in front of us.

We left Moose Jaw to come to Winnipeg about 1934. Dad was a travelling candy salesman at that time and sometimes, though not often, we all went with him. Living in a tent was an adventure. The Depression was really making itself felt, and the spring of 1939 found us living in two 9 x 9 tents in the old Granite Tourist Camp on Osborne Street as Dad switched from selling candy to selling cars for Breen Motors. Not too profitable as people were not buying either item as the Second World War inched closer. That was also the summer of the first Royal Visit of the King and Queen which was very exciting for us, as an uncle from Moose Jaw would be travelling with them.

Around 1938 we had left the Catholic Church and joined with Mother at St. Stephen's Broadway United. Here Mother and Dad became Sunday School Teachers and leaders in Young People's programs. I've heard it said that a convert often makes the strongest member and I think this was true for Dad. He loved the Church.

In November of 1940, Dad joined the RCAF earning the rank of Flying Officer. He did some training in Edmonton and Montreal before being posted to No. 3 Wireless here in Winnipeg. It was wonderful to have our Dad back home. Little did we know that six short months later he would die when his plane crashed just outside Winnipeg. We, his daughters were just 15, 13 and 11. Mother of course was devastated, but gamely took on the task of raising her three girls alone while returning to the work force for the first time since she and Dad were married.

I asked an aunt one time to tell me a little about my Dad, and she told me "Tom always loved to tell a good story." It is sad not to know the personality of one's Father. To us, he was loving, a gentle disciplinarian who always told us when he was leaving to "look after Mother." To quote from a letter from A. B. Shearer, Air Commodore of No. 2 Training Command to Mother 14 July 1941 following Dad's crash: "He was conscientious and willing in all his work, a man whose religion was very real to him, and his tolerance and understanding of others won for him the respect and admiration of the Officers of his Squadron."

Thomas Cook Lake (53 M/7), north of Knee Lake was named after him in 1995.

Cook, Lance Corporal **Wilfred M. B.** of Grand Rapids (H 101836). Calgary Highlanders, Military Medal. He died 29 August 1944 at the age of 20 and is commemorated at Bretteville-sur-Laize Canadian War Cemetery, France. He was the son of Solomon and Annie Cook of Grand Rapids. ***Cook River*** (53 N/4), which flows north into Gods River was named after him in 1995.

Cooke, Gunner **Hesketh** of Winnipeg (H 69899). Royal Canadian Artillery. He died 2 December 1942 at the age of 21 and is commemorated at Elmwood Cemetery in Winnipeg. He was the son of Christopher and Kate Cooke of Winnipeg. ***Cooke Esker*** (64 P/11), northwest of Caribou Lake was named after him in 1996.

Cooke, Craftsman **John C.** of Steep Rock (H 63634). Royal Canadian Electrical and Mechanical Engineers. He died 12 January 1945 at the age of 26 and is commemorated at the Groesbeek Canadian War Cemetery in Holland. He was survived by his mother Rose Cooke and by his wife Esther Cooke of Steep Rock. ***Cooke Hill*** (64 N/4), west of Quasso Lake was named after him in 1995.

Cooke, Private **Joseph** of Whitemouth (H 8017). Essex Scottish Regiment. He died 16 October 1944 at the age of 20 and is commemorated at Bergen-op-Zoom Cemetery, Holland. He was the son of Joseph and Elizabeth Cooke of Kenora. ***Joseph Cooke Peninsula*** (54 D/15) on Cygnet Lake was named after him in 1996.

Cooke, Private **Marshall** of Winnipeg (H 18544). Queen's Own Cameron Highlanders. He died 3 March 1945 at the age of 30 and is commemorated at the Groesbeek Canadian War Cemetery in Holland. He was survived by his wife Helen Cooke of Winnipeg and his two young daughters, Janice and Bernice. His daughter writes (26 November 2001):

Marshall "Peter" Cooke was born in Hartlepool, County Durham, England on September 25, 1914. He was one of six children. Before the war, Peter was employed at the *Winnipeg Free Press* as a Linotype Operator. He was a volunteer for the Red Cross Society and also belonged to St. John's Ambulance. He loved the outdoors and enjoyed activities such as hunting, horseback riding and canoeing.

Sisters Ricky and Joyce were teenagers when he went overseas and recall Peter as an easygoing man who was well liked and had a good sense of humour. They said he was very proud of his family and considered him to be a true family man. We will remember him.

Cooke Point (64 O/4) on Doig Lake was named after him in 1995.

Cooney, Private **Albert William** of Winnipeg (H 26013). Queen's Own Cameron Highlanders. He died 3 March 1945 at the age of 30 and is commemorated at the Groesbeek Canadian War Cemetery in Holland. He was one of the 11 children of Edward and Kristjana Cooney and was survived by his wife Jean Cooney of Winnipeg and their daughter. Private Cooney was wounded while a member of the Fort Garry Horse. Upon recovery, he returned to the fighting with the Camerons since his regiment had already gone on. ***Cooney Lake*** (63 I/16), east of Cross Lake was named after him in 1973.

Cooper, Flight Sergeant **Hector T. M.** of Plumas (R 80234). No. 101 Squadron. He died 3 April 1942 at the age of 20 and is commemorated at Lorient (Kerentrech) Communal Cemetery, France. He was the son of the Reverend Joseph E. and Mary Cooper of Oakville. ***Cooper Bay*** (64 P/12) in Nejanilini Lake was named after him in 1989.

Cooper, Private **Kenneth S.** of Mather (H 77726). Winnipeg Grenadiers. He died 21 December 1941 at the age of 20 and is commemorated at the Sai Wan Memorial in Hong Kong. He was the son of Thomas and Ethel Cooper of Mather. ***Cooper Island*** (64 N/8) in Shannon Lake was named after him in 1995.

Cooper, Trooper **Warren M.** of Winnipeg (H 101181). Calgary Tank Regiment. He died 2 October 1943 and is commemorated at Bari War Cemetery in Italy. ***Cooper Point*** (53 L/15) on Seller Lake was named after him in 1995.

Cope, Lieutenant **Alfred R.** of Winnipeg (CDN 480). South Lancashire Regiment. He died 18 September 1944 at the age of 20 and is commemorated at the Groesbeek Canadian War Cemetery in Holland. He was the son of William and Helen Cope of Winnipeg. ***Cope Island*** (53 L/4) in Nikik Lake was named after him in 1995.

Cope, Corporal **Francis P. F.** of Winnipeg (H 2985). 1st Canadian Special Services Battalion. He died 10 July 1944 at the age of 26 and is commemorated at the Holten Canadian War Cemetery in Holland. He was the son of Gilbert and Hilda Cope of Winnipeg. ***Cope Lake*** (63 K/13), southwest of Embury Lake was named after him in 1984.

Copeland, Rifleman **Edward J.** of Winnipeg (H 20177). Royal Winnipeg Rifles. He died 6 June 1944 and is commemorated at Beny-sur-Mer Canadian War Cemetery, France. ***Copeland Lake*** (64 O/2), southwest of Munroe Lake was named after him in 1975.

Coppins, Corporal **Frederick G.** (1987) 8th Battalion (Manitoba Regiment), Victoria Cross.

> On 9 August 1918 at Hackett Woods, near Amiens, France, Corporal Coppins' platoon came unexpectedly under fire of numerous machine-guns. It was not possible to advance or retire and there was no cover. Corporal Coppins, calling on four men to follow him, leapt forward in the face of intense machine-gun fire and rushed straight for the guns. The four men with him were killed and he was wounded, but going on alone, he killed the operator of the first gun and three of the crew and took four prisoners. Despite his wound, he then continued with his platoon to the final objective (Buzzell 1997).

He was 28 years of age at the time. This native of London, England enlisted at Valcartier, Quebec in September, 1914. He died in 1963 at the age of 73. ***Coppins Lake*** (63 P/7), east of Cauchon Lake was named after him in 2001.

Corbett, Pilot Officer **Ernest Clayton** of Winnipeg (J 6408). No. 60 Squadron. He died 17 May 1942 at the age of 21 and is commemorated at the Singapore Memorial. ***Corbett Lake*** (64 O/11), southeast of Nueltin Lake was named after him in 1961.

Corkett, Captain **George R. "Geordie"** of Winnipeg. Princess Patricia's Canadian Light Infantry. He died 22 September 1944 at the age of 28 and is commemorated at Coriano Ridge War Cemetery in Italy. He was the son of Colonel Cecil and Madeline G. Corkett and was survived by his wife Aileen M. D. Corkett (née Alley) and their unborn daughter. Captain Corkett graduated from Royal Military College in June, 1939 and accordingly was quickly shipped overseas and was given a number of diverse assignments.

> In December, 1942, familiar faces began disappearing in ones and twos from every Canadian officers' and sergeants' mess in the United Kingdom. Only those who packed their kitbags and disappeared knew why, or where they were going. It was four months after the disastrous Dieppe raid. Canadian soldiers had been slaughtered by the score in that half-day battle. They had fought bravely, but they lacked battle experience and paid the price for this deficiency. Every few weeks until March, 1943, the mini-drafts moved off. By then, 201 officers and 147 senior NCOs had silently departed from the Canadian hutted camps in southern England. They had been appointed to Q List. Their immediate destination was the Non-Effective Transit Depot (NETD) on Thursley Common; their final destination, a secret.
>
> NETD was the purgatory of the Canadian Army Overseas. People were usually posted to NETD for return to Canada with blots on their escutcheons. Drunks, black marketeers, chronic offenders against military discipline, misfits and crooks made up the main populations of NETD. That is why one Q List officer was greeted by an acquaintance with: "Good God Harry. You here? What did you do?" NETD was a cesspool of lost hopes and broken men, a stopping place on the way to perhaps dishonourable discharge, cashiering or at very least, 'adjutant-general's disposal' – an ominous and uncertain fate.
>
> But Q List did not contain those who had fallen afoul of military or civil authority. It was a select list, supposedly the best of the bunch. It just happened, so far as the Canadian Army Overseas was concerned, that they were temporarily 'non-effectives.' Hence, NETD was the only place they could be borne on ration strength and administered. In their case, it was a stepping stone to high adventure. They had been chosen to join the British 1st Army in North Africa to learn the trade of war by leading and commanding men in the heat of battle against Rommel and his *Afrikakorps*, then to return to lead their own men later in the war.
>
> Who were these chosen men? One was Major Frankie White, a curly-haired extrovert from Canada's Strathcona Horse. He became acting second-in-command of the swanky 17th/21st Lancers; their battle honours included Balaclava where they led the Charge of the Light Brigade, and Omdurman where Winston Churchill galloped against the [Dervishes] at the head of their troops. Another was George Corkett, a Princess Patricia's Captain. Posted to the Coldstream Guards, he was severely wounded in the head by enemy air action while on the way to join that regiment (Galloway 1979).

His obituary read in part:

> Member of a widely known military family, his wife is the former Aileen Maud Darracott Alley, daughter of Colonel and Mrs. H. R. Alley of Toronto. Mrs. Corkett resides in England. The young couple married in 1939 on the eve of his embarkation for England. His wife went overseas [with the] Voluntary Aid Detachment of the Red Cross [in 1940]. Assigned to a hospital in Basingstoke, Mrs. Corkett arrived to find her husband among casualties from the African Campaign. He had been assigned command of a company of the 2nd Coldstream Guards. Later he returned to the Princess Patricia's Canadian Light Infantry, his original regiment, for service in Italy (n.d.).

Corkett Lake (64 K/5), northeast of Reindeer Lake was named after him in 1972.

Cormack, Flying Officer **Douglas W. W.** of East Kildonan (J 12034). No. 45 Delivery Group. He died 13 October 1943 at the age of 21 and is commemorated at the Ottawa Memorial. ***Cormack Lake*** (64 O/11), east of Nueltin Lake was named after him in 1975.

Cormack, Flight Sergeant **John** of East Kildonan (R 59294). No. 405 Squadron. He died 15 April 1942 at the age of 22 and is commemorated at Rheinberg War Cemetery in Germany. He was the son of Frederick and Nora Cormack of Winnipeg. ***Cormack Island*** (63 N/13) in Sisipuk Lake was named after him in 1995.

Cormier, Private **Omer** of La Salle (H 16449). Princess Patricia's Canadian Light Infantry. He died 8 August 1944 at the age of 22 and is commemorated at Florence War Cemetery, Italy. ***Cormier Lake*** (64 F/2), southeast of Wells Lake was named after him in 1994.

Cornwall, Flying Officer **James Raymond** of Minnedosa (J 13599). No. 207 Squadron. He died 29 April 1943 at the age of 22 and is commemorated at the Runnymede Memorial in Surrey, England. He was the only son of Francis W. and Wilhelmina Cornwall of Minnedosa. He was patrolling the Bay of Biscay for submarines but failed to return. ***Cornwall Island*** (64 J/12) in Jamie Lake was named after him in 1989.

Cornwell, Private **Charles W.** of Winnipeg (H 103170). Canadian Scottish Regiment. He died 9 June 1944 at the age of 21 and is commemorated at Beny-sur-Mer Canadian War Cemetery, France. He was the son of Walter and Florence Cornwell of St. James. ***Cornwell Lake*** (63 O/5), southeast of Highrock Lake was named after him in 1973.

Cory, Private **Willis L.** of Winnipeg (H 17010). Princess Patricia's Canadian Light Infantry. He died 31 August 1944 at the age of 41 and is commemorated at Montecchio War Cemetery in Italy. He was the son of William and Ann Cory and was survived by his wife Annie L. Cory of Winnipeg. ***Cory Lake*** (64 K/7), northeast of Reindeer Lake was named after him in 1972.

Cosens, Private **William John** of Fisherton (H 59678). Algonquin Regiment. He died 27 October 1944 at the age of 22 and is commemorated at the Adegem Canadian War Cemetery in Belgium. He was survived by his wife Maud Cosens (née Gander) of Lewes, Sussex, England. According to his sister-in-law (1 May 1997):

> John liked carpenter work, plus wood carving and hunting deer and game birds. He carved a rolling pin and a wooden mixing spoon from a tree from his parents' farm which his mother used until she had a stroke at the age of 92 years.

Cosens Lake (64 G/15), northwest of Trout Lake was named after him in 1995.

Costello, Flying Officer **George A.** "Pug" of Stonewall (J 39820). No. 442 Squadron. He died 28 October 1944 at the age of 20 and is commemorated at the Reichswald Forest War Cemetery in Germany. He had been forced to bail out of his aircraft when it was hit by flak near Hennewig, Germany. The Nazi party member who shot him in the back while taking him prisoner was hanged following a war crimes trial in the post-war cleanup of Germany. He was one of the seven children of Valentine de Lacy and Marie Costello of Stonewall and was survived by his fiancée Mary Jepson of Toronto.

> Forty-two years ago, Stonewall's George Costello had just completed all his required flying missions. But seeing his buddy, Frosty, with one more to fly, the 20 year-old Spitfire pilot decided he'd wait for his friend and fly another mission himself. That final flight over Belgium turned out to be the fatal one for the Stonewall flyer. [He] was recruited while studying Grade 12 at Stonewall Collegiate. A long part of his service was spent on the Aleutian Islands protecting the West Coast. Later he was part of the first wing to land in Normandy and establish an Allied air force base in France (Reimer 1986).

His sisters remember that George was always called Pug at home, a nickname given by his paternal grandfather. A bright, hardworking student, he participated in all sports and excelled in gymnastics. He is also remembered by his wingman, Frosty Young, an American in the RCAF who risked staying over him until he was safely on the ground. His sister adds (7 January 2002):

> As Frosty Young returned to Canada, he was met in Halifax by his wife from Vancouver and as they returned home by train, they took time to visit with our parents as they passed through Winnipeg – a kindly, thoughtful thing to do. Frosty lives in Chico, California and keeps in touch with our family. He has been to visit twice in the last few years. We also meet him at the Canadian Fighter Pilots Reunion in Comox every other year.

Costello Island (64 G/12) in Big Sand Lake was named after him in 1986.

Côté, Private **Joe G.** of Winnipeg (H 27010). Canadian Provost Corps. He died 19 March 1941 at the age of 26 and is commemorated at Brookwood Military Cemetery in Surrey, England. He was the son of Frank and Frances Côté and was survived by his wife Norma Côté of Guelph. ***Côté Island*** (63 P/5) in Paint Lake was named after him in 1996.

Coté, Private **Paul A.** of Fisher Branch (H 1577). Royal Canadian Regiment. He died 6 September 1944 at the age of 25 and is commemorated at Coriano Ridge War Cemetery in Italy. He was the son of Alphonse and Malvina Coté (née Lambert) of Fort Frances, Ontario. His nephew's wife writes (15 February 1995): "While he lived in Fisher Branch he had made an attempt to farm – without much success. His brother Wilfred and sister May Ann resided in Fisher Branch. He then returned to Ontario where he joined the army." ***Coté Lake*** (64 N/16), west of Nueltin Lake was named after him in 1972.

Cottick, Private **Ernest A.** of Fishing River (H 17571). Lake Superior Regiment. He died 19 February 1945 at the age of 24 and is commemorated at the Groesbeek Canadian War Cemetery in Holland. He was the son of Mr. and Mrs. E. Cottick of Fishing River. ***Cottick Lake*** (64 O/10), west of Nejanilini Lake was named after him in 1975.

Cottier, Pilot Officer **Thomas G.** of Winnipeg (J 4885). No. 419 Squadron. He died 16 January 1942 at the age of 27 and is commemorated at Barton-upon-Humber New Cemetery in Lincolnshire, England. He was the son of Thomas E. and Sadie Cottier and was survived by his uncle Mr. G. F. Cottier of Bride, Isle of Man. ***Cottier Lake*** (63 P/15), southeast of Witchai Lake was named after him in 1996.

Cottingham, Lieutenant **David C.** of Swan River. Loyal Edmonton Regiment. He died 22 December 1943 at the age of 23 and is commemorated at the Moro River Canadian War Cemetery in Italy. He was the son of Edward and Anne Cottingham of Swan River and was survived by his wife Franklina S. Cottingham (née Pattison) and their daughter. His brother writes (4 October 2001):

> My brother was an officer in the Loyal Edmonton Regiment, an outfit that was badly decimated in what many consider the Canadian Army's Stalingrad. It was furious house-to-house fighting of the very worst kind. As my brother was leading his platoon from house to house, he threw a grenade into the adjoining house through a hole in the wall. The explosion brought most of what remained of the house down upon him. When his men managed to dig him out of the rubble, he was dead.

Cottingham Lake (62 N/15), southeast of Swan River was named after him in 1973.

Cotton, Pilot Officer **David N.** of St. Vital (J 87645). No. 427 Squadron. He died 29 June 1944 at the age of 22 and is commemorated at Juvincourt-et-Damary Churchyard in Aisne, France. He was the son of Sydney and Ada Cotton of Esquimalt, British Columbia. ***Cotton Creek*** (64 J/13), which flows north and west into Nicklin Lake was named after him in 1975.

Couling, Private **Kenneth W.** of Lauder (H 103188). Canadian Scottish Regiment. He died 15 September 1944 at the age of 22 and is commemorated at the Calais Canadian War Cemetery in France. He was the son of Harold and Louise Couling of Lauder and was survived by his wife Grace Couling and their son. His sister writes (13 December 2001):

> Kenneth ... was born at Lauder, Manitoba October 21, 1921 and got his schooling at Truro and Berry Hill school districts. He enjoyed farm life, friends, family, sports, dancing and all community affairs. He enlisted in the PPCLI in Winnipeg, November 1942, took his training at Fort Osborne and Shilo before going overseas in May, 1943.
>
> While in England, he was transferred to the Canadian Scottish Regiment. He saw duty in France and was wounded August 14, 1944. He returned to his platoon for active duty and then was killed in the line of duty a month later at Ambleteuse during the assault on Boulogne. He was buried at Herenval, France and later his body was transferred to the

Calais Canadian War Cemetery. Left to mourn Kenneth was his father, his brother Leonard, his wife Grace and their son Larry of Brandon and sister Audrey Bowen.

Couling Lake (64 K/7), northeast of Reindeer Lake was named after him in 1972.

Coull, Corporal **Leslie H.** (H 40974). Royal Winnipeg Rifles. He died 7 June 1944 and is commemorated at Beny-sur-Mer Canadian War Cemetery, France. ***Coull Lake*** (63 N/5), east of Kipahigan Lake was named after him in 1995.

Coull, Chief Radio Officer **William D.** of MacGregor. SS *Empire Hail*, Merchant Navy. He died 23 February 1942 and is commemorated at the Halifax Memorial. ***Coull Island*** (63 P/15) in Goose Hunting Lake was named after him in 1996.

Coulombe, Trooper **Albert A.** of Bénard (H 100590). Calgary Tank Regiment. He died 12 May 1944 at the age of 21 and is commemorated at the Cassino War Cemetery in Italy. He was the son of Oscar and Gertrude Coulombe of Bénard. ***Coulombe Lake*** (52 L/3), northeast of Brereton Lake was named after him in 1973.

Coulombe, Private **Edmond** of Pine Falls (H 615676). Mont Royal Fusiliers. He died 30 March 1945 at the age of 22 and is commemorated at the Groesbeek Canadian War Cemetery in Holland. He was the son of Ulric and Yvonne Coulombe of Pine Falls. ***Edmond Coulombe Lake*** (64 K/10), northeast of Reindeer Lake was named after him in 1984.

Coulson, Flying Officer **Robert F.** of Winnipeg (J 9324). No. 420 Squadron. He died 24 July 1943 at the age of 27 and is commemorated at the Malta Memorial. He was the son of Willard and Helen Coulson and was survived by his wife Phyllis Coulson of Winnipeg. ***Coulson Island*** (64 C/5) in Kamuchawie Lake was named after him in 1995.

Coulson, Pilot Officer **Ward D.** of Winnipeg (J 95264). No. 435 Squadron. He died 12 February 1945 at the age of 25 and is commemorated at the Singapore Memorial. He was the son of Willard and Helen Coulson and was survived by his wife Catherine Coulson of Norwood. ***Coulson Lake*** (63 N/1), northeast of Sherridon was named after him in 1970.

Coulson, Squadron Leader **William G. A.** of Winnipeg (29237). No. 220 Squadron, RAF. He died 15 August 1940 at the age of 37 and is commemorated at Elmwood Cemetery in Winnipeg. He was the son of William A. and Sarah Coulson of Winnipeg. According to a newspaper account:

"Bill" Coulson was born at Ottawa ... but had spent much of his life in Winnipeg. He flew with the Northwest Aeromarine at Winnipeg in late 1929 and early in 1930 went to England and joined the Royal Air Force. In 1936 the young man left the RAF to become a pilot for Imperial Airways. For two years he flew the big Imperial passenger planes back and forth over Europe, then in early 1938 he returned to Canada to become one of the pilots of Trans-Canada Airlines when the Trans-continental air service was first put into operation in this country. As a reserve Pilot Officer of the Royal Air Force he was called up for service when the war started and returned to England (n.d.).

His nephew adds that his aircraft hit a barrage balloon cable during the Battle of Britain. ***Coulson Bay*** (63 I/2) on the south shore of Molson Lake was named after him in 1988.

Coulter, Lance Corporal **John S.** of Selkirk (H 19389). Queen's Own Cameron Highlanders. He died 19 August 1942 and is commemorated at Brookwood Military Cemetery in Surrey, England. He was the son of Hugh A. and Edna Coulter (née Stewart) of Russell and the brother of Sergeant Robert L. Coulter (next entry). He was survived by his wife Ruth Coulter (née Hembroff) and their young daughter. He was severely wounded at Dieppe and died shortly thereafter in England. ***Coulter Island*** (64 C/8) in Granville Lake was named after him in 1995.

Coulter, Sergeant **Robert Leslie** of Winnipeg (R 157337). No. 115 Squadron. He died 25 March 1944 at the age of 34 and is commemorated at Gorssel General Cemetery in Holland. He was the son of Hugh and Edna Coulter (née Stewart) of Russell and the brother of Lance Corporal John S. Coulter (previous entry). His cousin writes (5 May 1997):

Leslie was born ... in the Rural Municipality of Silver Creek (near Russell, Manitoba). He attended Stratford rural school No. 814 for a very short time prior to the whole family of four boys moving to Vancouver. In 1923, Mr. Coulter died and Mrs. Coulter with Leslie, John, Harold and Wilson returned to make their home in Russell, Manitoba. There the boys continued their education, spending the summer holidays at the farm of Uncle Bob and Uncle Gav. Leslie worked for a few years in McDonald's Shoe Store in Winnipeg prior to enlisting.

Coulter Bay (53 L/6) in Joint Lake was named after him in 1995.

Counsell, Major **Ronald R.** of Winnipeg. Queen's Own Cameron Highlanders, Military Cross. He died 11 September 1944 at the age of 29 and is commemorated at the Adegem Canadian War Cemetery in Belgium. He was the son of Ronald and Margaret Counsell of Winnipeg. ***Counsell Lake*** (64 C/11), northwest of Granville Lake was named after him in 1947.

Courage, Sergeant **William R.** of Winnipeg (R 251499). No. 22 Elementary Flying Training School. He died 27 November 1944 at the age of 21 and is commemorated at Brookwood Military Cemetery in Surrey, England. He was the son of Nelson and Ada Courage and was survived by his wife Doris Courage of Winnipeg. ***Courage Lake*** (64 O/16), northwest of Nejanilini Lake was named after him in 1975.

Cousins, Private **Sidney J. "Jack"** of Bagot (H 16736). Princess Patricia's Canadian Light Infantry. He died 22 July 1943 at the age of 23 and is commemorated at Agira Canadian War Cemetery in Sicily. He was the son of William J. and Mabel E. Cousins of Bagot. ***Cousins Lake*** (64 B/15), east of Southern Indian Lake was named after him in 1948.

Coutts, Flight Sergeant **Lorne R.** of Newdale (R 123973). No. 428 Squadron. He died 27 April 1943 at the age of 23 and is commemorated at the Reichswald Forest War Cemetery in Germany. He was the son of Robert L. M. and S. Alma Coutts and was survived by his sister Marguerite E. Coutts of Newdale. She recalls (16 November 2001):

Lorne farmed and ran a trucking business with his father before joining the RCAF to train as a pilot. He went overseas and was attached to the RAF. Their Wellington aircraft crashed during a bombing trip over Dueilman, Germany. All crew members were lost except the bombardier who bailed out and was a prisoner of war for the duration. Lorne was the typical big brother "tease" but always there to help when one needed him.

Coutts Lake (64 P/15), northeast of Nejanilini Lake was named after him in 1974.

Coutts, Flying Officer **Russell Murray** of Neepawa (J 22152). No. 183 Squadron. He died 27 March 1944 at the age of 27 and is commemorated at Brookwood Military Cemetery in Surrey, England. He was the son of John and Lavina Coutts of Neepawa. His sister writes (23 October 2001):

> My brother Murray was a fun-loving guy. He was popular with his peers as well as with older people. He strove to please the customers in Fenwick's General Store in Neepawa where he worked. He was a member of the Lion's Club and was an avid curler. He was thrilled to be accepted into the RCAF in 1941. He seemed to love every minute of his training and made many good friends. According to letters received from friends after his death, he was always a practical joker amongst his air force buddies.
>
> He felt privileged to fly Mustangs and later joined the No. 183 Typhoon Squadron in England. During a training session, he was unable to bring his Typhoon out of a spin and crashed to his death. We were informed that this was a definite threat with this particular fighter plane. I firmly believe that although his death was untimely, he probably would have chosen to go doing what he really loved.

Coutts Island (64 F/2) in Wells Lake was named after him in 1994.

Couture, Private **Ernest V. J.** of St. Boniface (H 600257). Royal Canadian Army Service Corps. He died 31 July 1944 at the age of 22 and is commemorated at St. Boniface Cemetery. He was survived by his mother Mrs. A. Couture of St. Boniface, by his wife Jean M. Couture of Nanaimo, British Columbia and their son. ***Couture Island*** (64 F/6) in Wells Lake was named after him in 1994.

Couture, Private **Gaston J.** of St. Boniface (H 14575). Queen's Own Cameron Highlanders. He died 27 April 1945 and is commemorated at the Holten Canadian War Cemetery in Holland. He was the fifth of the 12 children of Pierre A. and Laura Couture (née Lamoureux). His sister recalls (2 April 2002):

> Gaston was the second oldest of five brothers and seven sisters. He was educated in Meyronne Separate School in Saskatchewan and furthered his education at the College Mathieu in Gravelbourg. He was very active in sports, won awards in jumping, running, swimming, baseball and loved to play his violin.
>
> He was an outdoor person. I remember him raising this baby coyote after its mother had been killed. He'd feed it and made a place on the farm for him. The howling at night frightened us youngest very much.
>
> Boy of many talents, he worked at the grocery store and at the drug store. He also baked his own bread for sale and made ice cream to sell at the bakery shop. He was a Jack of all Trades – a salesman for the Singer Sewing Machine Company and for Wearever Pots and Pans. At this time, he was working out of Moose Jaw, Saskatchewan. By the year 1942, the family had moved to Winnipeg and Dad was working for the CNR.
>
> Gaston enlisted in Winnipeg and was first posted to the barracks in Winnipeg for his training. From there, he was sent to Dundurn, Saskatchewan for more training. He then came home on a leave; three days later he was called to go to Nova Scotia and from there was sent overseas.
>
> It came to our attention that due to the inspiration of Lieutenant General G. C. Simonds, Commander of the 2nd Canadian Army, that the Holten area might be a suitable place for a Canadian War Cemetery. The soldiers who were killed in the spring of 1945 during the liberation of the eastern and northern parts of the Netherlands could be buried here. Every year on May 4th, a Service of Remembrance is held in this cemetery. On Christmas Eve, the school children put candles on the graves of all Canadians buried there. The more than 1500 candles give the place a fairy-like look.
>
> My younger sister, her husband and their three children visited the grave in 1977. My son, his wife and I went to Holten to visit in 1990. We signed the register, laid flowers on the grave and left a Canadian flag. This really helped to bring closure for all of us.

Couture Bay (53 M/1) in Semmens Lake was named after him in 1995.

Couture, Flight Lieutenant **Joseph A. L.** of St. Vital (J 20061). No. 578 Squadron. He died 21 July 1944 at the age of 23 and is commemorated at Uden War Cemetery, Holland. He was the son of Arthur and Albina Couture of Seattle, Washington. ***Couture Lake*** (53 M/6), southeast of Gillam was named after him in 1966.

Cowan, Lieutenant **John T.** of Winnipeg. 14th Canadian Hussars. He died 21 September 1944 at the age of 28 and is commemorated at the Holten Canadian War Cemetery in Holland. He was the son of the late Thomas H. and Robena Cowan of Winnipeg. A recent graduate of the University of Manitoba, he was in command of the first troop to enter Dieppe on 2 September 1944. ***Cowan Point*** (63 I/1) on Little Bolton Lake was named after him in 1995.

Cowan, Flight Sergeant **Robert J. A.** of Minnedosa (R 95345). No. 51 Squadron. He died 9 January 1943 at the age of 20 and is commemorated at the Runnymede Memorial in Surrey, England. He was the son of Frederick W. and Mabel B. Cowan of Minnedosa. According to his sister (14 November 2001):

> Bob was my younger brother and grew up with our brother Peter and me on the family farm north of Minnedosa. Bob attended Minnedosa schools and was very active in Scouting. I remember his hitchhiking to Winnipeg to receive his King's Scout award from King George VI in 1939. We were always very proud of him. I remember he was very active and full of fun. I particularly remember his fall off the barn roof, his love of horseback riding, his sense of humour and his honourable and fair nature. His memory has been an inspiration to his niece and especially to his great niece and great nephew who have also been very involved in Guiding and Scouting and have received the Canada Cord and the Chief Scout's award.

Cowan Island (64 O/9) in Gayoway Lake was named after him in 1995.

Cowie, Pilot Officer **Douglas G.** of Tuxedo (J 10626). No. 31 Recce School, RCAF. He died 7 August 1942 at the age of 22 and is commemorated at St. James Cemetery in Winnipeg. He was the son of George H. and Hannah T. Cowie of Tuxedo. ***Cowie Island*** (64 O/5) in Alyward Lake was named after him in 1995.

Cowie, Private **Robert** of Winnipeg (H 17169). Princess Patricia's Canadian Light Infantry. He died 13 December 1943 at the age of 27 and is commemorated at the Moro River Canadian War Cemetery in Italy. He was the son of George and Annie Cowie and was survived by his wife Phyllis Cowie of Peacehaven, Sussex, England. ***Cowie Lake*** (63 J/16), east of Setting Lake was named after him in 1972.

Cox, Sergeant **Harry K.** of Union Point (R 95453). No. 19 Elementary Flying Training School. He died 2 July 1942 at the age of 19 and is commemorated at Union Point United Church Cemetery, Manitoba. He was the son of James and Anne Cox of Union Point. ***Cox Point*** (53 L/6) on Touchwood Lake was named after him in 1996.

Cox, Stores Petty Officer **Henry J. M.** of Norwood (V 67950). HMCS *Alberni*. The *Alberni* was torpedoed and sunk by U-480, southeast of the Isle of Wight; 59 of her ship's company were lost. Petty Officer Cox died 21 August 1944 at the age of 30 and is commemorated at the Halifax Memorial. He was the son of Gerard and Cornelia Cox of Norwood and was survived by his wife Flora Cox of St. Vital. ***Cox Bay*** (64 G/12) on the south shore of Big Sand Lake was named after him in 1986.

Cox, Private **Jeffrey H.** of Swan River (H 103668). Argyle and Sutherland Highlanders of Canada. He died 12 August 1944 at the age of 30 and is commemorated at Bayeux War Cemetery, Calvados, France. He was the son of Harry and Alice Cox of Swan River. ***Cox Lake*** (62 N/15), southeast of Swan River was named after him in 1973.

Cox, Private **Leonard F.** of Winnipeg (H 1772). Queen's Own Cameron Highlanders. He died 13 September 1944 and is commemorated at the Adegem Canadian War Cemetery in Belgium. He was the son of Charlie and Charlotte Cox and was survived by his wife Ernestine Cox of St. Louis, Saskatchewan. ***Cox Rapids*** (64 P/5) in the Wolverine River was named after him in 1995.

Cox, Private **Melvin C.** of Winnipeg (H 23470). Lake Superior Regiment. He died 13 April 1945 at the age of 18 and is commemorated at the Holten Canadian War Cemetery in Holland. He was the son of Charles and Gladys Cox (née Kew) of St. James and was survived by his brothers Harold and Murray and sister Helen. ***Cox Peninsula*** (64 I/2) on Halldorson Lake was named after him in 1995.

Cox, Warrant Officer 1 **Stanley James** of Beresford (R 119595). No. 435 Squadron. He was presumed dead in Burma (Myanmar) 21 June 1945 at the age of 22 and is commemorated at Taukkyan War Cemetery, Myanmar. He was the son of Stanley and Mary Cox and was survived by his wife Barbara E. Cox (née Hinds) of London, England and their son. In 1990, a local hunter retrieved a watch inscribed with the name of one of the crewmen and five years later, a team was dispatched to recover the remains.

"We just want them to find enough remains for a proper burial," said Jack Barker, husband of Cox's only surviving sibling, May, age 80. The family has been waiting since November of last year when they first learned wreckage had been found. Barker knows the odds are slim that anything will be found. But just something, anything, to give Cox a proper burial would help end the heartache for May, who now suffers from Alzheimer's. "How do you think it feels when your brother has been missing for 50 years?" asked Barker, his eyes swelling with tears. "They were just like twins – they did everything together." (Purdy 1996).

It was Day 2 of the three-day recovery mission when wireless operator Stanley James Cox of Beresford, Manitoba sprang to life from the rich soil of the Burmese jungle. A watch, given to the Canadian airman on Boxing Day 1943, was the first personal belonging disgorged by the steaming jungle at the site of a downed Second World War supply plane. Moments later, a human bone appeared. "The watch just popped out," Master Corporal Steve Cruickshank of Fredericton said yesterday in Ottawa. "It was kind of a mixed emotional time." Cruickshank was one of 14 Canadians – 10 of them soldiers – who excavated the long-lost crash site last week in dense jungle so humid they could see their breath.

On June 21, 1945, Cox and all five others aboard were lost when their C-47 Dakota crashed in a storm during a supply mission. The wreck was first identified after a Burmese hunter emerged from the remote valley in 1990 carrying the inscribed watch of William Kyle of Perth, Ontario, the lost plane's co-pilot. Yesterday, Cruickshank was among the subdued military contingent recounting another mission – and another timepiece – they'll never forget. Cox's watch, inscribed with the words: Jim, from Mom, 26-12-1943 [his 21st birthday] brought the lost airmen of RCAF 435 Squadron to life. "You're happy to find something – you're working so hard, it's so hot, it's a little frustrating. I'm not an archaeologist," said Cruickshank, a signalman. "But when (a superior) read the inscription … it just became tangible. We've all got little children and it was from this guy's mom." Cox, the only married crew member, had sired a son Phillip David Cox only six months before his death. It was Cox's second air disaster of the war, having crashed and been interned in neutral Portugal in 1943. He was repatriated to England in 1944 just weeks after his mother had inscribed the Christmas watch. "The last day we had a ceremony on site and, well, there were 10 men there wearing the uniform who were all heads down trying to hide the tears," said Field (Cheadle 1996).

Phillip Cox (now Magee) was able to travel to Burma for the official ceremony:

Phillip Magee never knew his father, but that didn't stop him from making the long journey to see him buried in the land where he died. Cox, a 22 year-old wireless operator, died before he had a chance to see his son. Magee, who lives in Bakersfield, California, said the loss of his father struck him most emotionally on the plane coming to Burma, when he watched a segment of a documentary on the recovery of the remains. A kilted bagpiper, a trumpeter and a federal minister joined relatives, soldiers and veterans for the ceremony around a joint coffin and six headstones.

The lush green sward and foliage of Taukkyan, the Commonwealth War Graves cemetery 35 kilometres north of Rangoon is a far cry from the wintry home towns of the six airmen and their mourners. But familiar music filled the air during the ceremony: *Amazing Grace, Piper's Lament, Reveille, Last Post* played by Pipe Master Hugh MacPherson of Prince Albert, Saskatchewan and Warrant Officer Daniel Kean, the trumpeter from Peterborough, Ontario. "These six young men found themselves together at a moment in time that ended their lives and forever changed those of families and friends," said Lawrence MacAulay, secretary of state for veteran affairs. His voice sometimes cracking, MacAulay said there is a duty for Canadians to remember. He called the six airmen "every mother's son, every father's pride and joy, a hero to a brother or sister." "Magnificent" was how next-of-kin and veterans described the service (Altstedter 1997).

Cox Creek (64 A/16), which flows northeast into Assaikwatamo River was named after him in 1995.

Crabb, Flight Sergeant **William T.** of Souris (R 71397). No. 37 Squadron. He was killed in action 8 September 1942 while returning from a raid on Tobruk, Libya. He was 29 years of age and is commemorated at the Alamein Memorial in Egypt. Flight Sergeant Crabb was the son of Alfred and Gertrude Crabb and was survived by his wife D. Crabb and their young son Peter William of Souris. ***Crabb Lake*** (64 J/16), north of Tadoule Lake was named after him in 1975.

Crabtree, Lieutenant **John C.** of Winnipeg. Princess Patricia's Canadian Light Infantry. He died 23 May 1944 at the age of 24 and is commemorated at the Cassino War Cemetery in Italy. He was the son of George and Margaret Crabtree of Regina. ***Crabtree Lake*** (64 N/12), southwest of Nueltin Lake was named after him in 1972.

Craib, Corporal **Alexander W.** of Roblin (H 59003). Canadian Postal Corps. He died 24 November 1941 at the age of 47 and is commemorated at Brookside Cemetery in Winnipeg. This native of Keith, Scotland was the son of Mr. and Mrs. William Craib of Dufftown, Banffshire, Scotland and was survived by his wife Williamina Craib of Roblin and their son Corporal Thomas Craib (next entry). Craib Lake (64 P/1), southeast of Nejanilini Lake was named after him in 1974.

Craib, Corporal **Thomas** of Roblin (H 59048). Canadian Provost Corps. He died 3 January 1944 at the age of 22 and is commemorated at Brookwood Military Cemetery in Surrey, England. This native of Alves, Scotland was the son of Alexander W. (previous entry) and Williamina Craib of Winnipeg. ***Craib Island*** (64 N/11) in Jonasson Lake was named after him in 1995.

Craig, Telegraphist **Daniel A.** of Dauphin (V 24299). HMCS *Levis*. The *Levis* was torpedoed by U-74 120 miles off Cape Farewell, Greenland resulting in 18 lives lost. Telegraphist Craig died 19 September 1941 at the age of 28 and is commemorated at the Halifax Memorial. He was the only son of Daniel and Margaret Craig and was survived by his wife Vernice Craig of Dauphin. According to his niece (7 December 2001):

> Dan was the first casualty of World War II from Dauphin, Manitoba. News of his death arrived at the home of his parents in Dauphin on the wedding day of his only sister, Inez. As a young person, Dan is remembered for his outgoing personality, his mischievous character, his love of sports and his fondness for small children. His sister, Inez, kept his memory alive through the years, by telling stories of his fun-loving nature as a young man growing up in Dauphin. Dan is remembered often by his sister and his nieces for the sacrifice he made in World War II.

Craig Point (64 N/3) on Agerbak Lake was named after him in 1995.

Craig, Sergeant **Harold T. L.** of Brandon (L 59740). Royal Canadian Electrical and Mechanical Engineers. He died 11 September 1944 at the age of 30 and is commemorated at the Adegem Canadian War Cemetery in Belgium. He was the son of James and Edna Craig and was survived by his wife Marion Craig of Brandon and their daughter. ***Craig Island*** (64 H/6) in Northern Indian Lake was named after him in 1995.

Craig, Flying Officer **James** of Winnipeg (J 21466). No. 97 Squadron, Distinguished Flying Cross.

> This officer has taken part in numerous sorties against German targets including nine against Berlin. An excellent air bomber, by his determination in the face of heavy enemy opposition he has played no small part in the successful completion of many missions. On several occasions, his aircraft has been damaged by fire from the enemy defences (DFC Citation 1944).

He died 31 March 1944 at the age of 22 and is commemorated at the Hanover War Cemetery in Germany. The youngest son of John and Elizabeth Craig of Winnipeg, he was born in Ballymena, Ireland and had come to Canada with them at the age of 11. According to his brother who was stationed nearby, Flying Officer Craig had been given the option of doing two tours of 20 operations each with a month between tours or 30 operations straight. He chose the latter and was killed on his 29th mission. ***Craig Lake*** (64 C/12), east of Reindeer Lake was named after him in 1947.

Craig, Flight Lieutenant **John Ian** of Selkirk (J 16026). No. 407 Squadron. He died 27 September 1943 at the age of 20 and is commemorated at the Runnymede Memorial in Surrey, England. He was survived by his wife Bella Craig of Calgary. His widow relates that he had served several tours of duty and was due to come home on leave. Instead he flew for another airman who was ill; all crew were lost and never found. ***Craig Bay*** (63 I/7) in Molson Lake was named after him in 1995.

Craig, Gunner **Robert A.** of Roblin (H 800175). Royal Canadian Artillery. He died 21 November 1950 at the age of 22 and is commemorated at Foam Lake Cemetery, Saskatchewan. He was one of the five children of William and Ethel Craig of Foam Lake. His brother recalls (7 November 2001):

> Bob was too young to serve in World War II and felt somewhat cheated by that. When the Korean Special Force was formed, he saw it as his chance to serve his country in the same way his Father had done in World War I and two brothers in World War II. He was accepted into the Royal Canadian Horse Artillery and took his basic training at Camp Shilo.
>
> Bob was a native of Foam Lake, Saskatchewan. After his schooling, he decided to go to Flin Flon to work and enjoy the great outdoor activities it offered. He was an ardent fisherman and thrilled at landing a big pike or pickerel. It's fitting that a lake has been named in his honour. He spent many a winter night at the curling club and helped newcomers to the game in any way he could. Bob had time for anyone who wanted to get something off their chest and did all he could to help them through any problems they had. He had an uncanny knack for making friends.
>
> Bob's untimely and tragic death at age 22 cut short his desire to serve his fellow man. His spirit has been an inspiration to those who survived him and the lake that bears his name is a permanent reminder of his dedication to his friends and country.

He was a victim of the Canoe River train crash which claimed the lives of a number of servicemen:

> At 1035 hours, a train carrying troops of the 2nd Regiment, Royal Canadian Horse Artillery met another train, headed from Vancouver to Montreal in a head-on collision just east of Canoe River, BC. The engines and leading cars of both trains were derailed, but there were no passenger casualties on the civilian train. The leading cars of the military train were thrown down an embankment and demolished. Survivors pitched in at once to rescue their comrades, while Dr. P. J. E. Kimmett of Edson, Alberta and a civilian nurse volunteered their services. It was not until hours later that a specially organized train carrying much needed medical supplies, two doctors and eight nurses arrived. The injured were returned to Edmonton, Alberta and the uninjured to Wainwright, Alberta. Recovery of bodies was made extremely difficult; an oil fire rendered many of them unidentifiable. The final toll of dead was 17, including four soldiers whose bodies were never recovered. The remains of the other 13 were flown to the homes of their next-of-kin by RCAF aircraft or sent by train in the case of those who lived nearby (Korea Veterans Association of Canada 1999).

Robert Craig Lake (63 I/9), northeast of Lawford Lake was named after this Korean War casualty in 1998.

Craik, Warrant Officer 2 **Murray C.** of Baldur (R 110957). No. 467 Australia Squadron. He died 23 September 1943 at the age of 23 and is commemorated at Durnbach War Cemetery, Bavaria, Germany. He was the only son of George and Elsie Craik of Baldur. ***Craik Lake*** (63 N/2), south of Burntwood Lake was named after him in 1972.

Cram, Pilot Officer **John S.** of Morden (J 27370). No. 45 Delivery Group, RCAF. He died 7 September 1943 at the age of 26 and is commemorated at Christiansborg War Cemetery, Ghana. He was the son of William and Maddie Cram of Morden. ***Cram Lake*** (64 H/16), southeast of North Knife Lake was named after him in 1963.

Cramer, Trooper **David C.** of Winnipeg (H 26813). Fort Garry Horse. He died 6 July 1944 at the age of 23 and is commemorated at Beny-sur-Mer Canadian War Cemetery, France. He was the son of Oscar and Becky Cramer of Winnipeg. ***Cramer Island*** (64 N/13) in Tanuck Lake was named after him in 1995.

Crandell, Signalman **Augustus H. L.** of Winnipeg (H 68915). Royal Canadian Corps of Signals. He died 9 July 1943 and is commemorated at Brookwood Military Cemetery in Surrey, England. ***Crandell Lake*** (64 H/10), southeast of Buckland Lake was named after him in 1995.

Crane, Flight Sergeant **Beverley D.** of Winnipeg (R 100225). No. 20 Squadron. He died 29 September 1942 at the age of 21 and is commemorated at Lossiemouth Burial Ground Moray, Scotland. He was the son of Edward and Elizabeth Crane of Saskatoon. ***Crane Point*** (64 K/9) on Cantlon Lake was named after him in 1995.

Crane, Private **Gordon R.** of Makaroff (H 17224). Princess Patricia's Canadian Light Infantry. He died 24 January 1944 at the age of 23 and is commemorated at the Moro River Canadian War Cemetery in Italy. He was the son of Thomas and Maude Crane of Portage la Prairie. ***Crane Island*** (64 O/12) in Shannon Lake was named after him in 1995.

Crate, Bombardier **Leonard V.** of Koostatak (H 101037). Royal Canadian Artillery. He died 5 January 1945 at the age of 27 and is commemorated at Koostatak United Church Cemetery, Manitoba. He was the son of James and Margaret Crate of Koostatak. ***Crate Lake*** (64 J/7), southwest of Tadoule Lake was named after him in 1975.

Crave, Private **Donald L.** of Lillesve (H 102761). Perth Regiment. He died 10 December 1944 at the age of 22 and is commemorated at Ravenna War Cemetery in Italy. He was the son of Gilbert and Olga Crave of Lillesve. According to his sister, he was born at Bromhead, Saskatchewan and attended school there, completing Grade 8. At the age of 15, the family moved to Manitoba's Interlake where he enlisted at the age of 20. ***Crave Lake*** (54 M/14), northeast of Long Lake was named after him in 1984.

Crawford, Trooper **George B.** of Killarney, Manitoba (H 374). Lord Strathcona's Horse. He died 26 October 1946 at the age of 33 and is commemorated at the Holten Canadian War Cemetery in Holland. He was the son of William and Mary Crawford of Killarney. His brother indicates that he was serving with the occupation army at the time of his death. ***Crawford Rapids*** (64 P/3) in the Big Spruce River was named after him in 1995.

Crawford, Private **Gordon W.** of Dauphin (H 101552). Lanark and Renfrew Scottish Regiment. He died 5 September 1944 at the age of 22 and is commemorated at Gradara War Cemetery in Italy. He was the son of William and Winnifred Crawford and the brother of Flying Officer Kenneth Crawford (see entry). His sister, Florence writes (26 November 2001):

> Gordon is remembered for his strong Christian faith. He had a quiet, but genuine personality. He was loved by his fiancée Edna Hodges for 50 years. She never did marry and his picture remained on her bedside table until her death. Gordon was able to meet up with his brother Ken once during the war in England and it would be the last time they would see each other. Losing her only two sons, my mother grieved and cried almost every day of her life. His niece Lynda, has proudly framed their medals and has come to know them by reading their letters home from overseas. Missed by his sister Florence Arndt of Roblin, Manitoba, and his niece Lynda of Roblin, Manitoba.

Crawford Bay (64 P/12), on the north shore of Nejanilini Lake was named after him in 1985.

Crawford, Lance Corporal **Henry L.** of Erinview (H 63032). Canadian Provost Corps. He died 10 August 1943 at the age of 20 and is commemorated at Brookwood Military Cemetery in Surrey, England. He was the son of Garnet and Amelia Crawford of Erinview. ***Crawford Point*** (64 H/13) on Wishart Lake was named after him in 1995.

Crawford, Flying Officer **Kenneth** of Dauphin (J 25081). No. 432 Squadron. He died 3 January 1944 at the age of 19 and is commemorated at the Berlin 1939 - 1945 War Cemetery in Brandenburg, Germany. He was the son of William and Winnifred Crawford and the brother of Private Gordon W. Crawford (see entry). His sister Florence writes (26 November 2001):

> When the military recruiters came to the high school, Kenny was one of the first to sign up, even though he was only 17 years old. He had a vibrant, outgoing personality, always seeking adventure, and quickly rose through the military ranks. His brother Gordon, was also killed several months later, and their pictures remained on my Mother's bureau until her death. She was very proud of their medals, and showed them to every visitor to our house. Missed by his sister Florence Arndt of Roblin, and through pictures and stories, also by his niece Lynda of Roblin.

Crawford Island (64 P/12) in Nejanilini Lake was named after him in 1985.

Crawford, Flying Officer **William G.** of Lena (J 23127). No. 622 Squadron. He died 1 June 1944 at the age of 21 and is commemorated at Marissel French National Cemetery, Oise, France. He and his entire crew were lost during night operations near Trappes, France. His brother recalls (9 November 2001):

> Bill was very enthusiastic about everything he undertook. He took up fiddling at a young age and pursued this with great zeal and gusto. Our first radio was a small crystal set with one earphone and he would listen intently for hours if necessary to hear his favourite music from Nashville or wherever he could tune in some fiddling music. After working for various farmers in the district, he went to Winnipeg and worked at Canada Packers for two years before joining up in 1941. After two tours of duty with an RAF squadron (Lancasters), they were shot down about 30 miles south of Beauvais, France. The plane went down with a full load of bombs and only the tail gunner got out. Bill along with the rest of the crew are buried in a French Military Cemetery in the village of Marissel which is a suburb of Beauvais, France.

Crawford Peninsula (64 N/13) on Hasbala Lake was named after him in 1995.

Creba, Flying Officer **John F.** of Winnipeg (J 24044). No. 427 Squadron. He died 15 March 1944 at the age of 28 and is commemorated at Durnbach War Cemetery in Bavaria, Germany. He was survived by his mother Margaret Creba (née Gilchrist), a brother Glen and sister Wilma. His cousin writes (13 February 1996):

> Jack received his early education in Maple Creek, Saskatchewan and then attended the University of Manitoba after his mother, Mrs. Margaret Creba moved to Winnipeg following the death of her husband in 1931. Jack graduated with a Bachelor of Science degree (Agriculture) in 1938. He was Class Valedictorian. Always active in sports, he was a member of the YMCA. His interest in others is reflected by his membership with a then very well known popular young men's group called the Actimist Club. It had been organized by Stanley Jones, a prominent, respected businessman and it was an outstanding success. Although the club rooms and the club itself were in Westminster United Church, it was strictly an interdenominational organization. Jack was also a member of Westminster Church. His contribution to this group was recognized as he was elected its president. Jack was a personable young man, liked and respected by his peers. After casual employment, he joined the RCAF in 1941 as an Aircraftman, but received his commission prior to overseas service.

Creba Lake (64 N/9), southwest of Nueltin Lake was named after him in 1972.

Creber, Leading Aircraftman **Robert T.** of Newdale (R 162342). No. 11 Service Flying Training School. He died 5 July 1943 at the age of 22 and is commemorated at Newdale Cemetery, Manitoba. He was the eldest son of Thomas and Martha Creber of Newdale. His brother recalls (27 November 2001):

> Bob was born March 6, 1921 on the family farm at Newdale, Manitoba. His siblings were Fred (born 1923), Jack (born 1925) and Mary (born 1927). He received all his formal education at Newdale Consolidated School. Bob's cousin, Wilma who was an only child at that time, claimed that Bob and Fred were just like brothers to her. They always took her with them to dances and social outings.
>
> When Bob was very young, he received a model airplane for Christmas one year. His interest in airplanes and his mechanical ability prompted him to join the Air Force in Winnipeg in 1942. He began basic training at No. 2 Manning Depot, Brandon and furthered his training at Regina and Yorkton, Saskatchewan. Bob lost his life during flight training at Yorkton.

Creber Lake (64 P/16), northeast of Nejanilini Lake was named after him in 1974.

Creighton, Pilot Officer **John T.** of Winnipeg (J 9368). No. 31 Operational Training Unit, RCAF. He died 7 June 1942 at the age of 21 and is commemorated at the Elmwood Cemetery in Winnipeg. He was the son of William and Florence Creighton and was survived by his wife Joan Creighton of Winnipeg. ***Creighton Lake*** (64 O/8), southwest of Nejanilini Lake was named after him in 1975.

Cremeens, Rifleman **John W.** of Winnipeg (K 48936). Queen's Own Rifles of Canada. He died 9 September 1944 at the age of 17 and is commemorated at Calais Canadian War Cemetery, Pas de Calais, France. He was the son of H. O. and Norah Cremeens of Kenora, Ontario. ***Cremeens Lake*** (64 C/12), east of Reindeer Lake was named after him in 1972.

Creswell, Flight Sergeant **Ralph N. A.** of Winnipeg (R 59557). No. 22 Squadron. He died 31 May 1942 at the age of 22 and is commemorated at the Runnymede Memorial in Surrey, England. ***Creswell Lake*** (54 E/1), northeast of Split Lake was named after him in 1985.

Croll, Warrant Officer 2 **Arthur L.** of Nesbitt (R 104520). No. 38 Squadron. He died 12 December 1942 at the age of 32 and is commemorated at the Alamein Memorial in Egypt. He was the son of David and Edith Croll and was survived by his wife Eva Croll of Malton, Ontario. ***Croll Island*** (64 P/13) in Inverarity Lake was named after him in 1995.

Croll, Flight Lieutenant **Ian B.** of Nesbitt (C 312). No. 21 Squadron. He died 15 June 1944 at the age of 34 and is commemorated at the Runnymede Memorial in Surrey, England. ***Croll Lake*** (64 O/9), southeast of Nueltin Lake was named after him in 1961.

Crompton, Private **Kenneth C.** of Brandon (SH 61667). Princess Patricia's Canadian Light Infantry. He died 3 May 1953 at the age of 26 and is commemorated at the United Nations Cemetery in Pusan, South Korea. He was the fifth of the eight children of John and Edith Crompton (née Purley) of Brandon and was survived by his wife Emilie Crompton of Portage la Prairie. ***Crompton Lake*** (53 N/3), south of White Goose Lake was named after this Korean War casualty in 1998.

Cronk, Warrant Officer 2 **Gavin J.** of Winnipeg (R 152808). No. 15 Squadron. He died 12 May 1944 at the age of 29 and is commemorated at Leuven Communal Cemetery, Belgium. He was the son of John and Amy Cronk and was survived by his wife Annette Cronk of Vancouver. ***Cronk Island*** (64 G/8) in Southern Indian Lake was named after him in 1975.

Crossing, Flight Sergeant **John Keith** of Winnipeg (R 95095). No. 23 Squadron. He died 26 June 1942 at the age of 22 and is commemorated at Ambt-Delden General Cemetery, Holland. He was the son of Gerald P. and Christine T. Crossing (née Mowatt) of Winnipeg and was survived by his wife of eight months Ruth Crossing (née Bailey) of Winnipeg. It was over 50 years before his wife discovered the details of what had happened to him:

> It was only a small, yellowing photograph that Jaap Hulleman, a 52 year-old accountant from Zwolle, Holland, held in his hand. But he knew that it could easily awaken memories and cause distress in some Canadian home. In his other hand he held two Canadian addresses, the end result of a search that had taken years. What should he do? His father Joop, who had taken the photograph of a dead World War II Canadian flyer, had always rejected any suggestion that he should try to track down the man's family. But his father had died in 1989 and the son had finally felt free to search. He had the addresses of the man's widow and brother, but should he risk causing upset?
>
> Jaap made up his mind. In careful English, which he hadn't used since he was at school more than 30 years ago, he composed a letter in which he made an extraordinarily generous offer. If the man's widow, or any other member of the family, wanted to come to Holland to collect the photograph, Jaap and his wife Ena would pay for the trip. He mailed the letter to the airman's brother in Montreal. Months went by and he heard nothing. Then one day in April, there was a letter with a Canadian stamp on it. "He was so excited," says Ena, "he cried."
>
> They'd known each other since she was in high school in Winnipeg. There was never really anyone else for Ruth. His only flaw was that he couldn't dance, but he soon learned. "What did you like about him?" she says. "Just about everything." Keith Crossing joined the Royal Canadian Air Force early in the war. He was presented with his wings by the Duke of Windsor, married Ruth Bailey on October 10, 1941, and went overseas, all in two hectic weeks. Ruth says she doesn't really remember

much about saying goodbye to him at the train station "except that it was terrible. I have spent a lot of time not remembering."

On the night of June 25, 1942, Keith went on his first 1000-bomber raid over Germany. A telegram arrived a few days later informing Ruth that Keith was missing. He was 22. "We never did learn much more than that," she says. Ruth stayed with a friend in Ottawa for six weeks. "I smoked my head off," she remembers. Then she made up her mind that life had to go on. She went back to Winnipeg and, like so many other young women, put on a brave face and started going down to Moore's restaurant on Portage Avenue on Saturday nights, just the way she used to.

Her in-laws wanted her to meet a young fellow named Cecil Whiteside. In 1944, Ruth married Cecil, who would eventually found the publishing house Fitzhenry and Whiteside. "He was a real gentleman," Ruth says. They had four boys and were married for 45 years. Cecil died in 1989.

After the war, Ruth learned that Keith was buried in a war cemetery at Delden, Holland, and in 1973 she visited his grave. But his death still seemed unreal. Then, last spring, after holding on to Jaap's letter for months, Keith's brother called her from Montreal, told her about it and forwarded the letter. "Right away I said, 'I think it's too late for all this,'" Ruth recalls. "And yet I had to answer the letter after he had gone to so much trouble." "Mother was very upset," says her son Grant. "She didn't want to bring up the past. Yet she loved Keith. Dad (Cecil) was Dad, but she always loved Keith. I think she still feels one day he will walk through the door."

An exchange of letters began. Jaap offered to bring Ruth the photograph. Two weeks ago, he arrived in Toronto with Ena. They talked for hours at Ruth's house in Leaside – about the past, about Jaap's long search for her, and about Keith's death.

Joop, 19 that long-ago June morning in German-occupied Holland, was on his way to fetch milk from a farm when he saw planes fighting overhead. His hobby was photography and he had his camera with him. He saw a British plane hit by a German fighter. A parachute fluttered out. To his horror, Joop saw the German pilot strafe the parachute. (Jaap has since identified the German and discovered that he was killed 14 days later). The man, his parachute ripped, plummeted to earth. By the time Joop got to him, the airman, in Canadian uniform, was dead. Joop took a photograph and copied down the flyer's name and identification number. At that point, he heard German soldiers approaching and fled. Soon after, the Germans began house-to-house searches in Delden. Joop destroyed his negatives and buried the box containing the photograph in the garden just before he was sent to Germany as a forced labourer.

After the war, Joop dug up the box and, as his son grew up, would show him the sad momento. Originally, he had written the flyer's name on the back of the print, but he had scratched it out when he buried it. Uncovering the identity of the dead Canadian seemed a daunting job. He persuaded a forensic laboratory to X-ray the picture, revealing a couple of the letters on the back, and a friend, G. H. Van Ommen, who has a museum of war relics at Delden, came up with the name, John Keith Crossing. The most disgraceful aspect of this story is that when Jaap wrote to the Canadian Legion and the Veterans Affairs Department in Ottawa, both replied that they could find no trace of John Keith Crossing. Another contact, H. J. Egberink found a woman who, as a hobby, stores the names of Canadian wartime casualties and their families in her computer. She came up with the two addresses.

When I met them, it had been an emotional week for Jaap and for Ruth, who now has the photograph. "It was such a nice thing to do," says Grant. "They will be our friends for the rest of our lives." "These people came to our country and gave their lives to liberate us," Jaap said after giving Ruth a ceremonial candle from the mayor of Delden. "I'm inclined to get upset," Ruth says, apologetically, "but it was the right thing to do. It makes such a difference when you know" (Jones 1993; Reprinted with permission, *The Toronto Star Syndicate*).

Mr. and Mrs. Hulleman subsequently made plans to return to Canada for the 50th Anniversary of VE-Day. Mrs. Whiteside writes (26 November 1994):

Keith had one brother, Kennedy, who was in the army later living in Montreal. Keith's parents … for many years had the Dominion News Agency at 229 Portage Avenue in Winnipeg. In 1946-47, his parents retired to Vancouver BC, which explains why Keith was listed as from Vancouver in the book published by the Commonwealth Air Training Plan Museum Inc.

Keith went to Isaac Brock School and Kelvin High School in Winnipeg, then worked for his uncle John D. Mowatt at the Vulcan Iron Works until he joined the RCAF. I am also enclosing a copy of the write-up Frank Jones put in the *Toronto Star* after interviewing Jaap Hulleman and me. The photo Jaap brought to me was the original – 51 years old – clear, and definitely Keith. For a number of years a Dutch woman tended Keith's grave and wrote to Keith's mother. That was the only contact we had until Jaap and his wife located me after a great deal of effort.

Crossing Lake (64 G/6), northeast of McPherson Lake was named after Flight Sergeant Crossing in 1994.

Crosswell, Flying Officer **Percy B.** of Winnipeg (J 88362). No. 429 Squadron, Mentioned in Dispatches. He died 14 April 1945 at the age of 20 and is commemorated at the Runnymede Memorial in Surrey, England. He was survived by his mother Mary Crosswell. ***Crosswell River*** (54 L/1) which flows north into the Churchill River was named after him in 1948.

Crow, Warrant Officer 1 **Robert K. "Bert"** of Winnipeg (R 124020). No. 153 Squadron. He died 16 January 1945 at the age of 34 and is commemorated at the Runnymede Memorial in Surrey, England. He was survived by his wife Beth Crow of Winnipeg. His sister recalls (6 February 1995):

As I was the youngest in our family and do not have records, I am not certain – nor is his wife, but we think [he was born] in Antler, Saskatchewan. When [he] was very young the family moved to Manitoba [and he] attended an elementary school in Winnipeg called Bannatyne. [His interests included] photography, golf, travel and snowshoeing. [He] worked for the T. Eaton Company in Winnipeg before enlisting and was transferred to Fort William, Ontario as Assistant Manager. [His] parents were pioneers who came to Canada from Scotland.

Crow Lake (64 G/14), east of Big Sand Lake was named after him in 1994.

Cruse, Flying Officer **William Lorne** of Winnipeg (J 22072). No. 78 Squadron. He died 31 March 1944 at the age of 21 and is commemorated at Maubert-Fontaine Communal Cemetery, Ardennes, France. He was the son of William A. and Hazel M. Cruse of Winnipeg. His sister writes (13 June 1997):

[He] was born at the Grace Hospital in Winnipeg. He attended Wolseley, Isaac Brock and Gordon Bell Schools. Upon graduation in 1940, he joined the RCAF and trained in Canada as a navigator and left for England shortly after where he was commissioned as a Flying Officer. He served in England until his plane was shot down over France.

Cruse Lake (64 N/5), southwest of Nueltin Lake was named after him in 1972.

Culbert, Flying Officer **Frederick C.** of Winnipeg (J 13839). No. 408 Squadron. He died 26 June 1943 at the age of 33 and is commemorated at the Reichswald Forest War Cemetery in Germany. He was the son of George Arthur and Jean Culbert and was survived by his wife Margaret Culbert of Vancouver and their son. She writes (12 November 2001):

He was brought up in Boissevain, Manitoba. He started university in the east, but when his father's business burned down, he felt he must return home. Later he served with the RCMP and we married in 1939. When he

> left for overseas, he had a two year-old son. He was very close to his crew. They called him "Pop" because he was older and a father. He grieved over the fact that the others were so young that they had not had a chance to "live."
>
> At the time of their last flight, the tail gunner was in London on leave to get married. The rest of the crew was to go on leave the next day to attend the wedding. He later wrote to tell me that he went ahead with the wedding as he knew that that is what "the boys would want me to do." He said that Marty (the pilot) had worked out a dodging system that got them out of many a tight spot and he was sure that they could have done it again. He told me later that he had nightmares about it for years.

Culbert Lake (64 O/14), southwest of Nueltin Lake was named after him in 1975.

Cullen, Flying Officer **Clifford L.** of Brandon (J 13628). No. 39 Squadron. He died 25 September 1943 at the age of 23 and is commemorated at the Malta Memorial. He was the son of Stanley and Gertrude Cullen and was survived by his wife Doreen Cullen of Brandon. ***Cullen Lake*** (64 B/5), east of Granville Lake was named after him in 1995.

Culleton, Lance Corporal **Stewart R.** of Badger (H 1713). Royal Winnipeg Rifles. He died 8 June 1944 at the age of 24 and is commemorated at Beny-sur-Mer Canadian War Cemetery, France. He was the son of Richard and Blanche Culleton and was survived by his wife Jean Culleton. Lance Corporal Culleton was "executed" while a prisoner of war after the Normandy landing. ***Culleton Lake*** (64 N/14), north of Nueltin Lake was named after him in 1972.

Cumberland, Gunner **Roy R.** of Wellwood (H 92485). Royal Canadian Artillery. He died 30 December 1941 at the age of 18 and is commemorated at Riverside Cemetery in Neepawa. He was the son of John and Rose Cumberland of Wellwood. His sister writes (24 November 1996):

> My brother Roy … was born at Wellwood, Manitoba. He didn't have any special interests. He was only 19 years of age and worked on the farm until he joined the service in September of 1941. He was only in the service from September 1941 until December 1941.

He had only just begun his training and was home on leave at the time of his death. While demonstrating a drill to his family, his rifle accidentally discharged. ***Cumberland Lake*** (64 O/3), northwest of Tadoule Lake was named after him in 1975.

Cunningham, Pilot Officer **James A.** of Winnipeg (J 92036). No. 625 Squadron. He died 1 July 1944 at the age of 29 and is commemorated at Genouilly Communal Cemetery, Cher, France. He was the son of Charles and Margaret Cunningham and was survived by his wife Helen M. Cunningham of St. Vital. ***Cunningham Island*** (64 P/3) in Ogren Lake was named after him in 1989.

Cunningham, Lieutenant **Malcolm R.** of Winnipeg. Canadian Scottish Regiment. He died 5 July 1944 at the age of 27 and is commemorated at Beny-sur-Mer Canadian War Cemetery, France. He was survived by his mother Jean E. Cunningham and by his wife Doris Cunningham of Winnipeg. ***Cunningham Lake*** (64 K/11), northeast of Reindeer Lake was named after him in 1972.

Curle, Pilot Officer **John G.** of Winnipeg (J 88045). No. 427 Squadron. He died 5 October 1944 at the age of 32 and is commemorated at the Runnymede Memorial in Surrey, England. He was the son of James and Bertha Curle of Picton, Ontario. ***Curle Lake*** (64 N/5), southwest of Nueltin Lake was named after him in 1972.

Curphey, Flying Officer **Thomas G.** of Winnipeg (J 86491). No. 50 Squadron. He died 29 July 1944 at the age of 21 and is commemorated at Durnbach War Cemetery in Bavaria, Germany. He was the son of Thomas and Eva Curphey of Winnipeg. ***Curphey Lake*** (64 N/13), west of Nueltin Lake was named after him in 1974.

Currie, Lance Corporal **Cecil Harvey** of St. Vital (H 16591). Princess Patricia's Canadian Light Infantry. He died 22 July 1943 at the age of 23 and is commemorated at Agira Canadian War Cemetery in Italy. He was the son of Herbert and Vera Currie and was survived by his wife Eileen Currie (née Sally) of Winnipeg and their son whom he never saw.

> Eileen Sally celebrated D-Day as a 21 year-old widow with a toddler in her arms. Like many girls at the start of the Second World War, Sally was caught up in a whirlwind of romance, excitement and passion. She married her high school sweetheart in Winnipeg at age 17. Six weeks later, in March, 1940, Cecil Currie went overseas with the Princess Patricia's Canadian Light Infantry. Sally, who was pregnant, never saw him again. He was killed in action in Italy in 1943. "I was young and foolish and he was good looking," says Sally, now of Ottawa. "It was the thing to do. Everyone was getting engaged or married."
>
> The few moments of happiness seized in the face of uncertainty had ended with shattered dreams. The devastating news of her 22 year-old husband came on August 7, 1943 as she was looking after her son and living with her mother. Two uniformed men knocked at the door. Her mother immediately realized their significance and screamed. Sally looked on in stunned silence as one of them read a CN telegram from Ottawa addressed to her. "Regret deeply H16591 Private Cecil Harvey Currie officially reported killed in action 22nd July 1943. Further information to follow when received."
>
> "It was just a shock," Sally remembers. "It didn't sink in for a couple of days. I was so young that it never entered my mind that he could be killed. I had nightmares that he wasn't dead. My doctor thought I was going to have a nervous breakdown." She didn't truly absorb the fact of his death until three months later, when the army sent her his personal effects. These included a [bronzed] baby shoe she had sent him. It was in his breast pocket when he was shot.
>
> "I was a widow before I'd even grown up and I was saddled with a kid," says Sally. "It wasn't easy in those days. There was no day care." She is proud that she went out right away and found work as a federal government clerk, aware that she would have to look after herself and her child. She remarried in 1958 but it didn't work out. During the war years, women learned to cope with their fear and feelings of helplessness by carrying on with daily life with a stiff upper lip (Bohuslawsky 1994).

Currie Island (63 N/10) in Flatrock Lake was named after him in 1995.

Currie, Corporal **Robert N.** of Portage la Prairie (H 20427). Queen's Own Cameron Highlanders. He died 28 April 1945 at the age of 21 and is commemorated at the Holten Canadian War Cemetery in Holland. He was the youngest son of Archibald and Gertrude Currie of Portage la Prairie. According to his sister (16 May 1996):

> He was very young – 16 years old – when he joined the army and the only things I remember him doing was playing hockey in the winter and swimming in the summer. [He] never went very high in school – Grade 6, I believe. [He] swam in Crescent Lake around Island Park in Portage (although it was against the law). He escaped Dieppe by swimming six miles to a boat in the English Channel. He learned his swimming well!

Currie Bay (64 K/9) in Singleton Lake was named after him in 1995.

Curtis, Private **Ronald C.** of Kenton (H 41069). Essex Scottish Regiment. He died 21 July 1944 at the age of 23 and is commemorated at Bretteville-sur-Laize Canadian War Cemetery Calvados, France. He was the third of the 11 children of George B. and Gertrude Curtis of Kenton. His sister writes (13 November 2001):

> He was born at Birch River, Manitoba October 27, 1920 but spent most of his growing up years at Kenton. He had the usual childhood, growing up on a farm in a large family – went to work on other farms from age 15 till he joined the Royal Winnipeg Rifles on June 20, 1940, transferring to the Essex Scottish in 1942 while in England. He was killed outside Caen. Myself along with my mother and several siblings have visited the Brettville War Cemetery in France.

Curtis Island (64 O/4) in Blackfish Lake was named after him in 1975.

Cybuilski, Rifleman **Wasyl** of Winnipeg (H 17803). Royal Winnipeg Rifles. He died 8 June 1944 and is commemorated at Beny-sur-Mer Canadian War Cemetery in Calvados, France. He was the son of Mike Cybuilski of Rembrandt, Manitoba. ***Cybuilski Lake*** (63 I/7), north of Molson Lake was named after him in 1973.

Troops of the Highland Light Infantry of Canada embarking at dawn, 6 June 1944 at Southampton, England. Courtesy of the National Archives of Canada (PA-129059).

D

Daggitt, Sergeant **Munro J.** of Winnipeg (H 24148). Royal Canadian Artillery. He died 13 November 1944 at the age of 28 and is commemorated at Ancona War Cemetery in Italy. He was the son of Reginald and Mary Daggitt and was survived by his wife Winifred Daggitt of Lynton, Devon and their young son. ***Daggitt Lake*** (64 I/13), northwest of North Knife Lake was named after him in 1974.

Daigle, Sapper **Joseph** of Winnipeg (H 3688). Royal Canadian Engineers. He died 22 July 1943 at the age of 28 and is commemorated at Agira Canadian War Cemetery in Sicily. He was the son of Hugh and Mary Daigle and was survived by his wife Doris Daigle of Oxted, Surrey, England. ***Daigle Lake*** (64 O/8), south of Nejanilini Lake was named after him in 1995.

Daly, Flying Officer **John R.** of Crystal City (J 17612). No. 417 Squadron. He died 4 July 1944 at the age of 23 and is commemorated at Ravenna War Cemetery in Italy. He was the son of R. C. and Rita Daly of Crystal City. ***Daly Lake*** (63 K/16), west of Wekusko Lake was named after him in 1973.

Daniels, Rifleman **Walter** of Grosse Isle (H 41582). Royal Winnipeg Rifles. He died 8 June 1944 and is commemorated at Beny-sur-Mer Canadian War Cemetery in Calvados, France. ***Daniels Island*** (64 I/16) in the Seal River was named after him in 1974.

Danielson, Signalman **Norman S.** of Arborg (H 30639). Royal Canadian Corps of Signals. He died 12 November 1945 at the age of 23 and is commemorated at Ardal Lutheran Cemetery in Arborg. He had hopes of continuing his education and becoming an engineer when the war was over, but died in an accident on the family farm while home on leave. He was the son of Gudjon and Una Danielson (née Gislasson) of Arborg. His sister provided the following information for his obituary (translated from Icelandic):

> Norman's personality was of a strong and masculine nature. He seemed to approach everything with a reasonable calm and placid mind and a succinct manner, while at the same time being joyful and brave. I have been informed by those who knew him well that when he was leaving to join the army, his mother was very worried, but he soothed her and reassured her that there was nothing to fear and that he would come home again safe and sound.
>
> Norman loved to read and craved knowledge; he was particular in his reading and read mostly scholarly writings, uplifting tales and books. His intention was to gain more knowledge and education as would have been done.
>
> His death caused his parents, siblings and other family members tremendous sorrow and continues to live in their memories in spite of the passing of a year. All who knew him considered him an excellent person with great hope for the future. Loved ones are filled with memories which are all they have left. Yet, at the same time there is hope for a better world in the end, when "All loved ones shall return to the loving homeland." Rest in eternal peace (S. Ólafson 1946).

Danielson Lake (64 H/11), southeast of Small Lake was named after him in 1995.

Dann, Pilot Officer **Roland E.** of Portage la Prairie (J 4327). No. 407 Squadron. He died 22 January 1942 at the age of 25 and is commemorated at North Cotes (St. Nicholas) Churchyard, Lincolnshire, England. He was the eldest son of Roland and Ellen Dann of Portage la Prairie. According to a newspaper account:

> He was recently promoted acting adjutant of the reconnaissance squadron he was with. Around Christmas, this squadron was mentioned in a dispatch from Ottawa that told of the extensive work done by the fliers. Although he was born in Saskatoon, P/O Dann received his public and high school education here. He was responsible for the founding of the well-known Portage model plane club that took many trophies in provincial contests. Prior to enlistment he was employed by Lyons Garage as a bookkeeper, was a member of study, public speaking and several young men's organizations (*Winnipeg Tribune* 26 January 1942).

Dann Lake (64 I/7), northeast of North Knife Lake was named after him in 1974.

Danyliuk, Private **William** of Ward (L 20065). Winnipeg Grenadiers. He died a prisoner of war 1 December 1943 and is commemorated at the Yokohama War Cemetery in Japan. ***Danyliuk Lake*** (64 O/10), northwest of Nejanilini Lake was named after him in 1975.

Darby, Rifleman **Donald M.** of Winnipeg (H 42390). Regina Rifle Regiment. He died 28 September 1944 at the age of 21 and is commemorated at Calais Canadian War Cemetery, Leubringhen, Pas de Calais, France. He was the son of Jack and Marian Darby of Winnipeg. ***Darby Lake*** (64 I/1), east of North Knife Lake was named after him in 1974.

d'Arcis, Lance Sergeant **Frederick L. "Dick"** of Riverton (H 1918). Highland Light Infantry of Canada. He died 11 May 1945 at the age of 34 and is commemorated at Brookwood Military Cemetery in Surrey, England. He was the son of James and Maria d'Arcis of Riverton, Manitoba. Born at Washow Bay, he had been a fisherman on Lake Winnipeg before enlisting. ***d'Arcis Lake*** (64 P/1), southeast of Nejanilini Lake was named after him in 1974.

Davey, Warrant Officer 1 **Leonard F.** of Winnipeg (R 118243). No. 82 Operational Training Unit, RCAF. He died 29 May 1944 at the age of 22 and is commemorated at Brookwood Military Cemetery in Surrey, England. He was the son of Leonard C. and Edith Davey and was survived by two sisters and his wife Muriel G. Davey of St. Vital. She writes (10 November 2001):

> As his father worked for the CPR, Frank moved frequently with his family during his brief life. Schooling was in Brandon, Calgary and Vancouver where he graduated from Lord Byng Collegiate. During two summers of his high school years, Frank worked on the *Princess Louise* cruise ship of the Princess Line that plied the coastal waters from Vancouver to Alaska. Following his graduation, he joined the RCAF.

She adds (25 March 1998):

> Following his initial training in Edmonton, he was stationed at the No. 3 Wireless School in Tuxedo/Winnipeg for several months, during which time he met me. We were married just prior to his next posting back to Edmonton, where I accompanied him for a couple of months and then to his next posting to Patricia Bay, BC for five months. I returned to my parents' home in Winnipeg when my husband was posted to England, where he was killed the following May.

His Wellington aircraft was hit by "friendly fire" while returning from a night flying exercise in England. ***Davey Point*** (64 J/12) on Clisby Lake was named after him in 1995.

Davey, Flight Sergeant **Leslie G.** of Westbourne (R 177945). No. 433 Squadron. He died 24 March 1944 and is commemorated at the Berlin 1939 - 1945 War Cemetery in Brandenburg, Germany. ***Davey Bay*** (53 L/10) in Magill Lake was named after him in 1995.

David, Lieutenant **James A. V.** of Winnipeg. Winnipeg Grenadiers. He died 21 December 1941 at the age of 25 and is commemorated at the Sai Wan Memorial in Hong Kong. He was the son of Arnold and Enid David of Winnipeg. His sister recalls (10 February 1998):

Although Jim was a lot older than me (he being the oldest in the family and I was the youngest), I remember that he worked up in Gods Lake during the Depression in the 1930s. Our father was overseas in the first World War, a lieutenant with the Winnipeg Grenadiers. Dad was badly wounded in the leg so Jim grew up knowing about the 1914 – 1918 War, though like most Veterans, Dad rarely talked about it.

Although raised in the City of Winnipeg, Jim spent a lot of time in Killarney, Manitoba. He always wanted to be a farmer and before he went into the army, he farmed land near Killarney. He had a house, made his own bread, butter etc. I remember my mother taking prepared food, baking etc. to him. Jim was a top equestrian. Though I was very young, I remember his riding in the Eaton's Santa Claus parade as a teenager in the early thirties.

He graduated from Kelvin High School and took two years at the Agricultural College, University of Manitoba. Jim joined the Cameron Highlanders in 1940. He went to Gordon Head Officer's Training and got his first pip. When he returned to Winnipeg, he was stationed at Fort Osborne Barracks but was home a fair amount. In the Spring of 1941, the Winnipeg Grenadiers were looking for recruits to go overseas. Jim transferred from the Camerons to the Grenadiers.

I well remember them marching down Portage Avenue in the fall of 1941, Jim leading a Platoon. As they went to the Pacific, we figured it had to be the Orient. Pearl Harbour happened in December, 1941. Jim was in Hong Kong and on Christmas Eve we heard on the radio that Hong Kong had fallen to the Japanese. My mother visited Hong Kong in the sixties and saw the War Memorial with Lieutenant James V. David's name on it.

David Bay (63 I/16) in Kapechekamasic Lake was named after him in 1995.

David, Rifleman **Sylvio** of Lac du Bonnet (H 21067). Royal Winnipeg Rifles. He died 9 October 1944 at the age of 27 and is commemorated at the Adegem Canadian War Cemetery in Belgium. He was the son of Pierre and Georgina David of Lac du Bonnet. In 1943, Aileen Oder of Lac du Bonnet began writing "newsletters" to local men overseas which always began "Hello Soldier." Rifleman David responded:

Dear Miss Small: Please accept my thanks for your letters which I have received regularly and enjoy so much. The scenes depicted are so vivid and refresh memories which are not forgotten and the letters are so newsy. I missed meeting you in Lac du Bonnet but that will come soon we hope. We could have a cup of tea together. Believe it or not I am now quite English as far as drinking tea goes.

Letter number four pleased me very much as I have a great weakness for poetry. I always have a book of poetry with me wherever I go. Anything from Old English such as Palgrave's to the new Canadian. Cheerio now with many thanks for cigarettes and letters. Sincerely from one over there, Sylvio David (12 March 1944).

His sister adds (15 October 2001):

Sylvio was born in Carruthers, Saskatchewan January 20th, 1917, then moved to Lac du Bonnet in 1935 where his family started a farm. When called to service, he was attending the University of Manitoba. He joined the No. 10 Camerons of Canada (AF). Shortly thereafter, he was transferred to the Rifles as a rifleman. His training was in Portage la Prairie, Shilo and Winnipeg until the 31st of May, 1942 when he was transferred to the United Kingdom. In January, 1944 he was awarded the Canadian Volunteer Service Medal and Clasp. He disembarked in France on June 13th, 1944 and was killed in action on October 9th, 1944. Later, on October 22nd, 1944, he was awarded the France and Germany Star Medal and Clasp. Throughout his short life, Sylvio was a dedicated, honest, hard working and loving person, always placing family and duties first and himself last.

David Lake (64 K/10), northeast of Reindeer Lake was named after him in 1972.

Davidson, Gunner **Bryce D.** of Winnipeg (H 102662). Royal Canadian Artillery. He died 18 August 1943 at the age of 33 and is commemorated at Brookside Cemetery in Winnipeg. He was survived by his wife Doris Davidson of Winnipeg. ***Bryce Davidson Lake*** (64 C/13), south of McMillan Lake was named after him in 1996.

Davidson, Flying Officer **Edward I.** of Winnipeg (J 16866). No. 22 Operational Training Unit, RCAF. He died 30 November 1942 at the age of 22 and is commemorated at Stratford-upon-Avon Cemetery in Warwickshire, England. He was the son of Edward and Mary Davidson of Winnipeg. ***Davidson Rapids*** (64 I/14) in the Steel River was named after him in 1995.

Davidson, Flying Officer **Haraldur J.** of Winnipeg (J 6402). No. 47 Squadron. He died 26 October 1942 at the age of 29 and is commemorated at the Alamein Memorial in Egypt. He was the son of Mr. and Mrs. Haraldur F. Davidson and was survived by his wife Bertha Davidson of Winnipeg and their daughter. Prior to enlisting, he was employed with the T. Eaton Life Insurance Company. ***Davidson Point*** (64 N/8) on Shannon Lake was named after him in 1995.

Davidson, Flight Sergeant **Roy** of Neepawa (R 91650). No. 420 Squadron. He died 21 June 1942 at the age of 25 and is commemorated at St. Michael Churchyard in Waddington, Lincolnshire, England. He was the sixth of the seven children of George and Mary Davidson (née Ingram) and was survived by his wife Arleigh Davidson (née Sewell) of Toronto. According to his nephew (21 February 1998):

He grew up in the north end of this small town, his working class background and strong Scottish pride moulding him into a conscientious, outgoing lad. In the 1930s, economic conditions dictated that Roy find employment. His mechanical aptitude and people skills gained him a job at [the] Co-op service station. Roy's care of customers was evidenced one hot, July day by his purchase of ice cream cones for twins of an impoverished mother after she had spent all her money on gasoline. Roy's concern for things mechanical caused him to write from overseas to his brother Bill, reminding him to "please see to the car as cooler weather sets in, and be sure to add #10 oil."

Roy, who completed high school at the Neepawa Collegiate in 1932, was popular with his classmates, a friendly, helpful, musical fun-filled soul. Roy's talent on the violin attracted the attention of teacher and tutor George Burnett, himself an accomplished musician. In 1928, Roy won a chair in a Winnipeg "showcase" orchestra under the direction of Graham Padwick. Orchestra members were drawn from all over the Province. Another fun-loving musician from Neepawa, a young piano player named Arleigh Sewell caught Roy's attention and the two became inseparable, finally marrying on September 26, 1940 in the All Saint's Anglican Church in Winnipeg.

Roy enlisted in the RCAF in June of that year. On September 26, 1941 (his wedding anniversary) he was posted overseas, first to a British Training Squadron, then to operations in Waddington to fly with Canadian pilot Flight Lieutenant David S. Jacobs. Flying in an older Handley-Page Hampton bomber because time didn't permit delay of operations until the arrival of the larger, faster, modern Lancaster bombers on their base, Roy and his pilot took part in the 1000-plane raids in which every old, available aircraft was used to bomb German cities. One day, taking an extra "flip" (duty assignment) for a friend, Roy drew the belly turret for a major raid on the submarine base at Emden. Both plane and crew were badly shot up, limping back to Waddington minus the landing gear. The subsequent crash landing, with Roy trapped in the damaged belly turret, cost him dearly. He was rushed to hospital where, placed under a 24-hour nursing watch, he underwent a leg amputation in a vain attempt to save his life. He died on June 21, 1942. In the hours before his death Roy, who habitually put the concerns of others before his own, expressed regret for "the trouble he was causing" them. Roy is buried in the churchyard at Waddington, a well-treed district with soft, rolling hills very similar to Neepawa. Family members had the privilege of visiting his grave in 1978. His memory is perpetuated in the family through his great-nephew, namesake Roy Davidson, born in 1961 and now an RCMP constable in BC.

His sister adds (17 March 1998):

Our Dad, George Davidson, was an engineer on [the] CNR for many years. During the war years he worked out of The Pas, Manitoba on a "mixed train," conveying tanks and war materials to Churchill. He enjoyed being in Churchill, facing the ocean, as it reminded him of his home in Scotland, facing the North Sea. He loved the northern country, but found it hard to be away from his family in Neepawa. Those stressful years and losing his son Roy, no doubt led to a heart attack and untimely death ... [in] 1946.

Davidson Bay (64 C/8) in Granville Lake was named after him in 1995.

Davidson, Private **William A.** of Winnipeg (H 20323). Queen's Own Cameron Highlanders. He died 30 April 1941 at the age of 18 and is commemorated at the Halifax Memorial. He was the son of Alexander and Amy Davidson of Winnipeg. His sister writes (18 August 1997):

I would like to state that I not only lost my brother, but he was my best friend. We were a family of four children: Margaret, Jean, Bill and myself. Bill was only 18 and he was a bearer of kindness to all. It was depression years, so money was not one of our family assets. We had more – love – our parents Amy and Alex never drank, smoked or hit us and gave us a sense of value. I was 15 when Bill was taken. At 17, I joined the army and served four years and was discharged in 1946. Now, four children, 13 grandchildren and six great-grandchildren, one who has been in the Canadian Navy for 12 years, I feel God has blessed me. The last of the Davidsons.

Davidson Island (64 H/6) in Northern Indian Lake was named after him in 1995.

Davidson, Flying Officer **William Cameron** of High Bluff (J 10328). No. 424 Squadron. He died 13 July 1943 at the age of 26 and is commemorated at the Malta Memorial. He was the only son of William and Lucy Davidson of High Bluff, Manitoba and was survived by a sister, Merele Davidson of Fort William, Ontario. A family friend recalls that by trade, he was a printer before the war. ***Davidson Peninsula*** (53 L/2) on Island Lake was named after him in 1995.

Davie, Flight Sergeant **James A.** of Winnipeg (R 180070). No. 15 Squadron. He died 4 July 1943 at the age of 28 and is commemorated at the Runnymede Memorial in Surrey, England. He was the son of James and Margaret Davie. ***Davie Lake*** (64 H/15), north of Etawney Lake was named after him in 1995.

Davies, Rifleman **John R.** of St. James (H 40987). Regina Rifle Regiment. He died 12 August 1944 at the age of 25 and is commemorated at Bretteville-sur-Laize Canadian War Cemetery in Calvados, France. He was survived by his mother Mary E. Davies and stepfather Joseph Kisslinger of Winnipeg. ***Davies Island*** (64 F/3) in Goldsand Lake was named after him in 1994.

Davies, Lance Corporal **Robert L.** of Rivers (H 7116). Queen's Own Cameron Highlanders. He died 21 July 1944 at the age of 23 and is commemorated at Bretteville-sur-Laize Canadian War Cemetery, Calvados, France. He was the son of George Llewellyn and Janet Margaret Davies of Rapid City. His sisters report that (31 October 2001):

Bob was born and raised on a farm six miles from the town of Rivers. He helped his Dad on the farm until he joined the army. We had many good times in the years prior to the war, driving the old Model T in summer and the team and sleigh in winter. We learned to skate on the frozen sloughs in the middle of plowed fields. We would walk on our blades from slough to slough. (There were no skate guards in those days). My sister Ina and I have been blessed with the opportunity to visit his grave in the beautiful, peaceful French countryside.

She adds (8 March 1996):

He started his army training at Portage la Prairie, Manitoba in 1941, and from there to Terrace and Prince Rupert, BC. Went over to England in 1943 and was stationed near Canterbury, Kent. I don't think he was in France very long before he was killed, but I don't know a date.

Davies Peninsula (53 K/10) on Little Stull Lake was named after him in 1995.

Davies, Captain **Roslyn M.** of Winnipeg. Royal Canadian Army Paymaster Corps. He died 20 December 1941 at the age of 39 and is commemorated at the Sai Wan War Cemetery in Hong Kong. He was survived by his wife Lillian D. Davies (née Dundas) and their three children. His daughter writes (13 June 1997):

[He] was born in Wales June 1, 1902. Although he went by Ross, the Welsh spelling of his name was Rhoslyn Mailon Brychan Davies. He married Lillian Dorcas Dundas in Brandon, Manitoba. They had three children. His employment record included the Royal Bank, T. Eaton Company and other financial organizations and the last seven years with the City of Winnipeg as Executive Head, Department of Public Welfare in 1938.

For a number of years, he was a member of the Grenadiers Reserve and became active with the rank of Captain at the outbreak of war. He was recalled to Ottawa in 1941 for reassignment of responsibility and became a member of the Canadian Army Pay Corps as Field Cashier and prepared to embark for Hong Kong along with other Canadian forces including the Winnipeg Grenadiers. He was recommended for promotion to the rank of Major, but due to prevailing conditions at Hong Kong, the commission never became official before he was killed.

He was a loving father and a devoted husband. My Mom and Dad wrote to each other daily and because he was killed a year before [she was notified], all her letters were returned after the war. This was a very sad experience.

Davies Point (64 G/12) on Big Sand Lake was named after him in 1995.

Davies, Able Seaman **William T.** of Brandon (4242). HMCS *Ottawa.* The *Ottawa* was escorting Convoy ON.127 in the North Atlantic when it was struck by two torpedoes from U-91; 114 of her ship's company were lost. Able Seaman Davies died 13 September 1942 at the age of 20 and is commemorated at the Halifax Memorial. He was the son of Thomas and Katherine Davies of Brandon. ***Davies Lake*** (64 N/7), southwest of Nueltin Lake was named after him in 1972.

Davis, Private **Albert H.** of Winnipeg (H 6575). Winnipeg Grenadiers. He died 19 December 1941 at the age of 38 and is commemorated at the Sai Wan Memorial in Hong Kong. He was the son of Harry and Kate Davis and was survived by his wife Violet Davis of Winnipeg and their three children. ***Davis Island*** (64 J/1) in Chipewyan Lake was named after him in 1975.

Davis, Flight Lieutenant (Reverend) **Bernard D.** of Dauphin (C 4827). Royal Canadian Air Force. He died 29 March 1944 at the age of 39 and is commemorated at Riverside Cemetery in Dauphin. He was the son of Constantine Francis and Lily M. G. Davis (née Collins) of Dauphin. He had been ordained to the priesthood at St. Mary's Cathedral, Winnipeg in 1932. ***Davis Peninsula*** (64 C/8) on Granville Lake was named after him in 1995.

Davis, Rifleman **German C.** of Melita (H 422071). Royal Winnipeg Rifles. He died 2 February 1941 at the age of 46 and is commemorated at Melita Cemetery, Manitoba. He was the son of Mr. and Mrs. S. G. Davis and was survived by his wife Mabel Davis of Melita. ***Davis Hill*** (64 C/2), south of Granville Lake was named after him in 1995.

Davis, Rifleman **Herbert L.** of Winnipeg (H 41910). Royal Winnipeg Rifles. He died 8 June 1944 at the age of 21 and is commemorated at Beny-sur-Mer Canadian War Cemetery, Reviers, Calvados, France. He was survived by his wife Jeanette Davis of Horsham, Sussex, England. ***Davis Esker*** (64 I/4), east of Ashley Lake was named after him in 1995.

Davis, Private **John J.** of Winnipeg (H 6050). Winnipeg Grenadiers. He died 1 April 1943 at the age of 41 and is commemorated at the Sai Wan War Cemetery in Hong Kong. He was the son of George and Elizabeth Davis and was survived by his wife Alice Davis of Winnipeg. ***John Davis Rapids*** (53 M/10) in the Gowan River was named after him in 1995.

Davis, Trooper **Newton R.** of Winnipeg (H 26252). Fort Garry Horse. He died 17 April 1944 at the age of 24 and is commemorated at Brookwood Military Cemetery in Surrey, England. He was the son of S. and Irene Davis of Winnipeg. ***Davis Narrows*** (53 F/13) in Angling Lake was named after him in 1995.

Davis, Pilot Officer **Robert H.** of Winnipeg (J 19412). No. 429 Squadron. He died 26 November 1943 at the age of 21 and is commemorated at Hotton War Cemetery, Hotton, Luxembourg, Belgium. He was the son of Henry and Ethel Davis of Winnipeg. ***Davis Rapids*** (64 O/7) in the Anderson River was named after him in 1995.

Dawes, Able Seaman **James C.** of Portage la Prairie (V 16586). HMCS *Valleyfield.* The *Valleyfield* was torpedoed and sunk by U-548 50 miles south of Cape Race, Newfoundland; 125 of her ship's company were lost. Able Seaman Dawes died 7 May 1944 at the age of 23 and is commemorated at the Halifax Memorial. He was the son of William C. and Laura Dawes of Portage la Prairie and was survived by his wife Jeanie Dawes (née Campbell) of Paisley, Renfrewshire, Scotland. His brother recalls (2 December 1996):

> Small for his age, Jim played regularly with his younger twin brothers and so came to be known to many as "the third twin." He spent his school years and began his working life in Portage la Prairie, but enlisted in the Royal Canadian Navy at HMCS *Griffon* in Port Arthur, Ontario (now Thunder Bay) where his older sister was living.
>
> He served in many different areas including Murmansk on the frozen north coast of the USSR and in the Mediterranean. He was injured on one of these expeditions and was sent to hospital in Scotland. While there, he met and in July of 1943 married, Jean Campbell of Paisley, Scotland. Their married life was tragically short. He had leave at the time of their wedding and another time she met him in Londonderry, Ireland for a long weekend. With the rest of the crew, he was sent to Canada to pick up a ship at the Toronto Shipyard, but as he said at the time "this leave was on the wrong side of the Atlantic." Jean remarried and had a family and when last heard from was living in the Vancouver area.
>
> ... his family received the telegram which all servicemen's families had learned to dread. Red-haired and fun-loving, it's hard to believe that this light-hearted 23 year-old would now be almost 76. "They shall grow not old as we who are left grow old" is certainly true in these cases.

Dawes Lake (64 I/13), northeast of Tadoule Lake was named after him in 1957.

Dawson, Lieutenant **Alexander F.** of St. Vital. South Saskatchewan Regiment. He died 19 August 1942 at the age of 38 and is commemorated at Calais Canadian War Cemetery, Leubringhen, Pas de Calais, France. He was the son of the late Charles and Jeanie Dawson of Portage la Prairie and was survived by his wife Margaret S. Dawson of St. Vital, their daughter Enid and son Ronald. His father had died only three weeks previously. ***Dawson Lake*** (62 P/1), west of English Lake was named after him in 1982.

Dawson, Leading Aircraftman **Harry N.** of Winnipeg (R 59332). No. 2 Service Flying Training School. He died 7 January 1941 at the age of 22 and is commemorated at St. John's Cemetery in Winnipeg. He was the son of Sidney and Ethel Dawson of St. James. ***Dawson Rapids*** (64 N/5) in the Thlewiaza River was named after him in 1995.

Dawson, Sergeant **Leon W. J.** of St. Boniface (R 147410). No. 15 Squadron. He died 12 June 1943 at the age of 20 and is commemorated at the Runnymede Memorial in Surrey, England. ***Dawson Island*** (63 N/3) in Kississing Lake was named after him in 1994.

Dawson, Company Quarter Master Sergeant **William R.** of Winnipeg (H 7077). Winnipeg Grenadiers. He died 16 August 1944 at the age of 29 and is commemorated at Brookwood Military Cemetery in Surrey, England. He was the son of William and Jane Dawson and was survived by his wife Agnes Dawson of Winnipeg. ***Dawson Peninsula*** (64 O/15) on Blevins Lake was named after him in 1995.

Day, Lance Corporal **John W.** of Neepawa (H 20486). Calgary Tank Regiment. He died 10 July 1944 at the age of 29 and is commemorated at Foiano Della Chiana War Cemetery, Italy. He was the son of Arthur and Elizabeth Day of Neepawa and husband of Betty Day (née Armstrong) of Gladstone. His wife died in childbirth in 1940 and Lance Corporal Armstrong enlisted in the army shortly thereafter.

> John trained at Winnipeg, Hamilton, and Camp Borden. He was posted overseas with the Calgary Tank Regiment of the First Armoured Car Brigade in June, 1941 and took part in the Dieppe Raid 19 August 1942. John served with this Regiment in the Sicilian and Italian campaigns. His sister Mrs. Bert Graham received word from his Commanding Officer. John was driving his Captain's [he had just assumed command of the unit] tank when they met a fierce German counter attack. A shell from an anti-tank weapon directly hit the drivers seat. John was killed instantly (Pittman n.d.).

Day Lake (52 L/14), west of Tooth Lake was named after him in 1982.

Deacon, Flight Lieutenant **Arthur Allan** of Crystal City (41346). RAF. He died 24 November 1939 at the age of 22 and is commemorated at Wallasey (Frankby) Cemetery in Cheshire, England. A former member of the RCAF, he travelled to England before the war to join the RAF and was killed in a training accident. He was the son of Colonel Edgar A. and Olive M. Deacon of Crystal City. ***Deacon Lake*** (64 I/4), northeast of Ashley Lake was named after him in 1995.

Deakin, Flying Officer **Arthur K.** of Neepawa (J 18442). No. 407 Squadron. He died 13 November 1944 at the age of 27 and is commemorated at the Runnymede Memorial in Surrey, England. He was the son of Guy and Janey Deakin of Victoria, British Columbia. In his diary, he describes Southampton in early 1942:

> I caught the 10:30 Royal Blue Coach to Southampton, which for the price of four shillings, took me through the New Forest and some pretty country, leaving me at Grove Square at about noon. I started a tour of the town on foot. The damage in some parts is colossal, and it may be an exaggeration to say one out of every four dwellings was now occupied (and this is a cross section of town). St. Mary's Church was bombed completely. The four walls and arches and altar remain. I went in, and it is sights like these that make one realize the complete devastation that has been wrought in these parts. A tombstone in the adjoining churchyard bore the date 1660, verifying antiquity of the church and parish. I walked on. The railway yards did not appear to have suffered so heavily. A great portion of the docks was not approachable. Nowhere are there windows, and in one long deserted street I saw one woman emerge from a basement. I counted ten shelters in a public park and no less than 30 barrage balloons over the town. That portion of the dock which I did not see, and which contains the southeastern bastions of the old wall (a massive stone structure which defied a French attack by gun powder – probably one of the first times it was used – as long ago as 1459) now is in hideous shambles. The wreckage has been cleared of the streets, but wrecking crews were still visible cleaning up and for blocks, hardly a building stands. One large business house, gutted by fire and with only the walls left, had rather ironically I thought, a notice over the front door which read: "To be sold or Let". It had missed the flames (8 January 1942).

Deakin Lake (53 K/4), South of Red Sucker Lake was named after him in 1995.

Dean, Pilot Officer **George "Scotty"** of Pine Falls (J 88518). No. 18 Squadron. He died 7 February 1944 at the age of 23 and is commemorated at Beach Head War Cemetery in Anzio, Italy. He was one of the three children of John and Christina Dean of Pine Falls. His sister writes (23 October 2001):

> At the time of his death, he was attached to the RAF and was flying one of the few Boston bombers. His plane was shot down near Rome. George was listed as "missing in action" until his grave was discovered by the Graves Commission in 1945 at Campo Verano.
>
> George loved the outdoors – canoeing, swimming, tennis and golf in the summer and hockey in the winter. His last leave was spent in Scotland visiting relatives including his grandfather whom he had not previously met. It later transpired that his grandfather died the same night he did.

Dean Creek (52 L/6), which flows east into Parks Lake was named after him in 1978.

Dean, Aircraftman 1 **Herbert A. J.** of Winnipeg (R 100106). Rivers Air Observer School. He died 22 August 1941 at the age of 21 and is commemorated at St. Boniface Cemetery. He was the son of Walter and Ella Dean of Winnipeg. ***Dean Bay*** (64 N/5) in Snyder Lake was named after him in 1995.

Dean, Rifleman **Melvin J.** of Birch River (H 6975). Regina Rifle Regiment. He died 6 June 1944 at the age of 24 and is commemorated at Beny-sur-Mer Canadian War Cemetery, Reviers, Calvados, France. He was the son of John J. and Ella M. Dean of Birch River. Three weeks later, Rifleman Dean's father received the following letter:

> Dear Mr. Dean: I am Mel's chaplain. This is the time that I wish I were personally acquainted with the families of all my men. Expressions of sympathy are so cold when they lack the personal touch. However, I did know Mel very well and I write to you as his friend. He was with the Medical Section and I always travelled with them on schemes, and know them all very, very well. I can therefore pass on to you my genuine sympathy in the death of your son.
>
> I am going to tell you the circumstances of his death. I know that you would like to know them. He was killed on the beach, trying to get wounded men out of the water when we were landing on the beaches. He came in with the first company to land. His comrades speak with highest praise of his heroism and courage in carrying on his duties. As you know from accounts in the papers, the beaches were under very heavy Machine Gun and Mortar fire all the time that we were landing. You will be glad to know that his company went ahead to storm the beach defences, capture the village, finally reaching their objective inland and holding it against violent counter-attacks.
>
> You will be anxious about Mel's friends. His closest chum, Fred Weber, was killed at the same time, on the beach. Charlie Moorhead, the other medic with the company, was wounded in the arm but we had a letter from him to say that he is in hospital in England, doing very well. He hopes to be back with the regiment very soon.
>
> A letter is a mighty poor medium for conveying feelings of sympathy. My hope is that kind friends may help to lift the burden for you, the way our comrades in the regiment are holding one another up these days. The comradeship of the men is a grand thing and this unit is like one big, happy family.
>
> Mel was buried near the beach. Honorary Major Forth, Church of England padre and I conducted the service jointly. Ultimately all Canadians who lose their lives in France will be buried in one central cemetery and you will be informed of its location.
>
> May the comfort of the Christian gospel come home to you with fresh meaning, bringing comfort and strength. Please convey my sympathy and my kind regards to your family and to Mel's friends at home. Sincerely yours, Graham M. Jameson (26 June 1944).

Over a year later, his father received a letter from France:

This letter is written to you by a true Frenchman of the Resistance and I would have preferred writing you under different circumstances, but regretfully we cannot alter our destiny. On the 6th of June, 1944, we had the great joy to see all our young Canadians braced with their staunchest courage come to deliver us from the Nazi slavery. Unfortunately, there were a few of these young lads who fell in our territory. Your son was amongst them. The bodies were immediately buried near the property of my parents. These graves were tenderly cared for by my parents and their friends with blossoming flowers, while I was in England, a member of the voluntary Free French Resistance forces. Later on, the bodies of these soldiers were exhumed and interred in a large cemetery a few miles from home and these graves are still kept in perfect state of beauty and given loving care.

Since then, a committee has been formed and called France-England-Canada-and the United States of which we are all members. A plan has been decided by which each of us adopt one of these graves of our glorious Canadians who so valiantly fell in our country, your son's grave becoming my responsibility. May it give you some measure of comfort and consolation to know that my family care tenderly for your son's grave which is covered with flowers. I enclose this picture as a souvenir and may it bring to you some satisfaction to know that a grateful French family tends carefully your darling son's grave.

If some day there exists some service between Canada and France, I wish to extend a hearty hospitality to your family to visit here and the door of my home will be wide open for you as long as you wish to stay with us. I will continue to keep in contact with you as long as you desire, this friendship that I have vowed to your son, I wish to extend to all members of your family. Kindly accept, dear sir, the friendship that I have for your beloved son and may it be accepted by your family, so as to make it larger. Mr. and Mrs. A. Goupinet, Courseulles-sur-Mer, Calvados, France (12 October 1945).

Dean Lake (64 K/16), southwest of Nueltin Lake was named after him in 1961.

Dearle, Private **Robert H.** of Ninette (H 8810). Princess Patricia's Canadian Light Infantry. He died 12 February 1945 at the age of 21 and is commemorated at Ravenna War Cemetery in Italy. He was one of the eight children of Robert H. and Charlotte Dearle of St. James. His sister writes (5 November 2001):

Robert Henry Dearle [was] born February 8, 1924 in Ninette, Manitoba. He was named after his father who had served in World War I. Bob joined the PPCLI in March, 1943 in Winnipeg and trained at Shilo for a time and then Camp Borden. He departed overseas in September of that year. Bob served in England, North Africa, then Sicily. He was killed in action in Bagnacavallo, Italy.

Bob was a very happy, easy going person. He like to sing, whistle and yodel. He loved the outdoors and spent time at Carberry on his sister's and brother-in-law's farm before enlisting in 1943. Bob had just celebrated his 21st birthday on the 8th of February and was killed on the 12th. May he rest in peace.

Dearle Island (63 N/3), in Kississing Lake was named after him in 1972.

Dechief, Trooper **Earl F.** of Deloraine (H 1574). Lord Strathcona's Horse. He died 30 May 1944 at the age of 20 and is commemorated at the Cassino War Cemetery in Italy. He was the son of George and Eulalie Dechief of Deloraine. His sister reports that he was still in high school when he was called up. He enlisted at Portage la Prairie in 1943. ***Dechief Lake*** (64 K/8), northeast of Reindeer Lake was named after him in 1972.

Decloux, Flying Officer **Marcel A.** of Winnipeg (J 14440). No. 404 Squadron. He died 16 January 1944 at the age of 20 and is commemorated at the Runnymede Memorial in Surrey, England. He was the son of Justin and Pauline Decloux of Toronto. ***Decloux Lake*** (64 O/6), south of Corbett Lake was named after him in 1995.

Decruyenaere, Warrant Officer 1 **Albert J. "Bing"** of St. Boniface (R 59761). No. 136 Squadron. He died 15 March 1943 at the age of 22 and is commemorated at Taukkyan Cemetery, Myanmar. He was the eldest of the seven children of Alfred and Marie Decruyenaere of North Bay, Ontario. He enlisted in the RCAF when he was 19, but knowing that his parents would object, he joined while they were away on holiday. According to his sister (n.d.):

After completing his grade school at Provencher School in St. Boniface, Manitoba, he went on to further his education at St. Paul's College. He worked delivering milk for his brother-in-law, Omer Van Walleghem at Royal Dairies. He gained a reputation for being very popular with the young maidens on his milk route. In fact, he got along exceedingly well with the fair set.

He began his training in Trenton, Ontario and after only one furlough home he was sent overseas where his squadron joined forces with the Royal Air Force. Prior to leaving, he said to his mother "Think of me every day at 11 AM and I will do the same." They both did this faithfully until Bert's death.

Bert had always wanted to fly and he realized his dream in the African theatre and the India/Burma theatre. His Belgian heritage was very important to him and he honoured it by naming his plane *Leopold* after the King of Belgium. Even in the few short years he was in the war, he made many friends and was given the nickname "Bing." This was the result of the difficulty people had pronouncing his last name. They began to call him "de crooner" a nickname given to Bing Crosby and eventually it led to Bing. Owen Hearne, a resident of Calcutta, associated with one of the embassies in India, befriended Bert. They got to know each other very well on intermittent visits. After Bert was killed, Mr. Hearne wrote a book on his time with Bert. The title he gave it was "Bing."

Bert was a friendly, easygoing person with a zest for life. There was always laughter in his life, especially when he played practical jokes on those around him. He lived life to the fullest. He loved sports, hunting, fishing, cards and rolling dice. He enjoyed driving his Dad's "Buick Straight Eight" to see how fast it would go. Bert brought a special energy and excitement to any groups he joined. His death wasn't only a casualty of World War II; it was a great loss to his family and friends.

Decruyenaere Lake (64 I/7), northeast of North Knife Lake was named after him in 1974.

de Denus, Sergeant **George J.** of Winnipeg (H 42269). Regina Rifle Regiment. He died 8 July 1944 at the age of 31 and is commemorated at Beny-sur-Mer Canadian War Cemetery in Calvados, France. He was the son of Guy R. and Catherine de Denus of Winnipeg. His nephew reports (17 January 1998) that he:

... took part in the invasion of France on June 6, 1944 and it was with this regiment that he and fourteen other men liberated the town of Bretteville in France. When his commanding officer was wounded, George took over command of the platoon. On July 8, 1944 during the liberation of Caen, he was sent on a scouting mission and was brought down by a sniper.

George was truly loved by his family, extremely admired by his friends, highly respected by his regiment and sadly missed by anyone who knew him. Recently, I read many letters that were sent between George and his parents during that time. Despite the horror and hardships that the war caused, they had an amazing inner strength which came from their deep religious beliefs, a strong commitment to flag and country and the undying ideal of freedom for which so many men and women gave up their lives.

de Denus Lake (64 J/2), southwest of Tadoule Lake was named after him in 1975.

Delipper, Rifleman **John** of Russell (H 41206). Royal Winnipeg Rifles. He died 12 December 1944 at the age of 37 and is commemorated at the Groesbeek Canadian War Cemetery in Holland. He was survived by his wife Emma Delipper of Russell and their four children. ***Delipper Lake*** (64 O/5), east of Nueltin Lake was named after him in 1975.

Deller, Trooper **Walter J.** of Shoal Lake (H 1682). Lord Strathcona's Horse. He died 4 January 1945 and is commemorated at Ravenna War Cemetery in Italy. ***Deller Lake*** (64 K/12), northeast of Reindeer Lake was named after him in 1972.

Delorme, Private **George D.** of Carman (H 6758). Winnipeg Grenadiers. He died a prisoner of war 4 December 1944 at the age of 24 and is commemorated at the Yokohama War Cemetery in Japan. The official cause of death was listed as pneumonia. He was the son of William and Alice Delorme of Carman. ***Delorme Lake*** (63 O/4), north of Wekusko Lake was named after him in 1970.

Delorme, Sergeant **Léopold T. P.** of St. Adolphe (R 86322). No. 245 Squadron. He died 23 February 1942 at the age of 20 and is commemorated at Brookwood Military Cemetery in Surrey, England. He was the son of William and Philomene Delorme of St. Adolphe. ***Delorme Island*** (64 O/12) in Shannon Lake was named after him in 1995.

Delorme, Private **Lionel S. J.** of Winnipeg (H 21073). Essex Scottish Regiment. He died 8 March 1945 at the age of 20 and is commemorated at the Groesbeek Canadian War Cemetery in Holland. He was the son of Arthur and Amanda Delorme of Winnipeg. He seems to have enlisted when only 17 years of age by "altering" his date of birth on his attestation papers. ***Delorme Creek*** (62 P/16), which flows south into Leyond River was named after him in 1973.

Demeria, Corporal **Edward A.** (M 107541). Seaforth Highlanders of Canada. He died 12 April 1945 at the age of 22 and is commemorated at the Holten Canadian War Cemetery in Holland. He was survived by his wife Elizabeth A. Demeria and their young daughter. According to his wife (25 June 1996):

> My first husband was an inspiration to everyone; he was a wonderful husband, never thinking of himself. He was a very jovial man, always doing funny things to make me laugh and everyone else. We had a daughter ... just like her father, always making everyone happy but herself. Edward soon got to be Corporal and he was so proud. Also, he got to see his baby daughter before he left for overseas.

Demeria Lake (53 M/11), southeast of Ransom Lake was named after him in 1996.

Deniset, Captain **François A.** of St. Boniface. Royal Canadian Artillery. He died 8 May 1945 and is commemorated at the Brookwood Memorial in Surrey, England. He was the son of Mr. and Mrs. François Deniset of St. Boniface and was survived by his wife Joan Deniset of Farnham, Surrey. ***Deniset Lake*** (64 K/11), northeast of Reindeer Lake was named after him in 1972.

Denison, Major **Latimer Hugh** of Winnipeg. Royal Winnipeg Rifles, Distinguished Service Order and the Croix de Guerre.

> On the 21st February, 1945, D Company, Royal Winnipeg Rifles, commanded by Captain (Acting Major) Denison was ordered to capture the high ground which is thickly wooded and overlooks Moyland, Germany to the northeast. This attack was quickly pushed home despite the heavy defensive fire put down by the enemy and the few enemy that were left alive withdrew.
>
> Later in the day, D Company was ordered to pass through C Company and to seize the high ground at the eastern tip of the wood. This required a 1000-yard advance through an extremely thick wood which was being subjected to the full weight of the enemy's fire. Casualties amongst Major Denison's men were heavy, but ceaselessly moving from platoon to platoon, he kept control of his company and by his own personal courage inspired his men to go on. Machine gun fire from prepared positions on the hill feature was intense, but by skilfully manoeuvring his men he got his now depleted company into an assaulting position and stormed the hilltop with he himself leading.
>
> During the consolidation phase, they were counter-attacked twice by the enemy; both of these were successfully beaten off with heavy casualties to the Germans. When the enemy were seen forming up for a third attack, Major Denison, from the crest of the hill and in full view of the enemy, personally sited and directed the fire of a troop of tanks; the company and the tanks quickly broke up the enemy attack and they withdrew. By his initiative, leadership, courage and offensive spirit, Major Denison was able to inspire his men to hold their hard-won objective thus securing the left flank of the Brigade (DSO Citation).
>
> Captain Denison commanded a Canadian air liaison section and sailed with an advance party to Normandy on D-Day and acted as air liaison officer in contact cars which provided close air support during the pursuit across France. His work was often carried out under fire. His courage and determination in these operations led to the destruction of a great quantity of enemy material and men (Croix de Guerre Citation n.d.).

He died 30 March 1945 at the age of 24 and is commemorated at Groesbeek Canadian War Cemetery, Gelderland, Netherlands. He was the son of Alexander Latimer and Edith F. Denison (née Daly) of Winnipeg and the husband of Jean M. Denison (née Hay) of East Preston, Sussex, England. In a letter to his wife, Captain C. D. Shepard spoke of Major Denison:

> As I was walking back to the station in Aldershot, I spied a corporal in the Winnipeg Rifles and asked him if he had known Major Denison. It would have gladdened the hearts of the Denison family to have heard the respect and admiration with which this lad regarded Hugh. He was not in Hugh's company, but said that Hugh's company had passed through his own in the attack across the Rhine at Emmerich. Apparently Hugh's company was held up by a German self-propelled gun – a sort of semi-tank affair – and Hugh had crawled forward with a PIAT – the small armour-piercing weapon carried by the infantry – until he was only 50 or 75 yards from the Germans. The Germans had seen Hugh and he was killed instantly by a high explosive shell. The corporal thought that Hugh had been recommended for the DSO for his actions – which is a higher award than the MC and next to the VC; it was an action that Hugh had every right to delegate to one of his juniors but no doubt he appreciated its hazards and therefore decided to do the job himself. It is leadership like that that has won the war (11 May 1945).

Denison Lake (64 G/5), southeast of Big Sand Lake was named after him in 1948.

Denison, Flying Officer **Richard W.** of Winnipeg (J 15470). No. 403 Squadron. He died 18 March 1944 at the age of 25 and is commemorated at Brookwood Military Cemetery in Surrey, England. He was the son of R. Lionel and Celia Denison of Winnipeg and the second cousin of Major Hugh Denison (previous entry). The Denison family has a private cemetery in Toronto and the names of both men are inscribed on the cenotaph there. ***Denison Island*** (64 O/11) in John Osborn Lake was named after Richard Denison in 1975.

Dennis, Sergeant **Norman** of Birch River (L 36284). Governor General's Foot Guards. He was killed when an 88mm shell pierced the turret of his tank. While lying wounded, his only thought was reportedly for the well-being of his gunner and he died urging his troop to "carry on the fight." He died 9 August 1944 at the age of 22 and is commemorated at Beny-sur-Mer Canadian War Cemetery in Calvados, France. He was the son of Thomas and Jennie Dennis (née Watkins) of Swan River. Upon his arrival in England, he wrote to his mother:

Dear Mother: Well as usual we are all fine and like it here very much. We had a wonderful trip over and it was sure quite an experience. Wilfred got a leave a few days ago to visit relations and I expect to get one shortly. I don't know where I will go yet but I expect it will be to visit dad's relations. The weather and the country is just like dad said, and it sure is a wonderful place, what I have seen of it. I haven't received a letter from you since I've been here and this is the first letter I have written since I sent the cable. Well, I will be expecting a letter very shortly and write regularly. Your son, Sergeant N. Dennis (11 July 1943).

His last letter home had a reassuring tone:

Dear Mother: Well, as ever I am just fine and enjoying life very (very) much at the present time. I haven't received any mail from you for over two to three weeks. What is the matter with not writing? This is the first letter that I have written for quite some time. I am in France which makes news very scarce. Well, there isn't much I can say. I hope you are all well and don't worry because I am enjoying myself very much. Your son, Norman (30 July 1944).

The next communication she received was a telegram from the Department of National Defence:

Dear Mrs. Jennie Dennis: Minister of National Defence Deeply Regrets to Inform you that L 36284 Sergeant Norman Dennis Has Been Officially reported Wounded in Action on a Date Not Yet Available and Died of Wounds Ninth August 1944 Nature of Wounds Described As Traumatic Amputation right thigh wounds right Arm Stop When further Information Becomes available It will Be Forwarded As Soon As Received. Director of Records (15 August 1944).

According to his younger brother (3 April 1995): "Being only 10 years old in 1940, one memory that sticks was my mother writing letters to Norman at night with the light of a coal oil lamp at Birch River, Manitoba." ***Dennis Lake*** (64 I/12), northwest of North Knife Lake was named after him in 1974.

Dereworiz, Rifleman **Walter** of Winnipeg (H 204488). Royal Winnipeg Rifles. He died 8 June 1944 at the age of 24 and is commemorated at Beny-sur-Mer Canadian War Cemetery in Calvados, France. He was the son of Andrew and Anastasia Dereworiz of Winnipeg. ***Dereworiz Lake*** (64 J/1), south of Tadoule Lake was named after him in 1975.

Derksen, Private **Jacob** of Morden (H 69770). Royal Hamilton Light Infantry. He died 8 March 1945 at the age of 20 and is commemorated at the Groesbeek Canadian War Cemetery in Holland. Born at Rosenfeld, Manitoba, he was survived by his parents Jacob and Tina Derksen of Morden. ***Derksen Lake*** (64 N/3), southwest of Nueltin Lake was named after him in 1972.

de Rzonca, Sergeant **James R. W.** of Winnipeg (R 101835). No. 11 Elementary Flying Training School. He died 16 April 1942 at the age of 20 and is commemorated at Wellshill Cemetery in Perthshire, Scotland. He was the only son of Stanislaus J. and Helen de Rzonca (née Kiersnowska) of Winnipeg. The elder of his two sisters writes (17 August 2001):

Januszek (James) as he was called in Polish, was born in Warsaw, Poland August 29, 1921 at the General Hospital where my mother worked as a nurse. He became the centre of the universe for both my parents, although he was ill often as a child and needed a lot of care. I was born in 1923 and my sister followed in 1925. James and I actually were only a year and a half apart and grew up very close, always enjoying each other's company.

Our family emigrated from Poland to Canada in 1929, bringing enough money to last us for a few years as it was obligatory in those days, to buy and settle on a farm. My father having only worked as a "head cashier" in a large bank in Warsaw, knew little of a farmer's life, but managed to build bridges from logs on the farm, employ farmhands and bring in good crops. The depression years were a great struggle when wheat sold for 12¢ a bushel and he had to pay off help and the costly farm machinery. He bankrupted after three years of struggle. Mother and Father separated with Father leaving for Montreal to learn a new trade and Mother resuming her nursing career in Winnipeg. As Father spoke six languages including French, it helped.

Those three years on the farm during summer holidays were very memorable and happy for us children. The great freedom of the outdoors with over 600 acres to roam and play. My brother and I, hand-in-hand, running through the woods and fields exploring and picking wildflowers for Mother ... bareback riding one of the horses to a neighbour's swimming hole to cool off ... carrying lunches to the farmhands through golden, waving fields of wheat ... and then exploring places we missed on the way back. There were two rivers running through the property and many times we would catch minnows and I would segregate them in different jars. We also helped gathering berries and mushrooms in the woods along Mother's side, as she knew about herbs, wild mushrooms, berries etc.

At Christmas time, it was also much fun sliding down the river banks on our sleds. I recall one Christmas Eve when the snow was exceptionally high – 10 feet or so – and the whole family decided to attend Midnight Mass at the church in the village of Ste. Agathe. We were dressed warmly and bundled under wool blankets and fur rugs. Two horses pulled the big sled; little bells jingled merrily from the horses' harnesses. The sky was black but dotted with millions of stars shining like diamonds above. As we were only five miles away from the village and taking shortcuts through the snowy fields, it did not take too long to arrive and join the other neighbours and villagers in a memorable holy service; the candles, hymns, music and decorations impressed us greatly. However, on the way back it began to snow and Father got lost for a while, but after a neighbour gave him directions, we all arrived safely back home.

After Father's and Mother's departure from the farm, we became full-time boarders at the Convent and James boarded with the Lapalisse family close to the school. We only saw him during recess and/or summer holidays in Mother's home in Winnipeg. We were all very good students and it wasn't long before James, Teresa and I won provincial prizes for French and other subjects. I would like to mention here that we are very grateful to the sisters of the Infant Jesus and Mary for the excellent education received at Ste. Agathe and later at the St. Joseph's Academy in St. Boniface. James left the school after Grade 10 to take Greek and Latin at the College in St. Boniface. He mastered the four-year course in two years, then went on to University at St. Paul's College where he also played hockey. James wanted to become a Civil Engineer and worked very hard at his studies.

I must relate how kind and self-sacrificing James was and how much he cared and loved us. One early summer day, he decided to cycle from Winnipeg to Ste. Agathe, a distance of 35 miles one way, to deliver us a big box of fruit as a treat. Very basic fare in those days was served us at meals and this surprise was such a blessing. We were overjoyed to see him and he visited with us for a little while. He was anxious to start the journey back, as we could see he was already quite tired. Mother said later that when he arrived back home to Winnipeg he could hardly stand up. She massaged his cramped legs over the next few days as he had problems even walking. God bless him for that wonderful act of love.

It was about this time that James visited on many occasions the Trappist Monastery where they bred pure-bred dogs and made all kinds of cheeses for sale. One day, a pup with a bobbed tail became available for $25 and my brother cleaned out his bank account to buy him. When we first saw him, we thought it was fully grown, but as this was a Great Dane pup, he grew to be over three feet tall and 150 pounds, just like a small calf. We lost a lot of friends visiting over the next few years as this dog, although very gentle in nature, scared a lot of people away as he sat on the front steps of the house. James had dogs over many years, but Rex the Great Dane was his favourite.

James in his second year of University joined the RCAF in 1941. Apparently the same day another boy, Lloyd Armour also joined (from Chapman, BC). The two became fast friends and were transferred to the same locations across Canada as they received their training, and then onward overseas and then to be stationed in Scotland. They flew on missions many times as pilot and co-pilot and on that fateful day in April, fought the German planes attacking England and were shot down. They died together and their remains are mixed in two small caskets buried in Perth's cemetery, so flowers and prayers are always made and given to both graves, located side-by-side. Lloyd's father, Mr. Armour corresponded with my father over many years and also visited my mother and sister in Vancouver. I was away working that day and missed him.

On his last birthday in 1941, he was stationed out west – Comox or Lethbridge – I can't recall. I baked an Angel Food cake (13 eggs) for him with all the trimmings and along with candles mailed it AIRMAIL. He received it the next day for his birthday and as he wrote back, it was a wonderful surprise that was demolished by him and his friends in 10 minutes. My love for him is constant and never diminishes with his absence – only the pain of losing him is not so acute.

My mother never got over his death. She could not carry on nursing others; father became morose. He had been away nine years in Montreal before he came back in 1940 to Winnipeg. Of course, living apart, we did not see him too often. Mother raised us as a single parent with some monetary help from father, but far too little. As children of separated parents, we all turned out honest, hard-working, poor in monetary goods, but rich in love and memories. I married twice and have two wonderful daughters. My sister got a great University education and became a teacher. My dreams of becoming "a pharmacist or chemist" evaporated upon my brother's death. I had to take a secretarial course so I could earn my living and help mother financially. We all lost greatly when James died. Had James lived, our lives would have been so much better with his caring for us, his advice in all worldly matters and his protection. Mother always relied on him so even when he was a child. Her loss, especially as she grew older, was immeasurable.

In 1969, my husband Zak and I made a special detour on our European trip to visit my brother's grave in Perth. We also tried to trace my brother's girlfriend's family, but they had moved away. Some local people helped us find the cemetery and upon hearing of our difficulties, bought us dinner and gave us flowers. We became very fond of Scotland and its kind and gentle people. In 1997, my youngest daughter Karen and I toured the north of Scotland and visited Perth for a week, again planting flowers and laying potted flowers on both graves that are side by side. The military section of this cemetery is kept clean and tidy and we were impressed how this grateful, beautiful country of Scotland appreciated the sacrifices made by Canadians during the Second World War.

The younger sister Theresa added (30 August 2001):

In his last letter to my mother dated April 13, 1942, my brother wrote that he was supposed to leave for England in a week's time where he would be a Pilot Instructor as he was finishing his course in two days. Instead, what must have happened is that when there was that terrible attack by the Germans on April 16, all the graduate students must have been sent into battle where he was killed. I hope that God has a special, horrible place for monsters like Hitler that brought such horror to the world.

My brother was a wonderful human being, not only was he a responsible and caring person by trying to help mother during our difficult financial times by making lacy wooden ornaments which he sold door to door as well as other things – projects he picked from magazines to help pay for his books and tuition. He also had a marvellous sense of humour and was very handsome. I was most proud of him although he liked to tease me in a fun way. We often laughed at his antics.

Because the war was going so badly for the Allies during the two years after Poland was attacked and fell to the Germans, he decided to enlist (before conscription) instead of continuing with his studies in his second year of University at St. Paul's College. After he was stationed in Perth, Scotland he was pleasantly surprised to learn that many Polish pilots had joined the RAF to fight against the Germans to regain Poland's freedom. It is ironic that at the end of the war, Poland was betrayed by the Allies and handed over to communist Russia.

de Rzonca Lake (64 P/14), northeast of Nejanilini Lake was named after him in 1974.

Descôteaux, Leading Aircraftman **Louis J.** of Elmwood (R 116062). Royal Canadian Air Force. He died 12 January 1943 at the age of 22 and is commemorated at St. Boniface Cemetery in Winnipeg. He was the son of Romeo and Delphine Descôteaux of St. Boniface and was survived by his wife Hilda Descôteaux of Elmwood. ***Descôteaux Lake*** (64 J/12), west of Tadoule Lake was named after him in 1975.

Desieyes, Flight Sergeant **Jean G.** of Winnipeg (R 59777). No. 434 Squadron. He died 28 September 1943 at the age of 25 and is commemorated at the Runnymede Memorial in Surrey, England. He was the son of Frederic and Edith Desieyes of Winnipeg. ***Desieyes Lake*** (64 C/15), northwest of Arbour Lake was named after him in 1979.

Desilets, Flying Officer **Albert A.** of Norwood (J 26514). No. 206 Squadron. He died 15 July 1944 at the age of 23 and is commemorated at the Runnymede Memorial in Surrey, England. He was the son of Wilfrid and Lillian Desilets of Norwood. ***Desilets Lake*** (64 P/10), east of Nejanilini Lake was named after him in 1974.

Desjardins, Sergeant **J. A. Guy** of St. Boniface (SH 61667). Royal 22nd Regiment. He died 20 May 1953 at the age of 21 and is commemorated at the United Nations Cemetery in Pusan, South Korea. He was one of the 12 children of Alexander J. and Maria Desjardins of St. Vital.

The young Sergeant ... was last seen fighting the enemy with a pistol in his right hand and a sten gun in his left. [According to his commanding officer Lieutenant Colonel Poulin] "Desjardins wanted to do a really good show." He took his patrol up the forward slopes of the enemy's positions, found nothing and withdrew. He crossed and re-crossed the river several times looking for likely ambush spots. Then he got impatient, went downstream about 1500 yards. We were out of touch since he was ordered not to use his wireless unless he wanted help – lest he gave his position away. So he snooped around. He was just about to come back when his group was challenged by a Chinese standing waist high above a paddy dyke. Private Gilles Gibeault of Granby, Quebec threw a grenade and at once the enemy threw ten grenades among them. If we'd known where they were, we could have given them artillery and mortar support, but in the fight that broke out the signaller must have been hurt (*Winnipeg Free Press* 30 June 1953).

In one of his last letters home he wrote in part:

Dear Mom, Dad and Kids: How are you all? I'm fine except for a cold which is very easy to catch here because of the humidity and cold at night. It rained for a while, but now the sun shines again. I was glad to read your letter yesterday, Mom, it really helps our morale to get news. I'm glad to hear Dad is fine and still working ... also Julie working at the Manitoba Telephones. That's nice, Julie, I hope you keep this job. Oh yes, I received a letter from your boyfriend and I forgot what his address is, but would you thank him for me? It was very nice of him to write to me.

I guess dad will be taking his holidays soon. Well, Winnipeg certainly is a beautiful place to have a holiday. Dad, out here in Korea the sun shines bright but that's all. Mountains and valleys are all we see – no vegetation, just scrubby bushes here and there. The earth is a rusty brown colour and nothing grows around here except rice which is the Koreans' main dish.

It has been fairly quiet out here except for the artillery shelling at night and machine gun fire, but we are in a reserve position now. We expect to go up on the line, which is now about two miles from where we are now, in two weeks or maybe sooner – we never know. We have over 100 Koreans working for us. They are small men but can carry 200 pounds on their backs up a steep hill. They all wear surplus olive drab uniforms given to them by the American Army. All they eat is rice and tea. The earth is poisonous here; so is the water polluted. That is why they do not grow anything in the valleys. I must get back to work now, but will write again soon. Send me Ben's address. Love to Mom, Dad and Kids. Your son, Guy (30 April 1953).

Desjardins Lake (53 E/14), south of Fairy Rock Lake was named after this Korean War casualty in 1998.

Deslaurier, Private **Leon** of Winnipeg (H 6750). Winnipeg Grenadiers. He died 20 December 1941 and is commemorated at the Sai Wan Memorial in Hong Kong. The Sai Wan Memorial forms the entrance to Sai Wan War Cemetery and bears the names of more than 2000 Commonwealth servicemen who died in the Battle of Hong Kong, or subsequently in captivity, who have no known grave. ***Deslaurier Lake*** (64 I/15), northeast of North Knife Lake was named after him in 1974.

Desmarais, Sergeant **Benoit** of St. Boniface (R 124068). He served with No. 36 Operational Training Unit, RCAF. He died 8 October 1942 at the age of 19 and is commemorated at the Ottawa Memorial. He was the son of Louis and Marie Desmarais of St. Boniface. ***Desmarais Lake*** (64 O/6), southeast of Nueltin Lake was named after him in 1975.

Devenish, Lieutenant **Robert G.** of Winnipeg. Royal Canadian Engineers. He died 5 April 1941 at the age of 24 and is commemorated at Brookwood Military Cemetery in Surrey, England. He was the son of William and Jean Devenish of Winnipeg. ***Devenish Lake*** (53 F/13), east of Angling Lake was named after him in 1996.

Dewart, Flying Officer **Douglas Lyle** of Elva (J 44346). No. 19 Squadron. He died 29 January 1945 at the age of 21 and is commemorated at the Runnymede Memorial in Surrey, England. He was the son of Joseph and Annie Dewart of Elva, Manitoba. ***Dewart Lake*** (64 N/11), southwest of Nueltin Lake was named after him in 1972.

Dey, Pilot Officer **Robert** of Winnipeg (J 90571). No. 103 Squadron. He died 26 July 1944 at the age of 30 and is commemorated at Orleans Main Cemetery, Loiret, France. He was the second youngest of the 15 children of Fred and Marcianna Dey of Elmwood and was survived by his wife Ruth Dey of Winnipeg. She writes (5 March 1996):

He was a true gentleman, dedicated, an excellent craftsman, caring and thoughtful with a quiet sense of humour. He loved to read, was involved with the community club, ice skating and participated in roller skating at the Winnipeg Roller Rink. He will always be deeply loved and missed.

Dey Island (53 L/8) in Wapeeminakoskak Lake was named after him in 1995.

Diamond, Private **Norman A.** of Birtle (H 20745). Perth Regiment. He died 29 September 1944 at the age of 24 and is commemorated at Coriano Ridge War Cemetery in Italy. He was the son of Franklin and Leslie Diamond of Solsgirth, Manitoba. ***Diamond Island*** (64 I/1) in South Knife Lake was named after him in 1989.

Dickens, Ordinary Seaman **Alexander J. W.** of Winnipeg (V 9575). HMCS *Margaree*. The *Margaree* was lost in the North Atlantic after collision with the freighter *Port Fairy* while escorting the five ship Convoy OL.8; 142 of her ship's company were lost, many of whom were survivors of *Fraser's* tragic sinking. Ordinary Seaman Dickens died 22 October 1940 at the age of 19 and is commemorated at the Halifax Memorial. He was the son of James and Millicent Dickens of Winnipeg. ***Dickens Lake*** (54 L/6), southwest of Churchill was named after him in 1957.

Dickinson, Sergeant **Harry** of Winnipeg (R 157281). No. 11 Advanced Flying School, RCAF. He died 21 July 1943 at the age of 19 and is commemorated at Blacon Cemetery in Cheshire, England. He was the son of Frederick and Margaret Dickinson of Winnipeg. ***Dickinson Lake*** (64 G/4), west of Southern Indian Lake was named after him in 1985.

Dickinson, Private **Leslie W.** of Willen (H 20614). Queen's Own Cameron Highlanders. He died 23 July 1944 and is commemorated at Bretteville-sur-Laize Canadian War Cemetery in Calvados, France. He was survived by his wife Mrs. Lorna Dickinson. ***Dickinson Island*** (63 P/3) in Giffin Lake was named after him in 1995.

Dickson, Lieutenant **Chester S.** of Winnipeg. Ontario Tank Regiment. He died 12 May 1944 and is commemorated at the Cassino War Cemetery in Italy. Contemporary newspaper coverage described the circumstances of his enlistment:

A young married man who volunteered to join the army Wednesday, willing to give up an $1800-a-year job and his summer holidays, Chester Stuart Dickson, Winnipeg, route salesman for the Rumford Laundry, said he hoped other young men would do the same. Sometime ago he joined the 1st Cavalry Division, Winnipeg's reserve army service corps unit, on the understanding that when the call to active service came he would be ready, he explained. Now that additional units for the 4th Division Supply Column, army service corps, were being mobilized, he had determined to honour his pledge, he said.

Wednesday, he obtained one day's leave of absence from work and went down to the city army recruiting station in the Orpheum Theatre, 283 Fort Street. "I think every man in a reserve unit should volunteer," he said. "I'm giving up a good job and it's not fair that others should sit back. Some of my relations ask me why I should go when there are still young men unemployed and others who hang around pool rooms most of the day" (n.d.).

Dickson Island (64 O/16) in Hutton Lake was named after him in 1995.

Diehl, Private **Raymond J.** of Cypress River (H 1807). Canadian Scottish Regiment. He died 19 February 1945 at the age of 21 and is commemorated at the Groesbeek Canadian War Cemetery in Holland. He was the son of George A. and Maud E. Diehl of Cypress River. ***Diehl Lake*** (64 N/3), southwest of Nueltin Lake was named after him in 1972.

Digney, Flight Lieutenant **Roderick J.** of Winnipeg (J 9497). No. 424 Squadron. He died 31 March 1944 at the age of 29 and is commemorated at Durnbach War Cemetery in Bavaria, Germany. ***Digney Lake*** (64 C/11), northwest of Granville Lake was named after him in 1972.

Dillabough, Private **Lawson** of Transcona (H 18077). Princess Louise Dragoon Guards. He died 17 December 1944 at the age of 29 and is commemorated at the Cassino Memorial in Italy. He was the son of Duncan and L. Dillabough and was survived by his wife Mary Dillabough of West Selkirk and their four children. She writes (5 April 1998):

> Lawson was born in Selkirk, Manitoba; he attended school there. He was an excellent baseball player which got him employment at the Sturgeon River Gold Mine in Ontario ... also the Cordite war plant in Transcona. He enlisted in the Canadian Army on November 17 and was killed by machine gun fire exactly 13 months after enlisting.

Dillabough Lake (64 K/16), northeast of Lac Brochet was named after him in 1972.

Dingle, Pilot Officer **John T.** of Winnipeg (J 24270). No. 4 Service Flying Training School, RCAF. He died 30 May 1943 at the age of 22 and is commemorated at Elmwood Cemetery in Winnipeg. He was the son of Frederick and Kate Dingle of Winnipeg and was survived by his wife Isabel Dingle of Elm Creek. ***Dingle Lake*** (64 P/2), southeast of Nejanilini Lake was named after him in 1974.

Dingwall, Rifleman **George "Geordie"** of Deloraine (H 41607). Royal Winnipeg Rifles. He died 6 June 1944 during the invasion of Normandy. He was 33 years old and is commemorated at Beny-sur-Mer Canadian War Cemetery in Calvados, France. He was the third of the ten children of James and Mary Dingwall of Deloraine. His brother reports that he worked on farms and trapped and hunted in the Whitewater and Swan River areas prior to enlisting. ***Dingwall Lake*** (64 H/1), south of Hogg Lake was named after him in 1995.

Dinicol, Sapper **Louie** of Winnipeg (H 102623). Royal Canadian Engineers. He died 21 May 1944 at the age of 33 and is commemorated at the Cassino War Cemetery in Italy. He was the son of Saverio and Mary Dinicol of Winnipeg. ***Dinicol Lake*** (63 O/5), southeast of Highrock Lake was named after him in 1973.

Dion, Warrant Officer 2 **Walter L.** of The Pas (R 116350). No. 122 Squadron. He died 16 March 1943 and is commemorated at the Ottawa Memorial. The inscription there reads "1939 – 1945: In honoured memory of the men and women of the air forces of the British Commonwealth and Empire who gave their lives in Canada in the United States of America and in neighbouring lands and who have no known grave." ***Dion Island*** (64 N/10) in Tice Lake was named after him in 1995.

Dionne, Trooper **Philip** of Flin Flon (H 100244). Elgin Regiment. He died 1 May 1943 at the age of 20 and is commemorated at Brookwood Military Cemetery in Surrey, England. He was the son of Joe and Philomene Dionne (née Cursiteur) of Sturgeon Landing, Saskatchewan. According to his niece (24 July 1999): "... Philip took a short cut to get back to Base when he was killed. He had to cut across a field where the fighter planes were taking off at night. He was not missed until the next morning when they were doing roll call." ***Dionne Lake*** (64 H/9), north of Freeman Lake was named after him in 1995.

Dixon, Private **Alvin G.** of Swan River (H 10855). Essex Scottish Regiment. He died 1 March 1945 at the age of 35 and is commemorated at the Groesbeek Canadian War Cemetery in Holland. He was the son of John and Mary Dixon and was survived by his wife Grace Dixon of Swan River and by their four children. His Personnel Selection Record indicates that he was "appraised" as follows:

- Dixon, 34, A-1 category, is a quiet man, rather pleasant, straightforward and friendly. He talks easily and seems quite sensible and steady. His attitude seems good. "M" test indicates low average Army ability, has Grade 7 education and has had considerable experience driving tractors and trucks. Should make an efficient driver (31 July 1943).
- Getting along pretty well. His side bothers him in doubling, result of an old operation. Bit worried over one of his children who has sugar diabetes. Platoon Commander agrees that Dixon should have a medical recheck (24 September 1943).
- Drove a truck and did some garage work about 6 years. He says he is short of breath when doubling. His right index finger is deformed since it was cut in a mower (24 September 1943).
- Just returned from Woodstock where he qualified as Dvr. 1.C. 16 Feb 44. He said he liked it very much especially 1st week. He should be suitable now for overseas Service (24 February 1944).

From "Somewhere in Holland" he wrote:

> Dear Grace and Family: Here I am for a few lines as we are on the move again and I haven't very much time. But I got my pictures and I thought I would send them while I had a chance. They are not too bad. We have had a little more training which was supposed to be a rest. But I guess there is no rest till this is over, and I hope it's not too long. Things are going pretty good now. I am sure fed up on it. The weather is pretty miserable and wet all the time. So disgusted that it's even hard to write a letter. I thought when I got out this time I would be able to get the girls shoes, but with training and what not, I didn't get a chance. But some of these days I hope to get a chance. I shouldn't of promised them till I had them (15 February 1945).

He sent two letters to his family from "Somewhere in Germany" a week before his death:

> Dear Grace and Family: Well, here I am again for a few lines as I haven't been able to write these last few days. But I have a little while before dark, so this will be kind of short. I got your last letter a couple of days ago and was glad to get it and one from Bert. But I still haven't been able to answer it. I didn't lose my pen, but I did lose my ink so I am just about as bad as with no pen. No, I don't know of anything that I wish for over here unless you send a ticket for home is about all I ask for and hope for. Well, it shouldn't be so hard for you to be able to learn to drive a car as you used to be able. Yes, I guess it is a long wait for me coming home; I know it sure is for me. But it may not be so long. I sure hope not anyway. Well you will soon be able to go to dances again. Well there isn't very much to say that you don't hear over the radio any more than it is noisy here. I have never seen or heard from Stan Mault or saw any of the boys from [home] for a long time. It will be a big change for Stan; it is for us all. But all we can hope for is it to be over soon. The weather isn't quite so cold as it was, but still pretty wet and raining a lot. But the grass is turning green. I have a few more pictures here that I will send you soon. I am not able to get much stuff these days and to help things out I lost my small pack a couple of days ago and three or four hundred cigarettes. So I can start all over again. Well, I am glad that you are all feeling good, as I am pretty good. Will write in a

day or two or tomorrow if I get a chance at all and hope that this finds you all in the best of health. Love to all, Alvin (24 February 1945).

Dear Grace and Family: I don't know just how much time I have left so might not get done. Well for a change it is a nice day with a little sunshine which we all like to see as it gives the planes a chance to work. And do they ever. I had a letter from Bert last night. I had wrote him one on the 2 of Feb. and he had it and one back by the 24th, so that's good time. You should go and see about your eyes before they get too bad and get glasses if you need them. I guess [Jane] and Elva are quite the big girls now, but I suppose Sonny can look after himself. He must be quite a man now! How I would love to be with you all again and be able to see how the family are growing. But I guess it will be quite a while yet. The boys are getting pretty optimistic, saying that it will be over by Easter. I sure hope they are right. It can finish any time and it sure won't hurt my feelings any. But these [Germans] seem hard to convince they are beat and have been for a long time. And for good this time. Do you see Charlie at all and what does he think of it all? I guess he will be pretty satisfied to see them fall proper this time. Say, I got another picture of myself that I had taken when I was on my 48 but it looks like ... I hadn't ... shaved for a week. Which has happened a few times, but I was shaved when my picture was taken. But if you don't like it, it will always help to light the fire, and another post card and another bill of this useless money which there is a lot of amongst the boys these days. Have the girls got all the different kinds? I have sent them either 5 or 6 different ones and I hope they have got their hankies by this [time]. They sure have lovely stuff in the countries we have come through, but sure expensive. I can't think of much to say that you don't already know if your radio is still going. So I guess I will say By-by for this time. But will write every chance I get. Were the four letters you got in one week new? That's pretty good – 4 in one week. Well, I hope this finds you all in the best of health as I am fine. With lots of love to all and good luck. Love, Alvin (25 February 1945).

Dixon Island (63 P/10) in Armstrong Lake was named after him in 1995.

Dixon, Warrant Officer 1 **Gordon H.** of Winnipeg (533999). No. 12 Squadron, RAF. He enlisted in August, 1936 and died 27 April 1945. He was 31 years of age and is commemorated at Didcot Cemetery in Berkshire, England. He was the son of Joseph and C. Dixon and was survived by his wife Dorothy M. Dixon of Didcot, Berkshire, England. ***Dixon Point*** (64 P/12) on Nejanilini Lake was named after him in 1995.

Dobbs, Pilot Officer **Fernand W.** of Winnipeg (J 93872). No. 424 Squadron. He died 12 January 1945 at the age of 21 and is commemorated at the Runnymede Memorial in Surrey, England. ***Dobbs Island*** (64 N/9) in Nahili Lake was named after him in 1995.

Dobbyn, Flying Officer **Joseph L.** of Melita (J 18666). No. 50 Squadron, Distinguished Flying Cross.

This officer has flown on operations against such well defended German targets as Berlin, Hanover, Leipzig and Stuttgart. On three occasions, his aircraft has been attacked by enemy fighters while making the bombing run but each time, Flying Officer Dobbyn, undeterred, resolutely pressed home his attack. At all times he has displayed outstanding skill, courage and devotion to duty (DFC Citation 1949).

He died 23 March 1944 at the age of 22 and is commemorated at the Reichswald Forest War Cemetery in Germany. He was the son of Joseph and Helen Dobbyn. ***Dobbyn Lake*** (64 C/7), northwest of Granville Lake was named after him in 1947.

Dobesch, Flying Officer **Burghard H.** of Winnipeg (J 36379). No. 19 Training Unit. RCAF. He died 26 May 1944 at the age of 22 and is commemorated at Fettercairn Cemetery in Kincardineshire, Scotland. He was the son of Richard and Mary Dobesch of Winnipeg. ***Dobesch Lake*** (64 J/10), west of Tadoule Lake was named after him in 1975.

Dobson, Warrant Officer 1 **Amos R.** of Manitou (R 116474). No. 45 Squadron. He died 22 June 1944 at the age of 23 and is commemorated at Manitou Community Cemetery. He was the son of Amos and Hannah Dobson of Manitou. ***Dobson Lake*** (64 N/11), southwest of Nueltin Lake was named after him in 1972.

Dobson, Pilot Officer **Lorne G.** of Ninga (J 17746). No. 99 Squadron. He died 15 March 1943 at the age of 25 and is commemorated at Maynamati War Cemetery, Bangladesh. He was the son of George and Lazetta Dobson of Ninga. According to his sister (2 January 1995):

Early in 1942 he was assigned to the RAF and was sent to the Middle East where he remained for a short time and was posted to the Far East. He piloted Wellington bombers in the campaign waged against the Japanese who had infiltrated Burma and were at that time posing a very serious threat to India and peripheral areas.

Dobson Island (63 P/11) in Pikwitonei Lake was named after him in 1995.

Docking, Sergeant **Robert O.** of Minnedosa (R 59295). No. 115 Squadron. He died 17 June 1941 at the age of 21 and is commemorated at Marham Cemetery in Norfolk, England. He was the son of Clifford and Lilly Docking of Minnedosa. ***Docking Lake*** (64 C/3), east of Russell Lake was named after him in 1993.

Dodd, Private **Charles A.** of Ekhart (H 103756). Princess Patricia's Canadian Light Infantry. He died 11 May 1944 at the age of 22 and is commemorated at Bari War Cemetery in Italy. He was the son of Richard and Alice Dodd of Balmoral, Manitoba. He attended school there before enlisting in November, 1942. His niece remembers him (18 September 2001) as "... a fun-loving person who loved to tease and had many friends. He was raised on a farm and was very close to his family." ***Dodd Lake*** (64 G/4), northeast of Grandmother Lake was named after him in 1994.

Dodds, Pilot Officer **Vernon F.** of Winnipeg (J 89743). No. 405 Squadron. He died 21 July 1944 at the age of 23 and is commemorated at Tubbergen Roman Catholic Cemetery, Holland. He was the son of William and Dorice Dodds and was survived by his wife Eleanor Dodds of Winnipeg. She writes (6 June 1998):

[He was] educated at Gladstone, Earl Grey and Kelvin High School. He worked for [the] T. Eaton Company when he enlisted with the RCAF in 1942. He married in March of 1943 and graduated from AOS, Portage la Prairie in June of '43. He was shipped overseas in July of 1943.

Dodds Island (63 N/10) in Flatrock Lake was named after him in 1995.

Dodgson, Private **Arthur M.** of Portage la Prairie (H 14525). Calgary Highlanders. He died 6 April 1945 at the age of 25 and is commemorated at Brookwood Military Cemetery in Surrey, England. He was the eldest of the 10 children of John and Ivy Dodgson and the husband of Mabel Dodgson of Portage la Prairie. ***Dodgson Lake*** (64 K/11), northeast of Reindeer Lake was named after him in 1972.

Doerksen, Private **Henry** of Morden (H 1234). Royal Regiment of Canada. He died 3 March 1945 at the age of 25 and is commemorated at the Groesbeek Canadian War Cemetery in Holland. He was the eldest of the 10 children of Henry and Katharina Doerksen of Morden. His sister recalls their pre-war years together on the farm (5 May 1993):

My brother Henry and myself used to look after the children and Henry had to feed the four horses [and] get them ready and I would cook the meal and pack it and we would take it out to the field where mother and dad were, father on binder and mother stooking. Henry would bring home the other four horses and leave the ones he brought for dad to hitch up to the binder. I would bring the youngest one (for mother to nurse) and the other three boys and then take them all home and keep them busy and Henry would take the horses in the barn, water and feed them and then he'd come and help me with the children. Henry was a gentle person and always did his work.

When war broke out, I think we all had to go and fill out papers (or at least Henry did) and where the word "Nationality" was, he put "Dutch" instead of "Mennonite" so our parents were upset. But we did not like to be called Mennonite since we were teased in school being the only Mennonite family. My parents arranged for Henry to work in a [Conscientious Objector] camp since they did not believe in going to war, or rather, did not believe in killing. So when Henry joined the Army later, my mother was very sad but did not feel so bad about it after Henry went overseas and was asked to be a stretcher bearer.

"Stretcher Henry" as he came to be known to his comrades, was hit by machine gun and mortar fire while tending the wounded in the Hochwald Forest, Germany. ***Doerksen Lake*** (64 B/13), north of Opachuanau Lake was named after him in 1984.

Doig, Flying Officer **John** of Winnipeg (J 16112). No. 424 Squadron. He died 31 March 1944 at the age of 31 and is commemorated at the Hanover War Cemetery in Germany. He was the son of George and Isabella Doig of Winnipeg. ***Doig Lake*** (64 O/4), south of Nueltin Lake was named after him in 1961.

Dolding, Flight Sergeant **Arthur J.** of Winnipeg (R 101954). No. 405 Squadron. He died 17 November 1942 at the age of 22 and is commemorated at Saffron Walden Cemetery in Essex, England. He was the son of Frederick and Clara Dolding of St. James. According to his brother (3 April 1995), he:

... was born at the Grace Hospital in Winnipeg [and] grew up in the family home at 360 Olive Street, St. James. Art attended Bannatyne and Linwood Schools and played the usual high school sports. While attending high school, he worked for Carman Ruttan, former druggist and herbalist then located at Aldine Street and Portage Avenue.

Art joined the RCAF in 1940 and became Sergeant before going overseas. Following several flights over Europe, he was made Captain of a Halifax aircraft. While taking a test flight, the mid-upper gunner accidentally fired into the starboard engine causing complete hydraulic failure. Captain Dolding chose to stay with his aircraft thus enabling his crew to safely bail out.

Dolding Lake (64 P/3), southeast of Nejanilini Lake was named after him in 1974.

Domres, Private **Erdman** of Steinbach (H 616905). General List, Canadian Army. He died 1 January 1944 at the age of 29 and is commemorated at St. Johns Lutheran Cemetery in Steinbach. He was survived by his brother William Domres of Regina. ***Domres Lake*** (64 N/1), southwest of Nueltin Lake was named after him in 1972.

Donald, Private **James C.** of West Kildonan (H 59832). Canadian Forestry Corps. He died 12 December 1943 at the age of 39 and is commemorated at Old Kildonan Presbyterian Cemetery in Winnipeg. He was the son of Mr. and Mrs. Thomas Donald of West Kildonan. ***Donald Island*** (64 N/10) in Tatowaycho Lake was named after him in 1995.

Donald, Pilot Officer **James L.** of Grandview (J 87044). No. 419 Squadron. He died 15 February 1944 at the age of 25 and is commemorated at Magleby Churchyard, Langeland, Denmark. He was the son of Leo and Mary Donald of Grandview. ***Donald Bay*** (64 O/16) on Doney Lake was named after him in 1987.

Donen, Warrant Officer 2 **Samuel J.** of Winnipeg (R 110578). No. 45 Ferry Command. He died 7 September 1943 at the age of 22 and is commemorated at Christiansborg War Cemetery, Ghana. ***Donen Lake*** (64 I/14), northwest of North Knife Lake was named after him in 1974.

Doney, Warrant Officer 2 **Sydney R.** of Winnipeg (R 59859). No. 1664 Conversion Unit, RCAF. He died 22 November 1943 at the age of 22 and is commemorated at Stonefall Cemetery in Yorkshire, England. He was the son of Sydney and Jane Doney of Winnipeg. ***Doney Lake*** (64 O/16), north of Nejanilini Lake was named after him in 1975.

Donnelly, Assistant **Steward James** of Winnipeg. SS *Empire Comet*, Canadian Merchant Navy. The *Empire Comet* was lost 19 February 1942 and Steward Donnelly is commemorated at the Halifax Memorial. ***Donnelly Lake*** (63 P/7), south of Cauchon Lake was named after him in 2001.

Donogh, Lieutenant **Oliver Roland** of Rivers. Royal Winnipeg Rifles. He died 19 July 1944 at the age of 22 and is commemorated at Bretteville-sur-Laize Canadian War Cemetery in Calvados, France. He was the eldest son of Reverend Wallace R. and Mabel I. Donogh of Glenboro. He enlisted immediately upon completion of his third year of studies at the University of Manitoba. His brother writes (4 October 2001):

Roland was the eldest of five children and throughout his short life set a fine example for the rest of us. He was a first-rate athlete, a good musician and a scholarship student at university. He was highly principled, with a host of friends. While he and I served in the same Regiment, I was recovering from wounds in hospital and wasn't with him when he was killed in the fighting south of Caen. Before his death, he wrote glowingly of his engagement to a splendid English girl and was looking forward to "after the war." He is missed.

Donogh Island (63 J/13) in Wekusko Lake was named after him in 1972.

Donoghue, Flight Lieutenant **James Edward** "Ted" of St. Vital (J 20234). No. 409 Squadron. He died 13 January 1945 at the age of 24 and is commemorated at the Adegem Canadian War Cemetery in Belgium. He was the son of James Eugene and Hildagarde K. Donoghue of Winnipeg. Shortly after his death, his parents received a letter from his cousin:

Dear Hilda, Gene and Jack: This letter will leave many things unsaid simply because I can't find the words to express what I feel. I have just returned from Lille, France, where I paid our respects to Ted and visited his squadron. Ted and Mac were buried January 16th and the details should be a source of consolation to all of us. Flying Officer Rolly explained that Squadron Leader Conroy, Royal Air Force Catholic Padre, said the mass for Ted in the little village church of Lille, Veneville, about three miles southeast of Lille proper. It was the largest and most impressive funeral that Rolly has attended. There was a 100 per cent attendance of the squadron as well as a large number from the wing. As this I know will please you – a great number of civilians from the village attended the mass, dressed in their Sunday clothes to pray for these two men who had fought not only for Canada but for all Frenchmen. As a result, the village church was packed to the doors. It was a cold, bright day with snow on the ground. Despite the cold, every villager and the squadron accompanied the air force vehicles carrying the caskets to the cemetery for prayers at the grave. The villagers remained until the end.

Thus, Ted's funeral not only was one with full, military honours but what is more important, was intensely Catholic. The graves were banked with a mass of flowers from the Squadron, Wing and villagers. How or where the villagers obtained these in January is a mystery but they were sent through the mayor on behalf of the village. After learning these details from Flying Officer Rolly, I paid a visit to the cemetery which is on the northwest fringe of the village. Ted and Mac [Flight Lieutenant McPhail] are buried side by side – just as they flew – in the northwest corner of the cemetery. Lille Vendeville Cemetery is typical of most prosperous French villages. Its entrance is a wrought iron gate with a low red brick wall on each side. The cemetery is surrounded by a low green hedge and there is abundant evidence of attention and care characteristic of the French in this respect. It will interest you to know that Canadians are very popular with the villagers and I feel sure they will care for Ted's grave as if he were one of their own boys.

When Ted and I met in Normandy back in mid-August, he made a request that if anything happened he would like me to prepare his personal effects for shipment home. Neither of us had any premonitions at the time and we agreed to make the arrangement mutual. Unfortunately, in the rush of events in war he overlooked giving the adjutant my address. Thus, the first knowledge I had of the accident was contained in a letter from Colleen received January 30th and I left for Lille on the 31st. Since we had agreed to the arrangement, I took the liberty of enquiring about his personal effects and was informed that two fellow officers, supervised by the Adjutant, had packed them for shipment to you. Ted had made particular mention of his camera so I asked specifically about it and Flying Officer Rolly told me it was the first item that he had packed. Since it is of considerable value, Ted wanted to be sure that it reached you. You can rest assured that every personal item has been well taken care of by his friends.

There is something else I want to tell you. Ted loved flying and he had a strong sense of duty. Ted died not only doing his duty but doing a job he loved. He prayed each time he flew and I like to think that God wanted Ted with him because He knew Ted so well; after all, we want those we love best close to us – we overseas feel that very strongly. There's little more that I can say at the moment. The words to tell you how I feel just won't come. It is sufficient to say that since coming overseas I have considered Ted more of a young brother than a cousin. Love, Jask (3 February 1945).

Donoghue Lake (53 F/12), south of Hilton Lake was named after him in 1995. This feature was named in conjunction with nearby McPhail Lake (in Ontario) as Flight Lieutenants Donoghue and McPhail were close friends who died in the same aircraft.

Donovan, Private **Valentine A.** of Winnipeg (H 6527). Winnipeg Grenadiers. He died 19 December 1941 and is commemorated at the Sai Wan Memorial in Hong Kong. He was the son of Mr. and Mrs. Joseph Donovan of Winnipeg. ***Donovan Island*** (64 H/5) in Missinipi Lake was named after him in 1995.

Doran, Pilot Officer **William L.** of Neepawa (J 86233). No. 408 Squadron. He died 15 March 1944 at the age of 29 and is commemorated at Hilsenheim Communal Cemetery, Bas-Rhin, France. He was the son of William and Jessie Doran and was survived by his wife Marjorie Doran of Edmonton. ***Doran Lake*** (64 B/5), west of Ruttan Lake was named after him in 1995.

Dorrian, Private **James** of Winnipeg (291603). 44th Battalion (New Brunswick Regiment). He died 17 February 1918 at the age of 26 and is commemorated at Sucrerie Cemetery, Ablain-St.Nazaire, Pas de Calais, France. He was survived by his wife Elizabeth Dorrian of Ballywater, County Down, Ireland. According to his granddaughter (1 February 1988):

Sometime around 1909 at the age of 20 my Grandfather and his brother immigrated to Canada from Ireland, with my Grandfather eventually settling in the Norwood area of Winnipeg. The two brothers enlisted on February 10, 1916 and were assigned to the 222nd Regiment. They were later transferred to the 44th which was a New Brunswick regiment. They fought in the same battles in France until my grandfather was wounded. He went to his parents' home in Ireland to recover, but apparently he was worried about his brother so he went back to the battle before he really had to. As he was going back, his brother was being sent out on leave. The two lines passed each other and as far as I understand they had a chance to touch each other as they passed. My grandfather was killed shortly after this.

Dorrian Lake (64 I/11), north of Quinn Lake was named after this World War I casualty in 1989.

Dorval, Trooper **Oscar A.** of Morden (K 38108). Royal Canadian Armoured Corps. He died 3 July 1943 at the age of 31 and is commemorated at Brookwood Military Cemetery in Surrey, England. He was the son of Oscar A. and Ethel M. Dorval and was survived by his wife Gladys C. Dorval of Halifax, Nova Scotia. ***Dorval Lake*** (53 K/11), southeast of Edmund Lake was named after him in 1996.

Dorward, Flying Officer **David T.** of Killarney, Manitoba (J 14637). No. 10 Operational Training Unit, RCAF. He died 3 June 1943 at the age of 20 and is commemorated at the Runnymede Memorial in Surrey, England. ***Dorward Lake*** (64 P/4), south of Nejanilini Lake was named after him in 1974.

Douglas, Able Seaman **Albert** of Winnipeg (V 9393). HMCS *Ottawa*. The *Ottawa* was escorting Convoy ON.127 in the North Atlantic when it was struck by two torpedoes from U-91; 114 of her ship's company were lost. Able Seaman Douglas died 13 September 1942 at the age of 28 and is commemorated at the Halifax Memorial. He was the son of John and Elizabeth Douglas of Keewatin, Ontario and was survived by his wife Alma I. Douglas of Carlyle, Saskatchewan. ***Douglas Point*** (63 I/3) on Muhekun Lake was named after him in 1995.

Douglas, Private **Harry** of Ninette (H 20403). Queen's Own Cameron Highlanders. He died 19 August 1942 at the age of 29 and is commemorated at Dieppe Canadian War Cemetery in Seine-Maritime, France. He was the son of William and Ida Douglas and was survived by his wife Inez Douglas of Ninette. ***Douglas Peninsula*** (64 G/4) on Dickinson Lake was named after him in 1994.

Douglas, Private **Lyall F.** of MacGregor (H 8139). Royal Canadian Rifle Regiment. He died 7 September 1944 at the age of 22 and is commemorated at Coriano Ridge War Cemetery in Italy. He was the son of Edwin and Annie Douglas. ***Douglas Bay*** (64 J/15) in Stony Lake was named after him in 1989.

Douglas, Lieutenant **Robert H.** of Winnipeg. Royal Canadian Regiment. He died 19 December 1943 and is commemorated at the Moro River Canadian War Cemetery in Italy. ***Douglas Rapids*** (64 I/16) in the Lavallée Channel was named after him in 1995.

Dow, Rifleman **Roy H.** of Bethany (H 10159). Royal Winnipeg Rifles. He died 21 February 1945 at the age of 29 and is commemorated at the Groesbeek Canadian War Cemetery in Holland. He was the son of John R. and Charlotte Dow of Bethany and was survived by his wife Elizabeth Dow (née Leonard) of Bethany and their three daughters.

> Roy was born at Bethany December 24, 1915 and received his education there. He married Miss Betty Leonard from the same little village July 27, 1937. Prior to his enlistment in the Armoured Corps in June, 1943, Roy was employed with the Hudson Bay Smelting Works in Flin Flon. He was posted overseas with the Royal Winnipeg Rifles in June, 1944 (Pittman n.d.).

Dow Lake (63 K/15), southeast of Kississing Lake was named after him in 1958.

Dowds, Flying Officer **Herbert J.** of Winnipeg (J 20831). No. 420 Squadron. He died 17 August 1943 at the age of 20 and is commemorated at the Malta Memorial. ***Dowds Lake*** (64 O/12), south of Nueltin Lake was named after him in 1975.

Dowland, Sergeant **Frederick H.** of Bradwardine (R 106416). No. 22 Squadron. He died 7 September 1942 at the age of 19 and is commemorated at Bicester Cemetery in Oxfordshire, England. He was the son of Edward and Clara Dowland of Bradwardine, Manitoba and the brother of Warrant Officer Herbert L Dowland (next entry). ***Dowland Island*** (64 K/16) in Caron Lake was named after him in 1995.

Dowland, Warrant Officer 1 **Herbert L. "Bert"** of Bradwardine (R 124115). No. 114 Squadron. He died 25 August 1944 at the age of 25 and is commemorated at the Malta Memorial. He was the son of Edward and Clara Dowland of Bradwardine and the brother of Sergeant Fredrick H. Dowland (previous entry). ***Dowland Lake*** (64 P/13), north of Nejanilini Lake was named after him in 1974.

Dowling, Rifleman **Douglas K.** of Winnipeg (H 7125). Royal Winnipeg Rifles. He died 5 January 1945 at the age of 26 and is commemorated at Bergen-op-Zoom Canadian War Cemetery in Holland. He was the son of Archibald and Florence Dowling of Winnipeg. ***Dowling Lake*** (63 O/4), north of Wekusko Lake was named after him in 1970.

Downer, Private **Michael** of Transcona (H 200186). Queen's Own Cameron Highlanders. He died 8 August 1944 at the age of 27 and is commemorated at Bretteville-sur-Laize Canadian War Cemetery in Calvados, France. He was survived by his mother Mrs. A. Downer of McKenzie Island, Ontario. His brother writes (25 October 2001):

> [He was] killed on the day of his birthday. Michael graduated from St. John's Technical High School. He worked at the Starland Theatre as manager. His favourite actress was Betty Grable. My brother loved hunting with me. This poem was sent to me with his worldly belongings after he was killed in action:
>
> How sleep the brave who sink to rest
> By all their country's wished blest?
> When Spring, with dewy fingers cold,
> Returns to deck their sacred mold,
> She there shall press a nobler sod
> Than Fancy's foot has ever trod.
> And Freedom shall awhile repair
> To dwell, a weeping hermit, there.

Downer Lake (54 E/6), northeast of Split Lake was named after him in 1974.

Downing, Flying Officer **Albert E.** of Winnipeg (J 39340). No. 426 Squadron. He died 5 December 1944 at the age of 22 and is commemorated at Brookwood Military Cemetery in Surrey, England. He was the son of William G. and Mabel Downing of Toronto. ***Downing Lake*** (53 L/12), southwest of Laidlaw Lake was named after him in 1996.

Doyle, Captain **Charles J.** of Winnipeg. South Saskatchewan Regiment. He died 20 July 1944 at the age of 29 and is commemorated at Bretteville-sur-Laize Canadian War Cemetery in Calvados, France. He was the son of Peter and Margaret Doyle and was survived by his wife Kathleen E. Doyle of Winnipeg and their two daughters. His elder daughter recalls (12 November 1997):

> I was only two years of age when my father was killed in Normandy. My mother, my sister and I travelled with my father as much as we could in order to be together as he was a fitness instructor and was sent all over Canada to train men to go to war. After he was killed, a man came and told my mother that every time he trained new troops to go overseas he would ask to go as well. He hated to send such young soldiers and remain behind. He said he had a wife and children and had much to fight for. He was often sent away and mother did not know where, and then when he was allowed, he would again send for us. We moved 19 times in two years in order to be together. My grandparents did not want Mom to move around with two young children, but Mom was determined to be with my Dad. She was always so glad that she had done so.
>
> How I wish I had known my Father. My Mother loved him so very much and never married again although three times she was asked. I know life was hard for her but she managed to hire a housekeeper to help look after my sister and I when we were young and bought a wee house on Home Street in Winnipeg. It had two small bedrooms and she rented the second bedroom in order to make ends meet.

She still has the letter he sent her on the occasion of her second birthday:

> My Darling Wendy: How well I remember this day two years ago. Daddy always seems to be away on your birthday. When you were born, Daddy was in Nanaimo and a very worried Daddy he was. I didn't see you until you were almost two months old and what a surprise you were. You did an awful lot of travelling, my baby, so you could be with Daddy. Daddy remembers well how he and Mommy worried about you in Nanaimo when you had [w]hooping cough. Now my baby, Daddy is a long ways away but his heart is always with his three sweethearts. Say your prayers each night my precious one and next year Daddy hopes to be with you. I know he will be proud of you for Mommy has taken real good care of you. God Bless you my Dear and keep you safe (6 March 1944).

More than thirty years later, a friend of Captain Doyle wrote to the younger sister:

> Following our arrival in France, I saw your Dad occasionally and when we met we always had a warm but often brief visit. The last time I saw him was about ten days before his death. I had been wounded and was on my way back to hospital when he appeared on the scene with a cup of coffee for me. While I was in hospital a few days later, I was told of his death. It would be needless to say I was very saddened by the news, my memory of this great friendship has not diminished over the years.
>
> Prior to leaving England for France, your Dad and I exchanged badges in a gesture of friendship. I am enclosing the badge I believe this to be; I hope you will somehow find pleasure from the association. I am also giving you a book of poems called the *White Cliffs* written by an American in honouring the British and quite popular at the time. Also enclosed is a rather poor photo of myself at the time I knew your father, but it will give you an idea of your father's age at that time since our ages were only about a year apart. In closing, may I say how nice it has been for me to communicate with the daughter of such a dear friend and companion (25 January 1976).

Doyle Lake (64 N/1), northwest of Minuhik Lake was named after him in 1995.

Drake, Flying Officer **Howard R.** of Winnipeg (J 14815). No. 426 Squadron. He died 13 May 1943 at the age of 23 and is commemorated at Bergen-op-Zoom Canadian War Cemetery in Holland. He was the son of Howard and Lottie Drake of Winnipeg. ***Drake Lake*** (64 O/12), south of Nueltin Lake was named after him in 1961.

Drake, Sergeant **Richard E.** of Pipestone (R 60226). No. 57 Squadron. He died 25 July 1941 at the age of 27 and is commemorated at the Sage War Cemetery in Germany. He was the son of Thomas and Ione Drake and was survived by his wife Elizabeth Drake of Toronto. ***Drake Island*** (53 L/1) in Oneeskawaywin Lake was named after him in 1995.

Draper, Pilot Officer **Clarence O.** of Elgin (J 85398). No. 408 Squadron. He died 26 February 1944 at the age of 28 and is commemorated at Durnbach War Cemetery in Bavaria, Germany. He was the son of Albert and Clara Draper of Elgin. ***Draper Lake*** (64 N/14), west of Nueltin Lake was named after him in 1972.

Drascovich, Private **Robert A.** of Plumas (H 20564). Queen's Own Cameron Highlanders. He died at Dieppe 19 August 1942 at the age of 21 and is commemorated at Dieppe Canadian War Cemetery, Hautot-sur-Mer, Seine Maritime, France. He was the son of Mr. and Mrs. M. Drascovich of Plumas and the husband of Gladys Drascovich (née Hobson) of Winnipeg. According to his sister (28 November 2001):

My brother Bob, one of four boys (and me) was two years older than I and was quite mischievous and fun loving as a teenager. Being 6'3" and quite good looking, he was quite popular with the girls. We both left school early to help our parents in their business. Working together, Bob and I became quite close and as my "protector," he carefully screened any boy who may have been interested in me!

His first ten years of life were spent in Plumas, Manitoba, then in Winnipeg (West Kildonan) where he obtained most of his education and finally lived in south Fort Rouge. He was so pleased to find a number of friends from these communities were also stationed at the same place overseas. He wasn't quite 20 years old when he joined the Camerons in 1940. I was to be married in October that year, and Bob was unsure if he could attend the wedding let alone be in the wedding party. He was able to attend, coming in from Shilo, but left for the east two days later and then for overseas. I never saw him again.

Bob married Gladys Hobson in August, 1940. Her aunt and uncle in Winnipeg took in two young children from Scarborough, England as refugees – Michael and Shirley Morley. [The Children's Overseas Reception Board established in June, 1940, organized the evacuation of over 1530 children to Canada and more to other members of the Commonwealth]. Bob was immediately accepted into their family in England and spent most of his leaves with the Morleys. He became "their other son," and "brother" to their elder daughter. The Morley family loved him and felt his loss very deeply as indicated in all the correspondence kept up between the families.

Although he was treated well by the people in Britain, the weather left much to be desired and certainly increased his wish to "get on with it" so he could get back home to his loved ones and to meet the new little additions to our families, especially his namesake and god daughter (by proxy), Roberta, my first child. I'm sure he was expressing the sentiments of all "our boys" overseas.

I understand that Bob had fought all through the battle of Dieppe and was helping to shove the boat off the beach for their return when he was shot in the head by a sniper's deadly bullet. A business friend of my Mother was in France and visited the graves of the Camerons. Recognizing Bob's name, he thoughtfully took a picture of his grave and brought it home to my parents.

Drascovich Lake (64 O/1), north of Tadoule Lake was named after him in 1975.

Driedger, Private **John H.** of Altona (H 21112). Princess Patricia's Canadian Light Infantry. He died 7 December 1943 and is commemorated at the Moro River Canadian War Cemetery in Italy. ***Driedger Lake*** (64 K/7), northeast of Reindeer Lake was named after him in 1972.

Drummey, Sergeant **Robert Roy** of Lockport (H 21025). Queen's Own Cameron Highlanders. He died 1 October 1944 and is commemorated at Bergen-op-Zoom Canadian War Cemetery in Holland. ***Drummey Lake*** (52 E/14), northeast of Brereton Lake was named after him in 1974.

Drysdale, Flying Officer **Alan** of Neepawa (J 11030). No. 608 Squadron. He died 26 June 1943 at the age of 29 and is commemorated at El Alia Cemetery, Algeria. He was the son of James C. and Henrietta Drysdale (née McElroy). According to his cousin (23 January 1997):

His grandparents came from Sterling, Scotland in the year 1880. James C. Drysdale owned land on the same section (32-14-14) as his parents. When the Union School was built in 1883, many of the children were Drysdales. Alan's father died and his wife Henrietta kept the farm land but moved her family to British Columbia. Alan finished his education there and in 1934 or 1935, joined the British Columbia Provincial Police. In 1939, Alan enlisted with the RCAF and graduated as a pilot. He was sent to England for further training and to Coastal Command and later transferred to North Africa where he and his air crew were killed in an aircraft accident in 1943 in the month of June.

Drysdale Island (53 M/5) in Utik Lake was named after him in 1996.

Drysdale, Pilot Officer **James Leonard** of Winnipeg (J 17333). No. 44 Squadron. He was reported missing 23 May 1943 at the age of 21 and is commemorated at the Runnymede Memorial in Surrey, England. He was the eldest son of James and Mary Drysdale of Winnipeg. His nieces and nephews recall that in a letter home "Len" wrote:

I'm really looking forward to the next few days; at present I'm flying Manchester aircraft, and I was about to say, I'm being transferred to a new unit to take a try at the four-engine Lancasters. I expect it will only be another few weeks and I shall be a regular visitor over the continent and believe me, that will be none too soon for me. I have a very capable crew, seven in all. Only one other Canadian, a lad from Vancouver who is my tail gunner. I feel a lot safer knowing there is one of those "wild Canadians" back there (20 January 1943).

He had enlisted in the RCAF in May, 1941 and trained at Portage la Prairie and Dauphin where he received his wings in May, 1942. His Lancaster aircraft went missing in a night operation over enemy territory. It was his 21st mission (Allison and Hayward 1991). ***Drysdale Lake*** (63 N/1), southeast of Sherridon was named after him in 1970.

Dubinsky, Private **William H.** of Winnipeg (H 200121). Calgary Highlanders. He died 13 August 1944 at the age of 30 and is commemorated at Bretteville-sur-Laize Canadian War Cemetery in Calvados, France. He was the son of Shiyah and Reva Dubinsky of Winnipeg. ***Dubinsky Lake*** (63 I/16), east of Cross Lake was named after him in 1973.

Dubnick, Warrant Officer 2 **Edward "Harry"** of Winnipegosis (R 144401). No. 416 Squadron. He died 26 November 1943 at the age of 23 and is commemorated at Calais Canadian War Cemetery, Leubringhen, Pas de Calais, France. He was the son of McCauley and Annie Dubnick (née Tourdun) of Dauphin. His brother writes (3 November 2001):

> Harry Dubnick was born in Winnipegosis on September 10, 1920. He had three sisters and four brothers. His special interests were hunting, swimming, fishing and skating. Harry joined the armed forces in 1941. He was sent to England in early 1943 where he became a member of the Spitfire Squadron. On November 26, 1943 his squadron took part in a raid over Cambrai, France. As a result of enemy fire, Harry's plane crashed and he was killed trying to land his stricken plane. In 1987, relatives travelling in Calais, France located his tombstone. Harry Dubnick is sadly and fondly remembered. May the flowing waters of Dubnick Lake be a constant reminder of his dedication, courage and bravery.

In 1985, Warrant Officer Dubnick's brothers were presented with a replica of the aircraft which Harry had flown.

> A painful 40 year-old memory was rekindled recently for two brothers when they were given a model of the Spitfire their oldest brother flew in the Second World War. Harry Dubnick, 23, was shot down and killed November 26, 1943 in air action over France, where he is buried. The model, identical to the one flown by Dubnick, was given to Bill and John Dubnick during a tearful ceremony at the regional offices of the Department of Veterans Affairs in Winnipeg. The Spitfire, complete with ground crew and pilot, was built by Michael McHale, a mechanical maintenance fitter at the Jaguar Car Plant in England.
>
> The plant was an aircraft factory building Spitfires during the war and some of the materials in the model were taken from the factory, Veterans Affairs spokesman Liz Magnifico said. McHale, an amateur historian interested in the war, built the model to honour Canadian airmen who died in action, Magnifico said. She said Dubnick's name was picked at random from the cemetery where he is buried in France.
>
> McHale contacted Canadian authorities in Ottawa, who tracked down Bill Dubnick, the youngest brother in the family in Winnipegosis. John Dubnick, 63, said his brother's death was an open wound for many years, but it had healed over time. "He and I, we were very close." Dubnick said the gift was greatly appreciated, but added it had brought back a painful memory and some tears. He said the model will be donated to the Winnipegosis museum.
>
> Magnifico said the model's base was built from roofing felt taken from the original factory, located in Castle Bromwich, England. Another piece was constructed from the tarmac of an old Spitfire landing field, she said. The aircraft is made of wood, also taken from the original factory. The particular airplane was based at Digby, Lincolnshire, and Magnifico said the wheel chocks on the model are made from stone taken from Lincolnshire Cathedral. She said the toolboxes in the model are named after people who had some involvement in the project. Magnifico said McHale plans to honour another Canadian airman and perhaps a British pilot as well (*Winnipeg Free Press* 18 August 1985).

Dubnick Lake (63 K/13), northeast of Embury Lake was named after him in 1988.

Ducharme, Rifleman **Alphonse L. E.** of Woodside (H 41270). Royal Winnipeg Rifles. He died 17 July 1942 and is commemorated at Brookwood Military Cemetery in Surrey, England. **Ducharme Point** (64 O/10) on Kapusta Lake was named after him in 1995.

Ducharme, Private **James** of The Pas (H 1209). 48th Highlanders of Canada. He died 15 April 1945 at the age of 22 and is commemorated at the Holten Canadian War Cemetery in Holland. He was the son of Pascal and Virginia Ducharme of The Pas. His niece writes (11 December 2001):

> Jimmy was raised in the town of The Pas, Manitoba until he joined the army and went to war. He had several brothers and sisters, some of whom went overseas as well. Jimmy was an avid baseball player and an excellent musician. His brothers also played ball and just about any musical instrument around, consequently providing for a very active family.

Ducharme Lake (64 K/2), east of Reindeer Lake was named after him in 1961.

Ducharme, Private **Rupert R.** of Kinosota (H 87397). Royal Canadian Army Service Corps. He died 28 November 1942 and is commemorated at Brookwood Military Cemetery in Surrey, England. ***Ducharme Peninsula*** (64 I/1) on Condie Lake was named after him in 1995.

Duddles, Engine Room Artificer 4 **Stanley E.** of Winnipeg (V 24022). HMCS *Windflower*. The *Windflower* was rammed by Dutch freighter *Zypenberg* in dense fog off the Grand Banks while escorting Convoy SC.58; 23 of her ship's company were lost. ERA Duddles died 7 December 1941 at the age of 27 and is commemorated at the Halifax Memorial. He was the son of Daniel and Eliza Duddles of Winnipeg. ***Duddles Lake*** (54 L/12), west of Churchill was named after him in 1957.

Duff, Sergeant **Edwin C. "Ted"** of Winnipeg (H 5184). Royal Canadian Artillery. He died 24 November 1944 and is commemorated at Cesena War Cemetery in Italy. He was survived by his young son. ***Duff Lake*** (64 J/4), southwest of Tadoule Lake was named after him in 1975.

Duffield, Flying Officer **Kenneth V.** of Winnipeg (J 24048). No. 425 Squadron. He died 22 March 1944 at the age of 22 and is commemorated at Cologne Southern Cemetery, Germany. He was the son of Edward and Beatrice Duffield and was survived by his wife Georgina Duffield (née Frame). According to his brother (9 March 1995): "His only other relatives were cousins who lived in Horsham, England with whom he visited when he was posted overseas." His wife adds (15 October 2001):

> Ken grew up in West Kildonan and subsequently graduated from Lord Wolseley School. He went to work for the Canadian National Railway for a short time prior to joining the RCAF in 1942. The latter part of his training he received at Pearce, Alberta, graduating as a navigator in February, 1943, receiving his commission thereafter.
>
> Ken was an avid cyclist. He was an amateur boxer in the middleweight division and won some minor bouts. He was a member of the Kildonan Canoe Club and a member of the Anglican Church. As you can imagine, he had a very short time on Earth in which to leave his mark and I deeply appreciate that his name at least will live on in the lake named for him. Many years have passed, but I write this with tears in my eyes for "what might have been." Ken's memory has never been far from my thoughts despite the passage of time (30 April 1998).

She adds:

> Ken wrote from his station at Tholthorpe in England that he had bought a bicycle and loved to cycle through the English countryside. He loved the scenery and flower gardens of Devon in particular and promised to take me there at war's end. Much later, on a tour of England and Europe, one of the stops on tour was Cologne. Not speaking the language, I did not venture into the cemetery on my own, but I was able to light candles for him in the beautiful Cathedral that is famous in Cologne (15 October 2001).

Duffield Lake (64 N/5), southwest of Nueltin Lake was named after him in 1972.

Duffin, Pilot Officer **Edward Roy** of Winnipeg (J 89051). No. 427 Squadron, Mentioned in Dispatches.

This officer has proven himself to be an outstanding wireless operator. On several difficult operational sorties preceding and during the early stages of the invasion of France, his unfailing cheerfulness, courage and devotion to duty were an inspiration not only to his own crew but also to all air crew members of his squadron. On one occasion, his superb technical skill and mature judgement were largely responsible for the successful completion of a highly hazardous mission and the safe return to base of his entire squadron (25 October 1944).

He died 13 June 1944 at the age of 22 and is commemorated at Foncquevillers Military Cemetery, Pas de Calais, France. He was survived by his wife Margaret Duffin of Chatham, New Brunswick and their son. His wife writes (17 April 1998):

Roy was born in Thorndale, Ontario on October 13, 1921. He went to Saskatchewan in or about 1930, moving with the family back to Ontario in 1936. The family lived at Central Patricia Gold Mine from 1937 until early 1940 when they moved to Toronto and first Roy and later his father joined the Royal Canadian Air Force.

Roy and I first met in northern Ontario when he lived at "Central Pat" and I worked for his uncle and aunt a few miles down the road at another mine called "Pickle Crow." When Roy was posted to Winnipeg to the Wireless Air Gunnery School in what had previously been a school for the deaf, we re-established a relationship that had been carried on through correspondence. We married on June 20, 1942. We were posted to Chatham, New Brunswick in July of '42. Our son was born on July 6, 1943 and Roy got to see him only one time on his leave in August of 1943.

Roy was killed in a bombing raid over Arras, France on the night of June 12/13, 1944. He was 22 years old. He is buried with four others of his crew) in a British Cemetery at Foncquevillers, Pas-de-Calais, France. I had occasion to visit his grave last summer and was grateful to find it a peaceful, tranquil, well cared for place.

Duffin Lakes (64 P/4) were named after him in 1953 and Duffin River (64 P/3), which flows east into Wolverine River was named after him the same year.

Duffney, Sergeant **Peter** of Winnipeg (H 70113). Royal Winnipeg Rifles. He died 9 April 1945 and is commemorated at the Holten Canadian War Cemetery in Holland. ***Duffney Lake*** (64 J/14), west of Tadoule Lake was named after him in 1972.

Dufton Aircraftman 1 **John A.** of Winnipeg (R 253154). No. 10 Service Flying Training School. He died 8 December 1943 at the age of 21 and is commemorated at Brookside Cemetery in Winnipeg. He was the son of Wilbert and Elizabeth Dufton of Winnipeg. ***Dufton Lake*** (64 O/14), east of Nueltin Lake was named after him in 1975.

Duggan, Private **James A.** of Winnipeg (H 19967). Queen's Own Cameron Highlanders. He died 19 August 1942 at the age of 27 and is commemorated at Dieppe Canadian War Cemetery in Seine-Maritime, France. He was the son of John and Sarah Duggan and was survived by his wife Rhoda W. Duggan. ***Duggan Lake*** (64 O/7), west of Sandhill Lake was named after him in 1995.

Duke, Private **Andrew S.** of Elkhorn (L 9390). Royal Canadian Ordnance Corps. He died 5 June 1942 at the age of 22 and is commemorated at Brookwood Military Cemetery in Surrey, England. He was the son of Robert W. and Margaret J. Duke (née Stewart) of Elkhorn. His sister writes (31 October 2001):

Andrew was born in Wellbank, Scotland on March 1, 1921. He had ten brothers and sisters. The first five years he lived in the village of Wellbank, just outside Dundee. In 1925, he and his family immigrated to Canada; they sailed April, 1925 on the ship *Montreal* and landed in Halifax. His father had come to Canada two years earlier and was working in the Birtle area of Manitoba. It was to this area that the family came. Andrew took his schooling in Birtle, Wattsview and Elkhorn. After school, Andrew worked as a labourer and in 1941, he joined the Royal Canadian Ordnance Corps and was shipped overseas the same year. He lost his life in an accident in England. Andy was a likeable and mischievous child, but very caring. He had four brothers who served in the forces in World War II.

Duke Island (63 I/1) in Little Bolton Lake was named after him in 1995.

Duke, Private **John F.** of Woodlands (H 63640). Lake Superior Regiment. He died 16 February 1945 at the age of 24 and is commemorated at the Groesbeek Canadian War Cemetery in Holland. He was the son of Harry and Ivy Duke (née Smith) and was survived by his wife Ellen Duke of Winnipeg. His niece writes (24 November 2001):

John Frederick Duke was the son of Harry and Ivy Duke of England. He was a farm boy from the small town of Woodlands, just outside of Winnipeg. He was the only boy in the family with three sisters. He was a fun-loving tease and tormented his sisters at every chance. He taught himself to play the violin to the horror of all who heard him in his learning years. He mastered it though and enjoyed playing with his brother-in-law Jim (my father) on the guitar and another friend Russ on the banjo.

Jack joined the Lake Superior Regiment in 1940, I believe, where his mechanical knowledge was put to good use. He was sent to England and then to the battlefields of western Europe. He died just a few months before VE-Day, just one of many who gave their lives to protect our freedom and country. He is sorely missed by all whose lives he touched.

Duke Creek (64 J/5), which flows north into Sprott Lake was named after him in 1975.

Dumaine, Private **J. A. Gerard** of St. Norbert (H 77288). Winnipeg Grenadiers. He died a prisoner of war 17 February 1944 at the age of 21 and is commemorated at the Yokohama War Cemetery in Japan. His family only learned of his death shortly before the regiment was repatriated in 1945. He was the youngest of the seven children of Mr. and Mrs. Arthur W. Dumaine of St. Boniface. His sister recalls that (15 February 1995):

He was born ... in Ste-Geneviève, Manitoba about 10 miles north of Ste. Anne. His schooling started in Powerview (Pine Falls), Manitoba, then Lorette, Manitoba, then Ste. Anne. His hobbies were hunting rabbits and ducks. He liked skiing along the Seine River. In summer he loved to play baseball. Since we were living in the Depression, he was never able to find a real job. We still miss him very much.

Dumaine Lake (64 N/1), southwest of Nueltin Lake was named after him in 1972.

Dunand, Private **Marcel J. F.** of Val Marie (L 102437). Royal Regiment of Canada. He died 24 September 1944 at the age of 24 and is commemorated at Bergen-op-Zoom Canadian War Cemetery in Holland. He was the son of Antoine M. and Marie L. Dunand of Val Marie, Saskatchewan. ***Dunand Island*** (64 L/1) in Reindeer Lake on the Manitoba - Saskatchewan boundary was named after him in 1962.

Duncan, Lieutenant **Donald A.** of Winnipeg (CDN 450). Welch Regiment. He died 9 July 1944 at the age of 28 and is commemorated at Beny-sur-Mer Canadian War Cemetery in Calvados, France. He was the son of Ralph and Coral Duncan of Winnipeg. He had been an officer of the Winnipeg Light Infantry, but when the British Army called for Canadian junior officers last spring, he volunteered and went on loan to an Imperial regiment (*Winnipeg Free Press* 21 July 1944). In a letter to his sister he writes:

Eventually I'll get out of this hell-hole, either by a leave or by catching a piece of shrapnel. I can scarcely say I am leading the life of Reilly out here, but I'm getting enough to eat, enough to shoot at and the most modern, up-to-date slit trench with 20th century fixtures.

Perhaps I shall fall into your loving hands to be pieced together when I fail to duck in time. Will you handle me gently sister, "as the potter thumps his wet clay?" Or have you already lost your gentler nature amid the bestial duties of war-time nursing? Anyway we might manage a meeting, in which case I shall dine you at La Coquile in London and wine you at the Savoy and we will have a wonderful time, world without end. Amen (n.d.).

A letter was sent to his parents by Lieutenant Duncan's Platoon Sergeant:

My Dear Mr. and Mrs. Duncan: It is with my deepest regret that I have to write you a letter of this nature, please forgive me if I may sound brusque, but I must confess my surroundings are none too cheerful and secondly I'm not a very good writer of these types of letters. I shall have to be hard and I hope you will understand and realize the whole thing.

Your son was my Platoon Commander for a very short time and met with an accident which proved fatal. I know you will be informed through the War Office of his death, but it was his and our request that which ever met his fate or misfortune, we would write to the next-of-kin. It was an agreement between your son and us as a Platoon so I hope you don't mind me writing to you.

Well, I might say we all feel it very bad and can't quite realize that he has left us, as the boys of the old Platoon got on very well indeed with him and respected him in every way that was possible, he was and did prove to be a "Great Guy" and was known to us as "Dunc" – a little unusual maybe but he was one of us and a part of the team which had a job of work to do. I can say this with great pride that he will always be remembered by his boys and myself, that never once did he forget his duty to us, we were first and foremost in everything that concerned him and his Platoon, he was an Officer, which the lads take to.

The lads and myself buried him in an orchard which we now hold, it's not a very picturesque place, we buried him in as good a grave as is permitted under these conditions. It looked really nice even tho' we were at War, they turfed it and placed a pot of roses over the grave, then we secured some white wood from a nearby village and made a cross of it, really it is the best I've seen anyone do since I've been in this battle. You needn't worry about his burial, it was all in the very best of respect and honour to the dead. I am trying to get a photograph if possible of his burial ground, which I will forward to you without fail. I must close now with the regret of the whole Platoon and myself on your sad bereavement. Yours, M. Brimble, Pln. Sgt. (11 July 1944).

Sergeant Brimble also wrote to Lieutenant Duncan's brother:

… you may think me soft-hearted sir, but things like that get to me. All I can say is that your brother was avenged to the fullest … when we got to grips with the Boche a few days later … we didn't forget Dunc; it was "Don't forget one for Dunc" and sir let me tell you there were no prisoners taken by his old Platoon. We had that little satisfaction but what we wanted mostly was for Dunc to have led us. We have never had such a good officer in charge of the Platoon … no red tape if you know what I mean, that's what we appreciated and liked about him. Now I must close, as things are warming up and my slit trench is a favourite with the stuff flying around (25 August 1944).

Duncan River (53 M/14), which flows northeast into Dafoe River was named after him in 1985.

Duncan, Sergeant **Donald W.** of Winnipeg (R 134687). No. 7 Bombing and Gunnery School, RCAF. He died 2 September 1942 at the age of 24 and is commemorated at Brookside Cemetery in Winnipeg. He was the fifth of the six children of John M. and Jeanine W. Duncan of Winnipeg. His sister recalls (26 November 2001):

Don was born in Winnipeg [and] following his schooling, he was employed by the Coca Cola Company. He was a happy young man who enjoyed sports and music and was a bit of an entertainer. Don had leave for the last weekend in August, 1942 to attend his sister's wedding at St. Andrew's United Church on Elgin Avenue, August 29th. Don was an usher at the wedding and returned to Paulson on August 30th. His mother (a widow) received a letter from him dated September 1st and on September 2nd, she received the following telegram:

Deeply regret to inform you that your son R 134687 Donald Watt Duncan was killed in an aircraft accident this day while engaged in the performance of his duties. Further particulars being forwarded by letter. A. B. Muir, Flight Lieutenant, for Commanding Officer, No. 7 B&G School, Paulson, Manitoba.

What a weekend! The family was devastated. Don's funeral service was held the following Saturday at St. Andrew's Church and he was buried in Brookside Cemetery. A flypast by his fellow airmen honoured him. Don received the posthumous award of the air gunner's badge and sergeant chevrons along with a memorial bar showing his new rank. His mother received many tributes and a letter from the Station Chaplain at Paulson:

Dear Mrs. Duncan: May I offer my deepest sympathy to you on Donald's passing. He was so well known and so highly thought of here that this has been a great shock to us. We feel very much one with you in this hard experience. I knew Donald and admired him for his fine spirit. He was so bright and popular. Corporal Kelly told me that he was the most generous fellow he has ever met. All the lads in his class looked upon him as a natural leader. His instructors and officers tell me that he was one of the best students they have had for a long time. His influence on his classmates was always the best and he will be greatly missed.

You will find it very hard to understand why he has been taken, so young was he and so promising his future. But I am sure that you will feel akin to so many other mothers who have seen their homes emptied of their fine, straight sons. What a cost it is – but surely God will be gracious to such a one who has given his life for our cause. Indeed, he has just as surely done that as has any airman who has died in battle. We in the Service honour and respect him for it. May I call to see you when I come to Winnipeg? I would like to tell you how highly thought of Donald was, but written words seem so inadequate. Again, my sincerest sympathy. Faithfully yours, V. Lorne Stewart (n.d.).

Duncan Point (53 M/6) on Schwatka Lake was named after him in 1995.

Duncan, Warrant Officer 2 **Frederick C.** of Graysville (R 95497). No. 49 Squadron. He died 28 February 1943 at the age of 25 and is commemorated at Escoublac-la-Baule War Cemetery, Loire-Atlantique, France. He was the son of James and Louisa Duncan of Graysville. ***Duncan Lake*** (64 P/12), east of Nejanilini Lake was named after him in 1974.

Duncan, Corporal **Sydney C. "Buster"** of Winnipeg (H 16630). Princess Patricia's Canadian Light Infantry. He died 23 May 1944 at the age of 23 and is commemorated at the Cassino War Cemetery in Italy. He was the youngest of the seven children of Percival and Emily Duncan of St. Vital and the husband of Joan Duncan of Winnipeg. His sister recalls (12 April 1996):

He was always called [Buster] from the time he was born; even his comrades used his nick-name. Buster was a very loving person, [he] loved to play golf, baseball and skate. He was born on Hespeler Avenue, Winnipeg and we moved to 132 Sadler Avenue, St. Vital when he was a year old where he spent his entire life until he joined the army. He married a British war bride who remarried.

Duncan Bay (64 C/8) in Stag Lake was named after him in 1995.

Duncan, Pilot Officer **Stanley M.** of Winnipeg (J 95303). No. 435 Squadron. He died 12 February 1945 at the age of 22 and is commemorated at the Singapore Memorial. ***Duncan Peninsula*** (63 P/8) on Thom Lake was named after him in 1995.

Dunkin, Private **Walter** of Grandview (H 20273). Queen's Own Cameron Highlanders. He died 19 August 1942 at the age of 44 and is commemorated at Dieppe Canadian War Cemetery in Seine-Maritime, France. He was the son of Henry and Harriet Dunkin of Inglis. According to his sister (26 February 1997):

Walter Dunkin was an adventurous lad. World War I was declared so he never hesitated to enlist with the Fort Garry Horse. After completing his training in Winnipeg, he was slated for overseas. Arriving at Petawawa, he was sent to the hospital with measles and diphtheria. From there, he was discharged. Farming became his next adventure in life. World War II was declared. He joined the Queen's Own Cameron Highlanders. He saw action at Dieppe only to sacrifice his life for his family and country.

According to eyewitness Charlie McVey, he was killed while trying to get into one of the boats leaving Dieppe. ***Dunkin Lake*** (53 D/5), southwest of Carr-Harris Lake was named after him in 1980.

Dunlop, Sergeant **George Ernest** of Starbuck (R 123706). No. 10 Service Flying Training School. He died 11 January 1943 at the age of 30 and is commemorated at Starbuck Municipal Cemetery. He was the son of George and Tillie Dunlop of Starbuck and was survived by his wife Margaret Dunlop of West Kildonan and their two sons. ***Dunlop Lake*** (64 J/13), northwest of Tadoule Lake was named after him in 1973.

Dunn, Private **John** of Winnipeg (H 20514). Royal Canadian Electrical and Mechanical Engineers. He died 8 June 1945 at the age of 41 and is commemorated at the Groesbeek Canadian War Cemetery in Holland. He was the son of John and Agnes Dunn. ***Dunn Lake*** (64 K/5), northeast of Reindeer Lake was named after him in 1972.

Dunn, Pilot Officer **John H.** of Winnipeg (J 15859). No. 144 Squadron. He died 11 December 1941 at the age of 29 and is commemorated at Littlehampton Cemetery in Sussex, England. He was the son of Thomas and Grace Dunn of Winnipeg. ***Dunn Island*** (63 N/2) in Limestone Point Lake was named after him in 1995.

Dunn, Sergeant **Orval C.** of Portage la Prairie (R 134678). No. 2 Elementary Flying Training School. He died 22 March 1943 at the age of 28 and is commemorated at Moreton-in-Marsh New Cemetery in Gloucestershire, England. He was the son of George and Arabella Dunn of Portage la Prairie. Born in Vegreville, Alberta, he went to school at Salem and Amaranth and then attended Portage Collegiate. Following his schooling, he was employed in the municipal office of St. François Xavier and Elie before returning to work in the city municipal office in Portage la Prairie. ***Dunn Bay*** (64 O/16) in Courage Lake was named after him in 1995.

Dunnett, Private **David W.** of Winnipeg (H 103387). Essex Scottish Regiment. He died 11 July 1944 at the age of 21 and is commemorated at Bretteville-sur-Laize Canadian War Cemetery in Calvados, France. He was survived by his mother Mrs. M. Dunnett of Thurso, Caithness, Scotland. ***Dunnett Lake*** (64 I/11), northeast of North Knife Lake was named after him in 1974.

Dunphy, Flight Lieutenant **Roderick J.** of Winnipeg (J 13843). No. 426 Squadron, Distinguished Flying Cross.

Flight Lieutenant Dunphy has taken part in numerous operational sorties, the majority of which have been directed against major German targets. During a mission to Leipzig in October, 1943, his aircraft was twice engaged by enemy fighters and sustained in all seven attacks. The aircraft suffered severe damage and all the navigational instruments were destroyed. Despite this, Flight Lieutenant Dunphy, by superb navigation, directed the pilot to the target and back to base. This officer has invariably shown a high degree of skill and courage (DFC Citation 1943).

After this mission, his navigator's compartment was so bullet-shredded that it was sent to the Canadian War Museum in Ottawa (Allison and Hayward 1991). He died 20 December 1943 at the age of 20 and is commemorated at Rheinberg War Cemetery in Germany. He was the son of Kenneth A. and Ella Dunphy of Winnipeg. His friend, Murray Peden, DFC recalls their decision to enlist together:

I saw Air Marshall William Avery Bishop only once – at a recruiting rally in the Winnipeg Auditorium in the spring of 1941. I was seventeen, impatiently awaiting my eighteenth birthday so that I could join up. My classmate at Gordon Bell High, Rod Dunphy, sat beside me, both of us exhilarated by the pugnacious speech of the short, stocky flyer who, at that moment, was the greatest fighter pilot alive, with a score of seventy-two confirmed victories.

Eddie Rickenbacker, whose assessment in this field was based on solid credentials, once said that Billy Bishop was a man incapable of fear. Certainly the medal ribbons we could see on Bishop's chest afforded strong corroboration of Rickenbacker's assessment: Victoria Cross, Distinguished Service Order, Military Cross, Distinguished Flying Cross, to name only the ones we could identify. From the descriptions given by journalists and others, I had come expecting to see a gamecock, and in that respect Bishop certainly lived up to his billing. But he was much more than that; he exuded as much dignity as daring, doubling the impact he made on an impressionable audience. Dunphy and I came away convinced that our original intent had been right, and that we should join the Royal Canadian Air Force as soon as we could qualify, namely, at age eighteen (Peden 1988).

Dunphy Lakes (64 C/12), southwest of Lynn Lake was named after Flight Lieutenant Dunphy in 1947. Peden comments on the naming of geographical features after casualties of war:

The vivid and poignant recollections of war began to dim with one's return to civilian life. Memory's most deeply etched traces – the record of harrowing moments, or moments of blessed relief such as those when a safe return brought the knowledge that one would be alive for at least one more day – were gradually softened. The grist of a multitude of new, smaller scale experiences, like wind-driven sand, partially filled in the coarser impressions, and, over the years, obliterated completely the fainter trail of routine events.

But from time to time current happenings would reawaken fading memories, causing them to glow briefly with their old lustre. On May 6th, 1947, as one act in a program of naming previously unnamed geographical features after men who had given their lives for their country, the government assigned the name Dunphy Lakes to the extensive waters lying in Manitoba at Latitude 56 degrees 41' N., Longitude 101 degrees 34' W. If one opens the official Manitoba road map and glances at the upper left hand corner, the lake named in honour of Roderick J. Dunphy, DFC, is easy to find, some 30 miles southwest of the town of Lynn Lake (Peden 1988).

Dunsford, Sergeant **Edward C.** of Winnipeg (H 6382). Winnipeg Grenadiers. A native of Tiverton, Devon, England, he died 19 December 1941 at the age of 44 and is commemorated at the Sai Wan Memorial in Hong Kong. He had served with the Royal West Kent Regiment during World War I, but was discharged for medical reasons in 1916. Immigrating to Canada in 1920, he joined the militia in the 1930s. He was survived by a son. ***Dunsford Lake*** (63 I/7), north of Molson Lake was named after him in 1973.

Dunsheath, Regimental Sergeant Major (Warrant Officer 1) **Nathaniel** of Winnipeg (H 19798). Queen's Own Cameron Highlanders, Canadian Efficiency Medal and Member of the Order of the British Empire. He died 30 June 1945 at the age of 63 and is commemorated at Brookside Cemetery in Winnipeg. He was survived by his mother Mrs. N. Dunsheath of Neilston, Renfrewshire, Scotland and by his wife Elizabeth Dunsheath of Winnipeg. ***Dunsheath Lake*** (64 F/2), east of Reindeer Lake was named after him in 1961.

Durban, Pilot Officer **Nicholas F.** of Portage la Prairie (J 15038). No. 7 Squadron. He died 18 December 1941 at the age of 25 and is commemorated at the Runnymede Memorial in Surrey, England. He was the son of Mr. and Mrs. Fred Durban. According to a contemporary newspaper account:

> He was educated in the Portage public schools and the Collegiate, later taking a special course in refrigerator work in Chicago. [He] went to England in September, 1940 and was stationed there until reported missing in December, 1941 (n.d.).

Durban Lake (52 E/14), northeast of Brereton Lake was named after him in 1974.

Durston, Flying Officer **George H.** of Dauphin (J 24003). No. 578 Squadron. He died 19 March 1944 at the age of 22 and is commemorated at Durnbach War Cemetery in Bavaria, Germany. He was the son of Rowan and M. E. Durston of Dauphin. According to his brother (23 May 1997):

> George attended public school in the Durston School District in the town of Dauphin and completed his high school there. He was active in sports such as hockey, fast ball and track and field. At one time, he held the Provincial High School Mile Track Record. He belonged to the Dauphin Collegiate Drama Club and played violin in the orchestra. Following World War II his remains and those of the flying crew were located to a Canadian Cemetery south of Munich. They were on a bombing run over Frankfurt when they went missing.

He had been a teller at the Bank of Commerce in Gilbert Plains when he enlisted. ***Durston Lake*** (64 H/12), north of Wood Lake was named after him in 1995.

Dutchak, Flight Sergeant **Peter** of Angusville (R 190697). No. 630 Squadron. He died 18 March 1944 at the age of 28 and is commemorated at Coxyde Military Cemetery, Koksijde, West-Vlaanderen, Belgium. He was the only son of Harry and Dora Dutchak of St. James. His sister recalls (30 November 2001):

> His body along with his crew of seven washed up on the shores of the Strait of Dover near Ostend, Belgium. He was a mid upper gunner of a British Stirling bomber which was crippled from enemy aircraft fire and returning to England. However, this dear brother had eight younger sisters! We lived on a farm in the Silver Creek District at the edge of the beautiful Birdtail Valley. Peter was most outgoing and friendly. He loved playing hockey and baseball and Sunday afternoons found our farmyard full of friends playing ball on our pasture. Sometimes our father joined in. Mother was a wonderful cook and many stayed for the evening meal. He was skilful at woodworking, making fern stands and tables of willow and very musical, playing six instruments, violin being his first love. We were so proud of him. He made his own skis and poles and snowshoes and loved to hunt. He built us a boat and a windmill to wire our home on the farm for electric lights. My older sisters remember the Prairie Saturday Night Dances with real joy – all because of having a big brother for protection. He loved his horse 'Beauty' and his dog 'Rinty.' He did a lot of riding, hunting and fishing and loved the great outdoors. Though Dad was a farmer, Peter did not like farming and attended the National School of Engineering in Los Angeles. He graduated, the war broke out, he joined the RCAF. While in England, he met a lovely English girl; they were engaged to be married on his next leave. His untimely death came seven days before this planned, happy occasion. March 2, 1947 Peter was posthumously awarded the Operational Wings of the Royal Canadian Air Force in recognition of gallant service against the enemy.

Dutchak Lake (64 P/16), northeast of Nejanilini Lake was named after him in 1974.

Duthie, Sergeant **William Peter** of Winnipeg (R 58766). No. 419 Squadron. He died 3 February 1943 at the age of 21 and is commemorated at Sleen General Cemetery, Holland. He was the son of Robert M. and Lily E. Duthie (née Beckett) of Winnipeg. His brother was in Germany in May of 1945 and was able to visit the cemetery where Sergeant Duthie is buried. Later, his mother visited the site with a group of Silver Cross Mothers. Most recently, his niece paid her last respects there (1996). According to his brother (30 June 1997):

> He was about 18 when he enlisted in the RCAF to become an Aero Engine mechanic. The choice was probably because of his interest in mechanics, having worked on and overhauled at least two old cars with my brother, Les. His other interest was hockey, and he was the goal tender for a West End team in Winnipeg. Their second home in the winter was an open air rink behind the Canada Bread building just off Portage Avenue and Burnell Street at that time.

Duthie Lake (63 N/1), southeast of Sherridon was named after him in 1970.

Duthoit, Private **Raymond L.** of Winnipeg (H 9113). Royal Canadian Army Medical Corps. He died 2 July 1945 at the age of 21 and is commemorated at the Holten Canadian War Cemetery in Holland. He was the son of Albert and Verna Duthoit of Winnipeg. ***Duthoit Lake*** (52 L/3), northeast of Brereton Lake was named after him in 1973.

Dutka, Trooper **William** of Oak River (H 9905). Elgin Regiment. He died 9 June 1944 at the age of 33 and is commemorated at the Bayeux Memorial in Calvados, France. He was the son of Mickeal and Mary Dutka and was survived by his wife Mabel Dutka of Winnipeg. ***Dutka Lake*** (63 N/2), east of Kississing Lake was named after him in 1972.

Dutton, Corporal **Robert E.** of Gilbert Plains (R 152979). No. 5 Mitchell Operational Training Unit, RCAF. He died 23 December 1944 at the age of 22 and is commemorated at Eldon Cemetery in Gilbert Plains. He was the oldest of the four children of Thomas and Una Dutton (née Brooks) of Gilbert Plains. The father of the

pilot of the aircraft in which Corporal Dutton died wrote to his father: "You … and I … are loyal people of Canada. There are many, many like us whose wonderful boys are giving everything that our country may live. God bless those boys. God bless your Robert." His niece writes (20 September 1996):

> I am proud of the sacrifices that many of my family members made, and to me, Dutton Island not only represents my Uncle Bob, but my Great Uncle Edward Dutton, who was killed in World War I and is buried in France, and my dad, Lance Corporal John Irwin Dutton who served with the Calgary Highlanders in World War II. While serving in Holland, dad stepped on a land mine, losing one leg as a result. Dad died at the age of 66 years, and I don't think there were many days during his lifetime that he didn't suffer from the physical and emotional scars of war.
>
> I am 34 years of age, and since my father's death, I have marched in memory of what he, Uncle Bob and Uncle Edward gave, with the Gilbert Plains Legion on Remembrance Day. I hope I am instilling in my children the same respect and care for all those who fought in both world wars: those who died and those who fought, suffered and came home.
>
> Uncle Bob and Uncle Edward made the ultimate sacrifice – they died for Canada. My dad lived though physical pain, nightmares, depression and phantom pain of a lost limb. I will think of Dutton Island as being a tribute to Robert Edward Dutton, a young man that died before he had the chance to live – to Edward M. Dutton, a young man that died in a strange country and was buried among strangers – and to John Irwin Dutton, a young man who left home at the age of 18 and came home old beyond his years at age 19.

Dutton Island (64 F/1) in Melvin Lake was named after him in 1995.

Duxbury, Flight Sergeant **Thomas L.** of Elkhorn (R 59125). No. 40 Squadron. He died 12 October 1941 at the age of 25 and is commemorated at Dinant (Citadelle) Military Cemetery, Dinant, Namur, Belgium. He was the son of Thomas and Ethel Duxbury of Winnipeg. ***Duxbury Lake*** (64 P/7), east of Nejanilini Lake was named after him in 1974.

Dyer, Flying Officer **John Philip** of Minnedosa (39073). No. 99 Squadron, RAF, Distinguished Flying Cross. He died 22 May 1940 at the age of 27 and is commemorated at Belval Communal Cemetery, Ardennes, France. He was the son of John M. and Gertrude Dyer of Minnedosa. Flying Officer Dyer worked his way over to England on a cattle boat in hopes of joining the RAF. He began his training in 1935 and was the winner of a cup of honour in his pilot's course (1937). He flew his first mission in 1939. Flying Officer Dyer "was well on his way to RAF fame if fate hadn't intervened" (Allison 1978). ***Dyer Lake*** (53 L/1), east of Rochon Lake was named after him in 1995.

Dyker, Leading Aircraftman **Allan L.** of Holland, Manitoba (R 172957). No. 15 Elementary Flying Training School. He died 25 June 1943 at the age of 30 and is commemorated at Elmwood Cemetery in Winnipeg. He was the second of the seven children of Reverend Dr. George A. and Lulu Dyker of Holland, Manitoba. According to his sister (23 December 1995):

> His father was a Presbyterian and later a United Church minister who served congregations in several towns in Manitoba when the family was growing up. Allan received his elementary education at Belmont and secondary education at Waskada High School. After high school, he entered United College (now the University of Winnipeg) from which he graduated in 1933 with a Bachelor of Arts. In 1937 he graduated from the Manitoba Law School and was called to the bar that year. He was class president in his graduating year. Following graduation, he practised law in Winnipeg for two years and then became the solicitor for the Canadian Wheat Board until enlisting in the RCAF in July, 1942. He was killed in a flying training accident ... at Regina.

A contemporary newspaper account added that he was President of the Winnipeg Young Liberals association in 1935 and a member of the Ness Wise rink, a trophy winner in the 1942 Manitoba bonspiel (n.d.). ***Dyker Lake*** (64 O/15), east of Nueltin Lake was named after him in 1975.

Dykun, Sergeant **John** of Winnipeg (H 200049). 1st Canadian Special Services Battalion. He died 6 December 1943 at the age of 23 and is commemorated at the Cassino War Cemetery in Italy. He was the son of Peter and Tillie Dykun of Arran, Saskatchewan. ***Dykun Creek*** (63 K/16), which flows southwest into File River was named after him in 1973.

Chaplains aid in the evacuation of wounded soldiers at Caen, France 15 July 1944. Courtesy of the National Archives of Canada (PA-133244).

E

Eager, Flying Officer **William H.** of Norwood (J 17626). No. 61 Squadron, Distinquished Flying Cross.. He died 16 December 1943 at the age of 23 and is commemorated at Botley Cemetery in Oxfordshire, England. He was the son of Harry and Johanna Eager of Norwood and was survived by his wife Ada Eager of Todwick, Yorkshire, England and their twin daughters. Some of Flying Officer Eager's experiences (and that of his aircraft) were chronicled in a newspaper account:

> *K for Kitty* has gone missing. The legendary Lancaster which was piloted for the last 18 successful trips of her apparently indestructible career by Pilot Officer W. H. Eager, 151 Ferndale Avenue, Winnipeg, went down fighting on her 77th sortie over an enemy target. Eager and his crew were on leave when their veteran aircraft was borrowed by a new crew and took off on her last trip.
>
> "She went the night we got back," he said. "When we got up in the morning and found no *K for Kitty* it was like losing an old friend. We first took her over on her fifty-eighth trip when she was the oldest kite on the squadron and we were the youngest crew. She saw us through some pretty shaky times and we were looking forward to finishing our tour in her. There were four new engines waiting for her in the hangar, and the ground crew which had serviced her throughout all 77 operations figured she could go on forever. They were literally in tears when she didn't come back. Yes, *K Kitty* was a station institution. She must have delivered easily a million pounds of bombs in her career."
>
> Pilot Officer Eager finished his tour of operations in another K. It was *F Freddie* when he got it, but he and the ground crew lost no time in renaming it in honour of their favourite. "I think our shakiest experience was the raid on Peenemunde," he recalls. "It was the centre of German secret research and development and we bombed from an unusually low level in order to make absolutely sure of wiping it out first time. The flak was really terrific. It was *K Kitty's* seventy-sixth trip and she got pretty badly shot up, but none of us was hurt."
>
> Eager made 28 trips over Germany and Italy before he was awarded the DFC and sent as an instructor to a training station. He has seen rocket bombs come up at him over Hamburg and engaged ground defences from a height of 100 feet over Brest, but his only serious trouble was a flying accident at a conversion (training) unit in England. "We all got our hair singed that time," he remembers. "We were just coming in to land when our port engine caught fire at 800 feet and we made a crash landing. The bomb aimer got out through the smashed Perspex, and the rest of us got out through the escape hatches."
>
> His longest trip was to Turin, when he was in the air for ten and a half hours. Fifteen trips to the Ruhr and three to Berlin are included in his logbook, but good flying, good luck and a good aircraft have kept him from any notable mishap. "If I ever go back on 'ops' it will be in a *K for Kitty*," he says. "I've flown in three now, and you can take it from me that Ks are lucky" (12 February 1942).

He died when his Lancaster crashed in Nottinghamshire, England a month after he had been awarded the DFC. ***Eager Lake*** (64 C/12), southwest of Lynn Lake was named after him in 1947.

Eakins, Pilot Officer **Paris R.** of Minnedosa (J 7009). No. 411 Squadron. He died 19 August 1942 at the age of 27 and is commemorated at Neufchatel-hardelot (Neufchatel) New Communal Cemetery, France. He was the eldest son of George A. and May Eakins of Minnedosa.

> Paris was employed with the *Minnedosa Tribune* prior to moving to Winnipeg where he became a member of the Sports Staff for the *Winnipeg Free Press*. He enlisted in the RCAF in November, 1940, training at Sydney, Toronto, Victoriaville, Picton, Regina and Yorkton. Paris received his wings when he graduated from No: 11 Elementary Flying Training School in Yorkton, Saskatchewan on August 16, 1941. He was commissioned as a Pilot Officer four days later. While stationed at Yorkton, he became the first editor and editor-in-chief of *Wings*, the station's magazine. Paris was posted overseas, arriving October 1, 1941. He soon became known as an excellent fighter pilot and was an acting flight commander in charge of the many continental sweeps he made beginning May, 1942 in his Spitfire. He was slated for a permanent promotion prior to the Dieppe Raid, August 19, 1942. Paris had a premonition that he would not survive the sweeps over Dieppe and made his thoughts known to his public relations officer while on leave in London. His premonition became a reality when his Spitfire was shot down by a Messerschmitt that day. After signalling his commander that he had been hit, Paris's aircraft was seen going out of control and crashing near the racetrack behind Dieppe (Pittman n.d.).

Eakins Lake (52 M/12), southwest of Family Lake was named after him in 1980.

Earl, Pilot Officer **James** of Winnipeg (J 87615). No. 614 Squadron. He died 20 October 1944 at the age of 23 and is commemorated at the Malta Memorial. He was the son of Charles R. and Margaret Earl of Vancouver. Earl Lake (64 G/15), east of Trout Lake was named after him in 1995.

Earl, Corporal **Tom S.** of Winnipeg (M 102891). Seaforth Highlanders of Canada. He died 23 May 1944 at the age of 29 and is commemorated at the Cassino War Cemetery in Italy. He was the son of Sydney and Mary Earl of East Kildonan. ***Earl Bay*** (64 J/12) in Chornous Lake was named after him in 1995.

Earle, Pilot Officer **James Allan** of Winnipeg (J 19305). No. 408 Squadron. He died 14 January 1944 at the age of 29 and is commemorated at the Hanover War Cemetery in Germany. His sister visited the grave in the mid-1950s. He was the son of James R. E. and Edna E. Earle of Toronto. His niece writes (23 November 2001):

> Allan was born in China, the youngest son of a Methodist minister. The family finally moved back to Canada when he was nine. After living in Toronto, the family moved to Norway House and Cross Lake. He received his Bachelor of Arts degree from Wesley College (University of Winnipeg) and eventually worked as the assayer of the Gods Lake gold mine in the late 1930s. He joined the RCAF in the early 1940s hoping to be a pilot but finally graduated as a bomb aimer and was then sent overseas. In October, 1943, his aircraft was forced down in the North Sea but he survived that incident. On many flights he was a crewman on the famous aircraft known as the Ruhr Express – the first Lancaster bomber fully made in Canada. The crew affectionately called her "Q for Queenie" and thought of her as a good luck talisman. His last flight, not on Queenie however, was over Brunswick, Germany. The plane was reported missing and later confirmed as shot down.
>
> He was a loving and kind son, brother and uncle. His numerous letters to home are messages of a God loving, well thinking and understanding young man. To this day he is still revered by his relatives, especially on Remembrance Day.

He wrote a letter home after the crash mentioned above:

> Returning from a raid, our plane crashed into the North Sea. Somehow, all seven of us got out in the 20 to 30 seconds that the craft remained afloat. We struggled in the water for some time before we reached the rubber boat. Then we lay there exhausted, even though it was half full of water. Fortunately, there was a strong onshore wind that carried us on the fastest, wildest boat ride we've known, where we landed on a beautiful beach and waited for guides to lead us through the maze of land mines.
>
> After a week's leave, we still cannot believe it was really us who prayed in the water for strength. This we do realize – human power and

knowledge are but frail things. That alone cannot sustain us in our greatest trials. It is foggy and cold today, but there is sunshine and the joy of living in my heart – so be of good cheer (n.d.).

Earle Island (64 O/15) in Kapusta Lake was named after him in 1995.

Earley, Corporal **John** of Winnipeg (H 37326). Royal Canadian Army Service Corps. He died 7 November 1943 at the age of 23 and is commemorated at Brookwood Military Cemetery in Surrey, England. He was the son of Joseph and Sara Earley of Winnipeg. Earley Lake (64 J/3), southwest of ***Tadoule Lake*** was named after him in 1975.

Earp, Able Seaman **Ralph N.** of Winnipeg (V 68995). HMCS *Shawinigan*. The *Shawinigan* was torpedoed and sunk by U-1228 while on anti-submarine patrol in the Cabot Strait; all hands were lost. Able Seaman Earp died 24 November 1944 at the age of 18 and is commemorated at the Halifax Memorial. He was the son of William and Lillian Earp of Winnipeg. A local newspaper reported that:

A/B Earp enlisted with the RCNVR October 20, 1943, and after training at HMCS *Chippawa* and *Cornwallis*, served for two months on a minesweeper, before being transferred to the Shawinigan. Educated at Lord Roberts and Earl Grey schools and Kelvin high school, A/B Earp was employed in the accounting department, City Hydro Company before enlisting (*The Winnipeg Tribune* 7 December 1944).

Two years later, his parents received the following letter:

Dear Mr. and Mrs. Earp: You don't know me and have never heard of me so I start this letter as a stranger to you. I'm writing to express my deep sorrow on just receiving the news that your son is presumed dead. I knew Ralph, he was a couple of years younger than myself and not far behind in school and always impressed me as a lad destined to go places. I never really knew him well, just enough to say hello and a short chat at a hockey game or some similar incident, but I was really sorry when I read the sad news.

You mustn't give up hope though; war plays funny tricks and very often hurts us unnecessarily. There is still hope – hope that will linger a long time, and perhaps news will yet come through – good news, news you both will accept with joy in your heart. And if things remain black and no news does come through, I can assure you Mr. and Mrs. Earp, that Ralph has not given his life in vain. I have seen most of France, Belgium, Holland and now Germany, and I have seen what has happened to countries that went ... under. It is not nice. I may be next to go, but having seen what I have, I'm willing, and in the end we'll all have a free world. Sincerely, Private D. G. Rodger (16 March 1945)

Earp Lake (64 B/6), south of Southern Indian Lake was named after Able Seaman Earp in 1962.

East, Flying Officer **Ronald C.** of Rapid City (J 8202). No. 420 Squadron. He died 22 July 1943 at the age of 21 and is commemorated at the Cassino War Cemetery in Italy. He was the son of Thomas W. and Dorothy East of Winnipeg. His brother adds that he was a pilot who with his crew, died on a bombing mission to Naples, Italy. They had been stationed in North Africa. ***East Lake*** (64 K/1), north of Big Flat Lake was named after him in 1987.

Eastholm, Private **Eric E.** of Winnipeg (H 6160). Winnipeg Grenadiers. He died a prisoner of war 16 October 1942 at the age of 22 and is commemorated at the Sai Wan War Cemetery in Hong Kong. He was the son of Lars and Greta Eastholm of Winnipeg. ***Eastholm Lake*** (63 K/16), northwest of Wekusko Lake was named after him in 1973.

Eastland, Private **Jack** of Brandon (H 92438). Princess Patricia's Canadian Light Infantry. He died 20 December 1944 at the age of 22 and is commemorated at Cesena War Cemetery in Italy. He was the son of Axel and Ethel Eastland (née Pendlebury) of Sandy Lake and was survived by his wife O. Eastland (née McWilliams) of London, England and their daughter whom he never saw. Years later, his daughter attempted to make contact with her father's relatives:

Finding some of her long-lost relatives could be the key to a mended heart for a British woman who has traced her roots back to Manitoba. Valerie Groves has been trying for years to find relatives of her father, Jack Eastland, who served with the Princess Patricia's Canadian Light Infantry. He was killed in battle in December, 1944, only seven months after the birth of his only child, who never got a chance to know him. "I've always said if I could give up 10 years of my life to spend just 10 minutes with my dad, I would," said Groves who lives in London.

Groves has asked for help from the Canadian Veterans Association of the United Kingdom to try to locate her family in Canada. "I've re-united six families in the last nine years. It's something that should have happened years ago," said Cal Heywood, the association's secretary and past president. Groves knows little about her father and his family which has made her search difficult. She does know he was born at Sandy Lake, Manitoba in February, 1922 to parents named Alex and Elsie or Ethel, and he worked in Brandon as a mechanic before enlisting. His parents later moved to Cranbrook, BC, but his mother's two sisters stayed at Sandy Lake for some time, Groves said. "I know there must be family, because I know (the sisters) had children," she said. "I feel there's someone out there who knows something or has pictures."

If she met some of his relatives, she would finally feel like she belonged to someone, said Groves, who never had a good relationship with her mother and got little information from her about her father. "I've put this man on a pedestal who I've never known. I feel he's around me most of the time."

Groves hopes to visit Canada next year, but doesn't know where to start. She went to Italy several years ago to find her father's grave, which she called a very emotional experience. "There were 700 graves in the cemetery and I didn't know where he was. But I went in and walked straight to it" (Kubara 1998).

Through the efforts of the Manitoba Geographical Names Program and contacts in Erickson and Sandy Lake, she was in touch with her great uncle and family two months later. ***Eastland Lake*** (52 L/6), northeast of Lac du Bonnet was named after Private Jack Eastland in 1973.

Easton, Sergeant **George W.** of The Pas (H 75255). Royal Canadian Artillery. He died 7 September 1944 at the age of 22 and is commemorated at the Calais Canadian War Cemetery in France. He was the son of Fred N. and Elizabeth V. Easton of The Pas. His obituary in the local newspaper read:

Sergeant George Easton of the Royal Canadian Army has been killed in action in France, according to word received here by his father, Fred Easton, yesterday morning. Sergeant Easton, 22 years of age, was with Anti-Aircraft at the time of his death. He will be remembered here for his great interest in hockey at which he excelled. Born in Moose Jaw, Saskatchewan, he attended school there and at Yorkton. He was employed with the Western Grocers here, enlisting with the army in 1941. He had been overseas two years (n.d.).

A step-sister recalls (20 October 2001):

George was born in Moose Jaw, Saskatchewan and received his schooling there and in Yorkton. In his later teens, he worked at Western Grocers [and] later transferred to The Pas to be with his Dad Fred. His mother had passed away, at what date I don't know. George became part of our family after his Dad and my mother (Rose Aimee) were married in 1940. He continued to work at Western Grocers till he joined the army.

I remember him as always being cheerful and always whistling as he walked. He loved sports, especially hockey and he was a good hockey player. He often took me for a bike ride as I had just received a new bike. He loved to tease. One couldn't ask for a better brother and he would help anyone if need be.

While overseas, he often wrote to me. Sometimes the letters were sad and he seemed to be depressed and looking forward to coming home. He looked forward to the parcels my mother would send him. Soon after his death, we received a letter from his Padre telling us how he gave up his life saving others. His last letter to me was dated March, 1944. I still have it and others. I feel sure he is one of God's angels looking over us.

Easton Lake (64 K/3), east of Reindeer Lake was named after him in 1961.

Easton, Sergeant **Herbert R.** of Winnipeg (R 56846). No. 214 Squadron. He died 8 April 1941 at the age of 22 and is commemorated at the Runnymede Memorial, England. ***Easton Island*** (64 F/5) in Reindeer Lake was named after him in 1995.

Eby, Sergeant **Norris A.** of Carman (H 294). Lord Strathcona's Horse. He died 25 May 1944 at the age of 25 and is commemorated at the Cassino War Cemetery in Italy. He was the son of Levi and Ada Eby of Carman. ***Eby Lake*** (64 K/14), northeast of Reindeer Lake was named after him in 1972.

Eccles, Lance Corporal **Norman C.** of Flin Flon (H 6567). Winnipeg Grenadiers. He died 21 December 1941 at the age of 27 and is commemorated at the Sai Wan Memorial in Hong Kong. He was the son of Stanley and Katherine Eccles and was survived by his wife Ellen Eccles. ***Eccles Lake*** (64 J/14), northwest of Tadoule Lake was named after him in 1972.

Eddie, Sergeant **Lawrence E.** of Winnipeg (R 253389). No. 1653 Heavy Conversion Unit, RCAF. He died 3 November 1944 at the age of 28 and is commemorated at Brookwood Military Cemetery in Surrey, England. He was the son of William and Agnes Eddie of Winnipeg and was survived by his wife Margaret Eddie of Winnipeg. ***Eddie Lake*** (64 I/8), northeast of North Knife Lake was named after him in 1974.

Edgley, Private **Charles R.** of Winnipeg (H 6302). Winnipeg Grenadiers. He died 21 December 1941 at the age of 40 and is commemorated at the Sai Wan Memorial in Hong Kong. He was the son of Noah and Lily Edgley of Michigan. His sister wrote (16 September 1997):

Terrible to think he never had a proper burial. We were sending parcels all those years and he was gone. Sad. Poor mother sat at the table and cried wondering if he had any food. Was a terrible time. Mother was sending parcels all the time. Bert came home on the train with some of the soldiers. Poor guys, skin and bones. One soldier said he was standing beside Charley when he was shot. Their bodies laid in the ditches weren't even buried.

Edgley Lake (52 L/6), northeast of Lac du Bonnet was named after him in 1973.

Edgley, Lance Corporal **Harold V.** of Winnipeg (H 800152). Princess Patricia's Canadian Light Infantry. He died 6 June 1951 at the age of 30 and is commemorated at the United Nations Cemetery in Pusan, South Korea. ***Edgley Bay*** (53 L/4) in Kitchi Lake was named after this Korean War casualty in 1998.

Edgley, Corporal **Robert W.** of Winnipeg (H 42176). Loyal Edmonton Regiment. He died 18 September 1944 at the age of 31 and is commemorated at Coriano Ridge War Cemetery in Italy. He was the son of Cecil H. and Alice L. Edgley (née Ellard) of Winnipeg and was survived by his wife Margaret E. Edgley (née Miller) of Winnipeg and their two daughters. On the occasion of his daughter's first birthday, he wrote this letter to her:

Dear Bobbie: This note won't mean anything to you now, but maybe in later years, you can read it and remember it was the first letter you ever received from your Dad and it's to wish you many Happy Returns of your 1st birthday. I am thousands of miles away from you in Italy, but I'll be thinking of you and wishing I could have a piece of your cake. Later on when you're older, we'll read this together and I'll tell you all about where I am. Love, Daddy (13 September 1943).

Edgley Island (64 H/5) in Partridge Breast Lake was named after him in 1995.

Edmond, Flying Officer **Norman D.** of Winnipeg (41564). No. 242 Squadron, RAF. He died 20 April 1941 at the age of 21 and is commemorated at North Weald Bassett (St. Andrew) Churchyard in Essex, England. He was the son of Mr. and Mrs. Arthur Edmond of Calgary. Flying a Hurricane on patrol over the English Channel, he was in collision with two other Hurricanes of the same squadron when they were turning to avoid enemy aircraft. All three went down and all three pilots were killed (Allison 1978). ***Edmond Island*** (64 P/15) in the Caribou River was named after him in 1995.

Edmonds, Rifleman **Donald** of Hazelridge (H 42012). Royal Winnipeg Rifles. He died 15 August 1944 at the age of 30 and is commemorated at Bretteville-sur-Laize Canadian War Cemetery, France. He was the son of John H. and Catherine Edmonds of Hazelridge, Manitoba. His niece writes (19 December 2001):

He is fondly remembered by his niece and her sister and brother as a quiet and good natured man who worked very hard on the family farm. His interest in the repairing of farm equipment was only exceeded by his love for hunting. Often he would take his rifle and head out into the heavy bush areas and stay away for a day or two. His parents never worried about him as they knew he would come back safely.

Edmonds Lake (64 H/6), north of Northern Indian Lake was named after him in 1995.

Edmondson, Flying Officer **William** of Winnipeg (J 88640). No. 251 Squadron. He died 27 March 1945 at the age of 23 and is commemorated at Fossvogur Cemetery in Reykjavik, Iceland. ***Edmondson Lake*** (64 J/10), west of Tadoule Lake was named after him in 1975.

Edwards, Gunner **Edward W.** of Portage la Prairie (H 35538). Royal Canadian Artillery. He died 22 July 1941 at the age of 30 and is commemorated at Arnos Vale Cemetery in Bristol, England. He was the son of Edmund and Alice Edwards of Totterdown, Bristol and was survived by his wife Kathleen Edwards. ***Edwards Rapids*** (64 N/5) in an unnamed river which flows into Duffield Lake was named after him in 1995.

Edwards, Private **Frank R.** of Winnipeg (H 23192). Royal Canadian Infantry Corps. He died 25 April 1945 at the age of 21 and is commemorated at Brookwood Military Cemetery in Surrey, England. He was the son of Ernest and Rebecca Edwards of Winnipeg. According to his brother (4 May 1995):

Frank was born in the Birtle, Manitoba hospital 20 July 1923. After spending his first seven years on a farm and attending Solsgirth School, he moved to Winnipeg with his parents and brother. In the city, he attended Isbister, General Wolfe and Daniel McIntyre Collegiate. He was also a member of Knox United Church boys' group and Sunday School.

After high school he became an apprentice jeweller with Feldsted Jewellers in Winnipeg. He enlisted in the RCAF in 1942 and qualified as an instrument technician, working in St. Thomas, Ontario. He wanted action, transferred to the Canadian Army and received his paratroop wings in January, 1945. He was killed in a training accident in England with the 1st Canadian Paratroop Battalion.

Frank was a cheerful, fun-loving person with a host of friends. Being an athletic person, he enjoyed the rigorous training and the thrill of jumping and looked forward to being in the "battalion."

Edwards Peninsula (63 P/2) on Unwin Lake was named after him in 1995.

Edwards, Pilot Officer **Harry D.** of Winnipeg (41837). No. 92 Squadron, RAF. He enlisted in January, 1939 and died 7 October 1940 during the Battle of Britain. He was 24 years of age and is commemorated at Folkestone New Cemetery in Kent, England. He was the son of John H. and Emily M. Edwards of Winnipeg. Edwards was yet another of the young pilots who flew for the RAF at the beginning of the war. His squadron flew:

... air cover for the British forces once they had been squeezed back to the channel coast. Harry Edwards acquitted himself well in the fierce air battle over Boulogne and Dunkirk. Between May 23 and June 2, 1940, he downed two German aircraft and probably shot down three more. These combats were particularly confused; on one occasion, Edwards found a spent British bullet lodged in his cockpit. Like many other Canadians in the RAF, Edwards was subsequently killed a few months later (Halliday 1970).

Edwards Hill (64 P/6), northeast of MacLeod Lake was named after him in 1995.

Edwards, Flight Sergeant **John F.** of Portage la Prairie (R 91707). No. 9 Squadron. He died 21 December 1942 at the age of 27 and is commemorated at Oberschleisheim Churchyard, Germany. He was the son of Fred W. and Margaret Edwards of Portage la Prairie. Prior to the war, he had been director of the local horticultural society and past president of the Young People's Society of St. Mary's church. ***Edwards Point*** (63 I/8) on Robinson Lake was named after him in 1995.

Edwards, Sergeant **Robert W.** of Winnipeg (R 180425). No. 419 Squadron. He died 21 January 1944 at the age of 21 and is commemorated at the Berlin 1939 - 1945 War Cemetery, Germany. He was the son of John and Louisa Edwards of Winnipeg. ***Edwards Island*** (64 O/10) in Juice Lake was named after him in 1995.

Edwards, Ordinary Seaman **William J.** of Winnipeg (V 24127). HMCS *Levis*. The *Levis* was torpedoed by U-74 120 miles off Cape Farewell, Greenland resulting in 18 lives lost. Ordinary Seaman Edwards died 19 September 1941 at the age of 22 and is commemorated at the Halifax Memorial. He was the son of John E. and May Edwards of St. Vital. According to his sister (10 February 1995):

William John Edwards was born on April 5, 1919 at Dakota Siding, Manitoba. He attended Kirkfield Park School which was then located on Vimy Road. The family later moved to St. Vital where he attended Norberry School. Bill, as he was known to his family, played goalie for a neighbourhood hockey team. In addition, he played the guitar and mouth organ for a small band which performed at a local dance hall in St. Vital. He also delivered the *Winnipeg Free Press* and won a gold pocket watch for 18 months of perfect service. Prior to joining the Navy, he worked for the T. Eaton Company in the dispatch department. Today, his name is listed on the store's Honour Roll for those who fell while serving our country. Finally, he was a member of St. Mark's Anglican Church.

Edwards Bay (64 F/2) in Dunsheath Lake was named after him in 1994.

Edy, Flight Lieutenant **Allen L.** of Winnipeg (41566). No. 602 Squadron, RAF, Distinguished Flying Cross. He died 5 December 1941 at the age of 25 and is commemorated at Andreas (St. Andrew) Churchyard, United Kingdom. He was the son of John C. H. and Minnie L. Edy of St. Andrews. An article about him recently appeared in an Elmwood newspaper:

In a small church cemetery, Kirk Andreas, on England's Isle of Man, lie the mortal remains of a 25 year-old Elmwood pilot. Described by his colleagues as an absolute "wizard of the air," for his skills in the Spitfire fighter plane, Flight Lieutenant Allen Laird Edy, DFC, was killed in a tragic aircraft accident on December 5th, 1941. His obituary was prominently featured in the *Elmwood Herald* a few days later.

Allen Edy was one of twelve Manitobans who flew during the Battle of Britain with the Royal Air Force. They were among that small band of less than 3000 fliers of whom British Prime Minister Winston Churchill said: "Never in the field of human conflict was so much owed by so many to so few."

In this Millennium year 2000, which marks the 60th anniversary of that period, July 10th to October 31st 1940, a great turning point in history, it is appropriate that we honour the memory of Flight Lieutenant Edy. In doing so, we are also paying our everlasting respect to the memory of another Elmwood native son, Group Captain Johnny "Jack" Kent, who survived the war but died in England in September, 1985. It was due to pilots like these that Hitler's plan to invade England, code-named "Sea Lion," was thwarted.

Born on May 7th, 1916, Allen Edy attended Lord Selkirk School around the same time as Johnny Kent. Later, he crossed the Red River to continue his education at St. John's Technical High School. After graduation Allen joined his father's smallwares company, Valentine-Edy, as a prairies-region salesman. Prior to going overseas to train as a pilot with the RAF, he lived at 36 Hart Avenue, off Glenwood, next to Hespeler. By that time his parents lived much of the year in St. Andrews, in a place they named *Twin Oaks*. It was there that Allen said his last goodbyes. In the spring of 1938 Allen Edy and Curran Robinson, a fellow Winnipegger, bid farewell to their families and left Manitoba to see the world. They never came back.

Their original intent was to work their way across the Atlantic on a freighter but instead they paid the princely sum of $70 each for classless accommodations in the hold of a grain carrier. When they finally arrived in London, England, via Antwerp in Belgium, they were almost penniless. Edy and Robinson slept on park benches in Hyde Park and elsewhere, until rescued by the Salvation Army. They were given a warm bed and a hot meal and were introduced to Ian Davison, a writer, whose day job was picking hops. Ian and Allen became close friends.

Although neither Robinson nor Edy had shown any previous interest in flying, they soon followed the example of many other young, restless, unemployed Canadians in London and joined the Royal Air Force. By the end of October 1938 they were both training as pilots. Edy received his wings on January 14th, 1939 and was posted to 613 Squadron. Eighteen months later he used his new found skills to assist in the rescue of the British Expeditionary Forces from France. For his outstanding effort in dropping supplies to those trapped near Calais, the then Pilot Officer Edy was awarded the Distinguished Flying Cross (Williston 2000)

Ironically, it was later learned that the British troops in Calais had surrendered some time before and the ammunition and food which Edy had taken such pains to deliver had ended up in German hands (Halliday 1970).

On this operation he flew an obsolete Hawker Hector two-seater single engine biplane to bomb German field batteries in the area. Despite the chaotic circumstances in France that took the lives of several Manitoba pilots, Allen Edy somehow survived to fly ... and die ... another day. Twenty year-old Curran Robinson wasn't as fortunate.

On May 18th, 1940, while stationed at Bircham Newton in Norfolk, England, Pilot Officer Robinson failed to return from operations over Belgium. His Blenheim aircraft, belonging to 235 Squadron, with its three-man crew, was never found.

Sporting a second ribbon on his tunic sleeve, the newly promoted Flying Officer Edy was posted to 602 Squadron on September 8th and one week later the Elmwood pilot found himself making history. September 15th is now recognized as one of the most decisive dates in the Battle of Britain and is often referred to as the day the RAF finally got the upper hand on the Luftwaffe. For that reason it is now celebrated as Battle of Britain Day. It was also the day that Allen Edy claimed his first Luftwaffe victim, a Dornier Do17, as he related in his combat report.

"I was Red 2 and took off from Westhampnett at 1433 hours. When Red Section attacked a formation of enemy bombers on southerly course at 14,000 feet from quarter ahead I followed, selecting one enemy aircraft on starboard of enemy formation and separating from it. I attacked this enemy aircraft quarter ahead from 30 degrees above. Pilot Officer Hanbury, Yellow 3, saw this enemy aircraft pull up vertically, turn downward and dive into [the] sea."

Although the fate of the four-man German crew is unknown, it is likely that they all died. In his next letter home, Allen Edy wrote that shooting down the Dornier gave him "a queer feeling." But it had now become a matter of "who could outfly and outlive whom" and it wasn't long before Edy was again tested.

On September 21st he attacked a Junkers Ju88, 10 miles south of Brighton and severely damaged it. Five days later he engaged a Heinkel He111 near Southampton and set its port engine on fire. But before he could finish off this quarry, he was himself caught in a counter-attack by a Luftwaffe fighter over the Solent and sustained a bullet through the radiator of his Spitfire, X4411. The time was 1640 hours and he was forced to break off his attack and headed back to base.

In January, 1941 Flying Officer Edy was posted to 315 (Polish) Squadron and shortly thereafter was invited to Buckingham Palace to receive his DFC. He was subsequently awarded Polish wings, followed by a transfer to 457 (Australian) Squadron and a promotion to Flight Lieutenant.

Then came his final sortie. While testing a recently repaired Spitfire on December 5th, the aircraft developed mechanical problems which forced Edy to bail out. Eye-witnesses told different, somewhat conflicting stories. However, whether he was struck by the tailplane or if in fact he was hit by a falling piece of the wing, is now of little consequence. Allen Edy's body was found some distance from his Spitfire, which is said to have continued smouldering for four days after it crashed in flames near Ramsey. Mrs. Elsie Turner, who still lives on the Isle of Man which is situated in the middle of the Irish Sea, was a teenager at the time. She recalls how Edy's aircraft "screamed down" and crashed within 300 yards of her home.

I had an opportunity just recently to spend some time with Allen Edy's 81 year-old sister, Eileen McKeown. She told me about her warm memories of Allen and her April 1972 pilgrimage to his gravesite on the Isle of Man. Eileen has lived on Oakenwald Avenue in Fort Garry for the past 47 years and proudly displays on her living room wall a handsome framed picture of her older brother. On the back of it are pasted several newspaper clippings from December 1941 announcing his death, including the obituary clipping from the *Elmwood Herald*. Eileen remembered that on the afternoon of December 5th, 1941 a brief telegram arrived at the Edy residence: "Loving Christmas thoughts, best wishes, Love, Allen Edy." "That was just like Allen and the family was overjoyed, but within 24-hours our joy and laughter turned to tears," she recalled.

Next day, a second cable arrived. This one was from the Under Secretary of State at the British Air Ministry: "Deeply regret to inform you that your son, Flight Lieutenant Allen Laird Edy, DFC, is reported to have lost his life on active service on December 5th." Then, on Dec. 7, another Air Ministry message: "You would wish to know that your son will be interred with full military service honours at 10 o'clock on Tuesday, December 9th, 1941 at Andreas, Isle of Man."

How quickly it all happened. But to Eileen, the picture of her Errol Flynn look-alike brother is a fond reminder of a man who will live forever in her heart and mind. "He called me Chick and when he worked as a travelling-salesman he always brought me something special when he came home to our Hart Street [home] on the weekends." But as she recounted tales of their early childhood, I could see that it was difficult for her to maintain her composure, especially perhaps in view of her recent poor health. She added a note of regret that her brother never wrote much detail in his letters from overseas. "I don't know what happened to his log book, and most of the letters I had were destroyed when my basement was flooded many years ago."

Eileen's parents are long since dead but her brother, Harrington Edy, is still living. He was a member of the wartime Royal Canadian Air Force. The property in St. Andrews, still called *Twin Oaks*, is no longer owned by the Edy family. However, a lake in northern Manitoba now bears the Edy name. Eileen only learned of Lake Edy from the author of this article as the family had not been contacted since the Lake was named after her brother on March 31st 1995 (Williston 2000).

Edy Lake (53 F/13) is located southeast of Angling Lake.

Ehinger, Private **Fredrick** of Beausejour (H 16611). Princess Patricia's Canadian Light Infantry. He died 23 May 1944 and is commemorated at the Cassino War Cemetery in Italy. He was the son of Frank H. and Helen F. Ehinger of Beausejour. His brother recalls (26 November 2001):

> Fred was the eldest of nine children – eight boys and one girl. [He] enlisted in Winnipeg on January 5, 1940. Five brothers and his father served overseas during World War II. Fred was the only brother who did not return. Fred grew up during the difficult Dirty Thirties in Beausejour. Fred was married in England and was the father of one daughter, Patricia, whom he never saw.

Ehinger Lake (64 K/8), northeast of Reindeer Lake was named after him in 1972.

Einarson, Private **Sigurjon M.** of Winnipegosis (H 103507). South Saskatchewan Regiment. He died 20 July 1944 at the age of 23 and is commemorated at Bretteville-sur-Laize Canadian War Cemetery, France. He was the son of John S. and Vigdis Einarson of Winnipegosis. According to his brother (8 September 1996), he:

> ... was born and raised in Winnipegosis, Manitoba. He attended school there and then went up north to Flin Flon, Manitoba to commercial fish with his father Jack Einarson. They had trading posts in the northern areas. He enlisted in the army in 1942 ... [and] went overseas in June, 1943.

Einarson Lake (64 H/16), east of North Knife Lake was named after him in 1963.

Einarsson, Pilot Officer **Sigurjon** of Gimli (J 86556). No. 405 Squadron. He died 30 January 1944 at the age of 27 and is commemorated at the Runnymede Memorial in Surrey, England. He was the son of Einar and Anna Einarsson of Gimli. ***Einarsson Island*** (64 B/6) in the Rat River was named after him in 1981.

Eisthen, Private **Albert J.** of Tilston (H 18481). South Saskatchewan Regiment. He died 14 August 1944 at the age of 20 and is commemorated at Bretteville-sur-Laize Canadian War Cemetery, France. His brother and nephew visited his grave in May, 2000. He was one of the nine children of George and Jessie Eisthen of Tilston. A neighbour recalls (5 December 1984):

Mr. Eisthen was a veteran himself; he and his wife farmed in this area all of their lives on a very small acreage and raised a family of nine children. Realizing that the family was raised in the '30s will give you an idea of the struggles involved. Five of the nine children were in the armed forces – four boys and one girl. Albert was the only one who never came back. They were an honest, hard-working family and needless to say, received little help in making ends meet and when going about making their own way in life.

Eisthen Lake (64 K/9), northeast of Reindeer Lake was named after him in 1972.

Ekberg, Gunner **Clifford G. L.** of Brandon (L 18151). Royal Canadian Artillery. He died 2 November 1940 and is commemorated at Brookwood Military Cemetery in Surrey, England. He was the son of Alfred and Lena Ekberg. ***Ekberg Lake*** (64 I/6), north of North Knife Lake was named after him in 1974.

Elcheshen, Aircraftman 2 **Wilfred J.** of Winnipeg (R 210500). No. 3 Wireless School, RCAF. He died 25 July 1943 at the age of 20 and is commemorated at Elmwood Cemetery in Winnipeg. He was the son of John and Rose Elcheshen of Winnipeg. ***Elcheshen Lake*** (64 P/3), southeast of Nejanilini Lake was named after him in 1974.

Elder, Private **Luther W.** of Winnipeg (H 3533). Queen's Own Cameron Highlanders. He died 11 January 1945 and is commemorated at the Groesbeek Canadian War Cemetery in Holland. ***Elder Lake*** (63 I/7), north of Molson Lake was named after him in 1973.

Elders, Rifleman **James** of Winnipeg (H 20664). Regina Rifle Regiment. He died 10 July 1944 at the age of 23 and is commemorated at Beny-sur-Mer Canadian War Cemetery, France. He was the son of Bert and Margaret Elders. ***Elders Lake*** (64 O/9), northwest of Nejanilini Lake was named after him in 1975.

Elliott, Flight Sergeant **Lloyd G.** of Winnipeg (R 80244). No. 402 Squadron. He died 29 March 1942 at the age of 21 and is commemorated at the Runnymede Memorial in Surrey, England. His step-mother writes (9 May 1995):

After graduating from Daniel McIntyre High School, he worked at Eaton's until he enlisted. He received his wings in August, 1941 and was shipped out to England in September, 1941. On convoy duty, he had engine trouble and crashed in the [Bristol Channel]. Help arrived in minutes, but the rescue boats found nothing.

Elliott Lake (64 H/10), southeast of Buckland Lake was named after him in 1995.

Ellis, Private **Percy J.** of Wawanesa (H 6771). Winnipeg Grenadiers, Mentioned in Dispatches. He died a prisoner of war 23 August 1942 at the age of 25 and is commemorated at the Sai Wan War Cemetery in Hong Kong. His death and that of three other Grenadiers sparked a war crimes investigation after the war. It was determined that he had been executed after trying to escape. Nine of the ten Japanese military personnel involved were found guilty. See **Payne,** Sergeant **John O.** for additional details. He was the son of Ernest and Beatrice Ellis of Wawanesa. ***Ellis Island*** (52 E/13) in Brereton Lake was named after him in 1973.

Elmes, Trooper **Douglas** of Fisherton (H 26687). Fort Garry Horse. He died 8 August 1944 at the age of 21 and is commemorated at Bretteville-sur-Laize Canadian War Cemetery, France. He was the son of William and Helen Elmes of St. Vital. ***Elmes Island*** (63 K/16) in Morton Lake was named after him in 1973.

Elms, Pilot Officer **Francis J.** of St. James (C 19960). No. 434 Squadron. He died 29 January 1944 at the age of 21 and is commemorated at the Berlin 1939 - 1945 War Cemetery, Germany. He was the son of Frank and Elizabeth Elms of Winnipeg. In his last letter home he wrote:

Dear Evelyn [his cousin]: Received your swell and very interesting letter a short time ago and as tonight ops were scrubbed due to bad weather, I thought this would be a great time in which to get caught up on all my mail. To begin with, I'm keeping very well and getting quite a kick out of life at the moment what with going over Germany and blowing their cities up. But otherwise, when we are not doing anything we run about the country, visiting one town one night and another the next. When we stay in we generally hang about the mess and have quite a talk over a few beers.

I've now finished 13 trips and have about 14 more to go, at the end of which I'm hoping very much to get home and see you all for a month before returning to do another tour of ops. So far, things have been fairly quiet on my trips; we've had the fair share of bad ones, being shot up pretty bad and coming back on three engines, but otherwise it's been okay.

I'm flying with Squadron Leader Linnell who is from Alberta and he's really a good egg. By the way, he became a papa a short time ago. Boy was he ever worried that night on ops. Reminds me, he hasn't given me my cigar yet. I've had quite a number of leaves of which I spent most of them in London. London is quite a city, especially when you get to know it, but for a guy who don't, well he won't like the place.

I've been down and seen Uncle Ted several times; I was thinking about going and seeing them in the near future as the crew and myself are going to London to paint it red. I'm hoping to get my commission in about six weeks and I'll feel like I've got somewhere then, so here's hoping.

So very pleased Art and yourself are keeping well and for the photo of Susan. It's beyond words, it's really lovely, I'd really like to see her; give Susan a big kiss for me Evelyn. No, I'm not going to marry any of these girls over here. I'm going to marry a good-looking Canadian gal even if I have to wait here ten years. The girls over here and me don't get along after the first few hours.

Heard from mother the other day saying she was keeping well and that dad was feeling a little better. Say hello to Uncle Bill for me. Tell him I'll be dropping a line soon. Well I guess this is the end of the news but I'll drop you a line now and again. So for now, with all the best to you all. Love, Frank (25 January 1944).

He did not survive his next mission. His cousin reports that all of the crew's dog tags were found in the ashes but his. As a consequence, he remained "missing in action" for seven years before finally being declared dead. In the meantime, his father died of an illness he had contracted during the First World War. ***Elms Lake*** (64 O/13), on a peninsula in Nueltin Lake was named after him in 1975.

Elstow, Trooper **Charles S.** of Brandon (H 100120). Princess Louise Dragoon Guards. He died 21 May 1944 and is commemorated at the Cassino War Cemetery in Italy. ***Elstow Lake*** (64 I/2), east of North Knife Lake was named after him in 1974.

Elsworth, Able Seaman **Harold E.** of West Kildonan (V 24808). HMCS *Givenchy*. He died 22 March 1943 at the age of 21 and is commemorated at Esquimalt (Veterans') Cemetery in British Columbia. He was the son of Robert and Mabel Elsworth of Winnipeg. His sister recalls that he attended Centennial School and West Kildonan Collegiate and was particularly interested in hockey and fishing. ***Elsworth Lake*** (53 M/7), north of Knee Lake was named after him in 1966.

Elton, Captain **Walter R.** of Winnipeg. Royal Canadian Artillery. He died 24 December 1943 at the age of 57 and is commemorated at St. James Cemetery in Winnipeg. He was survived by his wife Florence Elton of Winnipeg. ***Elton Lake*** (52 L/11), northwest of Black Lake was named after him in 1982.

Eluke, Rifleman **William** of Charleswood (H 22894). Royal Winnipeg Rifles. He died 7 April 1945 at the age of 19 and is commemorated at the Holten Canadian War Cemetery in Holland. He was the son of George and Wasylka Eliuk (sp.) of Pacific Junction. ***Eluke Lake*** (64 B/1), northwest of Thompson was named after him in 1972.

Emberly, Private **Eldon L.** of Haywood (H 23196). Royal Canadian Infantry Corps. He died 27 February 1945 at the age of 19 and is commemorated at Brandon Cemetery. He was the son of Harvey and Alice Emberly of Haywood. His brother writes (17 December 2001):

> Eldon was an adventurous young man who enjoyed making things. He was very fond of animals and made pets of some of them. He began school at Emberly School and later Seaforth School to Grade 8.

Emberly Lake (64 F/6), north of Wells Lake was named after him in 1994.

Embleton, Corporal **W. J. Sidney** of Deloraine (H 87985). Royal Canadian Army Service Corps. He died 6 June 1945 at the age of 28 and is commemorated at the Holten Canadian War Cemetery in Holland. His sisters visited his grave in 1977. He was the son of William J. and Hessie Embleton of Deloraine and was survived by his wife Helen F. Embleton. His sister writes (7 November 2001):

> He was testing a jeep that he had just repaired. When he was at the crest of a hill, a lorry was on the wrong side of the road and it was a head-on collision. The passenger was screaming with pain, so Sid walked around the jeep and collapsed.

In a letter to Corporal Embleton's mother, his commanding officer wrote:

> I regret to have to write to you about the death of your son H 87985 A/Cpl Embleton, W. J. Cpl. Embleton died as a result of injuries sustained when a Jeep in which he was riding collided with another vehicle. An English Medical Officer, Capt. Marshall, who saw the accident immediately rendered medical treatment to Cpl. Embleton, but he died within a few minutes of the accident.
>
> Cpl. Embleton had always done an excellent job with this unit, and his recent promotion was a reward not only for good service in the past, but because he had the ability to lead others. The example that he set by hard work and honest endeavour was an inspiration to those working with him.
>
> As Cpl. Embleton's commanding officer, I know that I speak for all of the officers and men of my unit when I say that he will be greatly missed by all of us, and on their behalf I extend to you our deepest sympathy at this time of sorrow (18 June 1945).

Embleton Lake (54 E/4), northeast of Split Lake was named after him in 1964.

Embury, Trooper **Archer F.** of Oakville (H 185). Lord Strathcona's Horse. He died 24 May 1944 at the age of 24 and is commemorated at the Cassino War Cemetery in Italy. He was the son of Fred R. and Mabel Embury of Oakville. According to a contemporary newspaper obituary:

> Born in Portage, ... Archer moved to Oakville with his parents at an early age where he received his education. Prior to enlisting in 1940 with the Lord Strathcona Horse, he worked with his father on the Manitoba Telephone System. Training at Winnipeg, Listowel and Camp Borden, he went overseas three years ago. An outstanding athlete, Archer won the three mile race at the annual sports day in England last year. On being presented with a medal he was congratulated by General McNaughton (n.d.).

Embury Island (53 K/4) in Red Sucker Lake was named after him in 1995.

Emeno, Flying Officer **Lionel B.** of Winnipeg (41160). No. 269 Squadron, RAF. He enlisted in September, 1938 and was lost off the coast of Norway on 28 September 1940. He was 23 years of age and is commemorated at the Runnymede Memorial in Surrey, England. He was the son of David and Helen H. Emeno of Winnipeg. ***Emeno Lake*** (54 D/15), east of Myre Lake was named after him in 1996.

Emerson, Leading Aircraftman **Arthur Stanley** of Winnipeg (R 58784). No. 3 Repair Depot, RCAF. He died 23 August 1943 at the age of 22 and is commemorated at Elmwood Cemetery in Winnipeg. He was the son of John E. and Christina Emerson of Winnipeg. His brother writes (n.d.):

> The family moved to St. Vital, Manitoba in the 1920s residing at 929 St. Mary's Road. Stanley Emerson went to Norberry School and Glenlawn Collegiate. [He] joined the RCAF in January, 1940 and served as an air frame mechanic. [He was] stationed at Toronto and St. Thomas, Ontario, Saskatoon, Calgary, Boundary Bay and Pat Bay.

Emerson Island (63 N/13) in Sisipuk Lake was named after him in 1995.

Endert, Corporal **Edward** of Morden (H 20358). Queen's Own Cameron Highlanders. He died 14 August 1944 at the age of 24 and is commemorated at Bretteville-sur-Laize Canadian War Cemetery, France. He was the son of Edmund and Justina Endert (née Wirffel) of Morden and was survived by his stepmother Annie Endert of Morden. In a letter home he wrote:

> Dear Henry and Fritz: Received your letter today and was glad to hear from you'se again. So am answering rite away to show you I do write. And I'll have you know I write quite regular. I can't help it if you don't get my mail. As I'm not getting any of your'se neither. I haven't received the cigs you sent me in Feb. In fact, I haven't received any cigs for three months. I received the parcel and picture okay, as I told you in my previous letters.
>
> Well enough of that; so you've sold the farm and bought a house, from the address it seems to be out of the 'Peg apiece. What did you pay for it and how big is it? I reckon I'll probly never live to see the place.
>
> If I get back, my roving days will be over; I've had just about enough of this. By the way, I'm going to the hospital on Monday to have my tonsils taken out, which I should have done long ago. Another thing I had better mention is that I'm back to a Cpl. again, this time I got mad and told them where to get off, so they had me up before the major and he slapped me down a notch (12 May 1944).

His nephew recalls an old family story (30 September 1997):

> The story I heard and remember is that on a clear, cold night someone lit a small fire to make coffee. The corporal in charge, Uncle Ed, told him to put it out. The man poured the contents of the pot on the fire. The result was a column of steam; the result of that was mortar fire. A thoughtless mistake but a fatal one.

Endert Lake (64 N/3), southwest of Nueltin Lake was named after him in 1972.

Engen, Private **Samuel G.** of The Pas (H 20875). Lake Superior Regiment. He died 23 April 1945 and is commemorated at the Holten Canadian War Cemetery in Holland. ***Engen Lake*** (64 K/4), northeast of Reindeer Lake was named after him in 1961.

England, Flight Sergeant **William H.** of Winnipeg (R 177892). No. 1661 Conversion Unit, RCAF. He died 17 May 1944 at the age of 20 and is commemorated at Brookwood Military Cemetery in Surrey, England. He was the son of William L. and Cicely England of Winnipeg. He and Sergeant Allan W. Huppe (see entry) were friends who had attended Hugh John Macdonald School together in Winnipeg. They were killed in the same crash. According to his niece (26 November 2001):

> Although I never met my uncle Bill, my mom and nana would tell me stories about him. They told me my Uncle Bill had a friend named Allan Huppe. Bill and Allan grew up together, went to school together, were in the air force together and died together. From my understanding, Uncle Bill and his friend Allan are buried beside each other.

England Lake (64 H/6), northeast of Northern Indian Lake was named after him in 1995.

English, Flight Sergeant **George Cornwall** of Pipestone (R 86265). No. 1 Squadron. He died 3 June 1942 at the age of 23 and is commemorated at Chichester Cemetery, United Kingdom. He was the son of James C. and Ellen M. English of Pipestone and the cousin of Sergeant Marshall F. English (next entry). ***English Point*** (64 O/5) on Trohubiak Lake was named after him in 1995.

English, Sergeant **Marshall F.** of Virden (R 86298). No. 10 Squadron. He died 31 May 1942 at the age of 27 and is commemorated at Woensel General Cemetery in Eindhoven, Holland. He was the son of George and Nellie English of Virden and the cousin of Flight Sergeant George C. English (previous entry). ***English Peninsula*** (64 B/7) on Livingston Lake was named after him in 1995.

Enns, Flying Officer **Benjamin H.** of Morris (J 10008). No. 405 Squadron. He died 29 November 1942 at the age of 26 and is commemorated at Airth Cemetery, Stirlingshire, Scotland. He was the son of David and Gertrude Enns and was survived by his wife Helen Enns of Airth. ***Enns Island*** (64 C/12) in Laurie Lake was named after him in 1995.

Enns, Private **Gordon H.** of Winkler (K 67786). Westminster Regiment. He died 24 September 1944 at the age of 33 and is commemorated at Cesena War Cemetery in Italy. He was the son of Henry and Helena Enns and was survived by his wife Hersey Enns of Victoria, British Columbia. ***Enns Bay*** (53 L/12) in Laidlaw Lake was named after him in 1996.

Enns, Private **Jacob G.** of Morden (M 36300). Calgary Highlanders. He died 26 April 1945 and is commemorated at the Holten Canadian War Cemetery in Holland. He was the son of William J. and Katarina Enns of Altona and was survived by his wife Pade Enns. ***Enns Lake*** (64 K/8), northeast of Reindeer Lake was named after him in 1972.

Epp, Pilot Officer **Jacob A.** of Manitou (J 10878). Royal Canadian Air Force. He died 6 June 1942 at the age of 25 and is commemorated at Bournemouth North Cemetery, Hampshire, England. He was the son of Jacob and Susan Epp and was survived by his wife Ruth Epp. ***Epp Lake*** (63 K/16), west of Wekusko Lake was named after him in 1973.

Eppler, Ordinary Seaman **Clifford** of Winnipeg (V 73222). HMCS *Shawinigan*. The *Shawinigan* was torpedoed and sunk by U-1228 while on anti-submarine patrol in the Cabot Strait; all hands were lost. Ordinary Seaman Eppler died 24 November 1944 at the age of 19 and is commemorated at the Halifax Memorial. He was the son of Charles and Molly Eppler of Winnipeg. A local newspaper reported that:

> O/S Eppler was educated at Machray school and St. John's high school. He joined the navy September, 1943, receiving his training in HMCS *Chippawa*, Winnipeg and HMCS *Cornwallis*, Halifax. The Shawinigan was his first ship. A brother, Private Ernie Eppler, is with the Queen's Own Cameron Highlanders in Holland (*The Winnipeg Tribune* 7 December 1944).

Eppler Lake (54 L/13), northwest of Churchill was named after him in 1957.

Eppler, Pilot Officer **Edward W.** of Gretna (J 90181). No. 427 Squadron. He died 18 April 1944 at the age of 20 and is commemorated at Clichy Northern Cemetery, France. ***Eppler Island*** (64 G/12) in Big Sand Lake was named after him in 1995.

Erickson, Trooper **Aksel S.** of Ashern (H 186). Lord Strathcona's Horse. He died 24 May 1944 and is commemorated at the Cassino War Cemetery in Italy. His niece reports that he was born at Helsted, near Copenhagen in Denmark and came to Virden with his family in the 1920s. His father had formerly operated the creamery in Ashern. ***Erickson Island*** (64 N/9) in Nueltin Lake was named after him in 1995.

Erickson, Corporal **Charles G.** of Holland, Manitoba (H 33086). Queen's Own Cameron Highlanders. He died 27 October 1944 at the age of 22 and is commemorated at Bergen-op-Zoom Canadian War Cemetery in Holland. He was the son of Frank and Helen Erickson of Winnipeg. ***Erickson Creek*** (63 O/5), which flows north into Osborn Creek was named after him in 1973.

Erickson, Flight Sergeant **Harry A.** of Onanole (R 116318). No. 10 Squadron. He died 29 June 1943 at the age of 21 and is commemorated at Woensel General Cemetery in Eindhoven, Holland. He was the oldest son of Sapper Alex (RCE overseas) and Alvina Erickson of Onanole. His brother recalls that his main ambitions in life focussed upon becoming a pilot and furthering his education. ***Erickson Bay*** (64 K/1) in Chartrand Lake was named after him in 1995.

Erickson, Telegraphist **Ingvi S.** of Arborg (V 51886). HMCS *Alberni*. The *Alberni* was torpedoed and sunk by U-480, southeast of the Isle of Wight; 59 of her ship's company were lost. Telegraphist Erickson died 21 August 1944 at the age of 21 and is commemorated at the Halifax Memorial. He was the son of Ingvi and Herdis Erickson of Arborg. ***Erickson Lake*** (64 N/4), north of Lac Brochet was named after him in 1961.

Erskine, Private **John R. "Jock"** of Elmwood (H 9547). Royal Regiment of Canada. He died 13 October 1944 at the age of 29 and is commemorated at Bergen-op-Zoom Canadian War Cemetery in Holland. He was the son of Andrew and Mary Erskine and was survived by his wife Gertrude Erskine of Winnipeg. She writes (7 July 1998):

> Jock was born in Falkirk, Scotland and came to Canada at the age of six years. He went to Lord Selkirk School in Elmwood and worked at Simmons Bedding before going into the service. He played baseball for Simmons Bedding in a commercial league and also hockey. He was a goalie for [the] B. A. Oil Company in a commercial league.

Erskine Island (64 C/3) in the Laurie River was named after him in 1995.

Erzinger, Flying Officer **John D.** of Winnipeg (J 7023). No. 102 Squadron. He died 13 May 1943 at the age of 25 and is commemorated at the Runnymede Memorial in Surrey, England. He was the eldest of the three children of John A. and Mary Erzinger of Winnipeg. He had received the Governor General's medal for General Proficiency when he matriculated from St. John's College in 1934. He subsequently took a job with the Hudson's Bay Company, but was taking evening classes at a business school when he enlisted in 1940. ***Erzinger Lake*** (63 K/16), northwest of Wekusko Lake was named after him in 1973.

Esaruk, Lieutenant **John** of Stony Mountain. Royal Winnipeg Rifles. He died 25 September 1944 at the age of 27 and is commemorated at Calais Canadian War Cemetery, Leubringhen, France. He was the son of Alex and Irene Esaruk of Winnipeg and was survived by his wife Doris I. Esaruk (née Newman) of Stony Mountain and their son. He had seen his son only once and only for a few hours before his departure overseas. He had joined the Princess Patricia's Canadian Light Infantry in 1937 and worked his way through the ranks to earn a commission in 1941. He was held back in England as an instructor, but was sufficiently eager to get to France that he transferred to the Royal Winnipeg Rifles, reaching the Normandy Beach 10 August 1944. ***Esaruk Lake*** (64 K/12), northeast of Reindeer Lake was named after him in 1972.

Essar, Pilot Officer **William** of Winnipegosis (J 90741). No. 550 Squadron. He died 11 April 1944 at the age of 22 and is commemorated at Achiet-le-Petit Communal Cemetery, France. According to his sister (20 October 1996):

> William enjoyed hunting, fishing and the few sports that were available to him in his short life. When not in school, he busily searched for employment elsewhere. This took him to Sudbury, Ontario. Money was scarce and our family consisted of ten members including our parents. Throughout the 1930s, jobs were few and far between – the main reason William headed east. In 1941, he wrote home informing us that he had enlisted in the Royal Canadian Air Force.

Essar Lake (63 N/7), south of Takipy Lake was named after him in 1982.

Essenburg, Flying Officer **Edwin** of Winnipeg (J 36225). No. 427 Squadron. He died 21 February 1945 at the age of 23 and is commemorated at Rheinberg War Cemetery in Germany. He was the son of Ludwig and Else Essenburg of Winnipeg and was survived by brothers August and Herb and sister Irma. Born in Poland in 1922, he had come to Canada with his parents and a brother in 1927. His last mission was a bombing raid over Mannheim. According to his younger brother (29 November 2001):

> As a youngster, Edwin was active in sports. He was an excellent student and had an interest in flying so that joining the RCAF seemed appropriate for him. He receive his Pilot Officer commission in Manitoba and Flying Officer later in England. He was faithful in writing home and was the recipient of carefully wrapped parcels from home containing as many "goodies" as could be packed into a container the size of a shoe box!
>
> He had almost completed his allotted number of operations when his Halifax bomber was shot down near Mannheim and he was reported "missing in action." Herb and Irma, aged 12 and 10 at the time, vividly recall the shock of receiving the telegram. The family, after months of agonized suspense, were finally advised that he had been killed. Later, his pilot told the family that after the plane was hit and he had ejected, he saw that Edwin's 'chute had opened.
>
> After the war was over, the family learned that Edwin and another crewman had apparently landed safely but were killed by persons unknown. Their bodies were found in a shallow grave in a forest. The remains were exhumed and were reburied in the cemetery near Rheinberg. In 1970, Edwin's parents visited his grave and brought home a small vial of earth from it.

Essenburg Lake (64 P/10), east of Nejanilini Lake was named after him in 1974.

Evanchuk, Private **Peter** of Winnipeg Beach (H 7018). Queen's Own Cameron Highlanders. He died 28 August 1944 at the age of 27 and is commemorated at Bretteville-sur-Laize Canadian War Cemetery in Calvados, France. He was the son of Mr. and Mrs. William Evanchuk of Winnipeg Beach. ***Evanchuk Lake*** (64 K/6), northeast of Reindeer Lake was named after him in 1972.

Evans, Flight Sergeant **Clarence E. "Clarey"** of Winnipeg (R 91535). No. 35 Squadron. He died 26 July 1942 at the age of 27 and is commemorated at Uden War Cemetery, Holland. He was the son of James H. and Clara S. Evans (née Stitt) and was survived by his wife Merna J. S. Evans of Winnipeg. His widow recalls (24 April 1998):

> Clarey fished when he got the chance. We often went canoeing on the south Saskatchewan River. His great love was horse racing. We went every Saturday.

Clarence Evans Bay (63 O/1) in Halfway Lake was named after him in 1995.

Evans, Flying Officer **Earle R.** of Winnipeg (J 17548). No. 428 Squadron, Distinguished Flying Cross.

> When returning from his fifth operational sortie, Pilot Officer Evans was involved in a serious crash. Undaunted by this trying experience, he resumed operational flying and has since completed a number of operations against some of the enemy's major targets. At all times he has shown great courage in inspiring his crew with confidence (DFC Citation 1943).

He died 15 March 1945 on the 13th mission of his second tour of duty. He was 20 years of age and is commemorated at Nederweert War Cemetery in Holland. He was the son of Albert E. and Bessie Evans of Winnipeg. ***Evans Lake*** (63 N/2), east of Kississing Lake was named after him in 1950.

Evans, Trooper **Edward E.** of Norgate (H 26671). Fort Garry Horse. He died 9 June 1944 at the age of 26 and is commemorated at the Bayeux Memorial in France. He was the son of Ernest and Ethel Evans of Norgate, Manitoba. His sister recalls his youth (26 February 1997):

> Born ... in Gladstone, ... [in] 1924 he moved with his parents and a brother and sister to the little village of Norgate, Manitoba on the east side of the Riding Mountains. He took his schooling in a one-room school house there, through Grade 8. Very few farm boys went much further. He was a very outgoing young man and made friends wherever he went.
>
> He was a hunter and trapper. He was also an ingenious fellow. When we got our first radio we had to keep the battery charged. Living quite a piece from town, it wasn't always possible. So Ed built a wind charger on the roof of the house. It worked fine until one night we had a big west wind and it came crashing down. Not to be defeated, he took our old bike upstairs, raised the back wheel off the floor and hooked the generator to it. We all had to take turns peddling like crazy and going nowhere in order to get that battery charged up. By this time, he had two brothers and two sisters to take turns.
>
> He helped his Dad on the farm, breaking new land with an old Titan tractor. He worked part time at a filling station and garage at Norgate. The only car he ever owned was a Model T Ford. He lost his life on the beaches of Normandy. He has no known grave. We put his name on Stan's gravestone at McCreary.

He was the brother of Trooper Stanley C. Evans (see entry) of Norgate. ***Evans Peninsula*** (64 O/8) on Nejanilini Lake was named after him in 1995.

Evans, Private **Harold E.** of Winnipeg (H 40208). Veterans Guard of Canada. He died 28 January 1945 at the age of 63 and is commemorated at Brookside Cemetery in Winnipeg. He was survived by his wife Nellie M. Evans of Winnipeg and their six children. Private Evans was born in Yorkshire, England in 1881 and served in the Canadian army during World War I. He subsequently moved to Giroux, Manitoba where he worked as a grain buyer, enlisting again with the outbreak of World War II. He submitted an article to the *Winnipeg Free Press* in 1942, describing the Veterans Guard (Active) and their work:

> Quite frequently, your paper has a glowing account together with photographs, of the Veterans' Guard of Canada (Reserve) battalion of Winnipeg and Manitoba, photographs of their parades with bands though Winnipeg streets, insets of them saying good-bye to their wives when departing for their annual two weeks' training; photographs of church parades, photographs of inspections by some high army officer.
>
> It may come as a complete surprise to most Winnipeg people who have only seen the high pressure press publicity accorded these twice-a-weekers that there are two companies of Veterans' Guard of Canada (Active) from the city and province who have been on active service since late in 1940, unheralded and unsung. They have been keeping a watchful eye on the activities of enemies of the empire who have been gathered in by the navy, the air force and land forces of Great Britain and the Anzacs in the Far East, and such a watchful eye that the first Nazi has yet to register a successful escape from these forgotten ex-citizens of this Gateway of the West, famous for its smart, snappy Veterans' Guard of Canada (Reserve).
>
> The forgotten bleary-eyed old sweats now known as 22 and 23 companies, have rattled and humped their way from the eastern almost to the western seaboard, they have gazed upon the famous skyline of the largest city in America, they have stamped their half-frozen feet in drafty, ill-built internment camps in 50 below zero weather; their skin burned to a crisp in the summer, and every exposed part of their bodies eaten raw by everything that flew or crawled in that part of the dominion. They have at times run out on their commissariat and have had to tighten their belts up a notch or two to cover their none too slim waists, grousing like [censored] while doing it.
>
> But they are still carrying on. So, when you turn into your warm bed at night, give one kind thought to Manitoba's forgotten Companies 22 and 23 of the Veterans' Guard of Canada (Active), for they have homes and wives and children in Manitoba, and they gave it all up to do this thankless job that had to be done by someone. So, being without friends in the high places, it fell to the lot of 22 and 23 companies to do guard duty in all the God-forsaken, isolated spots in this fair dominion.
>
> To digress, if any one of your readers knows of a spot anywhere so far away that it would cost $10 to send a postcard to it, I am sure Ottawa would be glad to know of it so they can build an internment camp there and send 22 and 23 companies there on guard duty.
>
> Some day when this show is over, what's left of them will come home. They will be torn and dirty and haggard, but treat them kindly, they have done a good job that has brought them more kicks than ha'pence, and have done it well.
>
> Some day our province and our city will be as proud of 22 and 23 companies of the Veterans' Guard of Canada (Active) as they are now of their Veterans' Guard of Canada (Reserve) Battalion.
>
> I offer free an idea that a ladies' auxiliary to look after the comforts and interest of these forgotten legions be formed; it is needed and would be very much appreciated. H 40208, Ozada Camp, 20 June 1942.

Evans Narrows (64 I/12) in Hlowananatseda Lake was named after him in 1995.

Evans, Flying Officer **Horace A.** of Makinak (J 26336). No. 625 Squadron. He died 11 June 1944 at the age of 20 and is commemorated at St. Hilarion Communal Cemetery, France. He was the son of George and Annie Evans of Makinak, Manitoba. ***Evans Island*** (64 O/10) in Bangle Lake was named after him in 1985.

Evans, Private **Robert D.** of Winnipeg (H 17707). Winnipeg Grenadiers. He died 23 November 1943 and is commemorated at the Yokohama War Cemetery in Japan. ***Evans Rapids*** (64 F/1) in the unnamed river which flows into Barrington Lake was named after him in 1995.

Evans, Trooper **Stanley C. "Spud"** of Norgate (H 77045). 18th Armoured Car Regiment (12th Manitoba Dragoons). He died 7 June 1942 at the age of 22 and is commemorated at McCreary Cemetery. He was the son of Ernest and Ethel Evans of Norgate and the brother of Trooper Edward E. Evans (see entry). His sister recalls (26 February 1997) that he was:

> ... born in Gladstone Hospital, he took his schooling at Norgate till he finished Grade 8 – as far as they could go there. He was just the opposite to his brother Edwin [Edward]. He was very shy and bashful and very quiet. He was a good student at school. He was also a good worker and worked on a farm for one of our neighbours just a few miles from home. When he had enough money saved up, he bought a beautiful new CCM bicycle which was his pride and joy.
>
> He was not a hunter and I don't think he ever shot anything in his life – maybe partridge or a rabbit. His nick-name was "Spud" and he always called me "Sis." He never owned a car of any kind and I never heard him wish for one.
>
> On a foggy, rainy day, a train struck the truck that he and 19 other members of his regiment were riding in. He was thrown out and killed

instantly. They were scheduled to leave for overseas shortly. His body was brought home and buried with full military honours in McCreary Cemetery, just a few miles from Norgate.

Evans Esker (64 C/12), west of Craig Lake was named after him in 1995.

Evans, Pilot Officer **Thomas G.** of Winnipeg (J 86832). No. 106 Squadron. He died 29 June 1944 at the age of 21 and is commemorated at Feigneux Communal Cemetery, France. ***Evans Hill*** (64 O/12), north of Shannon Lake was named after him in 1995.

Evans, Private **Walton B.** of Bowsman (H 21142). Seaforth Highlanders of Canada. He died 23 May 1944 at the age of 23 and is commemorated at the Cassino War Cemetery in Italy. He was the son of Walton L. and Olga Evans of Bowsman. Walton Evans Rapids (53 M/14) in the Dafoe River was named after him in 1995.

Ewing, Flight Sergeant **Arthur C.** of Brandon (R 64755). No. 405 Squadron. He died 3 September 1942 at the age of 20 and is commemorated at Hotton War Cemetery, Belgium. He was the second oldest of the twelve children of William C. and Mabel R. Ewing (née McDermott) of Edmonton, Alberta. According to his brother (3 August 1998):

> He was born ... at Hampton, New Brunswick. Arthur graduated in June, 1939 from Hampton Consolidated School where he was an average student, a member of the cadet corps, soccer and hockey teams and a successful competitor in track and field events. He was also a Trooper in the reserve army, the 8th Princess Louise's New Brunswick Hussars. He enlisted in the RCAF June 26, 1940 and received his training as a wireless air gunner in Manitoba before proceeding overseas via Debert, Nova Scotia July 1st 1941.

Four brothers and his father also served in the armed forces during World War II. ***Ewing Island*** (64 P/12) in Nejanilini Lake was named after him in 1995.

Ewing, Flying Officer **William R.** of Winnipeg (J 38699). No. 434 Squadron. He died 14 October 1944 at the age of 24 and is commemorated at Blacon Cemetery in Cheshire, England. He was the eldest son of Robert S. and Eva G. Ewing of Winnipeg and the husband of Margaret Dorothy Ewing (née Shane) of Winnipeg. He had completed two years at the University of Manitoba in a Chartered Accountancy program and was articled to Glendenning, Gray and Roberts when he enlisted. He wrote a letter to his brother George a month before he was killed:

> Dear Dord: I meant to write you as soon as I came to this station but of course didn't get around to it. Anyway, this isn't a very good station to come to so I'd avoid it if you can. It's dispersed all over the country and the living quarters are extremely poor. In fact, it's a bloody poor station.
>
> We haven't done very much so far. We came up here on the 7th and didn't do any flying until the 13th. We did a few circuits and bumps in the morning and were scheduled for a Bullseye that night, but it was scrubbed on account of the weather. Then they changed the route to a cross-country. Then they changed the route once more and then after 2 1/2 hours of briefing, they cancelled the whole thing. Thursday afternoon we took off on a cross-country and when we got back to base about 7:00 Thursday night we were diverted to Dishforth. We had to spend the night there. They sent a servicing crew down from our own station to look after the aircraft that landed there. We could only get three of our engines started then in spite of having our own ground crew there. So about 5:00 last night they threw us in a truck and brought us back to Croft.
>
> Now this morning we are supposed to be flying back down to Dishforth to bring back our kite. It's 10:15 now, though, and no one has made a move in the direction of Dishforth yet so we may not be going down until this afternoon. I see my skipper is on his way now so I guess I don't have to go. I don't mind taking the morning off.
>
> I got the wedding cake all right before I left Topcliffe. Thanks for sending it on to me. Zach has done his second dickey stooge and the rear gunner also has one to his credit.
>
> I am now down at Dishforth waiting for them to fix up our kite. I'm sitting at my Nav. Desk writing and it's 3:30 PM. The ground crew are almost finished with the kite, so I guess we'll be going back to Croft pretty soon. I wonder if they will put us on flying tonight when we get back. I hope not. It looks to me as though the winds are pretty high today and I don't like flying when the winds are too high or too low. We are almost set to start now so I guess I had better close and mail this letter when I get back. Let me know where you are posted and take my advice about not coming to Croft. So long for now, Bill (16 September 1944).

His mother wrote to George after receiving word of Bill's death:

> Dordie Darling: Wish I was with you right now. Dorothy and I think of you alone over there – she has been wonderful, but feels everything has ended for her right now. Mr. Briggs, their Minister, went to see her and talked so nicely and told her the sun would shine again.
>
> I hope you have been able to get to the funeral and can tell me about it. I am so glad that Bill is having a burial, but we have not heard yet what happened. The telegraph company got in touch with Mr. Gray and he left the office and picked up the wires and came back and told Dorothy to come with him – he had some bad news for her and he took her in a taxi and started for here, but they went out and got her mother first – then came here. It was about three o'clock Monday afternoon. The wire just said Bill was killed on active service October 14th. Yesterday afternoon we had wires telling us he was to be buried in Chester at 2 PM today.
>
> Myrtle stayed with me Tuesday, but went to work yesterday as the boys were having an exam; she was over last night and is just broken-hearted. Everybody has been so kind to me and sent beautiful flowers and there has been a constant stream of visitors. Charlie sent a bunch of lovely dark roses but has not been able to come to see me yet, he feels so badly. The Stewarts were in Monday evening and Ross was in again yesterday and had your letter of October 5th in which you said you had not been so well – hope you are better. How about that tooth, is it out yet?
>
> Jean has been here every day, also Hartwells, they feel very badly too. Auntie Em was here all day yesterday and Herbert sent his sympathy.
>
> I have always prayed if one of you had to be killed in this war, it would be quick and there would be no suffering and it seems my prayer has been answered. Please God take care of you and bring you safely home.
>
> Tell me any news you can about Bill – we seem so far away – Dorothy will be so anxious to hear too. It is now 11:50 AM and I got your letter of October 5th and see you did get that tooth out and I hope your ear is better too. Jean is here for the day and we have just been talking about you and wondering if you got her box of candy and when.
>
> The days seem so long now, and I guess it will take me quite a while to get back to my routine, but I will though, Dordie, and I love you so much. So long, Mom (19 October 1944).

Flying Officer Ewing's widow wrote to his brother who was also stationed overseas:

> Dear George: The month of October is past now but the news it brought was so hard for us all to take. It seems so hard to believe that our Bill has gone. I had planned on writing you sooner, but I just hadn't words to frame a letter – as a matter of fact I still haven't, but I can try.
>
> We thought so much about you Dordie, particularly those first few days. The complete lack of privacy in the Air Force must have made the shock so hard and I'm sure your first thoughts were of worry for your mother as her thoughts were for you. She has been really wonderful, George and very brave. You would be very proud of her, and I know that you are. All the company that she has had lately has been quite an ordeal, coming as it did on top of the shock, but she has been able to laugh at the sudden influx of visitors, which is really something. I'm afraid I'd have been a lot less patient and shoo'd them out. However, Marjorie and Willis and the baby have gone now, so maybe she will be able to relax. The one

occupant of the house that would really make her happy would be you, and the day you return will really be a happy one for her, and for all of us. Your return will be doubly welcome to her, George. You don't need me to tell you how very proud she is of you – you can likely read between the lines of her letters.

We were all so happy together the night of Marion's wedding. I like to think that maybe Bill could see us that night. Ross and I had quite a chat during the course of the evening – comparing news from overseas, and speaking of Bill. As I'm never happier than when I'm speaking of Bill, I enjoyed myself. But that was the night my little personal life came to an end – when Bill crashed. I find it very difficult to speak of the tragedy, George. I know that it is one that is repeated in many homes these days of war, but that does not make the pain of separation any less. The prospect of a future stretching before me without Bill is a very lonely one, but maybe I can gain courage to face it by thinking of the courage that Bill showed, and that all you boys are showing, who are fighting for us at home.

In your letters to your mother you mentioned the padre's name and I wrote to him asking him to follow up [on] the delivery of some snapshots Bill took on his last leave and which he left in London for developing. They were to be mailed to him at the station. I hope so very much that these won't be sent back to the photo-finishing place unclaimed. We'll just have to wait and see. Bill had not had any snaps taken of himself since he went over there, so I'm very anxious to get these snaps. Bill had promised for a long time to have some taken, and I'm so glad he did find an opportunity on his last leave.

I've had several very nice letters from the wife of Bill's pilot and she seems to be a very fine, sensible girl. Living in Ottawa as she does, she had access to the RCAF records and was able to give us a few details. I'm sure your mother passed on these to you. Details are not so terribly important – are they? The fact that it all happened is in itself so overwhelming as to dwarf everything else in comparison. The only comforting fact is that it was sudden and conclusive. They tell me the concussion would be such as to make death instantaneous.

I don't have to tell you what Bill meant to me, George, we all loved him. He was a wonderful husband and made me very happy. I'm so glad that we were able to get married when we did – it scares me to think that we might have waited until after the war. Besides the memory of so many fine, personal qualities, Bill left me a very fine mother and brother-in-law – and they mean a great deal to me. The very best of everything to you George. Sincerely, Dorothy (9 November 1944).

Ewing Lake (64 O/11), southeast of Nueltin Lake was named after him in 1975.

Military personnel and civilians celebrating VE-Day on Sparks Street 8 May 1945. Courtesy of the National Archives of Canada (PA-114617).

F

Fabas, Private **Louis.** of La Broquerie (H 14784). Calgary Highlanders. He died 8 February 1945 at the age of 19 and is commemorated at the Groesbeek Canadian War Cemetery in Holland. He was the son of Eugene and Ella Fabas of La Broquerie, Manitoba. This was one of the names applied by the federal government without the knowledge of the family. When they discovered the name, Private Fabas' sister-in-law made an inquiry:

> Dear Sir: It was a great surprise to my husband and myself when we were shown that one of the many lakes in northern Manitoba has the same name as ours, namely Fabas Lake. As far as we know, the name "Fabas" is scarce. One of our daughters, Mildred, who happens to work for the government Finance Department, did some inquiring on our behalf. It seems that Manitoba had a lot of unnamed lakes, and recommendations for military service men, who died in the second World War was the name given to the lakes. This is a beautiful gesture to the now living, who have given their loved ones to the country. We found that Fabas Lake was named after my husband's brother, Louis Fabas, who died 8 February 1945 in Holland.
>
> As we have just learned of these facts within the last two weeks, could you verify this? The reason why we ask this request of you is because his mother, Mrs. Ella Fabas, who is now 94 years old often speaks of him and is very proud of him. She had three sons, Paul (my husband), Louis and Hector. Paul and Louis both were in the army as they were of age at the time (8 July 1983).

Fabas Lake (64 I/10), northeast of North Knife Lake was named after Private Louis Fabas in 1974.

Fagnan, Rifleman **Anthony A.** of Camperville (H 41980). Royal Winnipeg Rifles. He died 8 June 1944 at the age of 20 and is commemorated at Beny-sur-Mer Canadian War Cemetery in Calvados, France. He was the son of Joseph and Katherine Fagnan of Camperville. His niece writes (25 January 2002):

> My uncle was a Métis from Camperville, Manitoba. He lived with his family on a homestead along the North Pine River. He was the youngest child of five sisters, he had a sunny disposition, good natured with a great sense of humour. He was lovingly nicknamed "Waapishtikwan" because of his blond hair. He hunted and fished with his father to help with the family's livelihood. He was sadly missed by a large number of aunts, uncles, nieces and nephews. He is still missed and fondly remembered.

Fagnan Lake (64 K/6), northeast of Reindeer Lake was named after him in 1961.

Fahrni, Pilot Officer **Ross P.** of Gladstone (J 9903). No. 172 Squadron. He died 19 August 1942 at the age of 21 and is commemorated at Killay (St. Hilary of Poictiers) Churchyard, Glamorganshire, Wales. He was the son of Stanley Harrison and Edith J. Fahrni of Portage la Prairie. According to his sister (30 April 1996):

> Ross Pringle Fahrni grew up in Gladstone where he graduated from high school. Then he attended University of Saskatchewan, Regina Campus. He planned to study law. He enjoyed football, music and dramatics. He worked articling in my father's law office during the year he awaited call-up to the RCAF.

Fahrni Lake (63 K/14), north of Naosap Lake was named after him in 1982.

Fairey, Pilot Officer **Earl Roy** of Winnipeg (J 90956). No. 425 Squadron. He died 29 July 1944 at the age of 35 and is commemorated at the Runnymede Memorial in Surrey, England. He was the son of George and Louisa Fairey and was survived by his wife Edythe P. Fairey of Winnipeg. ***Fairey Island*** (52 H/10) in Lake Nipigon, Ontario was named after him in 1960.

Falardeau, Sergeant **William Leslie** of Winnipeg (R 80157). No. 82 Operational Training Unit, RCAF. He died 14 December 1941 at the age of 19 and is commemorated at Little Rissington (St. Peter) Churchyard in Gloucestershire, England. He was the son of Earl and Hilda Falardeau of Winnipeg. His obituary read in part:

> Born in Winnipeg, he was educated at Earl Grey and Kelvin schools. He carried his colours into sports arenas, and in 1939, won the half-mile event for Kelvin. He was an ardent tennis player. Photography and aviation were his hobbies. The former won him a position with the moving picture company that filmed *49th Parallel*. Sergeant Falardeau travelled with the company as an assistant at the camera and was also photographed in a few scenes as a substitute for Raymond Massey, star of the picture.
>
> He was a member of the Young Men's Club of the Crescent-Fort Rouge church. He won two cups in model aircraft contests and also received several rides in planes as prizes. He joined the Air Force November 6, 1940 and left for service overseas last August (*Winnipeg Tribune* December 1941).

Falardeau Lake (64 P/11), east of Nejanilini Lake was named after him in 1974.

Falconer, Flying Officer **Lloyd G.** of Winnipeg (J 29597). No. 10 Service Flying Training School. He died 17 August 1944 at the age of 27 and is commemorated at Old Kildonan Presbyterian Cemetery in Winnipeg. He was the son of Charles C. and Lena M. Falconer of Winnipeg and was survived by his wife Margaret A. Falconer of West Kildonan. ***Falconer Lake*** (64 F/3), northwest of Goldsand Lake was named after him in 1994.

Fallis, Flight Sergeant **George E.** of Carberry (R 86387). No. 418 Squadron. He died 3 May 1942 at the age of 28 and is commemorated at Brookwood Military Cemetery in Surrey, England. He was the son of William R. and Charlotte Fallis of Carberry, Manitoba. The Squadron Operations Record Book gives the following details:

> Departing RAF West Malling, Kent (19:25) with a full bomb load, the landing gear failed and broke away, shearing off part of the starboard elevator and rudder. The aircraft crashed, killing all three crew. Minutes later the bomb load exploded, killing another airman on the ground (1942).

Fallis Lake (64 P/6), east of Nejanilini Lake was named after him in 1978.

Falloon, Flying Officer **James Garnet** of Foxwarren (J 22895). No. 575 Squadron. He died 21 March 1944 at the age of 26 and is commemorated at Brookwood Military Cemetery in Surrey, England. He was the son of Albert S. and Mary Pearl Falloon of Foxwarren, Manitoba. ***Falloon Lake*** (64 P/15), northeast of Nejanilini Lake was named after him in 1975.

Farand, Private **Adelard J.** of Winnipegosis (SH 4942). Princess Patricia's Canadian Light Infantry. He died 19 November 1952 at the age of 19 and is commemorated at the United Nations Cemetery in Pusan, South Korea. ***Farand Lake*** (53 E/15), northwest of Island Lake was named after this Korean War casualty in 1998.

Farewell, Ordinary Seaman **Elmo R.** of Swan River (V 16395). HMCS *Windflower.* The *Windflower* was rammed by Dutch freighter *Zypenberg* in dense fog off the Grand Banks while escorting Convoy SC.58; 23 of her ship's company were lost. Ordinary Seaman Farewell died 7 December 1941 at the age of 19 and is commemorated at the Halifax Memorial. He was survived by his mother Maude L. Farewell of Swan River, Manitoba. ***Farewell Lake*** (64 N/14), west of Nueltin Lake was named after him in 1972.

Fargey, Lieutenant **Walter Henry G.** of La Rivière. Royal Canadian Artillery. He died 15 February 1945 at the age of 34 and is commemorated at the Groesbeek Canadian War Cemetery in Holland. He was the youngest son of Thomas L. and Isabella M. Fargey of La Rivière, Manitoba. Graduating from the University of Manitoba in 1937 with a degree in civil engineering, he had been employed in the mines at Sherridon, Manitoba prior to enlisting. ***Fargey Creek*** (54 B/14), which flows northwest into Mistikokan River was named after him in 1964.

Farnie, Flight Sergeant **Arthur Kingsley A.** of Reston (R 86310). No. 415 Squadron. He was shot down 2 July 1942 at the age of 20 and is commemorated at the Sage War Cemetery in Germany. He was the eldest of the three sons of Arthur and Ethel Farnie of Salford, Lancashire and nephew of George and Bella Harper (née Farnie) of Reston. According to his brother (22 October 2001), he:

> ... was born in Salford, England on 24th November 1921. Mother died in 1931 and Kingsley, aged 10 years, travelled alone to Canada to live with his uncle George Harper at Grove Creek Farm, Reston, Manitoba. Kingsley joined the RCAF on 4th January 1941, trained as an air observer and came to the UK in 1942 to serve in Coastal Command. On his first operational mission in a torpedo-carrying Hampden aircraft, he failed to return.
>
> I am Kingsley's brother, born in 1923. I've visited his grave at Sage; it's quite small, less than 1000 graves, all young men, mostly aircrew. What a terrible waste of life.

Farnie Lake (64 P/13), north of Nejanilini Lake was named after him in 1974.

Farquhar, Flying Officer **Allan R. A.** of Winnipeg (J 14805). No. 429 Squadron. He died 28 July 1943 at the age of 21 and is commemorated at Hamburg Cemetery in Germany. He was the son of Captain Allan A. and Dorothy M. Farquhar of Winnipeg and was survived by his wife and their unborn daughter. According to his grandson, he did not know he was going to be a father at the time of his death. ***Farquhar Lake*** (64 O/6), east of Booth Lake was named after him in 1995.

Farquharson, Trooper **Gordon** of East Kildonan (H 26118). Fort Garry Horse. He died 14 August 1944 at the age of 29 and is commemorated at Bretteville-sur-Laize Canadian War Cemetery in Calvados, France. He was the son of Patrick and Charlotte Farquharson of East Kildonan. ***Farquharson Lake*** (64 I/16), northeast of North Knife Lake was named after him in 1974.

Farrally, Flight Lieutenant **John** of Winnipeg (108623). No. 464 Squadron, RAF. He died 6 October 1944 at the age of 28 and is commemorated at Lille Southern Cemetery, Nord, France. He was the son of Albert E. and Edith Farrally and was survived by his wife Betty H. Farrally. ***Farrally Lake*** (53 N/15), northeast of Whitefish Lake was named after him in 1995.

Farries, Fireman **Richard N.** of Winnipeg. SS *Lom*, Canadian Merchant Navy. He died 3 December 1943 at the age of 21 and is commemorated at the Bari War Cemetery in Italy. He was the son of Thomas and Grace E. Farries and was survived by his uncle Mr. L. C. George of Chicago, Illinois. ***Farries Lake*** (63 P/8), north of Goulet Lake was named after him in 2001.

Faulconer, Sergeant **George M.** of Treherne (H 6799). Winnipeg Grenadiers. He died 31 March 1946 at the age of 29 and is commemorated at Woodlands Cemetery in Treherne. He was survived by his mother Harriet E. Faulconer (née Mulholland) of Treherne. ***Faulconer Lake*** (64 J/6), southwest of Tadoule Lake was named after him in 1975.

Favel, Gunner **Thomas G.** of Winnipeg (H 66972). Royal Canadian Artillery. He died 1 May 1946 at the age of 21 and is commemorated at Brookwood Military Cemetery in Surrey, England. He was survived by his father and stepmother John T. and Ethel H. L. Favel of Winnipeg. ***Favel Island*** (63 O/2) in Setting Lake was named after him in 1995.

Favel, Private **William** of High Bluff (H 60278). Algonquin Regiment. He died 3 March 1945 at the age of 25 and is commemorated at the Groesbeek Canadian War Cemetery in Holland. He was survived by his mother Mary Favel of High Bluff, Manitoba. ***Favel Bay*** (63 N/11) in Girouard Lake was named after him in 1995.

Fedak, Trooper **Stephen J.** of McCreary (H 77250). 12th Manitoba Dragoons. He died 6 December 1944 at the age of 23 and is commemorated at Bergen-op-Zoom Canadian War Cemetery in Holland. He was the son of Peter and Annie Fedak of McCreary, Manitoba. ***Fedak Lake*** (64 I/5), northwest of North Knife Lake was named after him in 1974.

Fedi, Flight Sergeant **Eric** of Winnipeg (R 172702). No. 77 Squadron. He died 7 September 1943 at the age of 19 and is commemorated at the Runnymede Memorial in Surrey, England. His nephew (14 June 2001) recalls that:

> ... [g]rowing up as a teenager on Ashburn Street, Eric spent most of Winnipeg's long, cold winter months playing hockey. He also worked weekends at the service station down the street. But his real passion was building model airplanes; this would most likely be the principal reason why he joined the Air Force.

Flight Sergeant Fedi was one of the many who managed to enlist while underage:

> Fedi falsified his age and was 16 years old when he enlisted; he was probably closer to 17 at the time of his death. Eric's sister, Mrs. Zornick of Winnipeg, explained how he got into the RCAF at 16: "A friend helped to falsify his birth certificate and his mother went along with it if he didn't go overseas. Eric graduated and went overseas without saying goodbye. A brother in the PPCLI in England threatened to expose his age, but Eric said he would never speak to his brother nor his mother if

that happened. Relatives in Glasgow, Scotland said he was very happy serving his country so nothing was said" (Allison and Hayward 1991).

Fedi Lake (63 H/1), east of Lake Winnipeg was named after him in 1974.

Fedirchyk, Flight Sergeant **Michael W.** of Winnipeg (R 86326). No. 22 Operational Training Unit, RCAF. He died 29 June 1942 and is commemorated at Stratford-upon-Avon Cemetery in Warwickshire, England. ***Fedirchyk Lake*** (52 M/13), northeast of Amphibian Lake was named after him in 1979.

Fediuk, Private **Nicholas** of Rorketon (H 67062). Highland Light Infantry. He died 25 July 1944 at the age of 20 and is commemorated at Beny-sur-Mer Canadian War Cemetery in Calvados, France. He was the son of Dmetro and Madeline Fediuk of Weiden, Manitoba. ***Fediuk Lake*** (64 O/10), northwest of Nejanilini Lake was named after him in 1975.

Feir, Sapper **Walter I.** of Basswood (M 36794). Royal Canadian Artillery. He died 27 August 1944 at the age of 23 and is commemorated at Bretteville-sur-Laize Canadian War Cemetery in Calvados, France. He was the son of Harry and Stella M. Feir of Basswood, Manitoba. ***Feir Lake*** (64 J/8), south of Tadoule Lake was named after him in 1975.

Felstead, Lieutenant **Robert C.** of Winnipeg (H 35540). Lanark and Renfrew Scottish Regiment. He died 3 December 1944 at the age of 26 and is commemorated at Ravenna War Cemetery in Italy. He was the youngest son of Tindal A. and May Felstead of Vancouver. ***Felstead Lake*** (64 K/12), northeast of Reindeer Lake was named after him in 1972.

Fenton, Bombardier **Fred I. N.** of Winnipeg (H 15154). Royal Canadian Artillery. He died 2 October 1941 at the age of 41 and is commemorated at Brookwood Military Cemetery in Surrey, England. He was survived by his wife Rita Fenton of St. Vital and their son. His obituary in the newspaper read:

> A drummer in the Great War and a member of the RCA in this one, ... [he] was employed in the utilities department of the Winnipeg School Board and took an active part in amateur trick skating. A memorial service will be held Monday at 3:00 PM at St. Thomas' Anglican Church, Weston (n.d.).

Fenton Creek (63 J/6), which flows east into the Hargrave River was named after him in 1972.

Fenwick, Flight Sergeant **William G.** of Norwood (784). Royal Canadian Air Force. He died 13 May 1944 at the age of 29 and is commemorated at Royal Oak Burial Park in Victoria, British Columbia. He was the son of Thomas and Edith M. Fenwick of Norwood and was survived by his wife Beatrice L. Fenwick of Victoria. ***Fenwick Lake*** (64 J/13), northwest of Tadoule Lake was named after him in 1975.

Fergus, Corporal **James** of Herb Lake (H 20947). Queen's Own Cameron Highlanders. He died 27 January 1945 at the age of 34 and is commemorated at the Groesbeek Canadian War Cemetery in Holland. He was the son of David and Mina Fergus (née Adams) of Herb Lake, Manitoba. ***Fergus River*** (64 J/14), which flows northeast into Bain Lake was named after him in 1961.

Ferguson, Sergeant **Charles E.** of St. Vital (H 6107). Winnipeg Grenadiers. He died 20 December 1941 and is commemorated at the Sai Wan Memorial in Hong Kong. ***Ferguson Peninsula*** (64 H/14) on North Knife Lake was named after him in 1995.

Ferguson, Lieutenant Colonel **Clarence William** of Winnipeg. Queen's Own Cameron Highlanders. He died 9 August 1944 at the age of 28 and is commemorated at Bayeux War Cemetery, Calvados, France. He was the only son of Reverend Clarence S. and Minnie M. Ferguson and husband of Lorraine J. Ferguson of Winnipeg. According to his sister (7 April 1995):

> My father died in Mortlach, Saskatchewan in 1922 where he was the rural dean. We then moved to Winnipeg. Bill attended St. John's College and while there became active in the COTC. Following gradation, he continued this interest and took courses at Sarcee ... as part of the Armoured Car Regiment Reserve where he held the rank of Lieutenant. When war was declared, he transferred to the Queen's Own Cameron Highlanders. He went overseas in March, 1940. He was sent to Camberley and when his course was finished, he became Aide de Camp of Major General Odlum. He then completed another course at Camberley and in August, 1942 was sent back to Canada to teach at RMC. He returned overseas in October, 1943, rejoined his regiment as Brigade Major. He was wounded on 8 August 1944 ... and died of his wounds 9 August 1944.

Ferguson Point (64 P/16) on Schwartz Lake was named after him in 1995.

Ferguson, Flight Sergeant **James M.** of Winnipeg (R 80008). No. 419 Squadron. He died 7 July 1942 at the age of 29 and is commemorated at Upavon Church Cemetery, Wiltshire, England. He was the son of Hugh and Jean Ferguson of Winnipeg. Flight Sergeant Ferguson was a wireless air gunner on Wellington Z1597 which took off from RAF Mildenhall on a mine-laying operation off Lorient. On return to base, it flew into the side of a hill near Oare, nine miles east northeast of Devizes, Wiltshire. All five crew, all RCAF, were killed. ***Ferguson Bay*** (64 I/6) in Gammack Lake was named after him in 1995.

Ferguson, Private **Robert G.** (L 22411). Queen's Own Cameron Highlanders. He died 19 August 1942 and is commemorated at Dieppe Canadian War Cemetery in Seine-Maritime, France. ***Ferguson Lake*** (64 K/4), north of Reindeer Lake on the Manitoba - Saskatchewan boundary was named after him in 1962.

Ferguson, Lieutenant **William S.** of Winnipeg. Royal Winnipeg Rifles. He died 6 June 1944 and is commemorated at Beny-sur-Mer Canadian War Cemetery in Calvados, France. He was survived by his mother Anne W. Pullen and by his wife Masala M. Ferguson of Vancouver, British Columbia. ***Ferguson Island*** (63 N/11) in Morin Lake was named after him in 1995.

Ferland, Rifleman **Norman P.** of Duck Bay (SH 5215). Queen's Own Rifles of Canada. He died 31 March 1954 at the age of 20 and is commemorated at the United Nations Cemetery in Pusan, South Korea. He was survived by his wife and their daughter. ***Ferland Lake*** (63 I/8), south of Robinson Lake was named after this Korean War casualty in 1998.

Fernstrom, Sergeant **Harold L.** of East Kildonan (R 218750). No. 27 Squadron. He died 8 November 1944 at the age of 19 and is commemorated at Blacon Cemetery in Cheshire, England. Born in Ridgedale, Saskatchewan, he moved to Winnipeg with his parents when he was two years old. He was the only son of Barry J. and Lena M. Fernstrom of East Kildonan and was survived by his fiancée Doreen Hitt. Prior to enlisting, he was an apprentice with the Bird Construction Company. An article in *The Chronicle* of Chester, England some years later read:

> A promise made some months ago in Winnipeg was fulfilled this (Friday) morning when Mrs. Melecey Taylor of Romas, California, at present spending a holiday in her native London, visited the grave of a 19 year-old sergeant of the Canadian Air Force in the RAF section of the Blacon Cemetery.
>
> The flier, Sergeant H. L. Fernstrom, who died on November 8th, 1944 was the only son of Mr. and Mrs. Fernstrom of Winnipeg, neighbours of Mrs. Taylor's elder sister.
>
> On her way to London from her home in California, where she has lived for the past three years, Mrs. Taylor called on her sister, and there met Mrs. Fernstrom who told her of her son's grave at Chester. "He is so very lonely," she said, and Mrs. Taylor immediately offered to visit the cemetery.
>
> On arriving in England, she wrote to the Mayor of Chester (Alderman A. H. Charmley) who invited her to visit the city. And this morning the Mayor accompanied Mrs. Taylor to the graveside.
>
> After prayers offered by Squadron Leader P. S. Greenwood, Chaplain at RAF West Kirby, Mrs. Taylor added a bouquet of golden chrysanthemums to one of mixed roses, placed there earlier by the cemetery authorities. She then noted the inscription on the simple headstone, "As we loved him, so we miss him," and took photographs to send to the airman's parents.
>
> Mrs. Taylor told the Mayor, "I am very pleased to see the great care shown for all the graves here," and added that she would write at once to the Mayor of Winnipeg and the Canadian Press to assure them of the way the graves of Canadians at Chester would always be cared for. There are 195 of them among 500 British and Commonwealth RAF graves at Blacon (12 December 1953).

Fernstrom Lake (52 L/6), northeast of Lac du Bonnet was named after him in 1973.

Ferrier, Corporal **Edwin J. M.** of Winnipeg (R 56640). No. 404 Squadron. He died 17 September 1943 at the age of 29 and is commemorated at Wick Cemetery, Caithness, Scotland. He was the son of John and Rachel A. Ferrier of Winnipeg. ***Ferrier Lake*** (64 I/14), northwest of North Knife Lake was named after him in 1974.

Ferris, Flying Officer **James B.** of Wawanesa (J 10785). No. 400 Mustang Squadron. He died 20 January 1943 at the age of 26 and is commemorated at the Runnymede Memorial in Surrey, England. He was survived by his mother Charlotte Ferris of Wawanesa, Manitoba. ***Ferris Lake*** (64 P/6), southeast of Nejanilini Lake was named after him in 1974.

Ferris, Private **Victor D.** of Dauphin (H 36512). South Saskatchewan Regiment. He died 14 August 1944 at the age of 25 and is commemorated at Bretteville-sur-Laize Canadian War Cemetery in Calvados, France. He was the son of Britton and Annie Ferris and was survived by his wife Gilberte "Betty" Ferris of New Westminster, British Columbia. She recalls (22 November 2001):

> In 1941, while in Winnipeg looking for a job I met my dream man – a tall, dark and handsome soldier named Victor D. Ferris on June 14th of that year. A short while later, he was transferred to Petawawa and then to Gander, Newfoundland. I had to follow my parents to BC soon after. All the while we corresponded.
>
> On February 14th, 1943 he proposed to me and I accepted. I got the wedding preparations ready, the Army gave him permission to marry so as soon as he arrived in BC, we were wed – September 14, 1943. So far, the number 14 was super, until he went overseas and two months later he was bombed by the RAF on August 14, 1944. I was widowed at 20 years of age and I got the telegram of his death on my 21st birthday.
>
> The authorities always refused to tell me how he died, but I know the RAF bombs fell at Bretteville-le-Rabet on August 14, 1944 – General Eisenhower wrote a book about it, so I have been hanging since then and wondering. So that's the whole story. I am still a very sad person, living alone for so long.

Ferris Island (63 N/13) in Sisipuk Lake was named after him in 1995.

Ferris, Warrant Officer 1 **Walter Harold** of Holland (R 110726). No. 608 Squadron. He died 27 January 1944 at the age of 22 and is commemorated at the Malta Memorial. He was the son of Lewis and Annie Ferris of Holland, Manitoba. ***Ferris Bay*** (54 D/7) on the north shore of Stephens Lake was named after him in 1982.

Ferro, Warrant Officer 1 **Carlo E.** of Winnipeg (R 86131). No. 511 Squadron. He died 23 March 1943 at the age of 20 and is commemorated at the Runnymede Memorial in Surrey, England. He was the son of Carlo and Katrina Ferro. ***Ferro Lake*** (64 H/11), south of Small Lake was named after him in 1995.

Feschuk, Trooper **William** of Vita (B 61215). 1st Hussar Tank Regiment. He died 6 June 1944 at the age of 26 and is commemorated at Beny-sur-Mer Canadian War Cemetery in Calvados, France. He was the son of Michael and Mary Feschuk of Vita, Manitoba. ***Feschuk Lake*** (64 O/11), south of Small Lake was named after him in 1995.

Fetherstonhaugh, Flight Sergeant **Charles B.** of Winnipeg (R 106063). No. 10 Squadron. He died 10 January 1943 at the age of 20 and is commemorated at Schiermonnikoog (Vredenhof) Cemetery, Holland. He was the son of Cuthbert F. and Dorothy F. Fetherstonhaugh of East Kildonan. ***Fetherstonhaugh Lake*** (64 P/14), northeast of Nejanilini Lake was named after him in 1974.

Fiddler, Chief Engine Room Artificer **Roderick** of Selkirk (A 1089). HMCS *Windflower*. The *Windflower* was rammed by Dutch freighter *Zypenberg* in dense fog off the Grand Banks while escorting Convoy SC.58; 23 of her ship's company were lost. Chief ERA Fiddler died 7 December 1941 at the age of 51 and is commemorated at the Halifax Memorial. This veteran of World War I was born in Mapleton, Manitoba. He was the son of Thomas and Eliza Fiddler and was survived by his wife Mary E. Fiddler of Selkirk, Manitoba. ***Fiddler Island*** (64 N/9) in Nueltin Lake was named after him in 1995.

Fidler, Rifleman **Garner** of Portage la Prairie (H 42060). Royal Winnipeg Rifles. He died 6 June 1944 and is commemorated at Beny-sur-Mer Canadian War Cemetery in Calvados, France. Sixty-nine Manitobans lost their lives during the Normandy landings that day. ***Fidler Lake*** (64 K/11), northeast of Reindeer Lake was named after him in 1972.

Fielding, Lance Bombardier **Donald R. J.** of Selkirk (H 3606). Royal Canadian Artillery. He died 4 February 1944 at the age of 43 and is commemorated at St. Clements Cemetery in Mapleton, Manitoba. He was the son of Mr. and Mrs. John R. Fielding of West Selkirk. ***Fielding Lake*** (64 A/11), northeast of Campbell Lake was named after him in 1996.

Fifer, Private **Roy V.** of Winnipeg (K 92337). Winnipeg Grenadiers. He died a prisoner of war 17 July 1944 at the age of 22 and is commemorated at the Sai Wan War Cemetery in Hong Kong. He was the son of Mr. and Mrs. Jack Fifer of Winnipeg. ***Fifer Lake*** (54 C/5), southwest of York Factory was named after him in 1964.

Finch, Flying Officer **Eldon Grant** of Winnipeg (J 24422). No. 184 Squadron. He died 13 February 1944 at the age of 21 and is commemorated at Brookwood Military Cemetery in Surrey, England. He was the son of Oscar J. and Bessie Finch of Winnipeg. His sister writes (22 August 1997):

> My brother ... was born in Elphinstone, Manitoba in 1923, but lived in Winnipeg since he was six years old. He graduated from Kelvin High School, then worked for the Bank of Commerce in Treherne for a year before joining up. He was a speed skater in high school and excelled in mathematics. In the Air Force, he passed a navigation course with the highest marks, but opted for pilot's training. He crashed in England returning from a training mission. He had just turned twenty-one.

Finch Point (64 N/1) on George Stewart Lake was named after him in 1995.

Finch, Squadron Leader **George H.** of Birtle (J 11101). No. 13 Squadron, Distinguished Flying Cross.

> Since joining his present squadron, Flight Lieutenant Finch has completed operations from North Africa, Sicily and Italy. On one occasion whilst on anti-submarine control [patrol?] he sighted a U-boat which he immediately attacked and straddled with depth charges. On another occasion, while taking part in a formation attack on a petrol dump in Italy, his aircraft was damaged by heavy anti-aircraft fire. In spite of the loss of power occasioned by this, Flight Lieutenant Finch remained in his place in the formation until his engine ceased to function. He has always shown the greatest keenness for flying (DFC Citation 1944).

He died 17 March 1945 at the age of 21 and is commemorated at the Alamein Memorial in Egypt. He was the son of Reverend Canon William J. and Mrs. Finch of Birtle Rectory, Manitoba. ***Finch Lake*** (64 C/10), northwest of Granville Lake was named after him in 1947.

Finch, Gunner **Glen A.** of Deepdale (H 75147). Royal Canadian Artillery. He died 7 August 1944 at the age of 34 and is commemorated at Bretteville-sur-Laize Canadian War Cemetery in Calvados, France. He was the son of John and Margaret Finch and was survived by his wife Jean A. Finch of Roblin, Manitoba. ***Finch Bay*** (64 A/12) in Baldock Lake was named after him in 1995.

Finch, Sergeant **Robert W.** of Winnipeg (H 26133). Fort Garry Horse. He died 13 April 1945 at the age of 33 and is commemorated at the Groesbeek Canadian War Cemetery in Holland. He was the son of Robert J. and Helene Finch and was survived by his wife Elizabeth M. Finch of St. Vital. ***Finch Island*** (64 O/12) in Shannon Lake was named after him in 1985.

Findlater, Sergeant **John** of Winnipeg (R 110760). No. 6 Bombing and, Gunnery School, RCAF. He died 16 February 1943 at the age of 23 and is commemorated at the Ottawa Memorial. He was the son of Thomas W. and Ida E. Findlater. ***Findlater Lake*** (64 O/16), northwest of Nejanilini Lake was named after him in 1975.

Findlay, Pilot Officer **Ernest Q.** of Winnipeg (J 18008). No. 418 Squadron. He died 23 June 1943 at the age of 25 and is commemorated at Bretteville-sur-Laize Canadian War Cemetery in Calvados, France. He was the only child of Lieutenant Ernest B. and Clara Findlay. His cousin writes (19 November 2001):

> On June 23, 1943, Boston III Intruder W8394 took off from RAF Station Ford in Sussex, England on a sortie of the Tours and Orleans area of France. The crew of this aircraft were Pilot Officer Findlay (Pilot), Flying Officer Carmichael (Navigator) and Sergeant Robertson (Air Gunner), all RCAF. The aircraft failed to return from this operation and was reported missing. No information is available as to the point reached by the aircraft in view of the strict radio silence.
>
> Ernest was born in Kilmacolm, Scotland on February 10, 1918. His father, Lieutenant Ernest Brainerd Findlay, British Army, was killed in action in September, 1918. Ernest was educated at Grosvenor School, Earl Grey School and Kelvin High School in Winnipeg. Following graduation, he worked for the *Winnipeg Free Press*, Prairie Cities Oil Company, Great West Life Assurance and the Hudson's Bay Company. His hobbies were photography and aeronautics. He enjoyed sports and participated in track, high jump, golf, bowling and horseback riding. Prior to joining the RCAF, Ernest was a Sapper with the Royal Canadian Engineers.

Findlay Island (64 B/1) in Harding Lake was named after him in 1995.

Findlay, Pilot Officer **Lloyd E.** of Kelloe (J 89738). No. 415 Squadron. He died 13 July 1944 at the age of 27 and is commemorated at the Runnymede Memorial in Surrey, England. He was survived by his father Mr. J. B. Findlay of Kelloe. His brother recalls (14 December 1995):

> Prior to enlistment, Lloyd farmed with his father at Kelloe, Manitoba. He was musically inclined but had no formal education in music. He was very fond of hunting and local sports of all kinds. He was particularly interested in wireless telegraphy.

Pilot Officer Findlay and the entire crew of his Wellington were reported missing while on a night anti-shipping patrol in the North Sea. ***Findlay Bay*** (64 K/9) in Singleton Lake was named after him in 1995.

Findlay, Private **Robert G.** of Kirkfield Park (H 19658). Queen's Own Cameron Highlanders. He died 19 August 1942 at the age of 21 and is commemorated at Coxyde Military Cemetery in West-Vlaanderen, Belgium. He was the son of William and Jessie Findlay and was survived by his wife Sheila Findlay of Seaford, Sussex and their one month-old son. His sister writes (20 January 1995):

> He was born at Lossiemouth, Scotland in 1921 and went to school there for a couple of years before coming to Canada in 1929 where he attended Norberry School in St. Vital. When war broke out, he and five of his St. Vital friends joined the Queen's Own Cameron Highlanders and went to Britain with the 2nd Division.
>
> In July, 1942, he married an English girl (about one month before Dieppe) and in May, 1943 a son was born. They, of course, remained in England after the war and she has since remarried, but we keep in touch.
>
> Four of the six friends who joined up together were in the Dieppe action, two were killed and two survived. It has been difficult to get the circumstances of my brother's death, but he was reportedly seen ashore and apparently drowned attempting to get back to the rescuing ships. His body was washed up on the Belgian coast in February, 1943 and he is buried in a very well-maintained Military Cemetery in Coxyde, Belgium which my husband and I visited a few years ago.

His wife adds (20 October 2001):

Rob volunteered for army service along with three of his school friends: Stan Child, Bob McKay and Garth McLure. On his arrival in England, Rob was stationed on the south coast in my home town of Seaford, Sussex. I first met Rob at a dance held in our local drill hall. After a period of courting, Rob and I were married in Seaford Parish Church. We spent our honeymoon at Lossiemouth in Scotland. We had time with his sister Willene and the family. After our return from Scotland, Rob was very busy and as it transpired, this turned out to be training for the Dieppe Raid. At this time I became pregnant and our baby boy was born after the tragic death of his father. I named our son Robert after his father. Robert married and has a daughter Sharon and a son, also named Robert after his Grandfather.

Findlay Lake (64 G/5), south of Big Sand Lake was named after him in 1994.

Finkbeiner, Flight Sergeant **Clarence H.** of Isabella (R 80168). No. 408 Squadron. He died 9 May 1942 at the age of 25 and is commemorated at the Berlin 1939 - 1945 War Cemetery in Brandenburg, Germany. He was the eldest son of Jacob Harry and Bertha A. Finkbeiner (née Chapman) of Isabella, Manitoba and is survived by a younger brother, Lorne of Pine Falls. He writes (22 November 2001):

Prior to his enlistment in the RCAF, he attended school at Isabella and Miniota and lived with his parents on the farm. Being an exceptional athlete, he won numerous athletic awards, but his chief enjoyment was pitching baseball at which he excelled. For several years prior to the war, he spent most of the summer pitching for various teams from Birtle, Hamiota, Miniota and other towns throughout western Manitoba.

He made 11 trips over enemy territory and was mentioned over the radio and in the press for his mine laying activities in enemy waters (Hill 1944). ***Finkbeiner Lake*** (64 P/16), northeast of Nejanilini Lake was named after him in 1974.

Finner, Lance Corporal **Russel L.** of Flin Flon (H 9607). Regina Rifle Regiment. He died 28 September 1944 at the age of 32 and is commemorated at the Calais Canadian War Cemetery in France. He was the son of John and Lillian Finner. ***Finner Lake*** (64 N/8), south of Nueltin Lake was named after him in 1961.

Finnie, Flying Officer **John M.** of Winnipeg (J 21882). No. 253 Squadron. He died 15 May 1944 at the age of 23 and is commemorated at Belgrade War Cemetery, Yugoslavia. He was the son of Alexander and Lizzie C. Finnie of Winnipeg and was survived by brother Alexander and sister Ileana. His nephew writes (11 November 2001):

I never met my uncle Jack, but have been told I have some of his characteristics. My aunt used to say she was their Dad's favorite, brother Alex was their Mom's favorite, and Jack was everybody's favorite. His last entry in his Pilot's log book was May 14, 1944 - after flying a Spitfire V on a dive bombing mission near Split.

Flying Officer J. W. "Duke" Munroe, a friend in the same squadron, wrote to Jack's brother Alex:

I was on the same mission with Jack and saw everything happen. We were strafing an enemy troop and motor transport concentration. Jack knew the place and led the attack at tree top level and we observed the strikes of his cannon and machine gun fire all over the target. He must have been hit by enemy fire, which was very intense, because his aircraft seemed to go out of control and crashed. It all happened in a split second. I know, from talking to him, that it happened the way he, or any of us, wished for – instantly and doing a vital job (31 May 1944).

Finnie Lake (53 D/5), south of Carr-Harris Lake was named after him in 1979.

Firman, Corporal **Roger J.** of Transcona (H 40587). Royal Winnipeg Rifles. He died 8 June 1944 at the age of 21 and is commemorated at Beny-sur-Mer Canadian War Cemetery, Reviers, Calvados, France. He was the son of Frederick F. and Emilie Firman of Transcona and was survived by his wife Vera J. Firman of Transcona. ***Firman Lake*** (64 K/9), northeast of Lac Brochet was named after him in 1972.

Firth, Private **Fred** of Winnipeg (H 16096). Princess Patricia's Canadian Light Infantry. He died 2 May 1942 and is commemorated at Brookwood Military Cemetery in Surrey, England. ***Firth Bay*** (64 O/7) in Kram Lake was named after him in 1995.

Firth, Flight Lieutenant **John R. B.** of Winnipeg (62009). No. 406 Squadron, RAF. He died 29 August 1942 at the age of 27 and is commemorated at Streatham Park Cemetery in Surrey, England. He was the son of Robert B. and Ruby K. Firth of Hove, Sussex. ***Firth Lake*** (64 N/3), west of Colbeck Lake was named after him in 1995.

Fisher, Warrant Officer 2 **Hugh A.** of Dauphin (R 116477). No. 9 Squadron. He died 8 April 1945 at the age of 24 and is commemorated at Botley Cemetery in Oxfordshire, England. He was the son of Arthur L. and Katherine I. Fisher of Dauphin. ***Fisher Point*** (64 K/16) on Burnie Lake was named after him in 1987.

Fisher, Flying Officer **Richard H.** of Winnipeg (J 40786). No. 429 Squadron. He died 31 March 1945 at the age of 22 and is commemorated at Becklingen War Cemetery in Germany. He was the son of Richard H. and Frances M. Fisher of Winnipeg. ***Fisher Peninsula*** (53 L/16) on Gods Lake was named after him in 1995.

Flamand, Private **Frederick** of Camperville (H 100883). South Saskatchewan Regiment. He died 8 August 1944 at the age of 21 and is commemorated at Bretteville-sur-Laize Canadian War Cemetery in Calvados, France. He was the eldest child of Peter and Annie Flamand (née Fagnan) of Camperville, Manitoba. His younger brother recalls (6 February 1998):

We were a large family with Fred being the first born. We all had our part to do and help to look out for each other and the younger ones. Our spare time during the summer months [was] often spent swimming and during the winter months we hooked fish on the lake.

His sister adds (25 January 2002):

Regarding my brother "Freddy" as we knew him, I just wanted to add that he was a Métis, the oldest of a family of ten who was helping with the family livelihood by hunting, fishing and trapping. He was only seventeen when he left to join the army. He is still remembered and sadly missed.

Flamand Lake (63 K/16), northwest of Wekusko Lake was named after him in 1973.

Fleming, Sergeant **Robert** of St. Boniface (H 19190). Queen's Own Cameron Highlanders. He died 19 August 1942 at the age of 36 and is commemorated at Le Portel Communal Cemetery, Pas de Calais, France. He was the son of James and Christina Fleming and was survived by his wife Mary M. Fleming (née McLean) of St. Boniface and their two children. His daughter writes (11 January 1995):

My father ... was a Scottish immigrant. He was born in Edinburgh to the best of my knowledge. This information may be vague as to the fact that my father was killed when I was 17 months old and my brother was six years old. My mother never spoke of my father in any detail during the remaining years of her life.

My father played soccer for the United Scottish during his pre-war years and enjoyed bowling and curling. He was the foreman in the Beef Cuts Department at Canada Packers before enlisting. My mother had also worked there in the egg grading section but was forced to leave because in those years man and wife were not able to work at the same place. My mother returned in 1947 to work at CP; [she] remained for 25 years.

His son adds (2 November 2001):

My father was born in Scotland in 1921 and after four children of my own and nine grandchildren, I have proudly told my father's horrific tale on his behalf, and instilled Scottish heritage in remembrance of him. Sergeant Fleming was not wounded; when last seen, he was helping the wounded after an attack when a bomb hit his destroyer; a number of men were killed and some were thrown overboard. That was the last time we had heard from my dad. I still have fond memories from when I was a child, birthdays and Christmases that I will always cherish in my mind.

Fleming Lake (64 G/5), south of Big Sand Lake was named after him in 1994.

Fletcher, Major **Charles W.** of McCreary. Fort Garry Horse. He died 23 October 1944 at the age of 32 and is commemorated at Bergen-op-Zoom Canadian War Cemetery in Holland. He was survived by his wife Jessie Fletcher and sons Denis and Allan of Winnipeg. His son reports (29 October 2001) that:

Charlie owned a dairy farm on the edge of McCreary, Manitoba and was a devoted family man. As a non-permanent militia officer prior to the war, he felt it was his duty to serve his country once war broke out. He was killed during the Battle of the Bulge and received the Croix de Guerre with Palm, the highest award given by the Belgian government.

Fletcher Lake (54 K/4), southeast of Churchill was named after him in 1948.

Flett, Trooper **Alfred James** of Victoria Beach (H 77346). 12th Manitoba Dragoons. He died 8 February 1945 and is commemorated at the Groesbeek Canadian War Cemetery in Holland. He was survived by his wife Irene Flett. ***Flett Bay*** (64 N/14) in Tice Lake was named after him in 1995.

Flynn, Lance Sergeant **Clifford G.** of McAuley (H 75155). Royal Canadian Artillery. He died 22 August 1944 at the age of 39 and is commemorated at Bretteville-sur-Laize Canadian War Cemetery in Calvados, France. He was the son of George and Mary E. Flynn of McAuley, Manitoba. Originally from Moosomin, Saskatchewan, he farmed there prior to enlisting. ***Flynn Lake*** (64 H/15), northeast of Etawney Lake was named after him in 1995.

Flynn, Flight Lieutenant **Harold L.** of Gunton (J 14851). No. 8 Operational Training Unit, RCAF. He died 15 December 1944 at the age of 23 and is commemorated at Dyce Old Churchyard, Aberdeenshire, Scotland. He was the only son of John H. and Muriel L. Flynn of Teulon, Manitoba. Born in Carlyle, Saskatchewan, Flight Lieutenant Flynn began his military career with the Fort Garry Horse in 1939, just prior to the declaration of war. He enlisted in the RCAF in 1940 and went to England later that year as an air gunner. During his tour of duty he was shot down twice, first breaking both his arms and on the second occasion landing in the North Sea where he was picked up by a passing ship. He returned to Canada and took pilot training, returning to England in 1944. He is believed to be the first to wear both air gunner and pilot wings on his uniform. ***Flynn Island*** (64 O/12) in Heuchert Lake was named after him in 1995.

Folster, Private **Donald Hector** of Winnipeg (H 70208). Winnipeg Grenadiers. He died 19 December 1941 at the age of 19 and is commemorated at the Sai Wan Memorial in Hong Kong. A descendant of Northwest and Hudson's Bay Company employees, he was the sixth son of William G. and Catherine F. A. Folster (née Wilson) of Winnipeg and the brother of Private Herbert T. Folster (next entry). His niece recalls (28 December 1996):

Hector was a fun-loving boy who loved to play pranks on his older brothers. His favourite hobby was building comical toys out of wood scrap for the amusement of his younger brother and sister. In 1936, at the age of 14, Hector left home to work on a farm in Woodside, Manitoba. When he was 18, he enlisted in the Winnipeg Grenadiers.

Folster Point (63 N/13) on Britton Lake was named after him in 1995.

Folster, Private **Herbert T.** of Winnipeg (H 6911). Winnipeg Grenadiers. He died 19 December 1941 at the age of 25 and is commemorated at the Sai Wan Memorial in Hong Kong. He was the fourth son of William G. and Catherine F. A. Folster (née Wilson) of Winnipeg and the brother of Private Donald H. Folster (previous entry). Like his brother, he was born at Folster's Landing near Herb Lake. His niece recalls (28 December 1996):

Herb was a pleasant, cheerful fellow who entertained family and friends with amusing stories and jokes. He loved the outdoors, hunting, fishing and trapping. Herb helped his father deliver freight and mail from the railway at Mile 82 to Herb Lake and Bingo Mine. After the mines closed, he worked for the government cutting timber for roads and bridges.

Folster Island (64 G/16) in Namaypin Lake was named after him in 1995.

Foord, Private **Frank M.** of Pierson (H 6113). Winnipeg Grenadiers. He died 22 December 1941 at the age of 23 and is commemorated at the Sai Wan Memorial in Hong Kong. He was the third of the eight children of William and Verna Foord of Pierson, Manitoba. His sister writes (15 December 1997):

Frank was born in Trossach, Saskatchewan on his Dad's homestead in 1918. He and his mother nearly didn't survive the bad flu of that year. Always exceptionally smart at school, he attended a little one-room country school that taught Grades 1 - 8. He was also very good at sports.

In the spring of 1931, he moved to Manson, Manitoba. The drought had already forced most of the homesteaders to lose their land. Already broke and being hit with the Depression, his life was always one of hard work, long hours and a struggle just to survive ... being hungry a lot of the time.

In 1934, a grasshopper plague hit that area and there were no crops to harvest. He went with his older brother and a friend to stook away north as they were hiring extra help to get their crops off before the plague reached there. At age fourteen, he stooked for three weeks, doing a daylight till dark, 12 - 13 hour day with only a half hour's lunch break in the field. For this he was paid $1.00 a day or eight cents an hour and board and a bed in the hayloft, making $2.00 – a fortune to him.

Finishing Grade 10 (that was as far as the school taught), the Principal talked him into attending school and to take his Grade 11 by correspondence. After passing this, he continued to take courses each year even after he joined up. Tired of the long hours, hard work and poor board with little pay, he left on the next train to Winnipeg after war was declared and joined the Grenadiers on September the sixth.

[He was] sent to Jamaica in March, 1940. On the trip over, an officer, noticing him studying, became interested [and] had him transferred to the Officer's Mess as his bat boy and taught him while in Jamaica till he passed his final exam.

The circumstances and date of his death were unknown to the family for quite some time:

At first, he was missing in the conflict between the 8th and 26th. Then, as he didn't draw rations on or after the 22nd of December, he was declared dead. In the [Book of Honour] his death is listed as 26th December because the fighting had stopped and he was never taken prisoner.

One of the boys that had returned said they were in the last days of the fighting and Frank and some others were sent out to clean up a machine gun nest. Frank was badly wounded in the chest and laying on a stretcher, he was asking for water. But the last three days of the fighting they had no water to drink and they finally ran out of food and ammo.

As the [Japanese] took no wounded prisoners, we were never sure how he met his end. They just buried all the dead in a trench. With no known grave he has always just been "Missing in Hong Kong." Now with a spot at last in Canada in his name, he will finally have a resting place. Of the five lads from McAuley that joined with Frank, he and Ralph Rees didn't survive. Ralph died in the Prison Camp just a few days before their release. I am sending this snap, all I have. Looking through old albums made me realize, no pictures were taken during "the Depression, the Lost Years." The uniform is from World War I as they had no new ones yet. Hoping you can use some of this, as there isn't much to say about these lads that never really had a life.

Foord Lake (64 J/14), northwest of Tadoule Lake was named after him in 1972.

Forbes, Private **James P.** of Winnipeg (H 6272). Winnipeg Grenadiers. He died 16 October 1942 and is commemorated at the Sai Wan Memorial in Hong Kong. ***Forbes Lake*** (64 J/1), south of Tadoule Lake was named after him in 1975.

Forbes, Pilot Officer **Roy B.** of Winnipeg (41391). No. 224 Squadron, RAF. He enlisted in October, 1938 and was lost while on coastal patrol 7 August 1940. He was 25 years of age and is commemorated at the Runnymede Memorial in Surrey, England. He was the son of James H. and Helen M. Forbes of London, Ontario. ***Forbes Island*** (53 E/14) in Begg Lake was named after him in 1995.

Ford, Leading Aircraftman **Herbert N.** of Winnipeg (R 59645). No. 400 Squadron. He died 29 May 1942 at the age of 22 and is commemorated at Brookwood Military Cemetery in Surrey, England. ***Ford Island*** (53 K/4) in Red Sucker Lake was named after him in 1995.

Forman, Flight Sergeant **John** of Reston (R 80334). No. 75 Squadron. He died 6 October 1942 at the age of 21 and is commemorated at Hardenberg Protestant Cemetery, Holland. His sister recalls (23 July 1995):

My brother John (Jack) was born in Reston, Manitoba, the youngest of four children. His mother and father came to Canada from Edinburgh, his father in 1910, followed by his mother and eldest brother in 1912. Dad first worked on a farm before going to work for the Canadian Pacific Railway. Jack attended school in Reston, graduating from the Reston Collegiate in 1940. He enlisted in the air force after graduation and while waiting to be called to service, he was employed at a local General Store as a clerk and delivery man. He received his call in November, 1940 and reported to Brandon Manning Depot. He graduated as a wireless operator at Calgary, Alberta August 17th, 1941 and then as an air gunner at No. 7 Bombing and Gunnery School at the air base in Paulson, Manitoba on September 13th, 1941. He went to Montreal and was with Ferry Command and proceeded overseas in December, 1941. My brother was killed in action ... on his 6th operation over Germany. He was reported missing in action, later presumed killed in action. The official confirmation of his death and location of his burial was December 1944. He and four other members of the crew, all Royal Air Force personnel are buried in the Protestant Cemetery in Hardenberg. I have visited Jack's grave which is well looked after by the people of this community in Holland. Jack was 6 ft. 4 in. weighing 142 lbs. when he enlisted. His main interest at the time of his enlistment and during his high school years was flying and aircraft.

Forman Lake (64 G/16), south of Cederlund Lake was named after him in 1995.

Forrest, Private **John** of Winnipeg (H 59672). Lanark and Renfrew Scottish Regiment. He died 2 September 1944 at the age of 33 and is commemorated at Gradara War Cemetery in Italy. He was the son of Arthur and Martha A. Forrest (née Hague) and was survived by his wife Mary Forrest (née Vizniak) of Starbuck, Manitoba and their daughter. According to his cousin (19 October 1999):

His parents were both [from] Denton, Manchester, Lancashire. They had emigrated to Canada from England just a few years before Jack's birth. Jack's father, Arthur, worked as a coachman carpenter for the CNR.

Jack was a well-built slender man, just under six feet tall. He suffered from a speech impediment that caused him to stutter; it didn't effect his enlistment in the army though. He had brown/black hair and blue eyes. He lived in Fort Rouge all his life, most of the time at 387 Brandon Avenue. He completed Grade 9 after attending Riverview Elementary School and Lord Roberts Junior High School.

Jack quit school during the depression because there was little hope of finding employment, even if one finished their high school education. He worked at many jobs including delivering meat for Law's Butcher Shop. His dad bought him a truck to supplement his income, hauling wood and coal for Mr. Romansky of Reliance Wood and Coal to the surrounding towns. He also trucked grain and hay at harvest time. He did a lot of work out of the Starbuck area. In 1940, he was employed by the CNR as a coach cleaner. He stayed in that position until his enlistment.

He met and married the girl next door who was working as a domestic. They then resided at Suite 6, Allan Apartments in Winnipeg. They were blessed with the birth of a girl October 19, 1940. They named her Joyce. Joyce had four children – one boy and three girls.

Jack's hobbies were ice skating, playing hockey and dabbling in auto mechanics. He also liked to ski a lot. He enjoyed ski-jumping at Old River Park near the Elm Park Bridge. During the summer, Jack and his cousins enjoyed swimming in the Red River at the foot of their street on hot summer days. Jack helped his dad make and repair cricket bats for the league run out of City (Assiniboine) Park. He also built crystal sets with his dad and cousins. They had many hours of enjoyment playing them late into the night when they should have been asleep. He also had a great love for animals that still runs in the family. He had dogs as a boy. He adopted an older kitten while in training in Woodstock, Ontario. It had kittens! ... and Jack was referred to as dad. He was also an accomplished accordion player. He played for dances some Saturdays at the Fort Rouge Labour Hall located at the corner of Osborne Street and Brandon Avenue.

Jack enlisted in the Canadian Army Active Service Force on January 10th, 1941. He felt it was his duty.

His cousin (19 October 1999) reports that his unit was one of many:

… trying to break the Gothic line during an advance from Ancona to Rimini. The troops were poised for a dash up the corridor between the Apennines and the Adriatic Sea to Bologna and the Po Valley in the northern end of Italy. Bitter fighting was occurring at a ridge north of the Foglia River four to five miles behind the Gothic Line. This is where we believe Jack lost his life. The Gothic Line was taken by the Allies on the 21st of September 1944.

Forrest Lake (53 N/12), southeast of Stupart Lake was named after him in 1995.

Forsberg, Private **Albert** of Sprague (H 40874). Loyal Edmonton Regiment. He died 23 May 1944 at the age of 32 and is commemorated at the Cassino War Cemetery in Italy. He was the son of Nils and Anna Forsberg of Winnipeg. ***Forsberg Lake*** (64 B/8), northeast of Shamattawa was named after him in 1964.

Forsman, Sergeant **Claude A.** of Neepawa (H 19164). Queen's Own Cameron Highlanders. He died 30 July 1944 of wounds suffered a week earlier and is commemorated at the Bayeux War Cemetery, Calvados, France. This former Erickson resident was survived by his wife.

He was born at Kinistino, Saskatchewan June 10, 1914. Claude moved to Erickson with his parents and later to Winnipeg where he received his education. After his schooling, he relocated to Neepawa. Enlisting in September, 1939, he trained at Winnipeg, Camp Shilo and Quebec. Claude was posted overseas in December, 1940 (*Neepawa Press* n.d.).

Forsman Lake (64 I/12), northwest of North Knife Lake was named after him in 1974.

Forster, Aircraftman 2 **Murray T.** of Beulah (R 116339). No. 3 Service Flying Training School. He died 17 November 1941 at the age of 19 and is commemorated at Birtle Cemetery, Manitoba. He was the son of Thomas E. and Millicent L. Forster of Beulah, Manitoba and was survived by his twin sister and an elder brother. According to his sister (17 February 1997):

Murray was an outdoors person and liked to fish and hunt with his .22 and his dog. He was a tennis player and a member of the local hockey team. He had no active service as he died as the result of an automobile accident while in training near Claresholm, Alberta.

Forster Island (64 C/5) in Kamuchawie Lake was named after him in 1995.

Forster, Sergeant **Thomas E. "Tim"** of Killarney, Manitoba (H 38362). Royal Canadian Corps of Signals. He died 23 June 1942 and is commemorated at Brookwood Military Cemetery in Surrey, England. ***Forster Lake*** (64 N/3), southwest of Nueltin Lake was named after him in 1972.

Forsyth, Private **Clifford G.** of Brandon (H 22107). Lake Superior Regiment. He died 11 April 1945 and is commemorated at the Holten Canadian War Cemetery in Holland. ***Forsyth Lake*** (64 G/11), east of Big Sand Lake was named after him in 1994.

Forsythe, Private **John A.** of Winnipeg (H 20491). Queen's Own Cameron Highlanders. He died 5 October 1942 at the age of 39 and is commemorated at St. Sever Cemetery Extension, Rouen, Seine-Maritime, France. He was one of nine children and the youngest son of James and Martha Forsythe of Winnipeg. His nephew writes (18 November 2001):

His father and eldest brother (who was killed in action at Vimy Ridge 9 April 1917) served in the 78th Battalion (Winnipeg Grenadiers) in the Great War and his second eldest brother served with the Royal Inniskilling Fusiliers (Imperial Army). Jack's father came to Canada with his eldest children from Londonderry, Ireland in 1913 with the intention of settling the family in Winnipeg. War intervened and the family remained separated until Jack's father was able to bring his wife Martha and the youngest children to Canada in 1919.

At the outbreak of war in 1939, Jack volunteered for active service and went overseas with the 2nd Canadian Division as a member of the Queen's Own Cameron Highlanders of Canada. The QOCH were selected to participate in Operation Jubilee and Jack landed with his regiment on the beaches of Dieppe on August 19, 1942. He was seriously wounded in the assault and taken prisoner. The family received several letters from Jack, indicating that he was recovering, however, word was later received that he had died on October 5, 1942 as a result of the wounds he had received. As with his father and brothers, when duty called, he served willingly.

In one of these heavily censored letters he wrote:

Dear Mother: We went into action August 19, but here I am in hospital doing very well. We have a very good German doctor and he is doing everything to help the boys get well. The nursing staff and food are very good. Don't worry about me as I will soon be all right. Do not send any parcels to this address as it is only temporary. I have lost all my tobacco and cigarettes. All I own now is my tunic. I had three pounds saved for my leave but that's gone. But I am lucky to be alive. The weather here is fine, just like summer. The French Red Cross sent us grapes, chocolate and cigarettes which were very nice. It sure was a treat when the grapes arrived. I hope this war ends soon. When I get back I will have a lot to tell you (n.d.).

Forsythe Lake (52 L/6), northeast of Lac du Bonnet was named after him in 1973.

Fortin, Corporal **Albert** of Clarkleigh (H 17910). Fusiliers Mont-Royal Regiment. He died 8 August 1944 at the age of 27 and is commemorated at Bretteville-sur-Laize Canadian War Cemetery in Calvados, France. He was the son of Ernest and Laura Fortin of Clarkleigh, Manitoba and was the brother of Sapper Alexis Fortin (next entry). ***Fortin Bay*** (64 G/12) in Big Sand Lake was named after him in 1986.

Fortin, Sapper **Alexis** of Clarkleigh (H 93476). Royal Canadian Engineers. He died 28 December 1943 at the age of 25 and is commemorated at the Moro River Canadian War Cemetery in Italy. He was the son of Ernest and Laura Fortin of Clarkleigh, Manitoba and was the brother of Corporal Albert Fortin (previous entry). ***Fortin Island*** (64 G/12) in Big Sand Lake was named after him in 1986.

Foster, Squadron Leader **Philip H.** of Flin Flon (87408). No. 404 Squadron, RAF. He died 26 May 1942 at the age of 30 and is commemorated at Egersund Churchyard, Norway. He was the son of Kadish and Rose Fenster (sp.) of Winnipeg. Squadron Leader Foster had owned Hudson's Bay Plumbing in Flin Flon until he joined the RAF early in 1940 (Allison 1978). ***Foster Rapids*** (53 M/14) in the Dafoe River was named after him in 1996.

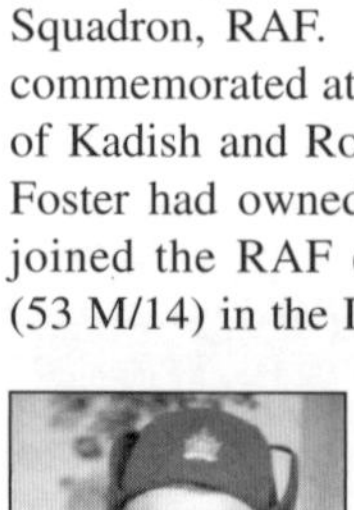

Foster, Private **Ray** of Mowbray (H 1190). Argyle and Sutherland Highlanders. He died 5 August 1944 at the age of 22 and is commemorated at Bretteville-sur-Laize Canadian War Cemetery in Calvados, France. He was the son of Ernest W. and Mary Foster of Mowbray, Manitoba. His sister recalls (13 February 2002):

When Ray left to fight for his country, he had known little other than the small farm and tight-knit community where he had been born and where he grew up in the Pembina Valley. He was a quiet, very shy young man, so none of us will ever really know how difficult it was for him to leave this safe, comfortable home and he [was] exposed to regimentation, strangers and war in far away countries. Since he never complained, we'll never know. However, we did get an idea from his letters how much news from home meant to him. He had obviously read and re-read these letters from home and would comment on each little detail about the farm, family and friends. Thoughts and warm memories of his home back in the pretty valley kept him going when the trenches were cold and muddy.

He carefully never spoke much of his dreams or plans for the future, but his family inherited a guitar which he ordered on his last leave – one of the many things in life he never got the chance to experience or fulfil.

His superiors said his quiet, good humour and willingness made him one of their best liked comrades. These also are two of the many wonderful qualities his family misses because of him being taken away from them in the prime of his life.

Foster Island (64 A/13) in Gauer Lake was named after him in 1989.

Foster, Sergeant **Russell M.** of Manitou (H 6477). Winnipeg Grenadiers. He died 21 December 1941 at the age of 27 and is commemorated at the Sai Wan Memorial in Hong Kong. He was the son of William L. and Evelyn Foster and was survived by his wife Bonnie L. Foster of St. Vital and their young son. ***Foster Bay*** (64 O/15) in Blevins Lake was named after him in 1995.

Foster, Private **Stanley P.** of Winnipeg (H 6533). Winnipeg Grenadiers. He died 28 October 1942 at the age of 20 and is commemorated at the Sai Wan War Cemetery in Hong Kong. He was the son of Percy S. and Bessie Foster of Winnipeg. ***Foster Peninsula*** (53 L/15) on Knee Lake was named after him in 1995.

Foster, Lieutenant **William M.** of Winnipeg. Loyal Edmonton Regiment. He died 18 October 1944 and is commemorated at Cesena War Cemetery in Italy. He was survived by his wife Anne M. R. Foster and their two children. She writes (25 March 1998):

Bill was very fond of Manitoba where he served after RMC and particularly Shilo. We have two children and five grandchildren of whom he would be very proud.

Foster Point (64 K/1) on Chartrand Lake was named after him in 1995.

Fostey, Pilot Officer **Allan M.** of Ridgeville (R 147033). No. 405 Squadron. He died 9 February 1945 at the age of 22 and is commemorated at the Runnymede Memorial in Surrey, England. ***Fostey Lake*** (63 K/16), west of Wekusko Lake was named after him in 1973.

Fournier, Flight Sergeant **Rene J. L.** of Lac du Bonnet (R 86362). No. 10 Operational Training Unit, RCAF. He died 30 October 1942 at the age of 22 and is commemorated at the Runnymede Memorial in Surrey, England. He was the son of Arthur and Alexandrine Fournier of Lac du Bonnet, Manitoba. ***Fournier Island*** (52 L/5) in the Winnipeg River was named after him in 1973.

Fowell, Warrant Officer 2 **Albert E.** of Oak Lake (R 91889). No. 408 Squadron. He died 15 June 1943 at the age of 22 and is commemorated at Rheinberg War Cemetery in Germany. He was the son of Frederick and Sarah E. Fowell of Oak Lake, Manitoba. The navigator, Flight Lieutenant Bruce Moore of Flin Flon recalls:

We were hit by flak and the bomb aimer jettisoned the bombs, we were hit again and the Halifax blew up almost immediately. When I came to, the ground was getting very close so I pulled the ripcord. I landed OK but was taken Prisoner of War. The next day I had to help bury my three Manitoba friends and was then taken to PoW camp where I helped in the Great Escape (Allison and Hayward 1991).

Fowell Lake (64 G/16), southeast of Chipewyan Lake was named after him in 1995.

Fowlow, Squadron Leader **Norman R.** of Winnipeg (J 15095). No. 411 Squadron, Distinguished Flying Cross.

This officer has taken part in a very large number of sorties and has proved himself to be a skilful and courageous fighter. He has destroyed four and shared in the destruction of another enemy aircraft (DFC Citation 1946).

He died 19 May 1944 at the age of 22 and is commemorated at Longuenesse (St. Omer) Souvenir Cemetery, Pas de Calais, France. He was the son of Reverend Ralph and Annie E. Fowlow and was survived by his wife Elsie M. Fowlow of San Francisco and their young son. Flying Officer Ross Linquist was on Squadron Leader Fowlow's last mission:

We dive-bombed Hazebrouck Marshalling Yards in the late evening of May 19, '44 – each of our twelve aircraft carrying a 500-pound bomb. We pulled into our dive at approximately 10,000 feet and came down through a heavy concentration of anti-aircraft fire. It appeared that Norm took a direct hit on his bomb, as his aircraft disintegrated before we reached release height. Fortunately, none of us were hit by the debris. I can still vividly recall the setting sun glistening off the horizontal curtain of anti-aircraft fire that we penetrated that night (Williston 1996).

Fowlow Lake (64 O/3), east of Blackfish Lake was named after him in 1995.

Fox, Pilot Officer **Albert Lloyd** of Desford (J 85331). No. 78 Squadron. He died 21 December 1942 at the age of 22 and is commemorated at Great Yarmouth (Caister) Cemetery, Norfolk, England. He was the son of Francis R. and Annie M. Fox of Desford, Manitoba. He kept a diary for his last year in the service. These are some of the entries:

- This day finds me at Rivers [Manitoba] having been presented with Air Navigator's wing and Sergeant stripes on December 20 and now studying astral navigation (1 January 1942).
- Weather bitterly cold today and our Australian comrades find it almost unbearable (2 January 1942).
- Received five-pound cake from Nell and "bright Card" from Les depicting me washing aircraft at Mossbank – the son of a gun (11 January 1942).
- Edith [his sister] came home for a few days – had dinner with Ida [his sister] and was given a farewell party by friends of the community – damned swell of them (29 January 1942).
- Ran into bush with Roy [his brother]. Roy got call – damn them. Said good-bye to dear old Mom and Dad. May God grant that I see both again (31 January 1942).
- Marched on board today. Boat a good passenger liner – cabin – an outside one. Here's hoping we have a good voyage. Boat's name: *Dominion Monarch* (9 February 1942).

- Felt rather punk all day. Had short church service. Meals are getting worse – plenty of food. Just poisoned in the preparation (15 February 1942).
- Meals horrible – booing CO every chance we get. He sits like a floorwalker in a woman's lingerie department (16 February 1942).
- Sighted land off port bow this morning – Aircraft circling overhead. That land looks mighty good and it should, it's Ireland [both sets of his grandparents were Irish] (18 February 1942).
- Went out to see the cathedral at Christchurch today. Built in 1092, it is still in use (24 February 1942).
- Arrived at Millom – it's an RAF outfit etc., etc. I don't like the look of things myself – expect plenty of trouble while here (21 March 1942).
- Started classes today – apparently plenty of crashes here – have to hold myself all along the line with these bloody English officers (22 March 1942).
- Went in bomb-teacher today. Went into town to see *49th Parallel* tonight – very good Canadian scenery (8 April 1942).
- Saw a beautiful sunrise while in the air. Ground dwellers miss this (17 April 1942).
- This English fool of a CO made us quit training while we "dig for Victory" [probably referring to "Victory Gardens"] (20 April 1942).
- Came down to Upper Heyford today. It appears to be a good station. Met Belgian soldier who escaped (5 May 1942).
- Tension very high in camp, nothing doing for us, but all others preparing for something big. My guess is invasion preparations (27 May 1942).
- Another "Big Night" being planned [this was the beginning of the 1000-plane raids]. There is great tension in the air. Those of us not going lay in bunks, watching the take-off and crossing our fingers for each crew. Essen will catch hell tonight (1 June 1942).
- Met Zack in Trafalgar Square. Went to see the Parliament Buildings and Big Ben, Westminster Abbey and Buckingham Palace. Saw Zack off at Waterloo Station and then went to see *Jungle Book* (21 June 1942).
- Dominion Day at home – hope I'm there for it next year. Had two three-hour flights in Wellington aircraft with my full crew (1 July 1942).
- Had the worst experience so far – flying with a hysterical man. Hit cloud at 200 ft. and he went crazy. Was lucky to get down (some of the Instructors were men who had a tour of operations and some had severe nerve problems at times, 13 July 1942).
- Flew on gunnery and bombing during day, then went on a five-hour cross-country at night. First experience with flak when Nottingham opened up on Jerries. Nearly collided with another aircraft (23 July 1942).
- Went on "Ops" tonight – dropped over a ton of incendiaries on Düsseldorf. Attacked by fighter coming back and punctured one gas tank. Caught by search lights and flak over Dutch coast – and another tank punctured and several holes in fuselage (31 July 1942).
- Another day of killing time. Went for pleasant bike ride by myself in evening – a lovely evening – saw a field filled with poppies. Thought of "In Flanders Fields" (7 August 1942).
- Here it is almost September and duck-shooting time again. I now know what the ducks feel like (30 August 1942).
- Reported sick again in the AM. Grounded for 48 hours. Read an article by Madam Kai Sheck (wife of China's Generalissimo). Put clipping of it in front of diary (6 September 1942).
- Went on a cross-country today. Tom went on Ops and failed to return (8 September 1942).
- Collected Tom's personal kit. Wrote home. Went on another cross-country (9 September 1942).
- Went cycling alone tonight as Ernst on "Ops" (25 September 1942).
- Ernst reported down in North Sea. Spent all afternoon out searching for the crew – no luck (27 September 1942).
- Started out for Flensburg tonight – got half way and had to turn back with turret unserviceable. Jonnie Canick, Gillian and Tommy Farr lost (30 September 1942).
- Raided Osnabrück tonight. Attacked twice by fighters – probably destroyed one (6 October 1942).
- Detailed to bomb Cologne, but bombed Bonn instead. Winds encountered were as high as 80 mph. Landed at Marston Moor on return (15 October 1942).
- Was introduced to Sir Archibald Sinclair by the CO. Was thrilled when the CO called me "a very good navigator." Jimmy Anderson died of his injuries at noon (17 October 1942).
- Had a couple of practise flights today. Nat came up. Squadron Leader Bennett told me that I was to be commissioned as an officer. Frankly I'm tickled (19 October 1942).
- Went to York to Jimmy's funeral this afternoon. Spent evening with Bill. Kid feeling pretty low (20 October 1942).
- Feverish preparation all day for flight to Genoa, Italy. Took off at 1800 hrs. and flew over the Alps. Saw Geneva all lit up and Mont Blanc and other Alps stood out plainly in brilliant moon light. Had perfect trip and topped navigation ladder (23 October 1942).
- Another quiet day. Skip and I went into York in evening. Jack Mills crashed when returning from mining operations. Harry Humphries killed, also Flight Lieutenant Turner (6 November 1942).
- Went on a raid to Genoa tonight – really "pranged" the town. Trip uneventful otherwise (7 November 1942).
- Watched boys take off for Turin tonight. "Good luck fellows" (28 November 1942).
- Took off for Frankfurt at 0130. The Gee unserviceable from take-off. Good trip to target, but both outer engines cut just after leaving it. Threw out all loose articles and finally landed at Tangmere after flying for four hours with only two engines (3 December 1942).

In his last letter home he wrote:

The first "op" we made after our leave we had a rather "shaky do." Two of our four motors conked out 400 miles inside enemy territory, and we had to limp home on the remaining two at about half our normal speed, with the result that we were still stooging over the continent in broad daylight and all alone – not a healthy thing. However, we eventually reached England and lobbed down at the first aerodrome. My pilot has been recommended for the DFM and I certainly hope he gets it. After that, the "powers that be" thought our nerves needed a rest so they gave us the boring job of ferrying aircraft from one station to another for a week or so – a job which no one likes. After a week, we were taken off the "nervous sick" list and again put on "ops," this time to Italy. This time we flew from northern France to the other side of the Alps in blinding snowstorms and rain, but we did reach and bomb our objective. I was later commended for my navigation on the trip by my squadron navigation officer. We had a good trip last night though for a change (15 December 1942).

Some two months after Pilot Officer Fox's death, fellow crewman Ralph Baillie wrote to Mrs. Fox about the incident:

Dear Mrs. Fox: I am writing first to express my sincere sympathy in the loss of your son Lloyd and to tell you what little I can about our crash. We were returning from an operational flight when something went wrong and Albert Hunter the Pilot ("Skip" as we called him) decided to ditch. Due to the bad weather, we crashed into the sea. That was the last I saw of Paul Kingsley, the tail gunner and Eddie Edwards the engineer. Albert must have drowned almost immediately, as I saw him come to the surface only once. Ted Malone, the wireless op. came up near me and in a few moments disappeared. I was unable to help him, due to the fact that I was injured and had all I could do to stay up myself.

In about an hour's time, a gunboat came along and picked me up, having already found Lloyd and Ashworth. They continued to search for the others for about two hours, but in vain. During those two hours the men in the gunboat were working on Lloyd, doing everything humanly possible to save him, but he died soon after. He was buried with full military honours in England and I am trying to find out just where he was buried so that I can let you know. If there is anything else you would like to know, please don't hesitate to write me c/o the Squadron. I am getting on well, but will be in hospital for another month or two. With renewed sympathy, I am, Yours sincerely, Ralph Baillie (4 March 1943).

Fox Rapids (64 I/14) in the Seal River was named after him in 1995.

Fox, Lance Sergeant **John E.** of Winnipeg (H 16002). Princess Patricia's Canadian Light Infantry. He died 24 January 1942 and is commemorated at Brookwood Military Cemetery in Surrey, England. He was the son of Fred E. and Kathleen I. Fox of Winnipeg. ***Fox Peninsula*** (64 F/6) on Wells Lake was named after him in 1994.

Foxall, Private **Reginald** of Winnipeg (H 6061). Winnipeg Grenadiers. He died 6 December 1942 at the age of 34 and is commemorated at the Sai Wan War Cemetery in Hong Kong. He was the son of James and Susan Foxall of Dublin, Republic of Ireland. ***Foxall Lake*** (63 K/16), northwest of Wekusko Lake was named after him in 1973.

Fradin, Gunner **Gabriel C. E.** of Notre Dame de Lourdes (B 144022). Royal Canadian Artillery. He died 14 August 1944 at the age of 19 and is commemorated at Bretteville-sur-Laize Canadian War Cemetery in Calvados, France. He was the son of Gustave and Juliene Fradin, of Notre Dame de Lourdes, Manitoba. ***Fradin Lake*** (41 O/1) in the Sudbury district of central Ontario was named after him in 1961.

Fradley, Private **Norman A.** of Flin Flon (H 19786). Queen's Own Cameron Highlanders. He died 24 July 1944 at the age of 29 and is commemorated at Beny-sur-Mer Canadian War Cemetery in Calvados, France. His brother visited the grave in 1995. This veteran of Dieppe and the D-Day landings was the son of the late Albert B. Fradley and Nellie Fradley of Stockport, Cheshire, England. According to his commanding Officer, Captain S. Gee:

> This man was posted as missing by this Unit after being left in enemy positions while engaged in street fighting. It is assumed that the body was robbed by them as no kit has been received by this Unit (n. d.).

Born in Manchester, England in 1914, he had been employed as a salesman prior to enlisting in September, 1939. ***Fradley Lake*** (64 I/1), northeast of Etawney Lake was named after him in 1974.

Frame, Flight Sergeant **George Murray** of Lenore (R 101501). No. 408 Squadron. He died 13 September 1942 at the age of 27 and is commemorated at Newark-on-Trent Cemetery, Nottinghamshire, England. He was the son of Allan and Gertrude Frame and was survived by six siblings. His brother writes (29 November 2001):

> He trained at Rivers, High River, Alberta and Dauphin. He went overseas in October, 1941 and was involved in many missions over Europe. Murray was noted for his sense of humour and also for his talent in music (fiddle playing) like his father before him.

Frame Lake (64 J/16), north of Tadoule Lake was named after him in 1975.

Francis, Private **Lindsay Leroy** of Norgate (H 103294). Princess Patricia's Canadian Light Infantry. He died 6 August 1944 at the age of 31 and is commemorated at Florence War Cemetery, Italy. He was the son of Harry and Elizabeth Francis of Norgate, Manitoba.

> He and several members of his regiment were sent to guard a bridge near Florence. The Germans had mined the bridge before leaving the region. Leroy was killed when one of the mines exploded. His twin brother Cecil, a member of the same regiment, was a short distance from the area and heard the explosion but was not aware his brother had been killed until later (Pittman n.d.).

Francis Bay (64 K/16) in the Seal River was named after him in 1995.

Francis, Pilot Officer **Richard W.** of St. James (J 92336). No. 419 Squadron. He died 13 June 1944 at the age of 19 and is commemorated at Meharicourt Communal Cemetery, Somme, France. He was the second of the five children of Hector W. and Marjorie M. Francis (née Drennan) of Medicine Hat, Alberta. "Dick" came from an aeronautical family, with his father and two brothers-in-law serving in the air. After schooling, he was an apprentice aeronautical engineer, and although this was declared an essential service from which employees were not drafted, he chose to volunteer with the Air Force. Four years after his death his mother received a letter from Ottawa:

> Dear Mrs. Francis: I would like to refer, please, to my letter of July 2, 1947, concerning the resting place of your son, Pilot Officer Richard William Francis, whose grave was located in the Meharicourt Communal Cemetery, Meharicourt, Department of Somme, France.
>
> A report has been received from our Overseas Headquarters that the re-arranging of the cemetery has been completed and the resting place of your son is with Flying Officer D. J. McMullen and Pilot Officer M. E. Gates (who could not be individually identified) in collective graves Nos. 48 and 49 which have been registered in their names. The other members of your son's crew are at rest with them, Sergeant White Grave No. 43, Flying Officer Pole Grave No. 44, Flying Officer McOrmond Grave No. 45 and Flying Officer Wilson Grave No. 47.
>
> The resting place of your son and his crew will be reverently and perpetually maintained by the Imperial War Graves Commission (of which Canada is a member). The Commission will also erect permanent headstones at the graves. Unhappily, there are great numbers of these headstones to be erected and it will quite naturally take considerable time. It is not necessary to write to the Imperial War Graves Commission as you will be contacted by them before the stone is prepared.
>
> May I take this opportunity of again extending to you and the members of your family my deepest sympathy in the loss of your gallant son. Yours sincerely, W. R. Gunn, Wing Commander (12 August 1948).

Francis Island (63 N/12) in Sisipuk Lake was named after him in 1995.

Franklin, Lance Corporal **Robert W.** of Swan River (H 39110). Royal Canadian Engineers. He died 8 December 1942 at the age of 22 and is commemorated at Brookwood Military Cemetery in Surrey, England. He was the son of James H. and Edna M. Franklin and was survived by his wife Violet D. Franklin of Bowsman River, Manitoba and their son Robert. ***Franklin Island*** (64 O/15) in Blevins Lake was named after him in 1995.

Franko, Rifleman **Harry** of Selkirk (H 10994). Royal Winnipeg Rifles. He died 6 June 1944 at the age of 19 and is commemorated at Beny-sur-Mer Canadian War Cemetery in Calvados, France. He was the son of William and Stella Franko of Selkirk, Manitoba. ***Franko Lake*** (52 E/11), southeast of Brereton Lake was named after him in 1974.

Fraser, Flying Officer **Alexander Donald** of Neepawa (J 90500). No. 76 Operational Training Unit, Distinguished Flying Cross.

> This, Pilot Officer has completed a large number of operational missions against targets in Austria and the Balkans. In July, 1944 his aircraft was detailed to mine the Danube. Despite opposition from ground fire and machine guns, he descended to a very low altitude and dropped his mines in the

required position. Pilot Officer Fraser has also attacked many important oil targets, all of which were heavily defended. In August, 1944 he completed a successful sortie against important railway sidings in Hungary although enemy fighters and adverse weather were encountered. Throughout his tour, this Pilot Officer has shown exceptional keenness and efficiency (DFC Citation 1945).

He died 3 April 1945 at the age of 22 and is commemorated at Ramleh War Cemetery, Israel. He was the son of Alex and Elizabeth Fraser of Winnipeg. According to a family friend (4 January 1996):

Don was born in Edrans, Manitoba. His parents ... emigrated from Scotland after the First World War, settling in the Edrans area and in 1939 they moved to Winnipeg. Don had a younger brother, William, who was physically handicapped and unable to attend school. He was educated at home by his mother, which was quite an accomplishment at that time. Bill later passed away in the late 1960s.

Don graduated from Daniel McIntyre Collegiate in 1941. He worked as an apprentice mechanic before enlisting in the RCAF on February 2, 1942. He graduated as a pilot from No. 10 SFTS, Dauphin on May 14, 1943. Two months later he was posted to England for Advanced Flying and Operational Training on bombers. On completion of his training he was posted to the RAF Squadron 23 based in Egypt. He completed a tour of operations and was awarded the DFC.

Don was then assigned to train bomber crews. On April 3, 1945, the aircraft he was in crashed with no survivors.

Fraser Lake (64 C/14), southwest of Lynn Lake was named after him in 1947.

Fraser, Third Mate **Edgar L.** of Winnipeg. SS *Bellerock*, Canadian Merchant Navy. The *Bellerock* was lost 15 July 1940 and Third Mate Fraser is commemorated at the Halifax Memorial. ***Edgar Fraser Lake*** (63 P/8), northeast of Goulet Lake was named after him in 2001.

Fraser, Corporal **Frederick W.** of Souris (H 59618). Queen's Own Cameron Highlanders. He died 21 July 1944 at the age of 21 and is commemorated at Bretteville-sur-Laize Canadian War Cemetery in Calvados, France. He was the son of Frederick and Sarah Fraser of Brooklands, Manitoba. ***Fraser Peninsula*** (64 G/12) in Big Sand Lake was named after him in 1995.

Fraser, Flight Sergeant **Iain** of Winnipeg (R 4236A). No. 50 Squadron. He died 17 January 1943 at the age of 22 and is commemorated at the Kiel War Cemetery in Germany. He was the son of John and Hannah N. Fraser of Winnipeg. His brother recalls (11 January 1998):

Iain was born on 7 June 1920 (me in 1921) so we grew up very close to each other. Growing up during the depression, we more or less did our own things, playing hockey on the road with road apples. This was in St. James; after we moved to West Kildonan we continued scrub hockey. Our summers were spent in northwestern Ontario where we have a cabin. Iain graduated Grade 11 at Centennial School. A short while later [he] got a job (unskilled labour) but when war was declared he was anxious to enlist in the air force. As I remember it, he was shot down over Denmark – a mid upper gunner in a Lancaster.

Fraser Creek (64 I/8), which flows northeast into North Knife River was named after him in 1974.

Fraser, Flying Officer **John C.** of Hamiota (J 21759). RAF Station Lyneham, England. He died 22 June 1943 at the age of 20 and is commemorated at Brookwood Military Cemetery in Surrey, England. Flying Officer Fraser was on leave when he fell from a hotel window. He died of his injuries in Charing Cross Hospital, London (Allison and Hayward 1991). He was the son of Clarence M. and Gladys Fraser of Hamiota, Manitoba. ***Fraser Island*** (53 D/13) in Gilchrist Lake was named after him in 1983.

Fraser, Private **John G.** of Norwood (H 70467). Canadian Army Corps of Military Staff Clerks. He died 26 February 1945 at the age of 29 and is commemorated at Brookwood Military Cemetery in Surrey, England. He was the son of Andrew and Amelia Fraser of Norwood. ***Fraser Point*** (53 L/16) on Semmens Lake was named after him in 1995.

Fraser, Flight Sergeant **Richard D.** of Winnipeg (R 119693). No. 12 Squadron. He died 13 May 1943 at the age of 22 and is commemorated at the Runnymede Memorial in Surrey, England. He was the son of Henry A. and Elizabeth M. Fraser of Winnipeg. ***Fraser Bay*** (64 O/13) in Nueltin Lake was named after him in 1995.

Frederick, Sergeant **Walter** of Winnipeg (R 147185). No. 17 Advanced Flying School. He died 28 July 1943 at the age of 21 and is commemorated at Blacon Cemetery in Cheshire, England. ***Frederick Lake*** (64 F/6), north of Wells Lake was named after him in 1994.

Frederickson, Flying Officer **Turner** of Glenboro (J 86863). No. 426 Squadron. He died 30 September 1944 at the age of 26 and is commemorated at the Reichswald Forest War Cemetery in Germany. He was the son of Frederick and Thora Frederickson of Glenboro and was survived by his wife Eileen D. Frederickson (née Dowd) of Glenboro. His wife recalls (4 December 1997):

He was born ... in Glenboro [and] lived [there] his whole life as did his brother Allen and two sisters. Turner received his education in town taking Grade 12. He enjoyed all sports – mainly golf and playing trombone with the Glenboro Brass Band. Sang in the Lutheran church choir. In his free time he worked in his father's general store. He was wonderful with people and so well liked by all who knew him.

Turner enlisted with the RCAF May 14, 1941. Spent a short while in Brandon – was sent to Regina ... for his basic training as a pilot. Portage la Prairie was his next move to start his flying instructions. I believe it was the Tiger Moth he trained on. Last move was Yorkton, Saskatchewan to fly the larger, twin engine Anson plane. He received his wings in late December 1941. He had 12 days before leaving for overseas (we married in that time).

[He] arrived in England January, 1942. He was chosen to be a flying instructor (pilot) and trained the boys for 18 months. [He] decided to go to Bomber Command to do his 30 trips over Germany and then return home for a month leave. It was so sad to lose him on his 27th trip. It was a bomb from one of their own aircraft that caused the crash. It was on the outskirts of Oberhausen returning home from a bomb mission over Düsseldorf.

Frederickson Lake (64 J/15), northwest of Tadoule Lake was named after him in 1975.

Freedman, Rifleman **Israel** of Winnipeg (H 20969). Royal Winnipeg Rifles. He died 5 July 1944 at the age of 21 and is commemorated at Beny-sur-Mer Canadian War Cemetery in Calvados, France. He was the son of Peter and Molly Freedman of Winnipeg. ***Freedman Lake*** (53 N/4), east of Fish Lake was named after him in 1995.

Freeland, Lance Corporal **Roy H. "Bugs"** of Roblin (H 3860). Royal Canadian Corps of Signals. He died 26 December 1942 at the age of 26 and is commemorated at Brookwood Military Cemetery in Surrey, England. He was the only child of Roy E. and Isabel Freeland of Roblin, Manitoba. He wrote the following poem shortly before his death:

When oft within my bunk I lie,
After Last Post goes slowly by,
I dream of home and all that's best,
Of workful days and peaceful rest,
O life unrolling like a road,
Broad and wonderful to behold,
Plans and dreams, unfurled, unspoiled,
By any gruesome pestilent coiled.

When from the darkness of the land
Comes morning, many close at hand,
Moaning their toil of grief and fear,
While onward rises a sound more near,
A grumbling, rumble, a thing of fear
Giving to Freedom's stand the lie;
Searchlights leaping; small men creeping,
Planes unloading, bombs exploding,
Hate and death to all those nigh,
I fearfully wonder, why?

Freeland Lake (63 I/11), southwest of Walker Lake was named after Lance Corporal Freeland in 1982.

Freele, Corporal **William O.** of Winnipeg (R 59167). Royal Canadian Air Force. He died 1 June 1945 at the age of 47 and is commemorated at Brookside Cemetery in Winnipeg. He was the son of William and Sarah Freele of St. Thomas, Ontario and was survived by his wife Louise J. Freele of Winnipeg. ***Freele Lake*** (64 H/11), southeast of Small Lake was named after him in 1995.

Freeman, Private **Edward J. A.** of Norwood (H 6075). Winnipeg Grenadiers. He died 26 October 1942 at the age of 41 and is commemorated at the Sai Wan War Cemetery in Hong Kong. He was the son of Mr. and Mrs. J. Freeman of Norwood and was survived by the two sons of his recently departed wife. He had been a musician and was a member of the Winnipeg Grenadiers regimental band before going overseas. ***Freeman Bay*** (64 P/16) in Nabel Lake was named after him in 1985.

Freeman, Flying Officer **Harold** of Winnipeg (J 22448). No. 198 Squadron. He died 24 May 1944 at the age of 26 and is commemorated at Bayeux War Cemetery, Calvados, France. He was the son of Arni M. and Elizabeth J. Freeman of Winnipeg. ***Freeman Lake*** (64 H/8), southeast of Etawney Lake was named after him in 1948.

French, Lieutenant **Charles D.** of Norwood Grove. Winnipeg Grenadiers. He died 19 December 1941 at the age of 20 and is commemorated at the Sai Wan Memorial in Hong Kong. He was the son of Charles D. and Clara E. French of Norwood Grove, Manitoba. ***French Island*** (52 L/4) in the Winnipeg River was named after him in 1973.

French, Lieutenant **William S.** of Winnipeg. Queen's Own Cameron Highlanders. He died 24 October 1944 and is commemorated at Bergen-op-Zoom Canadian War Cemetery in Holland. ***French Lake*** (63 N/4), southwest of Kississing Lake was named after him in 1982.

Friesen, Private **John U.** of Dauphin (H 6951). Winnipeg Grenadiers. He died 2 February 1944 and is commemorated at the Yokohama War Cemetery in Japan. He was survived by his mother Mrs. Henrietta Friesen of Winnipeg. ***Friesen Lake*** (64 H/7), north of Solmundsson Lake was named after him in 1995.

Frobisher, Private **Donald** of Winnipeg (H 6787). Winnipeg Grenadiers. He died 19 December 1941 and is commemorated at the Sai Wan Memorial in Hong Kong. He was the son of Mr. and Mrs. Roland Frobisher of Moore Dale, Manitoba. He:

> ... was born at St. Norbert, Manitoba on September 11, 1914 and was employed as a caretaker at Moore Dale, Manitoba when he joined the Winnipeg Grenadiers. He served in Canada and the West Indies and proceeded to Hong Kong in the fall of 1941. He was killed in action when the garrison at Hong Kong fell in December, 1941. Frobisher attended the local schools at Tamarack Lake (Hill 1944).

Frobisher Lake (63 I/16), east of Cross Lake was named after him in 1973.

Fruchtl, Flight Sergeant **John G.** of Killarney, Manitoba (R 101420). No. 9 Squadron. He died 19 July 1942 at the age of 26 and is commemorated at Hethe (Holy Trinity) Roman Catholic Cemetery in Oxfordshire, England. ***Fruchtl Lake*** (53 M/5), north of Utik Lake was named after him in 1996.

Fry, Sapper **Allan J.** of Winnipeg (B 110743). Royal Canadian Engineers. He died of injuries 20 September 1943 due to a land mine explosion. He is commemorated at Brookwood Military Cemetery in Surrey, England. He was one of the 14 children of Mr. and Mrs. W. E. Fry of Winnipeg. A contemporary newspaper account indicated that:

> Born in Saskatchewan, Sapper Fry came to Winnipeg with his parents while still a child. He attended Hugh John Macdonald and Gordon Bell schools. Prior to enlisting with the RCE in April, 1942, he was employed at the Pickle Crow Gold mines. He has been overseas a year (n.d.).

Fry Lake (64 K/5), northeast of Reindeer Lake was named after him in 1972.

Fryatt, Company Sergeant Major **Walter B.** of St. Vital (H 6062). Winnipeg Grenadiers. He died 21 December 1941 and is commemorated at the Sai Wan Memorial in Hong Kong. ***Fryatt Lake*** (52 L/3), northeast of Brereton Lake was named after him in 1973.

Fudge, Pilot Officer **Bruce S. "Candy"** of Winnipeg (J 17663). No. 431 Squadron. He died 22 June 1943 at the age of 21 and is commemorated at the Runnymede Memorial in Surrey, England. He was the son of Samuel and Lydia Fudge and was survived by his wife Anne M. A. Fudge of Maida Vale, London. ***Fudge Lake*** (64 O/12), south of Nueltin Lake was named after him in 1975.

Fuller, Lance Corporal **Austin Ralph** of Rapid City (H 41280). Royal Winnipeg Rifles. He died 8 June 1944 at the age of 26 and is commemorated at Beny-sur-Mer Canadian War Cemetery in Calvados, France. He was the son of Stanley and Dorothy Fuller of New Westminster, British Columbia. ***Fuller Lake*** (64 B/12), southwest of Opachuanau Lake was named after him in 1981.

Fuller, Trooper **Joseph W.** of Graysville (H 26654). Fort Garry Horse. He died 9 June 1944 at the age of 27 and is commemorated at the Bayeux Memorial in Calvados, France. He was the son of Joseph A. and Harriet M. Fuller and was survived by his brother and sister Gordon and Josie of Graysville, Manitoba. ***Fuller Island*** (53 K/13) in Gods Lake was named after him in 1995.

Fullerton, Rifleman **James H.** of Shortdale (H 41095). Royal Winnipeg Rifles. He died 8 June 1944 at the age of 31 and is commemorated at Bretteville-sur-Laize Canadian War Cemetery in Calvados, France. He was the son of Matthew and Jennie Fullerton and was survived by his wife Eveline A. Fullerton of River Hebert East, Nova Scotia. ***Fullerton Lake*** (53 D/12), northeast of Lewis Lake was named after him in 1989.

Fulton, Flying Officer **Roderick W.** of Dauphin (J 24683). No. 4 Squadron. He died 15 August 1944 at the age of 24 and is commemorated at Rosskeen Parish Burial Ground, Ross and Cromarty, Scotland. He was the son of Thomas and Katherine A. Fulton and was survived by his wife Agnes B. Fulton of Winnipeg. ***Fulton Lake*** (64 H/16), southwest of Condie Lake was named after him in 1995.

Furey, Private **Joseph** of Carberry (H 6384). Winnipeg Grenadiers. He died a prisoner of war 1 January 1944 at the age of 22 and is commemorated at the Yokohama War Cemetery in Japan. The official cause of death was listed as "killed in a typhoon." He was the son of James and Kate Furey of Carberry and was the brother of Lance Corporal Patrick Furey (next entry). ***Furey Island*** (52 L/4) in the Winnipeg River was named after him in 1973.

Furey, Lance Corporal **Patrick** of Carberry (H 17773). Princess Patricia's Canadian Light Infantry. He died 12 December 1943 at the age of 21 and is commemorated at the Moro River Canadian War Cemetery in Italy. He was the son of James and Kate Furey of Carberry and the brother of Private Joseph Furey (previous entry). ***Furey Lake*** (64 H/9), southeast of Etawney Lake was named after him in 1978.

Furness, Sergeant **Allan T.** of Winnipeg (1564511). RAF Volunteer Reserve. He died 30 June 1945 at the age of 27 and is commemorated at Old Kildonan Presbyterian Cemetery in Winnipeg. He was the son of Allan S. and Kathleen Furness of Winnipeg. ***Furness Lake*** (53 N/6), south of Patch Lake was named after him in 1995.

Fussey, Rifleman **John S.** of Clarkleigh (K 37792). British Columbia Tank Regiment. He died 3 March 1942 at the age of 22 and is commemorated at Prospect Cemetery in Toronto. He was the son of William L. and Gertrude L. Fussey of Clarkleigh, Manitoba. ***Fussey Lake*** (63 K/16), west of Wekusko Lake was named after him in 1973.

Futoranski, Flying Officer **Joseph** of Winnipeg. No. 419 Squadron. He died 23 October 1944 at the age of 21 and is commemorated at the Reichswald Forest War Cemetery in Germany. An orphan, he was survived by his aunt and uncle Mr. and Mrs. William Rapko of Winnipeg. ***Futoranski Lake*** (64 P/2), southeast of Nejanilini Lake was named after him in 1974.

Canadian troops enter San Pancrazio, Italy occupied only a week before by German soldiers 16 July 1944. Courtesy of the National Archives of Canada (PA-129763).

G

Gabor, Rifleman **Joseph M.** of Woodridge (H 1056). Regina Rifle Regiment. He died 18 June 1944 at the age of 20 and is commemorated at Beny-sur-Mer Canadian War Cemetery in Calvados, France. He was the son of Istvan and Ersebet Gabor of Woodridge, Manitoba. ***Gabor Lake*** (64 N/14), west of Nueltin Lake was named after him in 1972.

Gagnon, Trooper **Joseph E.** of East Kildonan (H 17041). Princess Louise Dragoon Guards. He died 29 January 1944 and is commemorated at the Moro River Canadian War Cemetery in Italy. ***Gagnon Lake*** (64 P/9), east of Nejanilini Lake was named after him in 1974.

Gair, Leading Signalman **Alexander M.** of Winnipeg (V 24028). HMCS *Guysborough*. The *Guysborough* was torpedoed and sunk by U-878 in the English Channel off Ushant, France; fifty-one of her ship's company were lost. Leading Signalman Gair died 18 March 1945 at the age of 25 and is commemorated at the Halifax Memorial. He was the son of Robert and Marjorie I. Gair of Winnipeg. ***Gair Lake*** (64 N/6), southwest of Nueltin Lake was named after him in 1972.

Galbraith, Private **Albert E.** of Miami, Manitoba (423023). New Brunswick Regiment. He died 18 September 1916 at the age of 26 and is commemorated at Contay British Cemetery, Contay, Somme, France. He was the son of James Galbraith of Miami and had been a Steam Engineer when he enlisted in April, 1915. ***Galbaith Lake*** (63 N/12), south of Sisipuk Lake was named after this World War I casualty in 2000.

Gallagher, Corporal **Chester** of Flin Flon (H 101411). Royal Winnipeg Rifles. He died 29 August 1944 at the age of 32 and is commemorated at Bretteville-sur-Laize Canadian War Cemetery in Calvados, France. He was the son of Angus and Mercy Gallagher and was survived by his wife Wilma E. Gallagher (née Le Doux) of Flin Flon, Manitoba. According to his wife (19 April 1995) he:

> ... was born in McCreary, Manitoba ... [and] worked as a farm hand till 1941; [he] came to Flin Flon [and] worked in the mill at Hudson Bay Mining and Smelting till he joined the army ... in July, 1942. [He was] sent overseas in December, 1942.

Gallagher Lake (64 C/15), east of Reindeer Lake was named after him in 1973.

Gallagher, Pilot Officer **James C.** of Winnipeg (J 86981). No. 432 Squadron. He died 16 September 1944 at the age of 21 and is commemorated at Aabenraa Cemetery in Denmark. ***James Gallagher Lake*** (64 F/5) east of Reindeer Lake was named after him in 1995.

Gallagher, Private **Patrick** of Winnipeg (H 1561). Perth Regiment. He died 17 January 1944 and is commemorated at the Moro River Canadian War Cemetery in Italy. ***Gallagher Island*** (63 I/6) in Butterfly Lake was named after him in 1995.

Gallant, Private **Harry J.** of Neepawa (H 9787). Lake Superior Regiment. He died 23 October 1944 and is commemorated at Bergen-op-Zoom Canadian War Cemetery in Holland. ***Gallant Island*** (64 C/5) in Kamuchawie Lake was named after him in 1995.

Gallant, Private **Lewis** of Angusville (H 530784). Lake Superior Regiment. He died 9 April 1945 at the age of 28 and is commemorated at the Holten Canadian War Cemetery in Holland. He was the son of Mike and Katherine Gallant and was survived by his wife Pauline Gallant of Angusville, Manitoba. ***Gallant Lake*** (62 N/15), southeast of Swan River was named after him in 1973.

Gammack, Trooper **Alexander J.** of Decker (H 232). Lord Strathcona's Horse. He died 25 May 1944 at the age of 34 and is commemorated at the Cassino War Cemetery in Italy. He was the son of James and Isabel Gammack of Decker, Manitoba. ***Gammack Lake*** (64 I/6), northwest of North Knife Lake was named after him in 1974.

Gamsby, Flying Officer **Austin G.** of Winnipeg (J 23114). No. 405 Squadron. He died 16 June 1944 at the age of 30 and is commemorated at the Calais Canadian War Cemetery in France. He was the son of Edgar and Jemima Gamsby of Winnipeg. ***Gamsby Lake*** (64 P/10), east of Nejanilini Lake was named after him in 1974.

Gant, Flying Officer **Maurice George** of Winnipeg (J 42505). No. 571 Squadron. He died 27 March 1945 at the age of 21 and is commemorated at Leek (Zevenhuizen) General Cemetery, Holland. He was the son of Maurice D. and Sophia Gant of Winnipeg. ***Gant Lake*** (64 O/7), southeast of Nueltin Lake was named after him in 1975.

Garand, Private **Clovis B.** of St. Norbert (H 64594). Cape Breton Highlanders. He died 13 September 1944 at the age of 20 and is commemorated at Coriano Ridge War Cemetery in Italy. According to his brother (1 June 1998):

> Clovis was born in Lewis, Manitoba in 1923. The family then moved to Ponteix, Saskatchewan where he became a 14 year-old orphan. He then went to live with an older brother in St. Jean Baptiste, joining the army in 1940. We are told he was a very sociable young person. He was active in the community and started a group of Lone Scouts in the village. He joined the army at a young age in 1940 and was sent overseas in 1941.

Garand Lake (64 N/2), southwest of Nueltin Lake was named after him in 1972.

Garand, Private Joseph **Edmond H.** of Dunrea (SM 9706). Princess Patricia's Canadian Light Infantry. He died 19 November 1951 at the age of 21 and is commemorated at the United Nations Cemetery in Pusan, South Korea. He was one of the 15 children of August and Rosanne Garand of Dunrea, Manitoba and the brother of Engineer Olivier Garand (next entry). ***Garand Peninsula*** (63 P/5) in Paint Lake was named after this Korean War casualty in 1998.

Garand, Engineer **Olivier J.** of Dunrea. Merchant Marine vessel *Vancouver Island*. The *Vancouver Island* was torpedoed by U-558 15 October 1941 in the North Atlantic while *en route* from Montreal to Cardiff; all 65 crew, eight gunners and 32 passengers were lost. Engineer Garand died 15 October 1941 at the age of 26

and is commemorated at the Halifax Memorial. He was one of 15 children of August and Rosanne Garand of Dunrea, Manitoba. Seven of the brothers joined the forces during the Second World War and an eighth died in the Korean conflict (see previous entry). ***Garand Island*** (63 P/5) in Paint Lake was named after him in 1995. His three remaining siblings and their families visited the island in 1996.

Gard, Private **James P.** of Fisher Branch (H 6776). Winnipeg Grenadiers. He died a prisoner of war 14 July 1945 and is commemorated at the Yokohama War Cemetery in Japan. Returning Grenadier Private Harry Atkinson reported that:

> "One month and 15 days ago seven of the fellows got stomach poisoning. They were in bad shape when they arrived back in camp that night. They were told to report to our [Japanese] commander. He ordered a stomach pump for them. Don't know why, probably saw the end of the war was near." Four of them died – Lance Corporal Malcolm Hawes, Private Jim Gard, Private Roy Kirk and Private Bob McLeod (*Winnipeg Tribune* September 1945).

Gard Lake (64 K/10), east of Lac Brochet was named after him in 1979.

Gardiner, Gunner **Harry** of Norwood (H 12022). Royal Canadian Artillery. He died 13 August 1944 at the age of 28 and is commemorated at Bretteville-sur-Laize Canadian War Cemetery in Calvados, France. He was the son of Frederick C. and Louise Gardiner and was survived by his wife Olga Gardiner of Norwood. ***Gardiner Island*** (63 N/13) in Loon Lake was named after him in 1995.

Gardiner, Sergeant **Melvin James** of Woodnorth (H 41092). Royal Winnipeg Rifles. He died 20 February 1945 at the age of 24 and is commemorated at the Groesbeek Canadian War Cemetery in Holland. He was the son of James R. and Annie E. Gardiner (née Duncan) of Woodnorth, Manitoba.

> A member of an anti-tank company, he landed in France on "D" Day last June and saw immediate action. In November, 1944, he was promoted to the rank of sergeant and made second in command of his platoon. Sergeant Gardiner took part in much of the fighting in Normandy and advanced with the Canadians into Holland. It was there on February 19th, just five days after his twenty-fourth birthday, that he was so seriously wounded that he died the following day (*Woodnorth News* 1945).

Gardiner Point (64 P/3) in Hoguycho Lake was named after him in 1995.

Gardner, Flight Sergeant **John** of Boissevain (R 101865). No. 106 Squadron. He died 20 December 1942 at the age of 20 and is commemorated at Amsterdam New Eastern Cemetery, Holland. He was the son of Alfred H. and Annie L. Gardner of Boissevain, Manitoba. ***Gardner Bay*** (64 K/16) in Caron Lake was named after him in 1995.

Gardner, Pilot Officer **William Alexander** of Gilbert Plains (J 26245). No. 45 Ferry Command. He died 7 September 1943 at the age of 22 and is commemorated at Christiansborg War Cemetery, Ghana. He was one of the two children of William and Lillie C. Gardner of Kelowna, British Columbia. Flying had been his major interest since childhood. ***Gardner Lake*** (64 H/10), southeast of Buckland Lake was named after him in 1995.

Garlick, Sergeant **William G.** of Emerson (H 19481). Queen's Own Cameron Highlanders. He died 16 August 1944 at the age of 25 and is commemorated at Bretteville-sur-Laize Canadian War Cemetery in Calvados, France. He was the son of George F. and Alice H. Garlick (née Daniels) of Winnipeg. ***Garlick Island*** (63 J/8) in Kiskittogisu Lake was named after him in 1971.

Garlinski, Private **Edward T.** of Ashville (H 100099). Queen's Own Cameron Highlanders. He died 17 August 1944 at the age of 23 and is commemorated at Bretteville-sur-Laize Canadian War Cemetery in Calvados, France. He was the son of Steve L. and Mary K. Garlinski of Ashville, Manitoba. His last letter home was from "Somewhere in France:"

> My Dearest Folks and Brothers: Well dear folks, how is everything? I sure hope everything is fine. I have had from you only one letter since we got here, but I haven't had much time to write as we were on the go all the time. They have just got us back of the Front Lines for a bit of a rest which is sure nice to have. As [to] when we are going in again, well we never know; as far as that goes, any time. I got a letter from Leo; he got over to England lately – just don't know when – just my luck. I always like to see him as he always writes me so often, but you never know what comes next. I don't know if I can get back to get married of not, sure wish I could. I get a letter from her every second day and so far everything is fine. She wrote you Ma. I wish, mother, I could see you just for a minute; it would mean the world to me. It's so long now that it's not funny – 2 1/2 years. I keep praying for God to keep me safe. Ma, don't worry, it won't be long before it's over now. We've got them where we want them. I guess no one knows what war is like till you're in it (2 August 1944).

Garlinski Lake (64 P/1), southeast of Nejanilini Lake was named after him in 1974.

Garman, Pilot Officer **Earle V.** of Winnipeg (J 8364). No. 208 Squadron. He died 29 September 1942 at the age of 24 and is commemorated at El Alamein War Cemetery in Egypt. Shortly after his death, his mother wrote down her recollections of Earle:

> Shortly after the declaration of war, Earle came home from Red Lake, Ontario where he had been in the forestry service. He was bewildered as were all our boys. We had taught them war was wrong and now we were sending them to the slaughter. They went with a smile and we praised them and wished them luck. We could not find jobs for them, but we put them into uniform and gave them as an ideal "Our Way of Life" on which to place their sacrifices. Earle could not see sense or reason in the war and "killing." I know that all through his training and when he left for overseas he had not overcome that feeling that there should be a "better way." On reaching the Middle East, he asked for and received training as a reconnaissance pilot. He was not allowed to attack, but was to evade. He wrote: "There will not be the glory of a fighter."
>
> As you know, he left England the first part of January and reached Cairo sometime the first part of March. He wrote: "The desert is an awful whole." (He never did spell properly). He also said there was nothing much to write about except sand and fleas and what he would say about the fleas would be censored, just one long blue line. Those were the only two things nearest to a complaint we ever heard from him. His letters, always so short, told us little and named only one boy, but from the time he left Canada, there is scarcely a message without the word "beauty" in it. Scotland was beautiful, England was lovely, Durban was a beautiful city. "I would like to tell you about it but being what I am it's just a beautiful city." The sunsets at sea and the tropical moon (he regretted being under its spell on a troop ship), his voyage around Africa – the last half especially was so wonderful he wished it would never end.
>
> From Cairo, he was sent into Palestine for three months for operational training. He must have had a wonderful time, but wrote that he felt like

a stooge because he had gone over there to fight a war instead of to enjoy life. Then he was sent to Syria near Beyrouth in the Lebanon mountains. Twice he wrote, saying his Dad and I must surely plan a trip over there after this mess is cleaned up. He had a horse and went riding a couple of times a day and told about the natives threshing their grain with an ox or a donkey hitched to a toboggan-like affair which was pulled round and round. He wrote: "From the mess hall, I can look out on beautiful mountains, some still capped with snow, and down into a beautiful valley filled with orchards of grapes, oranges and apples. Do not feel sorry for me over here. Since I left home, it has been one long holiday and a perfectly grand one." There too, he enjoyed champagne and sparkling wine.

On October second, I received a letter written July 10th in which he wrote: "Things were looking pretty shaky out here for a while and I figured I would be into it, but after sending us down to Alexandria where we were bombed a bit, they took our aircraft and sent us back up here (Beyrouth) by train. So here I am, still living a very wonderful life of peace and quiet. The only thing, it has been so good that when it breaks, I'm afraid I will really get a good dose of the opposite. But we have to expect that." He was sent back into the desert on operational duty about the middle of August, I think. That same afternoon, the message that read: "killed on active service September twenty-ninth" was handed to me.

When he went away, I wanted so much to tell him through it all to keep constantly in mind the twenty-third Psalm. My one fear was not that he would lose his life, but that bitterness would enter in. But I didn't have the willpower to say anything about it or any other religious thought. I knew he wouldn't want me to get sentimental or preachy and as you know so well, we are not a religious or church-going family. As the days passed and I kept "pulling for him" as all of us do for those dear to us, that one desire was strongest within me – I presume because that Psalm has been for me all the comfort and strength I ever seemed to need. Last Easter, I bought two copies of *The Song of our Syrian Guest*. (In case you don't know, it is an interpretation of the 23rd Psalm by a Syrian shepherd) and sent one to Aunt Etta who was very ill in Chicago and one to Aunt Myrtle in Spokane.

On the first Sunday after our message came, it was our privilege to attend a World Wide Communion Service, the contributions to which were to be given to Missions of the stricken countries. As we partook of Communion, the sunlight entered the window at the rear of the church [Westminster United] and slowly spread its beam of light in a widening arc over the congregation until it reached the altar. Afterwards, as we drove home down River Avenue, we saw another sight of rare beauty. In the glorious warm sunshine of that lovely autumn day, leaves of pure gold dropped from the trees like a shower of golden rain.

Last February, his Dad and I celebrated our silver wedding anniversary and knowing he had been posted to the Middle East, I wrote and asked him to some day send us the gift of a rug. On Monday, October fifth, a rug was brought to us, hooked by the mother of Helen's husband at Pugwash, Nova Scotia, not far from where the kid received his wings last October 25th. She has made these rugs for many years and sold them to American tourists. All the money she receives is contributed to her church. During August, she had written to Helen, telling her she was sending a rug to Winnipeg as there had been no tourists there last summer. I said I wanted the rug knowing that it was made of rags, home dyed. It is a very beautiful rug, a picture of the Three Wise Men on camels standing beside three palm trees on a green oasis and gazing at a beautiful star in the blue night sky. Below the star, the Sphinx can be seen in the desert background. In the border across the bottom of the rug are the words: "To Wise Men in the East the Star that Led."

On November eighth, ours will again be the privilege at another world-wide service, that of Armistice Day, to attend a special service at Regent's Park, a tribute to him and others he has joined in the service of their country and in the hope of a better way of life. A little book containing the names of the local boys in uniform was dedicated at the communion service. It will be rededicated on November eighth and the second Sunday of each month thereafter. I am asking Mr. Studd the minister to say: "He found peace and beauty in the hills of Lebanon, even in time of world-wide war," then sing the hymn *Unto the Hills Do I Lift Up Mine Eyes*. Somewhere in his sermon I want him to read the following little verse:

God with His million cares
Went to the left or right,
Leaving our world; and the day
Grew night.

Back from a sphere He came
Over a starry lawn,
Looked at our world; and the dark
Grew dawn.
(Norman Gale).

As I woke the morning of October sixth, I was facing the window and there in the darkness of the early dawn shone a beautiful star and the message that came from the Middle East seemed not to have been "killed on active service," but "a new day is being born" and the realization came to me that "the cross we have to bear" had been changed into "a star to guide us."

So we have been given the task of lifting the share of the burden he had to lay down and carry it on. Through the supreme sacrifice they make, their homes, like ours, so completely empty, receive a benediction and other's not so empty but wondering still, are filled with prayer and hope and faith. And in such a way are our prayers answered and our way made clear. It almost seems as if he had lived the 23rd Psalm and sent an answer to the whole wide world (n.d.).

Garman Lake (64 G/14), east of Big Sand Lake was named after Pilot Officer Garman in 1994.

Garonski, Leading Aircraftman **Alexander** of Morris (R 147125). Royal Canadian Air Force. He died 1 March 1943 at the age of 28 and is commemorated at Ashern United Church Cemetery, Manitoba. He drowned while assisting in a rescue of four airmen who were in a swamped dinghy at Langara Island (Allison and Hayward 1991). He was the son of Anthony and Nellie Garonski of Eriksdale and was survived by his wife Elfrieda E. Garonski of Regina. ***Garonski Lake*** (64 H/8), west of Hogg Lake was named after him in 1995.

Garritty, Lieutenant **Mervyn E.** of Winnipeg. Princess Patricia's Canadian Light Infantry. He died 20 December 1944 at the age of 30 and is commemorated at Ravenna War Cemetery in Italy. He was the son of Edward J. and Ellen T. Garritty and was survived by his wife Helen J. Garritty of Ottawa. ***Garritty Lake*** (64 H/9), southeast of North Knife Lake was named after him in 1978.

Gascoyne, Private **George** of Winnipeg (H 16574). Princess Patricia's Canadian Light Infantry. He died 20 July 1942 at the age of 35 and is commemorated at Brookwood Military Cemetery in Surrey, England. He was the son of Frank and Sarah Gascoyne of Derby, Surrey, England. ***Gascoyne Lake*** (63 O/4), north of Wekusko Lake was named after him in 1970.

Gates, Private **George A.** of Winnipeg (H 1303). Algonquin Regiment. He died 27 February 1945 and is commemorated at the Holten Canadian War Cemetery in Holland. ***Gates Lake*** (63 K/16), northwest of Wekusko Lake was named after him in 1973.

Gates, Flight Sergeant **William R.** of MacGregor (R 59718). No. 76 Squadron. He died 30 December 1941 at the age of 25 and is commemorated at the Runnymede Memorial in Surrey, England. He was the son of Ralph B. and Honora E. Gates of Centralia, Ontario. ***Gates Island*** (64 A/12) in Baldock Lake was named after him in 1989.

Gath, Corporal **Sydney** of Winnipeg (H 2203). 1st Canadian Special Services Battalion. He died 3 December 1943 at the age of 28 and is commemorated at the Cassino War Cemetery in Italy. He was the son of Norris and Agnes Gath of Winnipeg. His sister writes (1 November 2001):

Syd was born in Winnipeg on the 22nd of June, 1915. We belonged to St. Thomas Anglican Church. He was a member of the Cubs and later the Boy Scouts. In the summer, he would go on camping trips with them. He liked to draw and write and was a big fan of Bing Crosby and collected all his records and sang his songs. Syd joined the army September 3rd, 1939 – the day that England declared war on Germany. At first he was with the Royal Canadian Army Service Corps, but transferred to the 1st Canadian Special Service Battalion in 1942. He did most, if not all of his training in the States.

Gath Lake (64 J/2), southwest of Tadoule Lake was named after him in 1975.

Gauthier, Able Seaman **Joseph A. Richard R.** of Winnipeg (V 43226). Motor Torpedo Boat 459. He died 14 February 1945 at the age of 20 and is commemorated at the Adegem Canadian War Cemetery in Belgium. He was the son of Henri and Margaret Gauthier of Winnipeg. A flotilla of Motor Torpedo boats had been moored at Ostend, Belgium when an explosion of unknown origin began a chain of explosions and fires on twelve nearby boats. Twenty-eight Canadians and 35 British sailors lost their lives. A survivor of the incident, Napoleon Gagnon recounted his experience:

Something outside must have caught my attention and I looked out the porthole. All I saw was a wall of fire. I screamed "Fire" and ran upstairs. The others just laughed, thinking I was making a joke. I ran upstairs and tried to find a life jacket because I couldn't swim too good (*Winnipeg Free Press*, 14 November 1995).

Before Gagnon could get to a life jacket, a huge explosion hurled him overboard and smashed him into the water. Gagnon thinks a secondary explosion seconds later catapulted him onto a piece of floating debris and then into the water again.

I was sure I was about to die. Most of the water was on fire and I was under water and on the water and conscious and unconscious. At one point I saw my mother standing in our kitchen back home on Des Meurons Street, reading a telegram. I clearly saw the telegram in her hand. She was so real to me and I stood so close to her I could have touched her (*Winnipeg Free Press*, 14 November 1995).

As things turned out, Gagnon's boat was among the vessels which disintegrated in the Ostend inferno and Gagnon's mother in Winnipeg did indeed receive a telegram, saying that her son was missing in action. Gagnon ended up being dragged onto a jetty on the other side of the harbour by another sailor from Winnipeg.

I think his name was Richard or Joseph Gauthier. They lived on Flora Street and I visited his mom when I got home. They moved away after that and I lost track of them. I knew him the whole time I was in the navy. He wasn't hurt and kept going back into the water to get guys out. He was either hit or snagged on something or hurt by the fires that were still on the water. All I know is that he died that afternoon. In the morning we had been to church together (*Winnipeg Free Press*, 14 November 1995).

His brother recalls (4 December 1995):

Richard attended École Sacre Coeur [and] St. Paul's High School and was later employed by Kummen Ship Electric prior to his enlistment. His athletic interests were in hockey and swimming. He enlisted at HMCS *Chippawa* ... in 1941 and then trained in Esquimalt, British Columbia. He went overseas in August, 1943.

Gauthier Island (53 E/14) in Stone Lake was named after him in 1995.

Gauthier, Trooper **Omer L.** of Great Falls (K 65964). 1st Hussar Tank Regiment. He died 26 July 1944 at the age of 20 and is commemorated at Bretteville-sur-Laize Canadian War Cemetery in Calvados, France. He was the third of the six children of Jules R. and Irene E. Gauthier (née Bernard) of Great Falls, Manitoba. His sister recalls (10 August 1998):

Omer was a happy, active boy. In the winter he enjoyed hunting, skating, skiing and helping his father and brothers cut wood for the furnace. In the summer, he enjoyed swimming down at the beach and fishing for those beautiful sturgeon which mother canned for the winter.

Great Falls was a small town, but there was always things to do like shows and dances with his girlfriend. Ball games and hockey and of course there was school. When he was old enough, he left home to go to the Big City – Winnipeg.

In February, 1942 he took a Welding and Machine Shop training course. [He] moved to Vancouver [in] July, 1942 [and in] August, 1942, he enlisted in the Tanks Corps. He then went to Camp Borden, Ontario for his driver's certificate in operating a self-propelled vehicle.

Gauthier Bay (64 J/13) in Pope Lake was named after him in 1995.

Gayner, Lieutenant **Frank W. "Bill"** of Fort Garry. Regina Rifle Regiment. He died 18 June 1944 and is commemorated at Beny-sur-Mer Canadian War Cemetery in Calvados, France. His younger brother recalls (18 June 1997):

Born in Medicine Hat, Alberta in 1923, Bill and our mother and father, sister Helen and I came to Winnipeg in 1938 where our dad was manager of the then Manitoba Telephone System-owned radio station CKY.

In Winnipeg, Bill went to Kelvin Technical High School, graduated from Grade 12 in 1941 and went into second year Science at the University of Manitoba. We lived at the foot of Harvard Street and Bill's pals were a gang of six other kids in the neighbourhood including Bruce Hale, Beverly Best and John Wiley. When *Snow White and the Seven Dwarfs* came out, the gang decided each to take the name of one of the dwarfs. Bill came in at the end and so was known as Dopey Gayner despite his pretty good marks at school and his very warm good nature.

Bill was a big guy, six foot two, and as a teenager, rather scrawny. As he started to fill out he began playing football and in the fall of '42 played for the Manitoba Bisons. But if my memory is correct, there was a deal whereby he and the other Bisons played for the Winnipeg Blue Bombers. I can't remember the details, but it clearly had something to do with the manpower shortage.

While at University, Bill joined the Canadian Officers Training Corps, which was a basic army training operation for university students for part of the summer and weeknights during the winter. During the rest of the summer, Bill worked at the Manitoba (I think) Iron and Steel Works, turning shell casings on a lathe. The plant was near the Royal Alexandra Hotel in the North End, and we lived in Fort Garry. Bill used to ride his bike to work.

In the fall of '42 Bill joined up. He wanted to be a tanker but with his height they put him in the infantry, so he joined the Royal Winnipeg Rifles. He was ... sent to a camp at Maple Creek, Saskatchewan where he led a platoon of so-called Zombies – people who had been drafted and mostly didn't want to be in the army. Bill hated it and wanted to get overseas.

In the fall of '43, he was sent to Debert in Nova Scotia where he waited several weeks before being sent to England. Bill went in to Normandy on D-Day Plus Two or Three, as a reinforcement for the Prairie Rifle Brigade (the Royal Winnipeg Rifles, the Regina Rifles and the Loyal Edmontons). Bill was wounded very soon and died of internal injuries in a base hospital a few days later. Apparently, they hadn't realized how badly wounded he was internally.

Needless to say, it was a terrible blow to us all, but it was made worse by the fact that we heard that he was wounded but would be all right. Then several days later, we received the awful word. It is strange that although I am now 67 years old, I still see an older man in [his] photo.

Gayner Lake (52 L/11), south of Black Lake was named after him in 1982.

Gayoway, Private **Michael** of Winnipeg (H 17785). Princess Patricia's Canadian Light Infantry. He died 4 December 1943 at the age of 23 and is commemorated at the Moro River Canadian War Cemetery in Italy. He was the son of Michael and Louise Gayoway of Winnipeg. His sister recalls (21 June 1995) that:

... [he] was born [and] educated in Winnipeg, attending Margaret Scott, Faraday and St. John's High School. He enlisted in the PPCLI in 1940, went overseas in 1941 and served in England, Sicily and Italy.

She recalls too (26 October 2001) his artistic side:

As a teenage artist of considerable talent, he entered a painting in a USA contest and was informed by them that his skills warranted further training. Later, one of his paintings done on a wooden apple box was considered good enough to be kept as a momento in the Fort William Barracks. Before enlisting, he played the violin for his personal pleasure and enjoyed bowling and reading. He was a kind, generous person with a keen sense of humour and was the pride and joy of his parents. Martha, a former Winnipegger now living in Italy near the Moro River Cemetery, places flowers on his grave each November 11, for which we feel blessed and very grateful that people have not forgotten those who made the supreme sacrifice during the war.

Gayoway Lake (64 O/9), northwest of Nejanilini Lake was named after him in 1975.

Geddes, Quarter Master Sergeant **Stanley H.** of Winnipeg (H 3110). Canadian Dental Corps. He died 11 December 1944 at the age of 54 and is commemorated at Elmwood Cemetery in Winnipeg. He was survived by his wife Mary I. M. Geddes of Winnipeg. ***Geddes Lake*** (64 J/3), southwest of Tadoule Lake was named after him in 1975.

Gee, Flying Officer **Melsom H. W.** of Winnipeg (J 18681). No. 183 Squadron. He died 6 June 1944 at the age of 22 and is commemorated at Banneville-la-Campagne War Cemetery in Calvados, France. He was the son of Fred M. and Edith M. Gee of Winnipeg. His brother writes (4 September 1997):

He and four others were strafing armour south of Caen on D-Day. They were jumped by 12 Messerschmitts and a dogfight ensued. He radioed the Squadron Leader saying "am heading south to draw them off, so break for home." He crashed in an orchard and was buried by French peasants. Was "missing" for 15 months until War Graves Commission caught up. A survivor visited my parents at war's end. Brought his logbook and personal effects. He stated that none of the four who reached base would have survived without his sacrifice.

Gee Lake (64 O/8), southwest of Nejanilini Lake was named after him in 1975.

Geekie, Private **Victor E.** of Winnipeg (H 6555). Winnipeg Grenadiers. He died 19 December 1941 at the age of 31 and is commemorated at the Sai Wan Memorial in Hong Kong. His nephew visited the Memorial in 1997. He was the son of Thomas Y. and Jessie Geekie of Winnipeg and was survived by his wife Lillian Geekie and their five year-old son. He was born in Portage la Prairie and when the family moved to Winnipeg, he attended Earl Grey School. ***Geekie Lake*** (63 N/1), south of Burntwood Lake was named after him in 1972.

Gemmell, Private **David** of Winnipeg (H 17304). Winnipeg Grenadiers. He died 26 November 1942 and is commemorated at the Sai Wan War Cemetery in Hong Kong. ***Gemmell Creek*** (64 I/13), which flows southeast into the Seal River was named after him in 1974.

Genaille, Lance Sergeant **John H.** of Shortdale (H 41864). Lake Superior Regiment. He died 12 August 1944 and is commemorated at Bretteville-sur-Laize Canadian War Cemetery in Calvados, France. He was one of the six children of Frank and Mary Genaille of Shortdale, Manitoba. ***Genaille Bay*** (64 B/9) in Broughton Lake was named after him in 1995.

Genaille, Private **Lewis** of Russell (H 92488). Princess Patricia's Canadian Light Infantry. He died 27 December 1944 and is commemorated at Cesena War Cemetery in Italy. ***Genaille Island*** (64 O/5) in Booth Lake was named after him in 1975.

Genaille, Rifleman **Phillip A.** of Beaconia (H 100967). Royal Winnipeg Rifles. He died 6 June 1944 and is commemorated at Beny-sur-Mer Canadian War Cemetery in Calvados, France. He was the son of Mr. and Mrs. Peter Genaille and was survived by his wife Anna Genaille of Beaconia, Manitoba. ***Genaille Lake*** (64 K/10), northeast of Reindeer Lake was named after him in 1972.

Genest, Private **Armand J.** of St. Boniface (H 1576). Fusiliers Mont-Royal Regiment. He died 23 October 1944 at the age of 22 and is commemorated at Bergen-op-Zoom Canadian War Cemetery in Holland. He was the son of Charles and Angelina Genest of St. Boniface. ***Genest Lake*** (64 I/10), northeast of North Knife Lake was named after him in 1974.

Genest, Rifleman **Emile Y.** of Spearhill (H 10116). Royal Winnipeg Rifles. He died 10 October 1944 at the age of 20 and is commemorated at the Adegem Canadian War Cemetery in Belgium. He was the youngest of the 14 children of Ludger and Clara Genest. According to his brother (9 January 1998):

In 1917, my parents and family left Montreal to join my mother's parents who were proprietors of a hotel in Ashern. Emile ... was born on a homestead approximately ten miles from Ashern. Most of his later years were spent on a homestead near Spearhill, Manitoba where he attended Scandia School. He completed part of Grade 9 there, but decided to begin earning his living instead of continuing his education. He was not particularly interested in sports. After having worked at the local limestone plant for a short period, he joined the Royal Winnipeg Rifles and followed me overseas. I visited him only once in England, just before he crossed the Channel.

And later (27 October 2001):

When I heard that he had arrived in England, I was granted a weekend pass to see him. I tried to persuade him to ask for a transfer to my unit. He refused and said that he would prefer to transfer to a paratroop company.

When we were growing up, one of our pastimes was to build snow forts. We established two groups and threw snowballs for ammunition at one another. Before leaving our battleground late one afternoon, we made a provision of snowballs to take up the battle against the "foe" in the morning. That night, the low temperatures changed our harmless snowballs into lethal cannonballs. The youngest, Emile, received one on the head. He fell unconscious, but to our relief, soon recovered. Barely 16 years later, that which had been play became a sad reality. Now he lies in the Adegem Permanent Cemetery in Belgium.

Genest Island (63 I/2) in Mishepowistik Lake was named after him in 1995.

Gensorick, Private **Frank** (H 16225). Princess Patricia's Canadian Light Infantry. He died 6 December 1943 and is commemorated at the Moro River Canadian War Cemetery in Italy. ***Gensorick Lake*** (64 O/3), southeast of Blackfish Lake was named after him in 1995.

George, Flight Sergeant **William H.** of St. James (R 95479). No. 100 Squadron. He died 17 April 1943 at the age of 24 and is commemorated at Rheinberg War Cemetery in Germany. His sister recalls (27 November 2001):

> "Bill" George was born in Saskatchewan on June 7, 1918, one of three children of William and Lillian George. However, Bill lived most of his life in Manitoba. He spent his early years and attended school in Sifton. Spare time was spent playing hockey. Later, he worked with his father in the family retail business in Sperling. It was while he was in Sperling that Bill joined the forces. Bill trained in Virden. During the war, Bill flew on bombing runs over the continent from England. During his stay in England, Bill managed to surprise his father's relatives who still lived in Bath, Somerset. According to his aunt, one night there was a knock on the door of the house in King Edward Road. When his aunt answered the door, a young man in a Canadian uniform simply introduced himself as "Bill from Canada." Apparently a great evening followed.

George Bay (64 G/6) in McPherson Lake was named after him in 1994.

German, Flying Officer **Harold W.** of Pilot Mound (J 10730). No. 434 Squadron, Air Force Medal.

> This NCO has performed his duties as Navigation Instructor both in the air and as a lecturer in Ground Instruction School in an exemplary, whole-hearted and meritorious manner. He has shown exceptional keenness in his work and has constantly given instruction after normal working hours to improve the standing of his classes with most satisfactory results. He is possessed of a pleasing personality and his general relationship with all personnel has been of the highest standard. He has 650 flying hours (AFM Citation 1943).

He died 3 October 1943 at the age of 22 and is commemorated at the Hanover War Cemetery in Germany. He was the son of Arthur H. and Hazel German of Portage la Prairie. ***German Lake*** (64 C/11), southwest of Lynn Lake was named after him in 1950.

Gerrand, Pilot Officer **Norman H.** of Birtle (J 86559). No. 417 Squadron. He died 23 July 1944 at the age of 21 and is commemorated at Assisi War Cemetery in Italy. He was the son of Mr. and Mrs. Arthur W. Gerrand of Birtle, Manitoba. ***Gerrand Lake*** (64 K/1), north of Big Flat Lake was named after him in 1987.

Gerring, Pilot Officer **George W.** of Brandon (J 90925). No. 59 Squadron. He died 24 June 1944 at the age of 23 and is commemorated at Tamlaght Finlagan Church Of Ireland Churchyard, Londonderry, Northern Ireland. He was the son of David and Martha Gerring of Brandon. ***Gerring Lake*** (64 P/5), south of Nejanilini Lake was named after him in 1974.

Gertel, Private **Joseph** of Winnipeg (D 175522). North Nova Scotia Highlanders. He died 8 July 1944 at the age of 22 and is commemorated at Beny-sur-Mer Canadian War Cemetery in Calvados, France. He was the son of Israel and Miriam Gertel of Montreal. In a letter home he wrote:

> I must confess that I don't approve of your attitude to the army. Why should you be reluctant to joining [an] aircrew if you possibly can? You know damn well that the Jews have a great stake in the outcome of this war and I don't think that any of us should be hesitant in doing his share to the best of my capacity. I ... have no fears of being in [an] aircrew or in any dangerous branch of the service. I am looking forward to going overseas and am itching to get into the fight... I think each and every one of us ought to look at things that way. So why worry about being in [an] aircrew – after all (and I am sure that you will agree with me) there is something to fight for (30 May 1943).

He first enlisted with the artillery, but was later attached to the North Nova Scotia Highlanders prior to D-Day. His obituary added that:

> Gunner Gertel was born in Wodiwetz, Poland in 1921. He graduated from Baron Byng High School and the United Talmud Torahs. He was attending Sir George Williams College at the time of his enlistment, Gunner Gertel was a member of the Hashomer Hatzair (n.d.).

Gertel Lake (64 O/4), north of Egenolf Lake was named after him in 1995.

Geske, Rifleman **Gustave** of Camper (H 67511). Royal Winnipeg Rifles. He died 10 December 1945 and is commemorated at Brookwood Military Cemetery, Surrey, England. ***Geske Lake*** (64 J/7), southwest of Tadoule Lake was named after him in 1975.

Gibb, Private **Alexander** of Winnipeg (H 46412). Lake Superior Regiment. He died 6 December 1941 at the age of 40 and is commemorated at McCreary Cemetery in Manitoba. He was survived by his mother Annie Gibb of Aberdeen, Scotland. ***Gibb Lake*** (64 G/15), east of Little Sand Lake was named after him in 1995.

Gibbon, Trooper **Arthur W.** of Miniota (H 77706). 12th Manitoba Dragoons. He died 28 September 1941 at the age of 22 and is commemorated at Miniota Cemetery, Manitoba. He was the son of Mr. and Mrs. Hugh Gibbon of Miniota. ***Gibbon Lake*** (64 H/2), north of Holmes Lake was named after him in 1995.

Gibbons, Lance Corporal **Ernest W.** of Winnipeg (U 1857). Royal Canadian Engineers. He died 28 October 1944 and is commemorated at the Adegem Canadian War Cemetery in Belgium. He was survived by his father Edward W. L. Gibbons and by his wife Olive M. Gibbons of Winnipeg. ***Gibbons Lake*** (52 L/4), north of Brereton Lake was named after him in 1973.

Gibbons, Flight Sergeant **James R.** of Treherne (R 91886). No. 50 Squadron. He died 19 September 1942 at the age of 24 and is commemorated at Newark-on-Trent Cemetery, Nottinghamshire, England. He was the son of Thomas J. and Catherine Gibbons of Treherne, Manitoba. According to his niece (22 November 2001):

> I remember very little about my uncle. He had curly red hair and was a very kind and gentle man. I remember my Grandmother and Mother sending parcels to Uncle Jim and Grandmother would receive his letters. The day my Grandparents received the news, I saw my Grandma holding a picture of Uncle Jim and crying. I cried with her, not really knowing why. There was an older woman in England who would write to my Grandmother as she looked after my uncle's grave.

Gibbons Creek (53 M/14), which flows northeast into Duncan River was named after him in 1985.

Gibbs, Company Sergeant Major **Alexander L.** of Dauphin (H 41315). Royal Winnipeg Rifles. He died 30 March 1945 and is commemorated at Groesbeek Canadian War Cemetery, Holland. ***Gibbs Island*** (63 P/11) in Partridge Crop Lake was named after him in 1995.

Gibbs, Corporal **John T.** of Winnipeg (H 63509). Fort Garry Horse. He died 26 March 1943 and is commemorated at Brookwood Military Cemetery in Surrey, England. ***Gibbs Lake*** (64 G/16), southeast of Chipewyan Lake was named after him in 1995.

Gibson, Flying Officer **Gowan V.** of St. James (J 8415). No. 267 Squadron. He died 11 July 1943 at the age of 21 and is commemorated at Medjez-el-Bab War Cemetery in Tunisia. He was the son of Erling P. and Sophie Gibson and was survived by his wife Gwennie M. Gibson of Vancouver. She recalls (18 December 2001):

> Gowan spent his early years in Langruth, Manitoba. The family moved to St. James, a suburb of Winnipeg, where he graduated from high school. His father was a photographer, and the whole family - Gowan, his brother Orland and sisters Freda and Lois became involved in photography. When Ducks Unlimited was formed, Gowan became their first official photographer.
>
> He owned an Ariel 500 motorcycle which he loved to ride, and spent much of his spare time photographing his friends on Harley-Davidsons and Nortons performing at hill-climbs, sailing into space from the top of a hill. He spent his time in the Air Force attached to the RAF, fighting Rommel in Egypt, where his plane was shot down.

Gibson Lake (63 C/16), northeast of Swan Lake was named after him in 1977 and ***Gibson Point*** (53 L/8) in Webber Lake was named after him in 1995.

Gibson, Leading Aircraftman **Grant W.** of Winnipeg (R 116197). No. 12 Service Flying Training School. He died 8 July 1942 at the age of 21 and is commemorated at Brookside Cemetery in Winnipeg. He was the son of William H. and Jessie Gibson of Winnipeg. ***Gibson Island*** (64 C/8) in Granville Lake was named after him in 1995.

Gibson, Sergeant **Ralph P.** of Brandon (R 157276). No. 2 Air Observer School, RCAF. He died 29 October 1943 at the age of 23 and is commemorated at Brandon Cemetery. He was the son of John V. and Kate Gibson of Brandon and was survived by his wife Florence S. Gibson of Brandon. ***Gibson Peninsula*** (53 L/11) on Michikinabish Lake was named after him in 1995.

Gibson, Flight Sergeant **William Graham** of Winnipeg (R 86412). No. 10 Squadron. He died 20 July 1942 at the age of 21 and is commemorated at the Runnymede Memorial in Surrey, England. He was the son of Graham and Matilda Gibson of Winnipeg. His sister (30 November 1994) reports that he:

> ... had completed Grade 10 at Daniel McIntyre Collegiate in [the] early 1930s [but] my Dad's illness was such that he couldn't work any more. So Graham went to work as my sisters and I were doing. [He] had [a] few small jobs and then went to work for Lever Brothers. He rose to Office Manager and enlisted in the RCAF in January, 1941.
>
> [He] was stationed a several Manitoba towns and was awarded his Observer's Wings at Paulson, Manitoba in [the] fall of 1941 and went overseas to England [in] November 1941. His unit was attached to [the] RAF in England. He had completed one tour of duty and was on his second. His complete crew and plane disappeared over [the] North Sea on a bombing mission to Bremerhaven, Germany.

Gibson Bay (53 E/13) in Raven Lake was named after him in 1995.

Gidilevich, Flight Sergeant **Fred T.** of Dauphin (R 205426). No. 22 Operational Training Unit, RCAF. He died 28 May 1945 at the age of 21 and is commemorated at the Runnymede Memorial in Surrey, England. Gidilevich Lake (53 M/6), north of Oxford Lake was named after him in 1985.

Giesbrecht, Corporal **Frank** of Steinbach (H 42025). Royal Winnipeg Rifles. He died 16 April 1945 and is commemorated at the Holten Canadian War Cemetery in Holland. ***Giesbrecht Lake*** (64 N/2), southwest of Nueltin Lake was named after him in 1972.

Giffin, Flight Sergeant **Stephen G.** of Flin Flon (R 134457). No. 420 Squadron. He died 14 April 1943 at the age of 21 and is commemorated at Rocquigny Communal Cemetery, Ardennes, France. He was the son of Glen E. and Sue Giffin of Melfort, Saskatchewan. ***Giffin Lake*** (63 P/3), east of Sipiwesk Lake was named after him in 1968.

Gilbert, Flying Officer **Reginald C.** of Winnipeg (J 21298). No. 199 Squadron. He died 3 September 1943 at the age of 22 and is commemorated at Pornic War Cemetery, Loire-Atlantique, France. He was the eldest of the four children of David H. and Eva Gilbert of St. Vital. According to his sister (24 June 1995):

> He received his education at Windsor School and Glenlawn Collegiate. He always wanted to learn to fly and so joining the RCAF was his way to achieve that goal. As a young boy, he built airplane models as a hobby. He joined the air force at the age of 17, just before his 18th birthday. He was presented with his wings by His Royal Highness the Duke of Windsor 5 October 1941 at Claresholm, Alberta. He went overseas November 1941 and was shot down over France.

Gilbert Island (53 E/13) in Stevenson Lake was named after him in 1995.

Gilchrist, Flight Sergeant **David Ronald** of Miniota (R 152522). No. 77 Squadron. He died 26 May 1943 at the age of 25 and is commemorated at Heverlee War Cemetery, Leuven, Vlaams-Brabant, Belgium. He was the son of David and Margaret J. Gilchrist of Miniota, Manitoba. ***Gilchrist Bay*** (63 I/16) in Mowat Lake was named after him in 1995.

Gilchrist, Warrant Officer 1 **David R.** of Winnipeg (645). Winnipeg Repair Depot. He died 14 July 1944 at the age of 44 and is commemorated at Elmwood Cemetery in Winnipeg. He was the son of James and Margaret Gilchrist and was survived by his wife Charlotte M. Gilchrist of Winnipeg. ***Gilchrist Island*** (64 F/6) in Wells Lake was named after him in 1994.

Gildemaster, Corporal **Norman B.** of Gretna (R 162100). No. 2 Air Observer School, RCAF. He died 14 May 1944 at the age of 22 and is commemorated at Gretna Cemetery. He was the only son of Bernard and Minnie J. Gildemaster (née Piper) of Gretna, Manitoba. An Altona newspaper reported that he:

> ... was one of three airmen who lost their lives when their aircraft crashed before dawn Sunday morning May 14 in an isolated area near Barachois in the Gaspé Peninsula. The plane was one of three training aircraft which had been missing from the navigation school at the RCAF station in Charlottetown, PEI since May 13.
>
> Corporal Gildemaster was born in Winnipeg. He received his early education in Rosenort. Eight years ago, the family moved to Gretna and Norman attended the public school there, and in 1940-41 took his Grade 12 in the MCI. He took an active part in local sports including baseball and hockey, where he made himself beloved by all (31 May 1944).

Gildemaster Lake (52 L/6), northeast of Lac du Bonnet was named after him in 1973.

Gile, Sergeant **Ray J.** of Winnipeg (R 157466). No. 420 Squadron. He died 25 February 1944 and is commemorated at Ardennes American Cemetery, France. Sergeant Gile and his brother had grown up and enlisted in Winnipeg, but held dual citizenship. After joining No. 420 Squadron, he was asked to transfer to the USAF with a higher rank and pay but he was allowed to finish his tour of duty with his Canadian crew. While on a bombing raid over Germany, Sergeant Gile's aircraft was shot down and crashed with full bomb load near the village of Ostelheim. The Mayor was ordered to bury them as terrorists in the bomb crater. Contrary to orders, the German villagers gave them a formal burial and the Mayor addressed the participants as follows:

> My dear fellow citizens: At an unusual hour and under unusual circumstances, we are assembled here on our cemetery. Today, we meet not to mourn a fellow villager or a near relation, but the first common grave has been opened in our cemetery for the crew of seven men of an enemy plane.
>
> About the particulars of the deceased we know nothing as yet. What we know are but the names of an English or a Canadian Lieutenant Long and a Sergeant Major Cranley. The former presumably wanted to get out by means of a parachute which did not open. The latter was rescued with danger to life out of the burnt up plane in a completely unrecognizable state. Only two identification discs showing the name of a Canadian airman and John Gile were found. The names of the other three men are not known.
>
> The crew with their charge of bombs might easily have been fatal for our community if they had been shed over our village. Easily a common grave might have been opened for our inhabitants. I know that many people here, and certainly the leadership, reject a Christian and humane burial, but the prevailing majority of us Ostelheimers affirm it. We ourselves have sons of our community in the front and can sympathize with their parents, knowing how they would feel when they should learn that their sons were done away with as terrorists. Such a burial, as it actually has been ordered, would not give us any satisfaction.
>
> We are standing before this common grave with other feelings, it is true, than if they were our own people, but hatred certainly has to vanish in the face of Death. Every one of the deceased has a father and mother, perhaps also a wife and child in his native country, fretting in the same way as we do, for enemies by this action, but we simply act as Christians. If we would not act like this, we should not be a trifle better than those who know but hatred.
>
> We have now surrendered the seven men of the crew to the earth in our cemetery, not entirely without feeling and emotion and even tears in the face of Death. But let us all be thankful in this hour to our Lord that we have been spared from the charge of bombs, that very easily might have fallen on our village.
>
> As the deceased were probably members of a Christian creed, a Christian burial shall be apportioned to them which is now to be undertaken by our parson, the Reverend Helbling (Otto Gehring, Bürgermeister 1944).

Reportedly, "many inhabitants, particularly mothers, shed tears, probably in remembrance of their own sons" (Allison n.d.). ***Gile Lake*** (53 K/11), south of Edmund Lake was named after him in 1996.

Gillan, Lance Corporal **John J.** of Rorketon (H 103368). Hastings and Prince Edward Regiment. He died 23 May 1944 at the age of 23 and is commemorated at the Cassino War Cemetery in Italy. He was the son of James and Jessie Gillan of Rorketon, Manitoba. ***Gillan Lake*** (53 D/12), northeast of Lewis Lake was named after him in 1989.

Gillander, Warrant Officer 2 **David S.** of Elva (R 134421). No. 161 Squadron. He died 28 March 1944 at the age of 34 and is commemorated at Brookwood Military Cemetery in Surrey, England. He was one of the seven children of David and Catherine Gillander and was survived by his wife Myrtle E. Gillander (née Riddell) of Pierson, Manitoba and their two children. His widow, son and granddaughter (14 January 1998) report that:

> David loved farming and took a great interest in cattle, which started with the shipping of cattle to Winnipeg in the early 1940s. He farmed the home farm and continued in the cattle shipping business until he was accepted into the air force in the fall of 1941.
>
> David Gillander was a good friend to many and especially noted for his great personality. He enjoyed participating in community events, sporting events and reading books. His favourite event was the stage production of *The Gangster* where he played one of the gangster roles.
>
> Sergeant Gillander's interest in current events eventually led him to the Air Force where he trained at the Edmonton and Calgary wireless schools and at the B&G School at Paulson before going overseas with the Royal Canadian Air Force in May, 1943. He was stationed at Gibraltar as a Warrant Officer Class II Wireless Air Gunner then returned to England for the operations that ended fatally.

Gillander Lake (64 N/10), southwest of Nueltin Lake was named after him in 1972.

Gillespie, Flight Sergeant **Edward B.** of Winnipeg (R 133826). No. 160 Squadron. He died 26 October 1943 at the age of 22 and is commemorated at the Singapore Memorial. He was the son of Edward and Sarah M. Gillespie and was survived by his wife Barbara L. Gillespie of St. Vital. ***Gillespie Point*** (53 L/6) on Stewart Anderson Lake was named after him in 1995.

Gillespie, Rifleman **Glenn** of Winnipeg (H 103511). Regina Rifle Regiment. He died 10 October 1944 and is commemorated at the Adegem Canadian War Cemetery in Belgium. ***Gillespie Creek*** (63 O/14), which flows northeast into Rat River was named after him in 1975.

Gillespie, Lance Corporal **Hilton A.** of St. Vital (H 36832). 12th Manitoba Dragoons. He died 4 August 1944 at the age of 34 and is commemorated at Bretteville-sur-Laize Canadian War Cemetery in Calvados, France. He was the son of Archibald and Josie Gillespie and was survived by his wife Jean Gillespie of St. Vital. ***Hilton Gillespie Creek*** (64 I/2), which flows northwest into South Knife River was named after him in 1974. Commemorative Certificates for Lance Corporal Gillespie and seven fellow Manitoba Dragoons were issued c/o Herbert Nicholson, MM who explains:

> In 1946, the 12th Manitoba Dragoons returned from Europe, and with money from our Canteen Fund, furnished two wards in the Children's Hospital with a promise that as long as our Association lasts, we would continue to support the Children's Hospital Fund. Since 1946, we have contributed $1000.00 every year, with donations received from the members. Also, we had a plaque placed on the hospital's 2nd floor with names of our fallen comrades on one side and on the other side, the names of the departed comrades who have since passed away. This was done with the idea that one day the Regiment will again be together.
>
> Now this brings me to my request, that the Association's approximately 350 members, would after all your efforts to find next-of-kin, would like to become family and have the Name Certificate placed on the wall in the Children's Hospital in trust that if a next-of-kin comes forward, the Certificate would be handed over to them (16 December 1998).

Gillespie, Flight Sergeant **Hugh G.** of Winnipeg (R 95484). No. 405 Squadron. He died 14 November 1942 at the age of 31 and is commemorated at St. Columb Major Cemetery, Cornwall, England. He was the son of George M. and Ida J. Gillespie of Port Coquitlam, British Columbia. ***Gillespie Lake*** (52 L/5), east of Lac du Bonnet was named after him in 1973.

Gillespie, Sergeant **John** of Winnipeg (R 56637). No. 207 Squadron. He died 27 April 1943 at the age of 24 and is commemorated at Schoonselhof Cemetery in Antwerp, Belgium.

He was the son of Peter and Anne Gillespie of Toronto. ***Gillespie Bay*** (64 O/13) in Nueltin Lake was named after him in 1995.

Gillespie, Sergeant **William R.** of Winnipeg (R 196278). No. 8 Service Flying Training School. He died 23 March 1944 at the age of 21 and is commemorated at Elmwood Cemetery in Winnipeg. He was the son of Joseph L. and Johanna C. Gillespie of North Kildonan. ***Gillespie Island*** (64 C/2), east of McKnight Lake was named after him in 1995.

Gilliat, Lieutenant **Cecil R.** of Fort Garry. Lord Strathcona's Horse. He died 25 May 1944 at the age of 29 and is commemorated at the Cassino War Cemetery in Italy. He was the son of Edward C. and Blanche Gilliat and was survived by his wife Daisy M. Gilliat (née Douglas) of Fort Garry. A former Great West Life employee, he had enlisted in December, 1941 and went overseas in June, 1943. He was in North Africa the following December and reached Italy a month later. ***Gilliat Lake*** (54 D/6), south of Stephens Lake was named after him in 1996.

Gilliland, Rifleman **Alfred** of Winnipeg (L 28178). Regina Rifle Regiment. He died 4 July 1942 and is commemorated at Brookwood Military Cemetery in Surrey, England. ***Gilliland Lake*** (64 H/11), southeast of Small Lake was named after him in 1995.

Gilmore, Trooper **James A.** of Carberry (H 22022). British Columbia Tank Regiment. He died 2 May 1945 at the age of 22 and is commemorated at the Holten Canadian War Cemetery in Holland. He was the son of William and Jeannie Gilmore of Carberry. According to a friend (3 February 1997) who enlisted with him:

> Jim joined the Armoured Corps at Fort Osborne Barracks in January, 1944, took his basic training at Orillia and Advanced Training at Borden, Ontario. Upon completion of his training as a radio operator, he went overseas to England and then Europe where he joined the British Columbia Tank Regiment. Jim was killed ... when his tank was knocked out while the Division was clearing the highway ... *en route* to Oldenberg where the fighting stopped on the evening of May 7.
>
> I was in the Carberry Cemetery this summer and I found Mr. and Mrs. Gilmore's grave and on the back of the headstone the following was engraved:
>
> In Loving Memory
> *H22022 Tpr. Alexander James Gilmore*
> *Killed in Action May 2 1945*
> Aged 22 Years
>
> I mentioned this to some people in Carberry and they told me that Mr. and Mrs. Gilmore were concerned that when everyone was gone, there would be no record of Jim, so they arranged this which I thought was a lovely idea.

Gilmore Lake (52 E/14), southeast of Brereton Lake was named after him in 1974.

Gilmour, Pilot Officer **Gordon D.** of Winnipeg (J 5316). No. 4 Operational Training Unit, RCAF. He died 14 October 1941 at the age of 29 and is commemorated at the Runnymede Memorial in Surrey, England. He was the son of Dudley F. and Muriel C. Gilmour of Winnipeg. ***Gilmour Bay*** (64 N/7) in Tatowaycho Lake was named after him in 1995.

Gilmour, Leading Aircraftman **Wesley** of Brandon (R 134279). No. 7 Bombing and Gunnery School, RCAF. He died 18 September 1942 at the age of 31 and is commemorated at Brandon Cemetery. He was the son of Hugh and Eliza L. Gilmour of Brandon. ***Gilmour Island*** (64 I/15) in the Seal River was named after him in 1995.

Gimby, Private **Ronald G.** of Cartwright (H 100294). Princess Louise Dragoon Guards. He died 12 January 1945 at the age of 18 and is commemorated at the Cassino Memorial in Italy. He was the youngest of the four children of George B. and Anella M. Gimby of Killarney, Manitoba. His sister writes (6 November 2001):

> He enlisted 16 October 1943 [and] was in Brampton and Borden in 1943. He was transferred to Charlottetown, PEI in December of 1943. From there, he went overseas and notified us when he was in England with a letter. He was transferred to Italy in November, 1944 and killed in action. Ron has no known grave and his name is engraved ... on the memorial at Cartwright where he was raised.

Gimby Lake (64 J/2), southwest of Tadoule Lake was named after him in 1957.

Ginter, Private **Cornelius** of Plumas (H 28109). Royal Canadian Infantry Corps. He died 2 April 1945 at the age of 23 and is commemorated at Plumas Cemetery. He was the second of the 14 children of Isaac C. and Margaret Ginter of Plumas, Manitoba. According to his sister (25 November 1997):

> "Corny" as he was known to his family and friends loved to hunt and fish. He also enjoyed working out-doors. Corny never married. Corny died accidentally while in training at Camp Shilo.

His parents received this note shortly after his death:

> 1. Confirming our teletype of this date, it is with the deepest regret that I have been directed to inform you of your son's death at approximately 1500 hours on the 2nd of April, 1945, in the Battle Inoculation area of A-15, Canadian Infantry Training Centre, Shilo Camp, Manitoba.
> 2. Inquiries made of his Company Commander, his platoon commander and his fellow soldiers discloses the following information. On the 2nd of April, 1945, your son was in training on the Bullets and Bayonets course of the Battle Inoculation Area. In going over a fence, as he had been taught in training, he pushed his rifle over first, however, he caught one leg on the fence and as his leg came loose he fell forward, falling upon the bayonet. Immediate First Aid action was taken by members of his company. He was placed upon a stretcher and well covered up with blankets. The camp doctor and ambulance were sent for and your son made comfortable until their arrival. Shortly after the Doctor's arrival, at approximately 1600 hours, your son passed away.
> 3. Your son's death is a distinct shock to the men he was serving with. His self-discipline, good manners and Loyalty to the cause that he was serving is an outstanding example of Canadian youth. His friends, which would include the larger percentage of the Company he was training with, consider your son's death to be their own personal loss. His Company Commander and his platoon Commander have reported that Private Ginter's accidental death will be felt keenly by the whole Company with which he served.
> 4. Arrangements have been made for internment in Brandon, subject to your approval.
> 5. May we be advised at the earliest possible date, preferably by telephone ... in order to make the necessary arrangements and also for any further information that you may desire.
> 6. All applications regarding effects of the deceased should be addressed to the Administrator of Estates, Department of National Defence, Ottawa (2 April 1945).

Ginter Lake (64 B/12), southwest of Opachuanau Lake was named after him in 1981.

Girardin, Private **Edward Louis** of Winnipeg (H 8212). Seaforth Highlanders of Canada. He died 23 May 1944 at the age of 20 and is commemorated at the Cassino War Cemetery in Italy. He was the son of Edward J. and Marie Girardin of St. James and was the brother of Private Romeo Girardin (next entry). ***Girardin Lake*** (63 I/16), east of Cross Lake was named after him in 1973.

Girardin, Private **Romeo W.** of Ashern (H 22180). Algonquin Regiment. He died 28 February 1945 at the age of 19 and is commemorated at the Groesbeek Canadian War Cemetery in Holland. He was the son of Edward J. and Marie Girardin of Ashern and the brother of Private Louis Girardin (previous entry). ***Girardin Esker*** (63 I/16), west of Oxford Lake was named after him in 1995.

Girman, Sergeant **Lesa "Louis"** of Winnipeg (R 71250). No. 403 Squadron. He died 30 July 1941 at the age of 21 and is commemorated at Birmingham (Witton) Jewish Cemetery in Warwickshire, England. He was one of the six children of Joseph and Faith G. Girman of Winnipeg. ***Girman Point*** (64 H/8) on Hogg Lake was named after him in 1986.

Girouard, Flight Sergeant **Donald A.** of Somerset (R 101641). No. 42 Squadron. He died 22 September 1942 at the age of 24 and is commemorated at Dishforth Cemetery, Yorkshire, England. He was the son of David and Anne Girouard and was survived by his wife Lena Girouard of Winnipeg. ***Girouard Bay*** (63 N/12) in Sisipuk Lake was named after him in 1995.

Girouard, Warrant Officer 1 **Joseph E. G.** of Ile des Chênes (R 95332). No. 407 Squadron. He died 10 November 1943 at the age of 21 and is commemorated at the Runnymede Memorial in Surrey, England. ***Girouard Island*** (64 O/5) in Shannon Lake was named after him in 1995.

Gislason, Flight Sergeant **Magnus A. "Mike"** of Winnipeg (R 191413). No. 162 Squadron. He died 13 June 1944 at the age of 21 and is commemorated at the Runnymede Memorial in Surrey, England. He was the son of John H. and Eileen S. Gislason of Winnipeg. His sister Petrina writes (24 October 2001):

> While stationed in Iceland, my brother Magnus was able to visit his uncles, aunts and cousins when he had free time. Although his stay was cut short, he made the most of it by taking his fellow crew members out to ride Icelandic ponies and enjoying coffee and vinarterta. His Canso aircraft was lost while attacking an enemy submarine off Iceland. One of his young cousins, Gudmundur H. Gardarsson, admired Magnus so much that on learning of his death hid in the closet for a couple of days. Magnus was honoured by having a family member named after him.

Gislason Island (64 B/3) in Misinagu Lake was named after him in 1995.

Gislason, Rifleman **Robert M.** of Sandy Hook (H 16233). Royal Winnipeg Rifles. He died 6 June 1944 and is commemorated at Beny-sur-Mer Canadian War Cemetery in Calvados, France. He was the grandson of Mrs. Sigurlin G. Gislason of St. Boniface. ***Gislason Lake*** (64 P/9), east of Nejanilini Lake was named after him in 1974.

Gittins, Leading Aircraftman **Edward R.** of Winnipeg (R 196426). He died 26 January 1946 at the age of 23 and is commemorated at Brookside Cemetery in Winnipeg. He was the son of Thomas and Betsy Gittins of Winnipeg. ***Gittins Lake*** (63 P/2), northeast of Cotton Lake was named after him in 1996.

Gladish, Flying Officer **John J.** of St. Boniface (J 39988). No. 419 Squadron. He died 31 March 1945 at the age of 21 and is commemorated at Becklingen War Cemetery in Germany. ***Gladish Lake*** (63 J/3), east of North Moose Lake was named after him in 1973.

Gladu, Private **Leo P.** of St. Boniface (H 800129). Princess Patricia's Canadian Light Infantry. He died 3 April 1951 at the age of 19 and is commemorated at the United Nations Cemetery in Pusan, South Korea. According to a cousin (27 November 2001):

> Leo ... began his life as an underprivileged child born into a poor prairie family. His mother died when Leo was a young boy. Leo spent his young life looking for challenges and new adventures. He led a colourful life and while still a teenager, attempted to travel as much as possible. Leo sought to combine his desire to travel with his quest for adventure by joining the Canadian Armed Forces. His life was cut short while on duty serving his country during the Korean Conflict. Even in death, Leo was a blessing to his family. He provided financial assistance to his father via his military pension.

Gladu Lake (63 P/2), north of Wilkins Lake was named after this Korean War casualty in 1998.

Glasman, Private **Luverne H.** of Russell (H 18864). Queen's Own Cameron Highlanders. He died 21 February 1945 at the age of 32 and is commemorated at the Groesbeek Canadian War Cemetery in Holland. He was the son of Louis A. and Karoline M. Glasman and was survived by his wife Lillian A. Glasman of Russell, Manitoba. According to his wife (3 May 1996):

> He was born in Lafatte, Montana [and] came to Manitoba with his parents when he was six years old. The name Luverne was taken from a County Seat – a small town close to the border.

Glasman Lake (64 H/7), southeast of Solmundsson Lake was named after him in 1995.

Glass, Corporal **Ernest L.** of Winnipeg (H 128). Lord Strathcona's Horse. He died 9 March 1943 at the age of 21 and is commemorated at Brookwood Military Cemetery in Surrey, England. He was the son of Edwin W. and Christine M. Glass of Mount Royal, Quebec. ***Glass Lake*** (64 O/1), southwest of Nejanilini Lake was named after him in 1975.

Glass, Flight Sergeant **Ronald F.** of Kirkfield Park (R 180332). No. 102 Squadron. He died 10 July 1943 at the age of 20 and is commemorated at Florennes Communal Cemetery in Namur, Belgium. He was the son of Hilliard C. and Laura E. Glass of Kirkfield Park, Manitoba. ***Glass Island*** (64 N/1) in Egenolf Lake was named after him in 1987.

Glassco, Flight Lieutenant **Hugh S.** of Winnipeg (J 5131). No. 418 Squadron. He died 5 January 1945 at the age of 25 and is commemorated at Rheinberg War Cemetery in Germany. He was the son of John G. and Esther J. Glassco of Winnipeg. ***Glassco Lake*** (64 J/11), west of Tadoule Lake was named after him in 1974.

Glasspole, Gunner **Leslie G.** of Winnipeg (H 101366). Royal Canadian Artillery. He died 16 October 1944 at the age of 30 and is commemorated at Bergen-op-Zoom Canadian War Cemetery in Holland. His brother recalls (25 February 2002):

I can remember Les playing hockey each winter at the bottom of our street and in the summertime he could be seen riding his bicycle. He had many good friends and neighbours and never lacked someone to chum around with. Les must have had an inquiring mind as I remember one winter he dismantled the motor of Dad's 1929 Durant, but required assistance in putting it back together. I don't think Dad was too happy at the time.

One year, through a government-sponsored program, Les went to work on a farm for room and board and a small allowance. However, come spring, the farmer was unable to pay him in cash and instead, presented him with a pig (dressed of course). What a shock for Mom and Dad!

Les was apprenticing for a few years with a large printing firm to be a printer before he enlisted in the Army and went overseas. And the last time I saw him was the day before I left for Manning Depot in Toronto in the fall of 1941. Les was killed in Belgium.

Glasspole Lake (64 C/6), west of Granville Lake was named after him in 1972.

Glenn, Private **Harold J.** of Carman (H 20645). Queen's Own Cameron Highlanders. He died 19 August 1942 at the age of 21 and is commemorated at Dieppe Canadian War Cemetery in Seine-Maritime, France. ***Glenn Lake*** (64 I/10), northeast of North Knife Lake was named after him in 1974.

Glinz, Flight Sergeant **Donald F.** of Oak River (R 71415). No. 22 Squadron. He died 7 May 1942 at the age of 23 and is commemorated at the Runnymede Memorial in Surrey, England. He was the son of Arthur O. and Mabel A. Glinz of Oak River, Manitoba and was a cousin of Flying Officer Harvey S. Glinz (next entry). ***Glinz Lake*** (53 E/7), south of Island Lake was named after him in 1973.

Glinz, Flying Officer **Harvey S.** of Winnipeg (J 10212). No. 617 (Dam Buster) Squadron. The industrial installations and dams in Germany's Ruhr Valley had been seen as potential military targets even before the outbreak of the Second World War, but conventional bombing methods were not accurate enough to ensure success. The solution was to devise a "bouncing bomb" rotating at a speed of 700 RPM, released at precisely 360 miles per hour, 60 feet above the river. The bomb would bounce exactly 12 times over the defensive torpedo nets, sink to a depth of thirty feet at the base of the dams and then detonate. Nineteen crews were handpicked from all over the Commonwealth and the USA. Two dams were thus breached and an estimated 330 million tons of water was released into the valley destroying 125 factories and 25 bridges. Nearly half of the squadron failed to return and it became the most heavily decorated in RAF history. Flying Officer Glinz died 16 May 1943 at the age of 22 and is commemorated at the Reichswald Forest War Cemetery in Germany. He was the son of Ernest S. and Pearl E. Glinz of Winnipeg and was a cousin of Flight Sergeant Donald F. Glinz (previous entry). ***Glinz Bay*** (64 P/5) in Nejanilini Lake was named after him in 1989.

Glossop, Captain **Francis W. A.** Queen's Own Cameron Highlanders. He died 30 March 1945 at the age of 28 and is commemorated at the Groesbeek Canadian War Cemetery in Holland. He was the son of Walter H. and Margaret H. Glossop and was survived by his wife Beatrice Glossop. ***Glossop Lake*** (63 P/15), southeast of Witchai Lake was named after him in 1996.

Glover, Private **George R.** of Strathclair (K 50681). Seaforth Highlanders of Canada. He died 24 May 1944 at the age of 37 and is commemorated at the Cassino War Cemetery in Italy. He was the son of Benjamin and Mary Glover of Strathclair, Manitoba. Locally known as the coach of the girls softball team, he had found work in the mines in British Columbia when the war broke out. ***Glover Island*** (64 K/16) in Caron Lake was named after him in 1995.

Glover, Flight Sergeant **John** of St. James (R 56903). No. 102 Squadron. He died 7 September 1941 (his 25th birthday) and is commemorated at the Runnymede Memorial in Surrey, England. His aircraft was reported missing in the North Sea off the coast of Norfolk. He was the oldest of the five children of Samuel and Annie Glover of Winnipeg. According to his sister (30 November 1994):

... there's a lake named for him in northwestern Manitoba since 1974. I'm so sorry that his mother wasn't told of this; she always said she thought that she would feel better if she knew he had a resting place. All we know is that he's in the North Sea.

Glover Lake (64 P/14), northeast of Nejanilini Lake was named after him in 1974.

Gnutel, Private **Donald P.** of Menzie (H 601972). Lincoln and Welland Regiment. He died 29 April 1945 at the age of 25 and is commemorated at the Holten Canadian War Cemetery in Holland. He was the son of Harry and Kathrine Gnutel of Shoal Lake, Manitoba. His sister recalls (5 November 2001):

He grew up on the farm with four sisters and one brother; he was the second youngest. He was a quiet boy and very well liked by everyone. On the 29th April 1945, his parents got a telegram saying he was killed. On May 21st they got a letter saying that he was killed at Bad Zwischenahn in Germany by machine gun fire.

Gnutel Lake (64 J/8), south of Tadoule Lake was named after him in 1975.

Goddard, Gunner **Herbert** of Winnipeg (H 66579). Royal Canadian Artillery. He died 25 January 1945 at the age of 45 and is commemorated at Brookside Cemetery in Winnipeg. He was the son of Thomas and Lena Goddard of Brightside, Sheffield, England and was survived by his wife Jessie Goddard of Winnipeg. ***Goddard Island*** (53 M/5) in Utik Lake was named after him in 1996.

Goddard, Staff Sergeant **T. W. Sidney** of Winnipeg (H 95625). 11th Canadian Infantry Regiment. He died 2 September 1944 at the age of 23 and is commemorated at Montecchio War Cemetery in Italy. He was the son of Herbert and Jessie Goddard of Winnipeg and the husband of Muriel F. Goddard (née Bower) of Winnipeg. According to his wife (2 June 1996):

... I really didn't think anyone cared about the young men who gave their lives for our freedom. I will tell you all I know about Sid as we called him. He spent his life in the North End of Winnipeg. [The family] lived on Inkster Boulevard when I met Sid and they moved to 61 Lansdowne, I believe, in 1939. He went to Luxton, Machray and St. John's Technical High School. He started working at T. Eaton Company in the Warehouse Stove Department in 1939. He was later transferred to Eaton's on Portage Avenue in the Stove Department, 3rd Floor. He belonged to St. John's United Church. He was also associated with the Granada Speed Skating Club in the North End. He was a member of the Loyal Orange

Lodge 2311 (Friendly Lodge). Sid had a brother Douglas and sister Muriel (these two were twins). Sid's dad was in the RCA stationed at Shilo during the war.

An internal publication of the T. Eaton Company had the following to say about him:

Remember Sid Goddard? Sid was a typical Canadian boy ... high-spirited, carefree, clean and unafraid. He grew up in Winnipeg ... started to work at Eaton's ... married a girl from the mail order. As a salesman in the stove department his sunny smile won the hearts of all. Came the war ... Italy ... and Staff Sergeant Sidney Goddard in the thick of the fighting ... and then, on September 2nd, his lorry struck a Nazi mine on the roadside ... Sid was twenty-three.

Sid's best friend QMS [Fred] Burton wrote: He was my greatest friend and comrade. It is difficult to realize that I must go on without him. He rests with some of his comrades, of whom Canada's people can be proud!

And by the way, this photograph of Sid was his thoughtful way of showing his mother that he had received the pipe she had sent him to Italy.

Such is the price Sid Goddard paid ... the contribution of a gallant, loveable boy made to victory. It is for Canadian boys like Sid that we are asked again to buy Victory Bonds. To match his sacrifice with our dollars will certainly take the best we Eatonians can do, ALL we can do! "Buy one more Bond than before!" (T. Eaton Company Ltd. 18 October 1944).

According to Staff Sergeant Goddard's widow, when Sid's father received the news of his son's death, he died of a heart attack. ***Goddard Lake*** (64 I/15), north of North Knife Lake was named after him in 1974.

Godin, Private **Joseph Frederick** of Dauphin (703128). He died 28 November 1916 at the age of 34 and is commemorated at St. Sever Cemetery Extension, Rouen, Seine-Maritime, France. He was the third of the eight children of Joseph L. and Antoinette Godin (née Bercier). Private Godin was born in Three Rivers, Quebec and was working as a logger in Campbell River, British Columbia when he enlisted in December, 1915. ***Godin Creek*** (63 C/3), which flows northwest into the East Favel River was named after this World War I casualty in 1977. He had homesteaded in this area in 1902.

Godkin, Private **James C.** of Amaranth (H 1875). Lake Superior Regiment. He died 9 August 1944 at the age of 21 and is commemorated at Bretteville-sur-Laize Canadian War Cemetery, Calvados, France. He was the fifth of the nine children of William J. and Maggie M. Godkin of Ladysmith, British Columbia. His sister writes (28 November 2001):

Jim worked at farming in summer, ice fishing on Lake Manitoba and trapping in winter. He also worked in the copper mine at Berens River, Ontario. March, 1943, Jim joined the PPCLI ... in Winnipeg. [In the] fall of 1943, Jim went east, transferred to the Lake Superior Regiment and went overseas (6 December 1994).

While the four older brothers, Ed, Roy, Jim and Lorne were in training in the Army, the rest of the family moved to Saltair, Vancouver Island. Lenard joined the Army November 3, 1944 in Vancouver. When Jim had his last furlough in August, 1943, he travelled by train from Winnipeg to visit his family in BC. When Mum said goodbye, she felt it would be the last time she would see her son.

Lorne saw Jim March 30th, 1944 in Aldershot, England. The last time the three brothers Ed, Lorne and Jim met was in France. However, Ed saw Jim again in France 12 days after D-Day. Lorne saw Jim again just before Jim was killed at the Falaise Gap where the Canadian and British troops trapped a German armoured division. Years later, David travelled to France to find his brother's grave. He was overwhelmed by the number of white crosses – so many lads – 2791 Canadians are buried there.

Godkin Lake (63 J/12), east of Wekusko Lake was named after him in 1972.

Gohl, Flight Lieutenant **James G.** of Boissevain (J 8356). No. 440 Squadron, Air Medal. He died 12 June 1944 at the age of 24 and is commemorated at the Runnymede Memorial in Surrey, England. He was the son of Elijah and Philippa Gohl of Winnipeg.

Flight Lieutenant Gohl's aircraft crashed into the sea two miles southeast of Bournemouth, England after being damaged by flak while engaged on a bombing and strafing attack near Varaville, France. He bailed out but his parachute failed to open. He received his air medal for attacking a Japanese submarine and killing three of the sub's gun crews while flying with No. 111 Squadron off Alaska (Allison and Hayward 1991).

His brother recalls (30 November 2001):

Jim was two years older than I was and a great older brother. I remember him as quiet, well liked by his peers, and good in sports. He pitched on the school baseball team. He was a good student, an Isbister Scholar. Jim was born in Roland and at age eight he moved to Boissevain for the rest of his primary and his secondary education. He then attended the University of Manitoba for two years. He was well on his way to becoming a Chartered Accountant when he joined the Air Force. As a pilot, he served two tours in the US Army in the Aleutians, receiving the US Army Air Medal. Jim was mentioned in dispatches in the King's New Year List, January, 1944. He was leading his squadron in his second tour on a mission over France and on the way home went down in the English Channel. He died the day before his 25th birthday.

Gohl Lake (63 N/2), east of Kississing Lake was named after him in 1972.

Gold, Rifleman **David S.** of Pine Falls (H 16928). Royal Winnipeg Rifles. He died 8 June 1944 at the age of 26 and is commemorated at Beny-sur-Mer Canadian War Cemetery in Calvados, France. He was one of the five sons of Ernest S. and Beatrice E. Gold of Pine Falls, Manitoba. All served in the armed forces during World War II. He was the brother of Rifleman Ernest W. Gold (next entry). His brother recalls (26 May 1986):

David was born ... in Swan River, Manitoba and in July, 1926 the family moved to Pine Falls ... where Mr. Gold was involved in the construction of the paper mill. Dave enlisted in the PPCLI in Winnipeg and later transferred to the RWR. Following the D-Day invasion, David met his death in the "Kurt Meyer" infamy.

Gold Island (64 K/16) in Stevens Lake was named after him in 1989.

Gold, Rifleman **Ernest W.** of Pine Falls (H 82030). Royal Winnipeg Rifles. He died 16 February 1945 at the age of 21 and is commemorated at the Groesbeek Canadian War Cemetery in Holland. He was the youngest son of Ernest S. and Beatrice E. Gold of Pine Falls and was survived by his wife of four months Mary Gold (née Waldron) of Shropshire, England and their unborn son. After the war, she and her son moved to Pine Falls to live with their in-laws and later married Rifleman Gold's older brother George. Ernest was the brother of Rifleman David S. Gold (previous entry). ***Gold Point*** (64 K/16) in Stevens Lake was named after Rifleman Ernest Gold in 1989.

Gold, Corporal **Harold J.** of Bowsman River (H 26313). Fort Garry Horse. He died 14 August 1944 at the age of 28 and is commemorated at Bretteville-sur-Laize Canadian War Cemetery in Calvados, France. He was survived by his foster-father Herbert S. Gold of Swan River, Manitoba. ***Gold Bay*** (53 M/6) in Schwatka Lake was named after him in 1995.

Goldstone, Warrant Officer 2 **Vincent M.** of Brandon (R 106050). No. 228 Squadron. He died 13 June 1943 at the age of 25 and is commemorated at the Runnymede Memorial in Surrey, England. He was the son of Albert E. and Maude Goldstone of Brandon. According to his sister (3 July 1987):

Vincent was born ... in Brandon [and] joined the Air Force [there] in 1941. He took part of his training at the Manning Depot, Brandon and in Trenton, Ontario. Vincent went overseas in 1942 and was reported missing over the Bay of Biscay June 13, 1943. Six months later my parents were notified that Vincent was now presumed dead.

Goldstone Lake (64 P/12), west of Nejanilini Lake was named after him in 1974.

Gonroski, Flight Sergeant **Philip Felix** of Brandon (R 281969). No. 429 Squadron. He died 6 March 1945 at the age of 19 and is commemorated at Brookwood Military Cemetery in Surrey, England. He was the son of Tony and Frances Gonroski of Brandon. A childhood friend recalls (30 November 1989):

I went to school with F/S Gonroski for ten years. [He] completed Grade 11 at Moore Park – that was as far as Moore Park School went. He then went to Brandon and completed Grade 12. He joined the Air Force from there. F/S Gonroski's name is on the Minnedosa war monument, but it is spelled wrong; it is listed as Conroski with a "C" instead of a "G." My brother visited his grave in July, 1988. The cemetery is very well kept; all the crew are buried there. [H]e was a very dear friend.

His sister adds (18 November 2001):

Phil was born in Rivers, Manitoba on August 25, 1925 the only boy in the family of eight children. He took his Grade 12 at Brandon Collegiate. He was a good student and loved sports such as biking, skating, hockey and baseball. He loved to play his accordion and harmonica.

Soon after his 18th birthday, he enlisted in the RCAF and trained at several bases in Canada. On January 1, 1945 he was posted to 429 Bison Squadron at Leaming, Yorkshire. He went on his first operation March 1, 1945 as an air gunner on a Halifax 111 bomber; the target was Mannheim; this was a seven hour and twenty minute trip. His second mission was on March 2, 1945; the target was Cologne. His third mission was over Chemnitz in aircraft LV996. Upon returning to base in very heavy fog, the aircraft crashed near Halling, Kent and the entire crew were killed. In 1967, my husband and I visited Brookwood Cemetery.

Gonroski Lake (64 G/5), southeast of Big Sand Lake was named after him in 1994.

Good, Telegraphist **James H.** of Winnipeg (V 37733). HMCS *St. Croix*. The *St. Croix* was torpedoed and sunk by U-305 south of Iceland while escorting Convoy ON.202. Five officers and 76 men were rescued by HMS *Itchen*, but only one of these survived the loss of the *Itchen* two days later. See VanSickle, Ordinary Seaman Harold A. for additional information. Telegraphist Good died 20 September 1943 at the age of 21 and is commemorated at the Halifax Memorial. He was the son of Percy C. and Leah Good of Raith, Ontario. ***Good Lake*** (64 N/7), southwest of Nueltin Lake was named after him in 1972.

Goodall, Lieutenant **William B.** of Winnipeg. Queen's Own Cameron Highlanders. He died 19 August 1942 at the age of 28 and is commemorated at Dieppe Canadian War Cemetery in Seine-Maritime, France. He was the son of George and Iolanthe R. Goodall of Winnipeg and was survived by his wife Isobel M. Goodall of Winnipeg. ***Goodall Island*** (64 A/12) in Baldock Lake was named after him in 1995 and ***Goodall Lake*** (64 K/5), northeast of Reindeer Lake was named after him in 1972.

Goodburn, Sergeant **Wilfred** of Napinka (H 17155). Princess Patricia's Canadian Light Infantry. He died 16 February 1945 at the age of 23 and is commemorated at Argenta Gap War Cemetery, Italy. He was the son of John and G. Margaret Goodburn of Napinka, Manitoba. He had received mention in a newspaper article the previous autumn:

War takes a new turn when the enemy helps shoot up his own troops, but that is what happened after the Princess Patricia Canadian Light Infantry regiment routed the Germans out of Monte Santa Maria. German rearguards, mistaking some of their own stragglers for attackers, opened fire and helped the PPCLI and British troops wipe out more than 100 men. The stragglers, said Lieutenant John Koensgen, Winnipeg, commanding a PPCLI machine-gun platoon, were spotted fleeing up the valley between his regiment and Monte Godio which had been captured by the British.

It was too good a chance to miss. Platoons on the spot opened up with their own weapons while Vickers machine gunners under Corporals E. T. Douglas, Vancouver; J. E. Jennings, Coombs, Vancouver Island; Bill Goodburn, Napinka, Manitoba and Private A. S. Terry, Hamilton; pumped 14,000 rounds of ammunition into the Nazis. A field battery under Major Hervey B. Carswell, Vancouver and Ottawa, poured shells on them.

As Canadian fire became intense, German rearguard guns opened up, raining an agonizing fire on their own men. The stragglers then panicked right back into the fire of British troops. The actual number of dead was not known, but it was said to exceed 100 (25 September 1944).

Goodburn Lake (64 K/8), northeast of Reindeer Lake was named after him in 1972.

Goodchild, Corporal **William S.** of Winnipeg (H 16838). Argyle and Sutherland Highlanders. He died 3 March 1945 at the age of 27 and is commemorated at the Groesbeek Canadian War Cemetery in Holland. He was the son of George and Ida Goodchild of Oxbow, Saskatchewan. ***Goodchild Lake*** (64 J/4), southwest of Tadoule Lake was named after him in 1975.

Goodman, Pilot Officer **Benny B.** of Winnipeg (J 21746). No. 111 Squadron. He died 9 April 1943 at the age of 21 and is commemorated at the Ottawa Memorial. ***Goodman Lake*** (54 E/16), east of Bradshaw Lake was named after him in 1995.

Goodman, Private **Oscar** of Selkirk (H 64719). Winnipeg Grenadiers. He died 21 December 1941 at the age of 22 and is commemorated at the Sai Wan Memorial in Hong Kong. This native of Vestmannaeyjar, Iceland was survived by his parents Kristinn and Margaret Goodman of Selkirk, Manitoba. His parents did not receive confirmation of his death until July of 1945. His sister recalls (24 October 2001):

I had a letter from my brother written November 30, 1941. It was released in 1943. He said "don't worry about me, I am fine. My friend and I went out, there is much to see. We had to get back early, we are in the army now." He was talking about Christmas and how different it would be. But he did not see how different it would be as he was killed on December 21. I am sure he must have written letters to the rest of our family, but I have mine. The War Years were very sad years for all families of men that were killed and wounded.

Our brother was such a gentle person with tremendous patience – a brother to be proud of, a son so good to his parents. It was a sad day when we went to see our brother leave, as it was for all families. But they that served for Canada were so proud of the great country, a wonderful place to live.

Goodman Island (64 P/2) in Spruce Lake was named after him in 1989.

Goodmanson, Sapper **Johannes "Joe"** of Selkirk (H 82119). Royal Canadian Engineers. He died 12 September 1944 at the age of 27 and is commemorated at the Calais Canadian War Cemetery in France. He was the son of Mr. and Mrs. Gudrun Goodmanson of Selkirk, Manitoba. ***Goodmanson Lake*** (64 I/4), west of North Knife Lake was named after him in 1974.

Goodwin, Stoker 2 **George E.** of MacGregor (V 30924). HMCS *Avalon*, the Royal Canadian Navy shore establishment in St. John's, Newfoundland. He was awarded the Albert Medal for "supreme gallantry" in rescuing two women from the burning Knights of Columbus Hall in St. John's, Newfoundland in 1942 (Robinson 1996). He perished in the rescue. The Albert Medal was instituted by Queen Victoria in 1866 for gallantry on land or sea other than in the face of the enemy. He died 12 December 1942 at the age of 25 and is commemorated at Mount Pleasant Cemetery in St. John's, Newfoundland. He was the son of Everett and Florence E. Goodwin of Vancouver and was survived by his wife Mildred C. Goodwin of MacGregor, Manitoba. ***Goodwin Lake*** (64 B/4), southwest of Southern Indian Lake was named after him in 1969.

Goodwin, Private **Morris W.** (H 10962). Queen's Own Cameron Highlanders. He died 21 July 1944 at the age of 20 and is commemorated at Bretteville-sur-Laize Canadian War Cemetery in Calvados, France. He was the son of Clayton W. and Pearl M. Goodwin of Atikokan, Ontario. ***Goodwin Island*** (64 C/8) in Granville Lake was named after him in 1995.

Goodz, Gunner **Peter** of Portage la Prairie (H 92387). Royal Canadian Artillery. He died 16 February 1945 and is commemorated at the Groesbeek Canadian War Cemetery in Holland. He was survived by his mother Mrs. A. Goodz of Portage la Prairie, Manitoba. ***Goodz Lake*** (64 K/15), northeast of Lac Brochet was named after him in 1972.

Gordon, Sergeant **Bruce** of Winnipeg (R 152957). No. 82 Operational Training Unit, RCAF. He died 29 May 1944 at the age of 21 and is commemorated at Brookwood Military Cemetery in Surrey, England. He was the son of Robert B. and Georgina W. Gordon of Winnipeg. ***Gordon Island*** (63 N/10) in Flatrock Lake was named after him in 1995.

Gordon, Trooper **Frank R.** of Souris (H 26779). Fort Garry Horse. He died 6 June 1944 at the age of 24 and is commemorated at the Bayeux Memorial in Calvados, France. He was survived by his wife Gladys Eileen Gordon (née Patterson) of Souris. ***Gordon Island*** (64 O/4) in Egenolf Lake was named after him in 1975.

Gordon, Sergeant **James** of East Kildonan (R 59662). No. 11 Operational Training Unit, RCAF. He died 8 July 1944 at the age of 24 and is commemorated at Bassingbourn-cum-Kneesworth Cemetery, Cambridgeshire, England. He was the son of James and Christina Gordon of Winnipeg and was survived by his wife Ida M. Gordon (née Botterill) of Winnipeg. His brother-in-law writes (28 December 1994):

> James Gordon was born in East Kildonan on March 4, 1917. He attended Prince Edward School and East Kildonan Collegiate. After completing his schooling, Jim was employed as a printer at [the] J. H. Ashdown Hardware Company, Winnipeg. During this time, he met and fell in love with Ida Mary Botterill, also of East Kildonan. They were married on December 21, 1940.
>
> When war broke out, Jim, like so many sons of British immigrants, felt a duty to defend Canada and the country of his forefathers. He joined the RCAF in August, 1940 and began his flight training on Tiger Moths at EFTS Portage la Prairie. He soloed on January 6, 1941 and continued his training on Yales and Harvards at No. 6 SFTS Dunneville, Ontario. He graduated as a future fighter pilot on March 29, 1941 and was sent overseas.
>
> After arrival in England, Jim was switched from fighter training to bomber training at No. 11 OTU, Bassingbourn. He commenced training on Wellington bombers on June 23, 1941 and soloed on June 29, 1941.
>
> On July 8, 1941 at approximately 1:10 AM, Jim and his fellow airman, Sergeant Burnett crashed on a landing attempt. His widow, Ida M. Gordon passed away on January 7, 1994.

Gordon Bay (64 F/7) in Holiday Lake was named after him in 1995.

Gordon, Flying Officer **MacDonald S.** of Selkirk (J 21894). No. 199 Squadron. He died 3 September 1943 at the age of 23 and is commemorated at the Runnymede Memorial in Surrey, England. He was the son of William E. and Dorothea E. Gordon of Selkirk, Manitoba. ***Gordon River*** (64 P/8), which flows southeast into Caribou River was named after him and his brother Warrant Officer William F. Gordon (next entry) in 1974.

Gordon, Warrant Officer 2 **William F.** of Selkirk (R 66094). No. 7 Squadron. He died 10 November 1942 at the age of 27 and is commemorated at the Runnymede Memorial in Surrey, England. He was the son of William E. and Dorothea E. Gordon of Selkirk, Manitoba and was survived by his wife Maude E. Gordon of Selkirk. ***Gordon River*** (64 P/8), which flows southeast into Caribou River was named after him and his brother Flying Officer MacDonald S. Gordon (previous entry) in 1974.

Gorrie, Flying Officer **Charles G.** of Wawanesa (J 23996). No. 422 Squadron. He died 20 November 1943 at the age of 19 and is commemorated at the Runnymede Memorial in Surrey, England. He was the sixth of the seven sons of Charles C. and Evelyn Gorrie of Wawanesa, Manitoba. According to his elder brother (18 February 1998), he:

> ... attended school in Wawanesa and graduated with a Grade 12 Diploma. He worked a short time in the Wawanesa Mutual before entering the Royal Canadian Air Force.
>
> As you can imagine, a family of boys living in a small village alongside the Souris River would be a busy place. All of us took part in swimming, hunting, fishing, baseball, curling, hockey. Charles was good at them all. Hockey was his favourite and he was a star player on the midget team and later on the senior before he joined up.
>
> Music was another area where he excelled. In younger years he had a beautiful soprano voice. I remember all the talent concerts where we went together (I played the trombone in those days).
>
> Charles was a most personable young man, happy and outgoing and loved by his family and friends and everyone in our small village. He trained and graduated from No. 12 Air Training Base. He spent many hours visiting us in our home and we were sad to see him leave for overseas. This picture enclosed was taken as my Mother, Father and my wife were seeing him off to overseas from Winnipeg.

Gorrie Lake (64 P/6), east of Nejanilini Lake was named after him in 1974.

Gosselin, Private **Albert J. C.** of Winnipeg (H 101406). Princess Patricia's Canadian Light Infantry. He died 22 July 1943 and is commemorated at Agira Canadian War Cemetery in Italy. He was survived by his wife Ann Gosselin of Winnipeg. ***Gosselin Lake*** (64 K/6), northeast of Reindeer Lake was named after him in 1972.

Gosselin, Private **Louis J.** of La Broquerie (SL 4745). Royal Canadian Regiment. He died 22 June 1952 at the age of 23 and is commemorated at the United Nations Cemetery in Pusan, South Korea. ***Gosselin Bay*** (63 P/2) in Hermon Lake was named after this Korean War casualty in 1998.

Gosselin, Private **Roméo** of Winnipeg (H 2691). Queen's Own Cameron Highlanders. He died 12 April 1945 at the age of 24 and is commemorated at the Holten Canadian War Cemetery in Holland. He was the son of Philippe and Cora Gosselin of Winnipeg. ***Gosselin Island*** (63 I/2) in Molson Lake was named after him in 1988.

Gostling, Lieutenant Colonel **Alfred C.** of Winnipeg. Queen's Own Cameron Highlanders. He died 19 August 1942 at the age of 39 and is commemorated at Dieppe Canadian War Cemetery in Seine-Maritime, France.

> Meanwhile, Lt. Gostling had decided to postpone the Cameron's' landing [at Dieppe] ten minutes in order to give the Saskatchewans more time to clear the bridgehead through which the battalion was to pass. Navigational errors contributed to the delay when, a full 30 minutes late, the landing craft reached "Green Beach" led by a piper playing in full view of the enemy. The Commanding Officer, who encouraged his men on the run in, was killed as he leaped out on the shingle (Hunter 1982).

He was the son of Charles R. and Millicent Gostling of Toronto. His nephew writes (25 October 2001):

> "Alf" was my uncle and was born in England – probably in St. John's Wood, London. His older brother was Brigadier Guy S. N. Gostling. Guy was Honorary Colonel of the Toronto Scottish. Sometime in the early thirties, Alf and another fellow, Brock Windsor started a radio repair shop on Portage Avenue in Winnipeg. I believe the business still exists. Alf loved the outdoors and would spend weeks canoeing around the Manitoba north country. Just prior to going overseas, Alf was working on a large sail boat in Winnipeg. This boat was going to sail around the world. I don't know what happened to it. Alf was never married. Guy had three children who still live in Ontario.

Gostling Lake (63 P/13), northeast of Thompson was named after him in 1961.

Goszka, Flight Sergeant **Frank** of Winnipeg (R 59275). No. 8 Repair Depot, Winnipeg. He died 8 August 1944 at the age of 41 and is commemorated at Holy Ghost Cemetery in Winnipeg. He was the son of Frank and Verna Goszka and was survived by his wife Catherine Goszka of Winnipeg. ***Goszka Lake*** (64 O/14), east of Nueltin Lake was named after him in 1975.

Goulet, Private **Jean** of Richer (H 103961). Essex Scottish Regiment. He died 26 October 1944 and is commemorated at Bergen-op-Zoom Canadian War Cemetery in Holland. ***Goulet Island*** (53 E/15) in Island Lake was named after him in 1983.

Gow, Sergeant **George** of Winnipeg (R 210039). No. 9 Squadron. He died 23 May 1944 at the age of 20 and is commemorated at the Reichswald Forest War Cemetery in Germany. ***Gow Lake*** (52 M/13), northeast of Amphibian Lake was named after him in 1979.

Graafstra, Flying Officer **John W.** of Souris (39381). No. 242 Squadron, RAF. He died 23 May 1940 at the age of 27 and is commemorated at Wancourt Communal Cemetery, Pas de Calais, France. He was the son of Thomas and Sarah B. Graafstra of Souris, Manitoba. Flying Officer Graafstra had travelled to England in 1935 to study music, but enlisted in the RAF in December, 1936. When war broke out, he found himself flying Spitfires with No. 66 Squadron (Allison 1978). ***Graafstra Lake*** (53 N/10), northeast of Whitefish Lake was named after him in 1995.

Grabowski, Pilot Officer **Joseph** of Choiceland, Saskatchewan (J 47956). He died 4 November 1944 at the age of 27 and is commemorated at Woodlawn Cemetery in Nipawin, Saskatchewan. He was the son of Sam and Elsie Grabowski of Choiceland and was survived by his wife Jean L. Grabowski of Choiceland. ***Grabowski Lakes*** (64 N/12), north of Aniska Lake on the Manitoba - Saskatchewan border was named after him in 1968.

Grace, Private **Robert W.** of Winnipeg (H 6707). Winnipeg Grenadiers. He died 19 December 1944 and is commemorated at the Sai Wan Memorial in Hong Kong. He was the son of Mr. and Mrs. Harold P. Grace of Vancouver. ***Grace Island*** (64 C/8) in Granville Lake was named after him in 1995.

Graham, Sergeant **Alexander D.** of Winnipeg (H 24138). Royal Canadian Artillery. He died 7 September 1944 at the age of 28 and is commemorated at Montecchio War Cemetery in Italy. He was the son of Spence D. and Annie A. Graham and was survived by his wife Verna M. Graham. ***Alexander Graham Lake*** (64 A/16), south of Billard Lake was named after him in 1995.

Graham, Private **Carman B. "Stump"** of Neepawa (H 20178). Queen's Own Cameron Highlanders. He died 19 August 1942 and is commemorated at Dieppe Canadian War Cemetery in Seine-Maritime, France. He was the son of James and Eleanor Graham (née Birnie).

> Carman was born in Eden, Manitoba June 1, 1915 and received his education there. He worked at various jobs before enlisting with the Queen's Own Cameron Highlanders at Winnipeg in June, 1940. He arrived in England in December, 1940 and landed with his regiment for the Dieppe Raid on August 19, 1942. He was killed during these beach landings (Pittman n.d.).

Graham Hill (63 N/7), north of Burntwood Lake was named after him in 1995.

Graham, Rifleman **Cecil J.** of Minto (H 102663). Royal Winnipeg Rifles. He died 6 June 1944 at the age of 23 and is commemorated at Bretteville-sur-Laize Canadian War Cemetery in Calvados, France. He was the son of John and Theresa Graham of Minto, Manitoba. His sister-in-law (29 March 1995; 29 October 2001) reports that: "Cecil grew up on a farm with his parents and brother Harvey and was educated in a small country school called Dunallen. He enlisted in October, 1944 [and] was killed in action." ***Graham Rapids*** (64 I/15) on an unnamed river which flows into the Seal River was named after him in 1995.

Graham, Pilot Officer **Frederick George** of Oak Lake (J 88399). No. 207 Squadron. He died 16 July 1944 at the age of 21 and is commemorated at Lignieres-de-Touraine Communal Cemetery, Indre-et-Loire, France. He was the son of Joseph F. and Amy Graham of Oak Lake, Manitoba. Graham Lake (64 P/7), east of Nejanilini Lake was named after him in 1974.

Graham, Warrant Officer 1 **Harold R. "Gump"** of Dauphin (R 91900). No. 103 Squadron. He died 13 July 1943 at the age of 23 and is commemorated at the Runnymede Memorial in Surrey, England. He was the son of Mr. and Mrs. James Graham of Dauphin. According to his sister (19 May 1997): "He won a scholarship from Grade 11 and completed his Grade 12 with honours. He joined the Air Force the following February [1941]." ***Graham Peninsula*** (64 K/9) on Cantlon Lake was named after him in 1995.

Graham, Private **Jack E.** of Winnipeg (H 46086). Lake Superior Regiment. He died 31 October 1944 at the age of 23 and is commemorated at Bergen-op-Zoom Canadian War Cemetery in Holland. He was the son of Charles and Mattie A. Graham of Toronto. ***Jack Graham Lake*** (54 E/4), northwest of Embleton Lake was named after him in 1995.

Graham, Private **John A.** of Neepawa (H 19442). Queen's Own Cameron Highlanders. He died 19 August 1942 at the age of 42 and is commemorated at the Brookwood Memorial in Surrey, England. He was the son of Peter J. and Jennie Graham of Neepawa, Manitoba.

He was born in Neepawa, Manitoba January 11, 1900 and worked at various jobs until he enlisted with the Queen's Own Cameron Highlanders at Winnipeg September 11, 1939. He was killed during the Dieppe Raid August 19, 1942 while landing on the beach; his body was never recovered. His younger brother Peter with the same regiment, landed with him (Pittman n.d.).

John Graham Lake (64 B/8), west of Baldock Lake was named after him in 1995.

Graham, Corporal **John C.** of Winnipeg (H 19282). Queen's Own Cameron Highlanders. He died 22 July 1944 at the age of 26 and is commemorated at Bretteville-sur-Laize Canadian War Cemetery in Calvados, France. He was the only son of Mr. and Mrs. Harry Graham of Winnipeg. Corporal Graham had become engaged to be married while back in his native Scotland, but at the request of their parents, postponed the marriage until after the end of the war. ***Graham Esker*** (64 I/11), northeast of Quinn Lake was named after him in 1995.

Graham, Rifleman **John W.** of St. Vital (H 40925). Royal Winnipeg Rifles. He died 8 June 1944 and is commemorated at the Bayeux Memorial in Calvados, France. His execution by the SS shortly after D-Day sparked a war crimes investigation. ***Graham Bay*** (64 F/3) in Goldsand Lake was named after him in 1989.

Graham, Private **Johnston** of Winnipeg (H 20620). Queen's Own Cameron Highlanders. He died 26 October 1945 at the age of 24 and is commemorated at Elmwood Cemetery in Winnipeg. He was the son of Johnston and Betsie Graham of Winnipeg. ***Johnston Graham Island*** (53 E/16) in Island Lake was named after him in 1995.

Graham, Sergeant **Lewis R.** of Winnipeg (H 19542). Queen's Own Cameron Highlanders. He died 19 August 1942 at the age of 35 and is commemorated at Dieppe Canadian War Cemetery in Seine-Maritime, France. He was the son of Gordon M. and Florence R. Graham (née Mitchell). ***Graham Island*** (64 C/8) in Granville Lake was named after him in 1995.

Grahame, Flight Sergeant **John Howard J.** of Stonewall (R 106461). No. 1664 Heavy Conversion Unit, RCAF. He died 16 March 1945 at the age of 24 and is commemorated at the Runnymede Memorial in Surrey, England. He was the son of John E. and Elizabeth Grahame (née Brown) of Stonewall. His cousins recall (30 November 2001):

We were cousins, but Howard was much more like a brother to us. We grew up very close to each other in Stonewall. As a family, we were clearly bonded and had mutual feelings; we played together, discussed school and compared teachers, attended the same Sunday school, exchanged books, magazines, and catalogues, and revealed our heroes, our hopes and our dreams to each other.

Howard was scholarly, always an honour student and always wanted to know more about the big wide world around us. He studied and enjoyed photography and was an accomplished letter writer, interests which were enhanced by his time and service away from his home. He was a voracious reader and record keeper. He kept a detailed diary throughout his short life and continued with it while overseas. It is treasured by the family today. He was not overly athletic, but in high school, under the influence of a high school teacher named Harry Duckworth who played soccer actively in Winnipeg, became interested in the game and really enjoyed playing. He once expressed the wish to study geology and planned to attend a BC University, which in 1940, was the one that offered the courses which were not available in Manitoba.

Howard's mother Elizabeth died when he was fifteen and he took on added responsibilities early in life, helping his father John, and looking after his younger brother, Lloyd. He had a strong bond for his family and was very fond of older aunts and relatives of his parents, visiting them often.

He volunteered for service in the Air Force on September 4, 1939. He treated it as a job that had to be done before he could resume his interests and pursue his dreams. He initially had postings in Canada but was not content with this and kept applying for positions that would take him overseas. He eventually got his wish and was thrilled to become a Flight Sargent Air Gunner. He was soon flying bombing missions out of England, and went missing on such a mission.

One night in March, 1945, our mother and Howard's Aunt Susie were out walking and saw a brilliant shooting star cross the sky. She wondered to herself if that was Howard, and later it was confirmed that he went missing that night.

Grahame Point (64 O/15) on Blevins Lake was named after him in 1985.

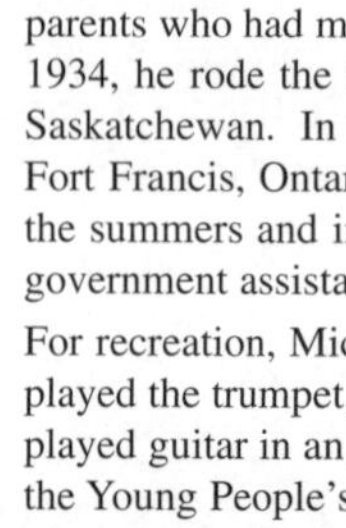

Grainger, Corporal **William A. "Mick"** of Beulah (H 6578). Winnipeg Grenadiers. He died 23 November 1944 at the age of 23 and is commemorated at the Yokohama War Cemetery in Japan. He was the son of Ezer and Ann Grainger of Beulah, Manitoba. According to his brother (4 February 1998):

Mick helped with the farm work, drove the school van, worked on neighbours' farms and went to Milestone, Saskatchewan the fall of 1933 to work before joining his parents who had moved to Beulah, Manitoba on September 23, 1933. In 1934, he rode the freights west to help with the harvest at Foam Lake, Saskatchewan. In the winter of 1935, he worked at a lumber camp near Fort Francis, Ontario. Mick continued to work on the farm at home in the summers and in the winter for farmers, getting five dollars a month government assistance.

For recreation, Mick enjoyed most sports, also hunting and fishing. He played the trumpet, guitar, mouth organ and chorded on the piano. Mick played guitar in an orchestra in Tilston and Beulah. He also belonged to the Young People's Group in Tilston and Beulah.

Mick joined the Winnipeg Grenadiers in the fall of 1939, taking his training in Winnipeg, Bermuda and Jamaica, returning to Canada in the fall of 1941. After a short leave home he was posted to Hong Kong, a British colony. Mick was wounded and taken prisoner of war.

Grainger Lake (63 I/7), north of Molson Lake was named after him in 1973.

Gramme, Corporal **William J.** of Winnipeg (H 50549). Royal Canadian Army Service Corps. He died 9 December 1944 at the age of 27 and is commemorated at Cesena War Cemetery in Italy. He was the son of Joseph T. and Ida M. Gramme and was survived by his wife Lillian L. Gramme of Winnipeg. ***Gramme River*** (64 B/2), which flows southeast into Leftrook Lake was named after him in 1972.

Granath, Fireman and Trimmer **David** of Winnipeg. SS *Keret*, Canadian Merchant Navy. The *Keret* was lost 22 August 1940. Fireman Granath was 45 years of age and is commemorated at the Halifax Memorial. He was the son of Gustave A. and Ida Granath of Vancouver. ***Granath Lake*** (63 P/9), north of Cauchon Lake was named after him in 2001.

Grant, Pilot Officer **Arthur G.** of Winnipeg (J 17223). No. 408 Squadron. He died 12 June 1943 at the age of 20 and is commemorated at the Rheinberg War Cemetery in Germany. He was the son of Dr. Keith G. and Marjory Grant and was survived by his wife Margaret Grant of Kirkcaldy, Fife, Scotland and their daughter. She writes (18 December 2001):

> Born in Montreal, he moved to Winnipeg in 1921 with his parents. He was educated at Montcalm and Hugh John Macdonald schools and Daniel McIntyre Collegiate. He played goal for the Winnipeg Rangers and the Winnipeg Monarchs and in 1939, came to Kirkcaldy, Fife, Scotland to play hockey for the Fife Flyers. During this period, he met my mother, Margaret Grant. Returning to Canada, he joined the RCAF in Winnipeg and was awarded his wings at Claresholm, Alberta in January, 1942. He then returned to Scotland and married my mother in September of that year. I was born August 1943, two months after my father was killed.

His Wing Commander wrote to his widow (in part):

> At approximately 10:50 PM on the night of the 11th instant "Art" (as he was known to the boys) and members of his crew took off from this Aerodrome to carry out operations over Düsseldorf, Germany but unfortunately, failed to return. He and his crew were due back at this Aerodrome at approximately 4 AM the next morning, but no news has been received from either the crew or aircraft since the time of take-off.
>
> It is with regret that I have to write to you this date to convey to you the feelings of my entire Squadron. The loss of your husband and other members of the crew is greatly felt by everyone in the Squadron. He was very popular with the boys especially in the Officers' Mess, where he was looked upon as "a good fellow."
>
> This war has caused grief to millions of people all over the world, and, it is a sorrowful state to know that so many fine young men must make great sacrifices in order to crush and erase from the face of the earth an infuriated enemy whose jealousy and hatred of our spirit and strength will eventually crush him and the members of his clique (13 June 1943).

Grant Bay (64 B/8) in Pakwaw Lake was named after him in 1995.

Grant, Flying Officer **John D.** of Winnipeg (J 11855). No. 45 Delivery Group, RCAF. He died 19 April 1943 at the age of 20 and is commemorated at the Ottawa Memorial. He was the son of John E. and Elizabeth M. Grant of Toronto. ***Grant Island*** (63 N/7) in Guthrie Lake was named after him in 1995.

Grant, Squadron Leader **John R.** of Winnipeg (40220). No. 115 Squadron, RAF, Mentioned in Dispatches. He died 12 May 1944 at the age of 29 and is commemorated at Wilsele Churchyard, Leuven, Vlaams-Brabant, Belgium. He was the son of Colonel C. R. and Beatrice L. Grant and was survived by his wife Ellena V. Grant of Oxford. ***Grant Point*** (54 D/15) on Little Cygnet Lake was named after him in 1996.

Grant, Flying Officer **William Angus** of Minnedosa (J 22204). No. 409 Squadron. He died 5 May 1943 at the age of 23 and is commemorated at the Runnymede Memorial in Surrey, England. He was the son of James M. and Hazel U. Grant of Minnedosa. His sister recalls (1 April 2002):

> Following high school where he was a Grade A student, he enrolled at the University of Manitoba in the Faculty of Science majoring in chemistry. He wrote to his mother that when he was in the science lab, he was in seventh heaven. However, it was a time of little money and few jobs, so on October 6, 1941, he enlisted in the Royal Canadian Air Force.
>
> At Ancienne Lorette, Quebec, he received his Navigator's Wings on August 28, 1942, standing second in his class. I travelled to Quebec to attend my brother's graduating ceremony and we returned together to Minnedosa for his last two weeks leave at home with his parents. In his memory, the family have endowed Minnedosa Collegiate with a scholarship called the William Angus Grant Memorial Award [for chemistry].

His mother wrote the following tribute:

In Memoriam

> And they cursed the god of battle who decreed that this should be in their time, but they never faltered. Many of these young men went missing and only the stars knew when and where or how they played their final scene on the grim stage of war. Through adversity to the stars was their motto and their creed, and near to the stars they met their end.

Grant River (53 M/9), which flows northeast into Stupart River was named after him in 1985.

Grant, Captain **W. Stanley.** of Portage la Prairie. Royal Canadian Engineers, Military Medal. He died 14 July 1945 at the age of 55 and is commemorated at Cataraqui Cemetery in Kingston, Ontario. He was survived by his wife Gertrude V. Grant of Portage la Prairie, Manitoba. ***Grant Creek*** (64 I/9), which flows northeast into North Knife River was named after him in 1974.

Grantham, Private **William Orville** of Sidney (H 77354). Winnipeg Grenadiers. He died 20 December 1941 and is commemorated at the Sai Wan Memorial in Hong Kong. ***Grantham Lake*** (64 I/5), southeast of Tadoule Lake was named after him in 1974.

Grassie, Flying Officer **Chesley R.** of Neepawa (J 39373). No. 44 Squadron. He died 11 November 1944 at the age of 22 and is commemorated at Stonefall Cemetery in Yorkshire, England. He was the son of Mr. and Mrs. Reginald Grassie of Neepawa.

> "Ches" as he was affectionately known by his pals, was educated in Neepawa Public School and Collegiate. He was employed in the Neepawa Post Office for a short time before taking a position with the local Canadian Bank of Commerce for a year and a half. He was transferred to Virden for a year before enlisting in the RCAF in September, 1942. He trained in Winnipeg, Brandon, Souris and Regina, rising to the rank of Flying Officer in a comparatively short time. In play as in work, "Ches" gave his best. He played on the collegiate hockey team. His clever, clean and gentlemanly conduct on the ice won the esteem of both players and fans (*Neepawa Press* 30 November 1944).

Grassie Lake (64 F/6), northwest of Wells Lake was named after him in 1994.

Gravel, Flying Officer **Louis Peter** of Norwood Grove (J 25273). No. 10 Squadron. He died 22 June 1945 at the age of 22 and is commemorated at Brookside Cemetery in Winnipeg. He was the son of Joseph W. and Rosa Gravel of Norwood Grove and was survived by his wife Margaret E. Gravel (née Ostrander) and their six month-old daughter. A newspaper obituary added that:

[He] was born at Terrebonne, PQ. He attended Queen Elizabeth and graduated from Norwood Collegiate in 1941. He enlisted in the RCAF early in 1942. After training at Brandon, Saskatoon and Virden, he received his wings at Dauphin. [He] was killed during a routine training flight at Pennfield Ridge, New Brunswick (n.d.).

Gravel Lake (63 J/3), east of North Moose Lake was named after him in 1973.

Graves, Rifleman **Raymond W.** of Mather (H 20717). Regina Rifle Regiment. He died 12 October 1944 at the age of 23 and is commemorated at the Adegem Canadian War Cemetery, Maldegem, Oost-Vlaanderen, Belgium. He was the son of William J. and Lydia J. Graves of Mather, Manitoba. His nephew writes (16 October 2001):

In the last week of September, 1944, the Allies held the city of Antwerp, but the Germans held both shores of the Scheldt Estuary so that the port of Antwerp could not be used. The task of clearing the southern shore of the estuary was allotted to the 3rd Canadian Division, aided by the 4th Canadian Armoured Division and the 52nd Division. The operations lasted from October until the beginning of November 1944; by 3rd November, the Germans had been cleared from the northwest corner of Belgium and the south shore of the Scheldt was free. There had been fierce fighting for two weeks for the crossing of the Leopold Canal. It was during this battle that Raymond was killed by a German sniper.

Five years later, the family received a letter from Belgium. In translation, it read:

This is after a large, patriotic ceremony in the Adegem Cemetery where your relative is buried. A religious service in English was held at Adegem. These pictures were taken on this occasion. As you know, our Society is interested in the regular visiting of the graves of Canadian soldiers. The tomb of your relative is one of these. We thought you would like to receive pictures of the Adegem ceremony. We assure you of our consideration for these very distinguished men (22 February 1949).

His last letter home was to his parents:

Hello Mother and Dad: Well here goes again. How is everything going over there? I hope you are well cause I haven't been feeling so good myself. I have had a cramp in the stomach for the last couple of days and that really raises hell with a man when he is working. I got a thousand smokes the other day and that sure helped a lot cause I have had to smoke English for a long time. There is a little of my mail catching up to me now. But I must have some more some place yet.

Ralph MacIntyre is up here now and I see him every once in a while. He told me of the old times he had back home and there is one of the Burns from Cartwright in the same section as I am in, so I hear a lot about the place. I guess I won't know nobody when I first get back there. I had a couple of letters from Belva. Lately she seems to be feeling OK. I guess it will be pretty quiet around home now that Loots has left.

How is the weather around there? It sure has been nice around here the last couple of days. Except for the odd chill, the land's pretty close. I suppose you are busy with the harvest around there. How are the crops this year? By the looks of things now, if they keep on going like we have, I might be back there for next fall.

I had a box of chocolates from Alice Munroe the other day. It sure didn't last long, but it sure was good while it lasted. I sure wish that I could BS so I could write a letter without all this trouble.

Have the girls been home much this summer? I guess Mae would be able to come home very often. I never heard from George for a hell of a long time. Well I guess I will close for this time. Hoping to hear from you soon. Love, Raymond (14 September 1944).

Graves Lake (64 N/10), southwest of Nueltin Lake was named after him in 1972.

Gray, Leading Aircraftman **Howard E.** of La Rivière (R 91905). No. 9 Repair Depot, RCAF. He died 4 July 1943 at the age of 38 and is commemorated at La Rivière Riverside Cemetery, Manitoba. He was the son of John S. and Annie Gray (née Charboneau) of Winnipeg and was survived by his wife Isobel Gray (née Moran) of The Pas and their daughter. His daughter reports that he was an avid writer and photographer and used both media to record his travels in northern Manitoba. On a trip from Ilford to Gods Lake he wrote:

The northern lights were out in all their colours and the night was real mild. Nothing much happened the first night, so I was on duty at five bells. The trail winds through tall spruce, some of them forty feet high. The land is nothing but moss, muskeg and rock – quite a combination don't you think?

This sure is wonderful country up here. And then one wonders what is wonderful about it – perhaps the scenery. There is nothing but a mine … now and then a few fur-bearing animals. I noticed quite a few peculiar formations of trees and rocks. We enter the jackpine now. It is a little lighter in colour than the spruce and there are odd groves of birch. The lakes are dotted with small islands, very thickly wooded and solid rock. I saw a few birds and fox running across the ice. Later on a plane flew over our heads. What a contrast in travel. We take two days, they take two hours. The trip being about 135 miles, but would be much shorter if not so crooked.

We leave Knee Lake and have a fifteen mile portage before getting to Gods Lake. We stopped for dinner and shortly after on the lake we passed the horse train (32 horses) from Gods Lake headed for Ilford. It was quite a sight, each outfit waving "good-day" and "good luck" and "farewell," not knowing each other (1935).

Gray Hill (64 I/1), east of South Knife Lake was named after him in 1995.

Gray, Bombardier **James C.** of Winnipeg (H 15045). No. 2 Heavy Anti-Aircraft Regiment, Royal Canadian Artillery. He died 7 January 1945 at the age of 24 and is commemorated at the Calais Canadian War Cemetery in France. He was the son of James A. and Doris Gray and was survived by his wife Lillian M. Gray of Edgware, Middlesex, England and their two children. His sister recalls (23 October 2001):

I was five years younger than my brother, but he used to take me to the movies (mostly scary ones) and also occasionally roller skating. Jimmie signed up when war was declared and he was at a vocational training camp in Marchand, Manitoba in September, 1939 when he received a letter telling him he was on active Battery strength and to report to Minto Armouries in Winnipeg. His outfit was sent overseas in July, 1941.

Jimmie loved sports and was on the boxing, football and basketball teams at Camp Petawawa. He married in England on June 3, 1942. His wife Lillian (Sonnie) Marriott was a gunner with the British 459th Anti-Aircraft Division. They had two children, Sonia Gail born June 25th, 1943 and James Frederick born October 7, 1944. Jimmie was serving in Holland when his son was born. His family was onboard ship on their way to Canada when he died. They arrived in Winnipeg in January, 1945 and spent a couple of years there before returning to England. Our Dad also served overseas with the Royal Canadian Artillery in World War I.

James Gray Rapids (64 A/11) in the Rasp River was named after him in 1995.

Gray, Corporal **James W.** of Winnipeg (H 101049). Lake Superior Regiment. He died 2 March 1945 at the age of 28 and is commemorated at the Groesbeek Canadian War Cemetery in Holland. He was the son of James W. and Jessie Gray of St. James. ***Gray Island*** (64 F/6) in Wells Lake was named after him in 1994.

Gray, Private **John A.** of Langruth (H 17704). Winnipeg Grenadiers. He died 13 December 1941 at the age of 20 and is commemorated at the Sai Wan Memorial in Hong Kong. He was the son of Robert and Isobel Gray. Private Gray was part of a contingent assigned to the Chinese mainland. When they were overrun, many tried to retreat to the main island. Private Gray and a friend were unsuccessful and became among the first of the Hong Kong casualties. ***John Gray Lake*** (53 N/3), northwest of White Goose Lake was named after him in 1995.

Gray, Private **John F.** of Gilbert Plains (H 18238). Queen's Own Cameron Highlanders. He died 26 February 1945 at the age of 20 and is commemorated at the Groesbeek Canadian War Cemetery in Holland. He was the son of Alfred G. and Elva M. Gray of Gilbert Plains, Manitoba. ***Gray Creek*** (64 N/8), which flows north into Seman River was named after him in 1995.

Gray, Flight Lieutenant **Kenneth M.** of Winnipeg (C 10383). No. 405 Squadron. He died 10 August 1943 at the age of 29 and is commemorated at Florennes Communal Cemetery, Florennes, Namur, Belgium. He was the son of William H. and Mollie A. Gray of Medicine Hat, Alberta. ***Gray Esker*** (53 L/1), east of Rochon Lake was named after him in 1995.

Gray, Flight Sergeant **Peter Richie** of Brandon (R 140935). No. 1664 Heavy Conversion Unit, RCAF. He died 2 December 1943 at the age of 25 and is commemorated at Stonefall Cemetery in Yorkshire, England. He was the son of Charles C. and Annabella Gray of Brandon. His brother recalls (30 November 1993):

> ... [he] was born on a farm three miles northwest of Brandon, Manitoba. He attended a rural school called Bloomsbury School. The teacher taught all grades from one to nine. Peter attended the Brandon Collegiate where he completed Grades 10 and 11. Before joining the Air Force in 1942, he worked at the Dominion Experimental Farm and lived at home during this time.
>
> I remember growing up with my older brother Peter, who certainly loved life and enjoyed many sports, such as horseback riding, skiing, swimming, cycling, fishing, hunting and baseball.

Gray Lake (64 G/4), northeast of Grandmother Lake was named after him in 1994.

Gray, Sergeant **Robert L.** of Lundar (H 41196). Royal Winnipeg Rifles. He died 8 June 1944 at the age of 36 and is commemorated at Bretteville-sur-Laize Canadian War Cemetery in Calvados, France. He was the son of Robert and Pearl Gray and was survived by his wife Hilda A. Gray of Winnipeg. ***Gray Peninsula*** (64 K/16) on Burnie Lake was named after him in 1995.

Gray, Craftsman **Robert M.** of Winnipeg (H 65005). Royal Canadian Electrical and Mechanical Engineers. He died 21 July 1944 at the age of 21 and is commemorated at Brookwood Military Cemetery in Surrey, England. He was the son of William H. and Sadie C. Gray of Winnipeg. ***Gray Rapids*** (64 N/5) on an unnamed river which flows into Kilpatrick Lake was named after him in 1995.

Gray, Warrant Officer 2 **William R.** of MacGregor (R 91855). No. 419 Squadron. He died 18 February 1943 at the age of 26 and is commemorated at the Runnymede Memorial in Surrey, England. He was the son of William R. and Elizabeth Gray of Winnipeg. ***Gray Bay*** (64 O/13) in Nueltin Lake was named after him in 1995.

Green, Corporal **Albert R.** of Brandon (H 6129). Winnipeg Grenadiers. He died of an illness 24 February 1942 at the age of 31 while in a prisoner of war camp and is commemorated at the Sai Wan War Cemetery in Hong Kong. He was the son of Robert and Viola Green and was survived by his wife Jennie L. Green of Edmonton. ***Green Point*** (64 I/5) on Legary Lake was named after him in 1995.

Green, Flight Sergeant **Hans A.** of Carman (R 147218). No. 467 Squadron. He died 23 September 1943 at the age of 32 and is commemorated at Durnbach War Cemetery in Bavaria, Germany. He was the son of Bodil A. and Bertal Green and was survived by his wife Veronica S. Green of Regina. ***Green Peninsula*** (64 N/8) on MacMillan Lake was named after him in 1995.

Green, Sergeant **William H.** of Churchill (R 225224). No. 432 Squadron. He died 2 December 1943 at the age of 32 and is commemorated at the Berlin 1939 - 1945 War Cemetery in Brandenburg, Germany. He was the son of Benjamin and Emily E. Green of Grimsby, Lincolnshire, England and was survived by his wife Mary Green (née Kasulratiak Ollybuk) and their two daughters. Titeraqti, as he was locally known, came to Canada from Lincolnshire as a seaman in 1930. He worked as a farm hand in the Boissevain area before becoming a trapper and clerk for the Hudson's Bay Company at Eskimo Point in the Northwest Territories. In 1938, he attempted to join the RCAF, but was put on a waiting list, so he joined the Engineers instead when war was declared. While in England, he transferred to the RCAF. ***Green Rapids*** (64 P/10) in the Caribou River was named after him in 1995.

Greenaway, Private **William J.** of Winnipeg (H 20189). Queen's Own Cameron Highlanders. He died 19 August 1942 at the age of 28 and is commemorated at Dieppe Canadian War Cemetery in Seine-Maritime, France. He was the fourth child of Thomas and Rachel Greenaway who had emigrated from Northern Ireland in 1905. He had originally enlisted with the Royal Winnipeg Rifles, but transferred to the Camerons while waiting for them to mobilize. While in England receiving training in commando tactics, he was able to visit his grandmother in Belfast. ***Greenaway Lake*** (63 J/16), east of Setting Lake was named after him in 1972.

Greenberg, Signalman **Hymie** of Winnipeg (H 38860). Royal Canadian Corps of Signals. He died 19 December 1941 and is commemorated at Stanley Military Cemetery, Hong Kong. ***Greenberg Lake*** (64 O/9), west of Nejanilini Lake was named after him in 1995.

Greengrass, Flight Sergeant **Roy S.** of Transcona (R 106204). No. 1659 Squadron. He died 10 March 1943 at the age of 19 and is commemorated at Ripon Cemetery in Yorkshire, England. He was the son of John H. and Mary H. Greengrass of Transcona. ***Greengrass Lake*** (64 N/10), southwest of Nueltin Lake was named after him in 1972.

Greening, Private **Albert** of Winnipeg (H 5088). Royal Canadian Artillery. He died 6 October 1944 at the age of 28 and is commemorated at Gradara War Cemetery in Italy. He was survived by his wife Barbara M. Greening. ***Greening Lake*** (64 O/2), northwest of Tadoule Lake was named after him in 1975.

Greenlay, Aircraftman 2 **Wallace B.** of Winnipeg (R 210475). No. 5 Bombing and Gunnery School, RCAF. He died 24 July 1943 at the age of 19 and is commemorated at Brookside Cemetery in Winnipeg. He was the son of Francis O. and Jensine Greenlay of Winnipeg. ***Greenlay Lake*** (53 D/6), south of Apisko Lake was named after him in 1979.

Greenwood, Ordinary Telegraphist **Clifford H.** of St. Vital (V 9888). HMCS *Trillium*. While on convoy duty in the North Atlantic on 12 April 1941, the *Trillium* was attacked by enemy aircraft resulting in three casualties. O/T Greenwood was 19 years of age and he and the two other sailors are commemorated at Sandwick Cemetery in Scotland's Outer Hebrides where they lie side by side facing the sea. His sister observed that there were 37 wreaths for these three boys – 22 from the people of Stornaway and 15 from their shipmates. His brother visited the grave in 1979. He was the son of Christopher H. and Helena M. Greenwood of St. Vital. His sister recalls that (3 April 1995):

> He was an A-student throughout his schooling and graduated in senior matriculation from St. Norbert Boys' School in 1939, crossing the Red River on the St. Vital ferry to attend. Clifford loved the outdoors and excelled in such sports as hockey, baseball and swimming. He studied piano and violin and played at numerous concerts in St. Norbert.
>
> After completing his Grade 12, Clifford enrolled in the radio course being offered by Russell Business Institute in Winnipeg. He joined the Navy at HMCS *Chippawa* in Winnipeg in the spring of 1940 and after further training in Halifax, was assigned to the new Canadian-built Corvette HMS (later HMCS) *Trillium*. The *Trillium* was the first of these Corvettes to cross the Atlantic, leaving in December of 1940.
>
> While the *Trillium* was undergoing completion in Scotland including the outfitting of guns, Clifford enjoyed shore leave with relatives in Blackburn, Lancashire.

A later officer of the *Trillium*, W. Ralph Moxley of London, Ontario recently gave Telegraphist Greenwood's older brother the ship's White Ensign for safekeeping. Following are some excerpts from some of his letters home to his brother:

> I'm getting on good in classes – this week so far I've got two 100% and one 99%. There were 960 English boys in the building (from the Royal Navy) for three days. They came over to bring back some of the destroyers given to Britain by the U.S. in exchange for air and sea bases. The English fellows left this morning. They sure were interesting to listen to. They talked about "air-raids," "blackouts," "Blackpool." The destroyers were brought here by American crews – there certainly were a lot of American sailors roaming around for a couple of days.
>
> The Governor General, the Earl of Athlone, was in Halifax and toured the dockyards and inspected all the sailors. He sure is a tall, good-looking fellow. The Minister of Defence or something was here today looking about.
>
> There are mouth organs, guitars and squeeze-boxes playing in different parts of the dorm. Lots of the boys are writing letters, others singing *Home, Sweet Home, Sweet Adeline* etc., others ironing their suits (9 September 1940).
>
> I'm still getting in the 90s, but the theory gives me a headache. The dope that is supposed to teach us just reads out of a book and explains nothing – I guess he doesn't know much anyway. I'm hoping to learn my theory by reading my book at night. It sure is a tough course. We're in our sixth week of it already and it is only a 12-week course.
>
> A week ago there were about 30 or 40 reporters and newspapermen from the United States come to Halifax. They looked over all us sailors and took pictures. Boy! We really have a wonderful band here. It is the best military band in Canada.
>
> About being lonesome – I was at first but not now. I will admit it would be swell to see all the folks at home again, but I like it here. I don't exactly miss you, but it would be swell if you were with me.
>
> P.S. I have a professional photo of Joe Spouler if you need one. He lived in St. Vital, joined the Air Force and lost his life as an air gunner. Others I can think of are the Tod twins of St. Vital and Sandy Hinds of Winnipeg. They were all Air Force as well (1 October 1940).

His brother adds (14 October 2001):

> Greenwood Avenue in St. Vital was named for my brother Cliff. I believe he was the first in St. Vital to lose his life in the war, or at least, in the Navy.

Greenwood Island (64 H/5) in Wood Lake was named after him in 1995.

Grenon, Able Seaman **Albert J.** of Somerset (4467). HMCS *St. Croix*. The *St. Croix* was torpedoed and sunk by U-305 south of Iceland while escorting Convoy ON.202. Five officers and 76 men were rescued by HMS *Itchen*, but only one of these survived the loss of the *Itchen* two days later. See VanSickle, Ordinary Seaman Harold A. for additional information. Able Seaman Grenon died 20 September 1943 at the age of 19 and is commemorated at the Halifax Memorial. He was the son of Joseph and Ida Grenon (née Filteau) of Somerset, Manitoba and the brother of Flight Sergeant Alfred J. Grenon (next entry). According to his sister (10 November 1997):

> ... [he] was born ... in Dumas, Saskatchewan. The parents and family of four moved to Radville, Saskatchewan shortly thereafter. His father ... was killed in a car-train accident in October, 1928. His mother remarried three years later and the family moved to Neepawa where the step-father taught school. In the later thirties, the family moved to Somerset, Manitoba. It was from here that Albert enlisted in the Royal Canadian Navy in 1940/41.

Grenon Lake (64 H/1), west of Hogg Lake was named after him in 1995.

Grenon, Flight Sergeant **Alfred J.** of Neepawa (R 119705). No. 428 Squadron. He died 22 May 1943 at the age of 25 and is commemorated at Dishforth Cemetery, Yorkshire, England. He was the eldest of the five children of Henry J. and Ida M. Grenon (née Filteau) and was survived by his wife Rosalie L. Grenon (née Barnes) of Neepawa and their young daughter whom he never saw. He was the brother of Able Seaman Albert J. Grenon (previous entry). According to his sister (10 November 1997):

> He received his elementary education at St. Oliver School in Radville, Saskatchewan where the family had moved from Dumas in the mid-twenties. At the age of 11, Alfred lost his father in a car-train accident. The tragic event affected "Fred" very deeply. In October, 1931, his mother remarried, and with her family moved to Neepawa, Manitoba. There Fred furthered his education until he lost interest in formal education and went to work at the Neepawa Flour Mills. He married Rosalie Barnes from McCreary, Manitoba. A little boy, Gary, was born from this marriage but lived only a few hours. The tragedy was a heartbreak for the young parents. World War II broke out in the fall of 1939 and Fred, then in his early twenties, joined the RCAF. He went overseas in November or December of 1942 as a wireless operator and air gunner stationed at Dishforth airbase. A daughter, Rosemarie, was born in June, 1943.

Grenon Island (64 N/8) in Shannon Lake was named after him in 1995.

Gresham, Major **Albert B. "Burt"** of Winnipeg. Winnipeg Grenadiers. He died 19 December 1941 and is commemorated at the Sai Wan Memorial in Hong Kong. According to a contemporary newspaper account:

> He was one of the leading authorities on wild life in the dominion and made many expeditions in search of rare kinds of birds and animals in the Grants Lake area and other parts of Manitoba. His outstanding photographs of geese and other birds, which appeared in the *Free Press* and in United States and Canadian magazines, were recognized as among the finest examples of their kind. Employed as both a cameraman and reporter on the *Free Press*, he pioneered in recording the development of aviation in Manitoba and made many flights with bush pilots engaged in rescue flights and other operations. On one occasion, he travelled for a considerable distance, standing on the wing of a plane in the flight, in order to get a photograph.
>
> He joined the staff of the *Free Press* in August, 1925, serving in the circulation department first for four years, becoming district manager. In 1929 he joined the editorial department as a reporter, showing a keen interest in aviation and becoming an expert in this field. He was noted for the kindly way in which he would show younger reporters the ropes.
>
> He was an expert outdoorsman, being able to find his way through the bush by the aid of the stars alone and frequently camping in the wilds during his natural history expeditions. He was happiest when following the geese in their migrations or flying over new territories.
>
> From the very first when the news of the grim fighting at Hong Kong came in, the people who knew Burt had a feeling that he would have been among the men who gave their lives, because he was the type of man who would fight to the end and never give up (*Winnipeg Free Press* January 1943).
>
> A hundred Manitoba families have received messages in the past few days addressed to the next-of-kin of members of the Winnipeg Grenadiers who were killed at Hong Kong or who are still missing. It is more than a year, now since Hong Kong fell and these families have gone through an agony of suspense, waiting even for the last, sad word.
>
> Among both officers and men killed at Hong Kong are many of the finest of the regiment. Every authentic report from observers who escaped records the fact that the Winnipeg Grenadiers and the Royal Rifles of Quebec put up a magnificent fight against hopeless odds. The story of Hong Kong is a tale of tragedy relieved only by the greatest heroism. The sympathy of this province goes out to all these Grenadier families of Manitoba.
>
> These men died nobly – all of them. All deserve honour. All their families merit the deepest sympathy. We of *The Tribune* believe that we will not be misunderstood if we single out two names for special mention. We wish to offer the deepest sympathy to our contemporary the *Winnipeg Free Press*, upon the death of Major Burt Gresham – a fine newspaper man, a true gentleman and a brave soldier. His attachment to his paper was all the closer since his widow is a member of the craft and is on the news staff of the *Free Press* (*The Winnipeg Tribune* 6 January 1943).

According to a contemporary newspaper account, he was shot while carrying a flag of surrender in an effort to save the lives of the men still with him (*The Winnipeg Tribune* September 1945). He was survived by his wife Margaret Gresham (née Marr) and by his mother Mrs. J. Gresham of Winnipeg. ***Gresham Lake*** (54 E/13), east of North Knife Lake was named after him in 1964.

Grevstad, Flying Officer **Melvin C.** of Winnipeg (J 24640). No. 463 Squadron. He died 18 March 1944 at the age of 23 and is commemorated at Durnbach War Cemetery in Bavaria, Germany. He was the son of Peter A. and Anna Grevstad. His brother writes (28 October 2001):

> My brother Melvin delivered groceries for Anderson's Food Store in Morse Place. One severe winter night, he returned home with both his ears solidly frozen. My parents used snowballs to aid in the process of reducing the pain and swelling.
>
> Prior to him heading overseas, he received his commission and had to acquire officer's garb – that was a rush job. A few days before leaving, he took me and my younger brother Bill downtown on the streetcar for a meal. He asked which restaurant. We both named the Exchange Cafe. We could have whatever was on the menu. We both chose liver and onions. For dessert we had our first Banana Split. That image is still strong in our minds and hearts.

Grevstad Lake (64 N/5), southwest of Nueltin Lake was named after him in 1972.

Grierson, Private **Hugh L.** of Winnipeg (H 6800). Winnipeg Grenadiers. He died 20 December 1941 and is commemorated at the Sai Wan Memorial in Hong Kong. ***Grierson Lake*** (52 L/11), northwest of Black Lake was named after him in 1982.

Grieve, Flying Officer **John M.** of Shoal Lake (J 22270). No. 427 Squadron. He died 21 December 1943 at the age of 23 and is commemorated at the Hanover War Cemetery in Germany. He was the son of John S. and Rena A. Grieve of Shoal Lake, Manitoba. His sister reports that before the war, his hobbies included mechanics, hunting, writing poetry and baseball. He was reported missing while on an operational flight over Frankfurt. His sister recalls (6 November 2001):

> As John grew from adolescence to manhood, it became obvious that this boy turned man was not to be trifled with. He became a mainstay of the operation of the family farm in its every day management. He excelled as head mechanic for farm machinery and in the use of farm animals. His fierce devotion to family and our collective love for him was evident in our daily lives. The many accomplishments of John included his passion for writing, his caricature drawings and his poems. Not to be omitted was his mischievous side that was the foundation of many of his practical jokes and humorous poems he composed complete with cartoons.

Grieve Lake (53 E/7), south of Island Lake was named after him in 1973.

Griffin, Private **Charles R.** of Winnipeg (148008). Canadian Machine Gun Corps. He died 26 September 1916 at the age of 23 and is commemorated at Courcelette British Cemetery at Somme, France. He was the son of Patrick and Nellie Griffin of Winnipeg and the husband of Alice M. Griffin (née Russell) of Winnipeg. He had been working as a clerk when he enlisted in August, 1915. ***Griffin Lake*** (63 G/12), north of Brackon Lake was named after this World War I casualty in 1985.

Griffith, Pilot Officer **Allan George** of Winnipeg (J 15231). No. 156 Squadron. He died 16 April 1942 at the age of 21 and is commemorated at Vlissegem Churchyard, De Haan, West-Vlaanderen, Belgium. He was survived by a wife. ***Griffith Lake*** (64 H/16), south of Condie Lake was named after him in 1995.

Griffiths, Pilot Officer **Charles A.** of Selkirk (J 18920). No. 426 Squadron. He died 3 January 1944 at the age of 21 and is commemorated at the Runnymede Memorial in Surrey, England. He was the son of Walter S. and Gladys V. Griffiths of Selkirk, Manitoba. ***Griffiths Lake*** (64 P/13), north of Nejanilini Lake was named after him in 1974.

Griggs, Private **Frederick T.** (H 16043). Princess Patricia's Canadian Light Infantry. He died 30 August 1940 at the age of 33 and is commemorated at Harrold (St. Peter and All Saints) Churchyard, Bedfordshire, England. He was the son of James and Ada Griggs. ***Griggs Lake*** (63 J/13), north of Wekusko Lake was named after him in 1972.

Grimble, Flying Officer **Henry** of Sturgeon Creek (J 36370). No. 433 Squadron. He died 17 August 1944 at the age of 20 and is commemorated at the Kiel War Cemetery in Germany. He was the third child of Sidney and Florence Grimble of St. James. This was his thirteenth mission and he was scheduled for leave the next day. His sister recalls (24 November 1995) that the family:

> ... lived in Ontario for six years, returning to Manitoba in 1936, settling permanently on a large lot at 167 Oakdean Boulevard, Sturgeon Creek, St. James. There were always animals around – cats, dogs, ponies, one cow and chickens. Henry loved the animals and he and his brother had the job of looking after them. Though a confirmed Anglican, Henry attended St. Paul's College for high school. He taught himself to play the piano by ear, but never had a lesson.
>
> Henry worked at the Royal Bank of Canada from age 16 to shortly after he enlisted in the Royal Canadian Air Force. He trained at Mossbank and Portage la Prairie, graduating as a navigator from the Portage base in October, 1943. He liked the Air Force and made many friends. Particular friends were three English airmen who trained with him at Portage. He went overseas immediately after graduation. He loved his family and wrote cheery, interesting letters home to all of them. His father (who won a Military Cross in the war of 1914 – 1918) and mother were born in England and he had many aunts, uncles and cousins there. Before going overseas, he said to his mother: "When I come back should I be a doctor or a minister?" So he didn't intend to return to banking.

On his final mission (to Kiel), his plane was shot down and crashed into the ocean. Five months later his remains washed ashore in Germany. ***Grimble Lake*** (64 H/16), west of Wells Lake was named after him in 1994.

Grimes, Private **Warren** of Winnipeg (H 3024). Princess Patricia's Canadian Light Infantry. He died 20 July 1942 at the age of 20 and is commemorated at Brookwood Military Cemetery in Surrey, England. He was the son of William and Gertrude Grimes and was survived by his foster-mother (aunt) Eliza Shanks of Winnipeg. ***Grimes Lake*** (64 J/12), west of Tadoule Lake was named after him in 1972.

Grimsdick, Flight Sergeant **Edward O.** of Winnipeg (R 71255). No. 152 Squadron. He died 27 October 1941 at the age of 19 and is commemorated at the Runnymede Memorial in Surrey, England. He was the son of Oliver V. and Florence Grimsdick of Winnipeg. ***Grimsdick Lake*** (64 P/11), east of Nejanilini Lake was named after him in 1974.

Grisdale, Flying Officer **Robert J.** of Winnipeg (R 89832). No. 433 Squadron. He died 10 April 1945 at the age of 22 and is commemorated at the Berlin 1939 - 1945 War Cemetery in Brandenburg, Germany. He was the son of Robert C. and Alice M. Grisdale of Winnipeg. ***Grisdale Lake*** (64 N/5), southwest of Nueltin Lake was named after him in 1972.

Grodecki, Pilot Officer **Joseph** of Erickson (J 85550). No. 405 Squadron. He died 23 April 1944 at the age of 20 and is commemorated at Conde-sur-Aisne Communal Cemetery, Aisne, France. He was the son of Mr. and Mrs. Mike Grodecki of Erickson. His obituary read in part:

> Joining the RCAF in 1942, Sergeant Grodecki trained at Brandon, Trenton and Macdonald where he graduated as an air gunner in June, 1943. He arrived overseas in July and went on active service almost immediately. After making 14 trips over enemy territory, he transferred to another arm of the RCAF from which he was reported missing. Sergeant Grodecki attended Erickson schools and prior to enlisting in the air force, he was employed in the box factory in Winnipeg (n.d.).

Grodecki Lake (64 O/12), south of Nueltin Lake was named after him in 1975.

Gronbeck, Sergeant **Norman** of Winnipeg (R 251698). No. 50 Squadron. He died 25 July 1944 at the age of 19 and is commemorated at Pontchateau Communal Cemetery, Loire-Atlantique, France. He was the son of Anders and Olive Gronbeck of Hudson, Ontario. ***Gronbeck Lake*** (64 P/16), northeast of Nejanilini Lake was named after him in 1978 and ***Gronbeck Island*** in northern Ontario was named after him in 1987.

Gross, Rifleman **Bernard B.** of Morden (H 41255). Royal Winnipeg Rifles. He died 6 June 1944 and is commemorated at Beny-sur-Mer Canadian War Cemetery in Calvados, France. He was survived by his mother Mary Gross of Morden, Manitoba. ***Gross Lake*** (54 M/5), southwest of Long Lake was named after him in 1984.

Gross, Lieutenant **Henry J.** of Winnipeg. Royal Winnipeg Rifles. He died 13 September 1944 at the age of 26 and is commemorated at the Calais Canadian War Cemetery in France. He was the son of Joseph F. and Barbara Gross and was survived by his wife Margaret A. Gross of Winnipeg. ***Gross Island*** (53 L/2) in Muche Lake was named after him in 1995.

Grossman, Sail Maker **Samuel** of Winnipeg (V 71410). HMCS *Cornwallis*. He died 30 July 1945 at the age of 31 and is commemorated at Shaarey Zedek Cemetery in Winnipeg. He was survived by his sisters Clara, Jennie and Beatrice of Winnipeg. ***Grossman Lake*** (64 N/8), southwest of Nueltin Lake was named after him in 1972.

Groves, Private **George H.** of Winnipeg (H 16927). Princess Patricia's Canadian Light Infantry. He died 14 July 1943 at the age of 23 and is commemorated at Enfidaville War Cemetery in Tunisia. He was the son of Henry and Lillian Groves and was survived by his wife Betty I. M. Groves of Haslemere, Surrey. ***Groves Island*** (63 N/3), in Kississing Lake was named after him in 1972.

Groves, Private **Gordon** of Winnipeg (H 100742). Princess Patricia's Canadian Light Infantry. He died 23 May 1944 at the age of 20 and is commemorated at the Cassino War Cemetery in Italy. He was the son of Henry and Lillian Groves of Dominion City, Manitoba. ***Groves Island*** (63 N/3), in Kississing Lake was named after him in 1972.

Grozik, Private **Mark P.** of Shortdale (H 9174). Canadian Scottish Regiment. He died 8 June 1944 at the age of 20 and is commemorated at Bretteville-sur-Laize Canadian War Cemetery in Calvados, France. Private Grozik was the son of Nicholas and Tillie Grozik of Shortdale, Manitoba. He was born near Kenora, Ontario where his father worked on the construction of the Backus-Brooks Paper Mill. They subsequently relocated to Chicago where Mr. Grozik was employed with the Chicago-Minneapolis-St. Paul Railroad, finally returning to the original homestead in Shortdale. It was here that the young Mark received his education. His brother recalls that his favourite pastimes were hunting, fishing and debating. He worked in the family business until enlisting 18 April 1943. He was killed in action during the Normandy invasion. ***Grozik Lake*** (52 L/11), southeast of Flintstone Lake was named after him in 1984.

Grundy, Captain **Howard** of St. Boniface. Queen's Own Cameron Highlanders. He died 20 July 1944 at the age of 26 and is commemorated at Bretteville-sur-Laize Canadian War Cemetery in Calvados, France. Captain Grundy and a friend took a jeep to rescue three of their wounded comrades whom the Medics had been unable to reach. On their return trip "all hell broke loose and all five were killed by concussion" (Ms. Joyce Grundy 1995). He was the son of Samuel and Jane Grundy of Winnipeg and was survived by his wife Catherine A. Grundy (née Beaton) of River Heights and their young son. His sister recalls (10 December 1994) that he:

> ... started school at Glenwood School [in] St. Vital, later went to King George V in Norwood and Norwood Collegiate Institute (now Nelson McIntyre Collegiate). There is a Memorial Plaque there with all the names of the Norwood boys who were killed in World War II. He also went to Success Business College.
>
> Howard enlisted with the Queen's Own Cameron Highlanders, transferred [and] had Commando Training in Courtney, BC. He was away on a tour of duty when the Grenadiers were sent to Hong Kong. He then transferred back to the Camerons; he wanted to serve overseas. He went overseas to join the Camerons in September, 1942. He spent some time lecturing officers in commando tactics at Sandhurst.
>
> He married Catherine Beaton September 7, 1940 at St. Philip's Church [in] Norwood. He had been a member there for most of his life [and] had been in Boy's Choir and other activities at the church.

Grundy Lake (64 K/14), northeast of Reindeer Lake was named after him in 1972.

Guay, Flying Officer **Gérard J.** of Winnipeg (J 47530). Royal Canadian Air Force. He died 19 February 1945 at the age of 24 and is commemorated at Brookwood Military Cemetery in Surrey, England. He was the son of Philippe and Alexandrine Guay and was survived by his wife Helen E. Guay of Winnipeg. He was the brother of Sergeant Lucien Guay (next entry). ***Guay Hill*** (63 N/1), southeast of Craik Lake was named after him in 1995.

Guay, Sergeant **Lucien P.** of Winnipeg (R 177647). No. 1 Central Navigation School, RCAF. He died 5 October 1943 at the age of 21 and is commemorated at St. Boniface Cemetery in Winnipeg. He was the son of Phillippe and Alexandrine Guay of Winnipeg. He was the brother of Flying Officer Gérard Guay (previous entry). One of his brothers, Joseph P. Guay later became a Member of Parliament and Senator. ***Guay Lake*** (63 N/1), southeast of Sherridon was named after him in 1970.

Guest, Flight Sergeant **George W.** of Stonewall (R 162319). No. 100 Squadron. He died 24 December 1943 at the age of 20 and is commemorated at Cambridge City Cemetery in Cambridgeshire, England. He was the eldest son of Oliver W. and Clara Guest of Stonewall, Manitoba. His brother writes (23 December 1997):

> You must realize that I was a twelve year-old when he went off to war overseas. In spite of my youth at that time and the passage of 54 years since his death, I still have a clear memory of my brother as a happy fellow who tried to make the best of things.
>
> George was born at Petersfield, Manitoba, the first son of Oliver and Clara Guest who married after Oliver returned from the First World War. Oliver Guest was awarded the Military Cross for bravery during the Battle of the Somme. In 1933, the Guest family moved to the farm north of Stonewall, Manitoba. George attended Stonewall Collegiate and graduated at age 18. His ambition was to study veterinary medicine and practice in rural Manitoba. These plans were put on hold when he joined the Royal Canadian Air Force in 1941.
>
> After training in western Canada and receiving his Bombardier's Wings in 1942, George was sent overseas in early 1943. He was killed in a mid-air collision near Cambridge, England ... and the family was notified of his death on December 26th.
>
> We were about to sit down at the dinner table when a local man named Dave Jackson came to the door with a telegram. I remember that my mother and father and myself knew immediately what the telegram would say. Dave was known to undertake the sad duty of taking similar messages to others in the Stonewall area.
>
> My brother George is buried in a well cared for civilian cemetery on the western outskirts of Cambridge. My wife and I visited the grave in the 1960s.

Guest Creek (64 P/8), which flows east into Gordon River was named after him in 1974.

Guest, Lieutenant **Robert** of Winnipeg. Lord Strathcona's Horse. He died 26 January 1945 at the age of 25 and is commemorated at Brookwood Military Cemetery in Surrey, England. He was the son of George C. and Ada B. Guest of Winnipeg. ***Guest Lake*** (64 K/13), northeast of Reindeer Lake was named after him in 1972.

Gugins, Sergeant **Clarence W.** of Winnipeg (R 191070). No. 1664 Heavy Conversion Unit, RCAF. He died 24 February 1944 at the age of 22 and is commemorated at Stonefall Cemetery in Yorkshire, England. He was the son of Herbert and Ruth Gugins of Winnipeg. Prior to enlisting he had been employed by the Picardy Candy Company. ***Gugins Lake*** (64 P/3), southeast of Nejanilini Lake was named after him in 1974.

Guiboche, Rifleman **Lawrence R.** of Camperville (H 42018). Royal Winnipeg Rifles. He died 8 June 1944 at the age of 21 and is commemorated at Beny-sur-Mer Canadian War Cemetery in Calvados, France. He was the son of William and Flora Guiboche of Camperville and was survived by his wife Cecilia Guiboche of Camperville. ***Guiboche Lake*** (62 N/15), southeast of Swan River was named after him in 1973.

Guiboche, Leading Aircraftman **Victor J. A.** of St. Laurent (R 121263). Royal Canadian Air Force. He died 22 March 1944 at the age of 30 and is commemorated at Mount Pleasant Cemetery in St. John's, Newfoundland. He was one of the 12 children of Toussaint and Rosalie Guiboche of St. Laurent, Manitoba. His youngest sister recalls (Goranson 1997): "Victor was 17 years older than me, but I remember he was so good to me, so kind. I still feel so sad when I think of losing him. He was my big brother and he was so special." ***Guiboche Island*** (53 L/12) in Windy Lake was named after him in 1995.

Guick, Private **Matt** of Riding Mountain (H 10618). Canadian Scottish Regiment. He died 7 October 1944 at the age of 23 and is commemorated at the Adegem Canadian War Cemetery in Belgium. He was the son of Tom and Vera Guick of Riding Mountain. ***Guick Lake*** (64 O/10), northwest of Nejanilini Lake was named after him in 1975.

Gulbis, Private **Charles J.** of Fork River (H 64531). Royal Canadian Ordnance Corps. He died 17 September 1944 at the age of 45 and is commemorated at Brookwood Military Cemetery in Surrey, England. He was the son of Chris and Olga Gulbis of Fork River, Manitoba. ***Gulbis Lake*** (64 H/3), west of Settee Lake was named after him in 1995.

Gunn, Company Sergeant Major (Warrant Officer 2) **Charles Allan** of Winnipeg (H 19900). Maisonneuve Regiment. He died 16 August 1944 and is commemorated at Bretteville-sur-Laize Canadian War Cemetery in Calvados, France. He was survived by his wife Ethel Gunn. ***Gunn Bay*** (64 N/15) in Putahow Lake was named after him in 1995.

Gunn, Signalman **Charles B.** of Winnipeg (H 38687). Royal Canadian Corps of Signals. He died 29 September 1944 and is commemorated at Cesena War Cemetery in Italy. ***Gunn Point*** (64 F/3) on Goldsand Lake was named after him in 1994.

Gunn, Private **Charles G.** of West Kildonan (H 19405). Queen's Own Cameron Highlanders. He died 19 August 1942 and is commemorated at Dieppe Canadian War Cemetery in Seine-Maritime, France. He was the son of Donald and Louisa Gunn of West Kildonan. ***Gunn Island*** (64 C/4), northwest of Choquette Lake was named after him in 1995.

Gunn, Corporal **George** of MacGregor (H 60489). Canadian Army. He died 24 August 1943 at the age of 38 and is commemorated at Woodstock Baptist Cemetery in Ontario. He was the son of John and Jessie Gunn of Wick, Caithness, Scotland and was survived by his wife Elizabeth E. Gunn of MacGregor, Manitoba. ***Gunn Hill*** (64 N/6), northwest of Choquette Lake was named after him in 1995.

Gunn, Sergeant **John C.** of Roland (R 86323). No. 13 Operational Training Unit, RCAF. He died 15 December 1941 at the age of 35 and is commemorated at Royal Oak Burial Park in Victoria, British Columbia. He was the son of James T. and Maggie G. Gunn of Goresbridge, Midlothian, Scotland. ***Gunn Peninsula*** (64 J/9), in Tadoule Lake was named after him in 1975.

Gunn, Private **John J.** of Winnipeg (H 6884). Winnipeg Grenadiers. He died 29 December 1941 at the age of 24 while a prisoner of war and is commemorated at the Sai Wan War Cemetery in Hong Kong. He was the son of Alfred and Emma Gunn of Fort William and was survived by his wife Muriel A. Gunn (née Randall) of Winnipeg. ***Gunn Rapids*** (64 I/13) in the McKay River was named after him in 1995.

Gunson, Rifleman **John T.** of Mulvihill (H 6981). Royal Winnipeg Rifles. He died 6 June 1944 and is commemorated at Beny-sur-Mer Canadian War Cemetery in Calvados, France. He was the son of Mr. and Mrs. T. Gunson of Eriksdale. ***Gunson Lake*** (62 O/2), west of Ashern was named after him and his brother, Private Wilfred A. Gunson (next entry) in 1972.

Gunson, Private **Wilfred A.** of Dauphin (H 6982). Queen's Own Cameron Highlanders. He died 20 July 1944 and is commemorated at Beny-sur-Mer Canadian War Cemetery in Calvados, France. He was the son of Mr. and Mrs. T. Gunson of Eriksdale. ***Gunson Lake*** (62 O/2), west of Ashern was named after him and his brother, Rifleman John T. Gunson (previous entry) in 1972.

Gurney, Private **James** of Badger, Manitoba (288306). 78th Battalion, Canadian Infantry (Manitoba Regiment). He died 1 February 1918 at the age of 41 and is commemorated at Fosse No. 10, Communal Cemetery Extension, Sains-en-Gohelle, Pas de Calais, France. This native of London, England was survived by his wife Florence M. Gurney of Badger. ***Gurney Lake*** (52 M/3), northeast of Bissett was named after this World War I casualty in 1976.

Gurr, Private **Ruebin J.** of Dauphin (H 20225). Lake Superior Regiment. He died 24 April 1945 at the age of 23 and is commemorated at the Holten Canadian War Cemetery in Holland. He was the son of Harry W. and of Lucille Gurr of Toronto. ***Gurr Lake*** (63 P/6), north of Landing Lake was named after him in 1981.

Gustafson, Sapper **Alver N. G.** (H 93384). Royal Canadian Engineers. He died 28 April 1945 at the age of 26 and is commemorated at the Holten Canadian War Cemetery in Holland. He was the son of Alphonse and Emma Gustafson and was survived by his wife Doris Gustafson of Stratton, Ontario. ***Gustafson Lake*** (63 O/7), southwest of Wuskwatim Lake was named after him in 1995.

Guthrie, Squadron Leader **Archibald J.** of Reston (34155). No. 9 Squadron, RAF. He died 18 December 1939 at the age of 28 and is commemorated at the Runnymede Memorial in Surrey, England. He was the son of William J. and Annie M. Guthrie and was survived by his wife Barbara A. Guthrie of Tamworth, Staffordshire, England. The Reston Roll of Honour includes the following inscription:

> Squadron Leader Guthrie led his squadron of bombers on a daylight raid on Heligoland in December, 1939. Many of them were shot down by enemy fighters. They were reported missing in action and later presumed dead.

Guthrie Peninsula (54 D/6) on Stephens Lake was named after him in 1995.

Guthrie, Private **Gordon** of Melford (H 42265). Loyal Edmonton Regiment. He died 28 May 1944 at the age of 22 and is commemorated at the Cassino War Cemetery in Italy. He was the son of James and Kathleen Guthrie of Vancouver. His sister recalls (13 October 2001):

> Gord was badly injured by a land mine and died in hospital. We were a very close family and enjoyed

our growing years. He was a quiet lad, but was comical and fun. He farmed after his schooling for a few years and when war broke out, he went to work in the Vulcan Iron Works in Winnipeg. He decided to join the army in '42 or '43. We all missed him dearly when he went overseas, but were happy to have letters back and forth.

Guthrie Island (64 P/12) in Inverarity Lake was named after him in 1985.

Guthrie, Flying Officer **Lindsay L.** of Winnipeg (J 29986). No. 625 Squadron. He died 9 November 1944 at the age of 23 and is commemorated at the Reichswald Forest War Cemetery in Germany. He was the son of William G. and Lilly Guthrie of Winnipeg. ***Guthrie Bay*** (64 A/12) in Baldock Lake was named after him in 1989.

Guthrie, Leading Seaman **Robert M.** of Brandon (4472). HMCS *Valleyfield*. The *Valleyfield* was torpedoed and sunk by U-548 50 miles south of Cape Race, Newfoundland; 125 of her ship's company were lost. Leading Seaman Guthrie died 7 May 1944 at the age of 20 and is commemorated at the Halifax Memorial. He was the son of Peter and Isabel Guthrie of Brandon. ***Guthrie Point*** (63 I/7) on Molson Lake was named after him in 1994.

Gutray, Squadron Leader **Joseph T.** of Winnipeg (C 768). Royal Air Force Ferry Command. He died 21 April 1942 at the age of 29 and is commemorated at St. Mary's Polish National Catholic Cemetery in North Kildonan. He was the son of Joseph and Francis Gutray of Winnipeg and was survived by his wife Margaret E. Gutray of Toronto. ***Gutray Lake*** (63 K/16), northwest of Wekusko Lake was named after him in 1973.

Guttormson, Pilot Officer **Hinrik** of Poplar Point (J 95307). No. 431 Squadron. He died 5 March 1945 at the age of 20 and is commemorated at the Hanover War Cemetery in Germany. ***Guttormson Lake*** (52 L/6), east of Lac du Bonnet was named after him in 1973.

Gyles, Rifleman **Richard F.** of Winnipeg (H 10911). Royal Winnipeg Rifles. He died 28 October 1944 at the age of 20 and is commemorated at the Adegem Canadian War Cemetery in Belgium. He was the son of Richard W. and Jean A. Gyles of Winnipeg. ***Gyles Lake*** (64 H/16), east of North Knife Lake was named after him in 1963.

Invasion craft en route to France on D-Day, 6 June 1944.
Courtesy of the National Archives of Canada (PA-116339).

H

Haacke, Flying Officer **Arthur Paul** of Elphinstone (J 25812). No. 1666 Heavy Conversion Unit, RCAF. He died 23 June 1944 at the age of 24 and is commemorated at Stonefall Cemetery in Yorkshire, England. He was the son of Arthur D. and Myrtle Haacke of Elphinstone, Manitoba and was survived by his wife Pauline R. Haacke (née Prosko) of Elphinstone. ***Haacke Lake*** (64 P/15), northeast of Nejanilini Lake was named after him in 1974.

Habiluk, Pilot Officer **Mike** of Winnipeg (J 86999). No. 434 Squadron. He died 17 June 1944 at the age of 21 and is commemorated at Ede General Cemetery, Holland. ***Habiluk Lake*** (63 J/3), east of North Moose Lake was named after him in 1973.

Hadfield, Private **Vincent G.** of Winnipeg (H 19558). Queen's Own Cameron Highlanders. He died 19 August 1942 and is commemorated at Dieppe Canadian War Cemetery in Seine-Maritime, France. ***Hadfield Lake*** (64 J/3), southwest of Tadoule Lake was named after him in 1975.

Hagel, Flight Sergeant **Francis E.** of Winnipeg (R 71111). No. 408 Squadron. He died 15 April 1942 at the age of 33 and is commemorated at the Reichswald Forest War Cemetery in Germany. He was the eldest of the five sons of Mr. and Mrs. Percy E. Hagel of Winnipeg. His youngest brother reports that he had been born in Winnipeg and later attended St. John's College and the University of Manitoba. He had worked as a driller in northern Manitoba and Ontario prior to enlisting (29 January 1998). His nephew writes (25 October 2001):

> Although I never met my Uncle Frank, my father Donald Hagel – my Uncle Frank's youngest brother – also served in the RCAF as an Observer/Navigator in the African Theatre and often spoke of him. Apparently, they were able to meet in London on several occasions prior to my father being transferred to Egypt. The events of those meetings as my father recalled, I hold very dear.

Hagel Lake (64 H/3), west of Fidler Lake was named after him in 1995.

Haider, Lance Corporal **Harry** of Pine Falls (H 26857). Fort Garry Horse. He died 11 June 1944 at the age of 34 and is commemorated at the Bayeux Memorial in Calvados, France. According to his sister-in-law, he was the son of John and Mary M. Haider (née Scheman) of Spear Hill, Manitoba and was survived by his wife Myrtle M. Haider (née Anderson) of Pine Falls, Manitoba (7 February 1997). He had moved to Pine Falls about 1930 and obtained employment with the Manitoba Paper Company. ***Haider Lake*** (64 N/16), west of Nueltin Lake was named after him in 1972.

Haigh, Lieutenant **Allen** of Transcona. 12th Manitoba Dragoons. He died 18 September 1945 at the age of 25 and is commemorated at the Groesbeek Canadian War Cemetery in Holland. He was the son of William and Kitty Haigh and was survived by his wife Mabel V. Haigh of Winnipeg. ***Haigh Lake*** (64 K/16), northeast of Lac Brochet was named after him in 1972.

Halasz, Trooper **George** of Sherridon (H 63773). Fort Garry Horse. He died 22 April 1945 at the age of 39 and is commemorated at Brookwood Military Cemetery in Surrey, England. He was the son of Joseph and Elizabeth Halasz and was survived by his wife Julia Halasz of Toronto. ***Halasz Lake*** (62 N/15), southeast of Swan River was named after him in 1977.

Hale, Lieutenant **William F.** of Winnipeg (O 29980). Motor Torpedo Boat 466, Mentioned in Dispatches. He died 14 February 1945 at the age of 21 and is commemorated at the Halifax Memorial. He was the son of Samuel Coffman and Helen A. Hale of Winnipeg. ***Hale Lake*** (64 A/9), east of Waskaiowaka Lake was named after him in 1950.

Hales, Corporal **Arthur C.** of Virden (H 40145). Veterans Guard of Canada. He died 9 July 1942 at the age of 51 and is commemorated at Virden Cemetery. He was the son of Arthur J. and Sarah Hales of Winnipeg and was survived by his wife Winnifred E. Hales of Virden and their three children.

> Corporal Hales was born in London, England … and came to Virden as a young man of 21 in 1911. He learned the trade of harness making in the old land, but never followed it after coming to Canada. He adapted himself to conditions here and being mechanically inclined, found employment as an auto mechanic and service man.
>
> As a youth he was associated with yeomanry and territorials in England. He served in the Canadian Expeditionary Force from 1915 to 1918, having joined the 79th Battalion. On returning to Canada and following his discharge from the active army he continued service in the 12th Manitoba Dragoons up to June 1940 when he again enlisted for active service in the Veterans' Guard of Canada.
>
> He was associated with the Formation of the Virden Branch of the Great War Veterans' Association of Canada and was one of its charter members. He continued his membership in this organization until it merged into the Canadian Legion … and had served several terms on the executive of both of these bodies (*Empire-Advance* 15 July 1942).

According to his daughter (3 February 1998):

> I know he learned the trade of a harness-maker and worked at repairing leather luggage in England. He also was very interested in anything mechanical and soon got working and training as a garage mechanic and parts man. This vocation was what I remember him earning a living at for many years through several changes of owners.
>
> Dad was very community-oriented and was always involved in activities – sports at the rink in the winter and baseball in the summer. He was also one of the founders of the rifle club at Virden – [one] which is still an active club even to date. Our home life was a very happy one and as a family we enjoyed exploring the countryside with Mother and Dad and we loved picnics. We were a very close family with our grandparents as well who used to visit very often.

Hales Lake (53 K/3), northeast of Red Sucker Lake was named after him in 1995.

Hall, Corporal **Archibald M.** of Winnipeg (H 19104). Queen's Own Cameron Highlanders. He died 28 August 1944 at the age of 25 and is commemorated at Bretteville-sur-Laize Canadian War Cemetery in Calvados, France. He was the son of B. E. and Matilda Hall of Winnipeg. ***Hall Bay*** (64 J/4) in Morand Lake was named after him in 1995.

Hall, Company Sargent **Major Frederick W.** of Winnipeg (1539). 8th Battalion, Canadian Infantry (Manitoba Regiment), Victoria Cross.

> On 24th April, 1915, in the neighbourhood of Ypres, when a wounded man who was lying some 15 yards from the trench called for help,

Company Sergeant-Major Hall endeavoured to reach him in the face of a very heavy enfilade fire which was being poured in by the enemy. The first attempt failed and a non-commissioned officer and private soldier who were attempting to give assistance were both wounded. Company Sergeant-Major Hall then made a second most gallant attempt, and was in the act of lifting up the wounded man to bring him in when he fell mortally wounded in the head (*London Gazette* 23 June 1915).

This native of Kilkenny, Ireland died 25 April 1915 at the age of 30 and is commemorated at Ypres (Menin Gate) Memorial, Ieper, West-Vlaanderen, Belgium. He was the son of Mary Hall of Leytonstone, London and the late Bombardier F. Hall. ***Frederick Hall Lake*** (63 P/8), south of Goulet Lake was named after him in 2001.

Hall, Private **Reginald A.** of Winnipeg (SH 800277). Royal Canadian Army Medical Corps. He died 4 January 1952 at the age of 21 and is commemorated at the United Nations Cemetery in Pusan, South Korea. ***Reginald Hall Lake*** (53 L/16), north of Gods Lake was named after this Korean War casualty in 1998.

Hall, Private **Victor W.** of Middlechurch (H 65930). Royal Canadian Army Service Corps. He died 22 June 1944 at the age of 21 and is commemorated at Brookwood Military Cemetery in Surrey, England. He was the son of R. V. and Ellen Hall of Middlechurch, Manitoba. ***Hall Lake*** (63 O/13), east of Highrock Lake was named after him in 1967.

Hall, Rifleman **William S.** of Winnipeg (H 18657). Royal Winnipeg Rifles. He died 28 February 1945 at the age of 19 and is commemorated at the Groesbeek Canadian War Cemetery in Holland. He was the son of William H. and Eva A. Hall of Winnipeg. ***Hall Island*** (64 F/1) in Barrington Lake was named after him in 1995.

Halldorson, Sapper **Bjarni** of Langruth (H 1324). Royal Canadian Engineers. He died 10 August 1944 on his 32nd birthday and is commemorated at the Bayeux Memorial in Calvados, France. He was the son of Bjorn and Jonina Halldorson of Langruth, Manitoba. According to his sister (3 February 1995) he was:

born ... at Langruth where he attended school and later did carpenter work in summer and fished on Lake Manitoba in winter. He also played the violin in the family orchestra. In November, 1942 he enlisted in the army at Portage la Prairie and later was sent to Chilliwack and Vancouver for further training. [He] left for overseas on December 23, 1942. He trained in England and shortly after the invasion in June, 1944, went to France taking part in warfare leading up to Caen. There he was reported missing ... and later presumed dead.

Halldorson Lake (64 I/2), east of North Knife Lake was named after him in 1974.

Hallek, Aircraftman 1 **Frank** of Winnipeg (R 177737). No. 113 Squadron. He died 23 March 1943 at the age of 22 and is commemorated at Elmwood Cemetery in Winnipeg. He was the son of Konstantin and Sophia Hallek of Winnipeg. ***Hallek Lake*** (64 O/16), north of Nejanilini Lake was named after him in 1975.

Hallen, Private **Edgar A.** of Neepawa (H 14472). 1st Canadian Parachute Battalion. He died 7 May 1945 at the age of 21 and is commemorated at the Holten Canadian War Cemetery in Holland. He was one of the ten children of George M. and Annie L. Hallen (née Dewar) of Neepawa, Manitoba. According to his brother (21 December 1994), this native of Rosetown, Saskatchewan:

Attended school at Bisley, Saskatchewan (1930 – 1936), then moved (November 1937) with family to farm at Neepawa. [He] completed high school at Neepawa Collegiate [and] enlisted in [the] artillery [in] September 1943 [at] Winnipeg. [He] trained at Petawawa [and] transferred into the 1st Canadian Parachute Battalion [in] March, 1944 and trained at Shilo. In April, he made a Victory Bond jump at Minnedosa and went overseas [in] July 1944.

In his letters he stated he would be getting married when he came home and would be taking over farming. He talked about how hard the going was:

- I'm now in Germany. We jumped over the Rhine River some time ago. Had a good jump, my eighteenth. I saw two planes go crashing into the woods, afire. When I hit the ground, two men were killed ten feet from me. Mortar shells were landing on us in the trench. One man was killed, some wounded, one beside me. I took him back to R.R. Quarters for treatment. It's hard slugging all the way, moving all day and half the night. You lay down where you stop and fall asleep, then get up in the morning and move on. You do not eat very often (March 1945).
- This is hell on earth and there is no glory in this, and do not let my brother join up. Hope this time it puts an end to War (May 1945).

By this time, the family felt relatively confident that "Tommy" would return safely (21 November 2001):

When VE-Day came, mother was excited. "Tommy" as he was called, was coming home. Plans were made to celebrate, but three weeks later, word came that he had died.

Hallen Lake (53 D/12), north of Harrop Lake was named after him in 1980.

Hallett, Private **Lawrence G.** of Fisherton (H 6895). Winnipeg Grenadiers. He died 2 February 1944 at the age of 30 and is commemorated at the Yokohama War Cemetery in Japan. He was the son of William and Mary Hallett of Fisherton, Manitoba. He was taken prisoner after the fall of Hong Kong and died in a prisoner of war camp. The official cause of death was listed as tracheal diphtheria. ***Hallett Lake*** (64 K/9), northeast of Reindeer Lake was named after him in 1972.

Hallett, Private **Lloyd M.** of Winnipeg (H 6842). Winnipeg Grenadiers. He died 19 December 1941 and is commemorated at the Sai Wan Memorial in Hong Kong. He was the son of Mr. and Mrs. L. Hallett of Winnipeg and was survived by his wife Dorothy Hallett and their two children. He had enlisted with the Grenadiers in March, 1940. ***Hallett Island*** (53 E/16) in Krolman Lake was named after him in 1995.

Hallett, Lance Corporal **Robert E.** of Poplar Point (H 21140). Royal Canadian Electrical and Mechanical Engineers. He died 5 September 1944 and is commemorated at Gradara War Cemetery in Italy. ***Hallett Bay*** (64 C/6) in Mounteney Lake was named after him in 1995.

Hallett, Flight Sergeant **Wilfred A.** of Poplar Point (R 166246). No. 53 Squadron. He died 17 April 1944 at the age of 20 and is commemorated at the Runnymede Memorial in Surrey, England. ***Hallett Point*** (64 J/12) on Descôteaux Lake was named after him in 1995.

Hallgrimson, Gunner **Peter H.** of Arborg (H 105272). Royal Canadian Artillery. He died 20 October 1945 at the age of 24 and is commemorated at the Holten Canadian War Cemetery in Holland. He was the son of Thorleifur and Elinborg Hallgrimson and was survived by his wife Svava S. Hallgrimson (née Palmason) of Winnipeg. According to his sister-in-law (20 August 1996) he:

... attended school in Riverton and then Success Business College in Winnipeg. [He was] employed by Booth Fisheries in Winnipeg before enlisting. Peter was stationed throughout Nova Scotia and Newfoundland before going to Holland in March, 1945.

His cousin recalls (6 November 2001):

He was tall, strikingly handsome, brimming with life, goodwill and joy, he was the brother I never had, he was my cousin, Pjetur Hoffman Hallgrimson. Pjetur was a strong athlete; I can still see him skating powerfully, playing defence for the Winnipeg Monarchs. But most of all, I remember him as a sensitive and caring man, going with him on the streetcar from Winnipeg to Selkirk to visit our grandmother, laden with Christmas goodies. He would hand her a small bottle of brandy and say, "Just in case you get a cold, Amma." Intermingled with those qualities was a man with a great sense of humour, always ready to laugh; it was uplifting and fun to be in his presence. The editor of the Icelandic newspaper in Winnipeg wrote on his death "We bid Pjetur Hoffman Hallgrimson farewell, in deep sorrow, and thank him for his friendship; his memory, warm and clean, will always be with us."

Peter's parents received a letter from a Dutch family two years after his death:

Dear parents of Peter: We read in the letter of Mrs. Hallgrimson also yours live in Winnipeg, and they are also most anxious to get to know the family who is so kindly looking after yours lovend one's grave. We promise you, we shall do us utmost for the grave of Peter, "your son." Hieby we send you a few snaps of the graves and ourselves, and we hope we does not hurt you woth these photographs. Please can you send us your address and a photograph of yourself and the birthday of Peter? English is a difficult language for us but we learn English and we hope that we with few weeks can send you a long letter. We remain, Yours sincerely, R. Kommer-Roskamp (26 August 1947).

Hallgrimson Lake (64 O/2), southwest of Nejanilini Lake was named after him in 1975.

Halliday, Sergeant **Alfred J.** of Winnipeg (H 417037). Veterans Guard of Canada. He died 20 November 1940 at the age of 48 and is commemorated at Mountain View Cemetery in Thunder Bay, Ontario. He was the son of James W. and Laura Halliday of London. ***Halliday Lake*** (64 I/1), northeast of Etawney Lake was named after him in 1974.

Halloran, Warrant Officer 2 **William R.** of Winnipeg (R 119691). No. 83 Squadron. He died 2 January 1944 at the age of 30 and is commemorated at the Sage War Cemetery in Germany. He was the son of Michael and Jean Halloran of St. Boniface. ***Halloran Lake*** (64 P/11), east of Nejanilini Lake was named after him in 1974.

Halperin, Flight Lieutenant **William L.** of Winnipeg (C 4234). No. 45 Transport Squadron, RCAF. He died 6 November 1943 at the age of 22 and is commemorated at the Ottawa Memorial. ***Halperin Lake*** (64 P/10), east of Nejanilini Lake was named after him in 1974.

Halstead, Sergeant **Glen E.** of Roland (R 59540). No. 10 Operational Training Unit, RCAF. He died 5 June 1941 at the age of 21 and is commemorated at Brookwood Military Cemetery in Surrey, England. He was the son of Arnold E. and Marion Halstead of Winnipeg. ***Halstead Lake*** (64 I/8), northeast of North Knife Lake was named after him in 1974.

Halstead, Flying Officer **Vernon H.** of Winnipeg (J 36270). No. 626 Squadron. He died 15 January 1945 at the age of 21 and is commemorated at the Berlin 1939 - 1945 War Cemetery in Brandenburg, Germany. He was the son of Carl N. and Jean E. Halstead of Winnipeg. ***Halstead Island*** (64 N/5) in Snyder Lake was named after him in 1987.

Haluik, Private **Mike** of Poplarfield (H 1683). Essex Scottish Regiment. He died 10 November 1944 and is commemorated at the Groesbeek Canadian War Cemetery in Holland. ***Haluik Lake*** (64 J/7), southwest of Tadoule Lake was named after him in 1975.

Hamalock, Trooper **Adam M.** of Virden (H 26789). Fort Garry Horse. He died 15 August 1944 at the age of 25 and is commemorated at Bretteville-sur-Laize Canadian War Cemetery in Calvados, France. He was the son of James and Nettie Hamalock. In his last letter to a friend, he wrote:

Dear Janet: I received your most welcome letter even if it did take such a long time to get here. You will notice by my address that I'm in France; I landed in France on D-Day and have been battling away with the Germans until this last week and my tank was knocked out so I'm waiting for another one. I had quite an experience since I landed and as far as the country goes, it's swell and the people are good to us and glad to see us. And when I do receive the parcel, I'll let you know for it's taking longer now for our mail to get through. There isn't anything special that I want and the less we carry the better. I had a lot of personal things but they all got burnt and that's how the war goes. I've seen a lot of Germans since I hit here and a lot of their equipment which was destroyed. I suppose you heard all about it over the radio or seen it in the paper. You'll be wondering how I get along with French over here, well I know a little of it, at least I can make them understand what I want. Well I better close now, and write soon again for I look forward to your letters, Adam (20 July 1944).

Hamalock Lake (64 C/13), south of McMillan Lake was named after him in 1982.

Hamelin, Private **François Frederick** of Fisher Branch (H 41694). Winnipeg Grenadiers. He died a prisoner of war 10 December 1943 at the age of 19 and is commemorated at the Sai Wan War Cemetery in Hong Kong. He was the son of Frederick and Helene Hamelin of Fisher Branch, Manitoba. ***Hamelin Island*** (64 C/3) in the Laurie River was named after him in 1995.

Hamelin, Warrant Officer 2 **Louis L.** of St. Boniface (R 106248). No. 81 Squadron. He died 23 March 1943 at the age of 21 and is commemorated at the Malta Memorial. He was the son of Joseph and Parmelie Hamelin, owners of the St. Norbert Hotel. Mr. J. Hamelin was MP for Ste. Rose du Lac for 16 years. ***Hamelin Lake*** (64 N/9), southwest of Nueltin Lake was named after Warrant Officer Hamelin in 1972.

Hamilton, Private **Alfred E.** of Boissevain (H 103770). Argyle and Sutherland Highlanders. He died 20 August 1944 and is commemorated at Bretteville-sur-Laize Canadian War Cemetery in Calvados, France. ***Hamilton Point*** (64 C/12) in Dunphy Lakes was named after him in 1995.

Hamilton, Private **Edward A.** (H 62711). Canadian Forestry Corps. He died 4 September 1941 and is commemorated at Brookwood Military Cemetery in Surrey, England. Edward ***Hamilton Island*** (64 O/13) in Nueltin Lake was named after him in 1996.

Hamilton, Sergeant **Hill** of Winnipeg (H 7091). Royal Winnipeg Rifles. He died 9 October 1944 at the age of 29 and is commemorated at the Adegem Canadian War Cemetery in Belgium. He was the son of David and Mary Hamilton of Winnipeg. ***Hamilton Rapids*** (64 N/9) in the Thlewiaza River was named after him in 1995.

Hamilton, Sergeant **James S.** of Winnipeg (H 2833). Canadian Army Corps of Military Staff Clerks. He was aboard the SS *Nerissa*, the only ship torpedoed while carrying Canadian troops to the United Kingdom. Sergeant Hamilton died 1 May 1941 at the age of 22 and is commemorated at the Halifax Memorial. He was the son of Walter H. and Lily Hamilton of Winnipeg. ***Hamilton Bay*** (64 O/5) on the north shore of Booth Lake was named after him in 1985.

Hamilton, Flight Sergeant **John** of Winnipeg (R 166270). No. 138 Squadron. He died 8 June 1944 at the age of 31 and is commemorated at La Ferte-St. Cyr Communal Cemetery, Loir-et-Cher, France. He was the son of Andrew and Sophia Hamilton and was survived by his wife Augusta Hamilton of Winnipeg. ***Hamilton Peninsula*** (64 O/2) on Greening Lake was named after him in 1995.

Hamilton, Warrant Officer 1 **Thomas B.** of Winnipeg (R 80109). No. 274 Squadron. He died 8 August 1942 at the age of 24 and is commemorated at El Alamein War Cemetery in Egypt. He was one of the seven children of Edward J. and of Elizabeth C. Hamilton (née McMaster) of Winnipeg. His sisters recall (20 November 2001):

Tom attended Earl Grey and Kelvin Technical High School. He enjoyed sports and was a fair jumper and enjoyed ice skating. He attended Crescent-Fort Rouge United Church and Sunday School. He played music by ear and enjoyed all types; one special favourite was *The Bluebird of Happiness.* This personified his outlook on life as he never came down the street, mostly on his bicycle, without whistling or singing. He rarely opened the gate, but jumped the fence when walking.

Tom received his training at Brandon, High River, Alberta, Fort William, Ontario and graduated at Moose Jaw in July, 1941. Leaving for overseas in late July, 1941, he was at sea for 16 days. The ship had to make a zigzag course trying to avoid detection of the German submarines. He wrote the poem *Convoy* during this crossing, sending it home by Air Mail. The poem was read on the CBC radio as well as recited at Kelvin Technical High School graduation exercises at Westminster United Church on June 9, 1943. This poem along with his *The Unknown Soldier* and *To My Mother on Mother's Day* are the family favourites.

Tom always enjoyed poetry and had a marvellous memory, often entertaining the family with his rendition of *The Highwayman* and many of Robert Service's poems, especially *The Shooting of Dan McGrew* and *The Cremation of Sam McGee*. He had a book of Service's poems, *Songs of a Sourdough* in his kit bag which we now have at home.

Stationed at Bournemouth, England for a time as well as in Scotland, he was sent to the Middle East where he did not like the heat, but found it very interesting. He was a fighter pilot.

Hamilton Island (63 P/4) in Sipiwesk Lake was named after him in 1995.

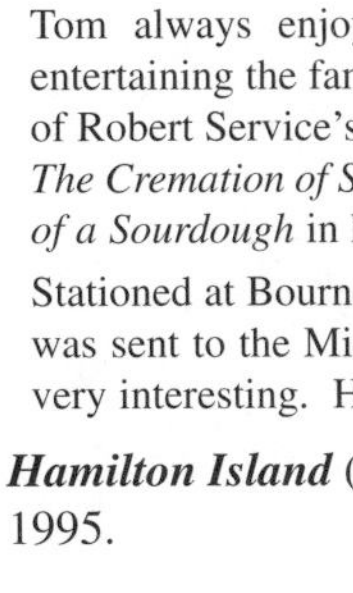

Hamilton, Gunner **William M.** of Ingelow (H 75308). Royal Canadian Artillery. He died 7 September 1944 at the age of 19 and is commemorated at the Calais Canadian War Cemetery in France. He was the son of William and Elizabeth Hamilton of Douglas, Manitoba. According to his brother (18 April 1995), he had been born in County Tyrone and arrived in Canada with his parents in 1927. ***Hamilton Hill*** (64 N/5), northwest of Snyder Lake was named after him in 1995.

Hammerberg, Private **Vernie W.** of Teulon (H 23291). Lake Superior Regiment. He died 22 April 1945 just weeks before VE-Day during the liberation of Holland. He was 20 years of age and is commemorated at the Holten Canadian War Cemetery in Holland. He was the son of Eley and Kathleen Hammerberg of Teulon, Manitoba. The people of Holland, including its youth, remember that time:

Victor Burak and Edward Petter went through hell in 1945 – but yesterday the Winnipeggers basked in the gratitude of 14 teenagers who grew up in a Dutch city Canadians liberated. "If it weren't for us, I guess they wouldn't be here. It's hard to believe what actually happened," said Burak, a 76 year-old veteran infantryman.

The 14 teenagers are members of a track and field club from Apeldoorn, one of the cities liberated in 1945 by Canadian troops. Last year, they invited several Canadian track clubs to Holland, and this month they're in Winnipeg with their hosts in the Winnipeg Optimist Athletic Club. They're running in track meets – including one today at the University of Manitoba – but the young athletes are paying special tribute to Canada's liberation of their home land.

Yesterday they visited veterans at Deer Lodge Centre and tomorrow they'll take part in a parade and wreath-laying ceremony at 2 PM that will involve hundreds of members of veterans organizations, active military units and cadets.

"It felt real good" to meet the Dutch athletes yesterday, said the 84 year-old Petter, who served with the 3rd Ammunition Company from Winnipeg. "I landed on D-Day. We ended up in Germany, but we had Holland in between," Petter recalled. "One place I remember is Remagen, where they had bridges. And I mean bridges, a mile long. We saved one of them from being destroyed by retreating Germans. The Dutch people were starving by the time the Canadians marched into their towns and villages," Petter said. "Everybody welcomed us, eh? They had a really rough time."

Nineteen year-old decathlete and future high school phys-ed teacher Daan Lammers said he grew up hearing stories about the war and the role that Canadian troops had played in freeing his country. "We're going to place flowers on veterans' graves," he said. "It means quite a lot to me. We owe a lot to these people. We see veterans here with a missing arm or a missing leg, and the people who died – this is the least we can do to show our appreciation."

Ben Zonnenberg, a track coach and one of the tour's organizers, said people in Holland want young people to maintain the country's bond with Canada. The trip is not only about sports, but also to "show Canadian children how our country is now. It's because of the high sacrifices Canadians made for us. For us, it's very emotional for us to be here on the soil of our liberators. They rebuilt our bridges, our roads, our hospitals, our schools" (Martin 2001).

Hammerberg Lake (52 E/11), southeast of Brereton Lake was named after Private Hammerberg in 1974.

Hammill, Sergeant **Arthur D.** of Winnipeg (R 80083). No. 4 Wireless School. He died 17 June 1942 at the age of 25 and is commemorated at Mount Pleasant Cemetery in Toronto. He was the son of Frank A. and Isabella Hammill of Winnipeg and was survived by his wife Florence Hammill of Toronto. ***Hammill Lake*** (64 F/3), north of Goldsand Lake was named after him in 1994.

Hammond, Pilot Officer **Albert E.** of Winnipeg (J 85187). No. 12 Squadron. He died 16 March 1944 at the age of 25 and is commemorated at Durnbach War Cemetery in Bavaria, Germany. He was the son of Albert and Alice M. Hammond of Winnipeg and was survived by his wife of six months Elizabeth W. Hammond (née Beveridge). She recalls (20 August 1998): "I loved [him] so very much.

We had such a short time together as I was in the WAAFs in England. I am enclosing three photographs of Albert; we never had time to take pictures." ***Hammond Lake*** (53 N/5), east of Swampy Lake was named after him in 1995.

Hammond, Trooper **Harvey R.** of Boissevain (H 379). Ontario Tank Regiment. He died 12 September 1944 at the age of 26 and is commemorated at Florence War Cemetery in Italy. He was the youngest child of Richard and Martha J. Hammond (née Kyle) of Boissevain, Manitoba. His nephew (6 October 1997) writes that:

> Harvey was born and raised on the family farm northeast of Boissevain in the Rural Municipality of Morton. Harvey's education was completed at the rural school of Hiawatha. After schooling, he continued to work on the farm until he enlisted in June, 1941 and went overseas that same fall. He and a cousin, Stan Hammond, joined up together with the Strathcona Horse. Later Harvey was somehow changed to Ontario Tank. Stan still resides in Boissevain, Manitoba.

Hammond Point (64 G/9) on Southern Indian Lake was named after him in 1963.

Hanan, Flight Sergeant **Brian H. H.** of Thornhill (R 100381). No. 11 Advanced Flying School. He died 3 December 1942 at the age of 20 and is commemorated at Shawbury (St. Mary) Churchyard in Shropshire, England. ***Hanan Lake*** (64 H/10), east of Buckland Lake was named after him in 1995.

Hancock, Private **Allan C.** of Stonewall (H 20647). Queen's Own Cameron Highlanders. He died 19 August 1942 at the age of 37 and is commemorated at Dieppe Canadian War Cemetery in Seine-Maritime, France. He was the son of Charles and Ellen Hancock of Stonewall, Manitoba and was survived by his wife Betty F. Hancock of Stonewall and their son. His obituary read in part:

> Born in South Wales, [United Kingdom] June 8, 1911, he attended school there and came to Canada in 1928. He farmed at Rossendale, Manitoba from where he enlisted in May, 1940. He received his training at Trenton, Montreal and Jarvis, graduating in the spring of 1941. He arrived overseas the following August (n.d.).

His son's widow writes (18 October 2001):

> Wayne always regretted not knowing his father; it was a source of pain to him. Wayne was born in 1941 so we are not sure if his father ever got to see him either. Wayne would not talk about it.

Hancock Lake (63 P/7), northwest of Bear Lake was named after him in 1972.

Hancock, Private **Donald M.** of St. Vital (H 9259). Essex Scottish Regiment. He died 28 August 1944 at the age of 22 and is commemorated at Bretteville-sur-Laize Canadian War Cemetery in Calvados, France. He was the son of Thomas H. and Doris M. Hancock of St. Vital. ***Hancock Bay*** (64 C/5) in Boulder Lake was named after him in 1995.

Hancock, Leading Aircraftman **Kenneth M.** of Roland (R 134775). No. 10 Service Flying Training School. He died 6 January 1943 at the age of 21 and is commemorated at Fairview Cemetery in Roland, Manitoba. He was the son of Luther S. and Clara M. Hancock of Roland. His sister writes (12 October 2001):

> [He] was born at Melville, Saskatchewan April 29, 1921, joined the service at Winnipeg in October, 1941. Hancock trained at Brandon, Regina, Virden and Dauphin where he was killed in an accident during his routine morning flight on January 6, 1943. Educated at Roland, Manitoba, he was engaged in farming when he enlisted. His hobbies were reading and aeronautics. He was a member of the Roland United Church.

Hancock Point (64 J/13) on Nicklin Lake was named after him in 1995.

Hancock, Flight Sergeant **Ronald** of Rossendale (R 59685). No. 407 Squadron, Distinguished Flying Medal. He died 28 April 1942 at the age of 31 and is commemorated at the Runnymede Memorial in Surrey, England. ***Hancock Island*** (63 N/6) in Kississing Lake was named after him in 1995.

Haney, Rifleman **Horace R. T.** of Winnipeg (H 195027). Regina Rifle Regiment. He died 9 July 1944 at the age of 17 and is commemorated at Beny-sur-Mer Canadian War Cemetery in Calvados, France. He was the son of George J. and Sarah Haney of Winnipeg. ***Haney Lake*** (64 O/8), south of Nejanilini Lake was named after him in 1995.

Hanna, Sergeant **Kenneth L.** of Rathwell (H 87394). Queen's Own Cameron Highlanders. He died 28 October 1944 at the age of 25 and is commemorated at Schoonselhof Cemetery in Antwerp, Belgium. He was the son of Sidney J. and Mable Hanna and was survived by his wife Hazel B. Hanna of Rathwell, Manitoba. ***Hanna Creek*** (54 M/10), which flows east into Hudson Bay was named after him in 1984.

Hannesson, Pilot Officer **Jack E. K.** of Winnipeg (J 87269). No. 514 Squadron. He died 30 June 1944 at the age of 21 and is commemorated at Brookwood Military Cemetery in Surrey, England. He was the son of Kari O. and Dorothy C. Hannesson of Vancouver. ***Hannesson Lake*** (64 O/4), north of Egenolf Lake was named after him in 1995.

Hanscom, Flying Officer **Harry R.** of Winnipeg (J 88672). No. 443 Squadron. He died 21 April 1945 at the age of 23 and is commemorated at the Berlin 1939 - 1945 War Cemetery in Brandenburg, Germany. ***Hanscom Lake*** (64 P/2), southeast of Nejanilini Lake was named after him in 1974.

Hansen, Private **Alfred E. R.** of Spear Hill (H 800265). Princess Patricia's Canadian Light Infantry. He died 26 February 1951 at the age of 23 and is commemorated at the United Nations Cemetery in Pusan, South Korea. He was the youngest son of Niels and Marion Hansen. ***Alfred Hansen Lake*** (53 L/4), southwest of Bolton Lake was named after this Korean War casualty in 1998.

Hanson, Private **Kenneth H.** of Selkirk (H 22375). General List, Canadian Army. He died 20 June 1944 at the age of 17 and is commemorated at St. Clements Cemetery in Mapleton, Manitoba. He was the son of Mr. and Mrs. Hjortur Hanson of Selkirk. His brother writes (3 March 1998):

> He was raised in Selkirk and went to school there. His favourite pastimes were swimming, baseball and hockey. There is not much a person can add to that. As with many others, his was a short life. We are forever grateful. He is not forgotten.

Hanson Island (64 C/9) in Eden Lake was named after him in 1995.

Haraczay, Flying Officer **Walter** of Baldur (J 29418). No. 17 Operational Training Unit, RCAF. He died 8 July 1944 at the age of 21 and is commemorated at Brookwood Military Cemetery in Surrey, England. He was the son of Peter Wodzinski and was survived by his step-parents Stephen and Katherine Haraczay of Winnipeg. ***Haraczay Lake*** (64 O/7), southwest of Nejanilini Lake was named after him in 1975.

Haralson, Sergeant **Oliver J.** of Erickson (R 131571). No. 419 Squadron. He died 14 May 1943 at the age of 20 and is commemorated at Rheinberg War Cemetery in Germany. He was the son of Mr. and Mrs. C. A. Haralson of Erickson. ***Haralson Lake*** (64 B/13), west of Southern Indian Lake was named after him in 1984.

Harbottle, Warrant Officer 2 **Ronald W.** of Winnipeg (R 91806). No. 134 Maintenance Unit, RCAF. He died 13 March 1943 at the age of 27 and is commemorated at Basra War Cemetery, Iraq. He was the son of W. A. and Jessie Harbottle of Dummer, Saskatchewan and was survived by his wife Irene G. Harbottle (née Hubbard) of Winnipeg. ***Harbottle Lake*** (64 P/3), southeast of Nejanilini Lake was named after him in 1978.

Hardesty, Flight Sergeant **Benedict J.** of Winnipeg (R 71321). No. 103 Squadron. He died 6 October 1942 at the age of 20 and is commemorated at Terschelling (Westerschelling) General Cemetery, Holland. He was the son of John B. and Theresa Hardesty of Winnipeg. ***Hardesty Lake*** (64 F/2), east of Wells Lake was named after him in 1994.

Hardesty, Flight Sergeant **Gilbert P. M.** of Winnipeg (R 59562). No. 103 Squadron. He died 15 January 1942 at the age of 27 and is commemorated at Becklingen War Cemetery in Germany. He was the son of John and Theresa Hardesty of Winnipeg. ***Hardesty Island*** (64 O/12) in Nueltin Lake was named after him in 1995.

Hardisty, Private **William L.** of Woodlands (H 6825). Winnipeg Grenadiers. He died 19 December 1941 at the age of 31 and is commemorated at the Sai Wan Memorial in Hong Kong. He was the son of Thomas A. and Juliet M. Hardisty of Langford, British Columbia. ***Hardisty Point*** (63 N/3) on Kississing Lake was named after him in 1972.

Harford, Private **Wilfred J.** of St. James (H 3215). Princess Patricia's Canadian Light Infantry. He died 17 September 1944 at the age of 23 and is commemorated at Coriano Ridge War Cemetery in Italy. He was the son of Wilfred and Amy Harford of St. James. ***Harford Lake*** (64 O/9), northwest of Nejanilini Lake was named after him in 1975.

Hargreaves, Private **John** of Winnipeg (H 36817). Winnipeg Grenadiers. He died 22 December 1941 at the age of 31 and is commemorated at the Sai Wan Memorial in Hong Kong. He was the son of Mr. and Mrs. George Hargreaves of Winnipeg and was survived by his wife Eva Hargreaves (née Shaw) of West Kildonan and their three year-old son. A contemporary newspaper account added that he:

> ... was born in Harrogate, England ... and came to Canada when only a baby. He had lived in St. James ever since. Prior to the war, Private Hargreaves was employed for four years by James Richardson and Sons. He was with the RCCS non-permanent force and went on a recruiting tour through rural Manitoba before transferring to the Winnipeg Grenadiers. Four days after the transfer, he left for Hong Kong (14 January 1943).

Hargreaves Lake (63 I/16), east of Cross Lake was named after him in 1973.

Hargreaves, Flight Sergeant **John B.** of Winnipeg (R 100108). No. 5 Operational Training Unit, RCAF. He died 3 September 1942 at the age of 19 and is commemorated at Oban (Pennyfuir) Cemetery, Argyllshire, Scotland. He was the son of Alfred and Sarah A. Hargreaves of Winnipeg. ***Hargreaves Island*** (63 I/16) in Kapechekamasic Lake was named after him in 1995.

Harkness, Flight Sergeant **Alexander** of Winnipeg (R 71459). No. 115 Squadron. He died 26 September 1941 at the age of 20 and is commemorated at the Runnymede Memorial in Surrey, England. He was the son of Alexander and Delina Harkness of Winnipeg. ***Harkness Island*** (63 I/10) in Lawford Lake was named after him in 1988.

Harkness, Rifleman **Gilbert H. L.** of Grandview (H 10567). Royal Winnipeg Rifles. He died 6 June 1944 at the age of 20 and is commemorated at Beny-sur-Mer Canadian War Cemetery in Calvados, France. He was the son of Herbert and Mary E. Harkness of Grandview, Manitoba. ***Harkness Bay*** (64 F/8) in Le Clair Lake was named after him in 1995.

Harkness, Private **William** of Winnipeg (H 6219). Winnipeg Grenadiers. He died 21 September 1942 and is commemorated at the Sai Wan War Cemetery in Hong Kong. He was survived by his sister Mrs. Olive Chapman of Winnipeg. ***Harkness Lake*** (64 K/7), northeast of Reindeer Lake was named after him in 1972.

Harms, Trooper **Gerhard** of Gretna (H 18288). Royal Canadian Armoured Corps. He died 27 December 1943 at the age of 18 and is commemorated at Rosetown (Blumenort Church) Cemetery, Manitoba. He was the son of David G. and Elizabeth Harms of Gretna. ***Harms Lake*** (64 N/3), southwest of Nueltin Lake was named after him in 1972.

Harney, Flight Sergeant **Edmund M.** of Winnipeg (R 74244). No. 419 Squadron. He died 15 September 1942 at the age of 30 and is commemorated at Cottesmore (St. Nicholas) Churchyard Extension, Rutland, England. He was the son of Edmund S. and Helen B. Harney and was survived by his wife Marie S. Harney of Winnipeg. ***Harney Lake*** (53 F/13), east of Angling Lake was named after him in 1996.

Harper, Able Seaman **Horace M. R.** of Winnipeg. SS *Cedarbank*, Canadian Merchant Navy. The *Cedarbank* was lost 21 April 1940 and Able Seaman Harper is commemorated at the Halifax Memorial. He was the son of Mabel Harper of Verdun, Quebec. Horace ***Harper Lake*** (63 P/9), northeast of Cauchon Lake was named after him in 2001.

Harper, Major **John T.** of Winnipeg. Princess Patricia's Canadian Light Infantry, Order of the British Empire. He died 15 October 1944 at the age of 51 and is commemorated at Brookwood Military Cemetery in Surrey, England. He was the son of John T. and Lucy Harper and was survived by his wife Alice P. Harper of Sidney, British Columbia. ***Harper Point*** (64 K/16) on Stevens Lake was named after him in 1995.

Harper, Driver **Owen** of Winnipeg (1250027). 6th Brigade, Canadian Field Artillery. He died 19 September 1917 at the age of 25 and is commemorated at La Targette British Cemetery, Neuville-St Vaast, Pas de Calais, France. He was survived by his mother

Winifred Harper of Winnipeg. This native of Seacon, Cheshire, England enlisted in 1916 at which time he indicated he was a "printer/pressman." ***Harper Bay*** (64 J/11), on the south shore of Clifton Lake was named after him in 1983.

Harper, Trooper **Ronald F.** of Winnipeg (H 32). 6th Duke of Connaught's Royal Canadian Hussars. He died 5 February 1944 at the age of 24 and is commemorated at the Moro River Canadian War Cemetery in Italy. He was the son of Frank Duckworth and Margaret E. Harper of Winnipeg. ***Harper Lake*** (64 J/4), southwest of Tadoule Lake was named after him in 1975.

Harrigan, Flying Officer **James F.** of Dauphin (J 21023). No. 115 Squadron. He died 29 January 1944 at the age of 23 and is commemorated at the Runnymede Memorial in Surrey, England. He was the son of Patrick and Agnes Harrigan of Dauphin, Manitoba. ***Harrigan Lake*** (64 G/14), east of Big Sand Lake was named after him in 1994.

Harris, Flying Officer **Dallas G.** of Brandon (J 20722). No. 36 Operational Training Unit, RCAF. He died 27 August 1943 at the age of 22 and is commemorated at Brandon Cemetery. He was the son of George E. and Leta I. Harris of Brandon. ***Harris Island*** (64 J/14) in Belsham Lake was named after him in 1975.

Harris, Sergeant **Frederick Maitland** of Winnipeg (R 59300). No. 2 Elementary Flying Training School. He died 14 February 1941 at the age of 24 and is commemorated at Elmwood Cemetery in Winnipeg. He was the son of Frederick W. and Isabell C. Harris of Winnipeg. His brother writes (10 December 1998):

> In October of this year, I was in Winnipeg for the Daniel Mac. High School reunion and was fortunate enough to see the Memorial Plaque situated in their hallway. I think this is a real tribute to all those great young men who unfortunately, did not get to enjoy the country they were fighting for.
>
> F. Maitland Harris was born ... in Tate, Saskatchewan. He moved to Winnipeg in 1929 with our entire family. He graduated from Daniel Mac in 1933 or 1934. His only hobby, to the best of my knowledge, was flying! He learned to fly at the Winnipeg Flying Club in 1937 and then became an instructor for the Connie Johanneson Flying School in Winnipeg. Maitland joined the Air Force in 1940 and was instructing "blind flying" at the Fort William Flying School in Ontario. He was killed ... while training a young serviceman. Their plane was hit by an unauthorized aircraft in their airspace. Maitland was my only brother.

Harris Rapids (64 P/5) in the Wolverine River was named after him in 1995.

Harris, Chaplain **George A.** of La Rivière. 1st Canadian Parachute Battalion. He died 7 June 1944 at the age of 34 and is commemorated at Ranville War Cemetery in Calvados, France. He was the son of Alfred and Blanche C. Harris of Solihill, Warwickshire, England. ***Harris Hill*** (64 I/15), south of Wither Lake was named after him in 1995.

Harris, Sergeant **Gordon J. "Hap"** of Kenville (H 95599). Princess Louise Dragoon Guards. He died 13 December 1944 at the age of 24 and is commemorated at Villanova Canadian War Cemetery, Italy. He was one of the six children of Henry Alfred and Nellie M. Harris of Kenville. His Commanding Officer, Major D. J. Burke, personally wrote to Sergeant Harris' mother:

> Dear Mrs. Harris: While it is usually the job of the junior officers under my command to write next-of-kin of soldiers who died in action while engaged with the enemy in one of the three troops, the writing of this letter of sincere condolences to you over the loss of your son, Gordon, is something I want to do personally.
>
> For, Mrs. Harris, I want you to know how much I appreciated this Sergeant son of yours, who became popularly known as "Hap" among the boys who fought alongside him on the Italian front-line. Mrs. Harris, I can truthfully say, that they do not come any better than "Hap" as senior NCOs in this Canadian Army.
>
> His coolness in the face of fire was a great inspiration to his fellow comrades in the ranks. And without stretching the point one bit I can say that if I needed an NCO, I could always find the material in Sergeant Harris' 9 Troop due to his leadership. He was highly respected by his men and was a fighting man through and through.
>
> I know his passing is a great loss to yourself, Mrs. Harris, but believe me, his passing was also a great loss to the Canuck Army for with more of his calibre in the NCO bracket, it would be a valuable help to the officers in the future operations of this Corps.
>
> I am quite sure, Mrs. Harris, that Gordon did not suffer. I hope that in some small part that will help to ease your suffering. Sergeant Harris went down fighting, in the heart of a tough mix with the Germans, and there was more than one pair of damp eyes in the squadron when news of his death was officially confirmed.
>
> I must close now, Mrs. Harris, God bless you and keep you well. I am not acquainted with whether Sergeant Harris had a father who is still alive. If so, my best wishes and blessings go his way also. In parting, Mrs. Harris, I might add that if all Canadian parents had sons born to them like Sergeant Harris "our Canada" would truly be a wonderful country (n.d.).

Harris Point (64 C/3) on McKnight Lake was named after him in 1993.

Harris, Flying Officer **Reginald B.** of Brandon (J 8360). No. 410 Squadron. He died 13 June 1943 at the age of 28 and is commemorated at the Runnymede Memorial in Surrey, England. He was the son of J. J. and Luella Harris of Rosetown, Saskatchewan. ***Harris Peninsula*** (53 L/6) on Beaver Hill Lake was named after him in 1995.

Harris, Flying Officer **Robert D.** of Binscarth (J 37989). No. 550 Squadron. He died 7 March 1945 at the age of 31 and is commemorated at the Runnymede Memorial in Surrey, England. He was the son of Robert W. and Ellen M. Harris and was survived by his wife Margaret M. Harris of Winnipeg and their eight month-old daughter. He had formerly been the naturalist in charge of wildlife management at Big Grass Marsh, Ducks Unlimited's first restoration project in Manitoba. ***Harris Bay*** (64 N/15) on Putahow Lake was named after him in 1989.

Harris, Lance Sergeant **Thomas H.** of Winnipeg (H 40728). Royal Winnipeg Rifles. He died 30 January 1943 at the age of 28 and is commemorated at Llanwonno (St. Gwynno) Churchyard, Glamorganshire, Wales. He was the son of Edward J. and Martha Harris and was survived by his wife Ellen J. Harris of Ferndale, Manitoba. ***Harris Creek*** (53 N/8), which flows north into Gods River was named after him in 1995.

Harrison, Lance Corporal **Albert** of Winnipeg (H 1517). Princess Louise Dragoon Guards. He died 13 December 1944 and is commemorated at Villanova Canadian War Cemetery, Italy. ***Albert Harrison Lake*** (53 K/12), east of Gods Lake was named after him in 1995.

Harrison, Flying Officer **Frank P.** of Hamiota (J 13416). No. 405 Squadron. He died 24 May 1943 at the age of 21 and is commemorated at the Runnymede Memorial in Surrey, England. He was the son of Percy and Amy F. Harrison of Hamiota, Manitoba and was survived by his brother Albert and sister Ruth. She writes (22 February 2002):

As I was only two years old when he went overseas, I have to go by what his friends and my parents told me about him. As soon as Frank finished his Grade 12 at Hamiota, he enlisted in the RCAF. He was stationed at Brandon No. 12, then on to Initial Training School in Regina where he was trained as a Navigator. He also trained at Neepawa air base. He was sent overseas in the fall of 1942.

I remember my parents remarking about his great leadership. My brother Albert and my Dad would be trying to fix a piece of equipment on the farm and Frank would come by and put them straight on how it should be done. He was a very well liked person as he enjoyed people. Reverend Tom Delgaty recalls Frank being called "Shorty" as he had to have blocks put on the foot controls during training in Regina. A school chum of Frank's, Dr. Roy Brown, mentioned they were stationed in Brandon together. One day, they hitch-hiked their way to the farm at Hamiota. My dad, Percy, was working in the east field. So they stopped at the house first and Frank picked me up into his arms and they walked out to see my dad in the field. In the spring of 1943, Roy recalls having this same scenario happening again after Frank was reported missing with only Roy and I walking out to the same field to see my Dad. What a feeling it was for both Roy and Percy.

Frank was a member of the Pathfinder Force operating a Halifax bomber. At the time of his death, it was a night trip over Dortmund, Germany with a crew of seven. The crew was reported missing on May 24th, 1943.

Harrison Lake (64 N/3), southeast of Colbeck Lake was named after him in 1979.

Harrison, Flying Officer **John L.** of Winnipeg (J 23750). No. 162 Squadron. He died 13 June 1944 at the age of 22 and is commemorated at the Runnymede Memorial in Surrey, England. ***Harrison Rapids*** (64 I/14) in the Steel River was named after him in 1995.

Harrison, Rifleman **John L.** of Roblin (H 20471). Regina Rifle Regiment. He died 8 June 1944 at the age of 42 and is commemorated at Bretteville-sur-Laize Canadian War Cemetery in Calvados, France. He was the son of John and Hannah S. Harrison of Peebles, Scotland. He had travelled from Scotland to reunite with friends in the Roblin area when war was declared and so he enlisted there. ***Harrison Hill*** (64 I/1), northwest of Condie Lake was named after him in 1995.

Harrison, Pilot Officer **Orton D.** of Winnipeg (J 25841). No. 158 Squadron. He died 22 September 1943 at the age of 28 and is commemorated at the Hanover War Cemetery in Germany. His Halifax aircraft was shot down at Groz Lobke, Germany while on a daylight operation to Hanover. He was the son of Orton B. and Elizabeth A. Harrison of Winnipeg and was survived by his wife Cora M. Harrison. His nephew writes (16 January 2002):

My father explained to me that his brother Orton left Canada to join the British RAF. Before his fatal mission, he shared a premonition with his brother Don that he would likely not return. My parents' tribute to their brother was to name their son Orton Douglas Harrison (born 1946) to maintain the family name of Orton. My mother often spoke of my uncle's happy go lucky personality and his popularity with his fellow workers at Eaton's in Winnipeg prior to the war.

Harrison Point (64 O/8) on Neuchay Lake was named after him in 1995.

Harrison, Corporal **Robert L.** of Cromer (H 38836). Royal Canadian Corps of Signals. He died 23 April 1945 at the age of 25 and is commemorated at the Holten Canadian War Cemetery in Holland. His brother writes (8 November 2001):

As a young man growing up in the Depression years, life was very quiet and rigorous. He worked for various farmers and did some trapping in the winter time. He was never married and left his parents, one sister and two brothers to mourn his loss.

Harrison Bay (64 G/6) in Denison Lake was named after him in 1994.

Harrison, Flying Officer **Robert W.** of Winnipeg (J 37741). No. 426 Squadron. He died 2 November 1944 at the age of 32 and is commemorated at Rheinberg War Cemetery in Germany. He was the son of William and Rachael Harrison and was survived by his wife Marie Harrison of Winnipeg. ***Harrison Island*** (52 M/12) in Sasaginnigak Lake was named after him in 1991.

Harrison, Deck Hand **Walter** of Winnipeg. SS *George L. Torian*, Canadian Merchant Navy. The *George L. Torian* was torpedoed and sunk by U-129 off British Guyana in the Caribbean. Deck Hand Harrison died 22 February 1942 at the age of 21 and is commemorated at the Halifax Memorial. He was the son of Mr. and Mrs. Michael Harrison of Winnipeg. ***Walter Harrison Lake*** (63 P/9), northeast of Cauchon Lake was named after him in 2001.

Harrison, Flying Officer **Walter D.** of The Pas (J 25314). No. 18 Advanced Flying Unit. He died 7 February 1944 at the age of 29 and is commemorated at Botley Cemetery in Oxfordshire, England. He was the son of Mr. and Mrs. Paul Harrison and was survived by his wife Helen Harrison of New Westminster, British Columbia. ***Harrison Peninsula*** (64 F/4) on Reindeer Lake was named after him in 1995.

Harrop, Pilot Officer **Frank G.** of Winnipeg (C 86741). No. 420 Squadron. He died 11 June 1944 at the age of 21 and is commemorated at Theuville Communal Cemetery, Eure-et-Loir, France. He was the son of George and Frances E. Harrop of Elmwood, Manitoba. ***Harrop Island*** (63 P/11) in Partridge Crop Lake was named after him in 1995.

Harry, Sergeant **William B.** of Winnipeg (H 16143). 1st Canadian Special Services Battalion. This was a special Canadian-American unit, trained in Montana as mountain/ski troops and the subject of the 1968 film *The Devil's Brigade*. He died 17 August 1944 at the age of 23 and is commemorated at Mazargues War Cemetery, Marseilles, Bouches-du-Rhone, France. His cousin visited the site in 1951. He was the son of Wilmot E. and Jean S. Harry and was survived by his wife Irene E. Harry of Vancouver and their son. His cousin writes (12 November 2001):

Billy grew up in Winnipeg (Wolseley School) and in Prince Albert, Saskatchewan. When their officer was killed, he led the chaps across the moat, which was dry at the time, and into Fort Lestissac. They passed through the portcullis and into the fortress, but the Germans were waiting for them. He managed to get his men stationed, then was hit by a grenade. He died shortly after being moved to the ambulance ship.

Harry Lake (63 K/16), northwest of Wekusko Lake was named after him in 1973.

Hart, Pilot Officer **Gerald C.** of Neepawa (J 15720). No. 419 Squadron. He died 3 September 1942 at the age of 25 and is commemorated at Warnant Communal Cemetery, Anhee, Namur, Belgium. He was survived by his mother Emily J. Hart of Neepawa, Manitoba.

He was born in Neepawa, Manitoba January 29, 1917 and following the death of his father in 1934, Charles took over his shoe repair business, leaving it in 1934 to join the Royal Canadian Air Force. He received his training in Winnipeg and Ottawa. He was posted overseas in May, 1940 where he received his wings and became a member of the famous Moose Squadron. Gerald participated in the raids on Osnabrück and the 3000-mile raids on Cologne and Bremen. Gerald and his crew were shot down 3 September 1942, six miles northwest of Dinant during an attack against Karlsruhe, Germany (Pittman n.d.).

Hart Island (53 M/12) in Diana Lake was named after him in 1985.

Hart, Pilot Officer **Norris** of Dugald (81879). No. 242 Squadron, RAF. He died 5 November 1940 at the age of 25 and is commemorated at the Runnymede Memorial in Surrey, England. He was the son of Robert S. and Mary A. W. Hart of Canada. ***Hart Peninsula*** (54 D/6) on Stephens Lake was named after him in 1995.

Hart, Flight Sergeant **Ralph E.** of Gilbert Plains (R 95244). No. 405 Squadron. He died 14 May 1943 at the age of 22 and is commemorated at Avereest (Oud Avereese) General Cemetery, Holland. He was the only son of J. Waddy and Gertrude Hart of Gilbert Plains, Manitoba. ***Hart Bay*** (63 P/10) in Armstrong Lake was named after him in 1995.

Hartog, Flying Officer **Martin "Jack"** of Winnipeg (J 40430). No. 431 Squadron. He died 31 March 1945 at the age of 21 and is commemorated at Becklingen War Cemetery in Germany. He was the son of Martin and Ida Hartog of Winnipeg. His sister writes (28 February 1998):

Jack was born in Winnipeg and attended Prince Edward School and East Kildonan Collegiate. After completing High School, he worked for Canadian Pacific Telegraphs ... until enlisting in the Royal Canadian Air Force in November, 1942.

Jack trained at Brandon, Saskatoon, Regina and received his Navigator's Wings and Commission on January 13, 1943 at Portage la Prairie. He was then posted overseas and left Winnipeg on March 15 of that year. We are currently in the process of trying to obtain further information as to where he was stationed in England etc.

Hartog Lake (52 L/6), east of Lac du Bonnet was named after him in 1973.

Hartwell, Private **Arthur G.** of St. Vital (H 101674). Royal Canadian Army Medical Corps. He died 8 August 1943 at the age of 30 and is commemorated at Agira Canadian War Cemetery in Italy. He was the son of Arthur J. and Rena Hartwell and was survived by his wife Helen C. Hartwell of St. Vital. ***Hartwell Lake*** (64 I/2), east of North Knife Lake was named after him in 1974.

Harvey, Flying Officer **Angus B.** of Rapid City (J 38162). No. 50 Squadron. He died 23 September 1944 at the age of 25 and is commemorated at Dalfsen General Cemetery, Holland. He was the son of Henry W. and Jannette E. Harvey of Winnipeg Beach, Manitoba. ***Harvey Point*** (64 P/13) on Bulloch Lake was named after him in 1995.

Harvey, Sergeant **Burt D.** of Winnipeg (H 35846). 1st Canadian Special Services Battalion. He died 3 December 1943 at the age of 19 and is commemorated at the Cassino War Cemetery in Italy. He was the son of Walter H. and Henrietta Harvey. ***Harvey Island*** (53 K/4) in Red Sucker Lake was named after him in 1995.

Harvey, Leading Aircraftman **Clifford A.** of Winnipeg (R 172898). Wireless Operator, RCAF Station Grande Prairie. He died 27 June 1945 at the age of 32 and is commemorated at Brookside Cemetery in Winnipeg. He was the son of Alexander and Emily Harvey of Winnipeg and was survived by his wife Florence K. Harvey of Winnipeg. She writes (29 March 1998) that he:

... enlisted in Winnipeg and is buried at the military cemetery there. During [the] years of the late '30s to '42, his interests were skiing and was for many years a member and competitor at the Assiniboine Golf Course.

A contemporary newspaper obituary added that:

Harvey was born in this city and prior to the enlistment with the RCAF in August, 1942 was employed with the Manitoba Pool Elevators company. He was active in sports organizations and in school athletic activities (n.d.).

Harvey Bay (64 N/1) in Slingsby Lake was named after him in 1995.

Harvey, Lieutenant **Denis F.** Royal Winnipeg Rifles. He died 16 February 1945 and is commemorated at Groesbeek Canadian War Cemetery in Holland. ***Harvey Peninsula*** (53 L/11) on Michikinabish Lake was named after him in 1995.

Hase, Flight Sergeant **Rudolf C.** of Souris (R 196364). No. 227 Squadron. He died 4 December 1944 at the age of 20 and is commemorated at Choloy War Cemetery, Meurthe-et-Moselle, France. ***Hase Lake*** (64 P/7), southeast of Nejanilini Lake was named after him in 1974.

Hatch, Corporal **Eldon T. P. "Kutch"** of Elgin (H 19954). Queen's Own Cameron Highlanders. He died 19 August 1942 at the age of 28 and is commemorated at Dieppe Canadian War Cemetery in Seine-Maritime, France. He was the youngest child of Jeffery H. and Beulah Hatch of Elgin, Manitoba. He had been employed as a telephone lineman before enlisting.

Eldon was known principally for his pleasant disposition and excellent baritone voice. He was a choir member and often soloist in the Hartney United Church choir. He is reported to have led the troops in songs many times (Royal Canadian Legion n.d.).

Hatch Lake (63 I/7), north of Molson Lake was named after him in 1973.

Hatch, Pilot Officer **George C.** of Winnipeg (J 88705). No. 434 Squadron. He died 20 February 1944 at the age of 25 and is commemorated at the Hanover War Cemetery in Germany. He was the son of Henry and Mary A. Hatch (née Arksey). ***Hatch Island*** (64 N/13) in Wakula Lake was named after him in 1995.

Hatton, Sergeant **Arthur T.** of Morris (R 4312A). No. 9 Squadron. He died 12 August 1941 at the age of 20 and is commemorated at the Runnymede Memorial in Surrey, England. He was the son of Arthur M. and Enid W. Hatton of Winnipeg. ***Hatton Lake*** (64 P/14), northeast of Nejanilini Lake was named after him in 1974.

Hauk, Corporal **Norman A. "Sandy"** of Virden (L 27470). Royal Canadian Corps of Signals. He died 6 June 1944 at the age of 23 and is commemorated at the Bayeux Memorial in Calvados, France. He was survived by his mother Mrs. Lena Hauk of Virden, two older brothers, his wife Muriel Hauk (née Mathews) of Wales and by their young son. In 1946, Norman's widow and their infant son Norman arrived in Canada and went to Virden to visit with the Hauk family. They resided there until 1967 when they moved to Winnipeg. ***Hauk Lake*** (64 H/11), south of Small Lake was named after Corporal Hauk in 1995.

Hawes, Private **Malcolm J.** of Selkirk (H 6204). Winnipeg Grenadiers. He died 15 July 1945 and is commemorated at the Yokohama War Cemetery in Japan. Returning Grenadier Private Harry Atkinson reported that:

> "One month and 15 days ago, seven of the fellows got stomach poisoning. They were in bad shape when they arrived back in camp that night. They were told to report to our [Japanese] commander. He ordered a stomach pump for them. Don't know why, probably saw the end of the war was near." Four of them died – Lance Corporal Malcolm Hawes, Private Jim Gard, Private Roy Kirk and Private Bob McLeod (*Winnipeg Tribune* September 1945).

Hawes Bay (64 N/5) in Snyder Lake was named after him in 1995.

Hawes, Corporal **Nelson S.** of Virden (H 26405). 14th Canadian Hussars. He died 23 August 1944 at the age of 36 and is commemorated at Bretteville-sur-Laize Canadian War Cemetery in Calvados, France. He was the son of the late John R. and Margaret A. Hawes and was survived by four brothers.

> He was born at Alexander, Manitoba in 1908, later moving to Two Creeks where he received his education. At the time of his enlistment, he was employed at Virden (Virden *Empire-Advance* n.d.).

Hawes Island (64 G/12) in Big Sand Lake was named after him in 1995.

Hawken, Trooper **George S.** of Miami (H 103747). 1st Hussar Tank Regiment. He died 6 June 1944 at the age of 21 and is commemorated at Beny-sur-Mer Canadian War Cemetery in Calvados, France. He was the second of the six children of Howard and Anna Hawken of Miami, Manitoba. His youngest sister (24 March 1998) writes that he:

> ... went to school in a small one-room school. He participated in all sports in school, no one in particular. He and his brother liked to go fishing with our Dad. George quit school at Grade 8; to go further he would have [had] to live away from home, and pay tuition and room and board which our parents couldn't afford. He remained home to help Dad run the farm until he enlisted in the army.

Hawken Lake (52 L/3), northeast of Brereton Lake was named after him in 1973.

Hawken, Warrant Officer 1 **Ralph E.** of Darlingford (R 81068). No. 148 Squadron. He died 4 November 1943 at the age of 30 and is commemorated at Belgrade War Cemetery, Yugoslavia. He was the son of William F. and Caroline E. Hawken of Darlingford, Manitoba. ***Hawken Island*** (64 C/10) in Chicken Lake was named after him in 1995.

Hawkes, Private **Douglas** of Selkirk (H 6837). Winnipeg Grenadiers. He died a prisoner of war 20 September 1942 and is commemorated at the Sai Wan War Cemetery in Hong Kong. ***Hawkes Lake*** (64 P/9), east of Nejanilini Lake was named after him in 1974.

Hawkins, Trooper **Lionel M.** of Winnipeg (H 195). Lord Strathcona's Horse. He died 24 May 1944 at the age of 32 and is commemorated at the Cassino War Cemetery in Italy. He was the son of Albert F. and Winifred M. E. Hawkins and was survived by his wife Ethel M. Hawkins of Port Arthur, Ontario. ***Hawkins Bay*** (53 L/8) in Webber Lake was named after him in 1995.

Hawkins, Private **Reginald J.** of Gilbert Plains (K 69867). Royal Hamilton Light Infantry. He died 22 November 1944 at the age of 32 and is commemorated at the Groesbeek Canadian War Cemetery in Holland. He was the son of James and Elizabeth Hawkins of Vancouver and was survived by his wife Elizabeth Hawkins of Vancouver. ***Hawkins Island*** (53 M/5) in Utik Lake was named after him in 1996.

Hawkins, Flying Officer **William B.** of Winnipeg (J 35828). No. 1666 Heavy Conversion Unit, RCAF. He died 8 June 1944 at the age of 28 and is commemorated at Stonefall Cemetery in Yorkshire, England. He was the son of William and Agnes E. Hawkins and was survived by his wife Muriel F. Hawkins (née Hooey) of Winnipeg. His cousin (18 February 2002) recalls that he was:

> ... born in Govan, Saskatchewan in 1915, the second eldest of five children. Mr. and Mrs. William Hawkins had immigrated from Scotland in 1908 and 1912 respectively. Three of the sons served in the Canadian Armed Forces in World War II. Bill graduated from Govan High School and was an ardent tennis player. During the Depression when it appeared there was little promise of a better future, Bill moved from the pioneer general store (1907 - late 1930s) in Govan owned by the much esteemed Donald Fraser, to Winnipeg where he found work with Shopeasy stores.
>
> Bill graduated as a navigator with a commission in Edmonton in September, 1943. He married Muriel Hooey from Cypress River, Manitoba and was posted overseas shortly thereafter. Bill was killed on active service 8 June 1944. Bill's grave is beautifully attended in the Harrogate Cemetery. It has been visited by members of his Canadian family and relatives. Muriel Hawkins is buried at Starbuck, Manitoba. The inscription on the grave stone bears the names of Muriel and William Hawkins.

Hawkins Lake (53 L/10), west of Gods Lake was named after him in 1961.

Hawrysh, Rifleman **Alexander** of Dauphin (H 95517). Royal Winnipeg Rifles. He died 6 September 1944 at the age of 22 and is commemorated at the Calais Canadian War Cemetery in France. He was the son of William and Annie Hawrysh of Dauphin. His niece writes (29 November 2001):

> My Uncle Alex, as he was called, grew up in Dauphin, one of five siblings. I feel a close connection with him, although I never had the opportunity to meet him, as I am his namesake. When any of the relatives speak of him it has always been positive. He was one of the young men who lied about his age so that he could go to war for his country. My father, his older

brother Steve, was in the air force and lucky enough to return to us, but Uncle Alex wasn't as fortunate. He was killed by friendly fire while overseas and is buried in the Calais Canadian War Cemetery in France. I understand he was a very genuine person, had a good sense of humour and was very kind to all that knew him. He had only started to live, as he died at age 23, and was looking forward to returning home to Dauphin to be with his parents, William and Annie, and his siblings, Steve, John, Betty and Pat. He is fondly remembered by school friends and neighbours, and I always feel humble when relatives who knew him tell me that I remind them of him.

Hawrysh Lake (64 H/4), north of Gauer Lake was named after him in 1995.

Hawthorne, Flight Sergeant **William Robert** of Oak River (R 68194). No. 172 Squadron. He died 15 December 1942 at the age of 23 and is commemorated at the Runnymede Memorial in Surrey, England. His sister (24 February 1998) recalls that:

Bob was born ... on our parents' farm ... one and a half miles northeast of the village of Oak River. He lived there until 1934 when our father died and mother sold the farm and moved to the village. Bob received his education at the local school where he took part in most sports but was not an avid sportsman. His one love was music and without any musical training, he could play any instrument he touched. The violin was his speciality and he started playing in public at age 8. In 1938, Bob came to Woodstock, Ontario where his older brother was working. He got a job at the Craig Machine Shop where he worked until the summer of 1940 when he joined the Air Force. On November 14th, 1941 he married Helen Cooke of Guelph and went overseas in January, 1942.

We never knew where he was in England because his letters were censored and ours to him went to a depot. On December 18th, 1942, Mother received the telegram that he was missing and it wasn't until after the end of the war that we learned that his plane went down in the English Channel.

Hawthorne Lake (64 H/7), north of Solmundsson Lake was named after him in 1995.

Hay, Flying Officer **Alan J. F.** of Winnipeg (J 21713). No. 88 Squadron. He died 13 August 1943 at the age of 22 and is commemorated at the Runnymede Memorial in Surrey, England. ***Hay Peninsula*** (64 O/2) on Munroe Lake was named after him in 1995.

Hay, Lieutenant Colonel **Dr. Arthur W. S.** of Winnipeg. Royal Canadian Army Medical Corps. He died 31 December 1944 at the age of 42 and is commemorated at Brookwood Military Cemetery in Surrey, England. He was the son of William and Viola W. Hay of Winnipeg and was survived by his wife Mary I. Hay of Winnipeg and their three children. During his undergraduate career, he was interested in the Students' Christian Movement and taught Sunday School in the Stella Mission. His summer holidays were spent preaching in the mission field.

After an intern year at the Winnipeg General Hospital, Arthur Hay graduated in 1928 and entered the Maclean-Thorlakson Clinic. In 1930 he went overseas for postgraduate study, obtaining his FRCS [in] Edinburgh in 1931, returning to Winnipeg after an absence of 18 months. Here, he resumed his practice with the McLean, Thorlakson Clinic (*Winnipeg Free Press* 1945).

In later years it was reported that he taught himself Ukrainian so that he might better serve his patients.

Dr. A. W. S. Hay was the gold medallist in the Manitoba Medical College Class of 1928. He joined the Maclean-Thorlakson Clinic immediately after graduation. He was an exemplary surgeon and an excellent teacher. At the outbreak of Work War II, he joined the Royal Canadian Army Medical Corps, and in 1944 was chief of surgery in a large military hospital just outside of London. Late in December of that year, the hospital had to deal with a disturbing number of cases of infectious hepatitis. Colonel Hay was active in the management of these cases and the efforts to control the disease. One day during the latter part of the month, after lecturing to the professional staff on the subject, he happened to look in a mirror and noticed the telltale yellowing of the eyes that marks the onset of hepatitis. He died on December 31, 1944, a tragic loss to his family and colleagues, and to the profession of medicine (Cunnings 1986).

In a letter home to his former partner, he wrote in part:

Dear Thor [Dr. P. H. T. Thorlakson]: ... When I left to join the army three and a half years ago, it was from a sense of duty to the cause of freedom throughout the world. There was no assumption on my part that when the war is over you should be hampered in post-war planning by any undue sense of obligation to those of us who have been over here. Certainly no one worth his salt would wish that a place be made for him just because he had served in one of the forces. This has been a "total war," and those of us who have stayed behind have certainly lived a much more strenuous and exacting life on the whole, than have officers in the RCAMC. Most of us are ready to admit that, and have done so repeatedly whenever the question has arisen. All of this is simply a fumbling attempt to express my sense of obligation to you and the group, my appreciation for most generous treatment and my hope that if your post-war plans do include me, these years of war service (which on the whole have been pleasant years) may not in any way affect your planning. Thank you for all you have done. It has indeed helped me to finally feel as though I can "close one door but open another." (17 September 1944).

His daughter established a scholarship in his name for graduates of Sturgeon Creek and Silver Heights collegiates. She adds (4 November 2001):

... I was only one when he joined the forces. My only surviving brother was just a year older, so he has few recollections as well. I do know that during my nursing years at the Health Sciences Centre, many Doctors, Nurses, Technicians, elevator operators and cleaning personnel shared several stories about him with me. The words "kind, energetic, very religious, brilliant, marvellous with his hands, asked by many to write speeches for them and sometimes tended to lose his temper" were repeated by those who knew him well. I did hear, as well, that when I was born he was delighted!

Hay Narrows (64 H/6) in Northern Indian Lake was named after him in 1995.

Hay, Flying Officer **Colin M.** of Winnipeg (J 39394). No. 432 Squadron, Distinguished Service Order.

One night in September, 1944, Flying Officer Hay was the navigator of an aircraft detailed to attack Bottrop. It was his third operational mission. Whilst over the target, the pilot was severely wounded and lost control of the aircraft which went into a dive. Displaying great promptitude, Flying Officer Hay took over the controls and succeeded in levelling out. Although inexperienced as a pilot and despite the fact that some of the instruments were unserviceable, he flew the aircraft back to an airfield and landed it. On touching down, the under-carriage collapsed and the aircraft caught fire but the crew got clear uninjured. This officer displayed great coolness and resource and was undoubtedly responsible for the ultimate safety of his comrades (DSO Citation 5 December 1944).

He died 6 March 1945 at the age of 31 and is commemorated at Brookwood Military Cemetery in Surrey, England. He was the son of Walter M. and Annie S. S. Hay (née Lyon) and was survived by his wife Bette A. Hay (née Rollins) of Winnipeg and their nine month-old daughter Heather whom he had never seen. He had been a salesman at the time of his enlistment. His daughter recalls (22 March 2002):

It means a lot to me that the Province of Manitoba has chosen to honour my father and others like him, whose lives were sacrificed for our freedom, by naming geographical places in the Province after them. The City of Winnipeg and surrounding area brings happy memories to my heart, as I'm sure it did for my mother and father.

Colin Maxwell Hay, my father, was born in Winnipeg on January 2, 1914. His parents were Annie Seton Steele Lyon and Walter Maxwell Hay, who had emigrated from Glasgow, Scotland. He had seven living siblings - four brothers and three sisters. They all lived at 368 Manitoba Avenue in Winnipeg.

He came from a family who enjoyed sports - track high on the list among them. Family games were organized easily with so many people available to play. The family attended St. Giles United Church and it was open house at their home every Sunday. He had a wonderful family life.

He delivered newspapers for the *Winnipeg Free Press* and the paper route was passed from brother to brother over a long period. He was given a pocket watch for perfect service, which is still in my possession.

On April 18, 1942 Colin was married to my mother, Bette Aileen Rollins, also from Winnipeg. I was born on June 10, 1944, when he was overseas. He was posted to Sydney, Nova Scotia and Mont Joli, Quebec before going overseas.

My father loved to sing. Both he and my mother sang in music festivals, scoring high marks and often being accompanied by Evelyn Gregory, my mother's sister, a well-known Winnipeg pianist and organist. I can attest to this love of music after discovering a trunk full of sheet music that belonged to them. He used to practise overseas with a pianist. I thought what a comfort it must have been to him. Margaret Jean Gresham, his oldest niece, told me that he was guest soloist on one occasion with the RCAF orchestra overseas. His dream was to be a professional singer and may not have been that unrealistic. Love of music was certainly passed on to me.

My mother didn't talk to me about him very often, as a person. It was too painful, I guess. She did bring out the medals and talked about his bravery and sacrifice for our freedom. Later in life, I asked her why she never re-married, and her reply was that she never loved anyone as much as Colin.

When I was young she would take me to the War Memorial on November 11th for the Remembrance Day services. When I was fourteen it became too painful for me and I never attended again. I seem to need something more personal and private. I watch the broadcast on television, but what gives me the most comfort is a visit to the Memorial Chamber in the centre block of the Parliament Buildings in Ottawa, every November 5th. That is the day that the page is turned to display my father's name, in the Memorial Book of those who sacrificed their lives in World War II. It is a quiet place, of ceremony and dignity, with inscriptions on the wall and the various books from the different wars on display and open.

I learned a lot about my Dad from my Uncle Joe, his brother, and wife Rita, when I visited Winnipeg in 1990 and 1992, after a long absence, and from my Aunt Margaret, his sister, who lived in Toronto. I became very close to her and learned from her that my father didn't tolerate injustice easily, and about his sensitivity and kindness. My cousin Margaret Jean's words come to mind in her vivid recollection of him: "He had a great sense of humour, was a kind, warm and loving man, a special individual, universally liked. I wish you had known him."

My understanding from my Uncle Joe was that it was on my father's last mission that his plane went down and the crew was killed. In order to get in his last operation so that he could come home to Winnipeg early, he had taken the place on a different crew, substituting for their navigator, who had been killed previously. You can imagine my mother's great anticipation at his coming home soon, only to receive a cable telling of his death. My father's death left a great void in my life, and when I think of him it is mostly with sadness and loss.

I lived in Winnipeg with my maternal grandparents and my mother until I was five years old. Then my mother worked for Senator Haig from Winnipeg and she lived in both Ottawa and Winnipeg according to his schedule. When I was nine years old we made the final move to Ottawa to live there permanently. She worked for the National Gallery of Canada, then as Secretary to Gordon Churchill, a Winnipeg MP, when he was Minister of Veterans' Affairs in the Diefenbaker years, and later she held a permanent job in the Department of Trade and Commerce.

Although we visited Winnipeg almost every year and I was well-loved by my mother and lacked for nothing, emotionally it was a lonely life for me away from family and relatives. I grew up feeling very insecure and in my late teens, when my maternal grandmother had a stroke and the open grieving was taking place for John F. Kennedy, all the grieving for my father came to the surface. My life has been one of coping with chronic depression and an anxiety disorder, but I'm thankful for the support I get from my doctors, my church and remaining close family and friends.

Following open heart surgery in 1969, my mother had a stroke in 1970 and lived until she was 67 years old in 1982. Although she was still active and involved in issues for the disabled, I know we both missed family support. Because the effects of war can be severe and long-lasting to families and some individuals, I do believe that peaceful means should be exercised until every possibility has been exhausted. That is why I wear a poppy on November 11th as well as the dove of peace pin. I do not regret that my father fought against evil for our country's freedom. It was courageous for everyone involved in the armed forces. My religious faith grows stronger as the years go by. I carry within me two written messages that have given me comfort and hope over the years: one is the inscription, part of which was written on the Memorial Chamber's wall before it was re-done. I discovered it comes from Hebrews Chapter 12 Verse 1 to 2a in the Bible.

> Let us run with patience the race that is set before us,
> looking unto Jesus, the author and finisher of our faith.

The other is the cherished words from an aerogram addressed to me by my father shortly after I was born. His personality just leaps from the page. In this letter he told me how happy he was to be my father and how much he loved me. He called me "wee snooks" and even asked my mom if he could take his turn pushing the baby carriage. He said, "Give the wee one a hug for me and I hope we three can get together some day soon."

In 1975, RAF cadets from Colchester, Essex discovered the buried remains of Flying Officer Hay's Wellington aircraft on a farm. Three years later, his widow was notified and invited to the dedication of a memorial in the Memorial Gardens at Walton-on-the-Naze. She recalls:

> And then a flood of memories came rushing back to that night in 1945, when, as a young girl with my baby daughter, I was living with my parents in Winnipeg while Colin was overseas. Dad had just fallen asleep after reading a fairy tale to Heather. I was in the hallway when a neighbour, Gladys Kellett, opened the front door and asked for my Mother who was in the kitchen. Gladys then persuaded Mother to go next door with her. I knew then that something had happened to Colin. Mother returned crying, holding the cable which told of the plane's crashing and that all crew members had been killed, specifically mentioning Colin's name and number.
>
> Mother hugged me as we read and reread the cable and then she ran upstairs to tell Dad. He came down slowly with Mother behind him. He held my hand and kissed me. Then we sat down in the kitchen and decided Dad should phone Mr. Hay, Colin's father. Dad was a strong man, but his hand shook as he picked up the receiver and his voice quavered as he explained the cable (Hay 1979).

Colin Hay Lake (64 H/12), north of Wood Lake was named after him in 1995.

Hay, Pilot Officer **Douglas N.** of Findlay (J 90944). No. 425 Squadron. He died 2 March 1944 at the age of 32 and is commemorated at Stonefall Cemetery in Yorkshire, England. He was the son of John and Sarah Hay and was survived by his wife Emilie Hay of Belleview, Manitoba. ***Hay Rapids*** (64 P/10) in the Cameron River was named after him in 1995.

Hayden, Trooper **Clifford H.** of Lyleton (H 103207). Fort Garry Horse. He died 9 June 1944 at the age of 21 and is commemorated at the Bayeux Memorial in Calvados, France. He was the son of Earl and Ada Hayden of Lyleton, Manitoba. Before the war, Trooper Hayden was an avid driver which possibly influenced his

decision to join a tank regiment. In the narrative of the Invasion of France for the 10th Canadian Armed Regiment, the entry for 9 June 1944 includes the following:

> The Commanding Officer and Adjutant visited the garrison of Les Buissons about 0900 hrs and found them somewhat shaken after a hard night. The enemy was still pressing his attack from two directions and had infiltrated mortars and machine guns forward into the grain fields a few hundred yards away from the positions. About this time, the enemy began a heavy bombardment by 88mm guns which were whistling through the whole area. The situation seemed somewhat tense so the CO ordered a counter-attack by tanks with fire from the east side of Les Buissons by two troops. This undoubtedly relieved the situation in the opinion of the infantry commanders, but several tanks were knocked out whilst engaging the enemy near Buron, by 88mm fire from near Galmanche. The CO and Adjutant's tanks were both lost by enemy fire, whilst trying to help the left flank with fire.

Trooper Hayden was the only member of his crew to be killed in this action; the other four crew members were taken prisoners of war. All went to visit his mother after the war. ***Hayden Creek*** (64 K/8), which flows northeast into Fergus River was named after him in 1972.

Hayes, Private **Harold** of Winnipeg (H 16233). Princess Patricia's Canadian Light Infantry. He died 13 December 1943 and is commemorated at the Moro River Canadian War Cemetery in Italy. ***Hayes Bay*** (64 B/9) in Naykownapiskaw Lake was named after him in 1995.

Hayes, Sergeant **James P.** of Souris (R 82352). No. 22 Operational Training Unit, RCAF. He died 6 July 1942 at the age of 21 and is commemorated at Hereford Cemetery, Herefordshire, England. He was the son of Edward E. and Mabel F. Hayes of Souris, Manitoba. His brother reports that his main interest before the war was Scouting and he attained the level of King's Scout. He had been employed as a shopman before enlisting in 1940. ***Hayes Lake*** (64 J/16), north of Tadoule Lake was named after him in 1975.

Hayhurst, Gunner **Cornelius "Connie"** of Oak River (H 92446). Royal Canadian Artillery. He died 29 August 1942 at the age of 19 and is commemorated at Nanaimo Public Cemetery, British Columbia. He was the son of John Thomas and Violet Hayhurst of Oak River, Manitoba. His youngest brother Frank, who was 10 years old at the time, recalls when Connie was at home on leave, a neighbour across the road gave him a plug of Big Ben chewing tobacco. "Connie told his mother to keep it for him for he knew his mission when he returned to barracks was overseas and he didn't know when he was going to be back home." ***Hayhurst Lake*** (63 N/2), east of Kississing Lake was named after him in 1972.

Hayman, Lieutenant **James Francis** of Winnipeg. Queen's Own Cameron Highlanders. He died 23 October 1944 at the age of 30 and is commemorated at Bergen-op-Zoom Canadian War Cemetery in Holland. He was the son of William F. and Georgina Hayman and was survived by his wife Greta N. Hayman of Winnipeg and their daughter. ***Hayman Lake*** (64 K/12), northeast of Reindeer Lake was named after him in 1972.

Haynes, Private **Orson A.** of Winnipeg (H 8754). Queen's Own Cameron Highlanders. He died 21 July 1944 at the age of 29 and is commemorated at Beny-sur-Mer Canadian War Cemetery in Calvados, France. He was the son of Anthony and Martha Haynes and was survived by his wife Kathleen P. Haynes of Winnipeg. ***Haynes Lake*** (64 J/1), south of Tadoule Lake was named after him in 1975.

Haywood, Lance Sergeant **Charles T.** of Norgate (H 26037). Fort Garry Horse. He died 4 July 1944 at the age of 23 and is commemorated at Beny-sur-Mer Canadian War Cemetery in Calvados, France. He was the son of Charles T. and Ethel Haywood of St. James. ***Haywood Lake*** (54 M/11), north of Long Lake was named after him in 1984.

Hazelton, Pilot Officer **William M.** of Winnipeg (J 51489). No. 1 Wireless School, RCAF. He died 5 August 1945 at the age of 23 and is commemorated at Brookside Cemetery in Winnipeg. He was the son of Josiah T. and Laura M. Hazelton of Ottawa. ***Hazelton Lake*** (64 J/11), west of Tadoule Lake was named after him in 1975.

Head, Flying Officer **Robert H.** of Winnipeg (J 17011). No. 38 Squadron. He died 6 January 1944 at the age of 22 and is commemorated at the Alamein Memorial in Egypt. He was the son of Cyril C. and Gladys C. Head of Sidney, British Columbia. ***Head Lake*** (64 O/14), east of Nueltin Lake was named after him in 1975.

Heaman, Rifleman **Raymond A.** of Hargrave (H 47029). Royal Winnipeg Rifles. He died 22 April 1945 at the age of 27 and is commemorated at the Holten Canadian War Cemetery in Holland. He was the son of Jerry and Ellen E. Heaman of Hargrave, Manitoba. ***Heaman Lake*** (52 L/11), east of Black Lake was named after him in 1982.

Heathfield, Sergeant **Gordon Basil** (H 14161). Lanark and Renfrew Scottish Regiment. He died 24 September 1944 at the age of 27 and is commemorated at the Cesena War Cemetery in Italy. He was the son of Reverend Harry and Pearl Heathfield (née Bolton) and was survived by his wife Eileen M. Heathfield of Kitchener, Ontario. His wife (20 November 2001) recalls that:

> Bas and I met at Port Arthur Collegiate Institute at about the Grade 11 level and until we were married in February, 1942, he was part of our already large family. When my second eldest brother Robert volunteered in 1940, they went to the recruitment office together. My brother was accepted into the Air Force at once, but because of poor eyesight, Basil was rejected by all. He worked at the Port Arthur Shipbuilding Company until 1943, when he said by then, if you could walk into the recruitment office, you were welcomed.
>
> He had a terrific sense of humour, was kind, generous and full of energy. I believe he was recruited by the Royal Winnipeg Rifles but his arm band in Italy was from the Perth Regiment. In six months he was overseas and was killed in September. I don't know where, but he had risen from Private to Sergeant and was well liked by the men under him, so another Sergeant wrote to me. At the time under fierce bombardment, he was the only one killed, somewhere along the Adriatic coast. This was their last siege in battle, the young Sergeant wrote.
>
> He and I were great pals and spent a great deal of time together. His father was the Reverend Harry Heathfield DD and at the time was minister of the large United Church in North Battleford, Saskatchewan. Basil had two brothers, Bolton who was older and Harold, younger, who was serving in the Army in the European theatre at the time. Basil

appeared to have nine lives at home and often challenged fate in doing and daring. Everyone assured me that he would be home again; most of them returned – three brothers, two brothers-in-law, a myriad of friends – but he lies in Cesena British Empire Cemetery.

I have his medals and other memorabilia. These great sacrifices are never forgotten and they should not be. My second marriage is as strong and loving as my first and we have a son and daughter which were a reward for the lack of children in my first. We have four grandchildren and I sometimes think that Basil looks down upon us and he smiles.

Thank you for naming the lake in Manitoba for him. We framed the lovely certificate and have it on our wall. It was an honour bestowed and greatly appreciated. I am now 86 and both Walter and I enjoy good health. Sometimes trials make you stronger and you realize how petty some things are – not worth a second thought. Life is good!

Heathfield Lake (63 O/7), southwest of Wuskwatim Lake was named after him in 1995.

Heathman, Private **Lester** of Winnipeg (H 19834). Queen's Own Cameron Highlanders. He died 19 August 1942 and is commemorated at Dieppe Canadian War Cemetery in Seine-Maritime, France. ***Heathman Lake*** (64 I/11), northwest of North Knife Lake was named after him in 1974.

Hebner, Gunner **Chester** of Riding Mountain (H 95535). Royal Canadian Artillery. He died 11 July 1944 at the age of 29 and is commemorated at Beny-sur-Mer Canadian War Cemetery in Calvados, France. He was the son of Frank and Minnie M. Hebner of Riding Mountain, Manitoba. ***Hebner Lake*** (64 P/1), southeast of Nejanilini Lake was named after him in 1974.

Heinrichs, Rifleman **Edward** of Halbstadt (H 14455). Royal Winnipeg Rifles. He died 5 July 1944 at the age of 19 and is commemorated at Beny-sur-Mer Canadian War Cemetery in Calvados, France. He was the third of the seven children of Anton and Margerith Heinrichs of Halbstadt, Manitoba. His sister reports that (29 April 1995):

Edward grew up in Halbstadt, Manitoba. [He] went to the country school to Grade 8, then took Grade 9 by correspondence. [He] attended the Bergthaler church in Halbstadt.

She adds (15 November 2001):

He went into action June 7th at Normandy Beach. He left behind his parents, two brothers and four sisters. He loved to read [and] as to what he planned for the future is hard to say with the war going on. He loved life and his friends.

Heinrichs Lake (64 N/4), southwest of Nueltin Lake was named after him in 1972.

Heinzig, Sapper **Paul** of Waskada (H 93494). Royal Canadian Engineers. He died 4 November 1944 and is commemorated at Schoonselhof Cemetery in Antwerp, Belgium. ***Heinzig Lake*** (64 K/7), northeast of Reindeer Lake was named after him in 1972.

Hellsten, Sergeant **Martin E.** (H 46137). Lake Superior Regiment. He died 4 April 1945 and is commemorated at the Holten Canadian War Cemetery in Holland. ***Hellsten Lake*** (64 O/3), southeast of Blackfish Lake was named after him in 1995.

Helman, Lance Bombardier **Allan J. "Sonny"** of Carman (SH 61952). Royal Canadian Artillery. He died 25 April 1953 at the age of 20 and is commemorated at the United Nations Cemetery in Pusan, South Korea. ***Helman Lake*** (63 O/1), east of Halfway Lake was named after this Korean War casualty in 1998.

Hembroff, Private **Earl** of Gladstone (532274). Royal Canadian Army Medical Corps. He died 9 April 1917 at the age of 27 and is commemorated at Quatre-Vents Military Cemetery, Estree-Cauchy, Pas de Calais, France. He was the son of Thomas Hembroff of Elderslie, Ontario and was survived by his wife Mabel Hembroff (née Dell) of Gladstone and their two children. His son died of diphtheria months later. Private Hembroff was hit by a shell fragment on the first day of the offensive at Vimy Ridge while carrying a wounded man to an Advanced Dressing Station. He kept a diary of his experiences while overseas. These are a few of the entries:

- Midnight. A million rounds of ammunition in one hour to celebrate Fritz's birthday (15 September 1916).
- St. Omer Rest Camp. Slept in a Fritz dugout 35 feet underground within 100 yards of Chamber of Horrors. Shells going over like hail and one continuous roar. Not many rats and Fritz too busy to put over gas. We have complete control of the air. Five Point 9s [five-pound nine-inch Howitzers] in goodly numbers in sight. All open country and trenches upon trenches in all directions. Advanced Dressing Station two miles behind lines. Very crude indeed. Just a couple of trenches with sand bag roof and a little trench matting. Dugout quite handy for emergencies. Very stuffy downstairs. Dead lying all over, especially in pieces as shells persist in bringing them to the surface. Bodies in Chamber all blackened from smoke bomb (26 September 1916).
- Trip to Galleries and Red Chateau in Courcelette. Road all shot to pieces and whole Company lost. Only 23 reported. Men lying all over and being walked over. Continuous shelling. Passed tanks. Tear shells. In dugout imprisoned for two days. Not much to eat as rations all lost. Beef picked up is bully. No water. Dugouts very elaborate. Arm chairs, telephones, electric lights, curtains, switchboards, cooking stoves, etc. Under monastery. Over week without wash. Clothes not off for about two months. Friends plentiful. Preachers bury dead at night (18 October 1916).
- Lost harness, belt bottle, rubber sheet, helmet, knife and mess tin coming out with a case. Shelled very heavily and road completely changed. Very dark and wet and muddy and especially hard going for tired boys. Slip and slide all over country and knee deep in mud. Not shaved or washed for 18 days today and ready to collapse. Boys all in and some of the biggest cried like babies (29 October 1916).
- From Terror Hill to Regina Trench via Chalk Pit rail head, Bell's Pit, Creightons Post and Red Chateau. After working hard from 6 AM to 10 PM putting through 44 – 50 – 54 – 73 – 87th casualties, over 800 in number, and about 90 Fritzes, we get orders to clear from "No Man's Land." Walked all the way through real good mud. Pretty well all in before we started. Roads very bad, especially to Regina Trench. Path literally lined with dead. Souvenirs of every description but more to worry about as time is precious (20 November 1916).
- Xmas 1916. Dinner at the front. Steak and onions, rice pudding, tea, sugar and milk, bread and an orange. Hut decorated with bandages and holly. No parcels from home. So quiet after the Somme that the story goes that they had to shoot a man to start a graveyard.
- Beginning to think the raid was a complete failure. Stories of 200 wounded lying in No Man's Land to our right. Talk of rest. About time, for all getting sick of this front (3 March 1917).
- "Great weather" – likely to snow, rain and shine all in one hour. Some good days, but few. Taking great pains fixing up camp. Looks as though we will be in tents any day now, for we are in one hut. Fritz evidently has a new type of aeroplane, for the last week he has had it all over our boys. The speed is marvellous, in fact so fast that anti-aircraft guns are useless. Big offensive raid today, another rank fizzle, as the

barrage cut our boys to pieces. Goodly number of casualties, all unnecessary through inefficiency of Corps Gunners (15 March 1917).

- Good news from the whole front, and by the preparations in our vicinity there is something going to be pulled off very soon. The guns and ammunition that is going our way makes us believe that it is going to be fiercer than the Somme. Until further orders, only one letter per week with no Greens, through someone's carelessness (21 March 1917).
- New news of the big push starting on our Front. Indications are not very promising for our boys and without exception we all dread the idea of going through another Courcelette or probably worse than that. About 1 AM, the preliminary bombardment opened up and the intensity, even to ourselves was a surprise. It lasted fully into dawn and Fritz retaliated by shelling the surrounding towns and villages as far back as Bouvigny, Grand Servins and Petit Servins. In the former place it struck the civilians pretty hard and I believe there are a good number of casualties. Today, those who are able are moving out with barrows, carts and improvised vehicles (5 April 1917).

This was his final entry. ***Hembroff Lake*** (63 N/8), south of Burntwood Lake was named after him in 1998.

Hemenway, Private **Howard Moore** of St. Vital (H 37411). Royal Canadian Army Service Corps. He died 7 October 1943 at the age of 23 and is commemorated at Brookwood Military Cemetery in Surrey, England. He was the only son of Howard H. and Essie J. Hemenway of St. Vital. His Graves Registration Card indicates the he died as a result of a fall from a motorcycle. His sister recalls (6 October 2001):

> Moore lived his entire life in St. Vital where he attended Windsor, Glenwood and Norberry schools. He was the oldest child and only son born to Essie and Howard Hemenway. Not only was he a loving and loyal son, but his two sisters were very special to him. Summers he could be found swimming in the Red River off the Elm Park Bridge or swimming with the Wrigley Swim Club at Winnipeg Beach. Skating daily and the odd curling game made the Manitoba winters pass by. When the war was declared, he was employed at the T. Eaton Company as a baker.

Hemenway Lake (52 L/3), northeast of Brereton Lake was named after him in 1973.

Hemmons, Pilot Officer **Robert T.** of Wawanesa (J 10243). No. 10 Service Flying Training School. He died 24 August 1942 at the age of 24 and is commemorated at Wawanesa Cemetery, Manitoba. He was the son of Henry E. and Eva M. Hemmons of Wawanesa. ***Hemmons Lake*** (64 P/6), southeast of Nejanilini Lake was named after him in 1974.

Hemphill, Sergeant **Albert S.** of Winnipeg (R 59759). Royal Canadian Air Force. He died 1 July 1941 at the age of 21 and is commemorated at Saffron Walden Cemetery in Essex, England. ***Hemphill Lake*** (64 H/2), south of Holmes Lake was named after him in 1995.

Henderson, Gunner **Clarence J.** of Winnipeg (H 5050). Royal Canadian Artillery. He died 20 May 1944 at the age of 27 and is commemorated at the Cassino War Cemetery in Italy. He was the son of William and Grace M. Henderson. ***Henderson Island*** (53 E/15) in Island Lake was named after him in 1979.

Henderson, Pilot Officer **David L. S.** of Winnipeg (J 87259). No. 407 Squadron. He died 14 August 1944 at the age of 23 and is commemorated at the Runnymede Memorial in Surrey, England. He was the son of George and Margaret Henderson of Winnipeg and was survived by his wife Gladys P. Henderson of Winnipeg. She writes (8 April 1998):

> The Commemorative Names Project ... is a very apt recognition of the sacrifice David made. I've been thinking for a long time that some individual memorial should be made for him, as he was one of the many airmen who were shot down and his body never recovered. [It's like] a proper burial.

Henderson Point (63 N/7) on Burntwood Lake was named after him in 1995.

Henderson, Flight Sergeant **Donald L.** of Winnipeg (R 59371). No. 408 Squadron. He died 10 January 1942 at the age of 20 and is commemorated at the Runnymede Memorial in Surrey, England. He was the son of James and Victoria Henderson and was survived by his wife Margaret I. Henderson of Winnipeg. ***Henderson Peninsula*** (64 I/3) on North Knife Lake was named after him in 1995.

Henderson, Signalman **Robert H.** of Winnipeg (V 9707). HMCS *Racoon*. The *Racoon* was torpedoed and sunk by U-165 while escorting Convoy QS.33 in the St. Lawrence River; there were no survivors. Signalman Henderson died 7 September 1942 at the age of 21 and is commemorated at the Halifax Memorial. He was the second of the three sons of John and Mabel Henderson of Winnipeg. According to his brother (7 November 2001), he was:

> ... one of three brothers who all joined the Navy within a space of one year of one another. Bob was a quiet fellow, but he was well liked by everyone he became acquainted with. He enjoyed hockey and baseball and became an enthusiastic ball player with the Navy teams in Halifax.
>
> While he was in high school, he became interested in the Sea Cadet movement in Manitoba. After high school, he joined the Navy in 1940. After his basic training and Visual Signalling School in Saint-Hyacinthe, PQ, he was drafted to the HMCS *Racoon*. We never saw Bob again after he left home, but we did keep in touch because of our closeness as a family.
>
> I knew him as a free-spirited person, subject to mischief, but a good person and hurt no one. It was a sad day for all of us at our house as the telegram of notification arrived on our wedding day.

He concludes (8 February 1995):

> The *Racoon* was an auxiliary vessel, refitted for coastal convoy duty. It was no match for the enemy submarines. Consequently, when his convoy was attacked, ... the *Racoon* was torpedoed with the loss of all hands. He will always be remembered as long as one of us is alive.

Henderson Bay (63 N/12) in Sisipuk Lake was named after him in 1981.

Henderson, Pilot Officer **Selby R.** of Winnipeg (40826). No. 206 Squadron, RAF, Distinguished Flying Cross. He died 4 July 1940 at the age of 22 and is commemorated at the Runnymede Memorial in Surrey, England. He was the only child of Selby and Elaine Henderson and was survived by his wife Joan L. Henderson of Hunstanton, Norfolk. He had enlisted in the RAF in April of 1938. ***Selby Henderson Lake*** (63 I/1), north of Little Bolton Lake was named after him in 1995.

Hendry, Gunner **David** of Goodlands (H 60106). Royal Canadian Artillery. He died 26 October 1944 at the age of 21 and is commemorated at Bergen-op-Zoom Canadian War Cemetery in Holland. He was one of the ten children of Alexander and Annie M. Hendry of Goodlands, Manitoba. His sister (October 19, 2001) recalls that: "His parents ... came from Scotland and located on the farm north of Goodlands. His picture was taken when he was visiting relatives up in Scotland." She adds (24 April 1994):

"Dave" was born on the family farm at Goodlands, Manitoba in the Municipality of Brenda. [H]e grew up on the family farm [and] got his schooling at Montefiore School. After that he was a farm labourer till he joined the army in 1942.

Hendry Lake (64 G/12), east of Big Sand Lake was named after him in 1963.

Hendry, Private **David** of West Kildonan (H 6583). Winnipeg Grenadiers. He died 13 February 1943 at the age of 35 and is commemorated at the Yokohama War Cemetery. He enlisted in September, 1939 and died of beriberi after being taken prisoner of war at Hong Kong. Private Hendry was survived by his parents David and Maggie Hendry, by his wife Sabina E. Hendry of West Kildonan and their two daughters Beth and Jessie. ***Hendry Island*** (64 I/2) in Clougher Lake was named after him in 1995.

Henfrey, Warrant Officer 2 **Jack** of Ninette (R 119823). No. 82 Operational Training Unit, RCAF. He died 2 January 1944 at the age of 24 and is commemorated at Stonefall Cemetery in Yorkshire, England. He was the son of Harry and Norah Henfrey of Winnipeg. ***Henfrey Lake*** (53 M/14), northwest of Hubley Lake was named after him in 1996.

Henry, Flying Officer **George E.** of Flin Flon (J 24106). No. 575 Squadron. He died 18 September 1944 at the age of 25 and is commemorated at Brookwood Military Cemetery in Surrey, England. He was the son of John and Dora Henry of Flin Flon, Manitoba. His aircraft was hit by flak while engaged in dropping supplies to troops at Arnhem, Holland; he was the only casualty (Allison and Hayward 1991). ***Henry Bay*** (63 P/2) in Cotton Lake was named after him in 1996.

Henry, Corporal **James Maxwell** of Brandon (H 70155). Royal Winnipeg Rifles. He died 15 August 1944 at the age of 27 and is commemorated at Bretteville-sur-Laize Canadian War Cemetery in Calvados, France. He was the son of Joseph E. and Margaret M. Henry (née Jones) of Brandon and was survived by his wife Margie E. Henry of Brandon and their daughter. She writes (19 November 2001):

When my mother received news of my father, I was one year old. Like many children of war victims, I never knew him. The only knowledge came from family, friends and pictures of his early life. Their memories of him showed me he was a compassionate and caring person who had everyone's interest at heart. This proved true to me a few years ago after being located by a long distance call from an old veteran who served with him. He had been reminiscing about the war and how fortunate he was to be alive thanks to my father who pushed him in a fox hole. Others weren't as fortunate. In 1956, I had the good fortune to visit his grave in France. This provided a bond that was not there before.

Henry Island (64 N/6) in Burch Lake was named after him in 1995.

Henry, Private **Joseph** of the Roseau Reserve (H 14123). Algonquin Regiment. He died 20 October 1944 at the age of 22 and is commemorated at the Adegem Canadian War Cemetery in Belgium. He was the son of Thomas and Philomene Henry and was survived by his wife Alice Henry of Roseau Reserve, Manitoba and by their two sons. ***Henry Lake*** (64 N/6), southwest of Nueltin Lake was named after him in 1972.

Hepburn, Flying Officer **Stuart A. W.** of Clandeboye (J 38441). No. 407 Squadron. He died 13 February 1945 at the age of 28 and is commemorated at Brookwood Military Cemetery in Surrey, England. He was the son of Alex and Mary Hepburn and was survived by his wife Florence Hepburn of Selkirk and their two children. His wife recalls (28 November 2001):

My husband, Stuart, joined the RCAF in Winnipeg on July 13th, 1942. After completing his training, he arrived in England in April of 1944. Stuart wrote to me every day but couldn't tell me much about his work. I spent the time between my parents' farm at Eriksdale, Manitoba and a rented cabin at East Hawk Lake, Ontario. My sister who kept the Hawk Lake Post Office, lived across the road from me. Her husband, Jack, was in the Navy at the time.

It was during my stay at East Hawk Lake I received the telegram notifying me of the plane crash that killed four of the crew. One man was picked up and survived. My daughter and I visited Stuart's grave at Brookwood Cemetery in 1978. Three other crew members are buried there – it is a beautiful place.

Hepburn Lake (53 L/10), west of Gods Lake was named after him in 1961.

Heppell, Lieutenant **John R.** of Winnipeg. Princess Patricia's Canadian Light Infantry, Mentioned in Dispatches. He died 23 May 1944 at the age of 32 and is commemorated at the Cassino War Cemetery in Italy. He was the son of John R. M. and Eleanor M. Heppell of Calgary, Alberta and was survived by his wife Lillian Heppell of Calgary. ***Heppell Creek*** (54 L/8), which flows east into Churchill River was named after him in 1948.

Herman, Sergeant **Donald L.** of Winnipeg (R 71231). No. 5 Reconnaissance Squadron. He died 20 May 1944 at the age of 32 and is commemorated at the Ottawa Memorial. He was the son of Charles and Molly Herman and was survived by his wife Diana Herman of Gimli, Manitoba. ***Herman Island*** (64 C/3) in McKnight Lake was named after him in 1995.

Hern, Private **Sidney A.** of Hamiota (4853). Canadian Army Service Corps. He died 9 December 1918 at the age of 42 and is commemorated at Mons Communal Cemetery, Hainaut, Belgium. He was the son of William and Rebecca Hern of Hamiota, Manitoba. Born in Perth County, Ontario, he enlisted in Togo, Saskatchewan in May, 1916. ***Hern Lake*** (53 M/14), southeast of Hubley Lake was named after this World War I casualty in 2001.

Hesp, Flight Sergeant **William J.** of Winnipeg (R 86357). No. 115 Squadron. He died 29 August 1942 at the age of 27 and is commemorated at Attigny Communal Cemetery, Ardennes, France. He was the youngest child of John and Annie Hesp of Winnipeg and was engaged to be married at the time of his death. ***Hesp Lake*** (52 E/14), northeast of Brereton Lake was named after him in 1974.

Hetherington, Gunner **Thomas** of Winnipeg (H 5018). Royal Canadian Artillery. He died 12 April 1945 at the age of 42 and is survived by his mother Jane A. Hetherington of Carlisle, England and by his wife Annie Hetherington of Winnipeg. ***Hetherington Lake*** (63 P/2), northeast of Cotton Lake was named after him in 1996.

Heuchert, Flying Officer **William R.** of Winnipeg (J 28950). No. 424 Squadron. He died 4 August 1944 at the age of 27 and is commemorated at Boran-sur-Oise Communal Cemetery, Oise, France. He was the son of Julius and Caroline Heuchert of Winnipeg and was survived by his wife Viola A. Heuchert of Winnipeg. ***Heuchert Lake*** (64 O/12), south of Nueltin Lake was named after him in 1975.

Heuft, Private **Ernest** of Winnipeg (H 6254). Winnipeg Grenadiers. He died 23 December 1943 at the age of 30 and is commemorated at the Yokohama War Cemetery in Japan. Private Heuft died while a prisoner of war at Niigata, Japan.

One of the toughest prison camps in which Canadians were held in Japan was at Niigata, a city of 1,000,000 population some 150 miles north of Tokyo, where starving prisoners performed hard labour under clubbings in coal yards, warehouses and a foundry. There were 250 Canadians there and 29 of them died of pneumonia, beriberi and dysentery during their stay there from September 1943 until they were liberated. The prisoners were undernourished and without medical supplies.

During winter, it was bitterly cold and the camp was swept by great snowstorms, one of which made it necessary to move from one barracks to another through snow tunnels. During one period, storms tied up railway traffic and the camp was isolated for three weeks. Practically until the moment they were freed, most of the prisoners believed they would spend their last days in Niigata. At various times the prisoners lost up to 60 pounds, some of which they made up by stealing food while on one warehouse job. When they were caught stealing the prisoners were clubbed until they couldn't walk (*The Winnipeg Tribune* 14 September 1945).

He was the son of Ernest L. and Anna Heuft of Winnipeg and was survived by his wife Lillian Heuft. Private Heuft had been a member of the Reserves since 1930 and went on active duty 12 September 1939. ***Heuft Lake*** (63 K/16), northwest of Wekusko Lake was named after him in 1973.

Hibbert, Private **Arthur** of Sylvan (H 6448). Lake Superior Regiment. He died 5 August 1944 at the age of 23 and is commemorated at Bretteville-sur-Laize Canadian War Cemetery in Calvados, France. He was the son of Arthur and Groa Hibbert of Winnipeg. ***Hibbert Lake*** (64 H/11), east of Southern Indian Lake was named after him in 1963.

Hickey, Lance Sergeant **Walter H.** of Winnipeg (H 16682). Princess Patricia's Canadian Light Infantry. He died 31 August 1944 at the age of 27 and is commemorated at Montecchio War Cemetery in Italy. He was the son of George E. and Esther L. Hickey of Winnipeg. His brother writes (17 October 2001):

Walter was born in Regina and came to Winnipeg at an early age. Until his enlistment in January, 1940, he lived in Elmwood, receiving his education at George V, Lord Selkirk and St. John's High School. He went overseas in May, 1940. In 1943 he participated in the invasion of Sicily, then to Italy with the Allied troops. The last letter received from him by his brother John was dated July 28, 1944, the day before his 27th birthday. He wrote: "Well I'll be 27 tomorrow. Quite an old man eh? I remember a year ago I celebrated my birthday in a slit trench – I wasn't at all sure I was going to last the day out." Sadly, as it turned out, it was the last birthday he would see.

The last letter written to his mother was dated August 10, 1944, just three weeks before he was killed. He understated the situation as follows: "We have been quite busy lately so I have not done much writing" and later in his letter: "... the war news is much brighter for us. I think it is safe to say that the end is in sight."

Walter was well respected by all the men he served with as the enclosed letter from his C/O written to his mother will testify:

Dear Mrs. Hickey: Please accept the heartfelt sympathy of myself and every man in the platoon on the death of your son, Walter. Your son was killed instantly by a sniper's bullet at about 0700 hrs. on the 31st August 1944 during the attack of the Battalion on the Gothic Line. He received a Christian burial with full military honours close by the spot where he was shot on the 1st September 1944.

The death of your son came as a blow to the platoon as he had gained an enviable spot in the men's esteem. Countless times he proved himself as a soldier and a man. He was an outstanding example to the men under his command.

Once more, I wish to convey our heartfelt regret of your great loss. May God bless you and assist you in this, your darkest hour. Sincerely, J. R. Koensgen (Lt.) OC, MMG, Pl. (2 September 1944).

Hickey Lake (62 N/11), northeast of Roblin was named after him in 1978. His brother and other relatives visited the lake in the early 1990.

Hicks, Sergeant **Allen F.** of Roblin (R 58819). No. 40 Squadron. He died 3 June 1941 at the age of 24 and is commemorated at Wyton (St. Margaret and All Saints) Churchyard, Huntingdonshire, England. He was the son of Arthur W. and Eva L. Hicks of Roblin, Manitoba. ***Hicks Island*** (63 N/15) in the Churchill River was named after him in 1995.

Hicks, Corporal **Francis R. G.** of Winnipeg (H 19945). Queen's Own Cameron Highlanders. He died 19 August 1942 and is commemorated at Dieppe Canadian War Cemetery in Seine-Maritime, France. He was the son of Gilbert and Emma Miniota Hicks (née Philpott) of Petersfield. According to a cousin (8 January 1998):

Francis attended Hartley School – a distance of three miles and attended Gunville Anglican Church, both in the Petersfield area. After his mother's death, his younger brother Kenneth went to live in the States with his Hicks relatives while Francis remained with his father Gilbert, eventually making his home with an aunt and uncle, George and Mable Heinricks of Petersfield.

Hicks Bay (64 F/4) in Carswell Lake was named after him in 1995.

Hicks, Warrant Officer 2 **Walter M.** of Portage la Prairie (R 91878). No. 55 Operational Training Unit, RCAF. He died 15 April 1943 at the age of 24 and is commemorated at Annan Cemetery, Dumfriesshire, Scotland. He was the son of George W. and Martha J. Hicks of Portage la Prairie and was survived by his wife Hilda M. Hicks (née Smith) of Portage la Prairie.

Walter was born July 31, 1918 at Portage la Prairie Hospital. He received his education at High Bluff elementary and high schools. Walter was a farm boy at heart and enjoyed working with his father on the farm. His pastime was participating in hockey and his favourite sport was baseball. He attended Sunday School regularly and was involved in the Young People's Organization. Walter attended university for two years prior to enlisting in the RCAF in 1941. He trained at Brantford, Victoriaville and No. 7 AOS, Portage la Prairie where he graduated and received his pilot's wings. He married his childhood sweetheart, Hilda Smith in 1941 and was posted overseas the same year. Walter piloted his Hurricane fighter aircraft in air operations over Egypt, England and later Scotland. During a reconnaissance mission, his Hurricane dove into the ground eight miles northeast of Longtown, England. Walter was posthumously promoted to the rank of Warrant Officer 2 (Pittman n.d.).

Hicks Lake (64 J/13), northwest of Tadoule Lake was named after him in 1975.

Hiebert, Private **David H.** of Kleefeld (B 138956). Lake Superior Regiment. He died 3 November 1944 at the age of 21 and is commemorated at Bergen-op-Zoom Canadian War Cemetery in Holland. He was the son of Jacob J. and Susanna Hiebert of Kleefeld, Manitoba. ***Hiebert Island*** (53 L/15) in Seller Lake was named after him in 1995.

Higginson, Private **James Stuart** of Eriksdale (H 200138). South Saskatchewan Regiment. He died 14 October 1944 and is commemorated at the Groesbeek Memorial in Holland. ***Higginson Lake*** (64 J/7), west of Tadoule Lake was named after him in 1975.

Higgs, Gunner **William A. "Jim"** of St. James (H 59534). Royal Canadian Artillery. He died 6 June 1944 at the age of 24 and is commemorated at Beny-sur-Mer Canadian War Cemetery in Calvados, France. He was the son of Arthur H. and Elsie Higgs of St. James. His niece writes (15 March 1995):

> He was born in Wrexham, North Wales ... and moved to Winnipeg approximately two years later. "Jim's" special interests included building and flying gas-engine model airplanes and he also loved working on cars, motorcycles and seemed to be the repairman for any broken bicycles in the neighbourhood. He always wanted to have his own motorcycle and ended up riding one in the war when he was a dispatcher. Jim also worked alongside his Dad who was in the painting and decorating business.

Higgs Lake (64 J/2), south of Tadoule Lake was named after him in 1975.

Hignell, Pilot Officer **Gordon K.** of Winnipeg (J 16808). No. 197 Squadron. He died 23 July 1943 at the age of 24 and is commemorated at Dieppe Canadian War Cemetery in Seine-Maritime, France. He was the son of Gordon K. and Margaret M. Hignell and was survived by his wife Marion Hignell of Saskatoon. ***Hignell Lake*** (53 L/10), west of Gods Lake was named after him in 1961.

Hildebrand, Flying Officer **Abram R.** of Winkler (J 22309). No. 162 Squadron. He died 29 July 1944 at the age of 27 and is commemorated at Lerwick New Cemetery, Shetland Islands, Scotland. He was the son of Peter and Tina Hildebrand and was survived by his wife Margaret Hildebrand of Chatham, New Brunswick. ***Hildebrand Lake*** (53 L/13), northwest of Oxford Lake was named after him in 1995.

Hill, Corporal **Harold J. E.** of MacGregor (H 16741). Princess Patricia's Canadian Light Infantry. He died 26 July 1943 at the age of 26 and is commemorated at Agira Canadian War Cemetery, Italy. He was the son of Walter and Katherine Hill. ***Hill Bay*** (64 K/5) on the southwest side of Whiskey Jack Lake was named after him in 1989.

Hill, Pilot Officer **Hugh E.** of Winnipeg (J 16537). No. 15 Squadron. He died 16 December 1942 at the age of 20 and is commemorated at Epe General Cemetery, Holland. ***Hugh Hill Rapids*** (64 A/11) in the Rasp River was named after him in 1995.

Hill, Lance Corporal **John W. "Jack"** of Winnipeg (H 40561). Royal Winnipeg Rifles. He died 8 June 1944 at the age of 27 and is commemorated at Beny-sur-Mer Canadian War Cemetery in Calvados, France. He was the son of Frederick J. and Hannah R. Hill of Winnipeg. His "execution" provided the impetus for a war crimes investigation after the war. ***Hill Point*** (63 I/7) on Molson Lake was named after him in 1995.

Hill, Trooper **Samuel W.** of Swan River (H 77762). Governor General's Horse Guards. He died 26 September 1944 and is commemorated at the Casino Memorial in Italy. ***Hill Peninsula*** (64 P/16) on Parrott Lake was named after him in 1995.

Hill, Flight Sergeant **William Leslie** of Lenore (R 140992). No. 5 Bombing and Gunnery School, RCAF. He died 26 November 1943 at the age of 23 and is commemorated at Breadalbane Cemetery at Lenore, Manitoba. He was the son of William A. and Margaret Hill (née Alexander) of Lenore. ***Hill Creek*** (53 N/16), which flows northeast into Yakaw River was named after him in 1995.

Hillhouse, Pilot Officer **James R.** of Winnipeg (C 8680). No. 76 Squadron. He died 3 October 1943 at the age of 20 and is commemorated at the Sage War Cemetery in Germany. ***Hillhouse Lake*** (64 N/5), southwest of Nueltin Lake was named after him in 1972.

Hilliard, Pilot Officer **Tom W.** of Winnipeg (J 19173). No. 408 Squadron. He died 3 November 1943 at the age of 29 and is commemorated at Rotterdam (Crooswijk) General Cemetery, Holland. He was the son of Tom A. and Daisy Hilliard of Winnipeg. ***Hilliard Lake*** (64 O/11), southeast of Nueltin Lake was named after him in 1975.

Hillman, Flying Officer **Victor J.** of Portage la Prairie (J 20621). No. 152 Squadron. He died 17 February 1944 at the age of 24 and is commemorated at Rawalpindi War Cemetery, Pakistan. He was the nephew and ward of Mr. and Mrs. David Little of the East Prospect district and was survived by his father Otto V. Hillman and sister Thelma of Loon Lake, Saskatchewan. She recalls (22 November 2001):

> Victor John Hillman was born in Penticton, BC, March 15th, 1920. After Mother's death, the family returned to Portage la Prairie. Victor was raised by an aunt and uncle, Mr. and Mrs. Dave Little of the Prospect District. He attended East Prospect School and graduated from high school in Portage la Prairie. After school, he worked as a farm hand and at various service stations. He also took a cabinet work course and was apprenticing when war broke out. He liked ice skating, roller skating, baseball and football. As I was older and finished school early, I went to live with our father in Saskatchewan. Unfortunately, we were apart for a period of his young life. After he joined the Air Force and was in Saskatoon training, he came to visit his Father and I at which time it gave us a chance to know him as a young man. He seemed to be a very happy and energetic young man, very excited about being in the RCAF and flying – one of his greatest ambitions.
>
> He left for overseas from Halifax in 1942. At a later date, he transferred to the RAF at which time he volunteered for service in India in 1943. On February 17th, 1944, he and his gunner Warrant Officer Tom Barlow along with two other planes left from Perhawa Base on a cross country formation flight. They ran into bad weather with violent air currents which effected their instruments so badly they lost control of the aircraft. It was reported by an eye witness that his aircraft was engulfed in flames before it crashed and was presumed to have been struck by lightning.

Hillman Lake (64 I/7), northeast of North Knife Lake was named after him in 1974.

Hilts, Private **Ervin L.** of Petersfield (B 118762). Algonquin Regiment. He died 10 August 1944 at the age of 28 and is commemorated at Bretteville-sur-Laize Canadian War Cemetery in Calvados, France. He was the son of Joseph H. and Jessie S. Hilts (née McMaster) and was survived by his wife Jean Hilts of Petersfield, Manitoba and their unborn son. ***Hilts Lake*** (64 O/10), northwest of Croll Lake was named after him in 1995.

Hindle, Leading Aircraftman **John F.** of Winnipeg (546994). No. 201 Squadron, RAF. He enlisted in December, 1937 and was lost while on patrol over the North Sea 9 July 1940. He was 21 years of age and is commemorated at the Runnymede Memorial in Surrey, England. ***Hindle Lake*** (64 N/8), south of Shannon Lake was named after him in 1995.

Hinds, Gunner **Milford F.** of Portage la Prairie (H 24165). Royal Canadian Artillery. He died 30 June 1942 at the age of 23 and is commemorated at Brookwood Military Cemetery in Surrey, England. He was the son of Frank and Ada P. Hinds of Portage la Prairie. Gunner Hinds was with the first group of Canadian soldiers to reach England following the outbreak of war and had been on active service since December 1939. ***Hinds Lake*** (64 O/1), north of Tadoule Lake was named after him in 1975.

Hinks, Warrant Officer 2 **Cecil C. D.** of Portage la Prairie (R 59536). No. 16 Squadron. He died 29 July 1942 at the age of 26 and is commemorated at Hamburg Cemetery in Germany. ***Hinks Lake*** (64 O/16), west of Baralzon Lake was named after him in 1987.

Hirak, Pilot Officer **Joseph M.** of Elphinstone (J 95284). No. 433 Squadron. He died 10 April 1945 at the age of 23 and is commemorated at the Berlin 1939 - 1945 War Cemetery in Brandenburg, Germany. He was the son of Michael and Rose Hirak of Elphinstone, Manitoba. ***Hirak Lake*** (64 P/16), northeast of Nejanilini Lake was named after him in 1974.

Hirst, Sergeant **Harvey E.** of Somerset (R 208993). No. 420 Squadron. He died 25 February 1944 at the age of 20 and is commemorated at Durnbach War Cemetery in Bavaria, Germany. He was the son of Arthur and Georgina D. Hirst of Somerset, Manitoba. According to his brother (18 November 1996), he:

> ... was raised on a farm in southern Manitoba in the Municipality of Lorne. He received his education in the Harmer School District [and] was one of four children. His ambition was to be a pilot. He joined the RCAF as an air gunner in December, 1942, went overseas in August, 1943 and was reported missing over Germany in February, 1944.

Hirst Lake (63 K/16), west of Wekusko Lake was named after him in 1973.

Hirst, Flight Sergeant **James F.** of Stonewall (R 71076). No. 101 Conversion Unit, RCAF. He died 13 July 1942 at the age of 32 and is commemorated at Buxton Cemetery in Derbyshire, England. He was the son of William and Gertrude L. Hirst of Stonewall, Manitoba. ***Hirst Island*** (64 B/16) in Chapman Lake was named after him in 1995.

Hjalmarson, Private **Gestur E.** of Winnipegosis (H 54406). Veterans Guard of Canada, Military Medal. He died 22 January 1942 at the age of 50 and is commemorated at the Veterans' Cemetery in Esquimalt, British Columbia. He was survived by his wife Winnifred Hjalmarson of Esquimalt and their four children. His son (9 November 1998) reports that:

> He was born in Hallson, North Dakota 11 August 1891 on a family farm. He moved to Pine River, Manitoba in 1910 to work in a General Store operated by his older brother John. It was during this period that he learned to speak Ukrainian.
>
> He joined the Canadian Army in 1915 and served with the 46th Battalion in France. On 26 October 1916, he was wounded in the right thigh and sent to hospital in Boulogne. Returning to join his unit at the Battle of the Somme, Gestur assumed leadership of the troops when his officer was killed and led a successful attack on an enemy machine gun emplacement. During the action, he received two serious wounds to the right arm and was sent to Bramley Hospital in England for surgery. Subsequently, he was awarded the Military Medal and Bar for "Bravery in the Field."
>
> Returning to Canada, he took a job as a forest ranger near Roblin, Manitoba. During this time, he married and the couple had a daughter and two sons. The next move was to Winnipegosis where he ran a General Store. Speaking both Icelandic and Ukrainian, his store was a popular meeting place in the town. In 1935, a second daughter was born. Gestur was active in local service clubs and was elected mayor in 1935. During his first term, he was instrumental in bringing in a hospital and having the road to Dauphin improved. He was subsequently re-elected for two more terms.
>
> A dedicated family man, he had many interests and hobbies – hunting, fishing, reading, poetry and chess were some of them. A man with a keen sense of humour, he also kept pace with the new technology and was among those who had a radio and car early in the thirties.
>
> When the Second War broke out, he joined the Veterans' Guard of Canada and died while serving as a weapons instructor in British Columbia.

Hjalmarson Lake (64 F/11), east of Reindeer Lake was named after him in 1961.

Hjartarson, Flying Officer **Frederick** of Winnipeg (J 23121). No. 1656 Conversion Unit, RCAF. He died 14 January 1944 at the age of 22 and is commemorated at Haycombe Cemetery in Bath, Somerset, England. He was the son of Ivar and Rosa Hjartarson of Winnipeg. His sister-in-law recalls (11 November 2001):

> Frederick was the youngest of Ivar and Rosa's four sons, all of whom served in the RCAF. After graduating from high school, he worked in a drug store and had dreams of going to University and becoming a pharmacist. War intervened and he enlisted. He was survived by his mother and three brothers.

Hjartarson Lake (64 J/10), west of Tadoule Lake was named after him in 1975.

Hlady, Private **John A.** of East Kildonan (H 9642). Royal Regiment of Canada. He died 10 October 1944 and is commemorated at Schoonselhof Cemetery in Antwerp, Belgium. He was survived by his wife Rita Hlady; it was their second anniversary. ***Hlady Lake*** (64 I/4), west of North Knife Lake was named after him in 1974.

Hnatiw, Corporal **Steve** of Olha (H 1444). Argyle and Sutherland Highlanders. He died 21 April 1945 at the age of 28 and is commemorated at the Holten Canadian War Cemetery in Holland. He was the son of Wasyl and Nastia Hnatiw of Olha, Manitoba. His cousin writes (16 October 2001):

When Steve Hnatiw enlisted in the army I was a little girl. I only remember when he came home on leave, he spent some time with us. This was with his Uncle and Aunt and us three kids. And I remember when he was trying to get a nap, we wouldn't let him because we wanted him to play with us. We were quite mischievous. And some time after he left, we heard that he was missing in action and later that he was officially killed.

Hnatiw Lake (52 E/14), southeast of Brereton Lake was named after him in 1974.

Hoagg, Flight Sergeant **Ernest A.** of Winnipeg (R 150850). No. 3 Advanced Flying School. He died 8 November 1943 and is commemorated at Blacon Cemetery in Cheshire, England. ***Hoagg Lake*** (64 O/5), southeast of Shannon Lake was named after him in 1995.

Hobday, Lieutenant **Leonard Manning "Babe"** of Winnipeg. Canadian Grenadier Guards. He died 21 August 1944 at the age of 22 and is commemorated at Bretteville-sur-Laize Canadian War Cemetery in Calvados, France. He was the son of Leonard Stanley and G. Tannis Hobday (née Manning) of Winnipeg. His brother writes (15 November 2001):

Prior to his enlistment, Babe was one of Winnipeg's outstanding athletes. In 1941, he was a member of the Winnipeg Rangers junior hockey team and played a major role in the Rangers' victory over the Montreal Royals in the Memorial Cup championship. Prior to this, he played minor hockey with the Winnipeg Panthers and Excelsiors, during which time he won the Shea Trophy for the most gentlemanly player. He also attended St. John's College where he was a leading quarterback, winning the Manitoba schools football league championship in 1940. On 6 October 2001, he was inducted into the Manitoba Hockey Hall of Fame.

Hobday Lake (64 K/12), northeast of Reindeer Lake was named after him in 1972.

Hobson, Pilot Officer **Kenneth E.** of Winnipeg (J 4903). No. 419 Squadron. He died 29 March 1942 at the age of 30 and is commemorated at the Sage War Cemetery in Germany. He was the son of William E. and Marion M. Hobson of Winnipeg. ***Hobson Lake*** (53 L/10), west of Gods Lake was named after him in 1960.

Hoddinott, Flying Officer **Arthur J.** of East Kildonan (J 22236). No. 407 Squadron. He died 14 August 1944 at the age of 26 and is commemorated at the Runnymede Memorial in Surrey, England. He was the son of Percy G. and Florence Q. Hoddinott of East Kildonan. His sister recalls (29 October 2001):

Art was born and educated at Birds Hill, Manitoba. He attended the University of Manitoba, receiving his Diploma in Agriculture in 1940. He served a year in the 10th Divisional Signals (Reserve), joined the RCAF in October, 1941 and went overseas in 1942.

Art enjoyed life. Besides working on the family farm, he enjoyed travelling and photography. He was a quiet, thoughtful person with an enquiring mind. During his time in the service, he was faithful in writing letters to his parents and sister on a weekly basis. Wherever he was stationed, and when he was off duty, he would explore the surrounding areas and learn the local history. He was especially fond of the British Isles.

His plans for the future were to further his education in Agriculture and settle down on the family farm. When word came that he was Presumed Dead, his parents sold the family farm and moved to East Kildonan.

Hoddinott Lake (52 L/6), east of Lac du Bonnet was named after him in 1973.

Hodge, Major **Frederick E.** of Norwood. Royal Winnipeg Rifles. He died 8 June 1944 and is commemorated at Beny-sur-Mer Canadian War Cemetery in Calvados, France. ***Hodge Bay*** (64 P/15) in Coutts Lake was named after him in 1989.

Hodgins, Craftsman **Welland J.** of Winnipeg (H 64651). Royal Canadian Engineers. He died 15 December 1944 at the age of 31 and is commemorated at Lambhill Cemetery in Glasgow, Scotland. He was the son of William W. and Annie Hodgins of Winnipeg and was survived by his wife Margaret Hodgins of Winnipeg and their daughter. ***Hodgins Lake*** (63 I/7), north of Molson Lake was named after him in 1973.

Hodgkins, Flight Sergeant **George A.** of Russell (R 134936). No. 166 Squadron. He died 25 July 1944 at the age of 32 and is commemorated at Durnbach War Cemetery in Bavaria, Germany. He was the son of Charles and Lillian A. Hodgkins of Russell, Manitoba. ***Hodgkins Lake*** (64 H/15), east of Etawney Lake was named after him in 1995.

Hodgson, Flying Officer **Edwin D. "Ed"** of Selkirk (J 26148). No. 90 Squadron. He died 6 November 1944 at the age of 21 and is commemorated at Enkhuizen General Cemetery, Holland. ***Hodgson Lake*** (53 M/3), west of Whitemud Lake was named after him in 1995.

Hodgson, Private **Wilfred** of Graysville (H 103972). Argyle and Sutherland Highlanders. He died 5 August 1944 and is commemorated at Bretteville-sur-Laize Canadian War Cemetery in Calvados, France. ***Hodgson Island*** (64 B/7) in Livingston Lake was named after him in 1995.

Hoffard, Private **Bernard A.** of Winnipeg (K 67853). 1st Canadian Special Services Battalion. He died 30 May 1944 at the age of 21 and is commemorated at Beach Head War Cemetery, Anzio, Italy. He was the son of Peter and Agatha Hoffard of Norwood. ***Hoffard Lake*** (64 O/6), east of Booth Lake was named after him in 1995.

Hogarth, Flight Sergeant **George A.** of Winnipeg (R 95351). No. 249 Squadron. He died 4 October 1942 at the age of 21 and is commemorated at Capuccini Naval Cemetery on Malta. He was the son of Edgar C. and Jean C. C. Hogarth of Winnipeg. His niece recalls (4 April 2002):

George was the third son born to Jean and Edgar, a druggist in Veteran, Alberta. His young life was very unsettling. His father died when he was five and his mother when he was only seven. The now-orphaned boys spent a period of time living with their maternal grandparents in Mitchell, Ontario where they were loved very much. However, their father had named his brother as their legal guardian so they were sent to live with their aunt and uncle in Winnipeg. The had only met Bruce and Grace Hogarth at their father's funeral, so they were strangers to them. Aunt Grace and Uncle Bruce had two daughters of their own and now had the responsibility of an additional three boys to raise. Uncle Bruce was a geologist and they received a very proper upbringing, with emphasis on education among all other normal activities. This was during the depression, so I'm sure it was a challenging time for all.

My mother, Arlean, met my father [Warren] shortly after George was killed and said his death had been devastating to him. My father kept every letter George had written to him from the time Dad left home until the last one arrived from Malta, until Dad died in 2000. After George's death, Warren had lost both parents and his youngest brother, leaving only his brother Campbell – Dad was only 24.

When Warren was in the advanced stages of Alzheimer's and still verbal, he talked about his brother George every visit, which was at least weekly. As Warren's children, we realized how greatly he had been effected by George's death. On one visit after he had been hospitalized, his youngest grandson who was 11 at the time was starting to leave and Dad got extremely agitated and wouldn't let him go. He thought it was his brother George and even after 58 years, he still felt protective of George.

George's other brother Campbell wrote to Warren upon hearing of George's death:

Dear Warren: I haven't acted much like a loving brother, have I? Upon hearing the news of dear George's death, I've been almost broken apart inside. I had to cry, yet even that failed to ease the pain in my heart. You and I will always remember what a wonderful fellow he really was and I promise you that someday, somehow I'll atone for his death or join him in the attempt. I've a letter which came yesterday from him which was written on October 3rd. Believe me, my heart nearly broke when I read the return address on the envelope. I'll keep it always, Warren and someday I'll be able to show it to you. I was the one who should have met his fate because he was a far better man than I'll ever be.

We are still awaiting our chance to do our part, but as yet have had to bide our time. I've been told that all my qualifications for procuring my commission are in order, but will not feel secure until I am [illegible] way back to Brockville. I've known too many setbacks already to base too much confidence in the future. The Army is like no other institution or force in the world Warren. There are so many things that have to be laid aside that one eventually becomes a totally different person than he was previous to his enlistment. Morals and character take a terrific bombardment every single day, and a fellow has to be pretty strong to maintain certain ideals that he knows are right, but that are being abused constantly. I've tried to adapt as much as possible dear Grandma's code for living, but until you've actually experienced it, you can never imagine how hard it is here.

We are so strictly censored, Warren that I am unable to give you any details as to where we are or what we do from day to day, but rest assured that I am absolutely alright and will pay back ten-fold that debt I owe the enemy before I am through. Take good care of yourself dear Warren and remember always, though I appear to be negligent and unthoughtful, you are ever in my mind and heart.

I don't go out very often as I've been taking courses in Trig and English and will need them if my appointment comes through. Write whenever you are able, Your loving brother Campbell. PS I say a prayer for him every night. He was a true hero I'm sure (n.d.).

Hogarth Lake (63 H/1), northeast of Weaver Lake was named after Flight Sergeant Hogarth in 1974.

Hogg, Flight Lieutenant **Mervin C.** of Warren (J 20942). No. 14 Squadron, Mentioned in Dispatches.

After reconnaissance near Marseilles, his Marauder was attacked by three ME 109s. His rear gunner, Warrant Officer Senior and turret gunner Warrant Officer Smith scored strikes on two of the enemy aircraft although both gunners were wounded. Flight Lieutenant Hogg flew his damaged plane 200 miles to base and although [the] aileron was out of action and the hydraulics were shot away, he landed without flaps (*London Gazette* 1 January 1945).

He died 19 April 1945 at the age of 24 and is commemorated at the Runnymede Memorial in Surrey, England. He was one of the five children of John and Mabel Hogg of Warren, Manitoba. ***Hogg Lake*** (64 H/8), north of Waskaiowaka Lake was named after him in 1948.

Hogue, Private **Joseph Alfred** of Portage la Prairie (H 21013). Loyal Edmonton Regiment. He died 12 May 1944 at the age of 20 and is commemorated at Brookwood Military Cemetery in Surrey, England. He was the son of Joseph E. and Julia Hogue of Winnipeg. ***Hogue Lake*** (64 K/11), northeast of Reindeer Lake was named after him in 1972.

Holditch, Flight Sergeant **Gordon W.** of Boissevain (R 140533). No. 23 Squadron. He died 17 August 1943 at the age of 20 and is commemorated at Botley Cemetery in Oxfordshire, England. He was the son of Reginald H. and Jane L. M. Holditch of Boissevain, Manitoba. His sister (8 March 1995) writes that he:

... was born on the home farm, attended our rural school – Royal No. 417, [and took] high school at Boissevain Collegiate. [He] participated in sports, namely hockey, ball and curling and [was] a good swimmer at the local lakes in summer. [He] enlisted after Grade 11, was a good student and well liked by other schoolmates.

Holditch Island (64 O/8) in Baird Lake was named after him in 1995.

Holdstock, Trooper **Stephen** of Jordan River (L 105454). Fort Garry Horse. He died 6 June 1944 at the age of 31 and is commemorated at Beny-sur-Mer Canadian War Cemetery in Calvados, France. He was the son of Mr. and Mrs. William Holdstock and was survived by his wife Lucille Holdstock of Jordan River, Saskatchewan. ***Holdstock Island*** (53 E/15) in Island Lake was named after him in 1983.

Hole, Rifleman **William J. S.** of Winnipeg (H 67403). Royal Winnipeg Rifles. He died 22 April 1945 at the age of 20 and is commemorated at the Holten Canadian War Cemetery in Holland. He was the son of William and Eva A. Hole of St. James. ***Hole Lake*** (64 H/13), north of Currie Lake was named after him in 1995.

Holenchuk, Pilot Officer **William** of Portage la Prairie (J 85619). No. 426 Squadron. He died 9 June 1944 at the age of 25 and is commemorated at Stonefall Cemetery in Yorkshire, England. He was the son of George and Sophie Holenchuk and was survived by his wife Anne Holenchuk of Sudbury, Ontario and their two children. In his last letter to his brother, he writes:

Dear George: Just a few lines to let you know I am getting along fine and hoping you are too. I was in hospital last week from Sunday morning till Wednesday noon due to a bad cold and a temperature of 101.2. But as soon as my temperature went down, I was let out of hospital and grounded for 24 hours. I missed a good operational trip to Essen. My crew went and took another bomb aimer with them who is a spare in our squadron. On Thursday, March 30th we went on the shakiest trip I have ever been on and it was the worst trip since the war started. Our target that night was Nuremberg. Bomber Command lost 96 heavy bombers that night. It was the worst loss since the war started. We were attacked by German fighters four times. The weather was 37 below zero at 22,000 feet and our electrically heated flying suits sure suited the purpose that night.

The losses in this game I am in are very heavy George. I am counting on you not saying much about the danger to my dear little wife. I keep telling her everything is rolling nice and smoothly and try to cheer her up as much as possible. I don't want her to worry because I may be here for about 9 or 10 months yet, and I would not want her to worry for that length of time. My Flight Sergeant has come through and it's back-dated to September 19th so I have six months back pay coming now and my crowns for my Warrant Officer 2nd class (WO2) have been overdue since March 19th. But it will take about two months to come through. But I have something better to look forward to than that. My commission will be through in about a month or a little more. I was strongly recommended for it by our Bombing Leader to our Commanding Officer and he gave me my forms to fill out. I had my medical already and had my interview with the Wing Commander and he told me definitely that he had my commission papers before him and that they are going into the Air Commodore's Office. I'll be called in for an interview by him. I was called up by the Captain when I was in hospital but I couldn't go for an interview because I was sick. So I'll be leaving any day now. It will mean a $2.25 a day more than I am getting now and better accommodation. Anne, being an officer's wife will get 10 dollars more in her allowance and whatever I can sign over to her more, which I expect will be about 25 or 30 dollars more.

My little baby son isn't feeling so good lately. He has a bad cold. I have received about 12 snaps in the month of March from Anne of herself and little Barbara and baby Allen. Little Barbara is sure going to be a good-looking little girl. Has Anne sent you any snaps of our little family? I hope you are dropping Anne a line often George. She will be very glad to hear from you. She might not be able to answer as soon as she would like to, but having two little kiddies to look after, she has lots of work. I received two snaps from Anne and Kenny and they look good. You sure were lucky to go home Christmas and to be able to see Fran too must have been a treat. At 5:45 PM yesterday [it] was exactly a year since Anne and I saw each other in the station in Winnipeg. It sure seems like a long time. Remember if you happen to come to Scotland, wire me where I can meet you and I'll get time off or go AWL and see you.

I guess the opening up of a second front soon will sure make a difference to our bombing and raids. My nine-day leave is due on April 8th. I will be going to London for part of the time and maybe Scotland for the rest. We had two aircraft go unserviceable one night on the ground before takeoff so we missed one of the raids on Frankfurt. And another time, we were at 21,000 [feet] coming near the enemy coast going to Berlin, the oxygen tube in our rear turret burst so we had to drop our bombs in the North Sea and return home. Well, I'll close now. Hoping to hear from you soon. Write Anne often. Best of luck kid and take good care of yourself. P.S. Tell Fran I send her my best regards. With Love, your brother Bill (2 April 1944).

Holenchuk Lake (63 I/1), southwest of Little Bolton Lake was named after him in 1995.

Holiday, Private **Joseph** of Winnipeg (H 8865). Algonquin Regiment. He died 10 August 1944 at the age of 31 and is commemorated at Bretteville-sur-Laize Canadian War Cemetery in Calvados, France. He was the son of Mr. and Mrs. George Holiday of Cleveland, Ohio. His sister writes (29 December 1996):

... he was an avid outdoorsman; hunting and fishing, seemingly always. Even his favourite inside activity had an outdoor theme, which was constructing beautiful scale model ships. [He] was born ... in Cold Springs, Manitoba. Three of Joseph's brothers were enlisted in the American armed forces. They represented the Holiday family in the US Army, Navy and Air Force.

Holiday Lake (64 F/7), east of Wells Lake was named after him in 1980.

Holke, Pilot Officer **Aldrene G.** of Winnipeg (J 88495). No. 619 Squadron. He died 8 May 1944 at the age of 24 and is commemorated at Orleans Main Cemetery, Loiret, France. He was the son of Max R. and Pearl T. Holke of Winnipeg. ***Holke Lake*** (64 O/6), southeast of Nueltin Lake was named after him in 1975.

Hollingworth, Warrant Officer 2 **Samuel** (P 34987). Royal Canadian Ordnance Corps. He died 7 September 1945 at the age of 37 and is commemorated at Elmwood Cemetery in Winnipeg. He was the son of Samuel and Mary Hollingworth of Winnipeg and was survived by his wife Margaret E. G. Hollingworth of Winnipeg. ***Hollingworth Lake*** (64 B/13), northwest of McBride Lake was named after him in 1982.

Hollis, Lieutenant **Oscar H.** of St. James. 43rd Cameron Highlanders. He died 23 October 1917 at the age of 23 and is commemorated at Tyne Cot Cemetery, Zonnebeke, West-Vlaanderen, Belgium. He was the son of Mr. H. W. and Mrs. K. Hollis of St. James. His brother recalls (21 November 1984):

Oscar graduated from the University of Manitoba with a degree in Law in 1916 and immediately following his admission to the Bar, entered the army with the 183rd Battalion of Winnipeg, later transferring to the 43rd Camerons. Prior to going overseas, Oscar had enjoyed our family cottage at Matlock and had, with one of his fellow law students, James Berg, purchased a lot at Matlock with the hope of developing it after the war.

He lost his life at Passchendaele. ***Hollis Lake*** (64 G/14), east of Big Sand Lake was named after him in 1986.

Holmberg, Flight Lieutenant **Carl Delbert** of Minnedosa (J 10169). No. 38 Squadron. He died 9 April 1944 at the age of 23 and is commemorated at the Phaleron War Cemetery in Athens, Greece. He was the son of Mr. and Mrs. O. Holmberg, formerly of Minnedosa. ***Holmberg Lake*** (64 N/4), southeast of Quasso Lake was named after him in 1995.

Holmes, Private **John A.** of Melita (H 8540). Seaforth Highlanders of Canada. He died 17 September 1944 and is commemorated at Coriano Ridge War Cemetery in Italy. ***Holmes Point*** (53 L/15) on Knee Lake was named after him in 1995.

Holmes, Private **John W.** of Winnipeg (H 1529). Saskatoon Light Infantry. He died 22 April 1945 at the age of 20 and is commemorated at the Groesbeek Canadian War Cemetery in Holland. He was the son of John and Alice A. Holmes of Winnipeg. ***Holmes Bay*** (64 F/1) in Melvin Lake was named after him in 1995.

Holmes, Trooper **Robert F. R.** of Middlechurch (H 26193). Fort Garry Horse. He died 11 June 1944 at the age of 23 and is commemorated at the Bayeux Memorial in Calvados, France. He was the son of James B. and Winnifred Holmes of Kleecoot, Vancouver Island. His nephew writes (18 December 2001):

Robert Francis Roger Holmes was born July 24, 1920 in the municipality of West St. Paul, in an area referred to as McNaughton's Corner, near Middlechurch. He died during the invasion of Normandy in a little hamlet called Rots. Robert was the brother of Jean and Reginald Holmes. I'm his nephew Harry Robert Holmes, and would like to recall what I can of his youth. He is commemorated at the Bayeux Memorial in France along with 14 others from the Fort Garry Horse. On the Bayeux Memorial are engraved the names of 1808 of the Commonwealth Forces who fell in the Battle of Normandy and the subsequent advance to the Seine, and who have no known grave. The connection with the Conqueror is recalled in the Latin inscription on the frieze of the memorial: "Nos A Gulielmo Victi Victoris Patriam Liberavimus" (we, once conquered by William, have now set free the Conqueror's native land).

Robert was a fun loving child who cared deeply for animals, always playing with the dogs and trying to take them with him wherever he would go. He was a good student, but did not have a passion for school.

When he reached the age of driving, this became his passion, but he was a reckless driver and had many minor accidents. One I remember in particular, occurred at the intersection of Main Street and Rossmore Road. He decided to see how fast the McGlaughlin Buick could take the corner. The results were very dramatic in that the car rolled three times before landing on its wheels. Bob was not injured and actually able to drive the car home. They had a part German Shepherd, part wolf dog who loved to ride on the roof of the car and would climb on whenever the car started. Bob would take him everywhere like that when possible. I don't know how that dog stayed on the roof. Might have been good training for driving a tank.

I have a letter he wrote to my father (his brother, Reginald) from "Somewhere in England May 23, 1944," just 18 days before he was killed. In it he talks about home, asking about his mother and father and all the family. He mentions how the beaches should be opening up and how nice that would be. He closes by saying "as ever, your loving brother, Bob." It is still difficult to think about this and the fact that he has no actual grave. My wife and I have visited the Memorial at Bayeux, and did appreciate the lovely site they have.

My wife's cousin, Russell (Bud) Hess was also in the Fort Garry Horse tank corps, and we found out many years later that they were good friends, and had gone ashore at Normandy together. Bud wrote us a bit of a description of the days and how rough it was. He said Rots, where Bob was killed driving his tank, had roads so narrow you could not maneuver the tanks, making them easy targets. I'm so very pleased that Manitoba has chosen to honour these brave men who gave their most precious gift of life to ensure our freedom. Robert would be thrilled to know an island is named for him.

The historian of the Chaudière Regiment described the scene in the village of Rots the morning after the battle there:

They fought like lions on both sides, so that the dead lay corpse by corpse. We searched every house, every courtyard to avoid ambush. And here is the confirmation of how ferocious last night's battle must have been. The Commandos lie dead in rows beside the dead SS. Grenades are scattered all over the road and in the porches of houses. Here we see a Commando and an SS man, literally dead in each other's arms, having slaughtered each other. There, a German and a Canadian tank have engaged each other to destruction, and are still smouldering, and from each blackened turret hangs the charred corpse of a machine gunner. Over here are a group who ran towards a wall for shelter and were shot down before they got there. And then near the church, as the advance guard of C Company and the carriers turn the corner, there are three Germans. Only three. But one of them instantly draws his pistol and hits one of our men. A Bren gunner kills two of the three SS men, but the survivor gets away. Now we understand with what kind of fanatic we have to deal (in Rempel n.d.).

Holmes Island (64 C/10) in Finch Lake was named after him in 1995.

Holmstrom, Private **Stuart** of Onanole (H 6940). Winnipeg Grenadiers. He died a prisoner of war 20 October 1943 and is commemorated at the Sai Wan War Cemetery in Hong Kong. He was the son of Alexander and Mary M. Holmstrom of Sandy Lake, Manitoba. ***Holmstrom Island*** (64 I/3) in North Knife Lake was named after him in 1995.

Holopina, Sapper **Christopher G.** of St. Claude. 23rd Field Engineers. He died 5 July 1996 at the age of 22 and is commemorated at Inglis Cemetery, Manitoba. He was killed in Bosnia – Herzegovina while serving with NATO forces in the Balkan States to maintain peace following the civil war in the former Yugoslavia.

Sapper Christopher Holopina was within days of returning to his family in southern Manitoba when he was killed in Bosnia. A husky 22-year-old who stood six-foot-four, Holopina died after his armoured vehicle overturned Thursday *en route* to help a British contingent trapped in a minefield. Six other Canadians were injured and were in stable condition. All were with the 23 Field Engineer Squadron from Petawawa, Ontario and stationed at the forward base in Kludj, Bosnia. Holopina is the 12th Canadian soldier to die in Bosnia, the first since Canada joined the NATO peacekeeping mission there this year. Earlier, Canada was in Bosnia under UN auspices (*Canadian Press* 5 July 1996).

His uncle added that he had a premonition about the tragedy:

We always told him it was too dangerous (in the military). But he said you could go here or go over there. When it comes, it comes. I just had a feeling he wasn't coming back. Just a couple days ago I was out in the field and I thought, maybe I'm wrong because he's pretty near done (*Winnipeg Free Press* 5 July 1996).

Camp Holopina, a military camp at Coralici, Bosnia-Herzegovina was named after him in 1997 and ***Holopina Lake*** (63 N/4), northwest of Duval Lake was named after him in 1996.

Holton, Sergeant **Eric A.** of Reston (H 60745). Royal Canadian Artillery. He died 9 September 1944 at the age of 23 and is commemorated at the Adegem Canadian War Cemetery in Belgium. He was one of the four children and the only son of Horace and Emily Holton of Reston, Manitoba. According to his sister (17 August 1998):

Eric was born in the small town of Reston. He was a joy to his family ... and his three sisters Gertrude, Florence and Reta. As a child, he was slower growing as he had been a premature baby. But with my mother's good care, he soon started to grow and develop. He had many friends and Saturday mornings, about five or six were around, helping him with his chores so they could get together and go gopher hunting or looking for crows' nests to collect the eggs. At that time, there was a bounty for both crows' eggs and gopher tails.

Eric was a good scholar at school and seemed to have little trouble. He played "scrub" at home in the Woodman's yard with the usual gang of boys and girls. He took part in some school activities and enjoyed them. Eric and his friend Bill Arthur chummed together as they grew up and Bill's father had a large yard with trees and let the boys build a small club house where they spent rainy days keeping themselves busy.

Every Saturday evening Eric listened to

with his father. They both enjoyed listening to and watching hockey. When war broke out, Eric joined up in January, 1941. I believe he joined with about eight other Reston boys – the South Saskatchewan Regiment – later the Royal Canadian Artillery. As I was in Winnipeg, I am not certain where he was moved, though I did write him when I knew where he was. He was in eastern Canada when he was moved to England. After a safe crossing, he took various courses and was eventually made a Sergeant. In this capacity he was well liked and got along with most of the men.

In 1944, some time in the summer, Eric and his unit were sent to France and Belgium. In Belgium he was almost instantly killed. The unit held services for him and buried him [on the] grounds of Loppem Castle. Later he was moved to the Belgian military cemetery near Bruges. I was able to visit his grave in 1969 along with my husband and one of my cousins who lives in England. God grant you Peace, dear brother.

Holton Lake (64 I/3), west of North Knife Lake was named after him in 1974.

Holyk, Sapper **Peter** of Middlechurch (H 36539). Royal Canadian Engineers. He died 5 November 1944 at the age of 26 and is commemorated at All Saints Cemetery in Middlechurch, Manitoba. He was survived by his mother Mrs. Jeryna Holyk of Winnipeg. ***Holyk Lake*** (64 A/11), northeast of Campbell Lake was named after him in 1996.

Hood, Rifleman **William C.** of Portage la Prairie (H 40685). Royal Winnipeg Rifles. He died 8 June 1944 and is commemorated at Beny-sur-Mer Canadian War Cemetery in Calvados, France. ***Hood Lake*** (64 H/3), south of Northern Indian Lake was named after him in 1963.

Hooey, Flying Officer **James D. C.** of Winnipeg (J 20237). No. 215 Squadron. He died 4 March 1944 at the age of 25 and is commemorated at the Singapore Memorial. He was the son of Hamilton C. and Meredith I. Hooey of Winnipeg and was survived by his wife LaVerne E. Hooey of Winnipeg and their daughter. His widow writes (1988): "… Jim was stationed in Calcutta. Their target was 28 miles north of Rangoon. Theirs was the only plane that was never heard of after they took off." ***Hooey Lake*** (64 N/13), west of Nueltin Lake was named after him in 1974.

Hook, Major **Harry W.** of Winnipeg. Winnipeg Grenadiers. He died a prisoner of war 7 July 1945 at the age of 45 and is commemorated at the Sai Wan War Cemetery in Hong Kong. The official cause of death was listed as "spinal meningitis." He was the son of Henry and Constance E. Hook of Winnipeg and was survived by his wife Jean L. Hook (née Bulloch) of Winnipeg and their son Flying Officer Robert Hook. ***Hook Island*** (63 N/8) in Burntwood Lake was named after him in 1995.

Hooker, Trooper **Winston G.** of Winnipeg (H 77619). 12th Manitoba Dragoons. He died 7 April 1945 at the age of 25 and is commemorated at the Holten Canadian War Cemetery in Holland. He was the son of Richard and Margaret Hooker of Winnipeg. ***Hooker Lake*** (62 P/9), southwest of Family Lake was named after him in 1978.

Hooper, Pilot Officer **George C.** of Winnipeg (J 16717). No. 142 Squadron. He died 30 July 1942 at the age of 22 and is commemorated at the Adegem Canadian War Cemetery in Belgium.

> Pilot Officer Hooper was born in Winnipeg on July 26, 1920. He enlisted on the 20th November 1940 at Winnipeg and trained at Brandon, Prince Rupert, Regina and Calgary. Hooper went overseas in September, 1941 and was attached to the RCAF in Great Britain. He was lost during an operational flight over Saarbrücken six days after he had been promoted to Pilot Officer. He was educated at Cecil Rhodes and St. John's Technical School. His hobbies were stamp collecting, drawing and wood working and was also a member of the St. John's rugby team during their three championship years. He is survived by his mother and stepfather Mr. and Mrs. J. C. Hill of Winnipeg, a brother P. A. Hooper in the armed forces and a step-sister Lenore (Hill 1944).

Hooper Point (64 P/9) on Gagnon Lake was named after him in 1995.

Hooper, Flight Sergeant **George T.** of Flin Flon (R 177542). No. 10 Squadron. He died 3 November 1943 at the age of 28 and is commemorated at the Reichswald Forest War Cemetery in Germany. He was the son of Hubert H. and Margaret Hooper of Winnipeg. ***Hooper Lake*** (53 M/1), east of Knee Lake was named after him in 1995.

Hooper, Private **Granger A.** of Winnipeg (H 41570). Saskatchewan Light Infantry. He died 22 July 1943 at the age of 19 and is commemorated at El Alia Cemetery, Algeria. He was the son of Frederick G. and Ella M. Hooper of McKague, Saskatchewan. ***Hooper Island*** (64 I/4) in Hlady Lake was named after him in 1995.

Hooper, Lieutenant **Ronald J.** of Winnipeg. Winnipeg Grenadiers. He died 21 December 1941 at the age of 26 and is commemorated at the Sai Wan War Cemetery in Hong Kong. He was the son of Charles S. and Isabella M. Hooper of Winnipeg and was survived by his wife Barbara Hooper of Winnipeg, two brothers and four sisters. His wife recalls (13 January 2002):

> He was born in Winnipeg 24 January 1915. As a boy, he was an enthusiastic athlete, excelling in many sports. He had a great love of music, playing the violin. He sang in his church choir and with the Winnipeg Light Opera. He was a Boy Scout at St. Jude's Anglican Church achieving the distinction of King's Scout and he was a cadet in the Cameron Highlanders Regiment. Later he joined the Royal Canadian Corps of Signals where he received his commission. After the outbreak of the Second World War, he transferred to the Winnipeg Grenadiers just before their departure for Hong Kong.

Hooper Bay (53 K/5) in Webber Lake was named after him in 1989.

Hope, Flight Sergeant **Donald W.** of Chater (R 59081). No. 11 Squadron. He died 13 July 1945 at the age of 27 and is commemorated at the Ottawa Memorial. His brother recalls (23 March 1998):

> My memory of Donald was that of a younger brother. Donald was 10 years older and due to the Depression was away a great deal of the later years of his life. Donald was born in Brandon; … we lived in the Chater area east of Brandon and he went to school there, completing Grade 9 and then he had to work. Don enlisted I believe in 1940 and was killed in a plane crash on Victoria Island.

He was survived by his wife Jean Hope of Ontario. ***Hope Bay*** (64 I/6) in Paragon Lake was named after him in 1995.

Hopkins, Sergeant **Douglas J.** of Selkirk (K 83922). Royal Canadian Ordnance Corps. He died 2 September 1944 at the age of 26 and is commemorated at Brookwood Military Cemetery in Surrey, England. He was the son of Albert and Dorothy Hopkins and was survived by his wife Muriel B. Hopkins of Selkirk, Manitoba. ***Hopkins Island*** (63 P/5) in Paint Lake was named after him in 1996.

Hopkins, Pilot Officer **Frederick R.** of Winnipeg (J 88421). No. 50 Squadron. He died 8 July 1944 at the age of 24 and is commemorated at Mesnil-Mauger Communal Cemetery, Seine-Maritime, France. ***Hopkins Lake*** (53 L/9), east of Gods Lake was named after him in 1961.

Horbatiuk, Private **Andrew** of Lac du Bonnet (H 14486). Queen's Own Cameron Highlanders. He died 28 October 1944 and is commemorated at Bergen-op-Zoom Canadian War Cemetery in Holland. ***Horbatiuk Lake*** (64 K/9), northeast of Reindeer Lake was named after him in 1972.

Horn, Warrant Officer 1 **Walter W.** of La Rivière (R 95448). No. 432 Squadron. He died 27 June 1943 at the age of 28 and is commemorated at the Runnymede Memorial in Surrey, England. He was the son of Robert F. and Sarah E. Horn of La Rivière, Manitoba. His younger brother recalls (30 August 1995):

Walter had a great interest in music. He played the trombone in the school band one year. He took violin lessons with a music teacher, got a violin, practised a lot and became proficient in playing the violin. The first banjo he played was one that he made himself. He sawed a board into an 11 inch diameter circular piece, mounted an inverted tin cake pan on the board, carved the neck from a piece of wood, bought the parts needed to complete it (i.e., bridge tailpiece, frets, tuning knobs, strings etc.). He made a guitar; a fellow student who was artistically inclined painted a Hawaiian picture on the front – palm trees, surf etc. – and he varnished it. He played in an orchestra with three other musicians in La Rivière. Later, he went on to be leader of an orchestra; played for dances at Archibald, Kingsley and Swan Lake.

I got catalogues from two large mail order radio stores in the USA. They sell all kinds of radio parts; they also sell radios and he saw that the prices of radios were quite a bit lower than in Canada, so he bought one and sold it to our uncle. That's how he got started selling radios. Later, he decided to get the radios from a wholesale house in Canada (Winnipeg). He would go around in the fall after the crops were in and sell radios to the farmers. He made quite a few sales.

He fitted a car generator with a propeller and mounted it on top of the granary and used it to charge the car battery and the storage battery used to power our battery radio. Later on, he bought a Wincharger power unit which consisted of a propeller and wind vane, mounted on a 40-foot tower, and a 32 volt set of batteries to supply lights for our house. He did the wiring of the house as well.

When he was in High School, he took an automotive course which was an option in place of Latin. After he finished school, he did a complete overhaul on our 1923 Essex car. This was about 1932. We drove the car for seven years after that. Then he took out the back seat and back of [the] car and made it into a truck which he used around the farm.

Horn Island (64 I/11) in Noguy Lake was named after him in 1995.

Horne, Able Seaman **Leslie "Buzz"** of Winnipeg (V 9632). HMCS *Nanaimo*. He died 16 June 1942 at the age of 26 and is commemorated at the Halifax Memorial. He was the son of Joseph B. and Elizabeth M. Horne of Winnipeg. His nephew recalls (28 November 2001):

Buzz will be most remembered as one of the finest local-born soccer players ever produced in Manitoba. He excelled both in playing and in coaching. He represented Canada, playing with the Irish club in the Pan American Games in Dallas, Texas. Buzz later played in Ontario with the Dome Mines soccer team prior to enlisting with the RCNVR.

His brief military career was summarized by a close friend:

Fifty years have passed since Leslie "Buzz" Horne strode into the Royal Canadian Naval Volunteers Reserve headquarters in that old, small building on Ellice Avenue and told the deputy petty officer he wanted to serve in the war on the high seas in defence of Canada. There were endless numbers of young athletes deciding to become sailors. They were thumping all over the parade square while awaiting orders to proceed to Esquimalt or Cornwallis.

Walt Ritchie, a pretty fair journeyman hockey player was one of them. He spotted Hugh Millen, also a junior star, and Bill Gibb, equally talented on skates. Walt decided these fellows would be his buddies. Bill and Buzz already were old friends from a mutual fondness for soccer around Atlantic Avenue. [He was considered one of the greatest soccer stars that Canada had ever produced].

But the struggle on the high seas was something else again. Nanaimo's look-outs spotted a freighter, all by itself, apparently disabled and Nanaimo's captain knew it likely had been torpedoed. The crew had taken to their life boats but their ship was still afloat. Nanaimo put a boat's crew over the side, including Buzz. They were examining the abandoned freighter for salvage purposes when they heard the ominous rumble of a ship beginning to capsize. The boat's crew went over the side but Buzz realized the officer in charge had not returned to the deck and went back to get him. This selfless gesture was his last mortal act. The freighter rolled over and went to the bottom. The admiralty in London sent a certificate of commendation to Buzz's family. His name would join the countless other young Canadians who gave their lives on the seas, in the skies and on the battlefields.

After the war, the federal government, knowing it had many unnamed lakes in Northern Canada, came up with the splendid idea of naming them after the war dead. Some months ago, Walt and Bill set out to get Buzz the honour he deserved. After much letter writing and tireless prompting, Buzz Horne Lake now appears on new maps of Manitoba. It is in the Leaf Rapids area.

It may be coincidence that Buzz and Andrew Mynarski, VC, lived a block or so apart. Their pictures hang in the main hall of Isaac Newton School and Mynarski Lake[s] is close to Buzz Horne Lake (Leah 1990).

Buzz Horne Lake (64 B/5), northwest of Pemichigamau Lake was named after him in 1990.

Horner, Private **Ernest W.** of Reston (H 20512). Queen's Own Cameron Highlanders. He died 13 September 1942 at the age of 23 and is commemorated at St. Sever Cemetery Extension, Rouen, Seine-Maritime, France. He was the son of William and Eva V. Horner of Winnipeg. ***Horner Lake*** (64 O/4), north of Egenolf Lake was named after him in 1975.

Horodyski, Leading Aircraftman **Kazimierz** of Beausejour (R 134141). No. 1 Initial Training School, RCAF. He died 12 September 1943 at the age of 23 and is commemorated at St. Mary's Cemetery in Beausejour, Manitoba. He was the son of Thomas and Regina Horodyski of Beausejour. ***Horodyski Lake*** (52 L/6), northeast of Lac du Bonnet was named after him in 1973.

Horsfall, Stoker 2 **Clifford** of Winnipeg (V 40851). HMCS *Mulgrave*. He died of diphtheria 24 January 1943 at the age of 25 and is commemorated at Brookside Cemetery in Winnipeg. He was survived by his mother Emily A. Horsfall of Winnipeg and by his wife Marion Horsfall of Winnipeg. ***Horsfall Island*** (63 J/8) in Kiskittogisu Lake was named after him in 1971.

Horton, Pilot Officer **Arthur L.** of MacGregor (C 85693). No. 426 Squadron. He died 9 May 1944 at the age of 24 and is commemorated at the Runnymede Memorial in Surrey, England. He was the son of Arthur and Florence E. Horton of Kirkfield Park, Manitoba. ***Horton Lake*** (64 J/15), northwest of Tadoule Lake was named after him in 1975.

Horton, Private **John Victor A.** of St. Vital (H 19119). Queen's Own Cameron Highlanders. He died 21 August 1942 at the age of 23 and is commemorated at the Brookwood Memorial in Surrey, England. ***Horton Island*** (64 C/4) in Tractor Lake was named after him in 1995.

Hosea, Pilot Officer **Russell L. G.** of St. Vital (J 15033). No. 115 Squadron, Distinguished Flying Cross.

Throughout the many sorties in which he has participated, this officer has displayed exceptional navigational ability combined with great determination not only to bomb his objective but to obtain photographs of the results. On several occasions during the winter months when navigation was rendered extremely difficult owing to bad weather, Pilot Officer Hosea never failed to navigate his aircraft back to base without difficulty. He has participated in attacks against a wide variety of enemy targets including raids on Berlin, Stettin, Brest, Kiel and Wilhelmshaven. His skill and tenacity have been outstanding (DFC Citation 1942).

He died 8 March 1942 at the age of 28 and is commemorated at the Runnymede Memorial in Surrey, England. He was the son of John W. and Margaret Hosea. According to his brother (14 April 1995), he:

... was raised on a farm northwest of Morden, Manitoba. He attended a rural school named Lloyd George and attended high school at Morden. He enjoyed playing sports especially baseball and hockey.

Upon entering the RCAF, he took basic flying instruction at Rivers, Manitoba. He took further training at Debert, Nova Scotia and graduated as an observer. He went overseas in 1941. Russell's crew made numerous bombing trips over Germany. In the winter of 1942, they took pictures of munitions and military factories.

Hosea Lake (53 O/16) in northwestern Ontario was named after him in 1949.

Hough, Sergeant **Frank B.** of Winnipeg (1074122). No. 142 Squadron, RAF. He died 25 October 1942 at the age of 28 and is commemorated at Bergen-op-Zoom Canadian War Cemetery in Holland. He was the son of Mr. and Mrs. F. H. Hough and was survived by his wife Mrs. F. B. Hough of Ottawa. ***Hough Bay*** (64 P/4) in MacLeod Lake was named after him in 1995.

Hough, Flight Sergeant **Franklin W.** of Winnipeg (R 91971). No. 118 Squadron. He died 9 May 1942 at the age of 20 and is commemorated at Dunkirk Town Cemetery in France. He was the son of James F. and Beatrice Hough of Winnipeg. ***Hough Island*** (64 J/12) in Tomchyshyn Lake was named after him in 1995.

Houghton, Gunner **Lawrence E.** of Selkirk (H 75278). Royal Canadian Artillery. He died 15 July 1944 at the age of 24 and is commemorated at Bayeux War Cemetery, Calvados, France. He was the son of Edward and Hilda E. Houghton of Selkirk, Manitoba. ***Houghton Lake*** (64 I/4), west of North Knife Lake was named after him in 1974.

Houlden, Sergeant **Eric** of Winnipeg (R 205200). No. 50 Squadron. He died 4 May 1944 at the age of 19 and is commemorated at Trouan-le-Petit Churchyard, Aube, France. He was the son of Sydney and Edna Houlden of Keewatin, Ontario. ***Houlden Lake*** (64 H/11), north of Small Lake was named after him in 1995.

Houle, Rifleman **Alfred** of St. Eustache (H 41988). Royal Winnipeg Rifles. He died 6 June 1944 and is commemorated at Beny-sur-Mer Canadian War Cemetery in Calvados, France. He was the son of Etienne and Adeline Houle of St. Eustache, Manitoba. ***Houle Lake*** (64 P/9, 16), east of Nejanilini Lake was named after him in 1974.

Hourie, Trooper **Lawrence** of Grand Marais (H 100534). Calgary Tank Regiment. He died 2 October 1943 at the age of 20 and is commemorated at the Cassino Memorial in Italy. He was the son of Peter and Mary Hourie of Grand Marais, Manitoba. According to his sister (21 February 1995):

He attended a one-room school where he got a Grade 8 education – this being the schooling available at the time. He was a commercial fisherman [and] also cut pulpwood for $1.50 a cord. He had to walk a distance of six or seven miles carrying his lunch and Swede saw and return six or seven miles. He then joined the Fort Garry Horse before he was 18 years old.

Hourie Lake (64 K/16), northeast of Lac Brochet was named after him in 1972.

Houston, Pilot Officer **Clifford E.** of Winnipeg (J 94145). No. 426 Squadron. He died 9 February 1945 at the age of 23 and is commemorated at Stonefall Cemetery in Yorkshire, England. He was the son of Elmer H. and Bessie G. Houston of Fort Garry. ***Houston Lake*** (64 H/16), southeast of Condie Lake was named after him in 1995.

Howald, Trooper **Wilbert** (H 94465). British Columbia Dragoons. He died 25 April 1945 and is commemorated at the Holten Canadian War Cemetery in Holland. He was survived by his wife Helen Howald of Dunecht, Aberdeenshire, Scotland. ***Howald Lake*** (64 O/14), east of Nueltin Lake was named after him in 1995.

Howanyk, Private **Michael** of Winnipeg (H 1439). Canadian Scottish Regiment. He died 12 August 1944 at the age of 20 and is commemorated at Bretteville-sur-Laize Canadian War Cemetery in Calvados, France. He was the son of Stephen and Katharine Howanyk of Winnipeg. ***Howanyk Lake*** (64 I/9), northeast of North Knife Lake was named after him in 1974.

Howard, Telegraphist **Frederick C.** of Winnipeg (3774). HMCS *Ottawa*. The *Ottawa* was escorting Convoy ON.127 in the North Atlantic when it was struck by two torpedoes from U-91; 114 of her ship's company were lost. Telegraphist Howard died 13 September 1942 at the age of 19 and is commemorated at the Halifax Memorial. He was the son of William C. and Gertrude M. Howard of Winnipeg. According to his sister (22 April 1995), he:

... was born in Burnley, Lancashire, England. He was educated at Principal Sparling Elementary and Daniel McIntyre Collegiate in Winnipeg. Fred was a former *Tribune* carrier. His special hobby was hockey and he was a player of note. Fred enlisted in the Navy in July, 1940. He trained in Esquimalt and Halifax, specializing in telegraphy.

She adds (28 February 2002):

There were three of us children in the family, my brother being the oldest followed by my sister Florence. I am the only surviving member of the family. Fred was ten years older than I, so I was quite young when he left home for the service. I am 71 and have scant memories of Fred. I wish I could have had him as a brother in my adult life where we could have had a closer relationship.

He immigrated to Canada with his parents in 1929. ***Howard Lake*** (54 L/14), northwest of Churchill was named after him in 1957.

Howard, Private **Harry S.** of Swan River (H 17032). Winnipeg Grenadiers. He died 22 October 1942 and is commemorated at the Sai Wan War Cemetery in Hong Kong. He had been taken prisoner of war after the fall of Hong Kong and died during his internment. He was survived by his wife Vera Howard of Swan River. ***Howard Bay*** (64 O/10) in Askey Lake was named after him in 1995.

Howarth, Captain **William H.** of Winnipeg. Royal Canadian Artillery. He died 1 September 1944 at the age of 29 and is commemorated at Montecchio War Cemetery in Italy. He was the son of Albert and Emily Howarth and was survived by his wife Alice Howarth of Winnipeg. ***Howarth Lake*** (64 K/6), northeast of Reindeer Lake was named after him in 1972.

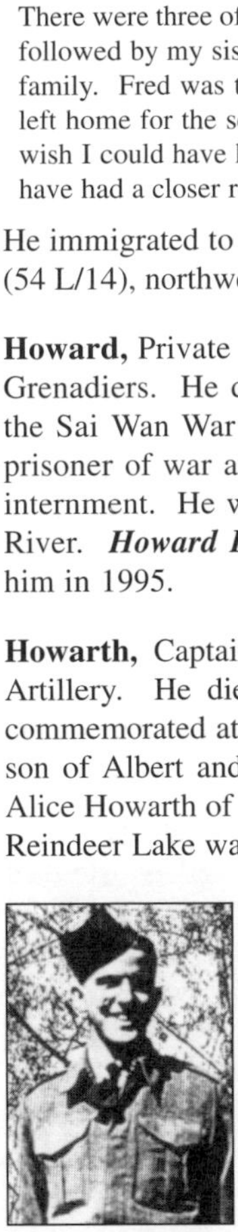

Howe, Private **George B.** of Swan River (K 1242). Canadian Scottish Regiment. He died 28 March 1945 at the age of 18 and is commemorated at the Groesbeek Canadian War Cemetery in Holland. He was the son of William George and Effie M. Howe of North Vancouver. ***Howe Island*** (54 D/6) in Gull Lake was named after him in 1996.

Howe, Lance Corporal **Harry L.** of Winnipeg (H 26566). Fort Garry Horse. He died 1 October 1944 at the age of 22 and is commemorated at Bergen-op-Zoom Canadian War Cemetery in Holland. He was the son of John H. and Minnie C. Howe of Toronto. ***Howe Peninsula*** (53 E/16) on Krolman Lake was named after him in 1996.

Hrehorak, Warrant Officer 2 **Nicholas** of Winnipeg (R 86111). No. 103 Squadron. He died 22 September 1942 at the age of 23 and is commemorated at Brigg Cemetery in Lincolnshire, England. He was the son of John and Anne Hrehorak of Winnipeg. ***Hrehorak Lake*** (53 D/5), southwest of Charron Lake was named after him in 1979.

Hrysko, Corporal **William** of Winnipeg (R 106466). No. 11 Squadron. He died 13 July 1945 at the age of 25 and is commemorated at the Ottawa Memorial. He was the son of John and Mary Hrysko of Winnipeg. ***Hrysko Lake*** (64 J/12), west of Tadoule Lake was named after him in 1975.

Hubick, (a.k.a. Hubicz, Hubiez) Sapper **Albert F.** of Winnipeg (H 36521). Royal Canadian Engineers. He died 15 June 1944 at the age of 19 and is commemorated at Holy Ghost Cemetery in Winnipeg. He was the son of Michael and Patricia Hubicz of Winnipeg. ***Hubick Lake*** (63 J/12), southeast of Wekusko Lake was named after him in 1972.

Hubley, Pilot Officer **Cecil D. B.** of Manitou (J 92593). No. 419 Squadron. He died 28 December 1944 at the age of 20 and is commemorated at Rheinberg War Cemetery in Germany. He was the son of James and Jean Hubley of Manitou, Manitoba. His sister recalls (10 October 2001):

> The crew was on its 18th mission to Opladen, Germany. I was twelve years old when we received word that my brother was missing, later presumed dead. I visited his grave in Germany in 1963.

Hubley Lake (53 M/14), southeast of Split Lake was named after him in 1966.

Hudson, Private **Donald T.** of Seven Sisters Falls (H 1795). Algonquin Regiment. He died 7 March 1945 at the age of 20 and is commemorated at the Groesbeek Canadian War Cemetery in Holland. He was the son of Harold and Dorothy Hudson of Seven Sisters Falls, Manitoba. ***Hudson Lake*** (64 C/5), southeast of Reindeer Lake was named after him in 1973.

Hudson, Private **Mitchell** of Winnipeg (H 204125). Princess Patricia's Canadian Light Infantry. He died 22 April 1945 and is commemorated at the Holten Canadian War Cemetery in Holland. ***Hudson Point*** (54 D/7) on Stephens Lake was named after him in 1995.

Hudson, Private **Thomas** of Neepawa (H 20328). Queen's Own Cameron Highlanders. He died 22 July 1944 and is commemorated at Bretteville-sur-Laize Canadian War Cemetery in Calvados, France. He was the son of Mr. and Mrs. E. Hudson and was survived by his wife Christine Hudson and their four year-old daughter. His brother writes (7 January 1997) that he was:

> ... born at Daisy Hill, County Durham in 1919. He was educated there and also at Neepawa, Manitoba. Prior to enlisting ... he was employed at Fenwick's Department Store in the grocery department. He took his military training at Winnipeg, Shilo and Quebec, arriving overseas in December, 1940. He was in the raid on Dieppe.

Hudson Island (64 O/15) in Younger Lake was named after him in 1995.

Huffman, Flying Officer **George L. "Huff"** of Winnipeg (J 21575). No. 426 Squadron. He died 24 November 1943 at the age of 26 and is commemorated at Stonefall Cemetery in Yorkshire, England. He was one of the six children of George E. and Ann E. Huffman of Winnipeg. He was employed at Central Patricia Gold Mines when he enlisted in March, 1942. ***Huffman Lake*** (64 O/8), southwest of Nejanilini Lake was named after him in 1975.

Hughes, Trooper **Albert J.** of Winnipeg (H 20764). Fort Garry Horse. He died 22 April 1941 at the age of 24 and is commemorated at Barrie Union Cemetery, Ontario. He was the son of Charles and Anne Hughes of Winnipeg and was survived by his wife Florence Hughes of Winnipeg. ***Hughes Peninsula*** (64 N/4) on Spencer Lake was named after him in 1995.

Hughes, Lieutenant **Glen W.** of Winnipeg. Royal Winnipeg Rifles. He died 12 August 1944 at the age of 28 and is commemorated at Beny-sur-Mer Canadian War Cemetery in Calvados, France. He was the youngest of the four sons and one daughter of Samuel and Annie M. Hughes, homesteaders at Grandview and Neepawa. His brother Ken (12th Manitoba Dragoons) writes (26 November 2001):

> Born in 1915 during the First World War, Glen was always interested in military matters and in listening to the stories told by the returning veterans of that war. When he finished his schooling, he joined the Militia Unit of the Royal Winnipeg Rifles and was very proud of his regiment. As a Captain in a Canadian Army Holding Unit in England in May, 1944, he reverted to Lieutenant when the Rifles required Lieutenants as reinforcements to take part in the D-Day invasion. I met him in Normandy twice in July, 1944 and he was full of praise for the men in his platoon and their performance in action. He wanted very much to return to Winnipeg to tell the people back there what great men their brothers, husbands and sons had proven to be when the going was tough. If he had to die, it is fitting that he is buried at Beny-sur-Mer where so many of his comrades lie.

His niece adds (26 November 2001):

> I had the honour of accompanying my father to Europe in 1995 for the VE-Day celebrations and we visited Glen's marker at Beny-sur-Mer. It was a very emotional experience, especially for my father, although he had been there before in 1945. I believe the army made it possible for relatives who were stationed overseas to visit.
>
> Our family has deep feelings for Glen, and even my grandchildren attend Remembrance Day ceremonies with me. My father also enlisted in the army and served overseas, so I do not have any memory of him until he returned in late 1945. I do remember the day the telegram came with the news about Glen because my mother spent the afternoon in her bedroom which she had never done before, and I was a worried three year-old.

Hughes Island (64 F/9) in Jordan Lake was named after him in 1994.

Hughes, Trooper **John H.** of Winnipeg (B 138442). Fort Garry Horse. He died 5 August 1944 at the age of 19 and is commemorated at Bretteville-sur-Laize Canadian War Cemetery in Calvados, France. He was the son of James W. and Alice Hughes of Toronto. ***John Hughes Lake*** (53 E/16), west of York Lake was named after him in 1996.

Hughes, Private **John L.** of Winnipeg (H 50558). Royal Canadian Army Medical Corps. He died 2 November 1944 at the age of 28 and is commemorated at the Holten Canadian War Cemetery in Holland. He was survived by his wife Irene Hughes of Winnipeg. ***Hughes Hill*** (64 I/15), northeast of Wither Lake was named after him in 1995.

Hughes, Private **Kenneth G.** of Winnipeg (H 8023). Algonquin Regiment. He died 17 November 1944 at the age of 22 and is commemorated at Bergen-op-Zoom Canadian War Cemetery in Holland. He was the son of Dwight and Mae Hughes of Winnipeg. ***Hughes Rapids*** (64 N/10) in the Thlewiaza River was named after him in 1995.

Hughes Petty Officer **Reginald A.** of Winnipeg (X 41099). HMCS *Avalon*, the Royal Canadian Navy shore establishment in St. John's, Newfoundland. He died 12 December 1942 at the age of 49 and is commemorated at Mount Pleasant Cemetery in St. John's. He was the son of Alfred J. and Eliza E. Hughes and was survived by his wife Mary T. Hughes of Vancouver. ***Hughes Point*** (63 I/16) on Dubinsky Lake was named after him in 1995.

Hughes, Pilot Officer **Trevor J.** of Winnipeg (J 17635). No. 544 Squadron. He died 15 May 1943 at the age of 30 and is commemorated at the Runnymede Memorial in Surrey, England. He was the son of John and Mary J. Hughes of Winnipeg. ***Hughes Bay*** (64 O/5) in Booth Lake was named after him in 1995.

Hughson, Corporal **Edward M.** of MacGregor (H 43008). Lincoln and Welland Regiment. He died 28 February 1945 at the age of 27 and is commemorated at the Groesbeek Canadian War Cemetery in Holland. He was the son of George H. and Susan Hughson and was survived by his wife Violet A. Hughson of MacGregor, Manitoba. ***Hughson Lake*** (64 O/3), east of Egenolf Lake was named after him in 1975.

Hugill, Gunner **Ernest L.** of Durban (H 54915). Royal Canadian Artillery. He died 17 January 1944 at the age of 22 and is commemorated at the Moro River Canadian War Cemetery in Italy. His nephew (20 January 1995) recalls that:

> ... he was born December 14, 1921 at Durban, Manitoba. He received his schooling at Durban as well. His most special interest was a love of music, playing the violin, banjo and guitar. He was killed by an artillery shell in Italy.

He adds (3 December 2001):

> While I was born several years after his death, my father Clarence would sometimes tell us about Ernie. He played the violin well and was keenly interested in sports. Though we didn't know him personally, he always had a place in our hearts. He wrote a letter home from Italy on December 9, 1943 to his oldest brother Jack. Parts of this letter read as follows:
>
> "You will most likely know long ere you receive this that I am in Italy and I must say, I haven't such a good opinion of it. It's been anything but 'sunny.' However, it may be nicer in the summer. But I'll take good old Regina any day and Simpson's [where he had worked]." In conclusion to his letter he writes: "Well folks, I'm just about out of space so I'll wish you (a little later perhaps) a very Merry Christmas and prosperous New Year. Love to you all and I hope to see you soon. Love, Ernie." He was killed in action less than a month later – apparently on his first day in battle.

Hugill Creek (64 N/7), which flows northeast into MacMillan Lake was named after him in 1961.

Hull, Private **Herbert J.** of Fort Garry (H 6601). Winnipeg Grenadiers. He died a prisoner of war 15 April 1944 at the age of 23 and is commemorated at the Yokohama War Cemetery in Japan. He was the oldest son of Herbert J. and Annie R. Hull and was survived by his wife Dorothy Hull (née Simpson) of Fort Garry. His sister reports (18 January 1996) that his family:

> ... lived in the west end of Winnipeg ... for 17 years and [he] got all his schooling in that district. At about 14 or 15, he started going to Minto Armouries twice a week with the Grenadiers and when war broke out, he enlisted right away. Everyone in the outfit knew him as he was the bugler.

Hull Lake (52 L/6), east of Lac du Bonnet was named after him in 1973.

Hullin, Captain the Reverend **William R.** of Winnipeg. Canadian Chaplains Service. He died 3 June 1945 at the age of 40 and is commemorated at the Adegem Canadian War Cemetery in Belgium. He was the son of George and Janet Hullin and was survived by his wife Gertrude G. Hullin of Winnipeg. ***Hullin Lake*** (64 K/11), northeast of Reindeer Lake was named after him in 1972.

Hume, Flight Sergeant **Raymond G.** of Flin Flon (R 116029). No. 77 Squadron. He died 21 April 1943 at the age of 20 and is commemorated at Fourfelt Cemetery in Esbjerg, Denmark. ***Hume Lake*** (63 O/15), north of Nelson House was named after him in 1979.

Hunt, Pilot Officer **James T.** of Winnipeg (J 16904). No. 106 Squadron. He died 11 February 1943 at the age of 25 and is commemorated at the Sage War Cemetery in Germany. He was the son of James and Mary E. Hunt of Winnipeg and was survived by his wife Vivian B. Hunt of Winnipeg. ***Hunt Island*** (64 K/15) in Maria Lake was named after him in 1989.

Hunter, Pilot Officer **Alvin J.** of Minnedosa (J 94317). No. 432 Squadron. He died 21 February 1945 at the age of 19 and is commemorated at Durnbach War Cemetery in Bavaria, Germany. He was the son of the late David B. and Anna M. Hunter of Winnipeg. ***Hunter Peninsula*** (64 F/9) on Jordan Lake was named after him in 1984.

Hunter, Private **Ferguson J.** of Crystal City (H 2554). Royal Canadian Ordnance Corps. He died 13 July 1940 at the age of 29 and is commemorated at Elmwood Cemetery in Winnipeg. He was the son of Mr. and Mrs. John Hunter of Crystal City and was survived by his wife Ethel Hunter of Winnipeg. ***Hunter Point*** (63 P/10) on Armstrong Lake was named after him in 1995.

Hunter, Private **Jack J.** of Neepawa (H 20326). Queen's Own Cameron Highlanders, Military Medal. The local newspaper bore the headline "Jack Hunter – First Local Boy to be Cited in this War." It read in part:

> Jack Hunter, 20 year-old son of Mr. and Mrs. Walter Hunter was awarded the Military Medal for bravery in the field. Jack was one of the first to land on the shore at Dieppe and under heavy fire from all sides, exposed himself while cutting a hole through the heavy enemy wire. When the wire was cut, Jack hauled his mortar over the beach and laid down a smoke screen while his platoon went over and through the sea wall. In this action, he showed total disregard for his own safety and his gallantry was of the highest order (*Neepawa Press* August 1942).

He died 19 August 1942 at the age of 20 and is commemorated at Dieppe Canadian War Cemetery in Seine-Maritime, France. ***Hunter Lake*** (64 C/10), northwest of Granville Lake was named after him in 1947.

Hunter, Private **Roy J.** of Fortier (H 67334). South Saskatchewan Regiment. He died 27 October 1944 and is commemorated at Schoonselhof Cemetery in Antwerp, Belgium. ***Hunter Creek*** (53 N/13), which flows northeast into Stupart River was named after him in 1995.

Hunter, Corporal **Stanley H.** of Winnipeg (H 6569). Winnipeg Grenadiers. He died 23 November 1943 and is commemorated at the Yokohama War Cemetery in Japan. He was taken prisoner after the fall of Hong Kong and died of malnutrition in a prisoner of war camp two years later. He was the son of Hamilton J. and Gertrude Hunter (née Labb). ***Hunter Bay*** (64 O/12) in Shannon Lake was named after him in 1995.

Hunter, Flying Officer **William G.** of Winnipeg (J 25758). No. 429 Squadron. He died 23 May 1944 at the age of 29 and is commemorated at Stonefall Cemetery in Yorkshire, England. He was the son of George and Emily Hunter of Winnipeg. ***Hunter Rapids*** (64 P/15) in the Caribou River was named after him in 1995.

Hunter, Sergeant **W. J. MacGregor "Mac"** of Swan River (H 25059). Royal Canadian Engineers. He died 1 October 1944 at the age of 33 and is commemorated at Schoonselhof Cemetery in Antwerp, Belgium. He was the son of Harry and Kate M. M. Hunter and was survived by his wife Nova K. Hunter of Winnipeg. He had been the first man from the Swan River area to enlist and had served overseas since August, 1940. According to his sister (22 January 1996): "... he was born in Killarney, Manitoba. Before the war he did work on the highway gang. He was involved in the United Church Choir." ***Hunter Island*** (64 O/4) in Szwec Lake was named after him in 1995.

Huppe, Sergeant **Allan W.** of Winnipeg (R 210041). No. 1661 Conversion Unit, RCAF. He died 17 May 1944 at the age of 20 and is commemorated at Brookwood Military Cemetery in Surrey, England. He was the son of Alexander and Jennie Huppe of Winnipeg. He and Sergeant William H. England (see entry) were friends, having attended Hugh John Macdonald School together in Winnipeg. They were killed in the same crash. ***Huppe Lake*** (63 N/1), southeast of Sherridon was named after him in 1970.

Huppert, Flight Lieutenant **Stanley B.** of Winnipeg (J 18426). No. 410 Squadron. He died 8 July 1944 at the age of 21 and is commemorated at the Runnymede Memorial in Surrey, England. His aircraft had just managed to sink a mine-laying ship in the mouth of the Seine River in France when it was hit by debris from the ship. The navigator bailed out safely, but did not see another parachute (Allison and Hayward 1991). He was survived by his wife Lorna Huppert. ***Huppert Lake*** (64 O/15), east of Nueltin Lake was named after him in 1975.

Hurlbut, Rifleman **Lewis** of Winnipeg (H 41455). Royal Winnipeg Rifles. He died 21 May 1945 at the age of 45 and is commemorated at Truro Cemetery in Nova Scotia. He was survived by his son James L. Hurlbut of Bow Island, Alberta. ***Hurlbut Lake*** (64 G/5), east of Hurst Lake was named after him in 1996.

Hurlin, Private **William R.** of Miniota (H 10521). Algonquin Regiment. He died 8 October 1944 at the age of 19 and is commemorated at the Adegem Canadian War Cemetery in Belgium. He was the son of William H. and Doris Hurlin of Miniota, Manitoba. ***Hurlin Lake*** (63 K/16), northwest of Wekusko Lake was named after him in 1973.

Hurst, Sergeant **Leslie E.** of Transcona (H 19286). Queen's Own Cameron Highlanders. He died 19 August 1942 at the age of 27 and is commemorated at Dieppe Canadian War Cemetery in Seine-Maritime, France. He was survived by his mother Elizabeth Hurst and by his wife Elspeth C. Hurst of Transcona. ***Hurst Lake*** (64 G/5), south of Big Sand Lake was named after him in 1963.

Hurton, Flying Officer **Roderick Harold** of Glenboro (J 9854). No. 268 Squadron. He died 12 May 1943 at the age of 23 and is commemorated at Newmarket Cemetery in Suffolk, England. He was the son of Roderick G. and Nellie Hurton of Glenboro, Manitoba. ***Hurton Lake*** (64 P/13), east of Baralzon Lake was named after him in 1987.

Hutchinson, Warrant Officer 2 **Gordon J.** of Winnipeg (R 918600). No. 101 Squadron. He died 31 January 1943 at the age of 28 and is commemorated at Amsterdam New Eastern Cemetery, Holland. He was the son of Fred and Olga Hutchinson of St. James. ***Hutchinson Island*** (64 N/4) in Maguire Lake was named after him in 1995.

Hutton, Flight Sergeant **Edsel R.** of The Pas (R 110037). No. 7 Operational Training Unit, RCAF. He died 28 September 1942 at the age of 20 and is commemorated at the Runnymede Memorial in Surrey, England. His niece writes (26 October 2001):

> Edsel Raymond Hutton was born on August 10, 1919 in The Pas, Manitoba. His father was employed by the Hudson's Bay Company as a store manager and trader and Edsel spent his early years in the communities of Wabowden, Graham, Ontario, then Red Earth, Saskatchewan and finally The Pas. Upon completion of his education, he was employed with the Dominion Bank in The Pas. Shortly before enlisting, he went into business with his father who had retired from the company and had started his own business in Red Earth.

Hutton Lake (64 O/16), east of Nueltin Lake was named after him in 1961.

Hutzcal, Trooper **Constantine N.** of Winnipeg (H 77705). 12th Manitoba Dragoons. He died 6 December 1944 at the age of 21 and is commemorated at Bergen-op-Zoom Canadian War Cemetery in Holland. He was the eldest of the six children of Nicholas and Vasilca Hutzcal (née Harrison) of Hairy Hill, Alberta. His sister reports (16 October 1998) that:

> My brother ... was born ... at Boian, Alberta. He left the farm at an early age and travelled to other farms working as a farm hand and was mechanically inclined, he loved repairing machinery and particularly favoured cars and motorcycles. He signed up with the Manitoba Dragoons in 1941.

Hutzcal Lake (64 C/7), west of Granville Lake was named after him in 1995.

Huzyk, Rifleman **Charles** of Winnipeg (H 102547). Regina Rifle Regiment. He died 8 July 1944 at the age of 22 and is commemorated at Beny-sur-Mer Canadian War Cemetery in Calvados, France. He was the son of Michael and Anna Huzyk. ***Huzyk Creek*** (63 J/6), which flows east into the Hargrave River was named after him in 1972.

Hyde, Private **David R.** of Newdale (H 66844). Royal Hamilton Light Infantry. He died 8 March 1945 at the age of 24 and is commemorated at the Groesbeek Canadian War Cemetery in Holland. He was the son of Robert A. and the late Mary Pearl Hyde of Newdale, Manitoba. According to his brother (29 October 2001):

> He was a quiet lad, kept mostly to himself. He grew up on the farm. Times were hard during his growing years. His mother died when he was nine. During the thirties, there weren't many jobs, so David and some of his friends rode the freight cars out west and went on harvest excursions, coming home the same way when harvest was over. In 1940, he joined the army at Camp Borden and trained as a truck driver and served in Canada until 1941 when he was shipped overseas. They were short of recruits for the infantry so he was put in the Royal Hamilton Light Infantry. He was wounded in France and sent back to a hospital in England. After he recuperated from his wounds, he returned to his unit in France and was killed in action.

Hyde Bay (64 O/3) in Canfield Lake was named after him in 1995.

Hyde, Warrant Officer 2 **Henry J.** of Lowe Farm (R 123526). No. 147 Squadron. He died 8 January 1944 at the age of 23 and is commemorated at the Ottawa Memorial. He was the son of Nicolai J. and Annie Hyde of Lowe Farm, Manitoba. ***Hyde Island*** (63 K/16) in File Lake was named after him in 1973.

Hyland, Flying Officer **George A.** of Winnipeg (J 39503). No. 415 Squadron. He died 31 May 1945 at the age of 28 and is commemorated at the Runnymede Memorial in Surrey, England. He was the son of Ernest N. and Margaret L. Hyland and was survived by his wife Emma M. Hyland of Detroit, Michigan. ***Hyland Lake*** (64 O/16), west of Baralzon Lake was named after him in 1995.

Hyndman, Pilot Officer **Orie F.** of Rapid City (J 85102). No. 179 Squadron. He died 22 February 1944 at the age of 22 and is commemorated at the Malta Memorial. He was the son of Frank S. and Laura M. Hyndman of Rapid City, Manitoba. ***Hyndman Creek*** (53 E/7), which flows northwest into Makepiece Lake was named after him in 1973.

Canadian soldiers returning from Vimy Ridge, May, 1917.
Courtesy of the National Archives of Canada (PA-001332).

I

Ibbott, Pilot Officer **Herbert** of Winnipeg (J 24024). No. 82 Operational Training Unit, RCAF. He died 9 August 1943 at the age of 21 and was buried in the family plot at Bedford Cemetery in Bedfordshire, England. He was the son of Arthur W. P. and Caroline Ibbott (née Whittle) of Winnipeg. Prior to enlistment, he had been a shipping clerk at Mitchell Copp Limited. His brother recalls (31 October 2001):

> We were five boys and three girls. Three of the boys wore the uniform; they were all in the RCAF. Herbert was the only one who ended up serving overseas. He was a Pilot Officer by rank, but he was training as a bombardier on August 9, 1943, the day his airplane crashed on a practice flight from England to Ireland and back. He died precisely one week after his 21st birthday.

The crash was later attributed to engine failure. ***Ibbott Lake*** (64 N/5), southwest of Nueltin Lake was named after him in 1972.

Ilasevich, Corporal **Harry** of Sadlow (H 17855). Princess Patricia's Canadian Light Infantry. He died 12 April 1945 at the age of 21 and is commemorated at the Holten Canadian War Cemetery in Holland. He was the son of Michael and Lena Ilasevich of Sadlow, Manitoba. According to his sister (12 August 1998):

> Harry ... was only 17 years of age when he joined the war effort on December 15, 1941. It was obvious that he was anxious to do his part so he told the recruitment office that he was older than he really was. As a boy, he was especially interested in music as well as baseball and fishing and other regular things that young boys were involved in during those years. Unfortunately, because of hard times he was only able to finish Grade 7 before he had to leave home to make a living for himself.

Ilasevich Lake (63 K/16), northwest of Wekusko Lake was named after him in 1973.

Iles, Private **Percy J.** of Arrow River (H 6650). Winnipeg Grenadiers. He died 11 October 1942 at the age of 25 and is commemorated at the Sai Wan War Cemetery in Hong Kong. He was the son of Percy J. and Sarah Iles of Arrow River, Manitoba. His sister writes (17 October 2001):

> I just can't remember much as I was away. Percy went to Arrow River School, [then] worked around as a hired man on different farms for next to nothing other than room and board. Times were hard. His name is in the memory book in Arrow River Church alongside his Dad's and we thank you for having a lake named after him.

Iles Lake (64 J/8), southeast of Tadoule Lake was named after him in 1975.

Illingworth, Electrical Artificer 4 **Joseph W.** of Winnipeg (V 24433). HMCS *Stadacona*. He was presumed dead 28 March 1943 at the age of 24 and is commemorated at Brookside Cemetery in Winnipeg. He was the son of Joseph and Helen Illingworth of Winnipeg and had been employed by the Vulcan Iron Works prior to enlisting. His obituary indicated that he had been missing since 25 March 1943 and was found floating in Halifax harbour 13 June 1943. The family later learned that his hands were tied behind his back. A court of enquiry was convened but the circumstances of his death were never resolved. ***Illingworth Lake*** (64 N/8), southwest of Nueltin Lake was named after him in 1972.

Ingram, Sergeant **Leopold A.** of Winnipeg (R 166212). Stationary Engineer, RCAF. He died 10 August 1945 at the age of 55 and is commemorated at Prairie Grove Cemetery, Manitoba. He was the son of George and Margaret Ingram and was survived by his wife Constance Ingram of Winnipeg. ***Ingram Lake*** (64 I/14), northwest of North Knife Lake was named after him in 1974.

Injates, Gunner **Louie** of Brandon (H 67223). Royal Canadian Artillery. He died 8 August 1944 and is commemorated at Bretteville-sur-Laize Canadian War Cemetery in Calvados, France. ***Injates Lake*** (64 J/5), north of Big Sand Lake was named after him in 1978.

Inverarity, Pilot Officer **John A.** of Wellwood (J 86381). No. 408 Squadron. He died 8 June 1944 at the age of 26 and is commemorated at the Runnymede Memorial in Surrey, England. He was the fifth child of James and Christina Inverarity and was survived by his wife Ethel I. Inverarity (née McIntosh) of Lucky Lake, Saskatchewan and their daughter. His brother recalls (17 November 1997) that he:

> ... grew up on the family farm. In 1941 he married. They had a daughter shortly before he went overseas. John was musically inclined and was a self-taught violinist. He played in an orchestra and this is where he met his future wife. John also enjoyed a variety of sports of which baseball was his favourite. John joined the air force in 1941 and went overseas in 1942. According to information received by the family, there is no known grave or marker in his memory and only a piece of his identification disc was found after he went missing and was presumed dead.

His wife adds (20 November 2001):

> We farmed the family farm three miles east of Wellwood. There were no tractors to farm with then, so it was done by horse power. We also had other livestock. Our farming didn't last long. Four months after we were married, he was called to report to Brandon Depot in July, 1941. So ended our farming and I moved home to live with my parents. John and I played in an orchestra for a couple of years, so I kept on with the music. My Dad passed away in June, 1944 and the following week I received word that John was listed as missing and believed killed in action. Indeed a sad time for all of us. I have a tree planted in the park at Wellwood in his memory.

Inverarity Lake (64 P/12), northwest of Nejanilini Lake was named after him in 1974.

Ireland, Flying Officer **Donald G. H.** of Killarney (J 88130). No. 101 Squadron. He died 17 December 1944 at the age of 22 and is commemorated at Durnbach War Cemetery in Bavaria, Germany. He was the eldest of the five children of George A. and Elizabeth M. Ireland of Killarney, Manitoba. The 101 was a secret squadron whose mission was to jam German fighter control communications. It lost more personnel on bomber operations than any other squadron in bomber command. According to his brother (9 February 1996):

> Immediately following the war, a member of a crew member's family (Sergeant Hartman) from England was able to go to Germany through the auspices of the Red Cross to visit the temporary grave site of the crew at Albeck. He was able to establish that the aircraft had crashed in the yard of a small inn north of Ulm. Ulm is a small city primarily noted for the highest cathedral in Germany. From the actual crash site at the inn, the crew members were removed to a cemetery in the nearby small town of Albeck and eventually to the Commonwealth military cemetery at Durnbach near Tegernsee in Bavaria.
>
> By using the information provided by Sergeant Hartman's family, I was able in 1971 to visit the cemetery at Albeck and to meet the family Schmidt who still occupied and managed the inn at the crash site. By

1971, it had become a hotel on the Autobahn with a service station and restaurant. The mother and daughter (then eight years old in December, 1944) had witnessed the Lancaster approach and crash in their back yard very close to the inn. Parts of the aircraft's aluminum structure were retrieved by Mr. Hartman in 1946 and sent to the other crew members' families. The villagers at Albeck recalled the incident and confirmed that the crew had indeed been transferred to the military cemetery. The Schmidt family were extremely courteous and observed that they did not know what the military target could have been and in any event, 80 per cent of the buildings in the city were destroyed by bombing although the cathedral was never damaged. I revisited the site and the Schmidt hotel in 1981. I believe that Ulm was not just an industrial target but also a Gestapo headquarters which might explain the extensive damage to the city. I have noticed in my visits to Ulm that almost every building apart from the cathedral is of post-war construction.

Ireland Island (64 O/10) in Askey Lake was named after him in 1995.

Ireland, Flight Sergeant **James Howard** of MacGregor (R 162102). No. 148 Squadron. He died 12 September 1944 at the age of 20 and is commemorated at Milan War Cemetery in Italy. He was the son of William H. and Jessie A. Ireland of MacGregor and the nephew of Olive M. Tarr of MacGregor. ***Ireland Lake*** (64 J/15), northwest of Tadoule Lake was named after him in 1975.

Ireland, Sergeant **Willard Vernon** of Holmfield (R 210291). No. 100 Squadron. He died 17 June 1944 at the age of 19 and is commemorated at Uden War Cemetery, Holland. He was the son of Willard N. and Agnes J. Ireland of Holmfield, Manitoba. The accompanying photograph is one which his brother had in his wallet since the time that it was taken. ***Ireland Bay*** (63 N/10) in Flatrock Lake was named after him in 1995.

Irvine, Warrant Officer 1 **Alfred "Fred"** of Winnipeg (R 95175). No. 277 Squadron. He died 27 May 1943 at the age of 22 and is commemorated at Brookwood Military Cemetery in Surrey, England. He was the son of William G. and Lillian M. Irvine of Winnipeg and was survived by his wife Hilda Irvine. His brother reports (8 May 1995):

Fred [was] born in Winnipeg March 1921. Lived at 867 Jubilee Avenue. Attended Lord Roberts and Kelvin schools. Worked for CNR before his enlistment. Fred had three brothers who served overseas. Harry with the QOCH of C. from 1939 - 45, Ted with the RCAF attached to RAF coastal command SEAC, 1942 - 46, George with the REME, 1944 - 46.

Irvine Island (64 O/11) in Corbett Lake was named after him in 1995.

Irvine, Private **Sidney** of West Kildonan (H 37760). Royal Canadian Army Service Corps. He died 15 September 1944 at the age of 38 and is commemorated at the Rome War Cemetery in Italy. He was the son of Hugh and Catherine Irvine (née Kirk) and was survived by his wife Gladys M. Irvine of West Kildonan and their two children. His daughter writes (15 November 2001):

My father joined the army (RCASC) in 1940. After training in Canada, he was shipped to England. He was an MP for a while and then transferred to Canadian Army Catering Group A. When Italy was invaded in 1944, he went to Anzio Beach Head. On September 5, 1944 he was burned over 40% of his body when a petrol cooker he was lighting exploded in the kitchen. At first, the doctor didn't think it was too serious, but he succumbed to his burns.

Bob and I were young when Dad joined up; we remember when he came home on his leaves. He looked so handsome in his uniform, he would show us his gun. He was a happy father and would play with us. He would take my brother to cowboy movies while mom and I went to a musical. A special event happened in October, 1999. My granddaughter Carolyn went to Italy with her mother and visited Rome, found the military cemetery and found his grave. She took pictures of the headstone and of herself sitting beside it. She looked in the book and found his name and my mother's as his widow. This was very touching to me and my brother. We are pleased to have a lake named after him.

Irvine Lake (52 E/14), east of Brereton Lake was named after him in 1974.

Irving, Lieutenant **Fleming Ladd** of Winnipeg. 1st Hussar Tank Regiment. He died on D-Day, 6 June 1944 at the age of 21 and is commemorated at Beny-sur-Mer Canadian War Cemetery in Calvados, France. He was the son of George F. and Ruth L. W. Irving of Winnipeg. His obituary in a newspaper read in part:

One of the few King Scouts in Manitoba prior to his enlistment with the Canadian Armoured Corps, Lieutenant Fleming Ladd Irving, 21, has been reported killed in action. He is the son of Mr. and Mrs. G. F. Irving, 137 Campbell Street.

Lieutenant Irving was one of four boy scouts chosen to represent the province at the reception at the Parliament Buildings during the time of the royal visit to Canada, 1939. He was the leader of a cub pack at St. George's church. Born in Winnipeg, he attended Queenston, Robert H. Smith and Kelvin schools and had completed two years in the Faculty of Science at the University of Manitoba where he joined the Canadian Officer's Training Corps. Lieutenant Irving enlisted in October, 1942, received his training at Gordon Head and Camp Borden and went overseas in May, 1943. He is survived by his parents and one brother, George, at home (n.d.).

Irving Lake (53 E/16), north of Island Lake was named after him in 1961.

Irwin, Sergeant **Clifford C.** of Miami, Manitoba (H 17564). Algonquin Regiment. He died 3 November 1944 at the age of 24 and is commemorated at Bergen-op-Zoom Canadian War Cemetery in Holland. He was one of the 12 children of Wilford and Anne Irwin and was survived by his wife Edith Patsy Irwin of Fort William, Ontario and their young daughter. His sister writes (8 February 1995):

He was born on a farm and went to a one-room school house called Mount Nebo and got an eighth grade certificate. He didn't have any real hobbies. On a farm you do the ordinary things, but he did love to hunt. All sorts of hunting – deer, wolves, geese, ducks etc.

He was born into a family of 12 – six brothers and five sisters. I am five years younger than him, so I can remember all our good times together and when he was gone, part of our lives went with him. He was a happy, carefree guy and certainly loved life which was far too short. We will always miss him.

Irwin Peninsula (53 F/13) in Angling Lake was named after him in 1995.

Irwin, Flight Sergeant **George K.** of Winnipeg (R 100416). No. 1 Advanced Flying Unit. He died 3 August 1942 at the age of 21 and is commemorated at the Runnymede Memorial in Surrey, England. He was the son of James A. and E. Merle Irwin (née Shropshire) of Winnipeg. They attended the opening of the Runnymede Memorial in 1953. His younger brother writes (7 November 2001):

During his short life, George lived at various times in Windsor, Peterborough and Toronto in Ontario and Brandon and Winnipeg, Manitoba. He was educated in Ontario schools and in Winnipeg after arriving there with his family in March, 1934. He attended Riverview School, Lord Roberts Junior High School and Kelvin High School prior to entering the Faculty of Agriculture at the University of Manitoba where he finished second year prior to enlisting in the RCAF in April, 1941.

As a university student, George was very active in athletics. He was awarded faculty crests in track and field, football and basketball, but his favourite sport was hockey. He was a better than average hockey player but truly had one overriding dream – to become a pilot and join the fight "for King and Country" overseas.

George was a quiet person with many close friends. We were told that there were young ladies who wished he were not so shy and quiet.

Upon joining the Air Force, George took initial training at Penhold, Alberta and Swift Current, Saskatchewan prior to travelling to Ontario to take Elementary Flying Training at Station Malton and on to Brantford for Service Flying Training. He was awarded his Pilot's Wings in late 1941.

After embarkation leave at home in Winnipeg over Christmas, 1941, George was in Britain at RAF Station Hastings for advanced training in early 1942 and serving in Scotland at the date of his untimely death in August of that year. Reports indicated that his aircraft dived into the sea following a mid-air collision near the Isle of Whithorn in southern Scotland.

As George's younger brother, Clare was 11 years his junior; it was 25 years before George's first and only nephew was born on May 8, 1967 in Vancouver, British Columbia and named George Irwin to honour the uncle he could never meet.

Irwin Bay (64 I/10) in Lovat Lake was named after him in 1995.

Irwin, Sergeant **James W.** of Virden (R 215775). No. 24 Operational Training Unit, RCAF. He died 24 September 1944 at the age of 19 and is commemorated at the Runnymede Memorial in Surrey, England. He was the son of Norman B. and Naomi R. Irwin of Virden. ***Irwin Island*** (63 O/12) in Nelson Lake was named after him in 1995.

Irwin, Private **Roy R.** of Melita (H 6592). Winnipeg Grenadiers. He died a prisoner of war 12 August 1944 at the age of 31 and is commemorated at the Yokohama War Cemetery in Japan. The official cause of death was listed as beriberi. He was the son of Wellington and Flossie Irwin and was survived by his wife Kay Irwin. ***Irwin Point*** (64 N/11) on Kasmere Lake was named after him in 1995.

Isaak-Derk, Regimental Sergeant Major (Warrant Officer 1) **Armand C.** of Norwood (H 33141). Royal Canadian Army Medical Corps. He died 17 October 1945 at the age of 38 and is commemorated at the Adegem Canadian War Cemetery in Belgium. He was the son of Frank F. and Aganetha Isaak (née Derksen) and the husband of Evelyn W. Isaak-Derk of London, England. His wife recalls (22 January 1998):

Abraham Isaak was born in Millirowa, Don, Russia. His family owned a flour mill which, after the Russian Revolution, was expropriated by the communist government. The family left the country in 1921, destined for security reasons to travel in two separate groups throughout Europe for the next two years until they came together in England, and finally arrived in Winnipeg in 1924.

In the early years of his education and in the course of his travels in Europe, Abraham Isaak, whose mother tongue was German, learned four languages, namely Russian, Polish, Czech and English. After attending secondary schools in Winnipeg, he continued his education at the University in Grafton, North Dakota.

With a growing identification to Canada, Abraham Isaak became a naturalized citizen [in] 1938 and on the same date had his name changed to Armand Cecil Isaak-Derk (Derk was his mother's maiden name). Armand enlisted in Winnipeg as a private in the Canadian Army at the outbreak of war in 1939 and with the Royal Canadian Army Medical Corps went to England the same year. He was stationed at No. 5 Canadian General Hospital, Taplow, Berkshire near London for the next four years and moved with that hospital to France in 1944 and was with it throughout the Canadian campaign in Holland and for five months after the war had ended in Europe.

Armand and I were married in London on October 19, 1940. Our circumstances were such that we were always able to live and work in close proximity, sharing our life together, until the Canadian Army with the Allied Forces invaded Europe in June, 1944. Thereafter, we were in frequent contact by letter and when the war ended we wrote of plans for our future. Almost exactly five years after our marriage date, Armand died, on October 17 in Nijmegen, Holland as a result of a traffic accident in a convoy of which he was an innocent passenger victim. The convoy was travelling to the port of embarkation to England and I was anticipating his arrival.

Writing of this event some 52 years after it happened, I am unfortunately still not reconciled as to what took place. I was not informed of Armand's death. Without word from him I had to inquire personally to the Canadian Army in London as to his whereabouts. A week after the accident, I was finally told Armand had died and had been buried at a Canadian cemetery in Nijmegen. I have never been given any of Armand's personal effects. I was told by a Canadian Captain that it had been planned that I would be flown over to Nijmegen for the funeral, but I received no such word. The Captain did volunteer the information, which I had no thought of asking, that there would be no point in suing the Air Force officer who had caused the accident.

Because this tragic event was so shocking and seemed so implausible, I continued to investigate and so can now attest to a Certificate of Death from the Department of Defence, Ottawa that "... No. H 33141, Regimental Sergeant Major Armand Cecil Isaak-Derk of the Royal Canadian Medical Corps, Canadian Army, died on the 17th of October, 1945 of injuries sustained in a vehicle accident." In the early 1950s, Armand's older brother Jake and his wife, living in Canada, journeyed to Nijmegen and visited Armand's gravesite.

When Armand and I lived together in England, and particularly during his leaves from duty, we took great pleasure in travelling to historic places in the British Isles. Armand was interested in the architecture and history of stately buildings and surrounding areas. He liked reading and in the process, discovered many books and writers. Armand was a relaxed, friendly person, kind, considerate and thoughtful. He had worked at Henderson's Directory in Winnipeg before the war and was interested in planning a directory of air travel for post-war use which he had patented. Together with an architect friend, he had full plans drawn up for the house we would build in Winnipeg.

As for myself, I came to Canada in May, 1946 to meet my in-laws, mainly Armand's mother (his father had died while Armand was overseas) and his brothers and sister, intending to return to England. However, I grew to like Canada and recognized opportunities the country affords and so have stayed here these many years. I know Armand would have felt gratified and proud to have a lake named in honour of him and I thank you on his and my own behalf.

Isaak-Derk Lake (64 K/6), northeast of Reindeer Lake was named after him in 1972.

Isfeld, Private **Einar Victor** of Amaranth (H 614129). Queen's Own Cameron Highlanders. He died 6 April 1945 at the age of 30 and is commemorated at the Groesbeek Canadian War Cemetery in Holland. He was the son of Einar and Jonina Isfeld and was survived by his wife Jean Lillian Isfeld (née Schive) of Amaranth and their young son. According to his wife (5 February 1998) he was:

... born at Big Point, Manitoba, east of Langruth. Victor was musically inclined, playing guitar and violin. He enlisted in the Queen's Own Cameron Highlanders in November of 1942. [He] received basic training at Portage la Prairie, then Dartmouth, Nova Scotia, then to Prince George, BC and Vernon, BC. [He] went overseas from Winnipeg on December 25, 1944. He was wounded crossing the Rhine on March 30, 1945.

Isfeld Island (63 N/5) in Kipahigan Lake was named after him in 1995.

Isfeld, Flying Officer **Ivan A.** of Baldur (J 16895). No. 139 Squadron. He was 21 years of age and is commemorated at the Reichswald Forest War Cemetery in Kleve, Germany. He was the fifth of the seven children of Holmgeir and Olive M. Isfeld of Fort Rouge. His sister writes (20 April 1995) that he:

... was born in Langruth, Manitoba. Ivan was four when the family moved to Argyle ... where they continued to farm. Ivan loved the farm and willingly assisted his father with the work, especially with the horses as he was very fond of horses.

Ivan was a slim six-footer but a very kind and gentle person. He did very well in school, receiving many honours. He took his Grade 9 in Arborg, Manitoba. While there, he stayed with his sister and brother-in-law Ethel and Bjarni Borgfjord. The family moved again, this time to Winnipeg where Ivan completed his Grade 11. By then, World War II was on and Ivan enlisted in the RCAF in Winnipeg and received his training in Regina. On completion of his training, he was transferred to England where he received his commission in April, 1943. Ivan was killed in action while on a night mission over Duisberg, Germany. [He] was found and buried by a German farmer. His grave was discovered in 1949 and reburied [at Kleve].

Isfeld Lake (63 O/4), north of Wekusko Lake was named after him in 1970.

Isfeld, Rifleman **Morris A.** of Winnipeg Beach (H 204114). Royal Winnipeg Rifles. He died 25 November 1945 at the age of 24 and is commemorated at the Holten Canadian War Cemetery in Holland. He was the son of Olafur and Helga Isfeld of Winnipeg Beach. ***Isfeld Peninsula*** (64 F/7) on Holiday Lake was named after him in 1980.

Isleifson, Trooper **Barney A.** of Glenboro (H 20375). 14th Canadian Hussars. He died 13 July 1944 at the age of 22 and is commemorated at Beny-sur-Mer Canadian War Cemetery in Calvados, France. He was the son of Thorstein and Sarah Isleifson of Cypress River, Manitoba. ***Isleifson Lake*** (64 J/6), southwest of Tadoule Lake was named after him in 1975.

Issett, Staff Sergeant Major (Warrant Officer 2) **Douglas H.** of Elmwood (H 26346). Fort Garry Horse. He died 30 April 1945 and is commemorated at the Holten Canadian War Cemetery in Holland. He was the only son of Mr. and Mrs. Samuel Issett and was survived by his wife Lilyan A. Issett. She writes (5 November 2001):

Doug enlisted in September, 1939 and was shipped overseas in November, 1941. He was wounded in action June 19, 1944 and returned to active duty when he recovered. Doug was affectionately known as "Doc" because of his extensive training with St. John's Ambulance.

Issett Lake (64 B/11), south of Southern Indian Lake was named after him in 1949.

Iverach, Pilot Officer **Donald M.** of Winnipeg (J 7768). No. 421 Squadron. He died 23 August 1942 at the age of 30 and is commemorated at Killay (St. Hilary Of Poictiers) Churchyard, Glamorganshire, Wales. He was the son of the Reverend David and Catherine M. E. Iverach (née Matheson) of Winnipeg. His brother John was overseas at the same time and described some of their experiences:

Don arrived overseas in 1941 and took a conversion training course for piloting Spitfires at Astondown near Chalford. He would survive a harrowing crash at Astondown in later 1941 and was hospitalized for several weeks. By March, 1942, Don had joined Spitfire Squadron 421 and was stationed at Fairwood Common near Swansea, Wales. He was five years senior to anyone else in his unit and was known as "Grandpappy." Just days before his death, he had flown as part of the Allied air cover during the Dieppe raids and was one of the few who came back without any holes in his aircraft.

During a training exercise on August 23, 1942, 11 days after his 30th birthday, Don was killed. About 11 AM, Don had been doing a simulated dog-fight exercise with a couple of other pilots using camera guns. He had just pulled out of a steep dive but instead of levelling off, he just kept going up and up until he finally stalled. He went into a spin and plowed right into the ground. As he would have had plenty of time to bail out if he wanted to, it was assumed that he had blacked out after pulling out of the dive and had never regained consciousness. He was the first member of No. 421 Squadron to lose his life.

Donald Munro Iverach was buried in the village of Killay, a suburb of Swansea, Wales. John attended the military funeral and later settled his brother's personal affairs. John kept his brother's clarinet with him for the duration of the war, finally returning with it to Canada in 1946. It and its story has since been passed on to John's children and grandchildren. All of Don's immediate family are now deceased (Iverach 1992).

Iverach Lake (63 K/16), northwest of Wekusko Lake was named after him in 1973. Members of the Royal Canadian Legion from Semans, Saskatchewan placed a commemorative marker at the lake on August 23, 1991, exactly 49 years after his death (*Last Mountain Times* 16 September 1991).

Iverach, Corporal **John A.** of Isabella (H 6693). Winnipeg Grenadiers. He died 30 September 1942 at the age of 35 and is commemorated at the Sai Wan War Cemetery in Hong Kong. He was the son of James and Maggie M. Iverach and was survived by his wife Margaret F. Iverach of Isabella, Manitoba. ***Iverach Creek*** (64 I/6), which flows southeast into Paragon Lake was named after him in 1974.

Troops leaving trenches during the Battle of the Somme, 1916. Courtesy of the National Archives of Canada (PA-207187).

J

Jack, Lance Sergeant **George J.** of West Kildonan (H 35339). Royal Canadian Artillery. He died 11 July 1943 in the Invasion of Sicily at the age of 47 and is commemorated at Agira Canadian War Cemetery in Italy. This veteran of World War I was the son of the late George P. and Annie Jack and was survived by his wife Alice Irene Jack of St. Vital and their two daughters. His eldest daughter recalls (7 November 2001):

> George John Jack served in both World War I and World War II. As an 'older' citizen with a wife and family (two daughters), he was not expected to enlist a second time. However, his patriotism prevailed and he badgered the recruitment office until they finally accepted him in early 1940. Following a signals course in Kingston, he was sent overseas just before Christmas 1940, leaving his wife and two young daughters (10 and two years). He spent two and a half years in Britain. A prolific letter writer, George described his daily activities in great detail – he could always see humour in everything. Some of his beautiful letters home are among our most treasured memories. To an avid fisherman, naming a bay in his honour is a beautiful way to keep his memory alive. He would have been so proud.

In a letter to his brother and sister-in-law two months before his death he wrote:

> Dear Winifred and Percy: Sincerest sympathy Winifred, for the loss of your brother [Major General Harry Salmon, see entry]. It was quite a shock to me too, as we were to be inspected by him the following week and I had been looking forward to seeing him again. I did not get any details here except that it was the result of a plane crash. Suppose the papers back home reported it in full. The whole division will feel the loss as he was responsible for the pick-up in training recently. We were beginning to think that we really were going to be a fighting division again. As to that, time will tell.
>
> Life is fairly quiet with us over here. Not much change from this regular routine of training. Have moved again, which makes the seventh time in a year. A soldier's life over here is surely unsettled so far as a billet is concerned. However, we can take it in our stride now. After so many moves it comes as nothing much to pack up and go somewhere, few care where, except those who have brought their English wives down to be near them. These usually pack up as soon as their month's rent is used up and tag along. Quite a sized community follows the Canadians wherever they go.
>
> Mail hasn't been so hot lately. Some followed us up, but the latest letter is about five to six weeks behind the date of mailing. Hope we stay settled long enough for the balance of it to catch up to us. There hasn't been any news of U-boat sinkings lately, so we cannot have lost much of it in that way lately. They have cut us in on some of the US cigarettes lately and the boys have been smoking Twenty Grands etc., but they don't seem to be sending over Camels, Chesterfields or any of the better brands. They are hard on the throat after our own brands.
>
> There are a couple of nice canteens in this town. The Sally Ann has one and the WVS run another. It means that we can get candies, chocolate bars and a variety of tasty things to eat as well as coffee, at very reasonable prices. The WVS is one of the best canteens I have seen over here. They have a very large, well fitted-out place and the boys patronize it in large numbers.
>
> There is only one picture show in town and that is usually packed to the doors. That is where I am heading for as soon as I finish this letter. Charlie Chaplin in the *Gold Rush* is showing. That will give you some idea of the dates of the films we get over here. Not all are as old as that, however.
>
> Haven't heard from you folks since you mentioned the big snow storm in March. Hope the resultant floods did no material damage to the old homestead. I suppose the dried out land would absorb quite a lot of moisture before it would get as miry as it did in the old days when there used to be things called muskegs around there.
>
> Hope all the youngsters are well and you oldsters also. The family must have increased in size since I last saw them. The young folks grow up so fast that it is pretty hard to keep track of them when home. Being away for three years is worse. Lots of love to all of you and I think you had better write oftener. Seem to get a letter at three month intervals only. Hope Mother and Cecil are doing OK also, George (19 May 1943).

Jack Bay (64 H/8) in Freeman Lake was named after him in 1995.

Jackson, Flight Sergeant **Alan B.** of Gladstone (R 116342). No. 434 Squadron. He died 7 September 1943 at the age of 21 and is commemorated at Durnbach War Cemetery in Bavaria, Germany. He was the son of Godfrey H. H. and Grace Jackson of Gladstone, Manitoba. ***Jackson Rapids*** (64 J/4) in the Mistay River was named after him in 1995.

Jackson, Pilot Officer **Alvin R.** of Neepawa (J 92355). No. 419 Squadron. He died 26 August 1944 at the age of 20 and is commemorated at Durnbach War Cemetery in Bavaria, Germany. His 13th and final mission was a bombing raid over Rüsselsheim, Germany. He was the son of Roy A. R. and Louisa V. Jackson of Norgate, Manitoba. According to his brother (28 March 1998) he:

> ... was born at Clarksville, Manitoba [and] attended school [there]. He worked on the family farm prior to his enlisting in the Air Force ... at age 18. He enjoyed local dances and skating. He didn't really have time to pursue many special interests.

Jackson Peninsula (64 O/9) on Gayoway Lake was named after him in 1995.

Jackson, Pilot Officer **Donald V.** of Dauphin (J 24626). Royal Canadian Air Force. He was lost at sea when Danish troop transport ship the MV *Amerika* was torpedoed. He died 22 April 1943 at the age of 21 and is commemorated at the Ottawa Memorial. He was the son of George A. and Muriel C. Jackson of Dauphin. ***Jackson Hill*** (64 H/7), north of Solmundsson Lake was named after him in 1995.

Jackson, Private **Melvin R.** of Neepawa (K 47737). Westminster Regiment. He died 24 May 1944 and is commemorated at the Cassino War Cemetery in Italy. ***Jackson Esker*** (53 M/11), northeast of Annesley Lake was named after him in 1996.

Jackson, Trooper **Stanley** of Selkirk (H 26279). Fort Garry Horse. He died 8 August 1944 at the age of 31 and is commemorated at the Bayeux Memorial in Calvados, France. He was the son of Herbert and Mary Jackson and was survived by his wife Isabel B. Jackson of Selkirk. ***Jackson Point*** (64 P/13) on Baralzon Lake was named after him in 1985.

Jackson, Pilot Officer **William J. "Jacko"** of Winnipeg (J 92936). No. 404 Squadron. He died 9 February 1945 over Fordeflord, Norway when the Beaufighter he was piloting was observed being shot down and crashing "with no one leaving the plane" at approximately 4:00 PM. He was 27 years of age and is commemorated at the Runnymede Memorial in Surrey, England. He was the son of William T. and Williamina Jackson of Winnipeg and was survived by four sisters. His nephew writes (15 November 2001):

> He was born at Holland, Manitoba in June, 1917 and grew up in Winnipeg where he attended Kelvin High School. He enlisted in the RCAF in December, 1941 and received his wings in 1942. He went

overseas with the Swordfish Squadron (No. 415) and later transferred to the Buffalo Squadron (No. 404) of Coastal Command.

According to Lieutenant Colonel C. W. Attwood of 14 Wing:

> ... our Roll of Honour shows ... Pilot Officer Jackson [was] lost during a sortie ... which became known as "Black Friday" due to the heavy toll the action took on the aircrews involved. It was to be the single worst day during the war for 404 Squadron (17 January 2001).

> Altogether, nine Beaufighters and one Mustang failed to return. Of these six were from 404 Squadron. The fact that the war in Europe was to be over in three months makes the sacrifice even more poignant. With hindsight, it is easy to query if this sacrifice was really necessary, but at the time, the war had still to be won and the young airmen of Britain and the Commonwealth could give little thought to these matters as they set out on their dangerous missions (*The Northern Scot* 3 February 1995).

Jackson Island (52 M/13) in Family Lake was named after him in 1979.

Jacob, Lance Corporal **Louis E.** of St. Boniface (L 93666). Westminster Regiment. He died 24 September 1944 and is commemorated at Cesena War Cemetery in Italy. ***Jacob Lake*** (64 K/11), northeast of Reindeer Lake was named after him in 1972.

Jacobs, Company Sergeant Major (Warrant Officer 2) **James** of Winnipegosis (H 17588). Regina Rifle Regiment. He died 8 July 1944 at the age of 25 and is commemorated at Beny-sur-Mer Canadian War Cemetery in Calvados, France. He was the son of Michael and Annie Jacobs of Mossey River and the husband of Agnes J. Jacobs (née Macfarlane) of Hillcrest, Renfrewshire, Scotland. On a brief leave prior to D-Day, he managed to get his first and only look at his new-born son. ***Jacobs Lake*** (64 G/16), east of Chipewyan Lake was named after him in 1995.

Jacobson, Sergeant **Edwin C.** of Winnipeg (H 62799). Canadian Forestry Corps. He died 16 October 1944 at the age of 44 and is commemorated at Brookwood Military Cemetery in Surrey, England. He was the son of Jacob and Kathryn Jacobson and was survived by his wife Elizabeth Jacobson of Abriachan, Inverness-shire, Scotland. ***Jacobson Lake*** (53 L/4), southwest of Kennedy Lake was named after him in 1995.

Jakeman, Pilot Officer **Colin I.** of Roblin (J 86240). No. 77 Squadron. He died 29 June 1944 at the age of 21 and is commemorated at Fourmetot Churchyard, Eure, France. He was one of the five children of Russell W. and Jessie T. Jakeman (née Paterson) of Roblin, Manitoba. His younger brother recalls (30 August 1995):

> Colin was born on a small farm two and a half miles east of Roblin. His mother (a Bruce through her mother) by the maiden name Paterson was a Queen's Nurse from Edinburgh, Scotland (Victorian Order) and she grew up in Oban, Scotland. His father grew up in Bethany, Ontario, the son of the local butcher who had left England when his father, a few miles north of Oxford, lost his inheritance. Colin was a friendly, outgoing, healthy boy who loved nature and the outdoors but was equally at home with his school work or some of the good literature provided by his mother who kept as many books on hand as a family could afford on a farm in the thirties. Dawn would find him up to help feed the livestock and milk the cows before catching the van for school. With two older and one younger brother and an older sister, the home was a busy place and usually the homework was done by coal oil lamp while keeping the house warm with a continuous supply of firewood cut from the farm by hand – an activity his generation knew very well. Ice for the ice well in winter and hay for the livestock in summer had to be ready on time, and what money could be gleaned from gopher tails or cowhides or the cream cheques had to be portioned carefully.

> Colin did well in school. A natural athlete, he excelled in almost all of the athletic events and I recall his mother telling of him bringing home the red ribbons and laying them at her feet saying: "There you are Mother!" As a scholar, he learned quickly and always took the honours in science and math while retaining a steady interest in literature and art. He was always well liked by his colleagues and later by his female classmates – his Grade 12 consisting of 17 girls and himself. He participated well in the oratorical events giving the class valedictory, winning the oratory contests and serving as class president and school president for the collegiate for several terms. He also competed in singing, for which he had a natural adaptation with a clear bass voice that rose and fell effortlessly, so that he became the local balladeer, at times playing the piano and singing some of the popular music of the times. As a junior sibling, I can't deny the odd tinge of jealousy that had to be squelched from time to time for a brother so well endowed.

> Upon graduation from Grade 12, Colin was now of military age so he enlisted with the RCAF after working with them in Dauphin for a few weeks. He progressed rapidly and with no difficulty received his wings in November, 1942. Our family saw little of him after that – the occasional visit on a three day pass and I remember well the last visit when he was *en route* to England. Mrs. Freeland gave a final party at her large house in town and everyone turned out to see him off on the train. He well knew of the horrors of war, but one could hardly have time to ponder such things as he kept up the bold and happy front for his parents and family. Such scenes don't require elaboration for those who have lived through those times as they were repeated endlessly in every village, town and city across the country. And so the promise of youth faced the pitiless demands of the war machine.

> After that, with his two older brothers also in the services in England, the letters came – always cheerful but quietly touching. Through the messages and hopes I recall his remark "Too bad about Charlie Ritchie but you know this is plain murder over here." Then another letter – his engagement to a lovely English girl (who long after continued to correspond with his mother). But then the telegram – "Missing in Action" – brought out to the farm by Mr. F. Y. Newton who though a diligent business person also had a heart and feeling for adversity. Dad was milking cows that morning and he just continued milking while he wept openly – a thing that I'd not seen before. Later the news was worse.

> Colin had been flying Halifax bombers and had made something like 30 or 40 "sorties" over Germany. On the fatal trip, a bomb dropped from another bomber knocked off a piece of his wing causing great difficulty flying. Colin was strong enough to maintain his course but, caught in the searchlights near Paris, he lost some altitude. Then near Le Havre a Messerschmitt fighter tore into his plane. Some of the crew parachuted to safety. I spoke to the flight engineer in London in 1961 and he described what happened. He attempted to bail out and Colin lost precious moments helping him out. Then Colin bailed out but his chute didn't open in time and he was killed by a branch of a tree on landing. The flight engineer was Jewish and spent the rest of the war as a guest of the Maquis, acting the part of a deaf and dumb French peasant worker. Colin was buried at Fourmetot in France in a place of honour at the front of the church by the local Maquis before the Germans found his body. I visited the site with my wife and mother in 1961.

> His was the role of the star of the family – Dad strove mightily to overcome the loss and Mother quietly accepted her grief, but it was evident any time *White Christmas* came on the radio. It was Colin's voice they really heard! He is remembered on the statue in Roblin in front of the United Church. He is now honoured by having a lake in northern Manitoba named after him. But best of all he is well remembered by all who knew him as a soldier, a scholar and a gentleman – a friend and loving brother, a son and a citizen well known for his abiding spirit. His life was brief, but it had purpose, and I and many others will not forget.

Jakeman Lake (64 G/11), east of Big Sand Lake was named after him in 1994.

James, Pilot Officer **Alan F.** of Winnipeg (J 7214). No. 150 Squadron. He died 24 April 1942 at the age of 29 and is commemorated at Pollington (St. John The Baptist) Churchyard in Yorkshire, England. He was the youngest son of Edward R. and Eleanor J. James of Winnipeg. His niece writes (9 January 2002):

> I did not know Fred, as I was only one when he left Canada. I have certainly heard all sorts of stories about the "scrapes" he got into when he was a young boy, according to his brother, Ren, my father. He was a mischievous kid, always inquisitive and was challenged to explore everything within his boundaries.
>
> Fred was born in Rosser in 1912 and lived with his mother, brother, four sisters and two cousins in the Grosse Isle area most of his life. Before entering the services, he farmed with his family in Grosse Isle. He was a charming, cheerful fellow who had lots of friends and he loved to play practical jokes on members of his family and his pals. He worked hard; he played hard and he enjoyed life to the fullest.
>
> Fred joined the RCAF in March, 1940 and trained at Brandon, Regina, Winnipeg, and Dafoe, graduating from the Rivers Navigation School in September, 1941. His last leave was spent with his brother, mother and friends in Grosse Isle in September, 1941 and he was sent overseas in October.
>
> In a letter from his Squadron Leader to Fred's mother after his death, the writer says: "He was truly a good pal who had made a good impression on all who knew him. He was every inch a courageous man who gave his all, without flinching. He was a splendid representative of Canada's forces in this terrible war."

James Island (64 N/9) in Shannon Lake was named after him in 1987.

James, Private **Arthur** of Winnipeg (H 95607). 1st Canadian Special Services Battalion. He died 20 February 1944 and is commemorated at the Cassino Memorial, Italy. ***James Rapids*** (64 I/7) in the North Knife River was named after him in 1995.

James, Trooper **Thomas W.** of Carman (H 287). Lord Strathcona's Horse. He died 18 April 1944 at the age of 22 and is commemorated at Bari War Cemetery in Italy. He was the son of Charles O. and Olive M. James of Winnipeg. ***James Peninsula*** (63 N/13) on Sisipuk Lake was named after him in 1995.

James, Lieutenant **William A.** of Grosse Isle (CDN 165). Durham Light Infantry, Military Cross. He died 1 July 1944 at the age of 34 and is commemorated at Hottot-les-Bagues War Cemetery in Calvados, France. He was the son of Alan and Mabel H. James of Grosse Isle and was survived by his wife Olive E. James (née Miller). His son recalls (23 December 2001):

> Bill grew up in the Rosser and Grosse Isle communities. He attended Grosse Isle School, then farmed in his home area. In 1934 he married Olive Miller of Argyle and they had a family of four children: Alan, Evelyn, Bob and Aileen. Early in World War II, Bill joined the armed services, took Officer's training before going overseas and became attached to a British regiment. He went to France shortly after D-Day. Although he was wounded, he returned to duty, but was killed July 1, 1944 near Caen, France. He was awarded the Military Cross for bravery posthumously.

James Lake (64 G/4), south of Big Sand Lake was named after him in 1948 and William James Lake (64 H/13), northwest of Currie Lake was named after him in 1995.

James, Sergeant **William P.** of Winnipeg (R 95238). No. 24 Operational Training Unit, RCAF. He died 12 August 1942 at the age of 24 and is commemorated at Barmby-on-the-Moor (St. Catherine) Churchyard in Yorkshire, England. He was the son of Eric W. M. and Ellen M. B. James of Winnipeg. ***James Bay*** (64 O/12) in Nueltin Lake was named after him in 1995.

Jamieson, Flying Officer **Donald S.** of Winnipeg (J 19863). No. 426 Squadron. He died 22 August 1944 at the age of 20 and is commemorated at the Runnymede Memorial in Surrey, England. He was the youngest son of Thomas and Diana Jamieson of Winnipeg. ***Jamieson Island*** (64 O/13) in Nueltin Lake was named after him in 1978.

Jamieson, Company Sergeant Major **James B.** of Winnipeg (H 41388). Royal Winnipeg Rifles. He died 19 January 1943 at the age of 36 and is commemorated at Brookwood Military Cemetery in Surrey, England. He was survived by his wife and daughter. She writes (27 November 2001):

> James grew up in Scotland and enlisted in a Scottish regiment at the age of 17. After some years of service, he emigrated to Canada. James settled in Winnipeg and worked for the Provincial Government until enlisting in the Royal Winnipeg Rifles in 1940. He enjoyed gardening and carpentry. His death came shortly before James was to return to Canada to attend Officers' Training School.

Jamieson Lake (52 L/6), northeast of Lac du Bonnet was named after him in 1973.

Jamieson, Corporal **John D.** of Killarney, Manitoba (H 22015). Essex Scottish Regiment. He died 1 March 1945 at the age of 37 and is commemorated at the Groesbeek Canadian War Cemetery in Holland. He was the son of Thomas and Margaret D. Jamieson and was survived by his wife Margaret Jamieson of Ninga, Manitoba. ***Jamieson Creek*** (54 B/16), which flows east into Comeault Creek was named after him in 1964.

Jamieson, Flight Sergeant **John Murray** of Gladstone (R 58352). No. 404 Squadron. He died 26 May 1942 at the age of 23 and is commemorated at Egersund Churchyard, Norway. He was the son of John J. and Olive Jamieson (née Beek) of Gladstone. According to his sister (3 October 1995) he:

> ... was born ... in Sceptre, Saskatchewan. He moved to Ogilvie, Manitoba in 1920 with his parents. He received his elementary education at Blake School, then to Gladstone for high school. During the thirties, he worked helping farmers that needed extra help through harvest. In 1937, he went to BC where he stayed with his grandparents to look for work. He joined the Royal Canadian Air Force in the spring of 1940. He was married in 1941 and left for overseas shortly after. Murray was reported missing on a flight over Norway in May, 1942; later we received word that he had been killed in action.

A family in Norway tends the gravesite to this day. ***Jamieson Bay*** (53 L/4) in Kitchi Lake was named after him in 1995.

Januik, Rifleman **Frank S.** of Whitemouth (H 22657). Royal Winnipeg Rifles. He died 10 April 1945 at the age of 19 and is commemorated at the Holten Canadian War Cemetery in Holland. According to his brother (15 December 1997) he was:

... born [and] went to school in Whitemouth. He left at 17 to join the army. While he was growing up he enjoyed playing hockey, baseball [and] football. He also enjoyed dancing, skiing and swimming. He used the Whitemouth River as his swimming pool.

Januik Lake (63 K/16), north of Reed Lake was named after him in 1973.

Janzen, Private **Menno** of Plum Coulee (H 64605). Essex Scottish Regiment. He died 19 February 1945 at the age of 20 and is commemorated at the Groesbeek Canadian War Cemetery in Holland. He was the son of Peter P. and Tina Janzen and was survived by his wife Phyllis B. Janzen of Keewatin, Ontario. ***Janzen Lake*** (64 F/3), east of Reindeer Lake was named after him in 1967.

Jarvis, Lance Sergeant **Reginald** of Winnipeg (H 19904). Queen's Own Cameron Highlanders. He died 11 November 1944 and is commemorated at Schoonselhof Cemetery in Antwerp, Belgium. ***Jarvis Lake*** (64 K/11), northeast of Reindeer Lake was named after him in 1972.

Jefferson, Rifleman **Robert M.** of Winnipeg (H 103882). Regina Rifle Regiment. He died 16 February 1945 at the age of 22 and is commemorated at the Groesbeek Canadian War Cemetery in Holland. He was the son of Robert E. and Mary A. Jefferson of Winnipeg. **Jefferson Lake** (64 G/6), northwest of Southern Indian Lake was named after him in 1984.

Jeffery, Sergeant **Basil** of Winnipeg (R 86347). No. 3 Advanced Flying School. He died 5 April 1942 at the age of 22 and is commemorated at Cirencester Cemetery, Gloucestershire, England. He was survived by his father Amos T. Jeffrey and his stepmother Lottie Hollingsworth of Winnipeg. His sister recalls (17 October 2001):

As a youngster, Basil was very air minded. As a 13-14 year-old, Basil saved all his money for flying trips around Winnipeg. Which he did every chance possible. Basil enlisted in the Air Force because of his very sincere love of flying. Even though Basil was a qualified mechanic, all he wanted to do was fly.

While on [a] flight over England, Basil was gunned down by German Air Force gunners Easter Sunday ... at the age of 22. Basil was buried in England's Airforce Field of Honour with full military honours. His brother Thomas, who was fighting with the 11th Heavy AA Battery on the White Cliffs of Dover, was rushed to Basil's funeral. Due to wartime conditions, [he] arrived too late for his brother's service but personnel in charge took Tom to his brother's burial plot and the Anglican Archbishop re-read the service at the graveside.

The Manitoba Geographical Names Program named a lake after him – Jeffery Lake in northern Manitoba. You will never be forgotten my beloved brother.

Jeffery Lake (64 J/13), northwest of Tadoule Lake was named after him in 1975.

Jeffrey, Private **Arnold F.** of Holland, Manitoba (H 10325). Lake Superior Regiment. He died 9 August 1944 at the age of 27 and is commemorated at Bretteville-sur-Laize Canadian War Cemetery in Calvados, France. He was the son of William and Florence Jeffrey and was survived by his wife Mary E. Jeffrey of Carberry. ***Jeffrey Island*** (64 I/13) in Shethanei Lake was named after him in 1995.

Jelly, Trooper **Arthur** of St. Vital (H 77808). Sherbrooke Fusiliers. He died 20 July 1944 and is commemorated at the Bayeux Memorial in Calvados, France. He was survived by his wife Norma Jelly. ***Jelly Lake*** (63 O/4), north of Wekusko Lake was named after him in 1970.

Jenkins, Warrant Officer 2 **Francis S.** of Shoal Lake (R 95049). No. 458 Squadron. He died 25 February 1943 at the age of 23 and is commemorated at the Malta Memorial. He was the son of W. A. and Margaret Jenkins of Shoal Lake, Manitoba.

He graduated from the Shoal Lake Collegiate in June, 1938 and was subsequently employed with the Royal Bank at Shoal Lake, Russell and Boissevain. Francis enlisted in the RCAF in January, 1941, completing his basic training at Brandon. He was then posted to No. 2 Wireless School at Calgary and then No. 7 Bombing and Gunnery School at Paulson, Manitoba where he was awarded his Air Gunner badge. Francis's last leave at home was in December, 1941. He was posted to Lachine, Quebec, Bermuda, Londonderry and Gibraltar. His next tour took him to Malta in 1943. His Wellington aircraft took off from Luqa Airdrome on 25 February 1943 for a shipping strike. It is believed the convoy or its escort damaged this aircraft. The plane crashed into the sea some distance from Capri. An Italian ship put out from port in a rescue attempt but could find the bodies of only four of the crewmembers. These were taken aboard the ship, identified and then buried at sea. The other two members including Francis were never recovered (Pittman n.d.).

Jenkins Lake (64 O/15), east of Nueltin Lake was named after him in 1975.

Jenner, Sergeant **John I. "Jack"** of Elkhorn (M 26984). Calgary Tank Regiment. He died 4 October 1943 at the age of 23 and is commemorated at Bari War Cemetery in Italy. He was the son of Frederick C. and Elizabeth Jenner of Rocanville, Saskatchewan. The local paper reported that:

We pause this week to pay tribute to the memory of another young man who helped to represent this district in the fight for freedom which is being waged against an unscrupulous aggressor. In so doing, we raise our thoughts to God, asking that in His good time this terrible affliction will be honourably ended and that the world will be cleansed of the blight which is destroying so much of the flower of the world's manhood.

Jack Jenner was born on August 10th, 1920 and received his early education at Buckingham and Parkland schools. He later went west to Red Deer, Alberta, and in February, 1941 enlisted there in the 14th Canadian Tank Regiment (Canadian Regiment).

He trained at Camp Borden and went overseas in June, 1941 to complete his course in England. Aptitude and ability brought him rapid promotion and when his unit became attached to the British First Army in North Africa he was a sergeant. Jack saw service in the Tunisian campaign and returned to England last May with his unit. In July he was in the thick of fighting in Sicily and to the great sorrow of us all we learned that he was killed on October 4th (*Elkhorn Mercury* n.d.).

Jenner Lake (53 L/12), northwest of Laidlaw Lake was named after him in 1996.

Jensen, Corporal **Knud** of Ostenfeld (L 1232). Saskatoon Light Infantry. He died 3 January 1944 at the age of 25 and is commemorated at the Moro River Canadian War Cemetery in Italy. He was the son of Hans and Thora Jensen of Ostenfeld. ***Jensen Bay*** (64 G/12) in Katimew Lake was named after him in 1995.

Jensen, Sergeant **Oscar K. L.** of Carman (R 95369). No. 20 Squadron. He died 9 August 1942 at the age of 26 and is commemorated at Fettercairn Cemetery in Kincardineshire, Scotland. He was the son of Einar B. and Anna C. Jensen of Carman. ***Jensen Island*** (53 M/1) in Semmens Lake was named after him in 1989.

Jensen, Rifleman **Robert L.** of Parkdale (H 41840). Royal Winnipeg Rifles. He died 16 February 1945 at the age of 21 and is commemorated at the Groesbeek Canadian War Cemetery in Holland. He was the son of Jens C. and Dagmar K. Jensen of Winnipeg. ***Jensen Point*** (64 N/11) on Kasmere Lake was named after him in 1995.

Jobin, Flight Lieutenant **Alfred Byrne** of Winnipeg (C 850). No. 1 CAC Flight, RCAF. He died 11 November 1941 at the age of 38 and is commemorated at St. Marys Cemetery in Winnipeg. He was the son of Thomas and Alice Jobin of Winnipeg and was survived by his wife Eldred G. Jobin. ***Jobin Lake*** (64 O/6), northeast of Egenolf Lake was named after him in 1975.

Jodoin, Sergeant **Daniel R.** of St. Boniface (H 19721). Queen's Own Cameron Highlanders. He died 8 August 1944 at the age of 25 and is commemorated at Bretteville-sur-Laize Canadian War Cemetery in Calvados, France. He was the son of Frederick and Antoinette Jodoin and was survived by his wife Mary V. Jodoin of Edinburgh, Scotland. ***Jodoin Lake*** (63 O/4), north of Wekusko Lake was named after him in 1970.

Johannesson, Flight Sergeant **Gudmundur "Arthur"** of Arborg (R 123858). No. 408 Squadron. He died 5 May 1943 at the age of 24 and is commemorated at the Runnymede Memorial in Surrey, England. According to his sister-in-law (12 January 1998) he:

> ... was born in 1918 in Arborg, Manitoba, the youngest of a family of nine boys and one girl, all of whom are now deceased. When he was about 10 years old, the family moved to Winnipeg and took up residence at 920 Sherburn Street. After completing high school, he attended the University of Manitoba but left before completing his degree to join the Air Force and went overseas in 1941 as a ... pilot. Early in 1943, he was reported missing in action.

Johannesson Lake (64 I/8), northeast of North Knife Lake was named after him in 1974.

Johannson, Lance Corporal **Sigurdur** of Riverton (H 1342). Black Watch (Royal Highland Regiment) of Canada. He died 23 August 1944 at the age of 23 and is commemorated at Bretteville-sur-Laize Canadian War Cemetery in Calvados, France. He was the son of Ingolfur and Juliana Johannson of Riverton. ***Johannson Lake*** (64 H/7), northeast of Solmundsson Lake was named after him in 1995.

Johannsson, Private **Fridfinnur Kjernested** (229352). 44th Battalion, New Brunswick Regiment. He died 3 February 1917 at the age of 24 and is commemorated at Villers Station Cemetery, Viller-au-Bois, Pas de Calais, France. ***Kjernested Lake*** (52 M/11), south of Dogskin Lake was named after this World War I casualty in 1983.

Johns, Private **Roy E.** of Winnipeg (H 16364). Princess Patricia's Canadian Light Infantry. He died 20 December 1943 and is commemorated at the Moro River Canadian War Cemetery in Italy. He was the son of Aaron D. and Mary J. Johns and was survived by his wife Vera Johns of Windsor, Ontario. ***Johns Bay*** (63 I/6) in Butterfly Lake was named after him in 1995.

Johnsen, Private **Peter L.** of Sprague (H 18173). Queen's Own Cameron Highlanders. He died 26 February 1945 at the age of 20 and is commemorated at the Groesbeek Canadian War Cemetery in Holland. He was the son of Ollie and Mary Johnsen of Sprague. ***Johnsen Lake*** (64 H/6), east of Northern Indian Lake was named after him in 1995.

Johnson, Private **Alfred I.** of Manson (H 8278). Algonquin Regiment. He died 8 March 1945 at the age of 22 and is commemorated at the Groesbeek Canadian War Cemetery in Holland. He was the son of Nicholis A. and Orpha E. Johnson of Manson, Manitoba. In a letter to Private Johnson's father, Company Sergeant Major K. M. Buffin wrote:

> My Company Commander has asked me to return to you the enclosed rings which were taken from a parcel addressed to H 8278 Pte. Johnson, A. I. of this Company who was a casualty of the recent fighting in Germany. He was expecting this parcel and had asked me to hang on to it for him should it arrive while he was on leave. Parcels containing food, candy etc. are opened and divided among the friends of the boys to whom the parcels were addressed, while any items of value or personal interest are returned to the sender.
>
> I am sure that you have already been told what fine work your boy was doing out here and how he would go out into battle looking for casualties and doing everything he could to help any wounded man, whether he belonged to this Company or any other, or even to other Regiments. Civilian wounded and enemy wounded were all carefully looked after by him and on the occasion of his last battle, when for twenty-four hours it was impossible to evacuate wounded, he gathered them up into the safety of a cellar and nursed them himself until they could be removed. On the same occasion, I saw him leave the comparative safety of our own lines and make many trips into a zone of heavy fire to carry out wounded men of another Regiment.
>
> You will understand that we are all proud to have known him and sorry to have lost him and please accept the most sincere sympathy and deep regrets of all members of "C" Company (n.d.).

Alfred Johnson Island (64 H/5) in Missinipi Lake was named after him in 1995.

Johnson, Sapper **Arthur H.** of Winnipeg (H 63745). Royal Canadian Engineers. He died 6 June 1944 and is commemorated at Beny-sur-Mer Canadian War Cemetery in Calvados, France. He was the son of Peter and Matilda Johnson of Winnipeg. ***Arthur Johnson Lake*** (54 E/9), northeast of Fly Lake was named after him in 1995.

Johnson, Rifleman **Ben** of Manson (H 18611). Royal Winnipeg Rifles. He died 19 February 1945 at the age of 20 and is commemorated at the Groesbeek Canadian War Cemetery in Holland. He was survived by his mother Stefania S. Johnson of Baldur, Manitoba. ***Ben Johnson Hill*** (64 P/13), southeast of Baralzon Lake was named after him in 1995.

Johnson, Private **Cecil H. J.** of Winnipeg (H 6862). Winnipeg Grenadiers. He died 19 December 1941 at the age of 33 and is commemorated at the Sai Wan Memorial in Hong Kong. He was the son of Mr. and Mrs. Cecil Johnson of Great Yarmouth, Norfolk, England and was survived by his wife Lily Johnson of Winnipeg. She writes (14 June 1995):

> Cecil emigrated from England about 1930. He spent two years in a training program with the Church Army of the Anglican Church. He worked in the Owen Sound area for two or three years and was then posted to Melita in southwest Manitoba. After a couple of years there, he was sent to Winnipeg to become an assistant to Canon Findlay of St. James Anglican Church. In 1940, he worked in Carcross [Yukon] at the residential school for a short period, returning to Winnipeg to join the Winnipeg Grenadiers. He went to Jamaica for 16 months and returned to Winnipeg in October for one month and left for Hong Kong with the unit.

Johnson Narrows (63 I/1) in Rushforth Lake was named after him in 1995.

Johnson, Private **Edward T.** of Otterburne (H 6440). Winnipeg Grenadiers. He died a prisoner of war 25 February 1944 at the age of 31 and is commemorated at the Yokohama War Cemetery in Japan. The official cause of death was listed as "cardiac beriberi." He was the son of Martin and Mary Johnson of Otterburne. ***Johnson Point*** (64 H/4) on Gauer Lake was named after him in 1995.

Johnson, Flight Sergeant **Frank E.** of Gladstone (R 95038). No. 22 Operational Training Unit, RCAF. He died 28 July 1942 at the age of 24 and is commemorated at the Kiel War Cemetery in Germany. He was the son of Leon L. and Christina I. Johnson of Fortier, Manitoba. Seven years later, his mother received a letter from the RCAF Missing Research and Enquiry Service which read in part:

Investigating officers of this service have ascertained that your son's aircraft was shot down by anti-aircraft fire and crashed at Kaiser Wilhelm Koog, Germany. Kaiser Wilhelm Koog is situated at the mouth of the Elbe River. Two of the crew had been buried by Germans in Brunsbuttelkoog Cemetery. Brunsbuttelkoog is nine miles up the river from Kaiser Wilhelm Koog. On excavating the wreckage of the aircraft, the remains of the other crew members were found.

In accordance with the agreed policy of the Nations of the British Commonwealth, that all British aircrew buried in Germany would be moved to British Military Cemeteries located in Germany, your son and the members of his crew were moved to the permanent British Military Cemetery 1 1/2 miles east of Kiel, Germany. The cemetery is known as the Kiel British Military Cemetery. Unhappily, individual identification could not be made on exhumation either at the scene of the crash or at Brunsbuttelkoog. They were therefore buried collectively in communal grave 14/15 in Row C., Plot 5 (5 May 1949).

His niece adds (18 October 2001):

My Uncle Frank had two bothers and two sisters. My Mom was one of his sisters and even though I was very young when my family got the message that Uncle Frank was missing, I remember what a sad time it was. His father passed away when he was a small child. The family was very close-knit and really enjoyed one another's company. Whenever they had the opportunity to get together, they would reminisce about childhood days that were fun-filled and happy. They were always amazed at how their mother was able to survive their antics being on her own.

Frank Johnson Lake (64 H/8), north of Hogg Lake was named after him in 1995.

Johnson, Flying Officer **Garth B.** of Birtle (J 27083). No. 4 Operational Training Unit, RCAF. He died 26 November 1944 at the age of 22 and is commemorated at Stonefall Cemetery in Yorkshire, England. He was the second of the four children of Morgan and Myrtle Johnson and was survived by his wife June M. Johnson (née Laycock) of Winnipeg and their son. His brother recalls (13 December 2001):

Garth was born in Miniota, Manitoba May 6, 1922 and attended school in Sonningdale, Saskatchewan, Beulah, Manitoba and Winnipeg. During his years in Beulah, he enjoyed the challenges of sports such as hockey, tennis and baseball. He also participated in the Miniota Municipal Field Days. He attended the United Church at Beulah and joined the Beulah Boy Scouts under the leadership of Joe Chisholm and George Heyhoe. Garth became an expert swimmer and would swim across Hoopers Lake (much to the anxiety of those on shore), rest on the far shore and then swim back. So often, he would arise before sunup in the summer months and walk in the countryside, searching for coyotes and gophers, not returning until later afternoon. He became an excellent marksman.

Garth also learned to play trumpet for ours was a musical family. Each member learned to play an instrument and it led to great family musical times around the piano in the 1930s. Garth had a love of jazz, something that the rest of the siblings acquired and share until this day.

Garth completed Grade 12 at Kelvin High School in Winnipeg and then entered the Faculty of Engineering at the University of Manitoba. During high school and while at university, he trained under ROTC (army). For two summers, he worked at MacDonald Aircraft in Winnipeg, building Avro Ansons. He then entered the RCAF in Winnipeg in 1942. He attended ITS in Edmonton and then No. 23 EFTS in Davidson, Saskatchewan, graduating June 10, 1943 from No. 12 SFTS, Brandon and received his commission a few days later. His Mother pinned on his Wings. For that reason, my wife Donna and I work as lifetime members of the Commonwealth Air Training Plan Museum in Brandon, Manitoba, walking in the same area where my Mother pinned on his wings and I stood with great pride.

Garth had married June Marie Laycock of Winnipeg in May, 1943 and when he was posted to a General Reconnaissance course in Summerside, PEI (Ansons), she accompanied him. He was posted to No. 160 Squadron, Yarmouth, Nova Scotia on anti-sub patrol. His son Garth Laycock Johnson was born on April 29, 1944 and grandson Garth Craig Johnson perpetuates the name into the current generation.

A posting to No. 4 OTU in Alness, Scotland in June, 1944 was next. On November 26, 1944, taking off in Sunderland aircraft DD851 resulted in a short flight before the aircraft crashed on the railway tracks at Saltburn, Scotland. The resulting fireball killed the entire Canadian crew of 11. We have visited the scene of the crash and met many inhabitants who lived there at that time, including the medical officer who attended. The entire crew was buried at Harrogate. We have visited the cemetery many times. Mr. George Heyhoe, Garth's Scout Master, also took time to pay his respects on a visit to England.

Sadly, the years pass, but "Time cannot erase the shadow of his smile." There is a void that could never be filled – the entire family was never quite so free again. Garth's wife June Marie later married again, but has since passed away. The fallacy of war lies heavily here. A life most nobly given for his country, a married father whose wife and infant son who needed him dearly, a budding career as a Civil Engineer ready to begin in the country that he loved and wanted so much to return to, so much to offer, so much dashed away in one blinding moment. Have we not held the torch high enough that those young men and women passed to us? Remember, and think of the frailty of our way of life and how dearly it was paid for by the lives of our dead. I have no problem remembering the faces of the young fallen – I just can't forget! At the going down of the sun, and in the morning, we will remember them.

Johnson Hill (64 N/8), southwest of Shannon Lake was named after him in 1989.

Johnson, Sergeant **Harvey** of Winnipeg (H 6019). Winnipeg Grenadiers. He died 19 December 1941 and is commemorated at the Sai Wan Memorial in Hong Kong. He was the son of Paul and Inga Johnson and was survived by his wife Edith F. E. Johnson (née Vance) of Winnipeg. ***Harvey Johnson Lake*** (64 N/16), northwest of Nahili Lake was named after him in 1995.

Johnson, Private **Herbert J.** of Lundar (H 20425). Seaforth Highlanders of Canada. He died 23 May 1944 at the age of 24 and is commemorated at the Cassino Memorial in Italy. He was the son of J. B. and Sigrun Johnson of Lundar and the foster son of W. H. and Helga G. Stinson of Lundar. His niece recalls (27 November 2001):

Herbert J. Johnson was born on August 21, 1919 in the Mary Hill District near Lundar. He was one of a family of seven. His siblings were: Gudjon, Bjorn, Paul, Gudrun Sigurlin (Lena Lindal), Herman and Herbert. At an early age he was taken in by his aunt Helga (J.B.'s sister) and uncle Bill Stinson. They raised him as one of their own. In the Stinson family he was a brother to Irene (Halldorson), Gwen (Wynnes), Clarence (Pat), Evelyn (Metcalfe) and Alvin. Bert lived most of his life in Lundar except for a couple of his first years which were spent at Kenton, Manitoba. He was a very happy-go-lucky man and his nickname was Tinny. Bert worked on a farm in the Silver Bay area before enlisting. Both his families were devastated by this loss.

Herbert Johnson Lake (64 F/1), northeast of Melvin Lake was named after him in 1995.

Johnson, Warrant Officer 2 **Jack L.** of Winnipeg (R 116340). No. 10 Squadron. He died 4 June 1943 at the age of 21 and is commemorated at Thames Ditton (St. Nicholas) Churchyard, Surrey, England. He was the son of Jon G. and Mickey Jonsson (sp. née Hanscom). ***Johnson Falls*** (64 C/3) in the unnamed river which connects Abrey Lake and McKnight Lake was named after him in 1995.

Johnson, Private **John Henry** of East Kildonan (H 1345). Canadian Scottish Regiment. He died 30 July 1944 at the age of 21 and is commemorated at Bretteville-sur-Laize Canadian War Cemetery in Calvados, France. He was the son of Joseph H. and Ellen Johnson of East Kildonan. His obituary read in part:

Born at Woodmore, Manitoba, ... he was resident in East Kildonan since 1927 and attended Polson School. He was also a member for a time of the Young People's Club at Washington Avenue Mission and was employed by the Memorial Marble and Tile Company. Private Johnson enlisted with the Active Army January 13, 1943 and subsequently joined the Princess Pats. He again transferred and went to France with the 1st Canadian Scottish, serving overseas since December 3, 1943 (*Winnipeg Free Press* n.d.).

According to his niece (28 October 1998):

He laughed when he told my Mom, how when he joined the army they had some papers for him to sign and told him: "Put your John Henry right here" and he said "That's exactly what I'm going to do!"

Although I never met my uncle Henry, my Mom often spoke to me of her younger brother. There were just the two children in the family and they were very close. She'd tell me about their growing up together, his sense of humour – good-natured joking and teasing, and how close they were; the ordinary things sisters and brothers do while growing up that bind them for life. Special times together like when the neighbourhood kids would gather and have bonfires and potato roasts in vacant land where the power lines ran. Mom would tell me so many little things she remembered about him with such love. Her father died only six weeks after Henry was killed and she never really got over losing the two of them.

Mom treasured a lovely pencil and ink sketch of a sailing ship Henry had drawn when he was young. He was artistic and loved music; at some point in time while growing up, he had some guitar lessons. He enjoyed singing and had a very nice voice; also apparently (from the letters he wrote) he enjoyed playing sports. Whenever I heard his Aunts, Uncles or cousins reminiscing about their times together with him, they always spoke so fondly of him and everything they said was to the effect that this was a fun loving, good, kind and loyal young man, someone you'd really like to have known.

My mother saved all the letters that Henry had written home to her and her parents while he was away in the army and she gave me the letters to read in 1996, about a year before she passed away. In reading the letters he wrote home from Shilo, Calgary and overseas in England and France, I got some insight about Henry. As I read, it was as though I was stepping back in time, privy to bits of intimate, personal conversation. The tone in his letters differs as he is speaking to each of the three of them. I'm so grateful to have these written words to glimpse this uncle I never knew and his loving relationship with my grandparents and mother.

In his letters, he speaks to them as he would if he were with them, just sharing with them the day-to-day events about his classes, training, free time and feelings. I would imagine most of the boys in the army, like Henry, were anxious to be close to their loved ones while apart through the letters they exchanged. The delivery seemed sporadic and sometimes he would have none for the longest time, and then get a pile all at once. He looked forward to each and every one he received and was eager to hear everything from home; he told them nothing would be boring, he was interested in it all. His parents weren't in the best of health and he worried about how they were managing, knowing it was a struggle for them in every way and he wasn't able to be with them to help out and make things easier for them.

He was in England for Christmas, 1943 and wrote to his parents:

Christmas over here wasn't the same as we had at home, but it was really a lot better than I expected. We had bacon and eggs for breakfast and chicken, Christmas pudding, bar cake, cookies, an apple, peanuts and mince pie for dinner. It was really good. We also got 50 cigarettes and a half-pound of Cadburys chocolates from the army. The day before Christmas, all the PPCLI received 50 cigarettes, two hankies, a bar of soap and a pair of shoelaces from the people of Winnipeg. It sure was swell of them, wasn't it? I think we were the only regiment that got such a gift in all the camp. It was sure appreciated by all of us. Christmas Eve, a few of the boys and I went down to the canteen and tipped a few and I decided we hadn't heard any carols as yet so we had better sing a few. I ended up by singing to a piano for the boys and they kept sending in requests until the canteen closed (26 December 1943).

In a later letter, he alludes to his father's poor health:

Dear Mom and Dad: Hello Folks. How goes the battle? I hope you are both well and enjoying yourselves as much as possible. I suppose it's pretty tough for you dad, getting to work on these cold days, but I know you are doing your best, but please don't go and kill yourself. Too bad I couldn't be there taking a little weight off your hands, but you understand how it is. There's a job to be done and a debt to be paid, more so now they have wounded Ellison and Don Griffin. Will do my best. Hope it is good enough. Goodnight for this time and keep all the letters coming that's possible. Your loving son, Henry. PS Keep your chin up, it won't be long now (19 January 1944).

His last letter was from France:

Just a few lines to let you know that I am still OK and hope this letter finds you both well and happy. You will have to excuse the writing as I am writing this in a hole and have hardly enough room to use a pen at all. I am happy to say I received a letter from you today. It sure is going to be quite a change for both Dad and you to have us home again, isn't it? Let's hope it's in the near future. Well, that was the last of the ink, but we're not licked yet! One of the boys had a pencil. Remember me to Uncle Frank and all the family and tell them I think of them often. Well, I must close now, with all my love. Your loving son Henry.

This letter was postmarked 29 July 1944, the day before he died. ***Johnson Rapids*** (64 F/3) in the Keewatin River was named after him in 1994.

Johnson, Sergeant **Julius B.** of Gimli (R 71026). No. 419 Squadron. He died 25 June 1943 at the age of 27 and is commemorated at Jonkerbos War Cemetery in Holland. He was the son of John B. and Josephine Johnson of Gimli. **Johnson River** (64 J/14), which flows northwest into North Seal River was named after him in 1985.

Johnson, Flying Officer **K. G. "Freeman"** of Gimli (J 43938). No. 159 Squadron. He died 9 February 1945 at the age of 21 and is commemorated at Taukkyan War Cemetery, Myanmar. He was the son of Valdimar and Gudrun Johnson of Gimli. His sister writes (26 June 1995):

... Freeman Johnson was an Honours student all his school years. After he completed his Grade 12, he enlisted in the Air Force, took his basic training, then officer training and graduated as a Pilot Officer (Bombardier). Freeman loved children and animals. He liked to dance and was interested in all sports, especially swimming and hockey. He played with the Gimli hockey team through his high school years until he joined up. He went overseas (Bombay) in December, 1944 and was killed in action shortly after his 21st birthday.

Freeman Johnson Lake (64 B/16), southwest of Chapman Lake was named after him in 1995.

Johnson, Pilot Officer **Leonard K.** of Manson (J 92014). No. 57 Squadron. He died 27 August 1944 at the age of 25 and is commemorated at the Runnymede Memorial in Surrey, England. He was the son of Andrew L. and Mary Johnson (née Ekman) of Manson. His niece writes (20 November 2001):

Leonard was born 23 June 1919 on his father's homestead NE 9-13-29W. The son of Swedish immigrants, he was the youngest of nine children and he attended Archie School. Lancaster LM278 left East Kirkby, England with six others on board. They were: Pilot Officer Austin T. Clarke, Montreal, Rear Gunner Sergeant Robert H. McNabb, Toronto, Mid-upper Gunner Sergeant Henry Winslade, England, Wireless Operator Sergeant H. Souci, England, Flight Engineer Francis J. Wilson, England and Navigator Sergeant Harold W. Lugg of Manville, Alberta. Rumour was that H. Souci became a prisoner of war. Leonard was posthumously given the rank of Pilot Officer.

Leonard Johnson Lake (53 N/11), northeast of Whitefish Lake was named after him in 1995.

Johnson, Lance Corporal **Nels D.** of Flin Flon (H 7103). Queen's Own Cameron Highlanders. He died 21 July 1944 at the age of 26 and is commemorated at Bretteville-sur-Laize Canadian War Cemetery in Calvados, France. He was the son of Charles P. and Jennie I. Johnson and was survived by his wife Gladys C. Johnson of London, Ontario. ***Nels Johnson Lake*** (64 K/1), southwest of Chartrand Lake was named after him in 1995.

Johnson, Trooper **Olie** of Selkirk (H 26274). Fort Garry Horse. He died 17 September 1944 at the age of 23 and is commemorated at the Calais Canadian War Cemetery in France. He was the only son of Jonas T. and Ina H. Johnson of Selkirk. Prior to enlisting, he had been employed as a timekeeper by Manitoba Rolling Mills. ***Olie Johnson Lake*** (64 O/4), west of Blackfish Lake was named after him in 1995.

Johnson, Flight Lieutenant **Sydney F.** of Winnipeg (91005). No. 256 Squadron, RAF. He died 26 February 1941 at the age of 25 and is commemorated at Cliveden War Cemetery in Buckinghamshire, England. He was survived by his mother Helen M. Johnson of Chelsea, London, England. ***Sydney Johnson Lake*** (63 P/10), north of Midnight Lake was named after him in 1995.

Johnson, Trooper **Thomas** of Souris (H 63737). Calgary Tank Regiment. He died 1 February 1945 at the age of 38 and is commemorated at Arezzo War Cemetery, Italy. He was survived by his wife Edith E. G. Johnson of Worthing, Sussex, England. ***Thomas Johnson Lake*** (63 N/12), south of Sisipuk Lake was named after him in 1995.

Johnson, Private **William** of Winnipeg (M 31507). Princess Patricia's Canadian Light Infantry. He died 23 July 1943 and is commemorated at Agira Canadian War Cemetery in Italy. ***Johnson Esker*** (53 M/8), northwest of Swampy Lake was named after him in 1995.

Johnson, Flight Sergeant **William H.** of Winnipeg (R 134935). No. 100 Squadron. He died 16 March 1945 and is commemorated at Durnbach War Cemetery in Bavaria, Germany. ***William Johnson Hill*** (64 N/12), north of Butterworth Lake was named after him in 1995.

Johnston, Warrant Officer 1 **Alan A.** of Stony Mountain (R 87222). No. 407 Squadron. He died 13 August 1943 at the age of 30 and is commemorated at Heanton Punchardon (St. Augustine) Churchyard in Devon, England. He was the son of J. Archibald and Ella M. Johnston (née Bradshaw) and was survived by his wife Minnie L. Johnston of Winnipeg. He was the brother of Flight Sergeant Clifford Johnston (see entry). ***Alan Johnston Bay*** (64 N/5) in Hillhouse Lake was named after him in 1995.

Johnston, Flight Sergeant **Arthur George** of St. Vital (R 59551). No. 58 Squadron. He died 7 August 1942 at the age of 27 and is commemorated at the Runnymede Memorial in Surrey, England. He was the son of Arthur F. and Lucy A. Johnston of St. Vital and was survived by his wife Margaret Johnston. ***George Johnston Lake*** (63 O/9), southwest of Ospwagan Lake was named after him in 1995.

Johnston, Pilot Officer **Arthur L. "Bud"** of Elm Creek (J 86171). No. 76 Squadron. He died 13 June 1944 at the age of 23 and is commemorated at Marissel French National Cemetery, Oise, France. He was the son of Joseph L. and Clara Johnston (née Cook) of Culross, Manitoba. His sister recalls (5 December 2001):

He was born August 27, 1920 at Sanford, Manitoba, later moving to Culross. He attended Giltedge School to Grade 9, taking Grades 10 and 11 at Wingham Consolidated School. He had to travel the two and a half miles by horseback or on skis to Dave Trumbla's to catch the van. He enjoyed sports and won the Travis North Shield for track and field at the Carman Fair. He also played hockey in the days when magazines were shin pads. The team was transported by team and sleigh.

Miss Phyllis Archibald had her high school Grades 9 – 11 put on three-act plays and concerts to assist the cast in spending a week at a cottage at Clear Lake. Of course the mothers, being great cooks, sent them off with full larders. Scotty Sisson and Bud were the only boys in a high school of girls. They joined up the same day.

After enlisting, he took all of his training in Alberta – Bowden, Penhold, Innisfail, Olds, Fort MacLeod and Edmonton, receiving a harvest leave to watch it rain. He was home for Christmas 1942, leaving before New Year's and embarking for overseas January 7, 1943. He was assigned to an RAF squadron and eventually served with an all British crew. He received notice of the awarding of his commission near the end of his first tour. He wrote: "Here I am a Pilot Officer. I don't know what [illegible] I got but it's dated March 12th. It came through yesterday [June 3]. I go on leave on the 14th so won't get my uniform till then. I had lunch in the Officers' Mess today which is quite a change to ours."

On the last trip of the tour, he and his crew departed on a night mission against Amiens, France and never returned. Much later, we learned that they had been buried by French peasants at Authieux and later reburied at Marissel. He was officially listed as "missing" for a year. His friend Scotty became a fighter pilot and was taken prisoner of war on June 12, 1944. When he returned to London, his first call was to find Bud; they were going on leave as planned. Just was not to be.

Johnston Peninsula (64 F/8) in Cline Lake was named after him in 1989.

Johnston, Flying Officer **Carl Donald** of Sanford (J 11449). No. 525 Squadron. He died 6 March 1944 at the age of 27 and is commemorated at Lisbon (St. George) British Churchyard, Portugal. He was the son of John M. and Pearl Johnston and was survived by his wife of one year Joan E. Johnston (née Cain) of Kingston-upon-Thames, Surrey, England. According to his brother (27 March 1985) he:

> ... was born on a farm southwest of Sanford, Manitoba. He lived there until joining the RCAF in 1940. He served by flying 44 missions and attained the rank of Flying Officer. On March 6, 1944 his plane crashed into the side of a mountain near Cintra, Portugal. This was to be his last mission before coming home.

Johnston Bay (64 F/8) in Le Clair Lake was named after him in 1989.

Johnston, Sapper **Charlie** of Great Falls (H 82322). Royal Canadian Engineers. He died 21 October 1944 and is commemorated at Schoonselhof Cemetery in Antwerp, Belgium. ***Johnston Creek*** (53 M/1), which flows south into Semmens Lake was named after him in 1995.

Johnston, Flight Sergeant **Clifford** of Birds Hill (R 119685). No. 283 Squadron. He died 18 October 1943 at the age of 26 and is commemorated at El Alia Cemetery, Algeria. He was the son of J. Archibald and Ella M. Johnston (née Bradshaw) of Birds Hill, Manitoba and the brother of Warrant Officer Alan A. Johnston (see entry). ***Johnston Esker*** (64 I/9), southwest of Nichol Lake was named after him in 1995.

Johnston, Private **David** of Letellier (H 6858). Winnipeg Grenadiers. He died 7 June 1943 at the age of 53 and is commemorated at the Sai Wan War Cemetery in Hong Kong. Private Johnston was born and raised in Edinburgh, Scotland. He came to Canada prior to the First World War, but returned with the Canadian Army when war was declared. He married in Jedburgh, Scotland and he and his bride returned to Canada. He enlisted with the Winnipeg Grenadiers immediately after Canada's declaration of war. After the fall of Hong Kong, he was taken prisoner and died in Sham Shu Po. He was survived by his wife Euphemia Johnston of Woodmore, Manitoba. In 1985, his daughter travelled to Hong Kong to take part in the memorial services there. ***David Johnston Lake*** (53 N/4), north of Fish Lake was named after him in 1995.

Johnston, Flying Officer **George P.** of Winnipeg (J 18128). No. 464 Squadron. He died 23 January 1944 at the age of 24 and is commemorated at Brookwood Military Cemetery in Surrey, England. He was the son of George W. and Anne Johnston of Winnipeg. ***Johnston Narrows*** (53 L/8) in Wapeeminakoskak Lake was named after him in 1995.

Johnston, Pilot Officer **James T.** of Brandon (43037). No. 151 Squadron, RAF. He died 15 August 1940 at the age of 26 and is commemorated at Folkestone New Cemetery in Kent, England. His sister visited his grave in 1964 and again in 1966, as did his brother. Pilot Officer Johnston fell at the height of the Battle of Britain when pilots were being rushed into service. He had completed his flying training one month before but had bypassed an Operational Training Unit. He was patrolling the English Channel near Dover when he was attacked by a number of Messerschmitts. By October, only one pilot of 151 Squadron who had participated in the 15 August skirmish survived. Pilot Officer Johnston is believed to be the first casualty of the war from Brandon. He was the son of Peter and Alice Johnston of Brandon. ***James Johnston Lake*** (64 C/12), northwest of Craig Lake was named after him in 1995.

Johnston, Flying Officer **John A.** of Minitonas (C 29783). No. 1659 Heavy Conversion Unit, RCAF. He died 22 October 1944 at the age of 27 and is commemorated at Blacon Cemetery in Cheshire, England. He was the son of William R. and E. Maude Armstrong Johnston of Carp, Ontario and was survived by his wife Janet I. Johnston. ***John Johnston Lake*** (53 L/3), north of Fairy Rock Lake was named after him in 1995.

Johnston, Able Seaman **Joseph N.** of Transcona (V 44249). HMCS *Skeena*. The *Skeena* was wrecked in a storm and grounded near Reykjavik, Iceland. Able Seaman Johnston died 25 October 1944 at the age of 22 and is commemorated at Fossvogur Cemetery in Reykjavik, Iceland. ***Joseph Johnston Bay*** (53 M/5) in Utik Lake was named after him in 1995.

Johnston, Able Seaman **Lawrence R.** of Winnipeg (V 51370). HMCS *Athabaskan*. The *Athabaskan* was sunk by a torpedo from a German destroyer while operating in the English Channel. Her captain and 128 men were lost, 83 taken prisoner and 44 men rescued by HMCS *Haida*. Able Seaman Johnston died 29 April 1944 at the age of 19 and is commemorated at Plouescat Communal Cemetery, Finistere, France. Lawrence Johnston Creek (54 A/11), which flows northeast into Kettle River was named after him in 1995.

Johnston, Flight Sergeant **Leroy V.** of Winnipeg (R 100116). Royal Canadian Air Force. He died 13 December 1942 at the age of 26 and is commemorated at the Runnymede Memorial in Surrey, England. He was the son of Fritz A. and Alma L. Johnston and was survived by his wife Edna E. Johnston of St. Boniface. ***Leroy Johnston Lake*** (64 H/3), northwest of Settee Lake was named after him in 1995.

Johnston, Sergeant **Lloyd G.** of Brandon (R 110817). No. 420 Squadron. He died 29 February 1944 at the age of 23 and is commemorated at Blacon Cemetery in Cheshire, England. He was the son of Robert J. and Alice B. Johnston of Beresford, Manitoba. His sister writes (2 May 1995):

> Lloyd was born in a farm house north of Brandon. The family moved to Brandon when Lloyd was six years old where he received his education, completing his Grade 12 at the Brandon Collegiate. He joined the RCAF, going overseas in 1943 as an air gunner. February 19, 1944 his plane was badly damaged, he and the crew except two were all killed, but they had managed to get to the English coast.

Johnston Hill (63 P/3), east of Sipiwesk Lake was named after him in 1995.

Johnston, Sergeant **Merritt E.** of Selkirk (H 75122). Royal Canadian Artillery, Military Medal.

> On September 18, 1944, 70 Canadian Light Anti-Aircraft Battery was employed in an infantry role holding an important sector of the Leopold Canal near Moerkerke, Belgium, with outposts established along the canal bank. One outpost occupying a house on the canal bank reported it was pinned down by machine gun fire from the enemy positions on both sides of the canal and surrounded by a strong enemy patrol on its own side of the canal.

Sergeant Johnston was dispatched with a patrol of ten men to clear the area. As he approached the outpost, he proceeded forward alone to reconnoitre and encountered a patrol of ten Germans who were blocking the route.

He personally attacked this patrol with his Bren gun, killed four of its members and took one prisoner. Then, still under machine gun fire from across the canal, Sergeant Johnston proceeded into the house which was burning. His prompt action, coupled with his complete disregard for his own safety was undoubtedly responsible for the withdrawal of the enemy patrol (MM Citation 1944).

He died 17 November 1944 at the age of 29 and is commemorated at Bergen-op-Zoom Canadian War Cemetery in Holland. He was survived by his wife Dorothy Johnston and their four children. His younger brother recalls (17 November 2001):

I was in the RCAF and had just returned to the United Kingdom from Italy, January of 1944 and was on furlough visiting relatives in Aberdeen, Scotland. Merritt was stationed in south England but could not make contact. My aunt said Merritt could drop in at any time. Next evening, I came in around suppertime and there was Merritt, what a great surprise! He thought I was still in Italy.

The balance of our furlough was just the greatest, exploring the Aberdeen countryside, walking along the River Dee. Pre-war, we spent a lot of enjoyable time along the Red River at Selkirk. Merritt was a keen duck and upland bird hunter. We had many conversations about the pre-war days.

Merritt missed his family dearly. He left a young family of four children ranging in age from two to eight, three girls, a boy and a wife. Merritt's mother never really got over his loss and his being buried so far away.

Merritt Johnston Lake (64 H/13), northwest of Currie Lake was named after him in 1995.

Johnston, Flying Officer **Percy H. W.** of Shoal Lake (J 11986). No. 200 Squadron. He died 27 August 1943 at the age of 31 and is commemorated at the Malta Memorial. He was the son of Captain Henry W. W. (Military Cross) and Flora H. Johnston and was survived by his wife Hilda M. W. Johnston of St. James and their five month-old daughter. His father was a veteran of both the Boer War and World War I. Prior to enlisting, Flying Officer Johnston had been an employee of the Royal Bank of Canada. ***Johnston Point*** (64 F/3) on Goldsand Lake was named after him in 1994.

Johnston, Private **Robert** (623165). 27th Battalion, Canadian Infantry (Manitoba Regiment). He died 6 November 1917 and is commemorated at Ypres (Menin Gate) Memorial, Belgium. He was survived by his wife Ella Johnston and was the father of Lance Corporal Vernon Johnston, a casualty of World War II (next entry). ***East Johnston Lak***e (64 O/9), northwest of Nejanilini Lake was named after this World War I casualty in 1995.

Johnston, Lance Corporal **Vernon A.** of Pine Creek (H 1098). Black Watch (Royal Highland Regiment) of Canada. He died 13 September 1944 at the age of 21 and is commemorated at the Calais Canadian War Cemetery in France. He was survived by his step-father and mother Ella Johnston of Pine Creek, Manitoba. He was the son of Private Robert Johnston (previous entry), a casualty of the First World War. ***West Johnston Lake*** (64 O/9), northwest of Nejanilini Lake was named after him in 1995.

Johnston, Trooper **William G. W.** of Fork River (H 613019). 31st (Alberta) Reconnaissance Regiment. He died 27 February 1944 at the age of 27 and is commemorated at Chilliwack (Royal Canadian Legion) Cemetery, British Columbia. He was the son of James W. and Sophie Johnston of Fork River, Manitoba. ***William Johnston Lake*** (64 I/13), north of Shethanei Lake was named after him in 1995.

Johnston, Flying Officer **William P.** of Brandon (J 26823). No. 407 Squadron. He died 7 June 1944 at the age of 22 and is commemorated at the Runnymede Memorial in Surrey, England. He was the son of Lloyd D. and Emily Johnston of New Westminster, British Columbia. ***Johnston Island*** (64 J/14) in the North Seal River was named after him in 1975.

Johnston, Flight Sergeant **William R. C.** of Winnipeg (R 86418). No. 23 Operational Training Unit, RCAF. He died 31 May 1942 at the age of 22 and is commemorated at Rotterdam (Crooswijk) General Cemetery, Holland. ***William Johnston Point*** (63 N/8) on Burntwood Lake was named after him in 1996.

Johnston, Sergeant **Wilson Thorburn** of Portage la Prairie (H 46051). Lake Superior Regiment. He died 19 September 1944 at the age of 24 and is commemorated at the Adegem Canadian War Cemetery in Belgium. He was the eldest son of Mr. and Mrs. John Johnston of Eden, Manitoba and was survived by his wife Helen Johnston (née Slade) of Cranberry Portage.

"Thorbie," as his friends better knew him, was born in Eden, Manitoba March 20, 1920. Of his own choice, he made his home with Mr. and Mrs. W. J. McCracken, formally of Eden and Neepawa, who moved to Amaranth where Mr. McCracken was the farming instructor on the Sandy Bay Indian Reserve. After rejoining his family, Thorbie received his education in Eden and Neepawa. He married Miss Helen Slade of Cranberry Portage on November 1, 1939. Wilson had worked with fishing crews in the northern lakes prior to his enlistment in the army in July, 1940. After his training at Fort William, Camp Borden, Ottawa, Debert and St. John, he was posted to England in 1942. He had a brother Garfield serving overseas and their father was a World War 1 veteran. Of this Canadian soldier it can be said: "Those who knew him best will miss him the most" (Pittman n.d.).

Johnston Rapids (64 C/9) in the Hughes River was named after him in 1995.

Jonasson, Pilot Officer **David Herman** of Baldur (J 19581). No. 427 Squadron. He died 20 February 1944 at the age of 31 and is commemorated at the Berlin 1939 - 1945 War Cemetery in Brandenburg, Germany. He was the son of Haraldur and Sigurveig J. Jonasson of Baldur, Manitoba. His nephew writes (18 February 2002):

Herman's parents were born in Iceland in the 1880s. They moved to Baldur where Herman was born May 3, 1913. His father was a veteran of World War I and was wounded in action in France. Herman grew up and took his schooling at Baldur. He was an average student, good athlete and a very good baseball pitcher. In addition to Baldur, he played for teams from Boissevain and Yorkton, Saskatchewan.

In 1936, Herman moved to the Sudbury, Ontario area where he played baseball and worked at the Copper Cliff Smelter for five years. Herman enlisted in the RCAF in July, 1941 with training at Winnipeg, Dafoe and Paulson. He went overseas in December, 1942 and was on his third tour when the plane was shot down over Leipzig, Germany in 1944.

Jonasson Lake (64 N/11), southwest of Nueltin Lake was named after him in 1972.

Jonasson, Sergeant **Leonard N.** of Pilot Mound (R 180403). No. 76 Squadron. He died 17 April 1943 at the age of 17 and is commemorated at Liesse Communal Cemetery, Aisne, France. He was the son of Otto and Asrun Jonasson of Point Roberts, Washington, USA. ***Jonasson Peninsula*** (64 O/4) on Gertel Lake was named after him in 1995.

Jones, Rifleman **Basil E.** of Winnipeg (H 100801). Regina Rifle Regiment. He died 18 July 1944 at the age of 20 and is commemorated at Beny-sur-Mer Canadian War Cemetery in Calvados, France. He was the son of George W. and Bertha Jones of Winnipeg. He had been employed by Royal Dairies prior to enlisting. His brother writes (20 August 1994):

> Basil was born in Miami, Manitoba ... and when his family moved to Winnipeg a few years later he received his education there. He enlisted with the PPCLI in Winnipeg and after going overseas in August, 1943, was transferred to the Regina Rifle Regiment on July 18th, 1944.

In a letter to Rifleman Jones' mother, Lieutenant L. Bergeron wrote:

> Dear Mrs. Jones: I am writing to give you an explanation as to how your son Earl came to his death. Earl volunteered for the scout platoon of this Regiment and came under my command on the 5th July, 1944; he had made a number of dangerous and successful patrols with me.
>
> On the 18th July, 1944, we were given a very important job to do, it being to make a crossing of the wire line south of Caen. Your son was one of the first men to get across this obstacle and to reach the objective given to him. All this was accomplished under enemy fire. Later, while he attempted to destroy an enemy machine gun post, he was killed. He died instantly. We were all very proud of your son and are proud to have had him as one of the platoon. We regret his loss very much. Hoping these few consoling words will help you in your recent, sad bereavement in the loss of your son Earl and you may feel very proud of your boy (22 August 1944).

Jones Island (64 G/11) in Denison Lake was named after him in 1994.

Jones, Leading Aircraftman **David A.** of Winnipeg (R 147315). Royal Canadian Air Force. He died 4 June 1943 at the age of 24 and is commemorated at Brookside Cemetery in Winnipeg. He was the son of Joseph and Sarah H. Jones of Winnipeg. ***Jones Rapids*** (64 P/3) in the Big Spruce River was named after him in 1995.

Jones, Sergeant **Edward J. "Teddy"** of Winnipeg (R 95236). No. 24 Operational Training Unit, RCAF. He died 1 August 1942 at the age of 20 and is commemorated at the Reichswald Forest War Cemetery in Germany. He was the youngest child and only son of Edward J. and Eleanor M. Jones (née Cresswell) of St. James. His niece recalls (16 February 1998):

> There were very few jobs when Teddy left school and he started a little book store that he left to join the Air Force. I ... remember the large dinner party my mother and father put on for him when he went away. He looked very handsome in his uniform and the whole family was there to kiss him and send him off. He left the next day for London and apart from letters, there was no contact until six months later when he was reported missing and then dead. Killed in a night raid over Düsseldorf I believe.

The family received conflicting information concerning the place of burial and a sister's trip to Belgium for that purpose proved unsuccessful. A cousin (26 February 1998) had better luck in 1995:

> I wrote a little note which said "Teddy: It took fifty-three years to get here, but we have not forgotten you. Your loving cousin, Stan." I put the note in a plastic ziploc bag with a Canada pin and buried it at the front side of the stone. I was just finished this and was starting to brush the dirt off my hands when a fighter jet on take-off roared by as if in a fly past. I did not see it as it was concealed by the trees. I was at Kleve maybe eight hours and I never saw or heard another fighter, so where it came from or where it was going are a mystery to me.

Jones Point (63 O/2) on Rosenberry Lake was named after him in 1995. His niece wrote (16 February 1998):

> His death meant that there was no one to carry on the family name and it ended with his death. And so, it is important and comforting to know there is a place in Manitoba called Jones Point. The family name did not die after all.

Jones, Sergeant **Frank H.** of Norwood (M 16385). Royal Canadian Army Paymaster Corps. He died 8 August 1942 at the age of 40 and is commemorated at Leeds (Armley) Cemetery in Yorkshire, England. He was the son of Edward G. and Sarah J. Jones and was survived by his wife Betty L. Jones of Norwood. ***Frank Jones Island*** (63 P/6) in Landing Lake was named after him in 1995.

Jones, Private **Harold B.** of Winnipeg (H 6483). Winnipeg Grenadiers. He died a prisoner of war 1 January 1944 and is commemorated at the Yokohama War Cemetery in Japan. The official cause of death was listed as "died in a typhoon." ***Jones Hill*** (64 I/16), south of Meades Lake was named after him in 1995.

Jones, Private **Harold J.** of Winnipeg (H 9639). Royal Canadian Armoured Corps. He died 28 August 1945 and is commemorated at Brookwood Military Cemetery in Surrey, England. ***Jones Esker*** (64 I/4), north of Ashley Lake was named after him in 1995.

Jones, Flying Officer **Philip C.** of Portage la Prairie (J 3761). No. 37 Squadron. He died 24 June 1942 at the age of 26 and is commemorated at Benghazi War Cemetery, Libya. He was one of the five children of Reverend Joseph and Florence Jones of Norway House, Manitoba. He had enlisted in 1940, immediately upon graduating from the University of Manitoba. His obituary read in part:

> Proceeding to England in April [1941], he took advanced training from April until August, taking part in many operations over France and Germany. Later in August, he navigated a plane from England to Egypt. Since then, he had been operating over Libya and from Malta, bombing military objectives along the North African Coast and off the Island of Sicily. In Libya, he was promoted to the rank of Flying Officer. An enthusiastic athlete, he was captain of the Science football team when it won the championship football shield. He was a member of the United Church (*Daily Graphic* 19 October 1942).

Jones Bay (64 N/10) in Tatowaycho Lake was named after him in 1989.

Jones, Leading Aircraftman **Richard C.** of Morris (R 281976). No. 7 Air Observers School, RCAF. He died 16 May 1944 at the age of 19 and is commemorated at Morris Cemetery. He was the son of Frederick W. and Violet Jones of Morris, Manitoba. His brother writes (13 July 1995):

> Richard was born in the small village of Ituna, Saskatchewan. This was a doubly-blessed event as it was accompanied by the birth of his sister

Elizabeth. They were the third and fourth children of Mr. and Mrs. F. W. Jones. In 1929, the family moved to Morris, Manitoba and it was here that Dick grew up and received his education. He was an excellent student who participated in sports; tennis and hockey were his favourites. After graduation from school, he began working for Price-Waterhouse, apprenticing for a degree in Chartered Accountancy. He travelled quite a lot in this capacity and the family received numerous letters from people he had met in various places expressing their regrets at his death and recalling how much they had enjoyed his visits.

Dick was injured at Portage la Prairie during a flying training session and passed away at Deer Lodge Hospital. He was interred at the Morris Cemetery May 20, 1944 where he now rests alongside his parents.

He added (18 March 1995):

I think this young man epitomizes the true volunteer that was the core of the Services in 1939/45. He left his position with an accountancy firm where he was well regarded and progressing so well, to join the Air Force even though his family was well represented in the Armed Services on Active Duty.

Jones Peninsula (53 N/3) on Red Cross Lake was named after him in 1995.

Jones, Flight Sergeant **Robert J.** of Winnipeg (R 106431). No. 406 Squadron. He died 7 April 1943 at the age of 23 and is commemorated at St. Martin-de-Re Communal Cemetery, Charente-Maritime, France. He was the son of Robert and Irene J. Jones of Winnipeg. ***Jones Creek*** (64 H/12), which flows southwest into Clee Lake was named after him in 1995.

Jonsson, Private **Theodore** of Baldur (H 6313). Winnipeg Grenadiers. He died in the "over the hill" battle 19 December 1941 at the age of 21 and is commemorated at the Sai Wan Memorial in Hong Kong. Born at Cypress River, he was one of the 13 children of Christian B. and Thordis Jonsson of Winnipeg. He enlisted in Winnipeg in 1939 and served in Jamaica prior to being sent to Hong Kong. ***Jonsson Creek*** (63 I/16), which flows southeast into Wakehao Lake was named after him in 1973.

Jordan, Flight Lieutenant **Ned** of Winnipeg (J 18919). No. 622 Squadron, Distinguished Flying Cross.

Flight Lieutenant Jordan joined the squadron in December, 1944 and quickly established himself as a captain and pilot of outstanding skill and determination. Trained in the use of special bombing equipment, he has been called upon to operate under most difficult conditions. His keenness to get at the enemy, and his skill and courage in the face of heavy opposition have made him a valuable leader and have contributed in no small measure to the success of the squadron's operational effort.

Operating almost continuously both by day and by night against heavily defended targets, Flight Lieutenant Jordan has completed a most successful tour without major incident.

His cheerful courage and fine captaincy have ensured a high standard of co-operation with his crew and this, combined with his flying discipline and skill as a pilot, has enabled him to evade combat with enemy fighters, which have on several occasions attempted to intercept him.

This officer's sustained operational effort and his courage and devotion to duty are worthy of the highest praise, in recognition of which I strongly recommend the award of the Distinguished Flying Cross (DFC recommendation 1945).

He died 15 September 1946 at the age of 26 and is commemorated at Elmwood Cemetery in Winnipeg. He was the son of Edward and Anna Jordan and was survived by his brother Edward M. Jordan of Winnipeg. After the formal cessation of hostilities, many pilots flew with No. 124 Ferry Squadron, returning lend-lease aircraft back to the USA. It was on one such return flight from Fargo, North Dakota to Estevan, Saskatchewan that Flight Lieutenant Jordan's Dakota aircraft crashed near its destination, killing all 21 passengers and crew. ***Jordan Lake*** (64 F/9), west of Big Sand Lake was named after him in 1961.

Josland, Private **Wilfred Arthur** of Clanwilliam (H 65403). Royal Canadian Army Medical Corps. He died 22 December 1944 at the age of 23 and is commemorated at Cesena War Cemetery in Italy. He was the son of Wilfred E. and Janet E. Josland of Clanwilliam, Manitoba. ***Josland Lake*** (63 K/16), north of Reed Lake was named after him in 1973.

Joslin, Squadron Leader **John D. C.** of Shellmouth (34158). No. 79 Squadron, RAF. He died 7 July 1940 at the age of 24 and is commemorated at Buckden Cemetery, Huntingdonshire, England. He was the son of Davies C. and Elizabeth Joslin and was survived by his wife Louisa M. Joslin of Buckden, England. Squadron Leader Joslin was killed when his aircraft was shot down while on patrol at 8000 feet over Dover, England. He had earlier flown with No. 56 Squadron and had shot down two enemy aircraft near Dunkirk. He was the Commanding Officer of No. 79 Squadron at the time of his death (Allison and Hayward 1991). ***Joslin Lake*** (54 D/6), south of Stephens Lake was named after him in 1996.

Joy, Private **Bertrand E.** of Winnipeg (H 28649). Royal Canadian Infantry Corps. He died 23 August 1945 at the age of 20 and is commemorated at Brookside Cemetery in Winnipeg. He was the son of Mr. and Mrs. A. E. Joy of Winnipeg. ***Joy Creek*** (63 K/16), which flows southeast into Squall Lake was named after him in 1973.

Joy, Squadron Leader **Douglas G.** of Winnipeg (C 1218). No. 160 Squadron. He died 1 May 1945 at the age of 25 and is commemorated at the Singapore Memorial. He was the son of Douglas G. and Beatrix E. G. Joy of Toronto and was survived by his wife Barbara G. Joy of Winnipeg. ***Joy Island*** (53 L/13) in Oxford Lake was named after him in 1995.

Joyal, Private **Joseph A. J.** of Winnipeg (H 17136). Princess Patricia's Canadian Light Infantry. He died 14 December 1943 and is commemorated at the Moro River Canadian War Cemetery in Italy. ***Joyal Lake*** (63 I/7), north of Molson Lake was named after him in 1973.

Joynson, Pilot Officer **Francis E.** of Winnipeg (J 90390). No. 424 Squadron. He died 29 June 1944 at the age of 22 and is commemorated at Marissel French National Cemetery, Oise, France. He was the son of William and Margaret Joynson of Winnipeg. ***Joynson Lake*** (64 P/4), south of Nejanilini Lake was named after him in 1974.

Justice, Corporal **Robert M.** of Dauphin (R 134275). No. 10 Service Flying Training School. He died 21 February 1942 at the age of 38 and is commemorated at Riverside Cemetery in Dauphin. He was the son of William and Christena Justice and was survived by his wife Hannah C. F. Justice of Dauphin. ***Justice Lake*** (64 P/16), northeast of Nejanilini Lake was named after him in 1978.

K

Kachor, Lance Corporal **John** of Hilbre (H 64122). Sherbrooke Fusiliers. He died 7 June 1944 at the age of 25 and is commemorated at Beny-sur-Mer Canadian War Cemetery in Calvados, France. He was one of the 10 children of Hnat and Paraska Pearl Kachor of Hilbre, Manitoba. His sister recalls (30 September 1992) that:

> My parents farmed in Hilbre, Manitoba. All 10 of their children were born there and raised in the local school house. He was interested in farming and I expect he would have continued in that field. He joined the service in the spring of 1942.

Kachor Lake (64 I/16), northeast of North Knife Lake was named after him in 1974.

Kadeniuk, Private **Walter** of Winnipeg (K 69461). Seaforth Highlanders of Canada, Military Medal. He died 17 September 1944 and is commemorated at Coriano Ridge War Cemetery in Italy. ***Kadeniuk Lake*** (64 C/6), east of Reindeer Lake was named after him in 1947.

Kaiser, Flight Sergeant **Walter Bruce** of Winnipeg (R 101947). No. 1659 Heavy Conversion Unit, RCAF. He died 25 July 1943 at the age of 25 and is commemorated at Dishforth Cemetery, Yorkshire, England. He was the son of Walter and Katherine Kaiser (née Bruce) and was survived by his wife Hazel A. Kaiser (née Reid) of Winnipeg. She recalls (21 January 2002):

> Born October 18, 1914 in Togo, Saskatchewan, he came to Winnipeg for employment with the Manitoba Wheat Board. Bruce enlisted in the Air Force in 1939 where he completed his training as an air gunner and married Hazel Reid on October 24, 1940. He was shipped to Halifax on November 3 and ten days later, he went overseas. The following summer, Bruce's Halifax aircraft crashed returning from his first operational mission over Germany. Rest in Peace.

Kaiser Lake (64 P/11), east of Nejanilini Lake was named after him in 1974.

Kaiser, Ordinary Seaman **William P.** of Winnipeg (V 35908). HMCS *Chippawa*. He died 27 December 1942 at the age of 21 and is commemorated at Brookside Cemetery in Winnipeg. He was the son of Henry and Martha Kaiser of Winnipeg. ***Kaiser Island*** (54 D/6) in Stephens Lake was named after him in 1996.

Kalyta, Pilot Officer **Peter** of Winnipeg (J 90760). No. 408 Squadron. He died 23 May 1944 at the age of 21 and is commemorated at the Reichswald Forest War Cemetery in Germany. He was the eldest son of Stephen and Frances Kalyta and was survived by his wife Aileen Kalyta of Winnipeg. His brother Bill recalls (27 February 2002):

> Peter was eight years older than myself and as his younger brother I always admired him because he excelled at anything he took an interest in. He attended Isaac Newton High School where the Isaac Newton Memorial Trophy was awarded in his name. The trophy was donated by a group of former students in Peter's memory and was awarded to the most outstanding male athlete. Peter continued his love for boxing and weight lifting during his years in the Air Force. After his training in Canada, Peter was assigned to RAF Linton-on-Ouse, England and then to the Dalton Battle School. He was reported missing and presumed dead as the result of air operations over Germany.

Kalyta Lake (64 O/11), east of Nueltin Lake was named after him in 1975.

Kamedish, Sergeant **John B.** of Winnipeg (R 59288). No. 10 Operational Training Unit, RCAF. He died 28 July 1941 at the age of 22 and is commemorated at Brookwood Military Cemetery in Surrey, England. He was the son of Peter B. and Louise Kamedish of Winnipeg. ***Kamedish Lake*** (54 E/1), northeast of Split Lake was named after him in 1985.

Kapusta, Corporal **Basil** of Winnipeg (R 71151). No. 418 Squadron. He died 8 February 1943 at the age of 21 and is commemorated at Pershore Cemetery, Worcestershire, England. He was the son of Michael and Anna Kapusta of Winnipeg. Corporal Kapusta was an aero engine or airframe mechanic who had hitched an unauthorized ride on Boston W8380 which was on a low-level training flight. It hit a tree and crashed one mile north of Vington Hall, near RAF Pershore. The pilot and observer were also killed. ***Kapusta Lake*** (64 O/15), east of Nueltin Lake was named after him in 1975.

Karaim, Sergeant **Anthony J. "Tony"** of Ashville (R 210272). No. 22 Operational Training Unit, RCAF. He died 14 February 1944 at the age of 22 and is commemorated at Stratford-upon-Avon Cemetery in Warwickshire, England. He was survived by his mother Verna Karaim of Winnipeg. Service records indicate that the pilot of his Wellington aircraft had only carried out six hours of solo night flying and crashed after making five attempts to land. The town of Wellesbourne in Warwicksire, England has built a museum to honour the 315 airmen who took off from the nearby Wellesbourne Mountford airfield and never returned. Of that number, 243 were Canadian, some as young as 19 (Sinclair 2001). In a letter home written a month before his death, he relates some impressions of his new surroundings in England:

> I am feeling strong and healthy so far, although this climate isn't very agreeable. I hope you spent your Christmas merrily, because it was very dull for me this year. I had a couple of days off so I went to the nearest town and indulged myself in drinking. Liquor and beer is plentiful here, that's why I'm afraid I'll be quite a drinking man when I come back home. Oh well, it's not as bad as it sounds because I've gained a couple of pounds since I've been here. I haven't seen much of this country yet, ... but from what I've seen it's not too bad. One thing I miss very much here is central heating. They warm their houses here with fireplaces in which half of the room would be cold (17 January 1944).

Karaim Lake (63 O/10), southeast of Nelson House was named after him in 1973.

Karlenzig, Sergeant **J. F. "Vincent"** of Winnipeg (R 71259). No. 1 Central Flying School. He died 3 June 1941 at the age of 21 and is commemorated at St. Vital Cemetery. He was the son of Frederick and Bentina M. Karlenzig of Winnipeg. His sister writes (22 October 2001):

> Vincent attended school for two years in Selkirk and one year in central Winnipeg. In 1929, he moved to St. Vital where he completed his education: four years at Windsor School, two years at Glenwood School and the final two years at Glenlawn Collegiate, completing Grade 11.
>
> Vincent was a quarterback with the St. Vital Bulldogs for several years and was to try out for the Winnipeg Blue Bombers in 1939 when war broke out. During 1938/39, he worked with two uncles fishing on Lake Manitoba. At the outbreak of war, Vincent tried to enlist in the RCAF for pilot training but was refused because he didn't have a university education. In the fall of 1940, he was accepted for pilot training and was sent to Manning Depot in Brandon. He was then transferred to Moose Jaw to begin his training. He received his wings in March, 1941. Vincent was recommended for training as a Pilot Instructor and was

transferred to Trenton, Ontario. He returned home for a short visit before going on to Trenton. On June 3, 1941, Vincent was flying solo in a Harvard near Frankford, Ontario when the aircraft developed problems. He crashed into a farmer's field.

Vincent was active in the Young People's Association of the St. Vital United Church. He was also a Boy Scout and became a King's Scout which he was very proud of, having received a scroll signed by Lord Baden-Powell. Vincent's parents received a Silver Memorial Cross from the Government of Canada.

Karlenzig Lake (64 O/14), east of Nueltin Lake was named after him in 1975.

Kashmar, Warrant Officer 2 **William** of Winnipeg (R 119924). No. 427 Squadron. He died 26 June 1943 at the age of 24 and is commemorated at Gorssel General Cemetery in Holland. He was the son of Roman and Eva Kashmar of Winnipeg. ***Kashmar Lake*** (64 I/8), northeast of North Knife Lake was named after him in 1974.

Kasijan, Private **Michael** of Portage la Prairie (H 6631). Winnipeg Grenadiers. He died 22 December 1941 and is commemorated at the Sai Wan Memorial in Hong Kong. He was survived by his wife Mary Kasijan. Private Kasijan enlisted only three weeks after Canada declared war. ***Kasijan Lake*** (64 K/15), northeast of Lac Brochet was named after him in 1972.

Kasik, Private **John** of Plumas (M 107115). Royal Canadian Regiment. He died 17 May 1944 at the age of 29 and is commemorated at the Cassino War Cemetery in Italy. He was the son of John and Judith Kasik. ***Kasik Lake*** (64 G/6), southeast of Big Sand Lake was named after him in 1985.

Kaspryzk, Private **Joseph** of Eden (H 14505). North Nova Scotia Highlanders. He died 17 September 1944 at the age of 29 and is commemorated at the Calais Canadian War Cemetery in France. He was one of the nine children of John and Verna Kaspryzk (née Prawdzik) and was survived by his wife Stella Kaspryzk (née Lavich) of Windsor, Ontario. ***Kaspryzk Lake*** (63 J/9), west of Cross Lake was named after him in 1981.

Kauk, Private **Jacob "Jack"** of Winnipeg (H 105126). Calgary Highlanders. He died 28 February 1945 at the age of 29 and is commemorated at the Groesbeek Canadian War Cemetery in Holland. According to his brother-in-law (27 August 1993):

> His father and mother were born in Bessarabiya, Russia and Austria respectively. They came to Canada around 1910. In Jack's younger days growing up in the depression years, jobs were scarce. He used to catch freight trains to Saskatchewan where he used to work on farms for the summer. He was a quiet and shy fellow, played a lot of sports, baseball and hockey on the neighbourhood rink in winter. He was well liked by everybody. Like so many other young fellows at that time, out of work, he joined the army.

His brother adds (16 November 2001):

> "Jack" was born sixth of nine children to Henri and Katherine Kauk (née Kendal) on 24 April 1915 in Elmwood, Manitoba (now a suburb of Winnipeg). Three of Jack's brothers also served in World War II – John (Peewee) with the Princess Patricia's Canadian Light Infantry, Phillip (Mickey) with the Manitoba Dragoons and Ludwig (Louis) with the Royal Canadian Artillery.
>
> Jack was in active service with the Calgary Highlanders in England, France, Belgium, Holland and Germany. He died of wounds in Kleve, Germany and was buried the next day by his younger brother Louis. His grave was later moved to Plot 7, Row B Grave 8 at Groesbeek, Holland as orders were not to leave Canadian dead in German soil.

Kauk Lake (52 L/6), east of Lac du Bonnet was named after him in 1973.

Kee, Warrant Officer 2 **Robert J.** of Graysville (R 86226). No. 61 Squadron. He died 3 January 1943 at the age of 21 and is commemorated at Bergen-op-Zoom War Cemetery, Holland. He was the third of the seven children of Matthew and Sarah M. Kee of Graysville. His brother writes (30 October 2001):

> Jim was the brother I never knew. Being the youngest of the seven children, I was not quite three when he left home to join the RCAF. From my sibling's stories, he was a good student, an excellent hockey player with great potential and a great brother. Not being able to know him has been one of my great regrets in life. We would have been great friends. We will remember him.

Kee Lake (63 N/1), southeast of Sherridon was named after him in 1970.

Keehn, Trooper **Robert H.** of Emerson (H 26531). Fort Garry Horse. He died 29 May 1945 and is commemorated at the Groesbeek Canadian War Cemetery in Holland. He was the son of Emil and Julia Keehn of Emerson, Manitoba. ***Keehn Lake*** (64 N/3), southwest of Nueltin Lake was named after him in 1972.

Keeler, Flight Sergeant **Russell R.** of Lauder (R 116462). No. 28 Operational Training Unit, RCAF. He died 12 August 1943 at the age of 21 and is commemorated at the Runnymede Memorial in Surrey, England. He was the son of Werden J. and Ethel F. Keeler of Hartney, Manitoba. His sister recalls (6 November 2001):

> Russell was in a ... Wellington aircraft which went down in the Channel returning from a leaflet raid. When the plane hit the water it broke in two and two of the crew members were thrown clear and picked up by rescue boats. A third body was washed ashore and was identified by family members. Russell had an all-English crew and had visited the homes of most of them. One mother wrote to my parents to say they would keep watch and if any further bodies were washed ashore, they would check as they knew my brother from him visiting in their home, but that never occurred.
>
> After the war was over, my mother received a letter from one of the surviving crew members telling her that he was now playing in a band on the Queen Mary which would be docking in New York. He would like to see Mother and Dad if possible. But in those days, New York was a long way from Lauder, Manitoba and Mother and Dad were no longer young! All of the parents and the two surviving crew members wrote to my Mother and Dad about Russell which was very kind of them.

In a letter to Flight Sergeant Keeler's parents, Group Captain Bell wrote:

> Your son was Captain of a Wellington aircraft detailed on a target in France. Their aircraft was hit over the target and damaged to such an extent that it reflects credit on the skill of the pilot in reaching the English coast on return, where he crashed offshore near Shoreham, Kent. There were two surviving members of the crew of six, from whom we learned that he had succeeded in pressing home the task and the operation had been accomplished.
>
> Your son was Captain of a very good crew which had just completed their training at this OTU. We have every confidence in their future success (n.d.).

Keeler Lake (64 F/2), east of Wells Lake was named after him in 1994.

Keeling, Flight Sergeant **Ralph A. W.** of Winnipeg (638360). No. 58 Squadron, RAF. He enlisted in March, 1939 and was killed 8 October 1940. He was of 29 years of age and is commemorated at Gloucester Old Cemetery, Gloucestershire, England. He was the son of Charles W. and Shirley Keeling of Camper, Manitoba. ***Keeling Lake*** (64 F/9), north of Jordan Lake was named after him in 1995.

Keir, Rifleman **James A.** of Winnipeg (H 40702). Royal Winnipeg Rifles. He died 8 June 1944 at the age of 23 and is commemorated at Bretteville-sur-Laize Canadian War Cemetery in Calvados, France. He was the son of James A. and Emma Keir of Winnipeg. His sister recalls (29 November 2001):

Although I am the last surviving member of his family and was seven years younger than him, the tragedy of losing a son and brother was very hard on our parents. Not knowing where and when his body was found was never really explained till I heard from a member of the RWR and on searching by members of that regiment. He was not buried where my parents had heard from the government at that time. One of the members of the regiment said that he was an easy going, likeable fellow with a good sense of humour, easy smile, trustworthy and liked horseplay. These are my memories of him also.

Keir Lake (64 I/11), southeast of Shethanei Lake was named after him in 1974.

Kell, Leading Aircraftman **Wilfrid R.** of Winnipeg (R 137818). No. 9 Service Flying Training School. He died 7 November 1942 at the age of 24 and is commemorated at Elmwood Cemetery in Winnipeg. He was the eldest son of Wilfrid R. and Mertie Kell (née Tupman) of Winnipeg. His brother recalls (11 December 2001):

Wilfrid Raymond Kell was born in November, 1917 in Saskatoon and moved with his family to Winnipeg in the early 1920s. He and his family lived on Rosedale Avenue and later, for several years at 266 Queenston Street. In 1935, at the age of 17, he joined the Hudson's Bay Company, Northern Stores Division and spent six years in its service in the James Bay area of northwestern Ontario. I believe his first posting was to Lansdowne House and for the last two years of service, he was manager of an isolated outpost at Caniapiscau [Quebec]. He was a well regarded employee and there is a letter on his personnel file from R. H. G. Bonnycastle inviting him back to company service after the war. One of his talents which intrigued me was that he was totally fluent in Ojibwa while he required the help of a translator in Cree.

In August, 1941, he joined the RCASC and in January, 1942, transferred to the RCAF. In November, 1942, he had completed his advanced flying training and was to get his Wings as a pilot in three week's time when he was killed on Saturday, 7 November 1942 in an accident involving a mid-air collision between two Ansons. He was an LAC but, presumably, would have been promoted to Sergeant upon receipt of his Wings. He was single, although my brother understands that he expected to become engaged to a Toronto girl within a matter of weeks.

Kell Lake (64 P/14), northeast of Nejanilini Lake was named after him in 1974.

Kellas, Private **William A.** of North Kildonan (H 6903). Winnipeg Grenadiers. He died 21 December 1941 at the age of 23 and is commemorated at the Sai Wan Memorial in Hong Kong. He was the son of Archie and Mary Kellas and was survived by his wife Ruth Kellas of Winnipeg and their unborn son. His wife recalls (12 November 2001):

Bill was born in Winnipeg on August 9, 1918. He grew up and lived in North Kildonan all his life. He was educated at Lord Kitchener School in North Kildonan. Bill was very family oriented, a loving son and brother. By nature, he was a very sincere and honourable man. He was very fond of sports.

Early at the start of World War II, he enlisted in the Winnipeg Grenadiers. He believed there was a job to do and he wanted to do his part. Early in 1941, he was sent to Sherbrooke, Quebec with part of his regiment. There he met his future wife, Ruth. On June 11, 1941, Bill and Ruth were married in Holy Trinity Church in Winnipeg.

But their happiness was to be denied them when on October 25, 1941, Bill left Winnipeg with the regiment, never to return. He was listed as "missing in action" as of December 21, 1941. With no news until the end of the war, he was then known to have lost his life.

His loss was devastating to his family and especially to his wife and the son he never knew, born after his father's death. After 60 years he is still loved and missed by his wife and son and surviving family. We are very proud of him.

Kellas Lake (64 P/9), east of Nejanilini Lake was named after him in 1974.

Kellie, Pilot Officer **James W.** of Oakbank (J 89392). No. 424 Squadron. He died 25 May 1944 at the age of 23 and is commemorated at the Runnymede Memorial in Surrey, England. He was the son of Raymond A. and Mary A. Kellie of Oakbank, Manitoba. His father recalls (27 September 1963):

... he was born at Virden on May 30th, 1920 and received his education in schools at Elkhorn and Oakbank. He started work as a telegraph operator for the CPR on September 1, 1939 and enlisted with the RCAF June 27th, 1941. He served as a wireless operator with No. 424 Squadron overseas and was reported missing, presumed dead after air operations over Aachen, Germany.

Kellie Lake (52 L/6), east of Lac du Bonnet was named after him in 1973.

Kelln, Trooper **Edward** of Winnipeg (H 70304). 8th Princess Louise New Brunswick Hussars. He died 6 October 1944 at the age of 24 and is commemorated at Cesena War Cemetery in Italy. He was the son of Gottlieb and Katie Kelln of Winnipeg. ***Kelln Lake*** (64 J/4), southwest of Tadoule Lake was named after him in 1975.

Kelly, Sergeant **Archibald B.** of Winnipeg (H 19512). Royal Winnipeg Rifles. He died 12 October 1944 and is commemorated at the Adegem Canadian War Cemetery in Belgium. ***Kelly Point*** (64 O/2) on Brownstone Lake was named after him in 1995.

Kelly, Captain **Bernard J. "Brian"** of Winnipeg (CDN 483). King's Shropshire Infantry. He died 18 July 1944 at the age of 34 and is commemorated at Ranville War Cemetery, Calvados, France. He was the son of Bernard J. and Frances M. Kelly. of Winnipeg. His nephew writes (31 January 1995):

Bernard was born in Ireland (Ballyjamesduff District, Union of Oldcastle, County of Cowan). He was the middle of five children, four brothers and a sister. The family moved to Canada in 1925 and lived in the West End ... on Maryland Street just south of Sergeant Avenue. All children finished their schooling in Winnipeg. All the brothers were in the services during World War II: Thomas (the eldest) in the US Merchant Marines died at sea. Grandma was notified by the Merchant Marines Association from New York. Edward, born 1914, served with the RCN. Frank (Francis), born 1917, served with the RCAF. Bernard (was called Brian because his father's name was Bernard also) was very athletic, a member of the Canoe Club, tennis, golf etc., and was employed as Assistant Manager at a local bank.

Kelly Rapids (64 I/10) in the North Knife River was named after him in 1995.

Kelly, Lieutenant Commander **Fraser J.** of Winnipeg. HMCS *Bytown*. He died 13 June 1942 at the age of 56 and is commemorated at St. John's Cemetery in Winnipeg. He was survived by his wife Muriel H. Kelly of Winnipeg. ***Kelly Reef*** (63 B/8) in Lake Winnipeg was named after him in 1976.

Kelly, Corporal **George A.** of Winnipeg (H 54118). Veterans Guard of Canada. He died 30 October 1944 at the age of 53 and is commemorated at Brookside Cemetery in Winnipeg. He was survived by his wife Elizabeth Kelly (née Batt) of Winnipeg and their eight children. A daughter wrote (5 June 1998):

> My father ... enlisted in the Canadian Expeditionary Force in November, 1914. He served in France with the 2nd Battalion, Canadian Machine Gun Corps.
>
> He married Elizabeth Batt in London, England before returning to Canada and was demobilized in August, 1919. They lived in Elphinstone, Manitoba for a few years, then moved to an area at the west end of Clear Lake when it was opened up as farms for retired soldiers. The area was eventually named Crawford Park. They had eight children, six girls and two boys. As it was a newly settled area, he was very active in the organizing of the start of the school, Legion and the building of the community hall.
>
> The land was very poor for farming. In the 1930s, he started working as a cook in the relief camps that had opened up in Riding Mountain National Park. After the relief camps closed, he went to work as a cook in boundary camps and construction of Highway 10 between Erickson and Wasagaming. He was Secretary Treasurer of the School District of Clear Creek for many years. He especially enjoyed involvement in a number of plays put on each year by the community and in concerts put on by men in the relief camps.
>
> He enlisted in the Veterans Guard of Canada in July, 1940. He served at prisoner of war camps in Flanders and Red Rock, Ontario. He received a medical discharge in January, 1942. He died in Deer Lodge Hospital in October, 1944.

George Kelly Lake (53 E/13), south of Stevenson Lake was named after him in 1996.

Kelly, Gunner **James M.** of Scarth (H 69614). Royal Canadian Artillery. He died 14 August 1944 and is commemorated at the Bayeux Memorial in Calvados, France. ***Kelly Bay*** (64 F/2) in Wells Lake was named after him in 1989.

Kelly, Private **Laurence B. J.** of St. Vital (H 6774). Winnipeg Grenadiers. He died 25 December 1941 and is commemorated at Stanley Military Cemetery, Hong Kong. He was the son of Benjamin and Elizabeth H. Kelly of St. Vital. ***Kelly Island*** (64 N/7) in Topp Lake was named after him in 1985.

Kelly, Pilot Officer **Ralph G.** of Winnipeg (J 88769). No. 408 Squadron. He died 20 February 1944 at the age of 21 and is commemorated at Choloy War Cemetery, Meurthe-et-Moselle, France. He was the son of George H. and Matilda E. Kelly of Winnipeg. ***Kelly Peninsula*** (64 N/1) on Minuhik Lake was named after him in 1995.

Kelsey, Captain **Kenneth J.** of Winnipeg. Royal Canadian Army Paymaster Corps. He died 9 September 1944 at the age of 26 and is commemorated at the Adegem Canadian War Cemetery in Belgium. He was one of the three sons of William and Mary Kelsey and was survived by his wife Bella Jean Kelsey of Vananda, British Columbia. She writes (8 November 2001):

> Ken was brought up in Winnipeg and after completing high school he articled with a Chartered Accountant firm to obtain his degree in 1942. He enlisted in July, 1942. On going overseas, he was attached to the 6th Field Regiment, Royal Canadian Artillery.

Kelsey Island (64 N/9) in Shannon Lake was named after him in 1989.

Kelso, Corporal **Henry** of Winnipeg (H 6499). Winnipeg Grenadiers. He died 19 December 1941 at the age of 25 and is commemorated at the Sai Wan Memorial in Hong Kong. He was the son of John L. and Mary Kelso of Winnipeg and was the brother of Corporal John R. Kelso. ***Kelso Lake*** (64 K/10), northeast of Reindeer Lake was named after him and his brother (see next entry) in 1979.

Kelso, Corporal **John R.** of Winnipeg (H 6038). Winnipeg Grenadiers. He died 19 December 1941 at the age of 21 and is commemorated at the Sai Wan Memorial in Hong Kong. He was the son of John L. and Mary Kelso of Winnipeg and was the brother of Corporal Henry Kelso. ***Kelso Lake*** (64 K/10), northeast of Reindeer Lake was named after him and his brother (see previous entry) in 1979.

Kelso, Pilot Officer **Stuart Ross** of Roblin (J 18860). No. 429 Squadron. He died 4 December 1943 at the age of 22 and is commemorated at the Sage War Cemetery in Germany. He was the son of Wilson R. and Mabel Kelso of Roblin, Manitoba. His sister (28 August 1995) describes him as "a Grade A student in school [whose] hobbies were making model airplanes and doing fine woodwork." A newspaper account described the mission he had flown a week before his death:

> An RAF Station Somewhere in England, Nov. 24 – Flaming, exploding Berlin was without strong defence Monday night when British and Canadian bombers struck it the most devastating aerial blow of the war. At this base, a returning RAF squadron, which includes many Canadians, reported no losses and said only one German night fighter plane was sighted – and that one didn't attack. Scores of RCAF Lancasters and Halifaxes from the Canadian Bomber Group were included in the 1000 aircraft that plastered Berlin. Four RCAF planes failed to return. "Berlin will be nothing but a Hamburg if we put on a couple more of these shows," said Flight Sergeant Emmett MacNeeley, Humboldt, Saskatchewan, who assisted in the pulverizing raids on Hamburg. He is a veteran of 17 operations.
>
> There were audible sighs of relief in the control room of this base as the first of the returning Halifaxes made their landings. And a cheer went up when *X for X-ray*, the last of them, came in safely. Flight Sergeant Tommy Schioler, Winnipeg; Flying Officer Frank Hurley, 1124 Grosvenor Avenue, Winnipeg and Flying Officer Frank Enfield, Hamilton, Ontario, agreed smilingly that the trip wasn't a difficult one. They called it "enjoyable." Hurley had been over Berlin four times before and had expected a rougher time. "Some flak exploded beneath the wing and knocked the controls from my hands," he said, "but we dived 2000 feet and I regained control." Canadian bomber group airmen on the raid included Pilot Officer S. R. Kelso, Roblin [and] Pilot Officer W. G. Crawford, 511 Home Street, Winnipeg (24 November 1943).

Kelso Island (64 A/12) in Baldock Lake was named after him in 1995.

Kemp, Corporal **James R.** of Winnipeg (H 10387). Royal Canadian Infantry Corps. He died 24 June 1945 at the age of 41 and is commemorated at Elmwood Cemetery in Winnipeg. He was the son of James and Christina Kemp of Winnipeg. ***Kemp Lake*** (64 J/1), south of Tadoule Lake was named after him in 1975.

Kendall, Pilot Officer **George Herbert** of Winnipeg (J 89860). No. 97 Squadron. He died 21 December 1944 at the age of 29 and is commemorated at Eiken Churchyard, Norway. His wife Doris was not officially notified until June 1945. From 1935 to 1942 he had been employed by National Drugs, a wholesale supplier for retail druggists. ***Kendall Island*** (63 N/6) in Tait Lake was named after him in 1995.

Kendall, Flying Officer **John M.** of Thornhill (J 14708). No. 227 Squadron. He died 23 December 1943 at the age of 21 and is commemorated at the Phaleron War Cemetery in Greece. He was the son of Percy G. and Mildred J. Kendall of Rivers, Manitoba. ***Kendall Lake*** (64 H/16), southeast of North Knife Lake was named after him in 1963.

Kendrick, Sergeant **John** of Winnipeg (936286). No. 16 Operational Training Unit, RAF. He died 2 April 1943 at the age of 25 and is commemorated at Elsworth (Holy Trinity) Churchyard, Cambridgeshire, England. He was the son of John and Edith Kendrick of Elsworth. ***Kendrick Island*** (53 M/5) in Bigstone Lake was named after him in 1995.

Kendyfore, Private **Peter** of Winnipeg (H 14650). Queen's Own Cameron Highlanders. He died 8 August 1944 and is commemorated at Bretteville-sur-Laize Canadian War Cemetery in Calvados, France. He was the son of Nickolas and Anna Kendyfore and was survived by his wife Nina E. Kendyfore of Winnipeg. ***Kendyfore Lake*** (64 I/10), northeast of North Knife Lake was named after him in 1974.

Kendzierski, Private **John** of Rorketon (M 53880). Queen's Own Cameron Highlanders. He died 18 January 1945 at the age of 20 and is commemorated at the Holten Canadian War Cemetery in Holland. He was the son of Peter and Mary Kendzierski of Rorketon, Manitoba and was survived by six brothers and two sisters. His brother recalls (9 November 2001):

> John was a carefree and easygoing person who loved the outdoors and enjoyed life as many teenagers. At the age of 18, he left the farm to work on a ranch in Alberta and in 1943 enlisted in the army in the Armoured Corps. John was sent to Camp Borden in Ontario for training and then on to New Brunswick. He was then transferred to the Queen's Own Cameron Highlanders and in 1944 sent on to England and combat. John served in the push through Belgium and Holland, but still wrote his family back home while receiving care packages from his parents including knitted socks made by his mom. Sadly, John died when he came upon a machine gun nest and now rests in Holten with other soldiers. His brothers visited there and found the area very well kept after local school children planted flowers by each headstone.

Kendzierski Lake (64 O/10), northwest of Nejanilini Lake was named after him in 1975.

Kennard, Private **John E.** (H 16964). Princess Patricia's Canadian Light Infantry. He died 12 December 1943 at the age of 29 and is commemorated at the Moro River Canadian War Cemetery in Italy. He was the son of John and Elizabeth Kennard of Cupar, Saskatchewan. ***Kennard Lake*** (74 O/8) in northern Saskatchewan was named after him in 1953.

Kennedy, Rifleman **Allan J.** of Brandon (L 103100). Regina Rifle Regiment. He died 6 June 1944 and is commemorated at Bretteville-sur-Laize Canadian War Cemetery in Calvados, France. ***Allan Kennedy Lake*** (53 M/5), west of Cuddle Lake was named after him in 1995.

Kennedy, Gunner **Cyril N.** of Neepawa (H 12076). Royal Canadian Artillery. He died 2 February 1944 at the age of 31 and is commemorated at Brookwood Military Cemetery in Surrey, England. He was the son of John L. and Elizabeth Kennedy of Neepawa. ***Kennedy Esker*** (53 M/4), north of Dobbs Lake was named after him in 1995.

Kennedy, Flying Officer **Frederick J.** of Eden (J 3762). No. 15 Squadron. He died 30 May 1942 at the age of 29 and is commemorated at the Runnymede Memorial in Surrey, England. He was the son of Alexander D. and Jean E. Kennedy of Eden, Manitoba.

> Frederick was born at Eden and completed his Grade 12 there. He continued his education in normal school at Winnipeg, graduating in 1931. At age eighteen, he became the principal of Springfield School in Transcona, a position which he held for one and a half years. He subsequently served as principal at Lidstone School, Swan River and Lyleton for two years each, completing his teaching career at Dugald. Frederick enlisted in the RCAF in September, 1939 and received his training at Toronto, Brandon, Camp Borden, Mossbank and Rivers, where he received his Pilot Officer's commission in February, 1941. Frederick was posted overseas in April, 1941; for the next year was a Navigator in a bomber squadron participating in operations over Germany. He was promoted to Flying Officer in March, 1942. Frederick's Stirling aircraft failed to return from a mine laying operation; all crew members were reported killed (Pittman n.d.).

Kennedy Island (64 K/4) in Engen Lake was named after him in 1987.

Kennedy, Flight Sergeant **Gerald W.** of Elm Creek (R 116232). No. 1660 Heavy Conversion Unit, RCAF. He died 12 February 1943 at the age of 20 and is commemorated at Thurlby (St. Germain) Churchyard, Lincolnshire, England. He was the son of John M. and Scilena M. Kennedy of Elm Creek, Manitoba. ***Kennedy Peninsula*** (63 I/7) on Molson Lake was named after him in 1995.

Kennedy, Private **Glen M.** of Graysville (H 8330). Queen's Own Cameron Highlanders. He died 29 July 1944 at the age of 22 and is commemorated at Bretteville-sur-Laize Canadian War Cemetery in Calvados, France. He was the son of John A. and Ruby Kennedy of Graysville, Manitoba. ***Kennedy Bay*** (64 O/8) in Lucki Lake was named after him in 1995.

Kennedy, Flight Sergeant **Jack M.** of Elm Creek (R 68661). No. 23 Operational Training Unit, RCAF. He died 8 April 1942 at the age of 23 and is commemorated at Pershore Cemetery, Worcestershire, England. He was the sixth of the 13 children of Dr. Matthew S. and Hattie E. Kennedy of Elm Creek. His older sister recalls (11 October 2001):

> He was a terror. At that time the girls had long braids and he'd tie the braids of the girl in front of him at school to the back of her desk so she couldn't get up. The girls liked Jack; I don't think he hated them either. He was a very popular boy with a mind that could see the funny side of everything. Dad wanted to make a lawyer out of him. He once told Jack

"if you don't want to study, you're going to have to work. When I come home at four o'clock, I want to see a pile of wood chopped." So my Dad took off but so did Jack. He got back just about five minutes before Dad and he had the axe and the root of a tree and he was hacking away on it. Dad said "That's it son, get a big root and woodpecker away on it all day." They went into Dad's office and he laid down the law. "Either you're going to do one thing or you're going to do another, but I have to know which it's going to be." So they shook hands and Jack went back to school.

Dad was a veterinarian. He died when Jack was 12 and I took over the family. My Dad had had a good business, but it was farm country, so they paid in meat or produce instead of money. When he died I think there was 3000 dollars, which didn't last very long. Counting Mom, there were 14 of us to feed and clothe. I made arrangements that Bud and Jack were to work and keep my mother and another three children because I had to work too to keep some money coming in. I took them all to Red Lake and got Jack a job in the Sullivan Mine and Bud a job at the hotel and one sister a job at the Post Office. I got Phyllis, another sister, a job as a babysitter.

In 1932, I got laid off. The boys had made friends with an old trapper and he suggested they try their hand at trapping. His trap-line was still registered in his name, but he was too old to go. He gave us the traps and snares and taught us how to use them. So I got groceries and supplies and paid for a plane and the three of us went way up north in Manitoba. We did it for two years. But when we tried to leave, we found that the government had confiscated all the planes. It took us two weeks to canoe out, but when got back to Red Lake we'd made enough money to buy a house. Jack practically lived around those planes in Red Lake. Some of the bush pilots would teach him and he knew how to fly them. I think that's why when he enlisted, he chose the Air Force and became a pilot.

We later learned that he had been shot down by an Allied aircraft. The Germans were bombing London and Jack was coming back from a raid over Germany. They had run into an electrical storm that knocked out their radio so they couldn't identify themselves. He and the six RAF airmen that were with him were killed. He had a "War Mother" in Pershore where he is buried and she sent me the buttons off his uniform. I had five brothers in the war. It killed them all to tell you the truth. My brother Ken came home and had to carry an oxygen tank around with him; he only had a quarter of a lung left. He only lasted two years. Our youngest brother Bud got through the war but he wasn't too well either; I think he lived five more years. Fortunately, I had arranged it so that my mother got a 30 dollar a month pension for Jack because he had been sending her money. They were having his memorial at Elm Creek when we learned that his nephew, Uncle Mitch's son, had been killed.

I saw the soldiers coming back from both wars. I was working the telephones at the CNR at the time and the boss let us go out onto the mezzanine to watch. Horrible. Young brides that had their husbands coming back ... some of them with no legs, some of them with no arms, some of them in baskets. It was a horrible thing to watch. They had a band there and it was playing *Mighty lak' a Rose*. To this day I can't hear that song without crying.

Jack Kennedy Lake (54 E/7), northwest of Fly Lake was named after him in 1995.

Kennedy, Flying Officer **James C.** of Winnipeg (J 22693). No. 424 Squadron. He died 10 July 1943 at the age of 20 and is commemorated at Enfidaville War Cemetery in Tunisia. He was the son of James A. and Ethel Kennedy of West Vancouver, British Columbia. ***Kennedy Point*** (63 N/6) on Crow Lake was named after him in 1995.

Kennedy, Private **Malcolm A.** of Napinka (H 19731). Queen's Own Cameron Highlanders. He died 20 July 1944 at the age of 23 and is commemorated at Bretteville-sur-Laize Canadian War Cemetery in Calvados, France. He was the son of John M. and Isabella Kennedy and was survived by his wife Joan B. Kennedy of Lewes, Sussex, England. ***Malcolm Kennedy Lake*** (53 K/13), northeast of Gods Lake was named after him in 1995.

Kennedy, Able Seaman **Robert M.** of Elmwood (3230). HMCS *Fraser*. The *Fraser* was lost in a collision with the British cruiser HMS *Calcutta* during the evacuation of France in 1940. Able Seaman Kennedy died 25 June 1940 at the age of 24 and is commemorated at the Halifax Memorial. He was the son of Herbert M. and Margaret S. Kennedy of Elmwood and was survived by his wife Agnes L. Kennedy of Winnipeg. ***Kennedy Rapids*** (64 I/9) in Grant Creek was named after him in 1995.

Kennedy, Pilot Officer **William J.** of Winnipeg (J 88743). No. 115 Squadron. He died 18 July 1944 at the age of 28 and is commemorated at Brookwood Military Cemetery in Surrey, England. He was the son of William D. and Mary A. Kennedy of Winnipeg. ***Kennedy Hill*** (64 O/13), east of Nueltin Lake was named after him in 1995.

Kenny, Ordinary Seaman **Norman W.** of Winnipeg (V 24383). Royal Canadian Navy. He died 8 May 1941 at the age of 34 and is commemorated at Elmwood Cemetery in Winnipeg. He was the son of George A. and Jennie Kenny of Winnipeg. ***Kenny Lake*** (64 N/7), southwest of Nueltin Lake was named after him in 1972.

Kenward, Gunner **Stanley F.** of Brandon (H 35209). Royal Canadian Artillery. He died 17 August 1944 at the age of 25 and is commemorated at Bretteville-sur-Laize Canadian War Cemetery in Calvados, France. He was the son of Albert T. and Dottie Kenward of Vancouver. ***Kenward Lake*** (64 F/6), north of Wells Lake was named after him in 1994.

Keown, Pilot Officer **John L.** of Boissevain (J 95371). No. 424 Squadron. He died 6 December 1944 at the age of 25 and is commemorated at Reichswald Forest War Cemetery, Germany. ***Keown Creek*** (63 N/2), which flows north into Moody Lake was named after him in 1972.

Kerek, Private **Albert** of Winnipeg (H 204425). Loyal Edmonton Regiment. He died 20 September 1944 at the age of 24 and is commemorated at Coriano Ridge War Cemetery in Italy. He was the son of Andrew and Ester Kerek of Winnipeg. ***Kerek Lake*** (64 I/13), northwest of North Knife Lake was named after him in 1974.

Kerman, Rifleman **Ronald S.** of Winnipeg (H 104091). Royal Winnipeg Rifles. He died 7 March 1945 and is commemorated at Groesbeek Canadian War Cemetery in Holland. ***Kerman Lake*** (64 I/11), northwest of North Knife Lake was named after him in 1978.

Kerr, Lieutenant **James C.** of St. Vital. Royal Winnipeg Rifles. He died 10 October 1944 at the age of 22 and is commemorated at Adegem Canadian War Cemetery, Maldegem, Oost-Vlaanderen, Belgium. He was the only son of Colin A. and Hilda H. Kerr and was survived by his wife Alice P. Kerr of Yarmouth, Nova Scotia. She writes (31 October 2001): "He was a very friendly, outgoing young man and enjoyed many sports activities including lawn bowling. He was also an avid bridge player." His sister adds (17 October 1998):

Jim left home at such an early age and there was nothing significant to relate that I can remember. He was a very kind and thoughtful person and I have been reading some of his letters sent to me and my parents that showed his deep love for his family. He was married to Alice, a lovely girl from Nova Scotia. Recently, we wrote for and received a tape in which the speaker mentioned Jim and told of a visit to my parents' home after Jim's death and spoke of the closeness of the family.

We have just received a video tape titled *The Ballad of Jimmy Kerr*. There was an article in the *Winnipeg Sun* which told of the memories of the young men who gave their lives. Chris Chadderton, who was a friend of Jim's heard the song and it reminded him of Jim and he asked that the song be titled *The Battle of Jimmy Kerr*. We were very moved by it.

Kerr Island (64 F/1) in Melvin Lake was named after him in 1995.

Kesselman, Pilot Officer **Murray** of Winnipeg (J 92274). No. 199 Squadron. He died 16 September 1944 at the age of 21 and is commemorated at the Runnymede Memorial in Surrey, England. He was the son of George and Martha Kesselman of Winnipeg. ***Kesselman Lake*** (64 P/2), southeast of Nejanilini Lake was named after him in 1978.

Ket, Trooper **Edward** of Winnipeg (H 9601). Fort Garry Horse. He died 29 September 1944 and is commemorated at Bergen-op-Zoom Canadian War Cemetery in Holland. ***Ket Lake*** (63 K/16), northwest of Wekusko Lake was named after him in 1973.

Keveriga, Flight Sergeant **William** of Grande Pointe (R 166294). No. 7 Air Observers School. He died 15 September 1944 at the age of 28 and is commemorated at Elmwood Cemetery in Winnipeg. He was the third child of Karl and Effle Kywyryga (sp.) of Grande Pointe. According to his sister-in-law (28 January 2000):

They were a very close and respected family in this farming community. Bill, as he was known to all, participated and helped on the family farm. Upon completion of school, he made it known to his father that he was interested in the Armed Forces, thus relinquishing the plans his father had for farming with his sons.

On his time of leave from the forces, he helped out on the family farm which he enjoyed. He loved spending time with his family and friends. He never married. Bill died in hospital in Winnipeg of a haemorrhage after tonsil surgery.

His sister adds (8 November 2001):

William ... successfully received his flight training at the Brandon Aero Association Limited. He received his wings in 1939. When war was declared, William enlisted. He received his training and was assigned overseas. En route, he was hospitalized in Winnipeg for minor surgery, which he did not survive. At the time, he was survived by his father, mother, three brothers and two sisters.

William was a fun loving individual with a great sense of humour. He was loved, admired and respected by all. Despite the years, his family still grieves his passing and wonders how their lives would have been changed had William survived.

Keveriga Lake (64 P/12), northwest of Nejanilini Lake was named after him in 1974.

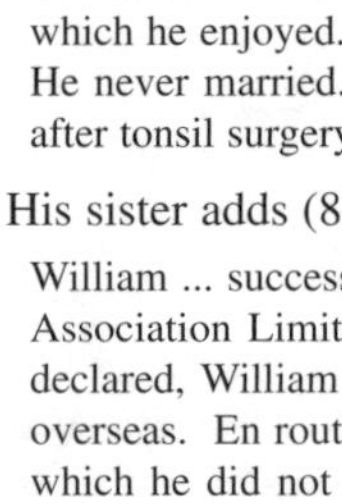

Keys, Private **Harvey I.** of Durban (H 1975). Queen's Own Cameron Highlanders. He died 3 March 1945 during the crossing of the Rhine. He was 34 years of age and is commemorated at the Groesbeek Canadian War Cemetery in Holland. He was the son of John and Prudence Keys and was survived by his wife Lillian Keys of Durban, Manitoba and their daughter. She writes (10 February 1997):

My Mom said he joined the army as a mechanic, which was his interest. Earlier, he drove a fuel delivery truck for his business which was The Durban Co-op store in Durban, Manitoba which he ran with my Mom; she graded eggs. We moved to Portage la Prairie where he trained. Then we were transferred to Red Deer, Alberta until he was shipped overseas. We returned to Durban.

She adds (3 November 2001):

He was a quiet farm boy who lived for his family. He felt it was his duty to enlist because his only brother had health problems and could not. After he married, he moved to town and drove a fuel truck for the local Co-op, hauling fuel to farmers. After he enlisted, he trained as a mechanic in his short stay before he was shipped overseas. After the war, a fellow soldier brought some of his belongings back to my mother and said that the whole platoon was wiped out at the crossing of the Rhine River in Germany. In his letters, he often mentioned what a beautiful country Holland was and that he's like to live there some day.

Keys Creek (62 N/15), which flows southeast into Pine River was named after him in 1980.

Kidd, Corporal **John S.** of Winnipeg (H 9628). Canadian Provost Corps. He died 1 February 1945 at the age of 32 and is commemorated at Brookwood Military Cemetery in Surrey, England. He was the son of James and Margaret C. S. Kidd and was survived by his wife Gladys M. Kidd of Winnipeg. ***Kidd Lake*** (63 O/5), southeast of Highrock Lake was named after him in 1973.

Kilborn, Sergeant **Allison Frank** of Virden (H 17047). Princess Patricia's Canadian Light Infantry. He died 11 March 1945 at the age of 36 and is commemorated at Virden Cemetery. He was survived by his wife Marion L. Kilborn (née McDonald) of Virden and their five children. His daughter writes (10 February 1997):

My Dad ... was born in Moosomin, Saskatchewan [and] had five brothers and two step-sisters. His father was Clinton Miles Kilborn, killed in action at Ypres, Belgium in 1916. My Dad loved sports, music, played the violin and piano and his great love was his family. His love letters to my mother are a treasure. He also was a great gardener, cook and always helped my Mom can all the fruit and vegetables. He loved to play ball.

He was stationed at Camp Shilo where he was an instructor; he used to bring convoys to Virden as I remember. He was on his way overseas when he died of a heart attack in Debert, Nova Scotia. I was nine when he died, the oldest of five. Although some of my younger siblings do not remember our Daddy, we try to remember him in many ways.

She concludes (12 November 2001):

I still remember that day the minister came to school to get myself (I was nine) and my brother Terry (7 1/2). I also had a sister Patricia, aged four. She was named after my Dad's regiment. Before he left, he had left a present for my sister to open on her birthday, March 19, and when his belongings came back in his writing case, there was an unposted birthday card for me for April 4. He was a great Daddy to us.

Kilborn Lake (52 E/11), southeast of Brereton Lake was named after him in 1974.

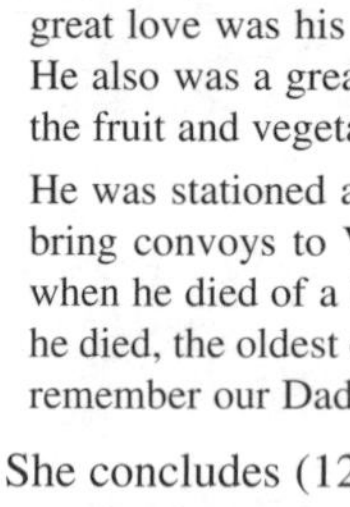

Kilfoyle, Private **Wesley N.** of MacGregor (H 6922). Winnipeg Grenadiers. He died 19 December 1941 at the age of 32 and is commemorated at the Sai Wan Memorial in Hong Kong. He was the second of the six children of John W. Kilfoyle and Mary J. Bazley. Many of the families who had relatives in Hong Kong after it was surrendered to the

Japanese never learned of their fate. In 1986, a niece was contacted by Harry Atkinson, President of the Hong Kong Veterans Association:

> I was with Wesley Kilfoyle in Jamaica and then on to Hong Kong. While prisoners in Hong Kong, they were shifted from place to place and as they were all getting much weaker, there were some who kept slipping behind. Those who could not keep up were shot. Wesley Newman Kilfoyle was one of those shot.

Kilfoyle Lake (64 H/6), northeast of Gauer Lake was named after him in 1963.

Kilgour, Midshipman **William G.** of Baldur (O 38950). HMS *Vernon*, the Royal Navy torpedo school in Brighton. He died 30 August 1942 at the age of 19 and is commemorated at Brighton (Bear Road) Borough Cemetery, Sussex, England. ***Kilgour Lake*** (64 C/7), north of Granville Lake was named after him in 1962.

Kiln, Leading Seaman **Alec D.** of St. James (2224). HMCS *Brandon*. He died 20 December 1942 at the age of 33 and is commemorated at the Halifax Memorial. He was the son of Harry and Mary Kiln of Weymouth, Dorsetshire, England and was survived by his wife Edith E. of Halifax, Nova Scotia. ***Kiln Creek*** (54 B/6), which flows east into the Kaskattama River was named after him in 1964.

Kilpatrick, Flying Officer **William F.** of Winnipeg (J 86304). No. 406 Squadron. He died 23 March 1945 at the age of 23 and is commemorated at Weerselo Roman Catholic Cemetery, Holland. He was the son of Charles F. and Wilhelmina Kilpatrick of Winnipeg. ***Kilpatrick Lake*** (64 N/5), southwest of Nueltin Lake was named after him in 1972.

Kines, Lance Corporal **Clare D.** of Roblin (H 41150). Royal Winnipeg Rifles. He died 8 June 1944 at the age of 29 and is commemorated at Beny-sur-Mer Canadian War Cemetery in Calvados, France. He was the son of W. Clarence and Hazel B. Kines of Chilliwack, British Columbia. ***Kines Lake*** (54 E/1), northeast of Split Lake was named after him in 1985.

King, Flight Sergeant **Arnold W. C. E.** of Winnipeg (R 71446). No. 106 Squadron. He died 22 April 1942 at the age of 37 and is commemorated at the Runnymede Memorial in Surrey, England. He was the son of William A. and Elizabeth King of Winnipeg and was survived by his wife Isabel P. King of Winnipeg. His obituary read in part:

> Born in Winnipeg, he was employed in the express office of the Canadian Pacific railway after graduating from St. John's technical high school. He joined the RCAF in October, 1940 and received his wings at Macdonald. He went overseas June, 1941 and transferred to the Royal Air Force (n.d.).

King Point (64 P/4) on MacLeod Lake was named after him in 1995.

King, Corporal **Earl D.** of Altamont (H 299). Lord Strathcona's Horse. He died 8 September 1944 at the age of 26 and is commemorated at Ancona War Cemetery in Italy. He was the third child of William T. and Maud King (née Brownell) of Altamont, Manitoba. His niece and nephew recall (27 November 2001):

> Earl received his schooling at Deerwood, Manitoba and farmed with his father and brother Norman before enlisting at the start of the war. Judging from reading his personal letters and from comments from his surviving peer group, he had a close relationship with his friends and family around Deerwood and Altamont.

King Island (63 I/2) in Molson Lake was named after him in 1995.

King, Flying Officer **Harold H.** of Newdale (J 35114). No. 101 Squadron. He died 1 July 1944 at the age of 24 and is commemorated at Chateaudun Eastern Communal Cemetery, Eure-et-Loir, France. He was the son of Reverend William J. and Edith L. King of Newdale, Manitoba. ***King Creek*** (64 P/4), which flows southeast into the Duffin River was named after him in 1974.

King, Sergeant **Robert A.** (H 19109). Queen's Own Cameron Highlanders. He died 26 September 1942 and is commemorated at St. Sever Cemetery Extension, Rouen, Seine-Maritime, France. ***King Bay*** (64 C/6) in Kaykayk Lake was named after him in 1995.

Kinnaird, Gunner **J. A. Elwood "Blackie"** of Portage la Prairie (H 66523). Royal Canadian Artillery. He died 8 June 1944 at the age of 22 and is commemorated at Bretteville-sur-Laize Canadian War Cemetery in Calvados, France. He was the son of Arthur J. and Mabel E. Kinnaird of Portage la Prairie. According to his sister (5 March 1995):

> The sport he loved mostly was hockey, in which he participated. He was also quite proficient in pole vaulting in his former years in school. He took an interest in all sports and was a willing competitor in many. His hobbies were performing in school plays and entertaining family, friends or whoever preferred to listen as he strummed on his tiny ukulele, often accompanying his Dad on the harmonica. He was a fun-loving person, dedicated to his family and friends and of course ultimately to his country.

Kinnaird Lake (64 O/3), southwest of Munroe Lake was named after him in 1975.

Kinney Stoker 2 **Glen E.** of Winnipeg (22790). Royal Canadian Navy. He died 16 March 1947 and is commemorated at Havana (Colon) Cemetery, Cuba. He was survived by his mother Mrs. Jean Kinney of Winnipeg. ***Kinney Lake*** (64 N/13), west of Nueltin Lake was named after him in 1972.

Kinsella, Gunner **James H.** of Norwood (H 12068). Royal Canadian Artillery. He died 17 May 1943 at the age of 21 and is commemorated at Brookwood Military Cemetery in Surrey, England. He was the son of Hugh F. P. and Nellie E. Kinsella of Winnipeg. ***Kinsella Lake*** (63 K/12), south of Manistikwan Lake was named after him in 1984.

Kinsley, Private **William F.** of Neepawa (H 95380). Black Watch (Royal Highland Regiment) of Canada. He died 1 November 1944 at the age of 26 and is commemorated at Bergen-op-Zoom Canadian War Cemetery in Holland. He was the son of David and Elizabeth Kinsley of Neepawa.

> He was born in Minto, Manitoba March 17, 1918. William joined the Royal Canadian Artillery on January 15, 1942, taking his training in Winnipeg, Brandon, Fort William and Kingston, Ontario. He was posted overseas in July, 1943, serving with the coastal command in England. William was transferred to the Black Watch prior to serving as a gunner during the battle in Antwerp, Belgium. He was wounded during this battle on October 1, 1944 and died a month later (Pittman n.d.).

Kinsley Lake (52 L/11), northwest of Bird Lake was named after him in 1982.

Kinsman, Rifleman **Harvey L.** of Darlingford (H 69959). Queen's Own Rifles of Canada. He died 10 August 1944 and is commemorated at Bretteville-sur-Laize Canadian War Cemetery in Calvados, France. He was the son of James and Annie Kinsman of

Darlingford, Manitoba. ***Kinsman Lake*** (64 J/7), southwest of Tadoule Lake was named after him in 1957.

Kipling, Private **Gilbert M.** of Winnipeg (H 103812). Royal Hamilton Light Infantry. He died 8 March 1945 at the age of 38 and is commemorated at the Groesbeek Canadian War Cemetery in Holland. He was survived by his mother Mary J. Kipling and by his wife Annie Kipling of Roland, Manitoba. ***Kipling Lake*** (64 J/3), southwest of Tadoule Lake was named after him in 1975.

Kippen, Captain **James Wendell** of Newdale. Royal Canadian Army Medical Corps. He was aboard the SS *Nerissa*, the only ship torpedoed while carrying Canadian troops to the United Kingdom. Captain Kippen died 1 May 1941 at the age of 25 and is commemorated at the Halifax Memorial. He was the son of Dr. Robert D. and Helen E. Kippen of Newdale, Manitoba and by his fiancée and was the brother of Private Robert S. Kippen (next entry). Captain Kippen graduated from Manitoba Medical College in 1939 and did his internship at Winnipeg General Hospital. He enlisted as a Medical Officer in 1940. ***Kippen Lake*** (52 L/11), west of Flintstone Lake was named after him in 1982.

Kippen, Private **Robert S.** of Newdale (H 35873). Royal Canadian Army Medical Corps. He died 21 May 1945 at the age of 33 and is commemorated at the Newdale Cemetery. He was the son of Dr. Robert D. and Helen E. Kippen of Newdale, Manitoba and the brother of Captain James Wendall Kippen (previous entry). The son of a country doctor, he graduated with an arts degree from Wesley College in 1935 and held a number of teaching positions before enlisting as a non-combatant. He contracted encephalomyelitis while on active service in northwestern Europe and was invalided back to England and thence to Deer Lodge Hospital where he died. ***Kippen Island*** (63 P/5) in Paint Lake was named after him in 1996.

Kirby, Sergeant **Alfred** of Transcona (R 95300). No. 20 Operational Training Unit, RCAF. He died 9 August 1942 at the age of 21 and is commemorated at Fettercairn Cemetery, Kincardineshire, Scotland. He was the son of Edmund C. and Catherine E. Kirby of Transcona. ***Kirby Lake*** (52 L/6), northeast of Lac du Bonnet was named after him in 1973.

Kirk, Private **Donald J. G.** of Stonewall (H 19277). Queen's Own Cameron Highlanders. He died 19 August 1942 at the age of 25 and is commemorated at Brookwood Military Cemetery in Surrey, England. He was survived by his wife Margaret H. Kirk of Stonewall and their daughter. ***Kirk Lake*** (52 E/14), north of West Hawk Lake was named after him in 1974.

Kirk, Warrant Officer 2 **James F.** of Hamiota (R 95108). No. 458 Squadron. He died 25 February 1943 at the age of 23 and is commemorated at the Malta Memorial. He was the eldest of the five children of J. E. and Katherine F. Kirk of Hamiota. His sister writes (8 November 2001):

> He enlisted in the Air Force in July, 1941 and went overseas on Christmas Day, 1942. He went missing in action while on routine patrol over the Mediterranean Sea. At the time of his death, he was engaged to an English girl. Our family has kept in contact with her all these years. After his death, he was promoted to Warrant Officer Second Class.

Kirk Island (53 D/13) in Gilchrist Lake was named after him in 1983.

Kirk, Lance Corporal **Roy L.** of Kelwood (H 6178). Winnipeg Grenadiers. He died 14 July 1945 at the age of 25 and is commemorated at the Yokohama War Cemetery in Japan. He was the son of Bernhard and Alice E. Kirk of Riding Mountain. Returning Grenadier Private Harry Atkinson reported that:

> "One month and 15 days ago seven of the fellows got stomach poisoning. They were in bad shape when they arrived back in camp that night. They were told to report to our [Japanese] commander. He ordered a stomach pump for them. Don't know why, probably saw the end of the war was near." Four of them died – Lance Corporal Malcolm Hawes, Private Jim Gard, Private Roy Kirk and Private Bob McLeod (*Winnipeg Tribune* September 1945).

Kirk River (54 M/12), which flows southeast into Caribou River was named after him in 1984.

Kirkpatrick, Lieutenant **Douglas A. W.** of Winnipeg. Royal Winnipeg Rifles. He died 28 August 1944 at the age of 25 and is commemorated at the Calais Canadian War Cemetery in France. He was the son of John A. and Dora Kirkpatrick and was survived by his wife Ella E. Kirkpatrick (née Draward) of Toronto and their daughter. She writes (17 June 1998):

> He graduated from Gordon Bell Collegiate in Winnipeg and became an employee of Eaton's mail order. He took accountancy at night school and was one year away from graduating when he enlisted. He enjoyed crossword puzzles and all sports – canoeing, baseball, biking.

Kirkpatrick Lake (64 I/9), northeast of North Knife Lake was named after him in 1974.

Kissick, Flight Sergeant **Victor R. D. J.** of Letellier (R 106357). No. 50 Squadron. He died 12 March 1943 at the age of 21 and is commemorated at Jonkerbos War Cemetery in Holland. He was the son of David and Eva M. Kissick of Norwood. ***Kissick Lake*** (64 J/9), east of Tadoule Lake was named after him in 1975.

Kitchen, Flying Officer **Harold Allan N.** of Winnipeg (J 14801). No. 198 Squadron. He died 17 September 1943 at the age of 23 and is commemorated at Lisieux Communal Cemetery, Calvados, France. He was the son of Harold W. and Edna J. Kitchen and was survived by his wife Elizabeth C. Kitchen of Winnipeg. ***Kitchen Lake*** (64 P/10), east of Nejanilini Lake was named after him in 1974.

Kitching, Trooper **Allan R.** of Roland (H 404). Lord Strathcona's Horse. He died 24 May 1944 and is commemorated at the Cassino War Cemetery in Italy. He was the son of William J. and Ida M. Kitching of Roland, Manitoba. His brother recalls (3 January 2002):

> Allan Raymond Kitching was born at Roland, Manitoba on June 7th of 1921 and took his schooling there. He was a healthy, outgoing boy and always played and worked hard. He had a great love of sports – skating, baseball and hockey. Allan was a good shot and spent many an hour chasing jackrabbits and gophers. Being raised in a farming area in the time of horse power, Allan had a great love for horses and the outdoors. He joined the army in the summer of 1941, standing five feet eight inches tall and weighing 127 pounds soaking wet.

Allan was in C Squadron of the Lord Strathcona's Horse. We left Camp Borden, Ontario in September, 1941 for overseas with the 5th Canadian Armoured Division and landed in England in November of 1941. Allan was a good soldier and took his training in England. He was a gunner on a Sherman tank. He went into action in Italy in 1943 and was killed in action May 24, 1944. We will not forget.

Kitching Point (63 B/10) on Lake Winnipeg was named after him in 1970 and ***Kitching Island*** (64 O/10) in Bangle Lake was named after him in 1995.

Kitching, Gunner **Lloyd E.** of Winnipeg (H 12050). Royal Canadian Artillery. He died 1 May 1945 at the age of 25 and is commemorated at the Holten Canadian War Cemetery in Holland. He was survived by his father and stepmother Robert B. and Eva L. Kitching of Winnipeg. ***Kitching Lake*** (64 J/2), southwest of Tadoule Lake was named after him in 1975.

Kite, Flying Officer **George R. Graham** of Pettapiece (J 87906). No. 10 Squadron. He died 23 September 1944 at the age of 22 and is commemorated at Leopoldsburg War Cemetery, Limburg, Belgium. He was the son of George R. and Janette B. Kite of Rapid City, Manitoba. According to his sister (22 April 1987):

Flying Officer Kite was on his 29th bombing mission as pilot of a Halifax bomber on the night of September 23, 1944. Their target was Krefeld, Germany. After releasing their bomb load on target, they turned for their home base and shortly afterwards the Halifax bomber was severely damaged by anti-aircraft fire. Flying Officer Kite ordered his crew of six to abandon aircraft and five of the crew members bailed out. They landed on German soil; four of them were taken prisoner and one is unaccounted for.

The navigator thought that the flight engineer did not have, or could not find his parachute, so Flying Officer Kite attempted to crash land the crippled Halifax in a field surrounded by trees. The bomber crashed into the trees killing both Flying Officer Kite and the flight engineer at the village of Zwier, Province of Limburg, Holland at 10:30 PM September 23, 1944.

His brother added that:

Graham was the eldest son in a family of four and was needed at home on the farm to help his father who had been seriously wounded in World War I. Like many sons of the region, he felt duty-bound to serve his country as his father had done. Graham was sent to Brandon Manning Depot in the winter of 1941 and then to Initial Training School in Saskatoon. As there was no immediate opening at a flying training school, he approached his commanding officer and was granted an extended furlough so that he could help his Dad on the farm. He completed his elementary flying training on October 8, 1942 with a total of 76 hours. Graham completed his service flying at Dauphin, where his Dad presented him his wings on February 18, 1943.

Kite Creek (53 E/7), which flows north into Lynx Lake was named after him in 1973.

Kitson, Flight Sergeant **Charles Albert "Bert"** of Austin (R 101804). No. 405 Squadron. He died 17 September 1942 at the age of 20 and is commemorated at Maubeuge-Centre Cemetery, Nord, France. He was the eldest child of Charles F. and Florence H. Kitson of MacGregor, Manitoba and was survived by his sisters Marie and Gene and brother Dennis. His brother writes (26 November 2001):

He was the rear gunner in a Halifax bomber which was shot down over France while returning from a bombing raid to Essen, Germany. Four other crew members were killed. Two of the crew survived, one was taken prisoner and one made his way back to England.

Bert, as he was generally known, was born on the family farm near Macdonald, Manitoba on July 18, 1922. The family moved to MacGregor in 1927, to Austin in 1934 and back to MacGregor in 1943. He received his education at MacGregor and Austin schools. In 1940, he enlisted in the non-permanent militia and entered his name for the navy in 1941. While waiting for call he was accepted into the RCAF on May 16, 1941 and trained at Dauphin, Edmonton, High River, Mountain View and Trenton. He graduated on November 21, 1941 and left for overseas the following month.

Bert was one of the popular young men in the community and was very fond of sports – swimming and hockey in particular. He belonged to the Boy Scouts and was a member of the Anglican Church. There is a Memorial Stone in his memory in the Air Force Association of Canada Garden of Memories on Air Force Way, Winnipeg. His name is also engraved on his dad's and mother's memorial in the Portage la Prairie cemetery.

Kitson Lake (64 J/15), northwest of Tadoule Lake was named after him in 1975.

Kitteringham, Private **John H.** of Gladstone (H 77628). Winnipeg Grenadiers. "Jack" Kitteringham enlisted when he was only 17 years of age by misrepresenting his year of birth on his Attestation Papers. Three months later he was shipped to Hong Kong and died 3 March 1944 at the age of 20 in a prisoner of war camp in Tokyo. The official cause of death was listed as chronic enteritis. He is commemorated at the Yokohama War Cemetery in Japan. Private Kitteringham was survived by his parents Alfred M. K. and Hettie E. Kitteringham of Gladstone, Manitoba. ***Kitteringham Lake*** (64 O/4), northeast of Egenolf Lake was named after him in 1975.

Klassen, Private **Dietrich Victor** of Myrtle (H 17884). Princess Patricia's Canadian Light Infantry. He died 23 July 1943 at the age of 20 and is commemorated at Agira Canadian War Cemetery in Italy. He was the son of George and Anna Klassen of Rivers, Manitoba. He was wounded in action at Leonforte and died of wounds two days later. According to his sister (16 May 1993):

He was born in a small hamlet in southern USSR somewhere near Odessa. In 1926 our parents emigrated to Canada, the destination here was Rosenfeld, Manitoba. Our dad worked briefly for the railroad and then for several farmers, finally settling in Myrtle (near Roland) where Dietrich received eight years of schooling. When war broke out, he was only 16 and he tried enlisting before he was 17, but was found out to be too young, so he returned to Myrtle to work for a farmer, and in the winter of '40 he worked in a sugar beet factory in Winnipeg. I'm not exactly sure of his enlistment date, but it was before Christmas of 1941. He enlisted with the PPCLI at Fort Osborne Barracks and trained at Portage la Prairie and later Shilo from where he was sent to England in June, 1942. There he was engaged in mopping up after German air raids. On July 9, 1943 he was with the division ... that landed in Sicily for the invasion. His regiment was engaged in heavy fighting and it was at the Battle of Leonforte where he was wounded in action and died of wounds two days later. He, along with 400 Canadian casualties are buried in the cemetery of Agira.

She adds (24 October 2001):

His letters home tell of frequent enemy bombings and his job to "clean up." Dietrich had a girl friend at home, Margaret Allen from Bagot, Manitoba, but several letters from England hinted at a girlfriend [there] that he might marry, but this did not happen. We sent frequent parcels and many letters, some of which he did not receive. In July of 1943, his regiment was sent to Sicily for the invasion and we received no further mail.

Klassen Lake (64 N/3), southwest of Nueltin Lake was named after him in 1972.

Klassen, Corporal **Gordon F.** of Plum Coulee (B 68196). Royal Regiment of Canada. He died 19 August 1942 at the age of 24 and is commemorated at Dieppe Canadian War Cemetery in Seine-Maritime, France. He was the son of Jacob and Helen Klassen of Morden, Manitoba. ***Klassen Island*** (53 L/11) in Michikinabish Lake was named after him in 1995.

Klippenstein, Corporal **Jacob** of Steinbach (H 17853). Queen's Own Cameron Highlanders. He died 18 August 1944 at the age of 24 and is commemorated at Beny-sur-Mer Canadian War Cemetery in Calvados, France. He was the son of Jacob and Tina Klippenstein and was survived by his wife Margaret M. Klippenstein of Winnipeg. ***Klippenstein Lake*** (64 N/2), southwest of Nueltin Lake was named after him in 1972.

Klohn, Company Sergeant Major (Warrant Officer 2) **Howard H.** of Winnipeg (H 41679). Queen's Own Cameron Highlanders, Mentioned in Dispatches. He died 15 October 1944 at the age of 24 and is commemorated at Schoonselhof Cemetery in Antwerp, Belgium. He was the son of Adolph and Emma Klohn and was survived by his wife Iris B. Klohn of Winnipeg. ***Klohn Lake*** (54 K/6), southeast of Churchill was named after him in 1948.

Klos, Corporal **Walter J.** of Brandon (H 41048). Royal Winnipeg Rifles. He died 6 June 1944 at the age of 26 and is commemorated at Beny-sur-Mer Canadian War Cemetery in Calvados, France. He was the son of Joseph and Antonia Klos of Brandon. ***Klos Lake*** (53 L/15), south of Knee Lake was named after him in 1983.

Klyne, Rifleman **Albert J.** of Portage la Prairie (H 41584). Royal Winnipeg Rifles. He died 27 August 1944 at the age of 22 and is commemorated at Bretteville-sur-Laize Canadian War Cemetery in Calvados, France. He was the son of Edward and Lena Klyne of Portage la Prairie. According to his niece (12 February 1996):

> My father advised that Albert loved to play horseshoes and was an avid swimmer. Dying so young didn't leave him much time to get involved in other things.

Klyne Lake (64 N/12), southwest of Nueltin Lake was named after him in 1972.

Klyne, Private **Joseph Ovide** of St. Laurent (H 46084). Lake Superior Regiment. He died 21 October 1944 at the age of 21 and is commemorated at Schoonselhof Cemetery in Antwerp, Belgium. He was the son of Joseph and Julienne Klyne of St. Laurent. ***Klyne Island*** (63 I/3) in Molson Lake was named after him in 1995.

Knight, Bombardier **Horace W.** of Cypress River (H 56851). Royal Canadian Artillery. He died 25 August 1944 at the age of 23 and is commemorated at Bretteville-sur-Laize Canadian War Cemetery in Calvados, France. He was the son of Thomas R. and Margaret M. Knight of St. James. ***Knight Island*** (64 H/6) in Northern Indian Lake was named after him in 1995.

Knight, Private **Robert A. J. "Pat"** of Eriksdale (H 10916). Essex Scottish Regiment. He died 31 July 1944 at the age of 19 and is commemorated at Bretteville-sur-Laize Canadian War Cemetery in Calvados, France. He was the eldest of the 11 children of Gwen Knight of Eriksdale and was survived by his wife Pearl Knight (née McKane) and their two children. His sister-in-law writes (11 April 1997):

> [He] attended primary school in East St. Paul and high school at Hugh John Macdonald in Winnipeg. The family then moved to a farm in the Eriksdale area. Pat liked music and was learning to play the fiddle. He drove a truck for Lightfoot's Transfer in Winnipeg [and] joined the army in the summer of 1943. He was nicknamed "Pat" by an Irish grandmother.

Knight Bay (63 I/2) in Molson Lake was named after him in 1995.

Knox, Sapper **William Howard** of Eriksdale (H 87717). Royal Canadian Engineers. He died 8 August 1944 at the age of 24 and is commemorated at Bretteville-sur-Laize Canadian War Cemetery in Calvados, France. He was the son of John H. and Barbara M. Knox of Eriksdale. His obituary read in part:

> Born in Weyburn May 28, 1920, he moved to Eriksdale the same year. He was educated in Eriksdale and United College, Winnipeg. He enlisted with the RCASC in January, 1942 and after his basic training at Portage la Prairie, he transferred to the Royal Canadian Engineers (n.d.).

Knox Lake (64 G/4), northeast of Grandmother Lake was named after him in 1994.

Koblun, Private **Albert** of Arborg (H 8882). Westminster Regiment. He died 11 November 1944 at the age of 39 and is commemorated at Cesena War Cemetery in Italy. He was the son of Herman and Amalie "Molly" Koblun of Arborg. His sister recalls (16 October 2001):

> Albert was the sixth of 13 children. He immigrated to Canada in 1911 with his family to the Arborg area. Ironically, the reason his parents wanted to emigrate was to avoid the compulsory military service in Germany. Two of Albert's brothers also served in war, one in the First World War and another in the Second.
>
> He was survived by many of his siblings and his parents. He was very good to us kids (the seven younger siblings). He would go away harvesting in the fall and when he came back he would buy all us girls a new dress for the Christmas concert.

Koblun Lake (63 K/16), west of Wekusko Lake was named after him in 1973.

Koester, Lieutenant **James V.** of Virden. Regina Rifle Regiment. He died 30 March 1945 at the age of 23 and is commemorated at the Groesbeek Canadian War Cemetery in Holland. He was the son of Theodore and Sarah A. N. Koester (née McDonald) of Oak Lake and husband of Gina Koester (née Kenward) of Shoreham-by-Sea in Sussex, England. According to his sister (28 November 1996):

> At Easter in 1941, all six boys in the Grade 12 class from Virden drove to Regina to enlist in the Regina Rifle Regiment. Of the group, Jimmy, a conscientious student, was the only one who returned to Virden to complete his high school education before going onto active service. He reasoned that he would have better credentials for the work force after the war if he had his Senior Matriculation certificate. He was the only one of the six to be killed in action.
>
> As a paperboy in the thirties and then throughout his service career, he helped support his mother with the proceeds of the paper route and also by assigning her part of his pay. He had started as a Private, Second Class but gradually rose through the ranks of NCOs and was sent back from Britain in 1943 to Gordon Head, BC where he took officer training. On his return overseas, he was posted to the Black Watch Regiment in

November of that year. He fought with them and was wounded in action at Caen in Normandy in 1944. Rejoining the regiment after recuperation, he took part in the bloody fighting at Nijmegen where the Allies were attempting to push forward against the Nazis. He was killed by a sniper's bullet in harsh house-to-house fighting in Emmerich. He is buried in the beautifully kept War Graves Cemetery in nearby Groesbeek, where throughout their school years, Dutch children each place a flower annually on the one particular grave they had "adopted" in gratitude to the Canadians who fought for Dutch freedom.

Two of Jimmy's older brothers had attended Normal School in Brandon in the thirties and had been befriended by a British couple who had close relatives in Shoreham-by-Sea near Brighton, England. The relatives took a keen interest in the Koester family, five of whom were in uniform. As each member of the Koester family came to Britain, they were invited to the Shoreham-by-Sea home where "Ma Ken" shared her meagre rations with them. On his first trip to Shoreham, Jimmy got onto the British Rail train and in the compartment was a young woman who saw the regimental tabs on his shoulder and struck up a conversation with him. Eventually she said "I'm Gina Kenward and you are coming to our house for your weekend off." They were married in the summer of 1944, but never had more than a few weekends together. They had no family and Gina kept working throughout the war. Jimmy's death was the most devastating blow of her life. She remained in England, but has kept in constant touch with members of the Koester family, offering generous hospitality to Jimmy's siblings and to his nieces and nephews for the past 50 years when they were visiting England.

Jimmy's name appears in Victoria Park, Virden on the War Memorial which had originally been built to honour those killed in the 1914 – 1918 War. It is also inscribed on the War Memorial in the church in Shoreham where he and Gina had been married.

Yet the continuity of the life cycle was evidenced when his brother Norman and his wife Evelyn, pregnant at the time of Jimmy's death, became the parents of a boy. They called their new-born James Victor Koester after his deceased uncle.

Koester Lake (64 H/1), southwest of Billard Lake was named after him in 1995.

Kokot, Private **William** of Minitonas (B 102735). Hastings and Prince Edward Regiment. He died 17 April 1945 at the age of 21 and is commemorated at the Holten Canadian War Cemetery in Holland. He was the son of Adolf and Lydia Kokot of Minitonas. ***Kokot Lake*** (62 N/15), southeast of Swan River was named after him in 1972.

Kolcun, Private **Peter** of Gilbert Plains (H 103967). Princess Patricia's Canadian Light Infantry. He died 23 May 1944 at the age of 23 and is commemorated at the Cassino War Cemetery in Italy. He was the eldest son of Nick and Cassie Kolcun of Gilbert Plains. His brother writes (19 July 1996):

My brother Peter was born ... near Valley River, Manitoba. He was raised on a farm and did mostly farm work for neighbours as we did not own any land. He had to leave school early to work out and help support us – my mother, three brothers and one sister – as our Dad had passed away in 1928. He was interested in sports, liked to fish and go rabbit hunting.

Kolcun Lake (64 C/4), west of Russell Lake was named after him in 1981.

Koleda, Flying Officer **Peter** of Winnipeg (J 37149). No. 427 Squadron. He died 13 June 1944 at the age of 21 and is commemorated at the Calais Canadian War Cemetery in France. A distant relative reports that because of his youth, his father had to co-sign his attestation papers. After Flying Officer Koleda's death, his mother blamed his father for the tragedy and subsequently had a "nervous breakdown." ***Koleda Lake*** (64 P/8), southeast of Nejanilini Lake was named after him in 1974.

Kolesar, Gunner **Charles** of Winnipeg (H 69860). Royal Canadian Artillery. He died 23 August 1944 at the age of 38 and is commemorated at Bretteville-sur-Laize Canadian War Cemetery in Calvados, France. He was the son of George and Anne Kolesar of Winnipeg. His brother writes (17 January 1996): "... he was born in Neepawa, Manitoba. As a young boy he was interested in Boy Scouts and also played baseball." ***Kolesar Lake*** (63 O/5), southeast of Highrock Lake was named after him in 1973.

Kolesar, Leading Aircraftman **Thomas N.** of Neepawa (R 148593). Service Police, No. 3 Flying Instructor School. He died 16 November 1942 at the age of 21 and is commemorated at Riverside Cemetery in Neepawa. He was the son of Steve and Elsie Kolesar of Neepawa.

He was born and educated at Springhill, Manitoba and on leaving school was employed by Collier's at Winnipeg and later Simpson's Department Store at Toronto. Thomas enlisted in the RCAF in December, 1941 and trained at Toronto, Kingston and Arnprior. He was accidentally killed during guard duties at Arnprior, Ontario (Pittman n.d.).

Kolesar Island (64 F/1) in Barrington Lake was named after him in 1995.

Kolomic, Flying Officer **Johnny P.** of Winnipeg (J 35077). No. 1666 Heavy Conversion Unit, RCAF. He died 11 July 1944 at the age of 20 and is commemorated at Stonefall Cemetery in Yorkshire, England. He was the son of Alexander and Helen Kolomic of Winnipeg. ***Kolomic Lake*** (64 J/10), west of Tadoule Lake was named after him in 1975.

Komarnisky, Rifleman **Walter** of Dauphin (H 41285). Royal Winnipeg Rifles. He died 18 November 1944 at the age of 26 and is commemorated at the Groesbeek Canadian War Cemetery in Holland. He was survived by his mother Annie Komarnisky of Dauphin. He had enlisted 25 May 1940 at Dauphin. ***Komarnisky Lake*** (64 J/7), west of Tadoule Lake was named after him in 1975.

Kontzie, Warrant Officer 1 **Herbert E.** of Waskada (R 101976). No. 458 Squadron. He died 2 August 1943 at the age of 24 and is commemorated at the Alamein Memorial, Egypt. He was the son of Edwin J. and Rose Kontzie of Waskada. ***Kontzie Lake*** (63 K/16), northeast of Reed Lake was named after him in 1973.

Kopp, Flight Sergeant **Benjamin P.** of Rennie (R 80078). No. 104 Squadron. He died 10 May 1942 at the age of 21 and is commemorated at the Alamein Memorial, Egypt. He was the brother of Pilot Officer John W. Kopp (next entry). ***Kopp Lake*** (64 N/10), southwest of Nueltin Lake was named after him in 1972.

Kopp, Pilot Officer **John W.** of Rennie (J 89848). No. 431 Squadron. He died 21 February 1945 at the age of 22 and is commemorated at the Reichswald Forest War Cemetery in Germany. He was the brother of Flight Sergeant Benjamin P. Kopp (previous entry). ***Kopp Island*** (64 F/5) in Reindeer Lake was named after him in 1995.

Korney, Sergeant **Michael** of Dauphin (H 41289). Queen's Own Cameron Highlanders. He died 11 September 1944 and is commemorated at the Adegem Canadian War Cemetery in Belgium. ***Korney Lake*** (64 H/11), northeast of Southern Indian Lake was named after him in 1973.

Korski, Flying Officer **George** of East Braintree (J 26959). No. 160 Squadron. He died 6 May 1944 at the age of 21 and is commemorated at the Singapore Memorial. He was the son of Mr. and Mrs. John Korski of Kings Park, Manitoba. According to his brother (18 May 2001):

> Born Jerzy Korowiakowski in Torczyn, Poland in 1923, George emigrated to Canada with his family in 1926. After the family settled on a farm in Stonewall, Manitoba, George attended Stonewall Collegiate. He quit school in 1941 to volunteer with the Royal Canadian Air Force.

Korski Lake (63 J/12), south of Wekusko Lake was named after him in 1972.

Koscielny, Private **Stanley F.** of Elphinstone (K 47685). Westminster Regiment. He died 22 May 1944 and is commemorated at the Cassino War Cemetery in Italy. He was the youngest son of Joseph and Mary Koscielny of Elphinstone. Private Koscielny received his education at Elphinstone Consolidated School. At age 16, he ran away from home and caught a train to British Columbia. He misrepresented his age once there so he could join the army without his parents' knowledge. ***Koscielny Lake*** (63 K/15), northwest of Elbow Lake was named after him in 1993.

Koscielski, Rifleman **Frank** of Birch River (H 102883). Regina Rifle Regiment. He died 11 September 1944 at the age of 20 and is commemorated at the Calais Canadian War Cemetery in France. He was the son of Mike and Annie Koscielski of Birch River. ***Koscielski Lake*** (64 I/12), northwest of North Knife Lake was named after him in 1974.

Koshelanyk, Private **Walter** of Caliento (B 146196). Royal Regiment of Canada. He died 24 October 1944 at the age of 22 and is commemorated at Bergen-op-Zoom Canadian War Cemetery in Holland. He was the son of Joseph and Helen Koshelanyk of Caliento, Manitoba and was survived by two brothers. Like so many other young men of that time, he was travelling across Canada looking for work. He was in Toronto when he enlisted. ***Koshelanyk Lake*** (64 C/6), north of Russell Lake was named after him in 1995.

Kosteck, Lance Corporal **John A.** of Plumas (H 77041). South Saskatchewan Regiment. He died 5 August 1944 at the age of 22 and is commemorated at Bretteville-sur-Laize Canadian War Cemetery in Calvados, France. He was the son of Joseph and Petronella (Pearl) Kosteck of Plumas, Manitoba. Born in Germakowka, Poland in 1922, he had come to Canada with his parents in 1929. ***Kosteck Lake*** (52 M/3), south of Aikens Lake was named after him in 1982.

Kostyk, Private **Andrew H.** of Transcona (H 20946). Queen's Own Cameron Highlanders. He died 29 August 1944 at the age of 25 and is commemorated at Bretteville-sur-Laize Canadian War Cemetery in Calvados, France. He was one of the 12 children of Fred and Eva Kostyk of Winnipeg and was survived by his wife Mrs. A. Kostyk of Transcona. He had been employed by Swift Meat Packers at the time of his enlistment. He was one of four brothers in the service. ***Kostyk Lake*** (64 K/10), east of Lac Brochet was named after him in 1972.

Kostyk, Lance Corporal **Peter** of Winnipegosis (H 42030). South Saskatchewan Regiment. He died 15 August 1944 at the age of 20 and is commemorated at Beny-sur-Mer Canadian War Cemetery in Calvados, France. He was the son of Mike and Mary Kostyk of Winnipegosis. His sister writes (17 January 1997):

> Peter left home at 16 after completing Grade 12 with Honours. He joined the Armed Forces as jobs were not plentiful. As a young boy he was a kind and considerate person – always helping out those who were in need. He loved animals, birds and all nature. He was always willing to help the elderly, e.g., he often put on storm windows for those who needed assistance.
>
> He loved his family and his love for them showed in always being the helping hand. In days when money was scarce, he managed to buy his baby sister a doll. He was a truly remarkable young man and was loved by those he touched. He was a strong believer in the teachings of his church and never missed Sunday School at Knox Presbyterian Church. His family was very proud of him.

Kostyk Island (53 L/8) in Webber Lake was named after him in 1995.

Kotchapaw, Lieutenant **William J.** of Winnipeg (CDN 270). King's Shropshire Light Infantry. He died 10 September 1944 at the age of 20 and is commemorated at the Groesbeek Canadian War Cemetery in Holland. He was the son of William G. and Bessie A. Kotchapaw of Winnipeg. ***Kotchapaw Lake*** (64 H/9), southeast of North Knife Lake was named after him in 1963.

Kotenko, Sergeant **William** of Winnipeg (H 17398). 1st Canadian Special Services Battalion. He died 3 December 1943 at the age of 20 and is commemorated at the Cassino War Cemetery in Italy. He was the son of Peter and Mary Kotenko of Winnipeg. ***Kotenko Lake*** (63 I/7), north of Molson Lake was named after him in 1973.

Kotowich, Private **Walter** of Winnipeg (H 43320). Essex Scottish Regiment. He died 19 February 1945 at the age of 20 and is commemorated at the Groesbeek Memorial in Holland. He was the son of John and Wanda Kotowich of East Kildonan. According to his brother (28 April 1998):

> Walter was born March 9, 1924 in East Kildonan. [He] received all of his education in East Kildonan at Polson, Prince Edward and Lord Wolseley schools. He enlisted in May, 1943 and trained for over a year in Canada, landing overseas in October, 1944.

Kotowich Lake (63 O/4), north of Wekusko Lake was named after him in 1970.

Kouk, Private **Henry** of Elmwood (H 3760). Royal Canadian Army Medical Corps. He died 18 January 1945 and is commemorated at Faenza War Cemetery in Italy. He was the son of Rudolph and Anna Kouk of Winnipeg. ***Kouk Lake*** (64 P/9), east of Nejanilini Lake was named after him in 1974.

Kovacs, Private **Alexander J.** of Winnipeg (H 42203). Irish Regiment of Canada. He died 24 February 1944 at the age of 19 and is commemorated at Caserta War Cemetery, Italy. He was the son of Florian and Julia Kovacs. ***Kovacs Lake*** (64 F/1), west of Melvin Lake was named after him in 1984.

Kowalchuk, Private **Peter** of Teulon (H 3709). Lanark and Renfrew Scottish Regiment. He died 31 December 1944 at the age of 24 and is commemorated at Villanova Canadian War Cemetery, Italy. He was the son of Marko and Isabella Kowalchuk of Teulon. His sister recalls (26 April 1995):

> He was a very good-natured person with an outgoing personality and a great sense of humour. His main sport was baseball and in those days everyone played horseshoes. He was only 18 when he went overseas, so he really didn't have time to do many things. His time here was so short. I'm sure the younger generation have no idea of the heartbreak war is.

Kowalchuk Lake (52 L/11), south of Black Lake was named after him in 1982.

Kozack, Gunner **Alexander** of Rossburn (H 67144). Royal Canadian Artillery. He died 11 October 1944 at the age of 28 and is commemorated at the Adegem Canadian War Cemetery in Belgium. He was the son of George and Irene Kozack (née Konyk) of Rossburn. ***Kozack Island*** (64 I/3) in North Knife Lake was named after him in 1995.

Kozak, Private **Stephen** of Scandinavia, Manitoba (H 37163). Royal Canadian Ordnance Corps. He died 12 March 1943 at the age of 33 and is commemorated at Brookwood Military Cemetery in Surrey, England. He was the son of David and Lillie Kozak and was survived by his wife Mary Kozak of Winnipeg. ***Kozak Lake*** (64 I/5), south of Shethanei Lake was named after him in 1974.

Koziarski, Lance Corporal **Edward Brownie** of Winnipeg (H 59577). Lanark and Renfrew Scottish Regiment. He died 6 October 1944 at the age of 25 and is commemorated at Cesena War Cemetery in Italy. He was the son of Mr. and Mrs. Frank Koziarski of Winnipeg and was survived by his wife Margaret Koziarski of Winnipeg. ***Koziarski Lake*** (64 O/1), south of Munroe Lake was named after him in 1975.

Krahn, Pilot Officer **George C.** of Winkler (J 85031). No. 415 Squadron. He died 13 June 1944 at the age of 24 and is commemorated at Flushing (Vlissingen) Northern Cemetery, Holland. He was the son of Cornelius B. and Maria Krahn of Winkler. His brother recalls (12 May 1984):

> George's parents immigrated to Canada from Russia in 1923. The family settled in the Winkler (Reinland) area. His father ... was a Minister in the Blumenorter Mennonite Church. George grew up in Reinland, a typical farm boy, with seven of his siblings. George completed elementary school in Reinland, took Grades 9, 10 and 11 in Winkler and Grade 12 at the MCI in Gretna, Manitoba. After graduating from high school until he joined the Air Force September 10, 1941, he worked as a clerk for his brother-in-law, Mr. A. C. Penner who was a general merchant in Arnaud, Manitoba.
>
> In Canada, George trained with the RCAF in Brandon, Macdonald, Saskatoon, Virden and got his pilot's wings in Dauphin. He also trained in Charlottetown, PEI and Victoria, BC and was posted overseas in the spring of 1943. In England, George was a member of the Swordfish Squadron. This squadron specialized in night operations against the enemy's light naval forces, particularly E- and R-boats in the English Channel and the southern part of the North Sea. The E-boat was a high-speed motor torpedo boat used by the enemy for attacks on coastal shipping. The R-boat was a small motor boat similar to the E-boat but slower and used for minesweeping and defensive escort of the E-boats as well as shipping. It carried anti-aircraft armament but no torpedoes.
>
> The Swordfish Squadron commenced its operational career as a Hampden torpedo-bomber unit in the spring of 1942 and changed over to Wellingtons (Wimpies) and Albacores in October, 1943. Night after night, the Wimpies (including P/O Krahn and his crew of six, co-operating with naval forces) patrolled over the North Sea on the watch for enemy convoys and E-boats while the Albacores maintained a lookout for shipping boats attempting to steal through the Straits of Dover during the hours of darkness. Many attacks were made on targets ranging from merchant vessels and destroyers to fleet little motor boats. Sometimes, specific results – a direct hit, explosions or fires – could be observed, but more frequently the darkness of the night and the violent evasive action necessary to avoid the intense flak barrages made it impossible for the crews to determine the outcome of their bomb attacks. P/O Krahn's experienced crew participated in many of these offensive activities successfully, but on the night of June 12, 1944, they had sighted and attacked a large group of E-boats in the neighbourhood of Ostend, and the Wimpy presumably was a victim of the intense flak concentration. His and two of his crew members' bodies were recovered by the Dutch Red Cross July 13, 1944 on the shore near the village of Zoutelande. P/O Krahn was buried on the 14th of July, 1944 in the graveyard called De Noorderbergraafplaats in the town of Vlissingen (Flushing). The activities of the Swordfish Squadron are detailed in a book called *The RCAF Overseas* (Royal Canadian Air Force 1949).

In a letter to his brother, he wrote:

> Hello Fred: I received your airgraph today. Thanks a lot. Look, *you* should talk about writing home and being worried about me out here. I've written twice as many letters home as I've received. When you get two or three ... at a time, you answer it with one.
>
> What I was going to write about mostly though, was that I received the Christmas parcel today. I guess it must have gone to the wrong squadron or something to take all this time. Anyway, I got it and I want to thank my parents for it. Seeing as I've written them two letters last week already, I'll have to make this letter do and you can thank them for me.
>
> I'm still getting along fine. I'm doing quite a bit of skating here. Last week we played two hockey games against different stations and we trimmed them on both occasions. Our team has seven players of my crew on it. In other words, every one of my crew is a good hockey player and can form a team of our own. Did you beat Winkler in the game you wrote you were going to have? Well old boy, this will have to do for now so cheerio and love to [you all] (14 March 1944).

Krahn Lake (64 K/16), northeast of Lac Brochet was named after him in 1972.

Kram, Pilot Officer **Meryn** of Winnipeg (J 43740). No. 86 Operational Training Unit, RCAF. He died 30 August 1944 at the age of 20 and is commemorated at Stonefall Cemetery in Yorkshire, England. He was the son of Leon and Anne Kram of Winnipeg. ***Kram Lake*** (64 O/7), northwest of Munroe Lake was named after him in 1975.

Krasnuik, Lance Corporal **Anthony** (H 16745). Canadian Provost Corps. He died 31 May 1944 and is commemorated at the Cassino War Cemetery in Italy. ***Krasnuik Lake*** (64 K/7), northeast of Reindeer Lake was named after him in 1972.

Krasny, Corporal **Walter** of Winnipeg (H 3025). Princess Patricia's Canadian Light Infantry. He died 25 January 1944 and is commemorated at the Moro River Canadian War Cemetery in Italy. ***Krasny Lake*** (63 K/13), east of Embury Lake was named after him in 1988.

Krause, Warrant Officer 2 **Joseph A.** of Altona (R 59132). No. 7 Squadron. He died 25 August 1942 at the age of 21 and is commemorated at Secheval Communal Cemetery, Ardennes, France.

> On June 21, 1941, WO Krause had made a forced landing in his #15 OTU aircraft off Audglas, Spain. He was interned in Spain for nearly a year and then returned to Gibraltar on April 11, 1942 (Allison and Hayward 1991).

Krause Lake (64 J/12), west of Tadoule Lake was named after him in 1975.

Krolman, Lieutenant **Norman M.** of Winnipeg. Three Rivers Tank Regiment. He died 23 May 1944 at the age of 24 and is commemorated at the Cassino War Cemetery in Italy. He was the eldest child of Martin and Emily Krolman of Winnipeg and was survived by his wife Meryl F. Krolman (née Smith). Like virtually all boys his age, Norman liked hockey and after enrolling at the University of Manitoba in 1939, he joined the team. According to a newspaper account, he excelled at the sport:

> Led by Norm Krolman, an unknown youngster who played his first Varsity hockey game Friday night, University of Manitoba took University of Minnesota hockey team into camp by the score 3-2. Krolman, gangling second string centre player, scored two of the Brown and Gold goals and played a sound all around game for the winners (*Winnipeg Tribune* 29 January 1940).

He enlisted in the Canadian Officer Training Corps while in a second year pre-med program at the University of Manitoba (March 1942) and was sent overseas that autumn. His wife recalls that while on a nine day leave, he married his college sweetheart, Meryl Frances Smith, also of Winnipeg. Both families had cottages at Gimli where they met while they were growing up. After over a year in Britain, he was transferred to the tank regiment for battle experience in Italy before the D-Day invasion. There he lost his life in a fierce tank battle between Pontecorvo and Aquino. A fellow officer, Major D. C. MacCallum wrote afterwards:

> Norm and I were in the same Brigade together in England and came to Italy on the same exchange. He became a troop leader in the same Squadron and was very much loved by all the ranks. His men feel his absence keenly (n.d.).

A letter from Captain D. S. Whiteford of his regiment indicated that:

> We served together in the Fort Garry Horse and came out here together. I have never met a more sincere and straight shooting man than Norm. He was liked by all, he was a real leader, he had the respect and friendship of his men, he was every inch a man, a soldier and officer.
>
> All I can do is state facts as I know them. We were both in the same action; we had destroyed one of Hitler's lines and were sent to aid an English armoured unit in difficulty against Hitler's second line. We were put in a tough spot. Here Norm got it, he got it fighting, he was leading his troops, he was responsible for success. Norm did not suffer. He is buried in a decent grave with his crew between Pontecorvo and Aquino. A few days later we were pulled out for a couple of day's rest – the Regiment held a ceremonial parade in full strength. Formed up in review order, the Colonel spoke, observed two minutes silence and then a church service (n.d.).

His wife adds (27 November 2001):

> Besides his wife, he left to mourn his loss his father and mother, his sister Marjorie Powell and his brother Dr. Gordon Krolman. Norm always wanted to be a Doctor, so his dream was fulfilled when his brother became an eye surgeon.
>
> Some years after World War II was over, his wife Meryl married a fellow officer Major Vernon Eriksson, also of the Fort Garry Horse. They went to Normandy for the 50th anniversary of the D-Day landing of the Fort Garry Horse Regiment. Vern Eriksson landed there on D-Day and fought with tanks through France, Holland and into Germany where he commanded the first squadron of Canadian tanks on to German soil during World War II.

Krolman Lake (53 E/16), north of Island Lake was named after Lieutenant Krolman in 1961.

Kropelnicki, Private **Philip** of Sifton (H 37366). Royal Canadian Army Service Corps. He died 11 June 1945 at the age of 27 and is commemorated at Sifton (Holy Trinity) Church Cemetery. He was the son of Paul and Antoslika Kropelnicki of Sifton. His sister recalls (13 June 2000):

> Philip loved the outdoors, loved the animals and the birds. In his early years, if he noticed a nest in the tree, he would climb the tree and if there were any eggs or young birds he would build a platform by the nest and always leave food for the birds; he continued to do it throughout his adulthood. The greatest love for the animals were snakes and frogs.
>
> He also was interested in honey bees. We had two neighbours that had honey bees. He would spend a lot of time with the beekeepers. Then he purchased a few hives and extracted the honey which he was able to sell in the neighbourhood.
>
> Many times he would bring wounded animals home and nurse them back to health and let them go back to the wild. Philip said when the war is over he will be back and build an animal shelter. I am sure he would have done so.

Kropelnicki Lake (53 M/14), northwest of Hubley Lake was named after him in 1996.

Krynski, Pilot Officer **Tony** of Gilbert Plains (J 90926). No. 460 Squadron. He died 28 June 1944 at the age of 20 and is commemorated at the Runnymede Memorial in Surrey, England. He was the son of Joseph and Elizabeth Krynski of Kemnay, Manitoba. This native of Tuczna, Poland immigrated to Canada with his parents in 1930. ***Krynski Lake*** (64 P/16), northeast of Nejanilini Lake was named after him in 1974.

Krysowaty, Private **Stephen "Sam"** of Shoal Lake (H 17829). Princess Patricia's Canadian Light Infantry. He died 23 May 1944 at the age of 29 and is commemorated at the Cassino War Cemetery in Italy. He was the son of Stephen and Sofia Krysowaty (née Sicharska) and was survived by his wife Mary M. Krysowaty of Shoal Lake. ***Krysowaty Lake*** (64 I/3), west of North Knife Lake was named after him in 1974.

Krywiarchuk, Private **Philip** of Winnipeg (H 14867). Essex Scottish Regiment. He died 13 August 1944 and is commemorated at Bretteville-sur-Laize Canadian War Cemetery in Calvados, France. ***Krywiarchuk Lake*** (64 O/9), northwest of Nejanilini Lake was named after him in 1975.

Kucera, Lance Corporal **Anthony J.** of Winnipeg (H 14476). Royal Winnipeg Rifles. He died 27 April 1945 at the age of 20 and is commemorated at the Holten Canadian War Cemetery in Holland. He was the son of Frank and Anna Kucera of Winnipeg. His mother received a letter from his commanding officer:

> Dear Mrs. Kucera: As your son's Company Commander, I want to write to you and offer my heartfelt sympathy to you in this, your great loss. Your son was a fine man and a good soldier. I was very close to him when he happened to be hit. At the time, the enemy artillery fire was heavy and several more boys received hits. We went on and gained one objective, silencing the guns. He had just been made a Lance Corporal and was doing a fine job. Please accept my condolences and those of the boys that knew your son. Sincerely, A. J. Cotton, Major (9 May 1945).

His brother recalls (20 December 2001):

> Anthony was the fourth son of Frank Kucera and Anna Kveton(ova). Born in East Kildonan, he grew up in Elmwood on Poplar Avenue and was a member of St. Alphonsus Church. Tony started school at the outbreak of the Great Depression. Having Czech parents, he was bilingual. He attended Lord Selkirk High School and St. John's Tech. Excelling in shops, he crafted his own skis. As a teenager, he had an interest in gardening, particularly in growing large watermelons – not common in the area at that time. He would walk miles, as far as Bird's Hill to go berry picking – particularly for Saskatoons.
>
> Before and while he was employed by Imperial Electric, he had a hobby of raising canaries, hoping eventually to crossbreed tame birds with wild goldfinches. For this purpose he built a number of his own flight cages and nesting boxes. When he enlisted, he left the canaries to a younger brother (not successfully). We still have a tree swallow birdhouse made out of a hollowed-out log – one of a number of his endeavours.
>
> I visited the cemetery at Holten in June of 1998, 53 years later. While there, a small yellow bird flew directly over my brother's grave and just past the central monument.

Kucera Lake (64 I/1), northeast of Etawney Lake was named after him in 1974.

Kullberg, Flight Sergeant **Elmer N.** of Brandon (R 162250). No. 619 Squadron. He died 22 June 1944 at the age of 23 and is commemorated at Rheinberg War Cemetery in Germany. He was the son of Nels S. and Anna E. Kullberg of Brandon. His younger sister recalls (29 July 1996):

> He was born November 24, 1920 in Brandon, Manitoba to Swedish parents. Both Mother and Dad immigrated to Canada in the 1910s (Mother in 1919, after World War I). They were married in Winnipeg during the 1919 strike and came to Brandon for their honeymoon and to live. Dad had a job upholstering here.
>
> Elmer was raised in Brandon. He took his elementary schooling at Park School and then Earl Oxford Junior High. Elmer wasn't the greatest scholar and left school after the 9th grade. What he did excel at was a jovial personality. He had a "Great Gildersleeve" (Fibber McGee and Molly) laugh, one that would bring anybody out of the doldrums. He belonged to First Presbyterian Church. He went up the scouting ranks from cub to King's Scout. He had a problem with weight but did manage to find a belt that fit him – which he wore at special functions and parades.
>
> He belonged to the Presbyterian young people and was always "centre stage" when they put on play. He was a salesman in Dad's furniture store. It was said of him he was such a good salesman he could sell the shirt off a customer's back. He had a lovely baritone voice and sang in the choir and at musical events in the city. Some of his chums are still living and have frequently told me he was a wonderful, reliable friend.
>
> Instead of being conscripted, Elmer joined the Air Force in 1942 (I believe). Before he went overseas – or was it on a leave – it was Easter – and when I came down for breakfast there was a brand new bike for me in the kitchen. He had sold his and with his pay he got me my first bike. I recall him being a terrible tease – yet he loved his family. Two days after he was reported missing (June 22/44) a parcel came in the mail for me. He had been on leave and bought me a ruby necklace. That was the last we ever heard from him.

Kullberg Lake (64 J/16), north of Tadoule Lake was named after him in 1975.

Kustra, Gunner **Jack** of Dauphin (H 100574). Royal Canadian Artillery, British Empire Medal. He died 22 November 1944 and is commemorated at the Groesbeek Canadian War Cemetery in Holland. He was the son of Mr. and Mrs. Joseph Kustra. ***Kustra Lake*** (64 F/16), west of Big Sand Lake was named after him in 1961.

Kuzenko, Able Seaman **Harry W.** of Winnipeg (V 60369). HMCS *Shediac*. He died 17 November 1944 at the age of 20 and is commemorated at the Halifax Memorial. He was the son of John and Pear Kuzenko of Winnipeg. Reportedly, before enlisting he said to his mother: "If I don't go to protect my country, the Germans will come and we won't have food on our table." ***Kuzenko Lake*** (64 N/8), south of Nueltin Lake was named after him in 1972.

Kuzina, Rifleman **Mike** of Cloverleaf (H 204672). Regina Rifle Regiment. He died 16 August 1944 at the age of 25 and is commemorated at Bretteville-sur-Laize Canadian War Cemetery in Calvados, France. He was the son of John and Nettie Kuzina of Winnipeg. ***Kuzina Lake*** (64 K/16), northeast of Lac Brochet was named after him in 1972.

Kwasny, Flight Sergeant **William** of Teulon (R 134910). No. 408 Squadron. He died 17 April 1943 at the age of 21 and is commemorated at Florennes Communal Cemetery, Florennes, Namur, Belgium. He was the youngest of the four sons of Lukas and Catherine Kwasny of Teulon. His niece writes (13 February 1998):

> Bill Kwasny was born February 15, 1923 on the family farm located four miles south of the town of Teulon. He grew up on the farm and attended McMillan elementary school and the Teulon High School. He enlisted in the RCAF during his last year of high school.
>
> Besides doing farm chores, Bill liked to play baseball, his favourite sport at the time. He also loved horseback riding which he did a lot of. He had a real love to fly and would always watch the planes from the Gimli airbase as their route was over the family farm. He had a great sense of humour and was always playing practical jokes on family members or just being foolish. At the time of his demise he was single but did have a school sweetheart.

Kwasny Lake (64 P/8), east of Nejanilini Lake was named after him in 1974.

Kwiatkowski, Private **Edward P.** of Garson (H 8144). Royal Canadian Regiment. He died 26 January 1944 at the age of 22 and is commemorated at the Moro River Canadian War Cemetery in Italy. He was the son of James K. and Annie Kwiatkowski of Garson, Manitoba. ***Kwiatkowski Lake*** (64 K/16), northeast of Lac Brochet was named after him in 1972.

Kyle, Corporal **James F.** of Novra (H 17557). Royal Winnipeg Rifles. He died 8 June 1944 at the age of 19 and is commemorated at Beny-sur-Mer Canadian War Cemetery in Calvados, France. He was the son of Harry and Jean Kyle of Novra, Manitoba. ***Kyle Lake*** (62 N/15), southeast of Swan River was named after him in 1973.

Kyle, Flight Sergeant **William T.** of Winnipeg (R 71497). No. 17 Squadron. He died 20 February 1942 at the age of 20 and is commemorated at Sutton Coldfield New Cemetery, Warwickshire, England. ***Kyle Bay*** (64 I/12) in Fersman Lake was named after him in 1995.

Kyle, Flight Sergeant **Wilton H.** of Winnipeg (R 106142). Royal Air Force Ferry Command. He died 9 February 1943 at the age of 22 and is commemorated at Gander Cemetery, Newfoundland. He was the son of Harold W. and Lucille Kyle of Winnipeg. ***Kyle Island*** (63 P/11) in Partridge Crop Lake was named after him in 1995.

Personnel of the Women's Royal Canadian Naval Service (WRCNS) embarking for the United Kingdom, February, 1944.
Courtesy of the National Archives of Canada (PA-108181).

L

La Bossière, Flight Sergeant **Jules J.** of St. Vital (R 119546). No. 12 Operational Training Unit, RCAF. He died 16 September 1942 at the age of 26 and is commemorated at the Groesbeek Canadian War Cemetery in Holland. He was one of the 12 children of Alex J. and Juliette Labossiere (sp.; née Savoie) of St. Vital. According to his brother (18 December 2000):

Jules had two brothers in the RCAF and one in the Navy who all served in Canada and overseas. He also left at home six sisters and two young brothers. He went to school in Somerset, St. Boniface and Fannystelle, Manitoba.

In 1938, Jules and his family moved to St. Vital. From that time on, Jules worked for different firms until he went to work for the CNR and was employed by the same company when he enlisted in the RCAF. Jules was devoted to his family and friends. Personable and well liked by everyone who knew him. He loved sports; he played hockey and baseball.

Jules' roots in Canada are long and firmly planted. Canada was his country, the country he loved and died for. Jules' body lies in Nijmegen, Holland. His spirit will live forever in the lake named after him in Manitoba, Canada.

Jules was an 8th generation Canadian on his father's side. First generation J. B. La Bossiere born in Nantes, France in 1695 came to Quebec in 1718 as a Subaltern Infantry Officer. Jules' grandfather Joseph LaBossiere, a 6th generation Canadian, came to Manitoba from Quebec in 1879. He obtained a homestead on 33-4-9 near St. Leon, Manitoba. The same land was still being farmed by Denis LaBossiere, a descendant in 1999. Jules was a 10th generation Canadian on his mother's side. Francoie Savoie came to New France (Port Royal, Acadia) around 1669. J. B. Savoie, Jules' grandfather moved to Ste. Anne from Quebec in the late 1800s.

Jules' uncle, Joe Savoie, was a fighter pilot in the 1914 to 1918 war. The name of General LaBossiere is written on the Arc of Triumph of Paris along with the name of the great Marshals and generals of Emperor Napoleon.

La Bossière Lake (64 P/4), south of Nejanilini Lake was named after him in 1974.

Lacerte, Flying Officer **Charles H.** of St. Boniface (J 10877). No. 5 Operational Training Unit, RCAF. He died 7 October 1942 at the age of 19 and is commemorated at Dunure Cemetery, Ayrshire, Scotland. He was the son of Origene and Charlotte Lacerte of Winnipeg. His sister writes. (23 March 1998):

My brother's full name was Charles Henri Lacerte, born April 5, 1923 in St. Boniface Hospital. He attended Provencher School for eight grades, then went to St. Boniface College, run by Jesuits for four years of high school. He was a Boy Scout while in grade school, liked baseball, hockey and swimming, and was also an altar boy for many years.

He enrolled in the Air Force right out of high school and took his first training in Paulson, Manitoba. He went on to Regina and Calgary to Bombing and Gunnery School before going overseas in May of 1942. He had further training in Dunmuir, Scotland as a rear air gunner and was on a training mission on October 7, 1942 when the plane developed trouble and the eight airmen aboard had to bail out over the ocean. He was the only one who didn't make it. He was an expert swimmer – he could swim across the Red River in Winnipeg in October.

They didn't tell us the exact cause of death. He was a Flying Officer at 19 1/2 at the time of his death. We received pictures of his funeral from a chaplain we had known for many years. His personal effects were also sent to us.

Lacerte Lake (64 I/7), northeast of North Knife Lake was named after him in 1974.

La Croix, Sergeant **George Richard** of Winnipeg (H 17245). 1st Canadian Parachute Battalion. He died 6 June 1944 at the age of 26 and is commemorated at St. Vaast-en-Auge Churchyard, Calvados, France. He was survived by his wife Elva O. La Croix (née Bruce) of Sturgeon Valley, Saskatchewan and their two children. According to his daughter (9 January 1998):

"Dick's" father was a Pharmacist who owned a drugstore in Marcelin, Saskatchewan, however, his father died in the big flu epidemic of 1918. Dick was eight months old at the time. He had two older sisters. The children were put in a convent and their mother, who was a nurse, went to work. He received a good education in the convent and grew up speaking both English and French.

He worked in a bank in Canwood, Saskatchewan after leaving school and it was there that he met his wife Elva Bruce of Sturgeon Valley, Saskatchewan. They were married and had two children. Dick loved to read and had learned to play the piano while in the convent. He was a loving husband and father and wrote many letters to his family while he was in training and while he was overseas.

Dick served with the Canadian Army (Militia) from April 11 to May 9, 1940 when he enlisted in the Princess Patricia's Canadian Light Infantry in Winnipeg. He transferred to the 1st Canadian Parachute Battalion on September 24, 1942 and was sent overseas on July 30, 1943. He was killed in action on June 6, 1944 – D-Day.

He wrote many letters home to his three year-old daughter:

Dearest Arlene: Received your letters today Sissy and thanks very much for the lovely pictures you drew. Hope you are being a good girl and that Dale is a good boy and that you eat your meals all up so that you will grow up and be a big girl and keep healthy. Give Mummy and Dale a big hug and kiss for me. I miss you very much Sissy and miss Mummy and Dale an awful lot too. Bye-bye for now honey. Sure wish I could be home with you. Love and kisses, Daddy (26 October 1942).

Dearest "Sissy:" Hello Arlene darling. Thank you for the letters you wrote to me dear. I liked them very much and always look for a letter from you. I sure miss you an awful lot Arlene and love you. I miss Mummy and Dale an awful lot too. Give them a hug and kiss for me, dear and tell them I miss them and love them.

Hope you are just fine and having lots of fun. Also, that Mummy and Dale are fine. I'm well. Can Dale talk yet and is he a good boy? I know you're a good girl and hope you eat your meals all up. Write to me again dear and give me all the news. Am sending a picture I drew for you and hope you like it. Bye bye for now Arlene dearest and tonight say a prayer for me (21 November 1942).

La Croix Lake (63 O/5), southeast of Highrock Lake was named after him in 1973.

Lafontaine, Private **Frank** of The Pas (H 102692). Queen's Own Cameron Highlanders. He died 21 July 1944 and is commemorated at Bretteville-sur-Laize Canadian War Cemetery in Calvados, France. He was the son of Joseph and Tillie Lafontaine of The Pas, Manitoba. ***Lafontaine Lake*** (64 C/9), southeast of Reindeer Lake was named after him in 1973.

Lafontaine, Private **Joseph** of The Pas (H 102246). Calgary Highlanders. He died 24 December 1944 and is commemorated at the Groesbeek Canadian War Cemetery in Holland. He was the son of Joseph and Tillie Lafontaine of The Pas, Manitoba. ***Lafontaine Island*** (64 C/9) in Eden Lake was named after him in 1995.

Laforte, Rifleman **Philip** of Pine Falls (H 41868). Royal Winnipeg Rifles. He died 7 April 1945 and is commemorated at the Holten Canadian War Cemetery in Holland. ***Laforte Creek*** (54 E/15), which flows northeast into the Croswell River was named after him in 1964.

Lagimodière, Sergeant **Donald R.** of Lorette (R 101688). No. 311 Operational Training Unit, RCAF. He died 13 September 1942 at the age of 21 and is commemorated at the Ottawa Memorial. He was the son of A. Lagimodière (MM) and Hester Lagimodière of Lorette, Manitoba. ***Lagimodière Lake*** (63 O/4), west of Setting Lake was named after him in 1979.

Lahoda, Private **Walter R.** of Winnipeg (H 10906). Lake Superior Regiment. He died 15 February 1945 and is commemorated at the Groesbeek Canadian War Cemetery in Holland. ***Lahoda Lake*** (52 L/3), northeast of Brereton Lake was named after him in 1973.

Laing, Private **Andrew J.** of Miami, Manitoba (H 19124). Queen's Own Cameron Highlanders. He died 19 August 1942 at the age of 23 and is commemorated at the Adegem Canadian War Cemetery in Belgium. He was the son of Alexander J. and Janet B. Laing of Winnipeg. ***Laing Bay*** (63 N/10) in Flatrock Lake was named after him in 1995.

Laing, Ordinary Seaman **Wallace W.** of Winnipeg (V 66845). HMCS *Alberni*. The *Alberni* was torpedoed and sunk by U-480, southeast of the Isle of Wight; 59 of her ship's company were lost. Ordinary Seaman Laing died 21 August 1944 at the age of 20 and is commemorated at the Halifax Memorial. He was the son of John A. and Mary M. Laing (née Waddell) of Winnipeg. ***Laing Lake*** (64 N/7), southwest of Nueltin Lake was named after him in 1972.

Laird, Bombardier **Douglas W.** of Winnipeg (H 12141). Royal Canadian Artillery. He died 14 August 1944 at the age of 25 and is commemorated at Bretteville-sur-Laize Canadian War Cemetery in Calvados, France. He was the son of Reginald W. and Nettie May Laird of Winnipeg. ***Laird Island*** (64 O/9) in Gayoway Lake was named after him in 1995.

Laird, Squadron Leader **George J.** of Winnipeg (J 4896). No. 427 Squadron, Distinguished Flying Cross.

> Rear gunner (P/O Jack Findlay, Toronto) and English wireless operator were killed in the Kassel incident when aircraft was half-way to target; night fighter raked Halifax from below. Aircraft caught fire; Laird did steep turn and lost 4000 feet but fire went out. Intercom knocked out and he learned by shouted reports that two were dead. Bomb aimer (Sergeant Joe Corbally, Toronto) unable to jettison bombs but fighter had shot away a cable that held 2000-pound "cookie" and during violent evasive action it fell off. Corbally checked for damage and applied tourniquet to Cardy. Mid-upper gunner (P/O James Moffat) found nine German bullets in the airplane, one of which passed between his own guns. While fire lasted in bomb bay, the mid-upper gunner could not see for flame and smoke but continued to direct evasive action. Navigator (Sergeant George Lorimer, Vancouver) laid down direct course for home and kept lookout in nose. Struggled home and advised by control tower to bail out. Cardy had been badly wounded (right arm and eye) and had been losing consciousness; Laird refused to commit him to a parachute and got permission to land. With hydraulics shot away and unable to lock down undercarriage, Cardy regained consciousness enough to direct axe and hack-saw work that finally got the wheels down. After touch-down the crew crawled clear just as incendiaries began to burn (Public Relations release of DFC award 1943).

He died 31 March 1944 at the age of 29 and is commemorated at Hotton War Cemetery in Luxembourg, Belgium. He was the son of George J. and Isabella M. Laird of Winnipeg and was survived by his wife Elma Laird. ***Laird Point*** (63 I/1) on Holenchuk Lake was named after him in 1996.

Laird, Trooper **Harry T.** of Winnipeg (H 63807). 17th Duke of York's Hussars (H 63807). He died 1 January 1944 at the age of 19 and is commemorated at Brookwood Military Cemetery in Surrey, England. He was the son of James and Rebecca M. Laird of Winnipeg. ***Laird Bay*** (64 I/11) in Noguy Lake was named after him in 1995.

Laird, Lieutenant **Wilson James** of Pilot Mound. South Saskatchewan Regiment. He died 23 October 1944 at the age of 25 and is commemorated at Bergen-op-Zoom Canadian War Cemetery in Holland. He was one of the seven children of Louis C. and Maude Laird (née Tait) and was survived by his wife of one month Doris Pat Laird (née Hall) of Toronto. His nephew writes (4 January 1998):

> He enjoyed drawing and writing as a boy. Mother states he always notated on the side of his drawing or writings how long it took him to do it. After completing school, he worked for a lawyer in Pilot Mound and intended to go to university to be a lawyer.

A newspaper obituary added that:

> He enlisted with the Winnipeg Grenadiers the day war was declared and served in Jamaica 16 months. He was attached to the commando force on his return to Winnipeg, training at Megantic, Quebec, finishing his training in England in October, 1942. He returned to Canada as an instructor at Prince Rupert and Courtney, BC, and then went back to England with the South Saskatchewan Regiment. He was commissioned at Aldershot (n.d.).

Laird Lake (53 L/11), west of Gods Lake was named after him in 1962.

Lake, Flight Sergeant **John W.** of Winnipeg (R 134599). No. 100 Squadron. He died 12 June 1943 at the age of 23 and is commemorated at Voorst (Terwolde) General Cemetery, Holland. He was the son of Harry and Lily A. Lake of Fort Rouge. ***Lake Island*** (64 H/5) in Missinipi Lake was named after him in 1995.

Lalor, Pilot Officer **Fintan H.** of Pine Falls (J 22229). No. 34 Operational Training Unit, RCAF. He died 13 March 1943 at the age of 21 and is commemorated at the Ottawa Memorial. He was the son of Patrick M. and Myrtle E. Lalor (née Wright) of Pine Falls, Manitoba. His brother writes (18 October 1995):

> Born November 16, 1921 at Welwyn, Saskatchewan. Commenced his schooling at Pine Falls, Manitoba to which community the family had moved in 1927. In 1936 he entered St. Paul's College High School in Winnipeg and there, in 1937, received the Governor General's Award for scholastic achievement. Following his graduation from high school, Fintan continued his education and completed two years of Science with a view toward entering medical college. During this period, Fintan became well known for both his scholastic and athletic ability. He was a better-than-average football player and boxer and his proficiency as a swimmer always assured him of summer employment as a lifeguard. He was also a fair musician, his favourite instruments being the banjo and violin.
>
> In 1939, Fintan, because of financial circumstances, was forced to take what he thought would be a temporary leave from his studies and take an office position with the Manitoba Paper Company at Pine Falls. He would remain in this position until a sense of duty to his country led him to enlist as a navigator in the Royal Canadian Air Force. He graduated from the school of navigation at Rivers, Manitoba in the winter of 1942 and there received his commission. Fintan, along with his crew went missing over the Bay of Fundy in March of 1943.

Lalor Lake (63 K/16), northwest of Wekusko Lake was named after him in 1973.

Lambert, Squadron Leader **James F.** of Winnipeg (J 15212). No. 421 Squadron. He died 20 December 1943 at the age of 26 and is commemorated at Cambrai (Route de Solesmes) Communal Cemetery, Nord, France. He was the son of Archie N. and Jessie Lambert of Winnipeg and was survived by his wife Peggy M. Lambert of Winnipeg. ***Lambert Lake*** (64 C/2), south of Granville Lake was named after him in 1995.

Lamirande, Rifleman **Gabriel** of St. Vital (H 41224). Royal Winnipeg Rifles. He died 14 April 1945 at the age of 35 and is commemorated at the Holten Canadian War Cemetery in Holland. He had enlisted in 1940 and served alongside his younger brother until he fell. ***Lamirande Lake*** (64 G/4), south of Grandmother Lake was named after him in 1994.

Lamont, Pilot Officer **Douglas P.** of Minto (J 24630). He was lost at sea when the Danish troop transport ship MV *Amerika* was torpedoed. He was presumed dead 22 April 1943 at the age of 24 and is commemorated at the Ottawa Memorial. He was the son of Daniel P. and Agnes M. Lamont of Minto, Manitoba. Prior to enlisting he had worked as a research officer with the Federal Department of Agriculture in Brandon. ***Lamont Bay*** (64 N/4) in Quasso Lake was named after him in 1995.

Lamont, Aircraftman 2 **Orville A.** of Brandon (R 258908). No. 2 Manning Depot. He died 3 July 1943 at the age of 19 and is commemorated at Brandon Cemetery. He was the son of Wallace M. and Isobel Lamont of Brandon. His sister recalls (18 January 1996):

The lilacs were in full bloom the time of the year our brother came into the world. That was June 5, 1924. The place was Virden, Manitoba. Our parents ... named him Orville Alvin. I was then ten years old and when Mother was busy, Orville became my personal charge. He would call for his "udder mama." He was an active, happy, loving little fellow.

As a young boy, he made fleets of airplanes and he and his little friends made pretend flights to many places in the world, all in our back yard. He would work for hours with a piece of wood and a jack-knife, to make a propeller, anywhere from two to five inches in length, and properly balance it so that when attached to the stick-winged plane, it would turn around swiftly when carried against the wind. Our back yard was filled with whirring sounds. Even then he longed to be an airplane pilot.

Orville was interested in skating, badminton, baseball and participated in these sports. He loved his rabbits and his bicycle which he found useful and enjoyed riding on his paper route. Orville attended Sunday School in Virden and became interested in Wolf Cubs. He progressed to the Boy Scouts and had many badges to show his promotion in this organization.

When Orville became of school age, he attended Virden Public School and Virden Collegiate. He made satisfactory progress and stored away a vast fund of knowledge. His friends and family would sometimes call him "The Encyclopaedia." Orville's aim throughout these years of schooling was always not to have more, but to be more, not for higher place, but for greater worth, not for fame, but for knowledge.

The family moved to Brandon in 1941 and Orville attended Brandon Collegiate from which he graduated with Honours from Grade 12 in June, 1942. In September of that year, Orville enrolled with The Wheat City Business College in Brandon in a course in Bookkeeping and Business Correspondence and English. He obtained his diploma in this business course in the spring of 1943. During these months he was clerking in a local drug store where his father, Wallace Lamont, was Manager. Orville continued in this job until June, when on his nineteenth birthday, he decided to serve his country and enlisted with [the] RCAF with the hope of becoming an Air Pilot. Then began a series of medical examinations with a local doctor, Winnipeg Air Force doctor, Brandon Air Force doctor. Orville passed all the medicals. He entered barracks in Brandon June 22nd. On the morning of July 3, 1943, his death came suddenly while he was participating in a ball game at the stadium. We found out later that Orville passed the final exam to permit him to enter the pilot training course with a high mark. Orville is sadly missed but we are proud he made the big decision to serve his country at war. Orville showed a quiet compassion to those in need and brought great happiness to those who knew him. The measure of life is, after all, not its duration but its donation.

Lamont Island (63 N/12) in Sisipuk Lake was named after him in 1995.

Lamontagne, Rifleman **Emelien** of Marchand (H 41931). Regina Rifle Regiment. He died 9 July 1944 at the age of 22 and is commemorated at Beny-sur-Mer Canadian War Cemetery in Calvados, France. He was the son of Raoul and Florence Lamontagne of Marchand, Manitoba. ***Lamontagne Lake*** (64 N/14), west of Nueltin Lake was named after him in 1972.

Land, Private **Gordon S.** of Carman (H 6289). Winnipeg Grenadiers. He died 19 December 1941 and is commemorated at the Sai Wan Memorial in Hong Kong. He was the son of John H. and Mary M. Land of Carman, Manitoba. ***Land Lake*** (64 K/14), northeast of Reindeer Lake was named after him and his brother (next entry) in 1972.

Land, Private **Roy C.** of Carman (H 6295). Winnipeg Grenadiers. He died 19 December 1941 at the age of 21 and is commemorated at the Sai Wan Memorial in Hong Kong. He was the son of John H. and Mary M. Land of Carman, Manitoba. ***Land Lake*** (64 K/14), northeast of Reindeer Lake was named after him and his brother (previous entry) in 1972.

Lane, Pilot Officer **Ernest A.** of Winnipeg (932746). No. 514 Squadron, RAF. He died 21 January 1944 at the age of 22 and is commemorated at Wonseradeel-(Makkum)-Protestant Churchyard, Holland. He was the son of Ernest A. and Nellie A. Lane (née Bark) and was survived by his wife Dorothy M. Lane of Winnipeg. He had enlisted in August, 1939. ***Lane Lake*** (64 I/14), northeast of Shethanei Lake was named after him in 1995.

Lang, Pilot Officer **Andrew Alexander** of Portage la Prairie (J 16053). No. 405 Squadron. He died 1 October 1942 at the age of 29 and is commemorated at the Kiel War Cemetery in Germany. He was the son of William J. and Grace M. Lang of Portage la Prairie. His brother recalls (23 August 1996):

Alex Lang grew up in Portage la Prairie, Manitoba where he graduated from the Portage Collegiate. He was active in sports and many community affairs. Alex was a charter member of the Portage Lion's Club and he frequently assisted in the United Church services while President of the Young People's Association.

Alex was one of the first in his community to enlist, joining the Royal Canadian Air Force when he was 26 years old in the spring of 1940 and a little over two years later he was killed in action. His active duty came early in the war effort, at a time when the Allied losses were heavy. Alex completed six operational trips including 34 hours over enemy territory before he was fatally shot down during a bombing raid over a submarine base in northern Germany.

The loss of Alex was devastating to his father and mother, William and Grace and to his younger sister Jessie and his younger brothers William and James who were also in active service. Alex's family knew him as an intelligent, warm-hearted, sociable young man with limitless potential. He was kind, generous, keenly interested in the welfare of others, proud of his Scottish ancestry, his country and his community. Words cannot express the loss of Alex to his family. He is a warm and loving presence in the hearts of our family.

On October 1, 405 Squadron participated in a raid with RAF bombers on the U-boat yards at Flensburg. The raids were carried out at less than 2000 feet and three aircraft and 23 members of the squadron were lost. ***Lang Peninsula*** (64 A/12) on Baldock Lake was named after Pilot Officer Lang in 1995.

Lang, Flying Officer **Francis H. "Sonny"** of Coulter (J 14144). No. 427 Squadron. He died 13 June 1944 at the age of 27 and is commemorated at the Calais Canadian War Cemetery in France. He was the son of Francis J. and Ethel J. Lang of Lyleton, Manitoba and was survived by his wife of four months Josephine I. Lang (née Cracknell) of Fort William, Ontario. He was the brother of Flight Sergeant James M. R. Lang (next entry). His niece writes (6 December 2001):

Francis ... was born July 24, 1916 at Lyleton, Manitoba and received his education at Coulter and Coultervale. He enlisted with the RCAF as a wireless air gunner in July, 1940. He trained at Toronto, Jarvis, Fort William, Regina and Mossbank. He went overseas April, 1941 and completed his required number of operational flights. He won his commission in May, 1943 in the field, for efficiency, meritorious service and display of qualities of leadership. He returned to Canada in February, 1944 on a month's leave where he was married on February 7, 1944 and then returned overseas for his second tour.

Lang Point (64 N/9) on the northwest shore of Creba Lake was named after him in 1989.

Lang, Flight Sergeant **James Murray R.** of Coulter (R 119753). No. 408 Squadron. He died 12 June 1943 at the age of 23 and is commemorated at Rheinberg War Cemetery in Germany. He was the son of Francis J. and Ethel J. Lang of Lyleton, Manitoba and was survived by his wife of 11 months Evelyn Lang (née Webb) of Browning, Saskatchewan. He was the brother of Flying Officer Francis H. Lang (previous entry). His niece writes (6 December 2001):

[He] enlisted in the RCAF in the fall of 1941 and took his training as a wireless air gunner at Trenton, Brandon, Winnipeg and Mossbank. He was married on July 7, 1942 and went overseas the same year.

Lang Island (64 N/9) in Creba Lake was named after him in 1989.

Langton, Private **Elmer L. W.** of Morris (H 200133). Saskatoon Light Infantry. He died 13 December 1943 and is commemorated at the Moro River Canadian War Cemetery in Italy. He was survived by his wife Jessie Langton. ***Langton Lake*** (63 J/12), south of Wekusko Lake was named after him in 1972.

La Peyre, Private **George** of St. Claude (H 200117). South Saskatchewan Regiment. He died 16 September 1944 at the age of 23 and is commemorated at Coxyde Military Cemetery, Koksijde, West-Vlaanderen, Belgium. He and his twin bother were the youngest of 11 children. He was survived by his wife Jessie D. La Peyre of Winnipeg and their daughter. She writes (10 April 1996):

He was ... of Métis origin, [born] at St. Claude, Manitoba in 1921. His ancestors had been displaced land owners on the Red River in the area of Letellier, Manitoba. George's father was an immigrant from Sarniguet, France who came to Canada to find a wife and obtain land of his own.

George is described to me as a wonderful man who was loved by all who knew him. He had a jolly nature, was fun loving and kind to all creatures. My maternal grandfather (Poppy) was a man who had not had many breaks in his life and who had, sadly, become somewhat bitter. However, his face would glow as he related stories to me that gave me such a good image of my dad. Poppy would visualize him as he arrived at the door with his beaming smile, showing strong, white teeth and a dark tan that hid any detail in his face, as it was framed by the light in the doorway. He met his wife Jessie when they were living in Charleswood as young adults. One story that my mother told me of him was that he would arrive by bus and walk the full way down the street on his hands. His friends of his youth regale in stories of his practical jokes and attempts at playing the guitar and singing. There are many photos of him helping his neighbours with their farming chores, helping his family with their yard work and house building, relaxing with friends and family.

Apparently my Dad worked for a builder in Charleswood as a carpenter until he enlisted to go overseas. He did not have to enlist as he was already a sergeant, but felt it was his duty. His letters home leave the impression of a very loving and loyal man with everything to live for, but who had chosen to do the honourable thing.

La Peyre Lake (64 J/5), southwest of Tadoule Lake was named after him in 1975.

LaPlante, Private **Gabriel** of Boggy Creek (H 41654). Winnipeg Grenadiers. He died a prisoner of war 22 November 1943 at the age of 23 and is commemorated at the Sai Wan War Cemetery in Hong Kong. He was the son of Private Joseph A. and Marie J. Laplante (sp.) of Boggy Creek, Manitoba. ***LaPlante Lake*** (64 F/2), east of Wells Lake was named after him in 1994.

Laplante, Private **Romain J.** of Marchand (H 75223). Winnipeg Grenadiers. He died a prisoner of war 17 October 1942 and is commemorated at the Sai Wan War Cemetery in Hong Kong. He was survived by his father Patrick LaPlante (sp.) of Marchand, Manitoba. ***Laplante Lake*** (53 L/11), west of Gods Lake was named after him in 1962.

Larche, Flight Sergeant **Joseph Armand** of Transcona (R 95499). No. 425 Squadron. He died 11 November 1942 at the age of 24 and is commemorated at Dishforth Cemetery, Yorkshire, England. He was the son of Alfred and Louisa Larche of Transcona. ***Larche Lake*** (52 L/6), northeast of Lac du Bonnet was named after him in 1973.

Larence, Lance Bombardier **Roy J. A.** of Makaroff (H 59984). Royal Canadian Artillery. He died 27 January 1944 and is commemorated at the Moro River Canadian War Cemetery in Italy. ***Larence Lake*** (64 K/15), northeast of Lac Brochet was named after him in 1972.

Large, Flight Lieutenant **George Russell** of Makaroff (J 9688). No. 408 Squadron. He died 16 April 1945 at the age of 25 and is commemorated at the Adegem Canadian War Cemetery in Belgium. He was the son of Alexander R. and Florence L. Large of Makaroff, Manitoba and was survived by his wife Isabelle K. Large and by his daughter Marilyn whom he had never seen. His brother writes (25 April 1995):

... known as Russell, [he] lived in Makaroff with his family and attended Makaroff School. In the late 1930s, [he] attended the University of Manitoba (Agriculture). After two years, he enlisted with the Air Force, got his wings at Yorkton and then went overseas. He was based in England [and] went on many bombing raids. In England [he] married Isabelle. Later, he was shot down and taken PoW. He never saw his daughter Marilyn.

Large Lake (64 H/9), northeast of Freeman Lake was named after him in 1995.

Larivière, Private **Ernest** of St. Vital (H 6506). Winnipeg Grenadiers. He died 2 November 1942 at the age of 22 and is commemorated at the Sai Wan War Cemetery in Hong Kong. He was the son of Fred and Mary Larivière and was survived by his wife Evelyn Larivière of Winnipeg. ***Larivière Lake*** (64 I/2), east of North Knife Lake was named after him in 1974.

Larkin, Corporal **Edwin E.** of Marquette (H 37796). Royal Canadian Army Service Corps. He died 20 October 1944 at the age of 24 and is commemorated at the Groesbeek Memorial in Holland. ***Larkin Lake*** (64 O/12), south of Nueltin Lake was named after him in 1975. His six brothers erected a plaque there in his honour in 1987.

Larocque, Lance Corporal **David** of Boggy Creek (H 101168). South Saskatchewan Regiment. He died 9 March 1943 and is commemorated at the Groesbeek Canadian War Cemetery in Holland. ***Larocque Lake*** (64 P/1), southeast of Nejanilini Lake was named after him in 1974.

Larsen, Rifleman **Nels** of Winnipeg (H 14959). Regina Rifle Regiment. He died 12 August 1944 at the age of 37 and is commemorated at Bretteville-sur-Laize Canadian War Cemetery in Calvados, France. ***Larsen Bay*** (64 P/6) in Jethe Lake was named after him in 1995.

Larsen, Private **Robert E. A.** of Winnipeg (H 6141). Winnipeg Grenadiers. He died 21 December 1941 and is commemorated at the Sai Wan Memorial in Hong Kong. ***Larsen Island*** (63 K/15) in Webb Lake was named after him in 1993.

Larson, Telegraphist **Norman A.** of Winnipeg (V 9684). SS *Avoceta*. He died 25 September 1941 at the age of 30 and is commemorated at the Halifax Memorial. It was his third Atlantic crossing. He was the only son of Nils and Alma Larson of Starbuck, Manitoba. His sister and niece recall (19 November 2001):

Norman was born in Winnipeg July 14, 1911. He grew up in Starbuck and worked several years in the grain commodity in Winnipeg. He enlisted as Telegraphist with the RCNVR in September, 1939 and made many crossings with the convoy across the Atlantic. On his last convoy, September, 1941, he was serving with the British Navy. On a return trip from Gibraltar, the convoy was attacked by an enemy submarine. Aside from the crew there were many children and women refugees aboard.

Rear-Admiral Sir Kenelm Creighton served for the first three years of the war as Commodore of ocean convoys and he remembers Telegraphist Larson:

All through the [church] service, my mind kept slipping back to the children and seamen drowned in the convoy. Particularly, I thought of the young Ulsterman who had been one of my signalmen and the Canadian wireless operator, Norman Larson. It had been Larson's third convoy. He ... was a fine, straightforward young man. Modest, shy, very keen on his duty, he was well-liked by his fellow men. Raised on a farm in the Middle West of Canada in the heart of the great wheat belt, the war in the Atlantic and Europe must have seemed far away.

One may wonder what it was that impelled him to go to sea and fight on an element he had never seen. For he was a volunteer. There was no compulsion. And his normal occupation on the land would have exempted him from conscription even if there had been any. But there is some magic in the word 'England.' He had heard that the old country, Mother of the Commonwealth needed help, so he was one of Canada's sons and daughters who came in their thousands to her aid.

And so he came, away from his family, his friends and all things dear to him to do his duty – and to die. I thought of him keeping his watch, all alone for hours each day and night at sea; hearing the hundreds of W/T messages in code which he could not read, occasionally picking up the call sign of a U-boat making her position to base. He saw the danger closing in on the convoy and ... he was all alone when it struck. I never saw him on deck in the brief flashes before *Avoceta* sank, but I have no doubt he was at his post and, when the end came, went down with her.

I wrote to his mother to send the deep sympathy of myself and those of my staff who survived, for the loss of a good shipmate and a gallant son. Part of his sister's letter in reply I have included here. It is a brave and courageous letter, typical of the grief, sadness and pride of so many families, whose husbands, fathers and sons gave their all in the cause of victory:

Dear Sir: My mother, sister and I wish to thank you very kindly for the information about Norman Larson, Telegraphist, RCNVR, a very dear son and brother. It is the first definite news we have had regarding this sad incident as Ottawa has only been able to tell us that he was missing, believed killed in action on September 25th and that he was on the *Avoceta*.

We find it very hard to believe that he is gone. We had a letter from him written on September 7th saying that he had acquired a good coat of tan in Gibraltar. My mother's heart is broken and we know it is so for all mothers who lose their sons in war. He always wrote faithfully to his mother and little souvenirs he sent us from England showed he thought of us at home. I tried to write him once a week as I know how much letters mean to the boys overseas and it was only yesterday I got back a letter written [by] him on September 25th, the very day of the sad happening.

In his last letter from England, just before sailing for Gibraltar, he mentioned one of the boys as having an accordion and they would have music on the way. I have wondered if that boy was among the survivors. I would love to hear if he is still on your staff or from any of the boys who spent any time with Norman at Gibraltar.

I will close now. May God protect you and give you the necessary strength to carry on in England's traditional way till victory is here. I remain, Yours very sincerely, (Mrs.) Robert Livingston, Starbuck, Manitoba, Canada (Creighton 1956).

The beginning of May, 1943 is generally recognized as the date when the tide turned in favour of the Allied convoys in the Battle of the Atlantic. With the arrival of a support group of the Royal Navy, 41 U-boats had been lost by the end of that month and subsequently all but a token number of submarines were removed from the main shipping lanes in the north. For that reason, the first Sunday in May is celebrated as Battle of the Atlantic Day. In 1992, the Atlantic Chiefs and Petty Officer's Association commissioned a bronze statue of a sailor to be erected at the foot of Sackville Street in downtown Halifax and Norman Larson's likeness was used. On the 50th anniversary of the Battle of the Atlantic the following year, ceremonies were held there to commemorate the more than 4000 Canadians who lost their lives supplying a beleaguered England with supplies and troops. The event began at the Sailors Memorial and included a 21-gun salute and a sailpast by the restored corvette *Sackville*. Fred McKee of the Atlantic Chiefs and Petty Officers Association dedicated the statue to wireless operator Norman Larson of Starbuck, Manitoba, who lost his life while on convoy duty. In concluding his address, Chief McKee said: "The Sailor Statue represents all the Norman Larsons and all the battles they fought ... Ready, Aye Ready." ***Larson Lake*** (64 C/16), south of Barrington Lake was named after Telegraphist Larson in 1957.

Laudrum, Aircraftman 2 **Ernest H.** of Oberon (R 205320). No. 6 Recruitment Centre, RCAF. He died 23 February 1943 at the age of 21 and is commemorated at Wellwood Cemetery, Manitoba. He was the son of Reginald and Edith Laudrum of Oberon, Manitoba. ***Laudrum Lake*** (64 P/12), northeast of Nejanilini Lake was named after him in 1972.

Laurila, Private **Sulo E.** of Pointe du Bois (H 18050). Algonquin Regiment. He died 22 October 1944 at the age of 21 and is commemorated at Schoonselhof Cemetery in Antwerp, Belgium. He was the son of Hjalmar and Lily Laurila of Pointe du Bois, Manitoba. ***Laurila River*** (64 K/16), which flows northeast into Stevens Lake was named after him in 1972.

Lavallée, Private **Ernest** of St. Laurent (H 41865). Winnipeg Grenadiers. He died a prisoner of war 27 February 1944 at the age of 23 and is commemorated at the Yokohama War Cemetery in Japan. He was the son of William and Elizabeth Lavallée of St. Laurent, Manitoba and was survived by a four year-old son. ***Lavallée Channel*** (64 I/16) on the Seal River was named after him in 1974 and ***Lavallée Island*** (64 C/6) in the Laurie River was named after him in 1995.

Lavallee, Private **Gustave** of Starbuck (H 17502). Essex Scottish Regiment. He died 20 September 1944 and is commemorated at Schoonselhof Cemetery in Antwerp, Belgium. ***Lavallee Lake*** (52 L/14), west of Tooth Lake was named after him in 1982.

Lavallee, Private **Henry J.** of Portage la Prairie (SH 493). Princess Patricia's Canadian Light Infantry. He died 19 July 1953 and is commemorated at the United Nations Cemetery in Pusan, South Korea. ***Henry Lavallee Lake*** (63 P/6), north of Landing Lake was named after this Korean War casualty in 1998.

Lavallee, Warrant Officer Class 2 **Thomas E.** of Pine Falls (R 117397). No. 178 Squadron. He died 27 April 1943 at the age of 32 and is commemorated at Bari War Cemetery in Italy. He was the son of Mr. and Mrs. Edward Lavallee of Montrock, Ontario. ***Lavallee Bay*** (53 M/5) in Bigstone Lake was named after him in 1996.

Lavarie, Private **Cecil F.** of Carman (H 6821). Winnipeg Grenadiers. He died a prisoner of war 14 February 1944 at the age of 30 and is commemorated at the Yokohama War Cemetery in Japan. The official cause of death was listed as pneumonia. He was the son of Hugh and Flora Lavarie. ***Lavarie Island*** (64 I/16) in the Seal River was named after him in 1974.

Lavigne, Private **Onizephore** (2381351). 22nd Battalion, Canadian Infantry (Quebec Regiment). He died 28 November 1918 and is commemorated at Elouges Communal Cemetery, Dour, Hainaut, Belgium. ***Lavigne Lake*** (53 L/5), north of Bolton Lake was named after this World War I casualty in 1999.

Law, Flying Officer **Albert C.** of Darlingford (J 20168). No. 405 Squadron. He died 10 July 1943 at the age of 28 and is commemorated at Cambridge City Cemetery in Cambridgeshire, England. He was the son of John O. and Sarah Law of Darlingford, Manitoba and was survived by his wife Betty J. Law of Darlingford. ***Law Point*** (64 P/12) on Nejanilini Lake was named after him in 1989.

Law, Private **George** of Winnipeg (H 6860). Winnipeg Grenadiers. He died 19 December 1941 at the age of 31 and is commemorated at the Sai Wan Memorial in Hong Kong. He was the son of Mr. and Mrs. R. J. Law of Winnipeg. His mother was not notified of his death until 1943. ***Law Bay*** (64 G/6) in Kasik Lake was named after him in 1994.

Law, Sergeant **James** of Winnipeg (R 58864). No. 9408 Servicing Echelon, RCAF. He died 27 June 1944 at the age of 24 and is commemorated at Stonefall Cemetery in Yorkshire, England. He was the son of John and Jessie Law and was survived by his wife Joyce E. Law of Walmgate, Yorkshire, England. ***Law Island*** (63 N/11) in Morin Lake was named after him in 1995.

Law, Private **William** of Morden (H 19566). Queen's Own Cameron Highlanders. He died 25 April 1943 and is commemorated at Brookwood Military Cemetery in Surrey, England. ***Law Lake*** (64 N/4), southwest of Nueltin Lake was named after him in 1972.

Lawlor, Flying Officer **James R. R.** of Kenton (J 18350). No. 18 Service Flying Training School. He died 27 October 1944 at the age of 26 and is commemorated at Kenton Cemetery, Manitoba. He was survived by his wife Bette Lawlor and by a son James, born ten days after his death. In 1941, he had flown Wellingtons out of England bombing Axis fortifications in the fjords of Norway. The following year, he flew Hudsons, protecting the convoys sailing from Gibraltar to Malta. In 1943, he trained on Lancasters as backup for the raid on the dams on the Ruhr in May of that year. Subsequently, he was posted back to Winnipeg to train as a pilot for the newly formed Trans Canada Airlines, while still in the RCAF. ***Lawlor Lake*** (64 P/7), east of Nejanilini Lake was named after him in 1974. In 1997, the family erected a plaque there in his memory.

Lawrence, Lieutenant **John C.** of Winnipeg (O 40910). HMCS *Shawinigan*. The *Shawinigan* was torpedoed and sunk by U-1228 while on independent anti-submarine patrol in the Cabot Strait; all hands were lost. Lieutenant Lawrence died 24 November 1944 at the age of 28 and is commemorated at the Halifax Memorial. He was the son of John H. C. and May L. Lawrence of Winnipeg and was survived by his wife Phyllis E. "Betty" Lawrence (née Dean) of Winnipeg. A local newspaper reported that:

> Lieutenant Lawrence attended Kelvin High school and graduated from the University of Manitoba in 1938. Before enlistment in 1942, he was employed at the Great West Life Insurance Company. He trained at King's College, Halifax and has been on active service for two years on the *Shawiningan*. His father, J. H. Lawrence, resides at 303 Waverley Street (*The Winnipeg Tribune* 7 December 1944).

Lawrence Reef (63 B/8), southwest of Reindeer Island in Lake Winnipeg was named after him in 1976.

Lawrence, Rifleman **Kenneth S.** of Crandall (H 1170). Royal Winnipeg Rifles. He died 8 June 1944 at the age of 21 and is commemorated at Beny-sur-Mer Canadian War Cemetery in Calvados, France. He was the son of Bertram K. and Mary Lawrence and was survived by his wife Ruth M. Lawrence of Crandall, Manitoba. ***Lawrence Island*** (53 E/16) in Island Lake was named after him in 1982.

Lawrence, Sergeant **Louie J. H.** of Winnipeg (H 40762). Queen's Own Cameron Highlanders. He died 7 August 1944 at the age of 25 and is commemorated at Bretteville-sur-Laize Canadian War Cemetery in Calvados, France. He was the son of John F. and Ena Lawrence (née Halpin) and was survived by his wife Mildred F. Lawrence of Winnipeg. ***Lawrence Bay*** (64 C/16) in Barrington Lake was named after him in 1995.

Lawrence, Flight Lieutenant **Richard C.** of Winnipeg (J 6228). No. 127 Squadron. He died 3 November 1942 at the age of 28 and is commemorated at the Alamein Memorial in Egypt. He was survived by his wife Norah F. Lawrence of Ottawa. ***Lawrence Point*** (64 N/11) on Kasmere Lake was named after him in 1995.

Lawrence, Sergeant **Ronald F.** of Winnipeg (1676060). No. 101 Squadron, RAF. He died 9 March 1942 at the age of 26 and is commemorated at the Runnymede Memorial in Surrey, England. He was the son of Louis F. and Edith Lawrence of Norwood and was survived by his wife Constance Lawrence. ***Lawrence Peninsula*** (64 C/13) on Macgregor Lake was named after him in 1996.

Lawrie, Private **Keith R.** of Morris (H 6301). Winnipeg Grenadiers. He died 21 December 1944 and is commemorated at the Sai Wan Memorial in Hong Kong. ***Lawrie Island*** (64 P/4) in MacLeod Lake was named after him in 1985.

Lawrie, Gunner **Norman R.** of Onanole (H 66722). Royal Canadian Artillery. He died 25 July 1944 at the age of 28 and is commemorated at Bretteville-sur-Laize Canadian War Cemetery in Calvados, France. He was the son of Andrew R. and Catherine J. Lawrie and was survived by a wife and son who recalls (16 April 1997):

> Norman is my real father. When Norman went in the army, my mother was pregnant and had five children from her first husband who died in 1937 due to problems from the First World War. The father I knew and [who] raised me – Edgar A. Lawrie (Norman's brother) – married my mother when he found out she was pregnant. I found this all out when my father was dying with cancer.

Lawrie Bay (64 B/1) in Harding Lake was named after him in 1995.

Lawrie, Warrant Officer 2 **Robert J.** of Winnipeg (R 124022). No. 53 Squadron. He died 17 April 1944 at the age of 21 and is commemorated at the Runnymede Memorial in Surrey, England. He was the son of Bruce W. and Margaret Lawrie of Winnipeg. ***Lawrie Lake*** (64 P/3), southeast of Nejanilini Lake was named after him in 1974.

Lawson, Gunner **Alfred Lorne** of Oak Lake (H 1248). Royal Canadian Artillery. He died 28 December 1944 at the age of 36 and is commemorated at the Groesbeek Canadian War Cemetery in Holland. He was the son of Alfred C. and Cassie Lawson and was survived by his wife M. Jean Lawson (née Stewart) of Lavinia, Manitoba. His sister writes (27 January 1997):

> Lorne was born in the farm home of his grandparents on August 2, 1908. Because of a Post Office in this home called Lippentott, ... that [is what is] on his birth certificate. Lorne kept in touch with us while he was in England, but we didn't hear about his whereabouts till we were notified of his death in Holland.
>
> Both my granddaughter and my cousin had the opportunity to visit his grave in Groesbeek, Holland and were aware of the fond feeling and appreciation the Dutch people had for the Canadians.

An employee of the *Oak Lake News* when he enlisted, the paper printed the following after his death:

> The above are the official facts and summary of Lorne's activities, but how bare and cold they look in print. Lorne was one of our staff for about two years and we got to know him pretty well. He was a good sport and one of the few top-ranking curlers in the district. No one ever saw him lose his good temper through a defeat. He was clever, obliging and quick to learn; good-natured and well-posted on current world affairs. Lorne was so alive and so enjoyed his work at the News Office that we always looked for his return and somehow never visualised the possibility that, when he left, his last type had been set and we should see him no more.
>
> The old office will never seem quite the same. Something young and vibrant is gone. God grant it may soon be our privilege and duty to report the news that Right has triumphed over darkest Evil and young lives like Lorne's have not been given in vain. The "News" joins in expressing the profound and sincere sympathy of the whole community to the Lawson families in their heavy sorrows (n.d.).

Lawson Lake (64 I/3), west of North Knife Lake was named after him in 1974.

Lawson, Flying Officer **Gordon H.** of Sherridon (J 9691). No. 458 Squadron. He died 15 July 1943 at the age of 24 and is commemorated at the Malta Memorial. He was due to go home on leave the following day. Flying Officer Lawson was survived by his parents W. A. and Mabel G. Lawson of Grandview, Manitoba. His brother recalls (9 April 1996):

> Gordon Herbert Lawson was born at home on the family homestead in the Tamarisk School District on June 6, 1916, the eighth child in the family of 11. He graduated from the Grandview School and was interested in further education. While working in Sherridon Hudson Bay Mining and Smelting, he was involved in bookkeeping and penmanship courses. He was athletic and participated in the district sports and social events. His special interest was in baseball. After he was employed, he financially assisted two younger sisters in furthering their education – one in nursing and one in a secretarial course. He flew Tiger Moth, Crane, Oxford and Wellington aircraft.

Lawson Island (63 P/4) in Bruneau Lake was named after him in 1995.

Lawson, Flight Sergeant **Kenneth W.** of Darlingford (R 147471). No. 76 Squadron. He died 12 June 1943 at the age of 22 and is commemorated at Woensel General Cemetery in Eindhoven, Holland. He was survived by his wife Marjorie Lawson. ***Lawson Bay*** (64 J/14) in Bain Lake was named after him in 1989.

Lawson, Flight Sergeant **Lloyd T.** of Flin Flon (R 58836). No. 57 Squadron. He died 3 September 1941 at the age of 19 and is commemorated at Whittlesford Churchyard, Cambridgeshire, England. He was the son of Samuel and Solveig M. Lawson of Piney, Manitoba. His niece writes (30 December 1996):

> Lloyd Lawson was born in Piney, Manitoba, the youngest of four children. His father died while Lloyd was a young child and he grew up helping his mother operate the Piney Hotel along with his sister and two older brothers. When his brothers decided to enlist, Lloyd was not to be left behind and, I believe, lied about his age in order to enlist. His brother Frank who was my father, served with the Goose Squadron as a rear gunner, returning safely home to Flin Flon where he lived until his death in 1979. His other brother Jack also saw the war out safely and lived in Swan River until his death in the mid-1980s.

Lawson Point (64 O/9) on Gayoway Lake was named after him in 1995. A family friend managed to fly into Gayoway Lake and mount a plaque on the point in 1996.

Layng, Flying Officer **William G.** of Winnipeg (J 38188). No. 419 Squadron. He died 4 October 1944 at the age of 21 and is commemorated at Stonefall Cemetery in Yorkshire, England. He was the son of George H. and Marjorie Layng of St. Boniface. His obituary read in part:

> He was active in sports, especially track, curling, tennis and badminton. While attending Norwood Collegiate he was business manager of the school's year book (n.d.).

His niece adds (21 March 1998):

> ... I have always felt a special bond with my uncle who was also my godfather and my father's only sibling. You see, Bill left Winnipeg on January 28th, 1944 and although he wasn't shipped overseas until February, that was the last day spent with his family. It was also the day I was born. Although we met only the once, he left me his memory in the safekeeping of the hearts and minds of those he loved and in a tiny gold locket inscribed simply, Uncle Bill. He was twenty-one. Not only did he miss Life; Life most certainly missed him.

Layng Lake (64 O/11), southeast of Nueltin Lake was named after him in 1975.

Layton, Pilot Officer **Frederick W.** of Winnipeg (J 90289). No. 432 Squadron. He died 8 June 1944 at the age of 20 and is commemorated at Marissel French National Cemetery, Oise, France. His sister visited his grave in 1956 and discovered that the LeRoy family had "adopted" it. Bernard LeRoy, a school boy in 1944, had been tending it for 12 years. Pilot Officer Layton was the son of Frederick George and Alma I. Layton of Fort Garry. His sister (14 February 1995) adds that he:

> ... attended Earl Grey and Kelvin Technical (KTHS) schools. [He] loved reading and seemed to retain most of what he read (history, Bible, true stories and fiction). [He] went to our uncle's farm in Saskatchewan for many summers and loved every minute of it even though it was hard work.

Layton Lake (64 N/5), southwest of Nueltin Lake was named after him in 1972.

Lazenby, Warrant Officer 2 **Thomas H.** of Plumas (R 124427). No. 420 Squadron. He died 17 August 1943 at the age of 32 and is commemorated at Agira Canadian War Cemetery in Italy. He was survived by his mother Mrs. Harry Lazenby of Foxwarren and by his wife Leona Lazenby. ***Lazenby Lake*** (64 P/13), north of Nejanilini Lake was named after him in 1974 and ***Lazenby Creek*** (64 P/13), which flows south into Wolverine River was named after him in 1987.

Leach, Leading Aircraftman **Douglas B.** of Winnipeg (R 91533). No. 15 Elementary Flying Training School. He died 10 June 1941 at the age of 21 and is commemorated at Brookside Cemetery in Winnipeg. He was the son of Neil G. and Margaret A. Leach of Winnipeg. ***Leach Lake*** (64 H/15), east of Etawney Lake was named after him in 1995.

Leask, Private **Richard L.** of Winnipeg (H 19970). Queen's Own Cameron Highlanders. He died 19 August 1942 at the age of 21 and is commemorated at Dieppe Canadian War Cemetery in Seine-Maritime, France. He was survived by his wife Shirley E. Leask of Winnipeg and their son. ***Leask Lake*** (64 K/7), northeast of Reindeer Lake was named after him in 1972.

Leathwood, Rifleman **George J. "Bud"** of Molson (H 42058). Royal Winnipeg Rifles. He died 15 August 1944 at the age of 21 and is commemorated at Bretteville-sur-Laize Canadian War Cemetery in Calvados, France. He was the son of Charles S. and Janet Leathwood of St. Thomas, Ontario. ***Leathwood Lake*** (64 N/16), west of Nueltin Lake was named after him in 1972.

LeBlanc, Signalman **Eugene W.** of Bélair (H 8714). Royal Canadian Corps of Signals. He died 17 December 1944 at the age of 20 and is commemorated at Bergen-op-Zoom Canadian War Cemetery in Holland. He was the son of Albert and Evelyn LeBlanc of Bélair, Manitoba. His niece (10 December 2001) reports that:

> He enlisted in March, 1943, going overseas in August, 1943. Besides his parents, he was survived by a brother, Colin, who was stationed overseas at the time. His father was a member of the Amputation Association, having lost a leg in World War I. He was sadly missed by all who knew him and his special character.

LeBlanc Lake (64 N/16), west of Nueltin Lake was named after him in 1972.

Lechowicz, Gunner **Z. Tadeus** of Angusville (H 35624). Royal Canadian Artillery. He died 9 September 1944 at the age of 23 and is commemorated at the Adegem Canadian War Cemetery in Belgium. He was the son of Anthony A. and Magdaline Lechowicz of Angusville, Manitoba. ***Lechowicz Lake*** (64 O/5), north of Egenolf Lake was named after him in 1975.

Le Clair, Rifleman **John** of Winnipeg (H 40939). Royal Winnipeg Rifles, British Empire Medal. He died 8 July 1944 while a prisoner of war and is commemorated at Bretteville-sur-Laize Canadian War Cemetery in Calvados, France. ***Le Clair Lake*** (64 F/8), southwest of Big Sand Lake was named after him in 1961.

Lee, Trooper **Albert P. "Bud"** of Portage la Prairie (H 46). Lord Strathcona's Horse. He died 24 May 1944 at the age of 30 and is commemorated at the Cassino War Cemetery in Italy. He was the son of James T. and Kathleen Lee and was survived by his wife Rita P. Lee (née James) of Portage la Prairie and their daughter. In 1995, she wrote:

> I will always wear a poppy. To me it honours the father I never met. Fifty-one years ago, he died at Monte Cassino. It also honours the mother who raised me alone. My mother's last glimpse of my father was as the troop train passed a field where she was waiting. She ran a mile across that field to wave goodbye. She was eight months pregnant. She had followed him from Portage la Prairie, Manitoba to Winnipeg after he enlisted in the Lord Strathcona Horse. She followed him to Camp Borden, Ontario, and if they had let her she would have followed him to war.
>
> Sometimes I wonder who sacrificed more, my dad, who died, or my mother, who lost the man she loved. She never remarried. My mother almost died giving birth to me. There was no one to sign the consent for a caesarean. She was unconscious. By that time my father was somewhere in England. I was a big baby. My mother was a tiny woman.

I was four months old before she was well enough to take the train trip back home to Portage la Prairie,

She and thousands of other Canadian women did what they had to do to keep their families functioning alone. Always with them was the dread of getting the fateful news that their beloved had been killed. When the news came, it was only confirmation. Mother told me years later that on the day of May 24, 1944, she sat down to write my dad and knew that he would not get the letter or parcel she was sending. She says she does not know how she knew. She just knew. He died that day.

Life as a war widow with a young child was not easy. The government in its wisdom and generosity provided a pension of $40 a month. There have been many celebrations this year to mark the 50th anniversary of the end of the war. There should have been more. The men and women who fought that war will always remember. But the generations that have followed have little consciousness of the sacrifices made so they could live in freedom.

The war generation is ageing. There are some who say that they were our last great generation. They lived through the Depression and fought and won the war. Those of us who follow them have never been put to the test as they were. We should ponder the fact that it is because of their tenacity and courage that we have been able to live in comfort and peace.

I will always wear a poppy (Hretchka 1995).

She adds (6 November 2001):

The stories I have been told all stressed that he loved to laugh. One of his mates who survived that day wrote my Mom that Bud would be missed by all because no matter how bad things were, he could always make them laugh. He had a serious side too. In a letter written three days before he died, he wrote to my Mother these words: "If anything should happen to me, I want you to remember that it was you that gave me the most memorable and precious moments of my life." Thank you for Lee Point.

Lee Point (53 L/2) on Island Lake was named after him in 1995.

Lee, Private **Ernest E.** of West Kildonan (H 40225). Veterans Guard of Canada. He died 11 March 1943 at the age of 53 and is commemorated at Old Kildonan Presbyterian Cemetery in Winnipeg, Manitoba. He was survived by his wife Jessie M. Lee of West Kildonan. ***Lee Bay*** (64 K/16) in Lake St. George was named after him in 1995.

Lee, Able Seaman **Frank E.** of Dickens (V 57850). HMCS *Valleyfield*. The *Valleyfield* was torpedoed and sunk by U-548 50 miles south of Cape Race, Newfoundland; 125 of her ship's company were lost. Able Seaman Lee died 7 May 1944 at the age of 24 and is commemorated at the Halifax Memorial. He was the son of Henry and Emma E. Lee of Dickens, Manitoba. ***East Lee Lake*** (52 M/4), northeast of Wanipigow Lake was named after him in 1986. West Lee Lake is named after his brother, Aircraftman 1 Frederick J. Lee (next entry).

Lee, Aircraftman 1 **Frederick J.** of Dickens (R 172591). No. 1 Flying Instructor School. He died 31 December 1942 at the age of 27 and is commemorated at Brookside Cemetery in Winnipeg. He was the son of Henry and Emma Lee of Dickens, Manitoba. West Lee Lake (52 M/4), northeast of Wanipigow Lake was named after him in 1986. ***East Lee Lake*** nearby is named after his brother, Able Seaman Frank E. Lee (previous entry).

Lee, Flying Officer **Jim G.** of Winnipeg (J 42216). No. 101 Squadron. He died 23 March 1945 at the age of 24 and is commemorated at the Sage War Cemetery in Germany. ***Lee Island*** (64 C/8) in Granville Lake was named after him in 1995.

Lees, Private **William** of Winnipeg (H 100646). Princess Louise Dragoon Guards. He died 15 December 1944 at the age of 27 and is commemorated at Villanova Canadian War Cemetery in Italy. He was the son of William and Clara Lees of Stalybridge, Cheshire, England. ***Lees Lake*** (64 I/15), northeast of North Knife Lake was named after him in 1974.

Lefort, Rifleman **Elmer J.** of Inglis (H 41815). Royal Winnipeg Rifles. He died 8 June 1944 at the age of 36 and is commemorated at Beny-sur-Mer Canadian War Cemetery in Calvados, France. He was the son of Frank and Tillie R. Lefort and was survived by his wife Doris Lefort of Inglis, Manitoba and their three children. ***Lefort Lake*** (64 I/6), north of North Knife Lake was named after him in 1974.

Lefurgey, Private **Allan J.** of Minnedosa (H 104041). Argyle and Sutherland Highlanders. He died 24 October 1944 at the age of 21 and is commemorated at Bergen-op-Zoom Canadian War Cemetery in Holland. He was the son of John and Mary Lefurgey and was survived by his wife Margaret M. Lefurgey of Minnedosa, Manitoba and their daughter. ***Lefurgey Lake*** (64 O/4), north of Egenolf Lake was named after him in 1975.

Légaré, Fireman **Raymond H.** of Dunrea. Merchant Marine vessel *Vancouver Island*. The *Vancouver Island* was torpedoed by U-558 in the North Atlantic while *en route* from Montreal to Cardiff; all 65 crew, eight gunners and 32 passengers were lost. Fireman Légaré died 15 October 1941 at the age of 23 and is commemorated at the Halifax Memorial. He was the son of Lucien and Emma Légaré (née Nadeau) of Dunrea, Manitoba. His brother recalls (27 November 2001):

Raymond was really loved by his family and friends. He is remembered as a kind, witty, cheerful and fun to be with person, also for his gentleness, whether he was playing with his kid brothers, shearing sheep or tending to his bees. He was a man of his word and generous, evident by keeping his promise to send money to buy a three piece suit and a little felt hat for his seven year-old brother who was also his godchild. His parents went to their grave unaware of their son's fate as he was merely reported missing in action. How we remember them, so sad, grieving, not knowing whether their son was dead, taken prisoner or perhaps there was a slight chance that they would be seeing him again? Losing a family member is terrible for any parents, but seemingly worse at such a young age and under such circumstances. More than forty years of enquiries were in vain until 1985 when the company that the ship was insured with provided complete details. It took fifty years for the Canadian government to recognize the members of the Merchant Marine who lost their lives and to honour them the same as other military forces. It is never too late.

Lac Légaré (62 F/1), southwest of Max Lake was named after him in 1988. Fireman Légaré spent his childhood near here and several relatives still reside in the vicinity.

Legary, Pilot Officer **Harvey A.** of Pilot Mound (J 92353). No. 427 Squadron. He died 29 July 1944 at the age of 22 and is commemorated at Hamburg Cemetery in Germany. He was the son of Edgar D. and Bethel H. Legary of Pilot Mound, Manitoba. ***Legary Lake*** (64 I/5), southeast of Tadoule Lake was named after him in 1957.

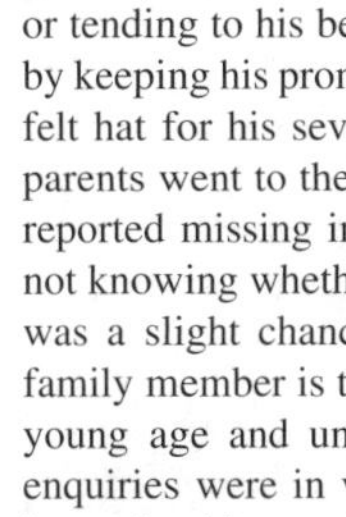

Legg, Trooper **Harry A.** of Brandon (H 26673). Fort Garry Horse. He died 12 April 1942 at the age of 18 and is commemorated at Brookwood Military Cemetery in Surrey, England. He was the son of Alfred and Daisy Legg of Brandon and was survived by two brothers and two sisters including Corporal James F. Legg (next entry). ***Legg Island*** (64 A/12) in Baldock Lake was named after him in 1995.

Legg, Corporal **James F.** of Brandon (H 40843). Fort Garry Horse. He died 14 August 1944 at the age of 21 and is commemorated at Bretteville-sur-Laize Canadian War Cemetery in Calvados, France. He was the son of Alfred and Daisy Legg of Brandon and had two brothers and two sisters including Trooper Harry A. Legg (previous entry). ***Legg Lake*** (64 O/3), west of Munroe Lake was named after him in 1975.

Leggo, Lieutenant **James G.** of Fort Garry. Saskatoon Light Infantry. He died 24 July 1943 at the age of 26 and is commemorated at Agira Canadian War Cemetery in Italy. He was the son of Gordon L. and Dorothy H. Leggo and was survived by his wife Marjorie C. Leggo of Fort Garry and their daughter. His wife recalls (26 October 2001):

> Jim joined the Cameron Highlanders in Winnipeg, 1940. He spent his training for an officer in Canada and his qualifying course at Gordon Head. He was sent overseas in 1943 and later transferred to the Saskatoon Light Infantry. Then on to Sicily where his carrier was blown up by a land mine.
>
> Jim was an avid horseman, owning two horses while still in his teens. We used to ride both summer and winter, joining up with other riders for paper chases, corn roasts and hunter trials. We married in 1939, so the horses had to go. We had a little daughter instead. He was very devoted to his parents, younger sisters and his own family.

Leggo Lake (64 K/5), northeast of Reindeer Lake was named after him in 1972.

Leguee, Sergeant **Frederick J.** of Winnipeg (H 16567). Princess Patricia's Canadian Light Infantry. He died 1 January 1944 at the age of 25 and is commemorated at the Moro River Canadian War Cemetery in Italy. He was the son of George A. and Bernadette Leguee of Winnipeg. ***Leguee Lake*** (63 I/16), northeast of Cross Lake was named after him in 1973.

Leguilloux, Private **Louis F. A.** of The Pas (H 100678). Loyal Edmonton Regiment. He died 29 August 1944 and is commemorated at Ancona War Cemetery in Italy. He was the son of Claude and Francoise Leguilloux. ***Leguilloux Lake*** (64 C/5), southeast of Reindeer Lake was named after him in 1973.

Leib, Private **Ernest** of Gladstone (H 25226). Royal Canadian Ordnance Corps. He was aboard the SS *Nerissa*, the only ship torpedoed while carrying Canadian troops to the United Kingdom. He died 1 May 1941 at the age of 24 and is commemorated at the Halifax Memorial. He was the son of Peter and Louise Leib of Gladstone, Manitoba. ***Leib Lake*** (64 B/1), south of Baldock Lake was named after him in 1972.

Leitch, Gunner **Charles R.** of Brandon (H 29076). Royal Canadian Artillery. He died 23 August 1945 at the age of 33 and is commemorated at the Holten Canadian War Cemetery in Holland. He was the son of William and Elizabeth Leitch and was survived by his wife Joyce M. Leitch of Coulsdon, Surrey, England. ***Leitch Island*** (64 N/2) in Whitmore Lake was named after him in 1995.

Leitch, Pilot Officer **John W.** of Winnipeg (J 89918). No. 429 Squadron. He died 23 May 1944 at the age of 21 and is commemorated at Stonefall Cemetery in Yorkshire, England. ***Leitch Lake*** (52 L/3), northeast of Brereton Lake was named after him in 1973.

Leithead, Flying Officer **Frank T.** of St. James (J 24304). No. 408 Squadron. He died 5 January 1945 at the age of 29 and is commemorated at the Sage War Cemetery in Germany. He was the son of Frank and Agnes Leithead and was survived by his wife Lillian L. Leithead of Winnipeg and their two children. ***Leithead Lake*** (64 J/11), west of Tadoule Lake was named after him in 1975.

Lelond, Private **Lyall T.** of Miniota (H 18884). Seaforth Highlanders of Canada. He died 12 April 1945 at the age of 29 and is commemorated at the Holten Canadian War Cemetery in Holland. He was the son of Jerimiah T. and Rose M. Lelond of Miniota, Manitoba. ***Lelond Lake*** (64 I/6), northwest of North Knife Lake was named after him in 1974.

Le Maistre, Pilot Officer **Arthur F.** of Winnipeg (41033). No. 210 Squadron, RAF. He died 9 April 1940 at the age of 26 and is commemorated at Sylling Churchyard, Norway. He was the son of Frederick F. and Edith H. Le Maistre of Winnipeg.

> In 1928 he was picked as the outstanding cadet from the Winnipeg Sea Cadets at age 14, to serve for two years on the HMS *Conway* in England. From 1930 – 1933 he was on the CPR *Empress of Japan*. In 1935 he joined the RCMP and in 1937 learned to fly at the Halifax Aero Club as a member of the Marine Division. A mid-air collision in January, 1938 made him the first person to successfully land two locked aircraft. When war started, he was flying Sunderlands with 228 Squadron at Pembroke Dock, Wales with Flying Officer L. Jones of Saskatoon. Transferring to No. 210 Squadron, he was on anti-sub patrols in the North Sea, but on April [9], 1940 was shot down near Oslo, Norway. Several Sunderland Flying Boats were lured there and shot down soon after the German invasion of Norway. He is buried there, with his crew of 10 (Allison 1978).

Pilot Officer Le Maistre was one of the many Canadians who travelled to England and joined the RAF before the outbreak of war (1938); his father had been born in Jersey. His younger brother joined the RAF two years later, achieved the rank of Flight Lieutenant and was awarded the Distinguished Flying Cross. ***Le Maistre Lake*** (53 K/11), southeast of Edmund Lake was named after Pilot Officer Le Maistre in 1995.

Lemay, Able Seaman **Marcel G. A.** of St. Boniface (V 54563). HMCS *Blairmore*. He died 7 August 1945 at the age of 22 and is commemorated at St. Boniface Cemetery. He was one of the 10 children of Mr. and Mrs. Arthur Lemay of St. Boniface. Ironically, he died at home due to drowning in his bathtub. ***Lemay Island*** (64 B/14) in Southern Indian Lake was named after him in 1962.

Lemerick, Flying Officer **George E.** of Winnipeg (J 23462). No. 419 Squadron. He died 29 January 1944 at the age of 21 and is commemorated at the Berlin 1939 - 1945 War Cemetery in Brandenburg, Germany. He was the son of George and Leta Lemmerick (sp.) of Traverse Bay, Manitoba. ***Lemerick Lake*** (64 H/2), east of Fidler Lake was named after him in 1995. Lemmerick Lake is named after his brother, Sergeant John A. Lemmerick (next entry).

Lemmerick, Sergeant **John A.** of Hillside Beach (R 123711). No. 14 Advanced Flying School. He died 8 April 1943 at the age of 22 and is commemorated at Cottesmore (St. Nicholas) Churchyard Extension, Rutland, England. He was the son of George and Leta Lemmerick of Traverse Bay, Manitoba. ***Lemmerick Lake*** (64 N/10), southwest of Nueltin Lake was named after him in 1972. Lemerick (sp.) Lake is named after his brother, Flying Officer George E. Lemerick (previous entry).

Lemon, Corporal **Harry** of Winnipeg (H 57907). Royal Canadian Army Service Corps. He died 18 September 1945 at the age of 39 and is commemorated at Burnsland Cemetery in Calgary. He was survived by his sister Violet Oakenfold of Calgary. ***Lemon Lake*** (63 O/4), north of Wekusko Lake was named after him in 1970.

Lennox, Rifleman **Gordon** of St. James (H 40814). Royal Winnipeg Rifles. He died 12 December 1944 and is commemorated at the Groesbeek Canadian War Cemetery in Holland. ***Lennox Lake*** (53 N/6), northeast of Knee Lake was named after him in 1972.

Leochko, Private **Michael W.** of Poplarfield (B 145617). 48th Highlanders of Canada. He died 28 August 1944 and is commemorated at Montecchio War Cemetery in Italy. ***Leochko Lake*** (54 D/15), northwest of Myre Lake was named after him in 1996.

Leonard, Lance Corporal **John G.** of Sperling (H 70488). Perth Regiment. He died 20 December 1944 and is commemorated at Villanova Canadian War Cemetery, Italy. He was the son of John H. and Rose H. Leonard. ***Leonard Lake*** (64 K/8), northeast of Reindeer Lake was named after him in 1972.

Leonard, Flight Sergeant **Roderick J.** of Portage la Prairie (R 213998). No. 354 Squadron. He died 22 April 1945 at the age of 20 and is commemorated at the Singapore Memorial. He was the son of John and Grace Leonard of Portage la Prairie. He gained some measure of celebrity while training in the Bahamas in 1943 by rescuing England's Prince Edward from a storm at sea. ***Leonard Island*** (64 F/8) in Chiupka Lake was named after him in 1989.

Lépine, Aircraftman 1 **Joseph George A.** of Winnipeg (R 140750). Royal Canadian Air Force. He was one of six Manitobans who lost their lives in the fire which swept through the Knights of Columbus Hostel in St. John's, Newfoundland on 12 December 1942. He was 29 years of age and is commemorated at Gander Cemetery, Newfoundland. He was the son of Edmund and Aldina Lépine of St. Boniface and was survived by his wife Amy S. Lépine of St. Boniface and their two young children. He had been a member of the Winnipeg Grenadier Cadets and Reserve, but missed being sent to Hong Kong because of being sick with the flu at that time. He was buried on his 30th birthday. His son writes (9 November 2001):

> My father died ... when I was three years of age. Even though I faintly remember him, I feel I do know a lot about my father through stories and the memories of him from family members and friends. Prior to enlistment in the RCAF, my father had been enlisted in the Artillery and then transferred to the Air Force.
>
> He was a physically strong, fun loving man and proud of his genealogy, being the grandson of Ambroise Lépine, a Lieutenant in the Provisional Government of Louis Riel in Manitoba. I am in possession of a letter written to me by my father as well as his identification tags and the telegram notifying my mother of his death. I cherish these items.

Lépine Lake (64 P/14), northeast of Nejanilini Lake was named after him in 1974.

Leppert, Flying Officer **Spencer E.** of Minto (J 40879). No. 24 Operational Training Unit, RCAF. He died 7 December 1944 at the age of 21 and is commemorated at Brookwood Military Cemetery in Surrey, England. He was the son of William L. and Hannah Leppert of Minto, Manitoba.

Spencer was born August 29, 1923 in Pine Falls. He received his education at schools in Pine Falls, Minto, and Brandon. He joined the RCAF and was posted overseas in 1944. It was during air operations over England when his Wellington aircraft crashed at Kiftsgate Court, Gloucestershire, killing all the crew (Pittman n.d.).

Leppert Lake (64 P/6), east of Nejanilini Lake was named after him in 1974.

Leroux, Pilot Officer **Adrian S.** of St. Claude (J 94407). No. 429 Squadron. He died 6 March 1945 at the age of 23 and is commemorated at Brookwood Military Cemetery in Surrey, England. He was survived by his mother Marie L. Leroux. ***Leroux Lake*** (64 G/15), west of Little Sand Lake was named after him in 1995.

Lesage, Gunner **Gerard R.** of McCreary (K 46317). Royal Canadian Artillery. He died 25 November 1944 at the age of 29 and is commemorated at the Groesbeek Canadian War Cemetery in Holland. He was the son of Noé and Eveline Lesage of Vancouver. He had been employed by The Caribou Gold Quartz Mine in British Columbia when he enlisted. He wrote home upon arriving overseas:

> Dear Brother and Family: Just a few lines to let you know I'm fine and hope all is well with you too. The weather here is swell and the people are nice too. I enjoyed my trip very much, wasn't sick at all on the way, and spent my time playing cards. I'll be glad though when it's all over. I'm anxious to celebrate the day when I get back. Write and tell me how things are going and how is your crop. Please keep in touch with Bert and let her know when you hear from me. Don't worry about me; I'll live through it. Sincerely, your brother, Gerry (August 1943).

Lesage Lake (53 M/11), southeast of Ransom Lake was named after him in 1996.

Leslie, Sergeant **James** of Winnipeg (H 26058). Three Rivers Tank Regiment. He died 17 May 1944 at the age of 34 and is commemorated at the Cassino War Cemetery in Italy. He was the son of George J. and Elsie J. Leslie and was survived by his wife Isabel Leslie of Winnipeg. Born at Tullynessle, Aberdeenshire, Scotland in 1909, he attended public school there. ***Leslie Lake*** (64 J/4), southwest of Tadoule Lake was named after him in 1975.

Leslie, Corporal **William** of Winnipeg (R 71320). No. 2 Air Observers School. He died 15 November 1944 at the age of 25 and is commemorated at Brookside Cemetery in Winnipeg. He was the son of William and Isabella Leslie of Winnipeg. ***Leslie Creek*** (54 D/8), which flows south into the Nelson River was named after him in 1977.

Letkeman, Lance Corporal **Theodore N.** of Winnipeg (H 800276). Princess Patricia's Canadian Light Infantry. He died 7 March 1951 at the age of 24 and is commemorated at the United Nations Cemetery in Pusan, South Korea. The first time he enlisted, his mother had him released because he was underage. ***Letkeman Lake*** (53 E/16), east of Krolman Lake was named after this Korean War casualty in 1998.

LeVasseur, Pilot Officer **Lucien C. "Louie"** of Lac du Bonnet (J 90129). No. 419 Squadron. He died 14 October 1944 at the age of 24 and is commemorated at the Reichswald Forest War Cemetery in Germany. He was the son of Albert and Carmen

LeVasseur of Lac du Bonnet. His brother writes (22 November 2001):

Pilot Officer LeVasseur was on his 26th operation when his Lancaster aircraft went down during a raid against Duisberg, Germany. He was buried in the Waldfriedhof Forest Cemetery, Lohmannsheide, exhumed and reburied at Reichswald near the Dutch border.

The crew of Lancaster B800 had started the daylight bomb run when they were hit by flak, knocking off a piece of the wing and setting both starboard engines on fire. The aircraft went out of control and just as the order to bail out was given, the aircraft exploded and crashed at Lohmannsheide. Miraculously, the pilot was blown clear, came to at about 5000 feet, landed near some gunners and was taken prisoner. He never knew what happened to the crew until after the war. Of the seven crew members, he was the only survivor.

Positive identification of some of the crew was difficult. On a trip to Europe, I found the grave site (Grave co-ordinates didn't match my information) and it was interesting to see that my brother's grave site and the one immediately next both had the cross and the Star of David engraved on the markers.

Growing up in Lac du Bonnet during those "depression" years was difficult to say the least. Louie was a hard working, astute young man, first learning the butcher trade from our self-employed dad, then joining the employ of the local Beaver Lumber Company just prior to joining the Air Force with a career seemingly assured.

Louie was an avid sportsman and excelled in hockey and baseball. He was very good natured and a loving brother in a close and very loving family. We will always cherish his memory.

LeVasseur Island (52 L/6) in Eaglenest Lake was named after him in 1973.

Leverrier, Sergeant **Gabriel C.** of Notre Dame de Lourdes (R 56912). No. 20 Operational Training Unit, RCAF. He died 30 July 1941 and is commemorated at Lossiemouth Burial Ground, Moray, Scotland. ***Leverrier Lake*** (64 J/15), northwest of Tadoule Lake was named after him in 1975.

Levins, Flight Sergeant **Milford G. T.** of Isabella (R 116417). No. 57 Squadron. He died 13 May 1943 at the age of 19 and is commemorated at Gendringen Roman Catholic Cemetery, Holland. He was one of the five children of Harry M. and Agnes C. Levins of Isabella, Manitoba and was survived by one sister Catherine and two brothers Jack and Fred. He was born at Haward, Saskatchewan and educated at Lenore and Lyleton, Manitoba. His brother writes (14 November 2001):

Milford joined the RCAF in July, 1941, trained in Canada, was posted overseas in July, 1942 and was attached to an RAF bomber squadron. He flew 26 missions over enemy territory as a mid-upper gunner on a Lancaster bomber. He was keenly interested in flying and on his return to Canada, hoped to take pilot training. He was active in sports, especially baseball, hockey and curling. Milford was personable, had a genial disposition and was a favourite among the young people in the district. He was family oriented and is sadly missed by his family and friends.

Levins Lake (64 I/7), northeast of North Knife Lake was named after him in 1974.

Lewicki, Gunner **Emil** of Renwer (H 42019). Royal Canadian Artillery. He died 19 September 1944 and is commemorated at the Calais Canadian War Cemetery in France. ***Lewicki Lake*** (62 N/15), southeast of Swan River was named after him in 1973.

Lewis, Warrant Officer 2 **Albert Bennett** of Muir (R 106451). No. 408 Squadron. He died 22 June 1943 at the age of 22 and is commemorated at the Reichswald Forest War Cemetery in Germany. He was survived by his parents Albert and Elizabeth Lewis and by his wife Arline A. Lewis (née Dukquits) of Gladstone, Manitoba. His brother recalls (2 November 2001):

Ben, as he was commonly known, was born at Chester, Cheshire, England on October 10, 1920. He emigrated to Canada with his younger brother Fred and his parents in 1926. They settled in the Golden Stream district nine miles southeast of Gladstone, Manitoba where Ben received his elementary education and his Grade 9 and 10 by correspondence. He was a lover of sports and took an active part in both softball and hockey. He was also a member of the United Church Young People's Group.

In the early part of 1941, Ben offered his service to his country, but was not accepted into the RCAF until June of that year. He received his training in both Manitoba and Alberta, graduating as a Wireless Operator. Shortly before being posted overseas, he married Arline Dukquits of Golden Stream.

Bennett Lewis Bay (63 P/6) in Landing Lake was named after him in 1995.

Lewis, Private **Dean E.** of Medora (H 103190). Princess Patricia's Canadian Light Infantry. He died 13 December 1943 at the age of 21 and is commemorated at the Moro River Canadian War Cemetery in Italy. He was the son of Evan and Catherine Lewis of Medora, Manitoba. According to his sister (15 May 1995):

Dean Edward Lewis was born on March 8, 1922 at the farm home in Medora. He obtained his education at Purple Hill School after which he farmed with his father and brothers. In November, 1942 he joined the Princess Patricia's Canadian Light Infantry, training at Fort Garry, Winnipeg and Shilo. In March of 1943 he was sent to England. After a few months of training he was sent to Sicily and then on to mainland Italy where he was killed in action on December 13, 1943 during the Moro River crossing at the Battle of Ortona.

During his short life, Dean was active in sports, enjoyed dancing and made many friends. Dean had a happy, sunny nature, always thinking of others rather than himself. He was dearly loved and is sadly missed by his family and friends.

Lewis Island (62 P/1) in Lake Winnipeg was named after him in 1980.

Lewis, Rifleman **Gordon J. W.** of Winnipeg (H 41029). Royal Winnipeg Rifles. He died 8 June 1944 at the age of 28 and is commemorated at Beny-sur-Mer Canadian War Cemetery in Calvados, France. He was the son of Samuel T. and Sarah Lewis of Winnipeg. His brother recalls (8 June 1988):

Gordy was working with Blue Ribbon at the time of enlistment, was affectionately esteemed by them and I believe regularly forwarded ... packages of treats [by them]. He was fully active in battalion sports, John, his brother, witnessing one of the inter-battalion [boxing] finals in [which] Gordy got a draw. Next morning at breakfast, the Mess Officer called attention to recommend Gordy on his fight the night before, upholding the prestige of the Winnipeg Rifles.

Gordon ... was killed in action ... after landing with invasion forces in France. Company "A" and [the] whole Battalion got entrapped and surrounded in farm land. On breaking out of the encirclement, some of A Company's men were captured and killed – 12 of them lined up and killed.

His niece adds (26 November 2001):

During our pilgrimage to Normandy in 1989, we were fortunate to learn more about exactly what happened. Most of the murders took place at the Chateau d'Audrieu, which was used as the headquarters of Kurt Meyers. Apparently, Gordy and three or four others that were among the captured, fully expecting what was about to happen, did try to make a run for it, but were gunned down. In total, there were 58 members of the Royal Winnipeg Rifles who were murdered on D-Day + 2 as well as several from other regiments.

One of the veterans who returned to Normandy for the 45th anniversary of the D-Day landings was former Captain Neil Mustard, age 73:

It was the tranquillity that most startled the retired civil engineer. His vivid memories were of the blood-stained countryside and the friends who fell in battle during the summer of 1944. "It's quite a shock not to recognize a bloody thing on the beach and just the odd street corner in the towns," he said yesterday as he returned to Bayeux. Mustard, who lives in Mississauga just west of Toronto, is one of the hundreds of Canadian veterans returning to Normandy for the first time since landing on the beaches in what historians call the greatest seaborne invasion of all time. Mustard ... said until this year he couldn't bring himself to return to Normandy. He said he has been filled with sad memories since he arrived Saturday. "I can't stop thinking of all my friends that were killed. Within three days of D-Day there were only seven of us left in our platoon that hit the beaches with 48 men. I trained with them, ate with them, and lived with them for four years before D-Day. I'm very sad" (*Winnipeg Free Press* 6 June 1989).

Lewis Bay (64 F/3) in Goldsand Lake was named after him in 1988.

Lewis, Sergeant **Gordon R.** of St. James (R 59848). No. 1 Advanced Flying School. He died 2 August 1942 at the age of 21 and is commemorated at Kirkinner Cemetery, Wigtownshire, Scotland. ***Lewis Esker*** (64 I/4), south of Ashley Lake was named after him in 1995.

Lewis, Leading Aircraftman **James F. B.** of Morden (644842). No. 40 Squadron, RAF. He died 14 April 1940 at the age of 21 and is commemorated at the Runnymede Memorial in Surrey, England. He was the youngest son of David L. and Margaret Lewis of Morden, Manitoba. According to his sister (14 April 1999):

When the Depression arrived, there was little work and he then rode the freights to Ontario. There he got work on a dairy farm and walked across the fields to the old Malton Airport where he took flying lessons. He was always athletic and took part in many sports and at one time was an amateur boxer.

After learning to fly, he took a freight to Vancouver and after visiting with Uncle Rob, who had lost a leg at Vimy Ridge, Jimmy got passage on a coal freighter. He worked his way over to England, passing through the Panama Canal. We have many letters of his experiences. This was in 1938. Arriving in England, he signed up for the RAF before the war broke out. He was stationed at several air bases in mid-England and wrote about the areas around Lancaster.

Despite his obvious determination to fly, when he arrived in England he discovered he had neglected to bring his pilot's licence. He was nonetheless admitted to the RAF as ground crew with the promise that he would be reclassified to aircrew. War was declared shortly thereafter and all trades were frozen. Frustrated, he "borrowed" a Blenheim and set out to prove that he could fly. He buzzed the Officers Mess at lunchtime before setting out towards Norway. He was never heard from again (Allison and Hayward 1991). A contemporary newspaper account added that:

His mother, Mrs. Lewis, who was visiting relatives in Winnipeg, Thursday, said she could hardly bring herself to believe there was no hope left that her son might still be alive, possibly a prisoner of war. Bravely facing the news, she said: "I suppose I am just one of thousands of mothers to whom news like this might come."

The last letter received by the mother from her son was dated March 22, at Wyton air force camp in England. "My squadron has been expecting to go abroad. I am gaining ground experience and expect to get flying before the year is out" (*Winnipeg Free Press* April 1940).

He was the brother of Leading Aircraftman David Earl K. Lewis, another World War II casualty. Lewis Lake in Saskatchewan was named in the latter's honour. ***James Lewis Bay*** (53 L/4) in Bolton Lake was named after LAC Lewis in 1995.

Lewis, Pilot Officer **James N.** of Winnipeg (J 7457). No. 3 Squadron. He died 31 May 1942 at the age of 20 and is commemorated at Folkestone New Cemetery in Kent, England. He was the son of George T. and Alix N. F. Lewis of East Kildonan. ***Lewis Peninsula*** (63 N/8) on Burntwood Lake was named after him in 1995.

Lewis, Private **Joseph M.** of Winnipeg (H 20871). Winnipeg Grenadiers. He died a prisoner of war 31 October 1942 at the age of 37 and is commemorated at the Sai Wan War Cemetery in Hong Kong. He was the son of Edwin and Lenora Lewis and was survived by his wife Dorothy L. Lewis of Fort Whyte. ***Lewis Rapids*** (64 I/8) in the South Knife River was named after him in 1995.

Lewis, Flight Sergeant **Richard H.** of Minnedosa (R 140521). No. 427 Squadron. He died 27 February 1943 at the age of 23 and is commemorated at North Luffenham (St. John The Baptist) Churchyard, Rutland, England. He was the son of Thomas C. and Henrietta J. Lewis of Minnedosa. ***Lewis Hill*** (64 F/4), west of Vandekerckhove Lake was named after him in 1995.

Lewis, Flight Sergeant **Richard J. H. "Lucky"** of Winnipeg (R 56879). No. 77 Squadron. He died 14 March 1942 at the age of 23 and is commemorated at Leeming (St. John The Baptist) Churchyard, Yorkshire, England. He was the only son of James H. and Grace H. Lewis of Winnipeg. According to a newspaper account:

He was wounded in action over Hamburg and crashed once into the North Sea after a raid on Berlin. By the time he had completed 13 trips into action over the continent, his numerous exploits and narrow escapes had won him the name of Lucky Lewis.

Lewis engaged actively in sports, winning a Manitoba speed skating championship in 1934 and being a member of the St. John's Roamers rugby team in 1933 - 34 (*Winnipeg Free Press* 18 March 1942).

His sister adds (20 July 1985) that on his final mission "the aircraft had been badly shot up and crashed when landing at their home base. He and one other of the crew were still alive when removed from the wreckage. Both died the same day." ***Lewis Point*** (64 B/12) on the Churchill River was named after him in 1989.

Lewis, Flying Officer **Thomas S.** of Winnipeg (J 40805). No. 415 Squadron. He died 31 March 1945 at the age of 22 and is commemorated at the Runnymede Memorial in Surrey, England. He was the son of Henry E. and Bertha Lewis of West Kildonan. ***Lewis Creek*** (64 P/3), which flows south into Big Spruce River was named after him in 1995.

Leyland, Flight Sergeant **John W.** of Petersfield (R 80045). No. 5 Operational Training Unit, RCAF. He died 30 August 1942 at the age of 28 and is commemorated at Dunure Cemetery, Ayrshire, Scotland. He was the son of John W. and Sarah Leyland and was survived by his wife Hilda Leyland of Brandon. ***Leyland Lake*** (64 H/9), north of Freeman Lake was named after him in 1995.

Lezun, Corporal **William** of Portage la Prairie (H 57903). Royal Canadian Army Service Corps. He died 26 August 1944 at the age of 28 and is commemorated at Bretteville-sur-Laize Canadian War Cemetery in Calvados, France. He was the son of John and Mary Lezun of Winnipeg and was survived by his wife Elsie M. Lezun of Winnipeg. His wife received the following letter from his commanding officer:

> Dear Mrs. Lezun: I regret very much that I must write you of the death of your husband. The loss of William Lezun is to us very real. His pleasant manner had made us all his friends, and the efficient way in which he performed all his duties made him a valuable member of our organization.
>
> On the night of August 25 we were subjected to an intense bombing attack and, as a result of injuries received that night, your husband died the following day. I realize that there is little I can say to ease the sense of great loss which I know you feel. I can assure you though that within a few minutes of the time he was injured, a Medical Officer was doing everything humanly possible to save his life and I am sure that he did not at any time suffer any pain.
>
> Please believe me when I say that you have my most sincere sympathy and that we here share in your sorrow. Yours sincerely, A. B. McFarlane, Staff Captain (12 September 1944).

Lezun Lake (64 K/14), northeast of Lac Brochet was named after him in 1974.

Lidster, Flying Officer **Perry D.** of Brandon (J 13829). No. 22 Operational Training Unit, RCAF. He died 28 June 1943 at the age of 23 and is commemorated at Botley Cemetery in Oxfordshire, England. He was the son of Wilbert M. and Louise Lidster of Brandon. ***Lidster Lake*** (64 P/5), south of Nejanilini Lake was named after him in 1974.

Lievense, Flight Sergeant **Semon** of St. Boniface (R 100278). No. 6110 Servicing Echelon, RCAF. He died 22 September 1944 at the age of 27 and is commemorated at Arnhem Oosterbeek War Cemetery, Holland. He was the son of Morris and Louise Lievense of St. Boniface. ***Lievense Lake*** (63 K/16), west of Wekusko Lake was named after him in 1973.

Lifman, Flight Sergeant **Thorhall B.** of Arborg (R 147416). No. 428 Squadron. He died 18 August 1943 at the age of 22 and is commemorated at the Berlin 1939 - 1945 War Cemetery in Brandenburg, Germany. He was the son of Bjarnthor J. and Margaret K. Lifman of Arborg, Manitoba. ***Lifman Lake*** (64 P/16), northeast of Nejanilini Lake was named after him in 1974.

Lightheart, Sergeant **Alvin E.** of Winnipeg (R 180436). No. 22 Operational Training Unit, RCAF. He died 19 April 1943 and is commemorated at Cirencester Cemetery, Gloucestershire, England. ***Lightheart Lake*** (63 N/1), southeast of Sherridon was named after him in 1970.

Lillyman, Ordinary Telegraphist **Raymond F.** of Winnipeg (V 38537). HMCS *St. Croix*. The *St. Croix* was torpedoed and sunk by U-305 south of Iceland while escorting Convoy ON.202. Five officers and 76 men were rescued by HMS *Itchen*, but only one of these survived the loss of the *Itchen* two days later. See VanSickle, Ordinary Seaman Harold A. for additional information. Ordinary Telegraphist Lillyman died 20 September 1943 at the age of 21 and is commemorated at the Halifax Memorial. He was the second son of Harry and Florence Lillyman of East Kildonan.

> He enlisted in June, 1942, going active in September and training at Toronto and Saint-Hyacinthe, Quebec before he was sent to eastern Canadian ports for convoy duty. He attended Prince Edward and Lord Wolseley schools and was an enthusiastic hockey and lacrosse player. Before enlisting, he was employed at the Winnipeg Bus Depot (*The Elmwood Herald* 7 October 1943).

Lillyman Lake (64 N/8), southwest of Nueltin Lake was named after him in 1972.

Lincoln, Gunner **Percy Charles** of Petersfield (H 66684). Royal Canadian Artillery. He died 12 July 1944 at the age of 34 and is commemorated at Beny-sur-Mer Canadian War Cemetery in Calvados, France. He was survived by his wife Lucy Lincoln. ***Lincoln Lake*** (52 L/11), east of Cole Lake was named after him in 1982.

Lindal, Lieutenant **Harold Earl** of Winnipeg. Essex Scottish Regiment. He died 25 October 1944 and is commemorated at Bergen-op-Zoom Canadian War Cemetery in Holland. ***Lindal Lake*** (64 K/6), northeast of Reindeer Lake was named after him in 1972.

Lindsay, Flying Officer **Alexander** of Winnipeg (J 27428). No. 630 Squadron. He died 27 July 1944 at the age of 26 and is commemorated at Clermont-Ferrand (Des Carmes-Dechaux) Communal Cemetery, Puy-de-Dome, France. He was the brother of Flying Officer James Lindsay (next entry). His niece reports that he had played for the Winnipeg Blue Bombers and boxed professionally prior to enlistment. ***Lindsay Island*** (64 F/8) in Le Clair Lake was named after him in 1995.

Lindsay, Flying Officer **James** of Winnipeg (J 19994). No. 153 Squadron. He died 14 October 1944 at the age of 22 and is commemorated at the Reichswald Forest War Cemetery in Germany. He was the brother of Flying Officer Alexander Lindsay (previous entry). ***Lindsay Bay*** (64 N/1) in Stephen Lake was named after him in 1995.

Lindsay, Sergeant **John** of East Kildonan (H 63527). Fort Garry Horse. He died 16 July 1942 at the age of 37 and is commemorated at Elmwood Cemetery in Winnipeg. He was survived by his wife Jane Lindsay of Winnipeg. ***Lindsay Lake*** (63 J/11), west of Cross Lake was named after him in 1972.

Linklater, Sergeant **William B.** of Selkirk (H 19751). Queen's Own Cameron Highlanders. He died 19 August 1942 and is commemorated at Dieppe Canadian War Cemetery, Seine-Maritime, France. He was the son of Violet Linklater. ***Linklater Lake*** (64 H/8), northwest of Hogg Lake was named after him in 1995.

Linn, Pilot Officer **Hubert J.** of Poplar Point (J 94444). No. 101 Squadron. He died 30 August 1944 and is commemorated at Dejbjerg Churchyard in Denmark. He was the son of John Linn and the brother of Helen Linn of Poplar Point. ***Linn Island*** (64 F/1) in Barrington Lake was named after him in 1989.

Lintick, Private **Stanley** of Sifton (H 1503). Queen's Own Cameron Highlanders. He died 14 August 1944 at the age of 21 and is commemorated at Bretteville-sur-Laize Canadian War Cemetery in Calvados, France. He was the son of Alexander and Magrethe Lintick of Sifton, Manitoba. ***Lintick Lake*** (64 O/10), northwest of Nejanilini Lake was named after him in 1975.

Lisowicky, Corporal **Jacob** of Winnipeg (H 14204). Royal Canadian Regiment. He died 5 December 1944 at the age of 20 and is commemorated at Ravenna War Cemetery in Italy. He was survived by his mother Mrs. Elsie Lisowicky of Winnipeg. ***Lisowicky Lake*** (64 J/2), southwest of Tadoule Lake was named after him in 1975.

Listmayer, Gunner **Andrew** of Sprague (H 20699). Royal Canadian Artillery. He died 9 October 1944 and is commemorated at Bergen-op-Zoom Canadian War Cemetery in Holland. ***Listmayer Lake*** (64 N/8), southwest of Nueltin Lake was named after him in 1972.

Litchfield, Flying Officer **Ralph F.** of Winnipeg (J 25734). No. 101 Squadron. He died 31 March 1944 at the age of 27 and is commemorated at the Runnymede Memorial in Surrey, England. He was the son of William and Magretta Litchfield of Burnaby, British Columbia. ***Litchfield Lake*** (64 O/6), southeast of Nueltin Lake was named after him in 1975.

Little, Rifleman **Earl R.** of Minto (H 43036). Regina Rifle Regiment. He died 25 September 1944 at the age of 24 and is commemorated at the Calais Canadian War Cemetery in France. He was the son of John A. and Janette Vera Little of Minto, Manitoba. ***Little Point*** (64 G/15) on Trout Lake was named after him in 1994.

Little, Private **Francis** of Winnipegosis (H 41796). Winnipeg Grenadiers. He died 21 December 1941 at the age of 24 and is commemorated at the Sai Wan Memorial in Hong Kong. He was the son of William and Agnes Little and was survived by his wife Della B. Little (née Carlson) of Owen Sound, Ontario and their two sons. His son Nels writes (18 October 2001):

Francis Little was born on June 18, 1913 in The Pas, Manitoba and moved with his family in 1918 to the Winnipegosis area. His parents were from a farming background. He had two brothers and two sisters. During the pre-war years, it was very hard to earn a living and this was done with odd jobs, commercial fishing and working for the local beef farmer. Frank was a hard working, happy man who loved his family. He was an emotional man with a temper that could be traced to his Irish ancestry. As a father and husband, he was missed and mourned for many years. His loss is eternal.

Little Island (64 H/1) in Billard Lake was named after him in 1995.

Little, Flying Officer **Gordon J.** of Selkirk (J 25849). No. 97 Squadron. He died 16 December 1943 at the age of 21 and is commemorated at the Berlin 1939 - 1945 War Cemetery in Brandenburg, Germany. He was the son of Charles A. and Sybil E. Little of Lorain, Ohio. ***Little Lake*** (52 L/3), northeast of Brereton Lake was named after him in 1973.

Little, Flying Officer **Thomas Bruce** of Dauphin (J 40372). No. 408 Squadron. He died 29 January 1945 at the age of 33 and is commemorated at Durnbach War Cemetery in Bavaria, Germany. He was the son of Magistrate Thomas and Eliza B. H. Little of Dauphin, Manitoba and was survived by his wife Dorothy I. Little (née Eyres) of Dauphin and their son. He writes (26 October 2001):

Bruce was born in Winnipeg and moved with his parents to Dauphin at the age of five. He received his education in the Dauphin public schools. At the age of 16, he became a cadet with the Canadian National Steamships and in the next year and a half visited Australia, New Zealand and South America. On his return, he graduated from Normal School in 1932 and taught for several years in Alonsa, Dauphin, Carman and St. James. He graduated with an Arts degree from Queen's University in 1941. Bruce was married to Dorothy Eyres of Carnegie, Manitoba and had one son, Gary, who resides in Portage la Prairie.

Bruce enlisted in the RCAF in 1942 and after training in Regina and Mountain View, graduated from Chatham, New Brunswick on January 20, 1944. Gary and his wife Gerry visited the Durnbach War Cemetery in 1996 and placed a bronze plaque on Bruce's headstone to commemorate their visit.

Bruce had a zest for life and adventure. He received great enjoyment from his travel experiences and the many friends he met along the way. Photography was an essential part of every trip and special occasion. He loved literature, poetry, drama and music. He had a special talent for the way he expressed his view of the world and life.

He wrote many letters home to his brother. These are a few excerpts:

Dear Harry: I received your epistle a few days ago but have just managed to make out the signature. I was able to read the letter alright – thanks for the printing. At last I have arrived at ITS where our training really begins. I have had my medical but have to have a re-check on my chest. I have had a very heavy cold and they seem to suspect that some lung trouble may be the result. If I wash out, I shall be in Toronto in a week or so to begin ground duties. However, I don't think there is anything wrong.

I like the Air Force very much but would be terribly disappointed if I couldn't continue as aircrew. There is lots of talk about the fellows on the ground being just as important – and it's true – but at the same time, everyone else in the Air Force is where he is in order to serve the air crews. And then there is something about being in the air that gets you and makes ground duties seem dull and ordinary.

As to your problem about enlisting, I know how you feel about the attitude of other people. But anyone who lets his decisions be ruled by what others think would be foolish. There are only two factors to be considered: 1. Yourself and 2. Your country. When I enlisted, I did so because I thought that I could do more good in the Air Force than in teaching. Teaching has gone to blazes since the war started – insofar as it is possible to teach such things as history and English from an unbiased point of view. Then too, I figured that I should act upon the convictions I had about the war. To me, it seemed that the war had to be won – not for the sake of Canada or Britain – but for the hope of a world in which nationalism will have disappeared and internationalism [will] have become the new spirit. It is a long story and like all thoughts which are wrapped up in ideals and emotions, very hard to express (n.d.).

Dear Harry: I thought that you might be interested in knowing something about what lies ahead of you if you come over here. Seems to me that I heard you were going thru' as a navigator. If so, you will probably be at an AOS by now and may have learned how to cook astro-shots already. I should also learn how to work them out quickly in a legal manner as the astrograph is out altogether here.

When you come to England, you will be sent to a Reception Centre where you await posting to an advanced flying school. Here you will go over your AOS work, brushing up and speeding up. Map-reading is of prime importance and very, very much more difficult here than in Canada. So be up on that part of your work. While at Reception Centre, you will take courses to keep you in trim pending posting.

You will have many surprises here – some pleasant, others unpleasant. The weather can be terribly duff at times and at others perfectly wizard. But the duff predominates. The food is very plain. You get plenty to eat, but miss sweets quite a bit. Clothes are rationed, so bring what you can and have a couple of good, warm sweaters and a scarf. You will like the afternoon teas which are a ritual here. Someone said that the British are winning the war because they know how to relax. That may not be the whole truth but it certainly is true that "Everything Stops for Tea."

England is a very lovely country – when the sun is shining. At other times, just now at any rate, it is cold and damp and terribly uncomfortable. There are lots of shows, dances and good pubs and one can have a fine time at "The Wagon and Horses" or "The Fox" or some other similarly named pub. Some wonderful leaves can be arranged here thru' service organizations or private individuals who go in for that sort of thing. I hope that the war will be over before you get here, but if not, you will find many pleasant people and places to keep you entertained in your spare time. Of course, there is a war on and you will have some work to do occasionally. Drop a line some time, Bruce (29 March 1944).

Dear Harry: Thought you might be interested in this article. The technique described is no longer in use, but the story of preparation for, and of an operation in very good. One detail which is most noticeable in fact, but which has been omitted in this article is that when there is a "hairy do" such as Berlin, the toilets work overtime just before take-off time.

Just noticed this in today's paper and decided to send it along to you. Had a bad trip last night and am tired. All my navigation aids "went for a Burton" before we left England so had to go in and out on estimation. Hit the target five minutes late but got home OK. Bruce (7 January 1945).

Little Bay (64 O/5) in Booth Lake was named after him in 1995.

Litynesky, Flight Sergeant **Stephen W.** of Ashville (R 157090). No. 1664 Conversion Unit, RCAF. He died 22 November 1943 at the age of 29 and is commemorated at Harrogate Cemetery, Yorkshire, England. He was the son of Vasil and Julia Litynesky of Ashville, Manitoba. His sister writes (15 March 1998):

He enjoyed being a grain farmer and hoped to return to it after his service was over. He also said he would have liked to own his own plane some day. His parents were originally from the Ukraine and upon arrival in Canada farmed in an area known as Ashville [near Dauphin] where he grew up.

Litynesky Lake (64 H/4), north of Gauer Lake was named after him in 1995.

Livingston, Lieutenant **Allan M.** of Winnipeg. Royal Canadian Artillery. He died 2 September 1944 and is commemorated at Gradara War Cemetery in Italy. ***Livingston Peninsula*** (64 F/9) on Jordan Lake was named after him in 1995.

Livingston, Lance Corporal **David I.** of Roblin (H 65999). Royal Canadian Artillery. He died 11 November 1944 at the age of 24 and is commemorated at Bergen-op-Zoom Canadian War Cemetery in Holland. He was the youngest of the four children of William A. and Agnes Y. Livingston of Roblin, Manitoba. His sister writes (15 May 1995):

David was a very quiet, friendly lad with a great sense of humour. Also very considerate of others. He seemed to enjoy life on the farm and the animals – particularly the horses. Of course he was into sports. A friend and I were fortunate in having a trip to Europe (1970) [and] we went to Holland and visited David's grave. It is in a quiet place, a ways out in the country, with a bluff of white poplars on one side.

Livingston Point (64 O/16) on Baralzon Lake was named after him in 1995.

Livingston, Pilot Officer **Robert A.** of Rosebank (J 17110). No. 405 Squadron, Distinguished Flying Cross.

This officer has taken part in a large number of operational missions as wireless operator air gunner. He has always shown the greatest determination to achieve his objective. On one occasion, during a daylight attack on Oldenburg, the aircraft in which he was flying was hit by cannon shells from two enemy fighters and fire broke out behind the navigator's seat. Pilot Officer Livingston promptly put the fire out, thus enabling the aircraft to return safely. At all times his devotion to duty and coolness under fire have set a fine example to his crew (DFC Citation 1944).

He died 22 June 1943 at the age of 21 and is commemorated at Rheinberg War Cemetery in Germany. He was the son of Mr. and Mrs. P. R. Livingston of Norwood. ***Livingston Lake*** (64 B/7), south of Southern Indian Lake was named after him in 1949.

Livingstone, Sergeant **Robert D.** of Winnipeg (R 180315). No. 158 Squadron. He died 21 January 1944 at the age of 30 and is commemorated at the Berlin 1939 - 1945 War Cemetery in Brandenburg, Germany. He was the son of William D. and Florence W. P. Livingstone of Winnipeg and was survived by his aunt Miss C. A. Walker of Winnipeg. ***Livingstone Bay*** (64 C/13) in McMillan Lake was named after him in 1995.

Livingstone, Pilot Officer **Samuel G.** of Winnipeg (J 86829). No. 419 Squadron. He died 13 May 1944 at the age of 21 and is commemorated at Brussels Town Cemetery in Belgium. ***Livingstone Island*** (53 D/5) in Carr-Harris Lake was named after him in 1989.

Lloyd, Sergeant **Hugh H.** of Winnipeg (401508). Royal Australian Air Force. He died 1 February 1943 at the age of 29 and is commemorated at Newark-on-Trent Cemetery, Nottinghamshire, England. He was the son of Thomas and Julie Lloyd and was survived by his wife Betty E. Lloyd of Victoria, Australia. ***Lloyd Island*** (53 L/13) in Oxford Lake was named after him in 1995.

Loader, Corporal **Thomas R.** of Winnipeg (H 101210). Regina Rifle Regiment. He died 12 September 1944 at the age of 22 and is commemorated at the Calais Canadian War Cemetery in France. He was survived by his mother and step-father Emily Loader (née Gifford) and Ben Morsette of Orient Bay, Ontario. His brother writes (25 April 1996):

Tom was born in Winnipeg in the fall of 1922 – I don't know the exact date. One of the things he loved was dancing, modern or old-time. At the time he joined the army he was working for the CPR at Douglas, Manitoba. He joined the army at Fort Osborne Barracks ... in June, 1942 and went overseas in June, 1943. He was killed in action in France.

Loader Lake (64 I/13), northwest of North Knife Lake was named after him in 1974.

Loat, Private **Norman J.** of Kenville (H 70606). Lake Superior Regiment. He died 14 August 1944 at the age of 24 and is commemorated at Bretteville-sur-Laize Canadian War Cemetery in Calvados, France. He was the son of Melvin and Margaret Loat of Kenville, Manitoba. ***Loat Lake*** (62 N/15), southeast of Swan River was named after him in 1973.

Lobb, Warrant Officer 2 **Benjamin J.** of Winnipeg (R 110978). No. 115 Squadron. He died 21 January 1944 at the age of 20 and is commemorated at the Berlin 1939 - 1945 War Cemetery in Brandenburg, Germany. He was the son of William H. and Norah E. Lobb of Edmonton. ***Lobb Lake*** (64 I/14), northwest of North Knife Lake was named after him in 1974.

Lochhead, Flying Officer **Hector** of Ridgeville (J 89692). No. 298 Squadron. He died 25 February 1945 at the age of 21 and is commemorated at the Runnymede Memorial in Surrey, England. He was survived by his mother Minnie Lochhead of Ridgeville, Manitoba. ***Lochhead Lake*** (63 J/8), north of Playgreen Lake was named after him in 1971.

Locke, Private **Elmer E.** of Dauphin (L 107548). Cameron Highlanders of Ottawa. He died 16 December 1944 at the age of 21 and is commemorated at Schoonselhof Cemetery in Antwerp, Belgium. He was the son of Charles E. and Euphemia Locke of Dauphin. According to his sister (4 February 1997):

> His schooling was in Dauphin Plains School. He liked to ride and break horses. He was a great person for teasing his mother. He was visiting his two sisters who lived in British Columbia when he joined up.

Locke Lake (63 N/12) near Sisipuk Lake was named after him in 1981.

Loeppky, Corporal **Peter** of Winnipeg (H 70516). Cape Breton Highlanders. He died 10 December 1944 and is commemorated at Ravenna War Cemetery in Italy. ***Loeppky Lake*** (62 P/16), west of Family Lake was named after him in 1973.

Loftson, Pilot Officer **Stefan A.** of Lundar (J 90278). No. 9 Squadron. He died 24 February 1944 at the age of 20 and is commemorated at Durnbach War Cemetery in Bavaria, Germany. He was the son of Bjarni M. and Thora Loftson of Lundar, Manitoba. According to his sister (Inga Einarson, 1995):

> Stefan was a lovely child with silvery hair. He was full of mischief and liked to get up on anything high and wave his arms as if he was going to fly off. He always wanted to fly and got his wish, but at what price.

Loftson Lake (64 P/15), northeast of Nejanilini Lake was named after him in 1974.

Logan, Warrant Officer 1 **Francis G.** of St. Boniface (R 101611). No. 59 Squadron. He died 24 June 1944 and is commemorated at Saffron Hill Cemetery, Leicestershire, England. ***Logan Island*** (64 P/5) in Little Duck Lake was named after him in 1989.

Logan, Flying Officer **Ray H.** of Winnipeg (J 17599). No. 109 Squadron. He died 28 May 1943 at the age of 21 and is commemorated at Rotterdam (Crooswijk) General Cemetery, Holland. ***Logan Point*** (53 L/12) on Windy Lake was named after him in 1995.

Logan, Rifleman **Robert J. G.** of Winnipeg (H 17736). Royal Winnipeg Rifles. He died 8 June 1944 at the age of 24 and is commemorated at Bretteville-sur-Laize Canadian War Cemetery in Calvados, France. He was the son of Charles and Albina Logan of Winnipeg. ***Logan Bay*** (64 I/12) in Pott Lake was named after him in 1995.

Long, Sergeant **John** of Winnipeg (H 6005). Winnipeg Grenadiers. He died 22 December 1941 and is commemorated at the Sai Wan Memorial in Hong Kong. ***Long Peninsula*** (63 I/4) on Playgreen Lake was named after him in 1995.

Long, Sergeant **Roy** of Varsity View (Charleswood) (H 35426). Royal Canadian Artillery. He died 12 September 1944 at the age of 28 and is commemorated at Gradara War Cemetery in Italy. He was the son of William C. and Lily Long. ***Long Hill*** (64 I/11), northeast of Quinn Lake was named after him in 1995.

Longley, Pilot Officer **Robert T. W.** of Winnipeg (J 92038). No. 433 Squadron. He died 5 July 1944 at the age of 22 and is commemorated at Laons Communal Cemetery, Eure-et-Loir, France. He was the son of Robert and Dorothy Longley of Winnipeg. His mother writes (9 September 1993) that he:

> ... was born in Winnipeg on June 8, 1922 at Misericordia Hospital. Robert attended Cecil Rhodes School and Daniel McIntyre High School where he completed his Grade 12 education. Robert loved to play hockey and baseball at school.
>
> When Robert was 18 years old he joined the Royal Canadian Air Force where he learned to be a pilot; he was sent first to Brandon and then on to Trenton and Kingston, Ontario (he joined in 1939). And when the world war broke, Robert was sent to Laons, France and went missing while on a mission.

Longley Lake (64 G/13), west of Big Sand Lake was named after him in 1994.

Longney, Private **Leonard V.** of Thornhill (H 103547). Princess Patricia's Canadian Light Infantry. He died 13 June 1944 at the age of 21 and is commemorated at the Cassino War Cemetery in Italy. He was the son of William H. and Jane M. Longney of Thornhill, Manitoba. His sister recalls (7 April 1995):

> Leonard Victor Longney attended school in Thornhill, Manitoba [and then] went to St. John's College in Winnipeg [for] one year. [He] stayed home on the farm with [his] parents until the fall, then went to Winnipeg to look for work. He was told to join up, 1942. His parents were farmers until he died. They then retired to live in Thornhill, then moved to Morden.

In his last letter home, he wrote:

> I guess you have heard we are at it again, so I guess the mail will be held up for a bit. There isn't much to say, you know as much as I do. I heard the BBC news and they mentioned just what we know as far as we are concerned (20 May 1944).

He had been wounded in Italy some three weeks before his death and his sister made enquiries about the circumstances. She received the following from the archives:

> After being wounded, he lay on the battle field for eight hours in the heat of the day. When he was finally moved by ambulance, there were maggots in his wounds and gangrene had set in. He had lost a lot of blood and was unconscious. He was given several blood transfusions

and underwent surgery. He did not respond to treatment for the first five days in hospital and then a slight response was noted. He finally passed away after 21 days. Shock was listed as the main cause of death (n.d.).

Longney Lake (64 K/7), northeast of Reindeer Lake was named after him in 1972.

Lonie, Pilot Officer **Jack M.** of Winnipeg (J 85164). No. 115 Squadron. He died 30 July 1944 at the age of 21 and is commemorated at Bretteville-sur-Laize Canadian War Cemetery in Calvados, France. ***Lonie Lake*** (64 O/13), south of Nueltin Lake was named after him in 1975.

Lopuck, Leading Stoker **Antoni** of Transcona (V 24712). HMCS *St. Croix*. The *St. Croix* was torpedoed and sunk by U-305 south of Iceland while escorting Convoy ON.202. Five officers and 76 men were rescued by HMS *Itchen*, but only one of these survived the loss of the *Itchen* two days later. See VanSickle, Ordinary Seaman Harold A. for additional information. Leading Stoker Lopuck died 20 September 1943 at the age of 30 and is commemorated at the Halifax Memorial. He was the son of Michael and Jessie Lopuck of Transcona and was survived by his wife Elsie Lopuck of Transcona and their son. He writes (14 November 2001):

> Antoni was born and raised in Transcona, the third eldest in a family of six children. Three of his brothers also served in the war. Antoni had started working on a CNR section gang when he was 14. He later worked for Dominion Malting before enlisting in June, 1941. He was survived by his wife and a six year-old son. Antoni's death was particularly hard on his mother who always hoped he had somehow survived and would return after the war. He had crossed the Atlantic on previous convoys without any major incident, but just prior to his last crossing, he felt very uneasy due to the aged condition of the *St. Croix* and the enemy's new use of acoustically-guided torpedoes.

Lopuck Lake (64 N/13), west of Nueltin Lake was named after him in 1972.

Lorentson, Rifleman **Raymond N.** of Winnipeg (H 18606). Royal Winnipeg Rifles. He died 29 March 1945 and is commemorated at the Groesbeek Canadian War Cemetery in Holland. ***Lorentson Lake*** (63 I/1), northwest of Little Bolton Lake was named after him in 1995.

Lough, Flying Officer **Spencer W.** of Winnipeg (J 20830). No. 431 Squadron. He died 17 June 1944 at the age of 29 and is commemorated at Uden War Cemetery, Holland. He was the son of William F. and Marion L. Lough of Winnipeg. ***Lough Lake*** (63 N/10), west of Flatrock Lake was named after him in 1995.

Lougheed, Flying Officer **Ralph James** of Winnipeg (J 40492). No. 103 Squadron. He died 7 January 1945 at the age of 20 and is commemorated at Munster Communal Cemetery, Haut-Rhin, France. He was the son of Dr. M. S. and Gladys Lougheed of Winnipeg. ***Lougheed Lake*** (63 J/3), northeast of North Moose Lake was named after him in 1973.

Lousier, Private **Ernie J.** of Bowsman (H 17470). Winnipeg Grenadiers. He died 19 December 1941 at the age of 19 and is commemorated at the Sai Wan Memorial in Hong Kong. He was the son of Daniel and Violet Lousier of Bowsman. His brother recalls (21 January 2002):

> He was raised in the small town of Bowsman where he attended school, played baseball and later worked as a grain elevator assistant and in the Caverly saw mill and lumber camp. He joined the PPCLI on June 25, 1940 and was stationed in Winnipeg. In March, 1941, he took a signalman course in Kingston and in October, 1941 he transferred to the Winnipeg Grenadiers to be with his brother, Arthur. After an embarkation leave at home for four days, they departed for Hong Kong.

Lousier Lake (64 C/5), southeast of Reindeer Lake was named after him in 1973.

Lovat, Engine Room Artificer 4 **Peter K.** of St. Boniface (V 27067). HMCS *Charlottetown*. The *Charlottetown* was torpedoed in the St. Lawrence River by U-517; ten seamen were killed. ERA Lovat died 10 September 1942 at the age of 23 and is commemorated at the Halifax Memorial. He was the son of Henry B. and Catherine S. Lovat of Norwood. The following is an excerpt from an Ontario newspaper:

> One of the most popular boys ever to come to Sudbury, his many friends here have taken a keen interest in his swift promotion since he joined the Royal Canadian Navy in the summer of 1941. Born in England, he came to Canada at the age of one, but after residing in four different provinces his family came to Sudbury, but since have moved to Winnipeg. While here, ... Lovat sang in the choir of the Church of the Epiphany. He was also active in the Boy Scout movement (n.d.).

Lovat Lake (64 I/10), east of Tadoule Lake was named after him in 1957.

Love, Sapper **George C.** of Winnipeg (H 25095). Royal Canadian Engineers. He died 23 April 1943 at the age of 48 and is commemorated at Edinburgh (Liberton) Cemetery, Edinburgh, Scotland. He was the son of William and Roberta Love and was survived by his wife Helen C. Love of Winnipeg and their two sons. His son writes (26 November 2001):

> Born in 1897 in Edinburgh, Scotland, he joined the King's Own Scottish Borderers (Royal Artillery) during World War I. He was discharged June 5, 1922 due to war wounds and came to Canada in 1928. At the outbreak of World War II he enlisted in the Royal Canadian Engineers and was sent overseas early in 1941. He died in his brother's home while on leave. At my mother's request, he was interred in the family plot in Edinburgh.

Love Island (64 J/13) in Nicklin Lake was named after him in 1995.

Love, Warrant Officer 2 **James H.** of Dauphin (R 95024). No. 103 Squadron. He died 20 December 1942 at the age of 29 and is commemorated at Bergen-op-Zoom Canadian War Cemetery in Holland. He was the son of William H. and Mabel Love of Dauphin. ***Love Creek*** (53 M/6), which flows northeast into Gowan River was named after him in 1985.

Love, Warrant Officer 2 **Roy J.** of Winnipeg (R 152695). No. 244 Squadron. He died 31 July 1944 at the age of 23 and is commemorated at the Alamein Memorial in Egypt. He was the son of Harold J. Love and Florence M. Love of Winnipeg. ***Love Bay*** (64 K/16) in Caron Lake was named after him in 1995.

Lovell, Corporal **Thomas Roy** of Darlingford (H 6654). Winnipeg Grenadiers. He died a prisoner of war 24 February 1944 at the age of 32 and is commemorated at the Yokohama War Cemetery in Japan. The official cause of death was listed as beriberi. He was the eldest son of Thomas and Jessie Lovell and was survived by his wife M. Madeline Lovell of Winnipeg and their young son. ***Lovell Lake*** (64 N/4), southwest of Nueltin Lake was named after him in 1972.

Lovell, Private **Walter** of La Rivière (874594). 8th Battalion, Canadian Infantry (Manitoba Regiment). He died 9 August 1918 at the age of 21 and is commemorated at the Manitoba Cemetery at Caix, Somme, France. He was the sixth child of Edward and Rebecca Lovell (née Cousins) of La Rivière, Manitoba. He wrote to his sister upon arriving in England:

> It was some ride on the boat we came over on, the *Empress of Britain*. It took us nine days to come across so you can see it was pretty rough. I wasn't sick at all but there was a lot that was feeding the little fishes quite often (1916).

He was wounded in the spring of 1917 and in another letter to his sister wrote:

> You asked where ... I got hit. Well, the arm the shrapnel went in the front just below the elbow and they took the shrapnel out the back of my arm. Well my leg next, the shrapnel went in the front of my leg that is about four inches above the knee and the four operations that I had they took it out the back. Gee but it was sore (10 July 1917).

Walter spent nine months hospitalized in England before returning to France after Christmas of 1917. His father later received notification that:

> Private Lovell was hit by an enemy machine gun bullet and instantly killed during the attack on the afternoon of August 9th, 1918. The Battalion advanced in the face of stout opposition from the enemy who placed a heavy barrage at the "jumping off" place, and from hidden nests poured machine gun fire into the ranks of the Troops who pushed forward (n.d.).

Walter Lovell Lake (53 F/13), east of Angling Lake was named after this World War I casualty in 2001.

Lovett, Sergeant **Donald A.** of Morden (H 41464). Essex Scottish Regiment, Mentioned in Dispatches. He died 13 August 1944 and is commemorated at Bayeux War Cemetery, Calvados, France. ***Lovett Lake*** (54 L/1), south of Churchill was named after him in 1948.

Low, Warrant Officer 2 **Douglas D.** of Grandview (R 91655). No. 9 Squadron. He died 8 November 1942 at the age of 25 and is commemorated at Lincoln (Newport) Cemetery, Lincolnshire, England. He was the youngest of the four sons of George and Jean Low of Owen Sound, Ontario. His nephew and sister-in-law write (1 November 2001):

> In January, 1941, Doug enlisted at Manning Depot No. 2 in Brandon, Manitoba. Training at Mossbank and Calgary gave him a rating of Wireless Operator and Air Gunner. After receiving his wings in September, 1941, Doug went overseas to England in October, 1941. Along with regular duties with his Lancaster crewmates, he also played the trumpet in the Air Force Band. He was stationed with the RAF at Waddington. On August 2, 1942, a letter written to his brother reads in part: "I have completed 16 trips to date. Our trips have all been fairly exciting. Have had a little damage to our kite, but none of the crew have been injured. There is a lot of luck to this business. Often the best crews fail to return."
>
> On November 8, 1942, while returning to base from another tour, there was a mid-air collision with an outgoing aircraft over an English airfield. The family at home in Canada received the dreaded telegram informing them of their loss. On November 11, 1942 Doug was interred in Newport Cemetery in Lincoln England.
>
> On his Mother's dresser, there stood a framed picture of Doug along with a poem. She surely must have taken comfort in the words of the poet:

Away!

I cannot say, and I will not say
That he is dead. He is just away.
With a cheery smile, and a wave of the hand,
He has wandered into an unknown land
And left us dreaming how very fair
It needs must be, since he lingers there.
And you - oh, you, who the wildest yearn
For an old - time step, and the glad return,
Think of him faring on, as dear
In the love of There as the love of Here.
Think of him still as the same. I say,
He is not dead - he is just away.
[James Whitcomb Riley]

Low Bay (64 H/2) in Fidler Lake was named after him in 1995.

Low, Flight Lieutenant **George "Mickey"** of Norway House (J 15406). No. 407 Squadron. He died 29 April 1943 at the age of 24 and is commemorated at the Runnymede Memorial in Surrey, England. He was the son of John W. and Phoebe R. Low of Norway House, Manitoba. ***Low Rapids*** (64 P/14) in the Caribou River was named after him in 1995.

Low, Flying Officer **George S.** of Winnipeg (J 22488). No. 427 Squadron. He died 24 August 1943 and is commemorated at Rheinberg War Cemetery in Germany. ***Low Peninsula*** (64 N/10) on Tatowaycho Lake was named after him in 1995.

Low, Sergeant **Leslie R.** of Flin Flon (R 100191). No. 8 Bombing and Gunnery School. He died 19 August 1942 at the age of 23 and is commemorated at Foxwarren Cemetery, Manitoba. He was the son of Thomas and Lillian M. Low of Foxwarren and was survived by his wife Estella M. Low of Flin Flon, Manitoba. ***Low Island*** (64 N/15) in Putahow Lake was named after him in 1989.

Lowe, Flight Sergeant **Francis John** of Ninette (R 50712). No. 12 Squadron, Mentioned in Dispatches. He died 26 March 1942 at the age of 32 and is commemorated at Bergen General Cemetery in Holland. He was the son of F. H. H. and Gertrude Lowe of Ninette, Manitoba. His sister writes (15 June 1995):

> Jack was born at Ninette, Manitoba on 10 May 1910. He grew up like any farm boy, with a lot of capabilities. In 1926 we moved south of Wawanesa to another farm where he helped in getting established. Then he left for the Turner Valley oil fields where he moved upwards from Roughneck to Driller. Once, when welding a connection to a new storage tank, he was blown up; someone had opened a valve allowing gas to enter. He was badly cut about the face but otherwise OK, which earned him the nickname of Lucky Lowe.
>
> Always interested in flying, he belonged to a glider club and was building his own plane. He also built for himself a trailer in which he pioneered the sleeping car principle of making up the bed in the dinette area – standard now for years in motor homes.
>
> He enlisted as Mechanic as soon as war broke out. He trained at Manning Pool, Toronto, St. Thomas, Camp Borden and Trenton. When the age limit for pilots was raised, he remustered and trained at Moncton, going overseas in 1941. His final posting was to No. 12 RAF Squadron flying Wellington bombers. In early March, 1942, he was Mentioned in Dispatches for bringing *V for Victory* home on one engine. He was shot down over Holland on 26 March 1942 with several other planes after the first heavy bombing of the Ruhr Valley.

Lowe Creek (53 N/14), which flows north into Stupart River was named after him in 1995.

Lowe, Corporal **George A.** of Winnipeg (H 6078). Winnipeg Grenadiers. He died a prisoner of war 18 February 1944 and is commemorated at the Yokohama War Cemetery in Japan. His sister recalls (6 November 2001):

George was the eldest of four children. There are two younger brothers and myself, his only sister. He was four years older than me. I remember our carefree childhood. We delighted in staging concerts in our garage. George would play his accordion or show Magic Lantern slides to the neighbourhood children. Roasting potatoes in bonfires in the vacant lot at the back of our house was also great fun. He taught me to ride a bike and watched out for me at school. He was my hero.

After attending high school, he started work at Stovel Press and was learning the printing trade. In 1939, when war was declared, George was in Grand Forks for the weekend playing baseball. He had been in the Reserves of the Winnipeg Grenadiers and had to report immediately on his return. He was the first in our community to join the army. He was sent to Jamaica and later to Hong Kong.

After the war, a good friend who was with him when he died, came to visit us. He told us George had been wounded during the fighting and although he recovered from his wounds, he later died of beriberi. It was hard not knowing where he was or if he was alive. Our mother sent many parcels and we did receive two letters from him. Still I grieve for my brother who died so young.

Lowe Point (63 N/2) on Batty Lake was named after him in 1995.

Lowe, Warrant Officer 2 **Irvin M.** of Bradwardine (R 134497). No. 76 Squadron. He died 4 December 1943 at the age of 24 and is commemorated at the Runnymede Memorial in Surrey, England. His occupation was listed as "farmer" when he enrolled in the militia in 1940. His niece and nephew write (23 December 2001):

Irvin, born January 28, 1919, was the son of William and Agnes Lowe, the youngest in their family of eight. My Mother was his eldest sister and as my Uncle, he was a super guy. He enjoyed sports, especially hockey. I remember him as a fun loving person and he would always be the one to be playing a trick on someone.

I always believed he enjoyed the air force and being a pilot, flying planes and doing stunt flying in the Tiger Moth. He was stationed at Virden, Manitoba where he took his training; during this time we "saw and heard" him often when he would fly over the home farm.

Lowe Lake (64 P/13), north of Nejanilini Lake was named after him in 1974.

Lower, Private **Douglas A.** of Lake Francis (H 17889). Lake Superior Regiment. He died 1 March 1945 at the age of 24 and is commemorated at the Groesbeek Canadian War Cemetery in Holland. He was the son of Richard H. and Rosie Lower (née Ford) of Lake Francis, Manitoba and was the brother of Corporal George Lower (next entry). According to his nephew (23 January 1996):

With three brothers already enlisted, he could have stayed home, but he wanted to go so his parents relented. He landed in Normandy shortly after D-Day and served in France, Belgium, Holland and Germany. He injured a knee in Holland and transferred to the Lake Superior Motor Regiment so he could ride. Their bivouac area just inside the German border was shelled during the night and he died the next day.

Lower Lake (64 P/9), east of Nejanilini Lake was named after him in 1974. Lower Bay is named after his brother, Corporal George E. Lower (next entry).

Lower, Corporal **George E.** of Lake Francis (H 17632). Regina Rifle Regiment. He died 9 June 1944 at the age of 27 and is commemorated at Beny-sur-Mer Canadian War Cemetery in Calvados, France. He was the son of Richard H. and Rosie Lower (née Ford) of Lake Francis, Manitoba. According to his nephew (23 January 1996):

He was over six feet two and before joining up he was very thin and usually unkempt. After joining up, he weighed over 200 pounds and was very fastidious about his appearance. He was a singer, mostly what was then called "cowboy" or "hillbilly" songs. He transferred to the Regina Rifle Regiment and as a corporal landed in Normandy on D-Day. He was killed a few miles inland on June 9, 1944. He was in charge of a Stokes mortar crew and a German tank blew up their position.

Lower Bay (64 I/13) in Shethanei Lake was named after him in 1989. Lower Lake is named after his brother, Private Douglas A. Lower (previous entry).

Lowry, Leading Aircraftman **Edward A.** of The Pas (R 86335). No. 2 Wireless School, RCAF. He died 11 December 1941 at the age of 25 and is commemorated at Riverside Cemetery in Dauphin, Manitoba. He was the son of William H. and Marguerite H. Lowry of The Pas. ***Lowry Lake*** (64 O/14), east of Nueltin Lake was named after him in 1961.

Lucas, Stoker 2 **Donald O.** of Winnipeg (V 60018). HMCS *Athabaskan*. The *Athabaskan* was sunk by a torpedo from a German destroyer while operating in the English Channel. Her captain and 128 men were lost, 83 taken prisoner and 44 men rescued by HMCS *Haida*. Stoker Lucas died 29 April 1944 at the age of 19 and is commemorated at the Halifax Memorial. He was the son of W. H. O. and Josephine Lucas of Winnipeg. ***Lucas Lake*** (64 C/16), south of Barrington Lake was named after him in 1957.

Luce, Private **Walter G.** of St. Vital (H 40187). Veterans Guard of Canada. He died 25 July 1942 at the age of 46 and is commemorated at Assumption Gardens in Winnipeg. He was the son of Fred M. and Margaret Luce of Winnipeg and was survived by his wife Agnes B. Luce of St. Vital and their two children. He was a veteran of the First World War. His daughter writes (23 June 1999):

[He] was born June 12, 1896 [at] Seacombe, Liverpool, England, [moving] to Winnipeg in 1904. [He] was associated with his father in the family's dry goods business in Winnipeg [and] was a member of his church choir and the Dramatic Society of Winnipeg. As [it] was a family trait, music and the stage were important aspects of his life. I understand he had a "happy-go-lucky" personality. He died at Ozada, Alberta ... of myocardial failure.

Luce Lake (52 L/3), northeast of Brereton Lake was named after him in 1973.

Lucemore, Corporal **William** of Winnipeg (H 195645). Queen's Own Cameron Highlanders. He died 24 April 1945 and is commemorated at the Holten Canadian War Cemetery in Holland. ***Lucemore Lake*** (64 O/16), west of Baralzon Lake was named after him in 1995.

Lucki, Pilot Officer **Albin** of Komarno (J 8342). No. 12 Squadron. He died 31 March 1942 at the age of 20 and is commemorated at the Runnymede Memorial in Surrey, England. He was the son of Mike and Katyzena Lucki of Winnipeg. ***Lucki Lake*** (64 O/8), northeast of Munroe Lake was named after him in 1975.

Ludwig, Corporal **Frederick** of Elmwood (H 26577). 17th Duke of York's Hussars. He died 23 October 1945 at the age of 33 and is commemorated at the Holten Canadian War Cemetery in Holland. He was the son of George and Matilda Ludwig of Elmwood. ***Ludwig Lake*** (64 P/9), east of Nejanilini Lake was named after him in 1974.

Lumgair, Pilot Officer **Norman A.** of Thornhill (J 86440). No. 408 Squadron. He died 15 March 1944 at the age of 22 and is commemorated at Hilsenheim Communal Cemetery, Bas-Rhin, France. He was the son of Robert W. and Hannah L. Lumgair of Thornhill, Manitoba. ***Lumgair Creek*** (63 J/16), which flows east into Sipiwesk Lake was named after him in 1972.

Lundmark, Sergeant **Victor D.** of Brandon (H 36857). Royal Winnipeg Rifles. He died 3 December 1941 at the age of 51 and is commemorated at Mountain View Cemetery in Thunder Bay, Ontario. ***Lundmark Lake*** (52 L/11), southeast of Flintstone Lake was named after him in 1992.

Lundy, Private **George V. J.** of Oak Point (H 18244). Algonquin Regiment. He died 14 September 1944 at the age of 27 and is commemorated at the Adegem Canadian War Cemetery in Belgium. He was the son of William A. and Ethel A. Lundy of Oak Point, Manitoba. ***Lundy Lake*** (64 H/3), west of Fidler Lake was named after him in 1995.

Lungstrum, Trooper **Edward A.** of Tyndall (K 50276). British Columbia Dragoons. He died 4 December 1944 at the age of 28 and is commemorated at Ravenna War Cemetery in Italy. He had travelled to British Columbia to find employment and enlisted there. ***Lungstrum Lake*** (53 M/11), east of Ransom Lake was named after him in 1996.

Lunney, Pilot Officer **Vernal N.** of Winnipeg (J 92324). No. 419 Squadron. He died 29 March 1944 at the age of 20 and is commemorated at the Runnymede Memorial in Surrey, England. ***Lunney Lake*** (64 J/11), west of Tadoule Lake was named after him in 1975.

Lunsted, Private **Adolph** of Dauphin (H 100284). Royal Canadian Infantry Corps. He died 17 April 1942 at the age of 32 and is commemorated at Riverside Cemetery in Dauphin, Manitoba. He was the son of Alfred and Anne Lunsted of Dauphin and was survived by his wife Elsie Lunsted of Dauphin and their two children. His wife writes (26 February 1998) that he:

> ... was born in Norway and moved to North Dakota with [his] parents. From there the family moved to Dauphin where he joined the army in April, 1942. I have no pictures ... as my house burned down three weeks after his death.

She recalls (6 November 2001):

> He was a very likeable person. He used to play the violin at dances at least once a month. He was very tall and thin, so everyone nicknamed him "Slim." He used to take his seven year-old son on hunting trips. He enjoyed that very much.

Lunsted Lake (62 N/14), south of Swan River was named after him in 1966.

Lupinsky, Pilot Officer **Jack** of Winnipeg (J 95174). No. 428 Squadron. He died 2 November 1944 at the age of 23 and is commemorated at the Reichswald Forest War Cemetery in Germany. ***Lupinsky Lake*** (64 O/10), west of Croll Lake was named after him in 1995.

Lussier, Lance Sergeant **Lawrence R.** of Oakburn (H 59640). Royal Canadian Artillery. He died 4 September 1944 at the age of 23 and is commemorated at Montecchio War Cemetery in Italy. He was the son of Romeo J. and Mae A. Lussier and was survived by his wife Gladys F. Lussier of Kelvington, Saskatchewan. ***Lussier Island*** (64 N/10) in Tice Lake was named after him in 1995.

Lychowich, Rifleman **John L.** of Garson (A 107694). Royal Winnipeg Rifles. He died 8 June 1944 at the age of 26 and is commemorated at Beny-sur-Mer Canadian War Cemetery in Calvados, France. He was the son of Szczepan and Rosalie Lychowich of Garson, Manitoba. ***Lychowich Lake*** (53 E/13), south of Stevenson Lake was named after him in 1997.

Lyne, Private **Vernon A.** of Rapid City (B 131472). Princess Louise Dragoon Guards. He died 27 September 1944 at the age of 27 and is commemorated at Cesena War Cemetery in Italy. He was the son of Albert E. and Hattie Lyne and was survived by his wife Dorothy L. Lyne of Brandon and their two children. He had been employed with a refrigeration company in Toronto when he enlisted. ***Lyne Island*** (53 M/5) in Utik Lake was named after him in 1996.

Lyons, Flight Sergeant **Gordon H. "Tiger"** of La Rivière (R 80184). No. 33 Squadron. He was reported missing in North Africa 28 May 1942 at the age of 25 and is commemorated at the Alamein Memorial in Egypt. He was the son of Howard T. and Sadie M. Lyons of Vancouver. His sister (18 June 1995) recalls that he:

> ... lived at La Rivière through most of his school years, then moved to Winnipeg and lived at 755 Ingersoll Street. Gordon enlisted with the RCAF in November, 1940. He received his training in Brandon, McLeod, Regina, Lethbridge and Dauphin and went to England in August, 1941.

Lyons Island (64 I/12) in Hlowananatseda Lake was named after him in 1995.

Lyons, Private **William J.** of Winnipeg (H 6615). Winnipeg Grenadiers. He died 23 September 1940 at the age of 24 and is commemorated at Kingston (Up Park Camp) Military Cemetery, Jamaica. He was the son of James H. and Mary Lyons (née Gwinn) of Saskatoon and was survived by his wife Lillian V. R. L. Lyons (née Forth) of St. James and their three children. His wife writes (30 April 1998):

> When war broke out, Private Lyons was laid off and was forced to join the army. He joined the Winnipeg Grenadiers in the spring of 1939 and they left for Kingston, Jamaica in the spring of 1940. At that time [we] were expecting the third child; it was a son. [He] never had the pleasure of holding [him] as he was born in August, 1940 and William passed away in September. His son carries his [father's] name and has a lovely family of his own.

Lyons Creek (64 I/15), which flows northeast into the Seal River was named after him in 1974.

Lysay, Private **John** of Winnipeg (H 101695). Princess Patricia's Canadian Light Infantry. He died 15 March 1943 at the age of 20 and is commemorated at Yorkton Cemetery, Saskatchewan. He was survived by his mother Nellie Lysay of North Battleford, Saskatchewan. ***Lysay Lake*** (62 P/15), west of Family Lake was named after him in 1978.

Lytle, Pilot Officer **Orville** of Roland (J 18694). No. 434 Squadron. He died 29 September 1943 at the age of 30 and is commemorated at the Hanover War Cemetery in Germany. He was the son of Joseph M. and Mable I. Lytle of Roland, Manitoba. ***Lytle Bay*** (64 J/9) in Tadoule Lake was named after him in 1975.

Victory in Europe Day celebrations, May, 1945.
Courtesy of the National Archives of Canada (PA-114626).

M

Mabb, Private **Herbert H.** of Fisher Branch (H 6530). Winnipeg Grenadiers. He died 7 October 1942 and is commemorated at the Sai Wan War Cemetery in Hong Kong. He was survived by his mother Mrs. Minnie Mabb of Fisher Branch. ***Mabb Lake*** (64 K/9), northeast of Reindeer Lake was named after him in 1972.

Macaulay, Gunner **Duncan A.** of Winnipeg (M 104654). Royal Canadian Artillery. He died 23 July 1944 at the age of 38 and is commemorated at Beny-sur-Mer Canadian War Cemetery in Calvados, France. He was the son of Duncan and Sarah Macaulay and was survived by his wife Gladys M. Macaulay of Winnipeg. ***Macaulay Island*** (64 O/12) in Shannon Lake was named after him in 1995.

MacAulay, Flight Lieutenant **Thomas H.** of Winnipeg (J 22098). No. 101 Squadron. He died 8 January 1945 at the age of 30 and is commemorated at Khayat Beach War Cemetery, Israel. He was the son of Donald L. and Margot Macaulay and was survived by his wife Georgina E. Macaulay of Santa Monica, California. ***MacAulay Point*** (53 L/1) on Rochon Lake was named after him in 1995.

Macaulay, Flight Sergeant **William J.** of Winnipeg (R 86116). No. 419 Squadron. He died 6 August 1942 at the age of 21 and is commemorated at the Reichswald Forest War Cemetery in Germany. He was the son of William G. and Pearl Macaulay of Winnipeg. ***Macaulay Lake*** (64 H/11), east of Small Lake was named after him in 1995.

MacCosham, Flight Sergeant **William R.** of Glenora (R 95723). No. 179 Squadron. He died 27 December 1942 at the age of 20 and is commemorated at the Malta Memorial. ***MacCosham Lake*** (64 F/16), southeast of Kustra Lake was named after him in 1995.

MacDonald, Lieutenant **Colin S.** of Winnipeg. Royal Canadian Artillery. He died 3 October 1942 at the age of 22 and is commemorated at Brookwood Military Cemetery in Surrey, England. He was the son of Colin S. and Margaret Macdonald and was survived by his wife Elizabeth M. MacDonald of Winnipeg. ***Colin MacDonald Lake*** (64 N/8), northwest of MacMillan Lake was named after him in 1995.

MacDonald, Trooper **Donald** of Roland (H 302). Queen's Own Cameron Highlanders. He died 3 August 1944 at the age of 22 and is commemorated at Bretteville-sur-Laize Canadian War Cemetery in Calvados, France. He was the son of Donald and Elspet McDonald (sp.) of Roland, Manitoba. ***MacDonald Rapids*** (64 I/15) in the Seal River was named after him in 1995.

MacDonald, Sergeant **Donald J.** of Winnipeg (R 225104). No. 419 Squadron. He died 18 November 1943 at the age of 22 and is commemorated at the Rheinberg War Cemetery in Germany. ***MacDonald Island*** (53 K/5) in Sharpe Lake was named after him in 1989.

MacDonald, Trooper **Donald J.** of Minto (H 103088). Royal Canadian Dragoons. He died 16 April 1945 at the age of 19 and is commemorated at the Holten Canadian War Cemetery in Holland. He was the son of Donald J. and Constance M. MacDonald of Minto, Manitoba. ***MacDonald Bay*** (64 N/15) in Tice Lake was named after him in 1987.

MacDonald, Corporal **John A. "Red"** of Stony Mountain (H 19565). Queen's Own Cameron Highlanders. He died 14 September 1944 at the age of 22 and is commemorated at the Calais Canadian War Cemetery in France. Born in Griffithstown, Wales, he had married earlier that year and his first child was born seven weeks after his death. His sister writes (19 May 1995):

> My brother took part in the Dieppe raid in 1942 but fortunately returned to England. He returned to Canada in July of 1943 to take an Instructor's Course at Shilo. He was married January 5, 1944 and went back to England in April. However, he did not enjoy instructing and asked to go into action. He went to France in August, 1944 and was killed in Belgium on September 14, 1944. His son James was born in November, 1944. He is so anxious to hear from anyone who knew his Dad. I have visited my brother's grave in the Calais Military Cemetery.

His son adds (23 October 2001):

> My father was a fun-loving, quick-witted jokester who became a little more serious after the Dieppe raid where he lost a lot of friends. His group apparently made it furthest inland that day – seven miles. Before the war, he loved to work at the Peircey's farm. Had he survived, we would likely have been farmers as he and my mother both loved that life. Some of his fun got him into trouble. A British officer was giving one of his friends a hard time and Dad apparently threw him over the bar onto some sort of a conveyor that carried empties to the cellar. Two Canadian Military Police standing at the door said they didn't see a thing and let Dad and his friends leave with no problem.

An older sister recalls (23 October 2001):

> Jack was a fun-loving pest and tease when he was younger. He apparently did something that really angered Dad who was not usually the disciplinarian of the family and never hit any of us kids. Dad chased Jack into the back kitchen where Jack quickly slid under the bed. Dad whipped off his belt and holding it up angrily said: "See this belt?" Jack popped out of the other side of the bed and whipped off his sock like it was a dangerous weapon and said: "See this sock?" Everyone broke down laughing and that was the end of the problem.

He wrote on the back of the photo of him and the horse taken in England in 1940: "I'm the short one in the hat."

> Jack had a real happy personality, was self-taught on the piano, guitar and harmonica and had a real nice singing voice. He was a real charmer, tease and was totally spoiled by myself, his other two sisters and Mom. He had lots of friends – male and female – because of his fun nature and gift of the gab.
>
> While on leave in Wales visiting his grandma and uncles, he suggested going to the pub for a drink. "Oh no!" everyone sad, "Women aren't allowed in the pub." Jack insisted that this was nonsense and away they went. When they arrived, Jack (Mr. Cheery Optimist) went immediately to work charming the landlord. "You don't expect me to come all this way and not be able to buy my own grandmother a drink, do you?" Grandma was allowed to stay and over the years overseas they had many drinks together.

MacDonald Peninsula (63 N/7) on Guthrie Lake was named after him in 1995.

MacDougall, Flight Lieutenant **Donald C.** of Winnipeg (C 549). No. 13 Operational Training Unit, RCAF. He died 15 December 1941 and is commemorated at the Ottawa Memorial. ***MacDougall Island*** (63 P/2) in Cotton Lake was named after him in 1995.

MacDougall, Private **John D.** of Elm Creek (H 103017). Lake Superior Regiment. He died 9 April 1945 at the age of 20 and is commemorated at the Holten Canadian War Cemetery in Holland. He was the son of Donald and Helen McDougall (sp.) of Elm Creek, Manitoba. ***MacDougall Bay*** (64 H/4) in Gauer Lake was named after him in 1995.

Macfarlane, Sergeant **Donald M.** of Winnipeg (1108340). No. 405 Squadron, RAF. He enlisted in 1940 and was killed in action 15 April 1942. He was 24 years of age and is commemorated at Rheinberg War Cemetery in Germany. ***Macfarlane Bay*** (63 O/1) in Halfway Lake was named after him in 1995.

MacFarlane, Private **George W.** of Winnipeg (H 6883). Winnipeg Grenadiers. He died 22 December 1941 at the age of 40 and is commemorated at Stanley Military Cemetery, Hong Kong. He was the son of David and Jessie Macfarlane and was survived by his wife Catherine E. Macfarlane of Winnipeg. ***MacFarlane Island*** (64 C/12) in Tod Lake was named after him in 1995.

MacFarlane, Ordinary Signalman **Robert J.** of Winnipeg (V 50139). HMCS *Chatham*. He died 12 October 1942 at the age of 18 and is commemorated at the Halifax Memorial. He was the son of Robert D. and Alma J. Macfarlane of Winnipeg. ***MacFarlane Lake*** (64 N/6), southwest of Nueltin Lake was named after him in 1972.

MacFie, Private **John G.** of Selkirk (H 1880). Queen's Own Cameron Highlanders. He died 30 March 1945 and is commemorated at the Groesbeek Canadian War Cemetery in Holland. He was the son of Claude and Victoria MacFie (née Taylor) and was survived by his wife Olive V. MacFie (née Harcus) and their seven children. His son recalls (23 February 2002):

John was born in Selkirk, Manitoba and was brought up on his parents' farm on the east side of the Red River. His dad, Claude MacFie married Victoria Taylor and raised one girl and four boys – Edward, Arthur, Agnes, Lawrence and John. John went to Kitchener School on the east side of the river. He had a seven-dog team and on his travels south to Lockport he met a girl by the name of Olive Victoria Harcus. They married and raised seven children: myself (John), Gerald, Allan and sisters Joyce, Doreen, Shirley and Victoria. John worked for the Manitoba Steel Foundries at Selkirk and hauled grain on weekends with his truck. On July 1st, he took all the Kitchener School kids to Winnipeg Beach for the day; we all had a good time. I live in Sundre, Alberta, Gerald lives in Prince Albert, Shirley lives in Winnipeg and Allan lives in Calgary. Joyce, Doreen and Victoria are deceased.

MacFie Lake (52 E/11), southeast of Brereton Lake was named after him in 1974.

MacGillivray, Pilot Officer **Arthur C.** of Warren (J 90365). No. 192 Squadron. He died 25 May 1944 at the age of 21 and is commemorated at Heverlee War Cemetery, Leuven, Vlaams-Brabant, Belgium. He was the son of William M. and Margaret C. MacGillivray of Warren, Manitoba. His nephew writes (31 December 2001):

He was born on November 28, 1922 and grew up on a farm in Warren, Manitoba. After school, he went to work at Eaton's where he enlisted at the age of 20. He was a bombardier in the Royal Canadian Air Force. He trained at different locations across Canada for a year before being sent overseas. He was eventually promoted to Flight Sergeant and then to Pilot Officer.

Arthur went overseas in March of 1943. He flew on ten different missions with his crew. On May 24, 1944 at 11:45 PM, they took off on what was to be their final mission. They were to have bombed Aachen, a city along the German border, but were shot down flying over Holland. Only one crew member survived.

MacGillivray Island (53 M/4) in Semple Lake was named after him in 1989.

MacGranachan, Flight Sergeant **Robert** of Foxwarren (R 106191). No. 119 Squadron. He died 25 December 1942 at the age of 23 and is commemorated at Foxwarren Cemetery. He and his crew lost their lives after volunteering for coastal patrol duty on Christmas morning (Hill 1944). He was the son of William and Lillian M. MacGranachan of Foxwarren. Flight Sergeant MacGranachan had been a third year engineering student at the University of Manitoba when he enlisted. ***MacGranachan Lake*** (64 C/13), southwest of McMillan Lake was named after him in 1989.

Macgregor, Pilot Officer **Alexander E.** of Winnipeg (J 10698). No. 10 Operational Training Unit, RCAF. He died 18 August 1942 at the age of 25 and is commemorated at Wick Cemetery, Caithness, Scotland. He was the son of Robert and Bella C. Macgregor of St. James. His brother reports that (3 May 1995):

Alexander was killed ... while defending over Dieppe. He served with the Canadian Army prior to transferring to the RCAF. He was born in Strasbourg, Saskatchewan, was educated in the St. James School Division and was employed with the T. Eaton Company as an Assistant Manager prior to joining the Canadian Army.

Macgregor Lake (64 C/13), southwest of McMillan Lake was named after him in 1995.

Machura, Private **Harry** of Riverton (H 615397). Lincoln and Welland Regiment. He died 23 April 1945 at the age of 22 and is commemorated at the Holten Canadian War Cemetery in Holland. He was the son of Maxim and Annie Machura of Riverton, Manitoba. His sister remembers (13 February 1996) that:

Harry left his family homestead at Hnausa in order to earn a little money to help support his six brothers and six sisters and two parents. Harry fully expected to return from his wartime experience and take over the family homestead.

Machura Lake (63 K/16), north of Reed Lake was named after him in 1973.

Macintosh, Gunner **Angus G.** of Winnipeg (K 70759). Royal Canadian Artillery. He died 4 September 1944 at the age of 20 and is commemorated at Montecchio War Cemetery in Italy. He was the son of William C. and Harriett H. Macintosh of Sydney, Nova Scotia. ***Macintosh Peninsula*** (54 D/15) on Cygnet Lake was named after him in 1996.

MacIntyre, Pilot Officer **Peter M.** of Winnipeg (J 85174). No. 179 Squadron. He died 21 February 1944 at the age of 22 and is commemorated at Tangier (St. Andrew) Churchyard, Morocco. ***MacIntyre Bay*** (64 B/8) in Barnes Lake was named after him in 1995.

Mack, Private **John D.** of Winnipeg (H 6317). South Saskatchewan Regiment. He died 19 August 1942 at the age of 20 and is commemorated at Dieppe Canadian War Cemetery in Seine-Maritime, France. He was the son of David F. and Ida L. Mack of Winnipeg. ***Mack Bay*** (64 O/15) in Blevins Lake was named after him in 1995.

Mack, Rifleman **John J.** of Makinak (H 9467). Royal Winnipeg Rifles. He died 9 July 1944 at the age of 20 and is commemorated at Beny-sur-Mer Canadian War Cemetery in Calvados, France. He was the son of Rosco and Mary E. Mack of Makinak, Manitoba. ***Mack Island*** (64 G/12) in Big Sand Lake was named after him in 1986.

Mackay, Flying Officer **George I.** of Garson (J 22602). No. 427 Squadron. He died 25 March 1944 at the age of 24 and is commemorated at the Reichswald Forest War Cemetery in Germany. He was the son of John A. and Janet S. Mackay of Port Nelson, Ontario. ***George Mackay Lake*** (54 E/2), south of Long Lake was named after him in 1995.

MacKelvie, Flight Lieutenant **James A.** of Winnipeg (J 5047). No. 44 Squadron. He died 18 June 1944 at the age of 29 and is commemorated at Bretteville-sur-Laize Canadian War Cemetery in Calvados, France. He was the son of Charles W. L. and Josephine E. MacKelvie and was survived by his wife Neila W. MacKelvie of Winnipeg. ***MacKelvie Lake*** (64 F/2), east of Wells Lake was named after him in 1994.

MacKenzie, Pilot Officer **Alan E.** of Winnipeg (J 18334). No. 428 Squadron. He died 3 November 1943 at the age of 18 and is commemorated at Cambridge City Cemetery in Cambridgeshire, England. He was the son of Kenneth B. and Margaret MacKenzie of Winnipeg. ***MacKenzie Rapids*** (64 N/2) in the unnamed river which connects Vanlerberghe Lake and Whitmore Lake was named after him in 1995.

Mackenzie, Pilot Officer **Jack D.** of Winnipeg (J 16924). No. 419 Squadron. He died 3 February 1943 at the age of 21 and is commemorated at Sleen General Cemetery, Holland. He was the son of Charles B. and Annie E. Mackenzie of Winnipeg. ***Mackenzie Lake*** (64 G/3), northeast of Mulcahy Lake was named after him in 1989.

MacKenzie, Warrant Officer 2 **Norman A.** of Winnipeg (R 86313). No. 405 Squadron. He died 1 September 1942 at the age of 27 and is commemorated at Dishforth Cemetery, Yorkshire, England. On 14 October 1944, the RCAF identified him:

> ... as the pilot of a Halifax bomber who gave his life recently in an attempt to save his crewmates, by keeping his burning bomber on a steady course while they jumped to safety. Four of the crew of seven were able to bail out before the plane crashed in flames. They were returning from a raid when the outer port engine caught fire. Only four had bailed out when the port wing and engines were blown off by an explosion and the machine crashed in flames (*Winnipeg Free Press* 14 October 1942).

Warrant Officer MacKenzie's Commanding Officer, Wing Commander L. G. Fraser wrote to his mother:

> The body of Norman was found at the controls of the aircraft. It is quite obvious that he was fighting to the last to bring the aircraft down safely. It is one of the most superb actions of heroism of which I know. To die like this, doing his duty to the very last, is given to but few of us and yet it is the hope of all of us here that if we have to go, we will go in the same manner as your boy. He was buried beside his two comrades ... Sergeant Harold Stone and Sergeant Gordon Eagles.... Sergeant Stone was a Jewish lad from a good family. In spite of their religion, his next-of-kin, who was his sister (his mother and father both being dead), requested that his body be buried by his comrades because that was his wish. This entailed burial on Saturday, which is contrary to Jewish religious beliefs. It also entailed burial by a Christian chaplain and in a Christian cemetery. We were all sincerely affected by their generous gesture. It is typical of the outlook of people in this country generally (n.d.).

A contemporary newspaper account added:

> Sergeant MacKenzie, a former constable on the Winnipeg police force which he joined in 1936, was reported in September as killed while on service overseas. He was born in Stornoway, Scotland in January, 1915 and came to Canada in 1923. He enlisted in the RCAF January 6, 1940 (n.d.).

He was the son of John and Mary MacKenzie of Winnipeg. ***MacKenzie Peninsula*** (64 O/12) on Shannon Lake was named after him in 1995.

MacKerracher, Corporal **Hugh J.** of Winnipeg (H 70411). Royal Winnipeg Rifles, Mentioned in Dispatches. He died 5 July 1944 and is commemorated at Beny-sur-Mer Canadian War Cemetery in Calvados, France. He was survived by his mother E. Mae MacKerracher of Arnprior, Ontario. ***MacKerracher Lake*** (64 G/6), east of Big Sand Lake was named after him in 1948.

Mackie, Flying Officer **Alexander M.** of Winnipeg (J 88245). No. 424 Squadron, Distinguished Flying Cross.

> This officer has completed, as pilot and captain of aircraft, numerous operations against the enemy in the course of which he has invariably displayed the utmost fortitude, courage and devotion to duty (DFC Citation 1947).

He died 12 January 1945 at the age of 30 and is commemorated at the Runnymede Memorial in Surrey, England. He was the son of George O. and May Mackie of Winnipeg and was survived by his wife Alice G. Mackie of Winnipeg. ***Mackie Lake*** (64 C/13), east of Reindeer Lake was named after him in 1947.

Mackie, Private **Charles C.** of Fisherton (H 20983). Queen's Own Cameron Highlanders. He died 8 August 1944 at the age of 32 and is commemorated at Bretteville-sur-Laize Canadian War Cemetery in Calvados, France. He was the second of the nine children of John and Sarah Mackie of Fisherton. His brother (10 November 2000) recalls that he:

> ... attended school in [the Fisherton] District for a short period of time. His labour was soon needed to help support such a large family on his dad's farm. He and his dad mixed-farmed together for quite some time. In later years, he owned some property of his own. Farming in those years was a lot of hard work with little pay. He farmed until he enlisted in 1941.
>
> He enjoyed playing cards, especially in the long evenings in winter. With no electricity, there was limited activity outside. Big game hunting was part of his life – as much for survival as sport. Fishing and trapping along a river that ran through our farm was also [a] pastime. Baseball and horseshoe games [were] part of [the] summer fun at home and at the local community hall [on] field days. Most of his short life was spent making a living in times that [were] hard.

Mackie Island (64 C/2) in Trophy Lake was named after him in 1995.

Mackie, Gunner **Ellwood B.** of Ochre River (H 100943). Royal Canadian Artillery. He died 15 August 1944 at the age of 23 and is commemorated at Beny-sur-Mer Canadian War Cemetery in Calvados, France. His half-brother writes (1 November 2001):

> Ellwood lived and went to school in Ochre River, Manitoba. After school, he worked with his older brother in a shoe and harness repair shop. Later, he worked at a garage, doing minor mechanical repairs. He was an accomplished harmonica player and was popular at local teen get-togethers. When he first attempted to enlist in the army, he was rejected on medical grounds (heart murmur). However, persistence won out and he proceeded to basic training in Winnipeg.

Mackie Point (64 N/10) on Tatowaycho Lake was named after him in 1995.

Mackie, Pilot Officer **William George** of Inglis (J 23631). No. 18 Operational Training Unit, RCAF. He died 27 May 1943 at the age of 26 and is commemorated at Rugby (Whinfield) Cemetery, Warwickshire, England. He was the son of William and Jane Mackie of Winnipeg. He had been employed at Sherridon prior to enlisting. ***Mackie Bay*** (53 K/4) in Red Sucker Lake was named after him in 1995.

Macksimchuk, Flight Sergeant **John T.** of Rosser (R 110747). No. 166 Squadron. He died 5 May 1943 at the age of 25 and is commemorated at Vlagtwedde General Cemetery, Holland. He was the third of the four children of Theodore and Mary Macksimchuk and was survived by his wife of nine months Anne Macksimchuk of Toronto. She writes (3 June 1998):

John was born ... in Rosa, Manitoba. [He] attended River Ranch public school and high school in Dominion City. [He] excelled in algebra. On one occasion, [he even] solved an algebra question that had the principal bewildered. After graduation, [he] worked for a while on the family farm and sold Watkin's products for a couple of summers. Then the war broke out and he enlisted in the Air Force on 20 June 1941. After graduation, we were married August 30, 1942 and on May 5, 1943 left for Halifax, Nova Scotia and then overseas.

His sister adds (20 November 2001):

It was depression time, so us older ones went job hunting; jobs were scarce. John and other young boys rode freight trains and got work on farms for $1.50 a day and meals. He almost got his leg broken on a freight train. He joined the Air Force about 1940 or 1941. His two older brothers were also in the armed forces. [In] October of 1942 he got orders to come to England.

He stopped in Toronto for a few days to see me and my family. We went to Niagara Falls which he enjoyed. He asked me to look after his wife as she was coming later on to Toronto, which I did my best. Then in May of 1943, we received a telegram that the plane that John was on was missing over in Holland. It was tragic news to his wife and the rest of the family – especially my mother and father.

Macksimchuk Lake (64 O/14), east of Nueltin Lake was named after him in 1975.

Maclean, Captain **Donald S.** of Winnipeg. 1st Canadian Parachute Battalion. He died 7 June 1944 at the age of 23 and is commemorated at Bretteville-sur-Laize Canadian War Cemetery in Calvados, France. He was the son of Dr. Neil J. M. and Frankie M. MacLean (sp.; née Taylor) of Winnipeg and was survived by his wife Dorothy G. I. MacLean (née Oliver) of Winnipeg. ***Maclean Lake*** (64 K/11), northeast of Reindeer Lake was named after him in 1972.

MacLean, Lance Corporal **Harold F.** of Elm Creek (H 1231). Canadian Provost Corps. He died 26 September 1944 at the age of 23 and is commemorated at Ancona War Cemetery in Italy. He was one of the 10 children of John D. and Frances MacLean of Elm Creek, Manitoba. His sister writes (18 November 2001):

He was born July 19, 1921 at Sperling, Manitoba. He had six brothers and three sisters, five of whom served in the Armed Forces in World War II. Harold joined the army with the Canadian Provost Corps in Winnipeg in January, 1943 and trained in Winnipeg, Debert, Nova Scotia and Windsor, Nova Scotia, then overseas to train at Aldershot and then he was on his way to Italy in October, 1943.

While he was stationed in Windsor, he had a visit from his brother Cameron who was serving on HMCS *Annapolis* and was in port on leave. They had a great time visiting and reminiscing together and Cameron was the last of the family to see Harold alive. He was injured on September 22, 1944 and died of injuries on September 26.

As a young boy, Harold attended Sperling School and participated in many sports. He was strong, tough and could run like the wind. He enjoyed fun, good natured teasing, being part of a large family and was always ready to go to a wiener roast or dance after the work was done.

MacLean Rapids (64 P/4) in the Wolverine River was named after him in 1995.

Maclean, Flying Officer **John O.** of Winnipeg (R 106786). No. 5 Operational Training Unit, RCAF. He died 30 August 1942 at the age of 21 and is commemorated at Dunure Cemetery, Ayrshire, Scotland. He was the son of John and Estella B. MacLean of Toronto. ***Maclean Hill*** (64 P/4), southwest of MacLeod Lake was named after him in 1995.

MacLean, Flying Officer **Norman J.** of Winnipeg (J 22150). No. 2 Repair, Evaluation and Maintenance Unit, RCAF. He died 9 June 1945 at the age of 24 and is commemorated at Elmwood Cemetery in Winnipeg. He was the eldest son of the six children of Norman and Margaret MacLean of Winnipeg. His sister writes (14 September 1998):

He grew up with two brothers and three sisters. He had a happy and busy childhood with interests in music (choral and piano) and also in all sport, especially hockey and basketball. Norman received his education at Gladstone, Earl Grey and Kelvin High School and was attending the University of Manitoba at the time he enlisted in the Air Force. He graduated as a pilot with a commission in December, 1942 and was then posted overseas and participated in active service until he came home on sick leave in 1944. After a short recovery period, he was reinstated to active duty as a test pilot in Moose Jaw, Saskatchewan where unfortunately, a fatal air crash claimed him. His death was a great loss to family and friends as Norman had always been a very outgoing, happy and caring individual.

A newspaper obituary reported that "an airplane he was testing 'cracked up.'" ***MacLean Bay*** (64 O/11) in John Osborne Lake was named after him in 1995.

MacLennan, Gunner **Lewis J.** of Roland (H 35554). Royal Canadian Artillery. He died 8 May 1942 at the age of 32 and is commemorated at Brookwood Military Cemetery in Surrey, England. He was the son of K. F. and Maude MacLennan and was survived by his wife Annie L. MacLennan of Roland, Manitoba and their son William. ***MacLennan Lake*** (64 N/2), southwest of Nueltin Lake was named after him in 1972.

MacLennan, Flight Sergeant **Stuart C.** of Winnipeg (R 172701). No. 76 Squadron. He died 31 August 1943 at the age of 19 and is commemorated at Roermond (Kapel in 't Zand) Roman Catholic Cemetery, Holland. He was one of the two children of K. A. and Ethel A. MacLennan of Winnipeg. A friend recalls (5 December 1996) that he:

... was born in Winnipeg [in] 1923. He attended Wolseley, Isaac Brock and Gordon Bell schools. Stuart was a *Free Press* carrier boy for many years. He was active in sports, an excellent swimmer and played hockey for the Monarch Hockey Club. He enlisted in June, 1942 and trained at Macdonald Bombing and Gunnery School where he graduated as an air gunner in December, 1942. He went overseas the following month.

MacLennan Island (63 I/7) in Molson Lake was named after him in 1995.

MacLeod, Rifleman **Angus M.** of Dunrea (H 40564). Royal Winnipeg Rifles. He was shot while a prisoner of war 8 June 1944 at the age of 27 and is commemorated at Beny-sur-Mer Canadian War Cemetery in Calvados, France. He was one of 34 Manitoba soldiers who were captured during the Normandy landing and executed by the SS. He was the son of Angus and Jessie MacLeod of Dunrea and was survived by his wife Leonora E. MacLeod of Dunrea. His sister recalls (29 October 2001):

He was my brother, my best friend, but we were not to have him long as he was taken prisoner and shot. When he was reported missing, I looked all over for him, but wasn't lucky enough to find him. He was one of the most kind persons you could find; he was kind and good to everyone. He loved to skate, play hockey and box. He was pretty well just finished school and not long after, [he] joined up. I still miss him and know he is happy in his new home.

MacLeod Rapids (64 I/8) in the South Knife River was named after him in 1995.

MacLeod, Flying Officer **John "Jack"** of Winnipeg (J 44992). No. 456 Squadron. He died 27 May 1945 at the age of 19 and is commemorated at the Singapore Memorial. He was the son of Mr. and Mrs. John MacLeod of Winnipeg. His last missions had been to several points throughout India. According to his sister (31 March 1995), he:

... was born at home at 1034 Empress Street. He was a very good student. He attended Isaac Brock School and Daniel McIntyre High School. He finished school and went to work for the Winnipeg Electric Offices, now known as the Winnipeg Transit Company. At that time, their offices were on Notre Dame and Portage. Jack was in the army reserve for a couple of years before joining the Air Force.

He loved skating, hockey, baseball [and] football. He always enjoyed fixing small appliances. When he was in the Air Force he earned the nickname "Gadget" as he fixed all the other boys' clocks, watches etc. He was an avid stamp collector and made many model aeroplanes, cars etc. When he joined the Air Force, he could hardly wait to fly the planes. He did become a pilot.

MacLeod Esker (64 B/9), north of Uhlman Lake was named after him in 1995.

MacMillan, Sick Berth Attendant **Duncan Ross** of Transcona (V 24847). HMCS *Avalon*, the Royal Canadian Navy shore establishment in St. John's, Newfoundland. He died 12 December 1942 at the age of 27 and is commemorated at Mount Pleasant Cemetery in St. John's, Newfoundland. He was the son of Archie and E. MacMillan of Ottawa and was survived by his wife Phyllis MacMillan of Transcona. ***MacMillan Lake*** (64 N/8), southwest of Nueltin Lake was named after him in 1972.

MacMurchy, Flying Officer **Edward D.** of Pilot Mound (J 20833). No. 428 Squadron. He died 27 September 1943 and is commemorated at the Hanover War Cemetery in Germany. ***MacMurchy Lake*** (64 H/3), southeast of Thorsteinson Lake was named after him in 1995.

MacNeil, Lieutenant **William J.** of Winnipeg. Princess Patricia's Canadian Light Infantry. He died 20 September 1944 and is commemorated at Coriano Ridge War Cemetery in Italy. ***MacNeil Lake*** (64 K/12), northeast of Reindeer Lake was named after him in 1972.

MacNicol, Pilot Officer **Donald K. I.** of Winnipeg (J 90988). No. 406 Squadron. He died 10 October 1944 at the age of 20 and is commemorated at Brookwood Military Cemetery in Surrey, England. He was the son of Donald D. and Charlotte G. MacNicol of Winnipeg. ***MacNicol Lake*** (64 N/13), west of Nueltin Lake was named after him in 1974.

Maconnell, Flight Sergeant **Walter Douglas** of Winnipeg (R 71384). No. 204 Squadron. He died 17 August 1942 at the age of 21 and is commemorated at the Malta Memorial. He was the son of Willis E. and Gertrude Maconnell of Field, British Columbia. His uncle made inquiries concerning the circumstances of his death and received the following reply from the Air Ministry:

Dear [LAC] Maconnell: With reference to your letter of 3rd October, 1942, addressed to the Record Office, I regret that I must confirm the information in the letter which you received. On 25th September at the time of the previous letter from Record Office no information had been received here, however, a report has been received from Air Headquarters, West Africa, which states that the survivors of the crew who returned safely to base reported that your [nephew] and three other members of the crew were dead. They are now listed as "missing believed killed."

The survivors reported that their Sunderland aircraft force landed in the sea after engine failure and sank almost immediately. Top deck crew were the only ones able to escape and landed at Portuguese Territory, Orango, after 105 hours in their dinghy. Please accept my deepest sympathy with you in the loss of your [nephew]. Yours sincerely, Flight Lieutenant Milton A. Joss (4 November 1942).

Maconnell Lake (64 H/10), north of Buckland Lake was named after him in 1995.

MacPhail, Sergeant **John F.** of Winnipeg (R 91524). No. 14 Operational Training Unit, RCAF. He died 8 March 1942 at the age of 22 and is commemorated at Cottesmore (St. Nicholas) Churchyard Extension, Rutland, England. He was the son of John and Ethel MacPhail of Winnipeg. ***MacPhail Lake*** (64 H/15), northwest of Etawney Lake was named after him in 1995.

Macpherson, Flying Officer **Donald J.** of Winnipeg (J 10329). No. 45 Squadron. He died 9 November 1942 at the age of 21 and is commemorated at Jonkerbos War Cemetery in Holland. He was the son of Evan and Hannah M. Macpherson. ***Macpherson Island*** (64 P/13) in Farnie Lake was named after him and his brother Warrant Officer Norman McPherson (next entry) in 1985.

Macpherson, Warrant Officer 2 **Norman** of Winnipeg (R 71487). No. 410 Squadron. He died 1 September 1942 at the age of 22 and is commemorated at Ayr Cemetery in Ayrshire, Scotland. He was the son of Evan and Hannah M. Macpherson and was survived by his wife of one month Isabella E. M. N. Macpherson of Edinburgh, Scotland. ***Macpherson Island*** (64 P/13) in Farnie Lake was named after him and his brother (previous entry) in 1985.

MacRae, Warrant Officer 2 **John** of Winnipeg (R 71345). No. 45 Ferry Command, RCAF. He died 7 September 1943 at the age of 23 and is commemorated at Christiansborg War Cemetery, Ghana. He was the son of Murdo and Hannah MacRae of Winnipeg and the husband of Rena MacRae. ***MacRae Lake*** (64 H/10), northeast of Buckland Lake was named after him in 1995.

MacRovic, Pilot Officer **Frank R.** of Winnipeg (J 58867). No. 425 Squadron. He died 31 March 1944 and is commemorated at Durnbach War Cemetery in Bavaria, Germany. He was the son of Lucas and Anna Majchrowicz of Winnipeg. He appears to have simplified his name at the time of enlistment. ***MacRovic Lake*** (64 P/10), east of Nejanilini Lake was named after him in 1974.

MacVicar, Private **Alexander "Sandy"** of Portage la Prairie (2842). 17th Battalion, Highland Light Infantry. He died 1 July 1916 at the age of 36 and is commemorated at Bouzincourt Communal Cemetery Extension, Somme, France. He was the fourth son of Donald and Susan MacVicar (née McLeod) of Portage la Prairie. He returned to his native Scotland at his own expense in 1915 to enlist. A Scottish newspaper reported:

> ... with characteristic Highland eagerness to get to his "job" with the least possible delay, [he] joined the HLI in Glasgow. He was one of many who distinguished themselves in the charge of 1st July when the HLI covered itself with glory. How proud he was the day he embarked for France with his sprig of Ross-shire heather snugly tucked away in his kit! (*Daily Graphic* n.d.).

His father travelled to France in 1920 to visit the grave. According to his niece (28 September 1999):

> Sandy was born on November 14, 1879 at Kiltearn Parish, Evanton, Ross-shire, Scotland. [His father] was the "dominie" or school master at Evanton until 1894-5 when he emigrated with his family of six sons and one daughter to Canada. They purchased farm land ... at Portage la Prairie and lived there until his and his wife's death in 1930.
>
> Two sons, Peter and Alexander, took positions with the railway and became CPR engineers. Peter was based in Kenora, Ontario. He joined the Merchant Marine and served all during World War I. [He] returned home and died in 1920 due to the effects of his war service according to family lore.
>
> Alexander was based at Outlook, Saskatchewan and ran west to Saskatoon, making his home at Portage la Prairie with his parents. He enlisted in January, 1915 in the 17th Highland Light Infantry. He went to France in November, 1915 and was killed [there]. The Brotherhood of Locomotive Engineers planted a tree with a plaque in his memory in the ... cemetery in Saskatoon.

MacVicar Lake (53 L/12), south of Max Lake was named after this World War I casualty in 1999.

MacWilliam, Pilot Officer **Walter A.** of MacGregor (J 92159). No. 7 Squadron. He died 6 October 1944 at the age of 24 and is commemorated at the Reichswald Forest War Cemetery in Germany. He was the son of William C. and Elizabeth McWilliam (sp.) of MacGregor, Manitoba. ***MacWilliam Lake*** (64 J/15), northwest of Tadoule Lake was named after him in 1975.

Madden, Private **John H. F.** of Roblin (H 20000). Queen's Own Cameron Highlanders. He died 19 August 1942 at the age of 34 and is commemorated at Dieppe Canadian War Cemetery in Seine-Maritime, France. He was the son of James L. and Mary Madden and was survived by his wife Anne Madden of Winnipeg. ***Madden Island*** (53 K/11) in Edmund Lake was named after him in 1989.

Madden, Pilot Officer **Joseph L. A.** of Winnipeg (J 86136). No. 410 Squadron. He died 11 February 1944 at the age of 24 and is commemorated at Brookwood Military Cemetery in Surrey, England. He was the son of Joseph L. and Ivy M. Madden of Winnipeg. ***Madden Lake*** (64 N/4), southwest of Nueltin Lake was named after him in 1972.

Madge, Flying Officer **Roy G.** of Winnipeg (J 13710). No. 428 Squadron. He died 26 May 1943 at the age of 23 and is commemorated at Heverlee War Cemetery, Leuven, Vlaams-Brabant, Belgium. He was survived by his mother Edna Madge of Varsity View (Charleswood). ***Madge Island*** (64 P/2) in the Porter River was named after him in 1995.

Madigan, Private **Charles L.** (H 87682). Princess Patricia's Canadian Light Infantry. He died 11 December 1943 and is commemorated at the Moro River Canadian War Cemetery in Italy. ***Madigan Lake*** (64 O/3), east of Blackfish Lake was named after him in 1995.

Madson, Pilot Officer **John E.** of Winnipeg (J 8950). No. 61 Squadron. He died 20 August 1942 at the age of 26 and is commemorated at Bilbao British Cemetery in Spain. He was the son of Mads E. and Edna M. Madson and was survived by his four sisters. They write (16 November 2001):

> Jack received his early education in Saskatoon, Regina, Edmonton and graduated from Kelvin High School in Winnipeg. Prior to his enlistment on January 14, 1941, he was employed by Bryce Bakeries and the Imperial Life Insurance Company. Jack had a very congenial disposition and good sense of humour. His RAF Squadron Leader described him as a keen, popular and capable member of his crew. During his training time at the Airbase in Dauphin, he would phone the family to say he was bringing some of the boys home with him on their weekend leaves. It was always entertaining to see how many chaps could squeeze into Jack's Pontiac coupe with a rumble seat, which was their mode of transportation. We were always pleased to meet young men from other parts of the Commonwealth.
>
> It was not until 1947 that the family learned the full details of what had happened. This was largely due to the efforts of Mr. William Harrad of England who's son, P/O John Harrad was the pilot of the Lancaster. He contacted a friend in Spain and ultimately the Parish Priest at Jornes who had conducted the services for the initial burial of the airmen. These details included this eye witness account:
>
> The aerial combat which I witnessed was that of the 20th August, 1942. On that day, at about three in the afternoon, in the direction of Cape S. Adrian (Malpica) there began to be heard outbursts of machine gun, and immediately after, towards the same place, three planes appeared in the air, travelling from south to north, inland, one of them, the largest, at a low altitude; the other two made persistent changes of position, placing themselves from time to time at the same level and taking advantage of such moments to direct their machine gun fire. They continued advancing overland 12 to 15 kilometres, but the largest, i.e., the British plane, continually lost height until it began to touch the highest tree-tops (pines) which it broke over a distance of some 200 meters, until it touched the ground. At this contact, and in a short interval, two tremendous explosions took place, followed by dense clouds of smoke. The other two planes turned back over the place of the incident, and changed direction towards the northeast, one of them left behind a column of smoke and it was reported afterwards that it had fallen into the sea (10 February 1947).

His sisters conclude (16 November 2001):

> A special plot was consecrated in the local churchyard of Jornes and the burial service was conducted by the local Parish Priest and attended by many of the villagers. The Parish Priest and villagers annually conducted and attended an anniversary "Service of Remembrance" on August 20th at this special plot from 1943 to 1952, when the remains of the boys were transferred to Bilbao. Funds provided by the families of the lost crew members were sent from time to time to the Parish Priest in Spain in appreciation of this care and services. The Priest specified that he did not wish any personal compensation, but that he hoped to use these funds to purchase land to enlarge his small churchyard. Jack's family and the Harrad family of England continued to correspond with each other for many years following the war.

Madson Lake (64 J/10), west of Tadoule Lake was named after him in 1975.

Magas, Rifleman **Henry** of Transcona (H 103502). Regina Rifle Regiment. He died 6 July 1944 at the age of 21 and is commemorated at Beny-sur-Mer Canadian War Cemetery in Calvados, France. He was the son of William and Nettie Magas of Transcona. ***Magas Lake*** (64 K/16), northeast of Lac Brochet was named after him in 1972.

Magnusson, Flight Sergeant **Clarence Norris** of Charleswood (R 124246). No. 428 Squadron. He died 22 May 1943 at the age of 27 and is commemorated at the Runnymede Memorial in Surrey, England. ***Magnusson Creek*** (63 I/11), which flows north into Walker Lake was named after him in 1988.

Magnusson, Private **Elmer A.** of Winnipeg (H 103840). Argyle and Sutherland Highlanders. He died 18 April 1945 at the age of 19 and is commemorated at the Holten Canadian War Cemetery in Holland. He was the son of Ari G. and Ruth Magnusson of Winnipeg. ***Magnusson Lake*** (62 P/16), west of Family Lake was named after him in 1973.

Maguire, Flight Lieutenant **Edward S.** of Winnipeg (J 20939). No. 432 Squadron. He died 21 February 1945 at the age of 25 and is commemorated at Rheinberg War Cemetery in Germany. He was the son of David A. and Alice M. Maguire of Winnipeg. ***Maguire Lake*** (64 N/4), southwest of Nueltin Lake was named after him in 1972.

Maguire, Flight Sergeant **James** of Winnipeg (R 106115). No. 489 Squadron. He died 23 January 1943 at the age of 22 and is commemorated at the Runnymede Memorial in Surrey, England. He was the son of John P. and Effie Maguire of Winnipeg. ***Maguire Island*** (64 H/4) in Gauer Lake was named after him in 1995.

Maguire, Flight Lieutenant **John G.** of Portage la Prairie (J 20876). No. 432 Squadron. He died 21 February 1945 at the age of 24 and is commemorated at Rheinberg War Cemetery in Germany. He was the son of John and Evelyn Maguire and was survived by his wife Phyllis E. Maguire (née Guay) of Jasper, Alberta and their young daughter whom he had never seen. Likewise, "Jack" had never known his own father; he was killed overseas during World War I before Jack was born. ***Maguire Bay*** (64 I/6) in Paragon Lake was named after him in 1995.

Mahon, Sergeant **James** (H 20449). Queen's Own Cameron Highlanders, Military Medal. He died 27 August 1944 at the age of 36 and is commemorated at Bretteville-sur-Laize Canadian War Cemetery in Calvados, France. He was the son of James and Louise Mahon and was survived by his wife Elizabeth D. Mahon of Fort Frances, Ontario. ***Mahon Lake*** (63 N/7), west of Guthrie Lake was named after him in 1995.

Mahr, Pilot Officer **Rudolph W.** of Winnipeg (J 95545). No. 101 Squadron. He was presumed dead 8 March 1945 at the age of 19 and is commemorated at the Runnymede Memorial in Surrey, England. He was the son of John and Anna Mahr of Winnipeg. His brother reports that he was born in Soldatskoje, Tashkent, Uzbekistan and emigrated to Canada with his family in 1928. He attended Egremont School near Swan River and Daniel McIntyre Collegiate in Winnipeg after the family moved there in 1939. His brother writes (14 November 2001):

His early years were spent on the family farm in the Swan River Valley near the town of Swan River. He received his junior education at Egremont School which was a one-room school located near the farm. He was a bright student and skipped a grade during his junior school years. This was an advantage for his younger brother because he could always rely on him for some help with his studies.

In 1940, the family moved to Winnipeg and Rudy completed his education at Hugh John Macdonald middle school and Daniel McIntyre Collegiate. After leaving school, he worked for about one year before enlisting in the RCAF on January 7, 1944. He enjoyed all sports and took an active part in boxing during his initial air crew training in Canada. After a short leave, he was transferred overseas in October, 1944.

In his letters home, he mainly commented on the various leaves he enjoyed visiting around England and Scotland and how well they were treated by the people they met. He also had the good fortune to spend some time with an old school chum, Ed Madden, who was in England on a naval training course. Rudy was a free spirit, enjoyed being with people and made friends easily.

According to his log book, he commenced operations with 101 Squadron on December 28, 1944 and completed ten operational sorties with his regular crew who all survived the war. About half of his regular crew were from Canada and one of them on his return to Canada telephoned us. He told us that on the evening of March 7, 1945, his regular crew were not scheduled for operations but for some reason Rudy was assigned to another all-British crew lead by Squadron Leader Gibbon. His regular crew were also mustered out at the last minute and Rudy tried to get transferred back to his regular crew but was told he could not for this sortie. No evidence or information was ever found concerning the Lancaster aircraft or any of the crew members.

Mahr Lake (64 O/11), southeast of Nueltin Lake was named after him in 1975.

Main, Lieutenant **Harold W.** of Winnipeg (CDN 174). Royal Welsh Fusiliers. He died 19 August 1944 at the age of 31 and is commemorated at Banneville-la-Campagne War Cemetery, Calvados, France. He was the son of William and Nan Main of Winnipeg. ***Main Lake*** (64 K/5), northeast of Reindeer Lake was named after him in 1972.

Mair, Flying Officer **Charles Maxwell** of Portage la Prairie (J 22694). No. 142 Squadron. He died 25 November 1943 at the age of 23 and is commemorated at Florence War Cemetery, Italy. He was the only son of Joseph and Grace G. Mair of Vancouver. His sister writes (18 October 2001):

Max was born and raised in Portage la Prairie. He was a member of Boy Cubs and Scouts and soloist in the Boys Choir at St. Mary's Anglican Church in Portage. He was fond of sports, playing tennis and hockey. He played for the Portage Collegiate hockey team until graduation of Grade 12 and then played for the Portage Terriers. He received a gold watch as winner of the "Most Popular Player" while with the Terriers. He kept up his hockey talent playing for the Air Force team at MacLeod, Alberta while he was in RCAF training school.

Four years after his death, his father received a letter from Gelluzo Ottavio of Agrigento, Italy:

Dear Sir: I am going to inform you what is still present at my mind even after so many years and regret the delay due to my long captivity. It was the evening of November 23rd or 24th, 1943 about eight o'clock; outside a terrible windstorm and snowstorm was raging and we were talking by the fireplace. All of a sudden, an aircraft was heard and all of us went out from the house fearing an air raid as had happened on other nights, though we were living well high on the mountains. A formidable blow was then heard and all houses all around shuddered. We were all frightened, but we had already understood what was happening and decided to go on the spot to give help in the case it was

> needed. We were, in those high mountains, the nearest human beings. A strong flame was seen two miles and a half far from us and shots were heard on account of the ammunitions which continually exploded. We had already made more than two miles under heavy wind and snow and it was very dark too and we had lanterns with us. The flame was still strong and ammunitions kept on exploding and so we could not get any nearer. Much to our regret, we went back to the village to report what we had seen.
>
> The following day at dawn, we went again on the spot. There was no more flame and no more shots were heard. We approached, but we could hardly recognize an aircraft out of the wrecks we saw. It had crashed against the slopes of Mount Gottero. The corpses were five and unrecognizable. All burnt out of your son who was intact from the trunk up. I, Gelluzo Ottavio, took his service book which contained some papers and snapshots. Soon after, we went back to Adelano to report the crashing of the aircraft to the Italian Military Police who sent three Carabiniers on the spot for four days until the German Court of Enquiry came; they ordered coffins to be made and burial to be effected at the cemetery of Adelano. Each family of Adelano gave one board and coffins were made; the mortal remains were piously gathered and all men, women and children of Adelano followed the five coffins to the cemetery telling their beads. No contribution from the Germans, not even one penny. Once the American troops arrived, they learned about the corpses of the five airmen and they brought them away. We do not know where. We did not understand if the aircraft was a bi-motor or a tri-motor; the wrecks were sent to Germany. If you need something else, will you please write (8 June 1947).

Mair Creek (64 N/10), which flows southeast into the Thlewiaza River was named after Flying Officer Mair in 1972.

Major, Private **William J. "Wilfred"** of Winnipeg (SH 4943). Royal 22nd Regiment. He died 19 August 1952 at the age of 18 and is commemorated at the United Nations Cemetery in Pusan, South Korea. ***Major Island*** (63 P/9) in Dafoe Lake was named after this Korean War casualty in 1998.

Majury, Private **William Murray** of Amaranth (H 18167). Essex Scottish Regiment. He died 5 October 1944 at the age of 20 and is commemorated at Bergen-op-Zoom Canadian War Cemetery in Holland. He was the son of Jack H. and Alice V. Majury of Amaranth, Manitoba. His sister writes (12 September 1998):

> He was born in Riding Mountain, Manitoba 29 August 1924 [and] went to school there, completing his Grade 10 education, then moving to Amaranth, Manitoba with his parents when he was 16. His interest was in western music; his sport was baseball.

Majury Lake (64 H/12), east of Southern Indian Lake was named after him in 1963.

Makarsky, Leading Writer **Lee W.** of Winnipeg (V 44967). HMCS *Miramiche*. He died 2 September 1945 at the age of 32 and is commemorated at Brookside Cemetery in Winnipeg. He was the son of Mr. and Mrs. G. W. Makarsky of Winnipeg and was survived by his wife Kathleen M. Makarsky of Winnipeg. ***Makarsky Lake*** (64 O/5), southeast of Shannon Lake was named after him in 1995.

Makay, Warrant Officer 2 **Albert G.** of Winnipeg (R 86164). No. 150 Squadron. He died 31 October 1942 at the age of 20 and is commemorated at Steenwijkerwold (Willemsoord) General Cemetery, Holland. He was survived by his mother Julia Makay of Winnipeg. ***Albert Makay Lake*** (64 I/14), east of Shethanei Lake was named after him in 1995.

Makepeace, Warrant Officer 2 **Thomas J.** of Basswood (R 157083). No. 148 Squadron. He died 31 May 1944 at the age of 21 and is commemorated at Belgrade War Cemetery, Yugoslavia. He was the son of Andrew and Mary Makepeace of Basswood, Manitoba. ***Makepeace Lake*** (53 E/7), south of Island Lake was named after him in 1973.

Makichuk, Corporal **Michael John** of Portage la Prairie (H 41223). Royal Winnipeg Rifles. He died 6 June 1944 at the age of 23 and is commemorated at Beny-sur-Mer Canadian War Cemetery in Calvados, France. He was the son of Mr. and Mrs. Saffron S. Makichuk and was survived by his wife Elizabeth A. Makichuk of Debert, Nova Scotia. ***Makichuk Lake*** (64 K/14), northeast of Reindeer Lake was named after him in 1972.

Maksymetz, Aircraftman 2 **Max R.** of Dauphin (R 250959). No. 2 Initial Training School, RCAF. He died 22 April 1943 at the age of 19 and is commemorated at Riverside Cemetery in Dauphin. He was the son of Roman and Dora Maksymetz of Dauphin. ***Maksymetz Lake*** (64 P/16), northeast of Nejanilini Lake was named after him in 1974.

Malbranck, Private **Jerome A.** of Norwood (H 8960). South Saskatchewan Regiment. He died 20 July 1944 at the age of 23 and is commemorated at Bretteville-sur-Laize Canadian War Cemetery in Calvados, France. He was the son of Daniel J. and Irma Malbranck of West Kildonan. ***Malbranck Lake*** (64 O/3), west of Munroe Lake was named after him in 1975.

Malcom, Bombardier **Philip G.** of Winnipeg (H 5141). Royal Canadian Artillery. He died 23 September 1943 at the age of 24 and is commemorated at Bari War Cemetery in Italy. He was the son of Reginald G. and Hildred Malcom of Winnipeg. ***Malcom Island*** (52 L/3) in Crowduck Lake was named after him in 1973.

Mallett, Flying Officer **Ronald F.** of Elkhorn (J 11451). No. 22 Operational Training Unit, RCAF. He was returning to Scotland from a training mission in a thick fog when his Wellington crashed killing all 11 crew members. Flying Officer Mallett died 30 November 1942 at the age of 23 and is commemorated at Stratford-upon-Avon Cemetery in Warwickshire, England. He was the son of George F. W. and Agnes E. Mallett of Elkhorn, Manitoba. He had been employed at the Canada Car Foundry Company at Fort William when he enlisted. His sister recalls (23 August 1995):

> His great love was his accordion and arriving overseas he purchased one, being unable to take his from Canada. He always felt that there were officers that went to the Mess Hall who might prefer to sing rather than drink.

Mallett Lake (64 J/16), north of Tadoule Lake was named after him in 1975.

Mallindine, Signalman **George Russell** of Winnipeg (H 3885). Royal Canadian Corps of Signals. He died 14 June 1944 at the age of 34 and is commemorated at Brookwood Military Cemetery in Surrey, England. He was the son of George A. and Isabella Mallindine (née Campbell) and the step-son of Mr. and Mrs. J. Smith of Winnipeg. ***Mallindine Lake*** (64 I/15), northeast of North Knife Lake was named after him in 1974.

Malofie, Pilot Officer **Daniel** of Fisher Branch (J 8596). No. 214 Squadron. He died 3 July 1942 at the age of 31 and is commemorated at Westernieland General Cemetery, De Marne, Holland. He was the son of Wasyl and Helen Malofie. ***Malofie Lake*** (64 C/7), southwest of Eden Lake was named after him in 1990.

Malone, Warrant Officer 2 **Edward C.** of Winnipeg (R 86225). No. 78 Squadron. He died 20 December 1942 at the age of 22 and is commemorated at the Runnymede Memorial in Surrey, England. He was the son of Cecil S. S. and Mary E. Malone of Vancouver. ***Malone Lake*** (64 P/12), north of Nejanilini Lake was named after him in 1974.

Maloney, Lieutenant **James E.** of Winnipeg. Queen's Own Cameron Highlanders. He died 20 July 1944 and is commemorated at Bretteville-sur-Laize Canadian War Cemetery in Calvados, France. He was survived by his wife Mary Maloney. ***Maloney Lake*** (64 K/6), northeast of Reindeer Lake was named after him in 1972.

Maltese, Private **James** of Winnipeg (H 6163). Winnipeg Grenadiers. He died 25 December 1941 and is commemorated at Stanley Military Cemetery, Hong Kong. ***Maltese Lake*** (64 O/1), east of Munroe Lake was named after him in 1975.

Maltman, Trooper **Johnstone M.** of Minitonas (H 63657). Three Rivers Tank Regiment. He died 14 October 1943 at the age of 23 and is commemorated at Bari War Cemetery in Italy. He was the son of Joseph H. and Gladys M. Maltman of Minitonas, Manitoba. ***Maltman Lake*** (63 N/3), east of Kississing Lake was named after him in 1945.

Mamchur, Trooper **Carl** (H 33). Lord Strathcona's Horse. He died 26 September 1944 at the age of 24 and is commemorated at Cesena War Cemetery in Italy. He was the son of Stanley and Tini Mamchur of Kenora, Ontario. ***Mamchur Lake*** (64 O/3), southeast of Blackfish Lake was named after him in 1995.

Manahan, Squadron Leader **James R.** of Winnipeg (41443). No. 100 Squadron, RAF, Distinguished Flying Cross. He died 12 June 1943 at the age of 26 and is commemorated at the Runnymede Memorial in Surrey, England. As a member of No. 148 Squadron, he flew 42 operations in the Western Desert, Crete, Greece and Malta (Allison 1978). He had enlisted in October, 1938. ***Manahan Lake*** (53 L/11), south of Munro Lake was named after him in 1995.

Manchur, Flight Sergeant **Carl A.** of Winnipeg (R 80326). No. 12 Squadron. He died 29 July 1942 at the age of 21 and is commemorated at Binbrook (St. Mary) Churchyard in Lincolnshire, England. He was the son of Joseph and Anna Manchur of Winnipeg. ***Manchur Lake*** (64 H/11), southeast of Small Lake was named after him in 1995.

Manders, Flight Sergeant **Clarence D.** of Winnipeg (R 124412). No. 426 Squadron. He died 24 November 1943 at the age of 20 and is commemorated at Stonefall Cemetery in Yorkshire, England. He was survived by his mother Maude E. Manders of West Kildonan. ***Manders Lake*** (64 P/14), northeast of Nejanilini Lake was named after him in 1974.

Mandzuk, Private **Mike** of Whitemouth (H 10124). Royal Rifles of Canada. He died 28 August 1944 at the age of 23 and is commemorated at Bretteville-sur-Laize Canadian War Cemetery in Calvados, France. He was the son of George and Mary Mandzuk of Whitemouth, Manitoba. ***Mandzuk Lake*** (64 I/12), northwest of North Knife Lake was named after him in 1974.

Manley, Bombardier **John** of Winnipeg (H 60565). Royal Canadian Artillery. He died 26 February 1945 at the age of 39 and is commemorated at the Groesbeek Canadian War Cemetery in Holland. He was the son of George H. and Nellie Manley and was survived by his wife Irene I. Manley of Winnipeg. ***Manley Lake*** (64 K/5), northeast of Reindeer Lake was named after him in 1972.

Mann, Private **George Westlake** of Medora (H 9892). Queen's Own Cameron Highlanders. He died 29 August 1944 at the age of 28 and is commemorated at Bretteville-sur-Laize Canadian War Cemetery in Calvados, France. He was the fifth child of James A. and Annie Melrose Mann and was survived by his wife Edythe Mann (née Sambrook) of Medora, Manitoba. His sister recalls (23 November 2001):

"Wes" was born on November 8, 1915 in Elgin, Manitoba. He started school in 1922 and showed musical talent at an early age, later playing violin in the string orchestra trained by the school principal, Mr. B. Thordarson. Wes graduated from the Elgin School in 1934, then attended Brandon College where he received his B.A. in Theology in 1939. Walter Dinsdale (later to become the Honourable Walter Dinsdale) was attending Brandon College at the same time and said: "If it had not been for Wes' help, I never would have passed the Math exam."

Wes held Pastorates at Kenton, Boissevain, Ninga and Medora – all located in Manitoba, before enlisting in the Army on May 18, 1943 in Winnipeg. He trained in Shilo and went overseas with the QOCH that same year.

Wes was a fun loving man who enjoyed singing, playing his violin and participating in sports. He did not believe in fighting, but wanted to do his part to save his country. We are told Wes' good humour encouraged his army comrades, especially the nervous one whom he coaxed into position. His platoon officer said he couldn't speak highly enough of him, stating Wes refused to take a "stripe." His wife Edythe of Medora is now deceased. His four remaining siblings will always cherish his memory.

Mann Lake (64 N/15), west of Nueltin Lake was named after him in 1972.

Mann, Lance Bombardier **William Eric** of Winnipeg (H 24162). Royal Canadian Artillery. He died 12 December 1943 at the age of 23 and is commemorated at the Moro River Canadian War Cemetery in Italy. He was the son of Harold and Anna M. Mann of Winnipeg. His brother recalls his last summer at home:

Eric went to work in a government forestry camp at Falcon Lake for the 1939 summer and took along his guitar to amuse himself in the evenings. I arranged to visit him on the Labour Day weekend. On the way to the bus depot, I saw newsboys selling "extras" and shouting "War with Germany." Germany had marched into Poland and Britain declared war on September 3rd. Eric and the other boys were uneasy; they fully expected to be called up for military service in a matter of days.

Nevertheless, I had a good visit as a guest in the camp. Eric and I entertained the lads and some vacationers around a campfire in the evening. But next day Eric decided to take his pay, quit the camp and return to Winnipeg with me on the bus. Within two weeks he voluntarily enlisted in the Fort Garry Horse Artillery.

The War seemed far away, but was very real. Germany overran Europe and some 350,000 troops were lucky to be evacuated at Dunkirk. My brother Eric was among the troops but his battery was pulled back before the main evacuation (Mann 2000).

Mann Island (64 P/8) in Koleda Lake was named after him in 1995.

Mannell, Private **John W.** (H 6757). Winnipeg Grenadiers. He died 1 November 1942 and is commemorated at the Sai Wan War Cemetery in Hong Kong. ***Mannell Lake*** (53 L/1), south of Rochon Lake was named after him in 1995.

Manness, Corporal **Leslie C.** of Winnipeg (H 16783). Princess Patricia's Canadian Light Infantry. He died 23 May 1944 and is commemorated at the Cassino War Cemetery in Italy. ***Manness Lake*** (62 P/16), west of Family Lake was named after him in 1973.

Manning, Sergeant **Percival T.** of Winnipeg (R 59283). No. 11 Squadron. He died 22 July 1941 at the age of 20 and is commemorated at Bassingbourn-cum-Kneesworth Cemetery, Cambridgeshire, England. He was the son of Herbert G. and Margaret M. Manning of Winnipeg. His aircraft was shot down while on a night flying training mission over England when it was shot down by another Wellington – one which had been captured by the enemy (Allison and Hayward 1991). ***Manning Lake*** (52 M/11), southwest of Dogskin Lake was named after him in 1983.

Manson, Corporal **Harold J.** of Winnipeg (R 59172). No. 3 Service Flying Training School. He died 26 August 1942 at the age of 29 and is commemorated at Elmwood Cemetery in Winnipeg. He was the son of William M. and Lena E. Manson of Winnipeg and was survived by his wife Eileen W. Manson of Calgary. ***Manson Lake*** (64 C/16), southwest of Barrington Lake was named after him in 1995.

Manson, Flight Sergeant **William M.** of Winnipeg (R 112619). No. 428 Squadron. He died 29 April 1943 at the age of 23 and is commemorated at the Sage War Cemetery in Germany. He was the son of William M. and Margaret M. Manson of Winnipeg. ***Manson Island*** (53 L/2) in Island Lake was named after him in 1995.

Marantz, Captain **Harry L.** of Flin Flon. Royal Canadian Army Medical Corps, Mentioned in Dispatches. He died 14 August 1944 and is commemorated at Bretteville-sur-Laize Canadian War Cemetery in Calvados, France. He was survived by his wife Eveline Marantz. ***Marantz Lake*** (54 K/4), southeast of Churchill was named after him in 1948.

Marchello, Private **John** (alias **Marchylo**) of Winnipeg (B 67550). Royal Regiment of Canada. He died 19 August 1942 at the age of 26 and is commemorated at the Brookwood Memorial in Surrey, England. He was the son of Dimytro and Annie Marchylo of Winnipeg. After the Dieppe Raid:

... the Royal Regiment virtually no longer existed. Of the 20 officers and 528 other ranks, only two officers and 63 other ranks got back, 31 of them wounded. Half of those who returned never landed as the landing craft turned away before unloading all of its soldiers (Leah 1992).

Marchello Lake (63 O/12), west of Apeganau Lake was named after him in 1995.

Marchisky, Trooper **Michael** of McCreary (H 26578). Fort Garry Horse. He died 8 June 1944 at the age of 27 and is commemorated at the Bayeux Memorial in Calvados, France. He was survived by his step-father Peter and mother Tilly Shura of McCreary, Manitoba. According to his brother (4 February 1998):

Trooper Marchisky landed in France on D-Day. Some days later his stepfather got a telegram notifying him that Trooper Michael Marchisky was missing in action as of 8 June 1944. A later telegram advised that [he] was presumed dead. After some time, the family got the story from eyewitnesses who were there on June 8th and saw his tank hit by an armour-piercing shell and immediately explode into flame. Because of the intense fire, bodies of the crew were burnt beyond recognition.

Marchisky Lake (63 N/2), east of Kississing Lake was named after him in 1972.

Marcotte, Able Seaman **Paul J. L.** of Transcona (2161). HMCS *Fraser*. The *Fraser* was lost in a collision with the British cruiser HMS *Calcutta* during the evacuation of France in 1940. Able Seaman Marcotte died 25 June 1940 at the age of 35 and is commemorated at the Halifax Memorial. He was the son of Joseph and Alma Marcotte of Transcona and was survived by his wife Alice M. Marcotte of Esquimalt, British Columbia. ***Marcotte Lake*** (63 N/12), south of Sisipuk Lake was named after him in 1981.

Markle, Flight Sergeant **Jack W.** of Shoal Lake (R 71494). No. 408 Squadron. He died 9 May 1942 at the age of 26 and is commemorated at the Berlin 1939 - 1945 War Cemetery in Brandenburg, Germany. He was the son of Mervyn C. and Lydia I. B. Markle of Shoal Lake, Manitoba and the brother of Pilot Officer Orin C. Markle (next entry). ***Markle Island*** (53 E/10) in Island Lake was named after him in 1995.

Markle, Pilot Officer **Orin C.** of Shoal Lake (J 91091). No. 1 Delivery Unit, RCAF. He died 7 March 1944 at the age of 24 and is commemorated at the Runnymede Memorial in Surrey, England. He was the son of Mervyn C. and Lydia I. B. Markle of Shoal Lake, Manitoba and the brother of Flight Sergeant Jack W. Markle (previous entry). ***Markle Lake*** (53 E/7), south of Island Lake was named after him in 1973.

Markoskie, Gunner **Lorne** of Winnipeg (H 616901). Royal Canadian Artillery. He died 10 January 1946 at the age of 20 and is commemorated at the Holten Canadian War Cemetery in Holland. He was the son of Mike and Edith Markoskie of Hyas, Saskatchewan. ***Markoskie Lake*** (64 I/11), north of North Knife Lake was named after him in 1974.

Marks, Private **Bert A.** of Portage la Prairie (H 102838). Lake Superior Regiment. He died 25 April 1945 at the age of 22 and is commemorated at the Holten Canadian War Cemetery in Holland. He was the son of William J. and Elizabeth Marks of Portage la Prairie. He had enlisted on his 18th birthday (3 September 1940). ***Marks River*** (64 K/15), which flows east into Chatwin Lake was named after him in 1972.

Marks, Warrant Officer 2 **Edward R.** of Winnipeg (R 134206). No. 426 Squadron. He died 18 August 1943 at the age of 23 and is commemorated at the Berlin 1939 - 1945 War Cemetery in Brandenburg, Germany. ***Marks Lake*** (64 G/14), east of Big Sand Lake was named after him in 1994.

Marks, Radio Officer **William K.** of Winnipeg. Royal Air Force Ferry Command. He died 10 August 1941 and is commemorated at Kilbride Old Churchyard, Buteshire, Scotland. ***Marks Island*** (53 K/11) in Edmund Lake was named after him in 1995.

Marsh, Flying Officer **Alfred J.** of Dauphin (C 8109). Ferry Training Unit, RCAF. He died 16 August 1942 at the age of 26 and is commemorated at Cirencester Cemetery in Gloucestershire, England. He was the son of William S. and Edythe E. Marsh of Dauphin. ***Marsh Island*** (64 N/10) in Tice Lake was named after him in 1995.

Marsh, Private **Clifford J.** of Winnipeg (H 41672). Winnipeg Grenadiers. He died a prisoner of war 12 February 1944 and is commemorated at the Yokohama War Cemetery in Japan. The official cause of death was listed as colitis. He was the eldest son of James Robert and Rena D. Marsh of Winnipeg. ***Marsh Rapids*** (64 A/11) in the Rasp River was named after him in 1996.

Marsh, Trooper **Gordon Glynn** of Souris (H 77260). 14th Canadian Hussars. He died 30 August 1944 at the age of 21 and is commemorated at Bretteville-sur-Laize Canadian War Cemetery in Calvados, France. He was the son of Ray and Violet Marsh of Souris, Manitoba. ***Marsh Peninsula*** (64 I/4) on Ashley Lake was named after him in 1995.

Marshall, Gunner **Stanley J.** of Roseisle (H 95440). Royal Canadian Artillery. He died 18 December 1943 at the age of 22 and is commemorated at the Moro River Canadian War Cemetery in Italy. He was the son of Robert E. and Maud T. Marshall of Roseisle, Manitoba. ***Marshall Creek*** (53 M/6), which flows northeast into Gowan River was named after him in 1985.

Marshall, Flying Officer **William J.** of Winnipeg (J 10778). No. 3502 Conversion Unit, RCAF. He died 30 July 1943 at the age of 21 and is commemorated at Llantwit Major Cemetery, Glamorganshire, Wales. He was the son of William and Blanche E. Marshall of Winnipeg and was survived by his wife Ruth M. Marshall of Winnipeg. ***Marshall Island*** (64 C/4) in Russell Lake was named after him in 1995.

Marten, Private **Lionel C.** of Winnipeg (H 19809). Queen's Own Cameron Highlanders. He died 19 August 1942 and is commemorated at Le Portel Communal Cemetery, Pas de Calais, France. He was survived by his mother Jessie Marten of Moose Jaw, Saskatchewan. ***Marten Rapids*** (64 P/14) in the Roberts River was named after him in 1995.

Martin, Flight Sergeant **Burnett H.** of Winnipeg (R 80218). No. 37 Squadron. He died 3 July 1942 at the age of 20 and is commemorated at El Alamein War Cemetery in Egypt. He was the son of Peter and Catherine Martin of Winnipeg. ***Martin Peninsula*** (64 N/16) on Nahili Lake was named after him in 1995.

Martin, Sergeant **Harold R.** of Winnipeg (904487). No. 102 Squadron, RAF. He had enlisted in 1939 and was killed in action 8 April 1941. He was 20 years of age and is commemorated at the Runnymede Memorial in Surrey, England. ***Harold Martin Hill*** (64 A/6), northeast of White Stone Lake was named after him in 1995.

Martin, Warrant Officer 1 **Lawrence G.** of Winnipeg (R 134391). No. 11 Squadron. He died 19 May 1944 at the age of 25 and is commemorated at the Ottawa Memorial. He was the son of George and Constance Martin of Winnipeg. ***Martin Bay*** (64 O/10) in Askey Lake was named after him in 1985.

Martin, Corporal **Thomas C.** (H 77700). 12th Manitoba Dragoons. He died 15 January 1945 and is commemorated at Bergen-op-Zoom Canadian War Cemetery in Holland. ***Thomas Martin Lake*** (53 L/2), south of Beaver Hill Lake was named after him in 1996.

Martin, Squadron Sergeant Major (Warrant Officer 2) **William** of Winnipeg (H 26157). Fort Garry Horse. He died 6 January 1945 and is commemorated at Bergen-op-Zoom Canadian War Cemetery in Holland. He was survived by his wife Mrs. I. M. Martin of Solihull, Warwickshire, England. ***Martin Hill*** (64 I/16), south of Meades Lake was named after him in 1995.

Martin, Lance Corporal **William John** of Marquette (H 40963). Royal Winnipeg Rifles. He died 6 June 1944 and is commemorated at Beny-sur-Mer Canadian War Cemetery in Calvados, France. In 1989, hundreds of veterans and their families returned to Normandy for the 45th anniversary of the D-Day landings:

> Stan Todd, 91 controlled six regiments of the Royal Canadian Artillery 45 years ago when he was a brigadier general. He also conducted the fire plan on the run into the beaches. "I can tell you within ten yards where we landed. I can visualize the sand, the guns, the ships," the Hamilton resident said. He said the worst moment was the morning after D-Day. "When I had to compile the casualty lists of the friends we'd lost during the night, it hit pretty hard. I became attached to men in my care and it hits me pretty hard now when I look at their graves and realize they were so young" (*Winnipeg Free Press* 6 June 1989).

Martin Island (64 O/12) in Nueltin Lake was named after him in 1975.

Martini, Gunner **Anton A.** of Winnipeg (H 8246). Royal Canadian Artillery. He died 24 October 1944 at the age of 24 and is commemorated at Cesena War Cemetery in Italy. He was the son of Frank and Katie Martini of Sand Hill, Manitoba. His sister writes (23 October 2001):

> Anton grew up on a small mixed farm and attended the local school for his elementary education. He was always anxious to help with the work on the farm, plus help his mother with her housework. He worked as a farm hand for many of the neighbouring farmers and thus earned some income. Anton loved horses and cared for them on the farm and trained them to be ridden. In his earlier years, he organized fastball games and picnics at the farm yard.
>
> His last leave was a short one, and it was for his eldest sister's wedding on October 12, 1942. With sadness in her heart, his mother arranged for a farewell party, including his ballplayer friends, neighbours and families.
>
> We had some correspondence from him, until his passing. We were told he was shot while having his lunch break in Italy. My husband's cousin visited his gravesite at Cesena and brought back pictures of the wooden cross and the lovely entrance of the British Empire Cemetery.

Martini Lake (63 O/4), north of Wekusko Lake was named after him in 1970.

Marych, Rifleman **Frederick** of Fisher Branch (H 41558). Royal Winnipeg Rifles. He died 8 June 1944 and is commemorated at Beny-sur-Mer Canadian War Cemetery in Calvados, France. ***Marych Lake*** (64 K/10), northeast of Reindeer Lake was named after him in 1972.

Mason, Gunner **Charles S.** of Glenella (H 103569). Royal Canadian Artillery. He died 24 February 1945 and is commemorated at the Groesbeek Canadian War Cemetery in Holland. ***Mason Creek*** (64 P/8), which flows south into Caribou River was named after him in 1985.

Mason, Rifleman **David** of Bagot (H 103845). Royal Winnipeg Rifles. He died 21 February 1945 at the age of 29 and is commemorated at the Groesbeek Canadian War Cemetery in Holland. He was the son of Ernest and Emily L. Mason of Bagot, Manitoba. His niece writes (15 January 2002):

> When my uncle joined the army, he really wanted to be a paratrooper, so he was sent to Shilo for training. But the tower was under repair, so after three weeks of sitting around, he asked for a transfer and soon after was sent overseas. He was a very good marksman and used to shoot a cigarette out of his cousin's mouth. I guess that's why he was a sniper for a while. I could tell by his letters he did not like being a sniper and was glad when they put him in a different unit. His mother died a few months after the news of his death. His brother said she died of a broken heart.

Mason Hill (64 J/5), west of Sprott Lake was named after him in 1989.

Mason, Corporal **Henry J.** of Winnipeg (H 6768). Royal Canadian Corps of Signals. He died 28 December 1943 at the age of 43 and is commemorated at Brookside Cemetery in Winnipeg. He was the son of J. H. and Barbara Mason of Winnipeg. ***Mason Peninsula*** (64 I/7) on Beganili Lake was named after him in 1995.

Mason, Flying Officer **Leonard E.** of Winnipeg (J 23153). No. 57 Squadron. He died 23 May 1944 at the age of 35 and is commemorated at the Reichswald Forest War Cemetery in Germany. He was the son of John T. M. and of Dorothy E. Mason (née Wakerley). ***Mason Rapids*** (64 P/8) in the Caribou River was named after him in 1995.

Matheson, Sapper **Arnie P.** of Winnipeg Beach (H 13252). Royal Canadian Engineers. He died 14 July 1940 at the age of 34 and is commemorated at Lundi Cemetery in Winnipeg Beach, Manitoba. He was the son of Mr. and Mrs. Thorstein Matheson of Winnipeg Beach and was survived by his wife Ingibjorg M. Matheson (née Thorkalson) of Winnipeg and their four children. His daughter recalls (22 November 2001):

> Dad was born in Iceland in 1906. After the death of his mother, Maria, he (aged two), his father, two brothers and sister immigrated to Canada. In 1931 he married Ingibjorg. Dad spent most of his short life as a commercial fisherman on Lake Winnipeg alongside his father. He volunteered for service to defend his new country in 1939. After his death in 1940, Ingibjorg had his remains shipped back to Winnipeg Beach. He now rests in peace alongside his father and one brother.

Matheson Bay (64 H/11) in Small Lake was named after him in 1995.

Matheson, Lieutenant **Donald J.** Royal Canadian Artillery, Military Cross. He died 10 September 1944 and is commemorated at Brookwood Military Cemetery in Surrey, England. He was the son of John C. and Ethel S. Matheson of Regina. ***Matheson Lake*** (64 C/5), south of Laurie Lake was named after him in 1947.

Matheson, Private **Dougal K.** of Kenville (H 18142). Queen's Own Cameron Highlanders. He died 3 March 1945 at the age of 19 and is commemorated at the Groesbeek Canadian War Cemetery in Holland. His sister visited his grave in 1960 and 1995. He was the son of John P. and Dorothy M. Matheson of Kenville, Manitoba. His sister writes (21 November 2001):

> My brother had only been working a few months on his first job when he decided to enlist in the army "to see the world." He was quite eager to join his friends who had already left home. He spent his war service in Belgium, Holland and lastly Germany where he was killed. His last letter to the family was dated February 3, 1945, just one month before he was killed.

Matheson Peninsula (63 N/4) on Duval Lake was named after him in 1995.

Matte, Private **Clarence F.** of Winnipeg (H 7147). Winnipeg Grenadiers. He died 30 July 1942 at the age of 19 and is commemorated at Assumption Gardens in Winnipeg. He was the son of Thomas and Eva Matte of Winnipeg and the brother of Private Thomas Matte (next entry). ***Matte Island*** (63 N/12) in Sisipuk Lake was named after him in 1995.

Matte, Private **Thomas** of Winnipeg (H 6014). Winnipeg Grenadiers. He died 20 December 1941 at the age of 17 and is commemorated at the Sai Wan Memorial in Hong Kong. He was the son of Thomas and Eva Matte of St. Boniface and the brother of Private Clarence F. Matte (previous entry). ***Matte Bay*** (63 N/12) in Sisipuk Lake was named after him in 1995.

Matthews, Private **Denis C.** of Winnipeg (H 6197). Winnipeg Grenadiers. He died 25 December 1941 at the age of 23 and is commemorated at the Sai Wan War Cemetery in Hong Kong. Born in Portsmouth, England, he came to Canada with his father in 1926. He was the son of Charles J. and Nellie B. Matthews of Winnipeg and the brother of Private Norman C. Matthews (next entry). He was survived by a wife. **West Matthews Lake** (53 M/1), west of Semmens Lake was named after him in 1995.

Matthews, Private **Norman C.** of Winnipeg (H 6044). Winnipeg Grenadiers. He died a prisoner of war 22 January 1944 at the age of 27 and is commemorated at the Yokohama War Cemetery in Japan. The official cause of death was listed as "cardiac beriberi." He was the son of Charles J. and Nellie B. Matthews of Winnipeg and the brother of Private Denis C. Matthews (previous entry). Born in Portsmouth, England, he came to Canada in 1929 with his mother. He was survived by his wife Irene M. Matthews of Red Deer, Alberta and their daughter. ***East Matthews Lake*** (53 M/1), west of Semmens Lake was named after him in 1995.

Matthews, Pilot Officer **Philip M.** of Langruth (J 11847). No. 408 Squadron. He died 9 November 1942 at the age of 22 and is commemorated at Ripon Cemetery in Yorkshire, England. He was the son of Gordon and Elizabeth Matthews of Langruth. ***Matthews Lake*** (64 F/2), south of Wells Lake was named after him in 1994.

Matthews, Flight Lieutenant **Stanley W.** of Winnipeg (J 5793). No. 403 Squadron. This was the squadron led by the legendary (Air Vice Marshall) Johnnie Johnston. Flight Lieutenant Matthews was presumed dead 18 November 1943 at the age of 24 and is commemorated at the Runnymede Memorial in Surrey, England. He was returning to England from a mission when he was shot down 25 miles inland from the French coast. He was the son of William H. and Ethel Matthews and was survived by his wife Rae L. Matthews (née Bull) of Fort Garry and their daughter Meredith Lynn. According to his sister (19 February 1996):

As a boy, Stan spent his summers at our cottage on Lac du Bonnet, just above what is now McArthur Falls power plant. It was here that he developed his love of the outdoors – particularly fishing, hunting, canoeing etc. He was married in 1941.

His daughter adds (19 November 2001):

He was a charming young man, intelligent and fun loving. He was a third year Engineering student at the University of Manitoba when he decided to join the RCAF. After receiving his wings in 1941, he was stationed at Yorkton, Saskatchewan as a navigation instructor. After a year and a half, Stan applied for overseas duty and realized his ambition to become a Spitfire pilot. He served in that capacity until 1943 when he went missing.

Matthews Island (64 J/12) in Jamie Lake was named after him in 1995.

Matynia, Flying Officer **George T.** of Poplarfield (J 13072). No. 427 Squadron. He died 26 June 1943 at the age of 20 and is commemorated at Gorssel General Cemetery in Holland. Born in Wierzbnik, Poland, George came to Canada with his parents and younger brother in 1928. His parents went to Winnipeg looking for work while George and John were brought up by their grandparents on a farm in Poplarfield. He received a Bachelor of Arts degree from the University of Manitoba before enlisting. His sister-in-law writes (10 December 1994):

I do hope your book will emphasize how the lives of families were shattered and not glorify war. My mother-in-law was destroyed by the loss of her brilliant son. She could never accept his death at such an early age. She refused the pension she was entitled to, calling it "blood money."

Matynia Lake (64 G/6), northeast of McPherson Lake was named after him in 1994.

Maughan, Leading Seaman **Edward J.** of Winnipeg (V 9377). SS *Cornwallis*. He died 3 December 1944 at the age of 32 and is commemorated at the Halifax Memorial. He was the son of Christopher and Elizabeth Maughan of Winnipeg and was survived by his wife Helen M. Maughan of Winnipeg. The *Cornwallis* was *en route* to Halifax when it was sunk by a U-boat off the New England coast. There were only five survivors. ***Maughan Lake*** (64 N/2), southwest of Nueltin Lake was named after him in 1972.

Mavor, Sergeant **Grant J.** of St. James (R 56873). No. 9 Squadron. He died 18 April 1941 at the age of 24 and is commemorated at Rheinberg War Cemetery in Germany. He was the only son of the late John and Clara P. Mavor of Winnipeg. According to his sister (23 October 2001):

Grant John Mavor was born in Winnipeg and attended Bannatyne School in Sturgeon Creek, St. James Collegiate and Wesley College (now the University of Winnipeg). He joined the RCAF on 17 April 1940 and graduated as Sergeant-Observer on 16 August 1940 at Malton, Ontario. This was the first class trained under the Commonwealth Air Training Plan. They proceeded overseas in the fall of 1940 and were attached to the RAF. After numerous missions, Grant was shot down one year to the day after he joined up.

Mavor Lake (64 N/9), southwest of Nueltin Lake was named after him in 1972.

Maw, Pilot Officer **Arthur Douglas** of Arrow River (J 19452). No. 76 Squadron. He died 31 March 1944 at the age of 30 and is commemorated at Durnbach War Cemetery in Bavaria, Germany. Pilot Officer Maw took part in the Nuremberg Raid of 30 - 31 March 1944. 111 Canadian airman lost their lives that night. RAF Bomber Command lists 95 aircraft as having failed to return with another 13 crashed or written off on home territory. An additional 46 were damaged. It has been referred to as the Dieppe of the strategic bomber offensive (Williston 1996). ***Maw Lake*** (63 K/16), northwest of Wekusko Lake was named after him in 1973.

Maw, Flying Officer **Franklin L.** of Winnipeg (J 37480). No. 20 Operational Training Unit, RCAF. He died 23 August 1944 at the age of 23 and is commemorated at Lossiemouth Burial Ground in Morayshire, Scotland. He was the son of Oscar F. and Margaret Maw of Winnipeg. ***Maw Island*** (64 C/6) in Kaykayk Lake was named after him in 1995.

Mawson, Flight Sergeant **James A.** of Sanford (R 116235). No. 1648 Conversion Unit, RCAF. He died 21 August 1943 at the age of 22 and is commemorated at Botley Cemetery in Oxfordshire, England. He was the foster son of Mr. and Mrs. George Jessen of Sanford and was survived by his wife Helen E. Mawson of Winnipeg. She recalls (12 November 2001):

After coming to Sanford, Manitoba at the age of 10, Jim had a very good home with his foster parents, Mr. and Mrs. George Jessen. Always a good student, he graduated from high school and then joined the Air Force. We were married in October, 1942. After finishing his pilot training, he was posted to England in November, 1942. These young men went overseas in great spirits! I was making a quilt for our home and Jim said "I will be home before you finish that quilt!" Sadly, it was not to be as he was killed as a result of a flying accident in 1943.

He had been a permit teacher at the time of his enlistment. ***Mawson Lake*** (64 P/4), south of Nejanilini Lake was named after him in 1974.

Maxwell, Flight Sergeant **Arnold G.** of Portage la Prairie (R 95390). No. 16 Operational Training Unit, RCAF. He died 6 May 1942 at the age of 20 and is commemorated at Kempston Cemetery, Bedfordshire, England. He was the son of Thomas E. and Mary Irene Maxwell of Portage la Prairie. His brother writes (17 August 1990):

[He] enlisted in the RCAF in Manitoba in January, 1941. He was posted first to Brandon Manning Depot and later for a time at Carberry RAF station before going to Sea Island at the West Coast for his preliminary training. In succession he trained as a flier at the RCAF Initial Training School at Regina and at the Service Flying Training School at Calgary where he earned his wings as a graduate flier in October, 1941. He went to Britain in November of the same year and was at an operational training school a time before taking his place in active air service.

Maxwell Island (52 M/12) in Sasaginnigak Lake was named after him in 1991.

Maxwell, Private **Ralph C.** of Transcona (H 6745). Winnipeg Grenadiers. He died 19 December 1941 and is commemorated at the Sai Wan Memorial in Hong Kong. ***Maxwell Lake*** (64 G/13), north of Big Sand Lake was named after him in 1963.

Maxwell, Captain **Robert Douglas** of Winnipeg. Royal Canadian Army Paymaster Corps. He was presumed dead 26 July 1944 at the age of 30 and is commemorated at Beny-sur-Mer Canadian War Cemetery in Calvados, France. This native of Belfast, Northern Ireland was the only son of Robert and Sarah "Jennie" Maxwell and husband of Margaret H. Maxwell (née Joss) of Winnipeg. Shortly after his death, his widow received a letter from Captain Maxwell's best friend, Lieutenant Bert Martin:

> Dear Mrs. Maxwell: In view of the close friendship which existed between Doug and myself, I feel that I should be the one to write to you after personally taking care of Doug's affairs over here. I know you will understand when I tell you that for obvious reasons, I can't give you complete details at this time, but will be only too glad to advise you or do anything you ask at a later date when I am at liberty to do so.
>
> I'm sure it will afford you some comfort to know that Doug didn't suffer for a minute and I sincerely believe that that is how he would have wanted it. You see his wounds were such that he would have been incapacitated for the rest of his life and given the choice, any of us would take the other alternative. He was devoted to you Margaret, if I may call you by name, and I know that I am more qualified to pass that on to you than anyone else as he was always talking to me about you and I was generally in his confidence as a pal.
>
> What personal effects of intrinsic value Doug had with him in the field, I have inventoried and forwarded to the O. I/C Estates as we are not allowed to forward them direct. His accounts in connection with pay were balanced in short order and personal cash has been credited to his bank account. We held a quiet funeral the following morning and Doug's resting place has been well cared for. Again, I can't tell you where it is located until later but I visit it once or twice a week to see that it is being looked after.
>
> If you want me to do anything further or if there is anything you want to know that I can tell you, please drop me a line. In the meantime Margaret, I would say, chin up and keep smiling because that's what Doug would want you to do. I am sure that you will be proud as we all are who knew him not only as a good friend to us but also as a man. In conclusion, may I offer you my deepest sympathy and trust that your grief will be mitigated in the knowledge that Doug went out just like the man and soldier that he was (n.d.).

Maxwell Bay (64 G/15) in Sandberg Lake was named after him in 1994.

Maxwell, Pilot Officer **Wallace Kingdon** of Winnipeg (J 19401). No. 434 Squadron. He died 29 January 1944 at the age of 29 and is commemorated at the Runnymede Memorial in Surrey, England. He was the son of Wallace K. and Mabel S. Maxwell of Victoria, British Columbia. ***Maxwell Point*** (64 A/11) on Campbell Lake was named after him in 1995.

May, Flying Officer **Alan E.** of Sprague (J 22859). No. 424 Squadron. He died 6 July 1944 at the age of 22 and is commemorated at St. Pol War Cemetery, Pas de Calais, France. He was the son of Edward O. and Mabel May of Sprague, Manitoba. ***May Bay*** (64 J/9) in Tadoule Lake was named after him in 1978.

May, Trooper **Harold** of Millwood (H 77402). 12th Manitoba Dragoons. He died 8 February 1945 at the age of 23 and is commemorated at the Groesbeek Canadian War Cemetery in Holland. He was the son of William M. and of Grace E. May (née Murdoch) of Millwood, Manitoba. His sister recalls (26 October 2001):

> Harold was born May 24, 1921 on a farm on the Manitoba-Saskatchewan border near Russell, Manitoba. Harold was always quick with a smile and always a tease. He is lovingly remembered by sister Edith Schrot whose husband (Ernie) was in the same regiment and was able to attend funeral services for Harold in Holland. Harold was part of a "Staghound" (armoured car) crew which consisted of Sergeant Donald M. Keele, Trooper J. E. Harkins, Trooper Charles E. Lisle and Trooper Victor G. Weippert.

May Island (64 C/8) in Granville Lake was named after him in 1995.

Maynard, Private **Percy** of Winnipeg (H 17726). Princess Patricia's Canadian Light Infantry. He died 23 May 1944 at the age of 33 and is commemorated at the Cassino War Cemetery in Italy. He was the son of Henry and Cecilia Maynard and was survived by his wife Irene T. Maynard of Edmonton, Alberta. ***Maynard Island*** (53 E/15) in Island Lake was named after him in 1995.

Mayo, Rifleman **Cyril A.** of Pointe du Bois (H 41535). Royal Winnipeg Rifles. He died 6 June 1944 and is commemorated at the Bayeux Memorial in Calvados, France. He was the son of Benjamin B. and Flora A. Mayo of Selkirk, Manitoba. ***Mayo Lake*** (63 O/4), north of Wekusko Lake was named after him in 1970.

Mayor, Pilot Officer **George W.** of Selkirk (J 91171). No. 424 Squadron. He died 25 April 1944 at the age of 19 and is commemorated at Rheinberg War Cemetery in Germany. He was the son of Harry J. and Ida V. Mayor of Crawford Park, Manitoba. His sister recalls:

> George was a well-built, good looking farm boy that enjoyed small community life. He had curly auburn hair that when he enlisted, soon got him the nickname "Red." He was an excellent shot and enjoyed hunting. He played hockey, ball and curled and enjoyed dancing. Since he had two brothers and a brother-in-law in the army, he anxiously awaited becoming old enough to join the Air Force. He began training on April 12, 1943 (n.d.).

Mayor Lake (64 B/13), west of Southern Indian Lake was named after him in 1979.

Mazick, Private **Joseph** of Winnipeg (H 43012). Royal Regiment of Canada. He died 25 July 1944 at the age of 22 and is commemorated at Bretteville-sur-Laize Canadian War Cemetery in Calvados, France. He was the son of Mike and Jessie Mazick of Montreal. **Mazick Lake** (64 J/1), south of Tadoule Lake was named after him in 1975.

Mazier, Sergeant **Michael W.** of Justice (R 119960). No. 19 Operational Training Unit, RCAF. He died 22 September 1942 at the age of 23 and is commemorated at Kinloss Abbey Burial Ground, Morayshire, Scotland. He was the son of Peter and Kathleen Mazier of Justice, Manitoba. ***Mazier Lake*** (64 P/6), southeast of Nejanilini Lake was named after him in 1974.

McAmmond, Company Sergeant Major (Warrant Officer 2) **Kenneth Ivan** of Winnipeg (H 19010). Queen's Own Cameron Highlanders. He died 29 August 1942 and is commemorated at Brookwood Military Cemetery in Surrey, England. ***McAmmond Lake*** (64 I/1), northeast of Etawney Lake was named after him in 1974.

McArthur, Flying Officer **William J.** of Winnipeg (J 92212). No. 103 Squadron. He died 7 January 1945 at the age of 28 and is commemorated at Munster Communal Cemetery, Haut-Rhin, France. He was the son of Dougald A. and Jessie B. McArthur of Winnipeg. ***McArthur Island*** (64 K/15) in Chatwin Lake was named after him in 1986.

McAuley, Sergeant **Douglas E.** of Winnipeg (R 78095). No. 2 Manning Depot, RCAF. He died 28 November 1941 at the age of 21 and is commemorated at Elmwood Cemetery in Winnipeg. He was the son of Oscar and Jean McAuley of Winnipeg. ***McAuley Island*** (53 E/15) in Island Lake was named after him in 1995.

McAuley, Private **Raymond H.** of Winnipeg (H 17352). Princess Patricia's Canadian Light Infantry. He died 23 May 1944 and is commemorated at the Cassino War Cemetery in Italy. ***McAuley Bay*** (63 P/8) in Goulet Lake was named after him in 1995.

McBain, Flying Officer **William E. J.** of Winnipeg (J 21879). No. 8 Squadron. He died 14 August 1944 at the age of 21 and is commemorated at Karachi War Cemetery in Pakistan. ***McBain Creek*** (63 J/3), which flows south into William River was named after him in 1973.

McBratney, Pilot Officer **William T. B.** of Flin Flon (J 85161). No. 22 Operational Training Unit, RCAF. He died 10 September 1942 at the age of 28 and is commemorated at Flushing (Vlissingen) Northern Cemetery, Holland. He was the son of Howard A. and Edith G. McBratney of Flin Flon. ***McBratney Lake*** (63 K/13), east of Manistikwan Lake was named after him in 1984.

McBride, Flight Lieutenant **Charles W.** of Winnipeg (J 22700). No. 619 Squadron. He died 17 March 1945 at the age of 26 and is commemorated at Durnbach War Cemetery in Bavaria, Germany. He was the son of Samuel and Susan McBride of Winnipeg. ***McBride Island*** (64 O/16) in Baralzon Lake was named after him in 1975.

McBride, Able Seaman **John L.** of Winnipeg (V 45461). HMCS *Athabaskan*. The *Athabaskan* was sunk by a torpedo from a German destroyer while operating in the English Channel. Her captain and 128 men were lost, 83 taken prisoner and 44 men rescued by HMCS *Haida*. Able Seaman McBride died 29 April 1944 at the age of 19 and is commemorated at Plouescat Communal Cemetery, Finistere, France. ***McBride Point*** (64 N/1) on George Stewart Lake was named after him in 1995.

McBride, Flying Officer **John L.** of Winnipeg (J 44088). No. 356 Squadron. He died 7 August 1945 at the age of 34 and is commemorated at Kranji War Cemetery, Singapore. He was the son of John L. and Elizabeth C. McBride of Winnipeg. ***McBride Lake*** (64 F/6), northwest of Wells Lake was named after him in 1994.

McBride, Private **William F.** of Carman (H 6143). Winnipeg Grenadiers. He died 21 December 1941 at the age of 29 and is commemorated at the Sai Wan Memorial in Hong Kong. His wife and mother did not receive notification of his death until January 1943. This native of Dervock, Northern Ireland was the son of William and Ann McBride and was survived by his wife Hilda M. McBride of Kirkfield Park, Manitoba. He enlisted the day that Britain and France declared war on Germany – a week before Canada followed suit. ***McBride Bay*** (64 I/11) on the northwest shore of Quinn Lake was named after him in 1989.

McCallum, Major **Douglas H.** of Carberry (R 106339). Royal Canadian Engineers, Distinguished Service Order. He died 25 July 1944 and is commemorated at Bretteville-sur-Laize Canadian War Cemetery in Calvados, France. He was the son of Mr. and Mrs. Fergus McCallum and was survived by his wife Hazel J. McCallum of Montreal. ***McCallum Lake*** (64 C/4), southeast of Reindeer Lake was named after him in 1947.

McCallum, Flight Lieutenant **Harvey G.** of Dugald (40309). No. 20 Elementary Flying Training School, RAF. He enlisted in September, 1937 and was killed 15 October 1940 in a flying accident while instructing in southern Rhodesia (Allison 1978). He was 27 years of age and is commemorated at Bulawayo (Athlone) Cemetery, Zimbabwe. He was the son of Duncan and Mary E. McCallum of Blenheim, Ontario. ***McCallum Island*** (64 I/13) in Shethanei Lake was named after him in 1989.

McCallum, Warrant Officer 1 **John M.** of Oakner (R 106339). No. 166 Squadron. He died 10 April 1944 at the age of 21 and is commemorated at Odden (Overby) Churchyard, Denmark. ***McCallum Bay*** (64 N/3) in Colbeck Lake was named after him in 1979.

McCallum, Flight Sergeant **Peter Thompson** of Winnipeg (R 172877). No. 429 Squadron. He died 26 November 1943 at the age of 21 and is commemorated at Carignan Communal Cemetery, Ardennes, France. He was the only child of Peter and Bessie McCallum of West Kildonan. ***McCallum Point*** (53 L/8) on Wechesawan Lake was named after him in 1995.

McCammon, Warrant Officer 2 **Samuel J.** of Winnipeg (R 91941). No. 200 Squadron. He died 6 January 1943 at the age of 28 and is commemorated at Fajara War Cemetery, Gambia. He was the son of Robert J. and Rachel McCammon and was survived by his wife Charlotte L. McCammon of Kenora and their child. ***McCammon Lake*** (53 L/12), east of Windy Lake was named after him in 1995.

McCann, Flying Officer **John W.** of Winnipeg (J 10138). No. 405 Squadron. He died 1 October 1942 at the age of 21 and is commemorated at the Kiel War Cemetery in Germany. He was the son of Dr. Albert S. and Jessie L. McCann of Winnipeg. ***McCann Lake*** (64 P/2), southeast of Nejanilini Lake was named after him in 1974.

McCann, Flight Sergeant **William A.** of Transcona (R 86355). No. 115 Squadron. He died 28 June 1942 at the age of 20 and is commemorated at Marham Cemetery, Norfolk, England. He was the son of Alexander and Florence McCann of Transcona. ***McCann Island*** (64 I/7) in Klazi Lake was named after him in 1995.

McCartney, Trooper **Joseph T. C.** of Winnipeg (B 421). Three Rivers Tank Regiment. He died 23 May 1944 at the age of 34 and is commemorated at the Cassino War Cemetery in Italy. He was the son of Terrence J. and Ida M. McCartney and was survived by his wife Flora A. McCartney of Winnipeg. ***McCartney Lake*** (53 L/2), north of Island Lake was named after him in 1995.

McCaskill, Sergeant **Richard L.** of Gladstone (R 287915). No. 24 Operational Training Unit, RCAF. He died 5 April 1945 at the age of 21 and is commemorated at the Runnymede Memorial in Surrey, England. He was the son of Daniel P. and Dora M. McCaskill (née Deveson) of Gladstone. His aircraft had been on a night cross-country exercise when it went down in the North Sea. His brother writes (23 January 2002):

I was stationed at 424 Squadron when I received a letter from my parents that Richard was posted to Stratford-upon-Avon. I got leave right away to go down and visit him. The day I left, I picked up my mail and received a wire from my parents that Richard was reported missing. I continued on to Stratford and when I arrived, I was escorted to the Commanding Officer. He explained the rescue procedures that had taken place and offered to fly me over the North Sea where they believed they went missing, but I decided that wasn't necessary. I was escorted everywhere I went – even back to the entrance gate. At the time, I thought I was being honoured, but [with] what happened since, I am beginning to wonder.

I was told the aircraft went missing on a training flight over the North Sea and they had no information as to what happened. They just disappeared. When my mother was in her 80th year, she decided to turn over Richard's belongings to me – that were sent back to her that I hadn't seen until then. One thing shocked me – both Dog Tags were sent home with his belongings. I passed this information on to a cousin of mine who was stationed at Stratford-upon-Avon a few months before Richard. He said that [on] some flights they made from that station, they were not allowed to wear their Dog Tags. I wrote a letter at that time to the DVA and they suggested there could have been duplicate Dog Tags.

Several months after Richard went missing, my parents received a letter telling them that one of the crew members' wallets [had been] found in a fisherman's net in the North Sea. When the book *They Shall Grow Not Old* came out, it said that Richard McCaskill's wallet was found in a fisherman's net. My parents were never told about this and if it was Richard's wallet, why wasn't it returned to his parents? The Dog Tags and the wallet raise questions in my mind as to what really happened.

Richard was born and raised on a farm near Gladstone, Manitoba along with two brothers, Neil and Kenneth. Our parents lived all their lives in the Gladstone area. Richard was witty and quick on the draw. One day in school, the teacher asked what he was going to be when he finished school. His answer was: "an old man I guess," which he never had a chance to be.

McCaskill Lake (64 P/13), north of Nejanilini Lake was named after him in 1974.

McCasky, Sergeant **Edward S. J.** of Winnipeg (R 110750). No. 22 Squadron. He died 11 September 1942 at the age of 20 and is commemorated at the Reichswald Forest War Cemetery in Germany. ***McCasky Lak***e (64 P/11), east of Nejanilini Lake was named after him in 1974.

McClarty, Pilot Officer **Edward J.** of Gilbert Plains (J 95360). No. 432 Squadron. He died 21 February 1945 at the age of 20 and is commemorated at Rheinberg War Cemetery in Germany. He was the son of Howard J. and K. Elizabeth McClarty of Gilbert Plains, Manitoba. ***McClarty Island*** (53 K/12) in Gods Lake was named after him in 1995.

McClarty, Flight Lieutenant **Stanley M.** of Winnipeg (J 14006). No. 411 Squadron, Distinguished Flying Cross.

This officer has displayed exceptional keenness for operational flying. He has taken part in a large number of varied sorties and has set a fine example of skill and tenacity. He has effectively attacked very many mechanical vehicles and several locomotives. In air fighting, he has destroyed three enemy aircraft (DFC Citation 1944).

Flight Lieutenant McClarty was the first Allied pilot to land on French soil after D-Day. He died 3 May 1945 and is commemorated at the Kiel War Cemetery in Germany. He was survived by his mother M. McClarty.

After strafing a train about 10 miles southeast of Newmunster, Germany, Flight Lieutenant McClarty reported by r/t that he had been hit in the legs by light flak. He climbed his Spitfire aircraft No. NH263 to about 4000 feet and was last seen diving into cloud, believed out of control (Allison and Hayward 1991).

McClarty Lake (63 K/8), north of North Moose Lake was named after him in 1948.

McClay, Flight Sergeant **Murton L.** of Belmont (R 147010). No. 102 Squadron. He died 31 August 1943 at the age of 20 and is commemorated at the Reichswald Forest War Cemetery in Germany. ***McClay Lake*** (63 I/9), northeast of Lawford Lake was named after him in 1988.

McClelland, Sergeant **David Stuart** of Stonewall (R 166291). No. 76 Squadron. He died 21 December 1943 at the age of 22 and is commemorated at the Runnymede Memorial in Surrey, England. He was the son of A. Hugh and A. Adella McClelland of Stonewall, Manitoba. His sister recalls (9 November 2001):

Stuart McClelland was my brother. Since he was 7 years older than I was, he was often too busy on the farm to play with me. However, when he had time, he played with me on his "farm" that he had carved out of a patch of ground under the trees of the shelterbelt beside our farm house. He had a metal toy tractor, but besides that his implements were found objects: meat bones served as a plough, for example. Eaton's catalogue furnished harnesses, even horses! My job was always to go to my playhouse and make dinner … not much to my liking. But he was my dearly-beloved big brother so I always went.

He dreamed of having a farm of his own and sent money home from overseas to my father to buy one for him and manage it in his absence. It was my parents' dream, too. A farm was purchased and occupied just weeks before he was missing. The heart was gone out of the enterprise for them.

I was one of three sisters (Agnes, Hughine, and Jean) that Stuart had. Hughine joined the Air Force the day he left for overseas, in the hope that she might join Stuart at some time, but that did not happen. They corresponded faithfully during those Air Force years, and Hughine still treasures the letters.

Stuart went missing on December 21, 1943. Since his body was never recovered, there is a sense of incompleteness surrounding his death. However, having a lake named after him has helped mitigate that feeling.

McClelland Lake (64 I/8), northeast of North Knife Lake was named after him in 1974.

McClelland, Flight Sergeant **Wilfred Glenn** of Killarney (R 208972). No. 576 Squadron. He was shot down over Munich 7 January 1945 at the age of 21 and is commemorated at the Runnymede Memorial in Surrey, England.

On the night of January 7, Saslove's Lancaster bomber had dropped its bomb-load on Munich and had turned toward home. Suddenly they were under attack by a German night fighter and the big bomber was raked from fore to aft with cannon and machine gun fire. With the outside engine aflame, F/O Saslove tried to contact the crew. He got no response from the two gunners Flt. Sgt. A. Campton of Montreal and Flt. Sgt. G. McClelland of Killarney, Manitoba.

F/O Chiswick was sent back to check. He found both gunners badly wounded and their gun-turrets jammed, making it impossible to get them out. F/O Saslove then ordered the remainder of the crew to bail out. Four of them did so, as the Ottawa pilot held the crippled aircraft steady.

In the words of F/O Chiswick: "Eddie was sitting at the controls, as cool as a cucumber and said quietly, So-long Max, I'll see you in a few minutes." But, as Chiswick floated safely toward the earth, he watched the fiery bomber disappear into the night and saw no other parachute.

Had F/O Chiswick realized that his pilot had no intention of abandoning ship, he would have tried to force him to do so, he said later. He told F/O Saslove's brother that he is certain that the heroic pilot had decided he would not leave the two wounded gunners to die in a pilotless plane and had tried to land the badly shot up and flaming bomber in mountainous terrain surrounding Munich. In fact, the wreckage of the plane was later found but there were no bodies reported (Mills 1967).

Flight Sergeant McClelland was the oldest child of Percy A. and Carrie L. McClelland of Killarney. ***McClelland Island*** (64 A/13) in Gauer Lake was named after him in 1995.

McClintock, Flight Sergeant **Archibald** of Winnipeg (R 80175). No. 408 Squadron. He died 15 April 1942 at the age of 24 and is commemorated at the Reichswald Forest War Cemetery in Germany. He was the only son of James L. and Elizabeth J. McClintock of Winnipeg and was survived by his wife Dorothy M. McClintock (née Armstrong) of Winnipeg and their unborn son. Mrs. McClintock wrote (14 April 1998):

Archie enjoyed the usual boyhood pursuits, cubs, scouts etc. His school days were spent at Riverview and Earl Grey elementary schools and Kelvin High School where he received his Grade 11 certificate. During the last years of the Depression, when work was hard to find, he delivered newspapers for the *Winnipeg Free Press*. Later he found work at Eaton's. Hockey and skiing were his favourite sports; he excelled at the latter.

On November 4, 1940 he joined the Royal Canadian Air Force. From the Manning Pool in Brandon he went to Penhold, Alberta and received his wings in Saskatoon in July, 1941, promoted to Sergeant Pilot, then assigned to Portage la Prairie for further training. On July 30, 1941 he married Dorothy Armstrong. Three weeks later he received his overseas orders.

In England, the crew which he piloted flew six operational flights over Germany. On April 14, 1942 [at] 10:00 PM, they departed on a bombing mission over Dortmund, Germany, due to report at 5:00 AM the following day. First listed as missing, all were later declared killed in action.

May 7, 1942, Archie's son Robert … was born. As an adult, he went to Reichswald Forest War Cemetery in Kleve, Germany to pay homage to the father he would never know. The cemetery gates bear the inscription "This land is donated by the German Government to honour soldiers, sailors and airmen who have sacrificed their lives."

She concludes (14 November 2001):

Archie and I pledged that each night at 10:00, wherever we were, we would look at the moon and say goodnight. Did he see the moon his last night? I always wondered.

McClintock Lake (64 F/3), north of Vandekerckhove Lake was named after him in 1994.

McCluskey, Able Seaman **Henry** of Winnipeg (V 39921). HMCS *Guysborough*. The *Guysborough* was torpedoed and sunk by U-878 in the English Channel off Ushant, France; fifty-one of her ship's company were lost. Able Seaman McCluskey died 18 March 1945 at the age of 21 and is commemorated at the Halifax Memorial. He was the son of John and Martha McCluskey of Winnipeg. ***McCluskey Lake*** (64 N/1), southwest of Nueltin Lake was named after him in 1972.

McColl, Private **Hugh** of Winnipeg (H 8304). Canadian Scottish Regiment. He died 14 October 1944 at the age of 21 and is commemorated at the Adegem Canadian War Cemetery in Belgium. He was survived by his mother Jennie McColl of Winnipeg. ***McColl Lake*** (64 O/9), north of Nejanilini Lake was named after him in 1975.

McColm, Sergeant **Harold W.** of Deloraine (R 56135). No. 77 Squadron. He died 30 September 1941 at the age of 20 and is commemorated at the Kiel War Cemetery in Germany. He was the son of Walton S. and Cora A. McColm. His sister recalls (14 November 2001):

He took all of his schooling (Grade 12) in Deloraine. He played the French horn and the bass drum in the marching band for five or six years. He played football and hockey. He also played the drums in a dance band, all in Deloraine. We moved to Montreal and Harold worked at Woolworth's store and that is where he joined the Air Force. He took most of his training at Winnipeg.

McColm Island (53 L/7) in Goose Lake was named after him in 1995.

McCormick, Private **George Albert** of Winnipeg (H 101409). Royal Hamilton Light Infantry. He died 19 February 1945 and is commemorated at the Groesbeek Canadian War Cemetery in Holland. ***McCormick Bay*** (64 N/9) in Shannon Lake was named after him in 1995.

McCormick, Flying Officer **John G.** of Flin Flon (J 9690). No. 172 Squadron. He died 24 July 1943 at the age of 22 and is commemorated at the Runnymede Memorial in Surrey, England. He was the son of Joseph and Mary T. McCormick of Flin Flon and the brother of Leading Aircraftman Joseph J. McCormick (next entry). ***McCormick Island*** (63 P/3) in McCormick Lake was named after him in 1995.

McCormick, Leading Aircraftman **Joseph J.** of Flin Flon (R 75487). No. 11 Service Flying Training School. He died 27 July 1941 at the age of 20 and is commemorated at Ross Lake Cemetery in Flin Flon. He was the son of Joseph and Mary T. McCormick of Flin Flon and the brother of Flying Officer John G. McCormick (previous entry). ***McCormick Lake*** (63 P/3), east of Sipiwesk Lake was named after him in 1968.

McCorrister, Private **Mervin S.** of Winnipeg (H 26247). Winnipeg Grenadiers. He died 19 December 1941 at the age of 20 and is commemorated at the Sai Wan Memorial in Hong Kong. He was the son of James and Jane Mary McCorrister of Winnipeg. His sister writes (22 May 1998) that he:

… was born … in Portage la Prairie. He attended the United Church and Victoria School until October 1934 when the family moved to Winnipeg. He then attended Somerset School. He enjoyed playing hockey. When Canada entered the war in 1939, he joined the Fort Garry Horse and later transferred to the Winnipeg Grenadiers. He played hockey for the army before being shipped to Jamaica. He returned to Winnipeg in 1941 for a short period before being shipped over to Hong Kong.

McCorrister Lake (64 J/3), southwest of Tadoule Lake was named after him in 1975.

McCowan, Leading Aircraftman **James G.** of Winnipeg (R 106175). No. 11 Flying Training School. He died 11 May 1942 at the age of 22 and is commemorated at Summerberry Cemetery in Saskatchewan. He was the son of James A. and May McCowan of Summerberry. **McCowan Lake** (64 F/2), southeast of Wells Lake was named after him in 1994.

McCrae, Private **George I.** of Grandview (H 103828). North Nova Scotia Highlanders. He died 17 September 1944 at the age of 28 and is commemorated at the Calais Canadian War Cemetery in France. He was survived by his step-father and mother James and Charlotte Coulter (formerly McCrae), sister Dorothy Stuart of Grandview and by his wife Freida McCrae (née Zimmer) and their daughter Judith. His sister recalls (25 November 2001):

> He was born in Winnipeg February 18, 1916 to Henry and Charlotte McCrae (née Farquharson). George received his education at Russell and Grandview. He liked farming, horses, hunting and calling at Square Dances. George trained at Portage, Fort Osborne Barracks and Ipperwash, Ontario. He married Freida Zimmer of Inglis and went overseas to England shortly after.

His mother received a letter from Private McCrae's commanding officer some months after her son's death:

> Dear Mrs. Coulter: I now approach a subject which grieves me and which I find hard to deal with, but feel it is my responsibility to write and tell you the facts concerning the death of your son. Your son was in 7 Platoon, "A" Company of the North Nova Scotia Highlanders and went into action on 17 September 1944. In the battle which followed, there were many casualties. We were attacking a hill called Mount Lambert which overlooks the city of Boulogne. We had just started up the mountain when we came under heavy mortar and machine gun fire and we had quite a few casualties as the enemy was in well protected dug-outs and could see us coming.
>
> George was hit by a machine gun bullet and he was just ahead of me when it happened. I immediately shouted for a First Aid man and George was taken back as soon as possible by vehicle to our RAP. He did not seem too bad when he left us but the shot had gone through his stomach. That night we were informed that he passed away. This news was very sad for us as we all knew George so well and he was a friend to all. It is so hard for us to lose our best friends that we have been working and playing with, but we must carry on and do our best as those like George who have paid the supreme sacrifice would want us to do.
>
> George was buried near Mount Lambert and our Padre performed the ceremony. He was a brave and courageous soldier and always did well what was expected of him. This job in which he received his fatal wounds was no exception. I send you my deepest sympathy which I know is small consolation, but know that you as a Canadian can be proud of the part that your son George played in this war. Hoping this will be of some condolence to you and may God bless you and keep you in your bereavement. Yours sincerely, Major A. W. Jefferson (22 December 1944).

Mrs. Coulter wrote back to Major Jefferson, but was informed that he too had been killed. ***McCrae Peninsula*** (53 L/8) on Murray Lake was named after Private McCrae in 1995.

McCruden, Flying Officer **Robert J. "Bert"** of Pointe du Bois (J 21389). No. 404 Squadron. He died 16 November 1943 at the age of 22 and is commemorated at Wick Cemetery in Caithness, Scotland. He was the third of the four children of Robert and Jen McCruden (née Petrie) of Pointe du Bois, Manitoba. According to his sister (15 June 1998):

> He was an excellent student and an avid reader who loved sports and nature. Tall (6' 2 1/2") and lean, quiet spoken, witty, a good companion, always willing to help, he formed close and lasting friendships and was very dear to his sister and younger brother.
>
> He had been an altar boy and was a devout young man of Roman Catholic faith who played hockey and tennis and even as a lad, was a patient and keen fisherman. Bert enjoyed hunting – game birds, big game etc. and loved the outdoors at all seasons of the year, with a companion or alone, communing with nature, trying to tame the whiskey-jacks and chickadees to eat out of his hand or just exploring the beautiful area around Pointe du Bois and the Winnipeg River.
>
> He had hoped to study aeronautical engineering and was very keen to be a pilot. His letters home after he soloed showed that he had found another great love. That his final resting-place was Wick was a little comfort to his Scottish parents.

McCruden Lake (52 L/6), east of Lac du Bonnet was named after him in 1973.

McCuaig, Flight Sergeant **Eric S.** of Bethany (R 132649). No. 247 Squadron. He died 15 August 1943 at the age of 20 and is commemorated at Brookwood Military Cemetery in Surrey, England. He was the son of Clarence N. and Judith McCuaig and was survived by his wife Joan E. McCuaig of Cornwall, Ontario. ***McCuaig Lake*** (63 I/16), west of Oxford Lake was named after him in 1995.

McCulloch, Warrant Officer 2 **Robert L.** of The Pas (R 134714). No. 158 Squadron. He died 20 December 1943 at the age of 21 and is commemorated at the Hanover War Cemetery in Germany. He was the son of Mr. and Mrs. R. W. McCulloch. Some time later his father received the following letter:

> I have for some time intended writing you a letter because my brother, Brian Hicks, brought your son "Mac" here to tea and dinner on the last day of their last leave and I thought you might like to hear about it. They came on December 10 and we had a very happy evening as the hours raced by. My Father and I, my sister and her husband and four of Brian's friends saw them off on the 11:30 PM train (to Lisset). It was quite a party on King's Cross Station platform. The boys were speculating whether they would be able to obtain 48 hours leave at Christmas and spend it here with us.
>
> But alas, it was not to be! Instead our hearts were stricken by the news on December 23 they were missing. We had a great affection for "Mac" and felt that our own beloved Brian was in excellent company. Listening to the conversation of the four crew members whom it was my privilege to know, I know they had the utmost confidence in one another's capabilities. In losing them, the Empire has lost four of her finest Sons (n.d.).

McCulloch Lake (64 G/11), east of Big Sand Lake was named after him in 1994.

McCumber, Trooper **Guy P.** of Selkirk (H 26277). Fort Garry Horse. He was fatally injured in England while trying to remove an unexploded bomb from a schoolyard. He died 12 April 1942 at the age of 21 and is commemorated at Brookwood Military Cemetery in Surrey, England. He was the son of Milton and Katie McCumber of Selkirk. ***McCumber Lake*** (64 I/4), west of North Knife Lake was named after him in 1974.

McCurdy, Flying Officer **Archibald R.** of Winnipeg (C 17966). No. 83 Squadron. He died 21 April 1945 at the age of 25 and is commemorated at the Runnymede Memorial in Surrey, England. He was the son of Archibald G. and Mary M. McCurdy of Winnipeg. ***McCurdy Lake*** (64 H/9), north of Freeman Lake was named after him in 1995.

McDennon, Flight Sergeant **Thomas Roy** of Winnipeg (R 162261). No. 53 Squadron. He died 17 April 1944 at the age of 20 and is commemorated at the Runnymede Memorial in Surrey, England. He was the son of Thomas J. and Isabel McDennon of Winnipeg. ***McDennon Lake*** (64 J/12), west of Tadoule Lake was named after him in 1975.

McDermott, Flight Lieutenant **Irving F.** of Winnipeg (41719). No. 104 Squadron, RAF, Distinguished Flying Cross. He died 1 November 1943 at the age of 27 and is commemorated at Biguglia War Cemetery, Haute-Corse, France. The son of Martin and Elsie McDermott of Winnipeg, he had enlisted in December, 1938. ***Irving McDermott Lake*** (64 O/7), east of Sandhill Lake was named after him in 1995.

McDonald, Trooper **Allan H.** of Kelloe (H 77820). 12th Manitoba Dragoons. He died 30 August 1944 at the age of 26 and is commemorated at the Calais Canadian War Cemetery in France. He was one of the six children of John D. and Annie E. McDonald of Kelloe, Manitoba. According to his brother (31 May 1995):

> Allan was born in Shoal Lake Municipality in January, 1918. He attended Culross School with his three brothers and two sisters, walking 3 1/2 miles in summer and with horse and toboggan in winter. He was a loving son, a trustworthy young man, a hard worker and he enjoyed social activities, especially picture shows, dancing and house parties. He was engaged to be married to a Scottish lass when he was killed in action.

Allan McDonald Lake (54 F/3), northeast of Dewar Lake was named after him in 1995.

McDonald, Flying Officer **D. Richard** of Minnedosa (J 16764). No. 432 Squadron. He died 3 August 1943 at the age of 21 and is commemorated at the Runnymede Memorial in Surrey, England. He was the son of Mr. and Mrs. R. T. McDonald of Minnedosa and the brother of Captain John W. B. McDonald (see entry). ***Richard McDonald Island*** (63 P/4) in Sipiwesk Lake was named after him in 1995.

McDonald, Leading Aircraftman **Daniel** of Winnipeg (R 61496). Royal Canadian Air Force. He died 20 September 1945 at the age of 51 and is commemorated at Assumption Gardens in Winnipeg. He was the son of Denis and Bridget McDonald of Curroghlane, Kilkenny, Irish Republic and was survived by his wife Elizabeth McDonald of Regina. ***Daniel McDonald Lake*** (64 F/16), west of Kustra Lake was named after him in 1995.

McDonald, Pilot Officer **Donald S.** of Selkirk (J 5093). No. 58 Squadron. He died 11 October 1941 at the age of 21 and is commemorated at the Runnymede Memorial in Surrey, England. He was the son of Donald and Donaldina McDonald and was survived by his wife Elizabeth McDonald. ***McDonald Point*** (64 O/3) on Mistahi Lake was named after him in 1996.

McDonald, Lieutenant **Dougald A. "Doug"** of Boissevain. Lanark and Renfrew Scottish Regiment. He died 24 September 1944 at the age of 26 and is commemorated at Cesena War Cemetery in Italy. He was the son of George W. and Jennie McDonald of Boissevain, Manitoba. ***McDonald Creek*** (64 I/2), which flows southeast into South Knife Lake was named after him in 1995.

McDonald, Lance Corporal **George M.** of Pilot Mound (H 37866). Royal Canadian Army Service Corps. He died 28 August 1943 at the age of 32 and is commemorated at Brookwood Military Cemetery in Surrey, England. He was the son of Mr. and Mrs. James McDonald of Winnipeg. ***McDonald Island*** (64 H/6) in Northern Indian Lake was named after him in 1995.

McDonald, Private **Harold J.** of Winnipeg (H 600532). Royal Canadian Infantry Corps. He died 19 May 1941 at the age of 21 and is commemorated at Elmwood Cemetery in Winnipeg. He was the son of Thomas J. and Rita McDonald of Winnipeg. Harold ***McDonald Creek*** (54 E/5), which flows northeast into Churchill River was named after him in 1995.

McDonald, Sergeant **Harry** of Winnipeg (R 56768). 1st Training Command, RCAF. He died 25 October 1940 at the age of 34 and is commemorated at Elmwood Cemetery in Winnipeg. He was the son of Clinton and Margaret McDonald of Winnipeg and was survived by his wife Gunhild McDonald of Winnipeg. Harry ***McDonald Lake*** (53 L/11), north of Munro Lake was named after him in 1995.

McDonald, Sergeant **Joffre K.** of Elkhorn (R 86943). No. 113 Squadron. He died 1 June 1942 at the age of 26 and is commemorated at the Ottawa Memorial. He was on patrol over the Bay of Fundy when he was shot down by a submarine. He was survived by his mother Matilda M. McDonald. According to his brother (16 February 1995):

> Joffre was born on a farm near Fleming, Saskatchewan. Our mother and family of seven children ages 1 1/2 to 11 moved to Elkhorn in March, 1919 following the death of our father during the flu epidemic in January, 1919. Joffre completed his Grade 11 at the Elkhorn public school in June, 1932. He was never married. His personal interests were family sports (baseball and hockey). He worked mostly as a farm labourer in the Elkhorn district, and occasionally as a carpenter's helper. No other employment was available during the 1930s in a small village of approximately 400 people. He went to Edmonton in 1939 in search of employment but was only able to find the same type of employment that he worked in Elkhorn. He enlisted in February, 1941 in Edmonton and was immediately sent to the Manning Depot in Brandon for his initial, basic training. Then he was transferred to Dafoe, Saskatchewan, then to Calgary, back to Dafoe, then to Macdonald Air Base in Manitoba.
>
> He graduated as an air gunner in February, 1942 and subsequently was posted to Yarmouth, Nova Scotia where he lost his life. Their aircraft was shot down over the Bay of Fundy by a German submarine. This incident happened so suddenly, they were unable to relay a message to their base. The only evidence found of the loss of the plane and the four airmen aboard was a seat from the plane which was later found on the shore of the bay. An airman from McAuley, Manitoba who was posted at the same base provided us with that information when he was home to McAuley near Elkhorn on his summer leave.

McDonald Hill (63 N/4), west of Kississing Lake was named after him in 1995.

McDonald, Lance Corporal **John Campbell "Cammy"** of Selkirk (H 1366). Royal Regiment of Canada. He died 8 March 1945 at the age of 18 in the Battle of the Rhineland and is commemorated at the Groesbeek Canadian War Cemetery in Holland. He was the eldest of the three sons of Allan and Isabella Mary McDonald of Hodgson, Manitoba. ***McDonald Lake*** (64 P/9), east of Nejanilini Lake was named after him in 1974.

McDonald, Captain **John W. B.** of Minnesdosa. 1st Hussar Tank Regiment. He died 27 February 1945 and is commemorated at the Groesbeek Canadian War Cemetery in Holland. He was the brother of Flying Officer D. Richard McDonald (see entry). ***John McDonald Point*** (63 P/4) on Sipiwesk Lake was named after him in 1995.

McDonald, Able Seaman **Richard A. A.** of West Kildonan (V 46463). HMCS *Valleyfield*. The *Valleyfield* was torpedoed and sunk by U-548 50 miles south of Cape Race, Newfoundland; 125 of her ship's company were lost. Able Seaman McDonald died 7 May 1944 at the age of 20 and is commemorated at the Halifax Memorial. He was the only child of Malcolm and Janet B. McDonald of West Kildonan. A friend writes (1 December 1995):

> Richard and I joined [the] Navy in Winnipeg [in] August, 1942. We received our call in December; after training in Winnipeg I was sent to the West Coast. Richard was held back to play hockey with the Winnipeg Rangers who went on to win the Memorial Cup that year. We never laid eyes on each other again. [I] named my first-born Richard in memory of him.

McDonald Narrows (63 N/6) in Kississing Lake was named after him in 1995.

McDonald, Rifleman **Robert J.** of Lakeland (H 69947). Queen's Own Rifles of Canada. He died 5 March 1945 at the age of 27 and is commemorated at the Groesbeek Canadian War Cemetery in Holland. He was survived by his mother Mrs. Lillian McDonald. His nephew writes (29 November 2001):

> Whereas I had never met my Uncle Bob, the following tribute to him is based on discussions I have had with extended family members, in particular my cousin Gladys. She knew our uncle quite well and informs me that he was an easygoing and good natured person who always championed the rights of the underdog. Bob, as he was known by his friends and neighbours, was of a very quiet nature, willing and kind. After Uncle Bob went overseas in June, 1944, he and my cousin Gladys corresponded on a regular basis. She remembers one letter in particular where Uncle Bob talked about his parcel of land he had been clearing and of his plans to build himself a home on it after he returned from the war. My cousin Gladys relates how our uncle never complained of the difficult times they all endured while overseas and would always end his letters to her with "it won't be long now and it will be all over, then we can get on with life." When news of his death finally reached home, it was discovered that Uncle Bob had been killed in action the same day that his father passed away in the Portage hospital.

McDonald Island (64 H/4) in Gauer Lake was named after him in 1995.

McDonald, Rifleman **William H.** of Deloraine (H 53445). Royal Winnipeg Rifles. He died 6 June 1944 and is commemorated at Beny-sur-Mer Canadian War Cemetery in Calvados, France. ***William McDonald Lake*** (54 E/3), west of Whiting Lake was named after him in 1995.

McDonald, Leading Aircraftman **William M.** of Winnipeg (R 59619). Clerk, RCAF. He died 16 June 1941 at the age of 36 and is commemorated at Old Kildonan Presbyterian Cemetery in Winnipeg. He was the son of Jeremiah and Hettie E. McDonald of West Kildonan. ***McDonald Esker*** (64 B/6), northeast of Pemichigamau Lake was named after him in 1995.

McDougall, Private **Donald J.** of Winnipeg (H 1860). Royal Canadian Regiment. He died 17 May 1944 at the age of 34 and is commemorated at the Cassino War Cemetery in Italy. This native of Dundurn, Saskatchewan was the son of Walter and Mary McDougall (née Flockhart) and was survived by his mother and step-father Robert Goodlass of Winnipeg. His sister wrote to his commanding officer requesting details of the circumstances surrounding his death. She received this reply:

> Dear Mrs. Moore: In reply to your letter of May 27th received this date. May I and other members of this Company express our deepest sympathy in the death of your brother Private McDougall. I shall endeavour to give you a short account, as much as I may, of the action which resulted in his death. Our unit went into action in the vicinity of Cassino and after crossing the Gari River, A Company made an attack on a small hill which was holding up our advance. Your brother was a member of #8 Platoon of A Company. After the Company had taken the hill, #8 Platoon came under heavy enemy shell and mortar fire and your brother, as well as several other members of his Platoon, including his Platoon Commander, Lieutenant [John L. Morgan] were killed. This hill has since been named Morgan's Hill in memory of #8 Platoon and their Platoon officer and for the fine work they did. Those who died were buried in a small cemetery made close by and they all lay in rest together a short distance from the scene of their battle in which they gave their lives. Most probably, they will be transported to another cemetery and no doubt you will be notified when this is done.
>
> As far as I know and can ascertain, he died instantly and did not suffer any pain. It is the custom of the officers of this Regiment to write to the next-of-kin at the earliest possible moment. So please forgive me if you think there has been a delay, as it was not possible to do so before. I sincerely hope this letter may be of help to you and your family and I am only too glad to do anything I can to help. Your brother was regarded highly in A Company and in #8 Platoon and although he has gone, he is not forgotten. Sincerely, J. E. Pickard, Capt. (8 June 1944).

His niece writes (20 November 2001):

> Donald McDougall was born on his family's homestead in Dundurn, Saskatchewan in 1910; the son of Scottish immigrants. My mother, Edith, was his younger sister. Although he was killed when I was nine, I remember him as a kind and gentle man with a wry sense of humour.
>
> In 1989, my daughters and I visited my uncle's grave site in the Cassino War Cemetery. This cemetery is situated in a beautiful location and well maintained. I have two letters written to my mother by his commanding officers and they state that Private Donald McDougall died courageously and instantly. When I visited Monte Cassino, I wondered how anyone could have been expected to take this hill from the enemy as the Germans were firmly dug in and anyone approaching would have been an easy target. I also have a telegram from my uncle to my parents dated November 17, 1943 from England sending us "Best Wishes for Christmas and New Year. Keep Smiling. Love, Donald McDougall." Donald's mother (my grandmother) went on to become President of the Silver Cross Mothers (of Manitoba, I believe) and I have a silver tray that was presented to her on December 6, 1956.

McDougall Lake (64 G/5), south of Big Sand Lake was named after him in 1994.

McDougall, Pilot Officer **George** of Transcona (J 87284). No. 106 Squadron. He died 10 May 1944 at the age of 21 and is commemorated at Clichy Northern Cemetery, Hauts-de-Seine, France. He was the son of John and Alice McDougall of Transcona. ***McDougall Peninsula*** (64 N/4) on Quasso Lake was named after him in 1995.

McEachnie, Corporal **Morell** of Winnipeg (H 26499). Royal Canadian Engineers, Military Medal. He died 6 June 1945 at the age of 35 and is commemorated at the Holten Canadian War Cemetery in Holland. He was the son of John and Mary McEachnie and was survived by his wife Tillie McEachnie of Winnipeg. ***McEachnie Lake*** (64 I/15), northeast of North Knife Lake was named after him in 1974.

McElroy, Pilot Officer **Lloyd W.** of Darlingford (J 90348). No. 415 Squadron. He died 29 July 1944 at the age of 22 and is commemorated at Becklingen War Cemetery in Germany. He had married Isobel Pearce just before he went overseas. ***McElroy Lake*** (64 O/16), northwest of Nejanilini Lake was named after him in 1975.

McEwen, Private **Seeley B.** of Winnipeg (H 13200). Royal Canadian Army Medical Corps. He died 17 September 1941 and is commemorated at Brookwood Military Cemetery in Surrey, England. ***McEwen Lake*** (54 M/12), northwest of Long Lake was named after him in 1984.

McEwen, Flight Sergeant **William T.** of Winnipeg (R 69829). No. 12 Squadron. He died 10 April 1942 at the age of 25 and is commemorated at the Runnymede Memorial in Surrey, England. He was the son of George A. and Alice M. T. McEwen of Toronto. ***McEwen Island*** (53 L/4) in Odee Smith Lake was named after him in 1995.

McFadden, Flying Officer **Hugh C.** of Rivers (J 14632). No. 168 Heavy Transport Squadron, RCAF. He died 2 April 1944 at the age of 30 and is commemorated at Monkton and Prestwick Cemetery, Ayrshire, Scotland. He was the sixth of the seven children of James and Albertha McFadden and the husband of Joan McFadden (née Mayhood) of Calgary. According to his nephew (23 December 1995):

> Hugh McFadden was born on the family farm at Pendennis, Manitoba (near Rivers). He received his elementary and secondary education at Rivers Consolidated School. He completed his Grade 12 in 1931 in the depth of the great depression. In October, 1932, he left Rivers on a freight train (Riding the Rods) destined for Flin Flon to look for employment to finance his further education. He found employment in the mine at Flin Flon and by 1939, he had graduated from United College (now the University of Winnipeg) with a B.A. degree. At university he excelled in sports and debating and was valedictorian in his graduating class. He was working on his M.A. in economics at the University of Toronto at the time of his enlistment.
>
> Hugh married ... on November 28, 1941, ... enlisted shortly thereafter and received his wings and commission in Regina in 1942. In late 1942 and part of 1943, he was a navigation instructor at No. 1 Central Navigation School at Rivers, Manitoba, near the place of his birth. In late 1943 he was assigned to the mail squadron which was ferrying mail to Canadian troops in Italy. He was the navigator on a Flying Fortress which crashed on take-off from Prestwick, Scotland.

McFadden Bay (63 N/9) in Highrock Lake was named after him in 1995.

McFadden, Captain **John A.** of Dauphin. Royal Canadian Army Medical Corps. He died 16 December 1944 at the age of 26 and is commemorated at Ravenna War Cemetery in Italy. He was the son of John N. and Madge P. McFadden and was survived by his wife Evelyn McFadden of Victoria, British Columbia and their two children. ***McFadden Island*** (64 C/16) in Barrington Lake was named after him in 1995.

McFeat, Private **Alexander R.** of Winnipeg (H 35380). Canadian Provost Corps. He died 19 September 1945 at the age of 26 and is commemorated at the Groesbeek Canadian War Cemetery in Holland. He was the son of Robert and Mary McFeat of Winnipeg and was survived by his wife Marjorie L. McFeat of Winnipeg. ***McFeat Lake*** (64 J/4), southwest of Tadoule Lake was named after him in 1975.

McFee, Private **Samuel** (H 16824). Princess Patricia's Canadian Light Infantry. He died 22 July 1943 and is commemorated at Agira Canadian War Cemetery in Italy. ***McFee Bay*** (63 K/12) in Athapapuskow Lake was named after him in 1984.

McFeetors, Pilot Officer **Albert S.** of Newdale (J 88901). No. 428 Squadron. He died 14 October 1944 at the age of 30 and is commemorated at Rheinberg War Cemetery in Germany. He was the son of Frederick and Annie Smith and was survived by his adoptive mother Susannah McFeetors and by his wife of ten months Marion L. McFeetors of Holland, Manitoba and their son. He writes (25 October 2001):

> "Bert" was born Albert Sydney Smith in Copper Cliff, Ontario. His mother died as a result of his birth and given the difficult times, the McFeetors family raised him. In 1939, he was officially adopted and took the surname McFeetors as there was no male heir to continue the name. Before the war, he was a mechanical foreman at Inco in Sudbury. Enlisting in North Bay in 1942, he travelled west to Brandon to the RCAF Manning Depot which was located in a former horse stable. He subsequently trained as a wireless air gunner in Winnipeg and Lethbridge.
>
> While in Winnipeg in 1943, he met Marion Rungay of Newdale on a blind date. Both had recently experienced failed love affairs and given their ages (29) and the pressure of war, no doubt were strongly attracted. After the completion of Bert's training, they were married on August 21, 1943 in Newdale. They honeymooned on Bert's embarkation leave aboard a Lake Winnipeg steamer and during that time conceived a son, Raymond born May 23, 1944. Bert and Marion never had a home together, but strong family bonds were formed between the extended families.
>
> Bert liked to fish and had a pet dog, Pal who was left behind when he went overseas. In letters home, he never complained and was always thankful for the "care" packages the family sent him. His last letter home was postmarked the day he died, October 14, 1944.

McFeetors Lake (53 N/1), east of Red Cross Lake was named after him in 1995.

McFetridge, Private **Henry H.** of Winnipeg (H 2964). Queen's Own Cameron Highlanders. He died 19 August 1942 at the age of 24 and is commemorated at Dieppe Canadian War Cemetery in Seine-Maritime, France. He was the eldest of the nine children of Mr. and Mrs. Henry McFetridge of West Kildonan. According to his younger brother (24 January 1998):

> We lived at 309 Newton Avenue in West Kildonan. Our family was large, four boys and five girls, Harry being the oldest and I the youngest of the boys. As I recall, before that terrible day in September, 1939, my brother Harry was already a soldier. He was in the militia with the Winnipeg Rifles for some two or three years at Minto Armouries. The day war was declared, he was called for guard duty at the Winnipeg Airport. A short time after, I remember him discussing with Mom and Dad that he was now in the regular army and had a choice between the Grenadiers or the Queen's Own Cameron Highlanders. He chose the Camerons since he was born in [Edinburgh] Scotland. After the airport duty, he was sent to Shilo. He had one or two days home and then was shipped to Montreal and then overseas to England. This is all I remember of my brother Harry. I was 12 years old at the time.

McFetridge Lake (64 J/2), southwest of Tadoule Lake was named after him in 1975.

McGavock, Flying Officer **John J.** of Winnipeg (J 17116). No. 426 Squadron, Distinguished Flying Cross.

This officer has taken part in numerous attacks against all types of enemy targets including such heavily defended areas as Hamburg, Mannheim, Essen and Cologne. He has also participated in several mine-laying operations. Pilot Officer McGavock's quiet determination to complete his allotted tasks, regardless of adverse weather or enemy opposition, has proved him to be an outstanding captain of aircraft who inspires the utmost confidence in his crew (DFC Citation 1944).

He died 21 December 1943 at the age of 24 and is commemorated at Stonefall Cemetery in Yorkshire, England. He was the son of Frank and Theresa McGavock of Winnipeg and was survived by brothers Frank in the Canadian Army Pay Corps, Vincent in the Royal Canadian Navy and Alexander, sisters Teresa and Rose. Rose writes (26 November 2001):

We were proud when John was awarded the DFC, also that McGavock Lake in northern Manitoba was named in his memory. John was happy to carry on his love of ice hockey by joining a team at his base in Dishforth, Yorkshire. The rink facilities were provided for Canadians by the Canadian YMCA. On his first leave, he was excited to travel to Glenarm, County Antrim, Northern Ireland where he met his maternal grandmother, also paternal and maternal aunts, uncles and numerous cousins. My husband Martin and I visited John's grave in September, 1976. We also visited the graves of a brother and a husband of two of our friends. So sad to read the young ages on so many of the graves. We also contacted Gerry Ruddock living in London. Gerry was the only English fellow in John's crew. We had a nice visit in his home with his wife and daughter. On his second tour, Gerry became a PoW. My nephew Neil (Alexander's son) has been very interested in John's RCAF career. We have sent him the DFC and service medals, log book, pictures, etc. His Dad had spoken much about his brother. Neil is a school teacher and one year in a Remembrance Day ceremony at the school, he gave a talk on his Uncle John's RCAF career. When he had finished, a Grade 12 student stood up and introduced himself saying: "I am Graham Rolfe and Vic Rolfe [a member of McGavock's crew] is my grandfather." The odds of the two of them crossing paths was incredible.

McGavock Lake (64 C/11), southeast of Reindeer Lake was named after him in 1947.

McGeachie, Sergeant **Donald W.** of Winnipeg (H 42183). Royal Winnipeg Rifles. He died 12 October 1944 at the age of 26 and is commemorated at the Adegem Canadian War Cemetery in Belgium. He was the son of C. Roy and Josephine E. McGeachie of Winnipeg. ***McGeachie Lake*** (64 O/1), east of Munroe Lake was named after him in 1975.

McGhee, Corporal **George W.** of Hamiota (H 20039). Queen's Own Cameron Highlanders. He died 19 August 1942 at the age of 24 and is commemorated at Dieppe Canadian War Cemetery in Seine-Maritime, France. He was the son of James and Isabella McGhee of Winnipeg. His sister writes (29 October 2001):

George was brought up in Hamiota and after attending public school, he worked on the family farm. Along with others from here, he enlisted on April 2, 1940 with the Queen's Own Cameron Highlanders of Canada. They were stationed at Shilo, Manitoba – a far different Shilo to what it is today. George was killed at Dieppe.

McGhee Lake (63 N/2), east of Kississing Lake was named after him in 1972.

McGibney, Electrical Artificer 4 **Frank** of Winnipeg (40569). HMCS *Fraser*. The *Fraser* was lost in a collision with the British cruiser HMS *Calcutta* during the evacuation of France in 1940. EA McGibney died 25 June 1940 at the age of 30 and is commemorated at the Halifax Memorial. He was the son of Francis and Sarah J. McGibney of Winnipeg and was survived by his wife Marie E. McGibney of Winnipeg. ***McGibney Lake*** (64 N/13), west of Nueltin Lake was named after him in 1972.

McGill, Flight Sergeant **Edmund Thomas** of Winnipeg (R 58817). No. 405 Squadron. He died 9 June 1942 at the age of 27 and is commemorated at Rheinberg War Cemetery in Germany. He was the son of N. Manuel and Helene E. McGill of West Kildonan and was survived by his wife Ilma H. McGill of West Kildonan. ***McGill Bay*** (63 I/6) in Butterfly Lake was named after him in 1989.

McGill, Lance Corporal **Harold E.** of Wingham (H 26525). Fort Garry Horse. He died 24 July 1944 at the age of 34 and is commemorated at Bretteville-sur-Laize Canadian War Cemetery in Calvados, France. He was the son of Richard and Alice McGill and was survived by his wife Gladys M. McGill of Winnipeg and their two daughters. His sister recalls (23 October 2001):

My brother ... worked on a farm for several years (after finishing school), then joined the army when war broke out. He trained at Camp Borden in Ontario, then went to England. In one letter home he said he was acting as machinist Sergeant and had 30 tanks and 30 trucks to look after. He spoke of staying in the army after the war.

In one of his last letters home before embarking for France he wrote:

Dear Dave and Hazel: I really feel ashamed of myself for not writing sooner. I have had the time alright, but just seem to keep putting it off. I find it harder all the time to sit down and write a letter. I received your lovely parcel OK and I got it Xmas eve. I had four parcels arrive the same day so it really made it seem like Xmas. I guess there must still be a Santa Claus after all. I had a lovely time over Xmas. We had a real good dinner with turkey and everything that goes with it including plenty of beer. I went out that afternoon to the home of an 8th Army soldier that was home on leave. They had a big party. They hold Boxing Day as much as Xmas Day over here. Some kept Sunday and others held it Monday depending on what days they could [get] off from their work. I was at a party each day so I did pretty well.

At the present, I am at a tank range. It is in a mountainous part and is very pretty even tho' it is winter. Nearly every day you can see the tops covered in snow. That is all the snow that I have seen for two years. I only have another week to put in here and I'm really glad it's nearly over. We convoyed up with trucks from the south of England and it was quite a trip. It is only 325 miles, but that is a lot of road to travel in this country. I have [seen] practically every county of England and Wales this past year on such trips. I usually go to Scotland on leave, so I've [seen] most of this island or at least, far more than the average Englishman sees in a lifetime. I saw Jim's and Nellie's county coming up on this last trip, Lancashire. I believe it would be a lovely place in the summer. You see pictures of old England with an old shepherd standing at a street corner with his dog and little herd of sheep. Well that is still the country in the north. I could not believe it could still be the same way until I saw it.

I guess it will not be so long until we will be seeing some new country. Well I guess the sooner the better and get it over with. Well I guess I'll close for this time, but I promise it will not be so long before I write again. So cheerio for now. Forever grateful, Harold (19 February 1944).

McGill Lake (64 K/14), northeast of Reindeer Lake was named after him in 1974.

McGill, Captain **Hugh R.** of Norwood. Queen's Own Cameron Highlanders. He died 17 August 1944 at the age of 26 and is commemorated at Bretteville-sur-Laize Canadian War Cemetery in Calvados, France. He was the son of Hugh and Jean McGill of Norwood. ***McGill Island*** (64 F/1) in Barrington Lake was named after him in 1995.

McGookin, Rifleman **Cecil J.** of East Kildonan (H 8282). Royal Winnipeg Rifles. He died 8 June 1944 at the age of 20 and is commemorated at Beny-sur-Mer Canadian War Cemetery in Calvados, France. He was the son of William J. and Elizabeth McGookin of Winnipeg. ***McGookin Lake*** (64 I/4), west of North Knife Lake was named after him in 1974.

McGorman, Private **Harvey A.** of Neepawa (H 95477). Royal Rifles of Canada. He died 28 August 1944 and is commemorated at Bretteville-sur-Laize Canadian War Cemetery in Calvados, France.

Harvey operated a mink ranch on his father's farm prior to enlisting in the Royal Canadian Ordnance Corps in January, 1941. He trained at Portage la Prairie and Camp Shilo. He transferred to the Royal Rifles of Canada before being sent overseas July 16, 1944. Six days later his regiment was shipped to France (Pittman n.d.).

McGorman Lake (64 I/5), south of Shethanei Lake was named after him in 1974.

McGowan, Flight Sergeant **John D.** of Carman (R 208585). No. 576 Squadron. He died 29 September 1944 at the age of 22 and is commemorated at Brookwood Military Cemetery in Surrey, England. He was the son of George A. and Alice E. McGowan (née Greenwood) of Winnipeg. Air Commodore D. E. MacKell wrote to Flight Sergeant McGowan's father:

It is with deep regret that I must confirm our recent telegram informing you that your son, Flight Sergeant John Douglas McGowan, died on Active Service.

Original advice received from the Royal Canadian Air Force Casualties Officer Overseas stated that your son was seriously injured on Active Service at Stenhow, Kettering, North Hampshire, England on September 24th, 1944, sustaining a gunshot wound in the left chest, when the aircraft of which he was a member of the crew was damaged by enemy anti-aircraft fire. The aircraft was detailed to attack Calais, France. A subsequent report states that your son died of his injuries at 12:43 AM on September 29th, in the No. 4203 United States Army Hospital. His funeral took place at 11:30 AM on October 3rd, at the Royal Air Force Regional Cemetery, Brookwood, Woking, Surrey, England.

You may be assured that any further information received will be communicated to you immediately. I realize that this news has been a great shock to you, and I offer you my deepest sympathy. May the same spirit which prompted your son to offer his life give you courage (5 October 1944).

McGowan Island (64 J/11) in Wilkie Lake was named after him in 1989.

McGowan, Private **Robert C.** of Gladstone (H 6938). Winnipeg Grenadiers. He died 19 December 1941 and is commemorated at the Sai Wan Memorial in Hong Kong and was survived by his parents Mr. and Mrs. James H. McGowan of Gladstone. He:

... was farming at Gladstone when he enlisted in the Winnipeg Grenadiers in April, 1941. He trained at Sherbrooke, the British West Indies and proceeded to Hong Kong in October, 1941. He was killed in action in December of the same year when the garrison fell (Hill 1944).

McGowan Bay (64 I/15) in Wither Lake was named after him in 1995.

McGowan, Captain **Samuel W.** of Winnipeg. 1st Canadian Parachute Battalion. He died 28 March 1945 at the age of 25 and is commemorated at the Holten Canadian War Cemetery in Holland. This native of Camelon, Scotland was survived by his wife Priscilla McGowan and their son. It is believed by some that he was the first Canadian paratrooper to jump on D-Day. ***McGowan Lake*** (53 E/16), north of Island Lake was named after him in 1961.

McGrath, Warrant Officer 1 **Denis B.** of Winnipeg (R 59351). No. 115 Squadron. He died 29 April 1942 at the age of 25 and is commemorated at Bievres Communal Churchyard, Essonne, France. He was the son of John and Isabella McGrath of Long Lake, Manitoba and the brother of Leading Seaman James D. McGrath and Flight Sergeant Robert K. McGrath (see entries). ***Denis McGrath Hill*** (64 N/2), northeast of Whitmore Lake was named after him in 1995.

McGrath, Leading Seaman **James Donald** of Winnipeg (V 652). HMCS *Alberni*. The *Alberni* was torpedoed and sunk by U-480, southeast of the Isle of Wight; 59 of her ship's company were lost. Leading Seaman McGrath died 21 August 1944 at the age of 20 and is commemorated at the Halifax Memorial. He was the son of John and Isabella McGrath of Winnipeg and the brother of Warrant Officer Denis B. McGrath and Flight Sergeant Robert K. McGrath (see entries). ***McGrath Lake*** (64 N/2), southwest of Nueltin Lake was named after him in 1972.

McGrath, Flying Officer **Joseph Earl** of Winnipeg (J 16363). No. 418 Squadron. He died 3 January 1944 at the age of 22 and is commemorated at the Runnymede Memorial in Surrey, England. He was the son of Major Joseph E. and Agnes McGrath of Winnipeg. According to his brother-in-law (5 February 1995), he:

... was born in Quebec City. He moved with his parents to Kingston for a few years and then in 1927 to Winnipeg where he resided until his enlistment in 1941. He resided with his family at the Fort Osborne Barracks and later, starting in 1939, at 1017 Strathcona Street. He was educated at St. Ignatius School and St. Paul's College – both in Winnipeg.

While attending school, he was a *Free Press* newspaper carrier for many years. For a few months after graduating from school in 1940 and prior to his enlistment, he worked as a civilian support staff worker at Fort Osborne Barracks. Earl ... always want[ed] to be a pilot.

Earl enlisted in the Royal Canadian Air Force in February, 1941 when a new recruit group was being assembled. He took his preliminary training at Regina and Yorkton ... and graduated as a pilot Flight Sergeant in September, 1941. He was posted overseas in October, 1941 where he underwent further training at Wigtown, Scotland and was commissioned as a Pilot Officer in December, 1942. He trained and served in and around the British Isles until he was commissioned Flying Officer June 11, 1943. In late August, 1943 he was assigned to flying Mosquito attack/bombers. Later, while attached to 418 Squadron, Earl and Flying Officer Donald Clifford Bissell, his flying partner, went missing in action on a raid into Germany. He was confirmed dead, missing in action about 12 months later.

McGrath Island (64 G/13) in Big Sand Lake was named after him in 1995.

McGrath, Flight Sergeant **Robert Kenneth** of Winnipeg (R 59361). No. 142 Squadron. He died 22 July 1942 at the age of 23 and is commemorated at the Runnymede Memorial in Surrey, England. He was the son of John and Bella McGrath and was survived by his wife Sadie C. McGrath of Verdun, Quebec. He was the brother of Warrant Officer Denis B. McGrath and Leading Seaman James D. McGrath (see entries). ***Kenneth McGrath Hill*** (64 N/2), northeast of Whitmore Lake was named after him in 1995.

McGregor, Sapper **Michael H.** of Winnipeg (H 25192). Royal Canadian Engineers. He died 17 March 1941 and is commemorated at Brookwood Military Cemetery in Surrey, England. ***McGregor Island*** (63 I/1) in Little Bolton Lake was named after him in 1995.

McGregor, Leading Aircraftman **Robert M.** of Winnipeg (R 253246). No. 23 Elementary Flying Training School. He died 8 October 1943 at the age of 18 and is commemorated at Brookside Cemetery in Winnipeg. He was the son of Roderick M. and Dovie Y. McGregor of Winnipeg. ***McGregor Bay*** (63 I/7) in Mukutasip Lake was named after him in 1995.

McHaffie-Gow, Corporal **James** of Rounthwaite (K 62060). Canadian Scottish Regiment. He died of wounds 14 October 1942 at the age of 28 and is commemorated at Brookwood Military Cemetery in Surrey, England. He was the son of James Gow and Jessie McHaffie-Gow and was survived by his wife Bertha M. McHaffie-Gow of Rounthwaite and their baby daughter. His widow writes (30 June 2001):

His father ... was killed in World War I when he was an infant. Born in Glasgow, Scotland, he came to Canada with his widowed mother at the age of eight years. Being in the militia, [he] went on active service when the war started. He spent time training in Nova Scotia, going overseas from there August, 1941.

McHaffie-Gow Lake (63 P/2), northwest of Cotton Lake was named after him in 1996.

McHugh, Flight Sergeant **Gerald F.** of Winnipeg (R 54884). No. 149 Squadron. He died 30 September 1942 at the age of 31 and is commemorated at the Runnymede Memorial in Surrey, England. He was the son of William and Rosa McHugh of High Wycombe, Buckinghamshire, England. ***McHugh Island*** (53 E/16) in Island Lake was named after him in 1996.

McInnes, Gunner **Gordon** of Killarney (H 60421). Royal Canadian Artillery. He died 2 November 1945 at the age of 25 and is commemorated at Killarney Cemetery in Manitoba. He was survived by his mother Annie Pratt of Lena. ***McInnes Lake*** (64 I/3), west of North Knife Lake was named after him in 1974.

McInnes, Flight Sergeant **John G.** of Carroll (R 128075). No. 149 Squadron. He died 8 October 1943 at the age of 29 and is commemorated at the Runnymede Memorial in Surrey, England. He was the son of John and Jessie M. McInnes of Carroll, Manitoba. At the time of his enlistment, he was the local druggist. ***McInnes Point*** (64 N/11) in Kasmere Lake was named after him in 1989.

McIntosh, Lieutenant Colonel **Forbes T.** of Winnipeg. Royal Canadian Artillery. He died 24 August 1944 at the age of 40 and is commemorated at Gradara War Cemetery in Italy. He was the son of John C. and Eva T. McIntosh and was survived by his wife Dorothy McIntosh of Winnipeg. ***McIntosh Point*** (64 O/13) on Nueltin Lake was named after him in 1996.

McIntosh, Pilot Officer **Garnet** of Brandon (J 86916). No. 219 Squadron. He died 19 March 1944 at the age of 22 and is commemorated at Blacon Cemetery in Cheshire, England. ***McIntosh Lake*** (64 J/14), northwest of Tadoule Lake was named after him in 1975.

McIntosh, Rifleman **James D.** of Headingley (H 102744). Royal Winnipeg Rifles. He died 8 June 1944 at the age of 20 and is commemorated at Beny-sur-Mer Canadian War Cemetery in Calvados, France. He was the seventh of the 10 children of William and Florence McIntosh of Headingley. Prior to enlisting, he had been an active curler and his rink won the Grand Challenge Cup in Manitoba Junior curling. His sister writes (2 January 1998):

His mother and father came from Scotland. His father was a carpenter and was active in community affairs. Jimmie received his schooling at Phoenix School, Alboro Street, Headingley. When he finished school, he worked for the railroad. When he was 18 he joined the Royal Winnipeg Rifles.

He was with a group of soldiers that penetrated the German line near Pavie, District of Calvados and were captured on June 8, 1944 by the 12th SS Hitlerjugend Division Commanded by Colonel Kurt Meyer. It was made up of Hitler Youth groups and veterans of the Russian Campaign. The Germans had to retreat and one of his officers asked Meyer what to do with the prisoners. He spoke to the officer in a low voice. The prisoners, with their hands tied behind their backs, were taken to a courtyard in a church and shot in the head. The excuse used [was that] the Canadians were shooting prisoners.

McIntosh Bay (63 N/10) in Flatrock Lake was named after him in 1995.

McIntosh, Sergeant **James W.** of Winnipeg (R 56908). No. 7 Service Flying Training School. He died 2 April 1941 at the age of 25 and is commemorated at Brookside Cemetery in Winnipeg. He was the son of Frederick and Elizabeth McIntosh of Winnipeg. ***McIntosh Island*** (53 M/2) in Seller Lake was named after him in 1995.

McIntyre, Aircraftman 1 **Alexander Donald** of Grandview (R 205452). No. 1 Central Navigation School, RCAF. He died 15 September 1944 at the age of 21 and is commemorated at Grandview Cemetery, Manitoba. His brother recalls (27 February 1996):

Don was on leave at the time of his death. He was at home and had an attack of appendicitis. He was taken to a doctor at Grandview who misdiagnosed the case. Don, who was still in pain, was taken to another doctor in Gilbert Plains by the family. The doctor there immediately had him transferred to the Dauphin General Hospital where he was operated on for a ruptured appendix. It was too late and he died there.

Don began his education in Grandview, then when he was 13 years old, the family moved to the Tamarisk School District south of Grandview where he completed his education. He worked with his father on the farm, then spent a short time in the mines at Sherridon, Manitoba before joining the Air Force on November 23, 1942. Don's interests were mainly in mechanics and farming. In sports he liked baseball and soccer.

Donald McIntyre Lake (53 N/1), east of Red Cross Lake was named after him in 1995.

McIntyre, Sergeant **Donald V. N.** of Winnipeg (R 196124). No. 101 Squadron. He died 31 March 1944 at the age of 23 and is commemorated at the Berlin 1939 - 1945 War Cemetery in Brandenburg, Germany. He was the son of Archibald and Helen M. McIntyre (née Van Norman) of Winnipeg. His nephew writes (5 April 2002):

Donny was born in Winnipeg on October 27, 1919 at the family home at the corner of Polson and St. Cross in West Kildonan. Donald was the youngest of six siblings. Donny left for war engaged to a lady from southern Ontario named Babe. Her family was kind enough to return Donny's portrait to the family. Donny was the tail gunner in a Lancaster bomber which failed to return from a raid on Nuremberg. Thanks to higher than expected winds, lack of cloud cover and a full moon, Bomber Command lost 104 aircraft that night.

McIntyre Lake (54 E/5), northeast of Embleton Lake was named after him in 1989.

McIntyre, Flying Officer **Robert J.** of Carman (J 19103). Royal Canadian Air Force. He died 15 September 1946 at the age of 23 and is commemorated at Greenwood Cemetery in Carman, Manitoba. He was the son of Peter and Mary Ann McIntyre of Carman. ***McIntyre Island*** (64 C/8) in Granville Lake was named after him in 1995.

McIvor, Private **Albert W.** of Carman (H 101464). Cape Breton Highlanders. He died 14 September 1944 at the age of 20 and is commemorated at Ancona War Cemetery in Italy. He was the son of William J. and Eva D. McIvor of Carman, Manitoba. ***McIvor Point*** (63 I/16) on Leguee Lake was named after him in 1995.

McIvor, Pilot Officer **John K.** of Winnipeg (107257). No. 4 Squadron, RAF. He died 10 August 1942 at the age of 28 and is commemorated at the Alamein Memorial in Egypt. He was the son of Dr. K. and Grace W. McIvor and was survived by his wife Patricia McIvor of Winnipeg. ***McIvor Peninsula*** (53 L/13) on Oxford Lake was named after him in 1996.

McIvor, Private **William** of Gladstone (H 17182). Princess Patricia's Canadian Light Infantry. He died 22 February 1944 and is commemorated at the Moro River Canadian War Cemetery in Italy. ***McIvor Island*** (53 M/4) in Bear Lake was named after him in 1989.

McKay, Sergeant **Alexander A.** of Lac du Bonnet (H 19344). Queen's Own Cameron Highlanders. He died 13 September 1944 at the age of 24 and is commemorated at the Adegem Canadian War Cemetery in Belgium. He was the son of James A. and Laura J. McKay of Lac du Bonnet, Manitoba. His brother John A. McKay also died in service. ***Alexander McKay Lake*** (53 L/1), southeast of Rochon Lake was named after him in 1995.

McKay, Gunner **Donald B.** of Killarney (H 102209). Royal Canadian Artillery. He died 31 October 1945 at the age of 27 and is commemorated at Killarney Cemetery in Manitoba. He was the son of William J. and Wilhelmina McKay of Killarney. ***McKay River*** (64 I/13), which flows south into Shethanei Lake was named after him in 1995.

McKay, Flying Officer **Donald G.** of Portage la Prairie (J 28933). No. 405 Squadron. He died 16 January 1945 at the age of 22 and is commemorated at Durnbach War Cemetery in Bavaria, Germany. He was the son of James Gordon and Florence M. McKay of Portage la Prairie and was the brother of Flying Officer Murray R. McKay (see entry). ***Donald McKay Lake*** (64 O/6), east of Booth Lake was named after him in 1995.

McKay, Flight Sergeant **Douglas G.** of Portage la Prairie (R 124347). No. 408 Squadron. He died 14 July 1943 at the age of 23 and is commemorated at Tilburg (Gilzerbaan) General Cemetery, Holland. He was the son of Robert G. and Dorothy L. McKay of Portage la Prairie. ***McKay Creek*** (53 M/11), which flows northeast into Bigstone River was named after him in 1989.

McKay, Flight Lieutenant **Douglas W.** of Rapid City (J 4246). No. 32 Squadron. He died 28 February 1944 at the age of 27 and is commemorated at Belgrade War Cemetery, Yugoslavia. He was the son of Howard E. and Etta C. McKay of Rapid City, Manitoba. ***Douglas McKay Lake*** (64 C/11), north of Glasspole Lake was named after him in 1995.

McKay, Lance Corporal **Eugene J.** of Portage la Prairie (H 16895). Princess Patricia's Canadian Light Infantry. He died 22 July 1943 at the age of 22 and is commemorated at Agira Canadian War Cemetery in Italy. He was the son of Mr. and Mrs. M. Fred McKay of Portage la Prairie and was survived by his wife Mary McKay (née Cruikshanks) of Portage la Prairie, currently residing in England. Born and educated in Portage, he enlisted in February, 1940 and went overseas in May of that year. ***McKay Hill*** (64 O/4), southwest of Blackfish Lake was named after him in 1995.

McKay, Private **George G.** of Roland (H 87806). Royal Canadian Army Medical Corps. He died 2 April 1944 at the age of 22 and is commemorated at the Moro River Canadian War Cemetery in Italy. He was the son of J. R. and Agnes McKay of Roland, Manitoba. ***George McKay Bay*** (64 P/12) in Nejanilini Lake was named after him in 1995.

McKay, Pilot Officer **Gordon O.** of Winnipeg (J 17179). No. 243 Squadron. He died 8 May 1943 at the age of 24 and is commemorated at Enfidaville War Cemetery in Tunisia. He was the son of Mr. and Mrs. G. C. McKay of Winnipeg. ***Gordon McKay Lake*** (64 A/13), southeast of Gauer Lake was named after him in 1995.

McKay, Warrant Officer 2 **Hugh R.** of Winnipeg (R 180114). No. 7 Squadron. He died 20 February 1944 and is commemorated at the Berlin 1939 - 1945 War Cemetery in Brandenburg, Germany. ***Hugh McKay Lake*** (53 M/7), north of Knee Lake was named after him in 1995.

McKay, Leading Aircraftman **James A.** of Winnipeg (R 71112). No. 1 Operational Training Unit, RCAF. He died 10 September 1942 at the age of 21 and is commemorated at Brookside Cemetery in Winnipeg. He was the son of John J. and Bessie M. McKay of Kildonan. ***McKay Narrows*** (53 L/5) in Bolton Lake was named after him in 1995.

McKay, Flight Sergeant **James P.** of St. Boniface (R 58824). No. 214 Squadron. He died 3 September 1941 at the age of 26 and is commemorated at Dunkirk Town Cemetery in France. He was the son of James and Brigid F. McKay (née Garvey). His sister writes (11 November 2001):

On September 3, 1941, they were returning from a raid on Frankfurt when they were shot down. They were believed to have gone into the sea. Prior to enlisting, Jimmy taught Science (Math, Chemistry and Physics) at the Dauphin Collegiate. He was the eldest of three brothers who served in the RCAF. He flew

Wellingtons. My husband and I visited his grave in France in 1992. The graves are very well kept and while we were, there were three gardeners tidying the grounds. Canadians are very well thought of in that area.

McKay Bay (52 M/14) in Family Lake was named after him in 1979.

McKay, Private **John A.** of Lac du Bonnet (H 19432). Queen's Own Cameron Highlanders. He died 21 July 1944 at the age of 28 and is commemorated at Bretteville-sur-Laize Canadian War Cemetery in Calvados, France. He was the son of James A. and Laura J. McKay of Lac du Bonnet, Manitoba. His brother Alexander A. McKay also fell. ***John McKay Lake*** (64 G/15), northwest of Trout Lake was named after him in 1995.

McKay, Private **John David** of Somerset (H 19886). Queen's Own Cameron Highlanders. He died 20 July 1944 at the age of 28 and is commemorated at Bretteville-sur-Laize Canadian War Cemetery in Calvados, France. He was the son of Mr. and Mrs. Alexander MacKay and was survived by his wife Marion H. McKay of West Worthing, Sussex, England. His sister recalls (3 January 1997):

He was a loving son and brother, always in a good mood. [He] loved to tease me as a kid sister. Whenever he could borrow a banjo or accordion, he would sit up in his room learning to play them. Of the three of us, he would have had the musical talent, given a chance.

I know someone who was nearby when David was hit. He said it was instantaneous, for which we are grateful. After all these years I still miss him. Ironically he died on July 20 and I lost my husband very suddenly on July 20, 1991.

David McKay Bay (63 I/1) in Vanular Lake was named after him in 1995.

McKay, Sergeant **Martin N.** of Selkirk (R 86317). No. 4 Squadron. He died 30 December 1941 at the age of 26 and is commemorated at St. Clements Cemetery in Mapleton, Manitoba. He was the son of Charles and Margaret A. McKay of Selkirk. ***McKay Peninsula*** (64 P/6), on Jethe Lake was named after him in 1985.

McKay, Flying Officer **Murray R.** of Portage la Prairie (J 38401). No. 49 Squadron. He died 9 April 1945 at the age of 20 and is commemorated at the Runnymede Memorial in Surrey, England. He was the son of James Gordon and Florence M. McKay of Portage la Prairie and the brother of Flying Officer Donald G. McKay (see entry). ***Murray McKay Island*** (64 O/6) in Donald McKay Lake was named after him in 1995.

McKay, Private **Norman H.** of Pilot Mound (H 10653). Royal Regiment of Canada. He died 28 August 1944 at the age of 20 and is commemorated at Bretteville-sur-Laize Canadian War Cemetery in Calvados, France. He was the son of Thomas Gordon and Beatrice McKay of Pilot Mound, Manitoba. His siblings recall (28 November 2001):

Our brother's nickname was "Nimby." He was very agile on his feet – therefore always in the middle of the action. Born and raised in Pilot Mound, he was a well liked boy who participated in many activities. He never liked controversy of any kind; he seemed to be guided by the joy of living. He enlisted on August 1, 1943 with the RCE, transferred to an armoured regiment and went overseas in April, 1944 with the RCA, serving with the artillery in France. He already had four of his seven brothers serving with the forces – one a PoW in Germany, two others in action and a fourth reported wounded in action.

Norman was only granted one leave, even when our Father died he was denied leave because they thought it was a gimmick to get away for a while. At this, Norm swore at the sergeant and almost got in trouble. After a few month's training in Winnipeg, he was transferred to Halifax and after seven more months, to England. In a letter to Mother he wrote "I just love London, the weather. Everyone else seems to think it miserable. I think it's great and the girls are gorgeous."

He was in England a short time before being sent to Normandy. He was officially reported slightly wounded on August 18 and hospitalized. Apparently he recovered quickly and returned to duty, meeting his death on August 28, 1944. For a young boy who had rarely been to Winnipeg let alone Europe, it must have seemed like a great adventure to him. He was killed at St-Ouen-du-Tilleul. In memory of their liberators, the citizens of Saint-Ouen erected a monument to the fallen on the exact spot where they were first buried. The 13 graves were later moved to the Canadian cemetery at Brettville-sur-Laize.

A memorial service was held at the monument on the 46th anniversary of the liberation of St-Ouen. The conclusion of the address read as follows:

What happened to the brothers in arms of those men? Did death find some of them on the road to the liberation of Belgium and the Netherlands? Who are those veterans who sometimes return anonymously to the sites of their battles? What do we owe to those men who, volunteers in the Canadian Army, returned to their towns and villages in Canada nearly fifty years ago?

Our lives today, thanks to the Allies, know better days than during the Occupation. In the Middle East, men and women are forced against their will to stay in a country which is not theirs ... Once more Freedom is ridiculed. To what purpose did our Canadian soldiers sacrifice their lives?

Everyone of you, everyone of us, must have as a mission to build for the future of our children. We must teach them to build their tomorrow. "Youth of France and Canada, the task is yours. You can do better than us: Build Peace..." (25 August 1990).

McKay Falls (64 I/10) in the North Knife River was named after him in 1995.

McKay, Lance Corporal **Reginald N.** of Flin Flon (H 42162). Hastings and Prince Edward Regiment. He died 18 April 1945 at the age of 23 and is commemorated at the Holten Canadian War Cemetery in Holland. He was the son of Arthur and Catherine McKay of Grand Rapids, Manitoba. ***Reginald McKay Lake*** (53 K/10), southwest of Kistigan Lake was named after him in 1995.

McKay, Sergeant **Wallace A.** of Winnipeg (P 10749). Royal Canadian Engineers. He was aboard the SS *Nerissa*, the only ship torpedoed while carrying Canadian troops to the United Kingdom. Sergeant McKay died 1 May 1941 at the age of 26 and is commemorated at the Halifax Memorial. He was the son of Andrew D. and Gertrude M. McKay of Winnipeg. ***Wallace McKay Island*** (53 K/6) in Sharpe Lake was named after him in 1995.

McKay, Lance Corporal **William J.** of Winnipeg (H 38607). Royal Canadian Corps of Signals. He died 25 July 1944 and is commemorated at Bretteville-sur-Laize Canadian War Cemetery in Calvados, France. He was the son of William J. and Miriam McKay of Moose Jaw, Saskatchewan. ***William McKay Lake*** (63 O/12), northwest of Apeganau Lake was named after him in 1995.

McKellar, Lieutenant **Alexander J.** of Winnipeg. Queen's Own Cameron Highlanders. He died 19 August 1942 and is commemorated at the Calais Canadian War Cemetery in France. ***McKellar Lake*** (64 K/7), northeast of Reindeer Lake was named after him in 1972.

McKellar, Flight Sergeant **Malcolm A.** of Winnipeg (R 157077). No. 419 Squadron. He died 22 November 1943 at the age of 20 and is commemorated at Diever General Cemetery, Holland. ***McKellar Island*** (64 C/13) in McMillan Lake was named after him in 1995.

McKelvie, Sergeant **Charles D.** of Winnipeg (1075572). No. 90 Squadron, RAF. He died 21 March 1943 at the age of 22 and is commemorated at Fourfelt Cemetery in Esbjerg, Denmark. This native of Glasgow, Scotland was survived by his parents William and Catherine McKelvie and by his uncle John D. McKelvie of Winnipeg. ***McKelvie Island*** (53 L/12) in Max Lake was named after him in 1995.

McKennie, Flight Sergeant **Gerald B.** of Winnipeg (R 110872). No. 21 Squadron. He died 5 April 1943 at the age of 23 and is commemorated at the Runnymede Memorial in Surrey, England. He was the son of Ansell W. and Elizabeth McKennie of South Burnaby, British Columbia. ***McKennie Lake*** (64 G/16), southeast of Chipewyan Lake was named after him in 1995.

McKenzie, Sergeant **David** of Winnipeg (H 19113). Princess Louise Dragoon Guards. He died 31 August 1944 at the age of 32 and is commemorated at Montecchio War Cemetery in Italy. He was the son of David and Mary McKenzie. ***David McKenzie Hill*** (64 A/14), southeast of Wernham Lake was named after him in 1995.

McKenzie, Gunner **Lewis C.** of Winnipeg (H 56989). Royal Canadian Artillery. He died 17 July 1944 at the age of 32 and is commemorated at Beny-sur-Mer Canadian War Cemetery in Calvados, France. He was the fourth of the nine children of Alexander and Annabella McKenzie of Winnipeg and was survived by his wife Cynthia Jean McKenzie of Norwood Grove, Manitoba and their son. His wife recalls (23 June 1998):

> Lew worked for the Orange Crush Company at his time of enlistment; he played the guitar and sang in an orchestra called the Barnyard Rascals, also at many get-togethers. Lew was a cadet in a highland regiment in his younger years, but didn't have the breath for the pipes. He was a wonderful husband and father; he worshipped his one year-old son.

McKenzie Esker (53 L/2), north of Island Lake was named after him in 1995.

McKenzie, Trooper **Lorne Kenneth** of High Bluff (H 276). Lord Strathcona's Horse. He died 30 May 1944 at the age of 25 and is commemorated at the Cassino War Cemetery in Italy. He was the son of Hugh and Florence McKenzie of St. James and was survived by his mother, two brothers and three sisters. Before enlisting in March, 1941 at Portage la Prairie, he was actively involved with the family farm. ***McKenzie Hill*** (64 I/7), north of Allan Lake was named after him in 1995.

McKenzie, Pilot Officer **Morris Allan** of Cartwright (J 86163). No. 426 Squadron. He died 20 February 1944 at the age of 23 and is commemorated at Woensel General Cemetery in Eindhoven, Holland. He was the son of Henry L. and Hazel B. McKenzie of Cartwright, Manitoba. According to his brother (18 April 1995):

> Allan was born November 7, 1920 on the family farm near Cartwright. He received his education at a country school called Chesterville, then attended Cartwright High School where he graduated from Grade 11. He worked on the family farm until he joined the Air Force in 1942.
>
> In November, 1943 he went overseas to England where he was with 426 Squadron. He attained the rank of Pilot Officer and was flying a Lancaster at the last. He and his crew were shot down over Holland on February 19 - 20, 1944 on a raid over Leipzig. They crashed on a golf course near Eindhoven, Holland. There were no survivors.

McKenzie Narrows (63 N/7) in Guthrie Lake was named after him in 1995.

McKenzie, Sergeant **Orville W.** of Winnipeg (R 80200). No. 408 Squadron. He died 2 June 1942 at the age of 24 and is commemorated at Amsterdam New Eastern Cemetery, Holland. He was survived by his parents Mr. and Mrs. M. N. Mackenzie (sp.) of Winnipeg. He:

> ... was born November 18, 1917 at St. Paul, Minnesota, making his home in Winnipeg where he was employed in a storage warehouse. McKenzie joined the RCAF in Winnipeg and trained at Brandon, Kamloops, Calgary and Macdonald, proceeding overseas in July, 1941. He was attached to the RCAF in Great Britain and was reported missing in action over Essen, Germany and subsequently presumed dead. McKenzie attended General Wolfe and Daniel McIntyre Collegiate. His hobby was golf (Hill 1944).

McKenzie Creek (64 P/7), which flows northwest into Guest Creek was named after him in 1995.

McKenzie, Sapper **Richard M.** of Winnipeg (H 3045). Royal Canadian Engineers. He died 3 April 1941 at the age of 38 and is commemorated at Tynemouth (Preston) Cemetery in Northumberland, England. He was the son of Thomas F. and Ann J. McKenzie of North Shields and was survived by his wife Tina McKenzie. ***McKenzie Island*** (64 H/5) in Missinipi Lake was named after him in 1995.

McKillop, Lieutenant **Orville W.** of Portage la Prairie. Winnipeg Grenadiers. He died 4 January 1942 at the age of 33 while a prisoner of war and is commemorated at the Sai Wan War Cemetery in Hong Kong. He was the son of Dougal and Jessie McKillop of Portage la Prairie. ***McKillop Lake*** (63 P/14), northeast of Paint Lake was named after him in 1961.

McKinney, Gunner **Bernard Eric** of Winnipeg (P 9971). Royal Canadian Artillery. He died 13 October 1944 at the age of 21 and is commemorated at Coriano Ridge War Cemetery in Italy. He was the second youngest child of Joseph H. and Florence N. McKinney (née Billings) of St. James. His brother writes (8 November 2001):

> Eric had normal childhood and education in St. James. At the age of 16, he followed in his father's footsteps; on 3 July 1939 he enlisted in 'C' Battery Royal Canadian Horse Artillery as a trumpeter. His father, deceased in 1927, was a Warrant Officer in 'C' Battery Royal Canadian Horse Artillery. Eric was always interested in the Military and before enlistment had been both a drummer and trumpeter in the Highland Cadets. He was a little "put out" when older brother H. V. McKinney enlisted in 'C' Battery Royal Canadian Horse Artillery and sailed for England in 1939. In 1942, Eric did catch up with his Regiment in England and in 1943 went to the Mediterranean.

McKinney Island (64 B/6) in Karsakuwigamak Lake was named after him in 1995.

McKinney, Pilot Officer **Robert F.** of Winnipeg (J 89964). No. 9 Squadron. He died 31 July 1944 at the age of 20 and is commemorated at Clichy Northern Cemetery, Hauts-de-Seine, France. His Lancaster aircraft and its RAF crew went missing from a night trip to Rilly le Montagne. He was the son of Frank J. and Annie Blanche McKinney of Winnipeg and was survived by his wife Nancy McKinney and by his sister Aldyne Adams. ***McKinney Lake*** (64 H/12), north of Wood Lake was named after him in 1995.

McKinnon, Flying Officer **Campbell A.** of Winnipeg (J 10893). No. 426 Squadron. He died 19 February 1943 at the age of 19 and is commemorated at the Runnymede Memorial in Surrey, England. He was the son of Mr. and Mrs. Peter McKinnon. His sister-in-law recalls (27 August 1998) that:

> Cam was a great athlete. He played with the St. Boniface Athletics [and] overseas he played with the RCAF teams. Baseball was another sport he enjoyed in the West End. [He] was a navigator with No. 426 Wellington Squadron. His loaded plane was over Wilhelmshaven, Germany when the Germans made a direct hit to his plane.

McKinnon Point (63 P/5) on Wintering Lake was named after him in 1995.

McKinnon, Lieutenant **George E.** of Arrow River. Royal Winnipeg Rifles. He died 19 August 1944 at the age of 27 and is commemorated at Bretteville-sur-Laize Canadian War Cemetery in Calvados, France. He was the son of John and Agnes McKinnon and was survived by his wife Helen M. McKinnon (née Tennant) of Miniota and their two children. According to his wife (22 February 1995):

> [He] joined the Royal Winnipeg Rifles June 7, 1940 and went to England in September of 1941. He studied and was promoted to an Officer Cadet and returned to Canada in 1942 to take his officer's training in Gordon Head, BC and in Shilo, Manitoba. He returned to England and France in June of 1944 and was assigned back to the same division and company in France. [He was] killed in action ... in the Battle of the Falaise Gap.

His nephew writes:

> Some time ago, I related how I'd returned to my roots, so to speak, and found a piece of history involving one of my uncles. He was Lieutenant George Edward McKinnon who was killed in action in France in 1944, shortly after D-Day. He was a member of the Royal Winnipeg Rifles and I was an eight year-old Manitoba farm kid at the time. I remember the day my aunt received the news from the federal government via telegram, that "the government regrets to inform you ..." It was a sad day in that wee farming town of about 40 and even more sombre a few days later at the memorial service in the tiny United Church.
>
> He was a strapping young man, so proud of his officer's bars and wore his uniform with the pride that only fits on those who truly believe in the right of their cause. I remember his last leave home. Most Canadian soldiers were given one final leave home before shipping overseas, because everyone knew a great many wouldn't be coming back. I remember his last leave when he would run every morning about three miles down to the CN station and back and the hours he spent polishing his brass, boots and Sam Browne belt. And the hours I followed him about like a wee puppy because he was everything I ever wanted to be. Then he was gone – forever.
>
> It's a comfort to know there's an island in Wells Lake in northern Manitoba that recognizes a Canadian and a Manitoban who paid the price for our freedom. It's McKinnon Island and someday I'll see it (Tennant 1999).

McKinnon Island (64 F/7) in Wells Lake was named after him in 1995.

McKinnon, Pilot Officer **Lloyd G.** of Winnipeg (J 95171). No. 206 Squadron. He died 28 September 1944 at the age of 29 and is commemorated at the Runnymede Memorial in Surrey, England. He was the son of Isaac J. and Teresa A. McKinnon. According to a contemporary newspaper account:

> One German submarine was destroyed and another probably destroyed recently in separate actions by two RAF coastal command Liberators, it was disclosed yesterday. Dates of the battles were not disclosed. The action in which the U-boat was destroyed was fought in daylight and the attack on the other was made at night with the aid of the bomber's searchlight.
>
> The destroyed U-boat was caught before its crew could do more than put up brief flak opposition and the airmen counted 21 dinghies full of German sailors who escaped before the submarine sank. Oil slicks containing debris from the blasted craft stretched for a half mile.
>
> Canadians on this attack were Flight Sergeant A. M. Cleland, Verdun, Quebec who fired 700 rounds as the bomber roared low over the target and Warrant Officer L. G. McKinnon of 533 Home Street who has since been reported missing stood by the wireless. Flight Sergeant J. A. Nadeau of Nassau, New Hampshire, an American member of the RCAF, was tail-gunner and fired 400 rounds.
>
> Both Cleland and Nadeau scored repeated hits on the conning tower and along the length of the submarine. Depth charges straddled the U-boat's stern on the first run and it started to sink. The aircraft was undamaged. The Canadian airmen ... were making their first operation against a submarine (*Winnipeg Free Press* 22 November 1944).

They were subsequently shot down off the coast of Stavanger, Norway. ***McKinnon Bay*** (64 O/2) in Munroe Lake was named after him in 1985.

McLachlin, Private **William J.** of Souris (H 54148). Veterans Guard of Canada. He died 10 May 1944 at the age of 45 and is commemorated at Glenwood Cemetery in Souris, Manitoba. He was survived by his sister Mrs. Edgar Taylor of Souris. ***McLachlin Lake*** (64 K/1), south of Chartand Lake was named after him in 1997.

McLaren, Leading Aircraftman **Alexander J.** "Sandy" of Clearwater (R 119706). No. 7 Service Flying Training School. He died 15 June 1942 at the age of 21 and is commemorated at Elmwood Cemetery in Winnipeg. He was the son of Alexander R. and Margaret M. McLaren of Clearwater. His brother writes (20 June 1995) that he:

> ... was born, raised and received his education in the Clearwater district. He was an excellent athlete and outdoorsman, playing hockey, baseball, skiing, swimming as well as ... hunting and was an excellent shot with a rifle.

McLaren Island (53 L/9) in Gods Lake was named after him in 1995.

McLaren, Private **John B.** of Portage la Prairie (H 18879). South Saskatchewan Regiment. He died 16 September 1944 at the age of 31 and is commemorated at the Calais Canadian War Cemetery in France. He was the son of Donald H. and Barbara A. McLaren of Portage la Prairie and was survived by his wife Daisy T. McLaren (née Bindas) of Portage la Prairie and their three children. His obituary read in part:

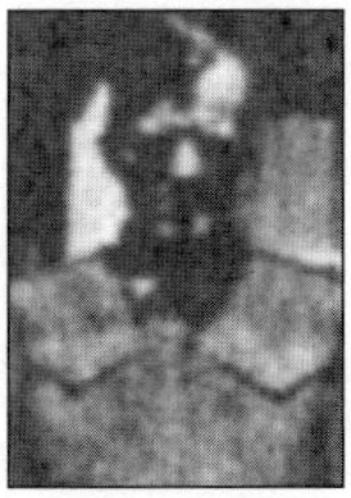

Eight months after enlisting in Winnipeg, Private John Bell McLaren has been reported killed in action. Word was received by his next-of-kin on October 7th. Enlisting with the transport, he went overseas shortly after and was transferred to infantry. Following one month's infantry training, he went into action. He was employed with the Gordon Webb bus service prior to enlistment (n.d.).

McLaren Bay (64 P/1) in Renault Lake was named after him in 1995.

McLaughlin, Private **George R.** of Hamiota (H 6686). Winnipeg Grenadiers. He died a prisoner of war 20 December 1943 and is commemorated at the Yokohama War Cemetery in Japan. ***McLaughlin Lake*** (53 L/14), southeast of Oxford Lake was named after him in 1983.

McLaughlin, Leading Aircraftman **Kenneth K.** of Winnipeg (R 110966). No. 5 Elementary Flying Training School. He died 29 December 1941 at the age of 24 and is commemorated at Old Kildonan Presbyterian Cemetery in Winnipeg. He was the son of Ray G. and Alice H. McLaughlin of Winnipeg. ***McLaughlin Island*** (64 O/13) in Nueltin Lake was named after him in 1995.

McLaurin, Flight Sergeant **George F.** of Brandon (R 205353). No. 50 Squadron. He died 8 July 1944 at the age of 20 and is commemorated at St. Sever Cemetery Extension, Rouen, Seine-Maritime, France. Flight Sergeant McLaurin had been on a mission bombing a V-1 launch site in France. He was the son of Mr. and Mrs. P. F. McLaurin of Brandon. ***McLaurin Lake*** (64 P/5), south of Nejanilini Lake was named after him in 1974.

McLean, Private **George I.** of Elphinstone (H 70486). Saskatoon Light Infantry. He died 16 December 1943 at the age of 23 and is commemorated at the Moro River Canadian War Cemetery in Italy. He was the son of Malcolm S. and Florence McLean of Elphinstone, Manitoba. ***McLean Island*** (63 P/3) in Sipiwesk Lake was named after him in 1995.

McLean, Lance Sergeant **Harold W.** of Brandon (H 102737). Lake Superior Regiment. He died 3 May 1945 at the age of 22 and is commemorated at the Holten Canadian War Cemetery in Holland. He was the son of Duncan and Alma A. McLean of Brandon. His sister writes (7 November 2001):

> His family remembers him for his sense of humour, good-natured joking and teasing and his ability to entertain with his accordion. He played for many dances at home and played for wedding dances in England and entertained the troops. Anyone who knew Harold enjoyed his music.
>
> Harold's brother was told by an officer of the Lake Superior Regiment that Harold was to receive the Military Medal, but it was never presented. Harold was a dedicated soldier and his officer told him on May 3rd to stay back and take charge of the camp, but being the soldier he was, he wanted to see the war finished to the end and therefore sacrificed his life. Harold was highly thought of by his comrades and all who knew him.

McLean Point (64 J/11) on Clifton Lake was named after him in 1989.

McLean, Private **Paul** of Newdale (H 10373). Princess Patricia's Canadian Light Infantry. He died 25 May 1944 at the age of 27 and is commemorated at the Cassino War Cemetery in Italy. He was the son of Peter and Annie McLean of Newdale, Manitoba. ***McLean Peninsula*** (64 N/9) on Turner Lake was named after him in 1995.

McLean, Sergeant **William J.** of Winnipeg (H 63027). Canadian Provost Corps. He died 4 December 1943 at the age of 47 and is commemorated at Brookside Cemetery in Winnipeg. He was survived by his mother Mrs. Christie Reynolds of St. Vital and by his wife Mae McLean of Winnipeg. ***William McLean Lake*** (64 K/1), northwest of Chartrand Lake was named after him in 1997.

McLean, Sergeant **William J.** of McCreary (H 26411). Fort Garry Horse. He died 6 July 1944 at the age of 24 and is commemorated at Beny-sur-Mer Canadian War Cemetery in Calvados, France. He was the son of James R. and Anne H. McLean of McCreary, Manitoba. He was the middle-weight boxing champion of the 5th Canadian Armoured Division in 1942. ***McLean Creek*** (53 N/9), which flows east into Gods River was named after him in 1995.

McLellan, Private **Earle** of East Kildonan (H 6324). Winnipeg Grenadiers. He died a prisoner of war 25 January 1944 at the age of 31 and is commemorated at the Yokohama War Cemetery in Japan. He was the son of Alexander F. and Mary J. McLellan of Winnipeg. ***McLellan Island*** (64 G/6) in Amiskoskotim Lake was named after him in 1994.

McLellan, Private **William Bernard** of Winnipeg (H 10153). Queen's Own Cameron Highlanders. He died 13 September 1944 at the age of 20 and is commemorated at the Adegem Canadian War Cemetery in Belgium. He was the son of Neil and Barbara McLellan of Winnipegosis, Manitoba. ***McLellan Bay*** (64 F/6) in Wachi Lake was named after him in 1994.

McLeod, Lieutenant **Alan A.** of Stonewall. Royal Air Force, Mentioned in Dispatches, Victoria Cross. He died 6 November 1918 at the age of 19 and is commemorated at Old Kildonan Cemetery in Winnipeg. He was the son of Dr. A. N. and Margaret L. MacLeod (née Arnett) of Winnipeg. According to a newspaper account:

> ... at the age of 18 [he] became the youngest Canadian to receive the prestigious Victoria Cross. At the age of 19, five days before Armistice Day 1918, he died in Winnipeg of influenza. This year, Lieutenant McLeod is honoured again by the naming of a new street at the northwest corner of Stonewall (*The Stonewall Argus/Teulon Times* 10 November 1982).
>
> ... Alan took to soldiering early. At the age of 14, he joined the Fort Garry Horse for their annual summer militia camp and although war broke out a year later, it wasn't until 1917 that he was accepted into the Royal Flying Corps school in Toronto and received his wings.
>
> By November of that year, McLeod had joined the Pilot's Pool at Saint Omer and found himself flying the Armstrong-Whitworth artillery spotter – a very slow plane. Eventually, McLeod teamed up with Lieutenant A. W. Hammond who had already received the Military Cross. When the Germans launched their spring offensive, the RFC put every available aircraft into the air to stem the advance around Bapaume.
>
> On March 27, 1918, McLeod and Hammond were on a bombing mission when they encountered a Fokker triplane which they shot down. The action attracted Lieutenant Hans Kirchstein and in a furious fight, one Fokker damaged McLeod's controls and Kirchstein got in a long volley that wounded both McLeod and Hammond and set the fuel tank ablaze.

McLeod swung the plane in the direction of the British lines as Hammond continued to fire. It became so fiery that McLeod climbed out onto the wing and flew the aircraft. Hammond climbed on the gun ring and shot down another enemy aircraft. Badly burned, McLeod crash-landed near the British lines.

Hammond was trapped in the wreckage and with enemy infantrymen firing at him, Alan McLeod dragged him to the safety of British trenches. Hammond was wounded six times, McLeod five. Hammond received a bar to his Military Cross and after months in hospital, Alan McLeod went to Buckingham Palace where King George V presented him with the Victoria Cross for one of the most amazing exploits in the annals of the Royal Air Force.

When he died November 6, 1918, he received lavish military honours at his funeral and six of his buddies from the newly-formed Royal Air Force carried him to his final resting place in Old Kildonan cemetery (Farmer 1978).

Alan McLeod Lake (63 P/2), northwest of Cotton Lake was named after him in 2001.

McLeod, Pilot Officer **Allister C.** of Balmoral (J 95367). No. 426 Squadron. He died 1 November 1944 at the age of 22 and is commemorated at Venray War Cemetery in Holland. He was the son of William and Mary Elizabeth McLeod of Balmoral, Manitoba and was the brother of Warrant Officer Norman S. McLeod (see entry). In a letter to Allister's childhood friend, Jack Verbrugge, Pilot Officer R. S. Goreham described what happened:

We had bombed our target in Germany and were *en route* home when we really got the works. I cannot say for sure whether we were hit six or seven times and they all came aboard in less than three minutes. The first hit was in our tail section which shot away part of my elevator control so our ship went into a dive. With that hit, the tail gunner, Andy Balfour groaned over his microphone so I felt sure he had been pretty badly hurt. I yelled into my mike to prepare to bail out and then with both feet and hands working on the controls, I managed to get the aircraft straightened out again into level flight. Then we got two or three more hits together, one in the mid-section and another beneath my feet where the wireless operator Jim Weedon was. I am not sure whether this killed Jim or not, but it started a fire that came up the control column and burned my face and neck. This also had knocked out our intercom and my mike went dead. I turned around in my seat and saw the mid-section was on fire too. (The escape hatch is out the bottom of the nose section). I am not too sure, but I think two or three of the boys passed by me through the cockpit to the nose of the plane to the escape hatch – Ed Curtis, Navigator, Al McLeod, Bomb Aimer and our Flight Engineer, the English lad. No sooner had they reached the nose, we took on another hit right below the escape hatch which I believe was now open. From then on I remember very little.

We were on fire and I was holding on to the controls while my face and hands were burning. I was waiting for our Mid-Upper Gunner, Ward Morrison to show up. I remember turning around again and seeing Ward crawling up towards me, he had been hit in the leg when the mid-section had got it. I remember praying he would make it. Seeing him crawling up towards me to get over the main spar is the last thing I remember clearly. I believe we had an explosion at that moment because the next thing I knew, I was falling through space, so I pulled my rip-cord and floated down. All was still when I came to and I began to think how peaceful and quiet things were when just a few seconds before it seemed we were going through hell (17 January 1949).

A young woman with the Resistance saw several airmen exit the aircraft but due to its altitude, there was insufficient time for their parachutes to open.

One fellow with a partially opened chute fell into a field close to where she was hiding. While the German soldiers were busy searching for those whom they had seen falling on the other side of the railroad embankment, she went into the field and found the young airman who had come down near her. She was able to locate him in the darkness for he was badly injured and she could hear him groaning. She released his chute and tried to comfort him as best she could. When the German search party began to spread out and come up on the railroad embankment with their lights, she carried and dragged this young airman into the bush where she continued to comfort him and keep him quiet as the German soldiers were gradually getting closer. They could not talk the same language, but she knew he was a Canadian airman from his shoulder tabs and later described him very well. Jack [Verbrugge] thought this just might be Allister McLeod. The girl reported that the young airman quietly died in her arms (Hornbeck 1979).

Three years later, Jack Verbrugge visited Holland, found the location where his friend's plane had crashed and met the woman who had tried to help him. Her brother told Jack that just that spring he had plowed up a watch near the crash site; on the back was engraved "Allister McLeod R205150." Jack was later invited to have tea with the Dutch Royal Family and Prince Bernhardt dictated a letter of sympathy to Pilot Officer McLeod's parents. ***McLeod Peninsula*** (64 H/4) on Gauer Lake was named after him in 1979.

McLeod, Private **Angus J. A.** of Kinosota (H 41743). Carleton and York Regiment. He died 1 March 1944 and is commemorated at the Moro River Canadian War Cemetery in Italy. ***McLeod Creek*** (63 O/2), which flows southeast into Ferguson Creek was named after him in 1995.

McLeod, Trooper **Donald C.** of Blackdale (H 26571). Fort Garry Horse. He died 6 June 1944 at the age of 24 and is commemorated at Beny-sur-Mer Canadian War Cemetery in Calvados, France. He was the son of Alexander and Wella M. McLeod of Stonewall, Manitoba. He was among the first to set foot on the beach at Normandy. ***McLeod Narrows*** (53 L/5) in Franklin Murray Lake was named after him in 1995.

McLeod, Sergeant **Donald M.** of Belmont (R 95290). No. 172 Squadron. He died 4 March 1943 at the age of 28 and is commemorated at the Runnymede Memorial in Surrey, England. He was the son of John H. and Effie J. McLeod of Belmont, Manitoba. ***Donald McLeod Lake*** (53 N/6), east of Patch Lake was named after him in 1995.

McLeod, Flight Sergeant **Ellis G. "Mac"** of Shoal Lake (R 119526). No. 106 Squadron. He died 28 July 1943 at the age of 19 and is commemorated at the Runnymede Memorial in Surrey, England. He was the son of Albert J. and Mabel L. McLeod (née Brockwell) of Shoal Lake, Manitoba. So eager was he to join the Air Force that at the age of 16, he ordered several copies of his birth certificate to practice altering his date of birth. His sister recalls (5 February 2002):

Ellis graduated from Shoal Lake Collegiate in 1941, age 17 years, enlisted in the RCAF in September and was stationed at Brandon, Saskatoon, Virden and Dauphin where he graduated as a Sergeant Pilot in August, 1942. He went to England in November and was posted to Lancaster bombers. On July 27, 1943, he and 17 planes left Systerton, Nottingham on a bombing mission to Hamburg. They encountered a severe storm over the North Sea and all planes and crew of 119 were lost. It was just his second mission.

Ellis was a very likeable young man. He loved dancing – especially the Jitterbug. On their way home from Dauphin, Ellis was driving. Dad said: "Son slow down, you aren't flying a plane now." He was doing 50 mph; Dad liked about 30 mph.

Ellis McLeod Lake (64 J/13), north of Nicklin Lake was named after him in 1995.

McLeod, Sergeant **Graham A.** of Winnipeg (R 56648). No. 405 Squadron. He died 8 November 1941 at the age of 21 and is commemorated at Becklingen War Cemetery in Germany. He was the son of John and Ida E. McLeod of St. James. His best friend recalls (26 November 1995):

Graham lived on the next street to me and we were in the same grades at school. The day the war broke out, Graham and I hitch-hiked to Selkirk to see some girls we had met at Clear Lake that summer. We told the girls some falsehoods that we were in the Air Force and would be soloing the next day. Little did we realize we would both end up in the Air Force.

Graham joined first and went over first and he was a gunner same as me. He was in 405 Squadron and we always corresponded. I went over in 1942, almost a year after Graham was killed and I was posted to 405 Squadron. So you see our paths always went in the same direction. I was lucky and was shot down and spent two years as a PoW.

Graham McLeod Creek (54 E/3), which flows northwest into Little Churchill River was named after him in 1995.

McLeod, Flying Officer **John C.** of Minnedosa (J 42059). No. 82 Operational Training Unit, RCAF. He died 5 January 1945 at the age of 20 and is commemorated at Brookwood Military Cemetery in Surrey, England. He was the son of Private Albert C. and Maud L. McLeod of Minnedosa, Manitoba. His brother writes (23 June 1994):

When he was in high school, he was very good in Track and Field [and] took part in all summer and winter sports that were available in our town, which were very limited in those years. He joined the RCAF in 1943 and graduated as a pilot in Brantford, Ontario in 1944.

McLeod Hill (63 P/3), east of Sipiwesk Lake was named after him in 1995.

McLeod, Warrant Officer 2 **Norman S.** of Balmoral (R 134200). No. 426 Squadron. He died 3 November 1943 at the age of 22 and is commemorated at Rheinberg War Cemetery in Germany. He was the son of William and Mary Elizabeth McLeod of Balmoral, Manitoba and was the brother of Pilot Officer Allister C. McLeod (see entry). When the youngest brother, Neil, came of age, he too was eager to enlist. His parents explained that they had already lost two sons and were "claiming" the last one. The Air Force "understood" and refused to admit him. Warrant Officer McLeod had been an employee of Swift and Company at the time of his enlistment. ***McLeod Bay*** (64 H/4) on the north shore of Gauer Lake was named after him in 1979.

McLeod, Private **Robert** of Winnipeg (H 6466). Winnipeg Grenadiers. He died a prisoner of war 15 July 1945 and is commemorated at the Yokohama War Cemetery in Japan. Returning Grenadier Private Harry Atkinson reported that:

"One month and 15 days ago seven of the fellows got stomach poisoning. They were in bad shape when they arrived back in camp that night. They were told to report to our [Japanese] commander. He ordered a stomach pump for them. Don't know why, probably saw the end of the war was near." Four of them died – Lance Corporal Malcolm Hawes, Private Jim Gard, Private Roy Kirk and Private Bob McLeod (*Winnipeg Tribune* September 1945).

His sister recalls (30 October 2001):

My brother was a baker by trade, so when he joined the army at age 19, he became a cook. He was sent to Jamaica June 6th, 1940 and returned September 23rd, 1941 and left for Hong Kong October 25th, 1941. On October 17, 1942, my mom received a telegram to say he was a prisoner of war. My mother and aunts went to the Red Cross and packed parcels for the PoWs. An American sailor came to visit my mom. His ship had picked up some radio messages from the PoWs. His message from my brother was August 4, 1944: "Well and happy, but would like to be home." The day the first Grenadier came home to Winnipeg, we got the telegram that Robert had died July 15, 1945. Such a sad time for our family.

McLeod Point (64 B/12), on the west shore of Opachuanau Lake was named after him in 1989.

McLeod, Flight Sergeant **Roderick M.** of Dugald (R 119623). No. 419 Squadron. He died 28 March 1943 at the age of 21 and is commemorated at Escoublac-la-Baule War Cemetery, Loire-Atlantique, France. He was the son of Robert and Mary McLeod (née Corrigal) of Selkirk. His sister writes (30 October 2001):

Rod and I were very close. We grew up together in the thirties and if that won't bond you, nothing will. The last months he was in Canada, he was stationed at Mont Joli, Quebec. I was at Barrie, Ontario where my husband was a soldier in the Tank Corps. He came down every month to see me.

Over the years there has been conflicting information as to what happened and every Remembrance Day I'd be heartsick thinking 'I'm not sure what happened to him.' Our trip over to France in May, 2000 finally brought closure. To meet the people who saw what really happened has made us all feel better – finally knowing.

She refers to the unveiling of a monument in France honouring "liberty heroes" who gave their life during World War II in that country:

Among the names was that of Roderick McLeod, ... brother of the before mentioned McLeod family members, originally from Dugald. The family lived in Ontario when they received the message that Roderick's plane, a Halifax, was shot down in France. For a couple of years, the telegram was repeated "missing in action," until finally, Roderick was "presumed dead." After the war, his grave was found near St. Lazaire.

The unveiling took place May 8, 2000 near the town of Trignac on the grounds of a steel factory where eyewitnesses saw the Halifax come down and recovered the bodies of the crew (five Canadians and two British). "The people of Trignac, St. Lazaire and area treated us with the utmost consideration. Meeting us at the train, arranging for lodging in the best hotel, chauffeuring us and even offering to pay part of our travelling expenses," remembered Mary Seller [a sister]. "Not to mention giving us the place of honour at the unveiling ceremony and providing an interpreter fluent in French and English. We were overwhelmed by their kindness and sensitivity, their empathy with the grief and pain of those who lost loved ones in the fight for France's freedom. It was a memorable trip indeed" (Clemens 2000).

Flight Sergeant McLeod wrote a letter to his sister and her husband the month before he was killed:

Dear Eileen and Bud: Received your two letters, October 5th and December 18th, the day before yesterday. I got 17 letters and actually found out how many people were wishing me a merry Xmas, which was quite unnecessary as I made it quite up to the point. No Johnny Dewars, but a fair substitute was available. Was glad to see the right attitude and starting the festivities a week ahead of schedule. Enough of that guff I imagine. Have you seen Kay lately? She said she was going to look you up but I think I sent her the old address. Her's is 19 Winchester Street, Suite 3, Toronto.

So Bud is thinking of coming over here in the spring? Well if I was him, I'd stay in Canada, but then you can't really appreciate the place till you get over here. Would kind of like to see the old devil over here though. Haven't been doing much except flying and looking over the present crop of debutantes – no hell either I might add. Nothing much to write about that the censor would like, so will close for now. Happy and healthy. Your loving brother, Rod (8 February 1943).

Roderick McLeod Lake (63 N/8), south of Burntwood Lake was named after him in 1996. His youngest brother erected a monument there in 1997.

McLeod, Flying Officer **Roydon H.** of Mather (J 44389). No. 356 Squadron. He died 18 August 1945 at the age of 20 and is commemorated at the Singapore Memorial. He was the son of Glenn H. and Mary J. McLeod of Mather. His brother recalls (31 October 2001):

> Roydon was born November 12, 1924 at Mather, Manitoba, raised on the family farm, attended Mather School and received his Senior Matriculation at Crystal City. He enlisted on his 18th birthday. [He] trained at Brandon and Virden and obtained his RCAF pilot's wings at Brandon. After Calgary and Boundary Bay, he went directly overseas.
>
> He was posted to India where he flew with the RAF and later with the South East Asia Air Force based on Christmas Island. His plane failed to return from a mission dropping supplies to PoW camps.

Roydon McLeod Lake (64 F/9), southwest of Jordan Lake was named after him in 1995.

McLeod, Corporal **Thomas D. G.** of Winnipeg (H 19701). Queen's Own Cameron Highlanders. He died 19 August 1942 at the age of 28 and is commemorated at Brookwood Military Cemetery in Surrey, England. He was the son of Donald and Ida M. McLeod of Winnipeg. ***Thomas McLeod Lake*** (53 L/13), northwest of Oxford Lake was named after him in 1995.

McLeod, Corporal **William** of Minnewakan (H 204543). Canadian Scottish Regiment. He died 15 August 1944 at the age of 24 and is commemorated at Bretteville-sur-Laize Canadian War Cemetery in Calvados, France. He was the son of Frederick and Mary E. McLeod and was survived by his wife Lucy J. McLeod of Lundar, Manitoba. ***William McLeod Island*** (53 L/8) in Gods Lake was named after him in 1995.

McMahon, Private **Edward E.** of Winnipeg (H 19206). Queen's Own Cameron Highlanders. He died 19 August 1942 at the age of 20 and is commemorated at Brookwood Military Cemetery in Surrey, England. He was the son of Alfred L. and Audrey M. McMahon of Winnipeg. ***McMahon Lake*** (63 I/7), north of Molson Lake was named after him in 1973.

McManus, Lieutenant **William W.** of Winnipeg. Queen's Own Cameron Highlanders. He died 19 August 1942 at the age of 25 and is commemorated at Brookwood Military Cemetery in Surrey, England. He was the son of Edward E. and Faustina McManus of Memramcook, New Brunswick. ***McManus Lake*** (64 K/5), northeast of Reindeer Lake was named after him in 1972.

McMillan, Flying Officer **Colin William** of Winnipeg (J 35127). No. 432 Squadron. He died 21 February 1945 at the age of 27 and is commemorated at Rheinberg War Cemetery in Germany. This native of California was survived by his parents Colin W. and Margaret H. McMillan. His family had been in Manitoba working on the construction of the Hudson's Bay Railway when he enlisted. ***McMillan Point*** (53 L/15) on Knee Lake was named after him in 1995.

McMillan, Warrant Officer 2 **John A.** of Winnipeg (R 100424). No. 411 Squadron. He died 21 January 1943 at the age of 22 and is commemorated at Scopwick Church Burial Ground in Lincolnshire, England.

> … his Spitfire aircraft No. AA754 collided with a Lysander aircraft and crashed in the sea 100 yards off shore two miles south of Skegness, Lincolnshire. [He] had been slightly injured on October 27, 1942 when he landed his No. 411 Squadron Spitfire aircraft with the wheels retracted (Allison and Hayward 1991).

His eldest brother recalls (22 November 2001):

> I can only say that John Alexander, known as Jack, was the best athlete of the four brothers including myself in the RCAF. I do know he was a fine running back for the Gordon Bell High School football team before joining the RCAF.

McMillan Island (63 N/7) in Guthrie Lake was named after him in 1995.

McMillan, Flight Lieutenant **Lawrence "Lorne"** of Miami (J 10231). No. 400 Squadron, Distinguished Flying Cross, Air Medal (USA).

> An exceptional pilot, this officer has participated in many successful sorties. He has always displayed the greatest determination to achieve his objective and a complete disregard of enemy opposition. On one occasion, during a heavy bombing raid on Essen, he experienced heavy and concentrated anti-aircraft fire before reaching the target. Nevertheless he secured some excellent photographs which were obtained during 200 minutes flying over the area (DFC Citation 1948).

He died 9 May 1945 at the age of 23 and is commemorated at the Runnymede Memorial in Surrey, England. He was the son of Frederick and Mary A. McMillan of Miami, Manitoba. According to his daughter-in-law he:

> … was a photo reconnaissance pilot in Spitfires. He was decorated in 1943 with the Distinguished Flying Cross and the American Air Medal for his work in photographing the damage following a large American daylight raid. Then he came back to Canada, then asked to return to active duty with the Toronto Squadron in northern Germany near the end of the war in Europe.
>
> The day after the war ended, May 9, 1945, he was shot down by a German boat. This boat had been attacked earlier in the day by a Russian plane as it was returning to port. Lorne was sent out to identify the ship and the Germans on board opened fire and shot him down. When his parents received the sad news, they wired my husband, also a pilot stationed near Cambrai, France.
>
> My husband Max was given permission to fly to Germany to find out the unusual circumstances surrounding Lorne's death. Lorne's parents never got to see the lake named after their son, but last summer my husband and I along with our friends Jim and Jean Murray decided to make the journey. I had brought along a small, covered cup. The pilot was kind enough to climb down on the pontoon and dip up some water into it. The four of us each drank a toast to Lorne from the cup, and you can imagine there were lumps in our throats as we did so.
>
> The rest of the water from the lake I brought home and divided it into three small containers which I gave to our own two sons, Lorne and Grant and daughter Lee. We feel very proud of Lorne McMillan and appreciate that such a wonderful way was found to acknowledge his contribution to Canada (in Telpner 1979b).

McMillan Lake (64 C/13), east of Reindeer Lake was named after him in 1947.

McMillan, Sapper **William D.** of Winnipeg (D 17025). Royal Canadian Engineers. He died 8 October 1940 at the age of 21 and is commemorated at Brookside Cemetery in Winnipeg. He was survived by his mother Dorothy McMillan of Winnipeg. ***McMillan Bay*** (64 A/4) in Rock Lake was named after him in 1995.

McMullin, Private **Walter G.** of Winnipeg (H 601390). Royal Canadian Infantry Corps. He died 29 July 1942 at the age of 22 and is commemorated at Brookside Cemetery in Winnipeg. He was the son of Hugh and Mary McMullin of Winnipeg. ***McMullin Lake*** (53 K/12), east of Gods Lake was named after him in 1997.

McMurachy, Private **A. S. David** of McConnell (H 100448). South Saskatchewan Regiment. He died 29 August 1944 at the age of 21 and is commemorated at Bretteville-sur-Laize Canadian War Cemetery in Calvados, France. He was the son of Joseph and Jennie McMurachy of McConnell, Manitoba. ***McMurachy Lake*** (52 L/11), west of Flintstone Lake was named after him in 1982.

McMurachy, Flight Sergeant **William D.** of Elphinstone (R 116366). No. 101 Squadron. He died 13 June 1943 at the age of 22 and is commemorated at the Runnymede Memorial in Surrey, England. He was the son of William J. and Anna C. McMurachy of Elphinstone, Manitoba. ***McMurachy Island*** (54 M/5) in the Caribou River was named after him in 1984.

McMurchy, Flight Sergeant **Kenneth C.** of Reston (R 253156). No. 424 Squadron. He was declared lost 15 February 1945 at the age of 21 and is commemorated at the Runnymede Memorial in Surrey, England. He had been on a mine laying operation in the Pomeranian area of Germany. ***McMurchy Lake*** (64 P/7), southeast of Nejanilini Lake was named after him in 1974.

McMurdy, Wing Commander **Gordon A.** of Winnipeg (J 4534). No. 419 Squadron. He died 22 October 1943 at the age of 25 and is commemorated at the Hanover War Cemetery in Germany. He had been appointed commanding officer of the squadron only 11 days earlier. He was the son of Archibald and Henrietta McMurdy of St. Vital. ***McMurdy Lake*** (64 F/6), west of Wells Lake was named after him in 1994.

McMurray, Sergeant **Gerald H.** of Winnipeg (R 95428). No. 2 Training Command, RCAF. He died 25 October 1941 at the age of 34 and is commemorated at Sunnyside Cemetery in Oakbank, Manitoba. He was the son of Thomas H. and Maria McMurray of St. Vital and was survived by his wife Helen McMurray of Winnipeg. ***McMurray Lake*** (52 M/12), southwest of Family Lake was named after him in 1980.

McMurtry, Sergeant **Allan F. "Bud"** of Winnipeg (R 250838). No. 1664 Heavy Conversion Unit, RCAF. He died 12 December 1944 at the age of 22 and is commemorated at Blacon Cemetery in Cheshire, England. He was the son of Clarence and Vera McMurtry of Winnipeg. ***McMurtry Lake*** (63 K/13), north of Kisseynew Lake was named after him in 1989.

McNab, Private **John** of St. Boniface (H 17341). Royal Canadian Ordnance Corps. He died 3 April 1944 at the age of 24 and is commemorated at Brookwood Military Cemetery in Surrey, England. He was the son of John and Amanda McNab and was survived by his wife Lucy M. McNab of St. Vital. ***McNab Bay*** (64 N/10) in Graves Lake was named after him in 1995.

McNabb, Flight Sergeant **Arthur Clark** of Minnedosa (R 116358). No. 407 Squadron. He died 31 May 1943 at the age of 24 and is commemorated at the Runnymede Memorial in Surrey, England. He was the eldest son of John Arthur and Margaret A. McNabb (née Thompson) of Minnedosa. He had hoped to return to Manitoba to complete his degree in agriculture, but failed to return from anti-submarine patrol in the Bay of Biscay. ***McNabb Island*** (53 M/5) in Atik Lake was named after him in 1985.

McNeil, Pilot Officer **William Y.** of Winnipeg (J 19838). No. 179 Squadron. He died 17 January 1944 and is commemorated at the Malta Memorial. His aircraft failed to return from an anti-submarine patrol off the coast of Gibraltar (Allison and Hayward 1991). ***McNeil Island*** (63 N/10) in the Churchill River was named after him in 1995.

McNeill, Able Seaman **Bernard J.** of Brandon (V 15283). HMCS *Valleyfield*. The *Valleyfield* was torpedoed and sunk by U-548 50 miles south of Cape Race, Newfoundland; 125 of her ship's company were lost. Able Seaman McNeill died 7 May 1944 at the age of 18 and is commemorated at the Halifax Memorial. He was the son of Hugh A. and Angela M. McNeill of Brandon. His sister recalls (24 October 2001):

> My older brother Bernie was the middle of seven children. His teenage photos indicate that he was a happy, fun-loving boy. He loved hockey and was a defenceman for the Brandon Elks Juvenile team. He must have been adventurous, as he joined the RCN at age 16 by falsifying his birth certificate. He was eleven days short of his 19th birthday when the *Valleyfield* was sunk. I recall our family's sadness when the "missing in action" telegram arrived at our home and during the following days of faint hope that Bernie would be found among the survivors. His last leave home was in 1943.

McNeill Lake (63 O/3), west of Setting Lake was named after him in 1967.

McNevin, Lance Bombardier **Earl D.** of Swan River (H 67282). Royal Canadian Engineers. He died 24 May 1944 at the age of 22 and is commemorated at the Cassino War Cemetery in Italy. He was the eldest of the five children of Milford A. and Beatrice K. McNevin of Swan River. His sister writes (26 October 2001):

> In 1965, his sister Marj visited Cassino and found it hard to describe the awe and serenity as she looked down on the cemetery from the rebuilt monastery on the hill that dominates the area. She was very impressed with the well-tended grave sites and the manicured lawns of the cemetery. His sisters recall their mother telling them that:
>
> As a boy growing up in Winnipegosis, Earl loved his dog "Sport" and how excited and proud he was to win the 1st Annual Dog Derby. Before enlisting in 1941, he worked at Watts Motors in Swan River. He trained at Shilo and Petawawa before going overseas in 1942. He arrived in Italy in 1943 and was a staff car driver while learning to be a mechanic. Letters from superior officers to his Mother after his death emphasized his gentleness and respectfulness.

McNevin Lake (62 N/15), southeast of Swan River was named after him in 1973.

McNicol, Sapper **Francis B.** of Cranberry Portage (H 20517). Royal Canadian Engineers. He died 10 July 1942 at the age of 32 and is commemorated at Brookwood Military Cemetery in Surrey, England. His nephew writes (14 February 1997):

> [He] was born ... in The Pas, Manitoba [and] attended the Catholic School in Otterburne, 35 miles south of Winnipeg from the age of 10 in 1929 until the age of 15 in 1934. When he returned to the North he worked with his father and brothers commercial fishing on Naosap Lake, 25 miles north of Cranberry Portage. Every winter before freeze-up, the boys and their father Frederick went out to their winter fishing camp and for five months, spent the days setting nets under the ice. In the evenings, the frozen fish were packed in snow and once a week were driven by horse five miles to the tracks and loaded onto a train to The Pas. This routine continued all winter until March, before break-up, when they returned home to Cranberry Portage.

Frank loved the north and enjoyed playing guitar for his friends and fishing for pleasure in the summer months. Frank enlisted in early July, 1940 and joined the army at Fort Osborne Barracks. [He] served at Aldershot, England. He died ... while instructing troops on the grenade range at Cove, England. At the time of his death, Frank had a brother James in Cove Camp and a brother Cecil in the Engineers, stationed in Chilliwack and later overseas.

McNicol Lake (64 H/16), southwest of Condie Lake was named after him in 1995.

McPhail, Private **Walter C.** of Selkirk (H 800030). Princess Patricia's Canadian Light Infantry. He died 19 March 1951 and is commemorated at the United Nations Cemetery in Pusan, South Korea. He was survived by his wife Lovina McPhail of Selkirk and their son. ***McPhail Island*** (53 E/16) in Island Lake was named after this Korean War casualty in 1998.

McPhail, Flight Lieutenant **William H. "Mac"** of Cromarty, Ontario (J 21326). No. 409 Squadron. He died 13 January 1945 at the age of 25 and is commemorated at the Adegem Canadian War Cemetery in Belgium. He was the son of Hector and Ada McPhail of Cromarty. Flight Lieutenant McPhail's "wingman" wrote a letter to his nephew many years later:

Dear Mr. Hocking: I believe I was the last person to see and talk with Mac just prior to his unfortunate accident. We were on duty the night of January 12/13 in Lille-Vendeville (the city of Lille in France). The weather on this night had deteriorated so badly that the flight was "stood down." However, two crews were designated to stand by for an emergency. This was Mac and myself with our navigators. We happily "hit the sack" believing we had it made for the night. Approximately three or four in the morning, the phone rang and the operational people advised there were "bogies" approaching Brussels and asked if we would take off. We looked at each other and Mac said "lets go!" We were airborne about 15 minutes later into extremely bad weather and were climbing out when operations advised the "bogies" had turned back and we could return to base.

Now we had a problem. There was approximately 8 to 12 inches of snow on the ground, although the runways were clear. After some difficulty, I finally was able to land. Knowing the difficulties Mac would encounter, I went up to the Control Tower to advise the conditions I had encountered. We had people on the runway to advise the tower and give assistance. I believe Mac made a couple of passes and then the ground crew advised he had overshot the runway. We immediately obtained a vehicle and drove down the runway and off the airport. The weather at this time had really deteriorated with blowing snow and fog. By this time, dawn was breaking and we were returning to the airport, we saw Mac's aircraft off to the side of the runway in an inverted position with a group of people and rescue vehicles present. It would appear that Mac had landed in the snow and this resulted in the aircraft being flipped over.

Mac was an exceptional pilot and this accident cannot detract from his ability. As I noted at the time "there but for the Grace of God go I." It was my privilege to serve with Mac and this night has always been in my thoughts. This is the first time I have put these thoughts into writing and I hope it will give your family a better understanding of his death.

The decision to go out that night was Mac's and I know he does not regret the decision. Perhaps you will find some peace in the knowledge that Mac was a brave and dedicated pilot. Sincerely, Lloyd M. Jones (10 July 1993).

See also the entry for **Donoghue,** Flight Lieutenant **James Edward.** ***McPhail Lake*** (53 F/12), south of Hilton Lake in northwestern Ontario was named after him in 1995. McPhail Lake was named in conjunction with nearby Donoghue Lake (in Manitoba) as Flight Lieutenants Donoghue and McPhail were close friends who died in the same Mosquito aircraft.

McPherson, Stoker 1 **Harold G.** of Winnipeg (V 24554). HMS *Algerine*. He died 17 November 1942 at the age of 21 and is commemorated at La Reunion War Cemetery in Algeria. He was the son of George and Bella McPherson of Winnipeg. ***McPherson Lake*** (64 G/6), southeast of Big Sand Lake was named after him in 1963.

McPherson, Sergeant **John R.** of Winnipeg (R 101638). No. 113 Squadron. He died 1 June 1942 at the age of 25 and is commemorated at the Ottawa Memorial. He was the son of Mr. and Mrs. Peter McPherson of Winnipeg and was survived by his wife Maeve McPherson (née Renahan). He had been on submarine patrol off the east coast of Canada when his aircraft was reported missing. He had been employed by the Inter-Ocean Grain Company at the time of his enlistment. ***McPherson Point*** (64 N/11) on Kasmere Lake was named after him in 1995.

McPherson, Pilot Officer **Murray L.** of Myrtle (J 89285). No. 626 Squadron. He died 25 April 1944 at the age of 22 and is commemorated at Brookwood Military Cemetery in Surrey, England. He was the son of Donald G. and Annie M. McPherson (née Langtry) and was survived by his sister Alma Mary of Myrtle, Manitoba. She recalls (24 May 1995):

Murray grew up on a farm at Myrtle [and] received his education at Myrtle Consolidated School. He liked to play baseball [and] played the piano by ear. He was a fine young man. He joined the RCAF in December, 1941. He loved flying. [He] lost his life on a return trip from a bombing mission over Germany [and] is buried along with his crew. [He] was promoted posthumously to the rank of Pilot Officer.

McPherson Bay (63 P/15) in Goose Hunting Lake was named after him in 1995.

McPherson, Rifleman **Rudolph** (H 10836). Royal Winnipeg Rifles. He died 27 September 1944 and is commemorated at the Calais Canadian War Cemetery, Leubringhen, France. ***McPherson Peninsula*** (64 O/14) on Nueltin Lake was named after him in 1995.

McPherson, Flying Officer **William H.** of St. Vital (J 22449). No. 434 Squadron. He died 15 February 1944 at the age of 22 and is commemorated at the Runnymede Memorial in Surrey, England. He was the son of George B. and Margaret M. McPherson of St. Vital and was survived by his wife Marguerite McPherson. ***McPherson Island*** (64 C/10) in Willis Lake was named after him in 1995.

McQueen, Lieutenant **Lewis J.** of St. James. Royal Winnipeg Rifles, Mentioned in Dispatches. He died 8 June 1944 on his 24th birthday and is commemorated at Beny-sur-Mer Canadian War Cemetery in Calvados, France. He was the second son of Heber L. and Gladys M. McQueen and was survived by his wife Iona E. McQueen of Winnipeg. According to his brother, "Lew" was born in Pullman, Washington in 1920, shortly before the family returned to Winnipeg:

Upon leaving school he worked for Schumacher-MacKenzie Limited, electrical contractors at 334 Main Street, Winnipeg. [He] joined the Royal Winnipeg Rifles in June, 1940. By early 1941, he had risen to the rank of Sergeant. While in England, he was recommended for a commission and was accepted. He returned to Canada and got his commission early in 1943. He was promoted to Lieutenant and served as a platoon commander at Shilo, Manitoba.

Lew returned to England to a holding unit. Several weeks before D-Day, he returned to the Royal Winnipeg Rifles. He was made platoon commander of 13 Platoon, "C" Company. Lew went in with his platoon with the first wave on D-Day. His platoon was attached to "B" Company for the landing.

Lew was killed in action … at Putot-en-Bessin. He was later found on the south side of the Caen - Bayeux railway. He, along with many others of the Royal Winnipeg Rifles, paid the supreme sacrifice this day (n.d.).

His brother found his grave 16 days later. ***McQueen Lake*** (54 K/12), southeast of Churchill was named after him in 1948. His brother erected a plaque there in 1988.

McRae, Gunner **Alexander** of Kelwood (L 350). Royal Canadian Artillery. He died 26 December 1944 at the age of 45 and is commemorated at Argenta Gap War Cemetery, Italy. He was the son of John and Isabella McRae of Kelwood, Manitoba. His sister-in-law recalls (26 February 1997):

I never had the pleasure of meeting my brother-in-law Alex, but by all reports he was a fine man. His parents and four of the oldest children immigrated from Scotland ... in 1905. I believe he was about two years old. He got his schooling in Plumas and Tenby, Manitoba. He worked as a lighthouse and buoy keeper along the BC coast on the ship *Newington* from Victoria to Prince Rupert until he enlisted. His father was a sailor in Scotland and ended up working with Alex tending and repairing lighthouses. He was accidentally killed while on active service in Italy.

Gunner McRae's mother received a letter from her son's commanding officer:

Dear Mrs. McRae: I wish to express to you my deep sympathy in the death of your son, Gunner Alex McRae. He was my personal orderly for the past two years so we knew each other very well. Alex was an uncommon soldier in that he was so friendly with everyone. Everyone knew him and everyone liked him. Not many people will pass away and leave fewer enemies than your son.

The night before he was killed was Christmas night. It is our custom for the officers and sergeants to give the boys their yearly treat and serve them their Christmas dinner. It was a jolly party with turkey and plum pudding and all the trimmings. There were only about 20 of us altogether in our little group. Everyone was in great spirits and no one appeared to enjoy it more than your son.

The next morning, shortly after breakfast, your son was helping one of the other boys to pack his kit as this other chap was going away for a few days. He picked up his gun and noticed that it was loaded. In trying to unload it, the gun accidentally went off and the bullet penetrated his abdomen. A doctor and ambulance were close by and came very quickly. His internal injuries were beyond medical aid, however, and he died in hospital a little more than two hours later.

His death was an awful shock to all of us and we feel we know in some measure the sorrow and grief that his death is causing you. On behalf of his many friends and especially the little group of 20 who were with him the night before, I offer you our deepest sympathy.

He was buried the next day in the little Canadian graveyard near Ravenna. About 15 of us attended the simple United Church service conducted by Captain Cowans, the United Church padre at the hospital. Some of the boys have taken pictures of his grave and we will send some to you when they are developed.

May your pride in knowing that your son was a good soldier and a grand comrade lessen your grief. Personally, I miss him very much as do all of us. Very sincerely, R. H. Wallace, Major (30 December 1944).

McRae Lake (63 J/9), west of Cross Lake was named after him in 1981.

McRae, Flight Sergeant **Christopher F. "Bud"** of Grande Pointe (R 147326). No. 75 Squadron. He died 23 September 1943 at the age of 26 and is commemorated at Rheinberg War Cemetery in Germany. He was the son of Christopher A. and Myrtle M. McRae of Grande Pointe, Manitoba and the brother of Flight Lieutenant William Gordon McRae (see entry). ***McRae Bay*** (64 O/10) in Askey Lake was named after him in 1995.

McRae, Engine Room Artificer 4 **Harry S.** of Souris (V 9884). HMS *Jervis Bay*. He was listed as "missing, presumably killed" on 5 November 1940 and is commemorated at the Halifax Memorial. The *Jervis Bay* was a converted passenger ship which was accompanying a convoy (HX.84) of 37 freighters from Halifax to Britain. The convoy was spotted by the captain of the German pocket battleship the *Admiral Scheer* which attacked immediately. The convoy scattered and the *Jervis Bay* engaged the *Admiral Scheer* for 24 minutes before the order to abandon ship was issued. This action was credited with saving 32 of the convoy ships. ERA McRae was 45 years of age and is commemorated at the Halifax Memorial. He was the son of William and Mary McRae and was survived by his wife Dorothy W. McRae (née Young) of Winnipeg and their three children. His daughter writes (27 March 1989):

Harry Smith McRae was born at Banff, Scotland. Soon after, he immigrated to Canada in 1905. He obtained his first class Power Engineer Certificate and spent most of his life working in Winnipeg. Harry joined the Royal Canadian Navy Volunteer Reserve as an ERA in June, 1940.

McRae Point (64 P/15), on the northwest shore of Arksey Lake was named after him in 1989.

McRae, Captain **Hugh S.** of Winnipeg. Queen's Own Rifles of Canada. He died 30 April 1943 at the age of 28 and is commemorated at Brookwood Military Cemetery in Surrey, England. He was the son of Hugh A. and Jessie E. McRae of Winnipeg. ***McRae Peninsula*** (53 E/13) on Stevenson Lake was named after him in 1996.

McRae, Gunner **John Alan** of Winnipeg (H 35696). Royal Canadian Artillery. He died 29 November 1944 at the age of 34 and is commemorated at the Groesbeek Canadian War Cemetery in Holland. He was the son of John A. and Minnie McRae (née Moore). His niece recalls (7 April 1995):

Alan was born in Morden, Manitoba in 1910 to a Scottish pioneer father and an English mother. He had one sister and a brother. His brother Charles served at Dieppe and Normandy. His early years were spent in Clandeboye, Manitoba. Prior to enlisting, he worked as a sign painter. Alan was talented in numerous artistic pursuits, an avid landscape artist and violinist.

McRae Island (64 C/12) in Laurie Lake was named after him in 1995.

McRae, Flying Officer **Lynds F.** of The Pas (J 7088). No. 102 Squadron. He died 5 October 1942 at the age of 20 and is commemorated at Brussels Town Cemetery in Belgium. He was the son of Lynds F. and Blanche A. McRae of New Westminster, British Columbia. ***McRae Hill*** (64 N/10), southwest of Sucker Lake was named after him in 1997.

McRae, Flight Lieutenant **William Gordon** of Grande Pointe (J 6834). No. 354 Squadron. He died 26 March 1945 at the age of 29 and is commemorated at the Singapore Memorial. He was one of the two sons and five daughters of Christopher A. and Margaret McRae and was survived by his wife Dulce E. McRae (née Gates) of Hamilton, Ontario and their one year-old son. His wife subsequently received a letter from his Commanding Officer who characterized the mission as "a great operational success:"

The aircraft fell into the Andaman Sea and exploded approximately 188 miles east of Little Andaman Island after being hit by enemy anti-aircraft fire while attacking enemy shipping. The Andaman Sea is part of the Bay of Bengal (n.d.).

Two of the crew escaped through the tail section before the aircraft exploded. McRae's tail gunner wrote:

Gordon McRae was one of the few real men that I had the good fortune to know. In his role as a British Officer, he was able to uphold a tradition and manner which made him a beacon. Never did he falter. He maintained his policy of good leadership by excellent example – more than often I had seen that trait in its dynamic action. Gordon fought with us and whenever the hour came, he fought for us with a val[our] which won him more than our mere respect (n.d.).

His wife adds (26 March 1998):

As a young widow with an infant son, the loss was heartbreaking; Gordon and I had made great plans for the future. After he went overseas, we wrote each other every day and letters used to arrive in bunches. The last entry in his diary – sent back to me from India – indicated he had received seven letters from me the day before the fateful flight.

The brother of Flight Sergeant Christopher F. McRae (see entry), he had hoped to attain a university degree in Business Administration after the war. ***McRae Rapids*** (64 P/10) in Adam Creek was named after him in 1995.

McTaggart, Corporal **Hugh P.** of Rathwell (H 6279). Winnipeg Grenadiers. He died a prisoner of war 5 December 1943 at the age of 29 and is commemorated at the Yokohama War Cemetery in Japan. He was the son of William and Elizabeth McTaggart of Rathwell, Manitoba. His sister recalls (22 October 2001):

He was the youngest of a family of eight. Hugh was born on October 30, 1914 at Starbuck where he lived until 1921. He then moved with his family to Rathwell where he was educated in a one-room school in the Cherry Valley district. After receiving his education, he worked as a farm hand in the area until he moved with his parents to the Hood district, half way between Rathwell and Portage la Prairie. There he farmed with his Father until September, 1939 when he enlisted with the Winnipeg Grenadiers, training in Winnipeg and Jamaica. Prior to leaving for Hong Kong, he was on leave and gave a white leather change purse to my daughter with five nickels which she still has.

McTaggart Lake (64 K/14), northeast of Reindeer Lake was named after him in 1972.

McTavish, Trooper **Donald J.** of Rapid City (H 103976). Lord Strathcona's Horse. He died 24 September 1944 at the age of 31 and is commemorated at Cesena War Cemetery in Italy. He was the son of Henry J. and Lillian M. McTavish of Rapid City, Manitoba. His niece writes (23 October 2001):

Don was born in Winnipeg July 25, 1913, travelled to Saskatchewan with his family and finally settled in [the] Rapid City area to farm. Don and a cousin, Ernie Ady met two hours before Don was killed. They planned to meet on their next leave but it was not to be. He was killed September 24, 1944 when his Algonquin II tank was blown up.

McTavish Bay (64 O/13) in Nueltin Lake was named after him in 1995.

McTavish, Lance Corporal **Stanley E.** of Solsgirth (H 3927). Stormont, Dundas and Glengarry Highlanders. He died 18 July 1944 at the age of 23 and is commemorated at Beny-sur-Mer Canadian War Cemetery in Calvados, France. He was the son of John E. and Ethel M. McTavish, of Solsgirth, Manitoba. ***McTavish Island*** (64 C/8) in Granville Lake was named after him in 1995.

McWhirter, Major **Samuel J.** of West Kildonan. Royal Canadian Artillery, Distinguished Service Order and the Canadian Efficiency Decoration. He died 9 February 1945 at the age of 36 and is commemorated at the Groesbeek Canadian War Cemetery in Holland. His sister visited his grave in 1995. This native of Belfast, Ireland was the younger son of Robert W. and Evelyn McWhirter (née Jones) and was survived by his wife M. M. McWhirter. The Padre wrote to his wife:

Dear Mrs. McWhirter: When I joined the regiment at Waldeshire Park in England, I promised your husband to write you at some time. It was to be a nice, friendly letter and I really intended to do so when I had the time. But I never, ever expected I would have to write to you like this and when I think back to the many times he sat writing beside me, it is hard to believe that he will not still be making a casual entrance into the Command Post.

I lost a twin brother in the Air Force a few years ago and not since then have I felt the sense of personal bereavement as in the loss of our beloved 2 IC. One is reluctant to form friendships over here, for if the break does come, one feels that much worse. But he had come through so much, facing without the flicker of an eyelash the heaviest fighting that had brought us so far. His courage became a bye-word in the division and his daring was known throughout the Canadian Army.

Yet it was not just that, great though the respect we had for him was. He was a soldier and a gentleman. Quietly devout in his life, uproarious in the Mess (where he provoked more arguments than everyone else combined) and fearlessly intrepid in action, he has been responsible for much of the efficiency and high morale of this splendid regiment. We all felt the same. He was our most tried warrior and had come through so much unscathed that we regarded him as indestructible. While he was in action he was on his mettle. In the mad dash across France he was in his element. I doubt if another jeep in the Canadian Army covered so much ground, did so much exploring, "discovered" so many chickens, and chased the Germans with such enthusiastic and close effect.

In the Breskens operation, while he was at Brigade as CO, we did not see so much of him and missed him accordingly. But in our three months by the Reichswald Forest, with a fine Mess and our best European accommodation and the 2 IC in charge of mixing drinks for several parties, we enjoyed his company to the full.

I was away in Brussels when the recent attack started. But already he was scenting battle and impatient to be off. For the long period of comparative inaction was irksome to him. He had been looking forward keenly to his leave in England which he appeared to greatly enjoy. But one could see that it was his great wish to get the war over and come home. Younger officers would be teasingly reminded that the Burma campaign would not be for veterans like him.

It may just have been that we got to know him better, but he spoke a lot of home lately and it was a pleasure to see the joy that your letters brought him. I think the happiness he received from you had much to do with the unshakeable courage with which he strengthened us all.

I got back on the Friday afternoon to see a greatly changed scene. Fields packed with guns, and heavy firing, and word on every side that the offensive was going well. The sun had broken through the clouds and the watery landscape was flooded with its welcome light.

The first thing I heard on my return was that Major McWhirter had been killed at the OP an hour or so before. He had gone up in the afternoon in excellent spirits to the hottest part of the front, telling his batman to have the water hot for a tub when he got back at 4 o'clock. The OP was a small one, with room for only two men, and as he went up with the Brigadier, he went out to lie beside the signaller, to one side of the OP. It was an old OP, and had been sniped at steadily but without effect, since the snipers could not fire down into it. Just as he lifted his head to look through his glasses, a sniper's bullet struck him at the side of the neck, just in the most vital spot, killing him instantly. They brought him out that afternoon and when I saw him, I couldn't believe at first that he wasn't still alive. His fine, dark eyes were unclouded, and with his jacket and famed necker-chief he looked just like himself.

The next morning was cold and wet. But in spite of that, there was one of the largest groups of his friends around that I have seen at any such occasion at which I have been present. He was buried as a Christian and a soldier in the second division cemetery between Nijmegen and Malden, beside one of the junior officers who had been killed on the same afternoon. A picture of his grave will be sent to you as soon as possible. The cemetery is on the side of a hill. He was buried in his complete fighting clothes, including the jacket in which he took such pride, and lay in state beneath the flag he served so well.

We have seen enough over here to know that this war is bigger than any of us. The sacrifice made by so many splendid men cannot be in vain. We know that "in Christ there is no death." For value such as contained in him cannot be destroyed. And in that spirit you will find his presence with you still. For you must know in your heart that love does not die. May God specially bless you at this time with the comfort and consolation of His near Presence. May He give you the courage and strength to carry on, as Sam would have you do. And may He help those of us who remain to see to it that his sacrifice may not have been made in vain. For he has earned the highest commendation – "Greater love hath no man than this ..." Yours very sincerely, John Fife, Padre (3 March 1945).

He had been employed at United Grain Growers when he enlisted. ***McWhirter Lake*** (64 C/12), southwest of Lynn Lake was named after him in 1951.

Meades, Private **Raymond A.** of La Rivière (H 6540). Winnipeg Grenadiers. He died 21 December 1941 and is commemorated at the Sai Wan Memorial in Hong Kong. ***Meades Lake*** (64 I/16), northeast of Shethanei Lake was named after him in 1957.

Meakin, Lance Corporal **Frank V.** of Birnie (H 95615). Royal Winnipeg Rifles. He died 8 June 1944 at the age of 20 and is commemorated at Beny-sur-Mer Canadian War Cemetery in Calvados, France. He was the son of John and Jennie Meakin of Birnie, Manitoba and the brother of Corporal George E. Meakin (next entry). Both he and his brother were taken prisoner shortly after D-Day and "executed" while prisoners of war. His nephew writes (20 May 1997) that he:

... was born in McConnell, located in the Municipality of Hamiota. He had four sisters [and] three brothers. He joined the Canadian Army at Winnipeg February 25, 1942 and took his training at Winnipeg, Brandon and Shilo and at Debert, Nova Scotia. As a member of the Royal Winnipeg Rifles, he embarked for the United Kingdom ... July 19, 1942, landing on Juno Beach (Courseilles-sur-Mer) with the Royal Winnipeg Rifles of the 3rd Canadian Infantry Division June 6, 1944 (D-Day). He was with that regiment when they liberated Graye-sur-Mer and later on Creully. On June 8, the Second Battalion German SS commanded by Oberst Bernhardt Siebkin attacked the Royal Winnipeg Rifles position at Putot-en-Bessin. [The] Company was surrounded and 24 RWRs and their commander, Major Fred Hodge were captured. Included in this group was Lance Corporal Frank Vernon Meakin and his brother Corporal George Edward Meakin. The prisoners were turned over to the 12th SS Recce Battalion, taken to their headquarters at the Chateau d'Audrieu, interrogated and subsequently, in small groups, taken into the woods behind the chateau and deliberately gunned down.

Meakin Lake (63 K/16), northwest of Wekusko Lake was named after him in 1973.

Meakin, Corporal **George E.** of Birnie (H 40752). Royal Winnipeg Rifles. He died 8 June 1944 at the age of 23 and is commemorated at Beny-sur-Mer Canadian War Cemetery in Calvados, France. He was the son of John and Jennie Meakin of Birnie, Manitoba and the brother of Lance Corporal Frank V. Meakin (see previous entry). Both he and his brother were taken prisoner shortly after D-Day and "executed" while prisoners of war.

It has been suggested the wounds on George's body indicated he might have jumped in front of his brother Frank to prevent him from being shot. In his final letter to his mother and sister (24 May 1944) he wrote: "This may be the last chance I get to write before the big day, so if you don't hear from me for a while don't worry. We will be OK and no matter what happens, I can always say I have the grandest mother and sister that anyone has, so keep on smiling and everything will turn out for the best" (Pittman n.d.).

Meakin Island (64 B/5) in Pemichigamau Lake was named after him in 1995.

Melnychenko, Private **Walter** of Shortdale (H 617137). Canadian Provost Corps. He died 19 September 1945 at the age of 25 and is commemorated at the Groesbeek Canadian War Cemetery in Holland. He was the son of Nick and Mary Melnychenko of Shortdale, Manitoba. ***Melnychenko Lake*** (64 F/6), north of Wells Lake was named after him in 1994.

Mencini, Private **Louis D.** of Winnipeg (H 16705). Princess Patricia's Canadian Light Infantry. He died 20 September 1944 at the age of 31 and is commemorated at Coriano Ridge War Cemetery in Italy. He was the son of Dominico and Josephine Mencini (née Deloli). ***Mencini Lake*** (64 K/10), east of Lac Brochet was named after him in 1972.

Mennell, Able Seaman **William Reginald** of Winnipeg (4469). HMCS *Wentworth*. He died 4 January 1944 at the age of 19 and is commemorated at the Halifax Memorial. He was the son of Edwin R. and Marjorie Mennell of Winnipeg. ***Mennell Lake*** (64 N/13), west of Nueltin Lake was named after him in 1972.

Mennie, Sergeant **William** of Reston (K 112). British Columbia Dragoons. He died 1 June 1945 at the age of 29 and is commemorated at the Holten Canadian War Cemetery in Holland. He was the son of William and Jane Mennie of Reston, Manitoba. Born in Ellon, Aberdeenshire, Scotland, he came to Canada with his family in 1921. ***Mennie Lake*** (64 O/6), east of Booth Lake was named after him in 1995.

Menzies, Flying Officer **James A.** of Carberry (J 27804). No. 42 Squadron. He died 22 February 1944 at the age of 27 and is commemorated at Brookwood Military Cemetery in Surrey, England. He was the son of Thomas and Margaret A. Menzies of Pratt, Manitoba. ***Menzies Island*** (64 A/13) in Gauer Lake was named after him in 1989.

Menzies, Private **James K.** of MacGregor (H 102791). Queen's Own Cameron Highlanders. He died 27 October 1944 at the age of 29 and is commemorated at Bergen-op-Zoom Canadian War Cemetery in Holland. He was the son of Donald and Catherine A. Menzies of Strathclair, Manitoba. His niece writes (3 December 2001) that he was:

... born March 14, 1915 in Oakburn, Manitoba, the youngest child in a Scottish immigrant family that consisted of seven sons and one daughter. He attended school at Shoal Lake prior to enlisting in October, 1942 with the Royal Canadian Engineers. He was employed at Shilo Camp before he transferred to the Rocky Mountain Rangers. He went overseas in February, 1944 and served with the Queen's Own Cameron Highlanders before being killed in action in Beveland, Holland.

Although he died long before I was born, I heard many stories of James. A picture of him was a permanent fixture on the living room wall at my great grandmother's house. According to my grandmother, he was very fond of old time dancing. In fact, she said that he was one of the best dancers in their area. He was a very humble person and was working on the family farm prior to enlisting. He was studying to be an electrician after he became a member of the Royal Canadian Engineers. Unfortunately, all of his brothers and his sister have passed on at the time of this being written, so many memories were not able to be passed on.

Menzies Lake (64 I/6), northwest of North Knife Lake was named after him in 1974.

Menzoski, Private **Mack** (H 17228). Princess Patricia's Canadian Light Infantry. He died 9 February 1942 and is commemorated at Brookwood Military Cemetery in Surrey, England. He was the son of Andrew and Annie Menzoski. ***Menzoski Lake*** (64 I/16), northeast of North Knife Lake was named after him in 1974.

Mercer, Rifleman **Stanley J.** of Wabowden (H 102381). Royal Winnipeg Rifles. He died 18 August 1944 at the age of 26 and is commemorated at Bayeux War Cemetery, Calvados, France. He was the son of Arthur and Bella Mercer and was survived by his wife Martha Mercer of Wabowden and their daughter Grace. ***Mercer Island*** (63 O/2) in Setting Lake was named after him in 1995.

Merkley, Flying Officer **Edwin A.** of St. Vital (J 28385). No. 57 Operational Training Unit, RCAF. He died 19 November 1943 at the age of 25 and is commemorated at Stonefall Cemetery in Yorkshire, England. He was the son of Ashton H. and Mary E. Merkley of St. Vital. ***Merkley Lake*** (63 I/1), south of Little Bolton Lake was named after him in 1988.

Merriam, Driver **Norman** of Winnipeg (H 52100). Royal Canadian Army Service Corps. He died 1 January 1941 at the age of 32 and is commemorated at Brookside Cemetery in Winnipeg. He was the son of Alan and Sadie Merriam of Winnipeg and was survived by his wife Doris W. Merriam of Winnipeg. ***Merriam Lake*** (64 I/1), northeast of Etawney Lake was named after him in 1974.

Merrick, Private **Charles E.** of Winnipeg (H 58014). No. 1 Motor Ambulance Convoy, Royal Canadian Army Service Corps. He died 27 August 1944 at the age of 21 and is commemorated at Ancona War Cemetery in Italy. He was the son of Ernest W. J. and Eleanor J. C. Merrick of Winnipeg and was survived by his wife Gladys A. Merrick. ***Merrick Lake*** (54 C/12), southwest of York Factory was named after him in 1964.

Merrifield, Flight Lieutenant **William E.** of Winnipeg (J 4776). No. 228 Squadron. He died 10 November 1943 at the age of 43 and is commemorated at Bilbao British Cemetery in Spain. He was the son of Charles and Elizabeth J. Merrifield and was survived by his wife Margaret J. Merrifield. ***Merrifield Lake*** (64 J/10), west of Tadoule Lake was named after him in 1975.

Metcalf, Gunner **Lyle E. "Bob"** of Virden (H 67245). Royal Canadian Artillery. He died 20 October 1944 at the age of 24 and is commemorated at Bergen-op-Zoom Canadian War Cemetery in Holland. He was the son of Robert H. and Margaret J. Metcalf of Virden, Manitoba. ***Metcalf Lake*** (52 L/11), northwest of Bird Lake was named after him in 1982.

Meyer, Sapper **Alex** of Winnipeg (H 13047). Royal Canadian Engineers. He died 23 July 1945 at the age of 48 and is commemorated at Brookside Cemetery in Winnipeg. He was survived by his wife Katie Meyer of Winnipeg. ***Meyer Island*** (53 E/16) in Island Lake was named after him in 1997.

Meyer, Pilot Officer **Melvin M.** of Winnipeg (J 17344). No. 427 Squadron. He died 23 June 1943 and is commemorated at the Reichswald Forest War Cemetery in Germany. He was survived by his mother Jennie Meyer of Winnipeg. ***Meyer Bay*** (63 N/6) in Kississing Lake was named after him in 1995.

Meyers, Private **Melvin H.** of Bowsman (H 1518). Westminster Regiment. He died 24 September 1944 at the age of 22 and is commemorated at Ravenna War Cemetery in Italy. He was the son of M. A. and Verna Meyers of Bowsman, Manitoba. ***Meyers Lake*** (64 J/5), southwest of Tadoule Lake was named after him in 1975.

Meyers, Flight Sergeant **Norman C.** of Winnipeg (R 95104). No. 150 Squadron. He died 10 October 1942 at the age of 19 and is commemorated at Brigg Cemetery in Lincolnshire, England. He was the son of Roy and Stella Meyers of Winnipeg. ***Meyers Bay*** (63 I/1) in Little Bolton Lake was named after him in 1995.

Michael, Pilot Officer **James P.** of Winnipeg (J 15439). No. 148 Squadron. He died 7 July 1942 at the age of 30 and is commemorated at the Fayid War Cemetery in Egypt. He was the son of Mr. and Mrs. George P. Michael and was survived by his wife Dorothy L. Michael (née Hall) of Vancouver. He:

... was born November 22, 1911 in Winnipeg where he was educated at the public schools and Daniel McIntyre Collegiate Vocational Institute to obtain his senior matriculation. He was employed in a brokerage office for a period and then engaged in mining and construction work in northern Canada and Pacific coastal areas. He was a member of the Non-permanent Militia, the Canadian Machine Gun Corps at Winnipeg for nine years before he joined the Perth Regiment. He was transferred to the RCAF in October, 1940 and trained at Calgary and Mossbank. He proceeded overseas in June, 1941 and served in Great Britain and the Middle East. He was killed in action over Tobruk while on active duty (Hill 1944).

Michael Lake (64 H/15), north of Etawney Lake was named after him in 1995.

Michalkow, Trooper **Orest** of Flin Flon (H 77499). 12th Manitoba Dragoons. He died 12 August 1944 at the age of 20 and is commemorated at Bretteville-sur-Laize Canadian War Cemetery in Calvados, France. He was the son of Martin and Julia Michalkow of Flin Flon, Manitoba. ***Michalkow Lake*** (64 I/12), northwest of North Knife Lake was named after him in 1974.

Michalski, Private **Boleslaus** of Arborg (H 43212). Royal Hamilton Light Infantry. He died 8 March 1945 and is commemorated at the Groesbeek Canadian War Cemetery in Holland. He was the son of Frank and Ann Michalski of Winnipeg. His sister-in-law writes (14 July 1995):

He was born in Winnipeg [and] lived [there] for five years with his father and mother. He went to Arborg School. He was a member of St. Philip's Church which his father built. He helped on the farm until 1940 [when he enlisted].

Michalski Lake (52 L/11), east of Black Lake was named after him in 1982.

Michie, Pilot Officer **Ernest W.** (J 86258). No. 420 Squadron. He died 4 May 1944 at the age of 23 and is commemorated at the Runnymede Memorial in Surrey, England. He was the son of George and Marian Michie and was survived by his wife Mary W. Michie of Toronto. ***Michie Island*** (63 I/8) in Harold Wilson Lake was named after him in 1995.

Michie, Sergeant **Stanley R.** of Souris (H 26486). Fort Garry Horse. He died 5 July 1944 at the age of 27 and is commemorated at Beny-sur-Mer Canadian War Cemetery in Calvados, France. He was the son of Norman and Rebecca J. Michie of Griswold and was survived by his wife Margaret H. Michie of Griswold, Manitoba and their daughter. His sister recalls (17 February 1997):

We both were born ... on the family farm one mile north of the village of Griswold, Manitoba. He was two years my junior. From our beginnings, we enjoyed a stable, happy life with loving parents and four grandparents as well as many relatives and friends of our family. The untimely death of our mother when we were eight and six years old respectively changed everything. All settled happiness disappeared from our lives and we barely managed to get along somehow.

For a few years, we took our unexpressed grief out in hostile behaviour – especially with each other. Then amazingly, in our teens, we became friends. Over time, I feel I witnessed the development of a very fine person in my brother. He was kind and courteous in every area of his activities, i.e., friends at school, team mates in sports such as baseball, hockey, curling and tennis. Individually, he swam well and was a keen, above average dancer at social functions. He and I often practised together as we tuned in the radio at noon hour to "The Happy Gang."

Far above average was his rich, baritone voice. He loved to sing and did so, in the fields as he worked, in the village choir and was in demand as a soloist for community functions. Sadly, his voice remained untrained as no teacher was available in that depression era.

A measure of happiness was regained over these years and he was popular with both female and male friends. At the beginning of World War II, he enlisted in the Fort Garry Horse regiment and before leaving for overseas, he married. A few months later, a daughter was born whom he never did meet.

As for me, I remember my brother as being sincere, unassuming, without guile or conceit. He was my confidante, my mentor, and when he was killed, I lost my dearest and best friend. My grief and loss have been compensated somewhat by meeting, over the years and at separate times, three friends of his who were in the same regiment. The reaction on each occasion was significant: "You're Stan Michie's sister?" I felt their respect and knew I must explain: "Yes, but wait a minute, don't expect too much of me – I would like to be like him, but that's impossible because I feel he was part angel." Named after him and all living are a grandson, a nephew and a second cousin.

Michie Lake (52 E/14), southeast of Brereton Lake was named after him in 1974.

Michlosky, Trooper **Steve** of Ladywood (H 101844). Royal Canadian Dragoons. He died 8 April 1945 at the age of 21 and is commemorated at the Holten Canadian War Cemetery in Holland. He was the son of Paul and Lena Michlosky (née Kyryluk) of Sherwood, Manitoba. His nephew recalls (16 October 2001):

Steve Michlosky's early years were typical of life on a subsistence mixed farm southeast of Lake Winnipeg in that era. He obtained his Grade 8 formal education in a one-room country schoolhouse and enjoyed playing baseball. He also showed an interest in motor mechanics and his trade was listed as "Truck and Tractor Man." He is remembered to have been a very nice person with many friends, a hard worker and a good dancer who was a regular at the Saturday night barn dances. He was a gentleman who showed respect to the ladies and they in turn adored him.

In 1942, he left home to join his brother John and sister-in-law Kay in Red Lake, Ontario. There he worked in the Hasaga Gold Mines until July, 1942 when at the age of 19, he joined the army.

He adds (11 October 2001):

I was only 5 1/2 years old when uncle Steve was killed but I still remember him quite well although I was only 3 1/2 when he boarded the train at the old CPR station at Higgins and Main in March, 1943. He was that kind of nice person who made such an impression you could never forget him, no matter how young you were then or how old you are now. Sophie's recollection is the same as my mother's who will be 88 years old soon.

He wrote many letters home to family and friends. These are a few excerpts:

- It was raining most of the time while I was on scheme and we were all wet. And to add to it, we had to swim through a river that was way over my head when we were making a make-believe attack on an armoured car camp. Don't think I liked it a heck of a lot. But it was all in a day's work so I didn't mind it much. At night, I dug myself into a farmer's haystack to keep out of the rain. Nobody could find me the next morning and I slept till 11 o'clock. But did I ever get hell when I showed myself up. I really felt bad about it because if it would have been an actual battle, that would have been deserting my comrades (16 July 1943).
- As you can see, I am not in England anymore, but somewhere in the Mediterranean area. It's quite a while now since I left dear old England and I miss the good times I had there. The only enjoyment I have over here is eating plenty of fruit and nuts. And the only drink here is wine and it's dynamite. And it acts like a time bomb (19 November 1943).
- I don't really know what to do with myself these days. I feel miserable and down for some reason. There is a girl in Portage la Prairie who writes me often, about every three days. I guess I told you about her when I was back in Canada. She's beautiful and good and she's in love with me very much. She has sent me parcels and cigarettes and she says she only lives for the day that I'll come back. I honestly don't know how I'll ever repay her for all her kindness and loyalty to a Soldier who is not worth any of it (n.d.).
- How's the twins and Bobby getting along? Gee, I'd sure like to see a picture of them now. I guess they won't even know me if I ever get back. Are you still working in the same place you used to? If you are, look up a girl by the name of Anne... She's a Ukrainian girl. She'll probably want to know a few things about me if you bump into her. Tell her some, but don't go too much into detail (11 February 1944).
- I'd really like to tell you some of the things we do around here. But I'm afraid the Censor would cut it all out anyway. So I'll save it till we get together again and I'm hoping it is not any later than the summer of '45 (14 February 1944).
- It's good to hear that you are feeling good and like your work. What are you going to do after you are finished in the bush? I sure wish I was back in the bush somewhere logging instead of slogging around in this Italian mud. Where I am now there are artillery shells going over day and night all the time. And it's good to know they are from our own guns (26 February 1944).
- The kiddies must be really getting big and strong now. I'd sure like to see them now. But I guess they'll be almost ready to go to school by the time I do. How's Bobby coming along? Tell him I miss him and that I think of him often (28 February 1944).

- You mentioned something in your letter about the girl in Portage la Prairie. Well my associations with her are finished, even though I still care for her. You may be wondering why, so I'll tell you. About a month [ago], she wrote me a letter which I haven't recovered from yet. In it she wrote me that she had a baby girl on Christmas Day. She gave the child away and still wants me to come back to her. No, the child is not any work of mine. If she'd [have] told me before the child came, I might have considered it, but she kept it from me till the last moment (6 March 1944).
- I went for a swim again this morning. The water is really lovely over here. I like it so much that I could stay in it all day long. How are the twins and Bobby? Gee, I miss them a lot. I guess when I first pop into the house, I'll be a kind of stranger to everyone. I've certainly changed a lot since you last saw me (11 May 1944).
- First of all, I want to say a big thanks for the second parcel I received from you last week. I did not as yet receive the pictures of the kiddies. They must be lost because they should be here by now if you sent them by airmail. The boys here got quite a few airmail letters in the last weeks and a lot of them were salvaged from air crashes, so that is why I am figuring the pictures are lost (16 May 1944).
- I'm working in the kitchen today. And am I ever black, worse than a coal miner would ever be. But it's all in the game and I have to like it. You know it seems funny to me, but Mike Tymchuk reminded me of the Christmas we had spent together back in Red Lake. And he said he hoped to God we spend another one like it this year together he says. It makes me feel really good when somebody writes something like that (23 May 1944).
- Did I tell you about the friend of mine who had his foot knocked off just above the ankle? It happened when a shell landed near our car. He was just getting inside and his foot was still outside. And "Bango!" the shell landed and a piece of shrapnel got him in the foot. It was not a pleasant sight. But as I have said before, this is war and more drastic things will happen. It could easily have been me for I was outside the car myself. But God was with me somehow and I got inside in the nick of time. Oh well, if it's only my foot they want, they can have it. But without it I'd be a complete failure, for you know how much I like dancing and without a foot I'm not much good (10 June 1944).
- In your letter you mentioned that mom received a telegram saying that I had been wounded. I'm glad it was only a mistake. But I admit I came very close to being hurt as two boys that were on either side of me got hit when that shell landed and exploded. The mistake was that my name went in instead of one of the others that got hurt and when the mistake was found, it was too late to rectify it. I hope mother has received the letter I wrote her saying so because I'm sure she must be worried sick (4 July 1944).
- Everything over here is pretty much the same – I mean as far as I'm concerned, although there [have] been quite a few changes. What with Florence liberated and a few gains on the Adriatic sector. And now the landings in southern France. As much news as I've heard so far, they're doing good. And let me tell you that that landing was certainly a surprise to me besides many others. It came off so quietly that I'm sure the Hun was caught with his pants down and before long we'll take them off altogether (16 August 1944).
- This is my first letter to you this year – I mean in 1945 and if you don't mind, I'd like you to keep it as a souvenir, as when I get back I will have a big story to tell you about the few days that have gone by previous to New Year's and after. I spent New Year's in the line and am still here. Jerry put up quite an assortment of tracer bullets when midnight came around; some of the boys claim they saw the letter "HNY" meaning "Happy New Year" made by tracer bullets. ... Well I must come to a close now. Please answer soon as the mail has been a little scarce for me lately. Good-bye and God Bless you all. Your ever loving brother, Stevie (2 January 1945).

This was his last letter. Trooper Orlando Segatore was a comrade of Trooper Michlosky's and recently (28 July 2001) related to his nephew the circumstances surrounding his uncle's death:

On April 8, 1945 most of Squadron "D" were once again in an infantry role. During a fire-fight with the Germans near a little town northeast of Deventer, they were running across open ground towards the cover of trees when the enemy opened up with their machine guns. They all dove for cover and Orlando saw uncle Steve dive into a ditch which was immediately raked with machine gun fire. Soon a Squadron "D" Staghound armoured car appeared and began to lay a smoke screen to provide cover for the troopers but was itself knocked out by a 75mm round killing the crew commander Cpl. W. J. Miller and wounding the remaining crew of four including a man from a northern Ontario Reserve named LaLonde who is still living.

After the Germans were routed, Orlando went to the ditch where he last saw uncle Steve. He said uncle Steve was obviously killed instantly by the machine gun fire. They picked up his body and carried it over to a yard that was surrounded by a wrought iron fence. There Orlando removed uncle Steve's dogtags and they buried him in the front yard between the house and the fence with his rifle barrel down into the ground and butt up with his helmet and dogtag as marker for the grave detail that always followed. He spoke a few words over the grave then they left, turning over the dogtag and details to the Regimental Padre who would have passed them on for the grave detail. The grave detail would later transfer uncle Steve's remains to the nearest cemetery. That would explain why his military record states he was buried in a temporary grave with religious rites on April 14, 1945 – six days later and four days after the breakthrough at Zwolle.

Michlosky Lake (64 K/15), northeast of Lac Brochet was named after him in 1972.

Middleton, Flight Lieutenant **Douglas D.** of Dauphin (39105). No. 9 Squadron, RAF. He died 20 July 1940 at the age of 26 and is commemorated at the Runnymede Memorial in Surrey, England. He enlisted in the RAF in September, 1936. He was the son of Reverend Fred C. and Nellie D. Middleton of Dauphin and was survived by his wife Olwen M. Middleton of Axminster, Devon, England. Two of his brothers were also in the RAF: Flight Lieutenant Donald Middleton was shot down 12 April 1940 and survived for five years as a prisoner of war at Colditz; and Wing Commander Bruce Middleton, AFC was in charge of all mail deliveries to and from Canada during the war. ***Middleton Island*** (53 L/15) in Seller Lake was named after Flight Lieutenant Douglas D. Middleton in 1995. An Imperial Order of the Daughters of the Empire (IODE) Chapter was also named after him in Dauphin.

Middleton, Sergeant **Melvin C.** of Winnipeg (H 40668). 1st Canadian Parachute Battalion. He died 29 June 1944 and is commemorated at Ranville War Cemetery, Calvados, France. ***Middleton Lake*** (52 L/3), northeast of Brereton Lake was named after him in 1973.

Middleton, (a.k.a. Mendelson) Lance Corporal **Norman C.** of Winnipeg (H 62683). Canadian Forestry Corps. He died 24 August 1942 and is commemorated at Urray New Parish Churchyard, Ross and Cromarty, Scotland. He was the son of Wilfred and Dora Mendelson. ***Middleton Point*** (64 O/13) on Nueltin Lake was named after him in 1996.

Middleton, Trooper **Robert** of Carberry (H 387). Lord Strathcona's Horse. He died 26 January 1944 at the age of 23 and is commemorated at the Moro River Canadian War Cemetery in Italy. He was the son of Alexander and Alice Middleton of Carberry and was survived by his brothers Sandy and George and sisters Bessie, Isabelle and Frances. His nephew writes (28 November 2001):

Although I never knew my uncle Bob, my mother has often spoken of her older brother. Bob was her favourite and excelled at anything that had to do with sports. He and a friend were scouted for one of the NHL teams, but due to the war, they never received a chance to play and neither returned home. Bob did his duty for his country and in his letters home to his mom he only had one wish and that wish was to be able to fight under our own flag, which at that time, we did not have. Bob will always be remembered by his friends in the Lord Strathcona Horse (RC) and his sister Frances. His sister's one regret is that he and all the others who served in Italy have never received "Their Just Due" from either our country or the Italians.

Middleton Bay (53 D/5) in Carr-Harris Lake was named after him in 1989.

Milburn, Flying Officer **Francis Lloyd** of Decker (J 20816). No. 408 Squadron. He died 13 June 1943 at the age of 23 and is commemorated at the Reichswald Forest War Cemetery in Germany. He was the son of Frank and Bena Milburn of St. Vital. His sister recalls that he was (28 November 2001):

... born in Woodnorth, Manitoba. We moved to Decker, Manitoba while he was a teenager. He loved sports, was a great curler and loved hockey. Although needed on the farm, at 21 he was called up to the RCASC in 1941, trained at Red Deer, Alberta, then remustered the same year into the RCAF. From the Brandon Manning Depot, he took bombardier instruction at Paulson and Portage la Prairie where he graduated in November, 1942. He arrived overseas December 24, 1942. He served with No. 408 Squadron at Leeming, Yorkshire on Halifaxes. On June 14, 1943, they were shot down over Bochum, Germany on their second trip. I talked to the navigator; they were on fire and told to bail out. Five survived as prisoners of war. Lloyd and the engineer died. He was buried in a local cemetery, then re-interred at the Reichswald Forest War Cemetery beside the engineer.

Milburn Lake (64 P/15), northeast of Nejanilini Lake was named after him in 1974.

Millar, Flight Lieutenant **George Glenn** of Winnipeg (J 20388). No. 442 Squadron. He died 28 September 1944 at the age of 22 and is commemorated at Uden War Cemetery, Holland. He was the son of George S. and Janet W. Millar of Winnipeg. ***Glenn Millar Lake*** (54 E/14), southeast of Braden Lake was named after him in 1995.

Millar, Flying Officer **James Brian** of Snowflake (J 44516). No. 357 Squadron. He died 1 April 1945 at the age of 20 and is commemorated at Chittagong War Cemetery in Bangladesh. He was the eldest son of John and Amy Millar of Snowflake, Manitoba and was survived by three sisters and one brother. His brother recalls (22 November 2001):

Brian grew up in a loving family in the village of Snowflake. He always had a great interest in airplanes and flying. His workshop had a series of model planes made by himself from scratch. At 18, he enthusiastically volunteered as a pilot in training with the RCAF. Overseas in England, his crew was transferred in 1945 to India to play a role in the defeat of the Japanese in Burma. As co-pilot of a B24 bomber, he and his crew were killed on a mission dropping paratroopers into Burma.

In 1975, I visited his war grave in Chittagong and with great emotion, left a maple leaf at the site. My heart was full of gratitude for his sacrifice and for that of his comrades buried nearby.

Millar Peninsula (64 C/3) on Elvyn Lake was named after him in 1993.

Millar, Private **Mary I**. of Brandon (W 10965). Canadian Women's Army Corps. She died 16 May 1943 at the age of 19 and is commemorated at Brandon Cemetery. She was the daughter of John S. and Elizabeth C. Millar of Brandon. ***Mary Millar Island*** (54 D/7) in Stephens Lake was named after her in 1995.

Millar, Warrant Officer 2 **Robert V**. of Manitou (R 106358). No. 425 Squadron. He died 26 June 1943 at the age of 20 and is commemorated at the Malta Memorial. He was the son of Leslie E. and Alice Millar of Vancouver. ***Robert Millar Lake*** (53 L/1), southeast of Rochon Lake was named after him in 1995.

Millen, Private **Howard V.** of Wawanesa (H 40712). Carleton and York Regiment. He died 15 December 1943 at the age of 29 and is commemorated at the Moro River Canadian War Cemetery in Italy. His sister writes (16 January 1988):

My brother was born in Wawanesa September 8, 1914 where he was raised and educated. He joined the army shortly after the outbreak of the war (Royal Winnipeg Rifles) and went overseas in 1941. He was killed at Ortona, Italy.

Millen Lake (52 E/11), southeast of Brereton Lake was named after him in 1972.

Miller, Corporal **Allen E.** of Winnipeg (H 19831). Queen's Own Cameron Highlanders. He died 20 July 1944 at the age of 25 and is commemorated at Bretteville-sur-Laize Canadian War Cemetery in Calvados, France. He was born in Minnedosa and raised in the Fortier area of Manitoba. ***Miller Esker*** (64 I/15), northeast of Wither Lake was named after him in 1995.

Miller, Leading Aircraftman **Charles M.** of Winnipeg (R 191243). No. 6 Elementary Flying Training School. He died 20 July 1943 at the age of 32 and is commemorated at Elmwood Cemetery in Winnipeg. He was the son of William and Mary A. Miller of St. Vital and was survived by his wife Catherine T. Miller of St. Vital. ***Charles Miller Lake*** (64 J/13), east of Nicklin Lake was named after him in 1995.

Miller, Private **Clifford L.** of Winnipeg (H 26725). Queen's Own Cameron Highlanders. He died 5 October 1944 at the age of 33 and is commemorated at Bergen-op-Zoom Canadian War Cemetery in Holland. He was the son of David M. and Mary-Anne Miller and was survived by his wife Mabel E. Miller (née Verhague) of Winnipeg and their daughter Joan. Prior to his enlistment, he had been employed by the CNR. His daughter recalls (21 November 2001):

He was a great letter writer and letters he sent home to his family chronicled the time spent in England waiting to be shipped over to France. Many poems were also sent, which more than anything, told of the anxiety, loneliness and torment suffered by the men. Following are two of the many received:

I read of deeds of bravery that are so often done
The parts you only get to know, that affect the mentioned one
Like pilots who have saved their kites and set them safely down
To be rebuilt and sent back out with crews so brave and young
Or watch the valiant bombardier as he staggers towards the door
Not knowing that the day is bright, for his eyes they are no more
Oh please, Dear God put an end to these sites which we behold
These things that send out men so young and bring them back so old.
(1943)

I am dreaming tonight of a land clear and bright,
Where the snow that falls is a pure crystal white.
Where the stars that shine from the heavens above,
Entwine in their shadows all things that I love
My home, my family, my all – Canada.
(1944)

Miller Bay (64 F/2) in Dunsheath Lake was named after him in 1989.

Miller, Private **David** of Winnipeg (H 616159). Prince Edward Island Highlanders. He died 18 May 1944 at the age of 30 and is commemorated at Brookside Cemetery in Winnipeg. He was the son of Mr. and Mrs. David Miller of Winnipeg and was survived by his wife Emma D. Miller (née Batters) of Winnipeg. This native of Winnipeg was educated at Luxton Junior High School and prior to enlisting, was employed as a meat cutter at Canada Packers Limited. His death was a result of a training accident; the cause was listed as "multiple shrapnel fragments to chest and abdomen." ***David Miller Lake*** (64 P/9), north of Caribou Lake was named after him in 1995.

Miller, Trooper **Everett W.** of Birdtail (H 1670). Highland Light Infantry. He died 12 October 1944 at the age of 22 and is commemorated at the Adegem Canadian War Cemetery in Belgium. He was the son of Henry A. and Eva C. Miller of Rossburn. His sister recalls (30 November 2001):

> Everett was a very happy young man who loved to whistle and play guitar. He loved to drive the car. Everett loved his parents and family and many letters stated how he would be glad to get home for his Mum's baking. Everett was wounded in Belgium. He went overseas in April, 1944 and was wounded in France. He was moved to Belgium where he died of his wounds. Everett enlisted in the army in January, 1942.

Everett Miller Lake (64 A/14), southeast of Wernham Lake was named after him in 1995.

Miller, Lance Sergeant **Harry G.** of Winnipeg (H 57952). Royal Canadian Army Medical Corps. He died 31 January 1944 at the age of 38 and is commemorated at Bari War Cemetery in Italy. He was the son of Robert and Kathrine Miller of Winnipeg and was survived by his wife Doris L. Miller of Winnipeg. ***Miller Island*** (53 E/15) in Island Lake was named after him in 1982.

Miller, Private **Howard G.** of Winnipeg (H 3547). Queen's Own Cameron Highlanders. He died 19 August 1942 at the age of 22 and is commemorated at Dieppe Canadian War Cemetery in Seine-Maritime, France. He was survived by his mother Annie Miller of Winnipeg. ***Miller Hill*** (64 O/8), south of Baird Lake was named after him in 1995.

Miller, Pilot Officer **Ivan A.** of Roland (J 15213). No. 138 Squadron. He died 21 April 1942 at the age of 29 and is commemorated at Brookwood Military Cemetery in Surrey, England. He was the oldest of the nine children of Archie C. and Annie M. Miller of Victoria, British Columbia. His brother recalls (23 September 2001) that he:

> ... was born in Nova Scotia [and] moved to Roland at about one year of age. He worked on [his] parents' farm at Roland and Myrtle and then moved with the family to Grandview about 1938. Ivan left from there and went to Winnipeg to take a mechanical course. He joined the RCAF from there.
>
> As I recall, he took his pilot's training at Uplands, Ontario before going overseas. As Pilot Officer, he flew mainly Halifax bombers. He was reported killed in action shortly after my 13th birthday. My memories of him are a little vague, but I remember him as a caring and helpful older brother.

Ivan Miller Lake (53 M/12), north of High Hill Lake was named after him in 1995.

Miller, Private **James** of Winnipeg (H 64717). Royal Canadian Ordnance Corps. He died 22 June 1943 at the age of 36 and is commemorated at Brookside Cemetery in Winnipeg. He was the son of Mr. and Mrs. James Miller of Perigord, Saskatchewan and was survived by his wife Agnes June Miller of Winnipeg. ***Miller Peninsula*** (64 H/6) on Northern Indian Lake was named after him in 1995.

Miller, Rifleman **Leonard H.** of Winnipeg (H 40565). Royal Winnipeg Rifles. He died 5 July 1944 at the age of 26 and is commemorated at Bretteville-sur-Laize Canadian War Cemetery in Calvados, France. He was the son of Harry D. and Agnes L. Miller of Winnipeg. ***Miller Creek*** (64 A/5), which flows southeast into Warnews River was named after him in 1995.

Miller, Private **Morris** of Winnipeg (H 37472). Royal Canadian Army Service Corps. He died 4 February 1945 at the age of 26 and is commemorated at Rome War Cemetery in Italy. He was the son of Frank and Mollie Miller of Winnipeg. ***Morris Miller Lake*** (53 N/5), east of Swampy Lake was named after him in 1995.

Miller, Leading Aircraftman **Vernon R.** of Reston (R 196677). No. 6 Elementary Flying Training School. He died 16 September 1943 at the age of 20 and is commemorated at South Hill Cemetery in Prince Albert, Saskatchewan. He was the son of Russell D. and Ena R. Miller of Smeaton, Saskatchewan. ***Vernon Miller Lake*** (64 N/3), southeast of Colbeck Lake was named after him in 1995.

Miller, Sergeant **William J.** of Sanford (R 91771). No. 1659 Heavy Conversion Unit, RCAF. He died 26 August 1943 at the age of 25 and is commemorated at Stonefall Cemetery in Yorkshire, England. He was survived by his step-parents George and Lily Miller of Sanford, Manitoba. ***Miller Rapids*** (53 E/14) in the Stevenson River was named after him in 1995.

Millidge, Warrant Officer 1 **Edwin G.** of Winnipeg (R 131449). No. 7 Squadron. He died 18 November 1943 at the age of 26 and is commemorated at Durnbach War Cemetery in Bavaria, Germany. He was the son of Edwin R. and Edith M. Millidge of Winnipeg and the stepson of Ethel M. Millidge of Winnipeg. He had been attending Veterinarian College in Guelph, Ontario, but dropped out to enlist with the RCAF. His sister writes (3 August 1998):

> Ed enlisted with the RCAF on October 17, 1941 at Hamilton, Ontario and went overseas on June 1, 1942. He joined No. 405 Squadron on January 16, 1943 and flew five anti-submarine patrol missions with that unit in the Bay of Biscay area. On April 30, 1943, Ed joined No. 7 Squadron, RAF, a Pathfinder squadron as an air gunner. The job of the Pathfinder force, with the aid of a new, secret radar, was to find targets in the dark of night and light them up with flares for the main bomber force. The Pathfinder squadrons had to fly at lower altitudes than the main bomber squadrons so that they were more vulnerable to enemy attack from the ground. On the night of November 18/19, 1943, Ed's aircraft, a Lancaster Mark II JA970 (*N for Nuts*) was shot down by anti-aircraft guns over Mannheim, Germany. All seven of the crew lost their lives and only two could be identified.

Millidge Lake (64 H/8), west of Hogg Lake was named after him in 1995.

Milliken, Private **John** of Winnipeg (H 8531). Princess Patricia's Canadian Light Infantry. He died 22 September 1944 and is commemorated at Coriano Ridge War Cemetery in Italy. He was the son of John and Agnes Milliken of Winnipeg. His sister recalls (7 December 2001):

John was born May 16, 1910 in Winnipeg. After a few years in Winnipeg, we moved to Mather, Manitoba. Dad wanted to raise his family on the farm; three sisters and four brothers were born. John got his schooling in a country school (Mount Prospect) and high school in Mather.

He was a member of the United Church, belonged to the Boy Scouts and was involved in skating and baseball. He liked mechanics and woodwork which was useful on the farm. He was always willing to help a neighbour and any community effort. When the war broke out, John went and signed up to go and fight for his country. Mother and Dad were saddened but also proud that he felt family was also important. John said: "We don't want the war in Canada," and said it was his duty as so many families felt the sadness for one another as other sons and brothers signed up. Later, he had two brothers join the army and the youngest brother went later on reserve. John was killed instantly in Italy. His friend nearby saw him blown to pieces in the front line as I'm sure many other brave men.

Milliken Lake (63 K/12), south of Embury Lake was named after him in 1982.

Millon, Sergeant **Lloyd F.** of Winnipeg (H 3121). Canadian Dental Corps. He died 1 November 1944 and is commemorated at the Groesbeek Memorial in Holland. ***Millon Lake*** (64 G/15), northwest of Trout Lake was named after him in 1995.

Mills, Private **Charles Edward** of Winnipeg (H 200025). Queen's Own Cameron Highlanders. He died 21 July 1944 at the age of 25 and is commemorated at Bretteville-sur-Laize Canadian War Cemetery in Calvados, France. He was the son of Charles E. and Elizabeth Mills of Winnipeg. ***Mills Lake*** (64 I/11), northwest of North Knife Lake was named after him in 1974.

Mills, Flight Sergeant **William F.** of Emerson (R 95119). Royal Canadian Air Force. He died 12 May 1944 at the age of 27 and is commemorated at Brookside Cemetery in Winnipeg. He was the son of Randle J. and Emma M. Mills of Sprague and was survived by his wife Emma Mills of Calgary. ***Mills Island*** (63 K/13) in Lac Aimée was named after him in 1997.

Milne, Lance Corporal **Arthur L.** of Winnipeg (H 16037). Princess Patricia's Canadian Light Infantry. He died 11 December 1943 at the age of 33 and is commemorated at the Moro River Canadian War Cemetery in Italy. He was the son of George and Agnes Milne of Winnipeg. His sister-in-law's daughter writes (31 January 1996):

Arthur was born and raised in Hartney, Manitoba of Scottish parents. He spent his early years as a farm hand on some of the surrounding farms. During the Dirty Thirties, work was scarce so Art enlisted in the PPCLI in 1939.

In a letter to his mother he wrote:

Dearest Mother: Here I am deep in the heart of Sicily attached to the 8th Army. I guess though, you will have heard all about us on the radio. We had quite a few news hounds with us getting all the news possible. Just at the present time we are resting for a couple of days just a few miles from the front line and still under Jerry's gun fire. It has been a very trying campaign for all of us; a very hot climate, lots of flies and fleas which gave us a very rough time. I would sure have loved to have had my camera and taken some pictures of us advancing across the hills. There are sure lots of hills. We had mule trains carrying our stuff. I had a slight wound for a few days, but am OK again and still with the push.

We are hoping it will be all over this week, as we are in need of supplies. There have been a few of my pals who have gone West, which makes it all the harder, but I am OK and looking forward to a rest when we finish the island. I will sure be glad when we reach the Mediterranean again so we can get a good swim and get into clean clothes again. Well, mother dear, here's hoping you are OK and not worrying too much because I have all good intentions of seeing this thing through and being able to give you a full account of my experiences. Your loving son, L/Cpl. Arthur L. Milne (26 August 1943).

In a subsequent letter from "Somewhere in Italy" he wrote:

Well mother, I have arrived back with the Regiment about one week ago just in time to get in the fight when the Jerrys are getting real tough. The Action has been rather hot these last few days. The Jerrys are sort of cut off and are throwing everything they have got at us in the line of artillery. I spent one night under a Jerry barrage just [a] couple of days ago. It really makes you keep your head down; it also tests one's nerves.

Well mother, we can smile again, the truck has just got through to us with our weekly rations of two chocolate bars, cigarettes, a box of matches also [a] bottle of beer. We get 40 cigarettes which we have to buy of course … amounts to about 3/3. It is sure a struggle to get by a week on so little. I am sure praying and hoping my smokes reach me soon. Seeing [as] I have received these two letters, maybe the smokes will be along any day now? I hope?…. (date illegible).

Milne Bay (64 J/13) in Nicklin Lake was named after him in 1995.

Milne, Company Sergeant Major (Warrant Officer 2) **James S.** of Portage la Prairie (H 32031). Canadian Intelligence Corps. He died 19 August 1942 and is commemorated at Dieppe Canadian War Cemetery in Seine-Maritime, France. His obituary read in part:

Sergeant-Major Milne was born in Aberdeenshire, Scotland, coming to Portage la Prairie in 1924 where he joined the city police force, receiving leave of absence in 1939 to enlist in the Intelligence Corps of the 2nd Division, going overseas in June, 1940. While in Portage, he was active in the Manitoba Mounted Rifles, winning the Efficiency Medal. Lieutenant-General A. H. Gammon expressed the regret of the whole Regiment this morning at the loss of their comrade, saying "He was highly esteemed by all the men and officers, and thoroughly merited the Efficiency Medal. We regret to hear of the loss of one of our members who has served so gallantly" (n.d.).

Milne Island (64 I/4) in Ashley Lake was named after him in 1995.

Milnes, Rifleman **Cecil A. "Bill"** of Brandon (H 40933). Royal Winnipeg Rifles. He died 15 August 1944 at the age of 27 and is commemorated at Bretteville-sur-Laize Canadian War Cemetery in Calvados, France. He was the son of Charles and Gladys Milnes of Souris. ***Milnes Lake*** (64 G/2), southeast of Numakoos Lake was named after him in 1983.

Milton, Aircraftman 2 **Gerald M.** of Sinclair (R 152726). Royal Canadian Air Force. He died 10 October 1942 at the age of 20 and is commemorated at Rapid City Cemetery in Manitoba. The son of Donald J. and Willena M. Milton of Moline, Manitoba, this new recruit died from an adverse reaction to the vaccination. ***Milton Peninsula*** (53 E/15) in Island Lake was named after him in 1997.

Milton, Sergeant **Thomas F.** of Norwood (9729). Black Watch. He died 9 May 1915 at the age of 31 and is commemorated at Le Touret Memorial, Pas de Calais, France. He was survived by his wife Fanny F. Milton (née Fraser) of Norwood and their three children. His youngest daughter whom he never knew writes (13 September 1999):

Thomas Milton was born in Scotland [in 1883] and as a young man joined the famous Black Watch regiment. While still in Scotland, he married Fanny Fraser and they had two little children, Fraser and Marion. As they desired to improve their circumstances, they decided to emigrate to Canada. It was a difficult choice as Canadian regulations required that [he] work in Canada for one entire year before his wife and children could join him. Sadly, they agreed to this long, painful separation.

In Winnipeg at this time, plans had been made for the building of the Legislative Building. Thomas worked on this project for the year of 1913 when the building of our beautiful Legislature, made with magnificent Manitoba Tyndall Stone, began being built.

Thomas Milton was then employed at the Winnipeg Post Office. His wife and children soon arrived in Winnipeg and the happy family was united again. As Thomas now had permanent employment, the family planned on buying a little home. His wife found she was expecting her third baby and they all looked forward to a happy future in Winnipeg.

Sadly, this did not happen as the Great War had begun in 1914 and Thomas felt it was his duty to return to his old regiment in Scotland – the Black Watch. He did so a few months before their third child was born – a daughter, Frances. Later, his wife received word that he was "missing in action" after a fierce battle in northern France.

Hoping for better news, his wife with her three little ones returned to Scotland. It was an extremely hazardous crossing, as many ships were torpedoed, but the brave ship's captain managed to make the crossing safely in 1915. Eventually, some time after peace had been declared, Thomas Milton's wife and children returned to Canada and began their life in Winnipeg once again.

Sergeant Thomas Milton's name is engraved on the beautiful monument on the Legislative Building grounds, erected by the soldiers' relatives in memory of those from Winnipeg who gave their lives in the Great War. This monument was dedicated on May 13th, 1923 after three years of labour and love. Years later, Winnipeg finally did erect the Cenotaph on Memorial Boulevard with the names of many battles where Canadian soldiers fell. Sergeant Thomas Milton now lies in a grave "Known only to God."

I never saw my father, nor did he ever see me. I yearned and ached for him all my life. I did visit the Le Touret Cemetery years ago and it was well maintained.

Milton Lake (53 L/5), north of Bolton Lake was named after this World War I casualty in 1999.

Minaker, Corporal **Ronald G.** of Morris (H 26560). Royal Winnipeg Rifles. He died 4 July 1944 at the age of 20 and is commemorated at Beny-sur-Mer Canadian War Cemetery in Calvados, France. He was the son of George L. and Sarah E. Minaker of Winnipeg and was survived by his wife Agnes V. "Jean" Minaker of St. Vital and their daughter. His wife writes (23 November 2001):

Ronnie joined the Fort Garry Horse at 17, then was sent back to Winnipeg. He was in the MD10 band, then when he was old enough, he went to the Winnipeg Rifles. He went to Signals School in Ontario, then Debert, Nova Scotia. We had a daughter that was five months old the last time we saw him.

He was raised in Morris, Manitoba. His father and uncle served in World War I and his father and his older brother served in World War II as well as many cousins. He loved his country and was very proud of his military background. I went to see his grave in France 49 years after his death. I finally was able to close that chapter of my life.

Minaker Creek (54 B/10), which flows northeast into Kaskattama River was named after him in 1964.

Minter, Flight Sergeant **Sidney A.** of Winnipeg (R 110879). No. 427 Squadron. He died 22 October 1943 at the age of 22 and is commemorated at the Reichswald Forest War Cemetery in Germany. He was the son of Harry and Catherine A. Minter of Winnipeg. ***Minter Lake*** (64 P/3), southeast of Nejanilini Lake was named after him in 1974.

Miskimmin, Private **Hugh** of Winnipeg (H 8856). Royal Canadian Army Medical Corps. He died 1 June 1945 at the age of 39 and is commemorated at Brussels Town Cemetery in Belgium. He was the son of Hugh and Charlotte Miskimmin and was survived by his wife Priscilla Miskimmin of Winnipeg and their son. He writes (9 November 2001):

My father served in Holland and Germany. He was cited for bravery for saving the life of a young boy from a pack of wild dogs while in Germany. His brother Joe also served in the Medical Corps in the Italian Campaign. In June, 1988, my son and I flew into Miskimmin Lake from Thompson for the weekend. While there, we caught a 10 – 12 pound lake trout.

Miskimmin Lake (63 P/2), north of Cross Lake was named after him in 1972.

Miskow, Sergeant **Wesley W.** of Shoal Lake (H 17455). Royal Winnipeg Rifles. He died 6 June 1944 on the beach at Normandy. He was 23 years of age and is commemorated at Beny-sur-Mer Canadian War Cemetery in Calvados, France. He was the youngest of the eight children of Phillip and Mary Miskow of Shoal Lake, Manitoba. ***Miskow Lake*** (64 J/8), southeast of Tadoule Lake was named after him in 1975.

Misztur, Rifleman **Frank** of Russell (H 42100). Royal Winnipeg Rifles. He died 16 June 1942 at the age of 43 and is commemorated at Russell Cemetery in Manitoba. He was survived by his wife Zena Misztur of Russell. ***Misztur Lake*** (64 O/5), northeast of Egenolf Lake was named after him in 1975.

Mitchell, Sergeant **Alexander** of Winnipeg (R 91993). No. 427 Squadron. He died 23 October 1943 at the age of 21 and is commemorated at the Reichswald Forest War Cemetery in Germany. He was the son of George and Margaret Mitchell and was survived by his wife Irene Mitchell. ***Mitchell Hill*** (64 B/3), west of Mynarski Lakes was named after him in 1995.

Mitchell, Flight Lieutenant **Alexander J.** of Winnipeg (C 7926). No. 427 Squadron. He died 27 July 1944 at the age of 30 and is commemorated at Elmwood Cemetery in Winnipeg. He was the son of Philip J. and Catherine Mitchell of East Kildonan and was survived by his wife Justine J. Mitchell of Ottawa. ***Alexander Mitchell Lake*** (53 E/14), west of Island Lake was named after him in 1997.

Mitchell, Warrant Officer 2 **Banks E.** of Winnipeg (R 80314). No. 58 Squadron, Distinguished Flying Medal.

Flight Lieutenant Sawtell and Sergeant Mitchell were pilot and rear gunner respectively of an aircraft detailed for a sortie in July, 1943. During the flight, a U-boat was observed on the surface of the sea and Flight Lieutenant Sawtell immediately went into the attack. Considerable anti-aircraft fire was encountered, but by skilful manoeuvring he enabled his gunners to rake the U-boat deck with machine gun fire. The enemy gun crews were put out of action and Flight Lieutenant Sawtell flew into close range to deliver a devastating attack. This officer displayed great skill and determination while the efforts of Sergeant Mitchell contributed materially to the success of the attack (DFM Citation 1943).

He died 23 August 1943 at the age of 26 and is commemorated at the Runnymede Memorial in Surrey, England. He was the son of James H. and Alice M. Mitchell and was survived by his wife Norma R. Mitchell of Winnipeg. ***Mitchell Lake*** (63 K/6), north of Cormorant Lake was named after him in 1979.

Mitchell, Private **Earl J.** of Morris (H 9258). Seaforth Highlanders of Canada. He died 23 May 1944 at the age of 37 and is commemorated at the Cassino War Cemetery in Italy. He was the son of Arthur T. and Jennie Mitchell and was survived by his wife Grace Mitchell (née Stoney) of Winnipeg. According to his niece (19 August 1996):

I was born in 1953 so I never had the privilege of knowing Uncle Earl. For me, he was a picture always placed in a position of importance in our home. It was always very difficult for my father to speak of him. Dad never missed a Remembrance Day service, a tear always shed and a longing for a brother that was sorely missed. Grandma Mitchell rarely spoke of Earl. Feelings of such deep sorrow, regrets and some anger and somewhere in all that some pride always remained so close to the surface, even after so many years.

Earl was born in Morris and moved to Winnipeg, living in the Elmwood area on Martin Avenue. In his early years, he worked at Canada Packers. He later owned and operated a couple of restaurants. One was called the "Greasy Spoon" and it was located across from the Free Press Building. Another (name unknown) was located on Main Street across from the Brunswick Hotel where he lived. Alice [another niece] remembers the clientele as being a number of police officers as the station was close at hand. He also used to feed a lot of those who had fallen on hard times. Alice says Earl was a very giving man. He always sent money home to his parents. The Depression had been hard on the Mitchells. Alice particularly remembers a very pretty taffeta dress that was given to her by uncle Earl. A silver tea service given to his parents still sits in my living room. Earl has been described to me as a very quiet, gentle man, a man of few words.

He married Grace Stoney shortly before leaving for the war. They were married only nine months before his death. There were no children. Aunt Grace never remarried. She remained always a part of our family. She died March 24, 1989 and is buried in Morris, Manitoba.

Mitchell Peninsula (64 C/11) on McGavock Lake was named after him in 1995.

Mitchell, Lieutenant **Eric L.** of Winnipeg. Winnipeg Grenadiers. He died 20 December 1941 at the age of 23 and is commemorated at the Sai Wan War Cemetery in Hong Kong. He was the son of Edmund A. V. and Charlotte E. Mitchell of Winnipeg. His brother William V. Mitchell (see entry) also fell.

Suddenly, others in his company opened fire. He too, began shooting. He could hear the Japanese commanders shouting orders below. He could hear the *whoompf* of the Japanese mortars and the staccato of their machine guns. Outnumbered 10 to one, the platoon's commander Lieutenant Eric Mitchell ordered a retreat. He and the remnants of his company dashed uphill, leaping from boulder to boulder, firing their First World War Lee-Enfield rifles at the pursuing Japanese.

On a ridge above Stanley Gap, the survivors joined a second group of fleeing Canadians and found themselves trapped. Bullets whined through the air and ricocheted off the rocks. The air smelled of cordite. Harry Atkinson was unaware that Sergeant Major John Osborn, just 20 metres behind him, was picking up Japanese hand grenades lobbed into the Canadian position and hurling them back. One grenade fell beyond his reach. He shouted a warning and threw himself on the grenade. It exploded into his stomach.

Through the stories of other Canadian survivors runs a recurring theme of terror and tragedy. They fought against impossible odds, mostly in the rain. They retreated in chaos. They ran out of ammunition. They ran out of food. They spent almost a week without sleep. They died in each other's arms. They died alone (Wood 1991).

Mitchell Esker (64 O/6), southeast of Shannon Lake was named after him in 1989.

Mitchell, Sergeant **George W.** of Brandon (R 258551). No. 330 Operational Training Unit, RCAF. He died 28 May 1944 at the age of 30 and is commemorated at Stonefall Cemetery in Yorkshire, England. ***Mitchell Rapids*** (64 N/1) in the North Seal River was named after him in 1995.

Mitchell, Flying Officer **William A.** of Winnipeg (J 23126). No. 115 Squadron. He died 26 November 1943 at the age of 20 and is commemorated at Durnbach War Cemetery in Bavaria, Germany. He was the son of Frank M. and Elizabeth Mitchell of Winnipeg. ***Mitchell Point*** (63 H/9) on Gunisao Lake was named after him in 1989.

Mitchell, Flight Sergeant **William G.** of Killarney, Manitoba (R 157293). No. 22 Operational Training Unit, RCAF. He died 28 June 1943 at the age of 27 and is commemorated at Botley Cemetery in Oxfordshire, England. He was the eldest of the seven children of Thomas A. and Grace L. Mitchell of Killarney, Manitoba and was survived by his wife of six months Katherine L. Mitchell (née Jones) of Hamilton, Ontario. His sister recalls (16 November 2001):

Bill joined the Air Force in Winnipeg in March, 1942. He trained at Brandon, Manitoba and Mossbank, Saskatchewan graduating from No. 2 Training Depot in Edmonton on December 24, 1942. Bill married Katherine Jones in Edmonton on December 17, 1942 before leaving for overseas. He received further training at Wellesbourne Airfield in England and it was flying from this airfield that his plane crashed and all of the crew were killed.

Bill was somewhat of a father figure for our family as our father was away much of the time during those depression years on whatever job he could find. He had a very caring and responsible nature. Following in his footsteps, two more brothers joined the Navy, one sister the Air Force (Women's Division) and another sister the CWAC.

Mitchell Bay (64 B/12) in Rusty Lake was named after him in 1989.

Mitchell, Lieutenant **William Vaughan** of Winnipeg. Winnipeg Grenadiers. He died 20 December 1941 at the age of 36 and is commemorated at the Sai Wan Memorial in Hong Kong. He was the son of Edmund A. V. and Charlotte Mitchell and was survived by his wife Doris B. Mitchell (née Tollington) of Winnipeg and their son. His brother Lieutenant Eric L. Mitchell (see entry) also fell. Prior to enlisting he had been employed in the Investments Department of the Great-West Life Assurance Company. ***Mitchell Island*** (64 O/4) in Blackfish Lake was named after him in 1989.

Mittler, Rifleman **Johan** of Sprague (B 139769). Queen's Own Rifles of Canada. He died 3 July 1944 at the age of 31 and is commemorated at Beny-sur-Mer Canadian War Cemetery in Calvados, France. He was the son of Joseph and Anna Mittler of Sprague, Manitoba. ***Mittler Lake*** (64 O/14), east of Nueltin Lake was named after him in 1995.

Moad, Flight Sergeant **Harold A.** of Clanwilliam (R 134973). No. 57 Squadron. He died 2 December 1943 at the age of 23 and is commemorated at the Berlin 1939 - 1945 War Cemetery in Brandenburg, Germany. He was the son of John A. and Ethel R. Moad (née Delmage) of Minnedosa. His nephew writes (n.d.):

He was born on December 16, 1920 in Clanwilliam where he received his education. Harold enlisted in the RCAF as a tradesman [in] November, 1941, training at Dauphin, Manitoba, Trenton, Ontario and Sea Island, British Columbia. He remustered as an Air Gunner, graduating from Macdonald on December 4, 1942. Harold and his brother Calvin were posted overseas and were together until the fall of 1943. The two brothers were gunners in two different Lancaster bombers participating in the same raid. Calvin was on his 16th operational flight when he was reported missing. Harold's Lancaster went missing over the target – Berlin.

Moad Lake (53 E/7), south of Island Lake was named after him in 1973.

Modeen, Rifleman **George** of Winnipeg (H 195591). Royal Winnipeg Rifles. He died 6 June 1944 at the age of 31 and is commemorated at Beny-sur-Mer Canadian War Cemetery in Calvados, France. He was the son of John and Emily Modeen of Minneapolis, Minnesota. ***Modeen Lake*** (53 K/11), south of Edmund Lake was named after him in 1996.

Moenaert, Lance Corporal **Robert L.** of St. Boniface (H 103482). Royal Winnipeg Rifles. He died 4 July 1944 at the age of 21 and is commemorated at Beny-sur-Mer Canadian War Cemetery in Calvados, France. He was the son of Camille and Helen Moenaert of Winnipeg. ***Moenaert Lake*** (64 K/14), northeast of Lac Brochet was named after him in 1972.

Moffat, Pilot Officer **Archibald Douglas** of Winnipeg (J 88479). No. 1666 Heavy Conversion Unit, RCAF. He died 24 July 1944 at the age of 21 and is commemorated at Stonefall Cemetery in Yorkshire, England. He was the son of Archibald and Jessie D. Moffatt (sp.) of East Kildonan. Prior to enlisting, he was employed in the instrument department of Trans-Canada Airlines. ***Moffat Point*** (64 P/13) on the northwest shore of Spratt Lake was named after him in 1985.

Moffat, Able Seaman **Cyril B.** of Winnipeg (V 24489). HMCS *Alberni*. The *Alberni* was torpedoed and sunk by U-480, southeast of the Isle of Wight; 59 of her ship's company were lost. Able Seaman Moffat died 21 August 1944 at the age of 26 and is commemorated at the Halifax Memorial. He was the son of David and Emmilene E. Moffat of Winnipeg and was survived by his wife Erica H. Moffat of Winnipeg. ***Moffat Peninsula*** (63 P/8) on Pritchard Lake was named after him in 1995.

Moffat, Lieutenant **John James** of Winnipeg. Irish Regiment of Canada. He died 22 December 1944 at the age of 24 and is commemorated at Villanova Canadian War Cemetery, Italy. He was the son of William J. and Mildred E. Moffat of Winnipeg. His brother writes (9 November 1984):

My brother ... enlisted in the Royal Winnipeg Rifles in 1941. He was commissioned as a lieutenant and in 1943 went to the UK as a reinforcement officer. In 1944, he was posted as a reinforcement to the Toronto Scottish Regiment in the Fifth Canadian Division and embarked for Sicily and later to Italy. On December 22, 1944 he was killed at Ravenna in northern Italy.

Moffat Bay (64 F/1), on the west shore of Barrington Lake was named after him in 1989.

Moffatt, Warrant Officer 2 **Bertrum A.** of Carberry (R 80237). No. 75 Squadron. He died 9 April 1943 at the age of 25 and is commemorated at Newmarket Cemetery in Suffolk, England. He was survived by his wife Lillian M. Moffatt of Littleport, Cambridgeshire, England. ***Moffatt Island*** (64 J/15) in Stony Lake was named after him in 1975.

Moffatt, Private **John A.** of Norwood (H 6599). Winnipeg Grenadiers. He died a prisoner of war 2 September 1942 at the age of 39 and is commemorated at the Sai Wan War Cemetery in Hong Kong. He was the son of John and Janet Moffatt and was survived by his wife Jewel M. Moffatt of St. Boniface and their two daughters, Margaret and Carol. His daughter Margaret writes (12 November 2001):

He was a painter by trade, but jobs at the time were scarce, so he worked at many things, whenever he could. He was one of the first to enlist when war broke out in 1939. He was first stationed in Jamaica and then returned briefly to Winnipeg before being shipped off to Hong Kong. I still have the one letter we ever received from him while he was a prisoner. He wrote of his love and concern for us all and how much he missed us. A great deal was sacrificed in this war and I am grateful my father and all the other brave men from Manitoba have been commemorated in this way.

Moffatt Rapids (64 P/14) in the Caribou River was named after him in 1995.

Mogey, Captain **Harold F.** of Winnipeg. Royal Canadian Artillery. He died 28 October 1944 and is commemorated at Bergen-op-Zoom Canadian War Cemetery in Holland. He was the son of Frederick J. and Christina F. Mogey of Regina, Saskatchewan. ***Mogey Lake*** (53 N/3), south of White Goose Lake was named after him in 1995.

Moggey, Corporal **James G.** of Ninette (H 228). Lord Strathcona's Horse. He died 24 May 1944 at the age of 19 and is commemorated at the Cassino War Cemetery in Italy. He was the son of Joseph and Susan Moggey of Ninette, Manitoba. According to his brother (10 October 2001):

He attended Ninette School and was active in sports, playing goal for the local junior and senior hockey teams. He worked odd jobs after school and on weekends and managed to save enough money to buy himself a bicycle. Jim spent the summer of 1940 at Shilo working for a Ninette man who was opening a restaurant there. This was his first contact with the military.

That year, Jim applied to the RCAF but was rejected because he was too young. The following year, he heard that Lord Strathcona's Horse was recruiting in Winnipeg, so he and three other local fellows decided to join up. Jim discussed it with Mother and convinced her that this was really what he wanted to do. Jim lied about his age at the recruiting office, telling them that he was 20 and although he was the youngest of his group of friends, he was the only one accepted. He took his basic training at Listowel and Camp Borden. After embarkation leave, he went overseas and spent his 18th birthday (1942) near Dundee, Scotland. This created a problem. He wrote that the army wanted to send him back to Canada for officer training. He later wrote that he had convinced them he was not about to come back until he was "finished."

Two of his last letters home were to his sister Alice who was with the RCAF in Ontario at the time:

Dear Sis: Hello little girl, how are you keeping these days? Is it cold where you are? What a pity; it is lovely here. The sun is nice and bright and we haven't had any rain for almost a week.

I am writing this from a very peculiar position. I am laying on my back on the back of my tank, just about two miles from the enemy lines, so if you see some sort of a scrawl, don't be excited as it will probably be my nervous reaction to an artillery gun, although I am quite used to them now. I didn't tell them at home that I was this far up as it would probably worry mum, so don't be too strong in what you write home.

I got your parcel the other day and look, don't you go sending me any more issue towels as I can get them for nought here. Boy, did I get a razzing when the fellows saw the issue towel. But I got back on one of them because when he opened his parcel he had a can of Bully Beef in it and was he mad.

I have been getting quite a bit of mail. I have been getting more than I have time to answer as we don't get much time to write in the daytime and at night we can't show a light. So if you don't hear from me for a while, don't get worried as I expect everything will turn out for the best.

How is everything over around there? Have you had a chance to get posted lately? You were telling me about giving a blood donation, well don't think you're so brave as I gave one about three weeks ago. I didn't have the reaction you did though; it never bothered me at all. Of course maybe it was the pint of beer we got after we gave the blood that kept me OK. So long for now. Lots of Love, Jim (24 January 1944).

Dear Sis: Well little butterfly, how the hell is the old lord treating you these days? Things are just the same here, no excitement as yet although we are living in hopes of seeing a little bit of action some day. It sure would be hell to go through a whole war without getting a crack at somebody.

I named the tank today, or rather, somebody else named it for me. The honourable name is *Screwball* and lord it sure fits the tank and the crew. The members of the crew range from Nova Scotia right through to BC. From east to west they are: Trooper MacDonald, Halifax, yours truly, Major Wattsford, Calgary, Signalman Derry, Vancouver and Sergeant Lovelock from Nanaimo. And you talk about a screwball outfit, well this tank crew is really it.

I had a letter from Miss [deleted] last night and from the way she writes, I think she is just like her mother, just a little bit cracked. She was telling me that [deleted] and [deleted] were back home again. I wonder what they are going to do now.

I also got the three hundred export cigs. from you last night. Thanks a lot. I don't know just when they were mailed as I threw the wrapper away without making sure. Well kid, by the time you get another letter from me, I may have a little more news, so as this is all the BS I can find for tonight, I will say so long for now. Love, Jim (16 May 1944).

The next letter the family received was from Major Wattsford:

Dear Mrs. Moggey: I have been wanting to write to you for some time now to tell you of the circumstances concerning your boy's death, but I have been unable to do so due to injuries, and regret to say that even now, my letter must be dictated. I know that Mr. Munroe has already written to you, but in view of the fact that your son was a member of the crew of my tank, I feel that I too want to write to you.

On the afternoon of the 24th of May, the Regiment was given the task of forcing a bridgehead over the Melfa River. This was a very important role as the Melfa formed the first chief obstacle after the Adolph Hitler Line and by securing it, we were to be the spearhead of the great push towards Rome. We hit heavy opposition on the Melfa, but the Regiment to a man lived up to its past, glorious tradition and in spite of fairly heavy losses, we secured our objective. About six o'clock in the evening, my crew and I were off a bit on the left flank of the Regiment. We noticed that an enemy gun still farther to the left was causing a lot of casualties amongst our troops both on this and on the far side of the river. As we were the nearest to it, it was obviously a job for us to take on and when I put it up to my crew, they agreed wholeheartedly to a man. Our plan was to get as close up in the rear of the enemy gun as possible so as to surprise him and also so as to be sure of a kill. The plan was working out well and we were just about ready to fire when we were spotted. The extraordinary thing that then happened was that both tanks fired at the same time, both registering direct hits.

I hope I am not being cruel in giving these details, but I feel that if I now tell you the absolutely true facts of your son's death that you will be spared the mental anguish of doubts and suspicions lingering on and on. The German shell came straight in the front of our tank, killing your boy instantly. I can honestly assure you that he would not know for even the fraction of a second what had happened. At least, thank God, he was completely spared all suffering. This is the first thing which I was most anxious that you should know.

The second point which I feel it is my duty to mention is that your Son's life was not needlessly thrown away, for our mission was successful and by knocking out the German gun, the task of consolidating the Regimental objective was considerably eased, in fact had the German gun remained there, the bridgehead could not have been maintained. This, I might say, is not only my own view, but also the view of our GOC. Last but not least, I want to tell you what a fine soldier and man your son was. The latter, I am sure, you already know, but maybe it will mean something to you to know that the goodness of your boy's character was not lost to others.

As my Corporal-Driver, he did a job which could not have been improved upon. In action he was calm, cool and entirely reliable, as I knew he would be. But I am really thinking now of day to day soldiering, when one has so often many tiresome tasks to do that a lazy man could say 'I'll do it tomorrow.' With your boy looking after my tank, I never had to give it a thought, knowing full well that should I need it in five minutes time, it would be ready for me and 100% battleworthy. Your boy was a leader and always a cheery influence with the rest of the crew, in fact, I think we had one of the happiest crews in the Regiment. I had always realized that your son was a very popular member of the Regiment, but this has been more forcibly brought home to me since his death, as countless lads who have come to see me in hospital have remarked on how sorry they are that Jim was killed and have mentioned how popular he was with everybody. You indeed may well [be] proud of your boy and can rest assured that he will always live in the memory of those of us who served with him.

I sincerely hope that this letter will not hurt you, but that you may derive some consolation from it. If I am fortunate enough to return to Canada when the war is over and if I am out your way, I will try and pay you a visit. If there are any questions you wish to ask me about your boy, please do not hesitate to write, for I may have left out some point which is worrying you. I pray that God will give you strength and comfort to help you with your great sorrow. Yours sincerely, G. J. H. Wattsford (23 June 1944).

Moggey Lake (64 N/15), west of Nueltin Lake was named after him in 1972.

Mokanyk, Sergeant **Alexander E.** of Winnipeg (R 71124). No. 130 Squadron. He died 11 October 1941 at the age of 23 and is commemorated at Illogan (St. Illogan) Churchyard, Cornwall, England. He was the son of Mr. and Mrs. William Mokanyk of Winnipeg and was survived by his wife Anne E. Mokanyk (née Klymkiw) of Winnipeg. His obituary read in part:

Born in Winnipeg, ... he was educated at St. John's Technical School and was a student at the University of Manitoba for three years where he took a pre-medical course. He obtained his private pilot's license before the war and joined the air force September 13, 1940. He left for England last May. He was a member of the Winnipeg Winter Club (n.d.).

Mokanyk Lake (64 G/15), west of Trout Lake was named after him in 1995.

Mollard, Flight Sergeant **William J.** of Stonewall (R 106468). No. 115 Squadron. He died 16 October 1942 at the age of 20 and is commemorated at the Runnymede Memorial in Surrey, England. He was the son of Albert J. and Marion Mollard of Stonewall, Manitoba. ***Mollard Lake*** (64 P/8), east of Nejanilini Lake was named after him in 1974.

Monaghan, Flight Sergeant **Allan D.** of Morden (R 133810). No. 57 Squadron. He died 13 May 1943 at the age of 22 and is commemorated at Reichswald Forest War Cemetery, Germany. He was the son of John and Elizabeth Monaghan of Morden and the great-grandson of Alvey Morden after whom the Town of Morden is named. He had originally joined the Queen's Own Cameron Highlanders, but due to an injury, he transferred to a mechanised unit (Fort Garry Horse). Later, he completed his Grade 11 and was admitted to the Air Force. ***Monaghan Lake*** (64 C/3), east of Russell Lake was named after him in 1993.

Monck, Flying Officer **Russell M.** of Winnipeg (J 9253). No. 12 Service Flying Training School. He died 26 September 1944 at the age of 22 and is commemorated at Brookside Cemetery in Winnipeg. He was the son of Russell M. and Mary M. Monck of Ottawa and was survived by his wife Rena M. Monck of Winnipeg. ***Monck Bay*** (64 P/2) in Thekakaya Lake was named after him in 1995.

Monette, Leading Aircraftman **Louis A. W.** of Marquette (R 152607). No. 3 Service Flying Training School. He died 4 December 1943 at the age of 27 and is commemorated at Hillside Cemetery in Portage la Prairie. He was the son of Patrick and Susan Monette of Portage la Prairie. ***Monette Lake*** (63 J/12), east of Wekusko Lake was named after him in 1972.

Money, Private **S. A. George "Geordie"** of Belmont (H 103460). South Saskatchewan Regiment. He died 9 March 1945 at the age of 23 and is commemorated at the Groesbeek Canadian War Cemetery in Holland. He was the son of Samuel G. and Lillian J. Money of Belmont, Manitoba. According to his sister (29 January 1998):

> He was very musical and could play almost any instrument, particularly piano, violin, banjo, guitar and played for dances in a small orchestra. He was fond of baseball and most sports in general.

Money Lake (64 K/7), southeast of Lac Brochet was named after him in 1972.

Monk, Flying Officer **Arthur J. B.** of Winnipeg (J 4692). No. 144 Squadron. He died 11 December 1941 at the age of 29 and is commemorated at the Runnymede Memorial in Surrey, England. He was the son of John B. and Beatrice L. Monk of Winnipeg. ***Monk Lake*** (64 C/7), north of Granville Lake was named after him in 1995.

Monk, Pilot Officer **William G.** of Winnipeg (J 17258). No. 90 Squadron. He died 29 April 1943 at the age of 21 and is commemorated at the Kiel War Cemetery in Germany. ***Monk Island*** (64 B/8) in Roe Lake was named after him in 1995.

Monkhouse, Flying Officer **William G.** of Winnipeg (C 2065). No. 4 Service Flying Training School. He died 12 December 1941 at the age of 38 and is commemorated at Elmwood Cemetery in Winnipeg. He was the son of Geoffrey and Augusta Monkhouse of Winnipeg and was survived by his wife Marjorie M. Monkhouse of Winnipeg. ***Monkhouse Lake*** (64 H/9), north of Freeman Lake was named after him in 1995.

Monnier, Flight Lieutenant **Henry C.** of St. Boniface (J 17208). No. 158 Squadron. He died 18 July 1944 at the age of 25 and is commemorated at Stonefall Cemetery in Yorkshire, England. He was the son of Roger H. and Helene Monnier of Norwood. ***Monnier Lake*** (64 O/15), east of Nueltin Lake was named after him in 1975.

Montgomery, Warrant Officer 2 **Richard G.** of Winnipeg (R 106426). No. 59 Squadron. He died 23 March 1943 at the age of 23 and is commemorated at the Runnymede Memorial in Surrey, England. ***Montgomery Lake*** (53 D/5), northwest of Carr-Harris Lake was named after him in 1979.

Mooney, Flying Officer **Frank W.** of Winnipeg (J 38975). No. 1659 Heavy Conversion Unit, RCAF. He died 15 January 1945 at the age of 21 and is commemorated at Stonefall Cemetery in Yorkshire, England. He was the son of Bernard R. and Elizabeth Mooney of Vancouver. ***Mooney Lake*** (64 H/16), southwest of Condie Lake was named after him in 1995.

Moor, Flying Officer **Maurice G.** of Winnipeg (J 10139). No. 464 Squadron. He died 6 December 1942 at the age of 23 and is commemorated at Woensel General Cemetery in Eindhoven, Holland. He was the son of Edward G. and Isobel Moor of St. Vital. ***Moor Island*** (63 N/3) in Kississing Lake was named after him in 1972.

Moorby, Pilot Officer **Robert G.** of Winnipeg (J 4674). No. 23 Operational Training Unit, RCAF. He died 10 March 1943 at the age of 23 and is commemorated at Brookwood Military Cemetery in Surrey, England. He was the son of Edward C. and Margaret Moorby of Winnipeg and was survived by his younger brother and sister Bill and Jean. His Wellington aircraft X3349 crashed at Keyham, Leicestershire; the entire crew was killed. Years later his brother wrote (6 December 2001):

> Bob was always interested in aviation and obtained his private pilot's license from the Winnipeg Flying Club at Stevenson Field at the age of 19. He interrupted his engineering studies at the University of Manitoba to work for a short time at the Canadian Car and Foundry factory in Thunder Bay which at the time was assembling Hurricane fighters before joining the RCAF. He took his navigator training in Summerside, PEI.
>
> He was at the family cottage for a brief time during his final leave to indulge in his favourite pastime – sailing. Bob then returned to Winnipeg for the remainder of his leave to be with family and friends. On arrival in England, he was assigned as a crew member on Wellingtons.
>
> In 1995, I visited my brother's grave to mourn the loss of so many of that generation of Canadians. All five members of the crew are commemorated together at Brookwood under a large maple tree.

Moorby Lake (64 N/6), southwest of Nueltin Lake was named after him in 1972.

Moore, Rifleman **Albert Henry** of Woodmore (H 40801). Royal Winnipeg Rifles. He died 5 July 1944 at the age of 32 and is commemorated at Brookwood Military Cemetery in Surrey, England. He was the son of John H. and Lillian L. Moore (née Hamblin) of Woodmore, Manitoba. His sister pressed the Department of National Defence for more details surrounding his death and received the following:

> Dear Miss Moore: Your correspondence with No. 21 Canadian General Hospital regarding your brother H 40801 Rfn. Moore, A. H. has been turned over to this unit as records of the case are now in our possession. He received extensive wounds of his thighs and buttocks in France on the 6th June 1944. The same day, he was treated in forward hospitals by operation, blood transfusion, penicillin, sulphonamide and anti gas gangrene serum. Some days later he was transferred to a base hospital in England where it was noted that though the wounds were extensive, they were healing fairly well. There was, however, some persisting infection and the patient had a fever. Treatment was continued with penicillin and

sulphadiazine. On the 4th July 44 he developed a blood clot in the veins of his legs. Some of this blood clot broke off and proceeded to his lungs resulting in the patient's death. This is not an uncommon complication in casualties severely wounded, and is one that can not be foreseen and once it has become established, does not respond well to any form of treatment. I wish to extend to you my deepest sympathy. Your brother was a brave man and his sacrifice has not been in vain. To such soldiers as he, Canada is deeply indebted. Lieutenant W. A. Oille, Royal Canadian Army Medical Corps (26 August 1944).

Henry Moore Lake (64 B/3), west of Mynarski Lakes was named after him in 1995.

Moore, Sapper **Alfred A. "Pat"** of Winnipeg (H 25157). Royal Canadian Engineers. He died 7 September 1944 and is commemorated at the Adegem Canadian War Cemetery in Belgium. He was the son of Walter H. and Edna M. Moore of Letellier and the brother of Pilot Officer Arthur F. Moore (next entry). ***Alfred Moore Bay*** (53 E/15) in Island Lake was named after him in 1995.

Moore, Pilot Officer **Arthur F.** of Winnipeg (J 93802). No. 172 Squadron. He died 19 February 1944 at the age of 24 and is commemorated at the Runnymede Memorial in Surrey, England. He was the son of Walter H. and Edna M. Moore of Letellier and the brother of Sapper Alfred A. Moore (previous entry). Fifty years later, the family received the following correspondence from Lieutenant Commander David Harries (Royal Navy, retired):

Very recently, and in connection with a Memorial Service being arranged to mark the 50th anniversary of those lost on HMS *Warwick*, it has come to light that on 20th February 1944, Wellington aircraft No. HF163 of 172 Squadron based at RAF Chivenor in north Devon, England ... was posted as overdue and at about 11:00 AM an Air/Sea rescue search was started and an Anson aircraft loaded with inflatable dinghies began searching the sea area off Padstow in Cornwall which is some fifty miles southwest of Chivenor.

On the same day and at the same time the destroyer HMS *Warwick* was on patrol in the same area, but just before midday she was torpedoed and sunk in about three minutes with very heavy loss of life. The pilot of the Air/Sea Rescue Anson actually saw the destroyer blow up and immediately came down above the survivors swimming in the chilling water and dropped among them the dinghies which he had ready for the crew of the Wellington for which he was searching. This action by him saved the lives of a number of HMS *Warwick's* company.

Sadly the airmen were never found but their deaths are very much connected with those of us who survived the sinking of the HMS Warwick because if their aircraft had not been posted overdue, no Air/Sea Rescue operation would have taken place and the warship's casualties would have been much higher.

Next year at 10:30 AM on Sunday 20th February 1994, a Memorial Service is being held at St. Merryn Church outside Padstow and where some of those who died in HMS *Warwick* are buried to mark the 50th anniversary of all those on her who were lost. A number of the next-of-kin and their families of those who were posted "Missing presumed killed" have been traced and will be attending the service.

During this Memorial Service, the names on the "Roll of Honour" of those who were lost will be read out by a group of those people from these families and included with the names of the naval personnel who were lost will be the names of the six airmen from the missing Wellington.

This will be done in memory of this group of aviators who, indirectly, are connected with the history of HMS *Warwick* and as a token of respect to the Royal Air Force, the Royal Canadian Air Force and the Royal Australian Air Force (1993).

Arthur Moore Island (53 E/15) in Island Lake was named after him in 1995.

Moore, Private **Bertrand C.** of Winnipeg (H 6621). Winnipeg Grenadiers. He died a prisoner of war 2 January 1944 and is commemorated at the Yokohama War Cemetery in Japan. ***Moore Point*** (53 M/4) on Utik Lake was named after him in 1995.

Moore, Corporal **Charles Robert** of Boissevain (R 80313). Radio Mechanic, RCAF. He died 19 July 1943 at the age of 32 and is commemorated at Ambon War Cemetery, Indonesia. He was the son of Charles H. and Ethel M. Moore of Boissevain, Manitoba. According to his brother (29 March 1995) he:

Enlisted in the RCAF as a radar mechanic November 1940 and in January, 1941 [was] posted to England where he was attached to the Royal Air Force. After training, [he] serviced ground radar equipment in Wales and Devon, England. In September, 1941 [he] was posted to Singapore and as the Japanese invaded, [he] escaped as far as Java when he was captured and later died as a PoW.

The official cause of death was listed as dysentery (Allison and Hayward 1991). ***Moore Esker*** (53 N/5), northeast of Swampy Lake was named after him in 1995.

Moore, Sergeant **David S.** of Flin Flon (R 182829). No. 3 Ferry Unit, RCAF. He died 23 April 1945 at the age of 21 and is commemorated at Dely Ibrahim War Cemetery in Algeria. He was the son of James and Margaret E. Moore of Flin Flon, Manitoba. His sister writes (12 September 1996):

He attended school in Birch River and moved to Flin Flon, Manitoba in 1938. David enjoyed hunting and fishing and numerous other outdoor activities.

His obituary hinted of unusual circumstances surrounding his death:

Sergeant David Stewart Moore ... was found dead on Blida Road, Algeria, North Africa, according to word received here Friday by his parents. The official message stated the time and cause of death were unknown. The body of a second airman was found at the same time, the message said. Sergeant Moore enlisted about three years ago and had been serving in Egypt (*Winnipeg Tribune* n.d.).

Moore Rapids (63 O/5) in Erickson Creek was named after him in 1995.

Moore, Private **Douglas H.** of Elgin (H 6371). Winnipeg Grenadiers. He died a prisoner of war 18 September 1942 at the age of 25 and is commemorated at the Sai Wan War Cemetery in Hong Kong. He was the son of Wilson and Elizabeth Moore of Birch River and was survived by his wife Johanna P. Moore of Winnipeg. She recalls (20 October 2001):

At the time of enlistment, Douglas was employed by Hudson Bay Mining and Smelting [in] Flin Flon, Manitoba. While on a pass – New Year's Eve, 1939 – at a dance he met his future wife while visiting his cousins. [In] June, 1940, he was sent on a tour of duty to Bermuda and Jamaica. Fifteen months later, while back in Winnipeg, he wed Johanna on Monday, 20 October 1941 and left for Hong Kong on Saturday. My wedding gift for him, a diamond signet ring sent to him shortly after, was returned in 1947. It had never reached him; what a disappointment.

Moore Island (64 O/9) in Croll Lake was named after him in 1985.

Moore, Private **Eric H.** of Winnipeg (H 102529). Westminster Regiment. He died 24 May 1944 at the age of 37 and is commemorated at the Cassino War Cemetery in Italy. He was the eldest of the six children of James and Janet Moore of Winnipeg. His sister-in-law writes (1 December 1994):

> We don't have too much to tell about his background. He was the oldest – 14 years old – when his mother passed away. [His] father took Eric to do farm work where they could find it and the oldest daughter was taken by an Aunt and Uncle; the next brother was adopted by the same couple; the three younger children were left in the Children's Home of Winnipeg, my husband being the youngest (11 months).
>
> Eric had trouble finding work before the war, but managed to get [on] with the Hudson's Bay Company in Winnipeg for a short time before he joined up. He said if his little brother could do it, so could he.

Eric Moore Lake (64 C/4), west of McCallum Lake was named after him in 1995.

Moore, Warrant Officer 2 **George W.** of Winnipeg (R 134338). No. 90 Squadron. He died 22 September 1943 at the age of 30 and is commemorated at Cambridge City Cemetery in Cambridgeshire, England. He was the son of George R. and Mabel F. Moore of Winnipeg. ***George Moore Lake*** (53 L/5), north of Bolton Lake was named after him in 1995.

Moore, Private **Howard D.** of St. Vital (H 102421). Royal Canadian Regiment. He died 4 September 1944 at the age of 30 and is commemorated at Ancona War Cemetery in Italy. He was survived by his mother Sadie Moore. His sister recalls (14 August 1990) that he was:

> ... born at Holland, Manitoba [and] moved to Winnipeg with his parents in 1918 at the age of four years. [He] started school at Earl Grey situated between Fleet Street and Garwood in Fort Rouge where he finished his education. In 1939, when war broke out, he was living at home with his mother, a widow. He was engaged to be married, but shipped out before he had a chance. He had been self-employed and was his mother's only support.

The family later learned that he had been shot while carrying a wounded soldier to safety. ***Moore Hill*** (53 M/7), north of Knee Lake was named after him in 1995.

Moore, Pilot Officer **James E.** of Winnipeg (J 24624). Royal Canadian Air Force. He was lost at sea when the Danish troop transport ship MV *Amerika* was torpedoed. He was presumed dead 22 April 1943 and is commemorated at the Ottawa Memorial. ***Moore Peninsula*** (64 C/9) on Eden Lake was named after him in 1995.

Moore, Warrant Officer 1 **John I.** of Brandon (R 80156). No. 8 Squadron. He died 10 July 1943 at the age of 21 and is commemorated at Maala Cemetery in Yemen. He was the son of Malcolm S. and Edith M. Moore of Brandon. ***John Moore Rapids*** (53 M/14) in the Dafoe River was named after him in 1995.

Moore, Private **Martin** of Lockport (H 19683). Queen's Own Cameron Highlanders. He died 19 August 1942 at the age of 38 and is commemorated at Dieppe Canadian War Cemetery in Seine-Maritime, France. He was the son of George and Mair Moore of Lockport and was survived by his wife Edna R. Moore of Lockport, Manitoba. ***Martin Moore Lake*** (64 O/7), southeast of Sandhill Lake was named after him in 1995.

Moore, Private **Norval H.** (H 18638). Royal Regiment of Canada. He was reported missing in action 19 February 1945 at the age of 19 and is commemorated at the Groesbeek Canadian War Cemetery in Holland. He was the third of the ten children of Percy and Grace Moore of Neepawa. His sister writes (5 March 1996):

> Norval Harvey Moore was born in [Neepawa] June 14, 1925. Norval was a very outdoors person and while living in Kenora, he and his friends built a small cabin on an island in the Winnipeg River. When he was a young boy he went to live with his grandparents, Mr. and Mrs. Walter Battershell on the farm near Birnie, Manitoba and went to school there as well. He later moved to Kenora with his family and worked at a small tourist camp at Granite Lake – also at a garage.

She adds (29 November 2001):

> He was a member of the Kenora Jaycees Juvenile Championship hockey team in 1942-1943 and while in Holland enjoyed skating on the canals, and even played in a hockey game. Norval loved to play the guitar and sing, and according to his letters he performed at amateur shows. One comment in a letter was that he saw a lot of things he never dreamed of seeing.
>
> He was enrolled in the Canadian Army January 4, 1944 and on October 12, 1944 left for the United Kingdom. I myself visited his grave in Holland in 1975 while on a personal vacation. The cemetery was very well kept.

Norval Moore Lake (53 M/10), east of Annesley Lake was named after him in 1995.

Moore, Warrant Officer 1 **Robert K.** of Winnipeg (R 124087). No. 1666 Heavy Conversion Unit, RCAF. He died 11 July 1944 at the age of 22 and is commemorated at Stonefall Cemetery in Yorkshire, England. He was the step-son of Thomas Kells and the son of Ethel S. Moore and was survived by his wife Doris M. Moore of Calgary. His brother writes (10 March 1995):

> Bob was known as "Red" by his close friends. He was an active speed skater and continually showed a zest and zeal for life's challenges. Commercial radio was another of Bob's special interests. He was enrolled in the Radio College of Canada prior to enlistment in the RCAF.
>
> Bob was very proud of his uniform, his crew and his accomplishments while in the service. Although his life was short, he lived each moment to its fullest. He lost his life on active service during a flying operation in a Halifax bomber. Bob remains alive today in the memory and hearts of his family.

Robert Moore Lake (64 I/5), west of Legary Lake was named after him in 1995.

Moore, Captain **Thomas W.** of Winnipeg. Royal Canadian Artillery. He died 20 July 1944 and is commemorated at Bretteville-sur-Laize Canadian War Cemetery in Calvados, France. He was the son of Lieutenant Colonel Thomas M. and Emily E. Moore and was survived by his wife Roberta M. Moore of Uplands, Ontario. ***Thomas Moore Lake*** (64 F/5), east of Carriere Lake was named after him in 1995.

Moore, Private **Wilfred S.** of Winnipeg (H 6674). Winnipeg Grenadiers. He died a prisoner of war 9 October 1942 and is commemorated at the Sai Wan War Cemetery in Hong Kong. ***Moore Narrows*** (64 A/12) in Baldock Lake was named after him in 1995.

Moore, Able Seaman **William W.** of Cypress River (V 54554). HMCS *Valleyfield*. The *Valleyfield* was torpedoed and sunk by U-548 50 miles south of Cape Race, Newfoundland; 125 of her ship's company were lost. Able Seaman Moore died 7 May 1944 at the age of 22 and is commemorated at the Halifax Memorial. He was the son of Wallace Moore of Cypress River. ***William Moore Lake*** (63 P/3), east of Sipiwesk Lake was named after him in 1995.

Moors, Sergeant **Arthur A.** of Sanford (R 119562). No. 14 Advanced Flying School. He died 8 April 1943 at the age of 21 and is commemorated at Cottesmore (St. Nicholas) Churchyard Extension, Rutland, England. He was the son of Walter A. and Gwendoline M. Moors of Sanford, Manitoba. ***Moors Lake*** (64 J/13), northwest of Tadoule Lake was named after him in 1975.

Moran, (alias Pollock) Private **Patrick J.** of East Lockport (B 145766). Irish Regiment of Canada. He died 5 May 1945 and is commemorated at the Holten Canadian War Cemetery in Holland. ***Moran Lake*** (53 E/16), north of Island Lake was named after him in 1997.

Morand, Private **George** of Marchand (H 21024). South Saskatchewan Regiment. He died 28 August 1944 at the age of 39 and is commemorated at Bretteville-sur-Laize Canadian War Cemetery in Calvados, France. He was the son of Joseph and Virginia Morand and was survived by his wife Ada Morand of Marchand, Manitoba. ***Morand Lake*** (64 J/4), north of Big Sand Lake was named after him in 1957.

More, Able Seaman **Andrew** of Winnipeg (V 9314). HMCS *Fraser*. The *Fraser* was lost in a collision with the British cruiser HMS *Calcutta* during the evacuation of France in 1940. Able Seaman More died 25 June 1940 at the age of 30 and is commemorated at the Halifax Memorial. He was the son of Andrew and Margaret More of Winnipeg. More Lake (64 C/16), south of Barrington Lake was named after him in 1957 and ***More Island*** (53 E/13) in Stevenson Lake was named after him in 1995.

Morfoot, Flight Sergeant **Lorne A.** of Beausejour (R 210350). No. 625 Squadron. He died 24 July 1944 at the age of 19 and is commemorated at the Runnymede Memorial in Surrey, England. He was the son of Thomas W. and Minnie E. Morfoot (née Nieman) of Beausejour. ***Morfoot Lake*** (64 N/10), southwest of Nueltin Lake was named after him in 1972.

Morgan, Lance Corporal **Albert W.** of Winnipeg (H 6731). Winnipeg Grenadiers. He died 19 December 1941 at the age of 33 and is commemorated at the Sai Wan Memorial in Hong Kong. He was the son of Mr. and Mrs. W. S. Morgan of Waltham Cross, Hertfordshire and was survived by his wife Elsie I. Morgan of Winnipeg and their son. ***Morgan Bay*** (64 H/2) in Fidler Lake was named after him in 1995.

Morgan, Rifleman **James B.** of Winnipeg (H 200064). Royal Winnipeg Rifles. He died 16 June 1944 at the age of 34 and is commemorated at Beny-sur-Mer Canadian War Cemetery in Calvados, France. He was the son of James and Agnes Morgan and was survived by his wife Olga Morgan of Winnipeg. She writes (4 May 1998):

> Jim was born in Paisley, Scotland, as well as his sister who is now deceased. His mother died and his father brought them to Canada at an early age. His father remarried and he had two sons: Jack who served in the Canadian Navy and William who served in the RCAF. Jim worked for the CNR up until he enlisted in May, 1942.
>
> I have letters from the Padre of his regiment during the Invasion and he spoke very highly of Jim. He had had many talks with him previously. I visited the Cemetery and saw where he is buried.

Morgan Point (64 K/1) on Chartrand Lake was named after him in 1995.

Morgan, Flight Lieutenant **J. A. Wynn** of Winnipeg (J 25000). No. 433 Squadron. He died 16 August 1944 at the age of 23 and is commemorated at Sonderby (Assens) Churchyard, Denmark. He was a student at the University of Manitoba at the time of his enlistment. His tail gunner recalls:

> Our captain was Wynn Morgan, a likeable Winnipegger in his early twenties. We all came to trust him completely. We may have grumbled sometimes, but we appreciated it when he worked us hard during training flights. Morgan was constantly trying to learn more about his plane and improve his skills as a pilot. The only mild criticism any of us had was that he always descended too quickly, bouncing us off the runway before putting the airplane down (Marchildon 1993).

His navigator, George Gill wrote to his parents after the war:

> Wynn and I roomed and spent many good times together as well as flying together. Both on and off the ground he was a great captain, a man who enjoyed the things he did in life. In the air, Wynn was a great pilot and captain, a job he loved no end. It was a privilege and pleasure to fly with your son who gave his life without regret doing the job he loved (n.d.).

Morgan Island (63 P/11) in Pikwitonei Lake was named after him in 1995.

Morgans, Warrant Officer 2 **Edward A. "Ted"** of Brandon (R 106093). No. 434 Squadron. He died 23 August 1943 at the age of 21 and is commemorated at Heverlee War Cemetery, Leuven, Vlaams-Brabant, Belgium. He was the youngest of the three children of John and Charlotte Morgans (née Irwin) of Brandon. His sister writes (4 January 1998):

> Ted was born in Richlea, Saskatchewan. He attended school in Richlea and Chater, Manitoba. He was an avid sports fan. He took many prizes in curling in Saskatchewan and played goalie for the Brandon Pee Wee hockey team and also in the Air Force. He walked two miles in sub-zero temperatures for practise and games. Ted loved ... hunting wild game such as duck hunting. As a boy of five, he used to go with his Dad. He was an animal lover; pet dogs were his shadow.

His obituary described him as:

> ... one of the finest young sportsmen to come along in juvenile and junior hockey circles. [He] was just as enthusiastic about his service in the Air Force. He was known to his companions in the service as "Tail End Charlie from Brandon" and he performed several heroic acts during his career in the service. A cannon shot tore a hole through the tail of his aircraft last June, but the young gunner hacked his way back to the body of the plane in some miraculous fashion, although suffering from wounds at the time (*Brandon Sun* n.d.).

Morgans Lake (64 P/5), south of Nejanilini Lake was named after him in 1974.

Morin, Leading Aircraftman **Joseph G. G.** of St. Boniface (R 119793). No. 8 Bombing and Gunnery School, RCAF. He died 19 August 1942 at the age of 20 and is commemorated at St. Boniface Cemetery. He was the son of Emile and Christina Morin (née Desroches) of St. Boniface.

Joseph was born 15 April 1922 at Beauchamp, Saskatchewan. He attended high school in Manitoba and took two years of classical studies at university prior to enlisting in the Royal Canadian Air Force 25 July 1941. Joseph was immediately sent to Penhold, Alberta for basic training. He was there about a month and was then transferred to Lethbridge, Alberta for a few days before going to Edmonton for further training. December 6, 1941, he was moved to Prince Albert, Saskatchewan. About three weeks later, he was sent to Trenton, Ontario. Valentine's Day, 14 February 1942, he was posted to Winnipeg and served there until the end of July. August 1, 1942 he was transferred to Lethbridge, Alberta for gunnery training. Seventeen days later, he was killed when the plane he was flying in crashed during gunnery practice one mile north of a town called Magrath at 10:45 August 18 (Morin 1997).

Morin Island (64 O/12) in Shannon Lake was named after him in 1985.

Morison, Major **Herbert C. J.** of Winnipeg. Royal Canadian Artillery. He died 8 February 1945 at the age of 27 and is commemorated at the Groesbeek Canadian War Cemetery in Holland. He was the son of Major J. B. and Lydia M. Morison of Winnipeg. ***Morison Lake*** (64 F/6), northwest of Wells Lake was named after him in 1995.

Moroz, Flying Officer **Hryhory "Harry"** of Flin Flon (J 12682). No. 408 Squadron. He died 22 March 1944 at the age of 20 and is commemorated at the Runnymede Memorial in Surrey, England. He was the son of Mr. and Mrs. Alexander Moroz of Transcona and the brother of Trooper Michael Moroz (next entry) and was survived by his wife. His nephew's wife writes (13 November 2001):

Harry Moroz was educated at Central School in Transcona. He was an active hockey player; in 1935 he played goal for the Winnipeg Monarchs, the Memorial Cup Champions. Harry also played senior hockey for Flin Flon in the Saskatchewan senior league for several years before enlisting. Moroz Street (formerly Royal Street) in the Regent Park area of Transcona was renamed after him and his brother in 1959.

Moroz Hill (64 K/15), southeast of Chatwin Lake was named after him in 1995.

Moroz, Trooper **Michael** of Transcona (H 101637). 12th Manitoba Dragoons. He died 9 August 1944 at the age of 28 and is commemorated at Bretteville-sur-Laize Canadian War Cemetery in Calvados, France. He was the son of Mr. and Mrs. Alexander Moroz of Transcona, the brother of Flying Officer Hryhory Moroz (previous entry) and was survived by his wife Margaret Moroz of Transcona and their son. His daughter-in-law writes (13 November 2001):

Mike Moroz was educated at Central School in Transcona. Prior to enlistment, he was an active hockey and baseball player. Mike enlisted in July, 1942 and was trained as a wireless operator at Dundurn, Portage la Prairie and Camp Borden, going overseas in June, 1943. He was killed in action at Normandy. His mother, who lost her only two sons during the war, unveiled the names on the Cenotaph in Memorial Park Circle in Transcona and served as the Silver Cross Mother during many Transcona Remembrance Day services.

The Moroz Cup (1945 - 1955), awarded to the Most Valuable Player in the Transcona Ball Club, was named after him in 1945 and ***Moroz Bay*** (64 K/15) in Maria Lake was named after him in 1979.

Morran, Sergeant **Laurence V.** of Winnipeg (H 19016). Queen's Own Cameron Highlanders. He died 14 March 1941 at the age of 37 and is commemorated at Brookwood Military Cemetery in Surrey, England. He was the son of David and Marion Morran and was survived by his wife Margaret I. Morran of Winnipeg. ***Morran Lake*** (64 O/2), southwest of Munroe Lake was named after him in 1975.

Morrice, Private **Neville E.** of Winnipeg (P 22305). Hastings and Prince Edward Regiment. He died 30 December 1943 at the age of 25 and is commemorated at the Moro River Canadian War Cemetery in Italy. He was the son of Walter W. and Mina A. E. Morrice (née Hall) of Vancouver and was survived by his fiancée Dorothy Featherstone. His niece writes (26 March 2002):

Neville was born in Misericordia Hospital, Winnipeg on February 25, 1918. His parents were thrilled and he was also welcomed by his older brother of 13 years, William, 10 year-old Katherine and five year-old Edith. His parents resided in the Hall family home. The Hall family had homesteaded here since 1858, where the "Hermitage" was well known in the area. It was run as a "home" farm and was also the first fruit growing business in the north west. In a tragic fire, the Hermitage was burned to the ground in 1920. The Morrice family stayed on the property for a number of years but eventually moved to Winnipeg and finally to Vancouver in 1941. Neville joined the PPCLI in 1939 and was sent to England on December 17th of the same year at 21 years of age. He arrived there safe and sound on December 30th to begin training.

It was in Vancouver where the family had all gathered for a holiday celebration that they learned Neville had been killed in action on Italian soil. I was born after this in May of 1945 and so I never met him but heard many family stories and I know he would be delighted that a lake carries his family name.

One of the family stories I do remember is that my grandmother had known Neville had been killed. She described it as a cold feeling, but calming and realizing what had happened filled her with grief. She stoically rejoiced in the family gathering and they all enjoyed themselves. Later, when the telegram arrived, she was not surprised.

Morrice Lake (64 H/3), east of Thorsteinson Lake was named after him in 1995.

Morrice, Private **Walter** of Winnipeg (K 85444). Canadian Scottish Regiment. He died 15 July 1944 at the age of 30 and is commemorated at Bretteville-sur-Laize Canadian War Cemetery in Calvados, France. He was the son of William and Katherine Morrice and was survived by his wife Anne Morrice (née Lukjaniuk) of Winnipeg. ***Morrice Rapids*** (64 I/14) in the Seal River was named after him in 1995.

Morris, Regimental Quarter Master Sergeant (Warrant Officer 2) **Alfred J.** of Winnipeg (P 9884). Royal Canadian Artillery. He died 8 August 1942 at the age of 41 and is commemorated at Brookside Cemetery in Winnipeg. He was the son of John H. and Edith M. Morris of Swansea, Wales. ***Morris Hill*** (64 H/7), north of Solmundsson Lake was named after him in 1995.

Morris, Flying Officer **Arthur John** of Winnipeg (J 10949). No. 402 Squadron, Air Force Medal.

This NCO has shown himself to be energetic and capable and his hard work and interest in his job have contributed materially to the success of the operations carried out at this unit. He has flown 966 hours 55 minutes day and 85 hours 10 minutes night on instructional flying between March 1941 and February 1942. He is cheerful and willing, giving his best at all times (AFM Citation 1 January 1943).

He died 21 March 1944 at the age of 25 and is commemorated at Scopwick Church Burial Ground in Lincolnshire, England. He was the son of David and Sarah W. Morris of Winnipeg. ***Morris Bay*** (64 G/15) in Trout Lake was named after him in 1986.

Morris, Gunner **Frederick A.** of Winnipeg (H 30657). Royal Canadian Artillery. He died 3 February 1946 at the age of 18 and is commemorated at Chapel Lawn Memorial Garden in Winnipeg. He was the son of Frederick J. and Hillevi C. Morris of St. James. ***Morris Esker*** (54 M/6), northeast of Long Lake was named after him in 1984.

Morris, Sapper **Frederick W.** of Winnipeg (SH 13071). Royal Canadian Engineers. He died 12 June 1952 and is commemorated at the United Nations Cemetery at Pusan, South Korea. He was survived by his wife Lillian Margaret Morris (née Murray) and their four children. A daughter visited his grave in 1994. ***Morris Rapids*** (53 L/4) in the Nikik River was named after this Korean War casualty in 1998.

Morris, Private **John I.** of Winnipeg (H 6162). Winnipeg Grenadiers. He died 20 December 1941 at the age of 23 and is commemorated at the Sai Wan Memorial in Hong Kong. He was the son of Charles H. and Margaret E. Morris of Horseshoe Bay, British Columbia. ***Morris Peninsula*** (53 L/11) on Colen Lakes was named after him in 1995.

Morris, Trooper **Willard J. "Windy"** of Winnipegosis (H 77206). 12th Manitoba Dragoons. He died 19 April 1945 at the age of 24 and is commemorated at the Holten Canadian War Cemetery in Holland. He was the son of John E. and Rose Morris of St. James. His brother recalls (17 January 1997) that he:

> ... loved life, loved nature, was an outdoor man who loved to fish and hunt; was fond of guns and loved nature. He was an excellent worker and strove to please.

Morris Point (64 C/6) on Kaykayk Lake was named after him in 1995.

Morrison, Flying Officer **Alexander J.** of Winnipeg (J 28801). No. 103 Squadron. He died 13 July 1944 at the age of 28 and is commemorated at Montiers-sur-Saulx Communal Cemetery, Meuse, France. He was the son of Angus and Isabella M. Morrison of Winnipeg. ***Morrison Point*** (64 N/6) on Catte Lake was named after him in 1987.

Morrison, Flying Officer **Colin Ross M.** of Winnipeg (J 38317). No. 76 Squadron. He died 25 April 1945 at the age of 21 and is commemorated at the Sage War Cemetery in Germany. He and the rest of the crew had completed their tour of duty, but were nonetheless dispatched one last time to a site north of Bremen. The German surrender occurred less than two weeks later and there is widespread belief that this was the last raid carried out by Bomber Command. He was the son of James and Dolina Morrison (née Sutherland) of Winnipeg. According to his brother (31 March 1995), he was:

> ... a first generation Canadian born in Portage la Prairie to Scottish parents. [He was] educated in Winnipeg, attending Wellington, General Wolfe and Daniel McIntyre schools. On leaving high school, [he was] employed at Dominion Bridge [and] MacDonald Brothers Aircraft. [He] enlisted at 18 years, ... taking basic training at Brandon Depot Manning Pool, Virden and Portage la Prairie Navigation School where he graduated as a Sergeant-Navigator. Before being posted overseas, he was promoted to the rank of Pilot Officer 12 November 1943.

Morrison Bay (64 O/12) in Larkin Lake was named after him in 1995.

Morrison, Private **Donald** of Hartney (H 9042). South Saskatchewan Regiment. He died 20 July 1944 at the age of 20 and is commemorated at Bretteville-sur-Laize Canadian War Cemetery in Calvados, France. He was the son of George Forbes and Mary E. Morrison of Hartney, Manitoba. ***Morrison Hill*** (64 I/13), north of Shethanei Lake was named after him in 1995.

Morrison, Flying Officer **Donald** of Winnipeg (J 19398). No. 419 Squadron. He died 17 June 1944 at the age of 21 and is commemorated at the Groesbeek Canadian War Cemetery in Holland. ***Morrison Peninsula*** (63 I/6) on Butterfly Lake was named after him in 1995.

Morrison, Trooper **Kenneth P.** of Minnedosa (H 103516). Governor General's Horse Guards. He died 3 September 1944 at the age of 22 and is commemorated at Gradara War Cemetery in Italy. He was the son of Roderick and Elizabeth Morrison of Minnedosa. ***Morrison Creek*** (64 P/16), which flows north into Nabel Lake was named after him in 1995.

Morrison, Private **Murdoch I. L.** of Russell (L 102692). South Saskatchewan Regiment. He died 15 November 1944 at the age of 23 and is commemorated at the Groesbeek Canadian War Cemetery in Holland. He was the son of Donald and Mary Morrison of Russell, Manitoba. ***Morrison Rapids*** (64 P/4) in the Wolverine River was named after him in 1995.

Morrison, Pilot Officer **Norman B. "Baldy"** of Deloraine (J 18881). No. 426 Squadron. He died 16 December 1943 at the age of 21 and is commemorated at the Hanover War Cemetery in Germany. He was born at North Battleford, Saskatchewan and moved to Deloraine with his parents in 1923. He enlisted in the RCAF in August, 1941 and went overseas in October, 1942. ***Morrison Island*** (64 O/13) in Nueltin Lake was named after him in 1975.

Morriss, Pilot Officer **John H.** of Winnipeg (J 90381). No. 9 Squadron. He died 21 July 1944 at the age of 22 and is commemorated at the Adegem Canadian War Cemetery in Belgium. He was the son of Howard J. and Mary Anne Morriss (née Alexander) and was survived by his wife Helena B. Morris (née Unger) of Winnipeg. Prior to enlistment, he had been the Manitoba Junior Swimming Champion in the 100 and 220 yard events and was on the Canadian Championship 200 yard relay team in 1938. He was the winner of the Parnell Trophy for best all-round swimming. He was employed at the Ogilvie Flour Mill in Winnipeg when he enlisted. Frank Raeman of Maldegem, Belgium has been researching the airmen buried in Belgium and contacted Pilot Officer Morriss' brother in 1998 with the following information:

> His aircraft was the Lancaster Mk I, serial LL884, code WS-H. The aircraft was on its 7th operation. His base was Bardney (England) and it

took off at 23:22 hrs (British time). The other six crewmembers were also killed, but they are still buried in Wevelgem (Belgium). His aircraft had a mid-air collision with a Lancaster of 101 Squadron. The crewmembers were also buried at Adegem (n.d.).

Morriss Lake (64 F/3), east of Goldsand Lake was named after him in 1994.

Morrisseau, Private **Edward J.** of Pine Falls (H 20809). Winnipeg Grenadiers. He died 23 December 1945 at the age of 27 and is commemorated at Fort Alexander Indian Reserve Roman Catholic Cemetery in Manitoba. He was the son of Mr. and Mrs. Albert Morrisseau of Pine Falls. ***Morrisseau Lake*** (64 K/15), northeast of Lac Brochet was named after him in 1979.

Morrow, Warrant Officer 1 **Frederick J.** of Melita (R 59815). No. 304 Squadron. He died 12 April 1943 at the age of 23 and is commemorated at the Runnymede Memorial in Surrey, England. ***Morrow Island*** (64 F/5) in Reindeer Lake was named after him in 1995.

Morrow, Captain **George D.** of Winnipeg. Royal Canadian Artillery. He was aboard the SS *Nerissa*, the only ship torpedoed while carrying Canadian troops to the United Kingdom. Captain Morrow died 1 May 1941 at the age of 56 and is commemorated at Ballinakill (St. Thomas) Church Of Ireland Churchyard, Galway, Republic of Ireland. He was the son of William and Esther A. Morrow. ***Morrow Lake*** (64 K/7), northeast of Reindeer Lake was named after him in 1961.

Morrow, Warrant Officer 1 **James P.** of Winnipeg (1251048). No. 466 Squadron, RAF. He died 20 January 1944 at the age of 23 and is commemorated at Becklingen War Cemetery in Germany. He was the son of Harold E. and Frances E. Morrow and was survived by his wife Anna B. Morrow of Winnipeg. ***Morrow Bay*** (64 P/7) in Wallbridge Lake was named after him in 1995.

Mortimer, Flight Sergeant **Arthur** of Winnipeg (R 106236). No. 97 Squadron. He died 20 December 1942 at the age of 20 and is commemorated at the Groesbeek Canadian War Cemetery in Holland. He was the son of Captain A. and Agnes G. Mortimer of Cumberland, British Columbia. ***Mortimer Lake*** (64 O/7), northwest of Sandhill Lake was named after him in 1995.

Moss, Private **Thomas** of Portage la Prairie (H 94307). Canadian Forestry Corps. He died 5 January 1942 at the age of 38 and is commemorated at Canadian Forces Base Military Cemetery, Quebec. He was survived by his wife Kathleen Moss of Portage la Prairie. ***Moss Bay*** (53 L/10) in Wanless Lake was named after him in 1995.

Mostowy, Flight Sergeant **Michael** of Domain (R 186675). No. 99 Squadron. He died 5 June 1945 at the age of 22 and is commemorated at the Singapore Memorial. He was the son of Joseph and Mary Mostowy of Domain, Manitoba. ***Mostowy Lake*** (64 P/12), northwest of Nejanilini Lake was named after him in 1974.

Motriuk, Warrant Officer 2 **Stanley A.** of Winnipeg (R 157271). No. 50 Squadron, Mentioned in Dispatches. He died 8 July 1944 at the age of 24 and is commemorated at Mesnil-Mauger Communal Cemetery, Seine-Maritime, France. He was the son of Sylvester and Anne Motriuk of Elmwood. ***Motriuk Lake*** (64 C/14), southwest of Lynn Lake was named after him in 1947.

Mouchet, Pilot Officer **Maurice R. N.** of St. Boniface (J 85366). No. 12 Squadron. He died 31 March 1944 at the age of 26 and is commemorated at Rheinberg War Cemetery in Germany. He was survived by his mother Suzanne Jacques of St. Boniface. ***Mouchet Lake*** (64 O/13), east of Nueltin Lake was named after him in 1975.

Moulson, Aircraftwoman 2 **Grace Audrey** of Rossburn (W 305964). No. 6 Recruiting Centre, RCAF (Women's Division). She died 8 August 1942 at the age of 25 and is commemorated at St. James Cemetery in Solsgirth, Manitoba. She was the daughter of William J. and Kathleen Moulson of Rossburn. Her sister writes (30 March 1998):

> Audrey (as she was known) was born January 24, 1917 at Rossburn, Manitoba. She grew up on a farm southwest of Rossburn. She took a hairdressing course in Winnipeg in the late 1930s [and] took over her sister's shop in Rossburn, maybe 1941. She was a fun loving, caring person with a lot of friends. She joined the WAACs in the spring of 1942, then went back to her shop to await her call-up. In August, she developed rheumatic fever and passed away at home, before she had a chance to serve her country.

Moulson Lake (64 H/2), south of Holmes Lake was named after her in 1995.

Mounteney, Gunner **William H.** of National Mills (H 103678). Royal Canadian Artillery. He died 20 July 1944 at the age of 21 and is commemorated at Bretteville-sur-Laize Canadian War Cemetery in Calvados, France. He was the son of Herbert and Ruth H. Mounteney of National Mills, Manitoba. ***Mounteney Lake*** (64 C/6), northwest of Granville Lake was named after him in 1973.

Mowat, Private **Charles A.** of Warren Landing (H 200155). Queen's Own Cameron Highlanders. He died 9 August 1944 at the age of 22 and is commemorated at Bretteville-sur-Laize Canadian War Cemetery in Calvados, France. He was one of the six children of Charles and Mary Mowat of Warren Landing, Manitoba. His brother recalls (13 December 1996):

> Charles was born ... at Norway House, Manitoba. In 1937 he found work on MS *Chickama II* and remained at this work for a couple of years. He left home in 1939 and took the ship down to where he could continue by road to Winnipeg and it was there that he joined the Queen's Own Cameron Highlanders and went off to war.
>
> Charlie was good to all us kids who were younger than he was. His spare time was devoted to all sports but mostly baseball and when he tired of that, he enjoyed recreational fishing.

Mowat Island (63 O/9) in Ospwagan Lake was named after him in 1995.

Mowat, Private **William J.** of Winnipeg (H 19540). Queen's Own Cameron Highlanders. He died 24 August 1942 and is commemorated at Dundee Western Necropolis, Angus, Scotland. ***Mowat Lake*** (63 I/16), east of Cross Lake was named after him in 1973.

Moyer, Lance Corporal **Abraham A. "Ack Ack"** of Winnipegosis (H 100971). Queen's Own Cameron Highlanders. He died 3 March 1945 at the age of 33 and is commemorated at the Groesbeek Canadian War Cemetery in Holland. He was the son of Abraham and Jennie Moyer of Winnipegosis, Manitoba. A brother who served with him recalls (21 March 1995):

> By family and friends he was called Abe. By his comrades in the army he was referred to as "Ack-Ack." Good-natured, well liked, played the violin and guitar, called square dance[s]. We got on well together overseas. When he had cigarettes, I had them and when I had them, he

had them. The same way with money. Seventeen days before he was killed, he and I helped our younger brother William Henry celebrate his 21st birthday in the City of Nijmegen. The last time I saw my brother we were together in Nijmegen, Holland in February of 1945. He was killed less than a month later.

Moyer Lake (64 C/4), southwest of Russell Lake was named after him in 1981.

Muir, Private **Archibald** of Winnipeg (H 20678). Queen's Own Cameron Highlanders. He died 19 September 1945 at the age of 22 and is commemorated at Brookside Cemetery in Winnipeg. He was survived by his mother Katie Muir of Winnipeg. ***Muir Island*** (63 I/1) in High Rock Falls Lake was named af er him in 1995.

Muir, Private **John R.** of Transcona (H 17400). Princess Patricia's Canadian Light Infantry. He died 14 December 1943 and is commemorated at the Moro River Canadian War Cemetery in Italy. ***Muir Bay*** (64 J/12) in Descôteaux Lake was named after him in 1995.

Mulcahy, Stoker 1 **Daniel** of Winnipeg (V 35412). HMCS *Valleyfield*. The *Valleyfield* was torpedoed and sunk by U-548 50 miles south of Cape Race, Newfoundland; 125 of her ship's company were lost. Stoker Mulcahy died 7 May 1944 at the age of 27 and is commemorated at the Halifax Memorial. He was survived by his mother Kate Mulcahy of Winnipeg. ***Mulcahy Lake*** (64 G/3), west of Southern Indian Lake was named after him in 1963.

Mullin, Flying Officer **Gordon J.** of Winnipeg (J 36947). No. 426 Squadron. He died 1 November 1944 at the age of 21 and is commemorated at Rheinberg War Cemetery in Germany. ***Mullin Lake*** (64 P/2), southeast of Nejanilini Lake was named after him in 1974.

Mullins, Sergeant **Patrick C. H.** of Winnipeg (R 191400). No. 30 Operational Training Unit, RCAF. He died 16 July 1944 at the age of 21 and is commemorated at Blacon Cemetery in Cheshire, England. ***Mullins Lake*** (64 H/16), southwest of Condie Lake was named after him in 1995.

Mumford, Pilot Officer **Arthur R.** of Winnipeg (J 90024). No. 407 Squadron. He died 22 June 1944 at the age of 21 and is commemorated at the Runnymede Memorial in Surrey, England. ***Mumford Lake*** (64 O/8), northeast of Munroe Lake was named after him in 1978.

Munday, Private **Donald Albert L. "Bert"** of Oakville (H 200166). Calgary Highlanders. He died 25 July 1944 at the age of 20 and is commemorated at Bretteville-sur-Laize Canadian War Cemetery in Calvados, France. He was the son of Albert R. and Myrtle H. Munday and was survived by his wife of six months Catherine B. Munday of Uddingston, Glasgow, Scotland. According to Mrs. Munday's brother, Private Munday (11 November 1994):

… was stationed in Scotland in 1943 where I and my family lived. As was done by so many families, from time to time we invited servicemen to our home and Don was one of those we welcomed.

He and my oldest sister "Rena" went out together many times and eventually decided to marry. After receiving permission from his army commander, the wedding took place in December, 1943 when "Don" as his Canadian relatives knew him ("Bert" to us Scots), had a week's leave from his unit which had been transferred to England.

From there, he received another short leave in March, 1944 and my sister travelled to England to be with him. She never saw him again as he was killed in Normandy in July, 1944. Rena never remarried but her son, named after his father, lives close to our home which Bert visited and in which my sister still lives.

My sister came to Canada immediately after the war to meet Bert's relatives but decided to return to Scotland, a decision she has often regretted. Since I emigrated to Canada [Brandon] in 1960, she has come to visit us many times.

Munday Lake (64 I/2), east of North Knife Lake was named after him in 1974.

Mundell, Flying Officer **Gordon** of Winnipeg (J 23368). No. 624 Squadron. He died 4 March 1944 at the age of 31 and is commemorated at Dely Ibrahim War Cemetery in Algeria. He was the son of Benjamin and Catharine Mundell (née Gannon) of Winnipeg. They originated in Stirling, Scotland and Maynooth, Ontario respectively. He had been an RCMP officer prior to enlistment and a participant in the "Musical Ride." His niece writes (12 September 1995):

Gordon attended Faraday, Ralph Brown, Sir Isaac Newton and St. John's High School. He loved to read and sports interested him greatly. He excelled in the discus and shot put. Gordon made his own weights and used them to build up his physique. During the 1930s, few jobs were available. Gordon was shy but had many friends and was very well liked.

Gordon joined the RCAF [on] April 14th, 1940. He flew with the RAF. Gordon was killed in action [when] his plane – a Halifax II – crashed shortly after takeoff on a special operation approximately five miles from his base at Blida, Algiers. The weather was bad with a low ceiling. Everybody on board was killed.

Mundell Lake (64 G/16), west of Namaypin Lake was named after him in 1995.

Munro, Private **Edward A.** of Birch River (H 102067). Royal Canadian Army Service Corps. He died 6 October 1945 at the age of 50 and is commemorated at the Holten Canadian War Cemetery in Holland. ***Munro Peninsula*** (64 P/3) on Pincock Lake was named after him in 1995.

Munro, Private **Walter** of Portage la Prairie (H 268). Royal Canadian Army Service Corps. He died 31 December 1944 at the age of 31 and is commemorated at Bergen-op-Zoom Canadian War Cemetery in Holland. He was the son of Mr. and Mrs. John Munro and was survived by his wife Hazel M. Munro (née Bird) of Portage la Prairie. ***Munro Bay*** (53 K/3) in Red Sucker Lake was named after him in 1995.

Munroe, Corporal **Hugh Archibald "Huck"** of Brandon (H 17414). Regina Rifle Regiment. He died 6 June 1944 at the age of 24 and is commemorated at Beny-sur-Mer Canadian War Cemetery in Calvados, France. He was the son of Hugh and Bessie H. Munroe of Brandon and was survived by his wife Constance Joan Munroe of Brandon. ***Munroe Island*** (53 M/2) in Knee Lake was named after him in 1995.

Munroe, Flight Sergeant **John A.** of Winnipeg (R 60371). No. 2 Radio School, RCAF. He died 23 November 1943 at the age of 20 and is commemorated at Haycombe Cemetery in Bath, Somerset, England. ***Munroe Rapids*** (64 I/12) in an unnamed river which drains Buckoski Lake was named after him in 1995.

Munroe, Sergeant **William A.** of Winnipeg (H 100354). Lake Superior Regiment. He died 10 August 1944 and is commemorated at Bretteville-sur-Laize Canadian War Cemetery in Calvados, France. ***Munroe Point*** (64 I/5) on Westman Lake was named after him in 1995.

Murdock, Gunner **Arthur** of Koostatak (H 67484). Royal Canadian Artillery. He died 27 August 1945 at the age of 25 and is commemorated at Koostatak United Church Cemetery, Manitoba. He was the son of Henry G. and Frances E. Murdock of Koostatak. ***Murdock Lake*** (64 J/7), south of Tadoule Lake was named after him in 1975.

Murphy, Aircraftman 2 **Gerald G.** of Winnipeg (R 59792). No. 7 Equipment Depot, RCAF. He died 17 September 1940 at the age of 23 and is commemorated at St. John's Cemetery in Winnipeg. He was the son of William A. and Constance Murphy of Winnipeg and was survived by his wife Lowry Murphy of Winnipeg. ***Murphy Point*** (54 E/4) on Embleton Lake was named after him in 1995.

Murphy, Flight Sergeant **Kenneth W.** of Grosse Isle (R 147182). No. 106 Squadron. He died 9 July 1943 at the age of 25 and is commemorated at Sutton Bridge (St. Matthew) Churchyard, Lincolnshire, England. He was the son of William H. and Ellen Murphy of Grosse Isle, Manitoba. ***Murphy Island*** (64 N/9) in Shannon Lake was named after him in 1987.

Murphy, Sergeant **Mervyn L. "Spud"** of Kelwood (H 26394). Fort Garry Horse. He died 6 June 1944 at the age of 27 and is commemorated at Beny-sur-Mer Canadian War Cemetery in Calvados, France. He was the son of Frank and Sarah Murphy and was survived by his wife Eileen M. Murphy (née Musgrave) of Kelwood, Manitoba and their unborn daughter. His wife recalls (13 November 2001):

> He was educated at Langruth, Manitoba before the family moved to Kelwood. He was a Boy Scout and a keen churchman and sportsman, playing hockey, softball and curling. Before joining up, he spent a year in the Forestry Service in the Riding Mountain National Park. After joining the 10th Army Tank Regiment, AFC Squadron, he spent four years in England where he married, in 1943, Eileen Musgrave from Ashford, Kent. His daughter, Carole Eileen, was born 30 June 1944. Eileen and Carole spent three years in Kelwood with Mervyn's parents, Frank and Sarah, after the war ended, but both now live in England. There are two grandchildren, Martin and Charlotte, and great grandsons Marcus and Timothy.
>
> Carole and I visited the cemetery at Beny-sur-Mer in 1994 – a very peaceful place surrounded by maple trees and perfectly cared for. Quite by chance, while browsing in a local bookshop, we found that there was, unknown to us, a fine memorial dedicated to the men from the Fort Garry Horse and other Canadian regiments who died on the beach that day. It is in the form of an open book on the sea front at St. Aubin-sur-Mer inscribed with the men's names and the fitting tribute: *Ils sont morts sur cette plage le 6 Juin 1944 pour notre liberté* [They died on this Beach 6 June 1944 for our liberty]. In 1999, I revisited Kelwood and Winnipeg and met a few of the friends I had made 50 years previously – it was indeed a very sentimental journey.

Murphy Lake (53 M/7), north of Knee Lake was named after him in 1995.

Murphy, Flying Officer **Robert G.** of Gypsumville (J 47080). No. 162 Squadron. He died 23 July 1945 at the age of 19 and is commemorated at Gypsumville Cemetery, Manitoba. He was survived by his mother Lillian Murphy of Gypsumville. Like many others, he had misrepresented his date of birth so that he could join the RCAF while under-age. His sister recalls (6 May 1997):

> Bob was born on October 13, 1925. When he was a young boy, most of his time was spent working around the rail station with our father. In his free time, he enjoyed skating and sledding during the winters. A lot of his time was spent playing with his dogs Fritz and Spot, who followed him wherever he went. Bob also enjoyed riding his bicycle and making things with his Meccano sets. A favourite hobby of his was collecting coins. He had worked at the Bay downtown for a short while before he left to join the Air Force. He lied about his age at that time; he was only 16. He was on his way home when his plane crashed in Ontario on July 23, 1945. Just prior to that, he was stationed in Reykjavik, Iceland.

Murphy Bay (64 C/3) in McKnight Lake was named after him in 1995.

Murray, Private **Albert T.** of Rivers (H 65624). Royal Canadian Army Service Corps. He died 26 February 1946 at the age of 32 and is commemorated at Rivers Cemetery, Manitoba. He was the son of Thomas and Emma Murray of Rivers. ***Albert Murray Lake*** (64 A/13), south of Gauer Lake was named after him in 1998.

Murray, Pilot Officer **Charles** of Winnipeg (J 17498). No. 83 Squadron. He died 17 June 1943 at the age of 25 and is commemorated at Rheinberg War Cemetery in Germany. He was survived by his wife Gwendolyne H. Murray of Saskatchewan. ***Murray Lake*** (64 C/5), southwest of Lynn Lake was named after him in 1951.

Murray, Flying Officer **Charles L.** of Winnipeg (J 15249). No. 434 Squadron. He died 20 February 1944 at the age of 25 and is commemorated at the Berlin 1939 - 1945 War Cemetery in Brandenburg, Germany. He was the son of Joseph F. and Evelyn Murray and was survived by his wife Catherine Murray of Fort William, Ontario. ***Murray Creek*** (64 B/5), which flows southeast into Pemichigamau Lake was named after him in 1995.

Murray, Private **Cyril** of Winnipeg (H 70151). Princess Patricia's Canadian Light Infantry. He died 7 December 1943 and is commemorated at the Moro River Canadian War Cemetery in Italy. ***Murray Esker*** (64 P/6), northeast of MacLeod Lake was named after him in 1995.

Murray, Flight Sergeant **Donald** of Winnipeg (R 95318). No. 22 Operational Training Unit, RCAF. He died 14 September 1942 at the age of 20 and is commemorated at Old Leusden General Cemetery in Amersfoort, Holland. He was the son of Charles and Katherine R. Murray (née Catto) of Norwood Grove, Manitoba – both natives of Aberdeen, Scotland. Aeroplane design and building had been his major hobby before enlisting and he had received a medal for attaining Dominion Marksman status while with the Queen's Own Cameron Highlanders cadets. ***Murray Hill*** (53 K/16), east of Edmund Lake was named after him in 1995.

Murray, Private **Franklin M. "Lanky"** of Stonewall (H 70574). Cameron Highlanders of Ottawa. He died 14 August 1944 at the age of 35 and is commemorated at Bretteville-sur-Laize Canadian War Cemetery in Calvados, France. He was the only son of Benjamin Frank and Sarah M. "Sadie" Murray of Hammond, British Columbia. His sister recalls (18 September 1995):

> Born in Neepawa, his family moved in 1916 to a farm in the vicinity of the town of Stonewall where he grew to manhood, assisting his father on the farm and attending the schools in Stonewall through the 11th grade. He was a good scholar, interested in the sciences and math, and assisted a number of young people, including some of his sisters, through their studies by working with them on their particular problems. In fact, a

number of his friends would help him with his chores so he could help them with their homework.

He had many interests and would have liked to continue his studies, but was needed on the farm. By the age of 15, he was his parents' mainstay. He took assorted correspondence courses in Chemistry and Physics and quoted poetry to the farm stock as he worked with them. Farming was not his choice of occupation but it was there to be done. He played ball with the local teens, both softball and hard; he participated in sports days in many activities, but excelled in track and was champion half-miler in the area.

The years of depression played havoc with his father's health and finances, and the farming came to an end in the late 1930s. Franklin then set off on his own in 1937, travelling by bicycle, with all his worldly goods on his back, to Geraldton, Ontario, where he found work in the Hard Rock Gold Mine – a very different type of work from what he was used to. He bought a small claim with a log cabin on it and settled in to being a miner, hoping in due time to be able to study further with an aim to becoming a teacher, and to work with the young people that he enjoyed so much.

Instead, in 1942 he joined the Army and was killed in action ... at the Battle of the Falaise Gap. The inscription on the headstone on his grave in Normandy, as suggested by his father reads: "A Friend to Man." This he was, a friend to men, women and children of every colour and creed, young and old.

Franklin Murray Lake (53 L/5), north of Bolton Lake was named after him in 1995.

Murray, Rifleman **George E.** of Solsgirth (H 8786). Royal Winnipeg Rifles. He died 6 June 1944 at the age of 20 and is commemorated at Beny-sur-Mer Canadian War Cemetery in Calvados, France. He was the son of Isaac and Dorothy H. Murray of Solsgirth, Manitoba. ***Murray Peninsula*** (64 H/5) on Missinipi Lake was named after him in 1995.

Murray, Stoker 1 **Glenn S.** of Winnipeg (V 55059). HMCS *Shawinigan*. The *Shawinigan* was torpedoed and sunk by U-1228 while on independent anti-submarine patrol in the Cabot Strait; all hands were lost. Stoker Murray died 24 November 1944 at the age of 19 and is commemorated at the Halifax Memorial. He was the son of Roderick J. and Irene L. Murray of Winnipeg. ***Glenn Murray Lake*** (53 M/5), west of Hackland Lake was named after him in 1995.

Murray, Pilot Officer **John K.** of Boissevain (J 86549). No. 550 Squadron. He died 17 June 1944 at the age of 26 and is commemorated at the Runnymede Memorial in Surrey, England. He was the son of Charles and Irene B. Murray of Stevens, Ontario. ***John Murray Creek*** (54 E/3), which flows west into Little Churchill River was named after him in 1995.

Murray, Flying Officer **Leo J.** of Portage la Prairie (J 10106). No. 5 Bomber Reconnaissance Squadron. He was reported missing 20 May 1944 at the age of 24 and is commemorated at the Ottawa Memorial. He was one of the seven children of Corporal Edward S. and Caroline Murray and was survived by his wife Jean Murray of Winnipeg and their son. He had been on anti-submarine patrol off the coast of Newfoundland. ***Murray Point*** (64 N/2) on Whitmore Lake was named after him in 1989.

Murray, Stoker 1 **Leon J. A.** of Winnipeg (V 41543). HMCS *Valleyfield*. The *Valleyfield* was torpedoed and sunk by U-548 50 miles south of Cape Race, Newfoundland; 125 of her ship's company were lost. Stoker Murray died 7 May 1944 at the age of 28 and is commemorated at the Halifax Memorial. He was survived by his father William A. Murray of Lac du Bonnet, his mother Stella B. Rheaume of Flin Flon and his step-father Gene Rheaume of Flin Flon. ***Murray Rapids*** (64 O/16) in the Andrew River was named after him in 1995.

Murray, Flight Sergeant **Ralph W.** of Winnipeg (R 90833). No. 147 Squadron. He died 22 April 1943 at the age of 25 and is commemorated at Brookside Cemetery in Winnipeg. He was the son of Walter T. and Rebecca Murray and was survived by his wife Pauline Murray of Winnipeg. ***Ralph Murray Lake*** (64 J/12), northwest of Grimes Lake was named after him in 1995.

Murray, Sergeant **Robert C.** of Winnipeg (H 433273). Queen's Own Cameron Highlanders. He died 25 July 1942 at the age of 47 and is commemorated at Elmwood Cemetery in Winnipeg. He was survived by his wife Ida M. Murray of Winnipeg. ***Murray Bay*** (64 C/12) in Laurie Lake was named after him in 1995.

Murray, Flying Officer **Ross M.** of Winnipeg (J 17209). No. 432 Squadron. He died 28 May 1943 at the age of 26 and is commemorated at the Runnymede Memorial in Surrey, England. He was the son of Marshal Murray of Penticton and the husband of Mildred Murray (née Way) of Penticton. He had been employed as a linotype printer with the *Penticton Herald* when he enlisted in 1940. He had completed the requisite 25 missions and normally would have been granted leave. Instead he was reassigned to another squadron and was on his second mission over Essen when he went missing. His younger brother writes (20 June 1998):

Ross was my hero. I was ten years his junior and when he left never to return, it was a very sad time. My father had died in 1939 and I had two brothers serving with the Seaforth Highlanders in the Italian Theatre. Both, now deceased, were seriously wounded in 1944. I myself joined the Canadian Navy in 1944 and saw service in the Atlantic and the Pacific.

World War II was a traumatic time for people of our generation and I am pleased that the memory of those who served and those who made the supreme sacrifice for their country are remembered in projects such as the Commemorative Names Program.

Ross Murray Lake (64 N/5), south of Snyder Lake was named after him in 1995.

Murray, Lieutenant **William.** Royal Winnipeg Rifles. He was awarded the Distinguished Conduct Medal for his service during World War I. Lieutenant Murray drowned in 1922 along with his companion Major Christopher P. J. O'Kelly (Victoria Cross, Military Cross). ***Murray Island*** (52 M/13) in O'Kelly Lake was named after him in 1983. See also O'Kelly Lake.

Mushumanski, Lance Bombardier **Victor** of Angusville (H 75187). Royal Canadian Artillery. He died 13 April 1943 at the age of 21 and is commemorated at Brookwood Military Cemetery in Surrey, England. His brothers visited his grave in 1993. He was the son of Charles and Annie Mushumanski of Vancouver. ***Mushumanski Lake*** (64 G/16), east of Cederlund Lake was named after him in 1995.

Musso, Flight Sergeant **Paul A.** of Winnipeg (R 140846). No. 619 Squadron. He died 1 September 1943 at the age of 20 and is commemorated at the Berlin 1939 - 1945 War Cemetery in Brandenburg, Germany. ***Musso Lake*** (64 P/11), east of Nejanilini Lake was named after him in 1974.

Mustoe, Sapper **William H.** of Winnipeg (H 101916). Royal Canadian Engineers. He died 17 June 1944 at the age of 35 and is commemorated at Beny-sur-Mer Canadian War Cemetery in Calvados, France. He was the son of Henry and Clara Mustoe and was survived by his wife Annie Marjorie Mustoe (née Buchanan) of Winnipeg. Sapper Mustoe was originally from Chilliwack, but was working in the mines at Sherridon when he enlisted. ***Mustoe Lake*** (63 J/16), east of Setting Lake was named after him in 1972.

Muswagon, Gunner **John A.** of Norway House (H 101790). Royal Canadian Artillery. He died 13 September 1944 at the age of 27 and is commemorated at Brookside Cemetery in Winnipeg. He was survived by his mother Margaret Muswagon of Norway House and by his wife Lydia Muswagon of Norway House. ***Muswagon Lake*** (53 F/13), south of Angling Lake was named after him in 1996.

Mutch, Rifleman **Andrew G.** of Reeve (H 42053). Royal Winnipeg Rifles. He died 6 June 1944 at the age of 24 and is commemorated at Beny-sur-Mer Canadian War Cemetery in Calvados, France. He was the son of James G. and Mary A. Mutch of Reeve, Manitoba and the brother of Rifleman Robert Mutch (next entry).

> He was born in Brookdale, Manitoba March 16, 1920. Andrew attended Tobarmore, Eden, and Union Schools. He was employed on farms until he joined the Royal Winnipeg Rifles at Winnipeg in December, 1941. Andrew landed on Juno Beach, D- Day June 6, 1944 with "A" Company Royal Winnipeg Rifles (3rd Division). He was washed overboard from his Landing Craft and the heavy load of equipment he was carrying sunk him quickly, making rescue impossible (Pittman n.d.).

Mutch Lake (64 I/5), northwest of North Knife Lake was named after him in 1974.

Mutch, Rifleman **Robert** of Reeve (H 1777). Royal Winnipeg Rifles. He died 8 June 1944 at the age of 21 and is commemorated at Beny-sur-Mer Canadian War Cemetery in Calvados, France. He was the son of James G. and Mary A. Mutch of Reeve, Manitoba and the brother of Rifleman Andrew Mutch (previous entry).

> He was born in Birnie, Manitoba August 6, 1922 and attended Union and Turtle Plains Schools. He was employed on farms until he joined the Royal Winnipeg Rifles at Winnipeg in January, 1943. Robert landed on Juno Beach, D-Day, June 6, 1944 with "A" Company the Royal Winnipeg Rifles (3rd Division). He was taken prisoner June 8, 1944 at Putot-en-Bessin France. He and several other prisoners were marched to the Chateau d'Audrieu, Head Quarters for the 12th SS Reconnaissance Battalion. It was under the command of SS Captain Gerd von Reitzenstein. SS Major Gerhard Bremer was also present. Major Fred Hodge, commander of "A" Company, RWRs, 21 soldiers from his regiment, two members of the Queen's Own Rifles and two soldiers from British Regiments were questioned by the SS Officers, marched out in small groups and subsequently shot. Robert was one of those (Pittman n.d.).

Mutch Creek (62 P/1), which flows west into Lake Winnipeg was named after him in 1982.

Mutcheson, Ordinary Seaman **John E.** of Portage la Prairie (V 83333). HMCS *Guysborough*. The *Guysborough* was torpedoed and sunk by U-878 in the English Channel off Ushant, France; fifty-one of her ship's company were lost. Ordinary Seaman Mutcheson died 18 March 1945 at the age of 19 and is commemorated at the Halifax Memorial. He was survived by his mother Margaret Mutcheson of Portage la Prairie. ***Mutcheson Lake*** (63 P/2), east of Sipiwesk Lake was named after him in 1968.

Muth, Private **Ervin** of Teulon (H 1333). South Saskatchewan Regiment. He died 13 January 1945 at the age of 22 and is commemorated at the Groesbeek Canadian War Cemetery in Holland. He was the son of Tofel and Eva Muth of Teulon, Manitoba. His sister recalls (26 November 2001):

> He loved working with motors, taking things apart and putting them back together in good running order. He was really good natured and a big tease. He loved his guitar and singing and yodelling his favourite songs. We could hear him from afar. I can remember him making skis for us, steaming the tips to get the right bend on them. It was awesome the time we had with them. He lost his life near the end of the war. While in Holland, he befriended a couple and they kept in touch with the family and also cared for his grave. My youngest sister and her husband did get over to see and visit his grave a number of years later. Tears came in remembering. We could finally put a closure to all this when we saw the photo of his grave.

Muth Lake (52 E/14), northwest of West Hawk Lake was named after him in 1974.

Mutz, Trooper **Wasyl** of Winnipeg (H 105046). British Columbia Regiment. He died 14 August 1944 and is commemorated at Bretteville-sur-Laize Canadian War Cemetery in Calvados, France. ***Mutz Lake*** (53 M/8), west of Swampy Lake was named after him in 1995.

Myers, Flying Officer **Frank M.** of Dauphin (J 39365). No. 426 Squadron. He died 5 March 1945 at the age of 20 and is commemorated at Stonefall Cemetery in Yorkshire, England. He was the son of Frederick J. and Jean F. Myers of Dauphin, Manitoba. His older brother reports (22 November 1995) that he:

> ... left the University of Manitoba and enlisted in the RCAF (I think this was in 1943). He was training as a pilot and washed out because of air sickness. He always had motion sickness – train, car, boat, whatever. So he was trained as a navigator. He continued to have this problem all the time on missions and wrote me (I was an MO in Italy). I advised him to parade sick and get out of flying, but he refused. He was killed in a mid-air collision.

He adds (11 October 2001):

> Frank was killed when his Halifax iced up and crashed 11 minutes after take-off from Linton. A total of seven bombers were lost within minutes due to icing conditions. His aircraft crashed 23 miles from the base.

Myers Lake (64 H/10), east of Buckland Lake was named after him in 1995.

Mynarski, Pilot Officer **Andrew Charles** of Winnipeg (J 87544). He was a tail gunner in No. 419 Squadron and was posthumously awarded the Victoria Cross.

> ... on the evening of June 12, 1944, he was relaxing a few hours before take off with his close friend and fellow gunner Pat Brophy. Just after midnight, they were to embark on a bombing raid of Cambrai in northern France. The men were more apprehensive than usual. This would be their 13th mission, scheduled for June 13. Feeling a little superstitious, Mynarski noticed a four-leaf clover on the lawn at his base and plucked it up. Laughingly, he handed it to Brophy, who threw it into his helmet without thinking twice.

At 12:00 AM June 13, the two men and the rest of the crew were aboard their Lancaster *A for Able*, crossing the coastline of France and keeping a look out for anti-aircraft artillery. Shortly after the Lancaster crossed into enemy lines, it was "coned" in searchlights and the pilot began evasive manoeuvres. But sure enough, within minutes Brophy spotted a German Junkers tailing them and firing rapidly. As he and Mynarski pivoted their guns to take aim, the Lancaster was hit. Brophy remembers looking at his watch; it was 13 minutes past midnight.

A burst tore through the fuselage, igniting the wing fuel tank, knocking out both engines. Fire ripped through the plane, separating the two gunners and destroying the intercom. The pilot gave the signal for all crew to bail out. Mynarski was half way out the rear hatch and about to jump when he looked back and saw Brophy struggling to get out of his turret. The hydraulic pivot system had been shot up, and Brophy was trapped. All the rest of the crew had already bailed, and the burning plane was bucking wildly. But Mynarski threw himself to the floor, and made his way through the flames to try to help Brophy escape. With his hair and clothing burning, Mynarski struggled in vain to turn Brophy's turret manually, but both men knew that it simply would not go. Brophy ordered Mynarski to get out while he could, and Mynarski made his way back through the growing wall of fire to the hatch, turned to salute his friend, and then made the leap. Mynarski's descent was clearly seen from below. His clothing and parachute were burning, and as he fell, the flames went higher. Although he survived the jump, he died within hours from his burns.

Incredibly, Brophy did not die. When the plane crashed moments later, his turret was thrown clear of the wreckage, and he was thrown from his turret with virtually no injury. When he came to, he picked up his helmet and out of it fell the clover. Years later Brophy reflected: "I'll always believe that a divine providence intervened to save me because of what I had seen, so that the world might know of a gallant man who laid down his life for his friend" (Bishop 1995:171-173).

Pilot Officer Mynarski died 13 June 1944 at the age of 27 and is commemorated at Meharicourt Communal Cemetery, Somme, France. He was the son of Stanley and Anna Mynarski of Winnipeg. ***Mynarski Lakes*** (64 B/3), south of Southern Indian Lake was named after him in 1949 and he was named a member of Canada's Aviation Hall of Fame in 1973.

Canadian infantry walking through ruins at Caen, France 10 July 1944.
Courtesy of the National Archives of Canada (PA-162651).

N

Nabozniak, Gunner **Ivan** of Caliento (M 1183). Royal Canadian Artillery. He died 26 November 1942 at the age of 32 and is commemorated at Brookwood Military Cemetery in Surrey, England. He was the son of Andrew and Antonia Nabozniak of Caliento, Manitoba. ***Nabozniak Lake*** (64 B/5), north of Rat Lake was named after him in 1995.

Nares, Lieutenant **Ramsey A.** of Winnipeg (O 54746). On loan to the Royal Navy aboard HMS *Fearless* in the Mediterranean. He died 23 July 1941 when the *Fearless* was sunk by bombs. He was 23 years of age and is commemorated at the Halifax Memorial. He was the son of Commander Hilary G. and Hazel F. Nares of Winnipeg. ***Nares Lake*** (64 I/8), northeast of North Knife Lake was named after him in 1957.

Nault, Warrant Officer 2 **Donat C.** of St-Pierre-Jolys (R 106380). No. 408 Squadron. He died 5 May 1943 at the age of 25 and is commemorated at the Runnymede Memorial in Surrey, England. He was the son of Amedee and Blanche Nault of St. Boniface. ***Nault Lake*** (64 J/9), east of Tadoule Lake was named after him in 1975.

Navis, Trooper **Zane R.** of Winnipeg (H 63979). Three Rivers Tank Regiment. He died 28 July 1944 at the age of 26 and is commemorated at Florence War Cemetery, Italy. He was the son of John and Mary Navis of Winnipeg and was survived by his wife Stella B. Navis of Winnipeg. ***Navis Lake*** (64 K/5), south of Lac Brochet was named after him in 1972.

Naylen, Gunner **William G.** of Birtle (H 60374). Royal Canadian Artillery. He died 8 October 1944 at the age of 21 and is commemorated at Bergen-op-Zoom Canadian War Cemetery in Holland. He was the son of Thomas A. and Ada E. Naylen of Butler, Manitoba. Some months later, his mother received a letter from the Padre of 2 Can A/T Regiment:

> My Dear Mrs. Naylen: For many weeks past I have been wanting to write you about your splendid son who gave his life in Holland on the 8th of October. They were days of fierce fighting and were followed by the drive up the Beveland Peninsula and the shift to the Nijmegen Salient. In order to write even a little as he deserved, I have had to wait till we were not so pressed. For in this and my other regiments, the casualties have been very high.
>
> There is nothing which can be said to make your loss seem less heavy, for only God and yourself can know how much you have given in him. But you should know that you are remembered in the memorial silence of our scattered services. This letter is a poor attempt to pay something of the tribute we feel due to him and to personally express to you, his mother, my deepest sympathy.
>
> You will have heard some official word of the action in which he was engaged. Our division was advancing on a wide front to close the neck of the Beveland Peninsula which, when cleared, could free the port of Antwerp for Allied use. Without too heavy fighting, we had advanced into Holland and were within sight of our objective. Then the enemy threw in an SS division in a desperate attempt to hold us off. The infantry had advanced north of Ossendrecht and your son's troop of anti-tank guns went with their allotted infantry. His gun, a big 17-pounder, was set up commanding the main road at a crossroads corner in ... a small village.
>
> Then the enemy counter-attack came in, driving our infantry back by superior numbers, supported by tanks and self-propelled guns. An enemy SP [self-propelled] gun broke through and advanced upon the village from the side road, covering the village with direct fire. Sergeant Finnie, Bombardier MacDonald and your son rushed out to take on the SP gun with their 17-pounder. While they manhandled the gun round, they were under direct fire, the enemy scoring two near-misses at point blank range. Still the boys stuck to their gun and they had just got it lined up and were prepared to fire when the enemy gun finally registered a direct hit. The three of them were killed instantly.
>
> The town had to be evacuated as the attack proceeded and heavy fighting took place before the enemy were finally driven out again. When it was possible to reach them, they were brought back to the town cemetery of Ossendrecht. There they were buried, with a score of their infantry comrades, by the Padre of the Black Watch, H. Capt. the Rev. E. Royle. Each man had a separate grave and they were given the full burial service with every honour possible due a Christian and a soldier.
>
> When I was able to see their graves, each was already marked with the white Canadian cross, with the blue patch of the division and the name, rank, number, date of death and unit painted on. Flowers had been placed on the graves by the Dutch people. When I saw the cemetery last, over a hundred of our Canadian boys had been laid away there.
>
> When the war is over, his grave will probably be moved to a permanent Canadian military cemetery similar to those of the last war in France and Belgium. And I can assure you from what I have seen of them that no effort or expense will be spared to make his final memorial as beautiful and impressive as possible. For his grave will be a shrine to Canadians as long as our country endures.
>
> He has made the supreme sacrifice in the service of his country. Yet it may not be as great as yours. For him, buoyed up by his great bravery, there was the excitement of battle and the precise actions of his long-practised gun drill. For him, it was sudden and complete, for he would not even know what had happened when his gun was hit. While for you, the sacrifice will be heavy and prolonged.
>
> You will not be able to help your grief, yet even that should not be permitted to be too great. Concern for those he loved should not be allowed to shadow the new adventures he faces now. Surely you must feel that the sacrifice of so many splendid men cannot be in vain. That value such as contained in him cannot be so destroyed. That "in Christ there is no death." And in that spirit, you may find his presence with you still. For you must know in your heart that love does not die.
>
> May God specially bless you at this time with the comfort and consolation of His near Presence. May He give you the courage and the strength to carry on, as your son would have you do. And may He help those of us who remain to see to it that his sacrifice may not have been made in vain. For he has earned the highest commendation: "Greater love hath no man than this ..." Yours very sincerely, John R. Fife (18 January 1945).

The Municipality of Ossendrecht, Holland personally thanked the families "of the 142 Canadian heroes who fell and were buried in the vicinity of Ossendrecht" (10 December 1945) and promised that a war memorial would be erected there dedicated to them. ***Naylen Lake*** (64 J/6), southwest of Tadoule Lake was named after him in 1975.

Nazarko, Leading Aircraftman **Walter** of Hazelridge (R 191412). No. 61 Base, RCAF Station Topcliffe. He died 28 November 1944 at the age of 21 and is commemorated at Stonefall Cemetery in Yorkshire, England. A brother with his wife and son visited the grave in 1982. In 1999, his sister's daughter offered to take her mother to England, specifically to visit her brother's grave. She wrote (28 October 2001):

> What an emotional, but rewarding experience – to know that Wally and 665 other Canadians, along with many servicemen from throughout the Commonwealth, a total of 992, were resting in such a peaceful and well cared for Cemetery.

He was the son of Adam and Ahafia Nazarko. His sister recalls (28 October 2001):

Wally enlisted from Grade 12 at 18 years of age. He was closely followed by his younger brother Joseph who also joined the RCAF. Although Wally was a fun loving homebody, he took defending his country most seriously. While training in Brandon, he was in the Precision Marching Squad. He continued his basic training at High River, Alberta before being sent overseas to England where he became a bomb aimer and was killed. His funeral was attended by his brother Joe, also stationed in England as a mid-rear gunner on bombers.

Wally was quite a prankster. When going for his driving license in a two-ton truck (he was 5'4 1/2" and 125 pounds), the examiner looked at Wally and remarked: "This little boy is going to drive that big truck?" Wally replied: "Why, do you have a problem with it?" He passed his test.

In July of 1939, our Dad was in a car accident, witnessed by many adults, but it took Wally's presence of mind to jump into our car and race down to the scene of the accident so that our Dad could be driven to the hospital some 40 - 45 miles away. Our Dad died on the operating table the next day. I am enclosing a copy of a letter Wally wrote to our older sister Ann three days before he was killed, which shows he had a premonition of his death:

Dear Toots: I just don't know how to start a letter like this. But here's hoping you'll understand what I'm trying to tell you. I'm not very good at expressing myself, so you must know by now. So if you think that this letter is a joke, don't laugh, because I'm very sincere, only don't know how to put it down on paper.

For a long time now, I've known that I have one of the nicest and sweetest sisters in the world. Have tried often to tell you, but I just couldn't. As I sit here at this desk by my lonesome (I'm on duty tonight), I'm going back and remembering all the little things that you did for me. Not only the little things, but big things also. And what did you get in return? Sometimes not even a thank you, and even sometimes I'd cause you trouble. But you'd always forget about that and do something nice again. It was just like returning good for evil. And do you know how I feel? Yes, just like hell. And now that I've begun to realize certain things, I can't do anything for you. But just remember Toots, that if anytime you should want anything – anything, don't be afraid to ask me, Toots, I'd do anything for you. Anything that is humanly possible. Because, I have one of the sweetest girls in the world for a sister. And always remember, Toots, that no matter where I am, I'll always be thinking of you.

Received a parcel from you this evening, with Paul's name on it. It was mailed October twenty-eight. In it you had everything. Also parcels for Buckleys and once again, all I can say is "Thanks Toots." You may say "Shucks, that's nothing." Well it may seem like nothing to you, but not so to me. It just goes to prove just what I said in the second paragraph. And I meant every word of it Toots.

Guess I'll sign off for now. Hope you're in the best of health and not working too hard. Also that Mom and [the] rest are keeping fine. And so till the next time, best of luck and cheerio. Your loving brother, just Wally. P.S. After reading this letter, you may as well start a fire with it. But just remember what I said about you. So long Sis (25 November 1944).

Nazarko Island (52 L/5), in the Winnipeg River was named after him in 1973. His brother and brother-in-law erected a granite monument and plaque there for a dedication ceremony on 16 August 1987. Twenty-eight family members were in attendance.

Neal, Flight Sergeant **Francis John** of Winnipeg (R 123716). No. 426 Squadron. He died 7 October 1943 at the age of 21 and is commemorated at Rachecourt-sur-Blaise Churchyard, Haute-Marne, France. He was the son of William M. and Frances J. Neal of St. Vital. His niece writes (15 June 1995):

"Jack" was born November 21, 1921 and attended Robert H. Smith School and Kelvin High School. He took one year at [the] University of Manitoba following which he worked at the Bank of Montreal. His special interests were hunting, fishing and horseback riding.

He joined the air force in 1941, training at Fort McLeod, Alberta. He was an operational training pilot with an experienced crew when they were shot down over France after an air attack on Stuttgart. Five others died while two survived.

Neal Lake (64 G/6), east of McPherson Lake was named after him in 1994.

Neal, Flying Officer **John M.** of Winnipeg. (J 27480). No. 50 Squadron. He died 24 July 1944 at the age of 21 and is commemorated at Nogent-le-Rotrou Communal Cemetery, Eure-et-Loir, France. He was survived by his wife Norma Neal (née Finch) and their daughter. They visited the gravesite in 1997. ***Neal Island*** (53 L/4) in Kitchi Lake was named after him in 1995.

Neff, Flight Sergeant **Lawrence B.** of Winnipeg (J 51440). RCAF Station Mountainview, Ontario. He died 18 March 1943 at the age of 41 and is commemorated at St. John's Cemetery in Winnipeg. He was survived by his mother Eve Neilson of Winnipeg. ***Neff Lake*** (64 I/14), north of North Knife River was named after him in 1974.

Negrich, Flying Officer **Tony** of Dauphin (J 22062). No. 51 Squadron. He died 30 June 1944 at the age of 22 and is commemorated at Bretteville-sur-Laize Canadian War Cemetery in Calvados, France. ***Negrich Lake*** (64 P/15), northeast of Nejanilini Lake was named after him in 1974.

Neill, Flying Officer **Robert W.** of Winnipeg (J 15441). No. 21 Squadron. He died 6 November 1942 at the age of 30 and is commemorated at the Runnymede Memorial in Surrey, England. He was the son of Dr. R. W. and Mary I. Neill. ***Neill Lake*** (53 N/4), north of Fish Lake was named after him in 1995.

Neilson, Flying Officer **Donald Maurice** of Erickson (J 42662). No. 420 Squadron. He died 18 April 1945 at the age of 20 and is commemorated at the Runnymede Memorial in Surrey, England. He was the son of Marinus and Mabel H. Neilson and was survived by his sister Ethel, all of Erickson. His nephew writes (8 January 2002):

I still have two of Maurice's toys. One is an old McGavins Bakery truck and the other is a hand-carved horse; I treasure these items. Even though I never met my Uncle, he continues to touch my life and the life of my family. Both my Mother and Maurice are gone, but I think they are still smiling.

Maurice was described by a friend as: "Good looking and smarter than the rest of us." As a youth, Maurice played hockey with the Erickson Cubs. He played forward. Maurice was also very interested in science. As a young boy, he amazed his friends by constructing a crystal radio and listening to the CBC from Brandon. He converted his older sister's playhouse into a science laboratory.

His last mission was over Heligoland, Germany. Halifax aircraft No. NP946 crashed into the North Sea off Norfolk, England during a daylight attack over Germany. A rescue plane was on scene within four hours and found three men, but they had succumbed to exposure and hypothermia. There were no survivors.

Many of these young men would have returned to their small towns and started businesses and families. The heart and soul of Erickson died with Maurice and others who were lost in the war. Many small towns lost their males of that generation. Think of the friends and family we never had because of the loss of these men.

Neilson Lake (53 E/7), south of Island Lake was named after him in 1973.

Neish, Signalman **James W.** of Winnipeg (J 36746). Royal Canadian Corps of Signals. He died 16 September 1945 at the age of 26 and is commemorated at Brookside Cemetery in Winnipeg. He was the son of James and Nellie R. Neish of Winnipeg; and was survived by his wife Angeline A. Neish of Outlook, Saskatchewan. ***Neish Lake*** (62 P/16), west of Family Lake was named after him in 1973.

Nelson, Private **Cecil M.** of Venlaw (H 45556). Royal Canadian Ordnance Corps. He died 21 April 1945 at the age of 36 and is commemorated at Brookwood Military Cemetery in Surrey, England. He was the son of Morris C. and Emma E. Nelson and was survived by his wife Lena E. Nelson of Venlaw, Manitoba and their two daughters. ***Cecil Nelson Lake*** (64 A/15), south of Christie Lake was named after him in 1995.

Nelson, Rifleman **John A.** of Carman (H 77215). Royal Winnipeg Rifles. He died 23 October 1944 at the age of 26 and is commemorated at the Adegem Canadian War Cemetery in Belgium. He was the son of George and Annie Nelson and was survived by his wife Marie Nelson of Plum Coulee, Manitoba. ***Nelson Island*** (53 E/15) in Island Lake was named after him in 1982.

Nelson, Trooper **Leo C.** of Winnipeg (H 87904). Sherbrooke Fusiliers. He died 18 July 1944 at the age of 32 and is commemorated at Beny-sur-Mer Canadian War Cemetery in Calvados, France. He was survived by his wife Jane S. Nelson of Winnipeg. ***Nelson Point*** (64 O/8) on Baird Lake was named after him in 1995.

Nelson, Private **Leslie W.** of Winnipeg (H 17786). Princess Patricia's Canadian Light Infantry. He died 17 January 1944 at the age of 22 and is commemorated at the Moro River Canadian War Cemetery in Italy. He was the son of Joshua and Edith Nelson of Winnipeg and was survived by his wife Emily Nelson of Winnipeg. ***Nelson Peninsula*** (64 H/2) on Holmes Lake was named after him in 1995.

Nelson, Private **Loren N.** of Sprague (H 22396). Lincoln and Welland Regiment. He died 10 April 1945 at the age of 19 and is commemorated at the Holten Canadian War Cemetery in Holland. He was the son of Nels J. and Christina Nelson of Sprague, Manitoba. His sister-in-law writes:

> Loren Nelson was the second son in a family of three boys and one girl. The rest of the family loved him dearly. As the third son, my husband, Harley says that he always looked up to his older brother, Loren, to teach him wisely. After Grade 8, Loren got a job as a carpenter along with his father. Together they built one of the original Canada Customs Buildings at the Middleboro crossing in southeast Manitoba. In his spare time, he also helped to break land on the newly acquired farm with his father and his brothers. There was also farm work and chores to be done. As a teenager, he helped his father build a home on the farm because all they had was a very cold log house to live in. He did most of the work himself because his father had to earn a living by working outside the farm.
>
> Loren proved that he was also very inventive by building and designing a sweep rake and a hay stacker. For recreation he also built a croquet set by hand. When there was time for musical enjoyment, Loren's older brother Evert would play the accordion and Loren would accompany him on his guitar.
>
> In 1944, when Loren was 18, he decided to join the Canadian Army and go overseas. The whole family was very sad when he joined the army, because his good humour and his help around the house was sadly missed. As a proud member of the Lincoln and Welland Regiment, Loren fought six battles in Holland and Germany from the fall of 1944 to the spring of 1945. Loren turned 19 while he fought overseas. Sadly, he was killed in action near Werlte, Germany on April 10th, 1945.

His nephew adds:

> It seems that this day was a day the same as any. The Regiment was near the end of its journey. The war would be over within a short month. There was an upbeat mood around the Regiment, many of the men were sure they would be home soon.
>
> As any war story often does, this one also ends in tragedy. No one is sure of what occurred on the 10th of April 1945. These recollections are lost. Clouded by time, bad memories, and certainly, a respect for fallen comrades (www.multipointproductions.com/heroes/loren/werlte.htm).

One of his comrades recalls:

> I can remember the morning well. We came up the road ... in trucks so far and then we got off and marched. It was pea-soup fog. It was thick and we were marching up and started to cross a ploughed field. And we hadn't got very far ... when suddenly, it was almost as if somebody had pushed a button and the curtain went up. The fog lifted and the sun came out, just burned it off. Here we are in the middle of a ploughed field going towards a bush. We got so far out and someone opened up from the bush with a machine gun and we hit the ground (Hayes 1986).

Nelson Rapids (64 N/1) in the North Seal River was named after him in 1995.

Nelson, Private **Thomas M.** of Carman (H 195179). Queen's Own Cameron Highlanders. He died 1 October 1944 at the age of 29 and is commemorated at Bergen-op-Zoom Canadian War Cemetery in Holland. He was survived by his wife Lorna P. Nelson of Carman. ***Nelson Hill*** (64 I/12), east of Tadoule Lake was named after him in 1995.

Nesbitt, Flight Sergeant **Gordon B.** of Neepawa (R 123738). No. 432 Squadron. He died 16 July 1943 at the age of 26 and is commemorated at Ripon Cemetery in Yorkshire, England. He was the son of John R. and Ida M. Nesbitt of Shoal Lake, Manitoba. ***Nesbitt Lake*** (64 F/3), north of Lynn Lake was named after him in 1967.

Neufeld, Private **Benjamin** of Winkler (H 6156). Winnipeg Grenadiers. He died 19 July 1945 at the age of 32 and is commemorated at the Yokohama War Cemetery in Japan. He was the son of A. A. and Helena Neufeld of Winkler and was survived by his wife Marion O. Neufeld (née King) of Altamont. His nephew writes (27 November 2001):

> Following Canada's declaration of war, Benny enlisted September, 1939 from Carman with the Winnipeg Grenadiers. Her served with this unit for 16 months in the West Indies and in the defence of Hong Kong where he was taken as a prisoner of war on December 25, 1941. Benjamin was moved to a prison camp in Tokyo where he died shortly before VJ-Day.

Neufeld Lake (54 B/9), northeast of Shamattawa was named after him in 1964.

Neufeld, Pilot Officer **Edmund** of Winnipeg (J 92280). No. 419 Squadron. He died 23 October 1944 at the age of 21 and is commemorated at the Reichswald Forest War Cemetery in Germany. He was the youngest of the 12 children of Peter and Anna W. Neufeld of Rossendale, Manitoba. ***Neufeld Bay*** (64 C/13) in McMillan Lake was named after him in 1989.

Neufeld, Trooper **John R.** of Winnipeg (H 77723). 12th Manitoba Dragoons. He died 18 August 1944 at the age of 21 and is commemorated at Beny-sur-Mer Canadian War Cemetery in Calvados, France. He was the son of David G. and Susan Neufeld of Winnipeg and the brother of Trooper Leonard G. Neufeld (next entry). ***Neufeld Island*** (64 N/16) in Nueltin Lake was named after him in 1995.

Neufeld, Trooper **Leonard G.** of Winnipeg (SH 62331). Lord Strathcona's Horse. He died 20 August 1952 at the age of 25 and is commemorated at the United Nations Cemetery in Pusan, South Korea. He was the son of David G. and Susan Neufeld and the brother of John R. Neufeld (previous entry). ***Leonard Neufeld Lake*** (53 L/11), south of Munro Lake was named after this Korean War casualty in 1998.

Neuls, Flight Sergeant **Philip C.** of Brandon (R 102474). No. 14 Squadron. He died 5 September 1942 at the age of 29 and is commemorated at Cottesmore (St. Nicholas) Churchyard Extension, Rutland, England. He was the son of Sigmund and Caroline Neuls of Melville, Saskatchewan. ***Neuls Lake*** (63 O/7), north of Setting Lake was named after him in 1973.

Neve, Trooper **Allan R.** of Teulon (H 65117). Fort Garry Horse. He died 13 April 1942 at the age of 18 and is commemorated at Brookwood Military Cemetery in Surrey, England. He was the son of Reginald T. and Ida C. Neve of Inwood, Manitoba. ***Neve Island*** (52 E/14) in St. Claire Lake was named after him in 1976.

Nevill, Flight Sergeant **John O. H.** of Glenboro (R 80124). No. 57 Squadron. He died 2 April 1942 at the age of 25 and is commemorated at Durnbach War Cemetery in Bavaria, Germany. He was the son of Thomas and Henrietta M. Nevill. ***Nevill Lake*** (64 P/7), east of Nejanilini Lake was named after him in 1974.

Neville, Pilot Officer **Robert T.** of Elgin (J 92282). No. 419 Squadron. He died 23 October 1944 at the age of 23 and is commemorated at the Reichswald Forest War Cemetery in Germany. He was survived by his wife Mrs. P. I. Neville. ***Neville Island*** (53 E/16) in Island Lake was named after him in 1984.

Newcombe, Warrant Officer 2 **Jack D.** of Winnipeg (R 58803). No. 426 Squadron. He died 16 December 1943 at the age of 22 and is commemorated at the Hanover War Cemetery in Germany. He was the son of Benjamin C. and Marjorie C. Newcombe of Winnipeg. ***Newcombe Lake*** (64 O/15), east of Nueltin Lake was named after him in 1975.

Newman, Aircraftman 2 **Daniel** of Winnipeg (R 258675). No. 4 Construction and Maintenance Unit, RCAF. He died 8 August 1943 at the age of 34 and is commemorated at Brookside Cemetery in Winnipeg. He was the son of William and Edith Newman of Winnipeg. ***Newman Bay*** (63 I/4) in Playgreen Lake was named after him in 1995.

Newman, Private **George A.** of McCreary (H 7137). Queen's Own Cameron Highlanders. He died 22 August 1944 at the age of 20 and is commemorated at Bretteville-sur-Laize Canadian War Cemetery in Calvados, France. He was the son of A. J. and Kate Newman of McCreary, Manitoba. ***Newman Island*** (63 P/4) in Sipiwesk Lake was named after him in 1995.

Newman, Private **Reginald W.** of St. James (H 16286). Princess Patricia's Canadian Light Infantry. He died 24 April 1943 at the age of 21 and is commemorated at Brookwood Military Cemetery in Surrey, England. He was the son of Ross and Agnes Newman and was survived by his wife Phyllis Newman of Winnipeg. ***Newman Point*** (64 P/16) in Thuytowayazay Lake was named after him in 1995.

Nichol, Private **David S.** of Darlingford (H 17410). Winnipeg Grenadiers. He died 12 October 1942 at the age of 20 and is commemorated at the Sai Wan War Cemetery in Hong Kong. He was the son of Walter M. and Olive E. Nichol of Darlingford, Manitoba. According to his brother (6 September 1988):

> Dave was born at Bateman, Saskatchewan December 12, 1921 [and] moved to Darlingford, Manitoba in November, 1927. Dave joined the Princess Pats in the spring of 1940 and joined the Grenadiers when they returned from Jamaica. He died in a prison camp in Hong Kong, but I am not sure of the date. The telegram that came to my parents said October 1942, but one Hong Kong veteran who knew Dave well said it couldn't have been later than March 1942.

Nichol Lake (64 I/9), northeast of North Knife Lake was named after him in 1957.

Nicholl, Flying Officer **Henry O.** of Winnipeg (C 2478). No. 3 Manning Depot, RCAF. He died 5 January 1942 at the age of 40 and is commemorated at Elmwood Cemetery in Winnipeg. He was the son of Samuel C. and Annie Nicholl of Winnipeg and was survived by his wife Gertrude A. Nicholl of Winnipeg. ***Nicholl Bay*** (64 I/4) in Podborochinski Lake was named after him in 1995.

Nicholls, Sergeant **Stanley F.** of Winnipeg (H 6081). Royal Canadian Artillery. He died 31 July 1945 at the age of 46 and is commemorated at Brookside Cemetery in Winnipeg. He was survived by his wife Ethel Nicholls of Winnipeg. ***Nicholls Bay*** (53 E/16) in Krolman Lake was named after him in 1997.

Nichols, Private **Stanley G.** of Pipestone (H 103624). Calgary Highlanders. He died 25 July 1944 and is commemorated at Hottot-les-Bagues War Cemetery, Calvados, France. ***Nichols Island*** (64 O/12) in Shannon Lake was named after him in 1995.

Nicholls, Flying Officer **William F.** of Winnipeg (J 89450). No. 426 Squadron. He died 13 January 1945 at the age of 23 and is commemorated at the Runnymede Memorial in Surrey, England. He was the son of William H. and Agnes Nicholls of Winnipeg. His aircraft suffered engine failure during a night trip to Stuttgart 15 March 1944. The crew were taken prisoners of war and Flying Officer Nicholls later died in a PoW camp (Allison and Hayward 1991). ***Nicholls Point*** (64 P/9) on Gislason Lake was named after him in 1995.

Nicholson, Trooper **Alfred** of Neepawa (H 77239). 12th Manitoba Dragoons. He died 14 August 1944 at the age of 32 and is commemorated at Bretteville-sur-Laize Canadian War Cemetery in Calvados, France. A fellow soldier witnessed him being killed by flying shrapnel. He was the son of Frederick J. and Lucy Nicholson of Charleswood. ***Nicholson Island*** (64 P/4) in Duffin Lakes was named after him in 1985.

Nicholson, Leading Aircraftman **Ronald K.** of East Kildonan (R 162418). No. 1666 Heavy Conversion Unit, RCAF. He died 17 June 1945 at the age of 21 and is commemorated at Manchester Southern Cemetery in Lancashire, England. He was the son of Roland D. and Beatrice Nicholson and was survived by his wife Jean Nicholson of Whalley Range, Manchester. ***Nicholson Lake*** (64 P/13), north of Nejanilini Lake was named after him in 1974.

Nicholls, Sergeant **James E.** of Souris (927758). No. 15 Squadron, RAF. He died 14 February 1943 at the age of 21 and is commemorated at Heverlee War Cemetery, Leuven, Vlaams-Brabant, Belgium. He was the son of James E. and Hilda Nicholls and was survived by his wife Mary E. Nicholls of Newtownards, County Down, Northern Ireland. ***Nicholls Peninsula*** (64 C/3) on McKnight Lake was named after him in 1995.

Nicklin, Lieutenant Colonel **Jevon A. "Jeff"** of Winnipeg. Commander of the 1st Canadian Parachute Battalion, Member of the Order of the British Empire. He died 24 March 1945 at the age of 30 and is commemorated at the Groesbeek Canadian War Cemetery in Holland. He was the son of Percy H. and Eva L. Nicklin and was survived by his wife Mary E. Nicklin of Port Credit, Ontario and their son. He had played for the Winnipeg Blue Bombers in 1935 and in 1946 his battalion donated a trophy to the Canadian Football League. The Jeff Nicklin Memorial Trophy was originally awarded to the player in the western division considered to be the most valuable to his team. ***Nicklin Lake*** (64 J/13), southeast of Egenolf Lake was named after him in 1957.

Nicolson, Gunner **Kenneth R.** of Winnipeg (H 9398). Royal Canadian Artillery. He died 17 April 1945 at the age of 27 and is commemorated at the Groesbeek Canadian War Cemetery in Holland. Greer Bosma adopted the grave in 1951 and has been placing flowers there ever since. He was the son of Kenneth and Jessie Nicolson of Winnipeg, and was survived by his wife Eileen L. Nicolson (née Marston) of Winnipeg and their two year-old daughter. His widow and daughter visited the grave in 1996. He had been employed by the City of Winnipeg Health Department when he enlisted. ***Nicolson Lake*** (64 I/15), northeast of North Knife Lake was named after him in 1974.

Nightingale, Flight Sergeant **Allan D.** of Winnipeg (R 71423). No. 80 Squadron. He died 1 April 1942 at the age of 22 and is commemorated at the Alamein Memorial in Egypt. He was the son of Samuel and Ellen E. Nightingale of Winnipeg. ***Nightingale Lake*** (63 N/1), south of Burntwood Lake was named after him in 1970.

Nile, Sergeant **Jack** of St. Vital (H 17036). Princess Patricia's Canadian Light Infantry. He died 22 October 1944 at the age of 25 and is commemorated at Cesena War Cemetery in Italy. He was the son of Edwin and Lilie Nile of Winnipeg and was survived by his wife Gertrude H. Nile of Winnipeg. ***Nile Lake*** (64 B/1), northeast of Nelson House was named after him in 1972.

Nisbet, Private **Neville W.** of Flin Flon (H 23245). Lincoln and Welland Regiment. He died 2 May 1945 and is commemorated at the Holten Canadian War Cemetery in Holland. ***Nisbet Lake*** (64 I/12), south of Shethanei Lake was named after him in 1974.

Nixon, Major **William B.** of Brandon. Royal Canadian Artillery. He died 27 February 1945 at the age of 29 and is commemorated at the Groesbeek Canadian War Cemetery in Holland. He was the youngest son of Rupert J. and Emily L. Nixon of Sooke, British Columbia. He received a personal citation from Field Marshal Montgomery:

> Temporary Captain W. B. Nixon, 12th Canadian Field Regiment, RCA: It has been brought to my attention that you have performed outstanding good service, and shown devotion to duty during the campaign in France. I award you this certificate as a token of my appreciation, and I have given instructions that this shall be noted in your Record of Service. B. L. Montgomery, Field Marshal, Commander-in-Chief, 21st Army Group (July 1944).

Nixon Lake (64 J/5), north of Big Sand Lake was named after him in 1975.

Niznick, Lieutenant **Harry** of Winnipeg (CDN 426). Durham Light Infantry. He died 9 September 1944 and is commemorated at Geel (Stelen) Churchyard, Geel, Antwerp, Belgium. ***Niznick Lake*** (64 K/11), east of Lac Brochet was named after him in 1972.

Noakes, Battery Sergeant Major (Warrant Officer 2) **Daniel H.** of Brandon (H 29004). Royal Canadian Artillery. He died 24 May 1944 at the age of 30 and is commemorated at the Cassino War Cemetery in Italy. He was the son of William and Mabel Noakes and was survived by his wife Violet B. Noakes of Waltham Cross, Hertfordshire, England. ***Noakes Lake*** (64 O/3), west of Munroe Lake was named after him in 1978.

Noble, Captain **David Stewart** of Winnipeg. Royal Canadian Army Medical Corps. He died 22 April 1945 at the age of 27 and is commemorated at the Holten Canadian War Cemetery in Holland. He was the son of David and Dora Noble of Winnipeg. Captain Noble graduated with a degree in Medicine at the University of Manitoba in 1943 and enlisted shortly thereafter. He was killed when the ambulance in which he was riding struck a land mine. ***Noble Lake*** (63 O/16), north of Paint Lake was named after him in 1967.

Nodrick, Corporal **Alexander** of Winnipeg (H 95567). Fort Garry Horse. He died 9 October 1944 at the age of 26 and is commemorated at Bergen-op-Zoom Canadian War Cemetery in Holland. He was survived by his mother Valerie Nodrick of Winnipeg. ***Nodrick Lake*** (64 I/10), northeast of North Knife Lake was named after him in 1974.

Noer, Private **Charles H.** (H 95678). Stormont, Dundas and Glengarry Highlanders. He died 27 February 1944 and is commemorated at Bergen-op-Zoom Canadian War Cemetery in Holland. ***Noer Lake*** (63 N/6), north of Kississing Lake was named after him in 1995.

Nordvall, Rifleman **George A.** of Birch River (H 9464). Royal Winnipeg Rifles. He died 21 February 1945 and is commemorated at the Groesbeek Canadian War Cemetery in Holland. ***Nordvall Lake*** (64 I/12), northwest of North Knife Lake was named after him in 1978.

Normand, Private **Emile** of St. Norbert (SH 62112). Princess Patricia's Canadian Light Infantry. He died 5 November 1951 and is commemorated at the United Nations Cemetery in Pusan, South Korea. ***Normand Island*** (53 E/16) in Island Lake was named after this Korean War casualty in 1998.

Normand, Rifleman **J. Lionel.** of St. Vital (H 42017). Royal Winnipeg Rifles. He died 8 June 1944 and is commemorated at Bretteville-sur-Laize Canadian War Cemetery in Calvados, France. ***Normand Lake*** (64 I/2), east of North Knife Lake was named after him in 1974.

Normandeau, Warrant Officer 1 **Alphonse J. P.** of St. Boniface (R 110699). No. 1664 Conversion Unit, RCAF. He died 16 March 1944 at the age of 22 and is commemorated at Stonefall Cemetery in Yorkshire, England. He was the second of the three sons of Emery and Alma Normandeau (née Rheault) and the brother of Sergeant Paul E. Normandeau (next entry). His sister writes (22 October 2001):

Alphonse was one of the first Scout Masters in St. Boniface. He graduated from Provencher School, attended Success Business College and joined the staff of the Manitoba Power Corporation in 1940 where he made many friends. In 1941, he signed up with the RCAF. He graduated as a wireless air gunner in June, 1942 and was promoted to the rank of Warrant Officer after he arrived overseas.

Normandeau Lake (52 E/11), southeast of Brereton Lake was named after him in 1974.

Normandeau, Sergeant **Paul E.** of St. Boniface (R 205216). No. 22 Operational Training Unit, RCAF. He died 20 August 1944 at the age of 20 and is commemorated at Brookwood Military Cemetery in Surrey, England. He was the youngest of the three sons of Emery and Alma Normandeau (née Rheault) and the brother of Warrant Officer Alphonse J. P. Normandeau (previous entry). His sister recalls (22 October 2001):

Paul was a fine athlete and was a member of Father Levesque's Junior Falcons winning hockey team of 1941. He attended Provencher School and Success Business College before joining Canadian Pacific in 1940 as a printer typist in the communications department. He enlisted in the RCAF and went overseas as a wireless air gunner in April of 1944. His brother Alphonse was killed overseas while Paul was on his way.

Normandeau Island (64 C/14) in Goldsand Lake was named after him in 1995.

Norquay, Flight Sergeant **Charles J. C.** of Selkirk (R 152593). No. 77 Squadron. He died 3 October 1943 at the age of 20 and is commemorated at the Hanover War Cemetery in Germany. He was the son of Thomas and Rose Norquay (née Cameron) and was survived by his wife Mildred L. Norquay (née Riley) of Winnipeg and their son whom he never saw. His brother recalls (22 November 2001):

Jack was born in May, 1923 at Selkirk, Manitoba, the first of the four sons of Tom and Rose Norquay. He married Mildred Riley on July 7, 1942. He and Mildred had met when they worked together at Belding Corticelli in Winnipeg. He had enlisted in the RCAF in January, 1942 and began training as a bomb aimer at Mossbank in July of that year, training which continued until September. Training meant flying in Avro Anson aircraft. Like most who flew Ansons, he was convinced that they only stayed aloft by flapping their wings.

Operations training in Britain began in March, 1943 and lasted until he joined with an all-RAF crew with No. 77 Squadron based at Elvington, Yorkshire. By then, he was aware that he had a son born July 26, 1943. His letters home to Mildred told how thrilled he was and that he hoped the baby would have blue eyes like its mother and not brown like his own.

He began "Ops" on September 22 in a brand new Halifax on which he had painted *Millie* on the nose. He made two operational flights over Hanover. His third mission was to Kassel on the night of October 3/4 and from which his aircraft did not return. This raid was comprised of 547 aircraft; 24 were lost. The H2S "Blind Marker" aircraft overshot the aiming point badly and the "visual markers" could not correct this because their view of the ground was restricted by thick haze. German decoy markers may also have been present. The main attack thus fell upon the western suburbs and outlying towns and villages. Even so, large fires were started at both the Henschel and Feisler aircraft factories, at the city's main hospital and at several other important buildings. The suburb of Wolfshaugen was devastated. Kassel's casualties were 118 dead – 68 civilians, 12 military and 38 foreigners – and 304 injured. Musgrove, in his book *Pathfinder Force* recorded that a large ammunition dump at Ihringhausen, just north of Wolfshaugen, was hit by a chance bomb load and that the resulting explosions attracted further bombs. Post-raid photographs showed 84 buildings at the military location destroyed and a great mass of craters in the area. The outlying townships of Bettenhausen and Sandershausen were also hit severely, but damage details for these places were not published.

Subsequently his family was notified that he and all his crewmates had lost their lives and were buried at Ihringhausen. After the war's end, they were re-interred at the British War Cemetery at Hanover.

Norquay Lake (53 M/8), west of Swampy Lake was named after him in 1995.

Norrie, Private **George M.** of Isabella (M 11583). Royal Canadian Army Medical Corps. He died 24 September 1944 at the age of 28 and is commemorated at Gradara War Cemetery in Italy. Private Norrie enlisted with the Calgary Highlanders in 1940 and went overseas the same year. He was with the Field Ambulance Corps when he died of wounds. He was the son of John and Helen Norrie of Isabella, Manitoba. ***Norrie Island*** (53 E/16) in Island Lake was named after him in 1984.

Noton, Flight Sergeant **Reginald F.** of Wawanesa (R 59356). No. 218 Squadron. He died 2 July 1942 at the age of 31 and is commemorated at the Runnymede Memorial in Surrey, England. He was the son of Frederick W. and Ethel M. Noton of Wawanesa, Manitoba. According to his younger brother (4 April 1996):

Reginald Frederick Noton was born May 18, 1911 in Newstead, Nottinghamshire, England. In 1912, at the age of one year, he accompanied his mother and father ... to Manitoba where he spent the rest of his life until joining the RCAF in January, 1940. Reg's grandfather C. W. Noton and uncles George and Alfred had immigrated to Boissevain in 1904 where they took up farming. Fred and Ethel Noton also farmed in this district until 1935 when they moved to Wawanesa. Reg attended school at Fairfax, Dunallen and Royal schools, the latter being four miles north and one mile west of Boissevain. After completing Grade 8 at Royal, he was kept home to work on the family farm.

Although of limited education, Reg was an avid reader and vitally interested in current affairs and politics. When 19, he campaigned with Eric Willis who was running for the Manitoba Legislature. Mr. Willis was a member for many years and later, of course, was appointed Lieutenant Governor of Manitoba. The Notons were members of the Anglican Church in Boissevain. Reg joined the Anglican Young People's Association and went on to become a Lay Reader in the Anglican Church. He taught Sunday School at various times, his last class being in Calgary when he was in the air force and attending wireless school.

At an early age, Reg became interested in airplanes and flying, however, any thought of becoming a pilot was thoroughly discouraged by his parents. He did get an early flight with a barnstormer who came to Boissevain. Out of a two by four, he made a model of Lindbergh's *Spirit of St. Louis*. In the early 1930s, Reg took a short course at the Manitoba Agricultural College, but his heart was not in farming. He soon left the farm and took over a motion picture business in Stonewall. This was eventually expanded to include a partnership in a theatre in the adjacent town of Stony Mountain. His connection with the church and his interest in politics continued. He was approached by the Conservative Party to run for the Legislature, but declined; by then, his politics had undergone some evolution. In January, 1940, Reg sold his theatre interests to his partner in Stony Mountain and joined the RCAF. He was now 28 years old with only a formal Grade 8 and a short course in agriculture, so he could not take pilot or navigator training. But he must fly; he took wireless air gunnery.

When he got to England in 1941, the RCAF was not yet completely organized in Britain and he was attached to the RAF and sent to Cranwell. Here he repeated some of his training because the RAF had little confidence in the RCAF. He liked neither the food nor the officers. Leaves were enjoyable because he was able to visit nearby aunts and uncles, relatives of his mother.

One night on operations, the crew was headed to France in a Wellington Bomber when, over southern England, both engines failed. All the crew parachuted safely. Later, Reg was assigned to Stirling Bombers with a crew from all over the Commonwealth. He, at five feet eleven inches, was the shortest man in the crew of five. They participated in the first thousand-bomber raids on Germany. Well into his first tour of duty in the spring of 1942, his letters said that city after city was being wiped out and surely Germany would not stand this devastation for long. How wrong he was. Into his second tour of duty on July 2, 1942, Reg's plane and crew were returning from a raid on Bremen when they sent out an SOS, undoubtedly sent by Reg. They did not return. Nothing more was heard or known of any of the crew, and in due course, they were presumed dead. Because of thousands of sacrifices such as Reg's, I enjoy life in a free country.

Noton Lake (64 P/6), east of Nejanilini Lake was named after him in 1974.

Nowell, Flying Officer **George R.** of St. Vital (J 26775). No. 21 Squadron, Mentioned in Dispatches. He died 23 April 1945 at the age of 21 and is commemorated at Schoonebeek (Oud Schoonebeek) General Cemetery, Holland. He was the son of Charles E. and Emmie Nowell (née Tritton) of St. Vital who visited his grave in 1968. He wrote several letters home to his parents, sister Pam and brother Ronald.

A letter from George, written April 22, 1945 (a day after his birthday and a day before he was killed), was found in his personal belongings and sent on by the squadron officer. There was also a letter to "Dear little brother" Ronald, serving in the Canadian Navy. He works today as a radio operator for the federal department of transport. A parcel with goodies that arrived too late for George was given to another mother's son, the officer wrote.

Octogenarian Emmie Nowell (she is six months short of 90) lives alone today in a self-contained suite in a senior citizens' apartment block. She reads, knits and does a bit of recycling of her wardrobe on her 1913 Seamstress treadle sewing machine. And as she knits, her memories, happy and sad, pass before her on the screen of her mind.

Son George's last letter is the most poignant. It begins "Dear mother and dad and Pam (his sister was seven at the time). Today (the day after his 21st birthday)," he wrote, "I am a man! Just a few lines from the new man in the family … I am getting 28 days leave pretty soon – sort of a rest when two thirds over a tour." He'd like to fly home but he knows that is out of the question. He didn't know that he was never to finish the remaining third of his "tour." He was killed the next day on his 48th mission.

A letter (no date) from the "little brother," Ronald, stationed in Canadian waters begins, "Dear mom, I hardly know what to say. I got your letter today telling me that George is missing. The signal that he was gone came through just a while ago. It seems hard to believe. I should be able to manage to get 14 days leave (to see you all). The 1st Lieutenant told me to put in a request.…"

Emmie Nowell, a native of Tilmanstone, Kent, England, came to Winnipeg with her parents Elizabeth and John Tritton and two brothers to improve their fortunes. At that early age she sewed in a sweatshop to help put bread on the table. Her father, a former keeper of the English Plough and Harrow Inn where miners stopped to get a tuppence of beer, found work in Canada as a maintenance man with the Canadian National Railway.

George's letters tell of visiting the quaint Kentish village and his grandfather's former inn. On one of his leaves, two of his mother's old classmates from the village school showed George around. He even visited the Wesleyan Chapel where young Emmie used to go sing with the temperance group: *Keep outside the public house; And take your money home.*

Before George enlisted, he worked in a chartered accountant's firm headed by a Mr. Reade. Thomas Sill (later to become a philanthropist millionaire) also worked there. George kept in touch with the two men and when Reade died suddenly, George sent his condolences to Sill (Emmie has the letter). "We here," wrote George, "have become used to losing friends. And thinking about it doesn't help." Then changing the subject, he reveals his sense of humour. "We're living here in a Chateau (French for big country home with inadequate plumbing) and we miss the good old Brussels sprouts and cabbage we used to get in England, for we don't have any fresh vegetables. However, I never had so many eggs in my life, for I know a French family across the road who keeps me supplied with 'oefs' in return for cigs and chocolate."

He notes that he is improving his French that he learned at home in St. Vital's Glenlawn Collegiate. "See you in four or five months! Sincerely, George Nowell."

Had George come back, his mother thinks he may have returned to become an accountant with the Reade-Sill firm, though she rather thinks he would have stayed with the Air Force. "He liked flying and was only biding time that year he worked as a junior accountant until his 18th birthday so he could join up."

George sensed the war was nearing its end. War for him came to an end sooner than expected.

Forty-seven Remembrance Days, counting this year, have passed since then. But to Emmie Nowell – like the many mothers who have lost dear ones in the services – every day of those years is for remembering. Mother Nowell's yellowed letters speak to her and comfort her. She is glad she visited his grave in Oud-Schoonebeek in 1968. "I could not have borne to do so sooner. Then I found it brought me peace. My son was not at this place – only his body. His spirit was with me and God. I pray for world peace, for the peace that men and women fought for in the war to end wars. May they not have died in vain."

Together we put the letters back into the embroidered folder that Emmie Nowell, Silver Cross mother, keeps them in (Barton 1987).

Nowell Lake (54 L/10), west of Churchill was named after him in 1948.

Nutter, Ordinary Signalman **Alexander** of Winnipeg (V 9625). HMS *Jupiter*. He died 25 January 1941 at the age of 20 and is commemorated at the Halifax Memorial. He was the son of William G. and Gwendoline Nutter of Winnipeg. ***Nutter Lake*** (64 G/7), southeast of Big Sand Lake was named after him in 1963.

Nutter, Pilot Officer **John V.** of Winnipeg (J 12476). No. 1 Reconnaissance Squadron, RCAF. He died 11 August 1942 at the age of 26 and is commemorated at the Ottawa Memorial. He was the son of John V. and Elizabeth A. Nutter of Winnipeg and was survived by his wife Carolan Nutter. She writes "... we had only been married a short time when he went missing in August, 1942 and was declared killed in action a few months later." ***Nutter Island*** (53 L/2) in Goose Lake was named after him in 1995.

Nykolaishen, Private **William** of Dauphin (B 43704). Highland Light Infantry of Canada. He died 25 July 1944 at the age of 23 and is commemorated at Bretteville-sur-Laize Canadian War Cemetery in Calvados, France. He was the son of Peter and Annie Nykolaishen of Zelena, Manitoba. His brother writes (10 April 1995):

William was born in 1921 in Shell River Municipality, Roblin, Manitoba. [He] received his education in Hillcrest School for nine years, then helped on his family farm until he moved to Toronto to find employment. There he enlisted into the army. He received his training in Winnipeg and Toronto. He then left for overseas and was killed in action.

Nykolaishen Lake (64 P/1), southeast of Nejanilini Lake was named after him in 1974.

A French veteran of the First World War greeting Universal Carriers of the South Saskatchewan Regiment during a Canadian advance in Normandy 20 July 1944. Courtesy of the National Archives of Canada (PA-131386).

O

O'Brien, Flying Officer **Wallace W.** of Winnipeg (J 14520). No. 428 Squadron. He died 13 May 1943 at the age of 24 and is commemorated at Dieppe Canadian War Cemetery, Seine-Maritime, France. ***O'Brien Island*** (64 J/12) in Descôteaux Lake was named after him in 1989.

O'Brien, Private **William E.** of Erickson (H 20595). Queen's Own Cameron Highlanders. He died 19 August 1942 and is commemorated at Dieppe Canadian War Cemetery in Seine-Maritime, France. He was the son of Mrs. Maud O'Brien of Erickson. ***O'Brien Lake*** (52 L/6), northeast of Lac du Bonnet was named after him in 1973.

O'Bryan, Flying Officer **William E. H.** of Winnipeg (J 45422). No. 571 Squadron. He died 19 March 1945 at the age of 29 and is commemorated at Brookwood Military Cemetery in Surrey, England. He was the son of William H. A. T. and Agatha M. O'Bryan of Winnipeg and was survived by his wife Helen L. O'Bryan (née Smith) of Winnipeg, their daughters Patricia and Lynne and his sister Sheila Hayward and families. His sister recalls (11 January 2002):

> My brother was a happy, fun loving person. He was born and raised in Winnipeg. He was an Observer flying with the RCAF attached to No. 8 RAF Squadron. As we have heard, his plane was hit on a mission over Germany, making it impossible to land safely. Both Bill and his pilot were killed in the attempt to land in England.

O'Bryan Lake (64 O/7), northwest of Munroe Lake was named after him in 1975.

O'Donnell, Flying Officer **Joseph Norman** of Killarney (J 39724). No. 1666 Heavy Conversion Unit, RCAF. He died 19 November 1944 at the age of 26 and is commemorated at the Runnymede Memorial in Surrey, England. He was the son of Mr. and Mrs. William O'Donnell of Killarney, Manitoba. ***O'Donnell Lake*** (63 I/3), southwest of Molson Lake was named after him in 1995.

O'Dowda, Pilot Officer **John F.** of Winnipeg (J 19976). No. 51 Squadron. He died 15 March 1944 at the age of 21 and is commemorated at Durnbach War Cemetery in Bavaria, Germany. He was the son of Robert T. C. and Hermina I. O'Dowda of Winnipeg. His sister writes (10 October 2001):

> He attended Laura Secord and Gordon Bell schools and was later employed at the Reliance Grain Company prior to his enlistment in 1942. Jack was a mid-upper gunner on a Lancaster bomber. He and his crew had almost finished their tour of duty when Jack developed a severe cold and could not fly. In the meantime, his crew finished their tour. Upon recovery from the cold, he joined another crew to complete his required flights. They were shot down on a raid in Stuttgart. His mother (a widow) and an uncle visited his grave in 1964.
>
> Jack was a happy spirit, liked by all who knew him and deeply loved by his family. He enjoyed skiing and the happy times at the family cottage at Laclu on Lake of the Woods.

O'Dowda Lake (64 P/2), southeast of Nejanilini Lake was named after him in 1974.

O'Kelly, Major **Christopher P.** Manitoba Regiment, Canadian Expeditionary Force, Military Cross, Victoria Cross. He was the youngest soldier in the Commonwealth to win both awards (aged 21).

> On 26 October 1917 at Passchendaele, Belgium, Captain O'Kelly led his company with extraordinary skill and determination. They captured six pill-boxes with 100 prisoners and 10 machine-guns. Later his company repelled a strong counterattack, taking more prisoners, and subsequently during the night they captured a hostile raiding party consisting of one officer, 10 men and a machine-gun (Buzzell 1997).

Major O'Kelly drowned in 1922 along with his companion, Lieutenant William Murray (Distinguished Conduct Medal). There is a monument to him at Camp Morton and ***O'Kelly Lake*** (52 M/13), north of Viking Lake was named after him in 1991. Murray Island, named after his friend in 1991, is located in O'Kelly Lake.

O'Neil, Trooper **Dennis P.** of Hartney (H 77261). 12th Manitoba Dragoons. He died 20 August 1944 at the age of 21 and is commemorated at Bretteville-sur-Laize Canadian War Cemetery in Calvados, France. He was the son of David H. and Beatrice O'Neil of Hartney, Manitoba. His sister recalls (5 December 1991):

> Dennis was as Irish as his name. He was a curly-haired, good-natured lad who was on friendly terms with young and old alike. His ready Irish wit and keen sense of humour were always enjoyed and sadly missed when they were no more. School was a bore for the boy who loved the outdoors – he often played the age-old game of hookey. He would wander the nearby fields catching gophers and selling their tails to the Municipality as so many youngsters were doing in those pre-war days.
>
> Dennis left school at an early age. Jobs were few, but being a willing worker, he always found something to do. He was particularly fond of farming, but having asthma, this was not a suitable occupation. Later, he took on a draying business. Before his 18th birthday, Dennis journeyed into Winnipeg to join the armed forces. Naturally, he was sent home until he became of age – he was so disappointed. He and his brother joined the 12th Manitoba Dragoons, Reserve force in Souris and drove over every week for training.
>
> His regiment was heavily involved in the fight to close the Falaise Gap, a battle we have read so much about. On the night of August 19, 1944, Dennis was delivering a message to headquarters. He met with a fatal accident and one can only guess what happened. Word was sent back to the family that Dennis died of head injuries. Major R. M. Mason was one of Dennis' officers and wrote a fine tribute to him: "An outstanding example of gallantry to duty. I have often seen him riding his motorcycle fearlessly on black, stormy nights with the ever-present danger of shelling. His cheerfulness and loyal obedience was an inspiration to his comrades. He was a great favourite among his associates."

O'Neil Lake (64 G/11), east of Big Sand Lake was named after him in 1963.

O'Neil, Pilot Officer **Grant M.** of Winnipeg (J 88853). No. 405 Squadron. He died 30 January 1944 at the age of 20 and is commemorated at the Runnymede Memorial in Surrey, England. ***O'Neil Bay*** (54 D/6) in Stephens Lake was named after him in 1996.

O'Neill, Private **Dori J.** of Winnipeg (H 6644). Winnipeg Grenadiers. He died 19 December 1941 and is commemorated at the Sai Wan Memorial in Hong Kong. He was the son of Patrick J. and Kristen O'Neill (née Olsen) of St. Peters, Manitoba and was survived by his wife Pearl O'Neill (née Smith) and their infant daughter. His wife recalls (8 April 1996) that he was:

... born at St. Peter's, Manitoba, growing up in Clandeboye [and] then moved to Winnipeg [where he] attended Strathcona and Champlain High School. Then he worked as a truck driver for Bell Bottling Company. He enlisted with the Winnipeg Grenadiers on September 26, 1939 in Winnipeg. He served in Canada, the Caribbean and Hong Kong. He married his High School girlfriend Pearl Smith and left May, 1940 for garrison duty to Jamaica, then came home October, 1941. He saw his daughter Brenda who was 10 months old for the fist time. He was to be home for six months, but all leaves were cancelled and the Winnipeg Grenadiers left for Hong Kong October 25, 1941. He wrote one letter home then the war broke out and nothing was known until February, 1943.

O'Neill Island (64 N/11) in Kasmere Lake was named after him in 1995.

O'Neill, Trooper **Thomas** of Magnet, Manitoba (H 100022). Calgary Tank Regiment. He died 25 August 1944 at the age of 20 and is commemorated at Florence War Cemetery, Italy. He was the son of Thomas J. and Della R. O'Neill of Three Hills, Alberta. ***O'Neill Lake*** (53 N/2), northeast of Red Cross Lake was named after him in 1995.

Oakenfold, Leading Aircraftman **Harold F.** of Winnipeg (R 186866). Headquarters of the Western Air Command, RCAF. He was lost at sea (aboard the *B. C. Star*) 24 July 1943 and is commemorated at the Ottawa Memorial. He was the son of Thomas F. and Violet Oakenfold of Calgary. ***Oakenfold Lake*** (64 P/11), east of Nejanilini Lake was named after him in 1974.

Oakes, Flying Officer **William H. "Buster"** of Swan Lake (J 40103). No. 420 Squadron. He died 5 March 1945 at the age of 25 and is commemorated at Stonefall Cemetery in Yorkshire, England. He was the son of William H. and Helen B. Oakes of Swan Lake, Manitoba. His obituary read in part:

F/O Oakes was born at Rosebank. He moved to Somerset with his family when three years old and in 1928 went to Swan Lake. He enlisted in August, 1941, and went overseas in March, 1944 after training at Winnipeg, Toronto, Paulson and Quebec. Prior to enlistment, F/O Oakes was [an] agent for the Pool Elevator company at Ninette, Manitoba (n.d.).

Oakes Lake (63 K/16), west of Wekusko Lake was named after him in 1973.

Oakley, Warrant Officer 1 **William H.** of St. Boniface (R 134130). No. 271 Squadron. He died 7 June 1944 at the age of 21 and is commemorated at the Runnymede Memorial in Surrey, England. He was the son of Mr. and Mrs. J. H. Oakley of St. Boniface. ***Oakley Creek*** (63 J/3), which flows southeast into McBain Creek southwest of Kiskitto Lake was named after him in 1973.

Oddy, Private **Herbert** of Thornhill (H 17792). Princess Patricia's Canadian Light Infantry. He died 27 July 1943 at the age of 21 and is commemorated at Agira Canadian War Cemetery in Italy. He was the only child of Jane Oddy of Thornhill, Manitoba. ***Oddy Lake*** (64 N/4), north of Lac Brochet was named after him in 1972.

Ogden, Corporal **Theodore J.** of Winnipeg (H 6985). Queen's Own Cameron Highlanders. He died 23 October 1944 at the age of 26 and is commemorated at Bergen-op-Zoom Canadian War Cemetery in Holland. He was survived by his wife Frances K. Ogden of Calgary. ***Ogden Lake*** (64 O/15), southwest of Blevins Lake was named after him in 1995.

Ogilvie, Flying Officer **James M.** of Portage la Prairie (J 22214.) No. 100 Squadron. He died 3 January 1944 at the age of 23 and is commemorated at the Runnymede Memorial in Surrey, England. He was the son of James M. and Caroline G. Ogilvie of Portage la Prairie. His brother recalls (29 November 2001):

Jim was the second of three brothers who went through most of their schooling in the same grade. This created a tremendous friendly rivalry. The year previous to their moving to Oakland, Jim and brother Fred bought an old Model T which they made over into a flat-deck pickup. They then took off from Durban, Manitoba to look for work. Their journey ended at Fort William, Ontario. They wrote home to say they had a really good trip and had only seven flat tires. Jim was survived by six brothers and sisters, two of whom served overseas in the air force.

Ogilvie Lake (64 O/13), east of Nueltin Lake was named after him in 1975.

Ogren, Sergeant **Carl E.** of Winnipeg (R 166219). No. 111 Squadron. He died 28 June 1943 at the age of 19 and is commemorated at the Ottawa Memorial. He was the son of Harold G. and Christina Ogren (née Lund) of Winnipeg. His sister and niece write (8 February 1995):

Carl was born in Elm Creek, Manitoba. [His mother] immigrated from Oslo, Norway and [his father] from the province of Värmland, Sweden. The family moved to Winnipeg ... after the death of his mother in a farming accident in May of 1929. Carl attended Hugh John Macdonald, Somerset and Lord Selkirk schools. He enlisted in the Air Force in May, 1942 and went overseas a year later as a wireless air gunner after training at Calgary and Fingal, Ontario. Carl was reported missing, then presumed dead ... at Nassau, Bahamas. It was said his plane went missing in the Bermuda Triangle. Carl enjoyed music, hockey and close family ties with his sister Edith (whom he listed as next-of-kin), brothers Evert and Herbert.

Ogren Lake (64 P/3), southeast of Nejanilini Lake was named after him in 1974.

Oige, Private **Joseph H.** of Selkirk (H 41666). Winnipeg Grenadiers. He died a prisoner of war 28 November 1942 at the age of 26 and is commemorated at the Sai Wan War Cemetery in Hong Kong. He was the son of Joseph A. and Clara Oige of Selkirk, Manitoba. ***Oige Lake*** (64 I/3), west of North Knife Lake was named after him in 1974.

Olafson, Private **Budvar P. "Bud"** of Portage la Prairie (H 6269). Winnipeg Grenadiers. He died a prisoner of war 1 January 1944 at the age of 25 and is commemorated at the Yokohama War Cemetery in Japan. Ten months after the fall of Hong Kong in 1941, Private Olafson was reported to be a prisoner of war; he died in a detention camp in Tokyo two years later during a typhoon. He had operated Bud's Barber Shop in Portage la Prairie prior to the war and was the son of John and Olive Olafson of Portage la Prairie. ***Olafson Lake*** (64 I/9), northeast of North Knife Lake was named after him in 1974.

Olenick, Rifleman **Theodore** of Reston (H 22815). Royal Winnipeg Rifles. He died 21 April 1945 at the age of 19 and is commemorated at the Holten Canadian War Cemetery in Holland. His older brother has visited the grave three times since 1990. Rifleman Olenick was the son of Andrew and Annie Olenick of Reston, Manitoba. His brother recalls (25 October 2001):

Ted was born October 21, 1925 at Reston, Manitoba. He was the sixth child of Annie (Diachuk) and Andy Olenick. As a young fellow, he was very popular and well liked. Like most of the Olenick children, he too was very athletic, his favourite sport being hockey. He served as a mascot for the hockey team when his older brothers were playing and eventually came to be a goaltender himself. He also enjoyed his time spent with the Boy Scouts. Ted was a good student and completed his Grade 10 at Reston High School. then worked for a short period with his Dad on the section and also at McDougall's Transfer in Reston. In the fall of 1943, Ted went to Winnipeg where he accepted a job with Liquidaire Craft of Winnipeg and at the same time he resumed his studies at night school.

Ted seemed to have a premonition about going overseas in World War II and was not nearly as anxious as his three older brothers were to pursue that avenue in life. However, he did become a member of the Royal Winnipeg Rifles on May 9, 1944. After training at Fort Garry, Shilo and Debert, Nova Scotia, he sailed for overseas on December 23, 1944. None of us will ever really know what all took place during those next three months after disembarking in Europe, but one thing we know for sure is that he would much rather have been back on the prairies than sailing to that far-off land, away from family and friends on Christmas Day, 1944.

We are told that he died about an hour after receiving wounds to the chest and thigh on the battlefields of northern Holland on April 21, 1945. He was 19 years old. He now lies in peace with 1400 other young Canadians in a beautiful military cemetery in the forest at Holten, Holland.

Olenick Lake (64 I/3), west of North Knife Lake was named after him in 1974.

Oliver, Lieutenant **Peter S.** of Holland, Manitoba. Canadian Provost Corps. He died 19 August 1942 and is commemorated at Dieppe Canadian War Cemetery in Seine-Maritime, France. First awarded at the Canadian Provost Corps School (now the Canadian Forces School of Intelligence and Security) in 1955, the Oliver Memorial Trophy is presented annually to the outstanding Military Police graduate from the Canadian Forces Military Police and Security Academy. ***Oliver Island*** (64 I/15) in the Seal River was named after Lieutenant Oliver in 1995.

Oliver, Sergeant **Roland Stanton** of Holland, Manitoba (1264816). RAF. He died 22 April 1942 at the age of 27 and is commemorated at the Runnymede Memorial in Surrey, England. He was the son of Roland and Lilian M. Oliver of Norwood. His brother recalls that (19 November 1996):

Sergeant Oliver was born in Stonewall, Manitoba and moved to Petersfield in 1919 with his family. He moved to Holland in 1929 where he completed his schooling. He then worked for three years in the dispensary of the General Hospital in Winnipeg before going to England in 1937. He joined the Royal Air Force in 1940. He was declared missing and presumed dead ... while flying a bomber from London to Cairo.

Oliver Point (53 L/15) on Magill Lake was named after him in 1995.

Oliver, Pilot Officer **William R.** of Killarney, Manitoba (J 88087). No. 405 Squadron. He was shot down 23 April 1944 at the age of 21. Pilot Officer Oliver is commemorated at Condé-sur-Aisne Communal Cemetery, Aisne, France. In 1981, his sister Mrs. Eileen Williston went to France to find her brother's grave and she recounts her experiences and the circumstances of his burial:

From March, 1944 to March, 1945 the bloodiest, most devastating aerial battles of all time were waged in Europe. During this time the Allied Bomber Command saw fit to send thousands upon thousands of planes to destroy the major cities of Germany at a cost in lives of 19,000 young [Canadian] airmen. On the night of April 21/22, 1944, the Lancaster on which my brother Bill was navigator received a direct hit from anti-aircraft fire over Laon, France, and crashed near the village of Condé-sur-Aisne. Like most of those 19,000, Bill was not yet twenty-one.

In 1981, I went looking for my brother's grave. I crossed from Dover to Calais by hovercraft, then took a train south to the city of Soissons. I asked the hotel desk clerk in English if there was a bus to Condé-sur-Aisne. He didn't know. I would have to get that information elsewhere. This was my first visit to France and I was apprehensive about my French. Would I understand anything, and could I make myself understood? I walked down a street crowded with market gardeners and bustling shoppers toting big canvas bags. It was "petit marche" day in Soissons.

For a block or two I wove my way amongst the shoppers. Surely some of these citizens would know the location of their bus depot. I looked for a friendly face, but all eyes were intent only on the mission at hand – to find the rosiest apples, the freshest loaves, the plumpest hen. As well, I was too timid to stop and ask. Suddenly I saw across the street a building with a sign over the door, "Bureau d'Industrie et Tourisme." Perhaps I could get help there. In my best broken French I asked the girl behind the desk if she knew how I could get to Condé-sur-Aisne. What was I looking for? Then, after listening intently to my laboured reply she said, "Ah, oui le cimetière militaire!" She told me the only way to get there was by taxi and that since the driver would have to wait for me there, then drive me back, she would phone and get a price for the return trip. Forty francs was settled on.

Within minutes, a small, white car came to a squealing halt outside. A dark-haired young man in a red sweater waved to us. "Votre taxi," said the girl. I thanked her and left the building, then got in beside the driver whose name was André. I gave him my understanding about the location of the grave: in a churchyard in Condé-sur-Aisne. *Non non*! He was sure it was a few kilometres beyond the village itself. He explained that there were many military cemeteries in this part of France and although he had never been to the one near Condé, he knew of it.

Off we went, winding along the country roads, in and out of tiny villages, until we came to one with the signpost CONDÉ-SUR-AISNE. In the village, André pulled up at one of the houses lining the street. He got out and knocked on the door. I expected to see the door open but instead I saw a peep-hole cover slide open, revealing part of a face. André exchanged a few words with the face, then got back into the car. "Trois kilometres," he said. I reminded him that the grave should be right there in the village. *Non non*! It was three kilometres further along! *These foreigners can be tiresome*, he must have said to himself as he changed gears and we sped off.

I wasn't prepared for the vastness of the cemetery or the melancholy I felt on seeing on one side the endless rows of identical white crosses and on the other endless rows of identical headstones. Servicemen by the thousands had been buried here. According to André, the crosses were for the French, the stones for the English. We began walking down the rows of headstones, noting that the engravings were all army emblems; there were no air force crests. André questioned an old man who was operating a power mower. He told us to consult the memorial book in the covered entranceway. Leafing through the alphabetically arranged names, it was soon evident that Bill's name was not there – and no wonder, for when we walked out of the cemetery I turned around and saw the words "La Guerre du Monde 1914 - 18" etched in the stone wall. Wrong war, wrong cemetery.

André now thought that perhaps I was right; the grave might after all be in the village itself. Pointing to the meter which read 60 francs, already more than what had been quoted for the whole trip, he asked me if 60 francs was agreeable, and when I said yes, he switched off the meter. Back in Condé-sur-Aisne, we drove up behind a large stone church. Nearby a man was hoeing his garden. When André spoke to him, he stopped his hoeing, then said a few words to a boy of about ten who had come up to listen in on the conversation. The boy immediately hopped on his bike and, motioning us to follow in the car, wheeled gracefully along until he came to a narrow lane. We followed him to the end where we saw a small cemetery.

It was situated on a slope facing south and was bounded on the north side by a high brick wall and on the remaining sides by low stone walls. Down the hill beyond the cemetery, fruit trees were in blossom, poplars were budding, and between the trees wound the river Aisne. In the graveyard, even before the boy led the way I sensed where my brother was buried for I could see seven identical markers in the far corner. As the three of us stood by those seven headstones, I felt an immediate sense of peace and relief that my brother was buried in this setting and not in that great impersonal "cimetière militaire." A carpet of mauve lobelia covered the ground and it touched me deeply to see that the graves were lovingly tended, even after so many years.

So moved was I by the experience that it wasn't until much later that I wished I had spoken to some of the people of the village. However, when I got home to Canada I wrote to the mayor of Condé-sur-Aisne to tell him of my visit and to ask him to pass along my gratitude to whomever tended those graves. I received a reply which in translation reads:

"I understand that you visited the grave of your brother in my village. It's a pity that you didn't come to see me because you would have been very well received. As for the plane in which your brother was killed, my wife and I saw it crash. I wasn't mayor at the time but I know that a civic official did everything she could to see that the airmen who were killed had an honourable burial. These airmen will always have a place in our village and their graves will always be well cared for. I say goodbye in the hope that if one day you come back to our village, I'll have the pleasure of meeting you."

It seemed a strange coincidence that this man I had written to had actually seen the crash. The cordiality of his letter reminded me of the friendly helpfulness of André, the taxi driver, who in reply to my farewell comment to him: "Vous êtes très galant," smiled and said "Tous les hommes de France sont galant!"

Only a month before that fatal night over France, Bill and his crew had been transferred from Squadron 434, known as Bluenose Squadron, to Pathfinder Squadron 405. The crew were young Canadians except for the mid upper gunner Johnny Tonkyn, RAF, whose family had befriended Bill and his crewmates. Also, just before 22 April, Ron Morrison of Winnipeg became ill and his place was taken by another member of the RAF. So it had been five Canadians and two British who climbed into their Lancaster to roar off into that black April night. It was their responsibility to fly to the target, then drop flares to guide the bombers that would follow.

Homeward bound through skies alive with anti-aircraft fire, a shell seared into our crew's plane, tearing it into two flaming sections, the main fuselage landing on the edge of the village of Condé-sur-Aisne, the rear turret and part of the tail three kilometres away. Five bodies were found in the fuselage, one in the tail section and one was missing. A huge yellow and black cat, the plane's mascot, walked away from the tail section, uninjured, and if today a yellow and black cat is seen sleeping on a window sill in the vicinity of Condé-sur-Aisne, who is to say it isn't a descendant of the only survivor from that Lancaster?

The Germans discouraged the villagers from snooping around the plane's wreckage and forbade them touching the bodies. However, during the night of April 25, four brave Frenchmen smuggled the dead airmen to their village where they were secretly buried at night. Then a week later a Catholic service was held for them (What did it matter that only two of the crew were Catholic?). One of the rescuers, Louis Hourblin, made six crosses out of metal scrounged from the aircraft but as only two of the bodies had been readily identifiable, he could put names on only two of the crosses. The other crosses were marked "aviateur inconnu de la RAF."

As soon as the war ended, an impressive service was held at the church and cemetery with the whole village, as well as a company from the American Army of Occupation in attendance. Bouquets and wreaths – one with a big 'C' for Canada – were brought to the graves. The mayor gave a speech and the captain of the American company, on behalf of the crew's families, thanked the villagers.

Two years later, an RAF officer and four British soldiers showed up at the village to disinter the bodies, put them in new coffins and try to make further identification. They were successful in identifying two more bodies. Thus, out of a crew of seven there were now four identified, two unidentified and one missing. The British then erected six white iron crosses. (As Bill hadn't been one of those identified, it was a long time before my family had stopped grasping at straws, hoping that he might have escaped the burning plane).

Years later, in place of the six white crosses, seven headstones bearing the name, number and rank of each of the airmen were erected.

In early spring, the bright carpet of lobelia covers the graves, then in summer roses come into bloom, and all the while the good villagers of Condé-sur-Aisne watch over the resting place of the strangers they adopted as their own (Williston 1993).

Oliver Bay (63 N/13) in the Churchill River was named after him in 1995.

Olmstead, Flight Sergeant **Leonard T.** of Carberry (R 134468). No. 434 Squadron. He died 7 September 1943 at the age of 25 and is commemorated at Durnbach War Cemetery in Bavaria, Germany. He was one of the four children of Albert W. and Mary J. Olmstead of Portage la Prairie. He completed his Grade 11 education at Wingham Consolidated School and then worked as a hired hand at Wingham and in the gold mines at Red Lake. He was employed at Macleod's Hardware in Portage la Prairie when he enlisted. ***Olmstead Lake*** (64 I/7), northeast of North Knife Lake was named after him in 1974.

Olshansky, Leading Aircraftman **Maxwell** of Winnipeg (R 177528). No. 6416 Servicing Echelon, RCAF. He died 12 October 1944 at the age of 22 and is commemorated at the Groesbeek Canadian War Cemetery in Holland. He was the son of Isaac and Mary Olshansky and was survived by his fiancée Ruth L. Harris of Winnipeg. His sister recalls (15 November 2001):

He was always in good humour, teasing, joking and adventurous. As a child, he never complained and didn't know the meaning of fear. His teacher had been telling the class about Canada, how big it was and about the Canadian Rocky Mountains. So at the age of 14, he hopped a freight train and went via roof top to British Columbia on October 31, 1936. The snow was already deep and the temperature was well below freezing. He found a job, worked for a year and came home.

He went back to school with some persuasion. At 18, he joined the Air Force. By the time he was 20, he went overseas, first to England and then to Holland.

Olshansky Lake (64 I/8), northeast of North Knife Lake was named after him in 1974. LAC Olshansky's fiancée commented (7 February 1985): "My wish of forty years of some memorial (which seemed an impossible dream) has come true."

Olson, Sergeant **Alvin G.** of Winnipeg (R 95308). No. 420 Squadron. He died 21 January 1943 at the age of 26 and is commemorated at the Runnymede Memorial in Surrey, England. He was the son of Gustaf A. and Jenny T. Olsen (née Carlson) of Winnipeg. ***Olson Peninsula*** (64 G/16) on Chipewyan Lake was named after him in 1995.

Olson, Corporal **Arthur** of Winnipeg (H 46271). Regina Rifle Regiment. He died 9 June 1944 and is commemorated at Beny-sur-Mer Canadian War Cemetery in Calvados, France. He was survived by his wife Blanche M. Olson of Kitchener, Ontario. ***Olson Rapids*** (64 I/7) in the North Knife River was named after him in 1995.

Olson, Pilot Officer **Ivor Donald** of MacGregor (J 90769). No. 3 Advanced Flying School. He died 16 September 1944 at the age of 26 and is commemorated at Worcester Park (St. Philip Churchyard) in Surrey, England. He was the eldest son of Anders Ivor and Nellie Olson and was survived by brothers John and Nelson and sisters Gloria and Hope. His sister recalls (26 November 2001):

> He was a flying instructor and was killed when his Anson aircraft lost its tail unit and spun into the ground after a mid-air collision with another Anson. The crash occurred at RAF Station Halfpenny Green, England.
>
> Donald, as he was best known, was born in Winnipeg October 20, 1918. In 1926, the family moved to a farm 1 1/2 miles north of MacGregor where he received his education. He first enlisted in the non-permanent militia, then in October, 1941 enlisted in the RCAF. He trained at Toronto, Edenville, Gooderich and Borden, then went overseas in November, 1942.
>
> Donald was prominent and popular in the life of the community and active in sports, being a member of the local hockey team. He enjoyed music and often played his guitar at dances and socials. There is a Memorial Stone in his memory in the Air Force Garden of Memories on Air Force Way in Winnipeg. His name is also engraved on his dad and mother's memorial in MacGregor Cemetery.

Olson Bay (64 H/13) in Currie Lake was named after him in 1986.

Olstead, Pilot Officer **George J.** of Neepawa (C 862). No. 1 Air Navigation School. He died 14 October 1939 at the age of 23 and is commemorated at Riverside Cemetery in Neepawa. He was the son of James M. and Mary A. S. Olstead of Sidney, British Columbia. Pilot Officer Olstead enlisted in 1938 after graduating from the University of Manitoba with a degree in science. He was one of six Manitobans chosen that year to train pilots overseas. It is unclear whether his aircraft crashed or exploded north of Kingston, Ontario. His commanding officer suggested the mishap may have been due to a snowstorm or sabotage. ***Olstead Lake*** (64 O/11), southeast of Nueltin Lake was named after him in 1975.

Olynyk, Private **Harry** of Selkirk (M 10653). Seaforth Highlanders of Canada. He died 6 October 1943 at the age of 24 and is commemorated at the Moro River Canadian War Cemetery in Italy. He was the son of Steve and Dora Olynyk of Winnipeg. ***Olynyk Lake*** (52 L/3), northeast of Brereton Lake was named after him in 1973.

Omand, Private **Thomas** (H 8701). Queen's Own Cameron Highlanders. He died 21 July 1944 and is commemorated at the Bayeux Memorial in Calvados, France. ***Omand Lake*** (64 I/16), north of North Knife Lake was named after him in 1974.

Onhauser, Private **John T.** of Morden (829685). 44th Battalion (Manitoba Regiment), British War Medal and the Victory Medal. He died 12 April 1917 at the age of 19 and is commemorated at the Vimy Memorial, Pas de Calais, France. He was the son of Adolf and Anna Onhauser (née Busch) of Winnipeg. His great nephew writes (20 December 1984):

> John was born December 4th, 1897 at Morden to Adolph and Anna, ... Austrian immigrants. John moved with his family to Langside Street in Winnipeg about 1908. John enlisted with his older brother Joseph on December 9th, 1915 in Winnipeg at the age of 17. In a newspaper column in the *Free Press* on May 21st, 1917, John's death is recorded: "His younger brother [John], however, is listed among the slain, having made the supreme sacrifice on April 12th, after getting safely through the Vimy Ridge fight. Previous to enlisting, he was attending the Winnipeg Collegiate Institute. The mother of these two boys is a widow residing at 525 Langside Street." No one in our family remembers or has written proof how exactly he died, but basically it seems he died after a blow to the head after falling from a horse while training in France.

His name appears on the plaque in Vimy Ridge Park on Portage Avenue and ***Onhauser Lake*** (64 O/16), west of Baralzon Lake was named after this World War I casualty in 1987.

Onysko, Flying Officer **Peter** of Winnipeg (J 24428). No. 257 Squadron. He died 27 October 1944 at the age of 22 and is commemorated at Brookwood Military Cemetery in Surrey, England. He was the son of Mr. and Mrs. George Onysko and was survived by his wife Irene M. Onysko of Blackheath, London. ***Onysko Lake*** (64 P/8), east of Nejanilini Lake was named after him in 1974.

Orieux, Captain **Achilles L. "Archie"** of St. Boniface (H 70450). Maisonneuve Regiment. He died 19 July 1944 at the age of 25 and is commemorated at Bretteville-sur-Laize Canadian War Cemetery in Calvados, France. He was the son of Aristide and Anna Orieux of St. Boniface. ***Orieux Lake*** (64 K/11), northeast of Lac Brochet was named after him in 1972.

Orlinski, Flight Sergeant **Casimir F.** of Winnipeg (R 134317). No. 429 Squadron. He died 22 June 1943 at the age of 19 and is commemorated at Flushing (Vlissingen) Northern Cemetery, Holland. He was the son of Joseph and Mary Orlinski and was survived by his wife Mary Orlinski. ***Orlinski Lake*** (64 O/14), east of Nueltin Lake was named after him in 1975.

Orr, Private **William H.** of Winnipeg (H 41741). Queen's Own Cameron Highlanders. He died 11 September 1944 at the age of 20 and is commemorated at the Adegem Canadian War Cemetery in Belgium. He was the son of Osmond R. R. and Anne B. Orr of Winnipeg. ***Orr Island*** (53 K/14) in Edmund Lake was named after him in 1995.

Orvis, Private **Harry** of Grand Marais (H 6932). Winnipeg Grenadiers. He died 27 December 1941 at the age of 22 and is commemorated at the Sai Wan Memorial in Hong Kong. He was the son of David and Annabell Orvis of Grand Marais, Manitoba. ***Orvis Lake*** (64 N/16), west of Nueltin Lake was named after him in 1972.

Osadchuk, Private **Nicholas A.** of Winnipeg (H 6887). Winnipeg Grenadiers. He died 23 December 1941 and is commemorated at the Sai Wan Memorial in Hong Kong. ***Osadchuk Lake*** (64 I/15), northeast of North Knife Lake was named after him in 1974.

Osadick, Private **Stephen** of East Kildonan (H 102461). Queen's Own Cameron Highlanders. He died 26 July 1944 and is commemorated at Bretteville-sur-Laize Canadian War Cemetery in Calvados, France. ***Osadick Lake*** (64 I/4), west of North Knife Lake was named after him in 1974.

Osborn, Company Sergeant Major (Warrant Officer 2) **John R.** of St. Vital (H 6008). Winnipeg Grenadiers, Victoria Cross. He died 19 December 1941 at the age of 42 and is commemorated at the Sai Wan Memorial in Hong Kong. He was the second of the four children of John R. and Harriet S. Osborn and was survived by his wife Margaret E. Osborn (née Nelson) of St. Vital and their five children. Osborn was born in Norfolk, England 2 January 1899 and joined the Royal Naval Reserve at the outbreak of the First War. He was captured but escaped two days later and rejoined his unit. Later, he was wounded and was medically evacuated. Upon release from hospital, he became the casualty of a mustard gas attack and was evacuated back to England. Poor health brought him to Ontario and thence Manitoba where he worked with a section gang of the CNR at Gregg. There he met his future wife whom he married 19 May 1926. With the outbreak of the Second World War, he joined the Winnipeg Grenadiers and served in Bermuda and then Jamaica. He was shipped to Hong Kong in October, 1941.

At Hong Kong on the morning of the 19th December 1941, a company of Winnipeg Grenadiers to which Sergeant Major Osborn belonged became divided during an attack on Mount Butler, a hill rising steeply above sea level. A part of the company led by Company Sergeant Major Osborn captured the hill at the point of the bayonet and held it for three hours when, owing to the superior numbers of the enemy and fire from an unprotected flank, the position became untenable. Company Sergeant Major Osborn and a small group covered the withdrawal and when their turn came to fall back, Osborn single-handedly engaged the enemy while the remainder successfully rejoined the company. Company Sergeant Major Osborn had to run the gauntlet of heavy fire and machine gun fire with no consideration of his own safety. He assisted and directed stragglers to the new company position, exposing himself to heavy enemy fire to cover their retirement. Whenever danger threatened, he was there to encourage his men.

During the afternoon, the company was cut off from the battalion and completely surrounded by the enemy who were able to approach to within grenade throwing distance of the slight depression which the company were holding. Several enemy grenades were thrown which Company Sergeant Major picked up and threw back. The enemy threw a grenade which landed in a position where it was impossible to pick up and return it in time. Shouting a warning to his comrades, this gallant Warrant Officer threw himself on the grenade which exploded, killing him instantly. His self sacrifice undoubtedly saved the lives of many others.

Company Sergeant Major Osborn was an inspiring example to all throughout the defence which he assisted so magnificently in maintaining against an overwhelming enemy force for over eight and a half hours and in his death he displayed the highest quality of heroism and self sacrifice (*The London Gazette* 2 April 1946).

Captain Njall O. Bardal gave a slightly different account:

The [enemy] were tossing grenades down into the trench from the higher ground and Osborn was catching them and throwing them right back at them. Then, two came at him at the same time. He yelled to one of the other men to throw the other one out, but when he turned round, he saw that the other man had hesitated and the grenade was about to explode so he threw himself on the grenade sacrificing his life to save the other two men (14 September 1945).

His son adds (22 October 2001):

I do think all the things have been said about Dad. He was a strict but fair disciplinarian and one of his sayings was "A man is as good as his word" and "A promise made is a debt unpaid." He believed in the Golden Rule and insisted on good manners. The day before he left for Hong Kong, my sister Patricia was severely burned and he gave a quart of blood before he left, not expecting her to live. She did and is living in Edmonton now. The night before he left, he sat my oldest brother John and I down and told us he was going to war and did not expect to return home. That our job was to take care of the family. We never received a letter from him and was not informed of his death until 1943/44 and that in 1946 he was awarded the Victoria Cross.

A plaque commemorating him was erected at Jardine Lookout in Hong Kong and Osborn Bay on Lake of the Woods bears his name. Osborn Hall at the St. Vital Hockey Rink and Osborn Tower at Deer Lodge Hospital were additionally named in his honour. The Royal Canadian Legion named their branch on Ellice Avenue in Winnipeg the John Osborn(e) VC Winnipeg Unit Branch No. 1 AN & AF of Canada. The British government honoured him by renaming Victoria Barracks in Hong Kong Warrant Officer 2 J. R. Osborn Barracks. A statue of Osborn based on family photographs was erected in Hong Kong's Victoria Park as a memorial to the Allied defenders of 1941. ***Osborn Creek*** (63 O/5), which flows north into Driftwood River was named after him in 1973 and ***John Osborn Lake*** (64 O/14), east of Nueltin Lake was named after him in 1986.

Ostir, Rifleman **Frank** of Shorncliffe (H 42014). Royal Winnipeg Rifles. He died 8 June 1944 at the age of 25 and is commemorated at Beny-sur-Mer Canadian War Cemetery in Calvados, France. He was one of the seven children of Mike and Kathrine Oster (sp.) of Shorncliffe, Manitoba. His nephew recalls (9 February 1995) that he was always "easy to talk to ... making people young or old smile." ***Ostir Lake*** (63 J/16), east of Setting Lake was named after him in 1972.

Otter, Trooper **Einar R.** of Gimli (H 167). Lord Strathcona's Horse. He died 1 September 1944 at the age of 23 and is commemorated at Montecchio War Cemetery in Italy. He was one of the nine children of Gustave and Hilda Otter of Gimli. He was a commercial fisherman at the time of his enlistment. ***Otter Bay*** (64 C/12) in Laurie Lake was named after him in 1995.

Ouelette, Private **Joseph P. A.** of Winnipeg (H 6526). Winnipeg Grenadiers. He died 25 December 1941 at the age of 37 and is commemorated at Stanley Military Cemetery in Hong Kong. He was the son of Frank and Anna Ouelette and was survived by his wife Patricia M. Ouelette of McKenzie Island, Ontario. ***Ouelette Lake*** (53 N/2), northeast of Red Cross Lake was named after him in 1995.

Ouellet, Signalman **Paul D.** of St. Norbert (H 101831). Royal Canadian Corps of Signals. He died 16 December 1944 and is commemorated at Schoonselhof Cemetery in Antwerp, Belgium. ***Ouellet Lake*** (64 N/4), north of Lac Brochet was named after him in 1972.

Outerson, Pilot Officer **Joseph Lawrie "Scrappy"** of Souris (J 95259). No. 76 Squadron. He died 25 April 1945 at the age of 20 and is commemorated at Sage War Cemetery in Germany. He was the only child of Archie L. and Annie E. Outerson of Souris. ***Outerson Lake*** (64 P/12), east of Nejanilini Lake was named after him in 1974.

Overby, Lance Sergeant **Carl O.** of Harperville (H 36242). Royal Canadian Engineers, Military Medal. He died 1 April 1945 at the age of 26 and is commemorated at the Groesbeek Canadian War Cemetery in Holland. He was the son of Otto K. and Ragna Overby of Harperville, Manitoba. ***Overby Lake*** (64 J/16), north of Tadoule Lake was named after him in 1957.

Owchar, Trooper **Russell W.** of Brandon (H 100115). 14th Canadian Hussars. He died 13 July 1944 at the age of 23 and is commemorated at Beny-sur-Mer Canadian War Cemetery in Calvados, France. He was the son of Alex and Annie Owchar of Brandon. ***Owchar Lake*** (52 E/14), northeast of Brereton Lake was named after him in 1974.

Owen, Private **Richard** of Winnipeg (H 6875). Winnipeg Grenadiers. He died 19 December 1941 at the age of 24 and is commemorated at the Sai Wan Memorial in Hong Kong. He was the son of Mr. and Mrs. Hugh Owen of Penysarn, Anglesey, Wales. ***Owen Lake*** (62 P/16), west of Family Lake was named after him in 1973.

Owens, Flying Officer **Dalton Harvey** of Winnipeg (J 16609). No. 176 Squadron. He died 25 December 1943 at the age of 22 and is commemorated at Chittagong War Cemetery in Bangladesh. He was the son of Dalton O. and Ann E. Owens of Winnipeg. ***Owens Island*** (64 N/10) in Sucker Lake was named after him in 1995.

Oxenforth, Gunner **John W.** of St. James (H 35601). Royal Canadian Artillery. He died 26 December 1944 at the age of 30 and is commemorated at Faenza War Cemetery in Italy. He was the son of Mr. and Mrs. Frederick W. Oxenforth and was survived by his wife Jean Oxenforth of Winnipeg. ***Oxenforth Lake*** (64 I/11), southeast of Shethanei Lake was named after him in 1974.

Mud and barbed wire through which the Canadians advanced during the Battle of Passchendaele, November, 1917.
Courtesy of the National Archives of Canada (PA-002165).

P

Pachkowski, Private **William F.** of Stonewall (H 22112). Queen's Own Cameron Highlanders. He died 6 March 1945 and is commemorated at the Groesbeek Canadian War Cemetery in Holland. He was survived by his mother Mrs. M. Pachkowski of Stonewall, Manitoba. ***Pachkowski Lake*** (64 O/12), south of Nueltin Lake was named after him in 1975.

Pachol, Sapper **Robert** of La Broquerie (H 82001). Royal Canadian Army Medical Corps. He died 4 August 1944 at the age of 23 and is commemorated at Bretteville-sur-Laize Canadian War Cemetery in Calvados, France. He was the son of Peter and Natlie Pachol and was survived by his wife Elsie M. Pachol of Applesham, Sussex, England. ***Pachol Lake*** (64 N/7), southwest of Nueltin Lake was named after him in 1972.

Padfield, Private **George H.** of Crandall (H 87484). Royal Canadian Army Medical Corps. He died 13 July 1944 at the age of 22 and is commemorated at Beny-sur-Mer Canadian War Cemetery in Calvados, France. ***Padfield Lake*** (64 I/6), north of North Knife Lake was named after him in 1974.

Pady, Private **Morris N.** of Ashern (H 200182). Queen's Own Cameron Highlanders. He died 8 September 1944 at the age of 28 and is commemorated at Brookwood Military Cemetery in Surrey, England. He was one of the 15 children of Edgar W. and Elizabeth Pady of Regina. His sister writes (18 December 1991):

> He was born in Edenwold, Saskatchewan on March 5, 1916, as were the rest of my family of 15 children. I married and came to Ashern in August, 1932. Due to the depression, my brother came to live with us in 1936. He made his home here until he enlisted in 1941.
>
> He enlisted with the Winnipeg Rifles and when they got to England, his outfit was transferred to the Queen's Own Cameron Highlanders to replace the losses of the Dieppe raid. He was wounded on the beaches of Normandy on August 8, 1944 in hand-to-hand Sten Gun fighting. He was flown to Hampshire, England and had three bullets in his body – two in the chest, one in the lower abdomen. They removed two bullets, but the one in his abdomen was poisoning him. He died during the last surgery in September, 1944.

Pady Lake (64 I/9), northeast of North Knife Lake was named after him in 1974.

Page, Trooper **Russell F.** of Oakville (H 64968). 17th Duke of York's Hussars. He died 14 August 1944 at the age of 31 and is commemorated at Bretteville-sur-Laize Canadian War Cemetery in Calvados, France. He was one of the eight children of Mr. and Mrs. Albert Page of Oakville. His obituary stated in part:

> ... educated in Oakville, Russell farmed with his father prior to his enlistment three years ago. He went overseas in 1943. Well-known in the district, he was a familiar figure at all sport meets (n.d.).

Page Lake (64 I/2), east of North Knife Lake was named after him in 1974.

Paillé, Lieutenant **Albert E.** of La Salle (ZD 3813). Royal 22nd Regiment. He died 21 October 1951 at the age of 24 while on night patrol and is commemorated at the United Nations Cemetery in Pusan, South Korea. He was one of the six children of François-Xavier and Blanche Paillé of La Salle. His brother writes (16 November 2001):

> Albert was born at La Salle 16 November 1926. He graduated with a Bachelor of Arts degree from the University of Manitoba 22 September 1948, having served for four years in the COTC at Currie Barracks in Calgary. He joined the Royal 22nd Regiment in Quebec City in 1949, transferring to its 2nd Battalion in August, 1950.
>
> Albert served at Fort Lewis, USA, then at Kure, Japan and finally Korea in October, 1950. As a Lieutenant, he was Platoon Leader of 5 Platoon, B Company. He was killed by a mine that blew up while on patrol in No Man's Land with several of his men who were wounded. The blast was heard by his brother Sergeant John E. Paillé of the PPCLI who had been in Korea since 16 December 1950. He was buried alongside the other Canadian soldiers in the United Nations Cemetery in Pusan. He left two brothers and three sisters.

Lac Paillé (54 E/12), south of North Norfolk Lake was named after this Korean War casualty in 1989.

Paillé, Private **Gérard J.** of St. Anne (H 195441). Highland Light Infantry. He died 19 September 1944 and is commemorated at the Calais Canadian War Cemetery in France. He was the son of Anthony and Marie Paillé of Ste. Anne-des-Chênes. ***Paillé Island*** (53 L/2) in Island Lake was named after him in 1995.

Palmason, Flight Sergeant **Stefan D.** of Winnipeg Beach (R 95316). No. 419 Squadron. He died 6 July 1942 at the age of 23 and is commemorated at St. John Churchyard in Beck Row, Suffolk, England. He was the son of Sveinn and Groa Palmason of Winnipeg Beach, Manitoba. ***Palmason Lake*** (62 N/11), northeast of Roblin was named after him in 1977.

Palmatier, Warrant Officer 2 **David E.** of St. James (R 116471). No. 429 Squadron. He died 22 June 1943 at the age of 22 and is commemorated at Jonkerbos War Cemetery in Holland. He was the son of Reo E. and Tryphena M. Palmatier (née Dyson) of Winnipeg. ***Palmatier Lake*** (64 P/14), northeast of Nejanilini Lake was named after him in 1974.

Palmer, Corporal **Frank** of Dauphin (H 70186). Winnipeg Light Infantry. He died 19 December 1941 at the age of 43 and is commemorated at Riverside Cemetery in Dauphin. He was survived by his wife Elsie Palmer of Dauphin. ***Palmer Island*** (63 P/4) in Sipiwesk Lake was named after him in 1995.

Palmer, Private **John H.** of Winnipeg (H 8830). Westminster Regiment. He died 3 September 1944 at the age of 24 and is commemorated at Gradara War Cemetery in Italy. He was the son of Joseph A. and Mary Palmer of Winnipeg and was survived by his wife Zoë M. Palmer of Winnipeg. ***Palmer Point*** (64 I/7) on Prosnyck Lake was named after him in 1995.

Palmer, Able Seaman **Ralph B. N.** of Winnipeg (V 9785). HMCS *Ottawa*. The *Ottawa* was escorting Convoy ON.127 in the North Atlantic when it was struck by two torpedoes from U-91; 114 of her ship's company were lost. Able Seaman Palmer died 13 September 1942 at the age of 25 and is commemorated at the Halifax Memorial. He was the son of John C. N. and Nora M. Palmer of Winnipeg and was survived by his wife Iva M. Palmer of Winnipeg. ***Palmer Lake*** (53 M/10), north of Knee Lake was named after him in 1966.

Palmer, Private **Robert F.** of Winnipeg (H 19895). Queen's Own Cameron Highlanders. He died 19 August 1942 at the age of 33 and is commemorated at the Boulogne Eastern Cemetery, Pas de Calais, France. He was the son of Alfred R. and Margaret M. Palmer and was survived by his wife Margaret J. M. Palmer of St. James. ***Palmer Peninsula*** (53 L/15) on Seller Lake was named after him in 1995.

Palmer, Flight Sergeant **Sidney A.** of St. James (R 91651). No. 419 Squadron. He died 5 October 1942 at the age of 20 and is commemorated at the Runnymede Memorial in Surrey, England. ***Palmer Bay*** (53 L/9) in Gods Lake was named after him in 1995.

Panco, Private **Michael** of Winnipeg (H 2058). Winnipeg Grenadiers. He died a prisoner of war 16 August 1943 at the age of 24 and is commemorated at the Yokohama War Cemetery in Japan. He was the son of Michael and Tekla Panco of Winnipeg. ***Panco Lake*** (54 C/11), southwest of York Factory was named after him in 1964.

Pangman, Rifleman **William** of Duck Bay (H 41890). Royal Winnipeg Rifles. He died 6 June 1944 and is commemorated at Beny-sur-Mer Canadian War Cemetery in Calvados, France. He was the son of Joseph and Sarah Pangman of Duck Bay, Manitoba. ***Pangman Lake*** (64 K/9), southwest of Nueltin Lake was named after him in 1961.

Pankiw, Ordinary Seaman **James** of Teulon (V 91702). HMCS *Cornwallis*. He died 17 August 1945 at the age of 19 and is commemorated at St. Stephen's Cemetery in Pleasant Home, Manitoba. His sister recalls (2 March 1998):

James Pankiw was born to Wasyl and Maria Pankiw on September 14, 1925 ... at Teulon, Manitoba. He was the eighth of nine children. James was a very kind and gentle person who was always thoughtful of others and willing to help out whenever possible. He attended McMillan School #1109, Grades 1 – 8 which was 1 1/2 miles away and walked to school every day, like everyone else did in those days. After completing Grade 8, he stayed at home to help on the farm as his mother was widowed early that year. This was during the "Dirty Thirties." The three oldest were working away from home.

When war was declared in September, 1939 the older brothers enlisted as soon as they were of age. When James reached the age to enlist in 1943, he joined the navy. When on leave, he spent his time visiting his mother and two brothers at home. [He] also visited his two oldest brothers and me, who were married so he could spend time with his nieces and nephews of whom he was very fond.

As far as being interested in sports and hobbies, he did take part in the annual Sports Day at school. There were not too many opportunities to take part in anything as we lived 4 1/2 miles from town with only a bicycle for transportation or walking. We often had pick-up ball games when family, friends and neighbours got together. [He] also listened to NHL games on a battery radio during the winter. This was before hydro or phones. He also hunted and snared rabbits to help supplement the food supply.

Pankiw Lake (64 N/1), southwest of Nueltin Lake was named after him in 1972.

Pannebaker, Trooper **Robert C. M.** of Roland (H 26760). Fort Garry Horse. He died 11 June 1944 at the age of 29 and is commemorated at Beny-sur-Mer Canadian War Cemetery in Calvados, France. He was the son of John and Mary E. Pannebaker. ***Pannebaker Creek*** (54 C/13), which flows north into Machichi River was named after him in 1964.

Paquin, Flying Officer **Felix F. F.** of St. Boniface (J 22094). No. 424 Squadron. He died 31 March 1944 at the age of 25 and is commemorated at Durnbach War Cemetery in Bavaria, Germany. He was the third of the six children of Wilfred and Georgina Paquin (née Savoie) of St. Boniface. His sister writes (6 March 1995):

My brother Felix was the third born of a family of six – five boys and myself. He was born ... at 612 St. Jean Baptiste Street, St. Boniface in the paternal house. He received his education first at Maison Chapelle, then went on to Provencher School under the direction of the Christian Brothers. He was in Scouts as a young lad, then played hockey for school. He was very musical, playing guitar, piano and loved to sing and dance. He was a very, very happy person.

He worked for the CNR prior to his enlistment. He joined up in 1940/41 and went overseas as a Flying Officer on the [RMMV] *Capetown Castle* which left Halifax January 7, 1943 and arrived in Liverpool January 14, 1943. After more training in England, he was sent to North Africa with 424 Squadron where they made many sorties over Italy. He then returned to England suffering from yellow fever and beriberi. After some time to recover, he was posted to Skipton, England. He made a total of 33 sorties with 424 Squadron, but on the evening of March 31, 1944, their plane was shot down over Nuremberg, Germany; 96 of our planes were shot down [that night].

In 1977, a Mr. Crawford wrote to me from Oshawa, Ontario regarding a museum they were setting up there for downed Canadian airmen. He sent inquiries in [to] different military magazines and he received a lot of correspondence from service airmen who remembered Felix and spoke most highly of him. He sent me copies of all the letters from across the country and it surely warmed our hearts to know he was so well liked. There's now a picture along with Felix's medals and a short history on one on the walls of the museum. Mr. Crawford has sent me a picture which I treasure.

Former comrade Ken Shedden recalls (25 March 1977):

Felix and I (and two others) shared the same cabin on the boat to England. Felix, myself and George Smith (one of the other cabin mates) became quite close friends and the three of us shared many a fun night in Bournemouth for the next four or five months until our turns came to commence further flying training elsewhere in England.

... we flew Halifaxes there [Skipton]. We loved the Halifax and though it wasn't quite the performer the Lanc was, it was a 'safe' plane in that you could get out of it faster and more easily than out of a Lancaster, as my own crew found out on January 28, 1944 when we were forced to bail out over England.

Felix was a smiling, pleasant, pure comedian as you well know and I have often laughed when I recall the many outings we enjoyed at Bournemouth, Ripon and Harrogate. Like all the other fine types we knew who were lost on ops, Felix was one of the best and I used to feel somehow that Felix would be one of the fortunate ones who would make it through their tours safely.

Paquin Lake (64 N/9), southwest of Nueltin Lake was named after him in 1972.

Parasiuk, Private **Metro** of Polonia (H 8404). Westminster Regiment. He died 26 September 1944 at the age of 21 and is commemorated at Ravenna War Cemetery in Italy. He was the son of Wasil and Mary Parasiuk of Polonia, Manitoba.

Metro attended school at Polonia and then worked on his father's farm. He enlisted in the army January, 1943 and was posted overseas in March, 1944. He served in France and the central Mediterranean, finally taking part in the Italian Campaign. It was during these battles that Metro lost his life (Pittman n.d.).

Parasiuk Lake (64 O/3), east of Blackfish Lake was named after him in 1985.

Paré, Private **Gabriel J.** of Winnipeg (H 6810). Winnipeg Grenadiers. He died 19 December 1941 at the age of 23 and is commemorated at the Sai Wan Memorial in Hong Kong. This native of Sedley, Saskatchewan was survived by his parents Joseph and Helen Paré of Winnipeg, two sisters and two brothers who both served in World War II. His brother recalls (17 December 2001):

Gabriel was a true sportsman, having a golden pitching arm in softball and walked many miles with hockey equipment over [his] shoulder. In his younger years, he showed a keen interest in marbles. We received one card from him in Hong Kong and treasure this card to this day. We shall not forget.

Paré Lake (64 I/13), northwest of North Knife Lake was named after him in 1974.

Parent, Company Quarter Master Sergeant **Nestor E.** of Winnipeg (D 61861). Fusiliers Mont-Royal Regiment. He died 19 August 1942 and is commemorated at the Brookwood Memorial in Surrey, England. ***Parent Lake*** (63 O/5), southeast of Highrock Lake was named after him in 1973.

Parfinuk, Private **Alexander** of Gladstone (B 78160). Royal Regiment of Canada. He died 13 April 1945 at the age of 21 and is commemorated at the Holten Canadian War Cemetery in Holland. He was the son of Jack and Natalie Parfinuk of Gladstone, Manitoba. ***Parfinuk Creek*** (64 I/16), which flows north into Seal River was named after him in 1974.

Pariseau, Flying Officer **Armand A.** of Winnipeg (J 14193). No. 427 Squadron. He died 23 June 1943 at the age of 31 and is commemorated at Warnsveld (Wichmond) General Cemetery, Holland. He was the son of Rene C. and Mary Pariseau of Winnipeg. ***Pariseau Lake*** (53 L/5), east of Bolton Lake was named after him in 1995.

Parisian, Rifleman **Percy** of the Peguis Reserve (H 100792). Royal Winnipeg Rifles. He died 8 June 1944 at the age of 20 and is commemorated at Beny-sur-Mer Canadian War Cemetery in Calvados, France. He was the son of William and Christine Parisian of Peguis, Manitoba. After the war, his mother received this letter:

Dear Mrs. Parisian: On December 10th, 1945, trials commence of German war criminals for the murder of a number of Canadian Army personnel. It is anticipated that publicity will be given to the trials through the medium of radio and press.

From recent information furnished by the Overseas War Crimes Investigation Committee, it seems quite probable that the name of your late son, H 100792 Rifleman Percy Parisian, will be mentioned. Therefore, it is considered advisable to prepare you in advance for the bad news that your son may have been murdered by the Germans and to allay somewhat the shock of hearing the news over the air or reading it in the press.

Please accept my sincere sympathy for any additional anxiety this may cause during your trying moments of bereavement. Yours truly, A. Gordon (Captain) for C. L. Laurin (Colonel), Director of Records for Adjutant-General (6 December 1945).

Parisian Creek (63 K/16), which flows south into Woosey Lake was named after him and his brother Private Sydney Parisian (next entry) in 1973.

Parisian, Private **Sydney** of the Peguis Reserve (H 100280). Queen's Own Cameron Highlanders. He died 2 October 1944 at the age of 30 and is commemorated at Bergen-op-Zoom Canadian War Cemetery Holland. He was the son of William and Christine Parisian of Peguis, Manitoba and was survived by his wife and three daughters. ***Parisian Creek*** (63 K/16), which flows south into Woosey Lake was named after him and his brother Rifleman Percy Parisian (previous entry) in 1973.

Parker, Flight Lieutenant **Allan B.** of Winnipeg (41610). No. 28 Squadron, RAF. He died 11 February 1942 at the age of 27 and is commemorated at the Runnymede Memorial in Surrey, England. He was the son of William and Edith M. Parker of St. Vital. Flight Lieutenant Parker was an alumnus of Wesley College and had completed three years at the University of Manitoba prior to travelling to England to enlist in December, 1938 (Allison 1978). ***Allan Parker Lake*** (53 K/11), southeast of Edmund Lake was named after him in 1995.

Parker, Private **Edwin W.** of Winnipeg (H 14043). Perth Regiment. He died 20 December 1944 at the age of 30 and is commemorated at Villanova Canadian War Cemetery, Italy. He was the son of Edwin G. and Mabel F. L. Parker of Winnipeg and was survived by his wife Evelyn S. Parker of Winnipeg. ***Parker Point*** (64 H/13) on Currie Lake was named after him in 1995.

Parker, Pilot Officer **Elbert F. "Fritz"** of St. Claude (J 18313). No. 408 Squadron. He died 28 July 1943 at the age of 22 and is commemorated at Hamburg Cemetery in Germany. He was the son of Mr. and Mrs. W. J. Parker of St. Claude. His obituary indicated that he was:

Reported missing in July, 1943, is now, for official purposes presumed dead, according to notice received by his parents. Born at Saint Claude, he joined the RCAF in October, 1940, training at Toronto, Camp Borden, Calgary and Macdonald. He went overseas in September, 1941, as wireless air gunner (n.d.).

Parker Peninsula (64 N/4) on Spencer Lake was named after him in 1995.

Parker, Pilot Officer **John Allen** of Minnedosa (J 19583). No. 419 Squadron. He died 15 February 1944 at the age of 23 and is commemorated at the Runnymede Memorial in Surrey, England. He was the son of Lewis A. and Roseina M. L. Parker (née Laver) of Minnedosa, Manitoba. His sister recalls that he:

... was born on June 10, 1920 in the Rural Municipality of Roblin – Cartwright, Manitoba. He joined the RCAF in September, 1941, going overseas in December, 1942 to serve Bomber Command over Europe. He failed to return from a mission over Berlin on February 15, 1944. His interests as he grew up were in Boy Scouts and in horseback riding and camping both winter and summer with a group of friends (4 April 1996).

He was employed in Burgess' Meat Market at the time of his enlistment. On one of John's first night training flights, his plane crashed, killing his instructor. John's Halifax aircraft was shot down in the Baltic Sea off Denmark during a mission to their target. This was the tenth operation of the entire crew and theirs was one of 42 allied aircraft lost that night (Pittman n.d.).

Parker Creek (53 M/14), which flows north into Cyril Lake was named after him in 1995.

Parker, Flight Sergeant **Robert L.** of Winnipeg (R 59576). No. 119 Squadron. He died 16 March 1942 at the age of 22 and is commemorated at St. John's Cemetery in Winnipeg. He was the son of Benjamin C. and Jessie C. Parker of Winnipeg. ***Parker Rapids*** (64 P/3) in the Big Spruce River was named after him in 1995.

Parker, Flight Sergeant **Thomas E.** of St. Laurent (R 59119). No. 142 Squadron. He died 21 October 1941 at the age of 23 and is commemorated at the Sage War Cemetery in Germany. He was the son of Henry G. and Ellen E. Parker of Winnipeg. ***Parker Island*** (64 I/3) in North Knife Lake was named after him in 1989.

Parker, Sergeant **Walter A.** of West Kildonan (H 26615). Fort Garry Horse. He died 12 August 1944 at the age of 23 and is commemorated at Bretteville-sur-Laize Canadian War Cemetery in Calvados, France. He was the son of Fitzgerald and Marie L. Parker and was survived by his wife Caroline E. Parker of Winnipeg and their daughter Bonita. His obituary read in part:

> A prominent Winnipeg athlete who enlisted ... in February, 1940 was killed in action in France. A well-known hockey and football player here, he was a member of the Fort Garry Horse team that won the service league championship in Scotland in 1942 – 43 (n.d.).

His daughter writes (22 November 2001):

> Shortly before I was born, my father had already begun the long journey overseas to fight for the freedom he so strongly believed in. I learned from my mother, family members and later on, the men from his regiment, that he was a generous, caring man with a *joie de vivre*. His older brother, Art told me that my father had been athletic and had excelled at hockey and football. From Art, I found out that when he and my father joined the Fort Garry Horse in 1940, my father was still under age, but he managed to convince the officials that he was old enough to fight for his country.
>
> My father lived for only 23 years, and he and I never had the chance to meet. Although his life was cut short, his memory will live on through his granddaughters and great granddaughter and all who knew him.

He had been employed by the T. Eaton Company at the time of his enlistment. ***Parker Bay*** (64 P/12) in Nejanilini Lake was named after him in 1989.

Parkes, Flight Sergeant **Charles** of Winnipeg (R 56777). No. 8 Repair Depot, RCAF. He died 21 May 1942 at the age of 40 and is commemorated at St. James Cemetery in Winnipeg. He was the son of Isaac and Betsy Parkes (née Oseland) and was survived by his wife Alice Parkes (née McLeod) of Winnipeg and their two sons. His great niece writes (22 February 1999):

> He was born in Birmingham, England in 1901 and immigrated to Canada with his parents, five sisters and one brother in 1919. Two other brothers remained in England. They resided in the municipality of Assiniboia which is now part of St. James at 275 Parkdale Avenue.
>
> He married Alice McLeod in 1924. She was born in De Tour, Michigan. They had two sons – Raymond born in 1926 and Leonard born in 1935. All three are now deceased. Raymond went to work for the railway in the US and had three sons who still reside there.

Parkes Bay (64 I/13) in Dawes Lake was named after him in 1995.

Parkes, Sergeant **Percy S.** of Winnipeg (H 26413). Fort Garry Horse. He died 6 June 1944 at the age of 31 and is commemorated at Beny-sur-Mer Canadian War Cemetery in Calvados, France. He was survived by his wife Rhoda M. Parkes. ***Parkes Lake*** (64 H/4), north of Gauer Lake was named after him in 1995.

Parks, Lance Corporal **Norman J.** of St. Vital (H 54303). Veterans Guard of Canada. He died 11 March 1944 at the age of 53 and is commemorated at Elmwood Cemetery in Winnipeg. He was survived by his wife Emmeline Parks of Winnipeg. ***Parks Lake*** (52 L/6), east of Lac du Bonnet was named after him in 1973.

Parliament, Flying Officer **George W.** of Winnipeg (J 47900). No. 11 Advanced Flying Unit. He died 20 June 1945 at the age of 26 and is commemorated at Blacon Cemetery in Cheshire, England. He was the son of William and Eva Parliament of Winnipeg and was survived by his wife Jean E. Parliament (née Whiting) of Winnipeg and their son. His brother recalls that "George attended Isaac Brock and Daniel McIntyre schools in Winnipeg. He was very interested in sports – particularly football" (6 April 1995). ***Parliament Lake*** (64 P/8), east of Nejanilini Lake was named after him in 1974. In August, 1996 his widow, son, grandson, sister, brother-in-law and a nephew flew to the lake and erected a marker there.

Parmeter, Lance Corporal **Benjamin H.** of Winnipeg (H 16410). Princess Patricia's Canadian Light Infantry. He died 20 February 1944 at the age of 26 and is commemorated at the Moro River Canadian War Cemetery in Italy. He was the son of Wally and Helen I. Parmeter (née Johnson) of Pasadena, California and was survived by his wife Evelyn Parmeter of Fort William, Ontario. The son of his wife's second husband writes:

> Benny and mother were only married for a short time before he left to go overseas in 1939. At one time mother considered taking a ship to England to visit him, but the peril from the German U-boats was too great. They were never to see each other again before his death in 1944. I was named after Benny's brother Glen.
>
> My son's middle name is Joseph in Remembrance of my uncle and grandfather. Uncle Joe was only on the European mainland for two days when he was killed. There is a picture of grandmother and grandfather Cooke at his grave in Holland and the pain and sadness of their loss is so clearly etched on their faces (n.d.).

Parmeter Lake (64 J/2), southwest of Tadoule Lake was named after him in 1975.

Parrott, Pilot Officer **Victor** of Grandview (J 19584). No. 76 Squadron. He died 20 January 1944 at the age of 26 and is commemorated at the Berlin 1939 - 1945 War Cemetery in Brandenburg, Germany. He was the son of Fleming and Elsie I. Parrott of Red Lake, Ontario. ***Parrott Lake*** (64 P/16), northeast of Nejanilini Lake was named after him in 1974.

Parry, Flying Officer **Richard C.** of Winnipeg (J 26844). No. 619 Squadron. He died 16 February 1944 at the age of 20 and is commemorated at the Berlin 1939 - 1945 War Cemetery in Brandenburg, Germany. ***Parry Lake*** (64 G/16), northeast of Cederlund Lake was named after him in 1995.

Parsons, Petty Officer **Howard N.** of Winnipeg (4470). HMCS *Shawinigan*. The *Shawinigan* was torpedoed and sunk by U-1228 while on independent anti-submarine patrol in the Cabot Strait; all hands were lost. Petty Officer Parsons died 24 November 1944 at the age of 20 and is commemorated at the Halifax Memorial. He was the son of Eli and Louise Parsons of Norwood. A local newspaper reported that:

> PO Parsons attended King George and Tache schools. He enlisted June 15, 1941 and trained in Esquimalt, BC and Halifax. His brother, Samuel, is with the RCAF at No. 8 repair depot. PO Parsons was a *Tribune* carrier for four years (*The Winnipeg Tribune* 7 December 1944).

Parsons Lake (64 N/13), west of Nueltin Lake was named after him in 1972.

Parsons, Sergeant **John** of Holland, Manitoba (R 596640). No. 2 Squadron. He died 1 November 1941 at the age of 20 and is commemorated at Brandesburton (St. Mary) Churchyard, Yorkshire, England. ***Parsons Bay*** (63 P/15) in Brannigan Lake was named after him in 1995.

Parsons, Sergeant **Owen** of Holland, Manitoba (R 110593). No. 434 Squadron. He died 14 October 1944 at the age of 24 and is commemorated at Blacon Cemetery in Cheshire, England. He was the son of James J. and Beatrice M. Parsons of St. James. ***Parsons Island*** (64 O/4) in Blackfish Lake was named after him in 1995.

Partridge, Flight Sergeant **Gordon J.** of Winnipeg (R 134563). No. 405 Squadron. He died 17 November 1943 at the age of 20 and is commemorated at the Rheinberg War Cemetery in Germany. He was the only child of John and Isabelle of Winnipeg and was survived by his wife of 11 months Elizabeth Partridge of Winnipeg. She recalls (31 March 1998):

> [He was born in] Winnipeg and raised in the West End (700 block of Lipton Street). He was the only son of John and Isabelle Partridge. Isabelle immigrated to Canada from Belfast, Ireland [and] John from England. [He was] employed by [the] Canadian Pacific Railway where he worked on the trains. [They were] members of Elim Chapel where Gordon was active in the Youth Group and where he was married December 26, 1942. [He] attended Daniel McIntyre Collegiate Institute. He loved the outdoors – skating, tobogganing, hiking, bicycling, also music and dancing at house parties.
>
> We were raised during the Great Depression and then when we reached our teens, Canada was at war. No one had aspirations regarding careers as it was expected that every able-bodied young man would enlist and serve his country. Gordon wanted very much to join the Air Force and become a pilot – which he did. We all grew up in a hurry. He was a super guy – tall, slim, handsome, outgoing, and would have been a great asset to our country had he lived.

Partridge Island (64 O/12) in Shannon Lake was named after him in 1995.

Pascal, Flying Officer **Stephen** of Selkirk (J 41525). No. 166 Squadron. He died 24 March 1945 at the age of 21 and is commemorated at the Reichswald Forest War Cemetery in Germany. His niece recalls (5 December 1996):

> Stephen Pascal was my uncle – my mother's youngest brother and a very special young man. He was a pilot officer and Bombardier in the RCAF. He was among the young RCAF officers who flew out of England with the RAF during the last year or two of World War II. He went down over Germany.
>
> He suffered with rickets as a child and had several operations by the Shriners' Hospital prior to six years of age. He had won a scholarship to go into medicine when he joined the RCAF at 18 years of age – along with his "buddies."

Pascal Lake (64 G/6), southeast of McPherson Lake was named after him in 1994.

Pash, Gunner **Charles W.** of Winnipeg (H 60391). Royal Canadian Artillery. He died 1 November 1944 at the age of 34 and is commemorated at Brookside Cemetery in Winnipeg. He was the son of Charles and Ellen Pash of Winnipeg and was survived by his wife Pearl P. Pash (née Banish) of Winnipeg and their two sons. They were eight years and five months old at the time. According to his wife (7 April 1998):

> He worked at Arctic Ice for a bit, then went to work for the Northern Paint Company on Gertrude Avenue for Mr. Lock. He was taught to make paint, varnish and soap as a chemist. He loved hockey and played right wing for the Winnipeg "Nifties." He loved to dance the one step. He also danced and called off the quadrille. He had a lovely tenor voice and he would sing along with anyone who would play the piano for him. His repertoire included opera, classics and just plain sing-along songs.
>
> He made application to enrol in the non-permanent active militia, 17th Field Battery, Royal Canadian Artillery in November, 1939, but was turned down because of poor eyesight. He was subsequently accepted into the Canadian Army May 29, 1941. He said it was a good way to help his country and feed his family at the same time. He took his basic training in Brandon and left for overseas March 17, 1942.
>
> On January 10, 1943, he experienced severe bronchial bleeding and was admitted to 8 Canadian General Hospital. As he was diagnosed with severe anaemia and he received three transfusions of blood. While medical examinations revealed no tuberculosis or other lung disease, he was determined to be unfit and transferred to the Non-effective training detachment. He was returned to Canada May 1, 1943 and admitted to Fort Osborne Military Hospital June 1, 1943 and later moved to Deer Lodge Hospital June 16. On June 22, 1943, he was released from hospital and granted an honourable discharge from the army the next day. He did not apply for a pension.
>
> He went to work for Canada Bread delivering bread until October 5, 1944. He came home and said he was ill and told me not to make supper as he would not be able to eat it. He asked for just a bowl of chicken soup and said if he finished that he would be doing well. I called Dr. Danzinger who had him sent to St. Joseph's Hospital. Three days later, the doctor phoned me and told me to get him transferred to Deer Lodge as he will be ill a long time and he was sure I could not bear the cost of his illness. His illness was war related and they could bear the cost and look after him. I had him transferred to Deer Lodge by ambulance.
>
> November 1 at 2:00 AM, the police awakened me and told me I was wanted at Deer Lodge Hospital. They said one of them would stay with the children and the other would take me to the hospital. They had phoned mother Pash also and she was on her way to my place. Mother Pash and his sister Kay came and Kay said she would stay with the boys. Mother Pash and I were taken to Deer Lodge Hospital by the police.
>
> We were ushered in to see Charles. He was very pleased to see us saying "Gee it's great to see you my sweet and you too mom. How are the boys?" I told him they were well and asleep and that Kay was with them. Mother and I kissed him. He was quite pleased and happy to see us and then said "My sweet, all at once I feel very, very tired. I think I can sleep now. Sweet, will you come by this afternoon?" I said, "I'll be here when you awaken." He went to sleep never to awaken. He went very peacefully and content. Under a marker inscribed "Asleep" he is buried in the military section of Brookside Cemetery in Winnipeg.
>
> He was a wonderful husband and a great father. He took the boys out for walks with him on weekends. His friends laughed at him and called him hen-pecked. He would just laugh and say "How else do you get to know your children if you don't spend time with them alone?" My mother – his mother-in-law – said he was too good for this wicked world. November 1 is All Saints Day and mother said the saints came and took him home as he was one of them.

Pash Lake (54 D/15), northeast of Myre Lake was named after him in 1996.

Pasowysty, Private **Peter** of Neepawa (H 101254). Princess Patricia's Canadian Light Infantry. He died 20 September 1944 and is commemorated at Coriano Ridge War Cemetery in Italy. He was the son of Mr. and Mrs. William Pasowysty of Eden, Manitoba.

> He was employed on his father's farm prior to joining the army in May, 1941. He was posted overseas with the Princess Patricia's Canadian Light Infantry in December, 1942. Peter hitched a ride on the school bus from his home into Eden after his embarkation leave, said his last good-byes and returned to service. His sister, Elsie Morosky recalls the sad feelings she had when they embraced, not knowing if this would be the last time she would see him. Peter was wounded in May, 1944 and after his recovery, continued to take part in the battles in Italy. Peter was also a veteran of North Africa and Sicily (Pittman n.d.).

Pasowysty Lake (64 O/4), northeast of Egenolf Lake was named after him in 1975.

Passey, Flight Sergeant **Thomas C.** of Winnipeg (R 205159). No. 267 Squadron. He died 19 September 1944 at the age of 32 and is commemorated at the Malta Memorial. He was the son of James and Agnes Passey of Winnipeg. ***Passey Lake*** (64 I/14), east of Shethanei Lake was named after him in 1974.

Patch, Corporal **Walter H.** of Winnipeg (H 70254). Winnipeg Light Infantry. He died 11 June 1943 at the age of 49 and is commemorated at Brookside Cemetery in Winnipeg. He was survived by his sister Ethel Patch of St. Helier, Channel Islands England. ***Patch Lake*** (53 N/6), northeast of Knee Lake was named after him in 1972.

Paterson, Lieutenant **Archibald** of St. Vital. 12th Manitoba Dragoons. He died 12 February 1943 at the age of 43 and is commemorated at the St. Vital Cemetery. He was survived by his mother Mrs. A. Paterson of St. Boniface and by his wife Marion C. Paterson of St Vital. ***Paterson Hill*** (64 O/5), south of Booth Lake was named after him in 1995. Commemorative Certificates for Lieutenant Paterson and seven fellow Manitoba Dragoons were issued c/o Herbert Nicholson, MM who explains:

> In 1946, the 12th Manitoba Dragoons returned from Europe, and with money from our Canteen Fund furnished two wards in the Children's Hospital, with a promise that as long as our Association lasts, we would continue to support the Children's Hospital Fund. Since 1946, we have contributed $1000.00 every year, with donations received from the members. Also, we had a Plaque placed on the Hospital's 2nd floor, with names of our fallen comrades on one side and on the other side, the names of the departed comrades who have since passed away. This was done with the idea that one day the Regiment will again be together.
>
> Now this brings me to my request, that the Association's approximately 350 members, would after all your efforts to find next-of-kin, would like to become family and have the Name Certificate placed on the wall in the Children's Hospital in trust that if a next-of-kin comes forward the Certificate would be handed over to them (16 December 1998).

Paterson, Sergeant **George H.** of Stonewall (H 6211). Winnipeg Grenadiers. He died 19 December 1941 and is commemorated at the Sai Wan Memorial in Hong Kong. ***Paterson Rapids*** (64 C/9) in the Hughes River was named after him in 1995.

Paterson, Private **John** of Winnipegosis (B 145563). Royal Regiment of Canada. He died 25 July 1944 and is commemorated at Bretteville-sur-Laize Canadian War Cemetery in Calvados, France. He was survived by his mother Anne Paterson of Winnipegosis. ***John Paterson Creek*** (54 E/6), which flows northwest into Little Churchill River was named after him in 1995.

Paterson, Signalman **Robert L.** of Winnipeg (V 24617). HMCS *Louisburg*. The *Louisburg* was attacked and sunk by Italian aircraft east of Oran while escorting a convoy from Gibraltar to Bone, Algeria; 38 of her ship's company were lost. Signalman Paterson died 6 February 1943 at the age of 25 and is commemorated at the Halifax Memorial. He was the son of Richard L. and Dorothy I. Paterson of Winnipeg. ***Paterson Peninsula*** (53 M/4) on Semple Lake was named after him in 1995.

Paterson, Flying Officer **William** of Winnipeg (J 39880). No. 622 Squadron. He died 24 December 1944 at the age of 27 and is commemorated at the Reichswald Forest War Cemetery in Germany. He was the son of Charles G. and Nellie M. Paterson of Winnipeg and was survived by his wife Jean M. Paterson (née Partridge) of Winnipeg. Her brother Flight Sergeant Gordon J. Partridge, was also a casualty of the war (see entry). His wife's second husband writes (29 March 1998):

> Well before the onset of Alzheimer's, however, she was careful to preserve all the letters from her husband, William Paterson, and to have them typed. I have these letters (in ten binders) and I plan to deposit them this summer, either in the military section of the National Archives in Ottawa, or in the Provincial Archives of Manitoba.

William Paterson Lake (53 L/16), south of Semmens Lake was named after him in 1995.

Patey, Pilot Officer **Jack D.** of Winnipeg (J 15251). No. 61 Squadron. He died 31 May 1942 at the age of 21 and is commemorated at Rheinberg War Cemetery in Germany. He was the son of John D. and Mary C. Patey of Vancouver. ***Patey Lake*** (52 M/14), southwest of White Eye Lake was named after him in 1982.

Patkau, Private **Jacob** of McCreary (H 14436). Royal Canadian Army Medical Corps. He died 26 August 1944 at the age of 24 and is commemorated at Bretteville-sur-Laize Canadian War Cemetery in Calvados, France. He was the eldest son of Jacob and Louise Patkau of McCreary, Manitoba. His sister recalls (16 October 2001):

> My last letter from Jake to a sister is dated February 24, 1944. I still have that letter in my possession. Jake believed in keeping fit – when he was at home on the farm, he would receive literature from Charles Atlas and he did a lot of body building. Jake was also very musical. He played guitar and violin. I remember him as a very kind-hearted brother.
>
> Overseas he was in the ... Medical Corps, picking up the wounded soldiers. This was where he apparently lost his life, when on duty, he was hit by a time bomb which they were not aware of. We as a family found it very hard to take when the "Telegram" came that Jake was killed in action. He was ready to meet his Maker, so we know we will see him again.

Patkau Lake (64 I/5), south of Shethanei Lake was named after him in 1974.

Patterson, Telegraphist **Cecil C.** of Dauphin (V 9696). HMCS *Windflower*. He died 1 April 1941 at the age of 24 and is commemorated at the Halifax Memorial. He was the son of Hugh and Laura Patterson of Dauphin. ***Cecil Patterson Creek*** (54 A/12), which flows northeast into Pikwataske Creek was named after him in 1995.

Patterson, Sergeant **David W.** of Shellmouth (H 7189). Queen's Own Cameron Highlanders. He died 17 August 1944 at the age of 26 and is commemorated at Bretteville-sur-Laize Canadian War Cemetery in Calvados, France. He was the son of William and May Paterson of Shellmouth, Manitoba. His sister recalls (10 January 1989):

> My brother and I were very close and our birthdays were on the same day, but born two years apart. That was also the day I got word of his death, so I have two memorial days every year. I was the last family member to spend time with him when he passed through Winnipeg where I was working.

Patterson Point (64 P/9) on Kellas Lake was named after him in 1989.

Patterson, Pilot Officer **John W. L. "Jack"** of La Rivière (J 92920). No. 427 Squadron. He died 25 November 1944 at the age of 22 and is commemorated at Bellie Burial Ground in Moray, Scotland. He was the son of John S. and Annie V. Patterson of La Rivière, Manitoba. His sister recalls (23 June 1995):

> We both were born in Winnipeg [and] lived in La Rivière and Winnipeg. Our Dad was a conductor with the CPR. Jack attended Daniel McIntyre Collegiate [and] enlisted in 1943 in Winnipeg. He graduated training at Paulson, Manitoba and approximately 10 months later he was killed with his crew ... laying mines near Norway. They crashed in the North Sea near northern Scotland. It was a heartbreaker for my parents. My Dad never got over the grief. He had served four years in France during the Great War. My Mother survived somehow. I hope my two sons and four grandchildren never have to be conscripted by any war.

Patterson Creek (63 O/6), southeast of Apeganau Lake was named after him in 1995.

Patterson, Corporal **Robert J.** of Roland (H 402). Lord Strathcona's Horse. He died 21 January 1945 at the age of 22 and is commemorated at the Argenta Gap War Cemetery in Italy. He was the son of John W. Patterson of Rosetown, Saskatchewan and the late Mary Patterson. Wounded in Italy the previous September, he had only just recently returned to active service. ***Patterson Esker*** (64 C/6), north of Russell Lake was named after him in 1995.

Patterson, Flying Officer **Wilfred N.** of Neepawa (J 27526). No. 626 Squadron. He died 21 February 1945 at the age of 22 and is commemorated at the Runnymede Memorial in Surrey, England. He was the son of Mr. and Mrs. Robert Patterson of Neepawa.

> Wilfred was born in Raymore, Saskatchewan. His family moved to Portage la Prairie and later Neepawa and he received his education there. In June, 1940, he joined the RCAF Medical Corps, later remustering to aircrew in June, 1942. Wilfred continued his training in Edmonton, finishing off at Calgary where he received his Commission and Wings in June, 1943. He was immediately posted overseas. He and his crew flew their first operational mission in a Lancaster bomber on 16 November 1944. On December 6, he piloted Lancaster PA990 UM-R2 – the only 626 Squadron Lancaster to complete over 100 operational missions. He failed to return from night operations over Dortmund and it was later confirmed his aircraft crashed in a wood near the village of Hagen near Dortmund. Six members of the crew were reported killed; one member Sergeant T. Whitby, survived the crash (Pittman n.d.).

Patterson Narrows (63 N/5) in Russick Lake was named after him in 1995.

Patteson, Pilot Officer **John G.** of Winnipeg (J 18092). No. 620 Squadron. He died 26 July 1943 at the age of 22 and is commemorated at the Groesbeek Canadian War Cemetery in Holland. He was the son of Harry and Jean M. Patteson of St. James. ***Patteson Lake*** (64 H/9), north of Freeman Lake was named after him in 1995.

Patton, Pilot Officer **Alvin A. J.** of Margaret (J 19028). No. 408 Squadron. He died 31 March 1944 at the age of 29 and is commemorated at Durnbach War Cemetery in Bavaria, Germany. He was the son of William J. and Christina A. Patton and was survived by his wife Jane Margaret Patton of Winnipeg. He had been working on the family farm prior to enlisting. ***Patton Island*** (64 C/7) in Granville Lake was named after him in 1995.

Patton, Flight Sergeant **Charles R.** of Petersfield (R 110977). No. 150 Squadron. He died 31 October 1942 at the age of 23 and is commemorated at Steenwijkerwold (Willemsoord) General Cemetery, Holland. He was one of the 12 children of George E. and Hannah M. Patton (née Bird) of Petersfield and the brother of Lance Corporal Victor E. Paton (next entry). His sister recalls (22 January 1985):

> Charles was the third youngest child, an RCAF air gunner. He had received a caterpillar pin. It was returned with his personal effects to our parents. [The Caterpillar pin was awarded to those who had successfully used a parachute]. Charles was very artistic and mechanically inclined. [He and his brother] enjoyed fishing and hunting. Both were near perfect at target shooting. Spring and summer they helped with seeding crops, attending the stock, gardens, berry picking. Summer and fall were busy times with harvesting, cultivating, haying and ploughing.

Patton Bay (64 O/2) in Brownstone Lake was named after him in 1985.

Patton, Lance Corporal **Victor E.** of Petersfield (H 20894). Queen's Own Cameron Highlanders. He died 14 August 1944 at the age of 19 and is commemorated at Bretteville-sur-Laize Canadian War Cemetery in Calvados, France. He was one of the 12 children of George E. and Hannah M. Patton (née Bird) of Petersfield and the brother of Flight Sergeant Charles R. Patton (previous entry). His sister recalls (22 January 1985):

> Charles and Victor were born and grew up on a farm at Petersfield, Manitoba. It was a dairy and grain growing operation – later a grain growing one. On a farm there was always plenty of work. From the time our brothers learned to walk, they were ardent workers. In winter there were card games, table tennis, crokinole, skating on a home made rink or on a little creek and sliding down large snow banks. Our parents were hard working, honest, just and wise. Many friends, relatives and neighbours often came to Dad for advice. There was lots of love, sharing and laughter in our home. Charles' and Victor's lives were brief, our memories of them long and cherished.

Patton Point (64 O/2) on Brownstone Lake was named after him in 1985.

Paul, Private **Ernest J.** of Carman (H 40700). Winnipeg Grenadiers. He died a prisoner of war 5 March 1945 at the age of 25 and is commemorated at the Yokohama War Cemetery in Japan. The cause of death was listed as tuberculosis. He was the son of Daniel and Agnes Paul of Carman, Manitoba. ***Paul Island*** (64 C/8) in Granville Lake was named after him in 1995.

Paul, Sergeant **Glen F.** of Winnipeg (H 3148). Canadian Army Dental Corps. He died 21 April 1944 at the age of 29 and is commemorated at the Sai Wan War Cemetery in Hong Kong. He was the son of Henry A. and Eliza E. Paul and was survived by his wife Evelyn L. Paul of New Westminster, British Columbia and their son. He was captured after the fall of Hong Kong and died in a prisoner of war camp. According to his widow (23 April 1998):

> He and his younger brother both joined the Dental Corps in the spring of 1940. We were married soon after and our son Glen Arthur Paul was born about 3 1/2 weeks before he was put on draft; [the] destination was unknown when he left, but it turned out to be Hong Kong. He was part of a dental team who were attached to the Winnipeg Grenadiers. They were only there for a few weeks when the Japanese attacked Pearl Harbor, then a few days later they attacked the Grenadiers who were stationed in Hong Kong.

Our soldiers had hardly any equipment and were completely taken off guard, so consequently a great many of them died. They surrendered on Christmas Day, 1941 and we did not find out whether they were prisoners of war or had died until August 19, 1942. During their imprisonment, they were very badly treated, with barely enough to eat. Anyway, he contracted malaria in April, 1944 and after much suffering he died, as the Japanese would not give him any medication as they said they needed it for their own men.

We hardly heard from him during the 2 1/2 years he was a prisoner, as they were seldom allowed to write. I think I heard from him twice in all that time and they were only allowed to print twelve words, so it was a very sad and lonely time for him as well as us who missed him so very much.

Paul Bay (64 O/13) in Nueltin Lake was named after him in 1995.

Paul, Trooper **Lavey** of Winnipeg (H 102284). British Columbia Dragoons. He died 25 May 1944 at the age of 20 and is commemorated at the Cassino War Cemetery in Italy. He was the son of Rubin and Ida Paul of Winnipeg. His sister recalls (6 May 1996):

My father ran a small business of manufacturing halters and other related items for a short period of time. I am not too clear on this as I was only four years old at the time. Lavey's special interest was sports, particularly football and skating. He worked at a bowling alley setting pins during his school years and also sold newspapers. After graduation from high school, he went to work learning the electrical trade. The name of the firm was S. Kleiman who has been credited [with] developing a water heater called the "Red Devil." The firm is no longer in business.

When Lavey enlisted, he trained at Camp Borden and then went overseas. At some point he was assigned to the British Columbia Dragoons as a radio operator and went from England to Italy where he was reported missing in action during the fighting at Cassino. His grave is located in a cemetery there. It had always been my wish to visit his grave, but I doubt I will ever get there.

Paul Point (64 P/3) on Naelin Lake was named after him in 1995.

Paul, Private **Louis** of Winnipeg (H 101914). Royal Canadian Army Service Corps. He died 9 August 1944 at the age of 29 and is commemorated at the Bayeux War Cemetery in Calvados, France. He was the son of Irving and Sarah Paul. ***Paul Peninsula*** (64 A/11) on Kiask Lake was named after him in 1995.

Paulson, Private **Edwin O.** of Bowsman River (H 9005). Princess Patricia's Canadian Light Infantry. He died 17 September 1944 at the age of 21 and is commemorated at Coriano Ridge War Cemetery in Italy. He was the son of Peter C. and Hannah N. Paulson of Bowsman River, Manitoba. ***Paulson Lake*** (64 K/10), east of Lac Brochet was named after him in 1961.

Paulson, Lieutenant **Frederick B.** of Winnipeg. 14th Canadian Hussars. He died 20 July 1944 at the age of 26 and is commemorated at Bretteville-sur-Laize Canadian War Cemetery in Calvados, France. He was the son of Gordon A. and Magnea B. Paulson of Winnipeg and the brother of Lieutenant Gordon Paulson (next entry). ***Paulson Bay*** (64 F/1) in Melvin Lake was named after him in 1983.

Paulson, Lieutenant **Gordon A.** of Winnipeg. Queen's Own Cameron Highlanders. He died 28 June 1945 at the age of 22 and is commemorated at Brookside Cemetery in Winnipeg. He was survived by his mother Magnea B. Paulson of Winnipeg and was the brother of Lieutenant Frederick Paulson (previous entry). ***Paulson Island*** (64 F/1) in Melvin Lake was named after him in 1983.

Paulson, Private **Roger Irvin** of Winnipegosis (H 1432). Stormont, Dundas and Glengarry Highlanders. He died 7 June 1944 at the age of 19 and is commemorated at Beny-sur-Mer Canadian War Cemetery in Calvados, France. He was one of the six children of Johann H. and Sarah Paulson of Winnipegosis, Manitoba. His sister writes (9 October 2001):

[He was] born August 30th, 1925 at Winnipegosis. Irvin enlisted in the Royal Canadian Artillery in February, 1943; after one furlough he was sent to England and shortly after transferred to the Stormont, Dundas and Glengarry Highlanders in preparation for D-Day. He was killed in action June 7th, 1944. According to his Captain, they had moved inland near Les Buissons, a little village not far from Caen, when he was hit by flying shrapnel and died instantly. Our parents were very grateful to have heard from his Captain.

He was always very good-hearted. Times were hard when we were growing up, but he loved to play a mouth organ, to dance and sang in the Church Choir.

Paulson Point (63 I/2) on Pinaysi Lake was named after him in 1995.

Payne, Sergeant **John O.** of St. Vital (H 6016). Winnipeg Grenadiers, Mentioned in Dispatches. He died a prisoner of war 26 August 1942 at the age of 23 and is commemorated at the Sai Wan War Cemetery in Hong Kong. He was the son of Benjamin O. and Margaret C. Payne of Fort Rouge. Much later, it was determined that he had been executed after trying to escape. Remarkably, a note written to his mother just prior to his escape attempt survived the war. It was delivered by close friend Sergeant Bob Manchester after he was repatriated in 1945:

Dear Mater: I have decided either fortunately or unfortunately as the case may be, to take a chance on getting through to Chunking. I've investigated as much as possible and feel sure we stand a jolly good chance of getting there. There are numerous reasons for this step, the chief being that the cholera season and fly season is starting, dysentery and beriberi are high in camp and anyway, I'm ruddy sick of Japanese hospitality.

You share, I know, my own views on fatalism, so for that reason I know you won't condemn my judgement. So just in case I shouldn't make it, you must remember that according to our beliefs, I have departed for a much nicer place (I hope) although it will grieve me to exchange the guitar for a harp even though there is a higher percentage of gold in the latter. But that's enough of this drivel, I'll be able to destroy this note myself I'm sure so bye-bye for now. Your devoted son, John.

P.S. Best regards to Di and Yvonne. Tell Ben to join the Air Force next war (19 August 1942).

Sergeant Manchester recalled:

As soon as we were taken prisoner, John started making plans and blueprints of how he would get out of the prison camp. About midnight, August 19, 1942, he was ready to go. There was a heavy rainstorm, almost a typhoon that night and it aided in the escape. Around the building, the Japanese had left ladders, and on two previous occasions, John had been over the hospital walls. He had got in touch with Chinese missionaries and others. Men who worked in the cookhouse supplied enough food to last them 10 days.

Before the boys slipped away, armed only with .45 calibre revolvers, they shook hands with the few of the 300 prisoners who knew of their plans and John gave me a letter for his mother. "Get that letter to my mother," he instructed me, "I'll meet you all in Winnipeg." We told them we hoped they'd make it. From North Point camp they had to cross four miles of water to the mainland. Once they got there, they would encounter Chinese guerrillas around Canton and up to Chunking.

It was later reported that they were recaptured when their boat was swamped in the storm. All four were summarily executed and this incident sparked a war crimes investigation after the war. Nine of the ten Japanese military personnel involved were found guilty and sentenced to death and life imprisonment in 1947. Two officers were sentenced to be hanged, but their sentence was commuted by a British officer to life imprisonment and twenty years respectively. This seemingly contravened the Geneva Convention's provision that a sentence that is to be commuted must have the permission of the country against which the crime was committed (Brioux 1998).

He had been a commercial photographer and Eaton's employee before enlisting on September 4, 1939, the day after Britain declared war on Germany. An article entitled "War's Waste of Genius" published by Eaton's had this to say about him:

> When in the West Indies with the Grenadiers, this gallant lad designed a cairn which was dedicated to his regiment at an official ceremony. Assisting him in the designing was Jack Kelso, an Eaton boy, who was later killed in the heroic defence of Hong Kong. Sergeant Payne, who was artistic to his fingertips, also carved a set of chessmen. They are exquisitely made from oak, rosewood and other woods in quaint oriental characters that took three years to carve. Experts value them at $2000.00 (n.d.).

Payne Lake (64 C/15), north of Cockeram Lake was named after him in 1979.

Peace, Sergeant **Leslie** of Brandon (524666). No. 106 Squadron, RAF. He died 29 July 1944 at the age of 27 and is commemorated at Durnbach War Cemetery in Bavaria, Germany. He was the son of George W. and Florrie Peace and was survived by his wife Ethel M. Peace of Brandon. ***Peace Lake*** (53 L/1), east of Rochon Lake was named after him in 1995.

Peacey, Captain **Harry J.** of Winnipeg. Fort Garry Horse. He died 25 July 1944 at the age of 32 and is commemorated at Beny-sur-Mer Canadian War Cemetery in Calvados, France. He was the son of Mrs. Maud Peacey, formerly of Minnedosa. ***Peacey Lake*** (64 K/11), east of Lac Brochet was named after him in 1972.

Pearce, Trooper **Alfred H.** of Dauphin (K 16498). Lord Strathcona's Horse. He died 17 April 1945 at the age of 28 and is commemorated at the Groesbeek Canadian War Cemetery in Holland. He was the son of Alfred R. and Bertha Pearce and was survived by his wife Evelyn M. Pearce of Vancouver. ***Pearce Bay*** (64 N/10) in Sandy Lake was named after him in 1995.

Pearce, Rifleman **Gordon R.** of Neepawa (H 19437). Royal Winnipeg Rifles. He died 24 January 1946 at the age of 30 and is commemorated at Brookwood Military Cemetery in Surrey, England. He was survived by his mother Evelyn Pearce of Winnipeg. ***Pearce Island*** (53 K/14) in Kenyon Lake was named after him in 1995.

Pearson, Private **Douglas E.** of Flin Flon (H 6958). Winnipeg Grenadiers. He died a prisoner of war 12 October 1942 at the age of 23 and is commemorated at the Sai Wan War Cemetery in Hong Kong. He was the son of Peter and Lillian Pearson of Austin, Manitoba. ***Pearson Island*** (64 H/4) in Gauer Lake was named after him in 1989.

Pearson, Private **Royal Blaine** of Birnie (H 800232). Princess Patricia's Canadian Light Infantry. He died 7 March 1951 and is commemorated at the United Nations Cemetery in Pusan, South Korea.

Blaine commenced his elementary schooling at Birnie, Manitoba. The family moved to Neepawa where Blaine continued his education, graduating from Grade 8 in 1946 at Central School. He was very active in sports and was awarded the Legion Trophy for Most Sportsmanlike Player in the Public School Hockey League in the spring of 1946. The family moved to Edmonton in 1950 where Blaine enlisted in the Princess Patricia's Canadian Light Infantry. His regiment became a special battalion based at Winnipeg where they completed more training prior to their departure for Korea. The PPCLI was the only Canadian Regiment to receive an American Presidential Citation for their involvement in the Korean Conflict (Pittman n.d.).

Blaine Pearson Lake (53 K/12), north of Sharpe Lake was named after this Korean War casualty in 1998.

Pearson, Lance Corporal **Thomas** of Dauphin (H 17051). Princess Patricia's Canadian Light Infantry. He died 22 July 1943 and is commemorated at Agira Canadian War Cemetery in Italy. ***Pearson Point*** (64 P/9) on Gagnon Lake was named after him in 1995.

Pearson, Rifleman **William T.** of Slave Falls (H 103283). Royal Winnipeg Rifles. He died 4 July 1944 at the age of 21 and is commemorated at Beny-sur-Mer Canadian War Cemetery in Calvados, France. He was the son of Robert and Lila O. Pearson of Slave Falls, Manitoba. ***Pearson Bay*** (64 O/16) in Hutton Lake was named after him in 1995.

Peden, Private **David** of Winnipeg (637). 8th Battalion, Canadian Infantry (Manitoba Regiment). This native of Maybole, Ayrshire, Scotland died 10 November 1917 at Passchendaele at the age of 30 and is commemorated at Ypres (Menin Gate) Memorial, Ieper, West-Vlaanderen, Belgium. He was the son of Mr. and Mrs. David Peden of Winnipeg. In a letter to his father, Solicitor General Arthur Meighen wrote (17 October 1916):

> Dear Mr. Peden: I have now gotten to the bottom of the difficulty with respect to reports as to the fate of your sons at the front. I find that you have no less than five sons in active service, and as a citizen of Portage la Prairie I want to tell you that I am proud of the family of David Peden. So far as I know, there is no record like this in the City or District and indeed very few like it in Canada. I am indeed sorry to learn that one son, James, has been killed and that the other two sons have been wounded. I sincerely trust they will reach an early and complete recovery. Most earnestly we all hope that you have heard the last of the bad news as to your boys and that you will live many years to enjoy the memory of the magnificent part your family has played in this great world struggle.

Private David Peden was killed the following year. ***West Peden Lake*** (64 F/5), northeast of Carriere Lake was named after him in 1996. East Peden Lake was named after his brother, Private James Peden (next entry).

Peden, Private **James** of Portage la Prairie (425195). 28th Battalion. This native of Maybole, Ayrshire, Scotland died 15 September 1916 at the age of 20 and is commemorated at the Vimy Memorial, Pas de Calais, France. He was the youngest son of David Peden of Portage la Prairie. According to a contemporary news account:

> The two brothers (James and John) were through the battle of the Somme, and in writing from a hospital at Oxford, England, to his parents, John, in a letter received a few days ago, stated that he presumed that his brother was "safe and sound." He told of the charge on the German trenches in which they both took part, stating that he saw his brother Jim, who was in the first party

to advance, reach the German trench. It was whilst John's section was rushing to the captured trench that he received a gunshot wound in the head (*Portage Graphic* 1916).

A nephew writes (7 July 1996):

I only wish my dad and grandparents were still alive to share our pride in these two boys who were killed in their prime. Naming the lakes after them helps ease the sense of loss of two uncles we never had the chance to know. The picture of my grandparents five sons who enlisted, two of whom were killed and two wounded, hangs prominently beside a picture of my brother who was a bomber pilot in World War II and survived. In those reflective moments when I contemplate what they went through defending this country, and the hell my grandparents suffered, I still get a lump in my throat.

East Peden Lake (64 F/5), northeast of Carriere Lake was named after him in 1996. West Peden Lake was named after his brother, Private David Peden (previous entry).

Peden, Sergeant **William Nelson M.** of Winnipeg (R 80475). No. 18 Service Flying Training School. He died 13 October 1944 at the age of 36 and is commemorated at Brookside Cemetery in Winnipeg. He was the son of Robert and Marion W. Peden of Rossburn and was survived by his wife Viola Peden of Gimli. ***Peden Island*** (64 P/4) in MacLeod Lake was named after him in 1974.

Pedersen, Flight Sergeant **Walter C.** of Clanwilliam (R 98793). No. 21 Operational Training Unit, RCAF. He was reported missing 14 September 1942 at the age of 35 and is commemorated at Terschelling (Westerschelling) General Cemetery, Holland. He was the sixth of the eight children of Marius N. and Bertha Pedersen of Clanwilliam, Manitoba. He received his Teaching Certificate in 1929, and for the next eight years taught at several schools in southwestern Manitoba. He enlisted in 1941 and while at Air Observers School in Regina, his Commander remarked that:

This airman is well matured as his age would indicate. He is dependable, serious and has a good sense of responsibility. He has had several years teaching experience and might prove better suited as an instructor (n.d.).

Nonetheless, he ended up serving with a British crew on a bombing raid to Bremen. His aircraft was shot down over the North Sea and his body washed up on the shore of a small island – Terschelling, Holland – a week later. A local resident named Van Der Weff had demanded of the German Commanding Officer that German casualties could only be buried at the Uredenhof Cemetery if the Allied dead were buried there also, and with full military honours. The Germans agreed and for the rest of the war, fallen Allies received full military services there. Jan Groendijk has tended the graves for many years and attempted to contact families of the deceased. His first attempt, dated 14 September 1942 was addressed simply to the "Mayor of Clanwilliam, Manitoba, Canada." A second attempt in 1990 came to the attention of Flight Sergeant Pedersen's brother and the family finally learned of their relative's fate. Groendijk claims:

... these planes have on board some very experienced crew members and some new airmen. The use of the OTU [Operational Training Unit] crews on a target like this (Bremen) was, to my mind, inexcusable. It was done on occasion to boost the numbers in the attacking force, but usually the introduction to operational flying before joining a squadron was against targets like the Channel ports or in France where the defences were not so strong (*Liverpool Star* 1 March 1991).

Commenting on his search for families, Mr. Groendijk adds:

When finally I make contact with their families I no longer feel that we are strangers. We are very grateful to the young men who lost their lives in the fight to gain freedom for Holland (*Liverpool Star* 1 March 1991).

Pedersen Esker (53 N/11), north of Whitefish Lake was named after him in 1995.

Peebles, Flight Sergeant **Francis G.** of Dauphin (R 59671). No. 102 Squadron. He died 17 June 1942 at the age of 22 and is commemorated at the Hardenberg Protestant Cemetery in Holland. He was the son of Mathew G. and Grace Peebles of Dauphin. ***Peebles Lake*** (64 H/7), southeast of Solmundsson Lake was named after him in 1995.

Pelechaty, Pilot Officer **Ignatius T.** of Winnipeg (J 90271). No. 426 Squadron. He died 30 September 1944 at the age of 22 and is commemorated at the Reichswald Forest War Cemetery in Germany. He was the son of John and Mary Pelechaty of Winnipeg. ***Pelechaty Lake*** (52 E/14), northeast of Brereton Lake was named after him in 1974.

Peloquin, Sergeant **Arthur C.** of Deerhorn (H 17491). Le Régiment de la Chaudière. He died 27 June 1945 at the age of 32 and is commemorated at the Groesbeek Canadian War Cemetery in Holland. He was the third of the eight children of Damase and Hermine Peloquin and husband of Marie A. Peloquin (née Lamblin) of Winnipeg and father of their two children. He wrote many letters home:

I was thinking of Leo [his son] all day today, thinking that he will be walking now. I hope the day will come when I will be with them again. You don't know the half of it, how hard it is to be so far away from home and don't know when you will ever see them again. Sometimes I try to get it out of my mind, but it just can't be done (9 January 1944).

I received your letter and it sure cheered me up. I was sure down and out. We just came back from digging graves for our boys. I tell you the days are long and the nights still worse. I never thought a man could go through such hell. I am writing this in a hole in the ground with the rumble of everything imaginable. I haven't lost hope to see you all someday and I really have faith in your prayers back home. I would like to see Leo with his hair cut. I bet he looks like a real little man. The vengeance of this war is terrible to keep us away from those kids (12 June 1944).

I somehow think it does a person a lot of good to go through this hell. We will know when we are well off. After this war is over, if I ever hear anybody "cheesing the rag" when I go back home I'll crown him. I am very lonesome but I don't worry as I know you are being well looked after. Hello Denise [his daughter], Daddy received your letters and likes to read them. Keep on praying for your Daddy to come back (14 February 1945).

According to his daughter (28 April 1998):

Arthur was raised on a small farm. His father laboured at mixed farming; his mother operated a small cheese factory on the family farm as well as raising her large family. Arthur, being the eldest, helped on the farm until June of 1940 when he enlisted in the army at the age of 27 years. He enjoyed carpentry and hunting when time allowed. He married on August 3rd, 1940. His bride ... lived on the neighbouring farm. She was 25 years old at the time. On June 25th, 1941, their first-born arrived, a daughter, Denise Marie Louise Patricia (Patricia after the "Princess Pats"). Eighteen months later a son was born. When my father left for overseas in the spring of 1943, I was two years old and my brother only six months. My Dad had purchased a small home near the Peloquin farm in order that my mother would be close to family during those difficult years.

My mother has kept all the letters that my father wrote during the war. It has given my brother and I and our families some insight into the war and our father's life during those years.

The sad part about this story is the fact that my Dad actually survived the war and was killed in a fatal motorcycle accident in Holland while completing their duties in June of that year. In his letters home he tells

> my mother to expect him in September. Thus when she received the telegram, she expected that it brought news of his return. As you can imagine, the news of his death was devastating. She has remained a widow since.
>
> My mother moved to the wartime housing in Winnipeg soon after the war was over in order to gain employment. In 1950, she moved the family to Burnaby, BC and bought a small home. My paternal grandmother came with us and helped care for us until my brother and I were in high school. Eventually, I graduated as a Registered Nurse from St. Paul's School of Nursing.

His wife and children visited his gravesite in 1986. ***Peloquin Lake*** (63 K/16), north of Reed Lake was named after him in 1973.

Penn, Flying Officer **Lloyd W. T.** of Winnipeg (J 21391). No. 6 Service Flying Training School. He died 22 July 1943 at the age of 22 and is commemorated at Elmwood Cemetery in Winnipeg. He was survived by his mother Gladys E. Penn of Winnipeg. His brother relates that he was a graduate of Champlain, Machray and St. John's Technical schools. He joined the reserve Air Force before the war and went on active service when war was declared. Initially trained as an air gunner, he remustered to pilot after the Battle of Britain and worked for a time in Canada as a navigational instructor. He was on an instrument flying training exercise when his Harvard aircraft went in to a spin and crashed one mile south of Canfield, Ontario (Allison and Hayward 1991). ***Penn Lake*** (64 N/6), southwest of Nueltin Lake was named after him in 1972.

Penner, Private **Bernard "Ben"** of Altona (H 18013). Princess Louise Dragoon Guards. He died 25 September 1944 at the age of 34 and is commemorated at Cesena War Cemetery in Italy. He was survived by his mother Mary Penner of Altona. ***Penner Lake*** (64 N/15), west of Nueltin Lake was named after him in 1972.

Pennie, Trooper **Robert M.** of Arden (H 9009). Fort Garry Horse. He died 1 September 1944 at the age of 19 and is commemorated at the Calais Canadian War Cemetery in France. He was the son of Robert O. and Olive M. Pennie of Minnedosa. His parents and a sister visited the gravesite in 1949 and the sister returned in 1989. She recalls (29 November 2001):

> Bob completed Grade 12 in 1942 and worked at the Commonwealth Air Training in Neepawa before he enlisted April 19, 1943. He was trained at Winnipeg, Portage and Camp Borden. He left for England December, 1943 and was stationed at Aldershot. He went to France July 19, 1944 where he served in the Caen and Falaise Gap actions as a radio operator in his tank crew. They were on their way to Dieppe when he was killed due to an accident.
>
> His interests as a boy were Boy Scouts, baseball and hockey. Bob had a great sense of humour. His many letters to our parents and myself (his sister) are full of light hearted comments and descriptions of the beautiful countryside as well as the difficulties of their lives.

Pennie Lake (64 I/5), south of Shethanei Lake was named after him in 1974.

Pennycook, Private **Paul N.** of Glenboro (H 20064). Royal Canadian Army Service Corps. He died 15 June 1944 at the age of 23 and is commemorated at Beny-sur-Mer Canadian War Cemetery in Calvados, France. He was the son of Robert and Jennie Pennycook of Glenboro, Manitoba. ***Pennycook Lake*** (52 E/13), east of Brereton Lake was named after him in 1973.

Penonzek, Private **Chester A.** of Winnipeg (H 42202). Saskatoon Light Infantry. He died 23 May 1944 at the age of 20 and is commemorated at the Cassino War Cemetery in Italy. He was the son of Frank and Lilian Penonzek of Vancouver. ***Penonzek Lake*** (63 I/7), north of Molson Lake was named after him in 1973.

Penonzek, Flight Sergeant **John M.** of Rossburn (R 180424). No. 3 Advanced Flying Training School. He died 31 December 1944 at the age of 22 and is commemorated at St. Patrick Churchyard in Jurby on the Isle of Man. He was the son of Bert and Margaret Penonzek of Rossburn, Manitoba. According to his cousin (9 November 2001):

> After graduation, he worked for one year at a General Store at Angusville, Manitoba. After that he went to teach at Bird School. He joined the Air Force in 1942 at the age of 20 and went overseas in 1943. He was killed ... when two planes collided over the Isle of Man off England.

Penonzek Island (53 L/8) in Wapeeminakoskak Lake was named after him in 1995.

Peppin, Private **Louis** of St. Lazare (H 20829). Winnipeg Grenadiers. He died 19 December 1941 and is commemorated at the Sai Wan Memorial in Hong Kong. He was the son of Benoit and Isabel Peppin of St. Lazare, Manitoba. ***Peppin Lake*** (63 K/16), northwest of Wekusko Lake was named after him in 1973.

Perederka, Private **P. William** of Winnipeg (H 7193). Queen's Own Cameron Highlanders. He died 21 July 1944 at the age of 26 and is commemorated at Bretteville-sur-Laize Canadian War Cemetery in Calvados, France. He was the son of William and Veronica Perederka of Winnipeg. ***Perederka Lake*** (53 M/5), north of Utik Lake was named after him in 1996.

Perkins, Warrant Officer 2 **Jack L.** of Winnipeg (R 101627). No. 306 Squadron. He died 23 August 1943 at the age of 21 and is commemorated at the Runnymede Memorial in Surrey, England. He was the son of Alexander B. and Cora M. Perkins of Winnipeg. ***Perkins Lake*** (64 H/16), southwest of Condie Lake was named after him in 1995.

Perron, Private **Gerald J.** of St. Anne (H 1230). Argyle and Sutherland Highlanders. He died 9 August 1944 at the age of 22 and is commemorated at Bretteville-sur-Laize Canadian War Cemetery in Calvados, France. He was the son of Alexandre and Edwardina Perron of Minaki, Ontario. ***Perron Lake*** (53 F/13), east of Angling Lake was named after him in 1996.

Perry, Private **Clarence A.** of Erinview (F 40825). West Nova Scotia Regiment. He died 2 August 1943 at the age of 33 and is commemorated at Agira Canadian War Cemetery in Italy. He was the son of Albert and Francis Perry and was survived by his wife Dorothy Perry of Cambridge Station, Nova Scotia. ***Perry Bay*** (64 P/4) in MacLeod Lake was named after him in 1995.

Perry, Flight Sergeant **Harry** of Winnipeg (R 58888). No. 15 Squadron. He died 4 September 1943 at the age of 24 and is commemorated at Frederikshavn Cemetery in Denmark. He was the son of Samuel and Priscilla Perry of Winnipeg. ***Perry Lake*** (63 H/1), northeast of Weaver Lake was named after him in 1974.

Perry, Flight Lieutenant **Robert R.** of Winnipeg (J 9503). No. 407 Squadron. He died 24 March 1944 at the age of 33 and is commemorated at the Runnymede Memorial in Surrey, England. He was the son of Edmund G. and Mary L. B. R. Perry of Winnipeg. He was a former employee at Great West Life and wrote a letter to his former co-workers from Malta:

We are stationed in what was a first class hotel, six of us in one room, formerly the lounge. It has a piano and lots of comfortable furniture so we are content. Can even swing from the chandelier if we've a mind to! Managed a trip to Egypt. Slept out on the desert one night in a tent and drank – of all things – ice cold Black Horse beer. That place was truly an oasis. Spent three days in Cairo, a wonderful place with fine, modern buildings, American cars, almost like walking down a street in Toronto except for bumping into the odd camel. Egyptians all wear fezzes and it looks like a Shriners Convention. Nothing is rationed there so brought back 48 jars strawberry jam, 48 jars apricot jam, 12 jars marmalade, 60 pounds sugar, 240 chocolate bars, tins of coffee extract and condensed milk which I am sharing with my Canadian cronies (n.d.).

Perry Island (64 N/7) in Topp Lake was named after him in 1995.

Persian, Flying Officer **Arthur T.** of Bowsman River (J 7328). No. 418 Squadron. He died 17 September 1942 at the age of 27 and is commemorated at the Runnymede Memorial in Surrey, England. He was the pilot of a Boston aircraft which made a forced landing in the sea off the coast of Essex. The observer and air gunner were also killed (Allison and Hayward 1991). ***Persian Lake*** (63 K/12), north of Athapapuskow Lake was named after him in 1970.

Pert, Gunner **John H.** of Vermette (H 69870). Royal Canadian Artillery, Mentioned in Dispatches. He died 23 December 1944 at the age of 29 and is commemorated at Ravenna War Cemetery in Italy. He was the son of Henry A. and Emily C. Pert of Vermette, Manitoba. ***Pert Lake*** (54 K/4), southeast of Churchill was named after him in 1948.

Peters, Pilot Officer **Donald H.** of Winnipeg (J 15202). No. 419 Squadron. He died 6 June 1942 at the age of 20 and is commemorated at the Runnymede Memorial in Surrey, England. He was the son of Henry and Sadie Peters of Winnipeg. ***Peters Bay*** (64 O/8) in Baird Lake was named after him in 1995.

Peters, Warrant Officer 2 **Frederick J.** of Winnipeg (R 172885). No. 4 Operational Training Unit, RCAF. He died 26 November 1944 at the age of 32 and is commemorated at Stonefall Cemetery in Yorkshire, England. He was the son of Alexander J. and Katherine Peters of Winnipeg. ***Peters Island*** (63 P/2) in Cotton Lake was named after him in 1995.

Peters, Sergeant **Kenneth F.** of Oak River (R 95372). No. 59 Operational Training Unit, RCAF. He died 20 December 1941 at the age of 19 and is commemorated at Carlisle (Dalston Road) Cemetery, Westmoreland, England. He was the eldest son of Harry B. and Eliza Peters of Oak River, Manitoba. His brothers remember (4 December 2001):

Ken grew up on the family farm with his parents, an older sister and three younger brothers. This was a typical farm of the 1920s – 1940s era. Land work was done with horses for the main part. Cattle, pigs and chickens were raised and during the Dirty Thirties provided not only food, but some income as well, although market values were poor. Many stories are recalled of the "adventures" of Ken and his brothers with the horses and other animals. Skating was the winter sport and ball games that of summer.

Ken obtained his elementary years of education at Poplar Grove, a small one-room country school and then rode seven miles on his bike in the summer time and horse back in the winter to get his high schooling at Cardale. He enjoyed his track and field activities at the small country school field days.

After finishing school, with the depression in full force and with no work to be found, Ken and his cousin "rode the rails" to the west. Shortly after returning, he enlisted in the RCAF. He enlisted October 1, 1940 and trained at Brandon, Winnipeg and Uplands, Ontario, receiving his wings on his 19th birthday – September 24, 1941. Word was received on Sunday, December 21, 1941 that Ken had been killed in action on December 20. A further cable received on the Monday stated that burial would be made at Carlisle on Wednesday, December 24, 1941. We wish we could have had more time together with him, but this was not to be.

Peters Point (63 N/10) on Flatrock Lake was named after him in 1995.

Peters, Flying Officer **Nicholas** of Steinbach (J 45525). No. 214 Squadron. He died 7 March 1945 at the age of 30 and is commemorated at Becklingen War Cemetery in Germany. He was the eleventh child of Isaac F. and Elizabeth Peters (née Reidiger) and was survived by his wife Emma Marguerite Peters (née Tustian) of Kagawong, Ontario and their two daughters. His nephew writes (22 October 2001):

Nicholas Peters was born in Bergtal, South Russia in his parents' home on April 8, 1915. In 1918, the family relocated to Landskrone, a village that was 75 miles south of Bergtal for safety reasons during the Russian Revolution. By 1925, the situation in the Ukraine was such that looting, starvation, disease, inflation and chaos reigned. It was at this time that the Peters family immigrated to Canada.

In Canada, the family settled on a farm in Grande Pointe, Manitoba. Nicholas' interests and studies centred on poultry farming. In 1935, he found employment in the coal mines in East Coulee, Alberta. From there, he moved on to the Pioneer Gold Mines in British Columbia. In 1937, Nicholas returned to Winnipeg to study agriculture at the University of Manitoba. He spent his summer working in Sudbury, Ontario and became active in youth work at the All Peoples United Church there. In November of 1940, he volunteered his services to the RCAF but was turned down because of a skin disease, so he went to work for DeHavilland Aircraft in Toronto.

On May 10, 1942, Nicholas married Marguerite Tustian. Two girls were born to this union, but neither lived. In November of 1942, he again offered his services to the RCAF and was accepted with a starting date in June, 1943. He did his early training in Toronto and on May 19, 1944, he graduated from Malton with his commission as Pilot Officer. The following July he left for England. Overseas, he was promoted to Flying Officer and had completed over half of his tour of flying missions over Germany when, on the night of March 7/8, 1945, their aircraft was struck by machine gun and anti-aircraft fire. On November 10th, word was received by his wife that he and two others of his crew lay buried at Elsdorf near Hamburg, Germany.

A book of his poetry entitled *Another Morn* was published by his wife in 1947. In large part it was written as a result on the condition of the world in 1939 and childhood memories of conflict, hunger and murder which arose when writing his speech to the young people in Ontario. These are some excerpts:

- On Humanity: There are things that make drunkards, just like there are circumstances that make accidents. They may be lessened but not offset by medicines or soup kitchens, but only remedied by getting at the cause.
- On War: How contradictory is life! We long for peace, yet if we never experienced war, we would not know what peace is. This does not only apply to world conditions, but also to conditions within ourselves ... Beauty consists of Unity, Variety and Harmony. About all that one may hope, then, is that our colours may enhance the Whole.

- On Marriage: And so we go on ... you in your work and I in mine, and yours and mine become ours and our future together is being formed. Then if we can extend into the community and the world at large, a better world is shaped. Not that you and I bring about this change, but we put our brick in the structure that makes up the world.
- On Hope: The dark war days of today will teach the world a lesson, temporary but nevertheless, it will teach it. For every two steps that we advance, we might slide back a step, but never all the way back. For the average human being is such that he learns from experience, and this experience gives reason for convictions, convictions that hold their light for a little while until greater lights show them up as shadows.

Peters Rapids (64 I/7) in the North Knife River was named after him in 1995.

Peters, Corporal **Robert P.** of Rapid City (H 20158). Queen's Own Cameron Highlanders. He died 29 July 1944 at the age of 35 and is commemorated at Bretteville-sur-Laize Canadian War Cemetery in Calvados, France. He was the son of Benson and Emma Peters. His nephew writes (7 July 1996):

After his education was complete, he worked in a bank and was transferred to a bank in Nassau in the Bahamas. When he came back to Canada, he helped his Uncle Rob who ran a small dairy and honey business in Rapid City until he joined up. He came to Winnipeg and stayed with my mother and I, where he helped me to plant our garden while awaiting results. He was turned down by the Air Force and joined the Queen's Own Cameron Highlanders. I remember him saying: " I hate the bagpipes and will look like hell in a skirt, but I guess I'll get used to it."

Peters Peninsula (63 I/1) on Little Bolton Lake was named after him in 1995.

Petersen, Wing Commander **Norman B.** of Winnipeg (C 170). No. 409 Squadron. He died 2 September 1941 at the age of 28 and is commemorated at Scopwick Church Burial Ground in Lincolnshire, England. He was the son of James and Meta Petersen. ***Petersen Lake*** (64 H/8), west of Hogg Lake was named after him in 1995.

Petersen, Private **P. J. Ernest** of Wellwood (H 7143). Queen's Own Cameron Highlanders. He died 13 September 1944 at the age of 29 and is commemorated at the Adegem Canadian War Cemetery in Belgium. He was the second of the six children of Peter John and Marguerite E. Peterson of Wellwood. His sister recalls (12 December 1994):

Ernie, as he was called, was born on the family farm at Wellwood, Manitoba. He attended school at Wellwood Consolidated School. I really don't know the extent of his education. He worked on the farm and helped out any neighbours that could use him. During the depression years, he worked where he could in Saskatchewan and Manitoba. When the road was being built through Riding Mountain Park, he worked on that. He enjoyed playing cards and taught me how to play crib. I do believe he enlisted with the Grenadiers, then joined the Camerons. He was wounded twice in August, 1944. He was a stretcher bearer. Due to the fire that destroyed my parents' home, most information from the war department was lost.

His nephew adds (26 November 2001):

Ernie enlisted in the Canadian Army (Active) on March 2nd, 1942 serving in Canada, Britain and northwest Europe. He was known to his comrades as 'Pete.' He was killed in action twelve days short of his 30th birthday. As written by the Chaplain of his unit: "he was buried in soil that his own faith and gallant service had helped to free."

Petersen Bay (64 G/5) in Unagimau Lake was named after him in 1994.

Peterson, Rifleman **Alfred M.** of Winnipeg (H 20430). Royal Winnipeg Rifles. He died 8 June 1944 at the age of 31 and is commemorated at Beny-sur-Mer Canadian War Cemetery in Calvados, France. He was the son of Martin and Anna Peterson. ***Peterson Rapids*** (64 P/15) in the Caribou River was named after him in 1995.

Peterson, Gunner **John** of Sandridge (H 100779). Royal Canadian Artillery. He died 2 October 1944 at the age of 30 and is commemorated at Ravenna War Cemetery in Italy. He was the son of Peter and Bina Peterson of Sandridge, Manitoba. ***Peterson Point*** (64 O/9) on Croll Lake was named after him in 1995.

Peterson, Flying Officer **Lawrence H.** of Winnipeg (J 8384). No. 33 Squadron. He died 30 October 1942 at the age of 21 and is commemorated at the Alamein Memorial in Egypt. He was the son of Lawrence and Ethel Peterson of Vancouver. ***Peterson Esker*** (53 L/7), north of Beaver Hill Lake was named after him in 1995.

Peterson, Flying Officer **Sidney G.** of Winnipeg (J 14208). No. 78 Squadron. He died 25 May 1944 at the age of 21 and is commemorated at Jonkerbos War Cemetery in Holland. He was the son of Lawrence A. and Ethel Peterson of Vancouver. ***Peterson Peninsula*** (53 K/14) in Kenyon Lake was named after him in 1995.

Pethybridge, Sergeant **William J. "Jack"** of Elm Grove (R 86320). No. 405 Squadron. He died 9 June 1942 at the age of 25 and is commemorated at Rheinberg War Cemetery in Germany. He was the son of E. J. and Alice Pethybridge of Carman. His brother writes (4 March 1997):

Born in Carman, Manitoba on May 28, 1917, he took his formal schooling at Lord Wolseley School in East Kildonan and was one of their top athletes. After graduating, he assisted at many farms in rural Manitoba until his enlistment. He took his basic training at Portage la Prairie and Regina where he received his LAC classification. Then stationed at St. Eugene, Ontario and Moncton, New Brunswick, he graduated as Sergeant-Pilot on August 20, 1941. He went to England in September, 1941 and was stationed at Welles near London. Out of here, he flew Wellington bombers. Later, he was transferred to the Midlands and flew Halifax bombers with the 405 Pathfinder Squadron. He was shot down over Cologne on a night bombing raid.

Pethybridge Lake (63 K/16), north of Reed Lake was named after him in 1973.

Petrie, Pilot Officer **David R.** of Winnipeg (C 26583). No. 1 Air Observers School, RCAF. He died 5 October 1943 at the age of 20 and is commemorated at St. James Cemetery in Winnipeg. He was the son of Archibald and Sophie I. Petrie of St. James. Pilot Officer Petrie was a fifth-year honours student at the University of Manitoba and had been awarded the Gold Medal by the Faculty of Science. A newspaper account revealed that:

Nine fliers of No. 1 Central Navigation School, Rivers, Manitoba were killed when two Anson planes collided in mid-air and crashed at approximately 10:50 PM Tuesday, one mile north of the station's airdrome, No. 2 Training Command, RCAF announced Wednesday. All occupants of both aircraft were killed in the accident, one of the worst that has occurred at a Canadian air school. The fliers were engaged on a night navigation exercise, air force authorities explained. Names of the dead fliers are withheld pending notification of next-of-kin (*Winnipeg Free Press* 6 October 1943).

Petrie Lake (64 P/10), east of Nejanilini Lake was named after him in 1974.

Petrow, Private **Maurice M.** of St. Boniface (H 1089). 1st Canadian Parachute Battalion. He died 2 February 1945 at the age of 21 and is commemorated at Venray War Cemetery in Holland. He was the son of John and Nattie Petrow of St. Boniface. ***Petrow Lake*** (64 N/12), southeast of Kasba Lake was named after him in 1972.

Pfeffer, Flying Officer **Francis A.** of Winnipeg (J 19700). No. 117 Squadron. He died 27 March 1944 at the age of 21 and is commemorated at the Singapore Memorial. ***Pfeffer Lake*** (64 J/11), west of Tadoule Lake was named after him in 1975.

Phelps, Warrant Officer 2 **Cephas Joseph** of Austin (R 86344). No. 221 Squadron. He died 4 April 1943 at the age of 20 and is commemorated at the Malta Memorial. ***Phelps Lak***e (64 P/13), north of Nejanilini Lake was named after him in 1974.

Phelps, Warrant Officer 1 **John S.** of Minnedosa (R 80093). No. 2 Air Delivery Unit. He died 9 April 1943 at the age of 23 and is commemorated at the Alamein Memorial in Egypt. He was the son of Mr. and Mrs. G. W. Phelps of Winnipeg. ***Phelps Bay*** (54 D/2) in Kettle Lake was named after him in 1992.

Philip, Private **Albert D.** of Scotland Farm (H 105699). South Saskatchewan Regiment. He died 28 August 1944 at the age of 32 and is commemorated at Bretteville-sur-Laize Canadian War Cemetery in Calvados, France. He was the son of Alexander and Helen A. Philip of Old Meldrum, Aberdeenshire, Scotland. ***Philip Hill*** (64 A/5), east of Baldock Lake was named after him in 1995.

Phillips, Flying Officer **Albert Thomas** of Winnipeg (J 42806). No. 12 Service Flying Training School. He died 9 March 1945 at the age of 28 and is commemorated at Old Kildonan Presbyterian Cemetery in Winnipeg. He was the son of Albert G. and Florence M. Phillips of Winnipeg and was survived by his wife Isabel J. Phillips of Winnipeg and their daughter. She recalls (15 October 2001):

> My Dad's name was Tom Phillips and he died when I was 18 months old. He was an instructor at the Commonwealth Air School in Brandon. I don't know why his plane went down, only that weather was very bad that day and he was killed. He loved to hunt and fish and canoe. He was a good photographer and an artist and a musician. People have told me that he was very intelligent and tons of fun. So I have his wings, his medals, the flag from his coffin that was given to my Grandma and a few pictures. I think I would have loved him.

Thomas Phillips Lake (53 L/8), south of Murray Lake was named after him in 1995.

Phillips, Leading Stoker **Caswell Ivan** of Winnipeg (V 51352). HMCS *Uganda*. He died 2 April 1945 at the age of 21 and is commemorated at the Halifax Memorial. He was the son of Caswell W. and Mary F. Phillips of St. James. His sister recalls (27 November 2001):

> Ivan was the third youngest in a family of five. Both our parents died in 1937 leaving our oldest sister, Merle, just 18 years old at the time, to bring up her younger sisters and brothers. These were tough times but we all received good educations and had some wonderful times. My brother Ivan helped to put me through school and his sister Neata through three years of nursing training. He was a very caring, fun loving person. He was always on the Honour Roll throughout his school years.
>
> Prior to joining the Navy, Ivan lived in St. James and graduated from high school there. He was employed by the CPR at the time of his enlistment. Ivan was posted to the HMCS *Uganda* which was somewhere off the coast of Japan when he passed away from natural causes. He was the first RCN volunteer to die in the Pacific theatre. He was buried at sea with full military honours.

Phillips Peninsula (63 N/2) on Hutchinson Lake was named after him in 1995.

Phillips, Pilot Officer **Cecil** of Myrtle (J 89468). No. 433 Squadron. He died 30 January 1944 at the age of 26 and is commemorated at the Berlin 1939 - 1945 War Cemetery in Brandenburg, Germany. ***Phillips Island*** (64 J/9) in Tadoule Lake was named after him in 1975.

Phillips, Quarter Master Sergeant (Warrant Officer 2) **Donald O.** of Winnipeg (P 35051). Royal Canadian Ordnance Corps. He was aboard the SS *Nerissa*, the only ship torpedoed while carrying Canadian troops to the United Kingdom. Quarter Master Sergeant Phillips died 1 May 1941 at the age of 25 and is commemorated at the Halifax Memorial. He was the son of Octavius and Mary A. Phillips of Toronto and was survived by his wife Olga M. Phillips of Toronto. ***Phillips Rapids*** (53 K/15) in the Stull River was named after him in 1995.

Phillips, Lieutenant **Ivan A. C. "Pip"** of Winnipeg. Essex Scottish Regiment. He died 8 March 1945 at the age of 27 and is commemorated at the Groesbeek Canadian War Cemetery in Holland. He was the son of Walter J. and Gladys Phillips and was survived by his wife Beatrice A. M. "Nancy" Phillips (née Taylor) of Moose Jaw, Saskatchewan and their three year-old son. The son of noted landscape artist W. J. Phillips, Lieutenant Phillips hoped to become a museum curator after the war. His wife reports that (19 May 1998):

> He was a member of All Saints Anglican Church. He also went through the ranks of the Boy Scouts to become a Scout Leader. He served in this capacity in Toronto also. Ivan enlisted in the Cameron Highlanders of Winnipeg. Later he was commissioned. He was adjutant at Shilo, an Acting Major overseas, but reverted to Lieutenant when he joined the Essex Scottish for the Battle of the Rhine.

She adds (23 November 2001):

> He had married Beatrice Taylor in All Saint's Church on September 18, 1940. Ivan enlisted in the Cameron Highlanders and soon became a Lance Corporal. By the time their son Walter David Arthur was born, on July 5, 1942, he had been commissioned as a Lieutenant. David was just walking when Ivan went overseas. He was attached to the Essex Scottish when they had lost so many of their officers in battle.

Phillips Esker (53 N/11), northeast of Whitefish Lake was named after him in 1995.

Phillips, Private **James E.** of Teulon (H 20702). Queen's Own Cameron Highlanders. He died 30 October 1942 and is commemorated at Brookwood Military Cemetery in Surrey, England. He was survived by his wife Edith Phillips of Winnipeg and their children. ***Phillips Bay*** (64 B/6) in the Rat River was named after him in 1983.

Phillips, Ordinary Seaman **James G.** of Norwood (V 64954). HMCS *Shawinigan*. The *Shawinigan* was torpedoed and sunk by U-1228 while on independent anti-submarine patrol in the Cabot Strait; all hands were lost. Ordinary Seaman Phillips died 24 November 1944 at the age of 20 and is commemorated at the Halifax Memorial. He was the son of Arthur W. and Lily Phillips of Winnipeg. A local newspaper reported that:

> OS Phillips was educated at Wellington and Greenway schools and was employed by the Western Glove Company before enlisting in June, 1943. He trained at HMCS *Chippawa* and HMCS *Cornwallis*, Halifax. His father ... and a brother serving with the RCOC are in Vancouver. Two sisters, Dorothy and Shirley are at home in Norwood (*The Winnipeg Tribune* 7 December 1944).

Phillips Creek (64 J/4), which flows southwest into Morand Lake was named after him in 1995.

Phillips, Ordinary Seaman **Ronald K.** of Transcona (V 64486). HMCS *Valleyfield*. The *Valleyfield* was torpedoed and sunk by U-548 50 miles south of Cape Race, Newfoundland; 125 of her ship's company were lost. Ordinary Seaman Phillips died 7 May 1944 at the age of 18 and is commemorated at the Halifax Memorial. He was the son of Samuel H. and Mabel M. Phillips of Transcona. Phillips Point (64 K/1) in Big Flat Lake was named after him in 1989.

Piasta, Private **Henry** of Rossburn (H 77410). Winnipeg Grenadiers. He died 22 December 1941 and is commemorated at the Sai Wan War Cemetery in Hong Kong. ***Piasta Lake*** (62 N/15), southeast of Swan River was named after him in 1973.

Picciano, Warrant Officer 1 **Raymond D.** of Winnipeg (R 140622). No. 214 Squadron. He died 6 November 1944 at the age of 20 and is commemorated at the Reichswald Forest War Cemetery in Germany. He was the son of Mr. and Mrs. Patrick Picciano of Winnipeg. His sister recalls (4 December 1997):

> Raymond had a fine personality. He was our jokester – could always put a smile on our faces. He went to Earl Grey School, then Kelvin High School. He played hockey [at] school and any other time he could. He went into the service right from school. He loved Strauss waltzes.

Picciano Lake (64 I/8), northeast of North Knife Lake was named after him in 1974.

Pickersgill, Captain **Frank H. D.** of Ashern (9992). Special Operations Executive, Canadian Intelligence Corps, Legion d'Honneur. He died 14 September 1944 at the age of 29 and is commemorated at the Groesbeek Memorial in Holland. He was the son of Frank A. and Sara C. Pickersgill (née Smith) of Vancouver. Together with his associate, Captain J. Kenneth Macalister from Toronto, Pickersgill was assigned to help organize the resistance in a particular part of France. They parachuted behind enemy lines the night of 15 June 1943, but unbeknownst to them, the resistance had been compromised and they were captured by the Gestapo. Pickersgill and Macalister were evacuated from Paris to Buchenwald in 1944, where they were executed. In April, 1945, the Canadian Ambassador to France, Georges Vanier, travelled to Buchenwald to investigate the fate of Canadians who had been taken there. He wrote in part (27 April 1945):

> The list [Macalister, Sabourin and Pickersgill] purported to be a record of the arrivals on the 27th August, 1944. The names were of men who had been doing special work, for example, the transmission of clandestine messages after having been parachuted, etc. They were known as the Robert Benoist group. I did not find any list which indicated that these men had been executed but I was told that the "X" opposite each of the above three names afforded proof of such execution. As a matter of fact, the records are most incomplete, many of them were either taken away or destroyed before the camp was liberated. I was assured, however, by a Captain Simms, sent by SOE [Special Operations Executive] to investigate, that there could be no doubt that these men had been executed. There were a few names (but not of Canadians) on the list, opposite which no "X" appeared and about which there is some doubt.
>
> I found an ex-prisoner who was able to give me some information. His name is Richard Rendl, an Austrian, whose permanent address is Sobieskigasse 9, Vienna IX; present address - Buchenwald Camp. He saw the three Canadians arrive at the camp. They were hand-cuffed and in civilian clothes. They were given other civilian clothes later but not the usual grey striped clothes of other prisoners. Rendl was quite sure that the three had been executed. He did not remember the exact date. They had been in Block No. 17 which was called the Quarantine Block. It was normal for them to be housed there because they were new arrivals and all newcomers were taken there. He saw them quite often up to and including the evening before they were executed. They were always in good humour, apparently not suspecting for a moment that they would be killed.
>
> Rendl reported that allied bombs fell in the camp towards the end of August (there was a factory nearby in which some of the prisoners worked). A few days later he heard Frank Pickersgill joking and wishing to wager a thousand pounds that they would all be home by Christmas.

Camp survivor Bernard Guillot wrote to Frank's brother Jack in 1946:

> I suggest that it wouldn't be a good idea to say anything to your Mother about the exact details of his execution, for a mother shouldn't know about such sufferings of her son. But I do want you, his brother, to understand what went on right to the end. The special report I've read says this: "The prisoners were brought into a basement of the crematorium on the night of September 11th. There they were beaten atrociously by a half dozen SS. They were then hanged on butcher hooks that had been cemented into the walls, until death came to them. Their bodies were immediately cremated in the furnaces." This is the sad truth, and the record can be verified (in Ford 1978).

Reportedly, Pickergill's and Macalister's last words were: "Long live France, long live England, long live Canada." Wing Commander Forest Yeo-Thomas, another SOE operative was a senior Allied officer at Buchenwald. Of Pickersgill he said (1951):

> Frank Pickersgill was a man who knew how to live and how to die. You don't come across many of them who can do both quite so well. You should not forget him in Canada.

Pickersgill Lake (53 M/11), southeast of Ransom Lake was named after him in 1996.

Pidlaski, Ordinary Seaman **Nicholas** of Winnipeg (V 41014). HMCS *St. Croix*. The *St. Croix* was torpedoed and sunk by U-305 south of Iceland while escorting Convoy ON.202. Five officers and 76 men were rescued by HMS *Itchen*, but only one of these survived the loss of the *Itchen* two days later. See VanSickle, Ordinary Seaman Harold A. for additional information. Ordinary Seaman Pidlaski died 20 September 1943 at the age of 28 and is commemorated at the Halifax Memorial. He was the son of Andrew and Mary Pidlaski of Winnipeg. His brother reports that this graduate of Beaver, Lord Selkirk and St. John's Technical schools was a calligrapher and an avid golfer. He had been employed at Sherwin Williams Paint when he enlisted. ***Pidlaski Lake*** (64 G/14), east of Big Sand Lake was named after him in 1963.

Piedalue, Lance Corporal **Ralph** of St. Boniface (H 43097). North Nova Scotia Highlanders. He died 16 October 1944 and is commemorated at the Adegem Canadian War Cemetery in Belgium. ***Piedalue Lake*** (64 K/13), north of Lac Brochet was named after him in 1972.

Pieper, Trooper **John W.** of Gretna (H 77722). 12th Manitoba Dragoons. He died 5 September 1944 at the age of 21 and is commemorated at the Calais Canadian War Cemetery in France. He was the son of Mr. and Mrs. C. A. Pieper of Plum Coulee. His sister recalls (15 May 1995):

> Jack was a very good-natured "happy go lucky" fellow – very good to his mother and very close to his twin sister. His hobbies were woodworking, helping farmers around the countryside, collecting and labelling pictures of Manitoba's wildflowers.

She adds (16 October 2001):

> I remember when he had his leave before going overseas and he spent some time teaching me how to polish shoes properly – the way he did it in the army. Then he paid me to polish his. It was a terrible day for all of us when the telegram arrived. He had a very charismatic personality and we all missed him terribly. When he was killed, he had been shot out of three armoured cars and got it in the fourth. He was on reconnaissance looking for new enemy positions and was surrounded by German Panzer divisions. They had fought through Caen all the way to Belgium and then were pushed back to Caen Canal when he was killed.

In a letter home he wrote:

> ... I have written a letter to Wynne and told her what I thought about everything concerning she and I and asked her to call it off because I thought it a no go. I told her I wanted it that way. I must be a coward because I'm scared to get married for fear I won't make the grade and anyway, I'm in no position to get married. I haven't seen many French homes over here as yet. I haven't seen so much destruction in my life as I've seen in one day in Normandy! (n.d.).

After the war, the Town Council of Ostend, Belgium renamed one of its streets Manitoba Avenue in honour of the 12th Manitoba Dragoons as the city was liberated by them 8 September 1944. ***Pieper Lake*** (64 N/3), southwest of Nueltin Lake was named after Trooper John Pieper in 1972.

Piercy, Flying Officer **James Wallace** of Selkirk (J 47376). No. 356 Squadron. He died 27 May 1945 at the age of 22 and is commemorated at the Singapore Memorial. He was survived by his wife Frances Piercy of Winnipeg and their son Roy Wallace. His wife recalls (22 November 2001):

> Wally joined up in 1939 along with his four brothers and was shot down over Burma on what was scheduled to be his final mission. Previously, Wally had worked in the Sherridon and Gods Lake mines.

Piercy Island (64 C/8) in Granville Lake was named after him in 1995.

Piercy, Flight Sergeant **Reginald Frank** of Rivers (R 253010). No. 429 Squadron. He died 25 February 1945 at the age of 20 and is commemorated at the Runnymede Memorial in Surrey, England. ***Piercy Lake*** (64 P/12), east of Nejanilini Lake was named after him in 1974.

Pildrem, Flying Officer **Robert A.** of Winnipeg (J 17738). No. 408 Squadron. He died 29 December 1943 at the age of 30 and is commemorated at the Reichswald Forest War Cemetery in Germany. He was the son of Alexander S. and Elizabeth M. Pildrem of Winnipeg. ***Pildrem Lake*** (64 O/7), southeast of Nueltin Lake was named after him in 1975.

Pilote, Lance Corporal **Joseph Donat** of The Pas (H 41436). Royal Winnipeg Rifles. He died 4 July 1944 at the age of 30 and is commemorated at Beny-sur-Mer Canadian War Cemetery in Calvados, France. He was survived by his foster parents Joseph H. and Florence Roy of Dauphin. ***Pilote Lake*** (64 C/9), southeast of Reindeer Lake was named after him in 1973.

Pincock, Warrant Officer 1 **Hugh** of Winnipeg (R 86428). No. 407 Squadron. He died 12 September 1943 at the age of 22 and is commemorated at Heanton Punchardon (St. Augustine) Churchyard in Devon, England. He was the son of Hugh C. M. and Ann G. Pincock of Winnipeg. ***Pincock Lake*** (64 P/3), southeast of Nejanilini Lake was named after him in 1978.

Piniak, Corporal **William** of Winnipeg (H 26400). Calgary Tank Regiment. He died 8 July 1944 at the age of 26 and is commemorated at Foiano Della Chiana War Cemetery in Italy. He was the son of Nicholas and Mary Piniak of Winnipeg. His cousin writes (23 January 1995):

> He attended his first venture in school work at a private Catholic school called St. Nicholas School run by Catholic nuns. The school's name was changed to Immaculate Heart of Mary School [at] 650 Flora Avenue. He stayed there until completion of Grade 5. Then he transferred to King Edward School for junior high education. From there, he was transferred to Isaac Newton Senior High to complete his education with graduation in 1935.
>
> William Piniak was a very good student and took great pride in achieving a high standard in his school marks. He was not a great athlete, but was very knowledgeable in baseball and hockey statistics. [He] joined a tank regiment in Winnipeg after Canada declared war on Germany in September, 1939. Being about two years younger, I entered the military in 1942 and completed my service with the Royal Winnipeg Rifles.

Piniak Lake (64 J/4), north of Big Sand Lake was named after him in 1975.

Pink, Sergeant **John Edward** of Winnipeg (R 4172A). No. 1 Air Observers School. He died 6 January 1941 at the age of 21 and is commemorated at Elmwood Cemetery in Winnipeg. He was the son of Edward T. and Frances Pink of Winnipeg. His sister recalls (14 April 1998):

> Eddie was born in Winnipeg on April 24, 1919. He lived in Fort Rouge until he joined the air force. He graduated from Kelvin High School, then worked for a time in the Canadian National Railway. He was interested in swimming and boating, particularly in the summer – he belonged to the Winnipeg Canoe Club. He enjoyed skiing in the winter and was a member of the DeMolay Lodge.

Pink Lake (64 G/16), southeast of Chipewyan Lake was named after him in 1995.

Pipe, Corporal **Oliver R.** of Dauphin (M 60875). Royal Canadian Regiment. He died 4 January 1946 and is commemorated at Brookwood Military Cemetery in Surrey, England. ***Pipe Bay*** (64 G/5) in Big Sand Lake was named after him in 1996.

Piper, Private **Togo** of Sprague (H 62811). Canadian Forestry Corps. He died 6 May 1943 at the age of 39 and is commemorated at Brookwood Military Cemetery in Surrey, England. He was the son of William A. and Ada J. Piper and was survived by his wife Julia Piper of Sprague, Manitoba. ***Piper Lake*** (63 N/12), south of Sisipuk Lake was named after him in 1995.

Pitkethly, Flying Officer **Alexander** of Winnipeg (J 14205). No. 424 Squadron. He died 6 September 1943 at the age of 31 and is commemorated at Salerno War Cemetery, Italy. He was the son of Alexander and Margaret Pitkethly of Winnipeg. His sister recalls (15 April 1995):

He was born December 9th, 1911 in Leith, Edinburgh, Scotland and our family came to Canada in May, 1924. He left school early and got a job with the insurance firm of Osler, Hammond and Nanton. He enlisted in September, 1941 and trained at Saskatoon, receiving his navigator's wings at Portage la Prairie in September, 1942. Two months later, he arrived overseas as a navigator with No. 424 Wellington Squadron of the Royal Canadian Air Force. He was on about his third mission when his plane was shot down and [he] was buried in the cemetery in Salerno. My son was over there many years ago and visited the grave site. His death was devastating as we were such a close family and he was such a wonderful person.

Recently, the "Flying Officer Alex Pitkethly Memorial RCAF Fund" was established by a former co-worker and friend of Alex's. The fund ensures his memory will be kept alive for years to come, as revenue from this fund will support a wide variety of community projects. ***Pitkethly Lake*** (64 O/11), southeast of Nueltin Lake was named after him in 1975.

Pitt, Flight Sergeant **Ernest W.** of Winnipeg (R 116161). No. 1659 Heavy Conversion Unit, RCAF. He died 18 April 1943 at the age of 21 and is commemorated at Dishforth Cemetery in Yorkshire, England. He was the son of Ernest and Dora Pitt of Winnipeg. ***Pitt Lake*** (64 O/16), south of Baralzon Lake was named after him in 1975.

Platson, Pilot Officer **Paul** of Winnipeg (J 11600). No. 31 Operational Training Unit, RCAF. He died 22 July 1942 at the age of 27 and is commemorated at Elmwood Cemetery in Winnipeg. He was the son of John and Anna Platson of Winnipeg. ***Platson Lake*** (64 O/8), northeast of Munroe Lake was named after him in 1975.

Ploschansky, Private **Joseph** of Ethelbert (H 102937). Hastings and Prince Edward Regiment. He died 26 August 1944 and is commemorated at Montecchio War Cemetery in Italy. He was the son of John and Tessie Ploschansky of Flin Flon. ***Ploschansky Lake*** (64 P/1), southwest of Caribou Lake was named after him in 1974.

Plumbtree, Private **Milton C.** of The Pas (H 1017). Queen's Own Cameron Highlanders. He died 28 March 1945 at the age of 19 and is commemorated at the Groesbeek Canadian War Cemetery in Holland. He was the son of Joseph B. and Mabel A. Plumbtree of Parry Sound, Ontario. ***Plumbtree Lake*** (64 C/5), south of Laurie Lake was named after him in 1973.

Podborochinski, Sergeant **Edmund** of Arborg (R 186875). No. 12 Squadron. He died 29 December 1943 at the age of 19 and is commemorated at Rheinberg War Cemetery in Germany. He was the son of Petro and Mary Podborochinski of Arborg, Manitoba. ***Podborochinski Lake*** (64 I/4), west of North Knife Lake was named after him and his brother Private Marion Podborochinski (next entry) in 1974.

Podborochinski, Private **Marion** of Arborg (H 42388). Queen's Own Cameron Highlanders. He died 2 October 1944 and is commemorated at Bergen-op-Zoom Canadian War Cemetery in Holland. He was the son of Petro and Mary Podborochinski of Arborg, Manitoba. ***Podborochinski Lake*** (64 I/4), west of North Knife Lake was named after him and his brother Sergeant Edmund Podborochinski (previous entry) in 1974.

Podruski, Private **Thomas P.** of Erickson (L 107851). South Saskatchewan Regiment. He died 28 August 1944 at the age of 21 and is commemorated at Bretteville-sur-Laize Canadian War Cemetery in Calvados, France. He was the son of the late Nicholas and Frances Podruski of Erickson, Manitoba. ***Podruski Lake*** (63 K/16), north of Reed Lake was named after him in 1973.

Pogue, Lance Corporal **David J.** of Winnipeg (H 67326). Lanark and Renfrew Scottish Regiment. He died 2 September 1944 at the age of 23 and is commemorated at Gradara War Cemetery in Italy. He was the son of David and Martha Pogue of Toronto. ***Pogue Lake*** (52 L/6), east of Lac du Bonnet was named after him in 1973.

Poho, Corporal **William** of Winnipeg (H 9437). Royal Winnipeg Rifles. He died 8 June 1944 and is commemorated at Beny-sur-Mer Canadian War Cemetery in Calvados, France. ***Poho Lake*** (64 O/14), east of Nueltin Lake was named after him in 1995.

Polanski, Trooper **Anthony** of Winnipeg (H 63928). Royal Canadian Armoured Corps. He died 6 September 1943 at the age of 48 and is commemorated at Holy Ghost Cemetery in Winnipeg. He was the son of Mikolaj and Katarzyna Polanski of Bialozurka, Krzemieniec, Poland and was survived by his wife Sophie Polanski of Winnipeg. ***Polanski Lake*** (64 I/1), northeast of Etawney Lake was named after him in 1974.

Polec, Corporal **Tadeusz L.** of Winnipeg (R 56918). No. 9 Construction and Maintenance Unit, RCAF. He was lost at sea (while travelling on the *B. C. Star*) 24 July 1943. He was 25 years of age and is commemorated at the Ottawa Memorial. He was the son of Casimir and Eugenia Polec of Winnipeg. ***Polec Lake*** (64 J/12), west of Tadoule Lake was named after him in 1975.

Polis, Gunner **Stanley J.** of Winnipeg (A 59597). Royal Canadian Artillery. He died 20 September 1941 at the age of 26 and is commemorated at Brookwood Military Cemetery in Surrey, England. He was the son of Joseph and Sofia Polis of Winnipeg and was survived by his wife Jean Polis (née Okopski). His niece recalls (30 November 2001):

Stanley and Jean met at a local dance where they were introduced by friends. Stanley had a good sense of humour and was the life of a party. He was well liked. During the war, Jean worked as an ammunition bench inspector in Winnipeg. Stanley died 1941 in central London near Custom House Station. He was survived by a brother Steven and two sisters Anne and Bernice.

Polis Lake (64 I/10), north of North Knife Lake was named after him in 1974.

Pollock, Pilot Officer **Albert L.** of McConnell (J 91136). No. 12 Squadron. He died 24 June 1944 at the age of 21 and is commemorated at the Runnymede Memorial in Surrey, England. He was the son of Andrew T. and Rose A. Pollock (née Armson) of McConnell, Manitoba and was the brother of Sergeant James A. Pollock (next entry). His brother recalls (15 October 2001):

Albert was my brother, four and a half years younger than myself. He took a great interest in sports and music. He played the violin, piano and piano accordion. He played hockey and baseball. He arrived overseas November, 1943 and we spent leave together as often as we could. Our brother Jim had been killed in action January, 1943 and many times we wished the three of us could have been together. I had met all the members of his crew and there were no survivors.

Pollock Lake (64 P/16), north of Caribou Lake was named after him in 1974.

Pollock, Sergeant **James A.** of McConnell (R 108564). No. 426 Squadron. He died 14 January 1943 at the age of 27 and is commemorated at the Runnymede Memorial in Surrey, England. He was the son of Andrew T. and Rose A. Pollock of McConnell, Manitoba and was the brother of Pilot Officer Albert L. Pollock (previous entry). His brother writes (15 October 2001):

Jim was my brother, three years older than I am. We will always remember what a gentleman he was and very kind to all members of our family. I had been in England five months before he arrived overseas. Every chance we got when we were on leave we spent together. Our last leave was in London. I remember saying goodbye to him as he left to return to his squadron. I did not know then that would be the last time I would see him.

Pollock Island (54 M/11) in Haywood Lake was named after him in 1984.

Pollon, Private **Douglas** of Clanwilliam (H 18275). Essex Scottish Regiment. He died 24 February 1945 at the age of 20 and is commemorated at the Groesbeek Canadian War Cemetery in Holland. He was the son of Private Arthur R. and Bertha Pollon of Clanwilliam, Manitoba. ***Pollen Island*** (64 B/12) in the Churchill River was named after him in 1981.

Pollon, Warrant Officer 2 **Ernest S.** of Dauphin (R 124287). No. 90 Squadron. He died 26 May 1943 at the age of 31 and is commemorated at the Runnymede Memorial in Surrey, England. He was survived by his mother Mabel Pollon of Dauphin. ***Pollon Bay*** (53 E/14) in Begg Lake was named after him in 1995.

Pollon, Sergeant **Joseph R.** of Minnesdosa (R 250815). No. 33 Operational Training Unit, RCAF. He died 28 May 1944 at the age of 17 and is commemorated at Stonefall Cemetery in Yorkshire, England. He was the son of Andrew and Lillian M. Pollon of Bethel, Manitoba. ***Pollon Lake*** (64 P/15), northeast of Nejanilini Lake was named after him in 1974.

Polnuk, Private **Adam E.** of Winnipeg (H 800003). Princess Patricia's Canadian Light Infantry. He died 31 May 1951 and is commemorated at the United Nations Cemetery in Pusan, South Korea. ***Polnuk Lake*** (53 K/10), south of Margaret Lake was named after this Korean War casualty in 1998.

Pontius, Private **Ira W.** of Moosehorn (H 6659). Winnipeg Grenadiers. He died 19 December 1941 at the age of 22 and is commemorated at the Sai Wan Memorial in Hong Kong. He was the son of Chester N. and Opal I. Pontius of Moosehorn, Manitoba. ***Pontius Lake*** (64 B/5), east of Granville Lake was named after him in 1975.

Pool, Flight Lieutenant **George Robert** of Edrans (J 16530). No. 431 Squadron, Distinguished Flying Cross.

As navigator, this officer has taken part in attacks on Berlin, Bremen, Duisburg and Cologne. In the low-level attack on Flensburg, extremely heavy anti-aircraft opposition was met. In the face of the enemy, Pilot Officer Pool invariably has displayed coolness and courage of a high order (DFC Citation 1943).

He died 6 January 1945 at the age of 25 and is commemorated at the Runnymede Memorial in Surrey, England. He was survived by his mother Isabelle Pool and by his wife Bernice Pool. According to his nephew (15 November 2001):

He enlisted with the RCAF in Winnipeg in February, 1941 and trained as a navigator. On his first tour of duty, he received the DFC for his bravery and quick thinking after being wounded on a night bombing mission over Germany. During the return flight to England, their plane was hit and Bob blacked out. When he regained consciousness, he realized that they were headed back over enemy territory when he noticed that the moon was suddenly on the wrong side of the plane. He was credited with the safe return of the crew as they were able to abandon the damaged bomber and parachute to safety over England. During his second tour of duty in 1944/45, his Lancaster bomber KB821 went missing during a night attack on Hanover, Germany, along with the crew of six.

Pool Lake (64 C/11), southwest of Lynn Lake was named after him in 1950.

Poole, Sapper **Brian T.** of Winnipeg (H 13209). Royal Canadian Engineers. He died 18 February 1941 at the age of 41 and is commemorated at Brookwood Military Cemetery in Surrey, England. He was the son of Thomas E. and Margaret Poole. ***Poole Lake*** (64 H/3), west of Settee Lake was named after him in 1995.

Poole, Private **James C.** of Winnipeg (H 195637). Highland Light Infantry. He died 20 September 1944 and is commemorated at the Calais Canadian War Cemetery in France. ***Poole Bay*** (64 P/5) in Little Duck Lake was named after him in 1995.

Poole, Flying Officer **Maxwell B.** of Winnipeg (J 6218). No. 1 Bombing and Gunnery School, RCAF. He died 18 August 1942 at the age of 30 and is commemorated at Elmwood Cemetery in Winnipeg. He was the son of George and Mabel Poole of Winnipeg and was survived by his wife Mary E. Poole of Toronto. ***Poole Island*** (64 C/12) in Dunphy Lakes was named after him in 1995.

Pooles, Telegraphist **Donald H.** of Winnipeg (V 9834). HMCS *Ottawa*. The *Ottawa* was escorting Convoy ON.127 in the North Atlantic when it was struck by two torpedoes from U-91; 114 of her ship's company were lost. Telegraphist Pooles died 13 September 1942 at the age of 24 and is commemorated at the Halifax Memorial. He was the son of William C. and Charlotte E. Pooles of Winnipeg and was survived by his wife Sarah C. Pooles of Winnipeg. She remembers (20 November 2001) him as:

"... a quiet young man with a great sense of humour. He was very well liked by all who knew him. He was very fond of music and had quite a collection of semi-classical records which was his hobby."

Pooles Lake (64 N/13), southeast of Kasba Lake was named after him in 1972.

Popaden, Lance Corporal **Steven** of Winnipegosis (H 41891). Royal Winnipeg Rifles. He died 5 July 1944 at the age of 27 and is commemorated at Beny-sur-Mer Canadian War Cemetery in Calvados, France. He was the son of Thomas and Mary Popaden of Winnipegosis, Manitoba. ***Popaden Lake*** (64 O/10), northwest of Nejanilini Lake was named after him in 1973.

Pope, Flight Sergeant **William J.** of Winnipeg (R 100460). No. 20 Operational Training Unit, RCAF. He died 9 November 1942 at the age of 24 and is commemorated at the Runnymede Memorial in Surrey, England. He was the son of William A. and Elizabeth D. Pope of New Westminster, British Columbia. ***Pope Lake*** (64 J/13), northwest of Tadoule Lake was named after him in 1975.

Popplestone, Flight Sergeant **William Maurice** of Pilot Mound (R 80033). No. 114 Squadron. He died 26 March 1942 at the age of 22 and is commemorated at Harlingen General Cemetery in Holland. He was survived by his mother, Mrs. Annie Wallace of Pilot Mound, Manitoba and brothers Lloyd, Gerald and Ross of Peace River, Alberta. His niece writes (26 November 2001):

> Maurice started his schooling in the Floral District and attended high school at Pilot Mound. He continued his education at Minnedosa Collegiate and enlisted while in attendance there. His Air Force training was completed at Souris and he took his first solo flight in May of 1941. Maurice loved sports. He played ball and was a goal tender for the Pilot Mound hockey team. One of his favourite pastimes on the farm was decorating show horses. Maurice was a well liked, down to earth, community minded young man.

Popplestone Lake (64 O/6), southeast of Nueltin Lake was named after him in 1975.

Porteous, Private **Louis** of Winnipeg (H 9784). Royal Canadian Army Service Corps. He died 27 January 1946 at the age of 29 and is commemorated at Assumption Gardens in Winnipeg. He was the son of Mr. and Mrs. Charles J. Porteous of Winnipeg. ***Porteous Island*** (63 N/15) in the Churchill River was named after him in 1995.

Porteous, Gunner **William R.** of Ashern (H 66450). Royal Canadian Artillery. He died 27 November 1944 at the age of 21 and is commemorated at Coriano Ridge War Cemetery in Italy. He was the son of Thomas and Josephine Porteous of Ashern, Manitoba. ***Porteous Lake*** (64 N/16), west of Nueltin Lake was named after him in 1972.

Porter, Aircraftman 1 **Albert E.** of Winnipeg (R 56893). No. 1 Central Flying School. He died 21 September 1940 at the age of 37 and is commemorated at Morris Cemetery. He was the son of Edward and Jane Porter of Winnipeg and was survived by his wife Kathleen Porter of Morris, Manitoba. ***Porter Lake*** (64 N/11), southeast of Kasba Lake was named after him in 1972.

Porter, Private **Allan L.** of Stonewall (R 152563). No. 419 Squadron. He died 26 July 1943 at the age of 20 and is commemorated at the Reichswald Forest War Cemetery in Germany. ***Porter Island*** (64 O/15) in Jenkins Lake was named after him in 1995.

Porter, Rifleman **Joseph N.** of Camperville (H 41228). Royal Winnipeg Rifles. He died 9 June 1944 and is commemorated at Beny-sur-Mer Canadian War Cemetery in Calvados, France. He was the son of Mrs. Eulalie Porter of Camperville, Manitoba. ***Porter Point*** (64 N/6) in Fort Hall Lake was named after him in 1995.

Porter, Warrant Officer 2 **Reginald F. C.** of Winnipeg (R 714280). No. 69 Squadron. He died 21 April 1943 at the age of 25 and is commemorated at the Malta Memorial. He was survived by a wife in Winnipeg and his mother in Teulon. ***Porter Bay*** (64 F/4) in Reindeer Lake was named after him in 1995.

Porter, Pilot Officer **Russell Lyle** of Carman (J 86838). No. 433 Squadron. He died 15 June 1944 at the age of 21 and is commemorated at Valenciennes (St. Roch) Communal Cemetery, Nord, France. He was the son of Russell H. and Elsie Porter of Carman, Manitoba. ***Porter River*** (64 P/8), which flows northeast into Caribou Lake was named after him in 1985.

Post, Flight Sergeant **Ralph A.** of Bradwardine (R 86124). No. 106 Squadron. He died 19 May 1942 at the age of 21 and is commemorated at the Runnymede Memorial in Surrey, England. He was the son of Stanley and Charlotte Post (née Nesbitt) of Bradwardine, Manitoba. His cousin writes (9 May 1994):

> Ralph enlisted at Winnipeg on December 16, 1940. He graduated in September of 1941 from [the] flight school at Brandon. Ralph was the pilot of a non-operational flight on May 19, 1942 over Wales and the Irish Sea. When the aircraft did not arrive at the expected time, an air-sea rescue search was implemented, however, no trace could be found of the plane.

Post Lake (64 P/7), southeast of Nejanilini Lake was named after him in 1974.

Pott, Private **Norman A. H.** of Birch River (H 6888). Winnipeg Grenadiers. He died a prisoner of war 11 February 1944 at the age of 22 and is commemorated at the Yokohama War Cemetery in Japan. He was the son of Francis and Elizabeth Pott of Birch River. According to his brother (4 February 1997):

> ... he received his education in the Dominion City and Steel School districts and enlisted in 1941. [The] family was told he died in Hong Kong. A personal search for his gravesite was done by family, but no information was turned up. The family was then informed that the gravesite might be in Japan. Norman had hoped to return to Manitoba and continue farming. Prior to his joining the army, he had slowly been purchasing livestock to be able to start up his own farm upon his return.

Pott Lake (64 I/12), northwest of North Knife Lake was named after him in 1974.

Potten, Trooper **Edwin H.** of Swan River (H 100186). Lord Strathcona's Horse. He died 30 May 1944 at the age of 27 and is commemorated at the Cassino War Cemetery in Italy. In 1972, his niece visited the grave. He was the son of Percy A. and Emma Potten (née Vetters) of Swan River, Manitoba. His brother writes (16 April 1996):

> When Edwin was 10 years old, his father passed away. His mother then moved the young family to Swan River. When she remarried, they moved to a farm one mile west of Swan River where the children could farm and work in town. Edwin also worked at Halliday's Garage and general trucking.
>
> Edwin loved to dance. He was a kind and loving-natured man. He loved children and adored the elderly and was fond of animals. He and his brother Stan both joined the army in 1942. While both were at Camp

Borden, Stan was in a bad accident and was discharged. Edwin then went to England to complete his training. In 1943, [he] went over to Italy. He was a tank driver. His last letter home was May 16, 1944 when he talked of the fierce battles. On May 30, 1944 he was killed in his tank at Pontecorvo, Italy.

Potten Lake (63 K/16), west of Wekusko Lake was named after him in 1973. On 30 May 1995, 51 years after Trooper Potten was killed, family members and an Honour Guard from the Royal Canadian Legion in Snow Lake gathered to witness the unveiling of a plaque to officially name Potten Lake (*The Snow Lake News*, 8 June 1995 Issue).

Potter, Sergeant **Charles E.** of Underhill (R 68604). Royal Canadian Air Force. He died 16 October 1944 at the age of 43 and is commemorated at Riverside Cemetery in Hartney, Manitoba. He was the son of Charles J. and Elizabeth Potter of Underhill, Manitoba and was survived by his wife Elsie Potter of Brandon. ***Potter Island*** (53 E/16) in Island Lake was named after him in 1997.

Potter, Flying Officer **James K.** of Pilot Mound (J 10323). No. 422 Squadron. He died 19 December 1942 at the age of 26 and is commemorated at the Runnymede Memorial in Surrey, England. He was the son of Robert A. and Amanda G. Potter of Pilot Mound, Manitoba. His sister recalls (21 November 2001):

> Our brother Jim was born on E 1/2 18-4-11W in Louise Municipality March 24, 1916, the second oldest in a family of four boys and one girl. He grew up on the farm in the Floral District where he took his early schooling and then high school in Pilot Mound. He helped on the family farm in the Floral District and then at Wood Bay as well as working for neighbouring farmers. For a short time he was employed at the Cartwright Creamery.
>
> Jim was always an avid reader and received the nickname "Bookworm" from his brothers and sister. We had no radio, so often he would walk two miles to a neighbour's to listen to the hockey game on Saturday night.
>
> In October, 1939 Jim was accepted into the Faculty of Agriculture at the University of Manitoba. While there, he took basic training and enlisted after completion of his second year. He trained at Penhold, Alberta and graduated from Navigation School at Rivers in March, 1942. He was at Charlottetown, PEI and St. John, New Brunswick and left from Halifax March 20, 1942 to go overseas.
>
> Jim was stationed in Scotland (we never knew exactly where) for a time, then Lough Erne, Ireland for a few weeks, then back to Scotland as an instructor. He wasn't at the base at Lough Erne very long before he was sent back to Canada in October, 1942. He spent his leave visiting family before he and his crew flew an aircraft across the Atlantic to the War Front. Soon after getting back, 422 Squadron was moved to Oban, Scotland. He was issued a bicycle and rode around Oban and up the coast to Fort William. The last letter we received from him was dated six days before his death.

Shortly thereafter, his parents received a letter from Wing Commander W. Shey:

> James was greatly admired by his comrades in the Canadian Airforce and his quiet and thorough knowledge of his work won the greatest respect of all ranks in his own Service and brought about his rapid promotion (n.d.).

Potter Lake (64 G/4), northeast of Grandmother Lake was named after him in 1994.

Poulsen, Private **Aage L. P.** of Winnipeg (H 6495). Winnipeg Grenadiers. He died 19 December 1941 at the age of 35 and is commemorated at the Sai Wan Memorial in Hong Kong. He was the son of I. P. and Laura Poulsen of Aarhus, Denmark. ***Poulsen Lake*** (64 O/2), west of Munroe Lake was named after him in 1975.

Pound, Able Seaman **Francis J.** of Winnipeg (V 63538). HMCS *Regina*. The *Regina* was torpedoed and sunk by U-667 off Trevose Head, Cornwall; thirty of her ship's company were lost. Able Seaman Pound died 8 August 1944 at the age of 19 and is commemorated at the Halifax Memorial. He was the son of Francis C. and Violet L. Pound of Winnipeg. ***Pound Lake*** (64 N/14), west of Nueltin Lake was named after him in 1972.

Powell, Flight Sergeant **Laurence A.** of Killarney (R 172914). No. 166 Squadron. He died 4 February 1944 at the age of 19 and is commemorated at Killarney Cemetery. He was the son of Oscar D. and Sarah E. Powell of Killarney, Manitoba. His sister recalls (11 April 1995):

> Laurence was born on the family farm ... in 1924. When his father died in 1929, the family moved to Ninga and later to Killarney where Laurence received his education. Laurence was a happy, fun-loving boy who enjoyed sports and also playing the trombone in the Killarney Band. When he completed his Grade 11 in Killarney Collegiate, he went to work in an aircraft factory in Fort William. When he became 18 on March 29, 1942, he joined the air force and started training in Brandon. From there to Winnipeg and later to Lethbridge where he received his WAG (Wireless Air Gunner) Badge and rank of Sergeant. His Norseman aircraft crashed shortly after take-off at Port Alice, British Columbia.

Powell Bay (64 H/13) in Currie Lake was named after him in 1995.

Powell, Flight Sergeant **Lloyd C.** of Virden (R 59709). No. 419 Squadron. He died 16 January 1942 at the age of 28 and is commemorated at Brandesburton (St. Mary) Churchyard, Yorkshire, England. He was the only child of Leslie L. and Mary L. Powell of Virden, Manitoba. ***Powell Lake*** (64 J/16), north of Tadoule Lake was named after him in 1975.

Power, Sergeant **Arthur T.** of Virden (R 203617). No. 19 Elementary Flying Training School. He died 8 August 1944 at the age of 19 and is commemorated at Virden Cemetery. He was the son of Guy T. and Marjorie Power of Virden. ***Power Bay*** (64 N/11) in Kasmere Lake was named after him in 1989.

Power, Lieutenant **James J.** of Winnipeg. Carleton and York Regiment. He died 20 March 1944 at the age of 27 and is commemorated at the Moro River Canadian War Cemetery in Italy. He was the youngest child of James A. and Katherine Maude Power (née Hefferman) of Winnipeg. While on leave in England, he wrote to his family:

> Dear Mother and All: Friday morning, lovely bright and sunny out, and as I feel in the mood I am going to use my last Air Mail form and let you know the latest. Have had no mail for two weeks, but if it does not catch up with me by Saturday, I am going down to the Unit and see what the trouble is. However, I phoned down Monday, so it may be here today.
>
> I purchased another Victory Bond today. I imagine you will be receiving the last one I bought next month as it will be paid for by then. I was in to see the Paymaster this morning and I have increased my assigned pay by $15.00 so it will bring my assigned pay up to $50.00. He tells me it cannot take effect until December 1st. However, as long as you get it, that is the main thing. I have had to buy a lot of extra equipment lately as well as pay insurance on all my equipment, but I have now got it all cleaned up. I have also had my leave so I will increase my assigned pay again.

Am not very busy at present, but am having a very good rest. I am only working a few hours a day and so spend the rest on the time wandering all over the country. Gee, I do hope I get a chance to see Art. I met a very nice girl and her mother last weekend. The girl is an actress on the London Stage. However, the mother lives in the town where Ralph is stationed. In fact, several of the officers stay at her house. So I gave her Ralph's name and she is going to look him up. They seemed to be very nice people and the Daughter was a beaut. So maybe Ralph will not do so bad. The daughter is a friend of one of the officers here and came down to spend her holidays near him.

Never felt better in my life. England agrees with me and I still have not seen any great deal of rain here. In fact, I like the climate very much. Find it very hard to write a letter these days as I get nothing from home to reply to. However, I guess when they catch up with me I will be swamped. There is so much of interest that happens to us, but which we cannot write about. However, after it is all over we shall have some great stories to tell.

Hope everyone at home is OK and enjoying life 100%. Tell Mary that she is next on my list for a letter. I am having a devil of a time to get these forms so I have to make every one count. How are all the kids? And the dogs? Hope this finds you well. Take care of yourself this winter and do not work too hard. Regards to Frank, Roy and all the kids. Excuse the writing but I am doing this on a book. Love, Jimmy (15 October 1943).

In one of his last letters home he writes:

Greetings to Mary, Roy, Allan, Eileen and Jerry: Hello! It's a long time since I was last around 292 Oak Street so I thought I had better drop in for a few minutes. Hope this finds you all well, the weather not too severe and still spending the money you won at the races (what a hope). As for myself, I am fine and am able to enjoy life. That is, the life we have here. It's not much but it's the simple things that count.

Have seen quite a bit of this old world since I was last in the Peg and must say, one who hasn't seen it hasn't missed much with the exception of England and Italy. Have had no mail for several weeks, but am eagerly awaiting the day it arrives. Am with a good regiment at present, have a fine bunch of boys under me and they will follow me anyplace. As they have already proven.

I have been lousy, deloused and am lousy again. In fact, I sort of missed the little blighters when they left me at the cleansing depot. However, their cousins moved in so everybody is happy again (excuse me for a minute while I scratch).

Italy must be a beautiful country in peacetime (but it sure is having its face lifted). It is very mountainous and the roads are like corkscrews. Nearly every town is on a hill. At present, I am living in a slightly bomb-happy building. However, it is dry and warm. We can pick apples outside the door and yet, not very far away, we can see the snow-covered mountains. Have really had my fill of olives since hitting this country. You can buy a pound for a few pennies. Oranges, apples and nuts are also plentiful. We can get all the wine we wish. But except for a little with the odd meal, I care little for it. As for the war, well we're giving Jerry hell and winning it. Nuff said.

Hope everything in the Peg is not buried under ten feet of snow and the weather is above forty below. Come to think of it, I believe I will try and spend next winter at home. These warm countries are not what they are cracked up to be.

Well, guess that this is all there is for today. Remember me to all and give Jimmy (to hell with that Allan stuff) and Eileen a big kiss for me. Regards to Roy and tell him I'll have some really good jokes the next time we meet. Oceans of love and a kiss on every wave. PS. That's really a smash ending eh? I must use it on Hazel next letter, Jimmy (15 January 1944).

A newspaper account described his last mission:

The patrol leader's orders as his men went out into the dark were "11 of us are going out and 11 are coming back." Two hours later, as first light was creeping in from the Adriatic, 10 men returned, bringing with them the body of the 11th. The patrol leader, a lieutenant from Winnipeg, had been killed.

The Adriatic battlefront where Canadian soldiers are fighting is furrowed with gullies. On the German side of one of these gullies is a house the enemy uses as an advance post and it was to this house that 11 men from the Carleton and York Regiment went out into the night. They included Ptes. N. G. Grabowski, Winnipeg and J. Powell, Hammond, BC.

Five went to the rear door of the house, were challenged and fired into the doorway with a Bren gun. The officer and five others opened fire from the front. Then both parties threw grenades through the door and windows. There were eight or nine Germans in the house and, said Powell "we could hear them mumbling and groaning." The grenades and bullets had been effective.

Enemy rifle grenades, the only answering fire, began to "pop" from about 100 yards to the rear of the house and shrapnel from one of them killed the lieutenant. Remembering his words that all would come back, three of the men crawled to the house, recovered his body and carried it back to their company observation post (Amaron 1944).

Power Lake (64 K/12), south of Lac Brochet was named after him in 1972.

Powers, Private **Wilfred S. "Pet"** of Brandon (H 1891). Essex Scottish Regiment. He died 21 July 1944 at the age of 35 and is commemorated at Bretteville-sur-Laize Canadian War Cemetery in Calvados, France. He was the son of Samuel S. and Helen Powers and was survived by his wife Margaret Powers of Elphinstone, Manitoba. His sister-in-law recalls (24 October 2001):

According to word his wife received, he was wounded and died on the plane back to wherever the wounded were taken. "Pet" as he was called, was called up in January, 1943, going overseas the same year. He worked at Rumford's Laundry in Brandon which was his last place of work. As a young man, he was very active in hockey and baseball in Nesbitt, Manitoba where he was raised.

Powers Point (53 L/12) on Laidlaw Lake was named after him in 1995.

Powers, Warrant Officer 1 **William Charles** of Brandon (R 71499). No. 403 Squadron. He died 20 July 1944 in a German hospital in France from wounds sustained in the crash of his aircraft a year before. He was 23 years of age and is commemorated at St. Charles de Percy War Cemetery, Calvados, France. He was the only child of W. L. and Jean Powers of Brandon and the husband of Joan M. Powers of Kent, England. Mrs. Powers' story was highlighted in a New Zealand newspaper:

Auckland, New Zealand, August 17: Having lost two husbands, one a New Zealander, the other a Canadian, in the war, an attractive English girl of 23 has reached New Zealand to start life afresh with her two sons. She is blond Mrs. Joan Powers of the Isle of Sheppey, Kent, and her story is one of shattered romances, wartime hardship and youthful courage.

At the age of 18, Mrs. Powers entered the WAAFs and while developing combat films at an RAF station met Pilot Officer Graeme Fenton of Auckland – a fighter pilot attached to a squadron there. They were married in 1942 but less than a month later her husband was killed in an air crash. Mrs. Powers' elder son, Graeme Fenton, was born and she returned to her duties with the WAAFs.

In May, 1943, she married her first husband's close friend, Warrant Officer Powers, a fighter pilot in the same squadron, who came from Brandon, Manitoba. The two men used to work together and were inseparables.

But just after D-Day when Warrant Officer Powers was engaged in combat with a Messerschmitt over France, some stray ack-ack shot up his plane and he was killed. He was the father of her second son Gary Powers.

Now with the future of her sons to consider, Mrs. Powers has accepted an invitation from her father-in-law B. C. Fenton of Auckland to start a new life in a new land free from blitzes, ruins and food shortages (n.d.).

Powers Island (64 N/5) in Snyder Lake was named after him in 1995.

Poyner, Stoker **Albert A.** of Souris (2191). HMCS *Chippawa*. He died 9 January 1944 at the age of 23 and is commemorated at Glenwood Cemetery in Souris, Manitoba. He was survived by his wife Mary Poyner of Winnipeg. ***Poyner Lake*** (53 M/11), southeast of Ransom Lake was named after him in 1996.

Pratt, Pilot Officer **Allan G.** of Winnipeg (J 6031). No. 10 Squadron. He died 26 July 1941 at the age of 22 and is commemorated at Gander Cemetery in Newfoundland. He was the son of Thomas G. and Anne Pratt of Winnipeg and was survived by his wife Helen M. Pratt of Winnipeg. ***Pratt Island*** (64 O/11) in Corbett Lake was named after him in 1995.

Pratt, Sergeant **Leslie H.** of Morris (H 20166). Queen's Own Cameron Highlanders. He died 19 August 1942 and is commemorated at the Brookwood Memorial in Surrey, England. ***Pratt Lake*** (64 I/9), northeast of North Knife Lake was named after him in 1974.

Prawdzik, Flying Officer **Charles J.** of Polonia (J 37535). No. 415 Squadron. He died 13 October 1944 at the age of 23 and is commemorated at Brookwood Military Cemetery in Surrey, England. He was the son of Jacob and Anna Prawdzik of Polonia, Manitoba.

Charles was born in Polonia, Manitoba on August 18, 1921. He completed his education in Winnipeg and worked for Canada Packers prior to enlisting in the RCAF in 1942. He trained in Brandon, Edmonton, and Regina before being posted overseas in November, 1943. Charles's Halifax aircraft NP935 was hit by enemy flak during a daylight raid over Wanne-Eickel, Germany and crashed upon return at Woodbridge, England; he was the only casualty (Pittman n.d.).

Prawdzik Lake (64 H/3), west of Settee Lake was named after him in 1995.

Prayzner, Corporal **Joseph** of Winnipeg (H 1759). Royal Winnipeg Rifles. He died 9 October 1944 at the age of 30 and is commemorated at the Adegem Canadian War Cemetery in Belgium. He was the son of John and Helen Prayzner and was survived by his wife Ann F. Prayzner of Winnipeg and their son. She went to Europe in 1995 for the VE-Day celebrations and wrote (7 April 1995):

At [an] early age, [his] family moved to Shoal Lake, Manitoba [where] Joseph attended school. During his youth he was active in sports: hockey, archery ... bowling and dancing. Joseph travelled for a few years [and] married in 1940, living in Winnipeg. He enlisted in 1943.

Prayzner Lake (52 L/13), south of Manigotagan Lake was named after him in 1982.

Preece, Corporal **Ralph B.** of Winnipeg (H 19666). Queen's Own Cameron Highlanders. He died 19 August 1942 at the age of 29 and is commemorated at the Adegem Canadian War Cemetery in Belgium. He was the son of Charles H. and Louise A. M. "Nancy" Preece of Winnipeg. ***Preece Lake*** (64 I/15), northeast of Shethanei Lake was named after him in 1974.

Prest, Aircraftman 2 **Frank B.** of Winnipeg (1408408). No. 44 Squadron, RAF. He died 31 August 1941 at the age of 20 and is commemorated at St. Michael Churchyard in Waddington, Lincolnshire, England. He was the youngest son of Frank B. and Elsie V. Prest of Winnipeg. This native of Arcola, Saskatchewan had joined the Royal Canadian Army Medical Corps before the war. He spent a year in England before transferring to the RAF and commencing pilot's training. His name appears on the Roll of Honour at Earl Grey School as he was formerly a student there. ***Prest Lake*** (53 E/14), south of Begg Lake was named after him in 1995.

Preston, Flight Sergeant **Charles William** of Portage la Prairie (R 119661). No. 158 Squadron. He died 4 July 1943 at the age of 19 and is commemorated at Heverlee War Cemetery, Leuven, Vlaams-Brabant, Belgium. He was the son of Charles and Ellen Preston of Portage la Prairie. A local resident found his body and removed the identity disc, and on the advice of the vicar, hid it from the Germans. Fifty-one years later his sister and the last survivor of the crash visited the site and were finally able to pay their last respects.

Fifty-one years after her brother's plane was shot down over Belgium, Florence Davies finally got a chance to bid him farewell. The Portage la Prairie woman recently made a pilgrimage to the site near Loncin, Belgium where her brother, Charles William Preston met his death at the hands of the Germans.

"It was like his funeral," she said, with traces of tears in her blue eyes. "I was young, just a teenager too, when this happened and it doesn't hit you the same."

Pilot Sergeant ... Charles William Preston – known as Bill to his friends and family – flew a Halifax Bomber for the Royal Air Force based out of Lissett, Yorkshire in England. He had already completed one tour of operations when he volunteered for another mission in early July of 1943. Preston and six other crew members were returning from skip-bombing a dam in Holland. The bombers would fly low over the water and drop bombs which would skip along the surface until they hit the dam and exploded. Preston's aircraft was shot down over Loncin by an enemy fighter disguised to look like an Allied aircraft. The flaming Halifax crashed at about 1:10 AM on July 4. Preston was only 19 years old.

Five years ago a retired Belgian police officer by the name of Patrick Henselaer began research on the crash and tracking down the families of the men who were killed there. Henselaer's father and uncle had been members of the Grateful People of Ans, a society which helped protect and hide downed Allied soldiers during the war. When Henselaer contacted the remaining Preston siblings, Florence was chosen to represent the family on the pilgrimage. She and husband Allen flew to England and Belgium for ten days at the end of September. In England, they hooked up with one of Florence's cousins and her husband; the foursome travelled to Belgium together. There they visited the grave of Bill Preston and the monuments which have been erected in memory of the men who died at Loncin.

The only surviving crew member, Bomb Aimer Warrant Officer John Redman also attended. Family members and some of the other men who were in the attack were on hand and the visitors were treated like royalty by local officials, Davies said. Reminiscing with Redman about her brother was an unusual experience for Davies since he has aged while she can only remember her brother as a young man. "We learned a few things about this that we didn't know (before)." It was also a touching way to celebrate the 50th anniversary of the invasion of Europe, she noted (*Portage la Prairie Daily Graphic* 10 November 1994).

Preston Bay (64 I/12) in Sattelberger Lake was named after Flight Sergeant Preston in 1995.

Preston, Lance Bombardier **Robert** of Portage la Prairie (H 54936). Royal Canadian Artillery. He died 17 April 1943 and is commemorated at St. John Churchyard in Upper Hopton, Yorkshire, England. ***Preston Island*** (64 C/2), southwest of Granville Lake was named after him in 1995.

Preston, Trooper **Thomas Wilby "Bill"** of Killarney (H 77415). 12th Manitoba Dragoons. He died 23 August 1944 at the age of 22 and is commemorated at Bretteville-sur-Laize Canadian War Cemetery in Calvados, France. He was the son of Walter W. and Helen Preston of Killarney, Manitoba. His sister recalls (26 November 2001):

> Bill was an "A:" student and graduated from Grade 12 at Killarney High School. He then went north to work for the Hudson's Bay and was training to be a fur trader. In those days it was quite a respectable profession. He joined the military in 1941 and was trained at Debert, Nova Scotia and Shilo, Manitoba before going overseas. We have all his letters home and it is somewhat comforting to know that Bill liked the military life and was planning to stay in and make it his career when the war was over. Bill's brother Bob and sister-in-law Phyllis have visited his grave in France. Bill's mother predeceased him in 1940. Left to mourn were his father, his sister Joan, his brother Bob and his aunt Marj Dickson whose continuous parcels and letters never stopped.

His brother adds that he (3 May 1995):

> ... was born at Dominion City, Manitoba. He joined the 12th Manitoba Dragoons in 1941. Bill later joined the 18th Armoured Car Regiment of the Dragoons. He was killed in Normandy ... when his armoured scout car was hit by German anti-tank fire.

Preston Lake (64 F/3), east of Reindeer Lake was named after him in 1967.

Price, Private **Maurice R.** of Winnipeg (H 54253). Veterans Guard of Canada. He died 3 August 1942 at the age of 46 and is commemorated at Fraser Cemetery in New Westminster, British Columbia. He was survived by his mother Polly Price of Ross-on-Wye, Herefordshire, England. ***Price Island*** (64 O/8) in Baird Lake was named after him in 1995.

Price, Rifleman **Sidney G.** of Petersfield (H 9932). Royal Winnipeg Rifles. He died 10 October 1944 at the age of 33 and is commemorated at the Adegem Canadian War Cemetery in Belgium. He was survived by his mother Henriette Price of Saltley, Birmingham, England. ***Price Lake*** (64 H/11), northeast of Small Lake was named after him in 1995.

Prieston, Corporal **Felix A.** of Benito (H 17554). Regina Rifle Regiment. He died 10 June 1944 at the age of 29 and is commemorated at Beny-sur-Mer Canadian War Cemetery in Calvados, France. He was the son of William H. and Eula P. Prieston (née Lindsey) of Benito, Manitoba and the brother of Private William Prieston (next entry). He enlisted with the Princess Patricia's Canadian Light Infantry 1 July 1940 and went overseas with the Regina Rifle Regiment in 1941 as part of the Normandy invasion. His sister recalls (1 November 2001):

> Before the war, Felix worked on a farm and at a sawmill in the bush. He and his brothers and sister moved from Ontario to Manitoba at a young age with his father. He was a nice man.

His brother, Riley Prieston, was taken prisoner of war there and was repatriated in 1945. ***Prieston Lake*** (63 K/15), east of Elbow Lake was named after him in 1958.

Prieston, Private **William A.** of Benito (H 41805). Winnipeg Grenadiers. He died 20 December 1941 and is commemorated at the Sai Wan Memorial in Hong Kong. He was the son of William H. and Eula P. Prieston (née Lindsey) of Benito, Manitoba and the brother of Corporal Felix Prieston (previous entry). His sister-in-law reports that he "enlisted at Swan River 14 June 1941 and hadn't had much time for military training prior to being shipped to Hong Kong." His brother, Riley Prieston, was taken prisoner of war there and was repatriated in 1945. ***Prieston Lake*** (62 N/15), southeast of Swan River was named after him in 1973.

Prince, Private **Albert** (A 22664). Royal Winnipeg Rifles (8th Battalion). He died 9 August 1918 and is commemorated at Manitoba Cemetery, Caix, Somme, France. ***Prince Lake*** (52 M/3), northwest of Wallace Lake was named after this World War I casualty and his brother Drum Major Lionel W. Prince (next entry) in 1987.

Prince, Drum Major (Sergeant) **Lionel W.** (830491). Royal Winnipeg Rifles (8th Battalion). He died 15 August 1917 and is commemorated at Rue-Petillon Military Cemetery, Fleurbaix, Pas de Calais, France. ***Prince Lake*** (52 M/3), northwest of Wallace Lake was named after this World War I casualty and his brother Private Albert Prince (previous entry) in 1987.

Prior, Sergeant **George T.** of Winnipeg (H 16780). Princess Patricia's Canadian Light Infantry. He died 14 December 1943 at the age of 29 and is commemorated at the Moro River Canadian War Cemetery in Italy. He was survived by his wife Marjorie G. M. Prior of Hampden Park, Sussex, England and their three year-old son. ***Prior Lake*** (63 I/16), east of Cross Lake was named after him in 1973.

Pritchard, Lieutenant **Kenneth P.** of Winnipeg. Royal Winnipeg Rifles. He died 21 February 1945 at the age of 21 and is commemorated at the Groesbeek Canadian War Cemetery in Holland. He was the son of Russell M. and Gladys E. Pritchard of Winnipeg. ***Pritchard Point*** (64 N/16) on Nahili Lake was named after him in 1995.

Pritchard, Gunner **Vernon R.** of East St. Paul (H 59546). Royal Canadian Artillery. He died 1 May 1944 at the age of 21 and is commemorated at Salerno War Cemetery, Italy. He was the son of Robert and Lenore Pritchard of East St. Paul. ***Pritchard Bay*** (63 I/1) in Little Bolton Lake was named after him in 1995.

Pritchard, Private **William Lawrence** of Rathwell (H 103566). Queen's Own Cameron Highlanders. He died 23 October 1944 at the age of 36 and is commemorated at Bergen-op-Zoom Canadian War Cemetery in Holland. He was the son of William and Mary Pritchard of Rathwell, Manitoba. ***Pritchard Island*** (53 K/3) in Red Sucker Lake was named after him in 1995.

Probizanski, Private **Maurice W.** of Gardenton (M 31573). Loyal Edmonton Regiment. He died 20 January 1944 at the age of 21 and is commemorated at the Moro River Canadian War Cemetery in Italy. He was the son of Wasyl and Todoska Probizanski of Gardenton, Manitoba. ***Probizanski Lake*** (64 N/1), southwest of Nueltin Lake was named after him in 1972.

Probizansky, Trooper **Nestor** of Stuartburn (H 77424). 12th Manitoba Dragoons. He died 11 April 1945 at the age of 22 and is commemorated at the Holten Canadian War Cemetery in Holland. He was the son of John and Catherine Probizanski (sp.) of Stuartburn, Manitoba. ***Probizansky Island*** (64 N/9) in the Seman River was named after him in 1995.

Procinsky, Private **Peter** of Winnipeg (H 6304). Winnipeg Grenadiers. He died 20 December 1941 and is commemorated at the Sai Wan Memorial in Hong Kong. **Procinsky Lake** (64 O/9), northwest of Nejanilini Lake was named after him in 1975.

Prokopchuk, Rifleman **Steve** of Dauphin (H 41330). Royal Winnipeg Rifles. He died 6 June 1944 and is commemorated at Beny-sur-Mer Canadian War Cemetery in Calvados, France. ***Prokopchuk Lake*** (64 J/7), west of Tadoule Lake was named after him in 1975.

Prokulivich, Private **Michael** (H 203107). Calgary Highlanders. He died 2 November 1944 and is commemorated at Schoonselhof Cemetery in Antwerp, Belgium. ***Prokulivich Lake*** (64 O/11), south of Corbett Lake was named after him in 1995.

Prosnyck, Flight Sergeant **John** of Portage la Prairie (R 110932). No. 428 Squadron. He died 5 May 1943 at the age of 24 and is commemorated at Zwolle (De Kranenburg) General Cemetery, Holland. He was survived by his mother, Mrs. H. Yaybak, his wife Elsie L. Prosnyck (née Munrosyck) and their young daughter Iris. His obituary read in part:

> According to German information received by Mrs. John Prosnyck of this city, her husband ... lost his life following air operations over Dortmund, Germany. Sergeant Prosnyck was born in Portage ... where he attended Victoria School and the Collegiate. He entered the Civil Service following his graduation. He was married in 1940 and enlisted with the RCAF in 1941. He received his basic training at Dauphin, Regina and London, Ontario and graduated from Rivers, Manitoba. He arrived overseas in 1942 (*Portage la Prairie Daily Graphic* n.d.).

Prosnyck Lake (64 I/7), northeast of North Knife Lake was named after him in 1974.

Prost, Private **Edward A.** of Winnipeg (H 87337). Royal Canadian Army Service Corps. He died 15 March 1943 at the age of 39 and is commemorated at Brookwood Military Cemetery in Surrey, England. He was the son of Adam and Kathrine Prost and was survived by his wife Emma C. Prost of Winnipeg. ***Prost Creek*** (54 C/10), which flows northeast into Hayes River was named after him in 1964.

Proteau, Private **Aimé** of Winnipeg (H 102767). Royal Canadian Army Service Corps. He died 20 April 1943 and is commemorated at Brookwood Military Cemetery in Surrey, England. ***Proteau Lake*** (64 J/1), south of Tadoule Lake was named after him in 1975.

Proulx, Private **Ernest** of Ste. Anne (H 41845). Winnipeg Grenadiers. He died a prisoner of war 11 December 1943 and is commemorated at the Yokohama War Cemetery in Japan. The official cause of death was listed as beriberi. He was the son of Onesime and Rose Proulx of St. Anne, Manitoba. His nephew reports (14 February 2002):

> He was inventive and very good with his hands. My great grandfather Paul Proulx was part of Louis Riel's provisional government. We still have his 12 gauge shotgun in the family and when the stock broke, Ernest carved a new one. All his brothers were in the armed services too. He enlisted July 18, 1941 with the Royal Winnipeg Rifles but was transferred to the Winnipeg Grenadiers shortly before their departure for Hong Kong. When I got out of the service in 1965, I met Frank Harding who was with Ernest when he died. He told me that there were beatings every day. If someone couldn't walk they were put to death with a bayonet while they lay in their bunks. Harding said they were very hungry all the time and cold in winter. I was overseas in Germany (1957 - 1960) when another man who had been with the medical corps was also with my uncle at Hong Kong. He told me pretty much the same story.

He wrote a letter to his mother after six months in captivity:

> Dear Mother: I guess you will be surprised when you receive this letter and I sure hope when this reaches you, it will find you all in good health. As for myself, I'm safe and well. How [is] everything back home now? I guess I will have to wait yet, as for here the weather is very nice. Mother, when you answer this letter, I want you to tell me how everyone in the family is getting along and the kind of crop you will get this fall. Here, what we do for a pastime is play ball and other games, and also on Saturday night, they hold a concert for us boys. We sing all kinds of old songs and it sure reminds me of back home. I will have to close my letter now, but before I do, I will ask you to tell all my friends if they're able to write [and] not to forget me. Give my best regards to dad and kiss everyone for me. Hope to see you all soon. Your loving son, Ernest (12 June 1942).

His mother received the letter nearly a year later by which time he had passed away. ***Proulx Bay*** (64 P/2) in Spruce Lake was named after him in 1989.

Pryde, Squadron Leader **David D.** of Winnipeg (39564). No. 77 Squadron, RAF, Distinguished Flying Cross. He enlisted in February, 1937 and was lost on 9 June 1942 over the Bay of Biscay while on patrol out of Devon (Allison 1978). He was 24 years of age and is commemorated at the Runnymede Memorial in Surrey, England. He was the son of Reverend John M. and Jean M. Pryde of Anstruther, Fife, Scotland. ***Pryde Lake*** (53 L/1), southeast of Rochon Lake was named after him in 1995.

Pryor, Ordinary Seaman **Albert L.** of Winnipeg (V 24421). HMCS *Spikenard*. The *Spikenard* was torpedoed and sunk by U-136 south of Iceland, while escorting Convoy SC.67; there were only eight survivors. Ordinary Seaman Pryor died 10 February 1942 at the age of 18 and is commemorated at the Halifax Memorial. He was the son of Leslie H. and Lily A. Pryor of Winnipeg. ***Pryor Lake*** (54 B/4), northeast of Shamattawa was named after him in 1964.

Prysiaznuk, Private **John** of Emerson (H 14764). Algonquin Regiment. He died 1 November 1944 at the age of 20 and is commemorated at Bergen-op-Zoom Canadian War Cemetery in Holland. He was the son of William and Lena Prysiaznuk of Emerson, Manitoba. ***Prysiaznuk Lake*** (64 N/3), southwest of Nueltin Lake was named after him in 1972.

Pullen, Flying Officer **Arthur Leslie** of Minnedosa (76016). No. 102 Squadron, RAF. He died 1 July 1941 at the age of 27 and is commemorated at Jonkerbos War Cemetery in Holland. He was the only son of Arthur N. and Ada Pullen (née Thompson) of Minnesdosa and the husband of Denise M. Pullen (née Wilson). "Les" had travelled to England in 1932 to study and became a Chartered Accountant, but joined the RAF at the outbreak of the war (Allison 1978). He had completed over 30 missions with No. 61 Squadron and had begun his second tour of duty. ***Pullen Lake*** (53 L/1), southeast of Rochon Lake was named after him in 1995.

Pulver, Rifleman **James E.** of Hamiota (H 14481). Royal Winnipeg Rifles. He died 4 July 1944 at the age of 19 and is commemorated at Beny-sur-Mer Canadian War Cemetery in Calvados, France. He was the son of Mr. and Mrs. E. E. Pulver of Hamiota, Manitoba. ***Pulver Lake*** (63 O/4), north of Wekusko Lake was named after him in 1970.

Purchase, Lieutenant **John R. "Jack"** of Winnipeg (CDN 284). Royal Welsh Fusiliers. He died 17 July 1944 at the age of 20 and is commemorated at Hottot-les-Bagues War Cemetery, Calvados, France. He was the eldest son of Algernon R. and Mabel F. Purchase (née Paull) of Swan River. According to his younger brother (7 September 1997):

The Purchase family moved from Swan River to Winnipeg in 1926/7 where his father held the position of Inspector, Soldiers Settlers Board, Mutual Life of Canada. In Winnipeg, the young Purchase family moved into an apartment and then into a rental house on Rathgar Avenue in Fort Rouge. About 1932, they moved successively to two larger rental houses on Ashland Avenue and about 1937 bought the house at 686 Fisher Street. Jack attended Riverview Public School and Gordon Bell High School where he completed Grade 12. Summer jobs for Jack included working in 1941 as a Telegraph Boy which involved delivering telegrams on a bicycle and as a taxi driver with Moore's Taxi in 1942.

In the fall of 1942, Jack attended the Broadway campus of the University of Manitoba where he took second year Science with the intent to specialize in Geology. As a member of the Canadian Officers Training Corps, Jack spent the spring of 1943 at Camp Shilo. Jack was then transferred to Chilliwack, BC after which he was posted to the Officers' Training School at Brockville, graduating in late 1943. Jack spent a month back at Camp Shilo and from there, in early 1944, moved to Military District No. 10 at the Infantry Training School located at the Fort Garry Campus of the University of Manitoba.

He volunteered to serve with CanLoan. This group of junior officers received further advanced training at Debert, Nova Scotia before proceeding overseas. Jack arrived in England in the spring of 1944 and was posted to the 4th Battalion, Royal Welsh Fusiliers. The regiment went to Normandy in late June, 1944 where Jack was killed.

There are two accounts of his death. His buddy, Jim Suttie, said that they had led patrols where Jack was spotted and killed by a Schmeisser with bullet wounds to the chest. Jim, who was subsequently killed while entering a field in Holland, said that Jack was a fine officer and a true gentleman. Later, the Commanding Officer wrote and said that Jack was killed leading his platoon in a set piece attack on Caen that turned out to be disastrous. The CO added that casualties were so severe that the Welsh Brigade never again went into action as a unit.

Jack was athletic and competitive, active in scouting (St. Alban's), enjoyed canoeing and skiing. He established close friendships and the group would bicycle to the outskirts of Winnipeg (e.g., Fort Whyte) and enjoy the outdoors both summer and winter. Sports-minded, Jack tried out for the Winnipeg Blue Bomber football team and enjoyed body-building and track and field. Adventuresome in building dugouts, forts, diving bells, a bow made of laminated oak flooring or carved out of oiled lemon wood and arrows with bullet casings for projectile points. Other activities included making gunpowder, stamp collecting and raising pets (pigeons, white rats). Jack was a natural leader, a wonderful older brother and a person who maximized his physical and intellectual potential.

Purchase Lake (64 K/5), south of Lac Brochet was named after him in 1972.

Purper, Rifleman **William** of Brandon (H 41015). Royal Winnipeg Rifles. He died 5 November 1940 at the age of 21 and is commemorated at Brandon Cemetery. He was the son of Mr. and Mrs. Henry Purper of Moose Jaw, Saskatchewan. ***Purper Lake*** (52 L/11), south of Black Lake was named after him in 1982.

Purvis, Private **Jack W.** of St. James (H 18598). Princess Patricia's Canadian Light Infantry. He died 11 April 1945 at the age of 19 and is commemorated at the Holten Canadian War Cemetery in Holland. He was survived by his mother Louise C. Purvis of St. James. His sister recalls (25 October 2001):

Jack was the second of three children. He was very outgoing, had lots of friends and played hockey and baseball. He joined the Lord Strathcona's Horse Cadets age 11 – 12 and remained with them till they disbanded due to war. Jack was 16 when our father, a CNR employee, passed away. Jack was offered a job with the CNR and he stayed for the next two years till he joined up – December 28, 1943.

As I am the youngest and sole survivor of three kids, I remember my brother Jack told me "I hope it (the war) lasts till I get there." In his last letter dated a day before he went into action, he said "the war should be over soon and I can hardly wait to get home." He sounded as if he had had enough of being a soldier.

Purvis Lake (64 H/5), east of Wood Lake was named after him in 1995.

German prisoners captured by Canadian troops at Juno Beach on D-Day.
Courtesy of the National Archives of Canada (PA-133754).

Q

Quasso, Guardsman **Louis** of Morris (H 10608). Canadian Grenadier Guards. He died 26 February 1945 at the age of 21 and is commemorated at the Groesbeek Canadian War Cemetery in Holland. He was one of the five children of Karl J. and Katherine Quasso of Lorette, Manitoba. His brother writes (13 December 2001):

> Our father, Karl Quasso, passed away in 1940. Louis was the oldest son at home and tried to keep the family farm going at age 16 when his father died. Later, Louis worked as a truck driver. He was a friendly, sociable young man who had many friends. He was survived by his mother, three sisters and one brother.

Quasso Lake (64 N/4), northwest of Lac Brochet was named after him in 1972.

Quaye, Private **Harold E.** of Brandon (H 59713). Queen's Own Cameron Highlanders. He died 3 March 1945 at the age of 24 and is commemorated at the Groesbeek Canadian War Cemetery in Holland. He was the son of Thomas H. and Laura Quaye of Brandon. His obituary read in part:

> He enlisted in February, 1941 and went overseas in June of that same year. Born in Brandon, ... he moved with his parents to Cornwallis district when seven years old. He attended Gorrie School and before joining the army he worked for a short time on farms in the district (n.d.).

His brother recalls (1 November 2001):

> I'm an old vet myself, 79 years old, two years younger than Harold would have been. We were quite close. We went overseas together, but were separated in England and I never saw him again. I was wounded in Italy in 1944; he was killed in Germany in 1945.

Quaye Lake (64 I/13), north of Shethanei Lake was named after him in 1974.

Quigley, Sergeant **Edward G.** of Winnipeg (R 191291). No. 32 Operational Training Unit, RCAF. He died 28 January 1944 at the age of 22 and is commemorated at the Ottawa Memorial. ***Quigley Lake*** (64 P/3), southeast of Nejanilini Lake was named after him in 1974.

Quinn, Captain **Richard H.** of Winnipeg. Veterans Guard of Canada, Colonial Auxiliary Forces Officers' Decoration. He died 19 October 1944 at the age of 59 and is commemorated at Mountain View Cemetery in Vancouver. He was survived by his wife Claude A. Quinn of Vancouver. ***Quinn Lake*** (64 I/11), east of Tadoule Lake was named after him in 1957.

Canadian troops in the English Channel en route to France 6 June 1944.
Courtesy of the National Archives of Canada (PA-132930).

R

Raban, Warrant Officer 2 **William E.** of Kildonan (R 100441). No. 428 Squadron. He died 29 December 1943 at the age of 23 and is commemorated at the Reichswald Forest War Cemetery in Germany. He was the son of Alfred and Charlotte Raban of East Kildonan. ***Raban Lake*** (64 P/8), northwest of Caribou Lake was named after him in 1974.

Radcliffe, Leading Aircraftman **Albert J.** of Rivers (R 177668). No. 10 Squadron. He died 20 October 1943 at the age of 21 and is commemorated at St. Donat Roman Catholic Cemetery, Quebec. He was the son of John and Ethel F. Radcliffe of Rivers, Manitoba and the brother of Sergeant Kenneth Radcliffe (next entry). His sister writes (17 December 1995):

Albert was the quiet one of the family and was referred to by our mother often as the "Oil on troubled waters." I remember one person telling her that he would probably reach a ripe old age because of his calm and relaxed nature. Little did they know he would not see his twenty-second birthday. Albert received his education at Rivers Elementary and High Schools. He played a viola which had been hand crafted by his father in one of Alex White's orchestras. There was little or no work in the Rivers area at this time and so he left home and "rode the rails" to South Porcupine where he gained employment in a gold mine until he was old enough to "join up."

Albert joined the Royal Canadian Air Force and took his basic training at No. 1 Manning Depot in Toronto. Albert became an aero-engine mechanic and his first [posting] was to Goose Bay, Labrador. He was later posted to Gander, Newfoundland which was overseas as Newfoundland had not yet joined Confederation. On October 23rd, 1943 he was coming home on leave aboard a Liberator Bomber being used to transport personnel from Newfoundland to Canada because of the German U-boat threat to shipping. The plane was *en route* to Mont-Joli, Quebec, but because of fog was ordered on to Dorval Airport. For some reason the aircraft strayed off course and struck Black Mountain about 20 feet below the summit. This mountain is located about 80 miles north of Montreal and the fate of the aircraft was not known for two years and seven months when it was located by some hikers in the area. All 24 men on board had perished on impact and the resulting fire, and after the discovery in 1946, a cairn was erected on the site. This site was later desecrated and a permanent site and cairn have been purchased and dedicated at St. Donat in Quebec. There is also a special plaque on Green Island in Ottawa, dedicated to the 24 men who lost their lives and on which Albert's name is inscribed. This was the largest air crash that Canada had experienced up to that point in history and Albert was the only Manitoban on board.

Unless one has been through this type of waiting and wondering, they cannot imagine the pain and suffering our parents went though. Fifty-two years ago there was very poor communication and often the news broadcasts on radio were inaccurate and misleading. Our parents went through a real roller coaster ride of emotions as the different news broadcasts were given. Our communication with the officials in Ottawa was all done by letter so you can imagine the endless days and weeks of meeting every new mail train as it came into Rivers. We were very grateful that one of the three Padres sent in to Black Mountain for the original funeral/memorial service was well known to our family and this brought us some comfort.

Radcliffe Island (64 J/16) in Stony Lake was named after him in 1975.

Radcliffe, Sergeant **Kenneth L.** of Rivers (R 184322). No. 44 Squadron. He died 25 March 1944 at the age of 19 and is commemorated at the Groesbeek Canadian War Cemetery in Holland. He was the son of John and Ethel F. Radcliffe of Rivers, Manitoba and was predeceased by his brother Albert (previous entry). His sister recalls (17 December 1995):

Kenneth Lloyd Radcliffe was born at the family farm in the Municipality of Daly. Ken loved to fish and often he and his older brother Albert would spend the whole day fishing up and down the Little Saskatchewan River. There was little money when Ken was a boy and as he did not like school very much, he started working for a neighbour at the age of 14. Ken was perhaps not as musical as some of his siblings, but his father hand-crafted a cello for him and he played for a time with one of the Rivers orchestras, led by Mr. Alex White who felt that every child should be able to play a musical instrument.

When Ken was 16, he decided to try nickel mining at Sudbury, Ontario and it was from there on his 18th birthday he enlisted in the Royal Canadian Air Force. Ken took his basic training at No. 2 Manning Depot at Brandon and his gunnery training at Macdonald. Ken went overseas before his 19th birthday and was assigned to a base in Lincolnshire where he served as a mid-upper gunner on a Lancaster bomber. Ken was one of two Canadians to be assigned to an RAF squadron and regularly flew with Captain Dunn of Toronto who was a navigator. On the eleventh flight over enemy territory, Captain Dunn was grounded for frost bite and a young Canadian man from Edmonton named Fedoruk took his place. This proved to be a great blessing for our family to later learn of the circumstances of Ken's last night. For that Lancaster bomber was shot down over the Ruhr Valley in Germany along with 97 others on the night of March 24/25, 1944 with the plane actually crashing in Holland. When the plane was fatally hit, the men were ordered to bail out although their altitude was about 28,000 feet. As Fedoruk prepared to jump, he heard the tail gunner say he could not get out of his turret. Fedoruk blacked out and it was not until after the war that he contacted our family and told us that he had spent fourteen months with the Dutch Underground and wanted to know the fate of the others. We know in our hearts that the regular crew had become closer than brothers – that none of them could jump and leave one to perish alone. This may seem a great waste, but those who knew Ken Radcliffe and the rest of the crew through him, knew they could not live with themselves if they did not do everything to help their friend. Kenneth was first buried with his crew mates and then later moved to the Canadian Cemetery. The verse of scripture that the family chose for his head stone reads: "Greater love hath no man than this, that a man lay down his life for his friend" (John 15:13).

Ken must have gone through great anxiety in the six months he was in England, for it was the October after his arrival that he learned of the disappearance of his older brother Albert, during a flight from Gander. Albert was still missing at the time that Ken was listed as "Missing in Action." These were very hard days and the anguish of our parents was a terrible thing to behold. Our family was truly shattered by the loss of Kenneth and Albert and it was a loss to be felt every time a veteran returned from overseas and whenever the young, returned men gathered and were honoured.

It is now over fifty years since Ken's death, but his face is as clearly etched on my mind as though it was only yesterday that he was home on his last leave. I sometimes look at men who would now be his age and often wonder – what might have been!

Radcliffe Lake (64 P/7), east of Nejanilini Lake was named after him in 1974.

Rae, Flight Sergeant **James D.** of Brandon (R 86314). No. 115 Squadron. He died 6 December 1942 at the age of 26 and is commemorated at Montcornet Military Cemetery, Aisne, France. He was the son of MacDuff and Laura M. Rae (née Pepper), and was survived by his wife Pearl M. Rae of Calgary and their young daughter. He was the brother of Flight Sergeant John M. Rae and Private Ronald A. Rae (next two entries). His sister recalls (n.d.):

Jim was born in Regina, Saskatchewan. He was active in sports; his favourite was golf. He was a member of Knox United Church. It was here that he had the opportunity to sing. He had a very good voice and took part in all concerts. He was married in September, 1939.

Rae Island (63 I/16) in Kapechekamasic Lake was named after him in 1995.

Rae, Flight Sergeant **John M. "Jack"** of Brandon (R 221847). No. 405 Squadron. He died 28 January 1945 at the age of 24 and is commemorated at Durnbach War Cemetery in Bavaria, Germany. He was the son of MacDuff and Laura M. Rae (née Pepper) and the brother of Flight Sergeant James D. Rae (previous entry) and Private Ronald A. Rae (next entry). His sister recalls that he: "... was born in Chater, Manitoba on the 8th of January 1921. He was also very active in sports, golf being his favourite" (n.d.). ***Rae Bay*** (63 I/16) in Kapechekamasic Lake was named after him in 1995.

Rae, Private **Ronald A. "Pete"** of Brandon (H 60451). Queen's Own Cameron Highlanders. He died 11 November 1944 at the age of 21 and is commemorated at the Groesbeek Canadian War Cemetery in Holland. He was the brother of Flight Sergeant James D. Rae and Flight Sergeant John M. Rae (previous two entries) and the youngest son of MacDuff and Laura M. Rae (née Pepper). He had been one of Brandon's better-known athletes, competing in provincial swimming meets. His sister recalls (n.d.) that he: "... was born in Chater, Manitoba. He excelled in swimming and hockey. He and John always had an old car that would run somehow." ***Rae Lake*** (52 L/3), northeast of Brereton Lake was named after him in 1973.

Raites, Private **Edward** of Winnipeg (H 6898). Winnipeg Grenadiers. He died a prisoner of war 29 September 1942 and is commemorated at the Sai Wan War Cemetery in Hong Kong. ***Raites Lake*** (64 J/12), west of Tadoule Lake was named after him in 1978.

Ralph, Corporal **Cecil A.** of St. Claude (R 152926). Royal Canadian Air Force. He died 3 February 1946 at the age of 27 and is commemorated at St. Denis Cemetery in Haywood, Manitoba. He had been part of "Exercise Musk Ox," a winter military training program on the site of a formerly secret American Air Force Base with a $10,000,000 airfield near Churchill, Manitoba. It was to have served as a refuelling station for planes flying from the American west coast to Europe. It was taken over by the federal department of transport the previous February. He was the son of Arthur and Margaret Ralph of Fort William, Ontario and was survived by his wife Germaine E. Ralph (née Richard) of Calgary. She recalls (n.d.):

> In the late 1930s, he worked as a telegraph operator with his father who was station agent for the CPR at St. Claude, Manitoba. [We were] married in Haywood, Manitoba where he was buried. In 1940, he went to work in the offices of Rouyn-Noranda Gold Mines in Quebec. We returned in 1942 where he joined the air force. [He] was posted at Shilo; from there he was posted to EFTS at Pearce, Alberta where we lived off-base in a little cabin in a farmer's field. From there, he was posted at No. 3 SFTS base in Vulcan, Alberta where he got his Corporal stripes, then to Calgary. In November, 1945 he was posted to Rockcliffe, Ontario where he was drafted into Exercise Musk Ox where he met his untimely death in a fire.

Ralph Island (64 O/12) in Nueltin Lake was named after him in 1995.

Ralph, Sergeant **Cuthbert Percy** of Elm Creek (R 95017). No. 22 Operational Training Unit, RCAF. He died 19 July 1942 at the age of 29 and is commemorated at Stratford-upon-Avon Cemetery in Warwickshire, England. He was the youngest son of Mr. and Mrs. C. J. Ralph of Elm Creek, Manitoba. His niece recalls (23 April 1996):

> Being as I spent a lot of time at the home of my grandparents, I can remember my uncle as a young man in his early twenties. He was a happy, healthy person who enjoyed a social life and when going out was always dressed to a "T" with never a hair out of place. He did not work full time at home on the farm, but did construction work with a local road gang in the RM of Grey, also spending a couple of winters in bush camps. He was a top-notch writer and printer, liked drawing and sketching plus was excellent at Math. He took up to Grade 11 at Wingham Consolidated School – the highest education in the family. He was tall and of slight build. I guess his adventure for life was why he chose to join the RCAF. I know his mother was proud and heartbroken when word of his death came. I can well remember the day.

Ralph Bay (63 N/5) in Russick Lake was named after him in 1995.

Ralph, Flying Officer **Howard P.** of Winnipeg (J 20738). No. 1414 Meteorological Flight. He died 25 October 1943 at the age of 24 and is commemorated at the Alamein Memorial in Egypt. He was the son of William P. and Edna R. Ralph of Ottawa. ***Ralph Point*** (53 E/16) on Island Lake was named after him in 1995.

Ramsay, Sapper **James S.** of Winnipeg (H 87541). Royal Canadian Engineers. He died 4 July 1944 at the age of 39 and is commemorated at Beny-sur-Mer Canadian War Cemetery in Calvados, France. He was the son of David and Margaret Ramsay of Edinburgh, Scotland. ***Ramsay Bay*** (64 N/14) in Rendall Lake was named after him in 1995.

Ramsay, Gunner **William M.** of Darlingford (H 75096). Royal Canadian Artillery. He died 7 September 1944 at the age of 20 and is commemorated at the Calais Canadian War Cemetery in France. He was the son of James D. and Annie Ramsay of Darlingford, Manitoba. ***Ramsay Island*** (64 P/12) in Nejanilini Lake was named after him in 1989.

Randall, Corporal **Milton E.** of Killarney (R 106107). Wireless Mechanic, RCAF. He died 22 May 1945 at the age of 29 and is commemorated at Killarney Cemetery. This native of Morse, Saskatchewan was the son of George G. and Elizabeth Randall of Killarney, Manitoba. He had been sent back to Canada from England for health reasons and died at Deer Lodge Military Hospital. ***Randall Island*** (53 L/12) in the Washikamow River was named after him in 1997.

Randall, Sapper **Vernon** of Winnipeg (H 13113). Royal Canadian Engineers. He died 2 October 1944 at the age of 36 and is commemorated at Schoonselhof Cemetery in Antwerp, Belgium. He was the son of Joe and Sarah Randall of Winnipeg and was survived by his wife Grace Randall of Winnipeg. She writes (25 May 1998):

> My husband ... was a family man. Like so many men in those depression times, he was occupied with trying to support his family so did not cultivate hobbies. He had an outgoing personality and enjoyed friends.

He also enjoyed reading and made use of the public library. He was born in Winnipeg and resided there all his life until he enlisted with the Royal Canadian Engineers in September, 1939.

Randall Lake (64 I/1), northeast of Etawney Lake was named after him in 1974.

Rankel, Private **William H. T.** of Moosehorn (H 43296). Queen's Own Cameron Highlanders. He died 27 February 1945 at the age of 21 and is commemorated at the Groesbeek Canadian War Cemetery in Holland. He was the son of John A. and Katherine Rankel of Moosehorn, Manitoba. ***Rankel Island*** (64 I/16) in the Seal River was named after him in 1974.

Rankine, Flying Officer **James Renton M.** of Winnipeg (J 9140). No. 162 Squadron. He died 6 April 1944 at the age of 22 and is commemorated at the Runnymede Memorial in Surrey, England. He was the son of William and Nina M. Rankine of Winnipeg. His nephew reports that he was born in McCreary and was raised there and later in Winnipeg. He was a member of Knox United Church and enjoyed sailing, building boats and woodworking. ***Rankine Island*** (64 I/15) in Wither Lake was named after him in 1995.

Rankine, Sergeant **William L.** of Winnipeg (H 19638). Queen's Own Cameron Highlanders, Mentioned in Dispatches. He died 19 August 1942 and is commemorated at Dieppe Canadian War Cemetery in Seine-Maritime, France. ***Rankine Lake*** (54 L/7), southwest of Churchill was named after him in 1948.

Rankmore, Flight Sergeant **Gordon J.** of Minnedosa (R 101981). No. 307 Operational Training Unit, RCAF. He died 28 May 1943 at the age of 23 and is commemorated at City Road Cemetery, Haverfordwest, Pembrokeshire, Wales. He was the fifth child of Fred and Emma C. Rankmore of Moore Park, Manitoba and was survived by his wife Elena Pearl Rankmore. His brother writes (3 November 1994):

He attended Moore Park Consolidated two-room school. He was a fun loving and happy individual and like a lot of other small town boys growing up during the Depression, there was not the opportunity to participate in sports like they do today. They had to make their own entertainment – no TV and few radios. They played baseball and football in the summer and skated on the outdoor rink and street hockey in the winter. He loved to sketch cartoons and animals. Playing cards and going to the local dances was very enjoyable to him. He worked on the construction of the Air Force training centre at Carberry before joining the RCAF.

His nephew adds (30 October 2001):

He died when the Boston aircraft in which he was a gunner approached the airport with the port engine unserviceable. The first landing attempt was aborted and the plane dived into the ground one mile from Talbenny, Wales as it turned to make a second approach.

In a letter to his brother, he wrote:

Well Hugh, I was up to London last week for the first time. I was one of about 120 Canadians representing Canada in a "Wings for Victory" campaign parade. We paraded for an hour and a half through the heart of London. My dogs were damned sore but we saw a lot of swell places: Fleet Street, Law Courts, House of Commons, Parliament Buildings, Westminster Abbey, Waterloo Bridge, Waterloo Station and Buckingham Palace etc. It was tiresome but fun. I sent Pearl a picture from the newspaper, but it's far too distant to recognize anyone. I've been watching all the news reels for days, but I haven't seen me yet. I know the movie camera was there 'cause I saw it. Maybe I've made my screen debut at last, eh? (12 March 1942).

Rankmore Lake (64 P/15), northeast of Nejanilini Lake was named after him in 1974.

Ransom, Sergeant **Alan H.** of Boissevain (H 29116). Royal Canadian Artillery. He died 24 May 1944 at the age of 27 and is commemorated at the Cassino War Cemetery in Italy. He was the son of Wilson and Edna Ransom of Mountainside, Manitoba. ***Ransom Lake*** (53 M/11), southeast of Split Lake was named after him in 1966.

Rapier, Gunner **Thomas A.** of Elmwood (H 101388). Royal Canadian Artillery. He died 1 May 1945 at the age of 31 and is commemorated at the Holten Canadian War Cemetery in Holland. He was the son of Harold G. and Minnie L. Rapier of Winnipeg. ***Rapier Lake*** (64 F/6), northwest of Wells Lake was named after him in 1994.

Rasmussen, Lieutenant **Carl E.** of Winnipegosis. Royal Canadian Armoured Corps. He died 8 August 1942 at the age of 22 and is commemorated at Brookwood Military Cemetery in Surrey, England. He was the son of Alfred and Albany Rasmussen and was survived by his wife Margaret E. Rasmussen (née Gosling) of Barrie, Ontario. She recalls (3 April 1998):

Lieutenant Carl Edward Rasmussen was born at Red Deer Point on Lake Winnipegosis. The family remained on the cattle and sheep ranch for about four more years before moving to Winnipegosis. Carl attended the schools there, completing Grade 11. That was as far as the schooling went.

During those years, the main sport was hockey and speed skating in the winter. Carl participated in these sports and enjoyed them. He enjoyed fishing in season. As well, all of the family liked to go out to the ranch in the summer to hay. It was like one big picnic after the day's work was finished. Also in the summer, since Winnipegosis is located on the lake of the same name, there were many water sports that Carl enjoyed. Rowing and swimming were the most common and a favourite. During the summer, it was always interesting to see the boats return from fishing, and help unload the fish and if you were lucky, get a job filleting them.

Carl loved to read. We had a small library in the town and there were many interesting books to enjoy, especially during those cold winter nights though we had lamp light by which to read.

After finishing high school, Carl applied for admission to Royal Military College in Kingston and was accepted in September, 1937. He did well scholastically. He also played hockey for the college team. He was on a winning team that played West Point Military College. He was pleased with that game!

He graduated six months early in December, 1940. The class was advanced because of the urgent need of the war effort. He married Margaret Gosling in 1941. He was attached to the Royal Canadian Armoured Tank Corp. After spending a short time in Petawawa and Camp Borden, he was sent overseas.

Rasmussen Bay (64 N/10) in Koona Lake was named after him in 1995.

Rasmussen, Ordinary Seaman **Clifford J.** of St. James (V 24916). HMCS *Ottawa*. The *Ottawa* was escorting Convoy ON.127 in the North Atlantic when it was struck by two torpedoes from U-91; 114 of her ship's company were lost. Ordinary Seaman Rasmussen died 13 September 1942 at the age of 20 and is commemorated at the Halifax Memorial. He was the son of John C. and Gladys Rasmussen of Winnipeg. ***Rasmussen Lake*** (64 N/7), southwest of Nueltin Lake was named after him in 1972.

Rasmussen, Private **Richard** of Dauphin (H 102997). Queen's Own Cameron Highlanders. He died 23 July 1944 and is commemorated at Bretteville-sur-Laize Canadian War Cemetery in Calvados, France. ***Rasmussen Island*** (64 C/9) in Stag Lake was named after him in 1995.

Rathert, Corporal **Herbert D.** of Starbuck (H 103768). Princess Patricia's Canadian Light Infantry. He died 4 March 1945 at the age of 23 and is commemorated at Assisi War Cemetery in Italy. He was the son of Henry and Louise Rathert of Starbuck, Manitoba. On 8 April 1944 he was wounded and spent two months in hospital. He was later killed when a truck overturned, pinning him underneath it 15 miles northeast of Faligno, Italy. ***Rathert Lake*** (64 I/2), east of North Knife Lake was named after him in 1974.

Ratinsky (alias Rohatynski), Rifleman **Walter** of Morden (H 41254). Royal Winnipeg Rifles. He died 4 July 1944 at the age of 25 and is commemorated at Beny-sur-Mer Canadian War Cemetery in Calvados, France. *Star Weekly* reporter M. H. Halton was on the scene for the assault on Carpiquet some months earlier in which Rifleman Ratinsky formed part of the "second wave:"

> There are no adequate adjectives for such a barrage. Tens of thousands of 25-pounder shells came over with the high wailing whistle of lost demons. The bigger shells came over with 10,000 maddened, warbling rushings. The huge naval shells came over like hell's express trains hurtling derailed through space with terrifying reverberations. Literally the earth shook and quivered and the noise was atrocious. For two hours it never ceased. The roaring of guns was bad enough, but worse was the explosion of the scores of thousands of shells just below us in an area only a mile wide and less than two miles deep. Within a few seconds and for the next hour we could see nothing but a dense fog of smoke and cordite fumes and flames. Vomit after vomit of flame and 10,000 flashes came from the enemy positions. Really, I was appalled and thought "Men just can't do this to each other, not even to Germans. It's monstrous." And even in that frantic excitement and evil exhilaration I kept thinking, "My God, if only we could harness this demonic energy to peace."
>
> I shook my head aghast but excited. Here was battle in all of its frightful reality – those were men down there! – so real that it seemed unreal. Men of flesh and blood attacking through that enemy shellfire and machine-gun fire, supported by a wall of fire and through a wall of fire. I forgot the microphone in my hand until MacDonald shouted: "Why aren't you talking?"
>
> I saw a terrible splendour. It was said in the last war and it is said in this that Canadians are superb assault troops. I knew this now for myself because I saw the superb in being before my eyes, a few hundred yards away, as the Canadians came towards us with their mothering tanks, in the maelstrom, through flame and steel. Nothing stopped them – NOTHING. No man stopped unless killed or wounded. I would fix my eyes on 15 or 20 men moving with a tank. Two or three mortar shells would burst among them and for a few seconds smoke would hide them from view. We would see the smoke and flame and then two seconds later hear the awful slow splitting carrumphs. But when the smoke lifted there were the easterners advancing like automatons. Not running; walking steady as robots. Perhaps they were shouting or swearing but I couldn't hear that. I could hear only the maelstrom.
>
> The wood from which the second wave of Canadians was coming was aflame. Some of our Bren carriers were hit and burst into flame; occasionally a tank was hit and stopped. But still the attackers bore down on Carpiquet – like fate – firing as they came. "My God, how do they do it?" I asked. "Because in war there's nothing for good men to do but go on," said Major Crofton. "You go on in spite of hell. War is like that. It's a hard and bloody thing" (*Star Weekly* 1944).

He was the only son of Clemens and Mary Rohatynski (sp.) of Morden, Manitoba. His commanding Officer, Captain D. B. Robertson wrote to his mother:

> Dear Mrs. Ratinsky: I would like to take this opportunity of giving what information I can on Walter's death and sending the sympathies of myself and the platoon in your loss. He was killed instantly by a mortar bomb during an enemy barrage. I was in the next trench and as soon as the barrage stopped I went over to him and I know that his death must have been instant and that he could have suffered no pain. We buried him the same day and the Padre came down and held a service which many of the lads in the platoon attended. His grave was carefully marked and as soon as the battle moves forward from that area he will be moved to a military cemetery.
>
> The loss to me was particularly great as he was part of my headquarters and as a result I knew him very well and know what a grand fellow he was. His work in the platoon was excellent and having been in the platoon for so long he was very well known and liked by everyone. Knowing what a loss his death has been to us, we know how much harder it must be for you and I hope that you will have some consolation in the fact that he has left us for a better world after doing his part in this great fight (13 July 1944).

Ratinsky Lake (64 N/4), north of Lac Brochet was named after him in 1974.

Ratner, Flying Officer **Harry** of Winnipeg (J 28242). No. 427 Squadron. He died 25 May 1944 at the age of 25 and is commemorated at Stonefall Cemetery in Yorkshire, England. He was the only son of Frank and Sarah Ratner of Winnipeg. His sister writes (29 December 1997):

> Being the youngest in the family I don't really remember all the activities he was involved in. He went to Machray School and then St. John's High School in Winnipeg. I know he loved sports; track and field was his thing. He was a star in the shot put, so they tell me and an active baseball player. He enlisted in the RCAF in 1941 ... overseas in 1942. He washed out as a flyer and became a bombardier. His last letter told us that he had completed his tour of ops and expected to be coming home. Unfortunately he never made it. He was a beautiful young man – the only boy with five female siblings and was loved by all who knew him.

Tragically, his death was an accidental one:

> Flying Officer Ratner was riding the pillion position on a motorcycle which ran into the rear end of a parked lorry on the Great North Road five miles south of Londonderry, Yorkshire. There was no guard posted to warn oncoming traffic and the lorry could not be seen in the dark. F/O Ratner was given first aid at the scene of the accident, but succumbed to his injuries in the RAF Hospital, Northallerton (Allison and Hayward 1991).

Ratner Lake (64 J/11), west of Tadoule Lake was named after him in 1975.

Raven, Pilot Officer **John A.** of Flin Flon (J 19271). No. 407 Squadron. He died 10 November 1943 at the age of 29 and is commemorated at the Runnymede Memorial in Surrey, England. He was the son of Albert and Louise Raven and was survived by his wife Agnes Raven and their daughter Beverly. She writes (14 November 2001):

> I never knew my father; I have only 'story' memories of him. I have one letter that he wrote to my mother on July 5, 1941. He thought he was on his way to Brandon, but ended up in Penhold, Alberta along with 18 of the 'air crew boys' from Flin Flon. The rest is history.
>
> From the stories I have heard, I know that he enjoyed his short life. He was a steel rigger by profession, loved to hunt, fish and party, with his

greatest love being his family. I have a letter which was sent to my mother from G. MacGregor Grant, Chaplain which states: "The day before he went on his last flight, he and I had a long talk sitting together on a log outside the crew room. We recalled days in Brandon when I was the minister of St. Paul's Church, when Jack ushered in the gallery and when his mother sang in the choir. He spoke with affection of both you and his mother and said he longed for the day when his tour of Ops would be over and when he could return to you."

This never came to be, but as I sit here and think of the devastating events of September 11 in New York, I realize that my father knew what he died for, the love of his country, his family and freedom. The closing paragraph of his letter says: "Well, I'll say so long sweetheart for now – say hello to everyone for me. All my love, J."

Raven Point (64 C/7) on Granville Lake was named after him in 1995.

Ray, Flight Sergeant **Kenneth F.** of Flin Flon (R 100210). No. 5 Operational Training Unit, RCAF. He died 18 January 1943 at the age of 30 and is commemorated at the Runnymede Memorial in Surrey, England. He was the son of Fredrick and Margaret Ray and was survived by his wife Anne Ray of Dauphin and their daughter. ***Ray Peninsula*** (53 E/14) on Dobbs Lake was named after him in 1995.

Ray, Private **Kenneth R.** of St. James (H 16498). Princess Patricia's Canadian Light Infantry. He died 11 September 1944 at the age of 25 and is commemorated at Ancona War Cemetery in Italy. He was the son of Tom and Eva P. Ray of St. James and was survived by his wife Lillian Ray (née Murray) and their son. ***Ray Point*** (64 N/11) on Kasmere Lake was named after him in 1995.

Rea, Gunner **Kenneth M.** of Russell (H 67088). Royal Canadian Artillery. He died while on leave 14 October 1945 at the age of 30 and is commemorated at Russell Cemetery. He was the son of John and Minnie Rea of Russell, Manitoba. His cousin recalls (11 May 1996):

He was most likely born at home in the Brightside District; he attended Brightside School. Kenny's special interest was always horses and the farm. The farm eked out a bare living in those days. After a devastating hail storm, about 1937 or 38, Ken and Leslie [his brother] gathered up wash tubs full of hail stones and we made ice cream. My sister and I were there.

Rea Lake (64 F/3), north of Goldsand Lake was named after him in 1994.

Reade, Captain **William M.** of Winnipeg. Lord Strathcona's Horse, Mentioned in Dispatches. He died 23 April 1945 at the age of 31 and is commemorated at the Groesbeek Canadian War Cemetery in Holland. He was the son of William E. and Vera Reade and was survived by his wife Dorothy Reade of Winnipeg. ***Reade Lake*** (64 H/3), northwest of Settee Lake was named after him in 1995.

Ready, Flying Officer **Robert F. "Bert"** of Reston (J 22628). No. 22 Operational Training Unit, RCAF. He died 29 June 1943 at the age of 22 and is commemorated at Weston-super-Mare Cemetery, Somerset, England. He was the son of James D. and Helen F. Ready of Reston, Manitoba. His brother writes (29 February 1996):

After graduating through the Reston Public and High School system, he worked as a printer at the *Reston Recorder*. Enjoying sports, he played baseball and hockey with the local teams. He enlisted in the RCAF at Regina in December, 1941. After training at several stations in Canada, he shipped overseas in February, 1943. He died in a plane crash in the Bristol Channel when the wing of the plane touched a wave while practising low-level flying.

Ready Lake (53 N/2), northeast of Red Cross Lake was named after him in 1995.

Reahil, Flight Lieutenant **Frederick J.** of Winnipeg (103568). No. 268 Mustang Squadron, RAF, Distinguished Flying Cross. He died 18 June 1944 at the age of 25 and is commemorated at the Runnymede Memorial in Surrey, England. He was the son of James G. and Mahala J. Reahil of Winnipeg. He travelled to England with the Royal Canadian Army Medical Corps in 1939 and transferred to the RAF the following year. His squadron flew support for the D-Day landings and for the army and navy in the weeks following. It was on one of these missions that he was killed (Allison 1978). ***Reahil Lake*** (64 P/3), northeast of Naelin Lake was named after him in 1989.

Reaney, Private **William H.** of Winnipeg (H 19869). Queen's Own Cameron Highlanders. He died 17 October 1940 at the age of 39 and is commemorated at Mount Hermon Cemetery in Quebec City. He was survived by his wife May M. Reaney of Winnipeg. ***Reaney Lake*** (64 O/1), east of Munroe Lake was named after him in 1975.

Rech, Flying Officer **Edward W.** of Winnipeg (J 26340). No. 12 Squadron. He died 14 January 1945 at the age of 22 and is commemorated at the Hanover War Cemetery in Germany. ***Rech Lake*** (64 O/16), southwest of Baralzon Lake was named after him in 1995.

Recksiedler, Signalman **Paul** of Morris (H 38899). Royal Canadian Corps of Signals. He died 8 January 1944 at the age of 25 and is commemorated at Sewell Cemetery, Manitoba. He was the only son of Henry and Elizabeth Recksiedler of Winnipeg and was survived by his wife of six months Katherine J. Recksiedler (née Golling) of Vancouver and their daughter whom he never saw. She writes (28 November 2001):

I am Paul's only child, Elizabeth Else, also at times called Paulette. For me he lives through his sister, Else Thomson (now deceased) and her family. Uncle Jim Thomson (who treats me as his own) has given me my Dad's high chair which he used as a child and also a bookcase he made from wooden produce crates. I'm also fortunate enough to have been given a copy of a "talking letter" my Dad sent to his family some five or six months before he died – it allows me to hear his voice long after he has been gone. These things, along with photos from Uncle Jim and Gramma Golling, I will always treasure.

Paul has three grandchildren: Gayle Cook, Robert Cook and Beverly (Cook) Ahola. He also has four great-grandchildren: Caitlyn and Connor Cook and Alisha and Victoria Ahola. Paul will also live through his niece Betty (Thomson) King and nephews Paul Thomson, Don Thomson and Ian Thomson (deceased) and their families.

My love and memories of my Father cannot come from the past, since he died two months before I was born. But they remain alive through the present and will into the future through my children and grandchildren and Aunt Else's family. They are his gifts to me.

Recksiedler Lake (64 O/2), west of Munroe Lake was named after him in 1995.

Reddie, Warrant Officer 2 **William J.** of Winnipeg (R 91868). No. 410 Squadron. He died 20 April 1943 at the age of 21 and is commemorated at the Runnymede Memorial in Surrey, England. ***Reddie Lake*** (64 H/4), north of Gauer Lake was named after him in 1995.

Reece, Flight Sergeant **Michael P.** of Winnipeg (R 86147). No. 80 Squadron. He died 10 August 1942 at the age of 20 and is commemorated at the Hadra War Memorial Cemetery in Alexandria, Egypt. ***Reece Lake*** (64 J/13), northwest of Tadoule Lake was named after him in 1975.

Reed, Lieutenant **Isaac T.** of Fort Garry. Royal Winnipeg Rifles. He died 5 July 1944 at the age of 35 and is commemorated at Beny-sur-Mer Canadian War Cemetery in Calvados, France. He was the son of John T. and Anne Reed and was survived by his wife Ina Reed of Victoria, British Columbia. ***Reed Rapids*** (53 K/10) in the Stull River was named after him in 1995.

Reekie, Lance Corporal **Arthur R.** of Killarney (H 41019). Royal Winnipeg Rifles. He died 6 June 1944 at the age of 26 and is commemorated at Beny-sur-Mer Canadian War Cemetery in Calvados, France. He was the son of Murdock and Emma M. Reekie of Killarney, Manitoba. His sister recalls (27 September 1995):

> Arthur was born [in the] Riverside Municipality near Margaret, Manitoba. He received his education at Pinkham, Alcester and Oakridge schools. Arthur like to dance, skate and play ball. He always lived on a farm and he farmed with his brother Bill until he joined the army in June, 1940. He received his training at Shilo, Manitoba and Debert, Nova Scotia. He went overseas in September, 1941. He was killed [on] invasion day.

Reekie Lake (53 L/11), west of Gods Lake was named after him in 1962.

Rees, Private **Ralph C.** of McAuley (H 6297). Winnipeg Grenadiers. He died a prisoner of war 14 March 1945 at the age of 34 and is commemorated at the Yokohama War Cemetery in Japan. This native of Monmouthshire, Wales was the son of Charles and Rose Rees and was survived by his wife Marjorie L. Rees of Virden and their daughter Marilyn. He wife recalls (18 October 2001):

> [He] enlisted with the Winnipeg Grenadiers on September 14, 1939 and served in Jamaica, British West Indies from March, 1940 to September, 1941. He arrived in Hong Kong in October, 1941 and was taken a prisoner of war on December 24, 1941. His cremated remains were buried at Yokohama.
>
> Ralph enjoyed singing. One time, a lady on a bus passed the hat around after he sang *Danny Boy* and he received $10.00. That was considered quite a sum in those days.

Rees Lake (64 I/5), south of Shethanei Lake was named after him in 1974.

Reeves, Trooper **Alvin** of Swan River (H 26669). Fort Garry Horse. He died 6 June 1944 at the age of 25 and is commemorated at Bretteville-sur-Laize Canadian War Cemetery in Calvados, France. He was the son of Edward and Pearl Reeves and was survived by his wife Evelyn M. Reeves of Toronto and their daughter. ***Reeves Lake*** (62 N/15), southeast of Swan River was named after him in 1973.

Reeves, Flight Sergeant **William N.** of Winnipeg (R 86394). No. 25 Operational Training Unit, RCAF. He died 21 May 1942 at the age of 27 and is commemorated at Darlington West Cemetery, County Durham, England. He was the son of Alfred and Ada Reeves of Winnipeg and was survived by his wife Jean E. Reeves of Winnipeg. ***Reeves River*** (64 J/4), which flows into the Mistay River was named after him in 1987.

Regimbal, Flight Sergeant **Léo J.** of Transcona (R 101761). No. 101 Conversion Unit, RCAF. He died 13 July 1942 at the age of 28 and is commemorated at Buxton Cemetery in Derbyshire, England. He was the son of Napoleon and Marie R. Regimbal (née Paquette) of St. Boniface. His aircraft was crewed by a mixed complement of Canadians and RAF officers on a training flight from Oakington, England. They flew into low cloud near Leek, Staffordshire and the aircraft was heard to explode a few minutes later. It had flown into high ground near a mountain; all crew were killed instantly. He had worked as a butcher for a large chain store in Transcona prior to enlisting. ***Regimbal Lake*** (52 L/6), northeast of Lac du Bonnet was named after him in 1973.

Regis, Flight Sergeant **Emile E. J.** of Fannystelle (R 102863). No. 122 Squadron. He died 15 October 1942 at the age of 28 and is commemorated at the Runnymede Memorial in Surrey, England. He was survived by his mother Rosa Regis of Drummondville, Quebec. According to his sister (10 January 1996):

> Emile was born ... at St. Henri, PQ. Our parents soon [moved] to a homestead in Gravelbourg, Saskatchewan and later moved to Fannystelle, Manitoba where our father worked on railway maintenance and care-taking of our church and school. Eventually there were 12 children in our family, seven boys and five girls.
>
> Emile was a good student early in life. He loved singing; yodelling was his favourite. He also played cornet in the town band. Everyone knew when he was practising on the back step. He also played the mouth organ and accordion very well. He sang in the choir. He enjoyed and was a member of the hockey and baseball teams.
>
> We lost our father when Emile was 17 years old. He was a great comfort to his mother. As finances became very low, our nun teachers helped him out as best they could financially. He was sent to St. Boniface College for his Grade 12. Apparently he was not happy there and set out to work – first in bush camps, then the mines. From there he joined the army; shortly after he joined the air force. Flying was in his blood immediately. He left for England on January 8, 1942; he was happy when in action. He was great at writing us all. His last letter to me was on September 19, 1942. Less than a month later, he was reported as missing in action. Then, a month later he was presumed dead which devastated our mother.

Regis Lake (64 P/4), south of Nejanilini Lake was named after him in 1974.

Reichert, Pilot Officer **Clifford C.** of Thornhill (J 18083). No. 408 Squadron, Mentioned in Dispatches. He died 22 June 1943 at the age of 23 and is commemorated at the Runnymede Memorial in Surrey, England. He was the son of William and Therese Reichert of Morden. According to ex-Pilot Officer George Pridham:

> We were badly hit by a night fighter aircraft so Cliff yelled for anyone who could to bail out. I was hit in the leg and lost it as a Prisoner of War. Pilot Officer J. C. Russell, the navigator also bailed out but the rest didn't make it. Cliff wasn't hit, I believe, but stayed with the aircraft not knowing who was hit or who could get out. In 1985, I was contacted by Mr. John Van Vleet of Lopek, Holland and he said our aircraft had been found by him and some diver friends in the mud of the Lek River at Lopek; one Rolls Royce engine was taken out and made to look like new. They built a six-foot by ten-foot steel and glass special memorial and put the engine in it along with a 20-foot wing pointing straight up; all of our names were put on it. I also contacted Cliff's relatives at Morden and in 1986 there was a get together there of some of the next-of-kin of those killed and those involved in Holland (Allison and Hayward 1991).

Reichert Lake (64 C/3), southwest of Granville Lake was named after him in 1947. His comrades placed a memorial there in his honour (Garland 1975).

Reid, Gunner **Clifford A.** of Virden (H 10335). No. 1 Radar Battalion, Royal Canadian Artillery. He died 24 February 1945 at the age of 20 and is commemorated at the Groesbeek Canadian War Cemetery in Holland. This native of Swift Current, Saskatchewan was survived by his parents James Leslie and Gladys Reid of Hargrave, Manitoba and siblings Olive, Gordon and Robert. His sister recalls (22 November 2001):

> Clifford always enjoyed his work on the farm. Whether he was harrowing with six horses or throwing hay down from the loft, you would hear him singing. When he was seeding wheat, he was figuring the yield and what it would buy. He rode horseback as if he were part of the horse. Once when he was riding bareback full tilt over hummocky ground rounding up a calf, I held my breath expecting he or the horse would end up with a broken neck.
>
> Cliff was very quiet but very responsive with his twinkly blue eyes and ready smile. There are so many good memories – our hikes in the river hills, skating on the rink that Dad made for us in the back yard, hunting rabbits, Hallowe'en pranks, running Meccano off the treadle sewing machine wheel to blow bran or paper pellets, like straw from a threshing machine. His generosity allowed him to assign $10.00 from his Army pay to his mother each month.
>
> He enlisted in the Royal Canadian Artillery at Winnipeg on June 16, 1943. He went on to become a wireless operator, driving a Bren Gun Carrier in the 1st Canadian Radar Battery. On August 4th, 1944, he embarked for the UK and on to Belgium and Holland to await his call to the front lines. He saw action for less than a week in Germany. Always remembered by his family and friends.

Clifford Reid Lake (53 N/3), southwest of White Goose Lake was named after him in 1995.

Reid, Lieutenant **Edward J.** of Winnipeg. Queen's Own Cameron Highlanders, Military Cross. He died 6 October, 1944 at the age of 28 and is commemorated at Bergen-op-Zoom Canadian War Cemetery in Holland. He was the son of Charles N. and Helena Reid of Souris. ***Reid Lake*** (64 C/3), southwest of Granville Lake was named after him in 1947.

Reid, Able Seaman **Edward R.** of Brandon (V 24959). HMCS *St. Croix*. The *St. Croix* was torpedoed and sunk by U-305 south of Iceland while escorting Convoy ON.202. Five officers and 76 men were rescued by HMS *Itchen*, but only one of these survived the loss of the *Itchen* two days later. See VanSickle, Ordinary Seaman Harold A. for additional information. Able Seaman Reid died 20 September 1943 at the age of 20 and is commemorated at the Halifax Memorial. He was the son of William and Lena Reid of Brandon. ***Reid Esker*** (64 I/16), south of Meades Lake was named after him in 1995.

Reid, Sergeant **James A.** of Onanole (H 40798). Royal Winnipeg Rifles. He died 8 June 1944 at the age of 26 and is commemorated at Beny-sur-Mer Canadian War Cemetery in Calvados, France. He was the son of Robert and Margaret Reid of Onanole, Manitoba. His brother recalls (6 December 1996):

> My brother ... joined the Royal Winnipeg Rifles on June 15, 1940. He was taken prisoner in Normandy and murdered by the SS. He was born in Transcona and moved to Clear Lake in 1923. He enjoyed singing, playing guitar, baseball and skating.

Reid Point (63 N/8) in the File River was named after him in 1995.

Reid, Sergeant **Joseph A.** of Fannystelle (H 59572). Royal Canadian Artillery. He died 17 September 1944 at the age of 26 and is commemorated at Gradara War Cemetery in Italy. He was the son of Bertram M. and Hannah Reid of Saskatoon. ***Reid Hill*** (64 I/8), north of the South Knife River was named after him in 1995.

Reid, Flying Officer **MacKenzie D. "Mac"** of Basswood (J 85448). No. 197 Squadron. He died 13 September 1944 at the age of 20 and is commemorated at the Calais Canadian War Cemetery in France. He was the son of William and Barbara A. Reid of Basswood, Manitoba. His brother recalls (6 November 2001) that Mac's youthful exuberance, enthusiasm and zest for life spoke for itself in his letters:

- Please excuse this letter if you can't read it, but I just 'soloed' and I can hardly sit still to write anything. Boy, oh boy!
- If I manage to get overseas, I will more than likely have a Spitfire to fly, whoopee!
- We've been doing a bit of flying lately and I've been over France five times. Sorry I can't mention the kind of work we're doing, but there's plenty of excitement. (Log Book entries: Bombing Crecy; escorting Marauders over Boulogne).
- Have done thirteen trips over France without mishap except for my first trip when my plane was hit a couple of times by ack-ack.
- I'm expecting to go on a 48-hour pass to England next week, so Bournemouth here I come. It's still my dream city in England and a lovely place for a holiday. Wish I could get to Clear Lake right now instead though.

> All of Mac's wartime letters were saved by his parents, and in his memory they were printed and published as a book titled *To a New Dawn* in 1994 by his brother Birnie, 50 years after his death. They provide engrossing details of an airman's life, insight into farm life in rural Manitoba and poignant reminders of the futility of war. Copies of the book are in the Library of the Canadian War Museum in Ottawa, the Library of the Commonwealth Air Training Plan Museum in Brandon and in the Legion at Minnedosa.

Reid Lake (53 E/7), south of Island Lake was named after Flying Officer Reid in 1973.

Reid, Flying Officer **Malcolm J.** of Winnipeg (J 22672). No. 83 Squadron. He died 20 February 1944 at the age of 25 and is commemorated at the Berlin 1939 - 1945 War Cemetery in Brandenburg, Germany. He was the son of Norman and Bella Reid of Vancouver. ***Reid Peninsula*** (63 N/12) on Sisipuk Lake was named after him in 1995.

Reid, Private **Nigel** of Onanole (H 46212). Lake Superior Regiment. He died 25 December 1942 at the age of 37 and is commemorated at Brookwood Military Cemetery in Surrey, England. He was the son of John and Sarah Reid and was survived by his wife Jessie Reid of Onanole, Manitoba and their two daughters. His daughter writes (31 May 1995):

> My father ... was born in 1904 at Clanwilliam, Manitoba. [He] served in the Canadian Army as a chef. He was remembered and loved dearly by [his] wife, brothers, sisters.

Reid Island (64 C/16) in Barrington Lake was named after him in 1995.

Reid, Flying Officer **Norman D.** of Durban (J 10353). No. 427 Squadron, Air Force Cross.

The above noted officer was employed as an NCO Flying Instructor at No. 11 Service Flying Training School, Yorkton, Saskatchewan, for a period of eleven months, after which he was appointed to a commission as Pilot Officer on 1 March 1942. During this period of eleven months, he logged nine hundred hours of instructional flying time. The quality of his work was outstanding in that his pupils always placed high in their respective classes and during the whole period, only one of his students was involved in an accident. His steadiness and persistent attention to duty furnished an excellent example to other NCO flying instructors. He has flown, while in the service, 1651 hours. His persistent efforts and devotion to duty have, if anything, increased since his appointment to commissioned rank (AFC Citation 1 January 1943).

The award was personally presented to him by the King at Buckingham Palace (*The Winnipeg Tribune* 1943). He died 23 June 1943 at the age of 28 and is commemorated at Warnsveld (Wichmond) General Cemetery, Holland. He was the youngest of the six children of George W. and Janet Reid of Durban, Manitoba. ***Reid Bay*** (64 O/12) in Shannon Lake was named after him in 1985.

Reid, Private **Ralph M.** of Birds Hill (H 102095). Royal Canadian Army Service Corps. He died 11 June 1944 at the age of 29 and is commemorated at the Cassino War Cemetery in Italy. He was the son of James and Elizabeth Reid and was survived by his wife Alma Reid of Winnipeg and their daughter. ***Reid Creek*** (64 P/5), which flows southeast into Wolverine River was named after him in 1995.

Rémillard, Private **Gérard** of St. Boniface (H 67385). Princess Louise Dragoon Guards. He died 23 September 1944 at the age of 19 and is commemorated at Cesena War Cemetery in Italy. He was the son of Alfred and Annie O. Remillard of St. Boniface. ***Rémillard Lake*** (64 K/13), north of Lac Brochet was named after him in 1972.

Rempel, Flying Officer **Walter E.** of Winnipeg (J 11436). No. 419 Squadron. He died 12 February 1944 at the age of 22 and is commemorated at the Runnymede Memorial in Surrey, England. He was the son of Gustave A. and Joanna I. Rempel of Vancouver. ***Rempel Lake*** (64 P/10), east of Nejanilini Lake was named after him in 1974.

Renaud, Private **Halfdan S. E.** of Riverton (H 17728). Princess Patricia's Canadian Light Infantry. He died 15 December 1943 at the age of 24 and is commemorated at the Moro River Canadian War Cemetery in Italy. He was the son of Emile J. and Gudlang J. Renaud of Riverton, Manitoba. ***Renaud Lake*** (64 O/10), west of Nejanilini Lake was named after him in 1975.

Renault, Private **Basil P.** of Ste. Rose du Lac (H 101549). Cameron Highlanders of Ottawa. He died 6 September 1944 at the age of 29 and is commemorated at the Calais Canadian War Cemetery in France. He was the son of Joseph and Félicité Renault of Ste. Rose du Lac, Manitoba. ***Renault Lake*** (64 P/1), south of Caribou Lake was named after him in 1974.

Rendall, Shipwright 4 **George W.** of Winnipeg (V 39429). HMCS *Stadacona*. He died 14 October 1942 at the age of 26 and is commemorated at the Halifax Memorial. He was the son of George and Isabella Rendall and was survived by his wife Elizabeth M. Rendall. ***Rendall Lake*** (64 N/14), west of Nueltin Lake was named after him in 1972.

Rennie, Rifleman **Russell** of Pierson (H 40716). Royal Winnipeg Rifles. He died 8 June 1944 at the age of 36 and is commemorated at Beny-sur-Mer Canadian War Cemetery in Calvados, France. He was the son of Alexander and Elizabeth Rennie of Pierson, Manitoba. ***Rennie Lake*** (63 K/12), south of Embury Lake was named after him in 1982.

Reske, Private **Reinholt** of Ladywood (H 105097). Royal Regiment of Canada. He died 24 October 1944 and is commemorated at Schoonselhof Cemetery in Antwerp, Belgium. He was the son of Julius and Mary Reske of Ladywood, Manitoba. ***Reske Lake*** (64 K/15), northeast of Lac Brochet was named after him in 1972.

Rewucki, Private **Edward** of Winnipeg (H 95676). General List, Canadian Army. He died 5 June 1944 at the age of 24 and is commemorated at Brookside Cemetery in Winnipeg. He was the son of John and Lena Rewucki of Winnipeg. ***Rewucki Lake*** (64 I/11), north of North Knife Lake was named after him in 1974.

Reynolds, Sergeant **James L.** of Killarney (H 45997). Lake Superior Regiment. He died 21 August 1944 at the age of 30 and is commemorated at Bretteville-sur-Laize Canadian War Cemetery in Calvados, France. He was the son of Bruce and Mary Reynolds and was survived by his wife Elena P. Reynolds of Toronto. ***Reynolds Bay*** (64 N/9) in Shannon Lake was named after him in 1987.

Reynolds, Flying Officer **William B.** of Winnipeg (J 13100). No. 170 Squadron. He died 6 August 1943 at the age of 26 and is commemorated at Evreux Communal Cemetery, Eure, France. He was the son of William and Litta I. Reynolds of Winnipeg and was survived by his wife of eight months Joan Reynolds. ***Reynolds Lake*** (64 O/6), southeast of Nueltin Lake was named after him in 1975.

Rheubottom, Flight Sergeant **James** of Winnipeg (R 196199). No. 300 Squadron. He died 25 July 1944 at the age of 19 and is commemorated at Orleans Main Cemetery in Loiret, France. He was survived by his mother Alice Nixon of Winnipeg. ***Rheubottom Lake*** (64 P/14), northeast of Nejanilini Lake was named after him in 1974.

Richard, Trooper **Gerard J. L.** of Winnipeg (K 1126). British Columbia Dragoons. He died 18 April 1945 at the age of 25 and is commemorated at the Groesbeek Canadian War Cemetery in Holland. He was the son of Alphonse and Bertha Richard and was the brother of Rifleman Lucien Richard (see entry) of St. Boniface. ***Richard Lake*** (63 K/16), west of Wekusko Lake was named after him in 1973.

Richard, Private **Henri J.** of Saltel (H 204685). Queen's Own Cameron Highlanders. He died 28 August 1944 at the age of 23 and is commemorated at Bretteville-sur-Laize Canadian War Cemetery in Calvados, France. He was the son of Henri L. and Elisabeth Richard of Ste-Geneviève. His sister recalls (26 October 2001):

My brother Henri had a happy childhood helping Mom and Dad in their general store. He was very energetic, ambitious, adventurous and always in a good humour. Since he was the eldest of the family, we all looked up to him. I remember following him whether it was, to build a log cabin, hunt blackbirds or gophers with his slingshot, go to watch him play baseball, or even get up very early to attend Mass and in the winter, start the fire in the wood stove at the school in order to warm up the one-room building. We played a guessing game, trying to locate various places on the big map of the world. Little did we think that he would be killed overseas one day...

He loved airplanes and had pictures of them everywhere. When World War II broke out, he tried to join the Air Force, but he could not be a pilot because he was colour-blind. He was so disappointed and did not want to be a gunner. Finally, he was accepted to be a Private in the infantry. While in service, he always volunteered for special duties such as scouting etc. In one of his last letters to Mother who had asked him if he prayed, he answered: "What else does a soldier think when he is in a fox-hole under bombardment?"

His nephew adds:

In August, 1944, Henri found himself overseas and joining the Allied effort just after D-Day. By this time, Henri had been in the army for over 18 months, of which he had prepared for and participated in an amphibious landing and spent many more months training back in Canada. The story is that he was "ready to go."

Back home in Ste-Geneviève, Manitoba, Henri's parents were worried about their eldest son, but proud enough to put up a map of France on the wall. Every day from the newspaper and radio news, Henri's parents would track the Allies' progress on the map.

Henri was killed sometime on the 28th. Henri was shot in the chest by a sniper on a mission which he had volunteered for. The letter received from Henri's commandant after his death said that Henri was the type of soldier who was always one to volunteer. Henri's tenacity was shown in his last words to his comrades. It was reported to be "Leave me here and go get those Germans" or words to that effect. To the end, his mission was clear, to fight the German army who had started this Great War, a huge atrocity against both his country and family.

Henri is buried ... near the very place he first joined the Camerons. When news of Henri's death came home, his father took down the map ... and threw it in the woodstove (www.multipointproductions.com/heroes/henri/henri4.htm).

Richard Peninsula (64 C/6) on Kadeniuk Lake was named after him in 1995. Three nephews and a brother erected a plaque there in July, 2000.

Richard, Leading Aircraftman **John F.** of Winnipeg (629318). No. 201 Squadron, RAF. He enlisted in December, 1938 and was lost while on patrol near the Shetland Islands on 21 August 1941. He was 23 years of age and is commemorated at the Runnymede Memorial in Surrey, England. ***Richard Rapids*** (64 I/13) in the McKay River was named after him in 1995.

Richard, Rifleman **Lucien J. A.** of Norwood (H 9166). Royal Winnipeg Rifles. He died 15 August 1944 at the age of 19 and is commemorated at Bretteville-sur-Laize Canadian War Cemetery in Calvados, France. He was the son of Alphonse and Bertha Richard of St. Boniface and the brother of Trooper Gerard Richard (see entry). ***Richard Bay*** (63 N/2) in Moody Lake was named after him in 1995.

Richardson, Flying Officer **Henry H.** of Winnipeg (J 17320). No. 50 Squadron, Distinguished Flying Medal.

By his excellent example, this airman has helped to maintain a high standard of efficiency among the pilots of his squadron. Many of the sorties undertaken by him were raids on strongly defended targets in Germany. On several of these, he avoided encounters with night fighters by skilful manoeuvring and flew his aircraft safely to base. Flight Sergeant Richardson also took some good shots. His courage and skill in pressing home his attack have invariably been worthy of high praise (DFM Citation 1943).

He died 14 April 1944 at the age of 28 and is commemorated at Botley Cemetery in Oxfordshire, England. He was the son of Henry R. and Elizabeth M. Richardson of Winnipeg. ***Richardson Creek*** (64 O/8), which flows northeast into Nejanilini Lake was named after him in 1975.

Richardson, Warrant Officer 2 **Jack G.** of McConnell (R 86416). No. 199 Squadron. He died 12 March 1943 at the age of 20 and is commemorated at the Runnymede Memorial in Surrey, England. He was the son of Jesse C. and Lottie Richardson of McConnell, Manitoba. ***Richardson Rapids*** (54 M/5) in the Caribou River was named after him in 1984.

Richardson, Coder **Jasper James** of Brandon (V 830). HMCS *St. Croix*. The *St. Croix* was torpedoed and sunk by U-305 south of Iceland while escorting Convoy ON.202. Five officers and 76 men were rescued by HMS *Itchen*, but only one of these survived the loss of the *Itchen* two days later. See VanSickle, Ordinary Seaman Harold A. for additional information. Coder Richardson died 20 September 1943 at the age of 21 and is commemorated at the Halifax Memorial. He was the son of Thomas and Sarah J. Richardson of Brandon. A childhood friend recalls (30 May 1995):

Jim was the only son the Richardsons had. His father was the steam engineer at Rumford's Steam Laundry (taken over years ago and now known as Perth's Dry Cleaning). The Richardson and Hamilton families both attended the old Knox United Church, formerly at the southeast corner of 15th Street and Victoria Avenue.

Richardson Bay (63 N/7) in Takipy Lake was named after him in 1995.

Richardson, Private **John W.** of Dauphin (H 103407). Calgary Highlanders. He died 25 July 1944 at the age of 30 and is commemorated at Bretteville-sur-Laize Canadian War Cemetery in Calvados, France. He was the second eldest son in a family of six boys and one girl born to Harold G. and Myrtle Richardson (née Blair) of Dauphin. His siblings and sisters-in-law write (16 November 2001):

Jack had a wonderful sense of humour; he was a big tease and enjoyed life to the fullest. Good times were had when he and his brothers and friends gathered at the neighbours' homes to enjoy an evening of music, dances or cards. He loved farming, hunting and his horses. Jack and his brother Lloyd had a very special, life-long relationship. They were inseparable as children and later as young men. They enlisted in November, 1942 with the Princess Patricia's Canadian Light Infantry, requesting to be together. They trained in Winnipeg and in Shilo, Manitoba. They were shipped overseas in June, 1943 and were transferred to the Calgary Highlanders. They were near each other when Jack died. Lloyd was wounded, but returned home after the war. Jack was first listed as missing in action. Weeks later, a taxi delivered a telegram to the farm – Jack had died in action.

He is fondly remembered by his family. He and his mother were very close and she never got over the loss. His Mother faithfully sent letters and parcels during the war. The letters she received had been censored before she got them, but she always looked forward to receiving them. Jack is not forgotten and his memory is kept alive by his many relatives. There have even been some of his nephews that have been to his gravesite near Caen, France.

Richardson Peninsula (64 N/11) on Kasmere Lake was named after him in 1995.

Richardson, Private **Joseph W.** of Winnipeg (H 98023). Veterans Guard of Canada. He died 6 March 1944 at the age of 51 and is commemorated at Brookside Cemetery in Winnipeg. He was survived by his sister Agnes Finch of Copco, California. ***Richardson Island*** (53 E/15) in Island Lake was named after him in 1983.

Richardson, Lieutenant **Leonard J.** of Winnipeg (CDN 191). Lincolnshire Regiment. He died 9 July 1944 at the age of 23 and is commemorated at Ranville War Cemetery, Calvados, France. He was the son of Charles L. and Ellen Richardson of Winnipeg. At the time of his enlistment, he was a fourth year student at United College and had planned to study for the ministry. ***Richardson Point*** (64 J/5) on Sprott Lake was named after him in 1989.

Richardson, Sergeant **William G.** of Winnipeg (1188860). No. 51 Squadron, RAF. He died 3 April 1943 at the age of 29 and is commemorated at the Reichswald Forest War Cemetery in Germany. He was the son of William and Lily Richardson and was survived by his wife Patricia P. Richardson of Kidlington, Oxfordshire, England. ***Richardson Hill*** (64 P/2), northwest of Meades Lake was named after him in 1995.

Richmond, Signalman **Wallace J.** of Winnipeg (V 9804). HMCS *Avalon*, the Royal Canadian Navy shore establishment in St. John's, Newfoundland. He died 12 December 1942 at the age of 22 and is commemorated at Mount Pleasant Cemetery in St. John's, Newfoundland. He was the son of John and Ada Richmond of St. James. ***Richmond Lake*** (64 N/8), northwest of Egenolf Lake was named after him in 1972.

Ridge, Flight Lieutenant **Raymond C.** of Brandon (J 24425). No. 404 Squadron, Distinguished Flying Cross.

> Since joining his present squadron, Flying Officer Ridge has completed a large number of operational sorties, many of which have been successful anti-shipping patrols against enemy naval and merchant vessels near the Dutch, French and Norwegian coasts. These convoys have been frequently accompanied by destroyers and anti-aircraft ships and have occasionally been protected by shore based guns. Flying Officer Ridge has always pressed home his attacks with great courage and fearlessness. He is a most experienced and capable pilot who has always given his leader every possible assistance (DFC Citation 1949).

He died 8 March 1945 at the age of 22 and is commemorated at the Runnymede Memorial in Surrey, England. He was the son of Ernest A. and Ethel M. Ridge (née Shepherd) of Brandon and was survived by his wife Olga E. Ridge of Toronto. She writes (5 November 2001):

> Raymond ... was born in Angusville on August 2, 1922. His fascination with planes started in public school where he made planes out of balsa wood and won prizes for his effort. Apparently, they hung in the school for many years. He worked for Winnipeg Electric Power Commission at Seven Sisters Falls before joining the RCAF in February, 1942.
>
> Virden Air School was his first posting. He graduated the most promising student in a class of 66, winning an engraved silver cigarette case. He received his commission in Borden, Ontario and then went on to train in the coastal command in Summerside, PEI. He went overseas in June, 1943 and flew many sorties over the Bay of Biscay. He died ... attacking U-boats in the North Sea. His plane went down in the fjords near Midtgulen, Norway. He received the DFC posthumously which was presented to his wife Olga (Ollie) by Lord Alexander of Tunis in Ottawa.

Ridge Lake (64 B/8), southwest of Baldock Lake was named after him in 1949.

Riel, Rifleman **Roland** of St. Vital (H 1572). Regina Rifle Regiment. He died 15 October 1944 at the age of 19 and is commemorated at the Adegem Canadian War Cemetery in Belgium. He was the son of Honoré and Yvonne Riel (née Vermette) and was survived by two brothers, two sisters and his wife of seven months Doris M. Riel (née Nickolson) of St. Vital. His sister and brother recall (13 November 2001):

> Private Roland Riel [was] born on December 8, 1924 at the family residence at 330 River Road in St. Vital, Manitoba. He was the great nephew of Louis Riel. The house where he was born and raised is now the Riel House Museum owned by Parks Canada. Roland was the eldest son in a very close knit family. He had a good sense of humour and was good natured. Hockey was his favourite pastime, with brothers, cousins and neighbours. They used the Red River as their rink.
>
> After graduating from Norberry School on St. Mary's Road, he went to work for a local sheep farmer. He also had employment with Globe Light Batteries until he joined the Regina Rifles in 1943. After basic training in New Brunswick, Roland returned to Winnipeg and married Doris Nickolson in March, 1944. Four months later, Roland left for Europe.
>
> In October of 1944, Rolly and his regiment were involved in the battle of the Leopold Canal in Belgium. While riding in a jeep with two other soldiers, they hit a landmine. Roland was severely injured and died shortly thereafter.

Riel Lake (63 O/4), north of Wekusko Lake was named after him in 1970.

Riesberry, Lieutenant **Donald L.** of Brandon. Royal Winnipeg Rifles. He died 11 October 1944 at the age of 30 and is commemorated at the Adegem Canadian War Cemetery in Belgium. He was the son of Ernest E. and Eva M. Riesberry and was survived by his wife Helen C. Riesberry of Brandon and their daughter whom he never had the chance to meet. She writes (4 April 2002):

> Donald Leach Riesberry was born February 20, 1914 and went on to study history and political science at Brandon University during the depression. He found summer work building the stone walls around Riding Mountain National Park. In his spare time he loved to play tennis and the trombone. He loved animals, particularly dogs and cats.
>
> He went overseas with the Royal Saskatchewan Regiment, later transferring to the Rifles. At one point, he studied history under noted local historian W. L. Morton at the University of Manitoba and was one of his top students. In Dr. Morton's book *The Kingdom of Canada*, the dedication reads: "For D. R., Normandy, 1944."

Riesberry Lake (64 I/2), east of North Knife Lake was named after him in 1974.

Riley, Captain **George Albert F. "Ab"** of Winnipeg. Royal Canadian Artillery. He died 5 September 1944 at the age of 26 and is commemorated at Gradara War Cemetery in Italy. He was the fifth of the eight children of Conrad S. and Jean I. Riley of Winnipeg and was survived by his wife Ailsa M. Riley (née Mathewson) of Winnipeg and their daughter. His widow wrote (29 May 1998) that prior to the war:

> He attended grade schools in Winnipeg followed by high school at Ridley College (a boys' school) in St. Catherine's, Ontario. Ab was a well set-up and well co-ordinated athlete. On returning to Winnipeg, he entered a course to become a Chartered Accountant. He was articled to Peat-Marwick and Mitchell for training and in the evening attended United College (now University of Winnipeg) graduating with a Gold Medal. He played interfaculty sports including rugby, but his main athletic interest was enjoyed at the Winnipeg Rowing Club. He was a very proficient oarsman being in winning four-oared crews and double sculling races over the years nationally and internationally. In 1939, as a result of winning in the double sculling, both in the American and the Canadian Henley Regatta in St. Catherine's, his double was selected to represent Canada at the Olympics in 1940, for which he was recognized

and honoured by the City of Winnipeg. However, due to the war, the Olympics were cancelled, of course.

On graduating in accounting in 1940, Ab immediately joined the army and was sent to Brandon as an artillery officer. At that time he married Ailsa Mathewson from Montreal; he found great joy in the birth of their daughter Ailsa Lynn on January 27, 1942. In July, '42, on graduation from the artillery training centre, he was sent overseas and was posted to the 8th Army Field Regiment, RCA, being an SP regiment attached to the 5th Canadian Armoured Division. The division joined the 1st Canadian Corps in Italy and fought battles in the area of Ortona and Rimini.

On September 5th, 1944, returning from forward artillery observation duty, his tank received a direct hit of enemy mortar fire and he was killed instantly. His family and friends were dear to him and he gave his life for the principles in which he so firmly believed. He was, is, and always will be a guiding influence for his descendants and all those who knew and loved him.

Riley Lake (53 N/4), northwest of Fish Lake was named after him in 1995.

Ringer, Flight Sergeant **James A.** of Winnipeg (R 162179). No. 10 Bombing and Gunnery School, RCAF. He died 9 June 1944 at the age of 24 and is commemorated at Assumption Gardens in Winnipeg. He was the son of William H. and Ethel H. Ringer of Winnipeg and was survived. by his wife Marion F. Ringer of Winnipeg. ***Ringer Lake*** (64 O/14), east of Nueltin Lake was named after him in 1975.

Rink, Gunner **Edward R.** of Gladstone (H 95563). Royal Canadian Artillery. He died 30 November 1943 at the age of 24 and is commemorated at the Moro River Canadian War Cemetery in Italy. He was the son of John and Flora Rink of Gladstone. His brother recalls (5 November 2001):

Edward was the oldest in a family of eight. At the age of 17, he worked for several farmers. He was always willing to help anyone who needed it and conscientiously performed his duties. The love of farming was in his blood and he intended returning home from the war to take up farming on the quarter of land he had already purchased.

In 1942, he joined the RCA and went overseas the following June. He went into Sicily, from there to Italy. While there, he took malaria fever and was hospitalized in North Africa. He recovered and joined his unit up the Italian boot. He was killed in action on November 30th. His parents received the sad news on December 13th. That was something they never got over.

Rink Lake (64 P/9), northwest of Caribou Lake was named after him in 1974.

Rissmann, Trooper **Burton F.** of St. Germaine (H 63952). Lord Strathcona's Horse. He died 26 May 1944 at the age of 22 and is commemorated at Naples War Cemetery in Italy. He was one of the eight children of Frederick T. and Minnie L. Rissmann (née Macloughlin) of St. Germaine, Manitoba. His nephew writes (25 November 2001):

Burt was born in Spooner, Minnesota and moved with his parents to Fort Frances then Dance, Ontario. In 1938, Burt went to live with his sister Emily and her family in Crozier, Ontario. Emily remembers Burt as being fun loving and very strong. She recalls a time when they were playfully competing for the same chair. Emily beat him to the seat and Burt, in one swift teasing moment lifted Emily, babe in arms, and the chair onto the table. There she sat while they all shared a good laugh. Burt would send money home so he could start farming after the war, recalls Emily. Burt's brother Mac recalls hunting together. Mac remembers Burt as being a practical joker and a very good marksman.

Rissmann Lake (64 K/15), northeast of Lac Brochet was named after him in 1972.

Ritchey, Lance Corporal **William H.** of Neepawa (H 20333). Queen's Own Cameron Highlanders. He died 26 July 1944 at the age of 39 and is commemorated at Bretteville-sur-Laize Canadian War Cemetery in Calvados, France. He was the fourth son of John W. and Marian Ritchey of Inkerman, Manitoba and was survived by his wife Margaret "Peggy" Ritchey (née Kerr). According to his niece (28 November 2001):

Bill and his wife Peggy took over his father's half-section of farm land and despite the depression, drought and grasshoppers, they found great pleasure in tilling the soil. Bill had a special rapport with animals and was very fond of them, especially his collie Bess and his huge dapple gray stallion, Jiggs. Bess independently went to the highway at the same time every evening, about three-quarters of a mile, and brought the cows home. Bill had a keen sense of humour and a hearty, infectious laugh. However, he strongly felt the need to defend our freedom from tyranny. He enlisted in June, 1940.

While Bill was stationed at Quebec City, his wife Peggy decided to visit him. She and their white terrier, Tiny, went by train. What a surprise when Bill saw Tiny running to meet him. What a joyous reunion! Bill found upstairs billets for them but after a few short days, he received notice that they were shipping out. Peggy said that as she listened to his footsteps going down the stairs and fading away, she felt that she would never see him again.

Bill left for overseas Christmas Day, 1940. Peggy returned home determined to run the farm until his return. She did so until after his death.

The shortage of farm labour was so great in England that Canadian soldiers who were experienced farmers could spend their leaves working on farms. The British farmers appreciated the help in growing more food and the Canadians, despite working eleven hour days plus after-work chores, had the time of their lives. Bill thoroughly enjoyed getting back to the land, but he also found time to visit his wife's relatives in Scotland.

From bits of information and a photograph, it seems he was in a motorcycle corps and was slated for the Dieppe Raid on August 19, 1942. However, he was injured in a practice manoeuvre and missed Dieppe. On July 7, 1944 the battalion landed on the Normandy coast. On July 16, he suffered minor shrapnel wounds from enemy fire, but walked to the first aid station and then returned to battle.

On July 18, 1944, the orders were to seize and hold the town of St. Andre-sur-Orne. Fighting was fierce. Casualties were heavy, but the Camerons held tenaciously to every bit of ground captured. My aunt later received a letter from Bill's company commander who was with him when he fell on July 26, 1944: "It was in the battle of St. Andre-sur-Orne, south of Caen. The battalion had been fighting night and day for a week without rest, against heavy enemy attacks. During all this, Bill did outstanding work, leading and encouraging his men and was always in the thick of things. His loss is deeply felt as he was very popular with everyone in his quiet, friendly way. His final sacrifice was made in the same unselfish manner he had always lived."

She adds (15 April 1995):

He was buried by the Chaplain at the field dressing station. The final burial site is Bretteville-sur-Laize. My aunt visited the grave with Madam Marcel Pelluet whom I believe was arranging for military graves to be adopted by local people. The grave has been adopted by Mademoiselle Paulette Boissais.

Ritchey Island (63 O/8) in Bison Lake was named after him in 1995.

Ritchie, Pilot Officer **Charles A.** of Roblin (J 85789). No. 420 Squadron. He died 16 March 1944 at the age of 23 and is commemorated at Durnbach War Cemetery in Bavaria, Germany. He was the son of Alex and Helen Ritchie and fiancé of Eva Burns. His sister recalls (n.d.) that:

Charlie was born and lived on a farm four miles from Roblin, Manitoba. He attended the elementary school and the high school there. He had two sisters and three brothers. This was a pleasant family unit that participated in sports (baseball, skating etc.) and community and social activities such as card games and dances. On completion of high school, he worked on his uncle's farm prior to joining the Air Force in 1941 and graduated as an Observer in 1942. He was with "Snowy Owl" Squadron, Halifax aircraft LW426. He served in England and in Africa. In 1943, he became engaged to Eva Burns and they had planned to be married on his next leave of absence. He did not return from a night operation to Stuttgart, Germany.

Ritchie Peninsula (64 F/8) on Unagimau Lake was named after him in 1995.

Ritchie, Flying Officer **John S. "Jack"** of Winnipeg (J 25867). No. 78 Squadron. He died 13 June 1944 at the age of 27 and is commemorated at Poix-de-Picardie Churchyard, Somme, France. He was survived by his fiancée Miss Kay Wood of Winnipeg. His aircraft was lost during a night attack against Amiens, France. Prior to enlisting, he was an agent at the Great-West Life Assurance Company. His twin brother reports (21 November 1994) that he was:

... born June 12, 1917 in Winnipeg's Grace Hospital and raised in the family's residence at 50 Evanson Street. He attended Laura Secord School, Gordon Bell High School and completed three years in the Faculty of Arts at the University of Manitoba. Prior to the war, he was employed at Great West Life Assurance at Head Office. A member of Young United Church (Sunday School teacher), the YMCA, the Winnipeg Chamber of Commerce, the Phi Kappa Pi Fraternity and the Winnipeg Canoe Club, he enjoyed tennis, soccer, lacrosse, hockey and basketball. His hobbies included the Winnipeg Boys' Choir (at that time directed by Davidson Kinley), the Male Voice Ensemble (directed by Davidson Thompson), the University Glee Club and the Great West Life Drama Club.

He wrote a letter to his work mates from overseas:

I am finding life over here very enjoyable and have seen quite a bit of the country. Spent my leave up in the highlands of Scotland at a very beautiful estate and sure enjoyed myself. Have just finished a four-week Commando course which entails crawling on hands and knees or stomach through thick undergrowth, supposedly stalking the enemy. They are apparently trying to toughen us up for our aircrew duties so I should be in pretty good condition soon. Just a few days ago I received word from my brother Dave informing me of the news concerning Bill Willard. It was an awful shock to us as I have been trying to contact him ever since my arrival. He was one of the finest chaps I ever knew. Please give my best wishes to all my friends in Head Office and Winnipeg Branch (*The Link* Issue 4, July 1943).

Ritchie Bay (63 N/7) in Burntwood Lake was named after him in 1995.

Ritchie, Warrant Officer 2 **Robert W.** of Winnipeg (R 119578). No. 431 Squadron. He died 4 December 1943 at the age of 21 and is commemorated at Becklingen War Cemetery in Germany. Four crewmembers were taken prisoner of war and later related that Warrant Officer Ritchie had maintained control of the aircraft long enough for them to bail out, but he stayed too long and went down with it (Allison and Hayward 1991). ***Ritchie Point*** (53 L/6) on Joint Lake was named after him in 1995.

Ritchie, Corporal **William** of Portage la Prairie (H 17367). Regina Rifle Regiment, Mentioned in Dispatches. He died 9 June 1944 at the age of 20 and is commemorated at Beny-sur-Mer Canadian War Cemetery in Calvados, France. He was the only son of Thomas Ritchie of Portage la Prairie. ***Ritchie Lake*** (54 K/12), southeast of Churchill was named after him in 1948 and ***Ritchie Rapids*** (64 P/10) in the Cameron River was named after him in 1995.

Ritzer, Stoker 1 **Edward R.** of MacGregor (V 35810). HMCS *Shawinigan*. The *Shawinigan* was torpedoed and sunk by U-1228 while on independent anti-submarine patrol in the Cabot Strait; all hands were lost. Stoker Ritzer died 24 November 1944 at the age of 29 and is commemorated at the Halifax Memorial. He was the son of Ferdinand and Florence B. Ritzer of MacGregor, Manitoba. ***Ritzer Lake*** (53 A/14) in northwestern Ontario was named after him in 1960.

Rivkin, Aircraftman 1 **Hyam I.** of Winnipeg (R 281554). Royal Canadian Air Force. He died 28 August 1945 at the age of 29 and is commemorated at Shaarey Zedek Cemetery in Winnipeg. He was the son of Samuel and Lena Rivkin of Winnipeg and was survived by his wife Anne Rivkin of Abbotsford, British Columbia. ***Rivkin Lake*** (64 P/11), east of Nejanilini Lake was named after him in 1974.

Robbins, Flying Officer **Ralph M.** of Brandon (J 26223). No. 1 Air Observers School. He died 11 March 1944 at the age of 23 and is commemorated at Brandon Cemetery. He was the son of John and Marjorie M. Robbins of Brandon and was survived by his wife Doreen F. Robbins of Rivers, Manitoba. ***Robbins Lake*** (64 P/4), southeast of Nejanilini Lake was named after him in 1974.

Roberge, Lieutenant **Victor E.** of Winnipeg (H 67594). South Saskatchewan Regiment. He died 9 March 1945 at the age of 23 and is commemorated at the Groesbeek Canadian War Cemetery in Holland. He was the son of Hector R. and Gertrude Roberge and was survived by his wife Marie A. Roberge of Burlingame, California and their son. ***Roberge Lake*** (54 F/6), northwest of York Factory was named after him in 1964.

Roberts, Pilot Officer **Charles A.** of Homewood (J 85903). No. 83 Squadron. He died 13 August 1944 at the age of 24 and is commemorated at the Hanover War Cemetery in Germany. He was the brother of Flight Sergeant Frank D. Roberts (see entry). ***Roberts Island*** (64 P/12) in Nejanilini Lake was named after him in 1974.

Roberts, Pilot Officer **Cyril E.** of Winnipeg (C 91052). No. 405 Squadron. He died 16 June 1943 and is commemorated at the Calais Canadian War Cemetery in France. He was the son of Edward I. and Kate Roberts of Winnipeg and was survived by his wife Margaret Roberts (née McKenzie). ***Roberts Creek*** (53 M/7), which flows south into Stupart River was named after him in 1995.

Roberts, Warrant Officer 1 **David R.** of Winnipeg (R 80174). No. 81 Operational Training Unit, RCAF. He died 11 January 1943 at the age of 22 and is commemorated at Wrexham Cemetery in Denbighshire, Wales. He was the son of Cecil R. and Barbara C. Roberts and was survived by his wife Margaret Roberts (née McKenzie) of Winnipeg. His brother writes (26 October 2001):

David ... was born in Winnipeg on March 1, 1920. He attended Earl Grey and Kelvin School and lived in west Fort Rouge. He was actively involved in social, sport and church groups, having been president of Crescent-Fort Rouge United Church Young Men's Club for two years and also an executive member of DeMolay for three years. His sports record included trophies for speed skating. He was first in the North-West Championship 10-mile race in 1938.

Warrant Officer Roberts enlisted in the RCAF in November, 1940 and received his wings at Saskatoon in July, 1941. He married Margaret McKenzie a few days later and was shortly thereafter posted overseas in England to complete training. He was assigned to a crew to fly a

Wellington bomber to North Africa via Gibraltar and Malta. He was stationed near Alexandria, Egypt.

When his tour of duty was completed in August, 1942, he flew his plane "Old Betsy" with his crew back to England from where he expected to return on leave to Canada. But this was not to be as he was needed as a pilot training instructor. During bad weather, he flew into a mountain in Wales and died in January, 1943.

While in Alexandria, Egypt, David described visiting the pyramids and Sphinx. He also had a short leave at the end of his tour of duty and along with two of his crew, by means of plane, taxi, bus and thumb, made it to Jerusalem. They met a Polish lorry driver who lived there and spoke at least seven languages including Hebrew and Arabic. This man, Benek by name, offered to show them around. They saw the new and the old Jerusalem, Bethlehem, Church of the Nativity, the Church of all Nations and the Mount of Olives just beside the Garden of Gethsemane. They also visited the tomb of the Virgin Mary. From the Mount of Olives they could just see the Dead Sea off in the distance and old Jerusalem with the wall surrounding. The most inspiring part was their walking tour through old Jerusalem including among other places, the Wailing Wall and the Church of the Holy Sepulchre. The last two days were spent in Tel Aviv.

Roberts Point (64 N/9) on Nahili Lake was named after him in 1987.

Roberts, Flight Sergeant **Frank D.** of Homewood (R 119606). No. 405 Squadron. He died 7 April 1943 at the age of 21 and is commemorated at St. Martin-de-Re Communal Cemetery, Charente-Maritime, France. He was the brother of Pilot Officer Charles A. Roberts (see entry). ***Roberts River*** (64 P/14), which flows northeast into the Caribou River was named after him in 1974.

Roberts, Private **Gerald D.** of Winnipeg (H 23638). Royal Canadian Army Medical Corps. He died 24 March 1945 at the age of 19 and is commemorated at Old Kildonan Presbyterian Cemetery in Winnipeg. He was one of the 12 children of Edgar and Jessie Roberts of Winnipeg and the brother of Flight Sergeant Norman W. Roberts (see entry). His nephew writes (3 December 2001):

> ... when Jerry was in his early teens, my Dad used to take him on the back of his motorcycle when he used to visit my mother at her parents'. My Grandma used to fatten him up with pie and ice cream. Just a few years later they got the letter that he was dead. He was so young.

Gerald Roberts Lake (63 P/2), north of Cotton Lake was named after him in 1995.

Roberts, Pilot Officer **John K.** of Winnipeg (J 5140). No. 59 Operational Training Unit, RCAF. He died 18 July 1941 at the age of 19 and is commemorated at Fairfield (St. Peter) Churchyard, Derbyshire, England. He was the son of John and Annie E. Roberts of Winnipeg. ***John Roberts Lake*** (53 K/12), east of Gods Lake was named after him in 1995.

Roberts, Flying Officer **John Murray** of Winnipeg (J 20417). No. 409 Squadron. He died 27 July 1944 at the age of 29 and is commemorated at Banneville-la-Campagne War Cemetery, Calvados, France. He was the son of Thomas and Hattie M. Roberts of Fort Garry. His sister recalls that (2 January 1995):

> My brother Murray was born in Winnipeg on October 9th, 1914. John Murray always used the name Murray. He was educated in Winnipeg attending elementary, junior high and high school before entering the University of Manitoba. As with many students during those times, it was frequently necessary for Murray to alternate university years with periods of earning so as to obtain the necessary funds. Much experience was gained through a variety of employment i.e., farming, night watchman, construction, renovating etc. Murray graduated from the University of Manitoba with a B.Sc. in Agriculture. He was employed by Canada Packers in the Food Sciences Laboratory until entering the RCAF in September, 1939.
>
> Murray started violin lessons when a young boy and his interest in music and his skills on violin, bass violin and trumpet remained with him as a source of pleasure and income. He was active in the University of Manitoba orchestra and Glee Club as well as in local bands which played for many Winnipeg dances in our two major hotels – the Royal Alexandra and the Fort Garry. Murray was always interested in sports and sporting events. He was active in the UMSU while at University.
>
> After enlisting in the RCAF, Murray trained in Canada, earning his Navigator's Wings and then his commission as a Pilot Officer. He was then stationed in England and assigned to duty as a navigator with a Mosquito night fighter squadron. Murray, with his pilot Jeff Jephson, flew many missions in the Mosquito, a two-man aircraft and participated in the air battles of D-Day, June, 1944. They remained in active combat constantly until the night of July 27, 1944. On that occasion, their Mosquito made a hit on a German fighter plane which exploded in front of them, damaging the Mosquito's engines. The family received all of this information through one of the operators of the radar connection back in England. She was in touch by voice as well. The two airmen indicated they were injured but were going to try for a landing. However, the altitude was only 1000 feet with the engines failing, so the aircraft crashed and burned with no one surviving. The site was Caen, France.

Roberts Bay (64 G/6) in Kapeetaukimak Lake was named after him in 1994.

Roberts, Flight Sergeant **Lloyd J. O.** of Winnipeg (R 74225). No. 419 Squadron. He died 7 May 1942 at the age of 21 and is commemorated at Durnbach War Cemetery in Bavaria, Germany. ***Roberts Peninsula*** (64 C/12) on Laurie Lake was named after him in 1995.

Roberts, Private **Louis C.** of Winnipeg (SB 153871). Royal Canadian Regiment. He died 30 May 1951 and is commemorated at the United Nations Cemetery in Pusan, South Korea. ***Louis Roberts Lake*** (53 L/13), north of Oxford Lake was named after this Korean War casualty in 1998.

Roberts, Flight Sergeant **Norman W.** of Winnipeg (R 110955). No. 408 Squadron. He died 30 March 1943 at the age of 22 and is commemorated at the Kiel War Cemetery in Germany. He was one of the 12 children of Edgar and Jessie Roberts of Winnipeg and the brother of Private Gerald D. Roberts (see entry). His nephew reports (3 December 2001) that:

> ... 22 Halifaxes from the 404, 408 and 419 squadrons were ordered on an attack at Berlin, the weather was poor with severe icing. Norm's plane failed to return. Six crew were killed and one [became a] PoW after being shot down by a nightfighter. The surviving crew member visited family of the men killed after the end of the war. He believed that Norm was dead before the plane went down as there had been no response from his gun position for some time after the initial attack.

Roberts Hill (64 B/5), north of Rat Lake was named after him in 1995.

Roberts, Flight Lieutenant **Warren A.** of Birtle (J 4566). No. 405 Squadron. He died 30 January 1944 at the age of 23 and is commemorated at the Berlin 1939 - 1945 War Cemetery in Brandenburg, Germany. He was the son of Joseph and Bessie Roberts of Birtle, Manitoba. ***Roberts Rapids*** (53 M/9) in the Gowan River was named after him in 1995.

Robertson, Major **David B.** of Winnipeg. Royal Winnipeg Rifles. He died 3 May 1945 at the age of 24 and is commemorated at the Holten Canadian War Cemetery in Holland. He was the son of David and Dorothy I. Robertson and was survived by his wife Kathleen M. Robertson of Toronto. ***David Robertson Lake*** (54 E/6), northwest of Fly Lake was named after him in 1995.

Robertson, Coder **Earl J.** of Winnipeg (V 9967). HMCS *Ottawa*. The *Ottawa* was escorting Convoy ON.127 in the North Atlantic when it was struck by two torpedoes from U-91; 114 of her ship's company were lost. Coder Robertson died 13 September 1942 at the age of 21 and is commemorated at the Halifax Memorial. He was the son of Robert and Mary Robertson of Winnipeg and the brother of Telegraphist Robert G. Robertson (see entry). ***Robertson Peninsula*** (64 C/3) on McKnight Lake was named after him in 1993.

Robertson, Private **Edward** of Carman (H 100251). Seaforth Highlanders of Canada. He died 6 October 1943 at the age of 29 and is commemorated at the Moro River Canadian War Cemetery in Italy. He was the son of Alexander and Margaret Robertson. ***Edward Robertson Lake*** (64 C/13), southwest of McMillan Lake was named after him in 1995.

Robertson, Private **Gilbert A.** of Winnipeg (H 41703). Winnipeg Grenadiers. He died a prisoner of war 29 November 1943 and is commemorated at the Yokohama War Cemetery in Japan. ***Robertson Falls*** (64 I/10) in the North Knife River was named after him in 1995.

Robertson, Pilot Officer **Harry K.** of Roblin (J 8649). No. 1 Flying Instructor School. He died 21 January 1942 at the age of 25 and is commemorated at Deer Park Cemetery in Tummel, Manitoba. He was the son of William H. and Elizabeth Robertson of Roblin and was survived by his wife Isabel C. Robertson of Roblin. ***Robertson Rapids*** (64 O/15) in an unnamed river east of Newcombe Lake was named after him in 1995.

Robertson, Pilot Officer **Ian** of Winnipeg (J 38435). No. 31 Operational Training Unit, RCAF. He died 2 April 1944 at the age of 22 and is commemorated at the Ottawa Memorial. He was the third child of Alexander and Annie Robertson of St. Boniface and was survived by his wife Violet H. Robertson (née Thorsteinson) of Winnipeg and their unborn son. His wife recalls (10 June 1987):

> [He was] born in St. Boniface [to] immigrants from Scotland. [He] lived in Norwood until enlisting in the RCAF. After graduating from Grade 12, [he] worked for Occidental Coal and Grain Company. On 3 April 1943 he married me [and] enlisted in the RCAF [the same year] and trained in eastern Canada as an Observer, obtaining top marks for his course and received a commission upon completion of his ground school. His final posting was to Debert, Nova Scotia where on 1 April 1944 he and his entire crew went missing over the Atlantic without a trace of either crew or aircraft ever being reported. At the time, I was four months pregnant. My son Ian Donald Robertson was born in Winnipeg [in] 1944.

Robertson Hill (64 N/1), northwest of Minuhik Lake was named after him in 1989.

Robertson, Private **James B.** of Winnipeg (H 37659). Royal Canadian Army Service Corps. He died 12 December 1942 at the age of 21 and is commemorated at Brookwood Military Cemetery in Surrey, England. He was survived by his mother Jeanne M. Robertson of Winnipeg. ***Robertson Narrows*** (53 L/8) in Webber Lake was named after him in 1995.

Robertson, Telegraphist **Robert Gordon** of Winnipeg (V 24172). HMCS *Guysborough*. The *Guysborough* was torpedoed and sunk by U-878 in the English Channel off Ushant, France; fifty-one of her ship's company were lost. Telegraphist Robertson died 18 March 1945 at the age of 25 and is commemorated at the Halifax Memorial. He was the son of Robert and Mary Robertson of Winnipeg, the brother of Coder Earl J. Robertson (see entry) and was survived by his wife Violet I. Robertson of Winnipeg. His sister-in-law writes (23 June 1993):

> Memories of these young navy men, the fun we all had when they returned on leave, are not easily forgotten. The heartache when they were reported lost at sea, to their parents who lost their only children, are still clear as they were when the telegrams arrived.

Robertson Island (64 C/3) in McKnight Lake was named after him in 1993.

Robertson, Corporal **Samuel D.** of The Pas (H 51772). 8th Princess Louise's (New Brunswick) Hussars. He died 25 May 1944 at the age of 22 and is commemorated at the Cassino War Cemetery in Italy. He was the son of John D. and Violet Robertson of The Pas. ***Robertson Esker*** (64 O/4), southeast of Nueltin Lake was named after him in 1975.

Robertson, Flight Sergeant **William Allan** of Reston (R 59266). No. 405 Squadron. He died 5 January 1942 at the age of 28 and is commemorated at Barmby-on-the-Moor (St. Catherine) Churchyard, Yorkshire, England. ***Allan Robertson Lake*** (53 L/15), west of Seller Lake was named after him in 1995.

Robidoux, Private **Marcel E. J.** of Headingley (H 6597). Winnipeg Grenadiers. He died a prisoner of war 7 October 1942 and is commemorated at the Sai Wan War Cemetery in Hong Kong. He was survived by his father Eugene Robidoux of Headingley. ***Robidoux Lake*** (54 C/8), south of York Factory was named after him in 1964.

Robinson, Trooper **Arthur E.** of Norgate (H 1982). Royal Canadian Armoured Corps. He died 3 February 1945 at the age of 20 and is commemorated at McCreary Cemetery. He was the second son of Harold and Janet C. Robinson (née McFarlane) of Norgate. His sister writes (3 February 1998):

> He was born ... at Minnedosa, Manitoba. As a baby, his parents moved to the USA for five years. A sister Ruth and a brother Robert were born there. In 1930, his parents came back to Canada and settled at Norgate, Manitoba. Arthur received all of his education at the Norgate School. He took part in all school activities such as ball, field days, Christmas concerts and learned to skate at the Norgate rink. His favourite pastimes were bicycle riding, singing with friends and hunting (he shot a bear when he was just 16). Sundays meant Sunday School and later the Norgate United Church young people's group.
>
> His older brother, Russell, had joined the Air Force and at age 18 Arthur joined the Army in Winnipeg. He took his other training in the armoured car at Camp Borden, Ontario. He was coming home on embarkation leave when he was killed by a CPR train in Otter, Ontario. The funeral was on February 8 at the Norgate United Church and he was buried at the McCreary Cemetery. The body was accompanied by Lieutenant Don Barwick of the Canadian Armoured Corp from Camp Borden. Pallbearers were all discharged servicemen.

Robinson River (64 P/15), which flows northeast into Caribou River was named after him in 1995.

Robinson, Pilot Officer **Curran S.** of Winnipeg (41470). No. 235 Squadron, RAF. He died 18 May 1940 at the age of 20 and is commemorated at the Runnymede Memorial in Surrey, England. See also Edy, Flight Lieutenant Allen L. His Squadron was in constant action over the English Channel in the spring and summer of 1940 in anticipation of a German invasion. It was on such a coastal patrol that his aircraft was lost (Allison 1978). ***Curran Robinson Lake*** (53 N/1), east of Red Cross Lake was named after him in 1995.

Robinson, Leading Telegraphist **Edmund C.** of Winnipeg (V 9661). HMCS *Charlottetown*. He died 16 September 1942 at the age of 22 and is commemorated at Brookside Cemetery in Winnipeg. He was the son of Herbert and Isabel Robinson of Winnipeg. ***Edmund Robinson Lake*** (53 L/3), northeast of Fairy Rock Lake was named after him in 1995.

Robinson, Flight Lieutenant **George D.** of Transcona (J 20412). No. 410 Squadron, Distinguished Flying Cross.

> As pilot and observer respectively, these officers have completed very many sorties. They have displayed the highest standard of skill and determination, qualities which were well illustrated in their first sortie when they destroyed a Junkers 88. Since then they have shot down another three enemy aircraft at night (Joint DFC Citation for Flight Lieutenant Robinson and Squadron Leader James D. Somerville 1944).

He died 26 December 1944 at the age of 26 and is commemorated at the Adegem Canadian War Cemetery in Belgium. He was the son of William G. and Flora M. Robinson of Transcona. ***Robinson Esker*** (64 J/1), east of Chipewyan Lake was named after him in 1989.

Robinson, Private **Henry** of Winnipeg (H 6637). Winnipeg Grenadiers. He died a prisoner of war 17 November 1942 and is commemorated at the Sai Wan War Cemetery in Hong Kong. ***Henry Robinson Lake*** (64 P/5), east of Little Duck Lake was named after him in 1995.

Robinson, Corporal **James Arnold** of Winnipeg (P 22332). Princess Patricia's Canadian Light Infantry. He died 15 December 1941 and is commemorated at Brookwood Military Cemetery in Surrey, England. He was one of the six children of Roderick J. and Florence L. Robinson of Portage la Prairie. ***Arnold Robinson Lake*** (53 M/3), west of Whitemud Lake was named after him in 1995.

Robinson, Gunner **John C.** of Portage la Prairie (H 92506). Royal Canadian Artillery. He died 22 July 1944 and is commemorated at Bretteville-sur-Laize Canadian War Cemetery in Calvados, France. ***Robinson Rapids*** (63 I/9) in the Lawford River was named after him in 1995.

Robinson, Private **Norman W.** of Souris (H 103308). 1st Canadian Parachute Battalion. He died 30 March 1945 at the age of 22 and is commemorated at the Holten Canadian War Cemetery in Holland. He was the son of Lemuel and Annie Robinson of Souris. ***Robinson Island*** (63 P/2) in Miskimmin Lake was named after him in 1995.

Robinson, Pilot Officer **Robert E.** of Ninga (J 5057). No. 122 Squadron. He died 26 August 1941 at the age of 21 and is commemorated at Stamfordham (St. Mary) Churchyard in Northumberland, England. He was survived by his mother Mrs. S. A. Robinson of Winnipeg. ***Robinson Peninsula*** (64 G/4) on Dickinson Lake was named after him in 1994.

Robinson, Leading Bombardier **Russell G.** of Manigotagan (H 66636). Royal Canadian Artillery. He died 12 April 1945 and is commemorated at the Groesbeek Canadian War Cemetery in Holland. He was the son of Mr. and Mrs. Dave Robinson of Manigotagan, Manitoba. ***Robinson Narrows*** (63 P/11) in Cuthbert Lake was named after him in 1995.

Robinson, Flying Officer **William Thomas** of Pine Falls (J 24161). No. 517 Squadron. He died 24 February 1944 at the age of 24 and is commemorated at Blacon Cemetery in Cheshire, England. He was the son of Albert B. and Sigurbjorg B. Robinson of Pine Falls, Manitoba. ***Thomas Robinson Lake*** (64 O/10), east of Corbett Lake was named after him in 1995.

Robson, Pilot Officer **Arthur E.** of Winnipeg (J 95463). No. 433 Squadron. He died 21 November 1944 at the age of 20 and is commemorated at the Reichswald Forest War Cemetery in Germany. He had received his commission the day before. He was the only son of William F. and L. Marjorie Robson of Winnipeg. The flight engineer on Pilot Officer Robson's last mission was Flight Sergeant J. Weir (RAF) of Lynemouth, Northumberland. He later wrote to Pilot Officer Robson's mother:

> Dear Mrs. Robson: I have just arrived back from Germany on the 13th of May, just a week ago. I would have written you sooner but I have been ill in bed since. Doris has not been able to write either because of looking after me. I know you must be very anxious for news of Art, so I am going to tell you all I can remember of the night of the 21st of November.
>
> I still remember it all so very vividly. We started out, quite a normal trip I thought, then things went wrong before we got away and we had to change our aircraft for another which may have spoiled our luck. Anyhow, near the target all was well again with us, a lovely night, moonlight and still, we were hit rather heavily by fighter or flak and began to burn in the air and pitch about. There was nothing I or anybody else of the crew could do but prepare to get out. We all had our chutes near us. I just managed to put on the skipper's chute before I was flung on the floor helpless. There was no panic, all had time to get out, I thought. Art was at his set to the last moment. The rear gunner Ken Slack was out first. Allan was hit and fell out of his turret and either unconscious or killed in the aircraft. I saw the navigator get out near Art. The bomb aimer Seymour, was standing by to do the same. The last I saw of Art was when he was standing up by his table making ready to jump, whether he did or not remains to be seen; somehow I don't think Art or Seymour did get out, I can't be sure. I don't know this, I never saw either of them after. This is what makes me think like I do. This all happened so quickly, all sorts of things could have happened. I don't think any of the others can tell you what happened to your dear son or the bomb aimer. We hoped to God that they were safe and that we might see or hear of them later during our travels. But none of us have. I have asked lots of other prisoners while in Germany if they have heard of Art or Seymour but the answer was always the same, surely, if they were still alive, somebody would have bumped into them at some PoW camp. Ken Slack was with me all the time after being shot down. I guess he is maybe in Canada now. The two officers Bond and Watson went to different Oflags [Officers' camps] together. We all had a rotten time at first, always being on the move, never got a chance to settle down as PoWs. I am in full sympathy with you about Art and Jimmie Seymour, also Allan, it is awful that it happened. I couldn't ever imagine it becoming our lot, we were so fine in the air, all knew our jobs well. Art

was the best wireless op I knew, he helped us out of lots of scrapes due to his skill. The others would say exactly the same, I assure you. I'm not much good at writing letters Mrs. Robson but this is in my own simple words.

I can only hope for the best about dear Art. I really got to admire him more than the others. God bless you all at the house (22 May 1945).

Three years later, she received the following from RCAF casualty officer F. F. Fatt:

It is with regret that I again refer to the loss of your son, Pilot Officer Arthur Edward Robson, but you will wish to know of a report received from our Missing Research and Enquiry Service.

Investigating officers of this service have ascertained that your son's aircraft had been shot down by a night fighter and crashed in a wood near Erkenschwick which is 17 miles northeast of Essen, Germany. Your son's aircraft had, in turn, apparently shot down the night fighter before it crashed as the wreckage of the night fighter was found 100 yards from your son's aircraft. The windshield which was three inches thick had five bullet holes through it. The remains of two of the three crew members who perished in the crash were recovered the following day and taken to Datteln, four miles east-northeast of Erkenschwick and buried in the local cemetery. The remaining member of the crew was not found until some time later when his remains were taken to Erkenschwick for burial.

The three graves were exhumed and Pilot Officer Allan was identified in the grave in Erkenschwick Cemetery and your son and Pilot Officer Seymour were identified in the two graves in Datteln Cemetery.

British Military Cemeteries have been located at a number of points in Germany and all Royal Canadian Air Force personnel buried in Germany will be moved to these cemeteries. This policy was agreed upon by the British and Dominion governments because it was felt that our Fallen in Germany should not lie in isolated cemeteries, but should rest in special War Cemeteries which have been carefully chosen for their natural beauty and peace of their surroundings and of which the soil will always be British. The graves will be tended in perpetuity by the staff of the Imperial War Graves Commission. Please be assured that when word is received of the re-interment of your son in a permanent Military Cemetery you will be advised.

May I again offer you my most sincere sympathy in you great loss (16 February 1948).

Robson Lake (64 O/11), southeast of Nueltin Lake was named after him in 1975.

Rock, Gunner **Robert O. D.** of St. James (H 14765). Royal Canadian Artillery. He died 22 April 1945 at the age of 22 and is commemorated at the Holten Canadian War Cemetery in Holland. He was the third of the eight children of Ann and Lewis Rock, immigrants from Northern Ireland and England respectively. He was survived by his wife Grace Rock (née McKenzie). His brother recalls (25 April 1995):

He grew up in St. James, at that time a suburb of Winnipeg, and was educated at Britannia School, Assiniboine School and St. James Collegiate. After completion of his schooling, he worked at various jobs before being employed at a cordite plant which manufactured war materiel. He endeavoured to enlist in 1941 but was rejected and subsequently went to work in the construction of the Alaska Highway. On returning from the Alaska Highway, he married Grace McKenzie, now deceased.

In the fall of 1944, he enlisted in the Canadian Army, trained in Canada and was posted overseas. He was killed in action on April 22, 1945 while serving with the 19th Field Regiment, Royal Canadian Artillery.

Rock Bay (63 N/7) in Burntwood Lake was named after him in 1995.

Rodd, Private **Orville W.** of Winnipeg (H 6330). Winnipeg Grenadiers. He died a prisoner of war 29 January 1942 at the age of 34 and is commemorated at the Sai Wan War Cemetery in Hong Kong. He was the son of Charles and Suzanne Rodd and was survived by his wife Ida J. Rodd of Winnipeg. ***Rodd Lake*** (64 J/2), southwest of Tadoule Lake was named after him in 1975.

Roddy, Flight Sergeant **William G.** of Winnipeg (R 95149). No. 156 Squadron. He died 7 July 1942 at the age of 22 and is commemorated at Lorient (Kerentrech) Communal Cemetery in Morbihan, France. He was the son of George J. and Harriet I. Roddy of Winnipeg. ***Roddy Lake*** (64 J/12), west of Tadoule Lake was named after him in 1975.

Rodgers, Sergeant **Edward H.** of Winnipeg (H 6086). Winnipeg Grenadiers. He died 21 December 1941 at the age of 30 and is commemorated at the Sai Wan War Cemetery in Hong Kong. He was the son of William E. and Jessie E. Rodgers of Winnipeg and was survived by his wife Vera I. Rodgers of Winnipeg. ***Rodgers Peninsula*** (64 F/16) on Bestick Lake was named after him in 1995.

Rodgers, Rifleman **Henry** of Giroux (H 8918). Royal Winnipeg Rifles. He died 8 June 1944 at the age of 22 and is commemorated at Beny-sur-Mer Canadian War Cemetery in Calvados, France. He was the son of Dan and Catherine Rodgers and was survived by his stepmother Pauline Rodgers of Giroux, Manitoba. According to his niece's husband (18 November 2001):

Henry ... was one of seven children in his first family. After Catherine's death, Dan Rodgers remarried and Henry's family grew by a further six. The family farm was modest but was in keeping with the fashion in which many people of that generation lived. Henry left school at age 14 with a Grade 8 education to work on a farm. He tried his hand as a machine man and helper in a gold mine. He drove a truck for a period of time and he worked as a logger in Ontario. Henry liked music and played the piano and accordion. He did not read much because his eyes sometimes bothered him. He enjoyed playing baseball and liked dancing. As did most rural Manitoba boys, Henry enjoyed hunting chicken, rabbits and deer.

After Henry joined the Canadian Army, he received his infantry training with the Royal Winnipeg Rifles. He left Winnipeg and went first to Montreal before deploying from Halifax to England on August 25, 1943.

Henry landed on Mike Beach in the Juno Beach Sector on D-Day, June 6, 1944. Henry was taken prisoner when members of the 12th SS Hitler Youth overran his position near Putot-en-Bessin. Henry was murdered as a prisoner of war on June 8, 1944. He and a number of other Royal Winnipeg Rifles were lined up, unarmed and machined gunned to death. Major General Kurt Meyer of the SS was later arrested, tried and convicted in a Canadian military court for being the officer that had been in charge of the SS troops that murdered Henry and numerous other Canadian soldiers.

Rodgers Lake (64 N/7), southwest of Nueltin Lake was named after him in 1972.

Rodgers, Pilot Officer **Herbert H.** of Macdonald (J 89733). No. 432 Squadron. He died 28 May 1944 at the age of 20 and is commemorated at the Runnymede Memorial in Surrey, England. ***Rodgers Rapids*** (64 I/16) in the Seal River was named after him in 1995.

Rodrigue, Private **Arthur L.** of St-Pierre-Jolys (H 19419). Queen's Own Cameron Highlanders. He died 20 January 1941 at the age of 38 and is commemorated at Brookwood Military Cemetery in Surrey, England. He was the son of Mr. and Mrs. Guillaume Rodrigue and was survived by his wife Flavie Rodrigue (née Rioux) of St-Pierre-Jolys, Manitoba and their nine children. His son writes (5 December 1996):

> My father was born August 26, 1902 in South Hanover, Connecticut [and] was married December 1, 1926. [He] enrolled as a volunteer September 11, 1939 [and] went to Shilo in July, 1940 [and] from Shilo he went to Quebec October 15th, 1940. From Quebec, he went to England December 12, 1940. He arrived in England December 25, 1940. He died accidentally on January 20th, 1941.

Rodrigue Lake (64 N/2), northwest of Egenolf Lake was named after him in 1972.

Roe, Private **Stanley** of Cartwright (H 1987). Royal Canadian Regiment. He died 5 December 1944 at the age of 32 and is commemorated at Ravenna War Cemetery in Italy. He was the son of Thomas Stanley and Edith Roe of Neelin, Manitoba. A family friend recalls (2 May 1995) that:

> The Stanley and Edith Roe family came from England and settled ... about five miles northwest of Neelin, Manitoba and about 10 miles southwest of Belmont. Fred went to a country school for Grades 2 to 8 – Huntley. Mrs. Roe and the boys were members of the Pentecostal Assemblies of Canada. Mr. Roe remained an [Anglican] Church man.
>
> Stanley enlisted in the Canadian Army February, 1943 and took basic training for 2 1/2 months at Portage la Prairie and then took advanced infantry training at Camp Ipperwash Infantry Training Centre near Forest, Ontario. When the training was complete, the company of 150 men went home by train to say goodbye to family. Some had to go as far as Kamsack, Saskatchewan and to The Pas, Manitoba. The Roe family had no car and Mr. Roe made the 20-mile trip with horses to meet them. They sat up all night to visit as next day they had to go back. A close neighbour, Henry Thompson was also there. They were two of the Canadian soldiers to take part in the landing on Sicily and later into Italy in the early fall of 1943.

Roe Island (64 O/15) in Newcombe Lake was named after him in 1995.

Rogers, Lieutenant **Arthur E.** of Winnipeg (H 26130). Fort Garry Horse. He died 6 July 1944 at the age of 26 and is commemorated at Beny-sur-Mer Canadian War Cemetery in Calvados, France. He was the son of Arthur A. and Mary A. Rogers (née Quarrie) and was survived by his wife Barbara E. Rogers (née Tingley) of St. Boniface and their daughter. ***Rogers Lake*** (64 G/4), north of Grandmother Lake was named after him in 1994.

Rogers, Gunner **Franklin W.** of Rapid City (H 67498). Royal Canadian Artillery. He died 10 October 1944 at the age of 25 and is commemorated at Brookwood Military Cemetery in Surrey, England. He was the son of Walter F. and Elizabeth M. Rogers of Newdale, Manitoba. His brother recalls (14 November 2001):

> ... we grew up together on a farm; he joined the army a year before I did. I was in England a year before he arrived. I was in Holland when I received word of his being killed. We spent one day together in England, but it seems so long ago to recollect what happened on that day. Letters from his officer indicate Franklin was a reliable soldier and a gentleman at all times. It was difficult for my Father as indications were that Franklin would take over the family farm. It was further difficult as our Mother had passed away one year before in October, 1943. Although I was in Army Signals, it was a bit of a shock to receive word of both of them one year apart. Recollections of over 50 years is a problem to bring up to date.

Rogers Bay (64 G/16) in Cederlund Lake was named after him in 1995.

Rogers, Private **Walter H.** of Winnipeg (H 14071). Perth Regiment. He died 20 December 1944 at the age of 26 and is commemorated at Villanova Canadian War Cemetery, Italy. He was the son of James A. and Eva Rogers of Winnipeg and was survived by his wife Doris M. Rogers of Winnipeg. ***Rogers Point*** (64 C/14) in Vandekerckhove Lake was named after him in 1995.

Rognan, Flying Officer **Everett R.** of Minnedosa (J 24589). No. 408 Squadron. He died 27 April 1944 at the age of 23 and is commemorated at the Runnymede Memorial in Surrey, England. He was the son of Albert and Abina Rognan of Erickson, Manitoba and was survived by his sister Mrs. J. E. Johnson of Minnedosa. His nephew recalls (5 February 2002):

> Flying Officer Everett Roy Rognan of Erickson was born August 20, 1920. He enlisted in the RCAF January 7, 1942, and received his pilot's wings at Uplands, Ontario, March 19, 1943. Nicknamed "Smiley" by his fellow crew members, he flew on several bombing missions over Germany with the 408 "Goose" Squadron, which was based at Linton-on-Ouse, Yorkshire, England. He was the pilot in a Lancaster II bomber that did not return from a sortie over Essen on April 27, 1944.
>
> Everett was the adopted son of Albert and Abina Rognan, immigrants from Norway who homesteaded in the Municipality of Clanwilliam in the early 1900s. They changed their surname from Andreasson to Rognan to commemorate their town of origin, a small town in northern Norway near Bode. Everett grew up on the family farm located about five miles north of the Village of Erickson. The six Rognan children included Everett's two brothers, Andrew and Fred and four sisters, Gunda, Alvhild, Inez and Gladys. Inez Rognan Johnson is the only surviving sibling in February, 2002.
>
> Everett's nephew, Dr. Harland Johnson (son of Alvhild) was six when Everett last visited before his overseas posting. He recalls: "Everett was a hero to me as a child, and my most vivid memories of him are playing with him in the snowy yard, and then the tragic family gathering the day the dreaded telegram arrived announcing he was Missing In Action. I will always remember him and we gave our son the middle name of Everett to carry on the memory. Three years ago, I was thrilled to discover a restored Lancaster bomber in a museum in Nanton, Alberta. I climbed through it, sat where Everett sat, and was humbled at the bravery of those young men heading out into the hostile skies to help win the life and death struggle. Only 25 of every 100 airmen survived those bombing raids. Much of the lifestyle that we take for granted is the legacy of the unselfish servicemen and servicewomen of that era."

Rognan Lake (53 E/7), south of Island Lake was named after him in 1973.

Rohloff, Private **Henry** of Winnipeg (H 203509). Canadian Provost Corps. He died 21 April 1945 and is commemorated at Brookwood Military Cemetery in Surrey, England. ***Rohloff Lake*** (63 O/5), southeast of Highrock Lake was named after him in 1973.

Roller, Sergeant **Lester W.** of Neelin (R 180492). Royal Canadian Air Force. He died 5 December 1944 at the age of 24 and is commemorated at Neelin Cemetery. He was the son of Walter B. and Olive C. Roller of Neelin, Manitoba. Roller Peninsula (64 F/3) in Roller Lake was named after him in 1996. ***Roller Lake*** was named in honour of his brother Flight Sergeant Ray C. Roller (next entry).

Roller, Flight Sergeant **Ray C.** of Cartwright (R 210007). No. 100 Squadron. He died 16 January 1945 at the age of 21 and is commemorated at the Berlin 1939 - 1945 War Cemetery in Brandenburg, Germany. He was one of the five sons of Walter B. and Olive C. Roller (née Greener) of Neelin, Manitoba. Some months later, the father of one of his crewmates received the following letter:

Dear Mr. Chapman: A few days ago I was at a reception held in Hamilton for repatriated Prisoners of War from the Royal Hamilton Light Infantry, who had been taken prisoner at Dieppe. One of the Officers who had returned from France, reported to me that he had secured particulars from a Frenchman concerning the death of your son. The Officer concerned is Captain T. J. Brown, RHLI, Hamilton, Ontario, but unfortunately he did not obtain the name and address of the Frenchman. Captain Brown was informed that what was thought to be a Liberator had crashed over Germany on or about the 17th of January, 1945. All members of the crew were reported to have been killed, and the only one identifiable was Flying Officer W. M. Chapman, Can. J 38421. His body was buried at 4:30 on January 18th, in the town of Dittichenrode, Kreis Saugerhausen, Germany. The Frenchman who gave the information stated that he had continued to care for the graves where your son and the others were buried. I am having an investigation made by our officials Overseas, and will send you any further information that becomes available. In the meantime I felt that you should have the information that I had received. May I extend to you my very deep sympathy in your loss. Yours very truly, Colin Gibson (5 July 1945).

Roller Lake (64 F/3), east of Reindeer Lake was named after him in 1967. Roller Peninsula was named in honour of his brother Sergeant Lester W. Roller (previous entry).

Ronahan, Pilot Officer **John M.** of Napinka (J 95100). No. 149 Squadron. He died 23 April 1944 at the age of 35 and is commemorated at Svendborg General Cemetery in Denmark. He was the son of William J. and Maude M. Ronahan. ***Ronahan Lake*** (64 N/11), southeast of Kasba Lake was named after him in 1972.

Roper, Private **Frank** of Winnipeg (H 1721). Westminster Regiment. He died 7 February 1945 at the age of 38 and is commemorated at Assisi War Cemetery in Italy. He was the son of Harry and Jane H. B. Roper of Winnipeg. ***Roper Island*** (64 C/5) in Kamuchawie Lake was named after him in 1995.

Rose, Flight Sergeant **Donald I.** of Stony Mountain (R 157415). No. 434 Squadron. He died 29 January 1944 at the age of 21 and is commemorated at the Berlin 1939 - 1945 War Cemetery in Brandenburg, Germany. His Halifax aircraft failed to return from a night raid on Berlin. He was the son of Herbert Cecil and Annie Marion Rose of St. James and the brother of Sergeant Thomas H. Rose (see entry). His brother writes (11 January 2002):

Donald Irwin Rose was born in Gladstone on April 19, 1923 and moved with his parents to Stony Mountain in 1924. He began school and completed his Grade 11 at Stony Mountain School and took his Grade 12 at St. Paul's College in Winnipeg. Don was always active in sports, particularly organized hockey. He was good in track and field sports as well as baseball. After completing school, he took a job with MacDonald Brothers Aircraft in Winnipeg, remaining with that company until he enlisted.

Donald applied and was accepted into the RCAF in February, 1942. He was sent to the Manning Depot in Edmonton and from there to the Initial Training School in Saskatoon. Some time was spent at No. 6 EFTS, Prince Albert for assessment as a pilot but there is no entry in his log book, although it is noted he flew in a Tiger Moth aircraft – the work horse of elementary flying training. Donald's next posting was to No. 8 Bombing and Gunnery School at Lethbridge where he began training as an Air Bomber. Part of this course was also conducted at No. 3 AOS Regina and Pearce, Alberta in October, 1942. His training besides bombing included air gunnery and navigation. His graduation ceremony was at No. 3 AOS Pearce where he received his Air Bomber Wing.

Upon arriving in England, he was posted to No. 6 OAS, Staverton, his course beginning May 19, 1943 and ending June 13, 1943. Transferred next to No. 23 OTU Pershore. He commenced flying on July 9 and finished August 25. On December 20, Donald had his first operational flight to Frankfurt.

Cousin Eleanor Becker remembers him as an energetic teenager who often rode his bicycle from Stony Mountain to St. James to visit with her family. "He was often into mischief," she recalls, "and would try the patience of a saint." ***Rose Bay*** (63 I/2) in Molson Lake was named after him in 1988.

Rose, Private **Kenneth V.** of Petersfield (H 66020). Queen's Own Cameron Highlanders. He died 8 August 1944 at the age of 27 and is commemorated at Bretteville-sur-Laize Canadian War Cemetery in Calvados, France. He was the son of Victor A. and Jane Rose of Petersfield, Manitoba. ***Rose Peninsula*** (64 O/11) on Nueltin Lake was named after him in 1995.

Rose, Sergeant **Thomas H.** of Stony Mountain (R 56850). No. 40 Squadron. He died 12 March 1941 at the age of 19 and is commemorated at Wimille Communal Cemetery, Pas de Calais, France. He was the son of Herbert Cecil and Annie Marion Rose of Victoria, British Columbia and the brother of Flight Sergeant Donald I. Rose (see entry). Doug Rose, elder brother of Tom, remembers him as a serious, quiet youngster who liked to cook and "could put together a very creditable jelly roll." His brother recalls (11 January 2002):

Thomas Herbert Rose was born in Gladstone April 6, 1921. He moved with his parents to Stony Mountain in 1924 and received his education at Stony Mountain School. In growing up he developed an artistic bent and worked with water colours and pastels. He was also very skilled at carving and model building. One of his best works was a model of the Queen Mary. This was exhibited at the T. Eaton Company in Winnipeg who sponsored a handicrafts exhibition in 1937. Tom was awarded first prize. Tom was also involved in sports, particularly baseball (he was a pitcher) and also in organized hockey with Stony Mountain and Salisbury House Juveniles and the Carman Intermediates.

When World War II began, it was Tom's ambition to join the Air Force. When he first applied he was rejected because of an eye problem. This was remedied and he was accepted in April, 1940. He left Winnipeg April 12, 1940 for No. 1 Initial Training School at the Eglington Hunt Club in Toronto. From there he moved to No. 1 Air Observer's School at Malton, Ontario where on June 5th, he completed his first training flight. He graduated as an Air Observer on October 25th, 1940. His class was the first trained under the British Commonwealth Air Training Plan. He arrived in London on November 25, 1940. He began operations training at No. 20 OTU, Lossiemouth, Scotland and his first flight was December 22, 1940. Training was completed on March 8, 1941. On his first operational flight over Berlin he was reported "Missing in Action." His death was later confirmed through the International Red Cross in Geneva. Prior to graduation, Tom was offered the opportunity to remain in Canada as an instructor, but he refused, stating he preferred being on active service.

Rose Point (63 I/2) on Molson Lake was named after him in 1988.

Rosenberg, Gunner **Dennis V.** of Brandon (H 35502). Royal Canadian Artillery. He died 6 September 1944 at the age of 23 and is commemorated at Gradara War Cemetery in Italy. He was the son of Carl V. and Lillian N. Rosenberg of Brandon. His brother recalls (11 March 1996) that he:

> ... was born in London, England ... and immigrated to Canada with his parents in 1921 and eventually settled in Winnipeg where the remainder of the family – five in total – were born and raised. He enjoyed camping and fishing and swimming very much. He enlisted in the RCA in Winnipeg and served in Italy with the 8th Field Regiment, 71st Field Battery.

Rosenberg Lake (63 K/13), east of Embury Lake was named after him in 1984.

Rosenberry, Warrant Officer 2 **Willard K.** of The Pas (R 91883). No. 90 Squadron. He died 16 February 1943 at the age of 21 and is commemorated at Blandford Cemetery in Dorset, England. He was the son of David D. and Rose K. Rosenberry of Vancouver. ***Rosenberry Lake*** (63 O/2), west of Setting Lake was named after him in 1973.

Rosenthal, Lieutenant **Hyman** of Winnipeg (CDN 653). Black Watch (Royal Highland Regiment) of Canada. He died 9 February 1945 and is commemorated at the Groesbeek Canadian War Cemetery in Holland. ***Rosenthal Lake*** (63 N/9), north of Burntwood Lake was named after him in 1995.

Roski, Pilot Officer **Antonio G.** of Tyndall (C 89022). No. 420 Squadron. He died 17 August 1944 at the age of 22 and is commemorated at the Runnymede Memorial in Surrey, England. ***Roski Lake*** (64 J/10), west of Tadoule Lake was named after him in 1975.

Ross, Sergeant **Alexander** of Winnipeg (H 36207). Royal Canadian Engineers. He died 14 January 1944 at the age of 40 and is commemorated at Brookwood Military Cemetery in Surrey, England. He was the son of John and Helen Ross and was survived by his wife Matilda Ross (née Bremner) of West Kildonan and their four children. His son reports (16 March 1995):

> Born in Rhynie, Scotland in 1903, he came to Canada in 1922. Initially, he settled in Nova Scotia, but came out west in 1925 to work on various farms in the Reston area. He moved to Winnipeg in 1927 where he married the following year. An avid golfer and soccer player, he was employed at City Dairy when he enlisted in October, 1939.

Alexander Ross Lake (54 E/13), northwest of Comeau Lake was named after him in 1995.

Ross, Rifleman **Allan S.** of Winnipeg (H 102423). Royal Winnipeg Rifles. He died 8 June 1944 and is commemorated at Bretteville-sur-Laize Canadian War Cemetery in Calvados, France. ***Ross Rapids*** (64 I/8) in the South Knife River was named after him in 1995.

Ross, Flying Officer **Floyd R.** of Elgin (J 28564). No. 356 Squadron. He died 12 June 1945 at the age of 24 and is commemorated at Taukkyan War Cemetery in Myanmar. He was the son of John A. and Ida M. Ross and was survived by his wife Joyce C. A. Ross of Vancouver. ***Ross Peninsula*** (64 F/1) on Barrington Lake was named after him in 1985.

Ross, Flight Lieutenant **John D.** of Elgin (J 12298). No. 423 Squadron. He died 11 February 1945 at the age of 25 and is commemorated at Irvinestown Church Of Ireland Churchyard, Fermanagh, Northern Ireland. He was the son of George D. and Elizabeth I. Ross of Elgin, Manitoba. ***Ross Esker*** (64 G/11), east of Big Sand Lake was named after him in 1985.

Ross, Flight Sergeant **L. J. Willis** of Rossburn (R 95429). No. 115 Squadron. He died 2 September 1942 at the age of 22 and is commemorated at Choloy War Cemetery, Meurthe-et-Moselle, France. ***Willis Ross Lake*** (63 I/1), southeast of Molson Lake was named after him in 1988.

Ross, Flight Sergeant **Samuel** of Winnipeg (R 71069). No. 78 Squadron. He died 28 August 1942 at the age of 26 and is commemorated at Tombeek Churchyard in Overijse, Vlaams-Brabant, Belgium. He was the son of Andrew and Agnes Ross of Winnipeg. His obituary read in part:

> Ross was born here and received his education at Hugh John Macdonald and Daniel McIntyre schools. He joined the RCAF here in March, 1940 and has served overseas since December the same year. He received his wireless air gunner's training at Toronto, St. John and Montreal. He had taken part in several raids over Germany (n.d.).

Ross Hill (63 N/1), east of Craik Lake was named after him in 1995.

Rothery, Private **Arthur** of Winnipeg (H 16952). Princess Patricia's Canadian Light Infantry. He died 1 September 1944 at the age of 32 and is commemorated at Brookside Cemetery in Winnipeg. He was the son of James and Susanna Rothery of St. James. ***Rothery Lake*** (53 K/11), southeast of Edmund Lake was named after him in 1996.

Rothnie, Private **Edwin G.** of Oak River (H 19961). Queen's Own Cameron Highlanders. He died 26 July 1944 at the age of 31 and is commemorated at Bretteville-sur-Laize Canadian War Cemetery in Calvados, France. He was the son of George and Jeannie Rothnie of Gardenstown, Banffshire, Scotland. ***Rothnie Lake*** (64 O/9), north of Nejanilini Lake was named after him in 1975.

Rothstein, Flight Sergeant **Irvine S.** of Winnipeg (R 123638). No. 75 Squadron. He died 7 August 1943 at the age of 21 and is commemorated at the Runnymede Memorial in Surrey, England. ***Rothstein Lake*** (63 N/1), northeast of Sherridon was named after him in 1970.

Roussin, Rifleman **Henri** of Dauphin (H 42069). Royal Winnipeg Rifles. He died 6 June 1944 at the age of 25 and is commemorated at Beny-sur-Mer Canadian War Cemetery in Calvados, France. He was the son of Paul and Elise Roussin (née Whiteford) of Dauphin. Born at Waterhen, Manitoba, he had been a farm labourer at the time of his enlistment. ***Roussin Lake*** (63 H/10), east of Lebrix Lake was named after him in 1982.

Rowe, Private **Herbert E.** of Elm Creek (H 20338). Queen's Own Cameron Highlanders. He died 19 August 1942 and is commemorated at Dieppe Canadian War Cemetery in Seine-Maritime, France. ***Rowe Bay*** (63 O/12) in Nelson Lake was named after him in 1995.

Rowe, Lieutenant **Terry F.** of Winnipeg. 1st Canadian Public Relations Department, General List, Canadian Army. He died 6 February 1944 and is commemorated at Anzio War Cemetery, Italy. ***Rowe Lake*** (64 K/12), south of Lac Brochet was named after him in 1972.

Roy, Leading Aircraftman **Charles J.** of Winnipeg (R 180188). No. 8 Repair Depot, RCAF. He died 14 July 1945 at the age of 36 and is commemorated at Elmwood Cemetery in Winnipeg. He was the son of James R. and Edith E. Roy of Winnipeg and was survived by his wife Florence H. Roy of Winnipeg. ***Roy Point*** (64 P/6) on Hemmons Lake was named after him in 1995.

Roy, Flight Sergeant **Charles N.** of Winnipeg (R 58798). No. 12 Squadron. He died 10 July 1943 at the age of 22 and is commemorated at the Reichswald Forest War Cemetery in Germany. He was the son of Frank and Mary J. Roy of Winnipeg and was survived by his wife Edith F. Roy of Winnipeg. ***Roy Lake*** (63 H/1), south of Gunisao Lake was named after him in 1974.

Roy, Private **Paul H.** of Morris (H 100002). South Saskatchewan Regiment. He died 29 August 1944 at the age of 22 and is commemorated at Bretteville-sur-Laize Canadian War Cemetery in Calvados, France. He was the son of George and Zelma Roy of Morris, Manitoba. ***Roy Island*** (64 N/15) in Putahow Lake was named after him in 1989.

Roy, Private **Victorien "Tifine"** of Winnipeg (H 43095). Le Régiment de la Chaudière. He died 13 January 1945 and is commemorated at the Groesbeek Memorial in Holland. Orphaned at a very young age, he had been raised by his aunt and uncle Mr. and Mrs. Celestin Girard of Dufrost. ***Roy Bay*** (64 C/14) in Vandekerckhove Lake was named after him in 1995.

Rozière, Sergeant **Lionel** of Winnipeg (H 105012). 1st Canadian Special Services Battalion. He died 24 May 1944 at the age of 23 and is commemorated at Beach Head War Cemetery, Anzio, Italy. He was the eldest child of Joseph E. and Emilie Rozière of Norwood. Sergeant Rozière had taken part in the invasion of Italy and was wounded and taken prisoner north of Rome. He succumbed to his wounds at the first aid station at Abadia, Italy. His brother recalls (7 November 2001):

> Lionel was the eldest of four boys and seven girls. He was in sports with a small group of boys and Father Levêque. In a letter written in a foxhole at the Anzio beachhead, Italy, he stated that in early mornings he would milk a cow in his helmet that was browsing nearby. He would share with the boys.

Rozière Lake (64 I/1), northeast of Etawney Lake was named after him in 1974.

Ruck, Bombardier **Rudolph** of Winnipeg (H 35287). Royal Canadian Artillery. He died 4 April 1945 at the age of 39 and is commemorated at the Groesbeek Canadian War Cemetery in Holland. He was the son of Godfrey and Bertha Ruck and was survived by his wife Rose Ruck of Winnipeg. ***Ruck Lake*** (62 P/16), west of Family Lake was named after him in 1973.

Rudick, Flight Sergeant **Peter** of Winnipeg (R 140995). No. 100 Squadron. He died 17 April 1943 at the age of 24 and is commemorated at Rheinberg War Cemetery in Germany. He was the son of Mr. and Mrs. G. Rudick of Winnipeg. According to his brother (1 April 1999), he was:

> ... born in the log cabin home on the family homestead [near] Poplarfield, Manitoba. The family moved to Rosser Municipality on the outskirts of Winnipeg in 1923, where he attended classes at Wentworth School for a short time until the family relocated to the permanent family home at 35 Kurt Avenue. Peter then attended Wordsworth School, another two-room school situated on the bald prairie at what is now the corner of Selkirk Avenue and King Edward. In order to continue one's education, it was necessary each day to hike to Brooklands School for Grade 8 and to Cecil Rhodes school in Weston for Grade 9.
>
> While at Isaac Newton, he became involved with and performed in the school's production of the operetta "Ju Ju." During this time he found he had great facility in wood working and produced three fine pieces which now grace the homes of his siblings. In addition to the prescribed scholastic classes, he studied and tried his hand at both forging and electrical. He found part time work at garages near home and worked his summer holidays for a repair shop in the city. He was interested in all new developments and built his own Cat's Whisker radio before the family acquired their first radio. After graduation, Peter first worked in the automotive trades. Along with a group of young men he spent a mandatory stint with the 2nd Battalion Winnipeg Grenadiers at Brandon. In June, 1941 Peter joined CP Rail's work force at Weston.
>
> His personal interest in the development of flight and his desire to fly prompted him to enlist in the Royal Canadian Air Force Special Reserve on July 17, 1941. Having passed his medical, he continued to work at Weston Shops while awaiting processing by the Air Force. On December 29, 1941, training began in earnest at No. 2 Manning Depot Brandon [and by] September 11, 1942 his training in Canada was largely completed; he had earned and was authorized to wear the Air Gunnery Badge. [He arrived] in England November 4, 1942 ... and on March 13, 1943 was posted to 100 Squadron.
>
> On April 16, 1943, 9 No. 100 Squadron aircraft took off from Grimsby, Lincolnshire; their target was Pilsen. Peter was the mid-upper gunner in Lancaster ED563 which took off at 21:22 hours into a night sky with about 80% illumination from a moon which was nearly full and nearly at its maximum height. Eight of the aircraft returned from the mission without experiencing anything unusual. Lancaster ED563 failed to return.
>
> The Red Cross reported receiving official German communications indicating that a Halifax aircraft had been shot down near Saarbrücken and that the crew had been buried in Reebach Cemetery. It named two of Lancaster ED563's crew and six unknown Canadians. A second report added Sergeant Peter Rudick to the named crew members at Reebach.
>
> In 1947, research was carried out to locate and identify isolated graves and to identify the buried individuals. An eye witness to the crash of Lancaster ED563 was located in the village of Rentrisch, three and a half miles northeast of Saarbrücken, Germany. He indicated that in descent, the aircraft hit a high tension cable and carried on into a hillside on the outskirts of the village where it burst into flames.
>
> The bodies were exhumed and five were successfully identified through laundry marks, brevets, badges of rank and the cross erected on the grave. The cross on Peter's grave was the only form of identification discovered for him on site. His identification disc had been found previously and resulted in the second communication to the Red Cross concerning the crash on the night of April 16/17, 1943. It was accepted that the cross bearing the name of Sergeant Peter Rudick did indeed mark his burial site. The seventh crew member was identified by elimination.
>
> In 1948, the bodies were moved to the Rheinberg British Military Cemetery, 11 miles northwest of Duisberg. Peter was laid to rest in Plot 8, Row J, Grave No. 25. His crew mates lie beside him in grave numbers 19 through 24. May they all rest in peace.

Rudick Lake (64 P/13), north of Nejanilini Lake was named after him in 1974.

Rudkawich, Private **Brunson** of Fork River (H 8860). South Saskatchewan Regiment. He died 16 August 1944 at the age of 28 and is commemorated at Bretteville-sur-Laize Canadian War Cemetery in Calvados, France. He was the son of Adolph and Frances Rudkawich of Fork River, Manitoba. ***Rudkawich Lake*** (64 O/5), south of Nueltin Lake was named after him in 1975.

Rudko, Private **Henry** of Dauphin (H 16124). Princess Patricia's Canadian Light Infantry. He died 30 January 1944 and is commemorated at the Moro River Canadian War Cemetery in Italy. ***Rudko Lake*** (64 O/4), east of Egenolf Lake was named after him in 1975.

Runner, Pilot Officer **Joseph M.** of Treherne (J 15172). No. 115 Squadron, Distinguished Flying Medal.

This airman has proved himself to be a cool and courageous air gunner when flying over well defended areas in difficult conditions. Apart from his duties as rear gunner, Sergeant Runner has always taken a keen interest in map reading and in obtaining intelligent [sic] information whilst over enemy territory. On several occasions, it has been largely due to his excellent pin-pointing that his crew have been able to identify and bomb their objective. The sorties in which he has participated have included many of the most important targets in Germany and occupied territory (DFM Citation 1944).

He died 9 March 1942 at the age of 24 and is commemorated at the Runnymede Memorial in Surrey, England. He was the son of John H. and Mabel M. Runner of Treherne. His sister-in-law writes (20 October 1995):

His father and mother were in the hotel business and moved frequently across the prairies. Joe was sent [from Winnipeg] to Treherne at about age ten. One of his older brothers, "Fish" operated the hotel there. Joe stayed with Fish and his wife Naomi during his formative years (i.e., elementary through high school). He was an average student but formal education was often delayed because of physical sports. All the boys were expected to take part in boxing, hockey, tennis, hunting etc. Joe was no exception and he also became interested and took lessons in flying.

When World War II began, he enlisted and went overseas early. At this time, he had just been accepted by an American college on a hockey scholarship. He wrote home ... on a more or less regular basis and always acknowledged the parcels he received.

He served with 115 Squadron, RAF. The crew was decorated by King George VI before the completion of their tour. Joe was promoted to Pilot Officer after this. As I recall, March 8, 1942 was Joe's final operational trip. I believe they were still flying Wellingtons at this time. My husband William [Joe's brother] served with No. 150 Squadron, RAF. He died in 1989, but during his lifetime he was always searching for Joe and seeking ways to honour his memory.

Runner Lake (64 C/4), south of Laurie Lake was named after him in 1947.

Rurak, Trooper **Peter** of Roblin (H 22616). Royal Canadian Armoured Corps. He died 27 September 1945 at the age of 21 and is commemorated at St. John's Cemetery in Shell Valley, Manitoba. He was survived by his mother Lena Rurak of Roblin, Manitoba. His family write (16 April 1998):

Peter was born in the Municipality of Boulton. [His] first years of schooling were at Shell Vale School and then in the town of Roblin at Goose Lake Consolidated School. He worked as a clerk at Starkman's General Store in Roblin. Previous to his enlistment, he worked for the Sherritt Gordon Mines.

Rurak Lake (63 I/10), southeast of Walker Lake was named after him in 1982.

Rush, Lieutenant **Mathew C. P.** of Winnipeg (CDN 279). Duke of Cornwall's Light Infantry. He died 9 July 1944 at the age of 22 and is commemorated at St. Manvieu War Cemetery, Cheux in Calvados, France. He was the son of Frederick L. and Susan E. Rush of Port Arthur, Ontario. ***Rush Island*** (64 F/4) in Carswell Lake was named after him in 1995.

Rushforth, Flying Officer **William J.** of Eriksdale (J 26291). No. 102 Squadron. He died 17 June 1944 at the age of 34 and is commemorated at the Reichswald Forest War Cemetery in Germany. He was the eldest son of Henry and Sarah J. Rushforth of Eriksdale, Manitoba. His brother recalls (13 February 1987):

William Rushforth was born in St. James on April 30, 1912. He started school at Britannia on King Edward Street and attended there until Grade 4. The family then moved to a homestead at Eriksdale. Intermediate studies were completed at Eastland School where Bill had the distinction of being the first student in that area to pass Entrance Exams. This was followed by high school in Eriksdale, driving seven miles there and back, with horse and buggy or cutter, as applicable.

A teaching profession appealed to Bill and he attended Provincial Normal School at Manitou, Manitoba where he won the Governor General's Award for General Proficiency in 1933. He taught school in the Eriksdale area during the 1934/35 season and then at Cold Lake, Manitoba from 1935 to 1939. In 1939, he accepted a position at Pikangikum, an Aboriginal school northwest of Red Lake, Ontario.

In 1942, Bill was able to leave Pikangikum School and join the Royal Canadian Air Force, one of four brothers serving their country overseas. Unfortunately, he did not return. Following a bomber raid over Germany on the night of June 16/17, 1944, Bill was reported "missing in action," and later "presumed dead." The later was confirmed when after hostilities ceased, local citizens (German) reported the location of a downed bomber and the gravesite of the crew. Bill's body was identified and later exhumed for reburial at his final resting place.

Bill was an avid reader and an excellent student. He was always interested in nature, people, outdoor life and sports. In the isolated areas where he chose to teach, he passed the time writing simple poetry about the people and their way of life. He put a lot of living into the short time he was allotted.

Rushforth Lake (63 I/1), east of Molson Lake was named after him in 1980.

Rusnak, Private **John** of Portage la Prairie (H 18116). Royal Canadian Ordnance Corps. He died 22 November 1945 and is commemorated at the Holten Canadian War Cemetery in Holland. ***Rusnak Lake*** (64 H/9), southeast of Etawney Lake was named after him in 1978.

Russell, Bombardier **Duncan** of Souris (H 60182). Royal Canadian Artillery. He died 22 July 1944 at the age of 23 and is commemorated at Beny-sur-Mer Canadian War Cemetery in Calvados, France. He was the son of John and Annie Russell of Kelso, Saskatchewan and the brother of Lance Corporal Melville Russell (see entry). ***Russell Island*** (64 I/3) in North Knife Lake was named after Bombardier Russell in 1974.

Russell, Flight Sergeant **John D.** of High Bluff (R 91885). No. 57 Squadron. He died 15 October 1942 at the age of 22 and is commemorated at the Runnymede Memorial in Surrey, England. He was survived by his stepfather and his mother Samuel and Clara Tuckey of High Bluff, Manitoba. Ken Thompson spent many years trying to get details of the last flight of his brother Duncan who was a crewmate of Flight Sergeant Russell. In 1993, he received a letter from E. G. Thale of Uxbridge, England which read in part:

289 aircraft (109 Wellingtons, 74 Halfaxes, 62 Lancasters and 44 Stirlings) took part in the attack on Cologne. Six Wellingtons, five Lancasters and two Stirlings were lost (6.2% of the force). This was not a successful raid. Winds were different from those forecast and the Pathfinders had difficulty in establishing their position and marking the target sufficiently to attract the main force away from a large decoy fire site which received most of the bombs. Cologne reports one "Luftmine" (out of 71 4000-pounders carried by the bombing force), three other high explosive bombs (out of 231) and 210 incendiaries (out of 68,590). 226 houses were damaged, but only two of these received what was classed as "serious" damage. Four people were injured.

Your speculation about the loss of the aircraft and the possibility of it going into the sea is quite reasonable, but I would suggest that it was hit either by AA or by a 37mm cannon shell. The Lanc carried 14,000 pounds of bombs and about 1500 gallons of gas on a short trip to Cologne. The Germans knew exactly where to cause disintegrating damage to a Lanc. Just one 37mm "cookie" and the aircraft just disappeared with no recognizable pieces of wreckage. The other possibility is that of a mid-air collision when both aircraft with combined bomb loads would blow up. This situation occurred quite frequently as Jim will tell you (29 June 1993).

A month before his death, Flight Sergeant Russell wrote a letter to his mother and left it with an aunt in London to be forwarded to her in case anything should happen to him. It read in part:

There is a favour I want to ask of you. I know this is going to be a hard blow for you to take, but don't shed too many tears over me. I like to see a person that can take it and I know you can. Remember I'm fighting for the things that make this old world better, sort of bearable to live in – freedom of speech, religion and being able to bring children up in the way we think best. Thank God I've got the opportunity to fight for these things. If I have to die I want to do it smashing out at Hitler's thugs. Even if I perish and hundreds more, the RAF is slowly but surely pulverizing city by city. Nothing can stop us now for it's God's will that we give these barbarians a good thrashing.

When we've won mother, greet the other boys who were more lucky than I. I want you to carry on and don't grieve too much. Just for you to be proud of me is all I ask. I could have got out of this position into a safer one without anyone knowing but the authorities, but I won't fail this job. I've got a conscience and besides, I've come from one of the best families whom I can't let down.

Well mother, this has been a hard letter to write as I'm not much good at putting my feelings down on paper. However, I've not done too bad this time, so good-bye and God bless you, the best mother a fellow ever had (n.d.).

Russell Bay (64 H/11) in Hibbert Lake was named after him in 1995.

Russell, Flight Sergeant **Leonard B.** of Winnipeg (R 147158). No. 431 Squadron. He died 22 October 1943 and is commemorated at the Runnymede Memorial in Surrey, England. ***Russell Rapids*** (64 I/14) in the Seal River was named after him in 1995.

Russell, Lance Corporal **Melville E.** of Griswold (H 26674). Fort Garry Horse. He died 19 February 1945 at the age of 26 and is commemorated at the Groesbeek Canadian War Cemetery in Holland. He was the son of John and Annie Russell of Kelso, Saskatchewan and the brother of Bombardier Duncan Russell (see entry). ***Russell Esker*** (54 M/6), south of Long Lake was named after Lance Corporal Russell in 1984.

Russell, Private **Robert W.** of MacGregor (M 11826). Royal Canadian Regiment. He died 5 December 1944 at the age of 28 and is commemorated at Ravenna War Cemetery in Italy. He was survived by his wife Gladys Russell of Austin, Manitoba. ***Russell Hill*** (64 N/3), northwest of Whitmore Lake was named after him in 1989.

Russell, Flying Officer **Walter** of Winnipeg (J 27639). No. 358 Squadron. He died 22 January 1945 at the age of 24 and is commemorated at Taukkyan War Cemetery in Myanmar. He was the son of Mr. and Mrs. Alexander Russell of Winnipeg. Prior to enlisting, he had played hockey with the Winnipeg Monarchs. According to his brother (10 April 1995), he: "[w]ent missing flying guerrilla troops into French Indochina. It was approximately seven years before his remains were found and buried in a military cemetery in New Delhi, India." ***Walter Russell Bay*** (64 O/7) in Bambridge Lake was named after him in 1995.

Russell, Private **William C.** of Winnipeg (H 17201). Royal Canadian Army Service Corps. He died 4 December 1942 at the age of 22 and is commemorated at Brookwood Military Cemetery in Surrey, England. He was the son of William C. and Mima H. Russell of Winnipeg. ***Russell Peninsula*** (64 N/2) on Weepaskow Lake was named after him in 1995.

Rutherford, Lance Sergeant **Archibald R.** of Winnipeg (H 6057). Winnipeg Grenadiers. He died a prisoner of war 5 December 1943 at the age of 34 and is commemorated at the Yokohama War Cemetery in Japan. He was the son of Hollis R. and Grace E. Rutherford of Truro, Nova Scotia. According to his brother, this native of Nova Scotia had been manager of the Truro Bearcats hockey and ball teams, a member of the Knights of Pythias and a sergeant with the local militia. In 1937, he left home to "go west on the grain excursions" and when war was declared he enlisted.

On Christmas Eve [1941], Private Frank Harding, an 18 year-old soldier from Winnipeg found himself with a couple of other Canadians trying to protect their company's flank on Bennet's Hill. A Japanese bullet caromed off his shoulder blade and lodged against his spine. Private Harding fell, half-paralyzed, screaming. Someone dragged him to a nearby rock. He asked to be propped up. And he asked for his .38 revolver.

He just sat there in the cold rain thinking, "When they come, I'll use it first on them and then put the barrel in my mouth and kill myself." The Japanese were just 50 metres away.

Then Sergeant Archie Rutherford … came along and carried Private Harding down the hill. In the darkness, Sergeant Rutherford – who had been shot in the thigh – stumbled several times beneath their combined weight and broke his ribs. As dawn broke over Hong Kong, Private Harding couldn't quite believe he was paralyzed yet alive. He wished himself a Merry Christmas. He doubted he'd see Boxing Day.

Frank Harding, too, gets tears in his eyes and cannot speak about the worst memories. A doctor at the PoW camp removed the bullet in his spine so he could walk, but no one can dislodge the thoughts of the price Archie Rutherford paid helping to save his life. Sergeant Rutherford lies in a Commonwealth War Graves Commission cemetery in Yokohama, along with 137 Canadian PoW dead. At his grave, Mr. Harding cries unashamedly and shakes his head. To this day it upsets him that Archie Rutherford's bones are interred in Japanese soil (Wood 1991).

In a letter home from the Hong Kong camp Lance Sergeant Rutherford wrote:

Dear Folks: Well it sure has been quite some time since we last communicated. It took quite a while to get a system inaugurated, but I should now be able to write at least once a month. Suppose you are all anxious to know how I'm feeling and how I look. Well let's see, want you all to relax and concentrate for a few minutes on how I looked to you when I was last home, then you will likely know that there has been no decided change, same losh (?) nothing changed. Sure, getting lots of pointers from this life, but nothing I hadn't already visualized before. You know the old attitude I take towards things etc. (ha ha). There are no hardships here that are not experienced in everyday life. The Nipponese show a very respectful attitude towards us and nothing we ask of them is too much for them to do. We have as recreation organized sports, organized card games and schools in languages and different vocations. Only allowed a limited number of words so will say so long for this time. Love to all and tell the Duchess better days are coming. Your loving son, Archie (3 June 1942).

Quite a few Winnipeggers received letters from family members interned at Hong Kong and other camps. These were universally cheerful although a few recipients were suspicious and attempted to "read between the lines." In some camps, it was customary to restrict letters to a specified number of sentences from a pre-approved list. The accounts of camp life as indicated in these letters was in stark contrast to the conditions described by repatriated Manitobans in 1945. ***Rutherford Lake*** (52 M/3), southwest of Aikens Lake was named after Lance Sergeant Rutherford in 1982.

Rutherford, Private **George A.** of St. Vital (H 6447). Winnipeg Grenadiers. He died 23 December 1941 at the age of 38 and is commemorated at the Sai Wan War Cemetery in Hong Kong. He was the son of James A. and Jennette S. Rutherford. His niece recalls (29 October 2001):

He lived with his family on a farm near Pilot Mound when he joined the Grenadiers. George was the youngest of a family of eight children and not married. My father was the second youngest and not home when George was with us as he was away with the Fort Garry Horse. My father survived the war, but Uncle George did not because he was sent to Hong Kong. I'm sorry I didn't know my Uncle George very well, but am glad I did meet him. I still have the small wax figure he brought for me from Jamaica where they went to train for Hong Kong.

I didn't know him well but I remember exactly what my mother said when George's mother wrote to tell her George was dead. Mother said: "I can't believe George is dead. He was such a happy go lucky fellow, I thought nothing would ever happen to him."

Rutherford Island (63 I/1) in Little Bolton Lake was named after him in 1995.

Ruthig, Trooper **Leonard A.** of Winnipeg (H 26103). Fort Garry Horse. He died 10 June 1944 at the age of 23 and is commemorated at the Bayeux Memorial in Calvados, France. He was the youngest son of Lorne and Anna Ruthig and was survived by his wife Viola L. Ruthig of Toronto and their son. His sister recalls (30 November 2001) that he:

... joined the Army with the Fort Garry Horse as a wireless operator. He was reported to have died of wounds in France. My brother Leonard was attending school at the time when the war started; our parents tried talking him out of enlisting, but his mind was made to stay in. At the Church where Leonard ushered, there was young woman named Viola, she sang in the choir, to whom he married. There were conflicting reports – in a letter from the Director of Records dated November, 1944, he died at a British Field Dressing Station, while on the Official Registration of Death, dated December, 1946, it stated that Leonard's body was not recovered. This was very confusing to the family.

Ruthig Lake (52 L/3), northeast of Brereton Lake was named after him in 1973.

Rutland, Corporal **Arthur J.** of Clearwater (H 41489). Royal Winnipeg Rifles. He died 12 October 1944 at the age of 25 and is commemorated at the Groesbeek Memorial in Holland. He was the son of Charles J. and Elizabeth Rutland of Clearwater, Manitoba. ***Rutland Lake*** (64 K/8), northeast of Reindeer Lake was named after him and his brother Rifleman William H. Rutland (next entry) in 1972.

Rutland, Rifleman **William H.** of Clearwater (H 42140). Royal Winnipeg Rifles. He died 12 December 1944 at the age of 22 and is commemorated at the Groesbeek Canadian War Cemetery in Holland. He was the son of Charles J. and Elizabeth Rutland of Clearwater, Manitoba. ***Rutland Lake*** (64 K/8), northeast of Reindeer Lake was named after him and his brother Corporal Arthur J. Rutland (previous entry) in 1972.

Rutledge, Rifleman **James E.** of Delta (H 9912). Royal Winnipeg Rifles. He died 13 July 1944 at the age of 23 and is commemorated at Beny-sur-Mer Canadian War Cemetery in Calvados, France. He was the son of Percy and Mary Rutledge of Delta Station, Manitoba. ***Rutledge Island*** (63 I/1) in Lorentson Lake was named after him in 1995.

Rutledge, Private **Percy M.** of Bowsman (H 65631). Royal Canadian Army Service Corps. He died 27 August 1944 at the age of 32 and is commemorated at Ancona War Cemetery in Italy. He was the son of L. W. and Annie R. Rutledge and was survived by his wife Elsie W. Rutledge of Birch River, Manitoba and their three small children.

Percy was born in Neepawa, Manitoba in 1912 and later moved to Bowsman, enlisting in the Army in 1941. He trained in Portage and Red Deer, Alberta prior to his posting overseas in January, 1942. Percy served throughout the campaign in Sicily and Italy with the Canadian Ambulance Corps (*Neepawa Press* 16 November 1944).

Rutledge Lake (64 K/14), northeast of Lac Brochet was named after him in 1961.

Ryan, Sergeant **Francis J.** of Flin Flon (H 41435). Royal Winnipeg Rifles, Military Medal. He died 6 July 1945 at the age of 31 and is commemorated at Ross Lake Cemetery in Flin Flon, Manitoba. He was the son of John C. and Mary V. Ryan of Prince Albert, Saskatchewan and was survived by his wife Sarah P. Ryan. ***Ryan Lake*** (64 J/10), west of Tadoule Lake was named after him in 1957.

Ryan, Leading Aircraftman **Gordon F.** of Winnipeg (R 56876). No. 2 Wireless School (Calgary), RCAF. He died 11 December 1941 at the age of 22 and is commemorated at Elmwood Cemetery in Winnipeg. He was the son of William H. and Jessie M. Ryan of Winnipeg. ***Ryan Island*** (64 H/11) in Small Lake was named after him in 1995.

Rychlicki, Private **Charles** of Silver (H 9515). South Saskatchewan Regiment. He died 20 July 1944 at the age of 20 and is commemorated at Bretteville-sur-Laize Canadian War Cemetery in Calvados, France. He was the son of Peter and Teenie Rychlicki of Silver, Manitoba and was survived by five siblings. His brother Nick recalls (28 November 2001):

In 1940, Charlie and I went to find work in Fort William, Ontario (now Thunder Bay). He was a generous, outgoing guy who made friends easily. He worked hard for the Highways Department and being young and away from home for the first time, sent some [money] back home. But he also enjoyed life – learning to play the guitar and proud of his first car – a well-used Model T Ford. Looking back now, I'm glad that Charlie was able to enjoy those experiences of his youth.

While growing up on the farm, he spent a lot of time helping Father clearing land and working the fields. It was only recently I found out that he was killed in action while attacking through ripened grain fields below Verrières Ridge, France.

Rychlicki Lake (64 J/7), southwest of Tadoule Lake was named after him in 1975.

Rye, Corporal **Ernest C.** of Winnipeg (H 40846). Royal Winnipeg Rifles. He died 19 February 1945 at the age of 38 and is commemorated at the Groesbeek Canadian War Cemetery in Holland. He was the son of Charles and Jessica E. Rye. A friend wrote (5 November 1996):

Ernie was born in England and I have no idea when he came to Canada [1935], but as a child in the 1930s, I remember him well as do former neighbours. He must have been very young when he came to work for Mr. and Mrs. Charles Kerr, now deceased. He was a good and reliable worker, very pleasant personality. I do not remember him socializing outside of the neighbours with whom he worked at times on threshing gangs or wood-sawing bees. He seemed perfectly content to work with the cattle and horses. Mr. Kerr had Clydesdale horses which he would show at the Toronto Winter fair and [which] won many ribbons.

Mr. and Mrs. Kerr were a Scottish couple who came to Canada in 1907. They had a charming farm home and Ernie was very comfortable with them. They had no children and have been deceased for many years.

I recall a visit Ernie made to England in the late 1930s to visit his mother. Before leaving, he spent an evening with each family in the district with whom he had worked in any capacity, playing cards, chatting and having a cup of tea. He returned from England and continued to live here until he joined the army. He was well respected by all.

Rye Lake (52E/11), northwest of Falcon Lake was named after him in 1974.

Ryne, Sergeant **Stanley E.** of Winnipeg (H 19946). Queen's Own Cameron Highlanders. He died 11 January 1945 and is commemorated at the Groesbeek Canadian War Cemetery in Holland. ***Ryne Creek*** (63 I/16), which flows northeast into Carrot River was named after him in 1973.

Eleanor Chartrand tightening nose plugs of 500-pound bombs, 1942.
Courtesy of the National Archives of Canada (PA-145665).

S

Saar, Trooper **Durward A.** of Pierson (H 8906). Elgin Regiment. He died 8 July 1944 at the age of 30 and is commemorated at Beny-sur-Mer Canadian War Cemetery in Calvados, France. He was the son of William C. and Bessie J. Saar (née McLauchlin) of Gainsborough, Saskatchewan. His brother writes (10 February 1997):

> He was born ... at Tunis, Montana. During the 1930s, [he] spent most of his time working on farms in Alberta. He was mechanically inclined and worked for some time in a garage. He loved music and played the mouth organ and some violin. He also enjoyed cards, especially cribbage. He never married. He enlisted, as far as I can remember, in Manitoba in 1942.

Saar Lake (64 N/15), west of Nueltin Lake was named after him in 1972.

Sabblut, Private **Aaron** of Winnipeg (H 200154). Saskatoon Light Infantry. He died 15 July 1943 and is commemorated at Agira Canadian War Cemetery in Italy. ***Sabblut Lake*** (64 I/1), northeast of Etawney Lake was named after him in 1974.

Sabiston, Rifleman **David H.** of Pine Falls (H 41262). Royal Winnipeg Rifles. He died 12 June 1944 and is commemorated at Bretteville-sur-Laize Canadian War Cemetery in Calvados, France. ***Sabiston Lake*** (64 N/16), west of Nueltin Lake was named after him in 1972.

Sadeski, Sergeant **John** of Souris (R 140616). No. 419 Squadron. He died 3 August 1943 at the age of 25 and is commemorated at Becklingen War Cemetery in Germany. He was the son of Nicholas and Rose Sadeski of Winnipeg. This was Sergeant Sadeski's first operation. His aircraft appeared to be hit by lightning just before it reached the target. All four engines failed and the electrical system went out (Allison and Hayward 1991). ***Sadeski Lake*** (64 P/12), east of Nejanilini Lake was named after him in 1974.

Sahaluk, Trooper **Walter** of Winnipeg (H 77803). 12th Manitoba Dragoons. He died 9 August 1944 at the age of 23 and is commemorated at Bretteville-sur-Laize Canadian War Cemetery in Calvados, France. He was the son of Kondrat and Katherine Sahaluk of Winnipeg. Commemorative Certificates for Trooper Sahaluk and seven fellow Manitoba Dragoons were issued c/o Herbert Nicholson, MM who explains:

> In 1946, the 12th Manitoba Dragoons returned from Europe, and with money from our Canteen Fund furnished two wards in the Children's Hospital, with a promise that as long as our Association lasts, we would continue to support the Children's Hospital Fund. Since 1946, we have contributed $1000.00 every year, with donations received from the members. Also, we had a Plaque placed on the Hospital's 2nd floor, with the names of our fallen comrades on one side and on the other side, the names of the departed comrades who have since passed away. This was done with the idea that one day the Regiment will again be together.
>
> Now this brings me to my request, that the Association's approximately 350 members, would after all your efforts to find next-of-kin, would like to become family and have the Name Certificate placed on the wall in the Children's Hospital in trust that if a next-of-kin comes forward, the Certificate would be handed over to them (16 December 1998).

Sahaluk Lake (64 C/12), east of Laurie Lake was named after him in 1972.

Sails, Pilot Officer **John C.** of Winnipeg (J 17062). No. 32 Squadron. He died 27 March 1943 at the age of 21 and is commemorated at the Alamein Memorial in Egypt. ***Sails Lake*** (63 J/13), northeast of Wekusko Lake was named after him in 1972.

Salmon, Major General **Harry L. N.** of Winnipeg. Hastings and Prince Edward Regiment, Military Cross (1916) and Bar (1918). He died 29 April 1943 at the age of 49 and is commemorated at Brookwood Military Cemetery in Surrey, England. He was survived by his wife Agnes L. Salmon (née Duncan) of Toronto. A contemporary newspaper account read in part:

> A good, honest youngster who was fond of games during his student days at St. John's College and went off to join the army in the last war when he was 20. This was the description given by W. Burman, headmaster of Maj.-Gen. H. L. N. Salmon, who was killed in an airplane accident in Britain, Thursday. Maj.-Gen. Salmon was born on a farm at Stony Mountain, Manitoba. He was a son of the late John L. Salmon [and his wife Louise] who first farmed in that district and later came to the city to work for some years as a meter reader for the Winnipeg Electric Railway Company. Both his parents died some years ago. The family resided for some time at 166 Cathedral Avenue.
>
> Salmon was educated in Winnipeg public schools and St. John's College from 1907 to 1910. In the latter year, he went into business in Saskatchewan. On his return from the last war, he was employed for a short time by General Motors in Regina but soon decided to make the army his career. About 18 years ago, he married a Winnipegger, the former Miss Agnes Duncan, daughter of the later Albert Duncan, former manager of the livestock department of the United Grain Growers in Winnipeg who died in Toronto in 1940. Mrs. Salmon is residing in Toronto (n.d.).

In later years, Salmon was credited with a dramatic turnaround in his battalion's morale and performance.

> He was an outsider; Lt.-Col. Harry Salmon, a Permanent Force soldier who might well have been insulted by the order to take over a militia battalion. Certainly the Regiment was grossly insulted by his appointment. Nevertheless, this man possessed the catalyst which was needed to transform the magnificent promise of the Regiment into reality. He knew the way, and he was ruthless.
>
> Heads rolled at once. A number of officers and senior NCOs found themselves on their way back to Canada within a week of the new CO's arrival. There was cruelty in their treatment, but cruelty was needed. Hard as a headsman, and as implacable, Salmon impressed his will upon the unformed human material of the unit. Fear was one of his weapons, used deliberately. Officers and NCOs hated him at first because they feared him, but they did what he said – either that or they were out.
>
> Salmon's guiding principle was a simple one. He believed that the private soldier was never wrong. If the soldier got in trouble, it was the fault of his officers or his NCOs. If, in battle, the officers were to expect the support of their troops, then they would have to give the men service during training, and give it so unstintingly that they would become little more than slaves to their men's needs. It was no new thesis, but Salmon made it a living fact (Stacey 1955).

See also the entry for **Jack,** Lance Sergeant **George J.** ***Salmon Lake*** (53 E/13), south of Stevenson Lake was named after Major General Salmon in 1996.

Samson, Private **Albert J.** of Piney (H 6909). Winnipeg Grenadiers. He died a prisoner of war 12 November 1943 and is commemorated at the Sai Wan War Cemetery in Hong Kong. He was the son of Mr. and Mrs. N. Samson of Piney, Manitoba. ***Samson Lake*** (64 J/3), north of Big Sand Lake was named after him in 1957.

Sandberg, Sergeant **Victor L.** of Bissett (H 39213). Royal Canadian Corps of Engineers. He died 8 May 1945 at the age of 29 and is commemorated at Bergen-op-Zoom Canadian War Cemetery in Holland. He was the son of Nils V. and Charlotte Sandberg and was survived by his wife Doris M. Sandberg. ***Sandberg Lake*** (64 G/15), east of Big Sand Lake was named after him in 1963.

Sanders, Trooper **Frederick R.** of Selkirk (H 26575). Fort Garry Horse. He died 24 July 1944 at the age of 26 and is commemorated at Bretteville-sur-Laize Canadian War Cemetery in Calvados, France. He was the son of William and Alice J. Sanders and was survived by his wife Clara F. Sanders of Winnipeg. ***Sanders Island*** (63 P/8) in Goulet Lake was named after him in 1995.

Sanders, Sergeant **G. A. Paul** of Carman (R 91798). No. 60 Operational Training Unit, RCAF. He died 18 March 1942 at the age of 20 and is commemorated at Haddington (St Martin's) New Burial Ground, East Lothian, Scotland. He was the son of Edward M. and Rowena O. Sanders of Carman, Manitoba. His brother recalls (22 November 2001):

It has been said so many times that the young men who gave their lives in the Great Wars were amongst the finest of our youth. Paul certainly fit this description – an exceptional athlete excelling in hockey, golf, baseball, a good student as well as being a sincere and considerate person in his association with others. One of Paul's high school teachers, Frances Mill, was so moved by the announcement of his death that she decided also to do her part in the war effort. She enlisted in the WRENs where she was trained to operate LORAN, a new type of radar locator.

Paul enlisted in Winnipeg early in 1942 and was sent to Ontario for Manning Pool and Initial Training School where the powers that be decided whether you were suitable for aircrew and if so, which category. On being chosen for pilot training, his next stop was the Elementary Flying Training School (No. 14) at Portage la Prairie, just 45 miles from Paul's home. He accumulated a total of 66 hours in Tiger Moths. From there, the next step was to No. 11 Service Flying Training School at Yorkton for advanced training on Harvard aircraft. He received his pilot's wings in November, 1941 with an "above average rating" and a total of 96 hours on Harvards.

On January 4, 1942, Paul was posted to No. 60 Operational Training Unit at East Fortune, East Lothian in Scotland for training as a night-fighter on the Boulton-Dent Defiant aircraft. This was a single-engine plane very similar in size, power and appearance to the famous Hurricane, but with the addition of a heavy, power gun turret behind the pilot's cockpit. This turret required another crew member to operate the guns so there was considerable extra weight involved. The theory behind this plane was that enemy fighter aircraft would assume this to be just a regular fighter and would therefore be vulnerable to the guns in the turret if attacking from the rear.

The theory seemed OK, but as Paul explained in his letters (somehow got by the censors), the extra weight of turret and gunner certainly hurt the performance of the aircraft. They did not prove effective and were soon discarded as night fighters and replaced with such planes as the Bristol Beaufighters. In one of his letters, Paul indicated that the maintenance of the Defiant aircraft left a lot to be desired and that he wished that the planes were looked after as well as the Harvards had been back in Canada.

By March 17, Paul had accumulated 65 hours of flying time on the Defiants, almost equally divided between daylight and night flying training. There was training scheduled for the night of the 17th; the weather apparently was terrible and Paul's aircraft was first in line. Whether it was an engine problem or weather related, he crashed shortly after take-off and died at the scene. His gunner, a Sergeant Roberts, survived with just a broken leg. I had the opportunity to meet a chap who was in the same course as Paul, and was also due to fly that night who told me that they should not have attempted to train that night. In fact, Paul's aircraft was the only one to attempt a take-off.

It is almost 60 years ago at this date that Paul died, but he, along with the thousands of other young men who were casualties of the war are still remembered by those of his family still alive as well as boyhood friends and acquaintances.

Sanders Lake (52 E/14), northeast of Brereton Lake was named after him in 1974.

Sanderson, Rifleman **Currie A.** of Fairford (H 41080). Royal Winnipeg Rifles. He died 22 August 1941 at the age of 21 and is commemorated at Brookside Cemetery in Winnipeg. He was the son of David and Mary Sanderson of Deerhorn, Manitoba. ***Sanderson Bay*** (53 E/13) in Stevenson Lake was named after him in 1997.

Sanderson, Private **Delmer Douglas** of Reedy Creek (H 14142). Princess Louise Dragoon Guards. He died 16 December 1944 at the age of 19 and is commemorated at Villanova Canadian War Cemetery in Italy. He was the son of Gilbert and Margaret Sanderson of Reedy Creek, Manitoba. ***Sanderson Island*** (64 C/14) in Motriuk Lake was named after him in 1995.

Sanderson, Private **Isaac** of Selkirk (H 41818). Winnipeg Grenadiers. He died 14 February 1946 at the age of 33 and is commemorated at Selkirk (St. Peter's Old Stone Church) Cemetery, Manitoba. He was survived by his mother Sophia Sanderson of Selkirk and by his wife Harriet J. Sanderson of Selkirk. ***Sanderson Lake*** (64 G/11), east of Big Sand Lake was named after him in 1994.

Sandison, Private **Walter John** of Lockport (H 37730). Royal Canadian Army Medical Corps. He died 20 October 1944 at the age of 25 and is commemorated at the Groesbeek Memorial in Holland. He was the son of Walter J. and Helena A. Sandison and was survived by his wife Pearl Sandison of Lockport, Manitoba. ***Sandison Lake*** (64 I/4), west of North Knife Lake was named after him in 1974.

Sanger, Lieutenant **Lewis John** of Winnipeg. HMCS *Valleyfield*. The *Valleyfield* was torpedoed and sunk by U-548 50 miles south of Cape Race, Newfoundland; 125 of her ship's company were lost. Lieutenant Sanger had just gone below decks with the change of the watch when it was torpedoed. He died 7 May 1944 at the age of 23 and is commemorated at the Halifax Memorial. He was the son of John W. and Lauretta A. Sanger of Winnipeg and was in his second year of university when he enlisted. ***Sanger Lake*** (63 N/12), east of Sisipuk Lake was named after him in 1981.

Sangster, Trooper **James** of Neepawa (H 18345). Lord Strathcona's Horse. He died 18 November 1945 at the age of 21 and is commemorated at Riverside Cemetery in Neepawa. He was the son of William and Mary Sangster of Neepawa. According to his brother (21 November 2001):

James had served with the Royal Canadian Armoured Corps in England and the European theatre and had volunteered for the Pacific. He died of carbon monoxide poisoning while at home on leave before going to the Pacific.

Before the war, James was raised on a farm in the Langford Municipality, Neepawa, growing up with two brothers and three sisters. With his older brother Bill, he did the usual farm boy antics – riding steers and harnessing them in the buggy, digging out fox's dens and shooting gophers. They also did stooking and hired out to neighbours to make their spending money. His sister Margaret served in the RCAC and brother Bill in the Armoured Car Regiment and Black Watch (1943-46) in England and Europe.

Sangster Lake (63 A/1), south of Wrong Lake was named after him in 1979.

Saruk, Rifleman **Emil** of East Kildonan (H 41473). Royal Winnipeg Rifles. He died 6 June 1944 at the age of 27 and is commemorated at Beny-sur-Mer Canadian War Cemetery in Calvados, France. He was the son of Michael and Emily Saruk of Winnipeg and was survived by his wife Lena Saruk of Winnipeg. ***Saruk Lake*** (63 J/11), southwest of Setting Lake was named after him in 1972.

Sattelberger, Private **Edmund A.** of Flin Flon (L 105785). South Saskatchewan Regiment. He died 8 August 1944 at the age of 18 and is commemorated at Bretteville-sur-Laize Canadian War Cemetery in Calvados, France. He was the son of Frederick and Mary R. Sattelberger of Flin Flon, Manitoba. ***Sattelberger Lake*** (64 I/12), northwest of North Knife Lake was named after him in 1974.

Saunders, Corporal **John H.** of Glenella (H 17213). Princess Patricia's Canadian Light Infantry. He died 27 August 1944 at the age of 22 and is commemorated at Montecchio War Cemetery in Italy. According to family tradition, he walked from Glenella to join the armed forces in Brandon:

> Jack and his brother Bob decided they wanted to join the army so took off walking to the recruiting depot at Brandon, some ninety miles away. They made it as far as Franklin the first day and were so tired they found a large barn in that little hamlet, climbed up into the loft and fell asleep. The next day they continued their journey and with the exception of a five-mile ride in a farmer's wagon, they walked the rest of the way to Brandon. John joined the Princess Patricia's Canadian Light Infantry, training with this regiment in Canada for a short period of time. The majority of his training took place at various bases in England after his posting overseas. John's brother Bob ended up being too young to enlist and had to wait another year before he was to be was in the army. Their mother often mentioned how bad she felt that Jack was only able to spend one leave at home before he went to England. She also felt the number thirteen to be an omen. Jack's regimental number included the number 13. He was born on the 13th day, joined the army on the 13th day and sailed overseas on the 13th day. As they embraced and said their farewells, Jack attempted to assure his mother everything would be OK and her fears would be unfounded (Pittman n.d.).

Saunders Lake (64 F/3), north of Vandekerckhove Lake was named after him in 1994.

Saunders, Private **Stanley W. G.** of Winnipeg (H 20851). Queen's Own Cameron Highlanders. He died 21 July 1944 and is commemorated at Bretteville-sur-Laize Canadian War Cemetery in Calvados, France. ***Saunders Island*** (63 N/11) in Morin Lake was named after him in 1995.

Saunders, Private **William G.** of Winnipeg (H 17763). Princess Patricia's Canadian Light Infantry. He died 1 December 1943 at the age of 20 and is commemorated at the Moro River Canadian War Cemetery in Italy. He was the son of George and Alexandria Saunders of St. James. ***Saunders Bay*** (63 I/16) in Breland Lake was named after him in 1995.

Saunderson, Lance Bombardier **Charles Edwin** of Dauphin (H 59696). Royal Canadian Artillery. He died 5 September 1944 at the age of 24 and is commemorated at Gradara War Cemetery in Italy. He was the only son of Major Bernard and Lily Saunderson of Winnipeg. ***Saunderson Lake*** (63 P/6), south of Landing Lake was named after him in 1981.

Saunderson, Third Radio Officer **John** of Winnipeg. SS *Hartington*, Canadian Merchant Navy. The *Hartington* was lost 2 November 1942 and Officer Saunderson is commemorated at the Halifax Memorial. ***Saunderson Island*** (63 P/7) in Cauchon Lake was named after him in 2001.

Savage, Sergeant **Emery** of Fisher Branch (R 2129). No. 82 Operational Training Unit, RCAF. He died 2 January 1944 at the age of 27 and is commemorated at Stonefall Cemetery in Yorkshire, England. He was the son of Mr. and Mrs. A. C. Savage of Fisher Branch, Manitoba. His obituary read in part:

> Sergeant Savage enlisted with the RCAF in 1937 and received his initial training at Winnipeg and was later posted to Calgary. Following training at Macdonald and Trenton as a bombardier, he was posted overseas in October, 1943 (n.d.).

Savage Lake (64 P/15), northeast of Nejanilini Lake was named after him in 1974.

Savage, Captain **James G. W.** of Brandon. Royal Winnipeg Rifles. He died 27 November 1944 at the age of 28 and is commemorated at Brookwood Military Cemetery in Surrey, England. He was the son of Reverend James and Jean E. Savage of Brandon and was survived by his stepmother Cynthia A. Savage of Brandon. He had been nominated an Isbister Scholar in 1933 and 1934. ***Savage Bay*** (64 O/3) in Blackfish Lake was named after him in 1995.

Sawatzky, Sergeant **John L.** of Kirkfield Park (H 7202). Seaforth Highlanders of Canada. He died 24 May 1944 at the age of 29 and is commemorated at the Cassino War Cemetery in Italy. He was the son of Cornelius and Elizabeth Sawatzky of Altona, Manitoba. ***Sawatzky Lake*** (64 K/8), northeast of Reindeer Lake was named after him in 1972.

Sawdon, Sapper **James E.** of Gilbert Plains (H 39159). Royal Canadian Engineers. He died 6 June 1944 at the age of 22 during the invasion of Normandy. He is commemorated at Beny-sur-Mer Canadian War Cemetery in Calvados, France. His brother writes (7 December 1995):

> In 1932, the Sawdon family moved [from Winnipeg] and took up residence in Gilbert Plains. Jim attended Brickburn School. He always had a strong interest in farming, primarily working with animals. In the early months of 1940 at the age of 18, he enlisted in the Canadian Army in Winnipeg, originally with the Second Pioneer Battalion, RCE. After the initial training, he proceeded overseas where he served in the defence of Great Britain. Shortly before the invasion of Normandy, he transferred to the Sixth Field Royal Canadian Engineers.

He adds (23 October 2001):

> Finally on D-Day, June 6, 1944, he landed on Juno Beach with the forward elements of the Royal Winnipeg Rifles. As engineers, their job was to clear mines, tank obstacles etc. While he was trying to accomplish this, he came under heavy mortar and shell fire, thus was severely wounded and died on the beach. He gave [his] life so that all Canadians may live in freedom as we do today. We all loved our brother very much and to us he is our hero!

He was the son of Ernest and Ivy G. P. Sawdon of Kirkfield Park, Manitoba. ***Sawdon Lake*** (52 M/6), southeast of Sasaginnigak Lake was named after him in 1980.

Scaife, Private **George A.** of Mather (H 20729). Queen's Own Cameron Highlanders. According to his sister, Hilda (22 November 2001):

> George was born in Yorkshire, England. He immigrated to Canada April, 1912 with his mother, brother (Tom) and sister (Janet). His father had immigrated in late 1911, settling in Gladstone. George's younger sister, Hilda and brother Chester were born in 1913 and 1915. George grew up and was educated in southern Manitoba. As a young man, George worked on local farms and then with the CPR. His other interests were limited as that was the "dirty thirties" and times were tough. George enjoyed playing baseball and going to the local dances.

His father and brother had both served with the Royal Winnipeg Rifles, but his father didn't want both of his sons to serve in the same regiment. Private Scaife was declared officially missing after the Dieppe raid and pronounced dead 19 August 1942 at the age of 31. He is commemorated at Bergen General Cemetery in Holland. Private Scaife was survived by his parents Albert and Jane Scaife (née Smith) of Mather, Manitoba. He was the brother of Corporal Lawrence C. Scaife (next entry). ***Scaife Island*** (64 N/15) in Putahow Lake was named after him in 1995.

Scaife, Corporal **Lawrence Chester** of Mather (H 40742). Royal Winnipeg Rifles. This had been the unit that his father had served in during the First World War. He took part in the Invasion of Normandy and died 6 June 1944 at the age of 27. Corporal Scaife is commemorated at Beny-sur-Mer Canadian War Cemetery in Calvados, France. He was the youngest child of Albert and Jane Scaife (née Smith) of Mather, Manitoba and the brother of Private George A. Scaife (previous entry). His sister Hilda writes (22 November 2001):

> Chester grew up and was educated in southern Manitoba. He enjoyed skating, baseball and attending local dances. Chester worked on neighbouring farms until June, 1940, when he enlisted. He trained at Shilo, Manitoba, Truro, Nova Scotia and then was sent overseas to Aldershot, England in 1941.

In a letter from "Somewhere in England," he wrote:

> Dear Mum and Dad: Received your air mail you wrote on March 28 on the sixth; you see how fast they come with the right connection. There isn't very much news, but you will understand. I was going on leave on the fifteenth, but one of our boys took mumps so we are [under] observation for 21 days. Yes, it seems everything happens to me. I am Orderly Sergeant for all this week, so that will pass some of the time. I met Elgin Melvin [also from Mather] today in camp for the first time; he has been just close and we didn't know it all this time.
>
> I understand our airmail letters are going by boat so there isn't any use putting a sixpence stamp on it. Did I ever mention a young fellow from Cartwright – RCAF – was buried at Ripon, Aitkens I think his name was. There has been very little regular mail in this last while for me, likely going to the field unit.
>
> Gosh, it sure is windy out today and it seems as if all the sand is moving. I wouldn't like this to be in Egypt or Shilo with a breeze like this. You would sure like it over here now Mum with the flowers and trees out in bloom and the grass is getting long enough to cut (10 April 1943).

Scaife Lake (64 N/15), west of Nueltin Lake was named after him in 1972.

Scali, Private **Samuel** of Winnipeg (H 203218). Hastings and Prince Edward Regiment. He died 24 May 1944 and is commemorated at Minturno War Cemetery in Italy. ***Scali Lake*** (64 A/11), north of Campbell Lake was named after him in 1996.

Scanlon, Private **Richard P.** of Winnipeg (H 26522). Canadian Army Corps of Military Staff Clerks. He was aboard the SS *Nerissa*, the only ship torpedoed while carrying Canadian troops to the United Kingdom. Private Scanlon died 1 May 1941 at the age of 23 and is commemorated at the Halifax Memorial. He was survived by his mother Mrs. Louisa Scanlon of Winnipeg. ***Scanlon Lake*** (64 J/4), north of Big Sand Lake was named after him in 1975.

Scarff, Flight Sergeant **Thomas D.** of Winnipeg (R 95040). No. 77 Squadron. He died 1 May 1943 at the age of 23 and is commemorated at Muiden General Cemetery in Holland. He was the son of Charles H. and Daisy K. Scarff of St. James. He was:

> ... born December 1, 1919 at Winnipeg and was employed by a large refrigerator company when he joined the RCAF. After training at Dafoe, Calgary and Brandon, he went overseas in June, 1941 to serve with the RCAF in Great Britain and over continental Europe. Scarff attended the local schools at Linwood and Assiniboine and the Dominion Business College (Hill 1944).

Scarff Lake (53 D/4), southwest of Family Lake was named after him in 1979.

Scarth, Sergeant **Arthur** of Winnipeg (R 106002). Royal Air Force Ferry Command. He died 29 May 1942 at the age of 21 and is commemorated at the Ottawa Memorial. He was the fifth of the nine children of Bert and Minnie Scarth of Winnipeg. According to his sister (3 February 1995):

> Born in Winnipeg, he attended Ralph Brown Elementary, Luxton Junior High and St. John's Technical High School. He worked delivering for a local grocery store with a carrier on his bike after school and eventually worked at the Woolworth's store across from Eaton's in downtown Winnipeg. One of his hobbies was building model airplanes and at one time he made models for Woolworth's to display in their hobby department. He also liked riding and was in a bike race to Kenora. Arthur also liked fishing and used to ride his bike out to Lockport with friends or some of his brothers to fish. He was very fond of the family pet dog.
>
> He joined the Canadian Air Force and after becoming a Sergeant, was attached to Ferry Command. He left Newfoundland ... as the radio operator on an aircraft being ferried across the Atlantic. Radio contact was lost about two hours after leaving and nothing more was heard of him. On June 1, 1942 he was reported missing ... and in December of that year was officially presumed dead. His parents have passed away as have two brothers, but his memory is still very much alive with the rest of the family.

Scarth Lake (64 G/5), south of Big Sand Lake was named after him in 1994.

Schacht, Private **Bernard** of Winnipeg (H 20238). Queen's Own Cameron Highlanders. He died 19 August 1942 and is commemorated at the Brookwood Memorial in Surrey, England. ***Schacht Lake*** (64 O/2), southwest of Munroe Lake was named after him in 1975.

Schellenberg, Flying Officer **Herman S.** of Morden (J 9154). No. 418 Squadron. He died 21 November 1943 at the age of 28 and is commemorated at Brookwood Military Cemetery in Surrey, England. He was the son of Jacob A. and Anna A. Schellenberg of Steinbach, Manitoba. He is believed to have been a crewman on Mosquito HJ742 which crashed after a single-engine approach near Lyminster in Sussex. ***Schellenberg Creek*** (52 L/6), which flows west into Bird River was named after him in 1973.

Schieve, Private **Otto L.** of Whitemouth (L 12233). South Saskatchewan Regiment. He died 14 August 1944 at the age of 23 and is commemorated at Bretteville-sur-Laize Canadian War Cemetery in Calvados, France. He was the son of Emil and Olga Schieve of Whitemouth, Manitoba. ***Schieve Lake*** (64 I/12), northwest of North Knife Lake was named after him in 1974.

Schioler, Pilot Officer **Thomas L.** of Winnipeg (J 86203). No. 78 Squadron. He died 24 March 1944 at the age of 20 and is commemorated at the Berlin 1939 - 1945 War Cemetery in Brandenburg, Germany. He was the son of Kai B. and Olina J. Schioler (née Magnusson) of Winnipeg and was survived by his fiancée Pamela Langdown of Bournemouth, England. His brother writes (19 November 2001):

> He was reported missing for several months until it was known that he lost his life. Tommy's aircraft crashed near Eckardtshausen approximately five miles south of Eisenach, Germany. He was buried in the Churchyard at Eisenach which was in Russian-held territory. In 1951, the graves of Tommy and five members of his crew and others were moved to the British Military Cemetery at Berlin.
>
> Tommy liked doing artwork, athletics and was a teaser. His favourite song was *When I Grow Too Old to Dream*. He would often ask his mother to play it on the piano and he would sing along with other members of his family. His mother wore his wings proudly and always kept a fresh red carnation beside his picture until her death in 1997. Tommy met and became engaged to a British girl, Pamela Langdown while he was stationed in England. Pamela wrote to Tommy's parents several times and they wrote and sent parcels to her. Her parents wrote to them as well. Pamela told them that she would hear from Tommy almost every day, sometimes saying only "Dear Pammie – Love Tommy" just to let her know that he was OK. Mr. and Mrs. Schioler wrote to the parents of other missing crew members and they replied. Tommy's mother and sister Elsa visited his gravesite in 1970 and his nephew Tommy A. Schioler visited the site in 1985.

He enlisted five months after his graduation from St. James Collegiate. ***Schioler Lake*** (64 H/7), south of Solmundsson Lake was named after him in 1995.

Schleihauf, Flight Sergeant **John W.** of Winnipeg (R 59578). No. 226 Squadron. He died 28 October 1944 at the age of 23 and is commemorated at Venray War Cemetery in Holland. He was survived by his wife J. D. Schleihauf and their four month-old daughter. ***Schleihauf Lake*** (64 H/11), southeast of Small Lake was named after him in 1995.

Schmidt, Stoker 2 **Alfred H.** of Prairie Grove (V 68505). HMCS *Guysborough*. The *Guysborough* was torpedoed and sunk by U-878 in the English Channel off Ushant, France; fifty-one of her ship's company were lost. Stoker Schmidt died 18 March 1945 at the age of 35 and is commemorated at the Halifax Memorial. He was the son of Gustave A. and Elise Schmidt and was survived by his wife Elinor J. Schmidt of Prairie Grove, Manitoba. ***Schmidt Lake*** (64 N/9), southwest of Nueltin Lake was named after him in 1972.

Schmitke, Private **Henry William** of Giroux (H 10936). Queen's Own Cameron Highlanders. He died 26 February 1945 and is commemorated at the Groesbeek Canadian War Cemetery in Holland. He was the son of Mr. and Mrs. Gustav Schmitke of Giroux, Manitoba and was survived by his wife Johanna Schmitke. ***Schmitke Lake*** (64 N/2), southwest of Nueltin Lake was named after him in 1972.

Schmok, Sergeant **Albert J. W.** of Winnipeg (R 56995). No. 330 Squadron. He died 5 June 1943 at the age of 23 and is commemorated at the Runnymede Memorial in Surrey, England. He was the son of Reinhold and Ida P. Schmok of Winnipeg. His sister writes (19 October 2001):

> I can't remember when Albert didn't want to fly. The walls in the bedroom he shared with his twin brother Carl (he didn't feel the same way!) were covered with posters and hanging planes. So when war was declared, he enlisted in the ground-crew with my dad's hope of him learning a trade. But when he reached England, he transferred to the flight crew (he wrote home and said he just had to fly) and received his wings as a flight engineer. It was so sad to think that he died on his first official mission.
>
> He also loved the summers we spent at our cottage at Brereton Lake, fishing and picking berries. Also liked cars and with some buddies "chipped in" and bought an old jalopy – spent most of their time pushing it around the block to the amusement of parents and neighbours – the girls got roped in to push as well, but we had lots of laughs. He was very protective of his "baby sister" and we missed him so much. Not having a proper burial, he was commemorated in Runnymede, England with my parents sailing overseas to attend. They would have loved to have known a lake was named for him.

Schmok Lake (64 P/14), northeast of Nejanilini Lake was named after him in 1974.

Schneeberger, Flying Officer **Walter** of Winnipeg (J 28601). No. 5 Operational Training Unit, RCAF. He died 4 February 1945 at the age of 24 and is commemorated at Brookside Cemetery in Winnipeg. He was the son of Philip and Adela C. Schneeberger of Winnipeg and was survived by his wife Joan E. Schneeberger of Winnipeg and their son. He writes (10 December 2001):

> Walter graduated from Gordon Bell High School in 1940. His sister Louise said that he loved railroads and spent hours building model HO layouts. He loved flying and worked as a time-keeper at Portage la Prairie Flying School before enlisting in May, 1942. His travels took Walter and Joan to Saskatchewan and Alberta where he was an instructor. Finally, Walter went to British Columbia for operational training while Joan, who was now pregnant, went back to Winnipeg. My father made it back to Winnipeg on leave in September, 1944 to see his new-born son. I have pictures of that occasion. It was the only time I saw my father. Walter was killed in the crash of a Liberator bomber that went down shortly after take-off from Abbotsford, BC.

Schneeberger Lake (64 O/6), northeast of Egenolf Lake was named after him in 1975.

Schneider, Squadron Leader **Murray S. F.** of Brandon (J 16432). No. 405 Squadron. He died 9 October 1943 at the age of 22 and is commemorated at the Hanover War Cemetery in Germany. Squadron Leader Schneider was on his second tour of duty and had only recently returned from a one-year stay in hospital due to serious burns incurred on an earlier mission. Only two of the crew survived his final flight and reported to his sister that he had been attempting to keep his aircraft on a level course to allow his crew to bail out. ***Schneider Lake*** (64 P/4), southeast of Nejanilini Lake was named after him in 1974.

Schnell, Fusilier **Walter R.** of Morden (H 103914). Princess Louise Fusiliers. He died 30 July 1944 and is commemorated at Caserta War Cemetery in Italy. His niece writes:

> Walter Roy Schnell was born on the family homestead to parents Louie and Kathleen Schnell in Morden in the year 1924. Walter attended Morden Elementary School and Morden Collegiate. He enjoyed all

sports but excelled in hockey. While attending Morden Collegiate, war was declared. Walter very much wanted to serve his country and without the consent or knowledge of his parents, lied about his age, enlisting at the early age of 16. Walter went directly overseas. Many letters were exchanged over the next several years. Mr. and Mrs. Schnell received the sad news that Walter died on July 30, 1944

One of his last letters home was to his brother:

Dear Phil: I received your letter and certainly was glad to hear from you. I guess you know I'm in Italy now. It's not bad over here, but sure is getting hot. I also received a letter and parcel from Carole and a letter from Erine; they're both fine. I haven't had a letter from home since I've been overseas. I guess they don't think of their sons who are far away. I didn't sign any pay over to Dad. I signed it over to Carole to put in the bank for me. I sign 20 dollars a month and I'm going to send money to Carole once in a while so my pay book won't have too much credit. I also bought a victory bond.

How are things going, Phil? I'm having a pretty good time myself – I could have a better time back home, but will have to take it as it comes. I sure have changed since I came to Italy. I guess it's because I worry too much of what is going to happen next.

I'll be closing for now until you hear from me again if nothing happens. God Bless You. Your loving brother, Walter (9 May 1944).

Schnell Lake (64 N/15), west of Nueltin Lake was named after him in 1972.

Schoenthaler, Flight Sergeant **Arthur L.** of Winnipeg (R 166151). No. 431 Squadron. He died 5 January 1944 at the age of 20 and is commemorated at Stonefall Cemetery in Yorkshire, England. He was the son of Mr. and Mrs. Nicholas Schoenthaler of Winnipeg. His brother recalls (30 November 2001):

He spent his early years (eight or nine) at St. Joseph's Orphanage in Winnipeg due to his father working at a lumber camp in Pine Falls and his (our) mother being sick at a hospital in Selkirk. Our mother died there; Art must have been 10 or 11 at that time.

Arthur attended school at Daniel McIntyre Collegiate Institute prior to his enlistment and was really sports minded, especially football and baseball. While there, he was involved in assisting the police in catching a felon and was awarded a police commendation. We were great friends, being a couple of years apart, we played hooky a couple of times together.

While I was overseas with the 48th Highlanders of Toronto, I went to visit Arthur outside of London, but he was on leave (that was in 1943). Early in 1944, I was at the front lines near Ortona, Italy when I received a telegram from the British Ministry of Defence regarding Arthur's death on January 5th.

Schoenthaler Lake (54 M/4), southeast of Pakulak Lake was named after Flight Sergeant Schoenthaler in 1984.

Schofield, Private **Joseph** of Portage la Prairie (K 74763). Essex Scottish Regiment. He died 13 August 1944 at the age of 21 and is commemorated at Bretteville-sur-Laize Canadian War Cemetery in Calvados, France. He was the son of Herbert S. and Harriet Schofield of Portage la Prairie. ***Schofield Lake*** (64 O/5), southeast of Shannon Lake was named after him in 1995.

Scholey, Private **John R.** of Winnipeg (P 22256). Princess Patricia's Canadian Light Infantry. He died 22 July 1943 at the age of 25 and is commemorated at Agira Canadian War Cemetery in Italy. He was the son of William A. and Clarice M. Scholey of Winnipeg. ***Scholey Island*** (52 L/3) in Crowduck Lake was named after him in 1973.

Schroeder, Private **Ernest** of Letellier (H 1626). 1st Canadian Parachute Battalion. He died 1 August 1944 and is commemorated at Ranville War Cemetery, Calvados, France. ***Schroeder Lake*** (54 B/11), northeast of Shamattawa was named after him in 1964.

Schultz, Rifleman **William G.** of St. Boniface (H 41462). Royal Winnipeg Rifles. He died 8 June 1944 and is commemorated at the Bayeux Memorial in Calvados, France. He was the son of Mrs. Gertrude Schultz of St. Boniface and was survived by a wife overseas. ***Schultz Lake*** (64 K/13), north of Lac Brochet was named after him in 1972.

Schurman, Flying Officer **George M.** of Winnipeg (J 16809). No. 3 Advanced Flying School. He died 11 July 1943 at the age of 26 and is commemorated at Cirencester Cemetery, Gloucestershire, England. He was the son of Claude M. and Annie R. Schurman of Winnipeg. ***Schurman Lake*** (64 J/11), west of Tadoule Lake was named after him in 1975.

Schwartz, Flying Officer **Frederick W. "Fritz"** of Flin Flon (J 13586). No. 524 Squadron. He died 13 July 1944 at the age of 33 and is commemorated at the Runnymede Memorial in Surrey, England. He was the youngest of the 10 children of Robert J. and Bertha A. Schwartz (née Mahlitz) and was survived by his wife Mary I. Schwartz of Indian Head, Saskatchewan. His nephew's wife writes (21 July 2000):

It is said he was born *en route* to Shell Lake, Saskatchewan where his parents were coming to from Kisbey, Saskatchewan. His father was born in Thorn County, Quebec and his mother was born in Frankfurt, Germany. They were the first white settlers in the Shell Lake area and upon their arrival, their first home was a tent. Frederick grew up in the Shell Lake area and attended school at Shell Lake Rural School No. 2903. His first teacher was Mrs. Alice (Bloss) Schwartz who was married to Frederick's brother Albert.

His childhood years were like every other young person's in those years. Hard work and hard times but lots of happy times with family and neighbours. He built the first hockey rink on the creek known as Stubbs Flats and was instrumental in starting the first hockey team in that area. He loved swimming and taught a young friend 15 years his junior to swim. Ironically, he later saved that same person's life (Jimmy Jackson) from drowning in that same waterhole.

He was known as a happy, full of fun young person. He also loved softball, dancing and playing the saxophone at which he was very adept. He was known as friendly and outgoing as well as a "Ladies' Man" and it was said when he smiled at the gals they all fell sideways.

He took a barber course with his older brother Eddie and together they cut hair in their barber shop back of the Chinese Café in the town of Shell Lake. He and a friend (Roy Cassidy) left Shell Lake for Flin Flon at a very young age. They worked in the mines there. Since Frederick was mechanically inclined, he got to work in the Machine Room. He was also a feisty young man which at times got him into trouble. This at times led to job demotions, but because he was an excellent mechanic, it would not take long to be promoted again.

He married a young red-headed gal from Winnipeg and was only home to Shell Lake, Saskatchewan once since moving to Flin Flon. He enlisted in the air force from Winnipeg ... and died ... while on a night operation over the enemy coast.

Schwartz Lake (64 P/16), northeast of Nejanilini Lake was named after him in 1974.

Schykulski, Private **Walter** of Dauphin (H 26828). Queen's Own Cameron Highlanders. He died 5 October 1944 and is commemorated at Bergen-op-Zoom Canadian War Cemetery in Holland. ***Schykulski Lake*** (53 M/3), north of Aikens Lake was named after him in 1984.

Scorer, Flying Officer **Jackson C.** of Winnipeg (J 26770). No. 148 Squadron. He died 31 March 1945 at the age of 22 and is commemorated at Bari War Cemetery in Italy. ***Scorer Lake*** (64 G/14), east of Big Sand Lake was named after him in 1994.

Scorgie, Rifleman **William G.** of Isabella (B 142526). Royal Winnipeg Rifles. He died 28 August 1944 at the age of 19 and is commemorated at Bretteville-sur-Laize Canadian War Cemetery in Calvados, France. He was the son of George and Sarah Scorgie of Toronto. A comrade recalls (7 February 1997):

His father had been badly gassed during World War I and suffered much from that during the years that I knew the family. I believe the father died during World War II. During the war, the family moved to the Toronto area. I was away in the army at that time as I was a couple of years older than William. He joined the army and came to our regiment as a reinforcement when we were in the Caen area. I saw him twice around that time, then I went out wounded on August 15 and returned to the regiment early in October. When I went to look him up I found out he had been wounded (I think) around Calais. He died from those wounds.

Scorgie Lake (53 L/5), north of Bolton Lake was named after him in 1995.

Scotland, Flight Lieutenant **William H.** of St. Vital (C 3789). No. 211 Group, Royal Air Force Headquarters, Middle East. He died 30 March 1943 at the age of 35 and is commemorated at Sfax War Cemetery in Tunisia. He was the son of William and Mary A. Scotland (née Leitch) and was survived by his wife Margaret A. Scotland of St. Vital. ***Scotland Lake*** (64 B/12), southwest of Southern Indian Lake was named after him in 1974.

Scott, Lance Corporal **Alfred H.** of Deloraine (H 1020). Calgary Highlanders. He died 9 October 1944 at the age of 21 and is commemorated at Bergen-op-Zoom Canadian War Cemetery in Holland. ***Scott Bay*** (63 C/3) in Wolfpack Lake was named after him in 1993. His family erected a commemorative bronze plaque there in 1996.

Scott, Gunner **Arland K.** of Carberry (H 35621). Royal Canadian Artillery. He died 8 June 1944 at the age of 26 and is commemorated at Brookwood Military Cemetery in Surrey, England. He was the son of David and Sarah Scott of Gregg, Manitoba and was survived by his wife Ellen "Nellie" Scott of Donemana, County Tyrone, Northern Ireland. ***Scott Island*** (63 I/6) in Butterfly Lake was named after him in 1989.

Scott, Corporal **David Herbert** of Wasagaming (H 17594). Regina Rifle Regiment. He died 14 October 1944 at the age of 32 and is commemorated at the Adegem Canadian War Cemetery in Belgium. He was the son of Thomas and Mable M. Scott and was survived by his wife Grace Winnifred Scott of Wasagaming and their son. His wife recalls (21 November 2001):

David Herbert Scott joined the PPCLI at Dauphin, Manitoba. Herb enjoyed the outdoors – hunting, hiking and horseback riding; for relaxation he played the violin and liked reading good books. On Herb's return, Peter Brodie had a [park] warden job waiting for him at Riding Mountain National Park at Wasagaming, Manitoba. Most of all, he looked forward to seeing his son Daniel for the first time.

Scott Point (64 G/6) on MacKerracher Lake was named after Corporal Scott in 1994.

Scott, Flying Officer **George E.** of Plumas (J 20850). No. 612 Squadron. He died 25 May 1944 at the age of 24 and is commemorated at the Runnymede Memorial in Surrey, England. This native of County Armagh, Ireland immigrated to Canada in 1926 and lived on a farm near Plumas throughout his youth. He had been employed as a truck driver and driller with International Nickel Mines at Sudbury, Ontario at the time of his enlistment. He was the son of Robert G. and Alice Scott of Plumas, Manitoba. Flying Officer Scott was declared missing in action while on an operational flight over the Bay of Biscay. It was his 39th mission and he would have returned to Canada on leave after his 40th. ***Scott Hill*** (63 N/2), southeast of Moody Lake was named after him in 1995.

Scott, Flight Sergeant **Gordon D.** of Brandon (R 140573). No. 29 Operational Training Unit, RCAF. He died 7 September 1943 at the age of 22 and is commemorated at Haycombe Cemetery in Bath, Somerset, England. He was the son of Sparling and Myrtle Scott of Brandon. ***Gordon Scott Hill*** (64 A/6), east of White Stone Lake was named after him in 1995.

Scott, Flight Sergeant **Jack K.** of Winnipeg (R 210098). No. 166 Squadron. He died 23 September 1944 at the age of 20 and is commemorated at the Runnymede Memorial in Surrey, England. He was the son of William F. and Annie W. Scott (née Mair) of Winnipeg. Born in Winnipeg to Scottish immigrants, Jack attended Aberdeen School and St. John's Technical High School. He was an active member of and Sunday School teacher at St. Giles United Church. He participated in the Tuxes Boys' Parliament in 1941. Prior to enlisting, he had been a Carrier Salesman for the *Winnipeg Tribune*. His ambition was to become an electrical engineer. ***Jack Scott Rapids*** (53 M/10) in the Gowan River was named after him in 1995.

Scott, Private **James R.** of Lenswood (H 1408). South Saskatchewan Regiment. He died 6 August 1944 at the age of 21 and is commemorated at Bretteville-sur-Laize Canadian War Cemetery in Calvados, France. He was the son of Elwyn and Mary Scott of Lenswood, Manitoba.

James was born in the Birnie district November 28, 1921. He attended schools at Glenholm and Orange Ridge. James moved with his parents to Lenswood in 1935 and enlisted in the South Saskatchewan Regiment in 1942. He was posted overseas early in 1944 (Pittman n.d.).

Scott Lake (62 N/15), southeast of Swan River was named after him in 1973.

Scott, Private **Orlin G.** of Neepawa (H 77179). Saskatoon Light Infantry. He died 6 October 1943 at the age of 26 and is commemorated at Bari War Cemetery in Italy. He was survived by his mother Janet Maud Scott (née Bowman) of Minnedosa, Manitoba.

"Orlie," as he was known locally, was born January 17, 1917 at Neepawa, Manitoba. He joined the Canadian Militia (12th Manitoba Dragoons) on May 12, 1941. Fifteen days later, he enlisted in the regular army, the 18th (Manitoba) Reconnaissance Battalion. His pay was $1.30 per day. He later transferred to the Saskatoon Light Infantry. Orlie embarked for overseas from Halifax August 21, 1942, disembarking at Glasgow on August 31. His regiment was posted to the Mediterranean and they arrived there twelve days later. Orlie's battalion had just finished digging in their trenches in anticipation of an enemy attack when shell fragments hit Orlie, killing him instantly. He was placed in a temporary grave situated on a hilltop near Gambatesa, Italy overlooking the river and valley below (Pittman n.d.).

Scott Esker (64 I/10), west of Lovat Lake was named after him in 1995.

Scott, Corporal **Robert** of Griswold (H 40931). Royal Winnipeg Rifles. He died 8 June 1944 and is commemorated at Beny-sur-Mer Canadian War Cemetery in Calvados, France. ***Scott Rapids*** (64 I/8) in the South Knife River was named after him in 1995.

Scott, Flight Lieutenant **Russell Clare** of Minnedosa (J 20438). No. 458 Squadron. He died 24 August 1943 at the age of 24 and is commemorated at the Malta Memorial. He was the son of John G. and Ester E. Scott (née Gash) of Brandon. ***Scott Peninsula*** (63 I/3) on Molson Lake was named after him in 1995.

Scott, Gunner **Sidney G.** of Spearhill (K 80514). Royal Canadian Artillery. He died 3 November 1944 at the age of 29 and is commemorated at Bergen-op-Zoom Canadian War Cemetery in Holland. He was the son of William D. and Rebecca Scott and was survived by his wife Lillian Scott of Spearhill, Manitoba. ***Sidney Scott Island*** (63 P/7) in Cauchon Lake was named after him in 1995.

Scotten, Sergeant **Jack C.** of Winnipeg (R 101980). No. 405 Squadron. He died 10 September 1942 at the age of 20 and is commemorated at Rheinberg War Cemetery in Germany. He was the son of Ralph and Diana Scotten of Winnipeg. ***Scotten Lake*** (63 H/1), south of Gunisao Lake was named after him in 1974.

Scoular, Sergeant **John** of Winnipeg (H 19766). Queen's Own Cameron Highlanders. He died 17 August 1944 at the age of 22 and is commemorated at Bretteville-sur-Laize Canadian War Cemetery in Calvados, France. He was the son of Robert and Mary Scoular of Winnipeg. ***Scoular Lake*** (63 I/7), north of Molson Lake was named after him in 1973.

Scribe, Private **Kenneth** of Norway House (H 101784). Highland Light Infantry. He died 11 October 1944 at the age of 23 and is commemorated at the Adegem Canadian War Cemetery in Belgium. He was the son of John and Jessie Scribe (née Keeper) of Norway House, Manitoba. ***Scribe Creek*** (64 I/16), which flows south into Lavallée Channel in the Churchill River was named after him in 1974.

Seagrim, Leading Aircraftman **Francis D.** of St. Vital (R 276956). No. 3 Bombing and Gunnery School, RCAF. He died 19 August 1944 at the age of 19 and is commemorated at St. Vital Cemetery. He was the son of Major Herbert C. and Florence E. Seagrim of St. Vital. His mother received a letter from Wing Commander G. R. F. Gross which read in part:

> As you know, Frank changed his course from pilot to air gunner because he could not brook the delay necessary to complete pilot training. This one fact in itself shows the type of lad we have lost. He joined the service, not as an adventure, but with the one idea that he must help in bringing about the end of this war as soon as possible. Both his classmates and instructors spoke highly of him. He was a keen student and was doing well on his course. The flying accident in which he met his death occurred about three miles from the station, shortly after he and two of his classmates had taken off on a training exercise (20 August 1944).

Air Vice-Marshal K. M. Guthrie added that:

> This war is no doubt a part of the age-long struggle between good and evil. We have arrayed against us powers, which if they were to prevail, would destroy all the highest values which we possess in life. To be found on the side of right, and to be willing to give one's life for it, is indeed deserving of commendation. Your son has made the supreme sacrifice for his King and Country, and all the things we hold most dear. He is worthy of the highest tribute of honour and praise (22 August 1944).

Prior to enlisting he had attended Norberry High School and had been briefly employed with Midwest Aircraft. ***Seagrim Island*** (64 N/16) in Nueltin Lake was named after him in 1995.

Seaman, Sergeant **William T. "Bud"** of Edrans (R 140842). No. 24 Operational Training Unit, RCAF. He died 10 June 1943 at the age of 21 and is commemorated at Pont-du-Cens Communal Cemetery in Nantes, France. He was the son of William J. and Ellen L. Seaman of Edrans, Manitoba. His sister recalls (28 November 2001):

> "Bud" as he was known to all, enlisted in the air force in Winnipeg on November 19, 1941. He was posted to No. 2 Manning Depot in Brandon and then to Saskatoon where he acted as a service policeman for 10 months. He then trained as an air gunner at Macdonald, Manitoba, graduating on January 22, 1943. He went overseas the following March and was attached to an RAF bombing crew. He and all his crew were killed in a leaflet drop over France. Several letters and poems were received by his family for some time after his passing.
>
> William was born at home on the family farm and received his elementary at Edrans School and then worked on the farm and at the Edrans brickyard until his enlistment. He was quite musical, playing the mouth organ and the accordion and also the kettle drum in the Edrans band. He also enjoyed hunting, trapping, fishing and other outdoor activities. One of his favourite pastimes was driving his old Model T Ford around the countryside.

Seaman Island (64 J/15) in Stony Lake was named after him in 1975.

Secter, Major **John M.** of Winnipeg. 1st Canadian Special Service Battalion, Mentioned in Dispatches. He died 28 May 1944 at the age of 30 and is commemorated at Beach Head War Cemetery in Anzio, Italy. He was the son of Peter and Jennie Secter of Winnipeg. According to his sister (21 November 2001):

> He was a track and field enthusiast [who] won [the] half-mile in a provincial track meet. [He was] also a lacrosse player with the YMHA ... and was an ardent horseback rider. His real forte was fencing. In 1938, he won the Manitoba épée championship [and] in 1939 both épée and sabre events in the Manitoba championship. The same year he placed second in both events in the Dominion championship which was held in Winnipeg.
>
> He won an "A" certificate which qualified him as a Second Lieutenant in the COTC. He joined the Royal Winnipeg Rifles in 1940 and went overseas with them. He returned to Canada in 1942 and was promoted to Captain and was then stationed in Vernon, British Columbia where he was attached to the Winnipeg Light Infantry for the purpose of training soldiers.

In the summer of 1942, the 1st Special Service Force was organized – a commando-paratroop unit manned jointly by Canadian and US personnel. He was the adjutant for the 3rd Brigade of the Canadian contingent and was promoted to Major. He saw service with this unit in Kiska, Monte Cassino and Anzio where he was killed.

Secter Lake (64 N/11), southeast of Kasba Lake was named after him in 1972.

Seddon, Corporal **Norman R.** of St. Vital (R 124273). No. 4 Bombing and Gunnery School, RCAF. He died of scarlet fever 24 January 1942 at the age of 20 and is commemorated at Elmwood Cemetery in Winnipeg. He was the son of Percy J. and Annie Seddon of St. Vital. ***Seddon Lake*** (64 J/15), northwest of Tadoule Lake was named after him in 1975.

Sedgwick, Rifleman **Gifford W.** of Sanford (H 66999). Royal Winnipeg Rifles. He died 18 October 1944 at the age of 27 and is commemorated at the Adegem Canadian War Cemetery in Belgium. He was the son of Wesley and Victoria Sedgwick of Winnipeg and was survived by his wife Ivy Sedgwick of Winnipeg. ***Sedgwick Lake*** (64 G/11), east of Big Sand Lake was named after him in 1963.

Seely, Pilot Officer **John C.** of Winnipeg (J 86749). No. 422 Squadron. He died 24 May 1944 at the age of 26 and is commemorated at the Runnymede Memorial in Surrey, England. He was the son of Reginald D. and Mary A. Seely of Winnipeg. Born in London, England, he immigrated to Canada in 1927. Prior to enlisting, he had been employed with the Burns Meat Packing Company. He enlisted with the RCAF in September, 1939 and departed for England the following year. He received his commission 13 days before his death. ***Seely Lake*** (64 O/14), east of Nueltin Lake was named after him in 1975.

Segal, Rifleman **Harry** of Winnipeg (H 10838). Royal Winnipeg Rifles. He died 8 June 1944 at the age of 25 and is commemorated at Beny-sur-Mer Canadian War Cemetery in Calvados, France. He was the son of Charles and Sarah Segal of Winnipeg and was survived by his wife Sylvia Segal (née Gutnik) of Winnipeg. ***Segal Lake*** (52 L/3), northeast of Brereton Lake was named after him in 1973.

Seifert, Flight Sergeant **Arnold A.** of Winnipeg (R 80202). No. 12 Squadron. He died 31 May 1942 at the age of 23 and is commemorated at the Reichswald Forest War Cemetery in Germany. He was the son of Adolph and Lydia Seifert of Winnipeg and was survived by his wife Patricia M. Seifert of Winnipeg. He was the brother of Flying Officer Harold Seifert (next entry). ***Seifert Island*** (64 A/12) in Baldock Lake was named after him in 1995.

Seifert, Flying Officer **Harold O.** of Winnipeg (J 16852). No. 5 Squadron. He died 8 November 1943 at the age of 21 and is commemorated at Ranchi War Cemetery in India. He was the son of Adolph and Lydia Seifert of Winnipeg and was the brother of Flight Sergeant Arnold Seifert (previous entry). ***Seifert Lake*** (52 E/13), northwest of Brereton Lake was named after him in 1973.

Sellar, Flight Sergeant **Ernest H.** of Winnipeg (R 101853). No. 405 Squadron. He died 21 February 1943 at the age of 22 and is commemorated at Boldre (St. John) Churchyard in Hampshire, England. He was the son of Raymond and Sara Sellar of Winnipeg. ***Sellar Lake*** (64 P/3), northeast of Shethanei Lake was named after him in 1974.

Sellgren, Aircraftman 2 Hjalmer **Sanford "Sammy"** of Inwood (R 186696). No. 1 Service Flying Training School. This native of Sweden died 26 August 1943 at the age of 21 and is commemorated at Inwood Municipal Cemetery, Manitoba. He was the son of Hjalmer and Hilda Sellgren of Inwood and was killed in a train accident on his way home on leave. His younger brother writes (31 October 1997):

Sammy ... left home and worked as a hired farm hand from about 1939/40 until he joined the RCAF in August of 1942, shortly after the death of our mother. We didn't see too much of him during the year he was in the RCAF as leaves home were few and far between – but being the eldest son and first born, my father took it very hard when Sammy died. To him it was such a useless death – if he had been serving overseas and it happened that he was killed, I think my father would have felt it was dying for his country and it took him a long time to get over it.

Sellgren Lake (64 P/15), northeast of Nejanilini Lake was named after him in 1974.

Seman, Private **Metro** of Brooklands (H 1704). Princess Patricia's Canadian Light Infantry. He died 20 September 1944 and is commemorated at Coriano Ridge War Cemetery in Italy. He was the son of Fred and Katie Seman (née Kosh) of Brooklands. ***Seman River*** (64 O/12), which flows northeast into Nueltin Lake was named after him in 1972.

Senchuk, Private **Michael** of Dauphin (H 17029). Essex Scottish Regiment. He died 15 August 1944 at the age of 24 and is commemorated at Beny-sur-Mer Canadian War Cemetery in Calvados, France. He was the son of D. and Annie Senchuk and was survived by his wife of Rosena M. A. Senchuk of Fredericton, New Brunswick. ***Senchuk Lake*** (54 E/16), east of Bradshaw Lake was named after him in 1995.

Senyk, Private **Walter** of Pulp River (H 14029). Lincoln and Welland Regiment. He died 2 April 1945 and is commemorated at the Groesbeek Canadian War Cemetery in Holland. ***Senyk Lake*** (63J/13), north of Wekusko Lake was named after him in 1972.

Serada, Sapper **John** of Winnipeg (B 19961). Royal Canadian Engineers. He died 10 April 1945 at the age of 22 and is commemorated at the Holten Canadian War Cemetery in Holland. He was the son of Peter and Anne Sereda (sp.) of Winnipeg. According to Nestor, John's youngest brother (28 October 2001):

My brother John was the oldest of four children. We lived in a small, rural community – Tolstoi, just outside Winnipeg. I was very young when John left home. I recall that when my brother joined the army, my mother wasn't very happy because he was not of age to enlist. I didn't see that much of John, but I was thankful that we had a family reunion in May of 1942 before he was sent overseas. That was the last time our family was together. John was a member of the Royal Canadian Engineers. It was close to the end of the war, only two months, when his division was hit by enemy gunfire while closing in on a barn. John was wounded and later died as a result of his injuries. He was so close to coming home to us alive and well. For his dedicated service to his country, we are sad but proud of his ultimate sacrifice.

Serada Lake (63 N/6), north of Kississing Lake was named after him in 1995.

Setlak, Rifleman **Joseph** of Hadashville (H 41952). Royal Winnipeg Rifles. He died 6 June 1944 at the age of 21 and is commemorated at Beny-sur-Mer Canadian War Cemetery in Calvados, France. He was the youngest of the nine children of Adam and Frances Setlak of Hadashville, Manitoba. His eldest niece writes (26 November 2001):

> I remember my mother making up many parcels of slabs of chocolate, gum, cookies and a few other items she knew her brother would enjoy. She mailed the parcel directly from the Eaton's store at their Post Office. When mother wrote letters, my short letters were always included. Uncle Joe wrote back in good spirits and thanked her for remembering him so far away. The whole family was devastated when the sad news arrived that we would never see Uncle Joe again. In loving memory, red poppies will always grow in my summer garden for my dear Uncle Joe.

Setlak Lake (64 C/6), west of Granville Lake was named after him in 1973.

Sexton, Flying Officer **Murray K.** of Regent (J 8974). No. 207 Squadron. He died 26 February 1943 at the age of 20 and is commemorated at Durnbach War Cemetery in Bavaria, Germany. He was the son of Justus J. and Annie C. Sexton of Regent, Manitoba. His obituary read in part:

> Born in Regent, Manitoba April 26, 1922, he graduated from Grade 12 in Boissevain Collegiate and March 8, 1941 joined the RCAF, training at North Battleford, Regina, Virden and Brandon. He received his wings November 21, 1941 and a week later, his commission. Promotion to Flying Officer came in October, 1942 and he was attached to an RAF squadron in England. He skippered a Lancaster bomber on operational flights (n.d.).

According to his sister (29 October 2001): "I can just add that he was handsome, loved hunting, fishing and singing. And we, his family, all loved him." ***Sexton Lake*** (63 K/15), northeast of Elbow Lake was named after him in 1993.

Shack, Rifleman **Joseph** of Winnipeg (H 10818). Royal Winnipeg Rifles. He died 26 June 1944 and is commemorated at Bretteville-sur-Laize Canadian War Cemetery in Calvados, France. ***Shack Lake*** (64 O/9), northwest of Nejanilini Lake was named after him in 1975.

Shakeshaft, Private **Ernest A. E.** of Winnipeg (H 19969). Queen's Own Cameron Highlanders. He died 19 August 1942 and is commemorated at Brookwood Military Cemetery in Surrey, England. ***Shakeshaft Lake*** (52 L/3), northeast of Brereton Lake was named after him in 1973.

Shanas, Private **Ben Z.** of Winnipeg (H 16497). Princess Patricia's Canadian Light Infantry. He died 7 December 1943 and is commemorated at the Moro River Canadian War Cemetery in Italy. He was the son of Isaac J. and Dorothy Shanas of Winnipeg. ***Shanas Lake*** (64 I/15), northeast of North Knife Lake was named after him in 1978.

Shand, Private **David T.** of Renwer (H 64989). North Shore (New Brunswick) Regiment. He died 23 August 1944 at the age of 26 and is commemorated at Brookwood Military Cemetery in Surrey, England. He was the son of J. W. and Catherine Shand of Winnipeg. ***Shand Lake*** (62 N/15), southeast of Swan River was named after him in 1973.

Shankland, Lieutenant **Robert** of Winnipeg. 43rd Battalion, Manitoba Regiment, Distinguished Conduct Medal, Victoria Cross.

> On 26 October 1917 at Passchendaele, Belgium, having gained a position, Lieutenant Shankland rallied the remnants of his own platoon and men of other companies, disposed them to command the ground in front and inflicted heavy casualties on the retreating enemy. Later he dispersed a counter-attack and then personally communicated to headquarters an accurate and valuable report as to the position on the brigade frontage. He then rejoined his command and carried on until relieved. His courage and splendid example inspired all ranks (Buzzell 1997).

He later achieved the rank of Lieutenant Colonel. ***Shankland Lake*** (63 P/8), south of Goulet Lake was named after him in 2001.

Shanks, Pilot Officer **Jack L.** of Brandon (J 86809). No. 432 Squadron. He died 17 June 1944 at the age of 20 and is commemorated at Gorssel General Cemetery in Holland together with his pilot and mid-upper gunner. He was the son of Robert C. and Norma H. Shanks (née Johnson) of Brandon. His brother reports that he enlisted in May, 1943 and was posted to Brandon Manning Depot. He graduated in September of that year and after three weeks embarkation leave, he was shipped overseas, first to Ossington and later to Dishforth. On May 24, 1944, he arrived with his crew (seven in all) at Group 6 Bomber Command at East Moore, Yorkshire to begin full operation flights on Halifax III four-engine bombers. On the night of June 16/17, his plane was shot down. Four of the crew successfully parachuted to earth and were taken prisoners of war. His last letter home was to his brother Charles and his wife congratulating them on the birth of their first child:

> Well how are the proud Mother and Father today? I'll bet you two are sure happy. I'm happy for you also. Sure hope that junior turns out to be a good boy like his Uncle Jack. Ha! Ha! Gee kids, I sure wish I could be home for a few days to see the little fella. I'll bet he's really cute. Likely by the time I get back he'll be quite a size. Time for me to scram. Have to DI [daily inspect] our kite [aircraft] for tonight. Be good and keep happy, Uncle Jack (16 June 1944).

That was his last operational flight. ***Shanks Lake*** (64 J/14), northwest of Tadoule Lake was named after him in 1975.

Shannon, Flying Officer **Arthur Melvin** of Winnipegosis (J 23708). No. 101 Squadron. He died 4 May 1944 and is commemorated at Dieppe Canadian War Cemetery in Seine-Maritime, France. ***Shannon Bay*** (64 N/4) in Ouellet Lake was named after him in 1995.

Shannon, Flight Lieutenant **Louis C.** of Winnipeg (J 9499). No. 271 Squadron. He died 27 March 1944 at the age of 29 and is commemorated at Brookwood Military Cemetery in Surrey, England. He was the son of Cecil H. and Rosamonde B. Shannon of Winnipeg and husband of Lilian A. Shannon (née Gillerlain) of Winnipeg. She writes (7 June 1998):

> My husband Louis Cecil Shannon was born in Winnipeg on June 22, 1914. On July 30, 1932 he joined the staff of the Bank of Nova Scotia in Winnipeg. He enlisted in the RCAF on November 7, 1940, trained as an observer and graduated with a commission in December, 1941 at Rivers. He then served briefly as a flight instructor at No. 5 AOS, Winnipeg.
>
> He married Lilian A. Gillerlain on June 8, 1942 and was posted overseas in November, 1942. He served in Africa before being sent back to Britain early in 1944. He was at Little Rissington, Cheltenham, Gloucestershire,

England while serving as a flight instructor. Lou was a devoted son and husband, very caring and sincere. He was an avid golfer, he had a great sense of humour, a ready wit. He had a host of friends and a great zest for life.

Shannon Island (63 P/11) in Pikwitonei Lake was named after him in 1995.

Shannon, Flying Officer **Robert A.** of Winnipeg (J 18167). No. 427 Squadron, Distinguished Flying Medal.

This airman has proved himself one of the keenest air gunners in the squadron. On every occasion he has displayed the utmost coolness and courage in the face of the enemy. Despite the fierce opposition which he has encountered over the most heavily defended targets in Germany and enemy occupied territory, Flight Sergeant [Shannon] has maintained an undiminished enthusiasm for operations. His courage, skill and determination in action have been an inspiration to his crew (DFM Citation 1943).

He died 31 March 1944 at the age of 21 and is commemorated at Rheinberg War Cemetery in Germany. He was the son of Thomas L. and Kate E. Shannon of Winnipeg. ***Shannon Lake*** (64 C/11), southwest of Lynn Lake was named after him in 1950.

Sharman, Lieutenant **Cyril D.** of Winnipeg. Royal Winnipeg Rifles. He died 23 April 1945 at the age of 33 and is commemorated at the Holten Canadian War Cemetery in Holland. He was the eldest of the five children of Harry and Gertrude Sharman of St. Vital and was survived by his wife Ada M. Sharman of Winnipeg. His brother writes (27 October 2001):

Cyril ... died 12 days before the end of the war. Cyril grew up in the North End of Winnipeg and attended Luxton and St. John's Technical schools. He was an avid hunter, curler, a very good golfer and loved to play bridge. Prior to the start of the war, Cyril was in the Winnipeg Light Infantry Reserve. He was one of the first groups of instructors at Portage la Prairie and Wainwright, Alberta. His nephew, Cyril R. Sharman is honoured to be named after him.

Sharman Lake (64 N/12), south of Kasba Lake was named after him in 1972.

Sharman, Flying Officer **Robert A.** of Winnipeg (J 6135). No. 116 Squadron. He died 9 December 1942 at the age of 26 and is commemorated at Elmwood Cemetery in Winnipeg. He was one of the four children of Bertram C. and Nellie M. Sharman of Winnipeg and was survived by his wife Joyce M. Sharman of Winnipeg. She writes (n.d.):

"Ro" was christened and confirmed in St. Alban's Church, but was a member of the Riverview United Church Men's Club and was their president late in the thirties. His father died so the boys went out to work. He spent the last two or three years prior to the war with the Ford Motor Company.

Tennis was his sport of choice. He was a member of St. Alban's, Fort Rouge and the Canoe Club. In winter, it was skating and skiing. Ro was an extrovert, outgoing and full of fun. If entertainment was being planned, he would be in the middle of it. Robert and a close friend edited a lease newspaper when they were in Catalina flying boats doing convoy duty out of Botwood, Newfoundland.

Sharman Island (63 N/10) in Flatrock Lake was named after him in 1995.

Sharp, Corporal **Harry T.** of Hilltop (H 41403). Royal Winnipeg Rifles. He died 4 July 1944 at the age of 36 and is commemorated at Beny-sur-Mer Canadian War Cemetery in Calvados, France. He was the son of Harry and Maude M. Sharp and was survived by his wife Irene L. Sharp of Toronto and their four children. ***Sharp Island*** (64 F/1) in Melvin Lake was named after him in 1984.

Sharp, Private **Harvey R.** of Portage la Prairie (H 9208). Princess Patricia's Canadian Light Infantry. He died 30 May 1944 at the age of 21 during the offensive on Rome. He was the son of Richard and Mary J. Sharp of Portage la Prairie and is commemorated at the Cassino War Cemetery in Italy. ***Sharp Peninsula*** (64 C/7) on Granville Lake was named after him in 1995.

Sharp, Warrant Officer 2 **Ronald** of Brandon (R 180338). No. 51 Squadron. He died 15 March 1944 at the age of 19 and is commemorated at Choloy War Cemetery, Meurthe-et-Moselle, France. He was the son of Arthur W. and Alice L. B. Sharp of Brandon. ***Sharp Rapids*** (63 N/7) in the Kississing River was named after him in 1995.

Sharpe, Flying Officer **George E.** of The Pas (J 21834). No. 61 Squadron. He died 2 January 1944 at the age of 23 and is commemorated at the Hanover War Cemetery in Germany. He was the son of the late Edward B. and Ethel M. Sharpe of Windsor, Ontario. His sister recalls (6 December 2001):

George was a good student, which was a mystery to me as he kept quite busy and never missed any new movie that came to town. But those wonderful years in The Pas came to an end when he became a student in Winnipeg at the University of Manitoba. He was in his second year of engineering when he moved on and joined the RCAF. The War was a cause he must have believed in or was he merely seeking a new adventure? This was a question not asked.

He completed his training as a pilot and left for overseas from Winnipeg. We were all there at the train station to see him off. And he did look mighty fine in his officer's uniform. George was a Pilot Officer by this time and his buddies made a point of coming by as we awaited the train so that he needed to answer their salutes with one of his own. It was great fun while it lasted, but all too soon it was over. He was soon part of the crowd of servicemen that were shipping out and I was never to see him again – alas, like many other wives and mothers that stood there and waved goodbye to their boys.

In England, George joined an RAF crew and as pilot, flew a Lancaster in the air raids over Germany. I believe they were over Berlin when their plane was shot down. It was in a village cemetery that George and his crew were buried originally. Their remains were moved by the military to a permanent site.

A woman in Scotland was a friend of the mother of one of the RAF airmen, and as she had a son stationed in Germany, she offered to ask him to locate and photograph the temporary graves of the crew. She kept the mothers of all seven airmen apprised of his progress. He wrote:

Dear Mother: Just a few lines to let you know that I received the message you gave to Jenny. I received it last week and on Sunday I started out to find the chap's grave, so here is the whole story from start to finish. On Saturday, just after dinner, the officer came along in his car and I found out that he was heading for a place called Wunstorf where the remainder of our flight is stationed and which is only three miles from the town of Neustadt, the place mentioned in the message. Well, I asked our officer if he would take me there to Wunstorf and after I explained the reason, he gladly said he would, so I put my best on, and without a wash or shave, I was on my way. We arrived about 4 PM and I saw my chum who put me up for the night as I didn't plan to go on to Neustadt that night, so after I got settled, I had a bite to eat and at night we went to an Ensa show in the camp. Well, the next morning I was up bright and early, and after breakfast, one of the lads had a camera which he gave me after I had explained why I wanted it, so at 9 AM I set off. It was a lovely morning, so I was in high spirits at the thought of getting some snaps of the lad's grave. Well, eventually I came to Neustadt and after making enquiries with some of the HD lads, I found there were three cemeteries, so for the next hour I was busy looking them over, but alas, the airman's grave wasn't there! I was disappointed and, to make sure there was only three burial grounds, I went to the Town Mayor.

His place was not open for business on a Sunday as a notice said; still, I knocked and I was rewarded by a clerk opening the door. I showed him the message and explained I had visited three burial grounds and couldn't find the grave, so he took me inside and we had a look at the map. It was then I got a shock – the village of Buren where the fellow was buried was nearly ten miles away. And what made it worse was the fact that I hadn't a chance of getting a lift as it was all country road where no military unit was stationed.

Still, I wasn't going back till I had found the poor chap's resting place, so off I went and I walked and walked till at last I was looking at the village of Buren; it was a lovely spot right out in the middle of the country. The village itself has only about 12 houses, but a very nice place and the people in it were very nice and did everything possible to help me which I will tell you about as the story goes on. Well, as I approached the village, nearly all the people came out to watch me. As there are no army units within miles of the place, I think I must have been the first British soldier they had seen. Anyway, I got to the centre of the village and had a look round to see if I had missed the cemetery.

As I stood there, I had an awful feeling that I wasn't going to find what I was looking for. Well, as I was standing there, one of the Germans came up to me, and before I could say anything, he said: "English flier." I knew then that I hadn't travelled in vain, and taking me by the arm, he led me up to the cemetery! It wasn't a big place as the village was very small, but I found the grave of the Seven Airmen! It was a communal grave. The German Air Force had buried the seven lads together. There was a cross placed in the middle and on it in block letters was the following:

Hierruhen 7 Englische Flieger
Gefallen AM. 2-1-1944

Which roughly means, Mother, "Seven English Fliers buried here. Befallen on the 2nd January 1944 in the early hours of the morning."

The grave was well taken care of by the village people. I took two snaps, one of the grave and cross, the other of the cross close up to it in the hope that the Mother of the airman may be able to read what was on it. All I am hoping for now is that the photos turn out alright.

After I had taken the snaps, I turned to head for home. By this time, half the village was standing silently round the cemetery watching me, so I thought it would do no harm to ask them if they knew anything about the crash and maybe I would be lucky and get some belongings of the airman and send home to his Mother. I asked them and they knew what I was wanting, but as their English was terrible and my knowledge of German ten times worse, we didn't get very far. At last, one of them said: "Fraulein speak English," so he sent one of the village lads to bring her and in a couple of minutes she arrived and believe me, she could speak better English than I can! Well, I explained that I would like to know as much as possible about the plane crash and if possible, to obtain anything which the villagers might have belonging to the airman so that I could send it home to his mother. She then asked all the villagers and after a while she said: "I am sorry, but all the clothing etc. which was on the airmen when they were lifted out of the plane had been taken by the German Military Authorities." She did say the plane did not catch fire, but every one was dead when the villagers arrived on the scene so that was that and I headed for Wunstorf.

That is the whole story Mother, and you can tell the airman's mother that her son is resting in peace with his six comrades and as long as there is someone in that village, the grave shall always have flowers. The people of the village are very nice. Well Mother, when the photos are developed, I will send them on straight away and just in case the first ones get lost in the post, I'll have some more developed.

I think that is everything, so I'll close now and get off to bed as it's freezing in our room. We have no stove so the warmest place is bed. Hoping this finds you in the best of health as it leaves me A-1. Love, Crighton, Your Loving Son (3 October 1945).

Sharpe Bay (63 K/12) in Athapapuskow Lake was named after Flying Officer Sharpe in 1984.

Sharples, Sergeant **Tom S.** of Winnipeg (R 59116). No. 11 Service Flying Training School. He died 6 June 1941 at the age of 20 and is commemorated at Elmwood Cemetery in Winnipeg. He was the son of Tom H. and Alice M. Sharples of Winnipeg. ***Sharples Lake*** (64 O/14), east of Nueltin Lake was named after him in 1975.

Shatford, Private **Howard E.** of Winnipeg (H 6446). Winnipeg Grenadiers. He died 20 December 1941 and is commemorated at the Sai Wan Memorial in Hong Kong. He was the son of Albert and Louisa Shatford of Gainsborough, Saskatchewan. ***Shatford Island*** (64 B/16) in Chapman Lake was named after him in 1995.

Shaw, Lieutenant **Harvey D.** of Cardale. Lord Strathcona's Horse. He died 5 January 1945 at the age of 27 and is commemorated at Ravenna War Cemetery in Italy. He was the son of George A. and Maria Shaw of Cardale, Manitoba. ***Shaw Bay*** (64 J/5) in Sprott Lake was named after him in 1995.

Shaw, Ordinary Seaman **Joseph** of Winnipeg. SS *Maplecourt*, Canadian Merchant Navy. The *Maplecourt* was lost through enemy action 6 February 1941. Ordinary Seaman Shaw was 24 years of age and is commemorated at the Halifax Memorial. He was the son of Mr. and Mrs. W. Shaw of Halifax. ***Joseph Shaw Lake*** (63 P/8), southeast of Goulet Lake was named after him in 2001.

Shaw, Gunner **Stanley A.** of Winnipeg (H 8268). Royal Canadian Artillery. He died 19 February 1945 at the age of 21 and is commemorated at the Groesbeek Canadian War Cemetery in Holland. He was the son of Edward H. and Anne B. Shaw of Winnipeg. ***Shaw Island*** (63 N/8) in Burntwood Lake was named after him in 1995.

Shayler, Private **Harry A.** of St. Vital (H 6309). Winnipeg Grenadiers. He died a prisoner of war 17 November 1944 at the age of 24 and is commemorated at the Yokohama War Cemetery in Japan. He was one of six brothers who served in the armed services during the second world war and was survived by a son. Private Shayler and a surviving brother (Lance Corporal William A. Shayler) had been used as forced labour in a nickel mine. ***Shayler Lake*** (52 L/4), southeast of Lac du Bonnet was named after Private Shayler in 1973.

Shea, Lieutenant **Cecil N.** of Winnipeg (P 22192). Princess Patricia's Canadian Light Infantry. He died 23 May 1944 at the age of 28 and is commemorated at the Cassino War Cemetery in Italy. He was the son of Nelson T. and Leita G. Shea of Deseronto, Ontario and was survived by his wife Mary Shea. ***Shea Lake*** (64 K/10), east of Lac Brochet was named after him in 1972.

Shean, Private **Walter A.** of Beulah (H 54202). Veterans Guard of Canada. He died 29 December 1940 at the age of 54 and is commemorated at Beulah Cemetery, Manitoba. He was survived by his brother Cecil D. Shean of Charlton Horethorne, Somerset, England, by his wife and their son. His obituary read in part:

> Walter Arthur Shean was a native of Yeovil, Somerset, England and was in his 57th year. In the year 1912 he came to Canada and was employed by C. E. Evans of Beulah, remaining there until he answered the call of duty in the first Great War in April, 1915, enlisting in the 44th Battalion. He saw active service and was severely wounded in the drive of 1918 when attached to the 3rd Brigade Machine Gun section, with the rank of Sergeant.
>
> Upon his return to Beulah, he went to reside with R. Reid and continued there until he again answered the call of duty and offered himself for service to his King and Country. His advanced age did not permit of his acceptance in a unit that might proceed to an actual theatre of war and he was attached to 10a company of the Veterans Home Guard in August last. Toward the end of that month, the unit went to Red Rock, Ontario to take guard duty at the internment camp. It was anticipated that Mr. Shean would spend a leave with Beulah friends about January 4th.
>
> During the many years residence in the Beulah district, Mr. Shean won the respect of a very wide circle of friends gained through his very pleasant disposition and a willingness to be of service to the community and his fellow man, and his kindly influence endeared him the hearts of those who came in contact with him in the many community undertakings that he interested himself in. He was a member of Miniota Masonic Lodge and has occupied the Master's chair for a term. As a returned soldier, he recognized his responsibility to his fellow comrades and became a member of the Miniota branch of the Canadian Legion and was honoured with the office of President on two occasions. At the time of his enlistment, he occupied the presidential chair and both these organizations have lost a valued brother and comrade. The death of this gentleman, for truly he was, in every sense of the word, inscribes his name on the roll of those who have died at the post of duty in the war that is now being fought to uphold the principles of justice and right (n.d.).

C. E. Evans' niece recalls (6 November 2001):

> He was very much a member of the family. I used to spend summer holidays on the farm as a child and to my young cousin and myself, he was always "Uncle Walter" and a big brother to my older cousin Lloyd. In the mid-1920s, Walter moved to the nearby Reid farm and as Lloyd eventually married their eldest daughter, Walter was doubly family.
>
> Walter was a quiet, sensitive and dedicated person and always more than ready and willing to help out wherever and whenever needed. He was very active in the Beulah community, particularly in the construction of the Community Hall where the building fund was started by a generous loan from him.
>
> I am 88 and Walter died 61 years ago. He must have been very special as I recall him vividly from my summers on the farm when I was between five and ten years old. He used to take my cousin and I in the buggy or wagon if he had to go pick up something and I remember this one time he had to take a team to pick up a wagon on a farm over a mile away – too far for two little girls to walk. The work horses were harnessed and so as not to disappoint us, he lifted us, one on each horse, made sure we were hanging on securely and he walked behind holding the reins firmly so the team couldn't walk too fast. We came back on the wagon.
>
> Another time when I fell into a fairly deep slough, he heard my cousin shouting and came running in time to save me from very possible drowning. He never mentioned the war (World War I) to us children, but often sang war songs to us while he was driving the wagon.
>
> When growing up, I did not get back to the farm often, but Uncle Walter always kept in touch with letters and cards as long as he lived and I can still feel the sense of loss on hearing of his death just after Christmas in 1940.

Shean Lake (64 J/8), south of Tadoule Lake was named after him in 1975.

Shelson, Flight Sergeant **Archie E.** of Beausejour (R 91663). No. 97 Squadron. He died 13 November 1942 at the age of 19 and is commemorated at Scampton (St. John The Baptist) Churchyard, Lincolnshire, England. He was the son of Joseph E. and Elizabeth Shelson (née Micklash) of Beausejour. He enlisted in January, 1941 and arrived overseas in February, 1942 following his training as a wireless air gunner at Calgary and Macdonald. ***Shelson Lake*** (52 L/5), northeast of Lac du Bonnet was named after him in 1973.

Shelton, Captain **Richard E.** of Winnipeg. Royal Canadian Artillery. He died 23 May 1944 and is commemorated at the Cassino War Cemetery in Italy. He had earlier served in the Army, but re-enlisted in 1939. He was the son of Corporal Arthur and Mrs. Vena Shelton of Winnipeg and was survived by his wife and two children. Born in Essex, England, he immigrated to Canada with his parents at the age of five. As a young man he was associated with the Holden Players and had his own theatrical troupe, the Shelton Players. He was also briefly employed with *The Winnipeg Tribune*. ***Shelton Lake*** (64 K/12), north of Lac Brochet was named after him in 1972.

Shepherd, Gunner **Robert S.** of Winnipeg (K 14034). Royal Canadian Artillery. He died 25 July 1941 at the age of 34 and is commemorated at the Veterans Cemetery in Esquimalt, British Columbia. He was the son of Edward and Margaret E. Shepherd of Winnipeg and was survived by his wife Doris M. Shepherd of Winnipeg. ***Shepherd Lake*** (53 K/6), east of Sharpe Lake was named after him in 1995.

Sheppard, Leading Signalman **David G.** of Winnipeg (V 9817). HMCS *Ottawa*. The *Ottawa* was escorting Convoy ON.127 in the North Atlantic when it was struck by two torpedoes from U-91; 114 of her ship's company were lost. Leading Signalman Sheppard died 13 September 1942 at the age of 20 and is commemorated at the Halifax Memorial. He was the son of Henry J. and Elizabeth Sheppard of Winnipeg. ***Sheppard Island*** (64 G/8) in Southern Indian Lake was named after him in 1963.

Sheps, Captain **Sam B.** of Winnipeg. Royal Canadian Artillery. He died 16 September 1944 at the age of 31 and is commemorated at Gradara War Cemetery in Italy. He fell at San Giovani near Romini during the assault on the Gothic Line. He was the son of Ben and Rose Sheps of Winnipeg and was survived by his wife Phyllis Sheps (née Cohen) and their daughter Roberta. His wife recalls (17 December 1996):

> Sam was born in Winnipeg, the son of Russian-born Jews. He was a graduate of the I. L. Peretz School and St. John's High School. Sam was a fine young man, warm and friendly and [had] a great capacity for enjoying everything. He was kind and generous. Sam liked sports, music and the arts – particularly the theatre – and played lead roles in several local productions.
>
> He was a recent, honours graduate of the University of Manitoba and Gold Medallist at the Manitoba Law School, but put a promising career on hold to join the army two days after Canada declared war on Germany. In his last letter to Rabbi J. Italiener, the Reform Rabbi of England, he wrote (n.d.):
>
> When I came to see you again, I was taking my leave of you all and silently saying good-bye. When I will see you again is something which only God Himself knows. To His wisdom I leave the resolution of when and where we may see each other again.

In his Tribute, the Rabbi said in part:

Sam Sheps was the kind of blessed man who unconsciously possessed the key to the hearts of others. His tall stature and his dark, bright eyes had an irresistible charm. In his home-town, Winnipeg, "Sammy" was one of the most popular figures, not least on the stage of the Winnipeg theatre.

But the same man who radiated so much cheerfulness also looked into the enigma of life with questioning eyes. His sincerity and reliability combined with the high standard of knowledge gained in a thorough education ... assured the young barrister of the high esteem of his colleagues as well as of those who sought him for advice and help. His keen interest in politics and his holy fervour for the solution of the social problem led his friends to hope he would be enabled to take an active part in the shaping of the post-war world.

He looked out on life and on the problems of the post-war world particularly from a Jewish aspect. He felt the responsibility of being a Jew. This man with the soft and child-like heart particularly appreciated the values of Judaism which had been created by the atmosphere of a real Jewish home. We recall his delight at the Seder evenings which he celebrated with us during the years of his sojourn in this country (December 1944).

Sheps Lake (63 O/4), north of Wekusko Lake was named after him in 1970.

Sherb, Private **Charles** of Brandon (H 18204). Princess Patricia's Canadian Light Infantry. He died 20 September 1944 at the age of 20 and is commemorated at Coriano Ridge War Cemetery in Italy. He was the son of Joseph F. and Lena Sherb of Brandon. ***Sherb Lake*** (52 E/14), northeast of Brereton Lake was named after him in 1974.

Sherman, Lieutenant **Laurence G.** of Winnipeg. Loyal Edmonton Regiment. He died 23 May 1944 at the age of 23 and is commemorated at the Cassino War Cemetery in Italy. He was the son of L. Ralph and Carolyn G. Sherman of Winnipeg.

Still youthfully energetic at 74, Louis R. (Bud) Sherman is a hard man to surprise. He has seen and heard and done a lot as a long time journalist and former federal and provincial politician. But Bud Sherman confesses he received "quite a jolt" when he happened to spot the name of his only brother in a recent edition of the *Prime Times News* listing of Second World War fatal casualties. "I was very moved to see his name on the list and to learn that a lake in Manitoba had been named after him," Bud recalled in an interview. "I didn't know about this program. It's very commendable of the province to do this. It's an impressive gesture which should be very gratifying to the next-of-kin." He and his wife Liz are sending copies of *Prime Times News* to his older sister in Toronto and younger sister in Kamloops. Bud says the discovery of his brother's name brought back a flood of memories.

When war broke out, Laurence, who was six years older than Bud, joined the Calgary Highlanders and became an officer. At the time, the family was living in Calgary where L. Ralph Sherman was the Anglican bishop. In 1943, the family moved to Winnipeg when The Most Reverend Sherman became Archbishop of Rupertsland. Laurence had gone overseas as a Calgary Highlander but he transferred to the Loyal Edmonton Regiment as a reinforcement officer. Bud reports that his post-war research showed the Edmontons were desperate for reinforcements "as they were badly cut up in the Battle of Ortona on the east coast of Italy. The regiment suffered 98 killed and many more wounded."

In May of 1944, the Edmontons were moved with other units of the 1st Canadian Infantry Division to support the Polish Corps in its attack on Monte Cassino, a pivotal point in the German defensive line south of Rome. The mountain was held by die-hard German paratroopers. "It was on May 23rd of 1944 that my brother was killed by a German sniper as the Edmontons were attacking," Bud says. "His body lies in the Commonwealth War Cemetery at Monte Cassino, which I have visited. It's a serene place, beautifully kept."

Bud Sherman was just too young to get into the war, but he joined the Canadian Officers Training Corps from 1947 to 1949 while attending the University of Manitoba. He was commissioned as an infantry officer with the rank of lieutenant. He maintains a military connection by serving (since 1984) on the advisory board of Manitoba's only kilted regiment, the Queen's Own Cameron Highlanders of Canada. "I'm a strong supporter of the militia as I consider it to be a crucial component of Canada's character," he says (Mardon 2001).

Sherman Lake (64 O/1), east of Munroe Lake was named after Lieutenant Sherman in 1995.

Sherrill, Flying Officer **John F. L.** of Winnipeg (J 35038). No. 434 Squadron. He died 29 July 1944 at the age of 22 and is commemorated at Hamburg Cemetery in Germany. ***Sherrill Lake*** (64 O/15), east of Nueltin Lake was named after him in 1975.

Sherritt, Private **Edward G. "Ted"** of Oakville (H 1140). Queen's Own Cameron Highlanders. He died 8 August 1944 at the age of 20 and is commemorated at Bretteville-sur-Laize Canadian War Cemetery in Calvados, France. He was the oldest son of Percival and Gertrude Sherritt (née Bray) of Oakville, Manitoba. His sister recalls (20 January 1995):

Ted took his schooling at Oakville. He had a keen interest in mechanics, often taking articles apart to assemble them again. He loved conversing with people. He was interested in their lives – especially the elderly. Ted loved sports, playing ball and skating in his youth. To Ted, fair play was essential. He was our tender-hearted brother who left high school to defend what he believed – freedom of his country. Ted joined the army in the fall of 1942, training at Portage la Prairie and Camp Borden. While in England, Ted volunteered for active duty in France with the Queen's Own Cameron Highlanders. He was killed at the Falaise Gap. In June of 1988, his three sisters visited his grave. We found the cemetery peaceful and well maintained. The epitaph on his headstone reads: "As we loved him, so we miss him."

Sherritt Bay (64 F/8) in Chiupka Lake was named after him in 1995.

Sherritt, Private **Eric W.** of Foxwarren (H 20715). Queen's Own Cameron Highlanders. He died 19 August 1942 at the age of 29 and is commemorated at St. Sever Cemetery Extension, Rouen, Seine-Maritime, France. He was the son of James T. and Jennett Sherritt of Foxwarren, Manitoba. ***Sherritt Lake*** (64 F/3), north of Goldsand Lake was named after him in 1988.

Sherwood, Corporal **Walter A.** of Dauphin (H 3938). Royal Canadian Army Service Corps. He died 1 March 1946 at the age of 45 and is commemorated at Lansdowne (Union) Cemetery, Ontario. He was the son of Earl and Sarah Sherwood of Quebec City and was survived by his wife Ethel M. Sherwood of Lansdowne, Manitoba. ***Sherwood Lake*** (64 C/11), north of Glasspole Lake was named after him in 1995.

Shewchyshyn, Private **Steven J.** of Lac du Bonnet (H 40817). Royal Canadian Army Supply Corps. He died 26 May 1944 and is commemorated at Salerno War Cemetery in Italy. He was survived by his wife Mary V. Shewchyshyn. ***Shewchyshyn Lake*** (63 O/2), north of Five Mile Lake was named after him in 1995.

Shewfelt, First Mate **Gordon.** SS *Lady Hawkins*, Canadian Merchant Navy. The *Lady Hawkins* was one of five Canadian ships that ran regular passenger service to Bermuda, the Bahamas, the West Indies and Guyana. First Mate Shewfelt died of pneumonia 16 January 1940. ***Shewfelt Island*** (63 P/6) in Landing Lake was named after him in 2001.

Shewfelt, Flight Lieutenant **Harold A.** of Winnipeg (J 915). No. 428 Squadron. He died 5 December 1944 at the age of 25 and is commemorated at the Runnymede Memorial in Surrey, England. He was the son of Lieutenant and Mrs. Shewfelt of Dauphin and was survived by his wife Shirley Shewfelt (née Blackwell) of Neepawa and their son. His Lancaster aircraft was involved in a mid-air collision with a Wellington from No. 426 Squadron. All 14 airmen were killed. ***Shewfelt Lake*** (64 J/10), west of Tadoule Lake was named after him in 1975.

Shiaro, Private **Arthur P.** of Selkirk (H 200181). Argyle and Sutherland Highlanders. He died 15 August 1944 at the age of 27 and is commemorated at Bretteville-sur-Laize Canadian War Cemetery in Calvados, France. He was survived by his wife Mary Shiaro of Selkirk, Manitoba and their son. He writes (15 November 2001):

> Due to the unfortunate timing of my father's death and my birth, we never saw each other. He knew of my birth, but never made it home to see me. He loved playing baseball and skating and in fact met my mother at a skating party on the Red River. By coincidence or heredity, when my son was younger, we enjoyed playing baseball and skating together. How I wish my father could have joined us.
>
> My wife and I had the experience of visiting the war graves in France. We felt a flood of various emotions, but none had the closeness of being down at the local skating rink. My uncle Charlie Shiaro, passed away on January 16, 2001. His last request was to have his ashes spread on Shiaro Lake.
>
> The picture I am enclosing is my parents' wedding picture. They were only married for about two years before my father was killed. Based on the letters he wrote to her, I'm sure he would like to be remembered as always being by her side.

Shiaro Lake (52 E/14), southeast of Brereton Lake was named after Private Arthur Shiaro in 1974.

Shiel, Private **Frederick G.** of Minitonas (H 77300). Saskatoon Light Infantry. He died 24 December 1944 at the age of 20 and is commemorated at Argenta Gap War Cemetery in Italy. He was the youngest son of William G. and Louise Shiel (née Godin). ***Shiel Lake*** (62 N/15), southeast of Swan River was named after him in 1973. His brother-in-law comments that the location seems particularly appropriate as his father had been a forest ranger in this area from 1913 to 1940.

Shields, Sergeant **Robert W.** of Waskada (R 166344). No. 22 Operational Training Unit, RCAF. He died 14 February 1944 at the age of 28 and is commemorated at Stratford-upon-Avon Cemetery in Warwickshire, England. He was the son of Walter E. and Clara E. Shields of Waskada, Manitoba and the brother of Sub-Lieutenant Walter Shields (next entry). He was survived by his wife Lorraine Shields and their daughter. He had been in Winnipeg working as a pharmacist when he enlisted. ***Shields Lake*** (64 N/13), south of Lopuck Lake was named after Sergeant Shields in 1995.

Shields, Sub-Lieutenant **Walter Edward "Ted"** of Waskada (O 66650). HMCS *Windflower*. The *Windflower* was rammed by Dutch freighter *Zypenberg* in dense fog off the Grand Banks while escorting Convoy SC.58; 23 of her ship's company were lost. Sub-Lieutenant Shields died 7 December 1941 at the age of 24 and is commemorated at the Halifax Memorial. He was the son of Walter E. and Clara E. Shields of Waskada, Manitoba and the brother of Sergeant Robert Shields (previous entry). At the time of his enlistment, he was studying law. ***Shields Creek*** (64 N/13), which flows north into Wakula Lake was named after Sub-Lieutenant Shields in 1972.

Shilliday, Flight Sergeant **Robert C.** of Winnipeg (K 263945). No. 153 Squadron. He died 16 January 1945 at the age of 19 and is commemorated at the Runnymede Memorial in Surrey, England. He was survived by his mother Ethel Shilliday of Winnipeg. ***Shilliday Lake*** (62 N/10), northeast of Roblin was named after him in 1973.

Shimmin, Leading Stores Assistant **Alfred G.** of Winnipeg (V 45064). HMCS *Strathadam*. He died 11 April 1945 at the age of 34 and is commemorated at Belfast City Cemetery, County Antrim, Northern Ireland. He was the son of Alfred G. and Rose Shimmin of Winnipeg. ***Shimmin Lake*** (64 N/7), southwest of Nueltin Lake was named after him in 1972.

Shineton, Corporal **William Edward** of McCreary (H 26568). Fort Garry Horse. He died 4 July 1944 at the age of 23 and is commemorated at Beny-sur-Mer Canadian War Cemetery in Calvados, France. This native of Kinlet, Shropshire, England was the son of Harry H. and Sophia Shineton of Norgate, Manitoba and was survived by his wife Bessie L. Shineton and their son whom he never saw. His brother writes (2 January 1997):

> The Shineton family moved to Canada in 1928. My Dad being a First World War veteran, moved onto a farm south of McCreary under the Soldier Settlement Plan. He also served as a Home Guard for several years in the second war. Brother John joined the service in 1939; brother Ed joined about 1940.
>
> As I remember, he liked hunting and sports although on the farm there wasn't much time for sports. But whatever the occasion, work or play, it was with determination to the fullest. Me being younger, I can remember when he and brother John came home on leave. And of course they had to initiate me to the Beer Parlour (under age too!). He was killed in the battle for Carpiquet air strip. Brother John was with him at the time.

Shineton Creek (63 N/2), which flows northwest into Limestone Creek was named after him in 1972.

Shinewald, Telegraphist **Sydney J.** of Winnipeg (V 42020). HMCS *Guysborough*. The *Guysborough* was torpedoed and sunk by U-878 in the English Channel off Ushant, France; fifty-one of her ship's company were lost. Telegraphist Shinewald died 18 March 1945 at the age of 20 and is commemorated at the Halifax Memorial. He was survived by his mother Jean Shinewald of Winnipeg. His obituary read in part:

> Telegrapher Shinewald joined the Navy in June, 1942 at the age of 17. He trained at HMCS *Chippawa*, Winnipeg, in Toronto and Saint-Hyacinthe. Later he was transferred to Halifax where he was posted to

the Corvette HMCS *Guysborough*, a Vancouver-built Bangor class ship doing minesweeping and anti-submarine operations. This ship's complement proceeded to England where it trained in preparation for its D-Day operations off the Normandy coast. Telegrapher Shinewald celebrated his twentieth birthday at home in Winnipeg while his ship was being refitted in Halifax.

Born in Winnipeg, ... he received his education at Norquay, David Livingstone and Machray Junior High Schools and the Jewish Workmen's Circle School. He was a member of the YMHA and YMCA and football and hockey teams which won city championships. Prior to enlistment, Telegrapher Shinewald was employed successively by a wholesale dry goods firm, the Hudson's Bay Company and a Manitoba shipping firm (n.d.).

Shinewald Lake (64 N/14), southeast of Kasba Lake was named after him in 1972.

Shires, Pilot Officer **Reginald A.** of Winnipeg (J 7532). No. 115 Squadron. He died 1 September 1942 at the age of 26 and is commemorated at Choloy War Cemetery, Meurthe-et-Moselle, France. He was the son of Horace and Harriett A. Shires of Vancouver. ***Shires Lake*** (54 D/15), southeast of Myre Lake was named after him in 1996.

Shkolny, Private **Max** of Winnipeg (H 6303). Winnipeg Grenadiers. He died 19 December 1941 and is commemorated at the Sai Wan Memorial in Hong Kong. He was survived by his wife Rose Shkolny of Vancouver. ***Shkolny Lake*** (64 O/1), east of Munroe Lake was named after him in 1975.

Shmigelsky, Warrant Officer 2 **Peter** of Komarno (R 86417). No. 502 Squadron. He died 22 March 1943 at the age of 25 and is commemorated at the Runnymede Memorial in Surrey, England. He was the son of Kasian and Nellie Shmigelsky of Winnipeg. ***Shmigelsky Lake*** (64 H/9), northeast of Freeman Lake was named after him in 1995.

Shnier, Flying Officer **Clifford C.** of Winnipeg (J 17452). No. 97 Squadron. He died 30 July 1943 at the age of 26 and is commemorated at Becklingen War Cemetery in Germany. In a contemporary newspaper account, he describes one of his bombing missions:

A one-time radio salesman from Winnipeg who took his initial training with the RCAF at Regina has just returned from a heavy raid on the Skoda works at Pilsen. He is Flight Sergeant Clifford Shnier, captain of a big Lancaster bomber. "We were flying through a wicked section of flak, searchlights, muck and corruption," Shnier told a *Sunday Express* man. "It looked absolutely solid, so we had no option. We just had to snake our way through. Then we were picked up by a blue searchlight and were immediately coned for seven minutes. It seemed more like seven hours. I lowered my seat and tried to sink my head into the cockpit, but the glare was blinding. It bathed the fuselage with a white light till it looked like a bottle of milk. We went into Pilsen between two concentrations of flak and searchlights that soon merged into a single cone. We saw our bombs go down. After being hit in the bomb bay and mainplane," said the Winnipegger, "I took advantage of a cloud and managed to escape into the dark." Shnier's crew has teamed together since October and have taken part in most of the heaviest raids over Germany and now have gone as far as Czechoslovakia. Shnier described the Pilsen raids as of real consequence (Cook 1943).

Shnier Lake (64 H/10), east of Buckland Lake was named after him in 1995.

Shore, Rifleman **Joseph** of Winnipeg (K 51093). Royal Winnipeg Rifles. He died 27 September 1944 at the age of 36 and is commemorated at the Calais Canadian War Cemetery in France. He was the son of Abraham and Rebecca Shore of Winnipeg. ***Shore Island*** (64 P/12) in White Rock Creek was named after him in 1995.

Shore, Private **William C.** of Winnipeg (H 6105). Winnipeg Grenadiers. He died 23 December 1941 and is commemorated at the Sai Wan War Cemetery in Hong Kong. He was the father of two sons. ***Shore Lake*** (63 K/13), east of Embury Lake was named after him in 1984.

Shtitz, Flight Sergeant **David J.** of Portage la Prairie (R 147012). No. 419 Squadron. He died 30 May 1943 at the age of 21 and is commemorated at Charleroi Communal Cemetery, Charleroi, Hainaut, Belgium. ***Shtitz Lake*** (64 I/7), north of North Knife Lake was named after him in 1978.

Shumsky, Warrant Officer 2 **William N.** of Winnipeg (R 68751). No. 7 Squadron. He died 25 August 1942 at the age of 21 and is commemorated at Gosselies Communal Cemetery in Charleroi, Hainaut, Belgium. ***Shumsky Lake*** (64 I/14), northeast of Shethanei Lake was named after him in 1974.

Shumyhora, Gunner **Michael** of Fork River (H 100893). Royal Canadian Artillery. He died 22 September 1944 at the age of 23 and is commemorated at Gradara War Cemetery in Italy. He was survived by his mother Annie Shumyhora and by his stepfather William Feschuk of St. Boniface. ***Shumyhora Lake*** (64 O/5), south of Nueltin Lake was named after him in 1975.

Shura, Corporal **John** of McCreary (H 1906). Essex Scottish Regiment. He died 1 March 1945 at the age of 22 and is commemorated at the Groesbeek Canadian War Cemetery in Holland. He was the son of Peter and Tillie Shura of Norgate, Manitoba. His brother writes (16 January 1998):

He was born in the Rural Municipality of McCreary [and] ... lived there until February, 1943 when he enlisted in the Canadian Army. He went over to England the latter part of 1943 as a member of an army reinforcement group. He was placed into the Essex Scottish Regiment from Windsor, Ontario. The Essex Scottish had fought at Dieppe in 1942 and required replacements. On July 25, 1944, he went into action with the Regiment as part of the Second Canadian Division.

Later, with the Essex Scottish Regiment, he was in the fighting to clear the Scheldt Estuary (the approaches to the port of Antwerp) in September, 1944 when he was wounded in action. After he recovered, he returned to his unit and fought in Holland. In late February, 1945, he was in the assault that entered Germany. On March 1, 1945, the Essex Scottish attacked in the Hochwald Forest in the push to the Rhine River. Corporal John Shura was killed that day.

Shura Lake (63 N/2), east of Kissising Lake was named after him in 1972.

Shusterove, Flying Officer **Sam Chester** of Winnipeg (J 10666). No. 221 Squadron. He died 23 January 1943 at the age of 20 and is commemorated at the Malta Memorial. ***Shusterove Lake*** (64 P/10), east of Nejanilini Lake was named after him in 1974.

Shuttleworth, Flying Officer **Leslie E.** of Minnedosa (J 14127). No. 407 Squadron. He died 30 June 1943 at the age of 23 and is commemorated at the Runnymede Memorial in Surrey, England. He was the third son of Norman P. and Sarah Shuttleworth (née Cameron) of Minnedosa. According to his brother:

Leslie's aircraft left the Chivenor base at 11:00 PM. It was a beautiful night and the stars were shining as the squadron Chaplain later recalled. Everyone was in good spirits as no trouble was anticipated, although every man knew each time he left the ground he took his life in his hands. That was the last time the aircraft or any of its crew were seen. When it failed to return to base at 8:00 AM on July 1st, the usual search procedures were carried out. No trace could be found and no prescribed messages of engaging the enemy or other perils had been issued after it left Chivenor the previous night. In view of the complete lack of communications, it has been assumed that an enemy JU 88 night fighter scored a direct hit off the coast of France, killing the crew before they could get a message away. Most of the German subs returning from the Battle of the Atlantic came into the Bay of Biscay and air cover was given by a series of JU 88 bases along the coast of France from Brest, south. The Bay was a theatre of supreme importance to both sides and the loss of life was indicative.

Leslie, like his two older sisters, Gertrude and Flossie, was profoundly influenced at a tender age by the exposure at the Lorndale Church to the life and teaching of Jesus. In one of his letters from Devonshire, Leslie wrote, "I've worshipped in huge city churches, in ancient parish chapels wreathed in mossy age, in a dispersal hut among roaring aircraft but God never seemed nearer to me than he did in the little old Lorndale schoolhouse back home" (Shuttleworth 1982).

Shuttleworth Lake (64 P/13), north of Nejanilini Lake was named after him in 1974. In 1986, his brother Bert and son Leslie (named after his uncle) flew into the lake and erected a cairn there in his honour (Neufeld 1987). Another brother adds (in Neufeld 1987):

The naming of Shuttleworth Lake, set as it is in the peace and quiet of the vast northland of this province brings to us a message that the peace and tranquillity of that place can be achieved by people of good will to work together in the future.

Shwaluk, Private **Wesley W.** of Oakburn (H 9595). 1st Canadian Parachute Battalion. He died 9 June 1944 at the age of 21 and is commemorated at Ranville War Cemetery, Calvados, France. He was the son of Steven M. and Catherine Shwaluk of Oakburn, Manitoba. ***Shwaluk Lake*** (64 I/6), north of North Knife Lake was named after him in 1974.

Shylega, Flying Officer **Bertram** of Rivers (J 26204). No. 53 Squadron. He died 4 January 1945 at the age of 23 and is commemorated at Stonefall Cemetery in Yorkshire, England. He was the son of Joseph and Mary Shylega of Rivers, Manitoba. ***Shylega Lake*** (64 P/7), east of Nejanilini Lake was named after him in 1974.

Shymkiw, Private **Anthony** of Makaroff (H 14948). Calgary Highlanders. He died 22 September 1944 at the age of 23 and is commemorated at Bergen-op-Zoom Canadian War Cemetery in Holland. He was the son of Mike and Nettie Shymkiw of Makaroff, Manitoba. His sister writes (25 November 2001):

I've read his letters and I feel so bad about how homesick he was. They weren't treated fair. The food that was shipped from Canada was not given to them. They were fed British substitutes. It was given to the British army. The boat they were shipped out in from Canada apparently had been used for shipping livestock. Wasn't even cleaned, and the food on the boat he was sure pigs wouldn't eat. He loved Canada and all he wanted was to come back. He was hoping very much the war would be over before he was sent on active duty. He was sent overseas in August, 1944. He was so sure that he could take care and survive. But a sniper's bullet got him while he was repairing some [telegraph lines]. My mother never got over his death.

Shymkiw Lake (64 I/2), east of North Knife Lake was named after him in 1974.

Shynkarchuk, Corporal **Peter** of Fraserwood (D 72309). 48th Highlanders of Canada. He died 25 March 1944 at the age of 25 and is commemorated at the Moro River Canadian War Cemetery in Italy. He was the son of Nick and Lena Shynkarchuk of Fraserwood, Manitoba. ***Shynkarchuk Lake*** (64 C/5), west of Kamuchawie Lake was named after him in 1995.

Sidebottom, Pilot Officer **George E.** of St. Vital (J 87992). No. 431 Squadron. He died 29 July 1944 at the age of 21 and is commemorated at the Kiel War Cemetery in Germany. He was the son of George W. and Ella Sidebottom (née Wopniford) and was survived by his wife Nora Sidebottom (née Hall) of St. Vital. She recalls (1 September 1998):

The family lived on Dunraven Avenue in St. Vital. When George was two, his mother died and George was looked after by his grandmother and family until George Sr. married Winnifred Harding. In 1929, George's brother Tom was born and the family moved to a home on Sherburn Street. George attended Glenwood School and Glenlawn Collegiate. He graduated in 1940.

George was a very active member of the Boy Scouts and was a Wolf Cub leader with the Fourth Troop of the Boy Scouts. He took part in the building of the Club House on St. Mary's Road at the corner of Morier Avenue. This building is still in use today.

While attending Junior and Senior high school, he delivered papers for the *Winnipeg Tribune* and on weekends he would deliver groceries for the local stores. When he graduated from high school, he went to work for the Consolidated Optical Company.

George met his lifetime sweetheart, Nora Hall, twin daughter of Mrs. Nora Hall and the late Jack Edward Hall in Grade 7 at Glenwood School. The two were inseparable and became formally engaged on April 8, 1942. They were married November 14, 1942 at St. Mark's Anglican Church in St. Vital.

In January, 1942, George joined the Pre-enlistment Course at the University of Manitoba so that he could become an Air Crew member of the RCAF. When the course was completed, he joined the Air Force with two friends, Thomas Fisher and George Nowell. The three were sent to No. 12 Manning Depot at Edmonton in June, 1942.

George was sent to No. 15 EFTS Regina in November. In January, 1942, he was transferred to Trenton where he was classified as a navigator. In April, he returned to No. 5 AOS at Portage la Prairie. During the summer months, George and Nora lived in accommodations in town and George travelled back and forth to the Air Base. George received his Navigator Wings at the end of August, 1943. In September, he left for overseas while Nora began teaching duties at Langside School in southern Manitoba.

In England, George was assigned to 431 Squadron at Malton, Yorkshire. He was commissioned on July 11, 1944. George was reported missing on a flight to Hamburg, Germany July 28/29. In 1952, the Commonwealth War Graves Commission indicated that his remains had been found in a common grave marked "Four English Airmen" at Busm, Germany. He is now buried in the Kiel Military Cemetery.

Sidebottom Lake (64 J/13), southeast of Egenolf Lake was named after him in 1975.

Sieffert, Flight Sergeant **Arthur J.** of Winnipegosis (R 119786). No. 429 Squadron. He died 22 June 1943 at the age of 28 and is commemorated at Bergen-op-Zoom War Cemetery in Holland. He was the son of John S. and Amanda M. Sieffert (née Parker) of Winnipegosis and the husband of Norma S. Sieffert (née Fredrickson) of Winnipeg. His sister recalls (2 December 1987):

> He was born in Winnipegosis and received his education there. He attended United College in Winnipeg for two years, then he returned to Winnipegosis and entered business – first fishing and then he started a garage and trucking route. His main route was north from Winnipegosis to Camperville and Duck Bay on Lake Winnipegosis and then east to Pine River. Art loved the great outdoors. He was a good athlete and excelled at hockey and baseball.
>
> He was well known throughout that whole area as our grandparents were among the first white settlers there. My grandfather Sieffert and family came from Ontario via North Dakota and arrived in Winnipegosis in 1891. My maternal grandparents came from New Brunswick in 1906.

Sieffert Lake (64 F/3), northwest of Goldsand Lake was named after Flight Sergeant Sieffert in 1988.

Sigurdson, Pilot Officer **Johann** of Winnipeg (J 19620). No. 1666 Heavy Conversion Unit, RCAF. He died 29 February 1944 at the age of 23 and is commemorated at Stonefall Cemetery in Yorkshire, England. He was the son of Sigurthor and Maria O. Sigurdson and was survived by his wife Mary E. Sigurdson of Winnipeg. ***Sigurdson Peninsula*** (64 P/13) on Nicholson Lake was named after him in 1995.

Sigurdson, Ordinary Seaman **John** of Vidir (V 88746). HMCS *Cornwallis*. He died 5 October 1944 at the age of 20 and is commemorated at Grafreitur Cemetery in Vidir, Manitoba. He was the son of Jon and Sigrun Sigurdson of Selkirk. His sister writes (22 November 2001):

> John and I were only a year apart. We came from a large, close-knit family. On September 19, 1944, I received a letter from him telling me he was on a train heading for Cornwallis, Nova Scotia. In October, my mother phoned my place of work to ask me to come home. I went to my apartment and picked up my mail and there was a letter from John. I said to myself, nothing has happened to him. He wrote about picking apples and that the country was beautiful around Cornwallis and he was happy to be in the Navy. But when I arrived at Mother's house, the news was that John, my pal, had died. I couldn't believe it. He had collapsed and died while taking part in a training exercise. He wanted to fight for his country.

Sigurdson Lake (64 N/1), northwest of Egenolf Lake was named after him in 1972.

Sigurdson, Rifleman **Kjartan** of Lundar (H 8899). Royal Winnipeg Rifles. He died 8 June 1944 at the age of 28 and is commemorated at Beny-sur-Mer Canadian War Cemetery in Calvados, France. He was the youngest son of Olafur and Olavia Sigurdson of Lundar, Manitoba. His niece recalls (6 May 1996):

> His parents were ... both from Iceland, immigrating to Canada in 1901. He had three sisters and two brothers and was the youngest in the family. He received his education in the Lundar Consolidated School and after Grade 8, he quit school like many did in those days. He was a likeable person, nice and friendly. He was good with tools and in repairing things. He loved to be near water when he was a kid and made little boats to sail on the water. He was a good person to work with. If he read something interesting, he would tell you all about it as he worked. As the dollars were pretty scarce on the farm, he took a job ice fishing on the lake. He made out all right and continued it. That is how he got to know Einar Olafson. He asked him to work for him winter fishing. So Kjartan went with him and they got along very well together. Einar even wanted him to stay there and start raising cattle too. Einar lived near Crane River. He had many cattle and fished in winter. He probably would have ended up permanently up there, but his call came to join the army and that was it. Last time he wrote home, he was in England. He liked it there, he said it was a pretty country. He was one of those Canadians who were taken prisoner when they went across and we never heard from him since.

Many of those taken prisoner on 8 June 1944 were "executed" by the SS. ***Sigurdson Bay*** (64 O/12) in Drake Lake was named after Rifleman Sigurdson in 1995.

Siha, Private **Tony** of Portage la Prairie (H 800150). Princess Patricia's Canadian Light Infantry. He died 20 March 1951 and is commemorated at the United Nations Cemetery in Pusan, South Korea. ***Siha Lake*** (53 K/5), southeast of Weber Lake was named after this Korean War casualty in 1998.

Silkey, Private **Samuel** of Selkirk (H 6561). Winnipeg Grenadiers. He died 19 December 1941 at the age of 35 and is commemorated at the Sai Wan Memorial in Hong Kong. He was the son of George and Millie Silkey and was survived by his wife Bessie Silkey (née Jefferson) of Selkirk. Born in Denmark, he came to Canada as a young boy and joined the Grenadiers in September, 1939. ***Silkey Lake*** (64 I/11), north of North Knife River was named after him in 1974.

Silver, Pilot Officer **Robert G. E.** of Winnipeg (J 95489). No. 432 Squadron. He died 2 February 1945 at the age of 24 and is commemorated at the Reichswald Forest War Cemetery in Germany. He was the son of Donald and Eugenie Silver of Winnipeg. ***Silver Island*** (64 N/1) in Minuhik Lake was named after him in 1995.

Simbalist, Flight Sergeant **Eugene** of Brandon (R 76610). No. 115 Squadron. He died 3 December 1942 at the age of 21 and is commemorated at Rheinberg War Cemetery in Germany. ***Simbalist Lake*** (64 P/5), southeast of Nejanilini Lake was named after him in 1974.

Simmons, Flight Sergeant **Hugh R.** of Winnipeg (R 134345). No. 1664 Heavy Conversion Unit, RCAF. He died 22 October 1943 at the age of 27 and is commemorated at Stonefall Cemetery in Yorkshire, England. He was the only son of James A. and Lydia Simmons of Portage la Prairie and was survived by his wife Margaret Simmons (née Knight) of Winnipeg. His obituary read in part:

> Sergeant-Pilot Simmons was born at High Bluff. He attended his first years of school at Leifur School District and High Bluff and later in Central School and the Portage Collegiate. For many years he was a member of the Portage Baptist Church, being active in the Young People's Society and the Sunday School. At the time of his death, he was a member of St. Andrew's Church, Elgin Avenue, Winnipeg (n.d.).

Simmons Peninsula (64 P/12) on Nejanilini Lake was named after him in 1995.

Simon, Gunner **Mervyn J. "Bud"** of The Pas (H 35456). Royal Canadian Artillery. He died 6 May 1942 at the age of 21 and is commemorated at Brookwood Military Cemetery in Surrey, England. Survived by his parents J. L. and Mary Simon of The Pas, he was the war's first casualty from that community. His obituary read in part:

He was well known in The Pas having attended both the Sacred Heart School and Collegiate and had four year's service with the Boy Scouts. He ... had been with the RCA for two years, serving with the 19th Battalion, 3rd Field Regiment at time of death (n.d.).

His death certificate listed the cause of death as "Multiple injuries caused through explosion of a land mine. Accidental, Instantaneous." ***Simon Bay*** (63 N/7) in Guthrie Lake was named after him in 1995.

Simpson, Private **John** of Winnipeg (H 58555). Royal Canadian Ordnance Corps. He died 5 December 1943 at the age of 42 and is commemorated at Elmwood Cemetery in Winnipeg. He was survived by his mother Harriet E. Simpson of Winnipeg and by his wife Charlotte M. Simpson of Winnipeg. ***Simpson Hill*** (64 P/1), south of Caribou Lake was named after him in 1996.

Simpson, Private **Kenneth** of Winnipeg (H 6088). Winnipeg Grenadiers. He died 19 December 1941 and is commemorated at the Sai Wan Memorial in Hong Kong. ***Simpson Rapids*** (64 P/3) in the Big Spruce River was named after him in 1995.

Simpson, Leading Aircraftman **Lawrence B. E. "Buzz"** of Winnipegosis (R 210365). Royal Canadian Air Force. He died 13 September 1946 at the age of 24 and is commemorated at Prospect Cemetery in Toronto. He was the son of John E. and Ruby F. Simpson of Winnipegosis, Manitoba. ***Simpson Island*** (64 O/1) in Maltese Lake was named after him in 1995.

Simpson, Leading Aircraftman **Walter H.** of Winnipeg (R 170035). No. 1 Central Navigation School, RCAF. He died 29 December 1943 at the age of 27 and is commemorated at Brookside Cemetery in Winnipeg. He was the son of Cherrie H. and Beatrice Simpson of Winnipeg and was survived by his wife Evelyn Simpson of Rivers, Manitoba. ***Simpson Peninsula*** (63 N/8) on Burntwood Lake was named after him in 1995.

Simpson, Lance Corporal **William G. E.** of Hargrave (L 27191). Lake Superior Regiment. He died 9 August 1944 at the age of 33 and is commemorated at Bretteville-sur-Laize Canadian War Cemetery in Calvados, France. He was the son of William G. and Jessie Simpson of Hargrave, Manitoba. ***Simpson Creek*** (64 P/2), northwest of Meades Lake was named after him in 1995.

Sims, Guardsman **Elven G. W.** of Pilot Mound (H 63960). Governor General's Foot Guards. He died 29 August 1944 at the age of 32 and is commemorated at Bretteville-sur-Laize Canadian War Cemetery in Calvados, France. He was the eldest of the nine children of Garnet H. and Frances M. Sims (née Lane) of La Rivière and was survived by his wife of nine months Janet E. Sims (née Goodchild) of Ramsgate, Kent and their unborn son. His son (also Elven) writes (5 July 1998):

For myself, growing up with only pictures and family reminiscences and recollections in place of a father, it is all too real. Multiply this by all the other war dead and one has a sense of the long lasting effects of war. They never returned to Manitoba but are buried in cemeteries far away.

Guardsman Sims' wife recalled (5 July 1998):

I met Elven in Reading, Berkshire. My mother, younger sister and I had been evacuated from Ramsgate, Kent. I had a job at International Stores in Reading. We were married in St. Mary's Church in Reading and went to Devon for our honeymoon, about a week. Elven could not get much leave and could not come to Reading, so I went and stayed several weekends in Surrey. We went for lunches, etc. He wrote to me after he crossed the English Channel and went through Normandy. I had been corresponding with Elven's mother and father and of course when the news of his death came in 1944. I had a lovely baby born on February 19, 1945 – Elven.

We visited my late husband's parents in the summer of 1947 in La Rivière, Manitoba. They have since both passed away, but did see their first grandson, Elven which made them happy after the loss of their son Elven in the Falaise Battle.

In a letter from Captain John Fraser, the Medical Officer with Guardsman Sims' unit, he describes "El:"

First let me tell you of the experiences we have gone through during the closing of the Falaise Gap and the mopping up which followed. We found [the First Aid Post] in some very uncomfortable positions. No matter how hot the going, El was ever the same cool and calm as though we were back in England, miles removed from the conflict.

I can see him yet on the first day of the big drive, calmly attending to one tank crew's casualties in the middle of a mine field with all hell breaking loose about us. He refused to take cover until he had given first aid to the wounded and got them safely under cover. In the Air Force, such courage would be rewarded by some decoration; in the Army and certainly to El, it was just a job to be done and for which he expected no reward. On several occasions, he showed the same calm courage displayed that day on the start of the drive which finally wiped out the resistance in that part of France.

On August 28, we crossed the Seine and pulled into a spot in the valley to [illegible] for the night. No sooner had we dismounted from our vehicles than the mortars arrived. Several casualties resulted. Elven was one of them. That it should have been El and not one of the others of my staff was entirely in the hands of fate. We were all together. I went to him immediately and he insisted that he was all right and that I should attend to the other casualties first. Although mortally wounded, I assure you that he was in no pain and was quite conscious. He asked both the Padre and myself to write to you and I am most ashamed that I have been so long in doing so.

In spite of his complaints, we attended to him first and he was evacuated to hospital immediately. When he left he was still the same El, waved goodbye to his friends and wished them luck. In spite of the prayers of Padre Latour, my own and I'm sure those of everyone of my staff, he died that night after reaching hospital (23 September 1944).

While in England he used his spare time to learn as much as he could about farming mechanisms and equipment because he thought it would be useful on his return to Canada; he planned to have his own farm. In one letter to his wife he wrote:

Have had a little break this afternoon, got out to town on my own and saw through the milk factory where they make powdered milk, sure was worth seeing, the old fellow showed me through the place. It was very interesting to see and know how it was done. Saw it all from the time it came to them in the can until it was powder in the tin and sealed. There are some very fine herds of cattle out here and it's nice to see them grazing in the fields (10 April 1944).

Sims Lake (64 K/7), southeast of Lac Brochet was named after him in 1972.

Sims, Flight Sergeant **George R.** of Pilot Mound (R 208935). No. 576 Squadron. He died 15 July 1944 at the age of 21 and is commemorated at Loches-sur-Ource Communal Cemetery in Aube, France. ***Sims Island*** (63 N/10) in the Churchill River was named after him in 1995.

Simundson, Sapper **Sigurd H.** of Winnipeg (H 19506). Royal Canadian Engineers. He died 1 December 1941 and is commemorated at Brookwood Military Cemetery in Surrey, England. ***Simundson Lake*** (54 M/12), northwest of Long Lake was named after him in 1984.

Sinclair, Private **Donald** of Souris (H 16214). Princess Patricia's Canadian Light Infantry. He died 22 July 1943 and is commemorated at Agira Canadian War Cemetery in Italy. ***Sinclair Peninsula*** (63 I/16) on Kapechekamasic Lake was named after him in 1995.

Sinclair, Private **Joseph W.** of Traverse Bay (H 65262). Royal Canadian Army Service Corps. He died 14 August 1944 and is commemorated at Bretteville-sur-Laize Canadian War Cemetery in Calvados, France. His adoptive brother writes (22 February 1998):

> Joe was educated at Elkhorn Boarding School. As far as I know, he was born in a little hamlet on the Hudson Bay Railway called Pikwitonei. After his schooling, he returned to Pikwitonei and started trapping. He was approximately 18 when he became like a brother and son to our family until he joined the army in 1941.

Joseph Sinclair Lake (53 L/6), south of Joint Lake was named after him in 1995.

Sinclair, Sergeant **Lloyd G.** of Elkhorn (R 59542). No. 77 Squadron. He died 21 September 1941 at the age of 23 and is commemorated at the Berlin 1939 - 1945 War Cemetery in Brandenburg, Germany. He was the youngest of nine children. According to his nephew (15 October 2001):

> Lloyd finished his first year of teaching in 1940 and couldn't wait to join up. In 15 months, he had been trained as a pilot, sent to England, flew about 25 bombing missions and was shot down in what was an early, if not the first, bombing raid on Berlin. Tragically, the RAF records show that the raid on Berlin had been cancelled in mid flight around 11 PM and while the other 10 bombers went to alternate targets and all returned to base, Lloyd's plane either didn't get or ignored the cancellation.
>
> Lloyd's letters home showed that he was exuberant, fun loving and enjoyed all the experiences in his short life. I was fortunate enough to have been able to visit his grave in Berlin in the early 1980s.

Sinclair Rapids (64 K/1) in the Mistay River was named after him in 1995.

Sinclair, Flight Sergeant **Marcel Stanley "Bud"** of Elkhorn (R 59701). No. 408 Squadron. He died 8 May 1942 at the age of 23 and is commemorated at Fourfelt Cemetery in Esbjerg, Denmark. He was the son of John M. and Alice W. Sinclair of Victoria, British Columbia. ***Sinclair Creek*** (64 P/7), which flows southeast into Guest Creek was named after him in 1995.

Sinclair, Major **Verner G.** of Winnipeg. Lanark and Renfrew Scottish Regiment. He died 19 September 1944 at the age of 28 and is commemorated at Caserta War Cemetery in Italy. He was the son of George and Mary Sinclair and was survived by his wife Dorothy R. Sinclair of Edmonton. ***Sinclair Hill*** (64 I/10), west of Lovat Lake was named after him in 1995.

Single, Corporal **John P.** of Brandon (H 66517). Royal Winnipeg Rifles. He died 25 October 1944 at the age of 37 and is commemorated at the Adegem Canadian War Cemetery in Belgium. He was the son of John and Elizabeth Single of Brandon. ***Single Lake*** (64 J/5), north of Big Sand Lake was named after him in 1975.

Singleton, Lance Corporal **Benjamin W.** of Eden (H 6256). Winnipeg Grenadiers. He died a prisoner of war 22 January 1943 at the age of 24 and is commemorated at the Sai Wan War Cemetery in Hong Kong. He was the son of Alfred and Agnes Singleton of Neepawa and was survived by an older brother Leslie and younger brothers Jim, Ken, Lawrence, and sister Shirley. A cousin recalls (13 March 1985):

> The Singleton family were early pioneers in Manitoba, arriving in 1889. Two sons, Arthur and Ben, enlisted in World War I. Arthur was badly wounded and Ben was killed. A third son, Alfred, named his second son after Ben. When World War II broke out, Alfred's two oldest sons enlisted.

A cousin's daughter adds (17 January 2002):

> Ben Singleton, born May 7, 1918 lived on a farm in the Birnie District and he attended the Glenholm School. The family was close, as was the community. Many of the neighbours were also aunts, uncles and cousins.
>
> Frequently on Sundays, there would be get-togethers, playing football and baseball as well as foot races. They also enjoyed singing and dances. When World War II started, Ben and his older brother Leslie went to Winnipeg to enlist. Ben joined the Winnipeg Grenadiers in September, 1939. He spent several months in basic training before leaving for Jamaica in 1941. After Jamaica, he went to Hong Kong where he was taken prisoner by the Japanese – Christmas of 1941. The family learned early in January, 1943 that Ben had died as a prisoner of war, probably of injuries. While he was able, he wrote to my mother (his cousin, eight years his junior). They wrote of parties and fun; he apparently never had a steady girlfriend. There were two letters from Jamaica; he talked of much hard work, no time for dances. My mother saved those letters, I gave them to his brother Ken who has recently passed away.

A brother adds that the cause of death was acute stomach problems brought on by the inadequate diet. ***Singleton Lake*** (64 K/9), east of Lac Brochet was named after him in 1972.

Sioux, Private **J. J. Anthony** of St. Laurent (H 41699). Winnipeg Grenadiers. He died a prisoner of war 16 November 1942 and is commemorated at the Sai Wan War Cemetery in Hong Kong. ***Sioux Lake*** (64 J/7), southwest of Tadoule Lake was named after him in 1975.

Sirett, Pilot Officer **Ebenezer A. "Ebb"** of Franklin (J 16946). No. 408 Squadron. He died 3 April 1943 at the age of 24 and is commemorated at Uden War Cemetery, Holland. He was the son of Frederick A. and Mabel A. Sirett of Neepawa. His brother recalls (12 December 1997) that he was:

> ... born and grew up on the home farm in the Gordon School District, 12 miles southwest of Neepawa. He received his elementary education at the Gordon School. He travelled to Franklin, eight miles by bicycle or horse and cutter to get his Grade 12 from Minnedosa Collegiate in 1938.
>
> In 1939, he entered the Faculty of Agriculture at the University of Manitoba. In 1941, Ebb answered the call to arms and joined the Royal Canadian Air Force. He took his elementary training at Ladner, BC and Claresholm, Alberta. In 1942, he went to England to continue training on Oxford and Halifax bombers. He was assigned his crew of Carter, Brice, Boyer, Kelly, McBride and Burke. They made their first operational flight to Hamburg February 3rd, 1943. They completed nine operational flights over enemy territory [but] never returned from their tenth flight. He had received his commission just weeks before he was shot down.

Sirett Lake (64 P/8), south of Caribou Lake was named after him in 1974.

Sirluck, Pilot Officer **Robert** of Winkler (J 86913). No. 76 Squadron. He died 1 March 1944 at the age of 22 and is commemorated at Stonefall Cemetery in Yorkshire, England. He was the son of Isaac and Rose Sirluck of Winnipeg. ***Sirluck Lake*** (63 K/16), west of Wekusko Lake was named after him in 1973.

Siwak, Flight Sergeant **Adolph A.** of Angusville (R 86398). No. 149 Squadron. He died 24 October 1942 at the age of 22 and is commemorated at Brookwood Military Cemetery in Surrey, England. He was one of the seven children of Dominik K. and Aniela M. "Nellie" Siwak of Angusville, Manitoba. His brother recalls that he had attended the country school at Lima and finished high school at Russell. He enlisted in 1941 and was returning from the last mission of his tour of duty when his plane crashed while making an emergency landing. ***Siwak Lake*** (64 P/16), northeast of Nejanilini Lake was named after him in 1974.

Skeet, Bombardier **Albert O.** of Edrans (H 67621). Royal Canadian Artillery. He died 10 August 1944 at the age of 35 and is commemorated at the Bayeux Memorial in Calvados, France. He was the fourth of the eight children of Albert C. and Olive V. Skeet (née Russell) of Edrans. His sister recalls (18 January 1988):

> Albert Ogle Skeet was born ... on a homestead in the Edrans district. His father ... had purchased homestead rights by 1903 when he married Olive Victoria Russell of Bruce County, Ontario. Father was from Colchester, Essex, England. Albert attended a nearby one-room school, completed his Grade 8 and helped on the farm for a few years. During the depression years, he worked wherever possible – as a farm hand, in lumber camps, in the Clear Lake Park building roads, etc., but eventually settling on a farm for himself. He left the farm in care of his brother Robert when he enlisted.
>
> He joined the 3 ATK Regiment, RCA and was sent to England for training for months. He was with the invasion forces for the assault on the French beaches, saw heavy assaults until August 10th when he was killed.

Major F. P. Boothe wrote to his parents:

> During the unsuccessful attack on Quesnay Wood, your son's troop was advancing behind the infantry. When his carrier was approaching the wood, it was hit by an enemy ATK gun. Your son died instantly and never knew what hit him. Willie Hudson and Holmes were killed at the same time.
>
> Your son had been with the Battery some time and was an excellent soldier and extremely popular with the men. He was very quiet and reserved and was always alert and on his job. He is very much missed by the rest of the battery and I can assure you he will never be forgotten by his friends here. He was a crack shot with an ATK gun and had come through with flying colours such hell holes as Carpiquet, Les Brissons and other such battles (9 September 1944).

Skeet Lake (64 I/5), northwest of North Knife Lake was named after him in 1974.

Skene, Private **William J.** of Deloraine (H 20708). Winnipeg Grenadiers. He died a prisoner of war 15 April 1944 and is commemorated at the Yokohama War Cemetery in Japan. The official cause of death was listed as "croup pneumonia." He was survived by his wife Gertrude Skene (née Sayer) of Grand Marais and their daughter. ***Skene Lake*** (64 K/7), southeast of Lac Brochet was named after him in 1972.

Skerritt, Rifleman **Clarence P.** of Camper (H 102152). Regina Rifle Regiment. He died 13 June 1944 at the age of 21 and is commemorated at Beny-sur-Mer Canadian War Cemetery in Calvados, France. He was the youngest son of Percy and Edith F. Skerritt of Winnipeg. His brother writes (4 March 1997):

> Clarence Percy Skerritt was born in Winnipeg on April 25th, 1923. [He] had his schooling in Winnipeg until 1935. [He] moved to Camper, Manitoba and farmed there on the family farm until September, 1942 at which time he joined the service and went overseas. Clarence loved the farm and dabbled with machinery and loved to hunt deer etc. His father [came from] Sheffield, England, his mother from Folkestone, Kent, England.

Skerritt Lake (64 J/7), southwest of Tadoule Lake was named after him in 1975.

Skidmore, Private **Torquil** of Brooklands (H 42108). Essex Scottish Regiment. He died 12 February 1945 at the age of 32 and is commemorated at Prague War Cemetery, Czech Republic. He was the son of James D. and of Mary Skidmore of Deer, Manitoba. ***Skidmore Lake*** (54 F/14), south of Cape Churchill was named after him in 1964.

Skinner, Lance Corporal **Allan R.** of Dauphin (H 17059). Princess Patricia's Canadian Light Infantry. He died 20 May 1944 and is commemorated at the Cassino War Cemetery in Italy. He was survived by his wife Joan I. Skinner of Reading, Berkshire, England. ***Skinner Island*** (64 H/14) in Knifehead Lake was named after him in 1995.

Skinner, Private **Walter T.** of Dauphin (H 42316). Lake Superior Regiment. He died 21 October 1944 and is commemorated at Bergen-op-Zoom Canadian War Cemetery in Holland. ***Skinner Lake*** (63 P/4), west of Sipiwesk Lake was named after him in 1995.

Skoblack, Flight Sergeant **Peter** of Brandon (R 59063). No. 55 Operational Training Unit, RCAF. He died 28 April 1943 and is commemorated at Annan Cemetery in Dumfriesshire, Scotland. ***Skoblack Lake*** (64 P/5), south of Nejanilini Lake was named after him in 1974.

Skromeda, Corporal **Stephen** of Winnipeg (H 19777). Queen's Own Cameron Highlanders, Mentioned in Dispatches. He died 19 August 1942 at the age of 37 and is commemorated at Dieppe Canadian War Cemetery in Seine-Maritime, France. He was the son of Elia and Clementine Skromeda and was survived by his wife Olga Skromeda of Winnipeg and their son. ***Skromeda Creek*** (54 L/6), which flows east into the South Knife River was named after him in 1948.

Skulmoski, Rifleman **Stanley** of Cormorant (H 10982). Regina Rifle Regiment. He died 24 April 1945 at the age of 20 and is commemorated at the Holten Canadian War Cemetery in Holland. He was the son of John and Mary Skulmoski of Cormorant, Manitoba. ***Skulmoski Lake*** (62 N/15), southeast of Swan River was named after him in 1973.

Skwarok, Lance Corporal **Anthony G.** of Dauphin (H 41130). Royal Winnipeg Rifles. He died 20 July 1944 at the age of 23 and is commemorated at Beny-sur-Mer Canadian War Cemetery in Calvados, France. He was survived by his mother Emily Skwarok and stepfather Steve Moroz of Dauphin. ***Skwarok Lake*** (64 O/4), northeast of Egenolf Lake was named after him in 1975.

Slack, Private **Eric G.** of Winnipeg (H 37226). Royal Canadian Army Service Corps. He died 28 November 1944 and is commemorated at Schoonselhof Cemetery in Antwerp, Belgium. He was survived by his wife Dorothy Slack of Winnipeg. ***Slack Lake*** (64 J/2), southwest of Tadoule Lake was named after him in 1975.

Slator, Lance Corporal **Michael J. "Danny"** of Stony Mountain (H 103032). 12th Manitoba Dragoons. He died 9 August 1944 at the age of 18 and is commemorated at Bretteville-sur-Laize Canadian War Cemetery in Calvados, France. He was the son of John J. and Mary J. Slator of Stony Mountain, Manitoba. ***Slator Lake*** (52 M/13), north of Amphibian Lake was named after him in 1979.

Slemmons, Private **Morton** of Grandview (H 63685). Princess Patricia's Canadian Light Infantry. He died 23 May 1944 at the age of 25 and is commemorated at the Cassino War Cemetery in Italy. He was the son of William and Della Slemmons of Grandview, Manitoba. ***Slemmons Bay*** (64 H/15) in Etawney Lake was named after him in 1986.

Slezak, Flight Sergeant **Henry M.** of Carberry (R 80198). No. 405 Squadron. He died 27 July 1942 at the age of 21 and is commemorated at the Runnymede Memorial in Surrey, England. ***Slezak Lake*** (64 P/6), southeast of Nejanilini Lake was named after him in 1974.

Slingsby, Able Seaman **Clifford F.** of Winnipeg (V 24618). HMCS *Columbia*. He died 29 November 1942 at the age of 23 and is commemorated at the Halifax Memorial. He was survived by his mother Rose Slingsby of Winnipeg. ***Slingsby Lake*** (64 N/1), northwest of Egenolf Lake was named after him in 1972.

Sloan, Private **Dempsey** of Winnipeg (H 16207). Princess Patricia's Canadian Light Infantry. He died 14 December 1943 at the age of 20 and is commemorated at the Moro River Canadian War Cemetery in Italy. He was the son of Allan and Agnes Sloan of Winnipeg. ***Sloan Lake*** (64 I/13), north of Shethanei Lake was named after him in 1974.

Slywchuk, Rifleman **Steve** of Winnipeg (H 21123). Royal Winnipeg Rifles. He died 8 June 1944 and is commemorated at Beny-sur-Mer Canadian War Cemetery in Calvados, France. He was the son of John and Helen Slywchuk of Ross, Manitoba. ***Slywchuk Lake*** (52 L/11), northwest of Black Lake was named after him in 1982.

Slyzuk, Private **John** of Ashville (H 204139). Princess Patricia's Canadian Light Infantry. He died 11 April 1945 at the age of 30 and is commemorated at the Holten Canadian War Cemetery in Holland. He was the son of Nicholas and Pearl Slyzuk of Ashville, Manitoba. ***Slyzuk Lake*** (64 O/5), northeast of Egenolf Lake was named after him in 1975.

Small, Flying Officer **Frederick G.** of Lac du Bonnet (J 20847). No. 434 Squadron. He died 9 October 1943 at the age of 26 and is commemorated at Ohlsdorf Cemetery in Hamburg, Germany. He was the only son of John Small of Winnipeg. He wrote a letter home to his sister just five days before his death:

Dear Aileen: Just came back from a week's leave spent at Marjorie's home in Boscombe. We celebrated her birthday and our engagement on the 1st. Had a grand party – just sort of a family "do" with a few close friends. Marjorie will be writing to you soon. Her holidays start next week so I'm hoping to get a place for her to stay so she can come here for a day or so. One evening we went to see the play *Wuthering Heights*. It was every bit as good as the movie. While we were there a sea mine exploded close by. Boy, did it shake the place, plenty of panic. We just stayed put although we thought the building was coming down on top of us.

Don't worry about me too much Ai. It isn't as bad as it's painted. Although you can get a false sense of security in these big kites when you are four miles up. But it sure is the thrill of a lifetime flying one. They're the size of a box car and have 80 times the horsepower of the plane I flew in Winnipeg. My crew is tops, even have a Frenchman, so if we land in France, he can parlez-vous for us. Last leave, three of them went to Belfast and haven't stopped raving since about the steak and chicken they had in Ireland. I must go there someday.

Glad to hear that school is going fine. It sure must be nice having Henry and Freda [Shipper] so near. Just like home to be able to visit them so often. Had a note from Gigs [Gisele] today. Nice of her to write. Please send me Russell's address.

Say, I had quite a chat with Group Captain Sampson. He was CO [Commanding Officer] at Lac du Bonnet in 1932. Don't forget to send chocolates and silk stockings for Margie, and my photo. Cheerio for now, Ai. Your loving brother, Fred (Oder 1975).

Small Lake (64 H/11), south of North Knife Lake was named after him in 1944. He was a former engineer with the Manitoba Air Division who joined No. 434 Squadron in Saskatchewan. CPCGN records (1944) indicated that the lake was named by the head of the Manitoba Government Air Service during the 23rd Base Line survey (1939 - 1940).

Small, Private **Glen C.** of Dauphin (SH 4778). Princess Patricia's Canadian Light Infantry. He died 14 July 1953 at the age of 18 and is commemorated at the United Nations Cemetery in Pusan, South Korea. He was one of the eight children of Milford G. and Lilian Small (née Peck). ***Glen Small Lake*** (53 L/6), east of Joint Lake was named after this Korean War casualty in 1998.

Small, Pilot Officer **John A.** of Winnipeg (J 3717). No. 401 Squadron. He died 27 October 1941 at the age of 24 and is commemorated at Dunkirk Town Cemetery in France. He was the son of David A. and Winifred M. Small of Toronto. Less than three weeks before his death, he sent a letter to his brother in Toronto:

Dear Bill: Well how goes the Air Force where you are? Guess by now you'll be out of ITS and either at the Observer's School or an EFTS. Wherever you are, I hope you're getting along well and enjoying the work. If you've been picked as an Observer, I wouldn't feel too badly – it's a damn important job and once on operations I'm sure you'll find it very interesting. Perhaps a little too interesting at times from what I hear. But I'd like to see you over here as a pilot in this squadron; it's a swell outfit and a grand gang of fellows in it. At present, we're not in a very attractive spot and the natives are rather hostile – however we're hoping to be moved.

Had some fun a little while ago. We were given some old "Spits" to train on before getting our new super-crates which, incidentally, are marvellous. Anyway, we were getting rather fed up and wanted to get them in action. Another Vancouver chap and myself decided we'd go looking for trouble, so we figured out a course to an aerodrome in one of the occupied countries. We knew we'd never get permission to go and beat it up "Dawn Patrol" fashion, so we didn't bother asking for permission. We got up before dawn and got a couple of Spits lined up – then got permission from Operations for some low flying practice over the sea. As soon as they'd allow us to take off we did and "went over." The weather was OK till we got there, then a thick fog came down and although we were only a hundred feet up, we couldn't see the ground. We buzzed around for a while, but couldn't find a hole in the fog so had to go home because our gas was low.

We couldn't quite make home, so landed at an aerodrome on the coast. Immediately, we were asked for a full explanation which we had thought up before. We said we'd sighted a German aircraft and chased it out to sea then lost it in the clouds. The explanation seemed OK because they didn't give us hell, although the Controller knew bloody well where we'd been. We hope to do it again soon with our new jobs. They'll surely give the Hun a surprise.

Well Bill, I guess I've covered the situation for the present. Best of luck and I'll be seeing you soon I hope. Love, Jack (8 October 1941).

Small Island (64 J/12) in Grimes Lake was named after him in 1989.

Small, Gunner **William A.** of Winnipeg (H 56958). Royal Canadian Artillery. He died 26 July 1941 and is commemorated at Brookwood Military Cemetery in Surrey, England. He was the son of William E. and Ethel Small of Winnipeg and was survived by his wife Pearl Small of Winnipeg. ***Small Bay*** (64 C/13) in McMillan Lake was named after him in 1995.

Smallpiece, Private **Ernest V.** of Portage la Prairie (H 16108). Princess Patricia's Canadian Light Infantry. He died 23 May 1944 at the age of 23 and is commemorated at the Cassino War Cemetery in Italy. He was the son of Arthur and Ellen Smallpiece and was survived by his wife Dorothy Smallpiece of Winnipeg. ***Smallpiece Lake*** (64 K/14), northeast of Lac Brochet was named after him in 1972.

Smart, Flying Officer **Wallace A.** of Winnipeg (J 18660). No. 64 Squadron. He died 3 July 1944 at the age of 26 and is commemorated at Brookwood Military Cemetery in Surrey, England. He was the son of Wallace V. and Evelyn J. Smart of Sidney, British Columbia. ***Smart Island*** (63 P/4) in Sipiwesk Lake was named after him in 1995.

Smelsky, Private **Michael** of Winnipeg (H 64587). Royal Canadian Ordnance Corps. He died 27 August 1942 at the age of 40 and is commemorated at Elmwood Cemetery in Winnipeg. He was survived by his wife Anne Smelsky of Winnipeg. ***Smelsky Lake*** (64 N/2), west of Egenolf Lake was named after him in 1972.

Smelts, Private **Edgar C.** of Elgin (H 6813). Winnipeg Grenadiers. He died 20 December 1941 at the age of 23 and is commemorated at the Sai Wan Memorial in Hong Kong. He was the eldest child of Charles W. and Ivy A. Smelts of Brandon. His sister recalls (16 October 2001) that:

He graduated from Grade 11 from Elgin Consolidated School No. 113. Following graduation in 1937, he secured employment as a painter. It may be hard to imagine now, but the firm who employed him kept busy every summer painting grain elevators in the three prairie provinces. He enjoyed outdoor activities, especially winter sports. He excelled in cross-country skiing and hockey.

As an aside, I must mention that my husband and I visited the memorial in 1991. Situated on an elevated site, it was evident that continuous care was being provided. Despite language barriers, the resident Australian was a perfect host and invited us to sign the guest register. Our family thanks those responsible for the decision to place our brother's name permanently on the map of Manitoba.

Smelts Lake (64 K/10), east of Lac Brochet was named after him in 1979.

Smith, Able Seaman **Alexander D.** of Winnipeg (V 24133). HMCS *Ottawa*. The *Ottawa* was escorting Convoy ON.127 in the North Atlantic when it was struck by two torpedoes from U-91; 114 of her ship's company were lost. Able Seaman Smith died 13 September 1942 at the age of 29 and is commemorated at the Halifax Memorial. He was the son of William and Ellen Smith of Winnipeg and was survived by his wife Margaret Smith of Winnipeg. ***Smith Narrows*** (63 O/2) in Fish Lake was named after him in 1995.

Smith, Private **Alfred L.** of Durban (H 42343). South Saskatchewan Regiment. He died 20 July 1944 and is commemorated at the Bayeux Memorial in Calvados, France. He was survived by his foster father Mr. G. Campbell of Durban, Manitoba. ***Alfred Smith Island*** (64 P/15) in Falloon Lake was named after him in 1995.

Smith, Petty Officer (Telegraphist) **Arthur J.** of Brandon (V 9368). HMCS *Louisburg*. The *Louisburg* was attacked and sunk by Italian aircraft east of Oran while escorting a convoy from Gibraltar to Bone, Algeria; 38 of her ship's company were lost. Petty Officer Smith died 6 February 1943 at the age of 20 and is commemorated at the Halifax Memorial. He was the son of Byron and Jessie Smith of St. James. ***Arthur Smith Hill*** (64 K/16), northwest of Stevens Lake was named after him in 1995.

Smith, Able Seaman **Arthur S.** of Brandon (4224). HMCS *Ottawa*. The *Ottawa* was escorting Convoy ON.127 in the North Atlantic when it was struck by two torpedoes from U-91; 114 of her ship's company were lost. Able Seaman Smith died 13 September 1942 at the age of 20 and is commemorated at the Halifax Memorial. He was the son of Ernest E. and Florence M. Smith of Brandon. ***Arthur Smith Lake*** (53 K/4), south of Red Sucker Lake was named after him in 1995.

Smith, Flight Lieutenant **Bert H.** of Winkler (J 11053). No. 608 Squadron. He died 16 September 1944 at the age of 22 and is commemorated at the Berlin 1939 - 1945 War Cemetery in Brandenburg, Germany. He was the son of Reverend E. Howard and Reita Smith. His brother recalls (19 October 2001):

Bert was born April 28, 1922 at Melita, Manitoba and was educated at Winnipeg, Killarney and Stonewall. After completing his high school and after brief employment with the Bank of Commerce at Stonewall, Bert joined the RCAF June 9, 1941. He earned his pilot's wings at age 18 and served as a flying instructor at various places in Manitoba, Saskatchewan, Ottawa and the Maritimes.

Bert was posted overseas in 1943 and in England he was attached to the RAF flying various bomber aircraft. Eventually, he piloted a Mosquito bomber. In a raid on Berlin September 16, 1944, his aircraft failed to return to base. It was later reported that it had crashed near a railway goods station at Rangsdorf, Germany. Both Bert and his navigator, a Sergeant Pegg of the RAF were killed. It was his first bombing raid in a Mosquito.

His pilot's log book shows he had flown 11 different types of aircraft for a total of over 1000 hours. His log book also contains a couple of interesting notes such as "rough weather, flew on deck, hit trolley wire – never again." It also contains the notation "In England – at last."

Bert Smith Lake (64 C/7), north of Granville Lake was named after him in 1995.

Smith, Private **Cecil E.** of Winnipeg (H 6598). Winnipeg Grenadiers. He died 19 December 1941 at the age of 21 and is commemorated at the Sai Wan Memorial in Hong Kong. He was survived by his mother Marguerite Smith of Winnipeg. He had enlisted with the Grenadiers in September, 1939. ***Cecil Smith Lake*** (64 H/16), south of Condie Lake was named after him in 1995.

Smith, Private **Charles W.** of Kenton (H 87381). Dispatch Rider, Royal Canadian Army Medical Corps. He died 5 April 1944 at the age of 21 and is commemorated at Brookwood Military Cemetery in Surrey, England. A native of Tipton, Staffordshire, he was survived by his parents Samuel J. and Louisa Smith of Kenton, Manitoba. ***Smith Falls*** (63 I/3) in the Keepeewiskawakun River was named after him in 1995.

Smith, Private **Clifford** of Boissevain (H 65903). Royal Canadian Army Service Corps. He died 24 May 1943 at the age of 22 and is commemorated at Brookwood Military Cemetery in Surrey, England. He was survived by his wife Jessie J. R. Smith of Boissevain and their daughter Frieda. His cousin recalls (25 April 1995):

Clifford's father was an American [who] lived in the Dunseith area of North Dakota. Clifford's parents were divorced when Clifford was only two or three years old. Clifford and his mother came back to live with her parents, Jacob and Elizabeth Daw. They lived in the Lake Max district in the Turtle Mountains. Clifford went to Lake Max School with me and most of my brothers and sisters.

After school, Clifford worked at several different jobs. Then he married a school teacher and they had one daughter, Frieda. Clifford's wife remarried and I haven't heard anything from Jessie for years.

Clifford Smith Creek (54 E/10), which flows south into Deer River was named after him in 1995.

Smith, Aircraftman 1 **David** of Winnipeg (R 56916). Eastern Air Command, Royal Canadian Air Force. He died 15 March 1941 at the age of 25 and is commemorated at Brookside Cemetery in Winnipeg. He was the son of Alexander and Mary Smith of Winnipeg and was survived by his wife Pauline Smith of Winnipeg and their daughter. Pauline Smith subsequently remarried to Flight Sergeant Ralph W. Murray (see entry) who was killed 22 April 1943. ***David Smith Lake*** (63 P/2), northeast of Cotton Lake was named after Aircraftman Smith in 1995.

Smith, Rifleman **Edward** of Beaconia (H 42084). Royal Winnipeg Rifles. He died 8 June 1944 at the age of 25 and is commemorated at Beny-sur-Mer Canadian War Cemetery in Calvados, France. He was the son of Joseph and Mary E. Smith of Beaconia. ***Edward Smith Lake*** (63 N/6), north of Kississing Lake was named after him in 1995.

Smith, Sergeant **Edwin** of Brandon (R 51480). No. 10 Squadron. He died 20 December 1943 at the age of 22 and is commemorated at Rheinberg War Cemetery in Germany. ***Edwin Smith Lake*** (54 E/1), northeast of Weir Lake was named after him in 1995.

Smith, Flying Officer **Edwin E. "Ted"** of Reston (J 12568). No. 159 Squadron. He died 12 August 1943 at the age of 28 and is commemorated at Ranchi War Cemetery in India. He was the son of Albert E. and Eliza Smith of Reston, Manitoba. His sister recalls (31 March 1995):

He joined at the outbreak of war. After spending a year in a cast with a broken back, he was able to return to training. When he transferred to the RAF, he was flying a plane to India. It was forced down by mechanical difficulties on the island of Bahrain. An RAF plane heading for India with a crew of men from "Down Under" required an extra pilot and so he made the switch.

He was killed in Burma while flying with the RAF. He was buried in a churchyard at Nudnapore near the site of the crash. The bodies were later moved to the cemetery at Ranchi when the separation of India and Pakistan made it impossible for the War Graves Commission to care properly for those buried in isolated areas.

Edwin Smith Island (64 N/9) in Nueltin Lake was named after him in 1995.

Smith, Rifleman **Frederick Cyril** of Winnipeg (H 21006). Royal Winnipeg Rifles. He died 23 October 1944 at the age of 19 and is commemorated at the Adegem Canadian War Cemetery in Belgium. He was the brother of Private Victor G. Smith (see entry). His daughter recalls:

I looked at the medals in the little white boxes and asked my Mother who they belonged to. They were so shiny and new, and being so young, I had no idea what they really meant. You see my father had died two and half months before I was born.

Like so many young boys in the very early '40s, my father enlisted in the armed forces, namely the Queen's Own Cameron Highlanders, in Winnipeg on the 5th of December, 1941 stating he was 20 years old. He was quickly discharged on the 26th of February 1942 for being under the age of seventeen.

Born Cyril Frederick Smith in Winnipeg on the 10th of May, 1925, he was the fourth youngest in a family of nine. Later, he would prefer to be called Fred. He spent much of his young life in that city, until his family moved to a homestead near Inwood, Manitoba. It was here the family learned the hard ways of the land. He was always a hard worker and when he realized people would pay to have work done, he was out there earning every penny he could. I've seen pictures of this rather handsome, large man with an axe in his hand standing on a pile of "scrub" he had just cut down, a dog at his side. I've seen other pictures of him with a team of horses pulling a hay rack with him standing tall on top.

He apparently had a very curious mind and a determination that one rarely finds in someone so young. As brothers are in families, they can do things that entice a young inquisitive mind. One day the older brothers made a makeshift wind vane from the radiator fan of an old car they had that no longer was in running condition, and hung it high on a pole in the farm yard. When Cyril came home and saw this he didn't believe his brothers when they told him the blades were turning, so he climbed up the pole and reached out to prove it for himself and as a consequence he cut the back of his hand quite badly; he was angry, but the brothers had a good laugh. And this accounts for the words "scar left hand back" that are written under "Marks or Scars" on his Record Card with the Armed Forces.

It seems there was some friction between Fred and his father and one day Fred decided it was time to leave home. He walked to the local school and took a friend's bicycle, rode it the 70 some miles into Winnipeg and promptly sold it. He was determined to make a life of his own from this day forth and once he turned 17, once again joined the forces, keeping his original Regimental number: H 21006.

My Mother and Father had a few months together before they received word that he would be transferred to Camp Borden, Ontario and eventually on to England 18 months later. In that short time, being as young as they were, they must have tried to enjoy every moment. I'm sure they danced in all the dance halls and saw every movie that came to town. I understand that my Mother was the only girl he ever brought home to meet the family, and the family were very fond of her from the start.

He embarked for England on the 3rd of August, 1944 and arrived nine days later. Two months after that, October 17th, he was in Belgium. What these brave young men must have thought, being in Europe.

Perhaps it was that they'd see the world. Perhaps they were somewhat fearful of what lay ahead. Perhaps they were unaware of what awaited them. In any case they went, did their duty to the best of their ability, and some paid a heavy price for our freedom.

There was no beauty in the world awaiting my father when he was sent up as a "reinforcement" for the Royal Winnipeg Rifles, 3rd Division, 7th Brigade that had been in heavy combat since D-Day. He met with only "wet and cold" conditions and strangers, and no combat experience. How lonely for a 19 year-old so far from home.

The Royal Winnipeg Rifles were into heavy fighting in the Scheldt Estuary better known as the "Breskens Pocket" in southern Holland. Part of General Montgomery's plan to free the way into Antwerp, the combat was very intense in this region. The weather was very wet and very cold, the ground was a slough of mud. There was no dry ground to gain some relief. The men fighting in this area become known as the "Water Rats" and have been touted by others in the forces as the men who really did the fighting to free Holland.

Frederick C. Smith – H 21006 – Rifleman – Royal Winnipeg Rifles, my father was Killed In Action October 23, 1944 near a small village called Boerenhol six days after setting foot on Belgian soil. He is buried in a War Cemetery in Adegem, Belgium. I have been twice to visit his grave.

My father whom I have never known or seen, who has never known or seen me will live forever in my heart as a true hero because I know he loved my mother and I was conceived in love and therefore he also loved me. I believe he is together with my mother this day. I will keep his memory alive to my son, and my son's children. He may be gone but he will never be forgotten. May he, and all the others who have sacrificed their young lives, forever rest in peace.

Frederick Smith Lake (53 N/7), east of Patch Lake was named after him in 1995.

Smith, Craftsman **Gordon R.** of Winnipeg (H 64733). Royal Canadian Electrical and Mechanical Engineers. He died 12 August 1945 at the age of 23 and is commemorated at Elmwood Cemetery in Winnipeg. He was the son of Mr. and Mrs. A. E. Smith of Winnipeg. ***Gordon Smith Lake*** (64 O/4), north of Egenolf Lake was named after him in 1995.

Smith, Private **John Spikula** of Winnipeg (H 6110). Winnipeg Grenadiers. He died a prisoner of war 12 September 1942 and is commemorated at the Sai Wan War Cemetery in Hong Kong. He was the son of Harry and Mary Spikula. ***John Smith Bay*** (53 F/13) in Angling Lake was named after him in 1995.

Smith, Pilot Officer **Kenneth** of Winnipeg (J 89042). No. 408 Squadron. He died 20 February 1944 at the age of 20 and is commemorated at Hoogezand-Sappemeer (Kropswolde) Protestant Church, Holland. ***Kenneth Smith Lake*** (64 N/11), west of Jonasson Lake was named after him in 1995.

Smith, Gunner **Leonard A.** of Winnipeg (H 2933). Royal Canadian Artillery. He died 25 July 1943 at the age of 22 and is commemorated at Agira Canadian War Cemetery in Italy. He was the son of Phillip and Rose Smith of Winnipeg. ***Leonard Smith Lake*** (64 I/11), northwest of Quinn Lake was named after him in 1995.

Smith, Gunner **Matthew Donald** of Hilltop (H 59763). Royal Canadian Artillery. He died 25 July 1944 at the age of 27 and is commemorated at Bretteville-sur-Laize Canadian War Cemetery in Calvados, France. He was the son of Sidney W. and Florence W. Smith of Scandinavia, Manitoba and was survived by his wife Winifred M. Smith of Sandy, Bedfordshire, England. ***Smith Peninsula*** (64 F/2) on Woodcock Lake was named after him in 1981.

Smith, Private **Melvin C.** of McCreary (K 75883). Queen's Own Rifles of Canada. He died 4 May 1945 at the age of 23 and is commemorated at the Holten Canadian War Cemetery in Holland. He was visiting an elder brother in Trail, British Columbia when he enlisted. He was the son of Raymond and Ada Smith and was survived by his wife Irene Smith and their daughter Edwina. His brother writes (9 November 2001):

He was raised on a farm along with 10 siblings and attended school in the Royal Oak district. He was a hunter, trapper and enjoyed playing basketball and listening to boxing on the radio.

Two years before his death, he gave his sister a letter to be given to his mother "should necessity arise:"

Dear Mum and all: Just a line to let you know that all is fine; am well, and hope this finds you all the same. Well Mum, here is my thought and what I think of fighting for Canada and also what I think of my home.

Let every Canadian fight to the last drop of blood in his body. Let him keep the golden fields and the busy streets clean and fresh and let him keep the air he breathes free from the stench of Nazism. I have no regrets of dying. Give this message to my friends and to the people of Canada if it is possible. I would like to thank you Mum and Dad for making my life a very happy one indeed, and for giving me every possible chance in life to make a success of it.

I have no regrets dying for my country; it is a grand country – any man who can call himself a Canadian should be proud to die in the struggle for freedom which I am sure Canada will always have. I am sure that our troops – the lucky ones – will march victorious through the streets of Berlin. I am proud of my country and proud of those brave lads of the Tank Corps with whom I had the honour to fight side by side.

So I will say good-bye and God bless you all. Love. Your son, Mel (n.d.).

Smith Esker (64 I/9), east of Nichol Lake was named after him in 1989.

Smith, Sergeant **Orville D. "Odee"** of Selkirk (H 17137). Royal Winnipeg Rifles. He died 12 October 1944 at the age of 23 and is commemorated at the Adegem Canadian War Cemetery in Belgium. He was the son of Ralph and Mildred Smith of Selkirk. "Odee" participated in the Normandy invasion and his unit proceeded inland to the Leopold Canal in Holland. Odee and part of his unit managed to cross it, but were held down for days by heavy fire. Finally, after several days, he was forced to go for rations and ammunition which enabled the enemy to pinpoint his slit trench. They subsequently focussed mortar fire upon it; he died of his wounds a few hours later. His brother writes (4 April 1995):

Orville, being the youngest, was a bit different than the two older brothers. We liked the farm and spent summers at Grandpa's or working at other farms in that area. Orville liked Selkirk. He had a friendly manner and smiled easily. Girls liked him and he had a wide circle of male friends. He was the best looking of the Smiths.

Getting a job was very difficult in the depression and he got a summer job in the local bakery. When they asked him to stay, he seized the chance although he hated the job. As more and more of his friends joined the forces, he became restless. Brother Russell joined the Fort Garrys and a short time later Orville joined the Royal Winnipeg Rifles and went to New Brunswick for training.

His friends always called him "Orville" without shortening his name. Underneath his character, a bit of steel could be sensed. This only got him more respect and deepened friendships. In the army with its numerous roll calls and other Smiths, his initials seemed to suit him; they turned it into his nickname Odee. Whenever I met a man from his unit during the war I would ask "How is OD doing?" and they always replied OD Smith is doing fine and fill me in with a funny story or a recent incident.

Odee Smith Lake (53 L/4), southwest of Bolton Lake was named after him in 1995.

Smith, Warrant Officer 2 **Richard C.** of Winnipeg (R 103690). No. 179 Squadron. He died 12 July 1943 at the age of 23 and is commemorated at the Gibraltar Memorial. He was the youngest son of Marshall G. and Vera B. Smith of Winnipeg. ***Richard Smith Bay*** (63 P/7) in Cauchon Lake was named after him in 1995.

Smith, Able Seaman **Robert** of Winnipeg (3317). HMCS *Margaree*. The *Margaree* was lost in the North Atlantic after collision with the freighter *Port Fairy* while escorting the five ship Convoy OL.8; 142 of her ship's company were lost, many of whom were survivors of *Fraser's* tragic sinking. Able Seaman Smith died 22 October 1940 at the age of 20 and is commemorated at the Halifax Memorial. He was the son of Peter R. and Emma Smith of Winnipeg. ***Robert Smith Hill*** (64 P/16), northeast of Nejanilini Lake was named after him in 1995.

Smith, Sergeant **Roderick G.** of Winnipeg (R 92555). No. 410 Squadron. He died 11 April 1942 at the age of 22 and is commemorated at the Runnymede Memorial in Surrey, England. He was the son of Victor O. and Grace E. Smith of Winnipeg. ***Smith River*** (64 H/9), which flows southeast into Beaver River was named after him in 1986.

Smith, Flying Officer **Stanley M.** of Winnipeg (J 23734). No. 115 Squadron. He died 22 November 1943 at the age of 22 and is commemorated at the Runnymede Memorial in Surrey, England. He was the son of Henry A. and Esther Smith of Winnipeg. ***Stanley Smith Lake*** (64 A/12), west of Jensen Lake was named after him in 1995.

Smith, Sergeant **Sydney William** of Sandy Lake (H 38644). Royal Canadian Corps of Signals. He died 8 August 1944 at the age of 26 and is commemorated at Beny-sur-Mer Canadian War Cemetery in Calvados, France. He was the son of Sydney and Jean Smith of Sandy Lake, Manitoba. ***Sydney Smith Lake*** (64 G/15), west of Little Sand Lake was named after him in 1995.

Smith, Leading Cook **Thomas Alfred "Alf"** of Winnipeg (V 24481). HMCS *Alberni*. The *Alberni* was torpedoed and sunk by U-480, southeast of the Isle of Wight; 59 of her ship's company were lost. Leading Cook Smith died 21 August 1944 at the age of 29 and is commemorated at the Halifax Memorial. He was the son of Thomas A. and Louise Smith of Norwood and was survived by his wife Letitia J. Smith (née McCallum) of Gaspé, Quebec. His brother writes (31 March 1995):

> He was born in 1915 in Rotherham, Yorkshire, England. Our family came to Winnipeg in 1923, lived on Lipton Street, then moved to St. Vital. He went to school there. In 1930 [we] moved to Norwood; while living there he worked for a soft drink bottling company that made a drink called Mexicola. After that, he worked at the Green Gables Restaurant on Academy Road and the Furby Grill next to the old Furby Theatre on Portage Avenue. [He] belonged to the Sons of England, was an avid golfer [and] was also in the Rovers at Holy Trinity Church on Donald Street.
>
> He joined the Navy in 1941 as a cook. Then he was sent to Gaspé. While there, he was a cook on an ocean-going tug – HMCS *Patricia McQueen*. He was married there to Lettie McCallum (no children). Then he was transferred to HMCS *Alberni* (a Corvette) as a Leading Cook. The *Alberni* went overseas some time in 1943 or 1944.

Alfred Smith Lake (64 K/8), southeast of Sims Lake was named after him in 1995.

Smith, Private **Victor G.** of Inwood (H 41690). Winnipeg Grenadiers. He died a prisoner of war 27 December 1944 at the age of 22 and is commemorated at the Yokohama War Cemetery in Japan. He was the son of Mrs. Florence Smith of Inwood and the brother of Rifleman Frederick C. Smith (see entry). According to his nephew (14 November 2001):

> He was very quiet and always the thinker. Victor, his older brother Robert and two younger brothers Fredrick (Cyril) and Thomas joined the service. Two of the boys went overseas and never returned. Cyril is buried in Belgium. Victor spent many hours building wooden model airplanes by lantern light with his brothers. He was the first boy to venture away from home. He liked hockey and played a bit in Red Lake, Ontario. He came back to Winnipeg in 1938 and met up with his older brother Robert who was in Winnipeg. They headed back to the family farm near Inwood, Manitoba and not long after, he followed his brother Robert back to Winnipeg and joined the Royal Winnipeg Rifles. He then transferred into the Winnipeg Grenadiers to be with his buddy. Victor was taken prisoner of war in Japan after the fall of Hong Kong. A couple of letters were sent from prison camp in Hong Kong. We are not sure how he died, but the information which has come out of the PoW camps leads me to believe his last days were horrific.

In 1942, his mother received a letter from Lieutenant Colonel F. W. Clarke which read in part:

> An arrangement for the despatch of letter mail to and from Canadian Prisoners of War in Japanese hands is now being negotiated and I will write you again giving full particulars as to addressing letters as soon as definite arrangements have been made. You will be pleased to know that the news we have received recently from unofficial sources would indicate that the treatment of Prisoners of War has improved materially, and that the conditions as to food supply are much better (7 July 1942).

In one of his last letters home he wrote:

> Dearest Mother and Dad: I am sure glad to have the chance to write you and let you know that I am in good health and that I have not received any letters from you as yet. Received one from Oscar Gullikson and Lorna Talbot, but have not given up waiting for one cause I know you will write. I was surprised to hear that Cyril is in the army. Would appreciate a few pictures from home as I lost all mine. Well I'll close now hoping that all are in good health. Please write and give my love and best regards to Miss Lorna Talbot, 383 Langside Street, Winnipeg. Goodbye for now. Your loving son, Victor (22 April 1944).

Victor Smith Lake (53 N/7), east of Patch Lake was named after him in 1995.

Smith, Sergeant **Walter G. "Smitty"** of Dauphin (R 86146). No. 120 Operational Training Unit, RCAF. He died 8 February 1942 at the age of 31 and is commemorated at Brookwood Military Cemetery in Surrey, England. He was the son of Richard M. and Maud H. Smith and was survived by his wife of seven years Marie L. Smith of Vancouver. She writes (22 November 2001):

> It was in the "Dirty Thirties" when doors were never locked. After completing high school and several courses, Walter Graham Smith (Smitty), my husband, decided to go into business. We began with a Service Station and to our dismay, found that there was a gas leak below the station. From there on, he established Smitty's Taxi and in 7 1/2 years of very dedicated work (night and day), operated three new cabs, four U-drives, the town ambulance, a four-seater Avro Avian plane and a snow plane built on skis and a propeller. We worked with doctors to service patients in outlying districts (around frozen lakes and rivers). He had the first snow plane license in Manitoba – S1.

> Then came the war. Every young man joined up. He was asked to instruct instead of going overseas but declined, saying: "After taking a crack at Hitler." He was transferred to the RAF in England. He loved the country and its brave people. We had a secret code telling me of his missions and that he had one more to make. He had five "squeaks" but on February 8, 1942, I received THE telegram, that his bomber came down over the station in flames. They were waiting for his return from Germany.
>
> He mentioned how the English were so brave, a mother who lost five sons still kept on volunteering as usual ... that if it came to pass, to look up at the sky and there would be another star shining.

Smith Rapids (53 N/12) in the Stupart River was named after him in 1995.

Smith, Flight Sergeant **Walter P.** of Edrans (R 178906). No. 90 Squadron. He died 28 June 1944 at the age of 20 and is commemorated at Brookwood Military Cemetery in Surrey, England. His brother, H. Fred Smith of Austin, Manitoba visited the site in 1955. Flight Sergeant Smith was the son of Horace E. E. and Lucretia "Lucy" M. Smith of Edrans, Manitoba. His brother recalls (27 November 2001):

> In the winter of 1941-42, Walter took an apprentice course with the Hudson's Bay Company. This course included grading and buying furs, radio, meteorology, carpentry, accounting, merchandising and cooking. He finished his course early in February, 1942 and signed a contract to work for the Hudson's Bay Company. He was posted to Aklavik, NWT and went by train to Edmonton, then by plane to Fort McMurray, Alberta. Here, he went to work in the HBC store and never did get to Aklavik.
>
> In July, he took leave from the HBC, went to Edmonton and joined the Royal Canadian Air Force. He took his air gunner's training in Brandon, Winnipeg and Mont Joli, Quebec, travelling overseas in September, 1943 on the *Queen Elizabeth*. On the night of June 28, 1944 [his] Lancaster aircraft returned from the target badly damaged by enemy cannon shell and machine gun fire. Flight Sergeant Smith was the only casualty.

Walter Smith's name is on the Hudson's Bay Company Honour Roll in Winnipeg and is also listed on the Cenotaph in the Edrans Cemetery. ***Walter Smith Bay*** (64 P/1) in Garlinski Lake was named after him in 1995.

Smith, Captain **Walter R.** of Winnipeg. 12th Manitoba Dragoons. He died 19 March 1942 at the age of 35 and is commemorated at Brookside Cemetery in Winnipeg. He was survived by his mother Mrs. T. Moorbey of Eriksdale and by his wife Margaret L. Smith of Winnipeg. Commemorative Certificates for Captain Smith and seven fellow Manitoba Dragoons were issued c/o Herbert Nicholson, MM who explains:

> In 1946, the 12th Manitoba Dragoons returned from Europe, and with money from our Canteen Fund furnished two wards in the Children's Hospital, with a promise that as long as our Association lasts, we would continue to support the Children's Hospital Fund. Since 1946, we have contributed $1000.00 every year, with donations received from the members. Also, we had a Plaque placed on the Hospital's 2nd floor, with names of our fallen comrades on one side and on the other side, the names of the departed comrades who have since passed away. This was done with the idea that one day the Regiment will again be together.
>
> Now this brings me to my request, that the Association's approximately 350 members, would after all your efforts to find next-of-kin, like to become family and have the Name Certificate placed on the wall in the Children's Hospital in trust that if a next-of-kin comes forward the Certificate would be handed over to them (16 December 1998).

Walter Smith Lake (53 M/2), northwest of Knee Lake was named after him in 1995.

Smith, Lance Corporal **William** of Mayfield, Manitoba (L 12857). South Saskatchewan Regiment. He died 6 August 1944 and is commemorated at Bretteville-sur-Laize Canadian War Cemetery in Calvados, France. He was survived by his wife Leila I. Smith of Moose Jaw, Saskatchewan. ***William Smith Island*** (54 D/6) in the Nelson River was named after him in 1995.

Smith, Private **W. A. Rule** of Swan River (H 41807). Winnipeg Grenadiers. He died a prisoner of war 27 November 1942 at the age of 18 and is commemorated at the Sai Wan War Cemetery in Hong Kong. He was the son of William R. and Hilda J. Smith of Pelly, Saskatchewan. ***Smith Lake*** (62 N/15), southeast of Swan River was named after him in 1973.

Smith, Private **William C.** of Winnipeg (H 102183). Seaforth Highlanders of Canada. He died 17 September 1944 at the age of 22 and is commemorated at Coriano Ridge War Cemetery in Italy. He was the son of Roland A. and Ethel R. Smith of Osoyoos, British Columbia. ***William Smith Lake*** (63 O/6), southeast of Apeganau Lake was named after him in 1995.

Smook, Flying Officer **Harry** of St. Malo (J 36168). No. 404 Squadron. He died 9 February 1945 at the age of 23 and is commemorated at the Runnymede Memorial in Surrey, England. ***Smook Lake*** (63 K/13), northeast of Embury Lake was named after him in 1988.

Smyth, Flight Sergeant **James W.** of Winnipeg (R 80105). No. 142 Squadron. He died 31 May 1942 at the age of 21 and is commemorated at the Adegem Canadian War Cemetery in Belgium. ***Smyth Lake*** (64 G/14), east of Big Sand Lake was named after him in 1994.

Snead, Sergeant **Frederick C.** of Winnipeg (R 58848). No. 15 Squadron. He died 16 September 1941 at the age of 20 and is commemorated at Becklingen War Cemetery in Germany. He was the son of Thomas and Sarah Snead of Winnipeg and was survived by his foster father Mr. F. D. Martyn of Winnipeg. He was the brother of Pilot Officer Samuel Snead (next entry). ***Snead Lake*** (64 G/15), west of Little Sand Lake was named after Sergeant Snead in 1995.

Snead, Pilot Officer **Samuel T.** of Winnipeg (J 26839). No. 1659 Heavy Conversion Unit, RCAF. He died 25 July 1943 at the age of 31 and is commemorated at Dishforth Cemetery in Yorkshire, England. He was the son of Thomas and Sarah Snead and the brother of Sergeant Frederick Snead (previous entry). ***Snead Bay*** (64 G/15) in Little Sand Lake was named after Pilot Officer Snead in 1995.

Sneath, Flying Officer **Robert H.** of Elgin (J 27589). No. 624 Squadron. He died 25 June 1944 at the age of 23 and is commemorated at Mazargues War Cemetery, Marseilles, Bouches-du-Rhone, France. He was the son of George and Mabel Sneath of Elgin, Manitoba. ***Sneath Lake*** (63 K/16), west of Wekusko Lake was named after him in 1973.

Sneesby, Trooper **Bruce A.** of Winnipeg (H 77329). 12th Manitoba Dragoons. He died 8 February 1945 at the age of 26 and is commemorated at the Groesbeek Canadian War Cemetery in Holland. He was the son of Albert H. and Jean Sneesby of Woodside, Manitoba. He had been employed for a few years on a ranch in Alberta and was with Holt Renfrew in Winnipeg at the time of his enlistment. ***Sneesby Lake*** (63 O/5), southeast of Highrock Lake was named after him in 1973.

Snell, Pilot Officer **Dennis E.** of Winnipeg (J 90078). No. 431 Squadron. He died 17 August 1944 at the age of 19 and is commemorated at the Runnymede Memorial in Surrey, England. He was the son of Edward and Mabel C. Snell of Winnipeg. ***Snell Lake*** (63 K/16), west of Wekusko Lake was named after him in 1973.

Snow, Flying Officer **Morley V.** of Winnipeg (J 16804). No. 431 Squadron. He died 4 December 1943 at the age of 23 and is commemorated at the Berlin 1939 - 1945 War Cemetery in Brandenburg, Germany. He was the son of Vivian M. and Evelyn M. P. Snow of East Kildonan. ***Snow Island*** (64 N/8) in Shannon Lake was named after him in 1995.

Snyder, Private **Blake F.** of Dauphin (H 21043). Queen's Own Cameron Highlanders. He died 21 July 1944 and is commemorated at Bretteville-sur-Laize Canadian War Cemetery in Calvados, France. He was the son of Charles H. and Elsie M. Snyder of Dauphin. and the brother of Flight Sergeant Charles W. Snyder (next entry). ***Snyder Island*** (64 B/3) in Mynarski Lakes was named after Private Snyder in 1995.

Snyder, Flight Sergeant **Charles W.** of Dauphin (R 146094). No. 434 Squadron. He died 24 August 1943 at the age of 26 and is commemorated at the Runnymede Memorial in Surrey, England. He was the son of Charles H. and Elsie M. Snyder of Dauphin and the brother of Private Blake F. Snyder (previous entry). ***Snyder Bay*** (64 O/10) in Askey Lake was named after Flight Sergeant Snyder in 1995.

Snyder, Leading Stoker **Robert B.** of Gilbert Plains (V 24772). HMCS *Stadacona*. He died 20 January 1944 at the age of 25 and is commemorated at Eldon Cemetery in Gilbert Plains. He was the son of David M. and Margaret Snyder of Gilbert Plains, Manitoba. ***Snyder Lake*** (64 N/5), southeast of Kasba Lake was named after him in 1961.

Soanes, Trooper **Gerald W.** of Flin Flon (H 77597). 12th Manitoba Dragoons. He died 6 April 1945 at the age of 22 and is commemorated at the Holten Canadian War Cemetery in Holland. He was the son of Simon and Helen Soanes of Flin Flon. ***Soanes Lake*** (64 I/12), south of Shethanei Lake was named after him in 1974.

Sobin, Flight Sergeant **Joseph S.** of Winnipeg (R 123719). No. 419 Squadron. He died 3 August 1943 at the age of 23 and is commemorated at Becklingen War Cemetery in Germany. He was the son of John and Melania Sopczyszyn (sp.) of Winnipeg. ***Sobin Lake*** (64 P/11), east of Nejanilini Lake was named after him in 1974.

Soderstrom, Pilot Officer **Clarence V.** of Winnipeg (J 90388). No. 434 Squadron. He died 17 June 1944 at the age of 21 and is commemorated at the Ruurlo General Cemetery in Holland. He was the son of Ture M. and Agnes L. Soderstrom of New Westminster, British Columbia. ***Soderstrom Lake*** (64 G/16), south of Cederlund Lake was named after him in 1995.

Sokalski, Private **George** of Winnipeg (H 6924). Winnipeg Grenadiers. He died a prisoner of war 30 May 1944 at the age of 41 and is commemorated at the Sai Wan War Cemetery in Hong Kong. He was the son of Vincent and Rosalie Sokalski and was survived by his wife Mary Sokalski (née Delinowska) of Winnipeg and their three children. He had been a shoemaker at the time of his enlistment. His son visited the grave in 1980.

> Rudy Sokalski was only eight when his mother received word of his father's prison camp death in 1944. Rudy's wife, Gloria, says the long awaited trip to the far away gravesite and the chance to meet men who knew Private Sokalski has been enlightening (*Victoria Times* 10 December 1980).

His sister-in-law adds (6 December 2001):

> Born in Poland, he came to Canada and married in Winnipeg ... in 1929. George had three children, now has 11 grandchildren and 16 great grandchildren. He joined the Winnipeg Grenadiers and served in the West Indies.

Sokalski Lake (64 O/9), west of Nejanilini Lake was named after him in 1975.

Sokol, Flight Sergeant **William** of Winnipeg (R 106059). No. 425 Squadron. He died 11 November 1942 at the age of 22 and is commemorated at Dishforth Cemetery in Yorkshire, England. He was the son of Mytro and Pearl Sokol of Winnipeg. ***Sokol Lake*** (64 P/14), northeast of Nejanilini Lake was named after him in 1974.

Solberg, Private **John A.** of Whitemouth (922825). 27th Battalion, Canadian Infantry (Manitoba Regiment). He died 21 August 1918 at the age of 19 and is commemorated at St. Sever Cemetery Extension, Rouen, Seine-Maritime, France. He was the son of Anton and Georgina Solberg of Winnipeg. Private Solberg was born 24 November 1899 and enlisted in the 200th Battalion in February, 1917. He went sent to England shortly thereafter and toured Scotland and England while on leave in the spring. He spent much of that summer in the trenches in France and was admitted to Rouen General Hospital and died the same day. ***Solberg Lake*** (63 I/2), south of Molson Lake was named after this World War I casualty in 1988.

Solmundson, Flying Officer **Oscar G.** of Gimli (J 27529). No. 162 Squadron. He died 3 April 1945 at the age of 32 and is commemorated at the Runnymede Memorial in Surrey, England. He was the son of Julius and Helga Solmundson and was survived by his wife Helen B. Solmundson (née Bothwell) and their son. He had been a high school teacher in Gimli before enlisting in 1939. ***Solmundson Island*** (64 P/15) in Falloon Lake was named after him in 1989. When notified of the naming, his eldest next-of-kin, sister Mrs. Lara Tergesen said:

> When I received the phone call, I got a lump in my throat and had to call back. It was such a surprise after 45 years and I was overcome with it. I think it is wonderful that we are not forgetting young men like my brother who gave their lives for this country (Newman 1989).

Solmundsson, Flying Officer **Kjartan A.** of Gimli (J 15190). No. 426 Squadron, Commemorative Medal conferred by the King of Norway. He died 28 January 1944 at the age of 22 and is commemorated at the Runnymede Memorial in Surrey, England. He was survived by his wife Margaret Solmundsson of Gimli and their son Keith. ***Solmundsson Lake*** (64 H/7), northeast of Gauer Lake was named after him in 1948.

Solnik, Trooper **Paul** of Selkirk (H 1288). 14th Canadian Hussars. He died 17 August 1944 at the age of 19 and is commemorated at Bretteville-sur-Laize Canadian War Cemetery in Calvados, France. He was the youngest of the seven children of Alexander and Nettie Solnik of East Selkirk. He had been a timekeeper at the Manitoba Rolling Mills in Selkirk when he enlisted in 1943 at the age of 17. ***Solnik Lake*** (64 O/12), south of Nueltin Lake was named after him in 1974.

Solodiuk, Rifleman **Michael** of Winnipeg (H 41512). Royal Winnipeg Rifles. He died 6 June 1944 and is commemorated at Beny-sur-Mer Canadian War Cemetery in Calvados, France. To many, the success of the Normandy invasion was seen as a vindication after the disastrous attempt at Dieppe two years earlier:

GHOSTS AT DIEPPE

Here on the shore beside the Channel waves
Where we have lain these two long, lonely years,
Within the confines of our troubled graves,
Faintly we heard a sound of ringing cheers.

Unseen, we rose, saw soldiers dusty-brown,
Led by the very men who saw us die,
The Essex Scottish, marching into town
With battle-flags of Canada on high.

The Royals of Toronto, tried and true,
With pride and confidence in every stride,
The boys who knew the hell that we went through.
In bullet-swept Dieppe, that day, we died.

The Hamilton Light Infantry went by,
The South Saskatchewans, erect and tall,
The men from Winnipeg and Calgary,
The Scottish and the Watch from Montreal.

Now we can sleep. Now we can dream of this,
No love of base revenge or foolish pride,
But just to know our boys came back to us,
To know they saved the cause for which we died
(Michael Foran)

Solodiuk Lake (63 K/13), east of Manistikwan Lake was named after him in 1984.

Soltowski, Private **Theodore** of Winnipeg (H 21130). Royal Canadian Regiment. He died 4 September 1944 and is commemorated at Ancona War Cemetery in Italy. ***Soltowski Lake*** (64 B/13), north of Opachuanau Lake was named after him in 1982.

Sombert, Sergeant **Edward** of Winnipeg (H 100005). Canadian Provost Corps. He died 5 August 1945 at the age of 29 and is commemorated at the Holten Canadian War Cemetery in Holland. He was the son of Frank and Emma Sombert of Winnipeg and was survived by his wife Ivy J. Sombert of Winnipeg. ***Sombert Lake*** (53 O/15), east of Shamattawa was named after him in 1949.

Somerville, Flight Sergeant **Gilbert E. "Stubb"** of Swan River (R 106330). Royal Canadian Air Force. He died 12 March 1943 when his aircraft went down off Gibraltar. He was 23 years of age and is commemorated at the Malta Memorial. He was the son of James M. and Mary Somerville of Swan River. His sister recalls (28 December 2001):

Gilbert or "Stubb" as he was affectionately known to family and friends, was born May 7th, 1919 in Moose Jaw, Saskatchewan. He began kindergarten there and continued his schooling in Swan River when his family was transferred to Manitoba by the Canadian National Railway. As a student, Stubb was active in sports and other extra-curricular activities. He was popular with his contemporaries and was a loving and loyal friend, brother and son.

Like a lot of young men of his generation, Stubb "rode the rails" looking for work after school. In 1942, he enlisted and Christmas that year was spent on the water *en route* to Africa. The rest is history.

Seventeen years after his death, his sister submitted a poem to the local newspaper. The last three stanzas read:

"He died for King and Country,"
This is what they say,
"To help create a better world
Than the one we have today."

Well, it won't be done by fighting,
For we've tried and tried again,
Before we change the world
We must change the hearts of men!

Yes, we know "they died in action,"
On land or sea or sky,
They tell us when and where and how,
But our hearts cry "Dear God why?"

Somerville Island (63 N/6) in Kississing Lake was named after him in 1995.

Somerville, Sapper **James G.** of Winnipeg (H 93525). Royal Canadian Artillery. He died 4 April 1944 at the age of 28 and is commemorated at Brookwood Military Cemetery in Surrey, England. He was survived by his wife Susan Somerville of Dominion City and their two children. ***Somerville Bay*** (63 N/9) in Kakinokumak Lake was named after him in 1995.

Somerville, Lieutenant **Richard L.** of Winnipeg. Queen's Own Cameron Highlanders. He died 14 September 1944 and is commemorated at the Calais Canadian War Cemetery in France. ***Somerville Lake*** (64 K/5), northeast of Reindeer Lake was named after him in 1972.

Sopko, Lance Corporal **Andrew** of Selkirk (H 46502). Lake Superior Regiment. He died 14 August 1944 at the age of 28 and is commemorated at Bretteville-sur-Laize Canadian War Cemetery in Calvados, France. He was the son of Michael and Agnes Sopko of Libau, Manitoba. ***Sopko Lake*** (64 I/12), northwest of North Knife Lake was named after him in 1978.

Sopuck, Flight Lieutenant **Vladimir J.** of Winnipeg (J 24247). No. 45 Squadron. He died 1 July 1945 at the age of 23 and is commemorated at Montreal (Mount Royal) Cemetery, Quebec. He was the son of Joseph P. and Marie Sopuck of Winnipeg and was survived by his wife Eleanore Sopuck of Verdun, Quebec. Prior to enlisting, he had been a violinist studying music at Chicago. He had returned from a leave home only a week before. The tail wheel of his Mosquito aircraft struck a fence upon landing causing it to somersault and crash (Allison and Hayward 1991). ***Sopuck Lake*** (64 O/16), northwest of Nejanilini Lake was named after him in 1975.

Soronow, Lieutenant **Morris M.** of Winnipeg. Royal Winnipeg Rifles. He died 28 August 1944 at the age of 33 and is commemorated at the Calais Canadian War Cemetery in France. He was the son of Max and Riva Soronow of Winnipeg. ***Soronow Lake*** (64 K/5), south of Lac Brochet was named after him in 1972.

Sorrenti, Flying Officer **Vincent A.** of Winnipeg (J 36937). No. 419 Squadron. He died 29 December 1944 at the age of 21 and is commemorated at the Reichswald Forest War Cemetery in Germany. He was the second youngest of the four children of Vincenzo and Euphemia "Effie" Sorrenti (née Andrew) of Fort Rouge. His sister recalls (15 February 1998):

Our parents both immigrated to Canada in the early 1900s, both settling in Winnipeg. Our mother came from Glasgow, Scotland and our father from Reggio, Calabria, Italy. They met and married in Winnipeg on October 16, 1915. The Sorrenti family lived in the Fort Rouge area during their lifetime and were a very close family, so Vincent grew up with a lot of love and support from parents and siblings. In his early years, he grew up like any normal child, rather quiet and serious but always had lots of friends.

When he was old enough, he delivered papers for the *Winnipeg Tribune* in his home area and was happy with the little bit of pocket money he made. Vincent did well at school, enjoyed music and sports but did not excel in any area, just an all-round person. The "dirty thirties" were hard years to grow up in, money wasn't too plentiful in the Sorrenti household, but our parents always encouraged us to bring friends home, and we did. Lots of card games, monopoly, etc. were played at our house. After skating and toboggan parties, Mother fed us pork and beans, bread and butter along with hot cocoa which everyone enjoyed.

After graduating from Kelvin High School, Vincent found a job with Canada Packers. However, he wasn't there too long as he and two of his best friends felt they should enlist and do their part for their country as there was a war on. He believed, as did our Father when he enlisted in 1916 with the 100th Battalion Winnipeg Grenadiers. The three friends enlisted in the RCAF and were accepted.

Vincent trained as a navigator and when his training finished, was sent overseas. The remarks in his log book by the Chief Navigator Instructor were that Vincent was a capable navigator and very keen. After Vincent enlisted in the RCAF, our Mother volunteered with the Women's Airforce Auxiliary, so we had many RAF trainees stay at our home on weekends until the war ended. Many lasting friendships were made.

Vincent and his crew, with the exception of the rear gunner, paid the supreme sacrifice on December 29, 1944 when their aircraft was hit by flak while on a mission over Germany. The rear gunner was blown clear.

She concludes (18 October 2001): "A Scottish friend of mine has visited my brother's grave recently and sent me pictures which I truly treasure." ***Sorrenti Lake*** (64 O/7), northwest of Munroe Lake was named after him in 1975.

Sosnowski, Trooper **Joseph** of Sifton (H 63810). Sherbrooke Fusiliers. He died 7 June 1944 at the age of 22 and is commemorated at Beny-sur-Mer Canadian War Cemetery in Calvados, France. He was the son of Wawro and Katyryna Sosnoski of Sifton, Manitoba. ***Sosnowski Lake*** (64 P/1), south of Caribou Lake was named after him in 1974.

Sothe, Private **Roland E.** of Winnipeg (H 35924). Royal Canadian Army Medical Corps. He died 16 August 1944 at the age of 23 and is commemorated at Beny-sur-Mer Canadian War Cemetery in Calvados, France. He was the son of John and Augusta Sothe of Hyas, Saskatchewan. ***Sothe Lake*** (54 M/3), south of Long Lake was named after him in 1984.

Southall, Able Seaman **Harry K.** of West Kildonan (V 24012). HMCS *Ottawa*. The *Ottawa* was escorting Convoy ON.127 in the North Atlantic when it was struck by two torpedoes from U-91; 114 of her ship's company were lost. Able Seaman Southall died 13 September 1942 at the age of 30 and is commemorated at the Halifax Memorial. He was the son of Henry A. and Barbara Southall of West Kildonan and was survived by his wife Jessie Southall of Winnipeg. A shipmate recalls (7 December 1984):

In the Army and Air Force, many of the dead were buried and their names engraved on markers, but not so in the Navy. The North Atlantic was so cold and the oil slicks after a torpedoing so deadly that a ship's crew had little chance of survival even if they made it to a Carley Float or lifeboat. At our Remembrance service at *Chippawa*, November 11th, the service brought back thoughts of my friends who went down in the North Atlantic. LTO Ken Southall, a chum from our youth in West Kildonan was one of these. He was lost when the destroyer *Ottawa* was torpedoed. Who knows, Ken could have been a hero, but whether he made it to a Carley Float or lifeboat, none of the survivors could tell me.

Southall Lake (64 N/14), southeast of Kasba Lake was named after him in 1972.

Sowerby, Private **Joseph M.** of Norwood (H 204123). Princess Patricia's Canadian Light Infantry. He died 20 December 1944 at the age of 23 and is commemorated at Ravenna War Cemetery in Italy. He was the son of Joseph and Agatha Sowerby of Winnipeg and was survived by his wife Laura M. G. Sowerby of Winnipeg. ***Sowerby Lake*** (64 B/1), northeast of Nelson House was named after him in 1972.

Spafford, Flight Sergeant **Alvin Leslie** of Winnipeg (R 59327). No. 103 Squadron. He died 3 July 1942 at the age of 33 and is commemorated at the Sage War Cemetery in Germany. He was the son of Alfred F. and Ida W. Spafford (née Porter) of Winnipeg and was survived by his wife Anne F. Spafford (née Malcom) of Winnipeg and their son. He was the brother of Nursing Sister Frances Spafford (next entry). His wife's nephew writes (1 November 2001):

Both Leslie and Frances were born in Winnipeg and attended Earl Grey and Kelvin schools. Leslie joined the RCAF and served on a flight crew. He was originally reported as lost but it was at a later date that a member of his squadron, who himself was shot down and imprisoned in a PoW camp, confirmed that Les' plane was blown up in mid-air.

Spafford Island (64 B/8) in Barnes Lake was named after him in 1995.

Spafford, Nursing Sister (Lieutenant) **Frances W.** of Winnipeg. Royal Canadian Army Medical Corps. She died 8 March 1941 at the age of 28 and is commemorated at Cliveden War Cemetery in Buckinghamshire, England. She was the daughter of Alfred F. and Ida W. Spafford (née Porter) of Winnipeg and the sister of Flight Sergeant Alvin Spafford (previous entry). Her sister-in-law's nephew reports that (1 November 2001):

Both Leslie and Frances were born in Winnipeg and attended Early Grey and Kelvin schools. Frances was a nursing sister and served in this capacity at Lady Ascot's estate which had been in part turned into a hospital during the early years of the war. Frances was diabetic and it was a diabetic reaction due to overwork that took her life.

Spafford Lake (64 K/6), northeast of Reindeer Lake was named after her in 1972.

Spall, Sergeant **Robert** of Winnipeg (475212). Eastern Ontario Regiment (Princess Patricia's Canadian Light Infantry), Victoria Cross. This native of Ealing, Middlesex died 13 August 1918 at the age of 28 and is commemorated at the Vimy Memorial, Pas de Calais, France. His great niece writes (25 October 2001):

... there was a ceremony a couple of years ago on Remembrance Day to add Robert Spall's name to the war memorial in Ealing which was attended by a member of the Princess Patricia's Canadian Light Infantry and also Lady Mountbatten. My sister-in-law in England and another Spall cousin also attended.

He was the son of Charles and Annie Maria Spall of Montreal. His father received a letter from Sergeant Spall's captain:

Dear Mr. Spall: I write on behalf of the officers and men of No. 3 Company to give you my deepest sympathy in your recent bereavement and loss of your Son, Sergt. R. Spall of our regiment; while you mourn the loss of a Son and loved one, we mourn the loss of a gallant comrade and a gentleman and one whom we shall never forget as Company commander. I'll give you an idea of how he met his death.

During this advance, your Son was acting as my Sergt/Major and was invaluable to the Company. On August 12th, our Company was selected to make a bombing attack by the flank on a position held by the enemy, and the attack was made at 8 PM up three different trenches; on getting to a certain cross trench, I found that the flank of two platoons was unprotected and to get in touch, I took a party of seven men and your Son and bombed up over 700 yards of the enemy trench, taking 14 prisoners and inflicting heavy casualties on the enemy; we ran into strong opposition and ran out of supplies necessitating our withdrawal down the trench to the cross trench.

About 5 AM on the morning of the 13th August, the enemy counter attacked my two platoons with over 600 men and practically cut us off; it amounted to a fight hand to hand to get out and we managed with surprisingly few casualties, but in order to do so, your boy calmly took a Lewis gun and climbed out of the trench and while the Bosch was about 200 yards away opened up and gave them terrible casualties; he came back into the trench and walked down cheering and encouraging the men and then went to another point in the trench, picked up another machine gun, got on top and at 75 yards range opened fire and held up the enemy attack and enabled us to withdraw to a better position and saved the situation. In doing this gallant and heroic action your boy was hit and instantly killed, and by his gallant action saved the lives of many of our men.

Words cannot express my sorrow and sympathy with you and yours, but it must be a source of comfort for you to know that your boy gave his life freely and fearlessly to save others. For this gallant action Sergt. R. Spall has been recommended for the Victoria Cross. The Commanding Officer has strongly recommended it, and no one earned it any more than your Son. He lies buried in a trench at Payne Wood near Parvillers. If there is anything I can do for you, please let me know. Sincerely yours, C. M. MacBrayne, Capt. (19 August 1918).

Two months later, his father received a letter from Buckingham Palace:

It is a matter of sincere regret to me that the death of No. 475212 Sergeant Robert Spall, Eastern Ontario Regiment (Princess Patricia's Canadian Light Infantry) deprived me of the pride of personally conferring upon him the Victoria Cross, the greatest of all rewards for valour and devotion to duty. George R.I. (31 October 1918).

According to a contemporary newspaper account:

It was in the first year of the conflict that he wrote home to his parents in Montreal, that he had donned khaki and it was three years ago in August when he passed through this city with the 90th Rifles of Winnipeg. A younger brother who has a position in a railway office was able to give the father and mother an hour's notice of the passing of the train through the city. So in the early hours of an August morning, there was a hurried packing of baskets of edibles for "Bob" and a little family gathering on a station platform where the young soldier was able to say a gay goodbye to his loved ones.

With the victories of the spring and summer months in their minds, Mr. and Mrs. Spall had almost persuaded themselves that "Bob" would be home for Christmas, when another August day brought them the news that their boy had died the death of the brave; that "Bob" would not be home for Christmas.

Bob Spall's father and mother are old country people. The boy was born ... in England and was brought by his parents to Canada when he was a little fellow of two. Brought up in a home where love of their motherland was inculcated in all the phases of daily life, it was no wonder that in the first year of the war, Bob Spall, grown up to healthy manhood, should hasten to answer the call of the land of his birth when that land found itself in the throes of the Great War.

The slender, gray-haired little mother spoke of it with mingled grief and pride. "Bob was a good boy," she said softly. "When I was ill he used to nurse me. I never had a nurse like Bob. He went away to Winnipeg four years before the war and we all missed him. He was always so happy and he laughed so much. I wouldn't have had it different for Bob wouldn't have it different. He was always a brave lad. His captain wrote us a letter about it. It was very good of him because they are so busy. I think it is wonderful that news can be sent to the families as quickly as it does come; there are so many boys dying over there" (29 October 1918).

Spall Lake (63 P/9), north of Cauchon Lake was named after him in 2001.

Sparrow, Sergeant **Bruce H.** of Winnipeg (R 86211). No. 16 Operational Training Unit, RCAF. He died 10 October 1942 at the age of 19 and is commemorated at Filey (St. Oswald) Churchyard in Yorkshire, England. He was the second youngest of the four sons of George W. and Flora Sparrow of Winnipeg. His sister-in-law recalls (14 September 1998):

He grew up in Winnipeg with three brothers and had a very busy and interesting childhood. He participated in all sports and especially loved skiing, swimming and horseback riding. Bruce received his education at Riverview, Lord Roberts and Kelvin High School. He was very interested in photography and also proved to be very gifted as an artist in both sketching and oil painting – in fact, he won a prize for oil painting at Kelvin High School. He was also an active member of the Winnipeg Sketch Club.

After high school, Bruce became a member of the Winnipeg Fire Department and in 1940 joined the Air Force, became an air gunner and was posted overseas in May, 1942. He participated in missions overseas until his untimely death in an air crash in England. This was a great loss to family and friends as Bruce had always been a happy and caring person to one and all.

Sparrow Lake (64 H/15), east of Etawney Lake was named after him in 1995.

Spearin, Flying Officer **James A.** of Brandon (J 23128). No. 426 Squadron. He died 29 July 1944 at the age of 21 and is commemorated at Hamburg Cemetery in Germany. ***Spearin Lake*** (64 C/9), west of Eden Lake was named after him in 1979.

Specht, Private **William J.** of Beausejour (H 6275). Winnipeg Grenadiers. He died 19 December 1941 and is commemorated at the Sai Wan Memorial in Hong Kong. He was the son of Joseph Specht of Beausejour. He wrote a letter to his father shortly before the fall of Hong Kong:

Dear Dad: Sorry in not writing sooner. Was pretty busy since we arrived here. Had a swell trip both on the train and on the boat. Seen quite a few ports, but we didn't get off at any. This place isn't bad, but I would rather have gone to England instead. The climate is pretty warm. It seems like we are going to spend another Christmas without snow. I've been out [a] couple of times, there is nothing I could write about of any great interest. I think this place is much worse than the last place we were. Also dad, I'm no longer working in the kitchen. I quit when we were on the boat. Now I'm in the motorcycle squad. I do like it much better. Also got a promotion as a Lance Corporal. That is one stripe with pay.

How are you dad and where are you staying at? Is your arm bothering you? I suppose it is in the cold weather. How is Elise and the rest of the family? Please give them my regards. Also, how is Joe Kubish? Will drop him a line with your letter, dad. Will you give it to him and ask him to write? Did Mary get married? Oh yes, you can tell her that I am not writing any letters to her as she was in Winnipeg and couldn't come to say goodbye.

I'm in the best of health, enjoying myself. But I must admit that I'm darn homesick and I sure miss Adie. Please write soon, dad. Closing with best of health and luck. Your son, Bill (December 1941).

Specht Lake (64 K/9), southwest of Egenolf Lake was named after him in 1972.

Spector, Flying Officer **Joseph** of Winnipeg (J 26649). No. 100 Squadron. He died 22 May 1944 at the age of 21 and is commemorated at the Reichswald Forest War Cemetery in Germany. He was the son of H. K. Spector of Winnipeg. ***Spector Lake*** (54 B/1), northeast of Shamattawa on the Manitoba - Ontario boundary was named after him in 1948.

Spence, Flying Officer **Herbert A.** of Winnipeg (C 4505). No. 163 Squadron. He died 22 September 1943 at the age of 21 and is commemorated at St. James Cemetery in Winnipeg. He was the son of John and Annie Spence of Winnipeg. ***Spence Island*** (64 G/13) in Big Sand Lake was named after him in 1995.

Spencer, Flight Sergeant **Hugh P.** of Flin Flon (R 100196). No. 51 Squadron. He died 1 May 1943 at the age of 20 and is commemorated at the Reichswald Forest War Cemetery in Germany. He was survived by his wife Hazel Spencer and their daughter. ***Spencer Island*** (63 P/4) in Sipiwesk Lake was named after him in 1995.

Spencer, Rifleman **Melville K. M.** of Winnipeg (H 10651). Royal Winnipeg Rifles. He died 9 October 1944 at the age of 20 and is commemorated at the Adegem Canadian War Cemetery in Belgium. He was survived by his wife Maevis L. Spencer of Winnipeg. ***Spencer Point*** (64 P/5) on Nejanilini Lake was named after him in 1995.

Spencer, Corporal **Ralph E.** of Morden (H 40660). Royal Winnipeg Rifles. He died 6 June 1944 at the age of 23 and is commemorated at Beny-sur-Mer Canadian War Cemetery in Calvados, France. He was survived by his wife Hazel E. Spencer (née Martindale) of Snowflake and their two children. According to his niece (1 August 1995):

Ralph was a little toughy as a wee man and never lost his zest for a good fight. He was considered Grandpa's favourite by some of the other siblings. Although he was an average student in school, Ralph loved to read. It was stated that he was a pretty good match as a hockey player. When his older brother Orval would take the horse and cutter into Morden, Ralph was all ready to go too. When he came home after that long drive, he would place those cold feet on his brother Mervin who had been in bed for a while and was toasty warm. Needless to say, he was not very popular for a few moments.

Ralph met Hazel, fell in love, and while working up in Snowflake, Ralph and Hazel were married. The same year, 1940, Ralph enlisted in the Royal Winnipeg Rifles, better known as the "Little Black Devils."

Ralph and Hazel lived in Ernest and Amanda's first homestead house. The arrival of their first born, Karen, delighted Ralph. Before he was shipped overseas, a second child, Bruce, was on the way. Ralph corresponded regularly with Mervin, Cora and his mother. Cora sent a picture to him while he was overseas of Hazel and the two children. Ralph was so proud of all of them that he showed that picture to anyone who would look at it. Ralph was killed … on the beaches at Normandy.

Spencer Lake (64 N/4), north of Lac Brochet was named after him in 1972.

Spencer, Warrant Officer 1 **Walter W.** of Winnipeg (R 110774). No. 206 Squadron. He died 21 April 1945 at the age of 22 and is commemorated at Aarestrup Churchyard, Denmark. He was the son of Oscar and Ethel M. Spencer of Winnipeg. After the war, a local newspaper reported that:

On the 20th of April, 1945 a British Liberator manned by members of the Flying Confederation with a crew of eleven men who, in the last years of the war flew many missions, crashed in Rold Forest near Norlund sawmill; all those on board were killed. The German occupation forces buried the crew in a mass grave and it was not until the 22nd of June 1947 that the men were given a proper burial attended by a large congregation in the Aarestrup Churchyard. The Airmen's Stone is a memorial consisting of a large stone with one of the propellers from the Liberator attached, erected at the crash site in August, 1945 by forestry workers from Norlund. The inscription reads: HER-FELDT EN-ALLIERET-FLYVER-NED D.20 APROL – 1945. IKAMPFOR-DANMARKS-FRIHED (Allison and Hayward 1991).

Spencer Bay (63 I/7) in Lawford Lake was named after him in 1995.

Spice, Flying Officer **Donald A.** of Flin Flon (J 43502). No. 19 Operational Training Unit, RCAF. He died 31 January 1945 at the age of 22 and is commemorated at the Runnymede Memorial in Surrey, England. He was the son of Edward and Jean B. Spice of North Kildonan. His sister writes (10 November 2001):

He graduated from high school in Kildonan and was enrolled at the University of Manitoba when he left to enlist in the RCAF. He qualified as a navigator. His plane was lost in the North Sea on the final flight of his training course. His logbook and some personal effects washed ashore and were sent to the family.

Don loved the outdoors, especially the family summer home on Cache Lake at Farlane, Ontario where he swam and canoed. He enjoyed fishing and climbing the hills to find blueberries. He was a happy and fun loving boy fondly remembered by family and friends.

Spice Lake (64 G/4), northeast of Grandmother Lake was named after him in 1994.

Spilchak, Rifleman **George "Eddy"** of Pine Ridge (H 10808). Royal Winnipeg Rifles. He died 6 June 1944 at the age of 22 and is commemorated at Beny-sur-Mer Canadian War Cemetery in Calvados, France. He was the son of Anthony and Teenie Spilchak of Pine Ridge, Manitoba. His youngest sister writes (8 November 2001):

Eddy came from a family of 10 children. When he was 18, his father died suddenly of a heart attack. Eddy, a very dedicated son and brother, helped his mother run the family farm along with his seven younger siblings who were still at home. When our mother remarried, Eddy then found work as a miner and in July, 1943, joined the army. When he would come home on leave, we saw that he was very proud of wearing his uniform.

He was a great role model, not only to his family, but to all who knew him. The very sad news of him being missing in action came on my ninth birthday. Two days later, we received confirmation of him being killed. Because there was no burial at home, our mother could not bring closure to his death. She believed till her dying day that maybe there was some mistake – that he was still alive. Perhaps when wounded, he suffered amnesia and lost his identification tag. After the war, a soldier that knew Eddy overseas said that he had died by drowning after being wounded as he disembarked from a landing craft on the Normandy beach.

Spilchak Lake (64 J/8), south of Tadoule Lake was named after him in 1975.

Spinks, Sergeant **Albert H.** of Neepawa (R 210945). No. 82 Operational Training Unit, RCAF. He died 29 May 1944 at the age of 18 and is commemorated at Brookwood Military Cemetery in Surrey, England. He was the son of Gordon F. and Gladys E. Spinks (née Shanks) of Port Coquitlam, British Columbia. His sister recalls (28 January 1997):

Albert was the first born of the six children of Floyd Spinks and Gladys (Shanks) Spinks. He was born in a hospital in Winnipeg on 14 June 1925. Albert was always Albert to adult relatives and friends, but he preferred "Al" as he grew up and so he was known to his peers. He was always cheerful, happy by nature, protective of his flock of five sisters and the pride and joy of his parents. He was always a practical joker, with many of his jokes often being tested on the closest, unsuspecting sister. He attended Neepawa Public School from Grade 1 to 8. He did not graduate to high school because of one of his practical jokes on the Principal – he was expelled and refused to apologise.

He found work in a sawmill where he worked until he enlisted in April, 1943 and left for basic training in Alberta on 29 May 1943 – 16 days before his 18th birthday. He was posted to Mont Joli in Quebec for his air gunner training, returned to Neepawa on embarkation leave late fall of '43 and went overseas early in 1944. Exactly one year to the day of his departure, 29 May 1944, we received the telegram advising that he had been killed, along with the rest of the crew, when their plane crashed near the base on return from a leaflet raid.

Spinks Lake (53 F/13), south of Angling Lake was named after him in 1996.

Spouler, Flight Sergeant **Joseph G.** of St. Boniface (R 71030). No. 214 Squadron. He died 14 September 1942 at the age of 20 and is commemorated at Rheinberg War Cemetery in Germany. ***Spouler Lake*** (64 H/10), north of Buckland Lake was named after him in 1995.

Spraggett, Lance Corporal **George E.** of St. Vital (D 77880). British Columbia Regiment. He died 14 August 1944 at the age of 33 and is commemorated at Bretteville-sur-Laize Canadian War Cemetery in Calvados, France. He was the son of John H. and Elizabeth Spraggett of St. Vital. ***Spraggett Lake*** (64 F/6), north of Wells Lake was named after him in 1994.

Spratt, Flight Sergeant **Cecil R.** of Kelwood (R 59112). No. 149 Squadron. He died 30 July 1942 at the age of 26 and is commemorated at Rheinberg War Cemetery in Germany. He was the son of William R. and Mary A. Spratt of Kelwood. His brother writes (25 November 1996):

My brother Cecil was born ... on March 15, 1916 on a homestead in the Glenhope district southeast of McCreary. The family moved over the years back to the Kelwood district where he received most of his education. He worked on farms [and] was in Ontario as a cook for some time before he enlisted in the Air Force at the start of the war. He was an air gunner when he was shot down over Saarbrücken.

Spratt Lake (64 P/13), north of Nejanilini Lake was named after him in 1974.

Spratt, Sergeant **Howard W.** of Brandon (617924). No. 27 Squadron, RAF. He travelled to England to enlist in August, 1938 and was posted to India the following year. He was killed 28 June 1941 when his aircraft hit a hill under heavy cloud cover near Akyab, Burma (Allison 1978). He was 22 years of age and is commemorated at Taukkyan War Cemetery, Myanmar. He was the son of Harry G. and Rosa Spratt of Brandon. ***Spratt Island*** (53 L/2) in Island Lake was named after him in 1995.

Sprott, Flying Officer **John C.** of Miami (J 24060). No. 433 Squadron. He died 17 August 1944 at the age of 31 and is commemorated at Aabenraa Cemetery in Denmark. He was the son of Walter and Blanche E. Sprott of Miami and the brother of Leading Aircraftman Ronald G. Sprott (next entry). ***Sprott Island*** (64 G/6) in Kapeetaukimak Lake was named after Flying Officer Sprott in 1994.

Sprott, Leading Aircraftman **Ronald G.** of Miami (R 119951). No. 10 Service Flying Training School. He died 3 August 1942 at the age of 21 and is commemorated at Miami Cemetery. He was the son of Walter and Blanche E. Sprott of Miami and the brother of Flying Officer John C. Sprott (previous entry). ***Sprott Lake*** (64 J/5), north of Big Sand Lake was named after Leading Aircraftman Sprott in 1957.

St. Croix, Private **William A.** of Winnipeg (H 19930). Queen's Own Cameron Highlanders. He died 19 August 1942 and is commemorated at Dieppe Canadian War Cemetery in Seine-Maritime, France. He:

... [w]as born at Barachois, Gaspé County, Quebec where he was engaged in mining. He joined the service in Winnipeg and trained at Shilo and Quebec City. He went overseas in December, 1940 and served in France and England. St. Croix was killed at Dieppe. He attended the local schools at Gaspé and is survived by his mother, brothers and sisters in Quebec (Hill 1944).

St. Croix Island (64 I/15) in the Seal River was named after him in 1974.

Stack, Sergeant **Arnold H.** of Flin Flon (R 59781). No. 16 Operational Training Unit, RCAF. He died 11 November 1941 at the age of 20 and is commemorated at Upper Heyford Cemetery, Oxfordshire, England. He was the son of Damas A. and Marie E. Stack of Vancouver. ***Stack Island*** (64 C/8) in Granville Lake was named after him in 1995.

Stack, Private **Walter** of Lorette (H 9555). Royal Canadian Regiment. He died 18 September 1944 and is commemorated at Gradara War Cemetery in Italy. ***Stack Lake*** (63 O/4), north of Wekusko Lake was named after him in 1970.

Stairs, Rifleman **Reginald J.** of Winnipeg (H 42172). Regina Rifle Regiment. He died 15 September 1944 at the age of 20 and is commemorated at the Calais Canadian War Cemetery in France. He was the son of Joseph and Dorothy E. Stairs of Winnipeg. His sister writes:

Reg was born in Winnipeg on May 19th, 1924. [He] attended Wellington and General Wolfe School in Winnipeg, getting his Grade 9. Reg was going to Sunday School, Cubs and Scouts at St. Matthew's Church (Anglican) [and] was confirmed in the same church. Reg liked to play baseball and was into ice skating (n.d.).

She adds (7 November 2001):

He was a loving and caring son and brother we were proud of. Loving thoughts are with you, may God give you rest. Thank you for helping your country.

Stairs Lake (64 H/9), northeast of Freeman Lake was named after him in 1995.

Stalker, Private **James W.** of Winnipeg (H 19247). Stormont, Dundas and Glengarry Highlanders. He died 18 July 1944 and is commemorated at Beny-sur-Mer Canadian War Cemetery in Calvados, France. His sister recalls (14 November 2001):

Jim was an Elmwood boy. He got his schooling at Lord Selkirk School, was a Cameron cadet and a bugler in the band. He worked after school and on weekends at the cemetery. He was the eldest of seven and was a great and caring brother.

Jim trained at Camp Shilo, then over in England as a Bren gunner. He was wounded at Dieppe where he lost two fingers. His second raid was in Normandy, but he lost his life in Caen, France.

Stalker Lake (52 L/6), southeast of Bird Lake was named after him in 1982.

Stamm, Rifleman **Roy D.** of Eriksdale (H 14669). Royal Winnipeg Rifles. He died 16 February 1945 at the age of 19 and is commemorated at the Groesbeek Canadian War Cemetery in Holland. He was the son of Charles A. and Agnes S. Stamm of Eriksdale. ***Stamm Lake*** (52 L/11), east of Cole Lake was named after him in 1982.

Stammers, Flight Sergeant **Ernest F.** of Transcona (R 59841). No. 115 Squadron. He died 6 December 1942 at the age of 21 and is commemorated at Rheinberg War Cemetery in Germany. He was the son of Frank and Susan E. Stammers of Transcona. ***Stammers Lake*** (64 N/10), southwest of Nueltin Lake was named after him in 1972.

Stanley, Private **Donald L.** of Portage la Prairie (SM 9538). Princess Patricia's Canadian Light Infantry. He died 21 June 1952 and is commemorated at the United Nations Cemetery in Pusan, South Korea. ***Stanley Rapids*** (53 K/10) in the Stull River was named after this Korean War casualty in 1998.

Stanley, Flight Sergeant **Frederick T.** of Kenton (R 134212). No. 419 Squadron. He died 5 May 1943 at the age of 19 and is commemorated at Zwolle (De Kranenburg) General Cemetery in Holland. He was the son of Charles and Gladys Stanley of Vancouver. His sister writes (22 October 2001):

Being quite young when he left home, I have very little memory of him. I do know that he was born and raised in the Kenton district and attended school there. He also played hockey for the Kenton teams.

Stanley Peninsula (64 P/5) on the Wolverine River was named after him in 1995.

Stanley, Corporal **Joseph F.** of Winnipeg (H 77720). 12th Manitoba Dragoons. He died 1 November 1944 at the age of 31 and is commemorated at Bergen-op-Zoom Canadian War Cemetery in Holland. This native of Aberavon, South Wales had immigrated to Canada in 1921 at the age of eight. He was the son of Ralph and Mary L. Stanley of St. James. ***Stanley Point*** (64 N/2) on Vanlerberghe Lake was named after him in 1995.

Stanley, Warrant Officer 2 **Richard Walter "Red"** of Brandon (R 95347). No. 149 Squadron. He died 30 May 1943 at the age of 25 and is commemorated at the Runnymede Memorial in Surrey, England. He was one of the four children of Richard and Phoebe Stanley (née Cole) of Brandon. A year later, his mother received a letter from a former friend of Red's:

Dear Mrs. Stanley: You will think me very rude for not replying sooner to the very nice letter which you sent to me. I know I was very pleased indeed at the time to get it. It was my first mail. I was not able to stay in Vancouver as it was too damp for my husband who has been suffering very badly with bronchial asthma. The doctors sent him on to Kelowna. He has been very ill and I have been so worried about him, but just this last week he seems to be on the mend and I am hoping the warm, sunny days will help him a lot.

Yes, my home was in England – London in fact – and I was through all the Blitz, but even so, I often feel quite homesick for it all. I love my parents and brother and sister very dearly and it was hard parting from them all. But my husband is a very dear boy and I like Kelowna and the people, so I am sure I shall be quite happy.

It was nice of you to tell me about all your family and I feel very deeply for you over the boy you are missing. I have been married before and my first husband was missing at Dunkirk; my little girl was only three weeks old and I know just how badly I felt because I had been married for six years and we thought the world of each other. I am now 32 and my little girl is just four years old.

One day, when we have a car, I will get my husband to bring me to see you and when we have built a house for ourselves, which we are hoping to do soon, you must come and visit me. At the moment, we have a five-roomed apartment.

Enclosed is a threepenny piece; your son gave it to me in England to pay for a stamp. I kept it because I thought you would like it as a souvenir. It came straight from him – his own hand. He gave it to me with your address. I wish you and your family safe and speedy return. It is so hard for all you poor mothers; I think you are splendid. I hope you are well and will write me again soon. Bye bye for now. Yours very sincerely, Mary Anderson (12 May 1944).

Six years later, his sister received the following letter:

Dear Mrs. Ross: It is with regret that I refer to the loss of your brother, Warrant Officer Class II Richard Walter Stanley, who lost his life on air operations against the enemy on the 30th of May, 1943, but a report has been received from our Missing Research and Enquiry Service giving the results of their investigation into the loss of your brother and the members of his crew.

Eye witnesses informed our Investigating Officers that your brother's aircraft approached the village of Dormagen from the direction of Neuss, just clearing the roof tops of the village and crashing into a field on the southerly edge of the village. Dormagen is 10 miles north, northwest of Cologne. The crash was of a very severe nature. The remains of only three members of the crew had been recovered, their graves were located in Cologne South Cemetery. Exhumation resulted in the identification of Pilot Officer Flack, your brother's pilot. Unhappily, individual identification could not be made in the case of the other two members of the crew. Their graves will therefore be marked as unknown. Pilot Officer Flack and the two unknown members of the crew have since been re-interred in the permanent British Military Cemetery, 11 miles north west of Duisberg, Germany. The cemetery is known as the Rheinberg Military Cemetery.

Unhappily, owing to the extreme hazards attending war in the air, there are many thousands of aircrew boys who, like your brother, do not have a known grave and their names will be commemorated on general memorials which will be erected by the Imperial War Graves Commission (of which Canada is a member).

I realize that this is an extremely distressing letter and that there is no manner of conveying such information to you that will not add to your heartaches. I am fully aware that nothing I may say will lessen your great sorrow, but I would like to express to you and the members of your family my deepest sympathy. Yours sincerely, Wing Commander W. R. Gunn (1 March 1949).

Stanley Bay (64 H/2) in Holmes Lake was named after him in 1995.

Stanley, Signalman **W. Harold** of Winnipeg (H 102710). Royal Canadian Corps of Signals. He died 16 June 1944 at the age of 22 and is commemorated at Beny-sur-Mer Canadian War Cemetery in Calvados, France. He was the son of William and Elizabeth Stanley of Winnipeg. ***Stanley Island*** (64 F/3) in Vandekerckhove Lake was named after him in 1994.

Staples, Pilot Officer **Murray C.** of Winnipeg (J 17698). No. 156 Squadron. He died 30 July 1943 at the age of 23 and is commemorated at Hamburg Cemetery in Germany. He was the son of Josiah C. and Mabel Staples of St. James and had recently begun his second tour of duty as a rear gunner. His nephew writes (27 November 2001):

> At 21:57 hours his Lancaster took off from England on a bombing raid over Hamburg. His plane was never heard from again. He was declared missing in action and presumed dead. [His] Manitoba Official Death Certificate dates his death as July 30, 1943.
>
> It's worth noting that these raids over Hamburg are well documented and were quite disastrous for both sides. Many lives were lost by both the Germans and the Allied Forces. In a few short days, hundreds of thousands of lives were lost.
>
> Many months later, there came information from German witnesses that his plane crashed near Wesseln, Germany (near Hamburg) and that his body and the bodies of the other six crew members were buried at Hemmingstedt Cemetery. He was not positively identified, but his parachute harness had the name "taples" on it so it was assumed that this was in fact Murray. The exact burial date is not known but it is assumed to be sometime in August. Many soldiers were buried at this cemetery and were later exhumed and re-interred at Ohlsdorf British Cemetery. Murray was one of these and he is currently buried ... four miles northeast of Hamburg.
>
> The last correspondence from the Federal Government regarding Murray was sent in July, 1950. That's quite a few years that Mabel and Josiah had to relive this most unfortunate time in their lives. I often wonder how Mabel was able to handle the emotions of this period.

Staples Lake (64 H/15), east of Etawney Lake was named after him in 1995.

Stapleton, Flying Officer **John W.** of Selkirk (J 23460). No. 582 Squadron. He died 6 July 1944 at the age of 28 and is commemorated at the Runnymede Memorial in Surrey, England. He was survived by his adoptive mother Winifred H. Stapleton of Selkirk, Manitoba. ***Stapleton Lake*** (64 H/16), southeast of Condie Lake was named after him in 1995.

Staradub, Private **Albert** of Selkirk (H 17858). Lake Superior Regiment. He died 26 February 1945 and is commemorated at the Groesbeek Canadian War Cemetery in Holland. He was the son of Mike and Annie Staradub of East Selkirk, Manitoba. ***Staradub Lake*** (52 E/14), southeast of Brereton Lake was named after him in 1974.

Stark, Lieutenant **Daniel D.** of Souris. Lake Superior Regiment. He died 4 November 1944 at the age of 31 and is commemorated at Bergen-op-Zoom Canadian War Cemetery in Holland. He was the son of Daniel and Barbara Stark and was survived by his wife Margaret A. Stark of Winnipeg. ***Stark Lake*** (64 H/11), south of Small Lake was named after him in 1995.

Starrett, Lance Corporal **Ewart G.** of Winnipeg (H 3031). Winnipeg Grenadiers. He died 19 December 1941 at the age of 27 and is commemorated at the Sai Wan Memorial in Hong Kong. He was the son of James and Jane Starrett of Winnipeg. ***Starrett Island*** (64 B/9) in Baldock Lake was named after him in 1995. Starrett Lake was named in honour of his brother Lance Corporal William J. Starrett (next entry).

Starrett, Lance Corporal **William J.** of Winnipeg (H 2970). Winnipeg Grenadiers. He died 20 December 1941 at the age of 23 and is commemorated at the Sai Wan Memorial in Hong Kong. He was the son of James and Jane Starrett of Winnipeg. His service record indicates that he had been "Killed outright" at Mount Butler after having been taken prisoner at 10:00 AM. ***Starrett Lake*** (64 I/4), north of North Knife Lake was named after him in 1974. Starrett Island was named in honour of his brother Lance Corporal Ewart G. Starrett (previous entry).

Stear, Pilot Officer **Victor** of Winnipeg (J 92357). No. 419 Squadron. He died 26 August 1944 at the age of 18 and is commemorated at Durnbach War Cemetery in Bavaria, Germany. He was the son of David and Amalia "Molly" Stear of Winnipeg. His brother writes (11 October 2001):

> Victor was born October 6th, 1925. He was schooled in Winnipeg's North End and was confirmed within Zion Lutheran Church April 6, 1941. Victor was a shy, quiet young man who worked for Zipursky's Grocery Store making deliveries with his bike; he was later employed by the MacDonald Aircraft Company. He had a passion to fly and April 22nd, 1943, he was sworn in as a member of the Royal Canadian Air Force. He was stationed in England and became a mid-upper gunner, flying sorties in Lancaster bombers. November 12, 1943, Victor was made a sergeant, receiving his wings.
>
> In 1943, Victor also took out a membership in Winnipeg for the Winnipeg Roller Skating Club, where he enjoyed roller skating. August 24th, 1944, Victor became a Pilot Officer; August 26th, 1944, after completing 10 sorties successfully, Pilot Officer Victor Stear was shot down over Germany. The plane in which Victor was flying was struck by an Allied plane which sheared off the tail section. The only survivor was the pilot who was ejected through the front windshield and managed to activate his parachute. All the remaining crew perished.

Stear Lake (64 C/11), southwest of Lynn Lake was named after him in 1979.

Stechyshyn, Lance Sergeant **John** of Winnipeg (H 20124). Queen's Own Cameron Highlanders. He died 14 August 1944 at the age of 26 and is commemorated at Bretteville-sur-Laize Canadian War Cemetery in Calvados, France. He was the son of John and Katherine Stechyshyn and was survived by his wife Margaret G. Stechyshyn of Port Hope, Ontario. ***Stechyshyn Lake*** (64 O/2), west of Munroe Lake was named after him in 1975.

Steeds, Lance Corporal **John H. F.** of Winnipeg (H 19521). Royal Canadian Corps of Signals. He died 25 December 1944 at the age of 24 and is commemorated at Bergen-op-Zoom Canadian War Cemetery in Holland. He was the son of Arthur H. and Norma Steeds and was survived by his wife Barbara E. Steeds of Winnipeg. ***Steeds Lake*** (63 N/4), southwest of Kississing Lake was named after him in 1982.

Steel, Major **Sunley G. H.** of St. Vital. Queen's Own Cameron Highlanders, Military Cross. He died 9 July 1941 at the age of 46 and is commemorated at Brookwood Military Cemetery in Surrey, England. He was the son of Thomas S. and Marion L. D. Steel (née Peters) and was survived by his wife Alice A. Steel (née Jones) of Winnipeg. ***Steel River*** (64 I/14), which flows north into the Seal River was named after him in 1957.

Steele, Private **James H.** of Flin Flon (H 16268). Princess Patricia's Canadian Light Infantry. He died 17 May 1944 and is commemorated at the Cassino War Cemetery in Italy. ***Steele Island*** (64 O/6) in Calder Lake was named after him in 1995.

Steele, Private **Norman L.** of Riding Mountain (H 200093). Queen's Own Cameron Highlanders. He died 27 October 1944 at the age of 30 and is commemorated at Bergen-op-Zoom Canadian War Cemetery in Holland. He was the son of John and Lavina Steele of Riding Mountain and was survived by his wife Marjorie Steele (née Charles) of Gilbert Plains, Manitoba. She writes (2 July 1996):

> In 1940, he enlisted in the Winnipeg Light Infantry. He trained there and in British Columbia. He later joined as a volunteer in the Queen's Own Cameron Highlanders. He trained in England and on October 27th, 1944 [he] was killed in action (after helping liberate Antwerp) at Wemeldinge, Holland.

Steele Bay (64 I/7) in Hillman Lake was named after him in 1995.

Steenson, Warrant Officer 2 **William J.** of Morden (R 106347). No. 7 Bombing and Gunnery School, RCAF. He died 14 April 1944 at the age of 23 and is commemorated at Darlingford Cemetery, Manitoba. He was the son of William and Maggie Steenson of Morden. ***Steenson Lake*** (64 J/9), east of Tadoule Lake was named after him in 1975.

Steeves, Gunner **Randolf E.** of Winnipeg (H 22277). Royal Canadian Artillery. He died 29 July 1945 at the age of 36 and is commemorated at the Holten Canadian War Cemetery in Holland. ***Steeves Lake*** (64 K/13), south of Embury Lake was named after him in 1984.

Stefanchuk, Flight Sergeant **John J.** of Stuartburn (R 58757). No. 408 Squadron. He died 10 July 1943 at the age of 22 and is commemorated at the Reichswald Forest War Cemetery in Germany. ***Stefanchuk Lake*** (64 H/11), south of Small Lake was named after him in 1995.

Stefanic, Trooper **Victor J.** of Selkirk (H 26272). Fort Garry Horse. He died 15 August 1941 at the age of 22 and is commemorated at Selkirk Ukrainian Catholic Cemetery. He was survived by his mother Jessie Adamoski of Selkirk, Manitoba. ***Stefanic Lake*** (64 O/3), southwest of Munroe Lake was named after him in 1975.

Stefanson, Private **Gisli S.** of Selkirk (H 9155). Princess Patricia's Canadian Light Infantry. He died 23 February 1945 at the age of 34 and is commemorated at Ravenna War Cemetery in Italy. He was the son of Stefan G. and Rannveig Stefanson of Selkirk, Manitoba. According to his sister (27 November 2001):

> "Gil" was born April 16, 1910 in Selkirk and received all of his schooling there. He was employed by the Booth Fisheries when he enlisted with the PPCLI in April, 1943, going overseas with them in December of that year. He was only in England for a short time before being shipped to Italy. He was wounded February 23, 1945 and passed away later that day. He was laid to rest in the 2nd Brigade Cemetery near Bagnacavaldo and later reinterred at Ravenna.
>
> Gil was a quiet type who loved and was loved by all his family. One of his favourite pastimes was playing softball and was the captain of a team called the Millionaires – the humour being that all the players were labourers at the Fisheries. He had a beautiful singing voice and while he was doing his chores he would sing to his heart's content. Many said that he sounded just like Bing Crosby. He never said no to anyone asking for help and was loved for his helpfulness. He was greatly missed when he went overseas.

Stefanson Lake (64 O/12), south of Nueltin Lake was named after him in 1975.

Stefansson, Rifleman **Eggert** of Winnipeg (H 1065). Royal Winnipeg Rifles. He died 8 June 1944 at the age of 21 and is commemorated at Beny-sur-Mer Canadian War Cemetery in Calvados, France. He was the son of Gusmundur A. and Johanna Stefansson of Winnipeg. ***Stefansson Island*** (64 O/13) in Nueltin Lake was named after him in 1995.

Stefanuik, Rifleman **Nicholas** of Selkirk (H 17371). Royal Winnipeg Rifles. He died 8 June 1944 and is commemorated at Beny-sur-Mer Canadian War Cemetery in Calvados, France. ***Stefanuik Lake*** (63 N/2), east of Kississing Lake was named after him in 1972.

Stein, Private **William** of Winnipeg (H 105100). Queen's Own Cameron Highlanders. He died 26 February 1945 at the age of 19 and is commemorated at the Groesbeek Canadian War Cemetery in Holland.

> By far the greater number of the men buried in this cemetery were Canadians, and many of them lost their lives in the Battle of the Rhineland, when the 2nd and 3rd Canadian Infantry Divisions and the 4th Canadian Armoured Division took part in the drive southwards from Nijmegen to clear the territory between the Maas and the Rhine, in February and March, 1945. Canadian casualties from 8th February to 10th March of that year totalled 5304 (Commonwealth War Graves Commission).

Stein Lake (64 I/1), northeast of Etawney Lake was named after him in 1974.

Steinberg, Pilot Officer **Hymie** of Winnipeg (J 46779). No. 162 Squadron. He died 19 December 1944 at the age of 19 and is commemorated at Fossvogur Cemetery in Reykjavik, Iceland. This former *Winnipeg Free Press* reporter may have been the youngest Canadian Pilot Officer at the time. ***Steinberg Lake*** (53 D/5), northeast of Carr-Harris Lake was named after him in 1975.

Steinke, Private **William** of Winnipeg (H 8912). Princess Patricia's Canadian Light Infantry. He died 21 December 1944 at the age of 29 and is commemorated at Coriano Ridge War Cemetery in Italy. He was the son of August and Matilda Steinke and was survived by his wife Iris L. W. Steinke of Banff, Alberta. She recalls (15 May 1998) that he was:

> ... born at Emerson, Manitoba, July 20, 1915. [He] grew up and received his education in Winnipeg. [He] joined the armed forces in April, 1943 – first the Lake Superior Tank Regiment, but soon was transferred to the PPCLI. [He] went overseas in early December, 1944 after training at Fort Garry, Shilo, Truro, Nova Scotia and Kingston, Ontario. Due to his ability to speak German fluently, he was chosen for a six-week course at Kingston in August, 1944. He spent a short time in England and then went to Italy where he was wounded ... and died.

Steinke Lake (64 F/6), west of Wells Lake was named after him in 1994.

Stephanson, Staff Sergeant **Magnus** of Selkirk (P 35405). Royal Canadian Ordnance Corps. He died 15 January 1941 at the age of 22 and is commemorated at Brookwood Military Cemetery in Surrey, England. He was survived by his mother Steinunn Stephanson of Selkirk, Manitoba. ***Stephanson Bay*** (64 O/11) in Corbett Lake was named after him in 1995.

Stephen, Leading Telegraphist **Donald** of Fort Garry (V 24255). HMCS *Alberni*. The *Alberni* was torpedoed and sunk by U-480, southeast of the Isle of Wight; 59 of her ship's company were lost. Leading Telegraphist Stephen died 21 August 1944 at the age of 27 and is commemorated at the Halifax Memorial. He was the son of Peter and Emily E. Stephen of Fort Garry. According to his brother (22 November 2001):

> Don was raised in the Fort Garry suburb of Winnipeg. He attended local schools, graduated and entered the business world with the Manitoba Telephone System. After his father's early passing, he took on the added responsibility of being the head of the family, overseeing the care of his two brothers as well as his mother.
>
> He was active in the outdoors, enjoying canoe trips with friends into the Whiteshell district. Following basic training in the RCNVR in 1941, he served on the HMCS *Restigouche* in the Atlantic Ocean and in the Mediterranean Sea theatres of war. He was later re-assigned to the HMCS *Alberni* serving in the English Channel. The *Alberni* was escorting the transportation of floating docks to the Normandy coast to assist the Allied troops. It was during this operation that she was sunk with the loss of two-thirds of her crew.

Stephen Lake (64 N/1), northwest of Egenolf Lake was named after him in 1972.

Stephens, Flight Sergeant **Robert F.** of MacGregor (R 59262). No. 19 Squadron. He died 12 September 1941 at the age of 27 and is commemorated at the Runnymede Memorial in Surrey, England. He was the son of Archibald and Emma E. Stephens of Westbourne, Manitoba. ***Stephens Bay*** (53 L/5) in Bolton Lake was named after him in 1995.

Stephenson, Lance Corporal **Frederick G.** of Souris (H 16313). Princess Patricia's Canadian Light Infantry. He died 20 September 1944 at the age of 22 and is commemorated at Coriano Ridge War Cemetery in Italy. He was the second of the four children of Frederick G. and Georgina D. Stephenson of Souris. His sister recalls (27 February 1995):

> All three boys served in the army and saw active service during World War II. Our father served in the army in World War I and was wounded twice. Fred grew up in Souris and attended school there. Dropping out at a young age, he went to work on the Collinson's farm. At the outbreak of the war, he and Glen Collinson enlisted in the army. Fred was only 17 at the time and our mother tried to persuade him not to, but he insisted he would be 18 the following March and would only re-enlist then. He was with the Princess Patricia's Canadian Light Infantry and was with one of the first groups to arrive in England in 1939.
>
> He spent most of his time in England and didn't see active service until the Italian Campaign. He was in various camps in England, but I can't recall them, or due to the censorship, I never knew. While he was on leave in London, he had the misfortune to be hit by a truck during a blackout and was hospitalized for quite a long time. My eldest brother Ted tried to persuade him to join his regiment, the Fort Garry Horse, but with no success. He eventually recovered and was sent on the Italian Front where he was killed by a sniper, about six months before the end of the war in Europe. My husband and I travelled to Italy in 1994, 50 years after his death and visited his grave. We were very impressed with the care given to the graves and saddened by the number of very young men buried there.

Stephenson Lake (64 G/4), northeast of Grandmother Lake was named after him in 1994.

Stern, Pilot Officer **Max** of Winnipeg (J 85923). No. 97 Squadron. He died 27 August 1944 at the age of 22 and is commemorated at the Runnymede Memorial in Surrey, England. Born in Ostoróg, Poland in 1922, he arrived in Canada in 1926. He was the son of Gabriel and Sophie Stern of Winnipeg. ***Stern Lake*** (64 H/16), south of Condie Lake was named after him in 1995.

Steuart, Rifleman **Guy** of Miniota (H 8269). Royal Winnipeg Rifles. He died 8 June 1944 at the age of 33 and is commemorated at Bretteville-sur-Laize Canadian War Cemetery in Calvados, France. He was the son of James H. and Louisa C. Steuart of Miniota, Manitoba. ***Steuart Lake*** (64 G/16), southeast of Chipewyan Lake was named after him in 1995.

Stevens, Trooper **Percival** of The Pas (H 101680). Fort Garry Horse. He died 4 July 1944 at the age of 29 and is commemorated at Beny-sur-Mer Canadian War Cemetery in Calvados, France. He was the son of A. James and Nellie Stevens of The Pas, Manitoba. ***Stevens Lake*** (64 K/16), south of Egenolf Lake was named after him in 1962.

Stevens, Pilot Officer **William G.** of Winnipeg (J 89945). No. 106 Squadron. He died 27 April 1944 at the age of 28 and is commemorated at Durnbach War Cemetery in Bavaria, Germany. He was the son of George and Beatrice M. Stevens of St. James and was survived by his wife Jean Stevens. ***Stevens Peninsula*** (64 N/14) on Farewell Lake was named after him in 1995.

Stevenson, Sergeant **Earle J.** of Winnipeg (R 59110). No. 104 Squadron. He died 3 August 1941 at the age of 20 and is commemorated at the Runnymede Memorial in Surrey, England. He was the son of J. H. J. and Florence Stevenson of St. Vital. ***Stevenson Hill*** (64 A/5), south of Baldock Lake was named after him in 1995.

Stevenson, Warrant Officer 2 **George E.** of Wawanesa (R 124239). No. 431 Squadron. He died 26 February 1944 at the age of 25 and is commemorated at Esbjerg (Fourfelt) Cemetery in Denmark. He was the son of Thomas and Margaret Stevenson of Wawanesa, Manitoba. ***Stevenson Creek*** (64 P/7), which flows into the Gordon River was named after him in 1974.

Stevenson, Pilot Officer **James** Douglas of Winnipeg (J 15340). No. 126 Squadron. He died 18 October 1942 at the age of 29 and is commemorated at Malta (Capuccini) Naval Cemetery in Malta. He was the son of Sidney S. and Alice H. Stevenson of Winnipeg. Pilot Officer Stevenson enlisted in August, 1940 and went overseas as a Sergeant-Pilot in April, 1941. He had served a total of 16 months of combat duty. ***Stevenson Bay*** (64 C/8) in Granville Lake was named after him in 1995.

Stevenson, Stoker 1 **Robert Gordon** of Flin Flon (V 60554). HMCS *Guysborough*. The *Guysborough* was torpedoed and sunk by U-878 in the English Channel off Ushant, France; fifty-one of her ship's company were lost. Stoker Stevenson died 18 March 1945 at the age of 20 and is commemorated at the Halifax Memorial. He was the son of Herbert and Nettie Stevenson of Flin Flon and was survived by his wife Jean L. Stevenson of Halifax. ***Stevenson Peninsula*** (63 I/2) on Molson Lake was named after him in 1995.

Stevenson, Lance Corporal **Robert J.** of Neepawa (H 26783). Fort Garry Horse. He died 6 June 1944 at the age of 26 and is commemorated at Beny-sur-Mer Canadian War Cemetery in Calvados, France. He was survived by his mother Cora M. Murdock of Franklin, Manitoba.

Robert joined the army in the early part of the war and was stationed overseas for three years. He landed with the Fort Garry Horse on Juno Beach on D-Day, 6 June 1944 and lost his life that day. He had two brothers, Clifford serving with the RCAF overseas and Lawrence with the RCAF at Vancouver (Pittman n.d.).

Stevenson Rapids (64 I/9) in the North Knife River was named after him in 1995.

Stevenson, Gunner **Robert M.** of the Peguis Reserve (H 66455). Royal Canadian Artillery. He died 24 October 1944 and is commemorated at Schoonselhof Cemetery in Antwerp, Belgium. ***Robert Stevenson Lake*** (53 K/3), southwest of Richardson Lake was named after him in 1995.

Stevenson, Leading Aircraftman **Thomas G.** of Belmont (R 116433). No. 14 Elementary Flying Training School. He died 30 October 1941 at the age of 18 and is commemorated at Belmont Hillside Cemetery. He was the son of Dr. William F. and Katherine A. Stevenson of Belmont, Manitoba. His sister-in-law writes (23 October 2001):

He was learning to fly at Portage la Prairie, I believe when another student came down through the clouds (where he shouldn't have been) and hit Tom. The other student survived but was badly injured. It was a tremendous loss for his family. I did not know Tom, but I was engaged to his brother Ken whom I later married.

Thomas Stevenson Lake (54 E/7), southwest of Fly Lake was named after him in 1995.

Steventon, Leading Aircraftman **Gordon M.** of Winnipeg (R 134543). No. 12 Service Flying Training School. He died 15 September 1942 at the age of 25 and is commemorated at Elmwood Cemetery in Winnipeg. He was the son of Alfred H. and Florence L. Steventon of Winnipeg. ***Steventon Lake*** (64 H/6), north of Northern Indian Lake was named after him in 1995.

Stewart, Sergeant **Clarence D.** of Manitou (1340810). No. 150 Squadron, RAF. He died 16 October 1943 at the age of 22 and is commemorated at Bolsena War Cemetery in Italy. He was the son of Duncan and Rose Stewart of Aberdeen, Manitoba. ***Clarence Stewart Creek*** (54 E/8) in Halfway Lake was named after him in 1995.

Stewart, Pilot Officer **Donald E.** of Manitou (42683). No. 44 Squadron, RAF. He died 11 September 1940 at the age of 27 and is commemorated at Becklingen War Cemetery in Germany. He was the son of John C. and Mary A. N. Stewart of Vancouver. He had enlisted in May, 1939. ***Donald Stewart Creek*** (53 N/9), which flows east into Gods River was named after him in 1995.

Stewart, Warrant Officer 1 **Donald D.** of Crystal City (R 116246). No. 148 Squadron. He died 4 July 1944 at the age of 21 and is commemorated at Budapest War Cemetery in Hungary. He was the son of David and Kathleen M. Stewart of Winnipeg. ***Donald Stewart Lake*** (54 E/11), west of Bradshaw Lake was named after him in 1995.

Stewart, Trooper **Donald H.** of Winnipeg (K 51228). Sherbrooke Fusiliers. He died 7 June 1944 at the age of 19 and is commemorated at Beny-sur-Mer Canadian War Cemetery in Calvados, France. He was the son of William J. and Florence E. Stewart of Vancouver. ***Donald Stewart Island*** (53 E/15) in Island Lake was named after him in 1997.

Stewart, Sapper **Elmer V.** of Kelwood (H 82066). Royal Canadian Engineers. He died 26 May 1944 at the age of 26 and is commemorated at the Cassino War Cemetery in Italy. He was the son of David E. and Beatrice Stewart and was survived by his wife Irene M. Stewart (née Gower) and their son.

Elmer was born in Kelwood in July of 1918 and remained there until his enlistment. Cheerful and a with a winning personality, his passing will leave a place which can never be filled. Elmer joined the army in 1941 and was posted overseas in April, 1942 with the Royal Canadian Engineers, 10th Field Regiment, serving in Italy for three months (Pittman n.d.).

Stewart Rapids (64 J/12) in the Johnson River was named after him in 1995.

Stewart, Private **George D.** of Oak Lake, Manitoba (H 1748). South Saskatchewan Regiment. He died 23 March 1945 and is commemorated at Prague War Cemetery, Czech Republic. He was the son of Duncan and Annie Stewart (née Joss) of Oak Lake. George had been taken prisoner of war 20 June 1944 and was last heard from in December of that year while interned at Stalag 8B Prisoner of War Camp. The cause of death was indicated to be "extreme physical decay." ***George Stewart Lake*** (64 N/1), north of Minuhik Lake was named after him in 1995.

Stewart, Lieutenant **Glen A.** of Austin. Royal Winnipeg Rifles. He died 4 July 1944 at the age of 30 and is commemorated at Beny-sur-Mer Canadian War Cemetery in Calvados, France. He was the son of John J. H. and Elizabeth Stewart was survived by his wife Wilhelmina M. Stewart (née Watters) of Austin, Manitoba. His sister-in-law recalls (10 April 1995):

Glen was born in Oakville and raised in Portage la Prairie. He was a good student and won the Governor General's medal upon graduation. Glen was a graduate pharmacist and worked in Hill's Drug Store in Portage prior to enlisting. He was married to Mina Watters of Austin. Glen and Mina had only one child, a son, Kenneth, born in 1941. While Glen was overseas, Kenneth fell into a well and was drowned. The family was later told that Glen was so devastated upon hearing of the death of his only child, that he volunteered for a dangerous mission and was himself killed, just five weeks later.

Stewart Peninsula (63 N/2) on Limestone Point Lake was named after him in 1995.

Stewart, Corporal **Harold W.** of Brandon (H 35633). Canadian Army Corps of Military Staff Clerks. He died 27 May 1943 at the age of 36 and is commemorated at Brookwood Military Cemetery in Surrey, England. He was the son of Wesley and Isabella Stewart and was survived by his wife Elsie M. Stewart of Winnipeg. ***Stewart Bay*** (64 H/15) in Etawney Lake was named after him in 1995.

Stewart, Rifleman **Jack** of Wabowden (H 20639). Royal Winnipeg Rifles. He died 6 June 1944 at the age of 31 and is commemorated at Beny-sur-Mer Canadian War Cemetery in Calvados, France. He was the son of James G. and of Virginia Stewart of Wabowden, Manitoba. According to a contemporary newspaper account:

Word has been received here by his mother, that Jack Stewart was killed in action in France on June 6th. Mr. Stewart is the first casualty on the Hudson Bay line and the first employee of the Hudson Bay Railway to give his life. He enlisted with the Queen's Own Cameron Highlanders on September 21, 1940 and later transferred to the Royal Winnipeg Rifles. A year after enlisting, he arrived overseas in September, 1941. A while ago, he received an injury to his thumb while on duty.

Mr. Stewart was not married, [his] father, James Stewart, at one time Hudson Bay post manager passed away some years ago and surviving Jack are his mother, living at Wabowden [and four siblings]. His father was a well-known pioneer of the north, serving for over thirty years with the Hudson's Bay Company in Labrador and the Northwest Territories. Before his death some 12 years ago, he was postmaster and magistrate at Wabowden. Jack's grandfather, Colonel James Stewart took part in the Northwest Rebellion (*The Pas, Northern Mail* n.d.).

Stewart Lake (62 N/15), southeast of Swan River was named after him in 1973.

Stewart, Pilot Officer **James Gordon** of Winnipeg (J 87408). No. 1664 Heavy Conversion Unit, RCAF. He died 24 February 1944 at the age of 20 and is commemorated at Stonefall Cemetery in Yorkshire, England. He was the son of James and Agnes Stewart of Winnipeg. An alumnus of Cecil Rhodes School and former member of the Winnipeg Boys Choir, Pilot Officer Stewart worked in the CPR Weston Shops as an apprentice machinist prior to enlisting. He was killed the day after receiving his commission. ***Gordon Stewart Lake*** (53 M/4), east of California Lake was named after him in 1995.

Stewart, Sergeant **James L.** of Winnipeg (H 58557). Royal Canadian Engineers. He died 19 December 1944 at the age of 61 and is commemorated at Beechwood Cemetery in Ottawa. He was the son of George and Agnes Stewart and was survived by his wife Cora J. Stewart of Ottawa. ***Stewart Hill*** (64 B/3), south of Mynarski Lakes was named after him in 1995.

Stewart, Rifleman **John Raymond M.** of Muir (H 1175). Royal Winnipeg Rifles. He died 8 June 1944 at the age of 21 and is commemorated at Bretteville-sur-Laize Canadian War Cemetery in Calvados, France. He was the son of Angus F. and Bertha M. Stewart of Muir, Manitoba. ***Stewart Creek*** (64 F/7), which flows west into Wells Lake was named after him in 1995.

Stewart, Flying Officer **Robert** of St. Vital (J 18281). No. 419 Squadron. He died 31 August 1943 at the age of 23 and is commemorated at the Runnymede Memorial in Surrey, England. He was the son of Robert and Margaret Stewart and was survived by his wife Winifred M. Stewart of Chester-le-Street, County Durham, England. ***Robert Stewart Lake*** (64 H/8), west of Hogg Lake was named after him in 1995.

Stewart, Private **Robert E.** of Winnipeg (H 20097). Queen's Own Cameron Highlanders. He died 19 August 1942 at the age of 22 and is commemorated at Dieppe Canadian War Cemetery in Seine-Maritime, France. He was the son of Robert D. and Gladys A. Stewart (née Sims) of Winnipeg. ***Stewart Island*** (64 F/2) in Wells Lake was named after him in 1994.

Stewart, Pilot Officer **William McGill** of Goodlands (C 86790). No. 429 Squadron. He died 25 May 1944 at the age of 37 and is commemorated at Bergen-op-Zoom Canadian War Cemetery in Holland. His nephew writes (11 April 1995):

He was always addressed as "Mac" by those who knew him. The special interest he cared most about was acting in local entertainment – in the days before television, this was an important part of community life and one in which he always took an active role. Uncle Mac joined the Royal Canadian Air Force, became a flight engineer and was killed over Aachen, Germany during a bombing mission.

I was not very old when he left to go overseas. I can remember, though, a cheerful, happy man, always joking and much loved by his family and all who knew him. I can remember too the terrible pain his loss caused my grandmother. This made an impression on me. I have never forgotten – an impression about the incredible waste and stupidity of all wars and a disgust with those, on both sides, whose criminal incompetence allows such things to happen.

McGill Stewart Lake (64 C/4), west of McCallum Lake was named after him in 1995.

Stillinger, Flying Officer **Roy E.** of Winnipeg (J 38395). No. 426 Squadron. He died 5 March 1945 at the age of 23 and is commemorated at the Berlin 1939 - 1945 War Cemetery in Brandenburg, Germany. He was the son of Clarence and Connie Stillinger of Vancouver and was survived by his wife Myrtle Stillinger (née Thompson). His sister writes (2 October 1993):

My brother ... was born in St. Boniface August 26th, 1921. His primary and high school were in the Norwood School Division from which he graduated in 1939. He secured employment with Manitoba Bridge and Iron Works and stayed there until enlistment in the RCAF in Winnipeg in 1943. [That year] ... he married Myrtle Thompson, a childhood sweetheart. There were no children from the marriage. Myrtle has since remarried and lives in Calgary, but we still keep in contact with her.

He was interested as a participant and spectator in nearly all sports, principally baseball, hockey and football. In addition to his interest in sports, my brother also loved the outdoors, particularly camping, fishing and canoeing.

Stillinger Lake (64 G/4), northeast of Grandmother Lake was named after him in 1994.

Stillman, Trooper **Basil** of Carman (H 77612). 12th Manitoba Dragoons. He died 6 December 1944 at the age of 20 and is commemorated at Bergen-op-Zoom Canadian War Cemetery in Holland. He was the son of Willis and Caroline Stillman of Carman, Manitoba. ***Stillman Lake*** (64 N/12), southeast of Kasba Lake was named after him in 1972.

Stinson, Pilot Officer **Lloyd A.** of Melita (J 17695). No. 408 Squadron. He died 14 May 1943 at the age of 21 and is commemorated at Flushing (Vlissingen) Northern Cemetery in Holland. He was survived by his step-parents Robert A. and Emma Stinson (née Thackeray) of Melita, Manitoba. His nephew writes (5 February 1997):

My recollections, though they seem fairly clear to me, are actually almost entirely second hand, i.e., from Grandpa's and my parents' recollections and from photographs. I remember him especially through my parents' stories as an always kind, smiling, good-natured young man whom everyone loved to have around, and I remember quite vividly Grandpa's grievous sense of loss when my Uncle Lloyd died.

Stinson Lake (64 H/11), southwest of Etawney Lake was named after him in 1963.

Stinson, Pilot Officer **William L.** of Fisherton (J 23811). No. 111 Operational Training Unit, RCAF. He died 28 June 1943 at the age of 19 and is commemorated at the Ottawa Memorial. He was the son of John C. and Edyth Stinson of New Westminster, British Columbia. ***Stinson Island*** (63 P/11) in Natawahunan Lake was named after him in 1995.

Stodgell, Corporal **Cyril A.** of Fisherton (H 20704). Lake Superior Regiment. He died 11 September 1944 at the age of 23 and is commemorated at the Adegem Canadian War Cemetery in Belgium. He was the son of Charles and Mary Stodgell of Fisherton, Manitoba. **Stodgell Islands** (64 P/8) in Caribou Lake was named after him and his brother Private Stanley F. Stodgell (see entry) in 1985. Stodgell Lake was named after their brother Garnett J. Stodgell in 1974 (next entry).

Stodgell, Private **Garnett J.** of Fisherton (H 6688). Winnipeg Grenadiers. He died a prisoner of war 20 March 1943 at the age of 26 and is commemorated at the Sai Wan War Cemetery in Hong Kong. He was the son of Charles and Mary Stodgell of Fisherton, Manitoba. ***Stodgell Lake*** (64 I/9), northeast of North Knife Lake was named after him in 1974. Stodgell Islands were named after his brothers Cyril A. and Stanley F. Stodgell in 1985 (previous and next entries).

Stodgell, Private **Stanley F.** of Winnipeg (H 6353). Winnipeg Grenadiers. He died 19 December 1941 at the age of 22 and is commemorated at the Sai Wan Memorial in Hong Kong. He was the son of Charles and Mary Stodgell, of Fisherton, Manitoba. ***Stodgell Islands*** (64 P/8) in Caribou Lake was named after him and his brother Corporal Cyril A. Stodgell in 1985. Stodgell Lake was named after their brother Garnett J. Stodgell in 1974 (previous entry).

Stone, Sergeant **Douglas B.** of Shoal Lake (R 59411). No. 428 Squadron. He died 27 September 1943 at the age of 28 and is commemorated at the Hanover War Cemetery in Germany. He was the son of William and Gertrude A. Stone and was survived by brother Alvin and by his wife Lydia Stone of Shoal Lake and their infant son Bryant. His wife recalls (14 November 2001):

"Stoney" had a very pleasant, outgoing personality and especially enjoyed playing hockey and working with motors. An old coupe was converted into "The Bug" which ran on noise, smoke and diesel fuel. Later, with the help of a friend, he built a snowmobile and then a snow plane. These were used as a means of transporting the RCMP and travellers on roads impassable to other vehicles. They also provided a source of winter income for him. Stoney was very ambitious and at the time he enlisted in the RCAF, he was studying diesel engines.

Stone Island (64 B/6) in Karsakuwigamak Lake was named after him in 1995.

Stoneham, Sergeant **Albert L. "Bert"** of Winnipeg (R 180231). No. 1660 Heavy Conversion Unit, RCAF. He died 22 April 1944 at the age of 29 and is commemorated at Stonefall Cemetery in Yorkshire, England. He was survived by his mother Annie E. Stoneham of Winnipeg. His sister recalls (28 November 1995):

Bert was the first-born and only son of Albert and Anne Stoneman who resided at 84 Carman Avenue in Elmwood. He grew up in this area and attended Lord Selkirk Elementary and High Schools. As a youngster growing up, he did all the things that young boys usually do – skated, played baseball, went swimming, rode his bicycle, etc. He was also a member of the Boy Scouts.

Upon completion of his education, he was employed by Canadian Pacific Telecommunications and latterly was a lineman with CP. He enjoyed working with his hands and showed a natural ability to be able to repair anything electrical. He also enjoyed woodworking. We still have two lamps, a foot stool and a card table that he crafted. Also, he along with a friend, built a boat and a canoe. Both boats were sold only when he enlisted. He was also an avid reader. He was baptised at St. Stephen's Anglican Church and attended Sunday School and church at that location.

Our Dad was killed while employed with the Canadian Pacific Railway when Bert was 12 years old and this left a void in his life. However, his best friend, Bill Leitch, lived across the street and it was his Dad that taught them how to handle their guns safely and they all went duck hunting every fall until the time Bert enlisted.

He enlisted on July 22nd, 1942 and left Winnipeg on October 2nd, 1943. Upon arrival in England, he was assigned to fly with the Royal Air Force. [T]hey were on their last training mission when two planes collided in mid-air, killing the crews of both.

Stoneham Lake (64 O/16), northwest of Nejanilini Lake was named after him in 1975.

Storey, Flying Officer **Harvey E.** of Brandon (J 25265). No. 12 Service Flying Training School. He died 26 September 1944 at the age of 30 and is commemorated at Brandon Cemetery. He was the son of George E. and Ruby V. Storey of New Westminster, British Columbia and was survived by his wife Joyce Storey of Brandon. ***Storey Bay*** (63 N/8) in Burntwood Lake was named after him in 1995.

Storey, Private **John H.** of Pierson (H 105087). Canadian Scottish Regiment. He died 12 August 1944 at the age of 27 and is commemorated at Bretteville-sur-Laize Canadian War Cemetery in Calvados, France. He was the son of George and Mary A. Storey of Pierson, Manitoba. ***Storey Island*** (62 P/1) in Lake Winnipeg was named after him in 1980.

Storozuk, Private **Joseph** of Seech (H 10452). South Saskatchewan Regiment. He died 20 July 1944 at the age of 27 and is commemorated at Bretteville-sur-Laize Canadian War Cemetery in Calvados, France. He was the fifth of the 11 children of John and Teenie Storozuk of Seech, Manitoba. His brother recalls (29 October 2001):

Joseph worked on his father's farm until he decided to travel east to Ontario. There he worked on SS Hamonic cruise ship as a waiter and later in a Hamilton restaurant as a chef. He loved to play the mouth organ, guitar, dance and many other talents that he had. He was terribly missed after we all received the bad news.

Another brother adds (23 April 2002):

Our brother went into war as an enlisted man with the South Saskatchewan Regiment on June 6, 1944 and managed to fight through Caen and just a bit beyond, past the city where at a village called Ifs, he was first listed as missing in action. By November of that year his parents received a telegram listing him as killed in action on July 20. The South Saskatchewan was practically decimated in that battle.

Storozuk Lake (63 K/16), northwest of Reed Lake was named after him in 1973.

Story, Lance Corporal **Rupert R.** of Dauphin (K 52299). Seaforth Highlanders of Canada, Military Medal. He died 29 July 1943 at the age of 25 and is commemorated at Agira Canadian War Cemetery in Italy. He was the son of Christopher and B. Story and was survived by his wife Phyllis Story of Milner, British Columbia. ***Story Lake*** (64 C/11), south of Lynn Lake was named after him in 1947.

Stowe, Private **Charles L.** of Miniota (SM 17956). Royal Canadian Regiment. He died 13 October 1952 at the age of 25 and is commemorated at the United Nations Cemetery in Pusan, South Korea. His niece writes (29 November 2001):

Charles Lorne Stowe was born June 17th, 1927 to Jack and Mabel Stowe of Miniota, Manitoba. He was their youngest son who grew up to be a hardworking, fun loving young man who enjoyed music, dances, sports and practical jokes. His winning smile charmed the young ladies and his easy going personality made him a favorite among his peers and co-workers. While Charlie's older brothers, Edwin and George were overseas taking part in World War II, Charlie remained at home to help with the family farm. When Edwin and George returned from the war, Charlie was eager to spread his wings and see the world around him. He tried his hand in the mining industry in northern Ontario and later headed north to Yellowknife for a time, then south to Alberta. Having been laid off from work, he decided to stop by a local pub in Forestburg, Alberta where he met Duke Elliot.

Mr. Elliott recalls (29 November 2001):

I lived in Forestburg, Alberta and was working on the CNR when I got laid off. So I went to the Forestburg Hotel for a beer to drown my sorrow. After a time, this good-looking lad came in and as there were only the two of us in there, he came over and introduced himself. As it turned out, he too had been laid off of the oil rigs where he had been working. Charlie had an old car and after a few beers, we decided to go to Edmonton to look for work. So after a week of looking, and what money we had was fast running out, it was decided we would go join the army. At least we would eat and have clothing etc.

After joining, we were sent to Petawawa, Ontario where we went through basic training together. That is where we got to know one another. When we finished our basic training, we were then shipped out to Wainwright, Alberta. After we were there a while, a few of us were asked if we would like to go on an NCO's course; we both said yes. After a few days on the course, I got kicked off cause I couldn't stand their BS, but Charlie stayed on. It was at that time that we got split up. He finished the course and I was shipped out to Korea. I did not see Charlie again until he finished his training at Kara Mura Battle Training School in Japan.

His niece recalls (29 November 2001) his embarkation:

Charlie took his last leave before shipping out in July, 1952. He spent the time with his family in Miniota where he would say his last good-byes. His older sister Norma who had been a nurse during World War II, remembered the day she last saw him. She related this story to niece Kathy (Stowe) Meekins saying: "I was walking into Mom and Dad's house with my heart in my throat, fighting my emotions. Although Ed and George had returned safely from World War II, I felt very strongly that Charlie would not return to us. I was angry at him for wanting to go to Korea. When he left, I wanted to go after him. It was the last time I saw him." Perhaps Charlie had the same feeling, for his young nephew, John Stowe recalled that final farewell, saying that Charlie was in full uniform and when he said goodbye to everyone at the farm that day, he said he wouldn't likely be coming back. Indeed it would be his final goodbye to his family. Charlie headed west to Vancouver, where on August 13th, 1952 he left the shores of Canada. He reached Korea on September 13th, 1952.

Letters home to his family were filled with stories of his experiences, some good, some bad. In one letter home he described the beauty of Korea and its people and noted that he would like to revisit Korea during peacetime and just be a tourist. It seemed he was in awe of its beauty.

Platoon Sargent John J. Worden and Private Duke Elliott later wrote letters to the family describing the circumstances surrounding Charlie's death (29 November 2001):

Charlie was a Private in 10 Platoon, D Company, 1RCR. The Platoon went to the position called Hill 355 on October 1st, 1952. The hill was known as Kwan-san, Little Gibraltar and The Gateway to Seoul. Anyone that held Hill 355 dominated the area. This was the site of some of the bloodiest battles of the Korean war. Platoon 10 was designated to the point position of the hill. They were closest to the Chinese Army. Charles was in No. 2 section under the command of Corporal John Kerr. Second in command was Lance Corporal Barney Rice.

The platoon started with 38 men, but as the numbers dwindled, the remaining men were sent to the outpost more frequently, which none were eager to do. It was obvious the enemy was planning to attack Hill 355 as they constantly dropped mortars day and night to inflict what casualties they could. Charlie's outpost was called Vancouver.

Duke Elliott recalls (29 November 2001) what happened next:

At about 9:30 PM, we were told that there was a large group of Chinese that was going to attack us. At 10 PM, all hell broke loose. They fired many rounds at Vancouver outpost; these men tried to fight their way back uphill to the main body of men. The men were screaming for help, but there was nothing you could do. Our officer told us to stay in our trenches and shoot Chinese. When I heard Charlie's voice, I went to him anyway, for which I got in trouble. But by the time I got Charlie in the trench, he was dead. And for my punishment, I was ordered to take a South Korean soldier and myself and carry Charlie down the back of the hill. They put him on a jeep and took him back to a Medic tent. That was the last I seen of my friend.

His niece concludes (29 November 2001):

The young farm boy who joined the army and became a soldier on the 13th, left Canada on the 13th, arrived in Korea on the 13th, died there on October 13th, 1952. He was 25 years old. Charlie was buried in the United Nations cemetery overlooking the city of Pusan, Korea. Duke Elliott and John Worden have both returned to the cemetery to pay their respects to Charlie and the others they fought side by side with. Charlie's sisters Norma and Dora visited Charlie's gravesite also, and Norma took with her a small container filled with soil from the farm where he grew up. It was placed by his grave so that he might always have a piece of his home with him. We, his family, remember Private Charles Lorne Stowe SM 17956. A cenotaph situated at the west end of the Miniota Park bears his name, so that we all shall remember him.

Stowe Lake (63 I/3), south of Molson Lake was named after this Korean War casualty in 1999. Duke Elliott adds:

I'm 75 now and don't write or spell good, so my wife re-writes my letters. I'm so happy they named a lake after Charlie, he earned it. He was the kind of man that could put on a pair of coveralls and still look good. I'm proud to have known him (29 November 2001).

Strachan, Telegraphist **Edward Eloi** of Winnipeg (V 50046). HMCS *Valleyfield*. The *Valleyfield* was torpedoed and sunk by U-548 50 miles south of Cape Race, Newfoundland; 125 of her ship's company were lost. Telegraphist Strachan died 7 May 1944 at the age of 20 and is commemorated at the Halifax Memorial. He was the son of Mrs. Helen M. Strachan of Winnipeg. According to his brother (26 February 1998):

He was named Edward after my father's brother who was killed in the trenches of World War I at St. Eloi in France, hence his second name of

Eloi. My father was also in World War I, as a Sergeant in the Cameron Highlanders, and received the Military Medal for "bravery in the field." His medal was presented to him after the war at the University on Broadway in Winnipeg by the Prince of Wales. He was wounded in battle, losing three fingers of his right hand from a machine gun bullet.

My brother Eddy attended George V School on Grey Street in Elmwood and later Lord Selkirk High School where he excelled in the Manual Arts. I still use a table he made in woodworking shop. After school, he joined the Remington Typewriter Company as a repairman. When Eddy was of age to join up, he tried the Air Force but was turned down because of his eyesight. He thought his eyesight was fine and never did wear glasses. He then tried the Navy and was accepted. My mother was pleased he missed the Air Force as she thought it was the [more] dangerous of the two. He was assigned to HMCS *Halifax*, a corvette, and spent his time on her until his transfer to HMCS *Valleyfield* in the spring of 1944.

Then in early May, 1944, the telegram … arrived and life in our family was never the same. The telegram was delivered to my brother Alex at his workplace of Osler, Hammond and Nanton Insurance Company. He took it, unopened, to my Dad who worked down Main Street at the Royal Bank on William Avenue. Dad then went home to break the news to Mother and told Alex to take his time getting home so as not to arrive before him. I was 11 at the time and as I was coming home from school, I was met by my sister Helen who told me Eddy was missing. I started to cry and she tried to console me by saying he was only missing and could still be found.

At first, we assumed that the *Halifax* had gone down because we had not heard from Ed about his promotion to the *Valleyfield*. Then the letter of May 11th arrived from the Defence Department naming the *Valleyfield*. My parents were quite confused about all this until Ed's letter arrived some time later telling about his transfer. He was happy about the move because a Frigate was much more comfortable than the smaller Corvette.

For a time, we all hoped and prayed he would be found afloat somewhere as in fact, two crew members were located some time after the torpedoing. However, as time passed and word came from Ottawa that he was now presumed dead, we knew he would not be returning. The *Valleyfield* was sunk just 100 miles off Newfoundland while heading for St. John's. She was just three or four hours from safety.

At the age of 13, after the close of the war, I joined the Sea Cadets at HMCS *Chippawa* and when my mother now saw me in the uniform, she burst into tears. One of my first classes when I joined was telegraphy and the instructor, Lieutenant Bill Rose, loved to tell stories of the war to relieve the monotony of learning Morse Code and he began telling the class about the sinking of the HMCS *Valleyfield*. He had no idea that one of his class had lost a brother on this ship. He proceeded to tell the story of a telegrapher who had stayed at his station sending the distress signal and their position until the ship went under. When class adjourned I approached him, introduced myself and told him my brother was a telegrapher on the *Valleyfield*. He was stunned and began to apologize but I assured him that I was pleased to hear the story and to think that it might have been my brother that he spoke about.

Strachan Lake (64 N/14), southeast of Kasba Lake was named after Telegraphist Strachan in 1972.

Strachan, Private **William Leslie** of Virden (K 800311). Royal Canadian Regiment. He died 30 May 1951 at the age of 21 at Chail Li while carrying out wounded under the auspices of the Red Cross. He is commemorated at the United Nations Cemetery in Pusan, South Korea. He was the son of Bill and Ina Strachan and was survived by four sisters and two brothers. His brother recalls (16 November 2001):

Les was born and raised in the Virden area of Manitoba. He received his education in rural schools east of Virden. In his teen years, he worked on farms, when not in school. Driving tractors was his favourite job. He enjoyed sports and liked to hunt. He was very generous and good to his parents. The family moved to Kelowna, BC in 1945 where Les worked on a fruit ranch. He worked there until 1950 when the family moved to town. He took a job in a juice factory but hated it and decided to join the special forces going to Korea. He trained at Petawawa for a short time and then was shipped to Fort Lewis, Washington. He liked it there and it was easy to get home on leave. He seemed to like army life. He went to Korea in April, 1951 and was killed May 30th while evacuating wounded.

Strachan Island (53 E/16) in Island Lake was named after this Korean War casualty in 1998.

Strain, Pilot Officer **John E.** of Winnipeg (J 86763). No. 460 Squadron. He died 25 February 1944 at the age of 20 and is commemorated at Durnbach War Cemetery in Bavaria, Germany. ***Strain Lake*** (63 N/7), northeast of Takipy Lake was named after him in 1988.

Strand, Trooper **Albert H.** of Gilbert Plains (H 100517). Calgary Tank Regiment. He died 13 May 1944 and is commemorated at the Cassino Memorial in Italy. ***Strand Lake*** (64 G/16), southeast of Chipewyan Lake was named after him in 1995.

Strandberg, Warrant Officer 2 **Edwin** of Garson (R 134019). No. 44 Squadron. He died 9 April 1943 at the age of 19 and is commemorated at Rheinberg War Cemetery in Germany. He was the eldest of the five children of John E. and Elvera E. Strandberg of Renton, Washington, USA. His sister recalls (30 October 2001):

The last time I saw my brother, I was only nine years old. As I remember Edwin, he was a very caring, optimistic and happy person. On his last leave before going overseas, our entire family had a day-long outing to a large amusement park in Winnipeg.

Edwin graduated as a wireless air gunner before departing to England. While a member of the RCAF he flew Lancaster bombers out of the RAF station at Blackpool, England. He was wounded on a bombing run and suffered some hearing loss and therefore volunteered to be retrained as a bomb aimer. He was promoted to Warrant Officer 2 and lost his life during his third tour of operations on a bombing run over Germany.

Strandberg Lake (52 L/6), northeast of Lac du Bonnet was named after him in 1973.

Strank, Corporal **George** of Rossburn (M 12307). 14th Canadian Hussars. He died 27 February 1945 at the age of 24 and is commemorated at the Groesbeek Canadian War Cemetery in Holland. He was the son of Wasyle and Annie Strank of Rossburn, Manitoba. **Strank Lake** (62 N/15), southeast of Swan River was named after him in 1973.

Stratford, Flying Officer **Frederick** of Brandon (J 29978). No. 227 Squadron. He died 6 December 1944 at the age of 32 and is commemorated at the Hanover War Cemetery in Germany. He was the son of Edward and Lucy Stratford (née Atherton) and the brother of Warrant Officer George H. Stratford (next entry). He was survived by his wife Jean Stratford (née Muirhead) of Brandon and their son James. He writes (3 December 2001):

Frederick was a member of the 45th Manitoba Rangers (Militia) from 1930 to 1935 and with the 59th Battery, RCA (Militia) Signals from 1939 to 1942 where he attained the rank of Sergeant. Prior to joining the RCAF, he was hardware manager at Eaton's Department Store. He enjoyed sports and played tennis, golf and hockey and also enjoyed hunting and fishing.

He flew with the 50th Squadron, Skellingthorpe and the 227th Squadron Balderton as a navigator in Lancasters. Frederick was shot down over Germany on his 19th mission and was listed as missing until the family was notified of his death in April, 1947.

There is a stained glass window in St. Mary's Anglican Church in Brandon in memory of George and his older brother Frederick, RCAF, killed in action 6 December 1944. It was donated to the Church by their parents in Loving Memory of their only two children.

Stratford Lake (64 P/5), east of Nejanilini Lake was named after him in 1974.

Stratford, Warrant Officer **George H.** of Brandon (642061). No. 78 Squadron, RAF. He died 19 July 1944 at the age of 28 and is commemorated at Neufmoulin Communal Cemetery, Somme, France. He was the son of Edward and Lucy Stratford (née Atherton) and was survived by his wife Betty K. A. Stratford (née Cowley) of Croydon, Greater London, England and their son George. He was the brother of Flying Officer Frederick Stratford (previous entry). His cousin recalls (17 February 1988):

When George joined the RAF in 1939, he was stationed at Cardington, Bedfordshire and my family lived within two miles of the base, so we saw a lot of George when he was off duty.

His nephew adds (3 December 2001):

Enlisting in May, 1939, he remustered and returned to Canada and graduated a Sergeant Pilot. Returning overseas, he joined No. 78 Squadron flying Halifaxes at Breighton, Yorkshire in 1943. Returning from bombing doodlebug (V1 rocket) pens on his 28th mission, they received a call for help from ground forces being held up by a German gun emplacement. They were on a low-level attack against the gun emplacement near Abbeville when they were shot down and killed.

Prior to enlisting, he served as a messenger for several years for the CPR telegraph office at Brandon. There is a stained glass window in St. Mary's Anglican Church in Brandon in memory of George and his older brother Frederick, RCAF, killed in action 6 December 1944. It was donated to the Church by their parents in Loving Memory of their only two children.

Stratford Island (54 D/7) in Stephens Lake was named after him in 1982.

Stratford, Pilot Officer **Gibson R.** of Pettapiece (J 7685). No. 6 Operational Training Unit, RCAF. He died 31 May 1942 at the age of 23 and is commemorated at the Runnymede Memorial in Surrey, England. He was the son of John P. and May R. Stratford of New Westminster, British Columbia. ***Stratford Bay*** (64 A/12) in Jensen Lake was named after him in 1995.

Stratton, Flight Sergeant **Keith R.** of Stonewall (R 140944). No. 30 Advanced Flying School. He died 28 April 1943 at the age of 20 and is commemorated at Bridgnorth Cemetery, Shropshire, England. He was the son of Mr. and Mrs. A. K. Stratton of Stonewall and the brother of Sergeant Ronald Stratton (next entry). His brother recalls (31 December 2001):

Keith was more serious and more handsome [than his brother Ronald; see entry]. His forte was in baseball. Keith also won the Governor General's medal in his final high school year and was the class valedictorian. As a pianist, he was not as accomplished as Grant, but passed on his skill at playing by ear to me, his younger brother. All his life, he teased me to distraction but was so much stronger than I that all my efforts to punish him were to no avail. It saddens me when I recall that on his last leave before going overseas, I had been doing some body building and challenged him to wrestle and was finally able to subdue him. He wrote me every week while overseas – interesting anecdotes on his adventures. I regret that when I learned of his death, in a fit of teenage frustration, I burned his letters. I have since found two and treasure them.

Stratton Lake (64 P/12), west of Nejanilini Lake was named after him in 1974. Stratton Island was named after his brother Ronald G. Stratton (next entry). A brother erected a cairn and plaque there in 1997.

Stratton, Sergeant **Ronald Grant** of Stonewall (R 59586). No. 10 Operational Training Unit, RCAF. He died 5 July 1941 at the age of 20 and is commemorated at Brookwood Military Cemetery in Surrey, England. He was the son of Mr. and Mrs. A. K. Stratton of Stonewall and the brother of Flight Sergeant Keith Stratton (previous entry). He was a member of the United Church choir, secretary of the Sunday School and assistant Boy Scout leader. His brother recalls (31 December 2001):

Grant carried clowning to a fault but usually had those around him in stitches. He was an excellent goal tender in soccer. He won the Governor General's medal in his final high school year and went on to achieve his teaching certificate in Normal School in Winnipeg before he joined the RCAF in 1940. As boys on the farm near Stonewall where we lived from 1935 to 1940, we formed a small orchestra with Grant at the piano, Keith on the guitar, the hired man with his mouth organ and me, the tag-along brother on the mandolin. This rather sorry group had the audacity to provide the music at several dances. We sure enjoyed it, but I can't speak for the dancers.

Stratton Island (64 P/12) in Stratton Lake was named after him in 1995. A brother erected a plaque there in honour of Keith and Ronald Stratton in 1997. The lake was named after his brother, Keith R. Stratton (previous entry).

Stringer, Able Seaman **Joseph** of North Kildonan (V 35344). HMCS *Valleyfield.* The *Valleyfield* was torpedoed and sunk by U-548 50 miles south of Cape Race, Newfoundland; 125 of her ship's company were lost. Able Seaman Stringer died 7 May 1944 at the age of 20 and is commemorated at the Halifax Memorial. He was survived by his foster-parents Charles and Caroline Collier of West Kildonan. The newsletter of the Knowles Home for Boys published a short article on him (n.d.) in which he is referred to as "Bill."

A Boy Named Bill

Bill was fourteen when he came to the Knowles Home for Boys. Some might call Bill a juvenile delinquent – if a youngster who never saw his father and was casually "given up" by his mother can be called delinquent. The school became a home to Bill, just about the first home he had known. He buckled down and did well. Not that he ever became letter perfect in keeping every last little rule. He was too full of life and pep to remember them all. But he did develop into a normal, healthy boy.

When the time came to leave the school he was found a job. He did not keep it long. You see, as soon as he became of age he joined the Navy. He loved the service. Ships and the sea became Bill's family. His home was still the Knowles School. He dropped in for a visit every time he came on leave. Bill used to write to the School to tell how he was getting along. In fact, he wrote from Halifax just before the *Valleyfield* sailed on her last trip. That was probably Bill's last letter. You see, he went down with the *Valleyfield.*

Bill was just one of the hundreds of boys who were given a chance to become good citizens at the Knowles School for Boys. Bill valued that chance. He valued it so much that he laid down his life in defence of the ideals which the School had taught him.

Stringer Lake (64 N/1), north of Egenolf Lake was named after him in 1972.

Striowski, Flying Officer **Albert G.** of Winnipeg (J 21814). No. 102 Squadron. He died 17 June 1944 at the age of 24 and is commemorated at the Runnymede Memorial in Surrey, England. He was the son of Julius and Matilda Striowski of Winnipeg and was survived by his wife Ethel Striowski. ***Striowski Lake*** (64 F/6), northwest of Wells Lake was named after him in 1994.

Strong, Trooper **Marvin** of The Pas (L 100854). Three Rivers Tank Regiment. He died 23 May 1944 at the age of 20 and is commemorated at the Cassino War Cemetery in Italy. He was the son of Elton E. and Hildred S. Strong of Moose Jaw, Saskatchewan. ***Strong Lake*** (64 A/4), northeast of Thompson was named after him in 1959.

Strood, Lieutenant **Percy S.** of Winnipeg. 1st Canadian Mounted Rifles (Saskatchewan Regiment). He died 8 October 1915 at the age of 34 and is commemorated at Ridge Wood Military Cemetery, Voormezeele, Heuvelland, West-Vlaanderen, Belgium. This native of Folkestone, Kent, England was the son of William and Elizabeth Strood of Folkestone and was survived by his wife Maud Strood of Winnipeg. Lieutenant Strood had extensive military experience with reserve and active regiments both in Canada and Great Britain when he enlisted in February, 1915. Prior to the war, he had been Inspector of Surveys in the Winnipeg Land Titles Office. ***Strood Lake*** (64 C/12), northeast of Laurie Lake was named after this World War I casualty in 1951.

Stroud, Pilot Officer **Claire D.** of Boissevain (J 90387). No. 192 Squadron. He died 25 May 1944 at the age of 22 and is commemorated at Heverlee War Cemetery, Leuven, Vlaams-Brabant, Belgium. He was the son of Douglas and Elsie Stroud of Boissevain. ***Stroud Lake*** (63 K/16), west of Wekusko Lake was named after him in 1973.

Stubbs, Sergeant **Kenneth E.** of Winnipeg (H 50503). South Saskatchewan Regiment. He died 7 April 1945 and is commemorated at the Holten Canadian War Cemetery in Holland. He was the son of Thomas H. and Violet Stubbs of Winnipeg. ***Stubbs Lake*** (53 L/14), north of Oxford Lake was named after him in 1979.

Stubbs, Pilot Officer **Stanley** St. George of Winnipeg (J 6021). No. 10 Squadron. He died 10 July 1942 at the age of 26 and is commemorated at Mount Pleasant Cemetery in St. John's, Newfoundland. He was the son of Lewis S. and Mary Stubbs of Winnipeg and was survived by his wife Elsie J. Stubbs of Winnipeg. ***Stubbs Island*** (64 K/16) in Burnie Lake was named after him in 1995.

Stubner, Flying Officer **Richard F.** of Rorketon (J 29635). No. 113 Squadron. He died 11 April 1944 at the age of 21 and is commemorated at Rabbit Walk Cemetery in Georgetown, Guyana. ***Stubner Lake*** (64 P/8), south of Caribou Lake was named after him in 1974.

Styne, Aircraftman 1 **Norman** of Stonewall (R 56981). No. 2 Service Flying Training School. He died 31 January 1941 at the age of 19 and is commemorated at Elmwood Cemetery in Winnipeg. He was the son of Horace and Edith E. Styne of Winnipeg. His sister writes (28 August 2001):

> Norman was born on September 18, 1921 in Binscarth, Manitoba. He grew up in Winnipeg and attended school there. He also sang in the St. Matthew's Church choir. He then moved to Balmoral, Manitoba.
>
> Norman trained at No. 2 Service Flying Training School. He did not get to see active service as the result of injuries received from a fall while working on a plane. Norman spent some time in Deer Lodge Hospital where he died on January 31, 1941.

Styne Lake (63 N/1), northwest of Wekusko Lake was named after him in 1970.

Sucharov, Flying Officer **Mortimer S.** of Winnipeg (J 37528). No. 428 Squadron. He died 2 December 1944 at the age of 29 and is commemorated at Bretteville-sur-Laize Canadian War Cemetery in Calvados, France. He was the son of Harry and Sophie Sucharov of Winnipeg. ***Sucharov Lake*** (64 J/11), west of Tadoule Lake was named after him in 1975.

Suddaby, Corporal **Gordon H.** of Souris (H 102740). Regina Rifle Regiment. He died 17 August 1944 at the age of 23 and is commemorated at Bayeux War Cemetery, Calvados, France. He was the son of Jerry and Lillian M. Suddaby of Souris and was survived by five brothers and a sister. His sister recalls (25 November 2001):

> He spent a lot of time as a young boy swimming, diving, and canoeing at the Souris River which was a favourite spot for the young people in the town. When winter came, he enjoyed playing goalie for one of the local hockey clubs as well as skiing. He also had a great love for music, the sound of the big bands such as Glen Miller and Tommy Dorsey and had a large collection of records and albums which he loved to play and enjoyed so much. He was employed at the Virden Air School before enlisting in May, 1942. He left for overseas on June 6, 1943 and arrived in France on D-Day where he died of wounds.

Suddaby Lake (64 J/6), southwest of Tadoule Lake was named after him in 1975.

Suffron, Lance Corporal **Gordon W.** of St. Vital (H 38526). Royal Canadian Corps of Signals. He died 8 August 1944 at the age of 22 and is commemorated at Bretteville-sur-Laize Canadian War Cemetery in Calvados, France. He was the son of Solon P. and Lillian L. Suffron of Winnipeg. ***Suffron Lake*** (64 K/12), northwest of Lac Brochet was named after him in 1972.

Sulyma, Private **Michael** of Dugald (H 10627). Royal Canadian Regiment. He died 6 September 1944 and is commemorated at Coriano Ridge War Cemetery in Italy. ***Sulyma Lake*** (64 K/10), northeast of Lac Brochet was named after him in 1972.

Sumner, Private **William J.** of Winnipeg (H 6815). Winnipeg Grenadiers. He died a prisoner of war 25 January 1943 at the age of 29 and is commemorated at the Sai Wan War Cemetery in Hong Kong. He was the son of Edward and Sarah E. Sumner of Winnipeg. ***Sumner Lake*** (64 J/3), northeast of Big Sand Lake was named after him in 1975.

Sumpton, Pilot Officer **John E.** of Pipestone (J 15454). No. 102 Squadron. He died 17 June 1942 at the age of 24 and is commemorated at the Runnymede Memorial in Surrey, England. He was the son of William and Nellie Sumpton of Pipestone, Manitoba. ***Sumpton Lake*** (64 H/7), south of Solmundsson Lake was named after him in 1995.

Sundeen, Private **Sven** (H 22282). Lincoln and Welland Regiment. He died 22 October 1944 and is commemorated at Bergen-op-Zoom Canadian War Cemetery in Holland. ***Sundeen Lake*** (53 M/5), north of Utik Lake was named after him in 1996.

Surrette, Flying Officer **Donald B.** of Winnipeg (J 15690). No. 142 Squadron. He died 13 July 1943 at the age of 21 and is commemorated at the Malta Memorial. His niece recalls (20 June 2001) that:

> Don went to Cecil Rhodes School and there is a plaque there today that hangs on the wall in honour of him. He was very shy and won awards for shot put, soccer and baseball. He was also an excellent artist. He thought the world of his mother, a stenographer who raised the three boys on her own. My uncle Bill saw him in the barracks in England and Don told his brother that he was dating a nurse. He went on approximately 20 missions and volunteered for his final mission. My uncle never saw him again. My dad received a letter from Don after he was shot down, congratulating him on his marriage to my mother.

His 10 year-old great niece Mandy wrote a story about him for a 1998 Remembrance Day presentation at her school (11 November 1998):

My Great Uncle Don

> A young man went off to fight in World War II. He flew a plane and would drop bombs. Other enemy planes would try to shoot at his plane. He didn't like killing people, but he was there to fight for freedom for his countrey.
>
> They told him his time in the war was over and that he could go home to be with his family. He had been there a long time.
>
> As a faver, the soldier told them he would make one more flight for them befor going home.
>
> On that assignment his plane was shot down over the ocean and he never made it home. They never found his body.
>
> The only things that went home were his belongings.
>
> His family were eagerly awaiting his retern and insed they got a telegram saying he would never be home agen. This is the true story of my Great Uncle Don, the great airman.

Surrette Lake (64 H/3), northwest of Settee Lake was named after him in 1995.

Sutcliffe, Lieutenant Colonel **John Louis R.** of Fort Garry. Winnipeg Grenadiers. He died a prisoner of war 6 April 1942 at the age of 44 and is commemorated at the Sai Wan War Cemetery in Hong Kong. He was the son of Benjamin and Sarah H. Sutcliffe and was survived by his wife Kathleen J. Sutcliffe (née Vincent) of Victoria, British Columbia and their two children. The news of his death elicited a lengthy memorial in the *Winnipeg Free Press*:

> Born in Elland, Yorkshire, England, ... he came to Winnipeg with his parents as a young boy. At 14, he started a military career which was to take him to France, India, Mesopotamia, Persia, Russia and the Far East. He first saw military service with the 18th Mounted Rifles, a militia unit, joining them at Portage la Prairie in the summer of 1912. At 16, when the last war broke out, he enlisted as a trooper with the Fort Garry Horse and went to England, joining the Royal Canadian Dragoons in 1915. After serving for one year in France and being wounded, he won a command in the Imperial Army with the 5th Worcestershire Regiment and was sent out to join the 9th "Woosters" in Mesopotamia in 1917 on the ill-fated troopship *Cameronia* which was sunk in the Strait of Messina while carrying 4000 troops. He first served with General Maude and later went to Baku as a member of the famous Dunster force, commanded by General Dunsterville, known to Kipling fans as "Stalky." After the Baku incident, he served with the army of occupation in Baku and Constantinople until November, 1919.
>
> Returning to Winnipeg to enter the provincial government service, he took an active part in the militia, joining the 10th Machine Gun Battalion in 1924 and rising to become company commander with the rank of major. In 1936, when the machine gun battalion merged with the Winnipeg Grenadiers, he became second in command of the new battalion. He was called to active service as second in command of the battalion on its mobilization in September, 1939.
>
> The cause of Colonel Sutcliffe's death is not revealed, a Canadian Press dispatch from Ottawa states. However, it is recalled that last Wednesday, in a return tabled in the House of Commons, T. L. Church (Con., Toronto-Broadview) was told that the food situation at Hong Kong and Kowloon, where Canadians are held, is unsatisfactory and that medical service and hospitalization there are inadequate. The staple diet of the prisoners and interned persons at Hong Kong and Kowloon was said to be soup and rice (*Winnipeg Free Press* 1942).

The official cause of death was later reported to have been beriberi. An editorial in the *Winnipeg Tribune* read:

> The whole community mourns the passing of Lieutenant Colonel Sutcliffe, who in civilian as well as military circles was widely known and highly respected. They are certain that to the last, in his own quiet, efficient way, he performed his duties with unflagging devotion and unhesitatingly sacrificed himself to the welfare of his men. Winnipeg will not forget a man, who from his 16th birthday onward was a gallant soldier, serving his King and country in many lands with a versatile intelligence and skill which unfailingly won the high esteem of his comrades (n.d.).

His daughter writes (1 November 2001):

> My father was a man of many interests: his family and church, gardening, drama (writing and producing plays) and of course, his regiment. It was difficult to put into a few words my love and respect for my father. The short time between the departure from Canada and the fall of Hong Kong left little time for letters written home or diaries.

Sutcliffe Lake (52 L/3), south of Crowduck Lake was named after him in 1973. The family used to vacation in this general area years before.

Sutherland, Flight Sergeant **Allan C.** of Winnipeg (R 196444). No. 207 Squadron. He died 8 July 1944 at the age of 27 and is commemorated at Haudricourt Communal Cemetery, Seine-Maritime, France. He was the son of George and Christine Sutherland and was survived by his wife Virginia B. Sutherland of Juliet, Illinois. ***Sutherland Point*** (53 N/11) on Whitefish Lake was named after him in 1995.

Sutherland, Corporal **John A.** of Flin Flon (H 9957). Lincoln and Welland Regiment. He died 27 April 1945 at the age of 28 and is commemorated at the Holten Canadian War Cemetery in Holland. He was the son of David R. and Ella S. Sutherland and was survived by his wife Catherine D. Sutherland of Winnipeg and their daughter. ***Sutherland Lake*** (64 I/12), south of Shethanei Lake was named after him in 1974.

Sutherland, Flight Sergeant **Peter** of Winnipeg (R 95344). No. 22 Operational Training Unit, RCAF. He died 14 September 1942 at the age of 21 and is commemorated at the Runnymede Memorial in Surrey, England. He was the son of William and Margaret Sutherland and was survived by his wife Florence C. Sutherland of Winnipeg. ***Sutherland Bay*** (53 L/16) in Semmens Lake was named after him in 1995.

Sutherland, Flight Sergeant **Roger J.** of Norwood Grove (R 177954). No. 692 Squadron. He died 17 December 1944 at the age of 26 and is commemorated at Brookwood Military Cemetery in Surrey, England. He was the son of Wilfred and Suzanne Sutherland and was survived by his wife Emilie Sutherland of Winnipeg. ***Sutherland Island*** (64 O/9) in Croll Lake was named after him in 1995.

Suttie, Captain **James M.** of Carberry (CDN 283). Royal Welsh Fusiliers, Military Cross. He died 22 October 1944 at the age of 28 and is commemorated at the Groesbeek Canadian War Cemetery in Holland. He was the son of John D. and Elizabeth Suttie of Wellwood, Manitoba. ***Suttie Lake*** (64 C/13), east of Reindeer Lake was named after him in 1947.

Swain, Rifleman **Arthur A.** of Selkirk (H 43099). Royal Winnipeg Rifles. He died 9 May 1945 at the age of 24 and is commemorated at Brookwood Military Cemetery in Surrey, England. He was the son of John and Flora Swain of Winnipeg. ***Swain Island*** (64 C/8) in Granville Lake was named after him in 1995.

Swanson, Flying Officer **Douglas M.** of Winnipeg (J 8153). No. 221 Squadron. He died 18 April 1943 at the age of 25 and is commemorated at the Malta Memorial. He was one of the five children of Mr. and Mrs. John J. Swanson of Winnipeg and was survived by his wife of five months Iris A. Swanson (née Roberts) of Nairobi, Kenya Colony. ***Swanson Lake*** (63 J/16), east of Setting Lake was named after him in 1972.

Swanson, Private **Edwin** of St. Martin (H 6675). Winnipeg Grenadiers. He died 22 December 1941 at the age of 34 and is commemorated at the Sai Wan Memorial in Hong Kong. He was the son of Adolph and Eileen Swanson and was survived by his wife Anna M. Swanson of St. Martin, Manitoba. ***Swanson Island*** (64 J/12) in Chornous Lake was named after him in 1989.

Swanton, Private **Elliott L.** of Brandon (H 63833). Cape Breton Highlanders. He died 13 September 1944 at the age of 21 and is commemorated at Coriano Ridge War Cemetery in Italy. He was the son of James and Susan E. Swanton of Transcona. ***Swanton Lake*** (64 I/2), east of North Knife Lake was named after him in 1978.

Swedberg, Rifleman **David R.** of Flin Flon (K 38570). Queen's Own Cameron Highlanders. He died 30 September 1944 at the age of 21 and is commemorated at the Calais Canadian War Cemetery in France. His sister recalls (17 July 1995):

> David was very quiet and shy and loved cars and motorcycles. He was born in Wadena, Saskatchewan on September 20, 1923 and came to Flin Flon with his parents and sister in 1926 and attended school there. He was active in sports and was a member of the Junior Bomber Hockey Club.
>
> Enlisting at Vancouver early in 1941, he trained there and at Prince Albert, Saskatchewan, Calgary, Alberta and Prince George, BC – arriving overseas in May of 1944. He was serving in France as a gunner in a tank. The following is an excerpt from a letter written to my mother by Padre A. J. Mowatt on November 28, 1944:
>
> "David was instantly killed while our troops were attacking the outskirts of Calais from the northeast. It was just before 2:00 PM on September 30th when his carrier suddenly hit a German mine. The explosion killed both lads. The rest of the attack went through successfully and Calais was freed early that evening."

He was the son of John E. and Inga Swedberg (née Nelson) of Flin Flon and was the brother of Flight Sergeant Dean Swedberg (next entry). ***Swedberg Lake*** (64 C/6), west of Granville Lake was named after him in 1979.

Swedberg, Flight Sergeant **Dean W.** of Flin Flon (R 177995). No. 1674 Heavy Conversion Unit, RCAF. He died 12 April 1944 at the age of 21 and is commemorated at Blacon Cemetery in Cheshire, England. This native of Washington, DC was survived by his parents Edward and Audrey Swedberg of Flin Flon and was the brother of Rifleman David Swedberg (previous entry). His sister recalls (17 July 1995):

> Dean was a happy-go-lucky tease. As kids growing up, I did not see that much of him. He was younger and had different friends than I had and as a result, the only picture that I can find is the enclosed newspaper clipping.
>
> He was killed along with eight other crew members ... in a Halifax MKII bomber aircraft. They were on a navigational training flight and had crashed in the northern Pennines, close to Cross Fell near Derbyshire, United Kingdom.
>
> The following is taken from a booklet which I received from Graham Doyle of Derbyshire, who tried to piece together information for the relatives. He then placed a memorial plaque with the names of all the crew at the crash site on May 1st, 1994. The article reads:
>
> "The accident report notes that the crew failed to request radio bearing fixes and, without knowing the circumstances or reliability of the navigational instruments, one can speculate that in poor weather conditions (there was a high wind) and in a vain effort to establish their whereabouts, a decision was made to fly below the cloud base and look for any recognizable features. In flying time, the aircraft was close to Longtown and was quite likely in direct radio contact with the control tower. However, BB310 did not have sufficient altitude to clear the summit of Little Dun Fell and crashed into the boulders of Blea Crag."

Swedberg Island (64 O/13) in Nueltin Lake was named after him in 1995.

Sweers, Rifleman **Everardus T.** of Winnipeg (H 104022). Royal Winnipeg Rifles. He died 4 July 1944 at the age of 42 and is commemorated at Beny-sur-Mer Canadian War Cemetery in Calvados, France. He was the son of Mr. and Mrs. Anthony W. Sweers. ***Sweers Lake*** (64 H/8), west of Hogg Lake was named after him in 1995.

Sweet, Chief Petty Officer **Charles E.** of Winnipeg (2563). HMCS *Athabaskan*. The *Athabaskan* was sunk by a torpedo from a German destroyer while operating in the English Channel. Her captain and 128 men were lost, 83 taken prisoner and 44 men rescued by HMCS *Haida*. Chief Petty Officer Sweet died 29 April 1944 at the age of 30 and is commemorated at Plouescat Communal Cemetery in Finistere, France. He was the son of William A. and Ethel M. Sweet of Plymstock, Devon, England and was survived by his wife Elsie Sweet. ***Sweet Lake*** (63 O/4), north of Wekusko Lake was named after him in 1970.

Sweet, Flying Officer **Lawrence T. E.** of Ostenfeld (J 14813). No. 427 Squadron. He died 30 March 1943 at the age of 23 and is commemorated at the Runnymede Memorial in Surrey, England. He was the son of Thomas E. and Violet C. Sweet of Ostenfeld, Manitoba. His sister writes (22 November 2001) Lawrence:

... [w]as born in Winnipeg on February 19, 1920. When he was eight years old, our parents moved to Monominto, Manitoba and lived there for five years, then moved to their homestead at Ostenfeld, Manitoba, about 35 miles east of Winnipeg. Lawrence worked for a short time at Canada Packers in St. Boniface, then enlisted in the Air Force at age 20. I think he was the gunner on a plane that was shot down over Germany, and none of the five men or the plane was ever found. His name is on a memorial statue in Oakbank and also in Regent's Park United Church in St. Vital.

Lawrence's passing was very devastating to his parents and grandparents. I have lost the names of the other boys, but they were sent to us and we did correspond for a while. Another brother, William also enlisted in the army and he returned safely. Both my brothers and their families still live in Ostenfeld.

Sweet Creek (52 L/5), which flows into Lac du Bonnet was named after him in 1973.

Swinton, Pilot Officer **Thomas R.** of Winnipeg (J 86402). No. 77 Squadron. He died 20 February 1944 at the age of 21 and is commemorated at the Runnymede Memorial in Surrey, England. He was the son of Thomas S. and Florence K. Swinton of Winnipeg. ***Swinton Lake*** (64 F/3), west of Goldsand Lake was named after him in 1994.

Switzer, Trooper **Cecil E.** of Fisher Branch (H 77570). 12th Manitoba Dragoons. He died 21 April 1945 at the age of 23 and is commemorated at the Holten Canadian War Cemetery in Holland. He was the son of William W. and Margaret A. Switzer of Fisher Branch, Manitoba. His sister recalls (27 November 2001):

Cecil was born in 1921 on his Dad's homestead where he resided until joining the army in 1941. He was the fourth child in a family of six siblings. He liked to hunt and trap, played baseball in the summer and hockey in the winter with his many friends and family. He was a very thoughtful and loving son and brother. Cecil loved tormenting and teasing his sisters. He farmed with his Dad and brother and had a great affection for horses.Cecil joined the army and was sent to the West Coast for almost one year of training. He returned home for a short time, then off to the East Coast in 1942 – his last visit home. From there, he was sent to England guarding the coast for a year, then to the front lines where he was wounded. Back to London to hospital and as he was convalescing there, he contracted diphtheria and remained in hospital for almost a year. While there, he met the love of his life, a CWAC from a town close to his home in Fisherton. They were engaged before he was once again sent back to the front lines where an explosion killed him when lighting a petrol stove in 1945.

Our mother saved all his letters and after she, my father and older brother passed away, the letters were passed on to me. They have been read by many of Cecil's nieces and nephews; they all feel they have got to know him in this way.

I, his sister Dorothy, went to Holland in 1995 with some fellow Veterans for the sole purpose of visiting his last resting place at the Holten Cemetery, Province of Cherysel. There I attended a memorial service. I returned later to place flowers and say a sad farewell, fifty years later. His family and friends will never forget this brave man.

Switzer Lake (64 I/16), south of the Caribou River was named after him in 1974.

Sykes, Pilot Officer **Robert F.** of Winnipeg (J 86398). No. 102 Squadron. He died 15 February 1944 at the age of 25 and is commemorated at the Berlin 1939 - 1945 War Cemetery in Brandenburg, Germany. He was the son of Arthur A. and Rachel M. Sykes of Winnipeg. ***Sykes Bay*** (64 N/10) in Tatowaycho Lake was named after him in 1989.

Symes, Flying Officer **George J. "Geordie"** of Winnipeg (J 28570). No. 106 Squadron. He died 1 November 1944 at the age of 22 and is commemorated at Bergen-op-Zoom Canadian War Cemetery in Holland. He was the second son of George and Louise Symes of Winnipeg. His sister writes (n.d.):

[He] joined the Air Force in the fall of 1939 – enlisted in the ground crew. In October, 1942, Geordie transferred to Air Crew. He took his Air Crew training at Belleville, Virden and Souris. On July 21st, 1943, he received his Pilot Wings and rank of Flying Officer. He proceeded overseas after graduation in the summer of 1943 (August 3rd).

Once in England, he was attached to an RAF Pathfinder Squadron where they flew Lancaster bombers. It was while attached to this squadron, Geordie and his crew were shot down ... over Hamburg, Germany. We (his family) were informed by the Canadian Government that Geordie was buried in a "collective grave" in a Canadian War Cemetery. We have since found out that he is buried in the Canadian War Cemetery in Bergen-op-Zoom, Holland. Here, each Canadian is identified by an individual headstone. This cemetery is cared for by the townspeople of this small village and is a marvellous tribute to our Canadian war Heroes.

Symes Island (53 E/12) in Bigstone Lake was named after him in 1984.

Symons, Flying Officer **Edwin G.** of Winnipeg (84907). No. 455 Squadron, RAF. He died 12 February 1942 at the age of 34 and is commemorated at the Runnymede Memorial in Surrey, England. He was the son of Ralph T. and Ethel Symons and was survived by his wife Hilda Symons. ***Symons Rapids*** (64 N/1) in the North Seal River was named after him in 1995.

Szumski, Rifleman **Mike L.** of Winnipeg (H 10709). Royal Winnipeg Rifles. He died 29 March 1945 at the age of 24 and is commemorated at the Groesbeek Canadian War Cemetery in Holland. He was the son of Joseph and Petronella Szumski. ***Szumski Lake*** (64 K/3), northeast of Reindeer Lake was named after him in 1987.

Szwec, Corporal **Ivan J.** of Dauphin (H 8143). Lake Superior Regiment. He died 10 November 1944 at the age of 20 and is commemorated at Brookwood Military Cemetery in Surrey, England. He was the son of William and Jessie Szwec of Dauphin. ***Szwec Lake*** (64 O/4), north of Egenolf Lake was named after him in 1975.

A Warrant Engineer of the HMCS Uganda at El Alamein Cemetery in Egypt 2 February 1945.
Courtesy of the National Archives of Canada (PA-166966).

T

Tagg, Engine Room Artificer 3 **James** of Winnipeg (V 24237). HMCS *St. Croix*. The *St. Croix* was torpedoed and sunk by U-305 south of Iceland while escorting Convoy ON.202. Five officers and 76 men were rescued by HMS *Itchen*, but only one of these survived the loss of the *Itchen* two days later. See VanSickle, Ordinary Seaman Harold A. for additional information. ERA Tagg died 20 September 1943 at the age of 43 and is commemorated at the Halifax Memorial. He was the son of Robert D. and Janet Tagg and was survived by his brother McLean Tagg of Glasgow. ***Tagg Creek*** (54 B/12), which flows northwest into Machichi Lake was named after him in 1964.

Taggart, Warrant Officer 2 **Garnett E.** of Brandon (R 86212). No. 502 Squadron. He died 26 March 1943 at the age of 21 and is commemorated at St. Columb Major Cemetery in Cornwall, England. He was the son of Raoul M. and Helen E. Taggart of Brandon. ***Taggart Lake*** (64 P/5), south of Nejanilini Lake was named after him in 1974.

Tait, Rifleman **Andrew** of Butler, Manitoba (L 105060). Regina Rifle Regiment. He died 4 July 1944 and is commemorated at Bretteville-sur-Laize Canadian War Cemetery in Calvados, France. ***Tait Bay*** (53 L/5) in Kakwusis Lake was named after him in 1995.

Tait, Captain **James Edward**. 78th Battalion (Manitoba Regiment), Victoria Cross, Military Cross.

> For most conspicuous bravery and initiative in attack [Battle of Amiens]. The advance having been checked by intense machine-gun fire, Lt. Tait rallied his company and led it forward with consummate skill and dash under a hail of bullets. A concealed machine gun, however, continued to cause many casualties. Taking a rifle and bayonet, Lt. Tait dashed forward alone and killed the enemy gunner. Inspired by his example, his men rushed the position, capturing twelve machine guns and twenty prisoners. His valorous action cleared the way for his battalion to advance. Later, when the enemy counter-attacked our positions under intense artillery bombardment, this gallant officer displayed outstanding courage and leadership, and, though mortally wounded by a shell, continued to aid and direct his men until his death (*London Gazette*, 24 September 1918).

He died 11 August 1918 at the age of 31 and is commemorated at Fouquescourt British Cemetery in France. He was the son of James B. and Mary J. Tait of Maxwelltown, Scotland and was survived by his wife Jessie S. A. Tait of West Arcadia, California. Captain Tait had worked on the original surveys for the Hudson Bay Railway and the CNR named a railway point ***"Jetait"*** (64 C/3) south of Lynn Lake after him in 1954.

Taite, Trooper **Cameron R.** of Winnipeg (H 101039). Three Rivers Tank Regiment. He died 6 October 1943 at the age of 18 and is commemorated at the Moro River Canadian War Cemetery in Italy. Like many other Canadians, he misrepresented his age on his attestation papers when he enlisted two years earlier; another Canadian casualty buried at Moro River was only 16. This is the largest Canadian war cemetery in Italy.

> What happened to Canadian troops during the winter of 1943 - 1944 has gone down as one of the most significant – and deadly – battles Canadians have ever fought. There are 1375 Canadians buried in this port city on the Adriatic Sea coast, but the headstones do not begin to tell the horrors of a battle that degenerated into house-to-house fighting throughout the city. Sam Witt, a Shilo resident who fought with the Royal Canadian Artillery at Ortona, said it was like a gang fight, but with heavy artillery. "Basically our guys would go into the top of a house, work their way down into the basement and then crash into the wall of the next house and work their way up that one," Witt recalls. "And you do that for an entire block" (*Winnipeg Free Press* 11 May 1994).

Trooper Taite was the son of John M. and Ellen A. Taite of Winnipeg. He wrote several letters home to his brother:

> Dear Ivan: I just received your letter dated the 16th and am very pleased to hear from you. So you're going to join the army eh? Well I want to tell you this much. When you go down and sign up, make sure you tell them that you want to go into the Canadian Armoured Corps and also tell them that you have two brothers in now and that you want to get with them. And I'll give you just one good tip about this man's army and that is "Don't try to buck it." Because if you do, you're not going to get anywhere. (Don't take this as an insult to you).
>
> Well I received the parcel OK as you probably know by now. We got a picture taken of the whole Gunnery Wing and as soon as I get it, I'll send it home. Well I certainly enjoyed myself in Toronto. But I guess you've heard about it by now. On my last weekend, I went to Barrie with Tom. We had a fairly good time. Well if you go to that party and drink that good old Manitoba beer, remember me because this beer down here is rank poison and I can't touch the stuff.
>
> And as far as Stalingrad goes, it's still holding out by to-nite's *Toronto Star*. Well Ivan, as far as overseas goes, it's either there or home again. I guess I'll say so long for now, hoping to hear from you soon. Your ever-loving brother, Cameron (16 September 1942).
>
> Dear Ivan: Well I am glad you had such a swell time at the party. It's too bad the car broke down. Guess what Ivan? Gracie Fields is appearing here in Camp Borden at the Lee Hall in person to-nite. I am going to see her if I can get in. They're broadcasting the show over a national hook-up, so if you've got the radio on to-nite (Sunday) you will hear her from here.
>
> I guess that was some parade, eh? I was in the one that they had in Barrie. There were 2000 of us altogether. Don't go fixing up any beds yet as I don't know when I'll be home. My furlough isn't due Until December 9 and I can't get it any sooner (1 November 1942).

Taite Lake (64 J/4), southwest of Tadoule Lake was named after him in 1975.

Takvor, Pilot Officer **Jack** of Winnipeg (J 16678). No. 260 Squadron. He died 19 December 1942 at the age of 20 and is commemorated at the Alamein Memorial in Egypt. He was the son of Mr. and Mrs. Archig Takvor of Winnipeg. ***Takvor Lake*** (63 O/4), north of Wekusko Lake was named after him in 1970.

Talbot, Rifleman **James S.** of Winnipeg (H 41252). Royal Winnipeg Rifles. He died 6 June 1944 at the age of 23 and is commemorated at Beny-sur-Mer Canadian War Cemetery in Calvados, France. According to his brother (21 December 1995):

> I can recall one incident that happened in the summer of 1938. It was the Depression and my brother Jimmy as he was called then seemed to have more spending money than was normal at the time. So my father asked him where he was getting it. He said that he made it on bets that he could swim from the icehouse (railroad) near the point where the Assiniboine and Red rivers meet to the ice breakers in Fort Garry. My father said "if you can do that I'll give you five dollars." So a date was set, father had borrowed a rowboat from a friend and off they went. Well without going into too much detail, father got some very nasty blisters on his hands and Jimmy got the five dollars.
>
> There were three girls and four boys in our family and Jimmy would put his arms outstretched and carry the six of us, apparently without any trouble. This ... does bring back some recollections to me of a brother that I was very proud of before as well as after the war.

Talbot Bay (63 I/7) in Lawford Lake was named after him in 1995.

Talbot, Private **John** of St. James (H 17133). Princess Patricia's Canadian Light Infantry. He died 16 October 1943 at the age of 21 and is commemorated at the Moro River Canadian War Cemetery in Italy. He was the son of John and Alice A. Talbot of St. James. His brother recalls (19 October 2001):

My brother John (Jack) and I were identical twins. We were in the same platoon. I was a few miles away when Jack was killed. Our Company Commander told me. It was hard to believe it had happened. I attended the temporary grave service.

People called us twins because they could not tell us apart. We kept a lookout for our sister and our two younger brothers during the school years. Jack and I were very active in sports – baseball, golf, hockey and horseback riding. We had our differences, but deep down we were very close. Fifty-eight years have passed. Rest in Peace. Always a Patricia.

Talbot Island (63 I/2) in Molson Lake was named after him in 1995.

Talocka, Flying Officer **Joseph P.** of Winnipeg (J 35641). No. 426 Squadron. He died 3 February 1945 at the age of 26 and is commemorated at Brookwood Military Cemetery in Surrey, England. He was one of the four children of John and Irene Talocka of Winnipeg. His sister recalls (6 June 1995):

He was born and educated in Winnipeg. He was a member of Holy Ghost Roman Catholic Parish and attended King Edward and Isaac Newton schools. He was very interested in hockey and hard ball and played for the Norwood Seniors Men's hard ball league. As there was no employment in Winnipeg, he left for Malartic, Quebec to work in the mines. From there, he enlisted in the Air Force in 1942. [He] went overseas in January, 1944. He was killed in action after returning from Germany. Their damaged plane crashed in England.

Talocka Lake (64 P/10), east of Nejanilini Lake was named after him in 1974.

Tanack, Private **Nicklas** of Winnipeg (M 56517). Lake Superior Regiment. He died 5 August 1944 at the age of 28 and is commemorated at Bretteville-sur-Laize Canadian War Cemetery in Calvados, France. He was the son of Harry and Caroline Tanack of Toronto. His brother writes (3 March 1996):

Nicklas was born in Winnipeg [and] grew up in La Broquerie. His father died when he was 10 years old. [He] left the farm to support his family (the Depression years) [and] went to Alberta to find work in the oil fields. So that would account for him enlisting in the province of Alberta. He left behind three brothers and two sisters.

Tanack Lake (53 M/11), southeast of Ransom Lake was named after him in 1996.

Tanner, Pilot Officer **John C.** of Winnipeg (J 43174). No. 145 Squadron. He died 6 July 1944 at the age of 30 and is commemorated at the Goose Bay Joint Services Cemetery in Newfoundland. He was the son of Charles A. and Laura W. Tanner of Winnipeg and was survived by his wife Edna M. Tanner of Winnipeg and their daughter Pamela. His brother recalls (20 November 2001):

My brother had completed his overseas tour and upon returning to Canada was stationed at Summerside, PEI with 145 Ventura Squadron flying coastal sweeps in search of U-boats. After refuelling at Goose Bay, observers to the Ventura lift-off have stated that the aircraft lost power in one engine at approximately 250 feet of altitude, fell to the runway and exploded. All on board died.

I have my brother's log book, maps of England and Europe and his training manuals. If he had lived out the war, I am sure he would be flying today; it was his great love. John attended Victory School and Wesley College in Winnipeg.

Tanner Island (64 O/12) in Shannon Lake was named after him in 1995.

Tanner, Pilot Officer **Walter A.** of Winnipeg (J 3764). No. 37 Squadron. He died 13 December 1941 at the age of 24 and is commemorated at the Alamein Memorial in Egypt. He was the son of William A. and Emma B. Tanner of Toronto. ***Tanner Bay*** (64 N/13) in Wakula Lake was named after him in 1995.

Tanuck, Pilot Officer **Gordon S.** of Winnipeg (J 90291). No. 420 Squadron. He died 8 June 1944 at the age of 19 and is commemorated at the Runnymede Memorial in Surrey, England. He was the son of William and Frances Tanuck of Winnipeg. ***Tanuck Lake*** (64 N/13), southeast of Kasba Lake was named after him in 1974.

Tapp, Private **Percy W.** of Brandon (H 46112). Lake Superior Regiment. He died 4 August 1944 at the age of 24 and is commemorated at the Bayeux Memorial in Calvados, France. He was the son of Percy and Ida Tapp of Brandon. His sister recalls (19 February 1996) that their parents:

... resided in Souris for two years where Mr. Tapp and his brother Bassett Tapp had a grocery store. When Bassett went back to England in 1922, Percy Tapp and family moved back to Brandon. Percy received his education in Brandon, going to King George School and Earl Haig Junior High. He worked on a farm for a year at $5.00 a month, then worked for a coal and wood dealer for 25 cents an hour. Percy enlisted with the Lake Superior Regiment in 1940.

Tapp Lake (64 F/3), north of Vandekerckhove Lake was named after him in 1994.

Tarbuth, Captain **Lyle T.** of Winnipeg. Winnipeg Grenadiers. He died 19 December 1941 and is commemorated at the Sai Wan Memorial in Hong Kong. He was survived by his wife Mildred J. Tarbuth and their unborn daughter. In 1993, the former Mrs. Tarbuth and her daughter visited the Sai Wan Memorial. She recalls (8 June 1995):

Captain Tarbuth and I were married in Jamaica. The Winnipeg Grenadiers were stationed there for six months after we were married, then recalled and sent to Hong Kong. It happened just after that as you know. Our daughter, Lyle Mildred was born the following January 11, 1942. As she never knew her father, you can imagine what this means to her.

Tarbuth Creek (64 K/6), which flows northeast into Cann Lake was named after him in 1972.

Tario, Private **Lloyd G.** of Austin (H 204479). Queen's Own Cameron Highlanders. He died 23 July 1944 at the age of 26 and is commemorated at the Bayeux Memorial in Calvados, France. He was the son of John and Mary Tario of Austin, Manitoba. ***Tario Lake*** (64 J/6), northeast of Big Sand Lake was named after him in 1975.

Tarnausky, Private **John J.** of Treherne (H 10044). Princess Patricia's Canadian Light Infantry. He died 16 December 1944 and is commemorated at Ravenna War Cemetery in Italy. ***Tarnausky Lake*** (64 J/6), southwest of Tadoule Lake was named after him in 1975.

Tarzwell, Pilot Officer **Herbert C.** of Grandview (J 93803). No. 419 Squadron. He died 29 December 1944 at the age of 23 and is commemorated at the Reichswald Forest War Cemetery in Germany. He was the son of Norman and Annie Tarzwell of Grandview. His niece writes (31 October 2001):

> Herbert Chester Tarzwell was born July 22, 1921 in Grandview, Manitoba. He completed his schooling in Tamarisk and worked around home until 1940 when he went to Rosetown, Saskatchewan (where his sister lived) looking for work. He also worked at different places in Alberta before travelling to Winnipeg to sign up as a pilot. He trained in Regina, Calgary and Edmonton and was sent overseas in 1941. He was killed in a mission over Essen.

Tarzwell Lake (64 P/16), northwest of Caribou Lake was named after him in 1975.

Tass, Warrant Officer 1 **Jack** of Winnipeg (R 106362). No. 82 Operational Training Unit, RCAF. He died 15 May 1944 at the age of 29 and is commemorated at Stonefall Cemetery in Yorkshire, England. He was the son of Eli and Pauline Tass and was survived by his wife Theresa Tass of Prince Albert, Saskatchewan. His niece writes (28 November 2001):

> Jack was the fourth of five children, six years younger than my father. They all loved music, loved to gather around the piano singing and playing, each one impatiently waiting his or her turn at the bench. Young Jack was also passionate about baseball and threw a truly wicked fastball.
>
> Although I was really too young to remember him when he died, two of my most poignant memories concern his death. I see my father sitting at my bedside, holding my hands, telling me that Uncle Jack was gone. I doubt that I understood what he meant, but I know he was so very sad. Years later, I heard this story. Their plane was crossing the Channel, returning to England. Near the coast, they were shot down by "friendly fire."

Tass Lake (64 H/7), north of Solmundsson Lake was named after him in 1995.

Tawns, Sergeant **Robert F.** of Winnipeg (H 12030). Royal Canadian Artillery. He died 15 June 1943 at the age of 29 and is commemorated at Brookwood Military Cemetery in Surrey, England. He was the son of Henry and Elizabeth I. Tawns of Winnipeg and was survived by his wife Eileen E. Tawns of Winnipeg. ***Tawns Creek*** (54 C/9), which flows north into Pannebaker Creek was named after him in 1964.

Taylor, Flight Sergeant **Donald A.** of Headingley (R 191422). No. 44 Squadron. He died 22 June 1944 at the age of 22 and is commemorated at Jonkerbos War Cemetery in Holland. He was the son of Rupert and Alice Ann Taylor of Headingley. ***Taylor Creek*** (64 B/7), which flows west into Rat River was named after him in 1995.

Taylor, Private **Edward S. J.** of Brandon (H 46089). Lake Superior Regiment. He died 25 February 1941 at the age of 40 and is commemorated at Brandon Cemetery. He was survived by his mother Ada Taylor of Birmingham, England and by his wife Marie E. Taylor of Brandon. ***Taylor Rapids*** (53 L/6) in the Wapawukaw River was named after him in 1995.

Taylor, Flight Sergeant **Herman J.** of Giroux (R 95405). No. 61 Squadron. He died 19 August 1942 at the age of 20 and is commemorated at the Runnymede Memorial in Surrey, England. ***Herman Taylor Creek*** (54 E/8), which flows east into Owl River was named after him in 1995.

Taylor, Flight Lieutenant **John R.** of Winnipeg (J 10787). No. 425 Squadron. He died 31 March 1944 at the age of 23 and is commemorated at Durnbach War Cemetery in Bavaria, Germany. He was the son of John C. D. and Bessie Taylor of Winnipeg. ***John Taylor Island*** (54 D/7) in Stephens Lake was named after him in 1995.

Taylor, Pilot Officer **Kenneth S.** of Winnipeg (83701). No. 71 Squadron, RAF, American Flying Cross (Pilot Officer Taylor was born in the United States). He died 9 August 1941 at the age of 21 and is commemorated at Brookwood Military Cemetery in Surrey, England. ***Kenneth Taylor Lake*** (64 N/4), west of Quasso Lake was named after him in 1995.

Taylor, Sergeant **Leslie Lawson** of Winnipeg (R 95172). No. 13 Elementary Flying Training School. He died 8 November 1942 at the age of 20 and is commemorated at Elmwood Cemetery in Winnipeg. He was the son of Leslie and Lillian Alberta Taylor of St. Boniface and was survived by his wife Dorothy W. Taylor of St. Boniface.

> He was born January 2, 1922 at Winnipeg. Leslie attended Isaac Brock and Daniel McIntyre schools. He thoroughly enjoyed visiting his cousin Roy Davie's farm in the Dumfries district during the summer vacation. It was a great thrill for a kid from the city. Prior to his enlistment with the RCAF, Leslie worked for a biscuit company in Winnipeg. Leslie was stationed at No. 13 Elementary Flying Training School, St. Eugene, Ontario where he was the only casualty when a Fleet Finch aircraft engaged in an instrument instructional flight crashed three miles southwest of St. Benoit, Quebec (Pittman n.d.).

Taylor Peninsula (64 C/16) on Barrington Lake was named after him in 1995.

Taylor, Private **Stanley E.** of Portage la Prairie (H 50654). Lincoln and Welland Regiment. He died 28 February 1945 at the age of 30 and is commemorated at the Groesbeek Memorial in Holland. He was the son of Daniel and Sarah Taylor of Portage la Prairie. ***Taylor Hill*** (53 K/16), east of Edmund Lake was named after him in 1995.

Taylor, Lieutenant **Thomas E.** of Winnipeg. 12th Manitoba Dragoons. He died 23 August 1944 at the age of 29 and is commemorated at Bretteville-sur-Laize Canadian War Cemetery in Calvados, France. He was the son of Francis W. and Emily Taylor and was survived by his wife Lillian M. Taylor of Winnipeg. Commemorative Certificates for Lieutenant Taylor and seven fellow Manitoba Dragoons were issued c/o Herbert Nicholson, MM who explains:

> In 1946, the 12th Manitoba Dragoons returned from Europe and with money from our Canteen Fund furnished two wards in the Children's Hospital, with a promise that as long as our Association lasts, we would continue to support the Children's Hospital Fund. Since 1946, we have contributed $1000.00 every year with donations received from the members. Also, we had a Plaque placed on the Hospital's 2nd floor, with names of our fallen comrades on one side and on the other side, the names of the departed comrades who have since passed away. This was done with the idea that one day the Regiment will again be together.
>
> Now this brings me to my request, that the Association's approximately 350 members, would after all your efforts to find next-of-kin, would like to become family and have the Name Certificate placed on the wall in the

Children's Hospital in trust that if a next-of-kin comes forward the Certificate would be handed over to them (16 December 1998).

Taylor Esker (64 I/12), east of Tadoule Lake was named after Lieutenant Taylor in 1995.

Teasdale, Private **Gowan C.** of Winnipeg (H 6338). Winnipeg Grenadiers. This native of Durham, England died 20 December 1941 at the age of 28 and is commemorated at the Sai Wan Memorial in Hong Kong. He was survived by his wife Marjorie Teasdale of Winnipeg. A year later, his wife received the following letter:

> Dear Mrs. Teasdale: The official lists of the Canadian prisoners of war at Hong Kong, furnished by the Japanese Government though the International Red Cross, have been coming in at intervals by cable during the past month. Some little time has now elapsed since the last list was received and it would appear likely that few, if any, more names will be reported.
>
> The next-of-kin of all the known prisoners of war have now been officially advised, and I regret very much to see that the name of your husband, of whom nothing has been heard since the fall of Hong Kong, is not among them. Every effort is being made to obtain definite information regarding those who are still missing and the International Red Cross has been asked to obtain all available particulars about them from the Japanese Government. You will be advised promptly as soon as there is anything to report.
>
> I am sorry indeed that I cannot give you better news at this time, or offer any encouragement that might help to relieve your anxiety, but if there are any questions in your mind regarding which you would care to write for me, please do not hesitate to do so. Yours very truly, Lieutenant Colonel F. W. Clarke (5 December 1942).

His service record was later amended to indicate that he had been "Killed outright" at Mount Butler after having been taken prisoner at 10:00 AM. ***Teasdale Bay*** (63 N/6) in Kississing Lake was named after him in 1978.

Teichrib, Private **William** of Manitou (H 20848). South Saskatchewan Regiment. He died 15 October 1944 at the age of 23 and is commemorated at Schoonselhof Cemetery in Antwerp, Belgium. He was the ninth of the 10 children of Jacob and Sarah Teichrib of Morden. According to his older brother Henry (12 October 2001):

> Bill was a sturdy young man, about five feet ten inches, rosy complexion, hazel eyes. He was wild, but a good guy; everything had to be moving. You could hear his loud, sharp voice across a crowded dance floor. He had a lot of friends and girlfriends. Our father died when Bill was a little boy and mother remarried and moved to Saskatchewan. He stayed with our older sister and her husband on their farm at Snowflake, Manitoba. He did farm work and received five years of school there, played hockey, football, baseball, skied and hunted. Later on, he stayed at our older brother's farm at Helston, Manitoba near Gladstone.
>
> In the summer of 1941, Bill enlisted in the army at Portage la Prairie. Said he wanted to see the world and when the war was over, he would be a farmer on the parcel of land his father left him. He was sent overseas in the fall of 1941 and learned the trade of shoemaker while stationed in England. In the summer of 1944, he was sent to France. By the fall, Bill was in combat in Belgium. His Canadian Army unit along with British and Polish units liberated the Scheldt Estuary in the autumn of 1944, after bitter fighting, thus opening the port of Antwerp. His letters home read that Canada was made of gold and was the best place to live. My daughter went to his grave site in 1998. She brought back photos and movie film so we could visit his grave site in some way too.

Teichrib Lake (52 L/14), south of Long Lake was named after him in 1982.

Teichrobe, Private **Isaac** of Altona (H 87539). Highland Light Infantry. He died 12 October 1944 at the age of 31 and is commemorated at Adegem Canadian War Cemetery, Maldegem, Oost-Vlaanderen, Belgium. He was the son of Jacob and Mary Teichrobe of Altona, Manitoba. ***Teichrobe Lake*** (64 K/7), southeast of Lac Brochet was named after him in 1972.

Temple, Sergeant **Albert J.** of Winnipeg (R 100369). No. 22 Operational Training Unit, RCAF. He died 7 September 1942 at the age of 27 and is commemorated at Bicester Cemetery in Oxfordshire, England. He was the son of John and Zita Temple of Winnipeg. His brother recalls (16 November 2001):

> As my brother, Albert was the oldest of his siblings, I have many fond memories of him. He was born on August 30, 1915. I have spent the past five hours re-reading his letters home and a large box full of sympathy cards and letters – all of them emphasizing his generosity. His gift to me was my first tennis racket during the depression of the 1930s. Albert wrote to Mother once a week and occasional letters to myself (Victor) and our sister Alice as well.
>
> Albert earned a Master's degree in chemistry from the University of Manitoba and moved to Manchester, UK to begin his career. He made some very good friends there and they were his happiest years. He loved to read (eating an apple at the same time) and also enjoyed playing chess.
>
> In 1940, Albert quit his job and returned to Winnipeg to enlist. He graduated from the RCAF as a Sergeant-Observer, being both a navigator and a bomber. His plane crashed of unknown causes. I often wonder about the happiness he could have added to our lives had he survived. I and my remaining sisters Alice and Rita remember him with love and sadness that we could not grow old together.

His niece adds (16 November 2001):

> But as I was growing up, [my mother] spoke of her brother Albert with almost a reverence. Albert and my father spent an evening in England together just before Albert's plane crashed. According to my Dad, Albert was a very kind, quiet man and their evening was spent talking about family back home and hoping the war would soon be over. Albert sent my mother a navy blue dress from England. She kept it all these years and gave it to me eight years ago (when I turned 50) to be handed down through the generations as a symbol of family, love, togetherness and to reinforce the fact that we must continue to struggle to keep our country free for generations to come.

Temple Lake (64 F/2), east of Dunsheath Lake was named after Sergeant Temple in 1988.

Tenklei, Company Sergeant Major (Warrant Officer 2) **Edward S.** of Carman (L 27835). Regina Rifles, Military Medal. He died 5 April 1945 at the age of 26 and is commemorated at the Holten Canadian War Cemetery in Holland. He was the son of John and Jessie Tenklei of Regina. ***Tenklei Lake*** (64 C/13), east of Reindeer Lake was named after him in 1947.

Tester, Trooper **Ernest** of Gladstone (H 77751). 12th Manitoba Dragoons. He died 5 March 1945 at the age of 22 and is commemorated at the Groesbeek Canadian War Cemetery in Holland. He was the son of George and Mae Tester. His sister-in-law writes (8 December 1945):

> He was the third born in a family of two girls and four boys. Prior to the war, he spent all of his life in Gladstone where he attended school, was a member of the United Church and the Boy Scouts group – all activities that he thoroughly enjoyed.

Ernest was a gentle and kind young man. He was very devoted to his family and had many friends. His keen interest in flowers, birds and animals was well known to all and he was affectionately nick-named "Nature Boy" by his family.

Before the war, Ernest worked at Slade's Greenhouse in Gladstone, and in 1941 he joined the active service. After training in Canada, he sailed for England with the 12th Manitoba Dragoons and saw action through France, Belgium, Holland and Germany beginning in July, 1944. On March 5, 1945 he made the supreme sacrifice near the Black Forest in Germany.

Tester Lake (64 P/9), north of Caribou Lake was named after him in 1974.

Tétrault, Flying Officer **J. O. A. Remi** of Transcona (J 23910). No. 425 Squadron. He died 23 May 1944 at the age of 26 and is commemorated at Le Mans West Cemetery in Sarthe, France. He was the son of Joseph O. and Caroline Tétrault of Transcona. His sister-in-law writes (24 April 1998):

[He] was born in Transcona on 1 October 1917. He enlisted 1939-40 and, since he had to help support the family, being the depression era, he was unable to go on and further his education. As far as sports go, they tell me that he loved to play hockey, but this was with neighbours and friends on outdoor rinks – not professional.

It was a very sad blow to our family when Remi died; his mother was indeed devastated. Later on, another son, Flight Lieutenant Joseph Wilfred Tétrault died along with 15 other airmen off San Juan, Puerto Rico – so much tragic loss for one family.

Tétrault Lake (52 L/6), northeast of Lac du Bonnet was named after Flying Officer Tetrault in 1973.

Tetroe, Flying Officer **Charles W. "Bud"** of Selkirk (J 39172). No. 1659 Conversion Unit, RCAF. He died 24 October 1944 at the age of 28 and is commemorated at Harrogate (Stonefall) Cemetery in Yorkshire, England. He was one of the four sons of Frank and Helen Tetroe of Selkirk. His half-brother writes (4 March 1995):

He attended school in Selkirk. Prior to the war, he worked in a mine at Favourable Lake, Ontario. He joined the Air Force in 1942 [taking] his training at Macdonald, Manitoba and at Mossbank, Saskatchewan. His father, Frank Tetroe was killed in the First World War. My father served with him in the 109th Battalion from Tyndall, Manitoba. After my father returned home, he married Frank's widow (my mother) in 1919. Bud's full brother, Frank Tetroe served with the Army Service Corps, 3rd Division.

Tetroe Lake (64 B/1), southwest of Baldock Lake was named after him in 1972.

Thachuk, Gunner **John** of Arbakka (H 59517). Royal Canadian Artillery. He died 26 August 1944 at the age of 24 and is commemorated at Bretteville-sur-Laize Canadian War Cemetery in Calvados, France. His sister recalls (16 May 2001):

He was born on a homestead in Arbakka to Domka [Doris] Thachuk. His father Gora [George] Thachuk would take the new-born names into the town of Vita where they were placed in the Hall of Records. John attended school in Arbakka until the 8th grade and then he went to Vita for the high school or till 12th grade living with a family. He would take a train from Vita to Pembina, North Dakota where his sister Helen lived and made plans for further education. Helen arranged for his tuition with room and board in Fargo. He enrolled in electrical engineering and was an excellent student. He was called into the Canadian Army in his second year of college and went into the Army Corps of Engineers. He was sent overseas almost immediately.

John Thachuk was known for being kind, always happy and a giving person. All of his friends described him as "a good man." He always had a smile for everyone and learned to play the violin. John and all his brothers Nick, Steve and Bill would get together on the front porch and play guitars, violins, drums and zither. They always wanted their sisters to dance. His sisters were Florence, Nellie, Mary, Verna and Helen. In their early years, everyone walked for miles to their house for these musical evenings on the weekends.

Thachuk Lake (64 N/3), northeast of Lac Brochet was named after Gunner Thachuk in 1972.

Thagard, Flight Lieutenant **Victor J.** of Winnipeg (J 8392). No. 260 Squadron. He died 20 December 1942 at the age of 22 and is commemorated at the Alamein Memorial in Egypt. He was the second of the three sons of Christian P. and Almeria Thagard (née Brabant) of St. James. His step-sister writes (11 December 1997):

Vic was brought up in Winnipeg's West End (Valour Road). He attended Isaac Brock School and Gordon Bell High School. Summers were spent at the family cottage at Victoria Beach where Vic and his brothers Ray and Gordie became excellent swimmers, saving a doctor's wife and family from drowning. Vic was the first of the brothers to join up followed shortly by Ray and Gordie. He went missing at El Alamein. Ray and Gordie returned to civilian life but have since passed away.

Thagard Lake (64 P/2), southeast of Nejanilini Lake was named after him in 1978.

Thibeault, Private **Cecil H.** of Dauphin (H 20952). Queen's Own Cameron Highlanders. He died 17 August 1944 and is commemorated at Bretteville-sur-Laize Canadian War Cemetery in Calvados, France. ***Thibeault Lake*** (64 I/16), northeast of North Knife Lake was named after him in 1974.

Thibedeau, Pilot Officer **Roy F.** of Pine Falls (J 90043). No. 50 Squadron. He died 31 March 1944 at the age of 23 and is commemorated at Durnbach War Cemetery in Bavaria, Germany. He was the son of Fred and Ruby Thibedeau and was survived by his wife Vera Thibedeau of Echo Bay, Ontario and their two year-old son. He writes (26 May 1998):

My Father was born in Sault Ste. Marie, Ontario on September 8, 1920. He married my Mother there and I was born on July 27, 1941. I believe he worked at several different jobs and I think his last employment was as a cab driver. Everything I have been told is that he was very well liked and was very good at anything he set out to do.

I am not sure of the exact date when he joined the Air Force. However, I did find out he fibbed about his age and joined the army first. He was posted to guard duty on the canal on St. Mary's River at Sault Ste. Marie. Needless to say, as soon as his Mother found out, she went to the post and had Roy removed from duty. He then joined the Air Force as soon as he could. He arrived in Toronto around December 28, 1942. He had hoped to be a pilot, but ended up as a tail gunner on a Lancaster aircraft. Roy left Canada for England around the fifth of August, 1943. I gained this information from a letter he wrote my Mother. I am lucky enough to have most of his letters. He sent my Mother a telegram on August 13, 1943 to tell her he had arrived safely in England.

His last letter to my Mother was on March 28, 1944. He wrote this letter in a locker room waiting for notice to take off on a bombing mission. The next official notice my Mother had was that my Father and his aircraft were missing during a mission over Nuremberg on the night of March 30/31, 1944. Some of the crew did survive, but I am not sure how many. I do know his Mother was in contact for awhile with his pilot and his pilot's family. This family lived in England.

My Mother told me the one wish my Father had was that if anything did happen to him and she remarried, he wanted her to try and have me keep the name Thibedeau. I was the last male in the family. My Mother was lucky and married a wonderful man who insisted I keep the same name. My Stepfather and Mother had three children and my Stepdad treated me as one of his own.

Thibedeau Lake (64 P/8), north of Caribou Lake was named after Pilot Officer Thibedeau in 1995.

Thickins, Private **Robert W.** of Ashern (722118). 78th Battalion (Manitoba Regiment). He died 13 April 1917 of wounds sustained at the Battle of Vimy Ridge. He was 20 years of age and is commemorated at Boulogne Eastern Cemetery, Pas de Calais, France. He was the son of John B. and Eleanor J. B. Thickens (née Green) of Ashern. His niece recalls (16 April 1996):

Robert's father ... was born in England and joined the British Army in India where he met and married Eleanor Green whose father was a tea planter. They had three children: Robert (Bob), Jessie and Sydney. Bob and Jessie were only two years apart and very close chums; in her eyes he could do no wrong. Syd was three years younger than Jessie. As retirement came near, John applied for work in several countries and was promised a job in Winnipeg. The position was filled and they stayed here until Jessie recovered from pleurisy and pneumonia, planning to return to England. Bob got a job with The Bay.

John's brother who farmed in Virden came to visit and talked him into going on a homestead in Ashern. It was a grim life for them but they still enjoyed it until Bob joined up. His death was hard on them all but especially his mother. She had a nervous breakdown, being so far from her family and losing Bob.

Thickins Lake (64 F/5), east of Carriere Lake was named after this World War I casualty in 1996.

Thirde, Flight Sergeant **William** of Hartney (R 80227). No. 233 Squadron. He died 1 November 1942 at the age of 21 and is commemorated at the Runnymede Memorial in Surrey, England. He was the son of Mr. and Mrs. J. R. Thirde of Hartney, Manitoba. His sister writes (17 March 1996):

Bill was born in Hartney [and] received his education there. He played minor hockey, was a member of Scouts, the local band and Army Cadets. He was on his first mission when the plane went down near Gibraltar. His body was never recovered from the Mediterranean. No. R 80227 is precious to us.

Thirde Lake (64 I/7), northeast of North Knife Lake was named after him in 1974.

Thomas, Pilot Officer **Arthur E. C.** of Winnipeg (J 88633). No. 106 Squadron. He died 28 June 1944 at the age of 21 and is commemorated at Dieppe Canadian War Cemetery in Seine-Maritime, France. He was the son of David C. and Mary J. Thomas of Winnipeg. ***Thomas Peninsula*** (63 P/15) on Witchai Lake was named after him in 1995.

Thomas, Private **Bertrum J.** of Albert, Manitoba (H 10481). Queen's Own Cameron Highlanders. He died 30 March 1945 and is commemorated at the Groesbeek Canadian War Cemetery in Holland. He was the brother of Private Clifford Thomas (next entry). His sister recalls (6 December 2001):

The youngest of six boys in a family of 12, Bert was great to have around. He was always happy, always joking and always ready to help with any chores at hand. In his teens, he worked in a bush camp, was a fisherman and a hunter as most young men were in his day. With so many brothers and sisters at home, the family was poor. Bert never hesitated to share his earnings or his bounty with not only his family, but his friends too. Bert was on the front lines in Germany just two weeks before he met his death.

Thomas Hill (64 I/1), east of Condie Lake was named after him in 1995.

Thomas, Private **Clifford** of Traverse Bay (H 75233). Winnipeg Grenadiers. He died a prisoner of war 9 December 1942 and is commemorated at the Sai Wan War Cemetery in Hong Kong. He was the brother of Private Bertrum Thomas (previous entry). His sister recalls (6 December 2001):

The second youngest of six boys in a family of 12, Clifford was fiercely proud and patriotic. In order to get into the army, you had to be 18 years of age. He lied about his age and was angry when he got found out and was released. About a month went by before he tried again with a different battalion. He was taken prisoner on Christmas Day in Hong Kong and died of starvation. He was very close to his younger brother Bert and worked with him in the bush camp as a fisherman and a hunter.

Thomas Point (64 O/14) on John Osborne Lake was named after him in 1995.

Thomas, Gunner **Edward I.** of Holmfield (H 103528). Royal Canadian Artillery. He died 17 May 1944 at the age of 21 and is commemorated at the Cassino War Cemetery in Italy. He was the son of Albert and Nellie Thomas of Holmfield, Manitoba. He was shipped overseas in July, 1943 and took part in the North African, Sicilian and Italian campaigns. He had been a farmer before he enlisted in November, 1942. ***Thomas Narrows*** (64 O/8) in Nejanilini Lake was named after him in 1995.

Thomas, Sergeant **George Stanley "Sonny"** of Neepawa (H 19436). Queen's Own Cameron Highlanders. He died 15 December 1944 at the age of 28 and is commemorated at the Groesbeek Canadian War Cemetery in Holland. He was the eldest son of George and Beatrice Thomas and was survived by his wife of 11 months Bettie Thomas (née Maddock) of Grimsby, Lincolnshire, England. His sister-in-law recalls (10 March 1997):

Stanley graduated from Neepawa Collegiate after which he was employed with the CNR and the Neepawa Power Plant. He received many ribbons at the local track meets for racing and high jump. He played the cornet in the Neepawa Town Band and played hockey with the high school team.

He enlisted within days of the declaration of war and was posted overseas the following year. In 1942, he enjoyed the distinction of leading the group that penetrated furthest inland during the ill-fated Dieppe raid. He was forced to return to the beach, by which time all the rescue ships had departed. He began swimming the Channel back to England; he and a few others were picked up before they arrived there. Ironically, his death two years later in Holland was accidental.

Thomas Bay (64 O/1) in Munroe Lake was named after him in 1995.

Thomas, Rifleman **Hector O.** of Beaconia (H 10854). Royal Winnipeg Rifles. He died 5 July 1944 and is commemorated at Beny-sur-Mer Canadian War Cemetery in Calvados, France. ***Hector Thomas Lake*** (54 E/16), east of Bradshaw Lake was named after him in 1995.

Thomas, Private **James O.** of Hodgson (K 51503). Seaforth Highlanders of Canada. He died 2 May 1945 at the age of 33 and is commemorated at the Holten Canadian War Cemetery in Holland. He was the son of Harry and Margaret Thomas of Hodgson, Manitoba. ***Thomas Esker*** (64 I/12), east of Tadoule Lake was named after him in 1995.

Thomas, Pilot Officer **Robert** of Winnipeg (J 86485). No. 433 Squadron. He died 14 May 1944 and is commemorated at Stonefall Cemetery in Yorkshire, England. Pilot Officer Thomas was killed when he fell out of a window of the Griffin Hotel in Leeds, Yorkshire (Allison and Hayward 1991). ***Thomas Rapids*** (64 P/8) in Caribou Lake was named after him in 1995.

Thomas, Rifleman **William D.** of Elphinstone (H 40697). Royal Winnipeg Rifles. He died 8 June 1944 at the age of 36 and is commemorated at Beny-sur-Mer Canadian War Cemetery in Calvados, France. He was the son of Edward J. and Mary A. Thomas of Winnipeg and was survived by his wife Anne Thomas (née Orr) of Winnipeg and London. Later information received by his family indicated that "he was shot as he lay in bed after having been taken prisoner" (*The Winnipeg Tribune* n.d.). ***Thomas Island*** (64 H/11) in Small Lake was named after him in 1995.

Thomasberg, Flight Sergeant **Balder** of Winnipeg (R 162252). No. 57 Squadron. He died 2 December 1943 at the age of 21 and is commemorated at the Runnymede Memorial in Surrey, England. He was the son of George and Hilda Thomasberg of Norwood. ***Thomasberg Lake*** (64 I/8), northeast of North Knife Lake was named after him in 1974.

Thomasson, Private **Thomas** of Baldur (H 6778). Winnipeg Grenadiers. He died a prisoner of war 14 October 1942 at the age of 24 and is commemorated at the Sai Wan War Cemetery in Hong Kong. He was survived by his father in New Westminster, British Columbia and by his sister Miss Helga Isfjord of Winnipeg. ***Thomasson Lake*** (64 J/3), northeast of Big Sand Lake was named after him in 1975.

Thompson, Lieutenant **Arthur P.** of Souris. Fort Garry Horse. He died 28 September 1944 at the age of 26 and is commemorated at Bergen-op-Zoom Canadian War Cemetery in Holland. He was the son of Arthur W. and Ethel I. Thompson of Winnipeg. Arthur ***Thompson Lake*** (64 O/9), northeast of Croll Lake was named after him in 1995.

Thompson, Lieutenant Colonel **Ernest P. "Tommy"** of Winnipeg. Queen's Own Cameron Highlanders, Distinguished Service Order.

> This youthful officer was 23 when, during the Canadian infantry brigade crossing of the South Beveland canal last October, he found himself acting as brigade commander when the latter became a casualty. It was for his leadership in this crossing – vital to the success of capturing the peninsula and freeing the port of Antwerp – that Colonel Thompson was awarded [by Field Marshal Montgomery] the Distinguished Service Order (*The Winnipeg Tribune* n.d.).

He died 26 February 1945 at the age of 24 and is commemorated at the Groesbeek Canadian War Cemetery in Holland. He was the son of ex-Alderman Frederick G. and Stella H. Thompson of Winnipeg and was survived by his wife Jean R. Thompson of Kirkcaldy, Fife, Scotland. His wife and sister write (24 October 2001):

> Growing up in Winnipeg, Tommy attended Lord Roberts and Kelvin high schools. He enjoyed paddling, camping, hunting and his involvement with the cadet corps of the Queen's Own Cameron Highlanders. He had completed pre-medical courses and had only recently received notice of acceptance to Manitoba Medical School when war was declared. Tommy enlisted with the Camerons and went overseas in December, 1940. He took part in the Dieppe raid in 1942, was reported missing and later turned up wounded. He received the Distinguished Service Order in October, 1944 when as Lieutenant Colonel of his regiment, he also assumed command of the 6th Brigade and was successful in directing the Brigade in a difficult and hazardous crossing of the South Beveland Canal. His widow came to Canada in 1946 and remains here.

Thompson Point (54 K/7) on the west shore of Hudson Bay south of Cape Churchill was named after him in 1948.

Thompson, Gunner **Ernest R.** of Stonewall (H 59937). Royal Canadian Artillery. He died 8 June 1944 at the age of 24 and is commemorated at Beny-sur-Mer Canadian War Cemetery in Calvados, France. He was born Ernest Robert Hebert and orphaned in Peace River, Alberta. He was adopted by Grace Thompson, a schoolteacher from Virden and raised on a farm near Stonewall. He was survived by his adoptive parents Mr. and Mrs. John Korski of Winnipeg and by his wife Annie A. Thompson of Napanee, Ontario. He had enlisted at the age of 20. ***Ernest Thompson Lake*** (64 B/6), northeast of Pemichigamau Lake was named after him in 1995.

Thompson, Trooper **Harold W.** of Winnipeg (H 27769). Royal Canadian Armoured Corps. He died 15 April 1945 at the age of 26 and is commemorated at St. John's Cemetery in Winnipeg. He was survived by his wife Irene Thompson of Winnipeg. Harold ***Thompson Lake*** (64 C/3), northwest of McKnight Lake was named after him in 1995.

Thompson, Private **James C.** of Whitemouth (H 2678). Royal Canadian Ordnance Corps. He died 29 January 1942 at the age of 31 and is commemorated at Whitemouth Cemetery in Manitoba. He was the son of James H. and Amelia Thompson of Oxford, Nova Scotia and was survived by his wife Charlotte B. Thompson of Winnipeg. ***James Thompson Lake*** (53 K/15), north of Atikamaykus Lake was named after him in 1995.

Thompson, Lance Corporal **James H.** of Swan River (H 20754). Royal Canadian Corps of Signals. He died 19 December 1943 at the age of 30 and is commemorated at the Moro River Canadian War Cemetery in Italy. According to his sister (20 November 1997):

> Jim was born in Strasbourg, Saskatchewan, the second child in a family that eventually increased to six. We lived at Strasbourg until 1927 when failing crops necessitated a series of moves – Indian Head, Sintaluta, Valeport. The Dirty Thirties with drought, dust storms and a grasshopper blight, forced many to seek areas farther north where conditions were somewhat better. Jim had his schooling in Saskatchewan in various schools, as we all did because of so much moving. He had Grade 11 standing, but did not have the opportunity of Grade 12.
>
> In the fall of 1933, he hired on with a neighbour, Mr. H. Niven, who was vacating his farm and trying to take his necessary machinery stock and household goods to the Swan River Valley, to locate on a farm at Minitonas where the drought had not struck. In 1934, our family headed in the same direction and our Dad took over the operation of a dairy farm. Jim helped for a time with the delivering of bottled milk. It was probably

in 1935 that he went to Ontario and worked in the woods near Dryden. Then for 1936 and 1937, he worked for a market gardener named Vanderhorst at Fort Frances. Our father's health was failing as a result of asthma and resulting heart complications, so Jim came back to Swan River to be a help to our parents. He operated a market garden in the area so he was able to live with our parents and help support them. Mother had taken up bee-keeping again (her occupation in Ontario before her marriage) to help in their support, so Jim was able to help in that too.

When war broke out in 1939, I think he enlisted very soon after. I think he first enlisted in the Queen's Own Cameron Highlanders, but soon transferred to the Signal Corps. Our youngest brother Robert also enlisted as soon as he was old enough. Both boys were home to Swan River for Christmas of 1940, the last time we saw Jim alive. Both went overseas in 1941, but were reunited at the Canadian camp at Aldershot. Our father died in October of 1941 though he had expressed the hope of living to see his two boys come home.

Jim was wounded on December 18, 1943 at Ortona and sent back to a hospital. Mother got news of his wounding promptly, but it was three weeks later that she got the news that he had died on December 19. The long lapse had raised her hopes that he was recovering, so it was a rude blow for a poor widow. I have often wondered how such a delay could have occurred.

James Thompson Point (53 M/1) on Semmens Lake was named after him in 1995.

Thompson, Flying Officer **John W.** of Winnipeg (J 28977). No. 619 Squadron. He died 27 September 1944 at the age of 22 and is commemorated at the Runnymede Memorial in Surrey, England. He was the second child of Arthur and Annette Thompson (née Supleve). His niece (6 April 1998) describes him as an:

... honours student who graduated from St. Paul's College, Winnipeg [and] worked at the Liquor Commission. [He] enlisted in the RCAF [and] trained as a navigator in Portage la Prairie. [He] enjoyed golf and played hockey at St. Paul's College.

John Thompson Lake (53 M/12), northwest of High Hill Lake was named after him in 1995.

Thompson, Lance Corporal **Lavern R.** of MacGregor (H 17166). Princess Patricia's Canadian Light Infantry. He died 21 December 1944 at the age of 24 and is commemorated at Coriano Ridge War Cemetery in Italy. He was the son of Bertram R. and Mabel I. Thompson and was survived by his wife Sarah E. Thompson of Winnipegosis. ***Thompson Peninsula*** (64 I/3), on North Knife Lake was named after him in 1989.

Thompson, Flight Sergeant **Ralph L.** of Glenboro (R 58545). No. 408 Squadron. He died 15 December 1941 at the age of 26 and is commemorated at the Runnymede Memorial in Surrey, England. He was the son of Albert E. and Rose E. Thompson of Burnaby, British Columbia. ***Ralph Thompson Lake*** (53 L/3), north of Fairy Rock Lake was named after him in 1995.

Thompson, Pilot Officer **Russell B.** of Winnipeg (J 86841). No. 158 Squadron. He died 3 June 1944 at the age of 23 and is commemorated at Ecquetot Communal Cemetery in Eure, France. He was the son of Harold B. and Edith M. Thompson of Winnipeg. ***Thompson Esker*** (64 B/9), south of Uhlman Lake was named after him in 1995.

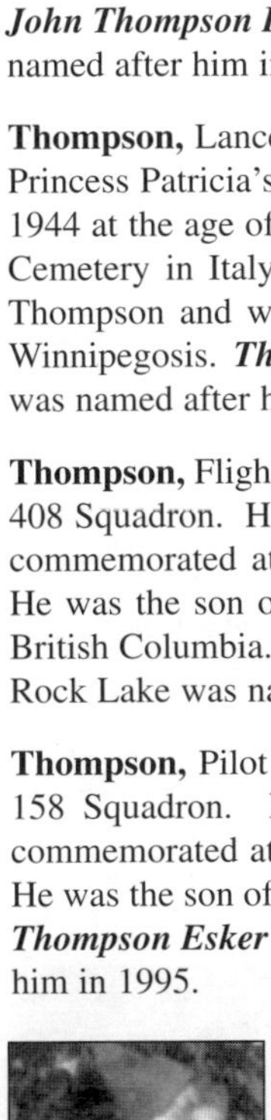

Thompson, Private **William Archie** of Sylvan (H 102809). Black Watch (Royal Highland Regiment) of Canada. He died 26 August 1944 at the age of 20 and is commemorated at Bretteville-sur-Laize Canadian War Cemetery in Calvados, France. Private Thompson had originally enlisted with the Royal Winnipeg Rifles, but was later transferred. He was one of the five children of Stanley and May Thompson of Sylvan, Manitoba. His sister writes (8 November 2001):

Archie grew up in a farming community north of Winnipeg and attended a one-room school house for his education. He loved picnics and enjoyed baseball. Following school, he worked on the family farm until he joined the Canadian Army in 1942. Shortly after the time that Archie was killed in France, back at the family farm his father got his brothers up at 0500 hrs. to start threshing at the neighbour's. His father had dreamed that night that Archie had been killed and he was unable to sleep further. At 1600 hrs. that afternoon, while they were still threshing, word was brought to them of Archie's death. We lost a son and a brother too early in his life.

Thompson Rapids (64 B/8) in the Pecheponakun River was named after him in 1995.

Thompson, Flight Sergeant **William C.** of Winnipeg (R 162116). No. 1658 Conversion Unit, RCAF. He died 4 January 1944 at the age of 21 and is commemorated at Blacon Cemetery in Cheshire, England. He was the son of George A. and Frances Thompson of Winnipeg. ***Thompson Hill*** (64 B/5), east of Granville Lake was named after him in 1995.

Thomsen, Gunner **Carl C.** of Sylvan (H 60706). Royal Canadian Artillery. He died 14 August 1944 and is commemorated at Bretteville-sur-Laize Canadian War Cemetery in Calvados, France. ***Thomsen Island*** (53 L/13) in Oxford Lake was named after him in 1979.

Thomsen, Trooper **Edward** of Winnipeg (H 26120). Fort Garry Horse. He died 8 August 1944 at the age of 27 and is commemorated at Beny-sur-Mer Canadian War Cemetery in Calvados, France. He was the son of Christian and Catherine Thomsen of Winnipeg. ***Thomsen Lake*** (64 F/2), southeast of Wells Lake was named after him in 1989.

Thomson, Lance Corporal **Alexander** of Stonewall (H 19216). Seaforth Highlanders of Canada. He died 14 December 1943 at the age of 26 and is commemorated at the Moro River Canadian War Cemetery in Italy. He was the son of Walter J. and Ann Thomson (née Milne) of West Kildonan. ***Alexander Thomson Lake*** (54 E/4), southwest of Embleton Lake was named after him in 1995.

Thomson, Flight Lieutenant **Alexander George** of Balmoral (J 14493). No. 162 Squadron. He died 3 April 1945 at the age of 33 and is commemorated at the Runnymede Memorial in Surrey, England. He was the son of David and Jane Thomson of Winnipeg. ***George Thomson Island*** (64 I/16) in the Seal River was named after him in 1995.

Thomson, Pilot Officer **James H.** of Winnipeg (J 9862). No. 426 Squadron. He died 27 April 1942 at the age of 21 and is commemorated at the Kiel War Cemetery in Germany. He was the son of William and Ellen J. Thomson of Winnipeg. James ***Thomson Lake*** (63 P/4), west of Sipiwesk Lake was named after him in 1995.

Thomson, Trooper **Robert M.** of Fort Garry (H 77104). 12th Manitoba Dragoons. He died 9 August 1944 and is commemorated at Bretteville-sur-Laize Canadian War Cemetery in Calvados, France. He was survived by his wife Mary Thomson of Fort Garry. Commemorative Certificates for Trooper Thomson and seven fellow Manitoba Dragoons were issued c/o Herbert Nicholson, MM who explains:

In 1946, the 12th Manitoba Dragoons returned from Europe, and with money from our Canteen Fund furnished two wards in the Children's Hospital, with a promise that as long as our Association lasts, we would continue to support the Children's Hospital Fund. Since 1946, we have contributed $1000.00 every year, with donations received from the members. Also, we had a Plaque placed on the Hospital's 2nd floor, with names of our fallen comrades on one side and on the other side, the names of the departed comrades who have since passed away. This was done with the idea that one day the Regiment will again be together.

Now this brings me to my request, that the Association's approximately 350 members, would after all your efforts to find next-of-kin, would like to become family and have the Name Certificate placed on the wall in the Children's Hospital in trust that if a next-of-kin comes forward, the Certificate would be handed over to them (16 December 1998).

Robert Thomson Creek (54 E/10), which flows south into Deer River was named after him in 1995.

Thomson, Pilot Officer **Thomas A.** of Rivers (J 88701). No. 426 Squadron. He died 28 January 1944 at the age of 23 and is commemorated at the Runnymede Memorial in Surrey, England. He was the son of Hugh and Caroline B. Thomson and was survived by his wife Hazel L. Thomson of Brandon. ***Thomson Lake*** (64 G/16), southeast of Chipewyan Lake was named after him in 1995.

Thordarson, Sapper **Harold G.** of Sinclair (H 36655). Royal Canadian Engineers. He died 13 July 1945 at the age of 26 and is commemorated at Sinclair Cemetery. He was the eldest of the five sons of Einar and Jonina Thordarson of Sinclair, Manitoba. His brother recalls (18 December 1996):

He was born May 14th, 1919 when [the family] lived north of Tilston, Manitoba. The family moved south of Tilston on what was known as the Crow farm. Harold started school there at the Beverly School. In the spring of 1930, the family moved north of Tilston on the Miller farm where Harold went to Crescent School and finished Grade 8.

Harold worked on the farm at home. After a couple of years, he started taking correspondence on motor mechanics. He went to Chicago to take his practical training in the fall of 1940. While he was there, his army call came to report for the thirty-day training as required at that time. The call was deferred to a later date. On his return home in late November, he was notified to report for his training in Brandon in January, 1941. After this, he remained at home until spring. At that time he went to Winnipeg looking for a job as a mechanic. Due to his age (22) he was unable to get a job. On May 16th, 1941, he joined the Royal Canadian Engineers. He took his training in Winnipeg, Camp Petawawa and Camp Borden in Ontario. He came home on a four-day furlough in October and later in October landed in England. He was stationed there until the summer of 1943 when he was moved to Italy where he was building and repairing bridges between the firing lines.

Due to illness, he was sent back to England and then back home to Canada. They landed in Canada around New Year's, 1945. On arriving in Winnipeg, he was detained for treatment. The diagnosis was that he had leukaemia. After a month of treatments he was able to come home for a few weeks. But his illness grew progressively worse, then took its toll on July 13.

Thordarson Island (53 E/16) in Island Lake was named after him in 1996.

Thordarson, Sergeant **Thordar** of Winnipeg (R 110768). No. 3 Bombing and Gunnery School, RCAF. He died 17 July 1941 at the age of 32 and is commemorated at Brookside Cemetery in Winnipeg. He was the son of Goodman and Gudlang Thordarson of St. James and was survived by his wife Eleanor Thordarson of Winnipeg. ***Thordarson Lake*** (64 O/15), east of Nueltin Lake was named after him in 1975.

Thoresen, Lieutenant **Raymond F.** of St. Vital (CDN 659). Seaforth Highlanders of Canada. He died 14 January 1945 and is commemorated at the Groesbeek Canadian War Cemetery in Holland. ***Thoresen Lake*** (52 L/6), east of Lac du Bonnet was named after him in 1973.

Thorinson, Rifleman **Sigfus L.** of Arborg (H 6764). Royal Winnipeg Rifles. He died 30 March 1945 and is commemorated at the Groesbeek Canadian War Cemetery in Holland. ***Thorinson Lake*** (64 O/14), east of Nueltin Lake was named after him in 1995.

Thorkelsson, Private **Harold** of Ashern (H 59029). Royal Canadian Army Service Corps. He died 3 October 1944 at the age of 29 and is commemorated at the Adegem Canadian War Cemetery in Belgium. He was the son of Halldor and Gudrun Thorkelsson of Ashern. ***Thorkelsson Lake*** (64 H/1), north of Waskaiowaka Lake was named after him in 1963.

Thornber, Flying Officer **Ernest Garfield** of Winnipeg (J 13792). No. 487 Squadron. He died 3 May 1943 at the age of 27 and is commemorated at Amsterdam New Eastern Cemetery, Holland. He was the son of Ernest J. and Laura M. Thornber of St. Vital. His sister recalls (n.d.):

He was a wonderful person and a great shock to our family when we lost him. He loved to play the guitar and entertain the family. He believed in good health and exercise and also did weight lifting. He was very interested in Morse Code and sat for many hours on what I believe he called a wireless radio. Later, he went up north to work for Canadian Airways and he was a radio operator. I remember Gods Lake as one of his work places.

Thornber Lake (63 P/3), east of Sipiwesk Lake was named after him in 1968.

Thornber, Sergeant **Fred A.** of Winnipeg (902836). No. 91 Squadron, RAF. He died 1 July 1941 at the age of 20 and is commemorated at Folkestone New Cemetery in Kent, England. He was the son of Hugh R. and Annie Thornber and was survived by his foster-daughter Eliza J. Usher of Hawick, Roxburghshire, Scotland. ***Thornber Island*** (63 P/5) in Wintering Lake was named after him in 1996.

Thorndycraft, Pilot Officer **Leonard A.** of Winnipeg (J 92417). No. 10 Squadron. He died 4 March 1945 at the age of 23 and is commemorated at Stonefall Cemetery in Yorkshire, England. He was the son of Harold C. and Amy A. Thorndycraft of Winnipeg. ***Thorndycraft Lake*** (64 J/11), west of Tadoule Lake was named after him in 1975.

Thorne, Private **Clifford** of Elphinstone (H 18007). Princess Patricia's Canadian Light Infantry. He died 20 September 1944 and is commemorated at Coriano Ridge War Cemetery in Italy. ***Thorne Lake*** (64 I/6), northwest of North Knife Lake was named after him in 1974.

Thorsteinson, Corporal **Norman K.** of Winnipeg (H 52136). Royal Canadian Army Service Corps, Mentioned in Dispatches. He died 26 March 1945 at the age of 31 and is commemorated at Bergen-op-Zoom Canadian War Cemetery in Holland. He was the son of Thorsteinn D. and Lilja M. Thorsteinson (née Lifman) and was survived by his wife Sigurros J. "Rosa" Thorsteinson (née Johnson) of Winnipeg. His niece writes (19 January 1998):

Norman's paternal grandparents ... had come from Iceland in 1876 and settled on a homestead in the Husavik area, a few miles south of Gimli, naming the farm Hvammi. Previous to his enlistment, Norman worked on the farm and also worked as a fisherman on Lake Winnipeg. In 1940, he enlisted with the RCASC, going overseas in 1941. He was killed in Holland as the unit was setting up camp for the night when a land mine exploded.

Thorsteinson Island (64 C/7) in Granville Lake was named after him in 1995 and Thorsteinson Lake (64 H/3), northeast of Gauer Lake was named after him in 1948.

Thorsteinson, Lance Corporal **Rurik W.** of Winnipeg (H 102861). Fort Garry Horse. He died 8 August 1944 at the age of 22 and is commemorated at Bretteville-sur-Laize Canadian War Cemetery in Calvados, France. He was the son of Adalstein and Kristin Thorsteinson of Winnipeg. His sister-in-law writes (15 May 1997):

... one of Rurik's favourite hobbies was bicycle racing for which he won many awards. He was also a member of the Rifle Club. He was a very happy and jovial person and we have nothing but fond memories of him.

Prior to enlisting, he had been employed by the Pioneer Grain Company. ***Thorsteinson Bay*** (64 N/1) in Minuhik Lake was named after him in 1995.

Thould, Warrant Officer 2 **Thomas F.** of Winnipeg (R 116497). No. 434 Squadron. He died 28 August 1943 at the age of 21 and is commemorated at Durnbach War Cemetery in Bavaria, Germany. He was the son of Frank and Ada M. Thould of Winnipeg. His bomb-aimer, Ken Reid, recalls their final mission:

It was getting dusk as our bomber roared down the runway. Takeoffs and landings required teamwork between Tommy and myself. When the control tower cleared our aircraft for takeoff, he would give the OK to open throttles. I called out air speeds as we roared down the runway. On lift-off my job was to lift the undercarriage and adjust flaps. He was doing the flying, but he needed both hands on that control column and his feet on the rudders. One miscue and it would be curtains for all of us, with those bombs and the fuel below.

As we climbed, the brown hues of earth gradually changed to total darkness. The only lights were the flashing beacons and the odd flash of gunfire ahead over the French coast. Our course took us straight down the centre of England to a point called Beachy Head on the south coast. As we approached the point, we were ahead of schedule so we did what we called a "dog's leg" to lose a few minutes. It turned out to be a mistake.

Over France, one of our engines started to lose power. We did everything we could, but slowly we were falling behind in the last wave of the attack, arriving a few minutes late. The Jerries were out in force. Oh, how we could have used those few minutes now!

When we entered the city's airspace [Nuremberg], we could see it had been well hit. Smoke was rising high from the fires below. I located our target ahead. We were suddenly aware no flak was coming up and the searchlights were not trying to cone us. We made our bombing run and dropped our bombs.

Now the searchlights were turned down on the high rising smoke. This made the smoke a giant screen for the night fighters above to pick out the bombers below. Almost immediately there was a fighter on our right side, then another on the port side. Our gunners each covered a fighter, who stayed just out of range. Each wanted the other to move in a cat and mouse game. While we tried desperately to get out of the city and into the night to have a better chance, those night fighters were just as determined to get the stragglers of this bombing raid. Just when our chances seemed good, a third fighter came up from below, firing shells through our bomber.

The aircraft shuddered as the shells ripped through the fuselage, then into the wing, and finally ricocheted off the outboard engine. As the tracers bounced off the motor, they came back toward the nose of the aircraft where I was positioned, then headed out into the night in front of the bomber. That was close enough. The outer gas tank was now burning furiously.

Tommy put the bomber into a steep dive while the flight engineer activated the fire extinguishers and managed to get the fire under control. By now we were out of the target area and we thought we had a reasonable chance of getting away. All the crew were heard from except Ray, our rear gunner. Perhaps his intercom had been knocked out in the attack. We still had three motors and the plane under control. We continued various evasive action while the Jerry fighters were equally determined for a kill.

Suddenly, cannon shells ripped through our aircraft from almost the same angle as before, from below the port side. This time the shells went through the centre of the aircraft, hitting the large gas tanks and bouncing off the inboard motor on the same side as before. Now both motors on one side were gone and the plane was a flaming torch. One shell had gone between the pilot and flight engineer, another between the flight engineer and the mid-upper gunner. Pieces of the tearing metal struck the engineer's legs, wounding him. The bullets passed through behind me, as I was in the nose of the bomber. I remember leaning to one side as the tracers whizzed by.

The main gas tanks were burning fiercely; flames flowed alongside and behind the aircraft. We thought the plane could blow up at any moment. No one was sure if all the crew was alive. Tommy gave the order for all to bail out as quickly as possible.

The escape hatch was on the bottom of the aircraft, near the navigator. Mac opened the hatch and jettisoned it. Tommy had by now trimmed the aircraft to fly with two engines on one side, to allow us to bail out. Mac, the navigator, went first, followed by Benny (wireless operator), Bob (flight engineer), Bill (mid-upper gunner), myself and finally Herb [novice pilot on a familiarization flight]. Herb glanced back and saw Tommy was ready to follow, but he never made it out.

One thought often expressed afterward was that when he let go of the control column, the aircraft went out of control and centrifugal force prevented him from getting out. It made us all realize how little time we had, and how we owed our life to him and his flying skills (Reid 2001).

Thould Lake (64 P/14), northeast of Nejanilini Lake was named after Warrant Officer Thould in 1974.

Thunder, Lance Corporal **Oliver L.** of Middlebro (H 20990). Queen's Own Cameron Highlanders. He died 22 July 1944 at the age of 25 and is commemorated at Bretteville-sur-Laize Canadian War Cemetery in Calvados, France. He was the son of Tom and Sarah J. Thunder of Middlebro. ***Thunder Lake*** (52 M/6), southeast of Sasaginnigak Lake was named after him in 1992.

Tice, Captain **Vernon E.** of Winnipeg. Royal Canadian Artillery. He died 9 June 1944 at the age of 29 and is commemorated at Beny-sur-Mer Canadian War Cemetery in Calvados, France. He was the son of Charles H. and Clara I. Tice and was survived by his wife Eileen E. Tice of Winnipeg. ***Tice Lake*** (64 N/14), west of Nueltin Lake was named after him in 1961.

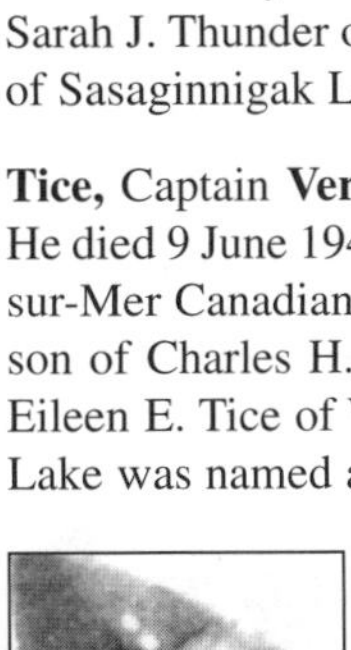

Till, Private **Earl B.** of Minitonas (H 41855). Winnipeg Grenadiers. He died a prisoner of war 1 January 1942 at the age of 28 and is commemorated at the Sai Wan War Cemetery in Hong Kong. He was the son of Charles and Mary E. Till of Minitonas, Manitoba. ***Till Lake*** (62 N/15), southeast of Swan River was named after him in 1973.

Tindall, Flying Officer **Charles E. "Ted"** of Winnipeg (J 20618). No. 425 Squadron. He died 22 March 1944 at the age of 22 and is commemorated at Cologne Southern Cemetery in Germany. He was the eldest of the three children of Charles and Thelma I. Tindall and was survived by his wife Georgette Tindall (née McLean) of Vancouver. His sister writes (8 February 1998):

> Ted attended Laura Secord School on Wolseley Avenue from Grade 1 to 9 and Gordon Bell High School where he was very active in sports: football, baseball, soccer and hockey. After graduating from Grade 11, he continued his interest in sports and while playing for the Elmwood Millionaires, was awarded the Shea Trophy for most gentlemanly player. He was a centre for the Winnipeg Monarchs in 1938-39.
>
> In 1939, he joined Trans Canada Airlines (now Air Canada) and worked in the office until he joined the RCAF in September of 1941. He trained at Edmonton, McLeod, Prince Albert and received his wings and commission at Saskatoon in November, 1942. After taking a course at Vulcan, Alberta, he returned to Saskatoon as an instructor. He married Georgette McLean on November 10, 1942. Georgette was the daughter of Mayor George McLean, long-time Mayor of St. Boniface.
>
> He requested overseas duty in 1943 and on March 6, 1944, he joined 425 Alouette Squadron. He was killed in 1944 on his first bombing run over Frankfurt, Germany (620 Lancasters took part, 26 were lost; 184 Halifaxes took part, seven were lost). Three members of his crew are buried with him. On Ted's gravestone is written:
>
> One of our pilots is safe
Rest in Peace
J 20618
>
> Ted was a fine gentleman, loved by all his family and remembered today with love.

Tindall Lake (64 H/16), southeast of Condie Lake was named after him in 1995.

Tinline, Flying Officer **John E.** of Brandon (J 26318). No. 424 Squadron. He died 25 April 1944 at the age of 24 and is commemorated at Werkendam Protestant Cemetery in Holland. He was the son of Milton J. and Mary M. Tinline of Brandon. ***Tinline Lake*** (64 P/4), southeast of Nejanilini Lake was named after him in 1974.

Tinndal, Private **Carl F.** of Lac du Bonnet (H 1957). Algonquin Regiment. He died 19 September 1944 at the age of 21 and is commemorated at the Adegem Canadian War Cemetery in Belgium. He was the son of John C. and Sophie M. Tinndal of Lac du Bonnet. ***Tinndal Creek*** (64 K/14), which flows northeast into Sandycheelay Lake was named after him in 1979.

Tippett, Trooper **Maurice William H.** of Minnedosa (H 171). Lord Strathcona's Horse. He died 30 May 1944 at the age of 24 and is commemorated at the Cassino War Cemetery in Italy. He was the son of Edward H. and Florence Tippett of Winnipeg. ***Tippett Lake*** (63 J/9), west of Cross Lake was named after him in 1981.

Titley, Private **David A.** of Winnipeg (H 20015). Queen's Own Cameron Highlanders. He died 21 July 1944 at the age of 31 and is commemorated at Bretteville-sur-Laize Canadian War Cemetery in Calvados, France. He was survived by his mother Florence S. Titley (née Cargill). After the death of her husband and son, she was forced to sell the family farm near Beulah and move to Winnipeg. ***Titley Island*** (63 K/16) in File Lake was named after Private Titley in 1973.

Titof, Pilot Officer **Leon A.** of Flin Flon (J 26842). No. 9 Squadron. He died 18 October 1943 at the age of 19 and is commemorated at the Hanover War Cemetery in Germany. He was the son of David A. and Fanny Titof of Flin Flon. ***Titof Lake*** (64 J/13), northwest of Tadoule Lake was named after him in 1972.

Titus, Flight Sergeant **Gerald R.** of Wellwood (R 86352). No. 405 Squadron. He died 27 July 1942 at the age of 28 and is commemorated at the Runnymede Memorial in Surrey, England. He was the son of Mr. and Mrs. C. E. Titus of Wellwood, Manitoba. ***Titus Lake*** (64 P/6), southeast of Nejanilini Lake was named after him in 1974.

Tkachuk, Private **Steve** of Sifton (H 21119). Royal Hamilton Light Infantry. He died 1 September 1944 at the age of 27 and is commemorated at Bretteville-sur-Laize Canadian War Cemetery in Calvados, France. He was the son of Michael and Mary Tkachuk of Sifton, Manitoba. ***Tkachuk Lake*** (63 I/8), south of Robinson Lake was named after him in 1995.

Tocher, Lance Corporal **John** of Hamiota (H 20073). Queen's Own Cameron Highlanders. He died 21 July 1944 and is commemorated at the Bayeux Memorial in Calvados, France. ***Tocher Lake*** (54 D/15), northeast of Myre Lake was named after him in 1996.

Tod, Private **James A.** of Sturgeon Creek (H 17112). Princess Patricia's Canadian Light Infantry. He died 23 May 1944 at the age of 30 and is commemorated at the Cassino War Cemetery in Italy. He was the son of David S. and Eva Tod (née Clark) and the husband of Anne E. Tod of Winnipeg. ***Tod Point*** (64 K/16) on Burnie Lake was named after him in 1995.

Tod, Warrant Officer 2 **Richard D.** of St. Vital (R 91741). No. 75 Squadron. He died 23 June 1943 at the age of 23 and is commemorated at Medemblik General Cemetery in Holland. He was the son of Alexander and Mary E. Tod of St. Vital. ***Tod Lake*** (64 C/12), east of Reindeer Lake was named after him and his twin brother, Warrant Officer Robert E. Tod (next entry) in 1947.

> It was unusual for two brothers to be on the same plane, but these young men, who were exceptionally close, asked special permission from the air ministry. Ironically, just a day before they were killed, the family here had received a note from the boys with the good news that they were both to be promoted from the rank of warrant officer to pilot officer.
>
> This was their 29th combat mission together on Lancaster bombers and both were decorated for bravery with the DSM and other military awards. Exactly a year after their death, another brother, John Tod, who is still called Jock by his friends, landed in Europe when allied forces stormed the continent on D-Day, June 6, 1944. Jock made headlines when he captured 27 German prisoners single-handed in a fantastic display of courage. But most of all, Jock wanted to find out about his two younger brothers because exact word of their fate wasn't known by the Tod family.
>
> During a break in the fighting, he went by motorcycle to the area of Holland where they had been shot down. He discovered there was a small burial plot where two or three Canadians were reportedly buried. When he got there, just by coincidence a 10 year-old Dutch girl was placing flowers on one of his brothers' graves. She told him that her family had "adopted" the graves and were looking after them. Jock also met members of the Dutch "underground" who had taken part in the service for the deceased twins.
>
> For years the Tod family kept in touch with the very fine Dutch people who tended the graves of the twins. As for Jock, a rugged outdoorsman, he now makes his home at West Hawk Lake. One family member told me that the twins were seldom apart in life. And so it was in death. Perhaps that's the way they might have wanted it had they been given the choice (Telpner 1979a).

Tod, Warrant Officer 2 **Robert E.** of St. Vital (R 91742). No. 75 Squadron, Distinguished Flying Medal.

This airman was the wireless operator of an aircraft which was damaged by anti-aircraft fire during an operational flight over enemy territory. The aircraft gradually lost height and the pilot was eventually compelled to bring it down to the sea. Meanwhile, Sergeant Tod worked coolly at his apparatus, maintaining wireless contact with base. His excellent work enabled the aircraft to be continuously plotted from the ground and plans for rescue to be made. The entire crew of the aircraft were picked up within fifteen minutes of coming down on the sea. This airman displayed great coolness and unswerving devotion to duty throughout (DFM Citation 1943).

He died 23 June 1943 at the age of 23 and is commemorated at Medemblik General Cemetery in Holland. He was the son of Alexander and Mary E. Tod of St. Vital. ***Tod Lake*** (64 C/12), east of Reindeer Lake was named after him and his twin brother, Warrant Officer Richard D. Tod (previous entry) in 1947.

Todd, Flying Officer **Frank G.** of Winnipeg (J 27271). No. 432 Squadron. He died 12 October 1944 at the age of 24 and is commemorated at Brookwood Military Cemetery in Surrey, England. He was the son of Frank S. and Barbara Todd of Winnipeg. ***Todd Island*** (64 O/13), in Nueltin Lake was named after him in 1961.

Todd, Flying Officer **Joseph C.** of Winnipeg (J 40382). No. 232 Squadron. He died 15 June 1945 at the age of 23 and is commemorated at Brookwood Military Cemetery in Surrey, England. He was the son of Joseph and Margaret H. Todd of Winnipeg. ***Todd Bay*** (53 K/11) in Edmund Lake was named after him in 1995.

Tokorow, Private **John** of Winnipeg (H 101998). Royal Canadian Infantry Corps. He died 2 May 1943 at the age of 20 and is commemorated at Brandon Cemetery. He was the son of Nick and Diana Tokorow of Sundown, Manitoba. ***Tokorow Lake*** (64 J/2), southwest of Tadoule Lake was named after him in 1975.

Toland, Wing Commander **Gerald T.** of Winnipeg (34033). No. 78 Squadron, RAF. He died 27 February 1941 at the age of 30 and is commemorated at St. Bartholomew Churchyard in Shropshire, England. He was the son of Thomas J. and Edna A. Toland of Fort Garry and was survived by his wife Kathleen M. Toland of Ardersier, Inverness-shire, Scotland. He was the brother of Corporal Keith L. Toland (next entry). Wing Commander Toland enlisted with the RAF in 1934 (Allison 1978). ***Toland Island*** (64 P/14) in Schmok Lake was named after him in 1995.

Toland, Corporal **Keith L.** of Fort Garry (H 16049). Princess Patricia's Canadian Light Infantry. He died 5 December 1941 at the age of 20 and is commemorated at Brookwood Military Cemetery in Surrey, England. He was the son of Thomas J. and Edna A. Toland of Fort Garry and was survived by his wife Ruby Doreen Toland (née Hull). This native of Eau Claire, Wisconsin enlisted the same week that Canada declared war on Germany, was married 2 December 1939 and left for England two weeks later. He was the brother of Wing Commander Gerald T. Toland (previous entry). ***Toland Lake*** (64 H/6), north of Northern Indian Lake was named after him in 1995.

Tomchyshyn, Flight Sergeant **Peter** of Winnipeg (R 110876). No. 1662 Conversion Unit, RCAF. He died 14 August 1943 at the age of 21 and is commemorated at the Runnymede Memorial in Surrey, England. He was the son of Harry and Anastasia Tomchyshyn of Winnipeg. ***Tomchyshyn Lake*** (64 J/12), southeast of Egenolf Lake was named after him in 1975.

Tomlin, Sapper **Arthur Mervyn** of Neepawa (H 101946). Royal Canadian Engineers. He died 22 November 1943 at the age of 25 and is commemorated at Brookwood Military Cemetery in Surrey, England.

He was the son of Fred and Katie Tomlin (née Tully) and was survived by his wife Marjorie U. Tomlin (née Holmes); they were married in 1943. Merv was born in Neepawa, Manitoba in 1914. He was educated in Neepawa and participated in several sports. Merv was a member of the Neepawa Collegiate Hockey Team when they won the Provincial Championship in 1939. He was also a member of the Neepawa Intermediate Hockey Team when they annexed the Provincial honours in 1936-37. Prior to his enlistment in the Royal Canadian Engineers in 1942, Merv worked as a brakeman with the CNR Railway. He was sent overseas in 1943. Merv passed away from a heart seizure during training exercises (Pittman n.d.).

Tomlin Lake (64 O/3), southwest of Munroe Lake was named after him in 1978.

Tomlinson, Corporal **David** of Winnipeg (H 87687). Queen's Own Cameron Highlanders. He died 12 September 1944 at the age of 23 and is commemorated at Brookwood Military Cemetery in Surrey, England. He was the son of James and Catherine Tomlinson of Winnipeg and was survived by his wife Caroline Tomlinson of Winnipeg. ***Tomlinson Bay*** (64 N/1) in Egenolf Lake was named after him in 1995.

Tomlinson, Flight Sergeant **James Gordon** of Winnipeg (R 157029). No. 434 Squadron. He was presumed dead 23 November 1943 on his first operational mission. He is commemorated at the Runnymede Memorial in Surrey, England. Flight Sergeant Tomlinson was survived by his wife Betty Tomlinson (née Ross) of Elmwood. Prior to enlisting, he had been employed by the Canadian Bank of Commerce. ***Tomlinson Island*** (63 N/8) in Burntwood Lake was named after him in 1995.

Tompkin, Corporal **Joseph J. E.** of Novra (H 17546). Royal Winnipeg Rifles. He died 6 June 1944 at the age of 23 and is commemorated at Beny-sur-Mer Canadian War Cemetery in Calvados, France. He was the son of Joseph L. and Lillian M. Tompkin of Winnipeg. His sister recalls (n.d.):

Three young soldiers from the small town of Novra, Manitoba would sacrifice their lives on the Normandy beaches that day. His letters home would tell us how they wished the war would start and be over so they could return home.

Joe was born in Bowsman River, Manitoba, moving to Novra in 1926, where he received his education. He loved to hunt in the flats, bush and Porcupine Mountains around Novra, making money for clothes by selling squirrel pelts. He also kept our table supplied with prairie chicken. Being the only son, he took responsibility of all the chores around our small farm. His Father was disabled from wounds sustained during World War I.

Tompkin Bay (62 N/15) in Wellman Lake was named after him in 1977.

Tompkins, Private **John E.** of Winnipeg (H 41649). Winnipeg Grenadiers. He died 19 December 1941 and is commemorated at the Sai Wan Memorial in Hong Kong. ***Tompkins Lake*** (64 F/6), north of Wells Lake was named after him in 1994.

Toon, Warrant Officer 1 **James W.** of Whitewater (R 74721). No. 103 Squadron. He died 14 April 1943 at the age of 23 and is commemorated at Le Mans West Cemetery in Sarthe, France. He was the son of Alphaeus and Eleanor E. Toon of Murrayville, British Columbia. He was:

... born April 24, 1919 at Whitewater, Manitoba and was employed as a storekeeper at Murrayville, British Columbia when he joined the RCAF in October, 1940. After training at Toronto, Dunnville, Winnipeg, Dafoe and Rivers, he went overseas in October, 1941, flying the Atlantic as a navigator on a Liberator aircraft. He served with the RCAF attached to the RAF in Great Britain and over continental Europe. Toon was shot down while returning from a bombing raid on Spezia, Italy. He attended public school at Murrayville and high school at Langley (Hill 1944).

Toon Lake (64 O/5), south of Shannon Lake was named after him in 1995.

Topolnistky, Rifleman **Frank** of Olha (H 102930). Regina Rifle Regiment. He died 9 June 1944 at the age of 30 and is commemorated at Beny-sur-Mer Canadian War Cemetery in Calvados, France. He was the son of Victor and Teenie Topolnitsky (sp.) of Olha, Manitoba. ***Topolnistky Lake*** (64 I/3), west of North Knife Lake was named after him in 1974.

Topp, Leading Stoker **Charles J.** of Winnipeg (V 516). HMCS *Valleyfield*. The *Valleyfield* was torpedoed and sunk by U-548 50 miles south of Cape Race, Newfoundland; 125 of her ship's company were lost. Leading Stoker Topp died 7 May 1944 at the age of 26 and is commemorated at the Halifax Memorial. He was the son of Charles R. and Margaret Topp of Winnipeg. ***Topp Lake*** (64 N/7), southwest of Nueltin Lake was named after him in 1972.

Toshack, Flight Sergeant **Robert H.** of Winnipeg (R 59108). No. 38 Squadron. He died 23 September 1941 at the age of 19 and is commemorated at the Malta Memorial. He was one of the three sons of Fred S. and Kathleen R. Toshack of Winnipeg. He had managed to join the RCAF when only 17 years old. On one of his earliest missions, he and much of the rest of the squadron were forced down *en route* to Malta by a severe storm and were later picked up off the coast of Portugal. He subsequently "escaped" back to England to be assigned another raid on Malta. He was shot down over Tripoli. His brother adds (27 April 1995): "Bob didn't live long enough to have many special interests other than he was an A student and was in University at age 15. He also loved football and hockey." ***Toshack Lake*** (64 I/14), northeast of Shethanei Lake was named after him in 1974.

Toth, Flight Sergeant **Leslie W.** of Flin Flon (R 213609). No. 419 Squadron. He died 24 November 1944 at the age of 27 and is commemorated at Stonefall Cemetery in Yorkshire, England. His sister visited it twice in 1945. He was the son of Leslie Steven and Rose Toth and was survived by his wife Adeline V. Toth (née Sebok) of Kipling, Saskatchewan and their daughter. His sister recalls (18 November 1998):

Leslie was born ... [at] Stockholm, Saskatchewan where his father was the Wheat Pool Grain Elevator agent. Leslie attended five years of elementary school there before the family moved to Regina in January, 1929. In Regina, his father worked for the Caterpillar Tractor Company while Leslie attended Sacred Heart Parochial School from which he passed his entrance examinations. During those three years, Leslie took violin lessons and later, in his teen years, taught himself the guitar and banjo.

In 1931, Leslie's family moved to a country place near Runciman, Saskatchewan where his father, a Stationary Engineer, worked on road maintenance for the Rural Municipality of Valparaiso. Leslie attended high school at Silver Stream School while his four sisters attended the Forester School. There were three consecutive winters when his father took a job pulling a series of huge bob-sleds with a Caterpillar Tractor between Churchill, Gods Lake and Ilford in northern Manitoba. Those winter evenings were enjoyable, when Leslie played his guitar and banjo and his sisters would sing, along with his mother and brothers.

During the summer holidays of 1936, the family travelled by Canadian National Railway to Flin Flon, Manitoba where their father was working for the Hudson Bay Mining and Smelting Company in the leaching plant. Later, Leslie worked in the HBM&S smelter. In June, 1939, Leslie married Adeline Joan Sebok from Kipling, Saskatchewan and in July, 1940, they had a daughter, Joanne Leslie Toth. Before Leslie joined the RCAF, he took his wife and daughter to Adeline's family home in Kipling in 1943.

Leslie died with his six crew members in a Lancaster bomber crash on November 24th, 1944 and they are buried beside each other in Harrogate [Stonefall] Regional Cemetery, irrespective of rank or religion. Leslie came from a devout Roman Catholic family which mourns him.

Toth Lake (64 G/16), north of Cederlund Lake was named after him in 1995.

Touchbourne, Lieutenant **Philip S.** of Eden. Fleet Air Arm, Royal Navy, Mentioned in Dispatches (1940 and 1941). He died 10 May 1941 at the age of 29 and is commemorated at Lee-on-Solent Memorial, Hampshire, England. His sister writes (14 November 1986):

Philip Sinclair Touchbourne was born in Powasson, Ontario in 1912; later the family moved to Eden, Manitoba. Mrs. Touchbourne remarried at Eden (after divorcing the children's father) and Philip and Hope received their education at Eden Consolidated School. Philip took his pilot's training at Stevenson Field, graduating with the lowest flying time record (at that time). He then went to England via a coal ship as a stoker. He joined the RAF and transferred to the Fleet Air Arm probably about 1938 or 1939. He served in the Singapore area and Middle East on the HMS *Eagle*. Shortly after World War II broke out, he was transferred to the HMS *Formidable*.

His mother received the following correspondence (n.d.):

The Secretary of the Admiralty presents his compliments and has pleasure in sending you the enclosed Bronze Oak Leaf Emblem which is in respect of the Mentions in Dispatches awarded to Lt. (A) P. S. Touchbourne, RN on the 11th September 1940 and 14th January 1941.

And later:

Madam: I am commanded by My Lords Commissioners of the Admiralty to send you the enclosed Certificate of a Mention in Dispatches, awarded by the King to your son, Lieutenant (A) Philip Sinclair Touchbourne, RN, for his steadfastness, courage and devotion to duty while serving in HMS *Eagle* in the Summer of 1940.

I am to express Their Lordships' pleasure at this mark of His Majesty's high appreciation, and Their deep regret that your son did not live to receive it. I am, Madam, Your obedient Servant, R. Gleadowe (19 December 1941).

A family friend added (14 November 1986):

In this day and age, it is very hard to imagine the sacrifice, dedication and hard work that led a young prairie boy to make such an effort to realize a dream of flying, in spite of the very depressed times of that day.

Touchbourne Lake (63 N/7), northeast of Takipy Lake was named after him in 1988.

Toupin, Private **René J. J.** of Winnipeg (H 102921). 48th Highlanders of Canada. He died 29 December 1943 at the age of 20 and is commemorated at the Moro River Canadian War Cemetery in Italy. He was the son of Mr. and Mrs. Edward Toupin and was survived by his wife Annis Toupin (née McIntyre). His sister writes (29 April 1996):

René attended Provencher School in St. Boniface and then went on to work for MacDonald Aircraft as a welder. He was interested in roller skating and joined clubs at the Winnipeg Roller Skating Rink where he learned fancy skating and was very good at it. He married Annis McIntyre before going overseas. Since his death we have lost all contact with her. We know that she remarried.

René had a favourite song – *Smoke gets in your Eyes*. When he left for overseas, he said that at the bottom of his letters, he would write "SGIYE." This would mean that everything was OK with him. If those letters were not there, it would mean he was going to the front lines. His last letter did not have SGIYE, so we knew he was moving somewhere. Shortly after, a telegram arrived bearing the sad news. This was very hard for my parents to accept; he was the only son.

My husband and I took a trip to Europe in 1979. Our tour had three days in Rome, so I wrote to the Commonwealth War Graves Commission in Ottawa and asked them if there was a way to get to Ortona from Rome in one day. The information we got back was just great – we could make it in one day. They told us what train to take and at what time and how much it would cost etc. We followed their instructions and had no problems at all.

At the train station in Ortona, we presented the letter from Ottawa explaining what we wanted. In no time, a gentleman drove us to the cemetery, gave us one hour to look around and brought us back to the station to catch the train back to Rome. We were very impressed with our visit on the shores of the Adriatic Sea and how beautifully kept the Canadian cemetery is. How sad it was to see rows and rows of identical monuments with the names, ages and dates of each soldier, mostly around 20 years old. This visit to Ortona was the highlight of our European trip.

Toupin Lake (64 I/15), east of Shethanei Lake was named after Private Toupin in 1974.

Tourand, Lance Sergeant **Charles E.** of Ste. Rose du Lac (H 42064). Royal Winnipeg Rifles. He died 4 July 1944 at the age of 25 and is commemorated at Beny-sur-Mer Canadian War Cemetery in Calvados, France. He was the son of John and Marie L. Tourand (née Houle) of Laurier. ***Tourand Lake*** (64 P/1), southwest of Caribou Lake was named after him in 1974.

Tourand, Rifleman **Joseph Leo** of Pine Falls (H 617421). Royal Winnipeg Rifles. He died 2 December 1945 at the age of 33 and is commemorated at the Holten Canadian War Cemetery in Holland. He was survived by his wife Irene Tourand (née Vinet) and their two sons. She writes (18 April 1998):

Leo was born in La Broquerie, Manitoba, the second youngest of five sons. The family later moved to Pine Falls, Manitoba. His mother died when he was nine years old and his father three years later. Following his father's death, he lived with different family members. He was a strong, healthy boy, able to do a man's work and was expected to work and contribute his earnings to the family. Leo loved the woods – camping fishing and hunting. He was considered an excellent marksman.

When he was 17 years old, he went to live with his brother Ernest who had fallen ill and was not able to work. It was agreed that Leo would take over Ernest's job at the paper mill in order to support his brother's family, and he did this until his marriage to Irene Vinet on July 5, 1937. They eventually had two sons born to them in 1938 and 1939. Leo continued working in the paper mill in Pine Falls until he was called to service and eventually stationed in Nanaimo, BC. He was sent overseas where he died, leaving a wife and two young sons.

Tourand Island (64 C/8) in Granville Lake was named after him in 1995.

Town, Flying Officer **John A.** of Brandon (J 16172). Royal Canadian Air Force. He died 10 April 1943 at the age of 25 and is commemorated at Houghton and Wyton Burial Ground in Huntingdonshire, England. He was the son of William R. and Winnifred M. Town and was survived by his wife Eileen A. Town of Brandon. His brother writes (2 February 1998):

John was born May 15th, 1917 in Brandon, Manitoba. In 1940, he enlisted with the RCAF and received his wireless air gunner's wings in Montreal. He went overseas in August, 1941 and for some time was attached to the coastal command, participating in operational flights. He received his promotion to Flying Officer early in 1942.

Town Lake (64 J/14), southeast of Egenolf Lake was named after him in 1975.

Townsend, Leading Aircraftman **Earl L.** of Winnipeg (R 134116). No. 18 Service Flying Training School. He died 15 December 1944 at the age of 23 and is commemorated at Brookside Cemetery in Winnipeg. He was the son of Bert and Amy E. Townsend of Winnipeg and was survived by his wife Lerena J. Townsend of Winnipeg. ***Townsend River*** (64 P/13), which flows east into Bulloch Lake was named after him in 1987.

Townsend, Corporal **George H.** of Selkirk (H 6135). Winnipeg Grenadiers. He died a prisoner of war 25 November 1944 at the age of 29 and is commemorated at the Yokohama War Cemetery in Japan. He was one of the three children of George H. and Elizabeth Townsend of Selkirk. His brother recalls (31 October 2001):

George was born and raised in Selkirk. He attended primary school at Mapleton (Old England) School and high school at Devonshire Collegiate in Selkirk. He spent his winters doing "Relief Work" in the bush in the Hungry 30s and worked with his Dad creating the golf course in Selkirk in the summer. He was fortunate enough to get a job gravelling the road from Clandeboye to Winnipeg Beach in 1937/38, then went to work for the Manitoba Rolling Mills in 1939. He was very active in local social circles, making the bobsled slide across the river, managing a "scrub" softball team of local players in their games against Cloverdale, Clandeboye, Petersfield, etc. He never missed any of the local school dances.

George was one of the very first from Selkirk to volunteer for military service. He was sworn in on either September 6th or 9th, 1939 at the Osborne Street Barracks in Winnipeg where he did his "boot training." He was posted to Jamaica where he became a full Corporal. He came home on leave in the summer of 1941 and then sailed out of Vancouver for Hong Kong, leaving behind a fiancée who was later to marry another Grenadier who had been in the same PoW camp as George.

Townsend Lake (52 E/14), southeast of Brereton Lake was named after him in 1974.

Towsley, Pilot Officer **Charles E.** of Winnipeg (J 93960). No. 120 Squadron. He died 13 July 1944 at the age of 20 and is commemorated at the Runnymede Memorial in Surrey, England. He was the son of Miron H. and Elizabeth R. Towsley of Winnipeg. ***Towsley Lake*** (64 P/10), east of Nejanilini Lake was named after him in 1974.

Traer, Gunner **Charles W. I. "Chuck"** of Winnipeg (H 10207). Royal Canadian Artillery. He died 22 April 1945 at the age of 20 and is commemorated at the Holten Canadian War Cemetery in Holland. He was the only son of Charles W. and Eleanor Traer (née Fleming) of Winnipeg. His sister recalls (16 November 1995):

"Chuck" as he was known, was born and raised in Winnipeg. At the time of his birth, his family resided at 252 King Edward Street in St. James. Chuck was a happy boy. My Mom lovingly called him Chucky-bird when he was small. Chuck attended Pinkham, Isbister, Victoria-Albert and Hugh John Macdonald Schools.

We were basically United Church but usually attended the neighbourhood church, Emanuel Baptist. Friday after school it was Grace Church; we attended many activities there. We also went to shows and Ice Capades with Grace Church. On Saturday afternoon, we went to the show for five cents each. The Beacon, Macs Province or the Wonderland. Chuck was always proud that Tom Mix, a western movie hero had his birthday the same day as his.

Chuck was a real worker. He earned money at a very early age doing errands or small jobs for neighbours. He was six when he painted the large stones along our walk for Mom. The neighbour admired them and Chuck quickly offered to paint his for 15 cents. He sold Liberty magazines for five cents a copy. He was a top salesman. You could earn coupons as well as money. The coupons could be used for prizes. When Chuck was 12, he received a certificate from MacFadden Publishers for exceptional sales achievements and outstanding character.

With the wagon he won from selling Liberty magazines, he made many trips to Arctic Ice in hot weather for blocks of ice. He delivered them to the neighbours. I can see him as he was, a little on the chubby side, and by the time he got home the perspiration would be rolling down his face. Sometimes he wore a red and white hanky on his forehead.

Chuck played hockey in the lane and was injured in the eye. He loved candy and would buy a bag of one-cent candy and always share with the kids. I remember the day he changed from a kid to a young man. We lived on Notre Dame Avenue. Northern Shirt was just up the lane. You could go there and buy shirts and pants. Chuck took his money and walked up the lane, a rather chubby boy in pants that were a little too large. The employees knew Chuck as he sold Liberty to most of them. They helped him pick out some new clothes which he wore home. He looked so tall and handsome and proud as he came down the lane to show me. He left a kid behind and came home a young man.

Chuck worked at Eaton's. He was employed at the CPR Express when he enlisted at 18. He was determined to serve his country. He was very proud of his uniform and his country. Chuck left behind a family who loved him, a sweetheart and many friends. Chuck was killed in action on April 22, 1945 in a forward position in Germany.

Traer Lake (64 I/10), north of North Knife Lake was named after him in 1974.

Trakalo, Lance Corporal **Pete** of Meleb (H 204478). Queen's Own Cameron Highlanders. He died 16 August 1944 at the age of 26 and is commemorated at Bretteville-sur-Laize Canadian War Cemetery in Calvados, France. He was the second of the five children of John and Tekla "Tillie" Trakalo (née Nosaty) of Meleb, Manitoba. He kept a journal before the war and continued to do so while overseas:

Dear Journal: Today was a hard day for many reasons. There hasn't been any rain for many days. The ground is very dry and crops haven't been growing well. Pasture hasn't been growing for the cattle. The farm work is really hard. We've been working long, hard hours and we are not pulling much money. We're barely getting by. Dad is very sick. It could be something very severe because he can't even get out of bed and work. I would get a job in repairing machinery, but it is very hard to find a job these days. To make things even worse, my youngest brother Paul has just been diagnosed with polio in both of his legs. Joe, Mike, Olga, Kate and I are all worried and praying for the best. The war has started; I'm curious and beginning to wonder when I will get my letter telling me where I am drafted will come. It could be anywhere. Wherever it will be though, I'll fight with honour (n.d.).

Dear Journal: I've finally received my letter and on January 10, 1941 I was drafted to the Winnipeg Light Infantry Unit. I've had to fill out countless forms about my life before the war, my health, my family, the condition I was in and many medical forms. I've had many tests and examinations on me as well. I had a physical, vaccinations and even a dental check-up. (Not surprisingly, they had been graded "neglected"). I have received an army soldier book that has all the information about the size and amount of clothes I have, my pay and the balance of my pay. I don't know for how long I will be staying here, but I know it will be hard work. I will learn many things. By the time I will leave, I'll know how to use weapons, be able to fight and probably strategy on how to defend ourselves from the enemy (n.d.).

Dear Journal: My days with the Winnipeg Light Infantry Militia are over. I trained there for 30 days, January 10 to February 10, 1942. I have some knowledge now on how to fight etc., but I have enlisted in the Canadian Active Service Overseas. I enlisted today which is September 10, 1942. The hard training that I have gone through will finally pay off. I am very nervous, yet excited, for I will be fighting in the real war with a real enemy and real weapons. When I was training, it didn't matter if you made a mistake because that was practice. Now, if I make a mistake it could mean the difference of life and death. But I will be brave and not back down and fight with honour for my country's freedom. Until another day (n.d.).

Dear Journal: I arrived in the UK quite a while ago and many things have happened since. I arrived in the UK on October 7, 1942. I reported here for active duty with the Camerons of Canada. I have been fighting with my unit for over a year now. My first battle was something I've never seen in my entire life. It was frightening and horrible, just seeing the true horror of the war with my own two eyes. Yet at the same time it was exciting and adventurous. I've been trying to write letters home to everyone but it has been very hard to. My pay is $1.50 a day. It's not much, but at least it's something. I have been working and fighting in the fields since I have arrived here. It is now the year 1944. Nothing really worthy of mention happened in '43. It's just been the same thing day in and day out. Fight, fight, fight. When will this ever end? But anyways, I am very proud to say that I received the Canadian Volunteer Service Medal and Clasp on January 15, 1944. And just a few days ago I was promoted from Private to Lance Corporal!!! I am so excited about this and very proud of myself. Goodbye for now (n.d.).

His great niece adds (22 March 2001): "Pete was killed only seven days after being promoted to Lance Corporal. He was shot by an enemy sniper when he volunteered to go and get supplies for his unit." His twelve year-old great nephew adds (n.d.):

I never actually met Pete Trakalo, but I know him very well from all the stories that were told by my family members and especially by my great uncle Joe and Auntie Jean Trakalo. My great uncle Joe was Pete's brother. Recently my Uncle Joe showed me all of Pete's documents from Pete's time in the Army. In the documents that my Uncle Joe had shown me, there was a military book that Pete always had to carry on him in his breast pocket. It was very sad to look at the book because the book had a bullet hole in it where Pete had been shot. I will continue to remember him and tell others stories about him so they will remember him because we can not ever forget about our war heroes.

In a letter home he wrote:

Dear Sister and Brothers-in-law: Received your most welcome letter and was glad to hear you are doing fine and well. I also received your parcel today which contained crackers, 6 packs chewing gum, packet cigs, razor blades, 4 choc. bars, sardines and a ribbon which you must have got in Church for it said "Souvenir, Holy Mass" in Ukrainian.

Say, you didn't mention in your letter about receiving my snapshot for I sent you one some time ago which I believe you should have received by now. I also received today 200 cigs from John Batik so I'll be well off for cigs for a while now.

Well I wonder how Joe made out about his postponement. It's too bad that he's got to go at the busiest time of the year with father unable to give any help. I haven't got very much to say for myself as I have been no place in particular since my last leave, except for an odd picture show. The other night the Canadian Concert party put on a play for us, a jolly good concert made up of a few soldiers and some CWACs.

I'm still waiting to get your picture for I'm eager to know how everybody has changed. I think I'll close my letter as the space is getting small.

With all the best wishes and kind regards to you and children and thanks a lot for the letters and parcel. Hoping to see you soon. Cheerio, Brother Pete (3 June 1944).

Trakalo Lake (64 I/4), west of North Knife Lake was named after him in 1974.

Travis, Private **William E.** of San Clara (H 8958). General List, Canadian Army. He died 15 February 1944 at the age of 41 and is commemorated at San Clara Cemetery, Manitoba. He was survived by his mother Rose Travis of San Clara and by his wife Mary L. Travis of Walkerburn, Manitoba. ***Travis Lake*** (64 P/1), south of Caribou Lake was named after him in 1974.

Treleaven, Flight Lieutenant **Errol H. W.** of Elm Creek (C 1499). No. 416 Squadron. He died 25 September 1944 at the age of 29 and is commemorated at Old Leusden General Cemetery in Amersfoort, Holland. He was the son of William K. and Laura L. Treleaven and was survived by his wife Ruby Treleaven (née Flett) of Glasgow, Scotland and their son James. His brother recalls (14 July, 1995):

Errol was born ... on a ranch at Langruth, Manitoba. He left Langruth in 1919 with his parents and older sister Margaret for Vancouver. After one year, the family motored from Vancouver to Winnipeg which took several weeks due to the lack of roads in BC. Part of the trip was through the northern USA and western Canadian prairies where roads were usually only trails.

The family settled in Poplar Point where they farmed until 1932 and where Errol took his primary and secondary schooling. Errol was a good athlete; he was asked to play junior hockey with the Portage la Prairie Terriers but his parents felt hockey would interfere with his education. He could have excelled at both as he bought the required books and completed his first two years toward a BA studying at home.

In 1934, he attended Normal School (teacher's college today). The following year, Errol taught at the one-room Hollywood School near Langruth. The next year (1936) he studied at Wesley College for one year then transferred to the University of Manitoba from where he graduated in 1938 with a BA degree. Errol then went to work for the Great-West Life Assurance Company where he studied for the actuary exams. While working there, he met his future wife Ruby, a fellow employee.

The war started on September 3, 1939 and Errol enlisted in the RCAF as a provisional Pilot Officer and was posted to the Brandon Flying Club for the elementary flying course with three other students. After elementary was completed, he was posted to Camp Borden for service flying where he received his wings in 1940. From Borden, he was posted to Trenton, Ontario where he took the instructor's course. His subsequent posting as an instructor was to Saskatoon.

Errol and Ruby were married April 19, 1941 and later that year were moved to Aylmer, Ontario where he was chief instructor. In 1942, his next posting took him and his family (they now had a son, James Willard) to Boundary Bay, BC where Errol flew Hurricanes with coastal patrol. A posting in early 1944 found Errol overseas and after further training, was assigned to No. 416 Squadron on Spitfires to take part in the Battle of Normandy. He lost his life in an air battle over Arnhem, Holland.

Flight Lieutenant Treleaven was with one of the aircraft taking supplies to the paratroopers trapped at Arnhem. ***Treleaven Lake*** (64 O/7), north of Munroe Lake was named after him in 1975.

Tremblay, Flight Sergeant **David Gerald** (a.k.a. Trumbla) of Elm Creek (R 123752). No. 9 Squadron. He died 16 June 1943 at the age of 27 and is commemorated at Schoonselhof Cemetery, Antwerp, Belgium. He was the son of David and Kate Trumbla of Elm Creek. His niece writes (21 November 2001):

When my uncle enlisted, his last name was incorrectly put down as Tremblay, so throughout the war he was known as Gerald Tremblay instead of Gerald Trumbla. My uncle Gerald was the oldest and only boy in the family. When he was called to serve in WW II he did not shirk his duty. Uncle Gerald died when the long-range guns of a fighter hit the plane he was the gunner on. The target was a war plant near Cologne and they completed their mission before being hit by enemy planes. The father of the pilot wrote my Grandfather and Grandmother a letter after Uncle Gerald's death. In it he stated: "Bertie the navigator, talked about what a good gunner this Canadian was and the pilot said you snap him up then." That is how Uncle Gerald came to join that crew. The father further continued in his letter: "You should be proud to have a son who flew straight into the most dangerous part of the fight and helped to break the heart of humanity's greatest enemy."

In his last letter home to my mother, a month before he was killed, he talked about flying his missions at night and how busy they were. He talked about missing home, family and friends. Our family will always remember Uncle Gerald as a war hero.

Tremblay Lake (64 J/15), northwest of Tadoule Lake was named after him in 1975.

Trenter, Warrant Officer 2 **George S.** of Winnipeg (SH 23473). Princess Patricia's Canadian Light Infantry. He died 11 October 1951 and is commemorated at the United Nations Cemetery in Pusan, South Korea. ***Trenter Lake*** (53 K/6), northeast of Sharpe Lake was named after this Korean War casualty in 1998.

Trewin, Flight Lieutenant **Thomas W.** of Bradwardine (J 8643). No. 406 Squadron. He died 5 April 1945 at the age of 26 and is commemorated at the Runnymede Memorial in Surrey, England. He was the son of Walter W. and Evelyn A. Trewin of Bradwardine, Manitoba. ***Trewin Lake*** (64 P/13), north of Nejanilini Lake was named after him in 1974.

Trimble, Private **Elmer** of Winnipeg (H 51889). Royal Canadian Army Service Corps. He died 11 October 1944 at the age of 33 and is commemorated at Coriano Ridge War Cemetery in Italy. He was the son of Harvey and Etta Trimble and was survived by his wife Helen A. Trimble. ***Trimble Lake*** (63 I/7), east of Molson Lake was named after him in 1973.

Trohubiak, Private **William** of Ethelbert (H 204660). Queen's Own Cameron Highlanders. He died 26 February 1945 at the age of 25 and is commemorated at the Groesbeek Canadian War Cemetery in Holland. He was the son of Peter T. and Annie Machnitsky of Ethelbert, Manitoba. ***Trohubiak Lake*** (64 O/5), south of Nueltin Lake was named after him in 1975.

Trojanoski, Rifleman **Kasimer S.** of Brokenhead (K 3141). Royal Winnipeg Rifles. He died 22 February 1945 at the age of 29 and is commemorated at the Groesbeek Canadian War Cemetery in Holland. He was the fifth of the 14 children of Steve and Victoria Trojanowski (sp.) of Brokenhead, Manitoba. His brother recalls (7 November 2001):

"Kasey" Trojanoski was born in Beausejour. He left the farm at an early age and journeyed to Mexico where he stayed for a period of time and then subsequently travelled to southern California and spent time as a chef in Hollywood. Rumour has it that he became a fishing companion of some of the prominent residents of Hollywood including Clark Gable.

Kasey attempted to join the US Army in an effort to follow in the footsteps of his brother Joe who had joined up in Philadelphia. However, as an illegal immigrant, Kasey was forced to return to Canada and ended up in Vancouver where he was successful in joining the Royal Winnipeg Rifles. After basic training, Kasey shipped out to Europe in October, 1944. The war ended in Europe on May 8th, 1945, but unfortunately Kasey died in Germany, in a Prisoner of War Camp of wounds received in battle.

A young life lost with the battle nearly won, he is loved and missed by all of his surviving brothers and sisters and many other relatives.

Trojanoski Lake (64 G/5), south of Big Sand Lake was named after him in 1994.

Troughton, Rifleman **Thomas B.** of Clearwater (H 41482). Royal Winnipeg Rifles. He died 4 July 1944 at the age of 25 and is commemorated at Beny-sur-Mer Canadian War Cemetery in Calvados, France. He was the son of Thomas B. and Ada T. Troughton of Altamont, Manitoba. His sister reports (15 August 1998) that he was:

... born February 5, 1919 in England [and] came to Canada with his parents and two older sisters in 1928. A third sister was born later in Canada. They lived at Clearwater, Manitoba from where he joined the Royal Winnipeg Rifles in 1941. He was killed in Normandy. Tom liked music and drawing things and was good at it. He was a quiet person and also loved reading.

Troughton Lake (64 K/8), northeast of Reindeer Lake was named after him in 1972.

Troup, Major **John G.** of Winnipeg. Queen's Own Cameron Highlanders, Military Cross. He died 13 February 1944 at the age of 57 and is commemorated at Brookside Cemetery in Winnipeg. He was survived by his wife Eleanor J. Troup of Winnipeg. ***Troup Lake*** (53 M/14), north of Hubley Lake was named after him in 1996.

Trudeau, Rifleman **Aimé P.** of Ile des Chênes (H 66938). Royal Winnipeg Rifles. He died 16 February 1945 at the age of 27 and is commemorated at the Groesbeek Canadian War Cemetery in Holland. He was the third of the four children of Théodore and Marie A. Trudeau of Ile des Chênes. His brother writes (19 December 1996):

Aimé received his education at the local school (No. 995) where he attended to Grade 8. He was a good student and a quick learner, but he could be strong-willed at times. All things mechanical interested him. He was a real wizard around the Meccano set his parents had got him and soon went beyond the models shown in the illustration provided with the set. A drag line he set up, complete with bucket fashioned from a copper tube, was modelled on a machine his uncle operated for the RM of Tache. (And it really worked!). Times were hard and money was scarce during his youth. He loved reading, but to him, a used copy of *Popular Mechanics* was a real treasure and was kept for future reference.

After his schooling, Aimé was active in operating his parents' farm. His outgoing disposition meant an active social life. His many friends included lots of girls. They liked his looks – five foot eleven, 150 pounds, blond hair, blue eyes and a ready smile. When in the mood, he could tell a good story.

Like many young people, Aimé had itchy feet. He had been trying to save money so he could take a course in diesel mechanics which meant quite a sum during the depression years. That project was set aside when World War II started. Early on, without a word to anyone, he went and joined the Canadian Army. Basic training in Winnipeg and advanced training in Camp Petawawa, Ontario. He went overseas with the 2nd Heavy Anti-Aircraft Regiment and almost immediately found himself on active service defending London from aerial attacks. The regiment had various postings including coastal locations. Aimé participated in the Normandy campaign where he was wounded. He later returned to front line duty where he was killed on February 16, 1945 in the Reichswald Forest.

Trudeau Lake (64 N/2), west of Egenolf Lake was named after him in 1972.

Truthwaite, Gunner **Murray A.** of Selkirk (SB 154368). Royal Canadian Artillery. He died 3 May 1953 and is commemorated at the United Nations Cemetery in Pusan, South Korea. ***Truthwaite Lake*** (53 M/8), west of Richardson Lake was named after this Korean War casualty in 1998.

Tucker, Lieutenant **Lewis Ord R.** of Winnipeg. Seaforth Highlanders of Canada, Mentioned in Dispatches. He died 25 October 1942 at the age of 36 and is commemorated at Brookwood Military Cemetery in Surrey, England. He was the son of Mr. and Mrs. Park B. R. Tucker and was survived by his wife Eleanor Tucker of British Columbia. She explains (24 March 1998):

His father, Park Benjamin Riddell Tucker was a bank manager and was killed in a bank hold-up in the 1920s or 1930s. The Tuckers were divorced and Ord and his brother Geoffrey went with their mother to live in British Columbia. Their stepfather was in the Provost Corps in World War I and the boys and their mother spent the war years in England.

Ord worked for an oil company in a town near Vancouver. He joined the militia unit of the Seaforth Highlanders and the regular Canadian Army in September, 1939. At the time I first met him, he had a "long service" medal, this was in 1941. I was a nursing sister in the Canadian Army Medical Corps when I met Ord in 1941. At that time, he was training for his commission, having previously held the rank of Company Sergeant Major.

We were married in April, 1942. In October, 1942 Ord was training a small group of soldiers in the use of the mortar. The mortar exploded prematurely and four of the soldiers were killed instantly; the NCO and Ord were seriously wounded. Ord was brought to the hospital where I was stationed and died of his wounds 24 hours later. He was awarded a posthumous "Mentioned in Dispatches" for his conduct at the time of the accident. According to his fellow officers, Ord was held in very high esteem. He was a very gentle person, well read and interested in history.

Tucker Island (53 L/4) in Otatakostikwan Lake was named after him in 1995.

Tugby, Private **Reginald G.** of St. James (H 1407). Calgary Highlanders. He died 5 September 1944 and is commemorated at Brookwood Military Cemetery in Surrey, England. He was the son of John D. and Daisy M. Tugby of St. James. ***Tugby Lake*** (52 L/3), northeast of Brereton Lake was named after him in 1973.

Tully, Private **John B.** of Winnipeg (H 20157). Queen's Own Cameron Highlanders. He died 19 August 1942 and is commemorated at Dieppe Canadian War Cemetery in Seine-Maritime, France. He was the son of Henry B. and Jemina M. Tully of Winnipeg. ***Tully Lake*** (54 M/7), east of Long Lake was named after him in 1984.

Turcotte, Private **Albert O.** of Alonsa (H 36713). Royal Canadian Army Service Corps. He died 4 January 1945 at the age of 41 and is commemorated at Assumption Gardens in Winnipeg. He was survived by his wife Catherine Turcotte of Alonsa, Manitoba. ***Turcotte Bay*** (53 E/16) in Irving Lake was named after him in 1997.

Turcotte, Private **George** of Transcona (H 1163). Royal Canadian Regiment. He died 16 January 1944 at the age of 20 and is commemorated at the Moro River Canadian War Cemetery in Italy. He was the son of Joseph and Marie R. Turcotte of Transcona. ***Turcotte Lake*** (54 E/10), northeast of Waskaiowaka Lake was named after him in 1964.

Turk, Sergeant **William O.** of Winnipeg (H 39). Lord Strathcona's Horse. He died 25 May 1944 at the age of 36 and is commemorated at the Cassino War Cemetery in Italy. He was the son of Nathaniel and Mary Turk and was survived by his wife Elsie E. M. Turk of Winnipeg. ***Turk Lake*** (52 L/11), southwest of Black Lake was named after him in 1982.

Turner, Able Seaman **Allan Thomas** of Winnipeg (V 50180). HMCS *Alberni*. The *Alberni* was torpedoed and sunk by U-480, southeast of the Isle of Wight; 59 of her ship's company were lost. Able Seaman Turner died 21 August 1944 at the age of 20 and is commemorated at the Halifax Memorial. He was survived by his mother Kathleen Turner of Winnipeg. ***Turner Point*** (64 N/11) on Kasmere Lake was named after him in 1989.

Turner, Flight Lieutenant **Charles Frederick** of Carman (40960). No. 126 Squadron, RAF. He died 22 July 1942 at the age of 27 and is commemorated at the Ottawa Memorial. He was the son of Charles E. and Fedelia E. Turner of Willowdale, Ontario. His sister writes (3 December 1997):

> Born in Carman in 1914, the family moved to Winnipeg in 1915 or thereabouts. He attended Laura Secord Elementary School and Gordon Bell High School. He played the piano well and had a great interest in building cars with his brother Douglas. He worked at Canadian Airways and always had dreams of flying. He left Winnipeg for England in [June] 1938 and joined the RAF. He flew in the Battle of Britain and was a member of the Caterpillar Club. He came back to Canada and was on operations off Halifax when his plane plunged into the ocean.

Membership in the Caterpillar Club was restricted to those who had successfully bailed out of a disabled aircraft. Certificates and gold lapel pins were provided by the Irwin Chute Company and by the end of the Second World War, there were 34,000 members. The incident in question occurred in 1941 when Flight Lieutenant Turner was flying with No. 145 Squadron. His Spitfire collided with another at 20,000 feet. Somehow he survived and returned to Canada as an instructor before returning to active service with No. 126 Squadron (Allison 1978). ***Frederick Turner Lake*** (64 K/1), southeast of Chartrand Lake was named after him in 1997.

Turner, Flight Sergeant **Clarence Alvin "Calvin"** of Ridgeville (R 134252). No. 1659 Conversion Unit, RCAF. He died 6 November 1943 at the age of 20 and is commemorated at St. Patrick Churchyard in Jurby on the Isle of Man. He was the son of George W. and Eva M. S. Turner of Ridgeville. His brother recalls (17 January 1997) that he was:

> ... the sixth child in a family of 10 children. Raised on a farm three miles south of the small town of Ridgeville, Manitoba – he took grade school and high school there. He loved to play hockey and was goal keeper for the local team. A few small towns not too far apart competed in a league of their own at that time. Calvin's life was that of the average Canadian country farm boy. He had a zest for life. Eager and ambitious, he looked to the future. His last letter to me (which I still have) mentions "when I get through this I will have a good vocation." The letter is dated October 12, 1943. On November 6, 1943, his plane crashed near Stradishall, Suffolk, England. He and six of his comrades are buried together.

Turner Rapids (64 I/7) in the North Knife River was named after him in 1995.

Turner, Rifleman **Cyril A.** of Winnipeg (H 9159). Royal Winnipeg Rifles. He died 21 February 1945 at the age of 36 and is commemorated at the Groesbeek Canadian War Cemetery in Holland. He was the son of Ernest A. and Ellen G. Turner. ***Turner Bay*** (63 O/2) in Five Mile Lake was named after him in 1995.

Turner, Sergeant **Ernest C.** of Flin Flon (H 77721). 12th Manitoba Dragoons. He died 30 October 1944 at the age of 28 and is commemorated at Bergen-op-Zoom Canadian War Cemetery in Holland. He was the son of Gordon and Gertie Turner and was survived by his wife Tena Turner of Elkhorn and their daughter. His sister Viney Reeves recalls (16 November 2001):

> He lived on the farm in Two Creeks, Manitoba until he was 17, then moved to Flin Flon where he lived until he enlisted. He was an only son with three sisters who all called him "son" and he hated that! He had rabbit cages in the back yard, teased his sisters and liked driving his Uncle Russell's Model T at the age of 14. He was so loved by his parents, sisters and daughter.

His daughter adds (8 November 2001):

> When my Grandmother was dying, I made a bedside promise to her that if it was in my realm of possibility, I would go to Bergen-op-Zoom in Holland and visit my father's grave. You see, she couldn't go herself because "if God had meant her to fly, he would have given her wings" (in other words, she was afraid of flying). The years have gone by too quickly and I've never had the means to travel to Europe. My youngest son who is now 30 has been for years now the keeper of the faith. He reads, collects military information, pictures etc., and keeps his grandfather's memory and what he and so many other young Canadians died for, alive and well in our treasure chest. He had the opportunity to travel to Europe the week of the tragedy in New York [11 September 2001]. He went out of his way and for the first time, a member of my family touched my father's headstone and Jeff told him how proud we were of him and how much we loved and missed him.

Turner Lake (64 N/9), southwest of Nueltin Lake was named after him in 1961.

Turner, Warrant Officer 2 **Frederick O.** of Wellwood (R 106197). No. 77 Squadron. He died 22 June 1943 at the age of 23 and is commemorated at the Runnymede Memorial in Surrey, England. He was the son of Oswald C. and Cora B. Turner of Wellwood and was survived by his wife Janet Turner (née Matheson) of Winnipeg and their nine month-old daughter Penny. His sister-in-law (19 April 1995) recalls that he was:

> ... born at Wellwood, Manitoba on February 8, 1920 [and] received his education (Grade 11) there. He was without a job before the war. He enlisted with the RCAF in Winnipeg on May 22, 1941 as a Wireless Telegrapher and arrived overseas on February 22nd of 1942.

Turner Peninsula (64 F/4) on Vandekerckhove Lake was named after him in 1995.

Turner, Flying Officer **Walter B.** of Winnipeg (J 38394). No. 405 Squadron. He died 28 January 1945 at the age of 21 and is commemorated at Durnbach War Cemetery in Bavaria, Germany. ***Turner Island*** (64 N/3) in Forster Lake was named after him in 1987.

Turrill, Rifleman **Austin H.** of Cartwright (H 103713). Royal Winnipeg Rifles. He died 18 November 1944 at the age of 21 and is commemorated at Brookwood Military Cemetery in Surrey, England. He was the son of Hubert W. and Marjorie J. Turrill of Cartwright. His sister notes (10 April 1995): "... [he] landed with the Canadian troops on the beaches of Normandy and was wounded twice in France. He died in England." ***Turrill Lake*** (64 K/8), southeast of Lac Brochet was named after him in 1972.

Tymchuk, Pilot Officer **Metro D.** of Garland (J 86662). No. 77 Squadron. He died 27 September 1943 at the age of 22 and is commemorated at the Runnymede Memorial in Surrey, England. He was the son of Mr. and Mrs. John Tymchuk of Garland, Manitoba. ***Tymchuk Lake*** (64 P/15), west of Baralzon Lake was named after him in 1974.

Tyndale, Flight Lieutenant **Lorne V.** of Winnipeg (J 13758). No. 582 Squadron. He died 29 August 1944 and is commemorated at Norre Vorupor Cemetery in Denmark. He was survived by his wife Helen D. Tyndale and their son. He writes (9 February 1999): "[He] lived at 45 Balmoral Place in Winnipeg when he enlisted. He was killed ... as part of No. 582 Pathfinder force in Lancaster PB202 near Vorupor during a night operation against Stetten, Germany." ***Tyndale Lake*** (64 O/8), northeast of Munroe Lake was named after him in 1978.

Tyshuk, Private **Samuel** of Winnipeg (H 615910). Royal Canadian Army Service Corps. He died 24 April 1944 at the age of 41 and is commemorated at Brookside Cemetery in Winnipeg. ***Tyshuk Lake*** (64 I/1), northeast of Etawney Lake was named after him in 1974.

Tytgat, Private **Armand P.** of Winnipeg (H 103903). Queen's Own Cameron Highlanders. He died 5 October 1944 and is commemorated at Bergen-op-Zoom Canadian War Cemetery in Holland. ***Tytgat Lake*** (63 I/7), north of Molson Lake was named after him in 1973.

German prisoners guarded by Canadian troops on Juno Beach on D-Day.
Courtesy of the National Archives of Canada (PA-136280).

U

Underhill, Trooper **George Holten L.** of Moline (H 1614). 1st Hussar Tank Regiment. He died 11 June 1944 at the age of 21 and is commemorated at Beny-sur-Mer Canadian War Cemetery in Calvados, France. He was the son of George H. and Mary L. Underhill of Moline, Manitoba. ***Underhill Lake*** (64 I/6), northwest of North Knife Lake was named after him in 1974.

Ungerer, Private **John C.** of Winnipeg (H 7167). North Nova Scotia Highlanders. He died 21 August 1944 at the age of 21 and is commemorated at Bretteville-sur-Laize Canadian War Cemetery in Calvados, France. He was the son of Christian M. and Annie V. Ungerer (née Johnston) of Winnipeg. His brother recalls (30 March 1998):

> John was born in Dauphin and received his early education there. The family moved to Winnipeg, so Jack continued his education there. He liked to play hockey and go fishing. He was a law-abiding citizen; the families were very proud of him. John first served with the Nova Scotia Highlanders, then transferred to serve in active battle in Kiska.

Ungerer Lake (52 L/6), east of Lac du Bonnet was named after him in 1973.

Unrow, Private **Edward N.** of Winnipeg (H 41036). Princess Patricia's Canadian Light Infantry. He died 23 May 1944 and is commemorated at the Cassino War Cemetery in Italy. ***Unrow Lake*** (64 J/4), north of Big Sand Lake was named after him in 1975.

Unruh, Pilot Officer **Victor A.** of Winkler (J 87613). No. 427 Squadron. He died 18 July 1944 at the age of 30 and is commemorated at Bretteville-sur-Laize Canadian War Cemetery in Calvados, France. He was the son of Dr. Abraham H. and Katherine Unruh of Winnipeg. ***Unruh Lake*** (64 H/10), east of Buckland Lake was named after him in 1995.

Urbanski, Private **William J.** of Traverse Bay (H 25300). Irish Regiment of Canada. He died 11 December 1944 at the age of 20 and is commemorated at Ravenna War Cemetery in Italy. He was the son of Jacob and Tena Urbanski of Traverse Bay, Manitoba and was survived by his wife Helen Urbanski. ***Urbanski Lake*** (64 O/11), east of Nueltin Lake was named after him in 1995.

Urquhart, Flight Sergeant **David S.** of Roland (R 119542). No. 425 Squadron. He died 7 December 1942 at the age of 21 and is commemorated at the Runnymede Memorial in Surrey, England. He was the eldest of the two sons of Charles and Elizabeth R. Urquhart (née Bain) of Carman. His niece writes (1 November 2001):

> David was an air gunner on a Wellington aircraft that took off from an air base in England at 5:00 PM, December 6, 1942 to carry out bombing operations over Mannheim. At 20 minutes past midnight, on its way back to base, an SOS was received from the aircraft as it flew over the Bay of Biscay but unfortunately, nothing further was heard from the aircraft after that time. David was listed Missing in Action December 7, 1942 and Presumed Dead December 23, 1942.
>
> I never met Uncle David as I was born four years after his death. I would have been his oldest niece. My remembrances are through his mother Elizabeth, my grandma. She remembers him as artistic (loved to paint with watercolours), academic (finished Grade 11), athletic (swam in the creek in the summer and played on the local hockey team in winter), congenial (enjoyed dancing at the town dances on a Saturday night and was engaged to be married when he went overseas). He was born and raised on a farm in southern Manitoba so riding horses and shooting crows and skunks was a common activity.
>
> My own memory is of a Silver Cross grandma received upon Uncle David's death. My job, as a young girl was to ensure there were fresh flowers on Uncle David's commemorative table, his picture was dusted and the Silver Cross cleaned. "Lest We Forget" is a part of me today due to this association.

Urquhart Lake (64 N/11), southeast of Kasba Lake was named after him in 1972.

The 9th Canadian Infantry Brigade lands on 'Nan White' Beach on D-Day. Courtesy of the National Archives of Canada (PA-137012).

V

Valde, Pilot Officer **Victor L.** of Transcona (J 90964). No. 415 Squadron. He died 2 November 1944 at the age of 20 and is commemorated at Rheinberg War Cemetery in Germany. He was the son of Lewis and Emma Valde of Transcona. ***Valde Lake*** (52 L/6), northeast of Lac du Bonnet was named after him in 1973.

Vancamp, Flight Sergeant **Ralph H.** of Winnipeg (R 134679). No. 619 Squadron. He died 15 June 1943 at the age of 20 and is commemorated at the Groesbeek Canadian War Cemetery in Holland. ***Vancamp Lake*** (64 P/11), southeast of Nueltin Lake was named after him in 1974.

Vance, Flying Officer **Gordon E.** of Winnipeg (J 24133). No. 290 Squadron. He died 15 April 1944 at the age of 22 and is commemorated at Eglantine Cemetery in County Down, Northern Ireland. He was the son of Samuel and Beatrice E. Vance of Winnipeg. ***Vance Lake*** (63 K/16), northwest of Wekusko Lake was named after him in 1973.

Vandekerckhove, Pilot Officer **George P. C.** of Stony Mountain (J 17326). No. 427 Squadron, Distinguished Flying Cross. The DFC was presented to his mother at Rideau Hall by the Governor General.

> This officer has successfully completed a number of operational bombing flights during which he displayed courage of the highest order. An exceptionally good captain, he has invariably pressed home his attacks with vigour and his success has been demonstrated by the photographs he has secured. In March, 1943, this officer was captain of an aircraft detailed for an attack on Essen. Nearing the target area, the aircraft was badly damaged by anti-aircraft fire but he flew safely back to this country, his rear gunner damaging a Junkers 88 on the return flight. On another occasion, Pilot Officer Vandekerckhove was testing an aircraft at 10,000 feet when the dinghy broke loose and severely damaged the tail of the plane. Ordering his crew to leave the aircraft by parachute, he regained control and made a successful landing in hazardous circumstances. This officer has always shown excellent judgement and superb airmanship (DFC Citation 1944).

This native of Neuville, France died 31 August 1943 at the age of 26 and is commemorated at the Reichswald Forest War Cemetery in Germany. He was the son of Basil and M. Vandekerckhove of Stony Mountain. He received mention in an unidentified English newspaper while there:

> Pilot Officer G. Vandekerckhove, RAF, a Canadian, was wearing the ribbons of the Distinguished Flying Cross at Durham City Ice Rink this week and was cordially congratulated upon his success. A bright-eyed young man, he has been in this country about two years and has taken part in more than 20 operational flights over enemy territory. He has one or two enemy fighters "in the bag."
>
> He has fallen in love with England and its people and speaks of the marked contrast of the wide open spaces of his own country and the typically English countryside. Asked if he finds domestic life much different in the two countries, he replied that he thought they were "pretty much the same" (n.d.).

Vandekerckhove Lake (64 F/3), east of Reindeer Lake was named after him in 1947.

Van Der Vennet, Private **Cyril** of St. Alphonse (H 204152). Argyle and Sutherland Highlanders. He died 26 February 1945 at the age of 25 and is commemorated at the Groesbeek Canadian War Cemetery in Holland. He was the son of Rene J. and Emilie Van Der Vennet (née Timmerman) of St. Alphonse, Manitoba. ***Van Der Vennet Lake*** (64 N/2), northwest of Egenolf Lake was named after him in 1972.

Vanlerberghe, Rifleman **Joseph** of La Broquerie (H 41522). Royal Winnipeg Rifles. He died 6 June 1944 at the age of 30 and is commemorated at Beny-sur-Mer Canadian War Cemetery in Calvados, France. He was the son of Contant and Evelyn Vanlerberghe of La Broquerie, Manitoba. ***Vanlerberghe Lake*** (64 N/2), northwest of Egenolf Lake was named after him in 1972.

Van Norman, Sergeant **Murray** of Brandon (K 18066). Royal Canadian Artillery. He died 20 September 1944 at the age of 30 and is commemorated at Coriano Ridge War Cemetery in Italy. He was survived by his mother J. B. K. Van Norman of Winnipeg. His obituary read in part:

> He was serving at the time with the British 8th Army in Italy. He enlisted in Vancouver in September, 1939 with the 7th Anti-Tank Corps, 111th Battery. He ... received his education in Fort Rouge, St. John's College and the University of Victoria. He was a member of the Vancouver Rowing Club (n.d.).

Van Norman Lake (64 K/1), north of Big Flat Lake was named after him in 1987. His nephew visited the lake in 2000.

VanSickle, Ordinary Seaman **Harold A.** of Swan River (V 39844). HMCS *St. Croix*. The *St. Croix* was torpedoed and sunk by U-305 south of Iceland while escorting Convoy ON.202. Five officers and 76 men were rescued by HMS *Itchen*, but only one of these survived the loss of the *Itchen* two days later. Ordinary Seaman VanSickle died 20 September 1943 at the age of 18 and is commemorated at the Halifax Memorial. He was the only son of Alex and Agnes VanSickle of Swan River. His sister recalls that: "As a young man who had never seen the ocean, he had a great desire to join the Navy and I'm sure he made a good seaman" (9 October 2001). The sole survivor of the *St. Croix* told his story in a newspaper account:

> "We were part of an escort detailed to a large convoy," [Stoker W. A.] Fisher related. "We received a signal that submarines were about. We stayed astern of the convoy, but on September 20, we had to come up and take on oil from a tanker in the convoy. On our way back to our position we saw a Canadian four-motored Liberator signalling us. We were told that they had spotted a submarine and dropped depth charges. We flashed two boilers and made for the spot at 24 knots. As we neared, we had to reduce speed. As we slowed up we were hit in the screws." Fisher said there was no panic and no one thought of abandoning ship. "But in two minutes another torpedo struck, this time near the mess deck, and water began to pour in," he went on. "The captain, Lieutenant Commander Dobson, then issued orders to abandon ship." That was just before 8 o'clock and dusk was gathering and a slight wind blew even though the sea was calm.
>
> Some men were injured by the explosions which followed the torpedoes, some were burned and cut. They were put in the motor launch before it was lowered over the side. The motor boat pulled away. Meanwhile attempts were made to lower a 60-passenger oar-driven whaler. Two attempts resulted in two large holes being gouged into the bottom of the whaler. Carley floats were dumped over the side and the men began jumping into the water. "No one seemed worried then," Fisher related. "Many of the crew laughed that they would be due for 29 day survivors' leave." The rowboat pulled away from the sinking destroyer, and picked men out of the water. "Even then I thought the ship would be saved," Fisher said. "Then I saw the captain dive off the boat. I knew everyone was off then and that the captain had given up hope."
>
> As Lieutenant Commander Dobson headed for the motor boat, he saw two men struggling in the water. He towed them to Carley floats and then made for the rowboat. Fisher was in charge of the motor boat. "No one in the boats died during the night," the survivor went on. "It was

morning that everything happened. Men on the Carley floats insisted on getting into the rowboat. As the men got in, it settled lower in the water. Just before the rescue ship came along, it sank. The whaler did not have any injured men aboard. They were oil-grimed and cold. I saw men who were tough, big men. They hung out all night in the hope a boat would pick them up. Then when the boat did not come into view they died. I guess they couldn't hang out any longer. We dropped them into the sea."

Sixty men were still alive on the whaler. The ship which headed to their rescue was the Royal Navy frigate *Itchen*, completed last September. As the frigate steamed through the lifting morning mist, the men in the whaler received the signal that the *Itchen* would come directly to their rescue. As the *Itchen* neared, a torpedo was seen to explode 30 yards to her stern. A message was flashed to the *Polyanthus*, a corvette of the Flower class, to come out of the convoy escort and circle the *Itchen* while the men were taken aboard. "The *Polyanthus* was just coming in and she was struck," Fisher said. "I guess she went down in about 10 minutes. We rescued 10 men in our whaler. The *Itchen* headed for the convoy," Fisher went on. "Some of us were given jobs to do. I did watch. On September 2, two days after we were rescued, we were ordered to our action stations because submarines were around. We had three orders. The first started at 6 at night. There was another one at 7 and again at 9. At 9 o'clock I was standing beside the funnel when a torpedo struck. I was knocked 30 feet and landed against a gun platform. As I crawled toward the rail I kept yelling for my pal, Stoker Rod MacKenzie, of Sydney. MacKenzie had been torpedoed six times before. He didn't answer and I jumped over the side. As I hit the water there was another explosion and I felt that my stomach was being squeezed through my ears. The water just cracked," said Fisher. When he reached down to tug off his boots, his left boot was missing. It had been blown off. Fisher grabbed a board and looked to see other men jumping from the ship. Most of them drowned. A Carley float drifted by and Fisher jumped on. During the night others jumped on, but most of them died (*Winnipeg Free Press* 1 October 1943).

VanSickle Island (64 F/9) in Jordan Lake was named after Ordinary Seaman Harold VanSickle in 1994.

Vanular, Flying Officer **John Henry** of Winnipeg (J 26359). No. 190 Squadron. He died 11 May 1945 at the age of 29 and is commemorated at Woensel General Cemetery in Eindhoven, Holland. He was survived by his wife Sonia Vanular. At the time of his enlistment, he was employed as an actuary by the Industrial Life Insurance Company in Quebec City. ***Vanular Lake*** (63 I/1), southeast of Little Bolton Lake was named after him in 1988.

Van Vliet, Group Captain **Wilbur D.** of Winnipeg (C 0094). Western Air Command, Victoria, British Columbia. He died 25 October 1942 at the age of 39 and is commemorated at Beechwood Cemetery in Ottawa. He was the son of George W. and Mary Ann Van Vliet of Winnipeg and was survived by his wife Audrey Van Vliet of Ottawa. ***Van Vliet Lake*** (64 O/8), east of Munroe Lake was named after him in 1975.

Vaughan, Private **Thomas W.** of Rackham (H 17834). Princess Louise Dragoon Guards. He died 1 September 1944 at the age of 20 and is commemorated at Montecchio War Cemetery in Italy. He was the son of Percy G. and Frances M. Vaughan of Rackham, Manitoba. ***Vaughan Island*** (64 F/6) in Wells Lake was named after him in 1984.

Veal, Rifleman **Herbert K.** of Dauphin (H 100961). Royal Canadian Corps of Electrical and Mechanical Engineers. He died 19 October 1945 and is commemorated at the Groesbeek Canadian War Cemetery in Holland. ***Veal Lake*** (64 N/13), southeast of Kasba Lake was named after him in 1961.

Venier, Warrant Officer 2 **Jack T.** of Gimli (R 152678). Royal Canadian Air Force. He died 20 April 1945 at the age of 29 and is commemorated at Assumption Gardens in Winnipeg. He was the son of Joseph and Angelina Venier of Belmont, Manitoba and was survived by his wife Viola A. Venier of Gimli. ***Venier Lake*** (53 M/11), northeast of Ransom Lake was named after him in 1996.

Venn, Sergeant **Frank J.** of Neepawa (R 59770). Royal Canadian Air Force. He died 26 June 1941 at the age of 24 and is commemorated at Stratford-upon-Avon Cemetery in Warwickshire, England. He was the son of Frank and Edith Venn of Edrans. According to his sister (n.d.):

Frank completed his Grade 11 schooling at the Edrans School whereupon he moved to Winnipeg where he joined the RCAF. After completing his training in Canada, he was posted overseas to continue upgrading his flight experience. It was on a training flight that his Oxford aircraft crashed at Loxley, Warwickshire killing all three members of the crew.

Venn Lake (64 P/6), east of Nejanilini Lake was named after him in 1974.

Verasky, Sergeant **William** of Winnipeg (H 19779). Queen's Own Cameron Highlanders. He died 11 October 1944 at the age of 32 and is commemorated at Bergen-op-Zoom Canadian War Cemetery in Holland. He was the son of John and Katie Verasky of Winnipeg and was survived by his wife Freda Verasky of Winnipeg. ***Verasky Lake*** (64 J/1), southeast of Tadoule Lake was named after him in 1975.

Vermette, Private **Antonio R.** of Ste. Rose du Lac (H 35754). Royal Canadian Army Medical Corps. He died 6 June 1944 at the age of 27 and is commemorated at Beny-sur-Mer Canadian War Cemetery in Calvados, France. He was the son of Antoine and Clarisse Vermette of Ste. Rose du Lac and the cousin of Private René Vermette (next entry). ***Vermette Lake*** (52 L/13), south of Manigotagan Lake was named after him in 1982.

Vermette, Private **René** of St. Germain (H 17742). Princess Patricia's Canadian Light Infantry. He died 31 August 1943 at the age of 24 and is commemorated at Agira Canadian War Cemetery in Italy. He was the son of Joachim and Marie Vermette of St. Germain, Manitoba and the cousin of Private Antonio R. Vermette (previous entry). ***Vermette Point*** (63 N/3) on Kississing Lake was named after him in 1972.

Verrall, Private **Walter H.** of Kenville (K 99750). Canadian Forestry Corps. He died 1 October 1942 at the age of 20 and is commemorated at Brookwood Military Cemetery in Surrey, England. He was the son of William W. and Rachel Verrall of Kenville. His sister writes (21 November 1996):

Walter was born April 2, 1922 at Strasbourg, Saskatchewan. He was a fun-loving boy and good natured. He attended a one-room school along with several of his siblings – seven in our family. He helped his father and brothers with the farm work.

In the winter, he loved to play hockey at the local rink. He played in goal and since "Turk" (Walter) Broda was the Leafs' hot goalie, everyone nick-named him "Brodie." He carried the name till he left to join the Canadian Forestry Corps at the tender age of 17.

He was stationed at Val Cartier, Quebec for some time before being shipped off to Inverness, Scotland. I do not know the dates of these moves, but he was becoming restless and wanting to see some 'action,' and was in the process of a transfer to the Air Force. But before he did, he was suddenly stricken with [an] apparent ruptured appendix and died on the operating table.

He loved music and had acquired a mandolin he loved to strum on. When his personal effects were shipped back to Canada, the ship was torpedoed and all was lost.

Verrall Lake (62 N/15), southeast of Swan River was named after him in 1973.

Viau, Private **Armand E.** of St. Boniface (H 33050). Royal Canadian Army Medical Corps. He died 29 January 1942 at the age of 34 and is commemorated at Brookwood Military Cemetery in Surrey, England. He was the son of Damase E. and Clara T. Viau and was survived by his wife Anna Viau of St. Boniface. He was the brother of Sergeant Joseph R. Viau (next entry). ***Viau Lake*** (64 K/13), northwest of Lac Brochet was named after him in 1972.

Viau, Sergeant **Joseph R.** of Winnipeg (R 86125). No. 12 Operational Training Unit, RCAF. He died 14 February 1942 at the age of 27 and is commemorated at Brookwood Military Cemetery in Surrey, England. He was the son of Damase E. and Clara T. Viau and the brother of Private Armand E. Viau (previous entry). ***Viau Bay*** (64 N/16) in Nueltin Lake was named after him in 1989.

Vick, Private **William G. A.** of Winnipeg (H 7120). Queen's Own Cameron Highlanders. He died 29 August 1944 at the age of 22 and is commemorated at Bretteville-sur-Laize Canadian War Cemetery in Calvados, France. He was the son of James A. and Victoria M. Vick of Winnipeg. His sister writes (12 March 1995):

Bill was born in Teulon November 1st, 1921 [and] attended school in Winnipeg to Grade 10. One special interest we remember was horseback riding. [He] worked for Brown and Rutherford until he joined the Winnipeg Grenadiers at the beginning of hostilities in 1939. Just prior to the Grenadiers leaving for Hong Kong, he had transferred to the Cameron Highlanders believing they would go overseas sooner, but he was fooled. He didn't get over to England until November, 1942 and went into France on D-Day. His photograph was sent to his mother by his English fiancée.

Vick Lake (63 K/13), east of Manistikwan Lake was named after him in 1984.

Vickers, Corporal **Jack F.** of Winnipeg (H 6443). Winnipeg Grenadiers. He died 23 December 1941 and is commemorated at the Sai Wan Memorial in Hong Kong. ***Vickers Island*** (64 P/12) in Nejanilini Lake was named after him in 1989.

Vickery, Pilot Officer **Clifford H.** of Makinak (J 94949). No. 419 Squadron. He died 16 March 1945 at the age of 24 and is commemorated at Nederweert War Cemetery in Holland. He was the only son of Christopher L. Vickery of Makinak, Manitoba. Prior to enlisting, he had worked with his father in the grain elevator at Makinak. His sister writes (15 November 2001): "Clifford was fond of music and loved to dance. He often took his sisters dancing. He was a good boy and never got into trouble. He was sorely missed by his father and two sisters." In a letter home he wrote:

Dear Dad: Well it's Sunday again, so will get a note off to you again. I got your letter in with the one you wrote from home. It was forwarded on from Lachine. I hope that I'll get another one from you soon. Tonight it is raining quite hard and has been raining off and on for the past few days. It rains an awful lot over here; you hardly go anywhere without a raincoat. The radio in the writing room is on and we heard the Jack Benny program which was transcribed from the United States via short wave.

I am going to try and get a bicycle, for the bus service is not so good for us. The roads are all very good over here so it won't be too bad for bikes. There are quite a few hills though and that's not so good, but we'll manage all right; all working people have bikes and very few have cars running now. I was into a good-sized town a few days ago and saw a show and tried to find a bicycle, but there weren't any in that day, so I'll have to wait until my next day off.

Well how are you keeping these days, and what are you doing? Is Mr. Basil putting up the hay on the hay farm? Are you getting any more cattle again? How much stock have you now? What is the weather, crops and everything around there [like] this year? I was home two months ago, but it seems like an awfully long time now. Is George still in the elevator? There was some talk of letting him go and he was talking of leaving. Do you know if Grandma has moved from Winnipeg yet? Fred was discharged from the army and was getting a job somewhere in Alberta and she was going to live with [illegible]. I was in to see her and took her some flowers. She seemed quite happy, but liked the idea of living with Fred.

Well I guess this is about all the room I have for this time, so will say goodnight for this time. Drop me a line soon and let me know all the news. Best of love and keep well. Love, Cliff (2 July 1944).

Vickery Lake (64 P/15), northeast of Nejanilini Lake was named after him in 1974.

Vickery, Leading Aircraftman **Leonard E.** of Wellwood (644401). No. 281 Squadron, RAF. He enlisted in May, 1939 and was killed in action 21 June 1944 while attached to an air-sea rescue squadron. He was 24 years of age and is commemorated at Brookwood Military Cemetery in Surrey, England. ***Vickery Bay*** (64 J/13) in Egenolf Lake was named after him in 1995.

Vickery, Rifleman **Nelson J.** of Rivers (H 100799). Regina Rifle Regiment. He died 9 June 1944 at the age of 28 and is commemorated at Beny-sur-Mer Canadian War Cemetery in Calvados, France. He was the son of Alfred and Rebecca A. Vickery of Rivers. ***Vickery Island*** (64 F/1) in Melvin Lake was named after him in 1995.

Vid (Vidomski), Pilot Officer **Frank J.** of Brandon (C 86521). No. 501 Squadron. He died 24 March 1944 at the age of 26 and is commemorated at the Calais Canadian War Cemetery in France. He was the son of John and Mary Vid of Saskatchewan and was survived by his wife Winnifred E. Vid (née Galloway) of Sudbury, Ontario. ***Vid Lake*** (64 P/4), south of Nejanilini Lake was named after him in 1974.

Vier, Private **Albert N.** of Starbuck (H 14969). Royal Regiment of Canada. He died 14 August 1944 at the age of 19 and is commemorated at Bretteville-sur-Laize Canadian War Cemetery in Calvados, France. He was the son of Herbert and Lillian M. Vier of Starbuck, Manitoba. ***Vier Lake*** (52 L/3), northeast of Brereton Lake was named after him in 1973.

Vince, Lance Corporal **Edward A.** of West Kildonan (H 63030). Canadian Provost Corps. He died 18 July 1944 at the age of 21 and is commemorated at Brookwood Military Cemetery in Surrey, England. He was the son of William and Ellen Vince of West Kildonan. His sister-in-law writes (22 February 1996):

> He was born February 14, a bouncing, big baby of 14 pounds. [He] grew up to be six feet four inches, the fourth in line of six boys. [He] had his schooling in Red River School in Old Kildonan [and] had a variety of jobs when available. He joined the army in 1941, went overseas in 1942 and the rest is history.

Vince Lake (63 O/4), north of Wekusko Lake was named after him in 1970.

Vince, Gunner **Irving L.** of Winnipeg (P 9908). Royal Canadian Artillery. He died 10 April 1940 at the age of 25 and is commemorated at Brookwood Military Cemetery in Surrey, England. He was the son of Benjamin and Charlotte Vince and was survived by his wife Edith M. Vince (née Anderson) of Winnipeg and their two children. ***Vince Island*** (64 C/8) in Granville Lake was named after him in 1995.

Vincent, Gunner **Henry J.** of Winnipeg (H 12075). Royal Canadian Artillery. He died 4 December 1943 at the age of 41 and is commemorated at the Moro River Canadian War Cemetery in Italy. He was the son of Joseph P. and Marie L. Vincent and was survived by his wife Belva Vincent of Oka, Quebec. ***Vincent Bay*** (64 K/16) in Stevens Lake was named after him in 1995.

Vincent, Gunner **Omer** of St-Georges (H 67097). Royal Canadian Artillery. He died 13 April 1945 at the age of 25 and is commemorated at the Holten Canadian War Cemetery in Holland. He was one of the 14 children of Fortunat and Marie-Louise Vincent of St-Georges, Manitoba. A Remembrance Day tribute read in part:

> Most Canadians will spend Saturday, November 11 morning in quiet reflection of wars gone past, of lives lost, of victories gained, and offer a few moments of silence in humble remembrance. For the families of lost loved ones, the remembrance has been a lifetime of reflection, a lifetime of memories, and they know only too well the priceless cost of war.
>
> On the very anniversary of his birth, April 13, Omer Vincent of St-Georges met his death, overseas while on a fateful mission to capture a German machine gun post. "He wasn't supposed to go on that mission," recalls sister Bella (Vincent) Kemball, who said her brother volunteered for the four-man manoeuvre. At 25 years of age, Omer Vincent would never return to Canada. He, alongside another comrade on the same mission were buried in Zutphen, Holland and later moved to a Permanent Canadian Cemetery in Holten.
>
> Bella Kemball remembers the telegram that arrived at the St-Georges Post Office that 1945 April day, "I'll never forget because I had to translate the bad news to French so my mother could understand." Brother Wilfred Vincent had not arrived home from his service and was quite upset by the news. The two brothers had met overseas and exchanged words shortly before Omer's death.
>
> "Omer was like a ray of sunshine," recalls Bella Kemball, the youngest of the 14 children, "he was always teasing us all the time." "Money was scarce, but he always shared with us. I remember he bought our first battery-powered radio. Mom cherished that radio and only allowed us younger children to listen to certain programs because batteries were expensive in those days" (n.d.).

Vincent Island (64 P/1) in Mullin Lake was named after him in 1995.

Vincent, Private **Stanley E.** of Stony Mountain (H 1531). General List, Canadian Army. He died 25 October 1944 at the age of 19 and is commemorated at Christ Church Cemetery in Stony Mountain. He was the son of Cyril S. and Gertrude Vincent of Stony Mountain, Manitoba. ***Vincent Lake*** (64 K/15), northeast of Lac Brochet was named after him in 1972.

Vinette, Private **Gabriel** of St. Boniface (H 8249). Princess Patricia's Canadian Light Infantry. He died 20 May 1944 at the age of 24 and is commemorated at the Cassino War Cemetery in Italy. He was the son of Philibert and Alma Vinette of St Boniface. ***Vinette Lake*** (64 K/13), northwest of Lac Brochet was named after him in 1972.

Vinie, Lance Corporal **Alfred J. "Guin"** of Winnipeg (H 19788). Queen's Own Cameron Highlanders. He died 19 August 1942 at the age of 23 and is commemorated at Dieppe Canadian War Cemetery in Seine-Maritime, France. This native of Middlesex, England was survived by his wife Daisy Vinie and their two children. ***Vinie Lake*** (64 I/13), east of Shethanei Lake was named after him in 1974.

Vinsky, Private **Gordon** of Winnipeg (H 204463). Princess Louise Dragoon Guards. He died 1 September 1944 at the age of 24 and is commemorated at Montecchio War Cemetery in Italy. He was the son of Samuel and Dora Vinsky of Winnipeg. ***Vinsky Lake*** (54 M/11), north of Long Lake was named after him in 1984.

Vivian, Pilot Officer **Jack K.** of Winnipeg (J 87751). No. 405 Squadron. He died 16 June 1944 at the age of 21 and is commemorated at the Calais Canadian War Cemetery in France. ***Vivian Lake*** (53 L/11), west of Gods Lake was named after him in 1983.

Vlassie, Flying Officer **Nickolas** of Winnipeg (J 28974). No. 619 Squadron. He died 27 April 1944 at the age of 25 and is commemorated at Landeville Churchyard, Haute-Marne, France. He was the son of Andrew and Photini Vlassie of Winnipeg. ***Vlassie Lake*** (63 J/13), east of Wekusko Lake was named after him in 1972.

Vogt, Gunner **Norman** of Winnipeg (H 101615). Royal Canadian Artillery. He died 17 April 1945 at the age of 29 and is commemorated at the Groesbeek Canadian War Cemetery in Holland. He was the son of Peter and Sarah Vogt and was survived by his wife Ann Vogt (née Ruta) of Winnipeg. She writes (21 September 1995):

> [He was] born [at] Aberdeen, Saskatchewan [and] worked at the *Winnipeg Free Press* and Canada Packers [before he] enlisted in July, 1942. [We were] married April 19, 1943 while he was on embarkation leave. He was in Italy, France, Germany, Belgium and Holland. On April 17, 1945 he was killed by a sniper.
>
> Norm was a very kind and gentle person. He loved to sing in his deep voice. He loved his chocolate Bars (Oh Henry!) and milk bars. He smoked, although his father didn't approve. His grandparents were Dutch and the name was Van Vogt, but someone shortened it. He was a religious person to a certain extent. We were married in [a] Lutheran church. I'm Catholic and he dropped out of his long before I met him. We decided to wait until he came back to join a church. We did not have any children. After Norm was gone, his family (sister) did not keep in touch and shortly after, his Dad forgot me!

Vogt Lake (64 J/3), north of Big Sand Lake was named after him in 1975.

W

Waddell, Sergeant **Ivan S.** of Winnipeg (R 100422). No. 8 Air Observers School. He died 24 November 1943 at the age of 25 and is commemorated at Assumption Gardens in Winnipeg. He was the son of Samuel G. and Ada B. Waddell of Winnipeg. ***Waddell Bay*** (64 C/5) in Plumbtree Lake was named after him in 1995.

Waddell, Rifleman **James A.** of Newdale (H 14688). Royal Winnipeg Rifles. He died 9 October 1944 at the age of 20 and is commemorated at the Adegem Canadian War Cemetery in Belgium. He was the second of the 11 children of Allan and Lillian Waddell of Newdale, Manitoba. His sister recalls (15 May 1991):

> Jimmy was born February 10th, 1924 at Newdale, ... raised on a farm and went to a one-room schoolhouse called Oldale. He had seven brothers and four sisters. He joined the Canadian Army October 20th, 1943 and served in Canada, Britain and the central Mediterranean area.

Waddell Island (52 M/12) in Sasaginnigak Lake was named after him in 1991.

Waddell, Sergeant **John B.** of Beausejour (R 95259). No. 33 Squadron. He died 24 July 1942 at the age of 20 and is commemorated at El Alamein War Cemetery in Egypt. ***Waddell Lake*** (52 L/6), northeast of Lac du Bonnet was named after him in 1973.

Wagner, Private **Frederick P.** of Winnipeg (H 7086). Calgary Highlanders. He died 30 September 1944 at the age of 19 and is commemorated at Bergen-op-Zoom Canadian War Cemetery in Holland. He was the son of Frederick and Mary Wagner of Winnipeg. ***Wagner Bay*** (63 N/11) in Morin Lake was named after him in 1995.

Wagner, Flight Sergeant **Gordon J.** of Winnipeg (R 59564). No. 70 Squadron. He died 26 June 1942 at the age of 21 and is commemorated at El Alamein War Cemetery in Egypt. The family visited his grave in 1984. He was the son of Montague F. and Florence Ethel Wagner of St. James. ***Wagner Island*** (63 H/16) in Stevenson Lake was named after him in 1985.

Waitt, Gunner **Arthur Stanley H.** of Winnipeg (H 35566). Royal Canadian Artillery. He died 11 October 1943 at the age of 20 and is commemorated at the Moro River Canadian War Cemetery in Italy. He was one of the eight children of Ronald V. and Mary Bertha Waitt of Vancouver and the brother of Gunner Norman Waitt (next entry) of Winnipeg. Their brother writes (7 December 1994):

> Our family grew up in south Wolseley – 511 Raglan Road. Stanley attended Wolseley, Isaac Brock and Gordon Bell schools. Norman did the same except he attended St. John's College as a theological student.

Waitt Lake (64 I/13), north of Shethanei Lake was named after Gunner Stanley Waitt in 1974.

Waitt, Gunner **Norman R.** of Winnipeg (P 9905). Royal Canadian Artillery. He died 29 November 1940 at the age of 27 and is commemorated at Brookwood Military Cemetery in Surrey, England. He was one of the eight children of Ronald V. and Mary Bertha Waitt of Vancouver and the brother of Gunner Stanley Waitt (previous entry) of Winnipeg. He enlisted in 1933 and was studying theology at St. John's College. The Padre wrote a letter to his mother:

> Dear Mrs. Waitt: Along with others in Barriefield Camp, I was saddened to hear that your son was recently killed in action in England. Stanley told me of his passing last Saturday. He seemed to feel the blow very keenly, but his chief thought was of you. We made reference to your son's death at the morning service in Barriefield Camp and prayer was offered for those that have been bereaved. After the Service, I had a long talk with Stanley and gave him what comfort I could.
>
> He is a splendid boy and regards his brother's death as a sacrifice offered to God for the preservation of freedom in the world. I know that the fact of his being killed while at the post of duty is a great consolation to you. Along with many of his fellows, he had made the supreme sacrifice and has entered into his heavenly reward.
>
> Hoping that you may receive divine strength in this time of loss and grief, I am, Yours very sincerely, W. F. Bannister, H/Capt. (3 December 1940).

Waitt Bay (64 I/13) in Shethanei Lake was named after Gunner Norman Waitt in 1995.

Wakefield, Corporal **Dorothy M.** of Forrest (W 300100). Royal Canadian Air Force (Women's Division). She died 11 May 1945 at the age of 25 and is commemorated at Brandon Cemetery. She was the daughter of Walter and Ingred Wakefield of Brandon. Her sister recalls (22 November 2000):

> Dorothy grew up in the area of Forrest, Manitoba. In her latter teens, she worked for different families in Brandon where she helped them with their household duties. She then had a chance to work in the kitchen of the Brandon Mental Hospital. She worked there as a cook. Dorothy was very dedicated to her job. She had a wonderful sense of humour and was a very kind and generous person.
>
> She was a great credit to her family. In the latter part of 1941, Dorothy joined the Royal Canadian Air Force (Women's Division). On January 3, 1942 until February 14, 1942 she was sent down to Guelph, Ontario to an RCAF school of cookery [at] No. 4 Wireless School. She passed her exams by obtaining 82% of the total marks. She was ranked first in a class of 24. We were all so proud of her. She was then posted to Dauphin, Manitoba where she spent the next 26 months cooking for all the Air Force personnel who passed through the station there.
>
> Dorothy's greatest wish was to be posted overseas, but she did not get her wish. From Dauphin, her next posting was to Clinton, Ontario. She was working there as a Cook-Chef when the German Forces surrendered. On May 11, 1945, Dorothy and one of her friends were riding their bicycles along Highway 4 between Clinton and the Air Force School. The girls had just come from visiting one of their co-workers who was sick in the hospital. At 9:15 in the evening, Dorothy was struck and killed instantly by a passing vehicle. Her bicycle was found in the ditch. The report was, that the driver was blinded by the glare of approaching lights and failed to see Dorothy in time and struck and killed her. Dorothy's remains were transferred to Brandon and on May 16, 1945, Corporal Dorothy Wakefield was buried in the Brandon Cemetery with full military honours.

Wakefield Lake (64 P/13), north of Nejanilini Lake was named after her in 1974.

Wakula, Private **John** of Sifton (B 116761). Westminster Regiment. He died 17 April 1945 at the age of 19 and is commemorated at the Groesbeek Canadian War Cemetery in Holland. He was one of the two sons of Fred and Polly Wakula of Sifton, Manitoba. According to his niece Gloria (27 November 2001):

> Although I never got to know my Uncle John, my Dad always spoke of him saying that his brother was a kind, gentle soul, loving, generous, loved life and that he died a hero. I still have a few of the letters he wrote to my parents and one in particular that stands out is the one he wrote April 13, 1945 in which says he "was sure glad to get out of Italy and get to a civilized country [Holland] where the people treat you as if you were their own son." I feel that because of this statement, we the family of Uncle John are truly grateful to the people of Holland, in particular to Jan and Fretty Bennemeer, who with the help of others have erected a memorial plaque honouring the three other lads along with Uncle John who were killed while liberating the town of Putten. Oh so young to die for his Country. My Dad was right, Uncle John was and always will be Our Family Hero.

Wakula Lake (64 N/13), east of Kasba Lake on the Manitoba - Nunavut boundary was named after him in 1974.

Walden, Able Seaman **Richard Willard** of Winnipeg (V 9456). HMCS *Niagara*. He died 5 June 1941 at the age of 29 and is commemorated at the Halifax Memorial. He was the son of William A. and Maud Walden of Winnipeg and was survived by his wife Verna M. Walden of Winnipeg and their one year-old daughter Dianne. He received his education at Earl Grey and Gladstone schools and was a member of Augustine United Church and Sunday School. His niece writes (5 February 1998):

> Prior to going on active duty, he worked for the CNR. Willard and his brother were both in the naval reserves. At the beginning of the war, they went on active duty – Willard to the east coast and Edward to the west coast. They didn't see one another again.

Walden Lake (64 N/14), southeast of Kasba Lake was named after him in 1972.

Walesiak, Private **Victor T.** of Winnipeg (H 101989). Royal Canadian Army Service Corps. He died 20 March 1944 at the age of 27 and is commemorated at Brookwood Military Cemetery in Surrey, England. He was survived by his wife Cecile M. Walesiak of Winnipeg and their son. His younger sister recalls (16 November 2001):

> Victor was a kind hearted, loveable person. He was a home builder, but his first love was hockey. He built a Club House and ice skating rink on Mountain and Galloway with hockey teams competing with one another. This Club House was for adults only and no kids were allowed. I remember when I was a small child, Victor used to sneak me in to sit behind the counter so I could watch the events and help myself to all the candy I could eat and pop I could drink. This was one of the best times of my childhood. Victor was the community's leader, bringing together people from all ethnic backgrounds in the neighbourhood to participate in this national sport and Club House activities. As my older brother, I looked up to him. Victor was my protector, my friend … my big brother. Symbolically, Victor was also the big brother of our community. I shall always miss him.

Walesiak Lake (64 B/7), southwest of Baldock Lake was named after him in 1979.

Walford, Private **James W.** of Souris (H 1769). Saskatoon Light Infantry. He died 12 April 1945 at the age of 20 and is commemorated at the Groesbeek Canadian War Cemetery in Holland. He was the son of Walter and Gladys E. Walford of Brandon. ***Walford Lake*** (64 I/3), west of North Knife Lake was named after him in 1974.

Walker, Leading Aircraftman **Edward G. C.** of Winnipeg (R 110680). Royal Canadian Air Force. He was being transported aboard the SS *Caribou* when it was torpedoed by U-69 in Cabot Strait with the loss of 136 lives. He died 14 October 1942 at the age of 39 and is commemorated at the Ottawa Memorial. He was the son of George C. and Kate Walker and was survived by his wife Sadie R. Walker of Winnipeg and their daughter. Born in England, he came to Canada with his parents, settling in St. James where he was educated. Prior to enlisting, he had farmed in the Riding Mountain district. ***Walker Bay*** (64 C/12) in Dunphy Lakes was named after him in 1995.

Walker, Private **Ernest A.** of Winnipeg (H 1102). Essex Scottish Regiment. He died 8 March 1945 at the age of 32 and is commemorated at the Groesbeek Canadian War Cemetery in Holland. He was the son of William and Annie Walker of Winnipeg and was survived by his wife Florence Walker of Winnipeg. His niece recalls (17 November 1997):

> He was born in Winnipeg 30 April 1912. At the time of his enlistment, he and his wife resided at Suite 2a, Assiniboine Court, Winnipeg. [His parents] resided at 396 Talbot Avenue. My uncle enlisted in the Canadian Army on 6 January 1943, completed his basic training with the 103rd C.A.(B)T.C. Fort Garry on 25 March 1943 and joined the Essex Scottish Regiment of Canada. He was killed in action ... during fighting around the Reichswald area in Germany.

Walker Point (64 J/13) on Dunlop Lake was named after him in 1995.

Walker, Corporal **Frank W.** of Winnipeg (H 102760). Royal Winnipeg Rifles. He died 4 July 1944 at the age of 29 and is commemorated at Beny-sur-Mer Canadian War Cemetery in Calvados, France. He was the son of William W. and Margaret Walker of Winnipeg. ***Walker Peninsula*** (53 L/4) on Kennedy Lake was named after him in 1995.

Walker, Private **Norman C.** of Miniota (H 6894). Winnipeg Grenadiers. He died 20 December 1941 and is commemorated at the Sai Wan Memorial in Hong Kong. ***Walker Island*** (64 F/3) in Vandekerckhove Lake was named after him in 1994.

Walker, Lance Corporal **William M.** of Brandon (H 25125). Royal Canadian Engineers. He died 28 September 1943 at the age of 32 and is commemorated at Brookside Cemetery in Winnipeg. He was the son of Robert and Jennie E. Walker of Winnipeg and was survived by his wife Mary Walker of Winnipeg. ***Walker Rapids*** (53 E/14) in the Stevenson River was named after him in 1997.

Wallace, Rifleman **Fraser F. W.** of Winnipeg (H 60567). Royal Winnipeg Rifles. He died 10 April 1945 at the age of 21 and is commemorated at the Holten Canadian War Cemetery in Holland. He was the son of William and Margaret Wallace of Winnipeg and was survived by his stepmother Gladys Wallace of Winnipeg. ***Wallace Bay*** (64 J/13) in Reece Lake was named after him in 1995.

Wallace, Pilot Officer **John M.** of Bagot (J 89880). No. 427 Squadron. He died 21 February 1945 at the age of 27 and is commemorated at Rheinberg War Cemetery in Germany. He was the son of James A. and Anne Wallace and was survived by his wife Kathleen Wallace of South Kensington, London. His sister recalls (3 December 2001):

John was born in the Bell Plain School District north of Portage on December 20, 1918 and the family moved to the Image Hill district northwest of Bagot later the same year. This was John's permanent home until he enlisted. He took his first eight grades at a small one-room school and the next three by correspondence, passing them all – including Latin – with good marks. He loved learning. He was in the Boys and Girls Club (gardening and poultry etc.) and had many hobbies including collecting arrowheads. He knew all the birds, trees and flowers and played ball and hockey. He even did some play acting in the winter. He loved the outdoors. John helped his Dad on the farm and also some of the neighbours. He did some carpentry and was a beekeeper for a few years. John read a lot of books but didn't have the opportunity to travel until he joined the Air Force. Then he got to meet his relatives in Ontario and Scotland.

My oldest son was in the Air Force and while he was in Germany, my daughter and I went to see him. He took us to see John's grave in Rheinberg. It is a beautifully kept cemetery and he lies beside his fellow gunner Eddy Essenburg [see entry] from Winnipeg, so he stayed with his friend. It was such a shock to see so many young men laid to rest there, some still in their teens.

Wallace Point (64 J/7) in Murdock Lake was named after him in 1989.

Wallace, Ordinary Seaman **Wilbert C.** of Wawanesa (V 24983). HMCS *Avalon*, the Royal Canadian Navy shore establishment in St. John's, Newfoundland. He died 12 December 1942 at the age of 22 and is commemorated at Mount Carmel Roman Catholic Cemetery in St. John's, Newfoundland. He was the son of Wilbert R. and Enid M. Wallace of Wawanesa, Manitoba. ***Wallace Island*** (64 O/12) in Dowds Lake was named after him in 1985.

Wallbridge, Leading Aircraftman **Harold R.** of Souris (R 116425). No. 6414 Servicing Echelon, RCAF. He died 8 June 1945 at the age of 23 and is commemorated at Hamburg Cemetery in Germany. According to his sister (1 May 1995):

He was born June 6, 1932 in Brandon, Manitoba. He joined the RCAF in 1941 [and] went overseas in 1942 and spent time in England, Italy and Holland.

Wallbridge Lake (64 P/7), southeast of Nejanilini Lake was named after him in 1974.

Walld, Flying Officer **Robert A.** of Bluff Creek (J 27582). No. 1664 Conversion Unit, RCAF. He died 16 March 1944 at the age of 20 and is commemorated at Stonefall Cemetery in Yorkshire, England. He was the son of Albin and Delia Walld of Bluff Creek, Manitoba. ***Walld Lake*** (64 G/15), north of Little Sand Lake was named after him in 1995.

Walley, Flying Officer **Keith M.** of Balmoral (J 13830). No. 426 Squadron. He died 5 April 1943 at the age of 20 and is commemorated at the Runnymede Memorial in Surrey, England. He was the sixth of the ten children of Cecil S. and Nina C. Walley (née Graham) of Balmoral and the brother of Flight Lieutenant Kenneth R. Walley (next entry). His sister recalls (19 September 2001):

Keith was a serious and sensitive youth. He liked school, did well and was intent on going to university. He preferred older people's company, enjoyed reading and participated in serious discussion resulting in close friendships with older people. At the completion of Grade 12 in 1941, he too felt he must sign up for war service and so joined his two brothers Bruce and Kenneth and his father Cecil in the Air Force. He trained as a navigator even though the Air Force would have liked him to be a pilot because of his youth.

But Keith was a sensitive youth. He loved animals and found the idea of shooting or being involved [abhorrent] and navigation at least removed him as far as was possible from that action. Such was his sensitivity that he refused to kill a chicken for a family dinner, leaving the job to a kindly neighbour.

His aircraft was disabled on the return trip from a bombing mission over Germany and crashed in the North Sea. The official report on the incident graphically described Flying Officer-Navigator Walley's last minutes:

Five minutes before the aircraft would have reached the East Anglian coast, the engines cut. The pilot ditched the [aircraft] but it went under the water and broke up at once. The bomb aimer and wireless operator P/O Leakey and Sgt. Anderson were able to swim to the overturned dinghy and each helped the other climb onto it. They could hear the cries of the navigator and rear gunner, but could not paddle to their assistance. Four and one-half hours later, the two survivors were picked up by a naval destroyer. F/O Kennedy's body washed up on shore but the other two bodies have not been discovered (5 April 1943).

The bomb-aimer later wrote to Keith's father and explained what had happened:

Dear Mr. Walley: It is my sad task to write you a few facts concerning the loss of your son, P/O K. M. Walley. As a crew member, I may be [able to] in some way cast a little light on the situation that must certainly be troubling you. Of course, censorship prevents exact details, but I shall endeavour to give a very brief picture of what happened.

On the night of Sunday, April 4th, we were returning from a bombing raid on Kiel when we encountered stiff enemy opposition. Our aircraft was severely damaged, but we managed to get away and make for home. Unfortunately, we were too severely damaged to reach England and had to make a landing on the sea. It was only due to the supreme co-operation of all members of the crew that we were able to get as far as we did, some thirty miles from our own coast. Our aircraft made a heavy landing and on breaking up, sank quickly. At this time the pilot, navigator and air gunner perished, being injured in the crash. The actual landing in the sea is still not yet clear in my mind, and neither the wireless operator nor myself can remember how we ever got out. All of the crew were thrown out of the aircraft, but their injuries were such that we only heard them once or twice and that was all.

Being one of those that escaped, I would like to say a few words for our crew and its particular members. On that fatal evening, every member did his job well in spite of the great difficulties that we were faced with. Particularly, the pilot and navigator did a magnificent job in bringing the aircraft as close to shore as they did. For your personal knowledge sir, [I] would like to say what a wonderful job in navigation Keith did, for when we landed in the sea, we were exactly on track – and this after 500 miles of flying over the sea with only the barest of navigational aids. Keith was one of the best navigators in the squadron and our crew had [the] utmost confidence in his work. We all owe him a great debt and feel his absence very severely.

As a man, P/O Walley was one of the best, having the highest character and strongest will of anyone I have ever met. Keith was respected everywhere he went and all looked upon him as a model character. His service record was outstanding and may well be an inspiration to those following him. He had a great interest in his environment and at all times displayed exceptional perseverance and keenness. Keith had great ambition and never let his surroundings affect him as so many other chaps do on operational life. He was the sort of fellow whose influence always lives on and I can truthfully say, sir, that I have never met a finer individual. However, the call of war is never sparing of any class of man and sooner or later they are taken. When this struggle is over, we may well take off our hats to such people who have sacrificed their own lives that we may live in peace. May God take care of all these fine fellows wherever they are and ease the hearts of those who are left behind. Yours sincerely, Dallas Leakey (n.d.).

Walley Lake (64 G/10), northwest of Southern Indian Lake was named after Flying Officer Walley in 1986.

Walley, Flight Lieutenant **Kenneth R.** of Balmoral (J 15873). No. 410 Squadron. He died 20 October 1944 at the age of 28 and is commemorated at the Calais Canadian War Cemetery in France. He was the second of the ten children of Cecil S. and Nina C. Walley (née Graham) and was survived by his wife Jean H. Walley of Winnipeg. He was the brother of Flying Officer Keith M. Walley (previous entry). His sister recalls (19 September 2001):

His early childhood was spent in England and in Winnipeg. On the threshold of his teens, the family moved to a farm near Balmoral, Manitoba. Most farms in the 1920s were mixed farms and such was the case with our parents'. With mixed farming, there were many chores, some arduous and unpleasant which had to be done, morning and night. Little mechanization in those days meant that the boys were expected to do their share. At seeding and harvest time, there was extra effort with long hours the norm.

At such times school was sporadic, but the older members of the family were expected to keep up their studies and prepare for provincial exams at the school year's end. Dropping out was not an option for members of our family. School was five miles distant and transportation was by horse-driven vans so the day was long, with the unpleasant prospect of all the barnyard chores awaiting them at the end of the day. At some point in his high school years, Kenneth had ruled out farming. Such was his distaste for the outdoor work that he persuaded our mother – and his sister who liked outside work – to exchange places for the winter. All of this is not to suggest that there was no time for leisure. Sundays were generally free, allowing for baseball and swimming in summer along with the occasional picnic outings. In the winter months [it was] skating but more frequently skiing behind a horse-drawn cutter, or better, a car or truck.

During this period, Kenneth had decided he wanted to be a doctor. By the time he had completed high school, the Great Depression had taken hold. Money was more difficult to come by and eventually Kenneth and his older brother would have to look elsewhere for work to enable them to go to university. He worked at a number of odd jobs and along with the proceeds from the sale of 100 tons of hay that he and his older brother had stacked one season, Kenneth was able to see his way clear for one year of school.

Having completed his first year, Kenneth decided to ride the freight trains along with his brother out west where there was a good prospect of work in the gold mines of BC. So with the absolute necessities to keep alive, they joined the nameless throngs atop box cars in search of greener pastures. It was risky and dangerous as they would have to hop on and off the train when it was moving on the outskirts of the train stops in order to avoid being caught by the police, because were they discovered and caught, they would proceed no further. Sometimes they would end up spending the night in a ditch, huddled around a small campfire to try and keep from freezing, preparing a meal as best they could under the circumstances. Those prairie nights could be very cold. Fortunately, Kenneth survived the experience unharmed and managed to get a job in one of the gold mines in BC. The work was hard, dirty and dangerous, but the pay was good. One year's work gave him sufficient funds to return to school.

At the completion of his second year of university, he was successful in gaining admission to medical school and from then on he never looked back. At last life became enjoyable. The future looked bright. He had time to enjoy friendships and pursue interests. I remember at one stage in his studies, he and a close friend became convinced that fish was good brain food. To the point where fish became the main staple of their diet as much as siblings, and parents tried to dissuade him and his friend from their position. This "fad" (so considered by family) did pass eventually.

The year Kenneth was to begin his internship, the war was in progress and not going well for the Allies. He decided that he must join his brother Bruce and father Cecil who were already in the Air Force. That was 1941. Kenneth trained as a pilot and was sent overseas as an instructor. Training future pilots was not his idea; he wanted to be in the action. Finally, in the spring of 1944, his request was granted. He was sent on a reconnaissance mission in advance of D-Day. His plane crashed and he was killed. A bright future cut short for our brother Kenneth!

Walley Island (64 F/3) in Vandekerckhove Lake was named after him in 1989.

Walmsley, Sergeant **Harold W.** of Bowsman River (H 40765). Royal Winnipeg Rifles. He died 4 July 1944 at the age of 27 and is commemorated at Beny-sur-Mer Canadian War Cemetery in Calvados, France. He was the son of James and Emily Walmsley of Bowsman River, Manitoba. ***Walmsley Lake*** (64 I/12), south of Shethanei Lake was named after him in 1974.

Walmsley, Corporal **James H.** of Winnipeg (H 103685). Royal Canadian Armoured Corps. He died 30 March 1944 at the age of 27 and is commemorated at Brookwood Military Cemetery in Surrey, England. He was the son of Frederick G. and Minnie Walmsley of Ewood in Lancashire, England. ***Walmsley Island*** (64 J/5) in Sprott Lake was named after him in 1995.

Walsby, Fourth Engineer Officer **George A.** of Winnipeg. SS *Fort Pelly*, Canadian Merchant Navy. He died 20 July 1943 at the age of 30 and is commemorated at the Halifax Memorial. He was the son of Mary Walsby of Kamloops, British Columbia. ***Walsby Lake*** (63 P/6), north of Landing Lake was named after him in 2001.

Walsh, Leading Aircraftwoman **Olive G.** of Winnipeg (W 301792). Royal Canadian Air Force (Women's Division). She died 7 January 1943 at the age of 37 and is commemorated at Brookside Cemetery in Winnipeg. She was the daughter of Charles and Sarah A. Bowd of Winnipeg. ***Walsh Lake*** (53 E/16), west of Krolman Lake was named after her in 1997.

Walters, Private **Frederick A.** of Winnipeg (H 200026). Queen's Own Cameron Highlanders. He died 24 July 1944 at the age of 24 and is commemorated at Beny-sur-Mer Canadian War Cemetery in Calvados, France. He was the son of George A. and Margaret Walters of Winnipeg. ***Walters Bay*** (64 O/16) in Baralzon Lake was named after him in 1995.

Walters, Private **George** of Winnipeg (B 73878). 48th Highlanders of Canada. He died 10 December 1944 at the age of 28 and is commemorated at Ravenna War Cemetery in Italy. He was the son of Godfried and Emily Walters of Old Kildonan. ***Walters Point*** (53 E/16) on Island Lake was named after him in 1995.

Walters, Sergeant **Ronald G.** of Winnipeg (R 95093). No. 29 Operational Training Unit, RCAF. He died 29 August 1942 at the age of 22 and is commemorated at St. John The Baptist Churchyard in Rutland, England. He was the son of George R. and Olive M. Walters of Winnipeg and was survived by his fiancée Rae Ledingham. His nephew writes (26 November 2001):

> I never met my Uncle Ron, but there were always pictures of him in my home and my grandparents' home. My father gave me the following information about his brother. My Uncle Ron attended Mulvey and Gordon Bell schools in Winnipeg. He enjoyed track and field and used to run five miles before classes to keep in shape. He also liked fishing and used to cycle out to Lockport, a distance of about 20 miles, with his friends to fish. His first job was as a machinist at Vulcan Iron Works. Ron and Rae Ledingham were engaged shortly before he went overseas. Ron met his Grandma Taylor and several other aunts and uncles when he got to England.

Walters Island (63 P/4) in Sipiwesk Lake was named after him in 1995.

Walters, Aircraftman 2 **Stewart F.** of Transcona (R 71348). No. 1 Technical Training School, RCAF. He died 13 January 1941 at the age of 28 and is commemorated at Elmwood Cemetery in Winnipeg. ***Walters Creek*** (52 L/6), which flows south into the Winnipeg River was named after him in 1978.

Walton, Warrant Officer 2 **Roy H.** of St. Vital (R 157319). No. 419 Squadron. He died 21 January 1944 at the age of 21 and is commemorated at the Berlin 1939 - 1945 War Cemetery in Brandenburg, Germany. ***Walton Island*** (64 P/1) in Ploschansky Lake was named after him in 1995.

Wanlin, Rifleman **Alphonse V.** of Notre Dame de Lourdes (H 614481). Royal Winnipeg Rifles. He died 10 April 1945 at the age of 24 and is commemorated at the Holten Canadian War Cemetery in Holland. His brother and nephew visited the site in 1986. They noted that the graveyard is very well maintained by the local Netherlanders who to this day, hold the liberation efforts of the Canadians in very high esteem. Rifleman Wanlin was survived by his father, Herman Wanlin, five brothers and two sisters. A veteran from the regimental Museum of the Royal Winnipeg Rifles provided these details of the battle of Deventer that claimed his life:

> The ancient city of 50,000 lies on the west bank of the Ijssel River. The river is about 100 yards wide and has a strong current. The Germans had an ATK ditch surrounding the town. The Allied attack started on April 6, 1945 with "C" Company leading. They found the bridge at the Schipbeek Canal "blown." The "pioneers" built a footbridge to cross the river and "D" Company secured the bridgehead under heavy fire. "A" Company led the assault on Deventer with artillery, tanks and Crocodiles (flame-throwing tanks) in support. 200 prisoners were taken by "A" Company. "B" and "D" Companies took over the battle, but were stopped by the ATK ditch. Though there was opposition to the obstacles, "B" and "D" companies were overcome. The position was consolidated on April 10, 1945 with 96 casualties suffered by the Winnipeg Rifles (n.d.).

According to his brother (16 November 2001):

> He is buried at Holten Cemetery near the town of Deventer where he died as one of the 96 casualties in the battle there. Alphonse was called up late to the war – September, 1944. He, along with a few other town lads, were taken to the train at Rathwell by L'Abbe Bourgar in late September. I recall how Alphonse cried at the departure because he really didn't want to go. He had heard how others had "hid in the wood" when the conscription notices came, or had delayed their departure as long as possible, but Alphonse had not done this. Had he left later, he may still be alive as he would have missed the war by catching a later boat.
>
> I received a letter dated January 19, 1945 (received January 29th) with a British stamp (written in French). He was not allowed to disclose where he was stationed, but he did relate how unprepared for war these young men were. He relates that he thought he was supposed to have further training in a place called Debut [Debert], but it never happened. Instead, he describes the journey from Winnipeg to Toronto where he spent four days. Then sent by train to Halifax where he was immediately shipped overseas to England by boat. He thought the voyage was "not too bad" as he was only sick for one day on arrival. He describes how terrible the damage was to areas around London and Liverpool and how pitiful the children appeared compared to those he left in Canada. He described how it was not safe to go outside with a "bare head" and how he missed the small things, like soap, that he failed to stock up on before leaving Canada. He related that living conditions in England were not as good as in Canada, but says things are okay and he hopes they will be in the future. He asked me to pass along his news and asked his family to write soon and send by airmail as stamps are hard for him to get. We learned of his death on April 22, 1945, when Father Champagne, the village Catholic priest, made the announcement in church to the Parish.
>
> Alphonse never knew much life beyond his rural upbringing and home town. He came from a farming family and his mother had died when he was only six years old. He had a generous nature and his war salary was more money than he ever saw in his early life. He mentioned in his letter that he hoped to send some money to his family as he knew it would help them, likely more than him. Needless to say, the money never arrived. He was a handsome-looking young man and it's a sad thing that he died without enjoying his full potential.

Wanlin Lake (52 E/11), southeast of Brereton Lake was named after him in 1974.

Wann, Flying Officer **John A.** of Winnipeg (J 9543). No. 10 Squadron. He died 4 April 1943 at the age of 22 and is commemorated at the Runnymede Memorial in Surrey, England. ***Wann Lake*** (64 C/11), southwest of Lynn Lake was named after him in 1979.

Warburton, Flight Sergeant **Eric** of Grosse Isle (R 56900). No. 51 Squadron. He died 31 October 1941 at the age of 21 and is commemorated at Den Burg Cemetery in Texel, Holland. He was the son of Mr. and Mrs. Albert Warburton of Poplar Point. His niece made him the subject of a Remembrance Day presentation at Yellowquill School (11 November 1992):

> In this time of remembrance, I'd like to focus our attention on one particular soldier; knowing his story is probably very typical of many who paid the supreme sacrifice on our behalf.
>
> May I introduce Eric Warburton, an uncle born October 24, 1918, killed in action in October, 1941 and buried in a war graves cemetery in Holland. From stories I hear from Eric's brothers and sisters, Eric was a very determined sort of young man. For instance, having a liking for western music, he took off one day to Winnipeg from his home in Grosse Isle and returned with a guitar, an instruction book and a western type of dress shirt. The next morning, he locked himself in his room with the guitar and came out at night a guitar player. One more story that accents his determination: Those were the years referred to as "the dirty thirties." In common with most young men of that time, he did not have or hope to have a dress-up suit of clothes. Somehow, the family had a suit given to them which proved to be too large for any of the boys. Eric asked his mom how to operate the sewing machine and in a very few days that suit was cut down to size and the finished product fit perfectly and was tailored as good as if it came off the rack.

He was making a name for himself as a goalie when war broke out in September, 1939, and he signed up almost immediately. Having his heart set on the air force and that part of it that was to be airborne, he soon came to realize that there were many ahead of him who hoped to be pilots, but there was a striking shortage of applicants to be wireless air gunners and it was easy to know why! It was recognized as the most dangerous of any in the air crew. One was almost locked in a cubicle in the rear of the plane with slim hope of getting out in time to parachute in case of fire or being shot down. Eric completed his training as wireless air gunner in Mossbank, Saskatchewan and was home for an overnight visit during very early December, 1940, and by the way, a full-fledged Christmas dinner. [He was] posted to Toronto for final briefing and to await departure overseas.

Several of his letters from England tell of visits with relatives over there and some had photos. In one of those letters to a brother, he let it be known that his chances of coming through alive were akin to zero and left it up to him as to tell that to Mom and Dad. The telegram that Eric was reported missing and presumed dead came shortly after that and some time later his body was found, identified and buried in Holland. A relative from England visiting here last summer identified some of the family places Eric had visited from the photos Eric had sent home.

A ... lasting momento was brought into being ... when Manitoba approved the naming of a lake after him. It is a family dream to someday fly in to that lake and leave a marker – In Remembrance.

Warburton Lake (64 P/13), north of Nejanilini Lake was named after him in 1974.

Ward, Private **Charles R.** of Dauphin (H 204621). Essex Scottish Regiment. He died 20 February 1945 at the age of 25 and is commemorated at Groesbeek Canadian War Cemetery in Holland. He was the son of Christopher J. and Ethel E. Ward of Dauphin. ***Ward Island*** (64 N/8) in Shannon Lake was named after him in 1995.

Ward, Warrant Officer 1 **Leslie** of Winnipeg (R 91945). No. 113 Squadron. He died 6 June 1943 at the age of 29 and is commemorated at Maynamati War Cemetery in Bangladesh. He was the son of James and Alice R. Ward of Winnipeg. ***Ward Lake*** (54 E/16), east of Bradshaw Lake was named after him in 1995.

Wardell, Trooper **Earl R.** of Winnipeg (H 61199). Lord Strathcona's Horse. He died 15 May 1944 and is commemorated at the Cassino War Cemetery in Italy. ***Wardell Lake*** (54 D/15), northwest of Myre Lake was named after him in 1996.

Wardrope, Sergeant **Calvin H.** of Winnipeg (R 191206). No. 431 Squadron. He died 3 October 1943 at the age of 19 and is commemorated at Hotton War Cemetery in Belgium. He was the son of Calvin C. and Ena U. Wardrope of Winnipeg. ***Wardrope Lake*** (64 P/14), northeast of Nejanilini Lake was named after him in 1974.

Wareham, Sergeant **Albert** of Rivers (R 110831). No. 19 Elementary Flying Training School. He died 30 July 1942 at the age of 23 and is commemorated at Rivers Cemetery in Manitoba. He was survived by his wife Norma L. Wareham (née Grummett). She recalls (9 October 2001):

When war broke out, Albert joined the Army and was sent to Portage la Prairie and while there, transferred to the RCAF. He was sent to Edmonton and on to Saskatoon where he received his wings in 1941. He was then transferred to Trenton, Ontario and back to Virden as a pilot instructor. He and his English student were both killed during a routine training flight ... and buried in the Service plot in Rivers Cemetery. It doesn't seem nearly 60 years – I have not forgotten the sacrifices made!

Wareham Lake (64 P/12), east of Nejanilini Lake was named after him in 1974.

Warkentin, Flying Officer **John H.** of Beausejour (J 23122). No. 429 Squadron. He died 24 March 1944 at the age of 21 and is commemorated at the Berlin 1939 - 1945 War Cemetery in Brandenburg, Germany. ***Warkentin Lake*** (52 L/6), northeast of Lac du Bonnet was named after him in 1973.

Warmington, Bombardier **William H.** of Winnipeg (H 35264). Royal Canadian Artillery. He died 12 May 1941 at the age of 45 and is commemorated at Elmwood Cemetery in Winnipeg. He was survived by his wife Mary Warmington of Fort Garry. ***Warmington Lake*** (53 F/13), southeast of Angling Lake was named after him in 1996.

Warne, Private **Bennett V.** of Winnipeg (H 20057). Queen's Own Cameron Highlanders. He died 19 August 1942 at the age of 25 and is commemorated at the Brookwood Memorial in Surrey, England. He was the son of Ole and Amy E. Warne of Pelly, Saskatchewan. His sister recalls (27 April 1997):

Bennett was born in Driscoll, North Dakota February 13, 1917. Our parents moved to Saskatchewan in 1926 and left for Manitoba in 1938. He was always called "Bennett." His life was so short, and he had to go to work so young [that] there wasn't much time for special interests. I am the only living family member now, but I do remember he had a crystal set and did enjoy playing the accordion and ukulele.

Warne Lake (62 N/15), southeast of Swan River was named after him in 1973.

Warner, Flying Officer **Lloyd O.** of Winnipeg (J 3251). No. 412 Squadron. He died 19 July 1942 at the age of 22 and is commemorated at the Runnymede Memorial in Surrey, England. He was the son of Edwin L. and Kathleen C. Warner of Hampstead, London. ***Warner Peninsula*** (64 H/8) on Freeman Lake was named after him in 1995.

Warner, Private **Ronald W.** of St. James (H 8090). Royal Canadian Regiment. He died 28 January 1944 at the age of 20 and is commemorated at the Moro River Canadian War Cemetery in Italy. He was the son of William F. and Salome A. Warner of St. James. ***Warner Lake*** (54 M/4), south of Pakulak Lake was named after him in 1984.

Warren, Pilot Officer **Gordon** of Winnipeg (J 93781). No. 576 Squadron. He died 28 December 1944 at the age of 20 and is commemorated at Brookwood Military Cemetery in Surrey, England. ***Warren Lake*** (64 H/13), northwest of Currie Lake was named after him in 1995.

Warrener, Gunner **James A.** of Baldur (H 9642). Royal Canadian Artillery. He died 15 September 1944 at the age of 21 and is commemorated at Coriano Ridge War Cemetery in Italy. He was the son of Clarence S. and Permilla A. Warrener of Baldur, Manitoba. His sister commented that (14 June 1995): "he enjoyed hunting but wasn't around long enough to have many other interests." ***Warrener Lake*** (64 K/10), east of Lac Brochet was named after him in 1972.

Warthe, Sergeant **George L.** of St. Boniface (R 210363). No. 24 Operational Training Unit, RCAF. He died 7 December 1944 at the age of 21 and is commemorated at Brookwood Military Cemetery in Surrey, England. He was the son of John and Olive Warthe of St. Boniface. ***Warthe Lake*** (63 K/16), west of Wekusko Lake was named after him in 1973.

Warun, Gunner **William A.** of Emerson (H 103864). Royal Canadian Artillery. He died 6 June 1944 at the age of 22 and is commemorated at Beny-sur-Mer Canadian War Cemetery in Calvados, France. He was the son of Alex and Annie Warun of Geraldton, Ontario. ***Warun Lake*** (64 N/3), southwest of Nueltin Lake was named after him in 1973.

Warywoda, Pilot Officer **Peter** of Winnipeg (J 86885). No. 9 Squadron. He died 23 March 1944 at the age of 21 and is commemorated at Brussels Town Cemetery in Belgium. He was the son of Michael and Annie Warywoda. ***Warywoda Lake*** (63 K/16), northwest of Wekusko Lake was named after him in 1973.

Washook, Pilot Officer **Michael** of Winnipeg (J 94448). No. 415 Squadron. He died 13 October 1944 at the age of 21 and is commemorated at Stonefall Cemetery in Yorkshire, England. He was the son of Alexander and Rose Washook of Winnipeg. ***Washook Lake*** (64 P/2), southwest of Caribou Lake was named after him in 1974.

Wasslen, Private **Theodore D.** of Binscarth (H 10628). Queen's Own Cameron Highlanders. He died 20 July 1945 at the age of 21 and is commemorated at the Holten Canadian War Cemetery in Holland. His sister writes (22 January 1997):

> Theodore was born on March 23, 1924. He was educated and completed his schooling in Binscarth. Theodore was very fond of sports – mainly hockey and baseball. Before joining the force, he worked for the North American Lumber Company in Binscarth.

Wasslen Lake (64 I/12), south of Shethanei Lake was named after him in 1974.

Waterbury, Flight Lieutenant **Orville R.** of Birtle (J 7520). No. 83 Squadron, Distinguished Flying Cross.

> On two occasions, despite the most adverse weather conditions, in daylight attacks on Germany, Pilot Officer Waterbury has displayed skilful navigation and as a result has successfully carried out his mission and brought his aircraft safely back to base. One night in September, when returning from an operational sortie on Wilhelmshaven, his aircraft was fired on by hostile aeroplanes and the wireless operator was severely wounded. Pilot Officer Waterbury successfully administered first aid, thereby saving the life of his colleague. He has completed numerous operational sorties, including attacks on the enemy's most heavily defended targets, and by his exceptional keenness and efficiency has set a fine example (DFC Citation, 29 September 1942).

He died 12 March 1943 at the age of 22 and is commemorated at the Reichswald Forest War Cemetery in Germany. He was the son of Ray D. and Edna Waterbury of Erickson, Manitoba. He had been a druggist at Prince Albert, Saskatchewan when he enlisted there in September, 1940. At the time of his death, he was on the last mission of his second tour of operations. ***Waterbury Lake*** (63 N/12), south of Sisipuk Lake was named after him in 1995.

Waterman, Lance Corporal **Ray C.** of Winnipeg (H 8767). Royal Canadian Army Service Corps. He died 20 May 1945 at the age of 34 and is commemorated at Bergen-op-Zoom Canadian War Cemetery in Holland. He was the son of Jesse and Mable Waterman and was survived by his wife Elizabeth Waterman of Winnipeg. ***Waterman Lake*** (64 J/6), southwest of Tadoule Lake was named after him in 1975.

Waters, Craftsman **Edward T.** of Winnipeg (H 63574). Royal Canadian Corps of Electrical and Mechanical Engineers. He died 1 July 1944 and is commemorated at Assisi War Cemetery in Italy. ***Waters Lake*** (64 H/2), northeast of Holmes Lake was named after him in 1995.

Watkins, Ordinary Signalman **Harry** of Winnipeg (3031). HMCS *Margaree*. The *Margaree* was lost in the North Atlantic after collision with the freighter *Port Fairy* while escorting the five ship Convoy OL.8; 142 of her ship's company were lost, many of whom were survivors of *Fraser's* tragic sinking. Ordinary Seaman Watkins died 22 October 1940 at the age of 20 and is commemorated at the Halifax Memorial. He was the son of George and Harriett Watkins of Winnipeg. ***Watkins Lake*** (64 N/7), southwest of Nueltin Lake was named after him in 1972.

Watson, Flight Lieutenant **Frederick S.** of Winnipeg (C 1372). No. 409 Squadron. He died 11 October 1941 at the age of 22 and is commemorated at Scopwick Church Burial Ground in Lincolnshire, England. ***Watson River*** (64 I/3), which flows north into Rocky River was named after him in 1974.

Watson, Private **George R. "Geordie"** of Balmoral (H 103598). Princess Patricia's Canadian Light Infantry. He died 23 May 1944 at the age of 21 and is commemorated at the Cassino War Cemetery in Italy. He was the fourth of the eight children of George A. and Isabell G. Watson of Balmoral, Manitoba. His nephew writes (3 April 1995):

> George was born at Rosser, Manitoba in 1923. He was working at a garage in Stonewall, training to be a mechanic when he enlisted in 1942. His hobby was anything mechanical. My uncle told me that George was an avid and good dancer who also enjoyed a good practical joke now and then. He was an all around "good guy."

George Watson Peninsula (53 M/14) on Hubley Lake was named after him in 1995.

Watson, Pilot Officer **James C.** of Winnipeg (J 7213). No. 206 Squadron. He died 25 June 1942 at the age of 21 and is commemorated at Hamburg Cemetery in Germany. He was the son of Alexander and Margaret Watson. ***Watson Creek*** (64 J/12), which flows northeast into Descôteaux Lake was named after him in 1978.

Watson, Flying Officer **Lloyd G.** of Napinka (J 38782). No. 429 Squadron. He died 30 November 1944 at the age of 27 and is commemorated at the Runnymede Memorial in Surrey, England. He was the son of Arthur H. and Faith E. Watson and was survived by his wife Verna Watson of Dauphin. ***Watson Peninsula*** (64 H/14) on North Knife Lake was named after him in 1995.

Watson, Stoker 1 **Norman R.** of Winnipeg (V 9654). HMCS *Louisburg*. The *Louisburg* was attacked and sunk by Italian aircraft east of Oran while escorting a convoy from Gibraltar to Bone, Algeria; 38 of her ship's company were lost. Stoker Watson died 6 February 1943 at the age of 21 and is commemorated at the Halifax Memorial. He was the son of Robert and Margaret Watson of Winnipeg. ***Watson Bay*** (64 O/5) in Atimkameskak Lake was named after him in 1985.

Watson, Warrant Officer 1 **Thomas Stewart** of Gladstone (R 116441). No. 271 Squadron. He died 25 May 1945 at the age of 22 and is commemorated at Choloy War Cemetery in France. He was the son of James H. and Annie G. Watson of Gladstone, Manitoba. His sister writes (26 October 2001):

Warrant Officer Watson was raised on a farm close to Gladstone, Manitoba. Prior to enlisting in the RCAF, he was helping his father with farm duties. He originally enlisted as a fireman, but soon after transferred to air crew as a pilot trainee. Stewart was the pilot of a Belgium-based aircraft that was carrying glider towing equipment to Salzburg, Austria when it crashed ten miles south of Trier, Germany. The entire crew perished.

Watson Island (64 K/10) in Maria Lake was named after him in 1989.

Watt, Flying Officer **Robert H.** of Winnipeg (J 18309). No. 415 Squadron, Distinguished Flying Cross.

Since January 1943, this officer has flown on most of the major operations undertaken by his squadron. He has often encountered very severe weather over the Dutch coast and has many times pressed home his mission in the face of heavy and light concentrated fire from enemy ships and in the presence of enemy night fighters. A skilful leader, he has been largely responsible for the fine efficiency and unerring operational ability of his detachment (DFC Citation 1946).

He died 19 January 1946 at the age of 23 and is commemorated at Elmwood Cemetery in Winnipeg. He was the son of Peter C. and Violet Watt of Winnipeg. ***Watt Lake*** (64 C/7), northwest of Granville Lake was named after him in 1947.

Watters, Pilot Officer **James F.** of Winnipeg (J 89106). No. 433 Squadron. He died 30 January 1944 at the age of 25 and is commemorated at the Berlin 1939 - 1945 War Cemetery in Brandenburg, Germany. He was survived by his mother Mrs. M. Watters of Vancouver. His brother writes (15 August 1995):

He went to school at St. John's Tech on Salter Street. In winter, he enjoyed playing hockey on the Olympic rink on Church Street. He was employed in one of the breweries and later at Vulcan Iron making shells when the war broke out. He went to Vancouver to work in an aircraft factory, but returned home to enlist in the RCAF and follow me overseas as a rear gunner. He was shot down on his first operational mission over Germany.

Watters Island (64 B/6) in Karsakuwigamak Lake was named after him in 1995.

Watters, Warrant Officer 2 **William J.** of Portage la Prairie (R 86348). No. 104 Squadron. He died 16 April 1943 at the age of 24 and is commemorated at Enfidaville War Cemetery in Tunisia. He was the son of Thomas G. and Elizabeth Watters and was survived by his wife Alice E. Watters of London, Ontario and their young son. His sister recalls (19 February 1998):

Bill was born October 6, 1918. He was the only boy among six girls, so his coming was a great joy to my parents. He was born in Portage, graduated from high school and then attended Business College in Winnipeg. Until he joined the Air Force, he worked in the same insurance company as I did, so we were very close.

During his school years, he was involved in sports – track and field, rugby and tennis being his favourites. He also worked in my Dad's grocery store after school hours. He loved music and seemed to enjoy life to the full.

When he joined up, he was posted to various stations in Ontario, St. Thomas, I think and Tilsonberg, and he met the girl in London, Ontario that he married before going overseas. She was an RN and she drew his name at a party the nurses held for the boys. He married her before going overseas and she had his son, David Anthony (Tony). Bill always loved little children, and to me it was so sad that he never saw his own son. The little boy died of leukaemia when he was 2 1/2 years old, but by that time, his father had been killed. Of all the people I have known in my life, she was and is one of the bravest I have known in the way she handled things. Last year on Remembrance Day she was asked to speak at a service they held in London, and she took her copy of the Commemorative Name Certificate in honour of Bill and gave a talk on what it was like for her during those sad times.

Bill was stationed on the Island of Malta at the time of his death. He was on a night flight when the plane they were on was hit. We were told by one of the other fliers that they all bailed out and their chutes all opened, but they were shot on their way down. There are six names on his grave: one from Australia, Great Britain, America and three from Canada.

Watters Lake (64 I/7), northeast of North Knife Lake was named after him in 1974.

Way, Flight Lieutenant **Wilfrid H. "Bill"** of Brandon (J 10777). No. 103 Squadron. He died 7 June 1944 at the age of 23 and is commemorated at Bretteville-sur-Laize Canadian War Cemetery in Calvados, France. He was the son of Edgerton S. and Helen Way of Edmonton.

His aircraft was approaching Vire, France at an altitude between 3000 and 4000 feet and was hit either by flak or an enemy night fighter and caught fire in both wings. The crew continued in their attack, dropping their bomb load on the target. The pilot turned the aircraft away from the target and flew back over Vire, gradually losing altitude. The aircraft crashed at Vire on Omaha Beach, and slid along the ground for about 200 yards breaking up into small, burning pieces (Allison and Hayward 1991).

The next morning the farmer inspected the wreckage and buried all seven members of the crew. He found the body of Len Zingellmann and the remains of three others in the main body of the aircraft. These three were Flight Lieutenant Way, my uncle Sergeant Jennings and Flight Sergeant Cooper. All four were buried next to the aircraft. I understand that the other three were buried some distance away, where they were found. The rear gunner Flight Sergeant Duns was still in his turret and two others were found along the line where the aircraft crashed and must have been thrown clear in the impact as it slid along and broke up.

The land battle in the area in the following weeks was very fierce and many of the residents dispersed to other areas for their own safety. Subsequently, when the Canadian soldiers came to remove the remains of the crew, they only found those of the four buried by the main part of the wreckage. Later, the farmer informed the authorities of the other three graves on his return to the area which accounts for the fact they are buried in different cemeteries and the confusion surrounding this at that time (Fell 1989).

Way Lake (64 P/4), south of Nejanilini Lake was named after him in 1974.

Waychuk, Flying Officer **Walter S.** of Brandon (J 29371). No. 408 Squadron. He died 11 July 1944 while returning from a bombing raid over Germany. He was 29 years of age and is commemorated at Brookwood Military Cemetery in Surrey, England. He was the son of Simeon and Katherine Waychuk of Brandon and was survived by sisters Anne Dunfield of Brandon and Mary Masciuch of Winnipeg. His sister writes (16 November 2001):

His parents were pioneer immigrants from western Ukraine. They built their home in Brandon on the north bank of a five-acre bend of the Assiniboine River. To attend school and all activities, Walter and his sisters had to use a boat in summer and the ice in winter. The popular Sixteenth Street Beach across the river provided them with fun and excitement throughout the dirty thirties.

Walter was known to be quiet and reserved, loyal and reasonable. He was an avid reader, had a good sense of humour, was concerned for others and serious far beyond his years. He spent a lot of time at the YMCA, was involved in swimming, diving and hockey and was an avid golfer. When his sister Mary Masciuch was seeing him off on his last leave, he wanted to stop at the corner of Portage and Main. "I don't know when I'll see this again," he said, then they walked from there to the CN Station – he was headed for Boston.

Walter is buried in Brookwood Cemetery in Surrey, England. His sister May, who visited his gravesite many times, describes it as a very extensive, peaceful, quiet place which has been beautifully kept. Close to home, at the Brandon Cemetery, Walter's name is inscribed on the Waychuk tombstone – the words "resting overseas," tell his story and move one to tears.

Waychuk Lake (64 J/14), northwest of Tadoule Lake was named after him in 1975 "to commemorate a son and brother who 'gave his life in Freedom's Cause.'"

Wayte, Private **Thomas L.** of Glenboro (H 20501). Queen's Own Cameron Highlanders. He died 23 July 1944 at the age of 26 and is commemorated at Bretteville-sur-Laize Canadian War Cemetery in Calvados, France. He was the son of Nichol and Linda Wayte of Glenboro and was survived by his wife Lena G. Wayte of Glenboro and their son. His wife recalls (15 October 2001):

He was raised on a farm which is now part of Spruce Woods Provincial Park and attended a small school in the area. He loved to hunt and was a good marksman. As a young man, his mode of travel was either horseback or bicycle. He enlisted in July, 1940 and was married the same year. He was stationed in Winnipeg and left for overseas in October, 1941. He took part in the Dieppe raid and was only in France three days when he was killed in the Battle of Caen. He believed that the war was a war to end all wars. He was a very caring person, both of family and Country. My son and I were able to visit his grave in 1999.

Wayte Lake (63 K/13), south of Mikanagan Lake was named after him in 1984.

Weaver, Private **Charles E.** of Birnie (H 77190). Saskatoon Light Infantry. He died 9 December 1943 at the age of 22 and is commemorated at the Moro River Canadian War Cemetery in Italy. He was the son of Sidney A. and Mary Weaver of Birnie, Manitoba and was the brother of Trooper Frederick Weaver and Pilot Officer Glen Weaver (next two entries). Private Weaver joined the 18th Canadian Armoured Car Regiment in June, 1942. In 1943, he was transferred to the Saskatchewan Light Infantry and participated in the landing on Sicily and the subsequent invasion of Italy. His brother recalls (22 November 2001):

Charles did exceedingly well in high school, especially in chemistry, algebra and geometry. His goal was to attend University. His favourite sport was baseball and he enjoyed the challenge of being a pitcher with local baseball teams. In the fall of 1942 when Charles and our brother Fred were home on embarkation leave, they wanted to take a roast turkey on the trip back with them. In those days, local farmers let their turkeys free range. So three days before leaving, along with a buddy, they went out and poached two local birds. The boys prepared them, so that when they returned home, Mother would unwittingly roast the birds the next day. One was served for supper and the other went along with them, all carved and wrapped *en route* to the East Coast!

He had been employed as a clerk when he enlisted in May, 1941. ***Weaver Point*** (64 J/15) on Stony Lake was named after him in 1989.

Weaver, Trooper **Frederick M.** of Birnie (H 77168). 12th Manitoba Dragoons. He died 5 September 1944 at the age of 21 and is commemorated at the Calais Canadian War Cemetery in France. He was the son of Sidney and Mary Weaver and was survived by his wife Jean C. Weaver (née Henderson). He was the brother of Private Charles Weaver and Pilot Officer Glen Weaver (previous and following entries). According to his brother (22 November 2001):

Fred joined the 18th Canadian Armoured Car Regiment, 12th Manitoba Dragoons in May, 1942 and went overseas in September of that year. Fred was married in May, 1944 to Jeanie Cochran Henderson. He landed in France in July, 1944 and was wounded and subsequently died September 5, 1944.

Fred had a natural instinct for sales and was the type of fellow who would do anything to have the satisfaction of closing a successful deal. Growing up in a rural environment, he loved to hunt and hockey was his favourite sport.

Weaver Island (64 J/15) in Stony Lake was named after him in 1989.

Weaver, Pilot Officer **Glen M.** of Birnie (J 19918). No. 405 Squadron. He died 4 May 1944 at the age of 24 and is commemorated at Montdidier French National Cemetery, Somme, France. He was the son of Sidney and Mary Weaver of Birnie, Manitoba and was the brother of Private Charles Weaver and Trooper Frederick Weaver (previous two entries). His brother writes (22 November 2001):

Glen initially joined the 18th (Manitoba) Reconnaissance Battalion in 1941 and later transferred to the RCAF where he trained as a wireless operator/air gunner. He went overseas in May, 1943 attached to 405 Squadron. When Glen was posthumously awarded the operational wings of the RCAF, he had completed one full tour of operations and had started on the second. He had a great love for curling and played in many rural Bonspiels as well as the Winnipeg 'Spiel.

Weaver Bay (64 J/15) in Stony Lake was named after him in 1989.

Weaver, Gunner **Robert F.** of Winnipeg (H 50536). Royal Canadian Artillery. He died 23 January 1944 and is commemorated at the Moro River Canadian War Cemetery in Italy. ***Weaver Peninsula*** (64 P/12) on Nejanilini Lake was named after him in 1989.

Webb, Sergeant **Edward C.** of Winnipeg (R 180232). No. 428 Squadron. He died 20 February 1944 at the age of 20 and is commemorated at the Runnymede Memorial in Surrey, England. ***Webb Peninsula*** (64 O/6) on Calder Lake was named after him in 1995.

Webb, Warrant Officer 2 **Francis A.** of Homewood (R 93492). No. 9 Squadron. He died 18 January 1943 at the age of 20 and is commemorated at the Runnymede Memorial in Surrey, England. ***Webb Rapids*** (64 I/13) in the McKay River was named after him in 1995.

Webb, Leading Seaman **Horace M.** of Winnipeg (2822). HMCS *Margaree*. The *Margaree* was lost in the North Atlantic after collision with the freighter *Port Fairy* while escorting the five ship Convoy OL.8; 142 of her ship's company were lost, many of whom were survivors of *Fraser's* tragic sinking. Leading Seaman Webb died 22 October 1940 at the age of 23 and is commemorated at the Halifax Memorial. ***Webb Bay*** (64 H/6) in the Churchill River was named after him in 1995.

Webb, Private **John** of Stonewall (H 98133). Veterans Guard of Canada. He died 23 April 1944 at the age of 50 and is commemorated at Stonewall Cemetery in Manitoba. He was survived by his mother Elizabeth Webb of Stonewall and by his wife Ruby Elizabeth Webb (née Whiteman) of Stonewall and their seven children.

He enlisted in the Canadian Army in World War I and was wounded in France. Following his return to Canada, he farmed until joining the Winnipeg Supply and Fuel Company Limited. Shortly after the outbreak of World War II, he joined the Veterans Guard of Canada and served at several points in western Canada until his death in Shaughnessy Military Hospital in 1944 (Webb 1995).

His eldest daughter recalls (17 December 2001):

Dad joined the Veteran's Guard of Canada with three of his Stonewall friends. Our parents raised seven children and we were a very closely knit family and still remain so today. We were upset about our Father wanting to enlist in the war, but thought we shouldn't worry too much as he wouldn't be involved in direct fighting as he was in the first war. He would be staying in Canada. It was such a shock to all of us when word came that he had died while guarding prisoners in British Columbia. His oldest son was training to be a pilot in Alberta and they allowed him to go to British Columbia to escort his father home. He is buried in the family plot in Stonewall.

Webb Island (52 E/13) in Brereton Lake was named after him in 1973. His eldest son and grandson erected a plaque there in 1995 (*The Argus* 6 November 1995). His daughter adds: "In 2000, his children, grandchildren and great-grandchildren gathered there for a family picnic and many stories, memories, tears and laughter were shared and enjoyed by all" (17 December 2001).

Webb, Colonel **Ralph H.** of Winnipeg. Royal Canadian Army Service Corps, Distinguished Service Order, Member of the Order of the British Empire, the Military Cross and the Efficiency Decoration. He died 1 June 1945 at the age of 59 and is commemorated at St. John's Cemetery in Winnipeg. He was survived by his wife Maud S. Webb. This veteran of the First World War had served two terms as the Mayor of Winnipeg (1925 - 1927, 1930 - 1934) and was instrumental in the creation of the Royal Canadian Legion in Winnipeg in 1925. ***Webb River*** (64 I/6), which flows southeast into Paragon Lake was named after him in 1974.

Webster, Pilot Officer **George H.** of Winnipeg (J 5471). No. 214 Squadron. He died 28 January 1942 at the age of 22 and is commemorated at the Runnymede Memorial in Surrey, England. He was the son of William and Ellen Webster of Elmwood. According to his sister (16 January 1995):

George was born August 1, 1919 in Winnipeg. He attended Salisbury School, Morse Place, Lord Selkirk and St. John's Technical schools. He worked for the Department of Education before enlisting. He always had a great love for airplanes; he used to drive me to the airport (then Stevenson's Field) and we would watch planes landing and taking off. George enlisted as a clerk in the Air Force in 1939 and was stationed at Manning Depot in Toronto. George and I were always very close, and I saved money to go visit him. Mother said: "His letters are different – keep your eyes open – perhaps he has a girlfriend!" The "girlfriend" turned out to be private flying lessons.

I went to Toronto Flying Club and watched innumerable of his take-offs and landings. At that time in history, the Air Force was taking only university graduates or those who were licensed pilots as air crew. With his commercial pilot license attained, George was able to remuster to air crew. George graduated from the flying training school at Dunnville, Ontario at age 21 and received the highest award at his class wings ceremony.

He was chosen for Bomber Command and trained at Lossiemouth, Scotland. He was then stationed at Stradishall, [Suffolk]. He piloted a Wellington bomber and he and the whole crew were reported missing in action during a raid on Muenster.

Webster Bay (64 G/6) in Jefferson Lake was named after him in 1994.

Webster, Warrant Officer 2 **Lloyd P.** of Roland (R 147246). No. 419 Squadron. He died 26 November 1943 at the age of 22 and is commemorated at Rheinberg War Cemetery in Germany. He was the son of S. Wilbert and Ethel G. Webster of Roland, Manitoba. His sister recalls (7 July 1982):

Lloyd Pierson Webster was born December 1, 1920 in Morden, Manitoba. He lived all his life on the family farm just south of Roland. His elementary schooling was in a one-room country school – Lowestoft No. 509. His high school education was taken at Roland Collegiate where he completed Grade 11. He joined the RCAF in January, 1942 and went overseas in December of that year. He served as an observer. He had just been raised to a WO2 shortly before his plane was shot down during a raid on Stuttgart, Germany. It's not a very colourful biography, but he wasn't around very long either.

She concludes (13 October 2001):

From the time he was quite young, he had a recurring ulcer in one eye, for which the doctors could find no cause. So the resulting scarring left him nearly blind in one eye. When he went to enlist, we did not think he would pass the medical exam, but he memorized the eye chart and I guess they didn't look in his eye.

He had a marvellous sense of humour which was reflected in letters home. There were rarely any "down" moments in these letters. This is an excerpt from a long letter that had no censor blackouts:

"Your little brother has had another shift and we are now flying the kite known to the world as Halifax. It is pulled along by four engines and floats lightly as a bird on a wing nearly 100 feet long. Boy, is there lots of room inside, two stories, hot and cold running water, bathtub and other toilet facilities. Games room downstairs with billiards and table tennis to amuse ourselves in our spare time when flying over Germany. Carpets on the floor, curtains and flowers in the windows. You should see my little office – mahogany desk, cushioned swivel chair, WAAF secretary to answer the phone and type out my log. Boy that kite's got everything. I'll tell you more about 'em next time."

That was written September 21, 1943 and there wasn't a next time. The letter closed with these lines which showed what was under all the bravado: "When you get this, I should be running over Germany and killing innocent little kids. Well, as the Squadron Leader told us, we're a bunch of trained killers and why not use the training?"

Webster Island (53 E/16) in Island Lake was named after him in 1982.

Webster, Sergeant **Robert W.** of Winnipeg (H 6045). Winnipeg Grenadiers. He died a prisoner of war 7 March 1944 at the age of 31 and is commemorated at the Yokohama War Cemetery in Japan. The official cause of death was listed as pneumonia. He was survived by his wife Ella May Webster of Winnipeg and their two children. ***Webster Lake*** (63 K/11), east of Athapapuskow Lake was named after him in 1976.

Weech, Private **Albert R. "Bert"** of Moore Park (H 1927). Royal Hamilton Light Infantry. He died 27 September 1944 at the age of 37 and is commemorated at Schoonselhof Cemetery in Antwerp, Belgium. He was survived by his wife Alice M. Weech of Moore Park, Manitoba and their six children. She writes (25 November 1995):

> Albert R. Weech was born in Poland [and] came to Canada as a young child. He lost his father at an early age as he died in Poland. "Bert" as he was known to most people, was raised in the Russell-Angusville district [and] went to work at an early age. He took up carpentry, painting and bricklaying. He built many barns, etc. around Moore Park, Manitoba where we lived when he went into the army. There are many barns still standing and still in pretty good shape after 50 years. He helped build Shilo Army Base, also No. 12 Airport at Brandon.
>
> You might wonder why he joined the army when we had six children. But when he was working at Shilo, he hurt himself and developed a hernia. At that time, ... you had to get a pink slip stating you were not fit for active service as they needed men badly. So Bert went to Dr. Harold Evans who was the servicemen's doctor for the Brandon area and he said go to Winnipeg because he had just had the hernia operated on and they won't pass him "as you are not an A1 man." Well, he went through as A1 and that was it. He was killed in Holland – a sniper got him and he died instantly. That's the way it was told to me [by someone] who knew Bert and told me a couple of years later.

After his death, his wife and six children were awarded a Widow's Pension of $95.00 per month. ***Weech Lake*** (63 K/16), northeast of Reed Lake was named after him in 1973.

Weeks, Flight Sergeant **Edward H.** of Winnipeg (R 166149). No. 20 Operational Training Unit, RCAF. He died 26 August 1943 at the age of 20 and is commemorated at Lossiemouth Burial Ground, Morayshire, Scotland. He was the son of Edward G. and Ruby I. Weeks of Winnipeg. ***Weeks Lake*** (64 P/11), east of Nejanilini Lake was named after him in 1974.

Weidenhamer, Lance Corporal **Hubert C. "Ham"** of Dand (H 1406). Princess Patricia's Canadian Light Infantry. He died 23 November 1944 at the age of 21 and is commemorated at Ancona War Cemetery in Italy. He was the only son of Roy and Nellie Weidenhamer of Dand, Manitoba. His sister recalls (5 April 1995):

> Hubert was born at his farm home with a midwife July 8, 1923. He enlisted in January, 1943 and trained with the RCA at Fort Garry, Camp Ipperwash, Ontario and went overseas in December, 1943. He transferred to the PPCLI in England and went to Italy in March, 1944. He was seriously wounded in September, 1944 and passed away [in] November. He is remembered by school mates as "Ham."

She concludes (15 October 2001):

> Chaplains wrote letters for him to keep in touch with parents. None of his personal things were returned. He had spent a few years after school on the farm with his parents. He was athletic and loved sports.

Weidenhamer Lake (64 K/10), east of Lac Brochet was named after him in 1972.

Weidner, Rifleman **Adolph** of Moosehorn (H 59101). Regina Rifle Regiment. He died 18 August 1944 and is commemorated at Bretteville-sur-Laize Canadian War Cemetery in Calvados, France. ***Weidner Lake*** (64 I/16), south of Caribou Lake was named after him in 1974.

Weir, Flight Sergeant **Alexander C.** of Winnipeg (R 123705). No. 102 Squadron. He died 21 April 1943 at the age of 26 and is commemorated at Fourfelt Cemetery in Esbjerg, Denmark. He was the son of Hugh P. and Hattie K. Weir of Minaki, Ontario. ***Weir Peninsula*** (63 P/5) on Wintering Lake was named after him in 1995.

Weir, Pilot Officer **Ivan A.** of Belmont (J 86890). No. 102 Squadron. He died 24 April 1944 at the age of 22 and is commemorated at Svino Churchyard in Denmark. He was the son of John S. and Mary C. Weir of Belmont, Manitoba. His sisters write (26 November 2001):

> He trained at Brandon Manning Depot followed by Regina for his ITS, Mossbank for EFTS and received his Air Bomber Wings at Pearce, Alberta. He went overseas in April, 1943. His crew was 1st Class Reserve and engaged in many missions over Europe. He was commissioned as a Pilot Officer on April 22, 1944, reported missing on April 24, 1944 and later presumed dead. On his first operational trip, Ivan became a fully qualified member of the Caterpillar Club when he was forced to make his successful parachute jump.

Weir Island (64 N/5) in Hillhouse Lake was named after him in 1989.

Weir, Pilot Officer **James C.** of Winnipeg (C 15021). No. 97 Squadron. He died 24 June 1942 at the age of 22 and is commemorated at Bergen General Cemetery in Holland. He was survived by his mother, Mrs. Anne E. Weir of Winnipeg. He:

> ... was born at Regina on January 12, 1920. Before joining the service in September, 1939, he was employed in a Winnipeg grocery business. Weir received all of his training in England after arriving overseas in February, 1940. While attached to the RAF, he was reported missing in action over Holland. Weir attended Gordon Bell High School where he played on the rugby team. He was one of those in the first group of airmen to go overseas with the 110th RCAF Squadron (Hill 1944).

Weir Point (64 F/4) on Carswell Lake was named after him in 1995.

Weir, Flight Sergeant **Robert N.** of Winnipeg (R 152759). No. 427 Squadron. He died 22 January 1944 at the age of 23 and is commemorated at the Berlin 1939 - 1945 War Cemetery in Brandenburg, Germany. He was survived by his mother Eva Weir of Vancouver. ***Weir Bay*** (64 H/6) in Northern Indian Lake was named after him in 1995.

Welbanks, Sergeant **Charles E.** of Winnipeg (H 26297). Fort Garry Horse. He died 10 June 1944 and is commemorated at Beny-sur-Mer Canadian War Cemetery in Calvados, France. He was the son of Charles M. and Mary A. Welbanks of Winnipeg. ***Welbanks Lake*** (63 I/7), north of Molson Lake was named after him in 1973.

Welburn, Rifleman **Francis W.** of Winnipegosis (L 105672). Royal Winnipeg Rifles. He died 20 April 1945 at the age of 20 and is commemorated at the Holten Canadian War Cemetery in Holland. He was the son of Charles and Winnifred Welburn of Winnipegosis, Manitoba. His younger sister recalls (23 June 1997):

> We were born at the farm home at Rokeby, Saskatchewan, a few miles from Yorkton. My family moved to [the] Camperville – Winnipegosis area in 1937. Although it's many years since he has been gone, it is very painful to me. I was fourteen years old at the time and remember very vividly the day we received the sad word. He was so alive in all the letters, relating the bad times of war. He was wounded in February, 1945

but was back till … he was killed in action. He talked so optimistic about coming home in all his letters. He had a girl friend whom he loved dearly and mentioned her fondly in all of his letters. Her name was Margaret … from Gull Lake, Saskatchewan. She also lost her brother just shortly before Francis was taken, so it was a bad time for her too.

Welburn Lake (64 O/10), west of Nejanilini Lake was named after him in 1975.

Welch, Flight Sergeant **Robert T. J.** of Boissevain (R 101969). No. 1679 Conversion Unit, RCAF. He died 23 December 1943 at the age of 24 and is commemorated at Stonefall Cemetery in Yorkshire, England. He was the son of James A. and Clara W. Welch of Boissevain, Manitoba. ***Welch Lake*** (63 K/16), west of Wekusko Lake was named after him in 1973.

Weldon, Private **Luther P. L.** of Carlowrie (H 7090). 1st Canadian Special Services Battalion. He died 21 May 1944 and is commemorated at the Cassino Memorial in Italy. He was survived by his mother Vina Weldon. ***Weldon Lake*** (52 L/13), south of Manigotagan Lake was named after him in 1982.

Wellar, Lance Corporal **Lloyd D.** of Strathclair (H 8870). Royal Hamilton Light Infantry. He died 8 March 1945 at the age of 21 and is commemorated at the Groesbeek Canadian War Cemetery in Holland. He was the second youngest of the nine children of John Nelson and Mary J. Wellar of Strathclair, Manitoba. His sisters write (26 November 2001):

Lloyd was born October 16, 1923 in Strathclair. [He] received his education in Strathclair and upon graduating from high school, went to work for Reliance Elevator at Glossip, Manitoba. He enjoyed skating, baseball, curling and hunting. Lloyd joined the army in March, 1943 and was stationed in Winnipeg, then to Orillia, Ontario in December, 1943 where he made the move to [the] Hamilton Light Infantry. From Orillia, he went overseas in 1944. He was killed going into Germany March 8th, 1945. This was in the final days of the last major German offensive.

Wellar Lake (63 J/9), west of Cross Lake was named after him in 1981.

Wells, Leading Aircraftman **John T.** of Carberry (R 116413). Royal Canadian Air Force. He died 8 November 1946 at the age of 59 and is commemorated at Carberry Cemetery. He was the son of John O. and Eliza Wells of Wellwood and was survived by his wife Mabel E. Wells of Carberry, Manitoba. ***Wells Island*** (63 P/2) in Cotton Lake was named after him in 1995.

Werbenuk, Lance Corporal **Joseph** of Winnipeg (H 22078). Queen's Own Cameron Highlanders. He died 11 November 1944 at the age of 19 and is commemorated at the Groesbeek Canadian War Cemetery in Holland. He was the only son of Alex and Mary Werbenuk of Winnipeg. His aunt recalls (23 July 1991):

Joe enlisted in March, 1944 and by May he was in England. He was sent over without embarkation leave because of the upcoming June invasion. He came home on a 48-hour leave before he went over. Joe has been greatly missed by his family and all who knew him; he was a very kind, gentle and noble person. We all miss Joe very much.

Werbenuk Lake (64 I/1), east of North Knife Lake was named after him in 1974.

Werner, Sapper **George C.** of Ashern (H 616999). Royal Canadian Engineers. He died 1 November 1945 at the age of 21 and is commemorated at Ashern Cemetery. He was the son of Mr. and Mrs. Adolph Werner of Ashern, Manitoba. ***Werner Lake*** (64 N/16), west of Nueltin Lake was named after him in 1972.

Wernham, Flight Lieutenant **James C.** of Winnipeg (J 6144). No. 405 Squadron, Mentioned in Dispatches. He died 30 March 1944 at the age of 27 and is commemorated at Poznan Old Garrison Cemetery, Poland. He was the son of James C. and Flora Wernham of Winnipeg. According to a newspaper account:

Flight Lieutenant Wernham was one of 47 Allied airmen shot by the Germans following an escape from Stalag Luft 3 prisoner-of-war camp on March 26, 1944. He had been taken prisoner after being shot down during a raid on Bremen in 1942. He was later mentioned in dispatches.

Born in Gourock, Scotland in 1917, Flight Lieutenant Wernham came to Winnipeg with his parents at the age of 18 months. He was educated at General Wolfe and Daniel McIntyre Collegiate. The escape attempt, and the subsequent execution of the airmen was headlined all over the world at the time and is the subject of the book *The Great Escape* by Flight Lieutenant Paul Bricknell (*Winnipeg Tribune* 18 February 1954).

The book was made into a motion picture in 1963.

A few minutes later, Jimmy Wernham came in and went to change bunks with a fellow Canadian. Jimmy was in high spirits, his eyes shining with excitement at the prospect of his first escape, and he joked about the hospitality they would receive from friendly Czechs once they crossed the border. "The Dodger and I probably won't make it all the way, but I'm sure we'll have a pretty good outing!" (Vance 2000).

Wernham Lake (64 A/14), east of Gauer Lake was named after him in 1950.

Werry, Corporal **Everet Gordon** of Crystal City (H 40633). Royal Winnipeg Rifles. He died 15 October 1944 at the age of 24 and is commemorated at the Adegem Canadian War Cemetery in Belgium. He was the son of Luther E. and Margaret J. Werry of Winnipeg. ***Werry Lake*** (64 J/5), north of Big Sand Lake was named after him in 1972. A commemorative certificate was presented to his cousin and former Royal Winnipeg Rifles commanding officer Lieutenant Colonel Ron E. Werry by the Honourable Gil Molgat on 28 April 1995. The event was the annual dinner of the Royal Winnipeg Rifles commemorating the Battle of Fish Creek (1885).

Wesley, Flying Officer **Ralph E.** of Winnipeg (J 10523). No. 106 Squadron. He died 3 March 1943 and is commemorated at the Kiel War Cemetery in Germany. His aircraft was involved in a mid-air collision during a bombing raid over Hamburg. Flying Officer Wesley and six RAF crewmen all perished instantly (Allison and Hayward 1991). His daughter writes (28 December 2001):

My father was born in Winnipeg and educated at Lord Roberts and Kelvin High School. His brother has told me that my father was very athletic and participated in all sports as a youngster. As he grew older, he settled on weight lifting, eventually winning the lightweight championship of Manitoba.

He was working for the City of Winnipeg when war broke out and tried to enlist in the RCAF for pilot training, but was told that he did not weigh enough. He tried many diets to gain weight, finally settling on a banana diet, apparently popular at the time. He gained the necessary weight, reapplied and was accepted in May of 1941.

He received his wings and commission in February, 1942 and arrived in England the following April. He continued his flight training, was finally assigned to No. 106 RAF Squadron and promoted to Flying Officer in February, 1943. He was reported missing in March, 1943. His death was subsequently confirmed by the German Red Cross.

Wesley Lake (64 B/13), west of Southern Indian Lake was named after him in 1985.

Wess, Private **William** of Ukraina (M 17211). Loyal Edmonton Regiment. He died 5 August 1943 at the age of 35 and is commemorated at Agira Canadian War Cemetery in Italy. He was the son of Nickolas and Barbara Weslowski (sp.) and was survived by his wife Eswynne C. Wess of Whitton, Middlesex, England and their son. She writes (29 November 2001):

William came from a large, loving family. He loved hunting and enjoying the countryside around Canada ... where he worked on the family farm. He loved ice sports. He was born in Manitoba on the 11th November and his parents have died, but they still have grandfather's old house. After his death in Sicily, we had a son, Lawrence Wess who has since passed over. He was a tremendous character, like his father, and worked in Canada. He was a Canadian and always remembered his father's sacrifice in the war which affected him with a nervous illness. Let us hope those men will be remembered always.

Wess Lake (64 B/5), west of Ruttan Lake was named after him in 1995.

Westland, Sergeant **John J.** of Winnipeg (1100628). No. 10 Squadron, RAF. He died 26 February 1942 at the age of 19 and is commemorated at the Runnymede Memorial in Surrey, England. He was the son of Mr. and Mrs. J. W. Westland of Boston in Lincolnshire, England. ***Westland Lake*** (53 L/3), northeast of Fairy Rock Lake was named after him in 1995.

Westman, Rifleman **Cecil O.** of Glencairn (H 1319). Royal Winnipeg Rifles. He died 16 February 1945 and is commemorated at the Groesbeek Canadian War Cemetery in Holland. He was the son of Mr. and Mrs. Enoch Westman of Glencairn, Manitoba.

Cecil was born June 9, 1921 at Lonsdale, Minnesota. He moved to Glencairn with his parents where he received his education. Cecil was employed at Birnie and later Brandon prior to enlisting in the Tank Corps in January, 1943. He trained at Fort Garry Barracks, Portage la Prairie and Camp Borden before his overseas posting in August, 1943. He transferred to the Rocky Mountain Rangers and later the Royal Winnipeg Rifles with whom he served during the campaign in Holland. He was killed on the German front. Cecil had one brother, Guardsman Harold who was a patient in Deer Lodge recovering from wounds he had received while serving in Belgium in October, 1944 (Pittman n.d.).

Westman Lake (64 I/5), northwest of North Knife Lake was named after him in 1974.

Whalen, Private **Bernard B.** of Winnipeg (H 6140). Winnipeg Grenadiers. He died 19 December 1941 at the age of 23 and is commemorated at the Sai Wan Memorial in Hong Kong. He was the son of Peter and Cecelia Whalen and was survived by his wife Florence A. Whalen of Fort Garry and their children. He had enlisted with the Grenadiers in September, 1939. ***Whalen Creek*** (54 C/4), which flows northeast into the Pennycutaway River was named after him in 1964.

Wheadon, Flight Sergeant **Albert E. G.** of Gypsumville (R 80179). No. 407 Squadron. He died 29 April 1942 at the age of 26 and is commemorated at the Runnymede Memorial in Surrey, England. He was the son of Albert and Susan Christina "Tina" Wheadon of Gypsumville, Manitoba. His cousin writes (22 November 2001):

He was an only child and grew up in a very loving family atmosphere. He attended school at St. John's School and continued at St. John's College in Winnipeg. He had a great sense of humour and was always playing jokes and teasing friends and family. Although he had no siblings, he had a number of Uncles (one of which was my dad) who were not much older than him, and when he came home they all partied and had a great time. Mom told me lots of stories of their antics.

Al always thought of his parents. Just prior to his leaving for overseas he bought a 1940 Ford sedan and brought it out to Gypsumville for his parents to use. It was the greatest car I had ever seen. I was only eight or nine and the first ride he took my brother and I on was one we would never forget!

I could not find any letters that he wrote to his mother, but I found this letter that she received from a friend after his loss. I found it very touching as is probably what Al would say to his mother:

He stood before me – oh so big and strong. I could scarcely believe he was my child. My little boy who had never grown up always seemed so carefree, young and wild. But in his air force blue and his solemn thought had brought a world-old sorrow to his eyes, as tenderly he whispered, "dear mom be brave, the Mother of a Soldier never cries."

And all alone in ceaseless agony I try to hope and work, to wait and pray. But oh, how hard it is to sit at home with all my fears and hopes so far away. Then comes a letter – What a wondrous joy, and trembling I read with tear-dimmed eyes. "Just keep on smiling mom, don't forget – the Mother of a Soldier never cries."

He's dead – just numb, I sit and try to think; all I can realize is big dull pain. The world's so empty, robbed of all life's joys. How can I go on living just the same, and keep up courage when my heart is lead? With nothing left to live for or to prize. But hark, his dear voice whispers, "Don't give up mom, the Mother of a Soldier never cries."

No, I will not give up, for there's a thought that gives me strength to live my empty life. A man must die someday. The noblest death is surely in the glorious heat of strife, where man by courage and true sacrifice, can prove to God his manhood as he dies. And so my heart is glad and I see why "the Mother of a Soldier never cries!"

Wheadon River (63 N/8), which flows northwest into Burntwood Lake was named after Flight Sergeant Wheadon in 1972.

Wheatcroft, Flying Officer **Leslie R.** of Winnipeg (C 50187). No. 7 Photo Wing, Mentioned in Dispatches. He died 6 July 1945 at the age of 27 and is commemorated at Brookside Cemetery in Winnipeg. He was the youngest of the three sons of Arthur and Gertrude Wheatcroft of St. James and was survived by his wife Violet M. Wheatcroft (née Cormack) of St. James and their unborn son. She recalls (6 February 1998):

Typical of many teenagers of his generation, he left school seeking employment in the "Dirty Thirties." The goal was to earn enough … to be self-sufficient no matter how personally unsatisfying or menial the employment. I know that Leslie and a brother "rode the rails" for a time, often being temporarily employed by farmers. He told of helping at harvest time. The hours were dawn to dusk and the food often meagre. With amusement, he recounted a story of riding a boxcar to Montreal on one occasion and applying for the position of a chauffeur in a Westmount home without benefit of a driver's licence. And he was hired!

It was a considerable improvement when he obtained employment with the T. Eaton Company in Winnipeg. It offered a permanent 5 1/2 day week. For the first time he could enjoy a few pleasures – one of which was the purchase of a motorcycle. When war was declared, the three Wheatcroft brothers enlisted. One joined the Winnipeg Grenadiers and was taken prisoner when Hong Kong fell to the Japanese. He barely survived the subsequent treatment he experienced. Leslie and his oldest brother, Reg enlisted on the same day in 1940. They enlisted as ground crew, but Leslie was one of the first flight engineers to become air crew when that category was established.

He served with No. 5 Bombing and Reconnaissance Squadron on the east coast of Canada and Newfoundland. He completed two tours of operations (about 50 missions) in that posting. On one mission, the crew ended up on their rubber life rafts in the Atlantic. This was never discussed. I only knew of it because Leslie developed pneumonia from the exposure prior to being rescued and was granted sick leave. This was a bonus – an extra leave which delighted us both!

Leslie was a member of the crew of a Catalina Flying Boat which was credited with damaging and probably destroying an enemy U-boat. For this the crew received a "Mentioned in Dispatches" award. The newspaper report at that time stated that the attack occurred off the East Coast, but I believe the U-boat was actually in the mouth of the St. Lawrence River.

In January, 1944, Leslie and I were married. We had met in 1938 and dated often, but not steadily. When Leslie enlisted, I promised to correspond with him. Our relationship developed through three years of correspondence and his brief annual leaves. Because it was wartime, because we were together so briefly, we rarely spoke of the past – or indeed of the future. We lived in the present. The one gesture my husband made toward our future was to insist on purchasing all our china, crystal [and] silver prior to our marriage.

After our marriage, Leslie rejoined his unit and I remained in Winnipeg working on staff at the Winnipeg General Hospital. In November, 1944 my husband was posted to No. 7 Photo Wing in Ottawa where he successfully rented one room in the overcrowded capital and I was able to join him. We were there six months and witnessed the excitement of VE-Day in Ottawa.

The mission of No. 7 Photo Wing after VE-Day was to engage in Canada's first extensive geographical air survey of the Northwest Territories. This was to begin in June, 1945. We decided that I would spend the summer with my family in Winnipeg and I returned there before the end of May.

Leslie's crew left Ottawa on June 3 to establish a base on Nueltin Lake. The crew spent an overnight in Winnipeg. It was my husband's 27th birthday. I was able to tell him the exciting news that he was going to be a father in about six months.

In early July, Leslie and a fellow officer were reported missing presumed drowned following an accident on Nueltin Lake. On August 6th, his body was recovered. This was the day the first atomic bomb fell on Hiroshima. It was also my 24th birthday. My husband's body was flown to Winnipeg and following a military funeral, was buried on August 9th, 1945 – the day after the second atomic bomb fell on Nagasaki. On January 4, 1946 our son was born. I named him Leslie after his father.

In 1950, we moved to Toronto where I pursued my nursing career, bought a home and raised our son. Young Les grew up knowing he could have the advantage of a University education through the grant made available to children of war widows. Both of us are so grateful that this opportunity was assured. He did credit to that program. He graduated from York University in 1970 as an Honours Student and was awarded a Woodrow Wilson Fellowship. His father would have reason to be proud.

Wheatcroft Lake (64 C/2), south of Granville Lake was named after Flying Officer Wheatcroft in 1962.

Wheeler, Trooper **John F.** of Winnipeg (H 1563). Fort Garry Horse. He died 25 July 1944 at the age of 21 and is commemorated at Bretteville-sur-Laize Canadian War Cemetery in Calvados, France. He was the son of Joseph and Mary I. Wheeler. ***Wheeler Lake*** (63 O/4), north of Wekusko Lake was named after him in 1970.

Wheeler, Pilot Officer **John W.** of Winnipeg (J 19486). No. 434 Squadron. He died 15 February 1944 at the age of 22 and is commemorated at the Runnymede Memorial in Surrey, England. He was the son of Arthur F. and Elizabeth Wheeler of Winnipeg. ***Wheeler Island*** (64 P/15) in Savage Lake was named after him in 1989.

Whillier, Sapper **Joseph C.** of Brandon (H 17222). Royal Canadian Engineers. He died 26 October 1944 and is commemorated at Bergen-op-Zoom Canadian War Cemetery in Holland. ***Whillier Lake*** (52 E/14), southeast of Brereton Lake was named after him in 1974.

Whillier, Lance Corporal **Walter C.** of Brandon (H 6901). Winnipeg Grenadiers. This World War I veteran died a prisoner of war 9 September 1942 at the age of 43 and is commemorated at the Sai Wan War Cemetery in Hong Kong. He was the son of Lieutenant Colonel C. J. and Ada A. Whillier of Brandon and was survived by his wife Hilda F. Whillier (née Baker) of Brandon and their two daughters. A daughter writes (7 July 1998):

Walter Clifford Whillier was born in Brandon on July 31st, 1899. At the age of 17 years he joined the infantry and served in France until the end of the First World War. In 1924 he married ... and subsequently had two daughters, Gladys Maureen (McWilliam) and Kathleen Patricia (Wightman). Walter was an active member of the IOOF Lodge and also served as an officer of the 45th Regiment of the non-permanent army force in Brandon.

He re-enlisted for active service in September, 1940 [and] was stationed at A4 Barracks, Brandon until 1941 when he transferred to the Winnipeg Grenadiers. In November, 1941, his regiment was shipped to Hong Kong. They fought there until Christmas Day when they were taken prisoners of the Japanese. Walter subsequently died of diphtheria in that prison.

Whillier Island (64 H/1) in Billard Lake was named after him in 1995.

White, Able Seaman **Clayton L.** of Brandon (V 68792). HMCS *Shawinigan*. The *Shawinigan* was torpedoed and sunk by U-1228 while on independent anti-submarine patrol in the Cabot Strait; all hands were lost. Able Seaman White died 24 November 1944 at the age of 19 and is commemorated at the Halifax Memorial. He was the son of Percy and Myrtle White of Brandon. A subsequent article in a Regina newspaper read in part:

A brilliant and energetic young hockey player who was taking his bows at Queen City Gardens only last spring, Clayton White will lace up his skates no more. He has been lost at sea with the Royal Canadian Navy. It seems only yesterday that Mrs. Wes Champ was hugging this clean-cut, pink-cheeked athlete and the fans were roaring acclaim when she presented him with the Champ Memorial trophy. Clayton was the most valuable player in last winter's junior league, was the circuit's leading scorer and not a fan in town denied him the honours. White was terrific on skates last year when he had his last fling at the ice pastime with Navy. His prolific goal scoring and dynamic play made him the most compelling figure in the league. Professional scouts agreed he was NHL timber in post-war days.

But Clayton went down with his ship a few paltry months after completing training with the Navy. He was originally a Brandon product, coming to Regina with Dick Slifka and Toby Brown to join Commandos. He was an immediate hit, but last winter was at his best. He had just arrived in hockey when war took its toll. If there is a place set aside up there for hockey players, then surely White and Abe Tilson will get together and maybe look on wistfully when the National league teams bolster their line-ups with young talent after the war. They belonged in hockey's big time but gave it up for something bigger and something finer (*Regina Leader-Post* 14 December 1944).

Clayton White Island (63 P/9) in Cauchon Lake was named after him in 1995.

White, Lance Bombardier **Francis "Bush"** of Grandview (H 75172). Royal Canadian Artillery. He died 18 September 1944 at the age of 23 and is commemorated at the Adegem Canadian War Cemetery in Belgium. His sister visited his grave in 1961. He was the son of Frank and Lizzie J. White of Grandview, Manitoba. His eldest sister recalls (1 December 2001):

> He joined the army 8 June 1941 and trained at Shilo, Ile-Maligne, Quebec and Debert, Nova Scotia prior to going overseas in August, 1942. At the time of his death, his father was stationed with the Veteran's Guard at Riding Mountain National Park. His two sisters were in the service: Leading Aircraftwoman Iris White at No. 8 Repair Depot and Private Aldyth White in the CWAC, Fort Osborne Barracks.
>
> While attending school, Bush was goalie for one of the hockey teams. On weekends, the team would travel to towns surrounding Grandview. He enjoyed the fun and comradeship. He also learned to curl on the 'curling sheet' Dad made in the back yard. The neighbourhood kids joined in and had hours of fun competing. Prior to enlisting, Bush worked on a farm. He loved the environment, the cattle and horses. Had he lived, I'm certain he would have returned to farming.
>
> On 7 May 1961, Iris (oldest sister) visited Adegem Cemetery while on a European tour. Such a quiet, beautiful spot surrounded by trees and shrubs. Mr. Harrison, the head gardener, lived near the cemetery. As Iris went by on the road, he asked her to have tea with he and his wife. This gesture made her day as it gave a link between Bush and his family in Canada. Later in the year, he sent photos and info on the cemetery.

White Esker (64 P/1), north of Meades Lake was named after Able Seaman White in 1995.

White, Rifleman **George T.** of Gilbert Plains (H 41139). Royal Winnipeg Rifles. He died 8 June 1944 at the age of 27 and is commemorated at Beny-sur-Mer Canadian War Cemetery in Calvados, France. He was the son of William S. and Alma E. White of Gilbert Plains, Manitoba. His brother, Rifleman Robert E. White, also fell (see entry). ***White Point*** (63 I/2) on Molson Lake was named after him in 1988.

White, Warrant Officer 2 **John D.** of Hartney (R 91819). No. 405 Squadron. He died 3 April 1943 at the age of 21 and is commemorated at the Groesbeek Canadian War Cemetery in Holland. He was the son of Abram J. and Agnes M. White of Hartney, Manitoba. After his first tour of duty had been completed:

> ... he had earned a trip home, but it was late in 1942 and air force personnel could not be spared, so [he] was given three months "rest" on coastal command and then returned to the 2nd tour. The night of his final trip, his co-pilot of the regular crew was sick and unable to make the trip. The co-pilot survived the war and wrote to John's mother regularly (Royal Canadian Legion n.d.).

White Island (64 O/13) in Nueltin Lake was named after him in 1975.

White, Flying Officer **Kenneth** of Winnipeg (J 5085). No. 149 Squadron. He died 30 June 1942 at the age of 21 and is commemorated at Amsterdam New Eastern Cemetery, Holland. He was the son of Henry G. and Elsie White of Winnipeg. He:

> ... joined the service at Winnipeg in May, 1941 and trained at Toronto, Jarvis, Regina, Moncton and Malton. After arriving overseas, he was attached to the RAF Ferry Command in Great Britain. On the 29th of June, 1942, he was reported missing in action over northwest Germany. On September 8, his body was recovered from the sea. White was born on January 18, 1921, and was a student at the University of Manitoba when he enlisted. He received his secondary education at Isaac Brock and Daniel McIntyre schools. Before enlisting, he worked for a short time with Imperial Oil Limited (Hill 1944).

White Creek (64 B/5), which flows southeast into Pemichigamau Lake was named after him in 1995.

White, Rifleman **Robert E.** of Gilbert Plains (H 41628). Royal Winnipeg Rifles. He died 8 June 1944 at the age of 24 and is commemorated at Beny-sur-Mer Canadian War Cemetery in Calvados, France. He was the son of William S. and Alma E. White of Gilbert Plains, Manitoba. His brother Rifleman George T. White also fell (see entry). ***White Bay*** (63 I/2) in Molson Lake was named after him in 1988.

White, Private **Ronald O.** of Winnipeg (SB 7611). Royal Canadian Regiment. He died 1 October 1952 and is commemorated at the United Nations Cemetery in Pusan, South Korea. ***Ronald White Lake*** (53 N/6), south of Patch Lake was named after this Korean War casualty in 1998.

White, Rifleman **Roy** of Novra (H 200069). Royal Winnipeg Rifles. He died 8 June 1944 at the age of 20 and is commemorated at Beny-sur-Mer Canadian War Cemetery in Calvados, France. He was the son of William J. and Lizzie White of Novra, Manitoba. ***White Peninsula*** (64 C/3) on McKnight Lake was named after him in 1993.

White, Private **Thomas C.** of Brandon (H 17693). Winnipeg Grenadiers. He died 22 December 1941 and is commemorated at the Sai Wan Memorial in Hong Kong. ***White Narrows*** (64 B/7) in Kinwaw Lake was named after him in 1995.

White, Private **Wesley M.** of Winnipeg (H 37493). Royal Canadian Army Service Corps. He died 1 July 1943 at the age of 24 and is commemorated at Brookwood Military Cemetery in Surrey, England. He was the son of William L. and Emily V. White of Winnipeg. ***White Rapids*** (64 O/4) in the North Seal River was named after him in 1995.

Whitecross, Flying Officer **James A.** of Winnipeg (41888). No. 50 Squadron, RAF, Distinguished Flying Cross. Flying Officer Whitecross enlisted with the RAF on 4 January 1939. He died 15 August 1941 at the age of 24 and is commemorated at the Runnymede Memorial in Surrey, England. He was the son of James W. and Isabella J. Whitecross (née Anderson) of Winnipeg. Details of an earlier crash and escape are chronicled in his debriefing notes:

> In the evening of 28 April 1941 I set out with my crew Sergeants Martin, Ross and O'Hare from Lindholme for the La Rochelle area. At 00:30 hours we developed engine trouble and soon after crashed near Loudeac. The aircraft burned up and all the contents including papers were destroyed.
>
> I made my way, on landing with a parachute, to Redon through Josselin and by the canal footpath. I then went on through Blain and Ancenis, where I got some civilian clothes from a farmer. Here they told me that two of my crew (Ross and O'Hare) had been killed and the third (Martin) had leg injuries and was a P/W. There was a reward of 3500 francs for my capture. My route later was through Doue, Loudin, Richlieu, Poitiers and Ruffec to La Chignole (4 May). I crossed the Line of Demarcation on 5 May between Montemboeuf and La Rochefoucauld, passing through a large wood in company with fifteen French refugees from Paris. I should add that I had lost sight of Sergeant Martin, who had been taken off to a French hospital after bailing out.
>
> The Dutch and Belgian money with which I had been issued at my station, I was able to exchange for French francs. I had not been issued with a compass, although I knew of this escape adjunct and had attended

a lecture on escaping in March, 1941 at Lindholme. Soon after crossing into Unoccupied France I was stopped at the first gendarme post where papers were requested. As I was unable to produce any, I was sent under escort to St. Hippolyte du Fort.

On 17 May I got away from this concentration camp, took the train to Nimes and then to Perpignan, where, in a hotel, I met two Royal Army Medical Corps Captains (Plant and McPartland). On 25 May we crossed the Pyrenees and, unnoticed, reached Barcelona by train. Here we were arrested and spent three weeks in jail before our release by the Embassy (14 July 1941).

He eventually made his way to Gibraltar and got a ride back to England aboard the aircraft carrier HMS *Furious*. Upon arrival at his base in England, he was chastised for not turning in his parachute. According to his brother (6 March 1996):

James completed his first full tour of operations including a trip to Rotterdam on the night of August 11/12, 1941. One of the tasks of No. 50 Squadron on that raid was to drop 500 bags of tea from the Dutch West Indies for the civilian population. Three nights later, F/O James Whitecross was ordered into the air (from Swinderby) to participate in an air-sea rescue for the crew of a Wellington (possibly R1500 from 115 Squadron) that had crashed in the North Sea while returning from a raid on Hanover. At 15:30 hours, F/O Whitecross signalled that his engines were failing. Nothing more was heard from Hampden P4408, but some time later, two bodies were recovered from the icy waters. F/Sgt. N. Gray, DFM and Sgt. R. Taylor are buried in Sage War Cemetery (Oldenburg) as are Sgt. C. C. Alway, the Wellington skipper and Sgt. R. W. Duke.

On August 15, 1941, the North Sea became the watery grave for F/O James Whitecross and Sgt. M. O. Fisher. It was also the final resting place for three members of the Wellington crew including Sgt. James G. Park, the RCAF wireless- air gunner from Cornwall, Ontario. All of their names are inscribed on the Runnymede War Memorial.

His brother concludes (16 November 2001):

Jim Whitecross, son of Mr. and Mrs. James Whitecross of 183 Ash Street, Winnipeg, was born in Winnipeg on March 3, 1917 at the height of the last war when aviation was in [its] early stages of development. He grew up in this city, a typical healthy school boy, fond of games, enjoying the companionship of his friends, looking forward to the time when he would be a man making his own way in the world. He went to R. H. Smith public school and St. John's college where he matriculated in Grade 11 and was studying engineering at the University of Manitoba when he decided to answer the call for intrepid young Canadians who were needed to help build up the Royal Air Force. At that time, the threat of German aggression was growing month by month.

Jim went to England in January, 1939 [enlisting on January 4]. By the time war was declared he had won his wings and as the danger drew steadily closer to Britain, he was already a Pilot Officer, trained and fit, ready for the hard task and the great adventures which lay ahead.

No. 6 "Jim Whitecross" Squadron of the Royal Canadian Air Cadets was created and named after him on 24 September 1941 and ***Whitecross Lake*** (64 O/16), west of Baralzon Lake was named after him in 1987.

Whitehead, Flying Officer **William A.** of Winnipeg (J 28941). No. 207 Squadron. He died 15 October 1944 at the age of 22 and is commemorated at Laastrup Churchyard in Denmark. ***Whitehead Lake*** (64 H/12), north of Wood Lake was named after him in 1995.

Whiteside, Private **Edwin E.** of Winnipeg (H 6584). Winnipeg Grenadiers. He died 20 December 1941 at the age of 26 and is commemorated at the Sai Wan Memorial in Hong Kong. He was the son of William E. and Dorothy F. Whiteside of Winnipeg. ***Whiteside Lake*** (64 O/9), north of Nejanilini Lake was named after him in 1975.

Whitmore, Able Seaman **Gordon S.** of Dauphin (4471). HMCS *Naden*. He died 15 November 1943 at the age of 20 and is commemorated at Riverside Cemetery in Dauphin. He was the son of John and Ethel Whitmore of Dauphin.

A six-footer, Gordon was a very likeable and outgoing person who enjoyed excitement. He attended Gartmore rural school and Dauphin's St. Paul's Anglican Church, liked hunting, baseball and soccer, working on the family farm.

As soon as turning 18 in 1941 and believing the Navy [to be the] fastest route for getting into action against Japan, he enlisted to serve on the West Coast. [He] served as a gunner on defensively equipped merchant ships prior to returning to Esquimalt base for further training. "He served in this capacity for some time" naval chaplain L. M. Outeridge later wrote Gordon's mother. "It is one of the most heroic duties that can be performed by a Naval gunner, for the safety of a merchant ship and the crew are so largely dependent upon the small crew of Naval personnel which attend the guns. [They] carry a larger responsibility [than] would fall on them when serving as part of a large ship's company" (Neufeld 1989).

Whitmore Lake (64 N/2), west of Egenolf Lake was named after him in 1961.

Whittaker, Corporal **Charles R.** of Winnipeg (H 16191). Princess Patricia's Canadian Light Infantry. He died 18 December 1943 at the age of 31 and is commemorated at the Moro River Canadian War Cemetery in Italy. He was the son of Harry and Lillian M. Whittaker and was survived by his wife Helena Whittaker of St. Paul, Minnesota. ***Whittaker Island*** (64 I/14) in the Seal River was named after him in 1995.

Whittaker, Sergeant **John** of Winnipeg (R 250965). No. 15 Squadron. He died 12 May 1944 at the age of 20 and is commemorated at Leuven Communal Cemetery in Belgium. He was the son of Harry and Hilda M. Whittaker of Winnipeg. ***Whittaker Lake*** (64 P/14), northeast of Nejanilini Lake was named after him in 1974.

Whyte, Sapper **Bernard C.** of Winnipeg (H 36295). Royal Canadian Engineers. He died 16 October 1940 at the age of 26 and is commemorated at Brookside Cemetery in Winnipeg. He was survived by his mother Annie Whyte of Winnipeg and by his wife Annabella Whyte of Winnipeg. ***Whyte Hill*** (64 O/7), west of Sandhill Lake was named after him in 1995.

Whyte, Able Seaman **John W.** of Roblin (V 50134). HMCS *Alberni*. The *Alberni* was torpedoed and sunk by U-480, southeast of the Isle of Wight; 59 of her ship's company were lost. Able Seaman Whyte died 21 August 1944 at the age of 31 and is commemorated at the Halifax Memorial. He was the son of John W. and Jessie A. Whyte of Roblin and was survived by his wife Marguerite L. Whyte of Fort Frances, Ontario. ***Whyte Lake*** (64 N/1), northwest of Egenolf Lake was named after him in 1972.

Wickes, Trooper **Arnold F.** of Dauphin (H 26304). Fort Garry Horse. He died 4 July 1944 at the age of 22 and is commemorated at Beny-sur-Mer Canadian War Cemetery in Calvados, France. He was the son of Harry and Harriet A. Wickes of Dauphin. ***Wickes Lake*** (64 J/8), south of Tadoule Lake was named after him in 1975.

Wicks, Sergeant **Philip F.** of Winnipeg (R 180285). No. 434 Squadron. He died 29 January 1944 at the age of 20 and is commemorated at the Berlin 1939 - 1945 War Cemetery in Brandenburg, Germany. ***Wicks Island*** (53 K/3) in Red Sucker Lake was named after him in 1995.

Wickstrom, Flying Officer **Fred E.** of Erickson (J 9642). Royal Canadian Air Force. He died 25 October 1942 at the age of 21 and is commemorated at the Malta Memorial. He was the son of Mr. and Mrs. O. A. Wickstrom of Erickson. ***Wickstrom Lake*** (53 E/7), south of Island Lake was named after him in 1973.

Wickstrom, Trooper **Karl J. C.** of Winnipeg (M 44863). South Alberta Tank Regiment. He died 8 April 1945 at the age of 36 and is commemorated at the Holten Canadian War Cemetery in Holland. He was the son of Sigmund and Hildua Wickstrom and was survived by his wife Rachel Wickstrom of Winnipeg. ***Wickstrom Island*** (53 L/15) in Cinder Lake was named after him in 1995.

Widlake, Trooper **Thomas H.** of Transcona (H 63525). Ontario Tank Regiment. He died 24 June 1944 at the age of 26 and is commemorated at the Assisi War Cemetery in Italy. He was the son of Edward H. and Mattie W. Widlake of Transcona. ***Widlake Lake*** (64 N/15), west of Nueltin Lake was named after him in 1972.

Wiebe, Private **Henry** of Winnipeg (H 77148). Winnipeg Grenadiers. He died 21 December 1941 at the age of 19 and is commemorated at the Sai Wan Memorial in Hong Kong. He was the son of Mr. and Mrs. G. Wiebe of Winnipeg. ***Wiebe Lake*** (64 J/6), southwest of Tadoule Lake was named after him in 1975.

Wiebe, Private **Peter D.** of Winnipeg (H 3582). Princess Patricia's Canadian Light Infantry. He died 20 December 1944 at the age of 31 and is commemorated at Ravenna War Cemetery in Italy. His wife and brother visited his grave in 1993. He was the son of Mr. and Mrs. John Wiebe and was survived by his wife Irene Wiebe (née Daigneault) of St. Boniface and their daughter Louise. His brother writes (31 October 2001):

> Peter D. Wiebe was born February 12, 1912 in Giroux, Manitoba where he went to grade school. In 1929 when Peter was 17, the stock market crashed and the great depression began. Peter quit school when his father went bankrupt from his general store business, having given too much credit to the local farmers who were unable to pay. Peter worked in the woods, cutting cordwood and pulp for the railways and for farmers during harvesting to help support a family of 10. In depression days, you had a better chance for a job if you were good in sports or could play an instrument and entertain, [so] Peter learned to play a guitar and joined a local band. There were two special occasions of note. Once at his parents 25th anniversary in 1935 and again at his sister Helen's wedding in 1937.
>
> In 1939, shortly after the war started, Peter joined the army. On June 1st, 1940, Peter married Irene Daigneault, shortly after which he was shipped overseas.
>
> Shortly after arriving overseas, Peter developed ulcers and other stomach complications. He was further educated and trained, then worked in an administration office while healing his stomach during most of the war. Meanwhile, his wife Irene had a baby girl born on April 3, 1941 and they named her Louise. During the war, Irene worked in an ammunition factory where they made gun powder for ships. This helped supplement her income to raise a child and send gifts to Peter. In his correspondence, Peter often mentioned that when the war would be over, he would like to start a general store business. In 1944, Peter was transferred with a PPCLI unit to Italy. He was only in the front lines a short time when he was killed near Ravenna, which is not far from Venice.

His last letter home was posted six days before his death:

> Dearest Irene: Hello my Darling. I am well as I hope this finds you and Louise. It's ages since I had a letter; guess it's delayed somewhere, however, I am hoping to hear from you soon. It certainly would cheer me up a lot at a trying moment. Darling, please don't worry if you don't hear from me for a couple of weeks. I will be OK and soon as possible, I will write again. I feel very tired and would like a rest, but we must go on and get this thing finished; we'll rest later on. Guess you will be busy preparing for Xmas. Here's hoping you have a good one. Next one we will have together and it will be a real one.
>
> Louise must be getting quite excited now with Xmas so close. She sure has a good memory for her age. I love you Irene and my thoughts are always with you and home and happy days to come soon. My pen is nearly dry, so this will have to do for now. Remember Irene, I Love you and always will to the end. Best regards to all with all my Love and Kisses, Always your Loving Husband, Peter.
>
> Dear Louise: I hope Santa brings you and mother a lot of presents. I will be home soon. Love and Kisses, Daddy (14 December 1944).

Wiebe Island (64 G/6) in McPherson Lake was named after him in 1986.

Wightman, Leading Aircraftman **John K.** of Emerson (R 177675). No. 8 Repair Depot, RCAF. He died 5 June 1945 at the age of 30 and is commemorated at Emerson Cemetery in Manitoba. He was the son of Sidney D. and Kate E. Wightman of Emerson and was survived by his wife Annette Wightman (née Dionne). He had operated the barber shop and pool hall in Emerson before he enlisted and had been actively involved in sports, playing goalie in the Old States Dominion League. ***Wightman Lake*** (64 J/9), east of Tadoule Lake was named after him in 1975.

Wigle, Pilot Officer **Robert E.** of Winnipeg (J 8393). No. 33 Squadron. He died 8 July 1942 at the age of 22 and is commemorated at the Alamein Memorial in Egypt. ***Wigle Lake*** (63 J/3), northeast of North Moose Lake was named after him in 1973.

Wilkie, Lieutenant (Nursing Sister) **Agnes W.** of Carman (O 78010). Royal Canadian Navy. She died 14 October 1942 at the age of 30 while on active service aboard the SS *Caribou* when it was torpedoed by German submarine U-69. Despite the efforts of her companion, Sub-Lieutenant (Dietician) Margaret Brooke, Sister Wilkie died following more than two hours of struggling to hold on to the ropes of an overturned lifeboat. Margaret Brooke was later named a Member of the Order of the British Empire for her efforts. She recalls the incident:

> "[We] were asleep at 2:21 AM when a torpedo struck the ferry *Caribou* in the Cabot Strait between Nova Scotia and Newfoundland. I was pitched right cross the cabin and landed on her. We just got up and grabbed our naval raincoats," recalled Brooke, 71, in a phone interview from Victoria. The two prairie women grabbed their lifejackets and attempted to open the cabin door, but it was jammed. Brooke forced the door open and they joined other passengers streaming down the pitch-black hallway. They made their way upstairs onto the deck, but their assigned lifeboat was gone.
>
> "Within a few minutes the ship went down – and we went down with it." The two nurses were sucked under as the vessel sank only four minutes after being torpedoed. "I thought we would never come up, but we did eventually," says Brooke, recently retired University of Saskatchewan geology instructor. The two naval sub-lieutenants, clinging to each other and floundering in the icy water grabbed a passing overturned lifeboat. About 10 other survivors pulled them on top of it.
>
> The cold night and icy waters caused hypothermia in the survivors clinging to the lifeboat and it weakened them. Huge waves crashed down on them and one by one they were washed away. Wilkie, who only

weighed about 100 pounds, eventually lost consciousness and let go of the lifeboat. Brooke hauled her back on top. She held her friend for a while with one hand and clutched the lifeboat with the other. "Another wave came and I wasn't strong enough to hold her and it yanked her out of my hands, I couldn't pull her back." Two men on the lifeboat also grabbed for Wilkie but also had no strength left. Only Brooke and two or three other survivors were left at daybreak when they were rescued by a minesweeper (*The Edmonton Journal* 11 September 1986).

Agnes Wilkie, a graduate of Misericordia Hospital, worked as an OR Nurse there until enlisting. She became the only Canadian Nursing Sister to die due to enemy action during the war and a picture of her was subsequently hung in all Canadian Naval Hospitals. She is commemorated at Mount Pleasant Cemetery in St. John's, Newfoundland and was survived by her parents John and Helen Wilkie (née Usher) of Carman, Manitoba. ***Wilkie Lake*** (64 J/11), west of Tadoule Lake was named after her in 1957.

Wilkinson, Pilot Officer **Einar T. "Buster"** of Gimli (42663). No. 3 Photo Reconnaissance Unit, RAF. He died 14 February 1941 at the age of 26 and is commemorated at the Runnymede Memorial in Surrey, England. He was the son of Walter J. and Karin A. Wilkinson (née Peterson) of Winnipeg. His niece recalls (22 November 2001):

> Buster was born in Gimli, Manitoba on February 9, 1916. Buster was educated in Gimli and Winnipeg where he attended General Wolfe School and Daniel McIntyre Collegiate, following which he moved to British Columbia where he worked in a paper mill for three years. Buster went to Britain in the spring of 1939 to pursue his ambition to become a pilot in the Royal Air Force. Buster joined the RAF in May, 1939 and received his commission 11 days after war was declared.
>
> Buster piloted both fighters and bombers in action and participated in the air battles over Dunkirk during the evacuation. Buster was reported missing in action and presumed killed while on a photography reconnaissance mission over the Ruhr Valley on February 14, 1941. He is listed at the Memorial at Runnymede along with 20,000 other airmen who were lost in the Second World War during operations from bases in the United Kingdom, Northern and Western Europe and who have no known graves.
>
> For the surviving members of our grandparents' extended family, even for those of us who never knew Buster personally, he has always been an integral part of our families and has been remembered with love. There has always been a sadness that he went missing and was never found. We were always left wondering what actually happened to him. He has given us an appreciation of the sacrifices these young men made for us.

Wilkinson Island (53 L/15) in Seller Lake was named after him in 1995. In the summer of 2001, Buster's nephew, Joseph Thor Wilkinson, who was named after him, visited the island and placed a plaque on a tree there to commemorate him.

Wilkinson, Flight Sergeant **Gordon L.** of Brandon (R 78711). No. 206 Squadron. He died 26 June 1942 at the age of 20 and is commemorated at Hamburg Cemetery in Germany. ***Wilkinson Bay*** (53 K/11) in Margaret Lake was named after him in 1996.

Wilkinson, Private **Thomas Donald** of Oakbank (H 7172). Queen's Own Cameron Highlanders. He died 8 August 1944 at the age of 25 and is commemorated at Bretteville-sur-Laize Canadian War Cemetery in Calvados, France. He was the eighth of the nine children of George and Lillian A. Wilkinson (née Beresford) and was survived by his wife Christina J. Wilkinson (née Finnie) of Portage la Prairie. He was employed by the Canada Car and Foundry in Fort William at the time of his enlistment in February, 1942. ***Wilkinson Lake*** (64 F/6), northwest of Wells Lake was named after him in 1994.

Willems, Gunner **Elie J.** of St. Boniface (H 615043). Royal Canadian Artillery. He died 4 June 1943 at the age of 19 and is commemorated at Belgian Sacred Heart Church Cemetery in St. Boniface. He was the son of Paul and Elodie Willems of St. Boniface. ***Willems Lake*** (64 K/11), east of Lac Brochet was named after him in 1972.

Williams, Flight Sergeant **Arthur R.** of Winnipeg (R 71274). No. 408 Squadron. He died 14 January 1944 at the age of 23 and is commemorated at the Hanover War Cemetery in Germany. He was the son of Arthur W. and Annie G. Williams of Winnipeg. ***Williams Rapids*** (53 M/9) in the Gowan River was named after him in 1995.

Williams, Cadet **Donald L.** of Winnipeg (H 88197). Royal Canadian Army Service Corps. He died 23 December 1942 at the age of 26 and is commemorated at St. James Cemetery in Winnipeg. He was the son of Ernest H. and Clara F. Williams of St. James and was survived by his wife Emerald A. Williams of Winnipeg. ***Williams Narrows*** (64 O/12) in Nueltin Lake was named after him in 1995.

Williams, First Radio Officer **Geoffrey Dean** of Winnipeg. SS *Empire Progress*, Canadian Merchant Navy. The *Empire Progress* was lost 13 April 1942 and Officer Williams is commemorated at the Halifax Memorial. ***Dean Williams Lake*** (63 P6), north of Landing Lake was named after him in 2001.

Williams, Warrant Officer 2 **Gordon I.** of Elkhorn (R 119950). No. 97 Squadron. He died 31 January 1944 at the age of 21 and is commemorated at Zwanenburg General Cemetery in Holland. He was the only son among the four children of Fred and Daisy Williams of Elkhorn, Manitoba. His sister recalls (3 December 2001):

> Gordon longed to be a pilot but instead, he was to train for an observer. He grew up on a farm and loved all the animals, but his heart was not in farming. When we used to put up hay in the summer, we would have to stop and watch a plane as it passed over every day around 4 PM. He spent the two years after his schooling helping his dad with the cattle and horses. His father was wounded in the First World War and found it very difficult to say goodbye to Gordon when he left for overseas. He is buried in the cemetery near where his plane was shot down. Five of the crew were recovered when the plane was dug up in 1999 or 2000.

Williams Point (64 J/15) in Copeland Lake was named after him in 1989.

Williams, Lance Corporal **Jack G.** of Stonewall (H 6564). Winnipeg Grenadiers. He died 19 December 1941 at the age of 36 and is commemorated at the Sai Wan Memorial in Hong Kong. He was the son of Drury and Jane Williams of Stonewall. He:

> ... was born November 4, 1907. Joining the Winnipeg Grenadiers in September, 1939, he received his training in Winnipeg and the British West Indies. Proceeding to Hong Kong in October, 1941, he was killed in action in December. Williams was doing labouring work at Stonewall when he enlisted. He attended the local schools and played baseball with the school team. His hobbies were hunting and general sports (Hill 1944).

Jack Williams Lake (53 N/12), south of Stupart Lake was named after him in 1995.

Williams, Flight Sergeant **James H.** of Teulon (R 106082). No. 50 Squadron. He died 6 August 1944 at the age of 22 and is commemorated at Pontoise Communal Cemetery in Val d'Oise, France. ***James Williams Lake*** (64 A/14), southeast of Wernham Lake was named after him in 1995.

Williams, Corporal **John A.** of Winnipeg (H 94571). Canadian Forestry Corps. He died 4 March 1945 and is commemorated at Brookwood Military Cemetery in Surrey, England. ***John Williams Lake*** (53 N/11), northwest of Whitefish Lake was named after him in 1995.

Williams, Pilot Officer **Leslie Llewellyn** of Foxwarren (J 85857). No. 1667 Heavy Conversion Unit, RCAF. He died 1 June 1944 on his 23rd birthday and is commemorated at Sleepyhillock Cemetery in Angus, Scotland. He was the son of Edwin and Ethel I. Williams (née Honey) and was survived by his wife Mary H. Williams (née Mark) of Toronto. ***Llewellyn Williams Lake*** (63 P/6), north of Landing Lake was named after him in 1995.

Williams, Battalion Sergeant Major (Warrant Officer 2) **Lewis J.** of Brandon (H 29046). Royal Canadian Artillery. He died 24 May 1944 at the age of 35 and is commemorated at the Cassino War Cemetery in Italy. He was the son of John and Annie Williams and was survived by his wife Leonora Williams of Brandon. ***Williams Falls*** (63 N/7) in the Kississing River was named after him in 1995.

Williams, Private **Orville H.** of Portage la Prairie (H 9455). Queen's Own Cameron Highlanders. He died 23 October 1944 and is commemorated at Bergen-op-Zoom Canadian War Cemetery in Holland. ***Williams Bay*** (64 P/2) in Mullin Lake was named after him in 1989.

Williams, Warrant Officer 2 **Percy G.** of Harrowby (R 116322). No. 207 Squadron. He died 25 February 1943 at the age of 20 and is commemorated at Durnbach War Cemetery in Bavaria, Germany. He was the son of William and Dora S. Williams of Neepawa, Manitoba. ***Williams Peninsula*** (64 C/16) on Barrington Lake was named after him in 1995.

Williams, Flying Officer **Ronald Lenard** of Foxwarren (J 17347). No. 272 Squadron. He died 22 November 1944 at the age of 22 and is commemorated at the Alamein Memorial in Egypt. He was the son of Edwin and Ethel Williams of Foxwarren, Manitoba. ***Williams Esker*** (64 I/2), southwest of South Knife Lake was named after him in 1992.

Williams, Flight Lieutenant **Stanley Smith** of Oak Lake (J 15283). No. 413 Squadron, Mentioned in Dispatches. He died 20 August 1943 at the age of 20 and is commemorated at Liveramentu Cemetery in Colombo, Sri Lanka. He was the son of Thomas E. and Hazel E. Williams of Oak Lake and was survived by his wife Dorothy S. M. Williams of Dundee, Ontario. ***Williams Hill*** (64 J/5), west of Sprott Lake was named after him in 1989.

Williams, Pilot Officer **Tracy A. T. "Red"** of Stonewall (J 18908). No. 78 Squadron. He died 24 August 1943 at the age of 21 and is commemorated at the Berlin 1939 - 1945 War Cemetery in Brandenburg, Germany. He was the son of Arthur D. and Topsy P. Williams (née Prime) of Stonewall, Manitoba. In his last letter home to his mother he wrote:

> I had a good time in London when I was there on leave. While I was there, there were three air raids, but nothing much happened. I have some really bad news which I picked up in London and sure hate to tell you this, but you might as well know that Rusty Peryman is dead. He was shot down in France. I met one of his pals who trained with him in Canada and he told me all. There isn't a lot to say, for all the news I've had lately is bad. For every raid, another pal doesn't come home. But don't worry about me Mom, I was born under a lucky star, or at least it seems that way (May 1943).

Two years later, his mother received a letter from one of Tracy's crewmates:

> Dear Mrs. Williams: I hope you will forgive me for not writing to you sooner than this. I have paid a visit to the rest of the crew's people all except Mrs. Lovery whom I shall visit as soon as I can. I'm only sorry that you live so far away from me as it would give me the greatest pleasure to be able to see you in person. At the moment I have been demobilised and am working with my old firm Shanks and Co. once more.
>
> Well, Mrs. Williams, as you no doubt know, I was blown out of the plane and luckily my parachute opened by some means unknown to me. I was taken to hospital on the 24 of Aug. 43 and the doctor there told me the names of the crew and also said that they were all dead. I'm sorry if I have said that too abruptly, but it was the only way I could say it. I shall try and tell you now as near as I can what happened from the time of our leaving England on that fateful night.
>
> We went to the briefing room and were told our target for that night was Berlin, but that wasn't a very big surprise as we were quite expecting it. We then collected our equipment and climbed aboard the transport for our plane which was *J for Johnny*. After checking our guns and instruments, it was time for take off, so everything was going well. Our take-off was perfect and we started circling to gain height. At 10,000 feet, we set our course for Berlin and so we were on the way. As we came towards the French coast we could see the searchlights and the flak coming up, but this was nothing new to us by now and quite frankly, we thought nothing of it.
>
> Things still went well for us as we flew over Holland and so into Germany with the pilot calling us up every hour to see that everything was still OK. Finally our target came in sight with I'm quite sure over a thousand searchlights ringed round it. We could see some of our own boys caught in the searchlights and being shot down, so I can assure you as a crew, we were all on the job. We arrived over the markers or flames marking the bombing spot and bombed successfully, as just after the bombing, a black pall of smoke arose up to nearly 10,000 feet. By this time, we were flying at 24,000 feet.
>
> Everything had gone well and so we set course for home. Just then, Tracy sighted a fighter on our starboard and gave us notification of it. At the same time, I spotted one on the port side and told the pilot also. Tracy and I then arranged to watch one each, he taking the one on the starboard and me the one on port. We kept watching them but they didn't attempt to make an attack and stayed just outside our range. The next thing, we were riddled with cannon fire from one that had sneaked underneath whilst we were watching the other two. Tracy must have spotted him as I could hear his guns firing, but they stopped after a second or so. I called to him but received no answer. The plane on the starboard side started to make an attack next, and I gave the pilot instructions for evasive action, but the plane would only fly straight and would not turn, so we were just a sitting target for Jerry.
>
> We had three more attacks by them in as many seconds. By now we were burning furiously and my ammo was starting to go off with the heat. I had a bullet wound in the head at this time from the last attack. The Pilot then gave orders to bail out so I came out of my gun turret, put my chute on and the last thing I remember was the explosion which must have blown me out of the plane. When I regained consciousness, I was only a few feet above the ground and feeling pretty low. When I landed, I destroyed my chute and started to walk. Unfortunately, my boots had been blown off and my head was bleeding badly and I was passing out every few minutes until the Germans picked me up. They took me into a farmhouse and kept me there until the ambulance arrived and then I was taken to hospital to lie there for three months. I am sorry I could not tell you more about Tracy, but all I can tell you is what the German doctor told me.
>
> I will sign off now, Mrs. Williams with the sincerest wish that I shall see you and your family at some future date. With kindest regards and best wishes, Sincerely Yours, David Lamb (3 March 1946).

Fifty years later, Sergeant Lamb contacted Pilot Officer Williams' sister (Glen Sheldon) in Stonewall by mail.

Sheldon had kept much of the information and letters about Tracy including the letter Lamb had sent to her mother after the war. She was so excited to talk to Lamb, she picked up the phone and dialled the long distance number. "I couldn't wait, I had to phone," she said excitedly. At the other end of the line, thousands of miles away, an elderly voice responded to her call. "You could just hear it in his voice that he was as excited as I was," said Sheldon of her conversation with her brother's war buddy. During the phone call, Lamb recalled as much as he could about Tracy or "Red" as everyone referred to him. After suffering four strokes and five heart attacks, the 74 year-old veteran could still recall the red-headed Canadian who he considered his best friend in the squadron, as most gunner pairs were in bomber flight crews. Each had to watch each other's back and rely on each other's skill and competence under fire.

Sheldon and Lamb also shared stories of family, friends and health over the past 50 years. Lamb was the only crew member of the Halifax who was married and had a daughter. He considered himself fortunate to live through the ordeal and return to his wife and family. After the phone call, Sheldon sent a letter with pictures of Tracy and his squadron members. She is also considering sending his medals to the Yorkshire Air Museum where Tracy was based. Sheldon says she is grateful for the letters she has kept for so many years, for they have kept the memory of Tracy Williams alive in her heart. And for the letter from Squadron 78, which has kept her in touch with someone who remembers Tracy just as fondly (*The Argus* 6 November 1995).

Tracy Williams Lake (64 O/5), south of Shannon Lake was named after him in 1995.

Williamson, Private **Donald D.** of Dauphin (H 98108). Veterans Guard of Canada. He died 8 March 1945 at the age of 66 and is commemorated at Riverside Cemetery in Dauphin. This native of Glasgow, Scotland was survived by his wife Elizabeth B. Williamson (British Empire Service League) of Dauphin and was the father of Private Donald Williamson of Roblin (next entry). Mrs. Williamson was awarded two Silver Crosses – one for her husband and one for her son. ***Williamson Island*** (64 O/5) in Booth Lake was named after him in 1995.

Williamson, Private **Donald** of Roblin (B 38300). Argyle and Sutherland Highlanders. He died 1 August 1944 at the age of 20 and is commemorated at Bretteville-sur-Laize Canadian War Cemetery in Calvados, France. He was the son of Donald and Elizabeth B. Williamson of Dauphin (see previous entry). His sister recalls (20 November 1995):

My parents were both in the service; they came over from Scotland after the First World War. Donald, my brother, was born over there in Glasgow. When he left Roblin to enlist, I was only about five years old, so I only have memories. But we do have all his medals ... and I have his dog tag. He was a dispatch rider at the time of his death and I do know that he changed regiments somewhere along the line. My mother had two Silver Crosses as my father passed away while serving with the Veterans Guard at Lethbridge.

Williamson Lake (64 H/1), south of Billard Lake was named after him in 1995.

Williamson, Flight Sergeant **John A.** of Brandon (R 95454). No. 487 Squadron. He died 4 April 1943 at the age of 33 and is commemorated at the Runnymede Memorial in Surrey, England. He was the eldest of the ten children of William H. and Dorothy G. Williamson of Brandon. His sister writes (15 February 1996):

[He was] born September 23, 1909 in the Rural Municipality of Whitehead. He attended Roseland Rural School and graduated from the Brandon Collegiate. His interests were sports (hockey and baseball) and reading. He worked for a neighbouring farmer for $5.00 a month before joining the air force in March, 1941. He also loved horseback riding and was an excellent scholar and continued to self-educate himself.

He wrote home to his sister two weeks before his death:

Dear Estella: Just a few lines to let you know that I am well and on leave again. I am back in London for a few days. We are supposed to get nine days every six weeks but get gypped out of a few days every time. I received your parcel with writing paper and toilet articles in it. I have enough till Christmas now. Thanks a lot. Next time send some black socks size 10 and canned eats or cake. I don't want much do I? But pass the word along where it will do the most good. I did not get Alice's parcel. There is one back at camp for me now, but I do not know who it is from yet. I am going to spend a very quiet week here. Have over fifteen pounds saved up but am going to see if I can buy a second-hand bike. Wish I had yours. It is worth about fifty dollars now (over here). Remember me to all at home, also those away from home. Take care of yourself and don't get married till I get back to see you. Love, Johnny (22 March 1943).

Williamson Bay (64 N/5) in Ibbott Lake was named after him in 1995.

Willis, Private **Charles** of Winnipeg (H 6319). Winnipeg Grenadiers. He died 21 December 1941 and is commemorated at the Sai Wan Memorial in Hong Kong. He was the son of Mr. and Mrs. H. J. Willis of Winnipeg. ***Willis Rapids*** (64 P/3) in the Big Spruce River was named after him in 1995.

Willis, Major **Charles J.** of Winnipeg. Royal Canadian Artillery. He died 16 October 1944 at the age of 30 and is commemorated at Schoonselhof Cemetery in Antwerp, Belgium. He was the son of Harold S. and Amy J. Willis of Winnipeg and was survived by his wife Lauretta M. Willis. ***Willis Peninsula*** (63 I/2) on Molson Lake was named after him in 1995.

Willis, Private **Frank** of East Kildonan (874980). 8th Battalion, Canadian Infantry (Manitoba Regiment). He died 15 August 1917 at the age of 31 and is commemorated at the Vimy Memorial in Pas de Calais, France. This native of Dorset, England was the son of John E. and Jessie Willis and was survived by his wife Sadie Willis (née Armstrong) of East Kildonan and their two children. ***Willis Bay*** (64 J/14) in Clifton Lake was named after this World War I casualty in 1989.

Willis, Squadron Leader **Frank C.** of Winnipeg (40332). No. 421 Squadron, RAF. He died 8 November 1942 at the age of 24 and is commemorated at the Runnymede Memorial in Surrey, England. Having assumed command of No. 421 Squadron only five months earlier, he was lost on a "sweep" over the English Channel (Allison 1978). ***Willis Creek*** (53 K/6), which flows north into Richardson Lake was named after him in 1995.

Willis, Leading Stoker **Stanley T.** of Dauphin (21989). HMCS *Valleyfield.* The *Valleyfield* was torpedoed and sunk by U-548 50 miles south of Cape Race, Newfoundland; 125 of her ship's company were lost. Leading Stoker Willis died 7 May 1944 at the age of 24 and is commemorated at the Halifax Memorial. He was the son of Sidney R. and Dorothy Willis of Dauphin. ***Willis Island*** (53 M/12) in Silsby Lake was named after him in 1985.

Willson, Captain **William W.** of Winnipeg. Queen's Own Cameron Highlanders. He died 22 July 1944 at the age of 31 and is commemorated at Bretteville-sur-Laize Canadian War Cemetery in Calvados, France. He was survived by his wife Lois Willson. She writes (4 May 1995):

Captain William Wright Willson was born in Winnipeg on June 16, 1913. After graduating, he spent some time in Hamilton where he was associated with the YMCA. He returned to Winnipeg in 1938 and was engaged in the insurance business, enlisting in the army in 1940. He joined the Queen's Own Cameron Highlanders and took his COTC at Tuxedo Barracks. His regiment went overseas in December, 1940 and was stationed in England, being part of the second Canadian Division.

In August, 1942, the Queen's Own Cameron Highlanders participated on the infamous raid on Dieppe, France where the casualties were devastating. Fortunately, he and his commanding officer escaped capture by swimming to a destroyer – dive-bombed while they swam. However, they were taken aboard the destroyer and got back to England unharmed.

In early 1943, he was returned to Canada and was posted to the Infantry Training Centre at Camp Borden, Ontario where he remained until the fall of that year. He toured southern Ontario, addressing factories and businesses in connection with the Victory Bond drive that year.

Captain Willson returned to England in December, 1943, sailing on December 25th on the *Louis Pasteur* – the same day and same ship as in 1940. After arriving in England, he rejoined his regiment and began arduous training in southern England for the eventual invasion of Europe.

The 2nd Division did not participate in the June landing on the coast of France, having never been fully reinforced after Dieppe. However, the division went into action in late July at Caen, which was reduced to rubble and where the casualties were enormous.

Willson Lake (64 H/6), west of Northern Indian Lake was named after him in 1995.

Wilman, Leading Aircraftman **Richard H.** of Carman (R 191061). No. 440 Squadron. He died 16 July 1944 at the age of 30 and is commemorated at Beny-sur-Mer Canadian War Cemetery in Calvados, France. He was the son of Frank B. and Clara E. Wilman of Portage la Prairie, Manitoba. ***Wilman Lake*** (64 P/12), west of Nejanilini Lake was named after him in 1974.

Wilmot, Squadron Leader **Brian E.** of Winnipeg (J 23777). No. 415 Squadron, Distinguished Flying Cross and Bar.

This officer has completed many sorties during which he has attacked such well-defended targets as Berlin, Frankfurt and Düsseldorf. One night in April, 1944, in a sortie against the last named target, Flying Officer Wilmot displayed the greatest determination in pressing home his attack although one engine failed and some height had been lost before reaching the target. His fine fighting spirit has always been apparent and he has set a most commendable example (DFC Citation 1944).

Since the award of the Distinguished Flying Cross, Squadron Leader Wilmot has completed numerous sorties against a variety of targets. On a recent operation against Brunswick, although his aircraft was attacked and severely damaged by enemy night fighters, Squadron Leader Wilmot displayed great skill and determination in pressing home his attack and in bringing his damaged aircraft safely back to base. He has set a worthy example (Bar to DFC 1944).

He died 21 August 1944 at the age of 21 and is commemorated at Stonefall Cemetery in Yorkshire, England. He was the son of John H. A. and Bertha A. Wilmot of Winnipeg. ***Wilmot Lake*** (64 C/11), southwest of Lynn Lake was named after him in 1947.

Wilmot, Pilot Officer **Earl D.** of Winnipeg (J 95499). No. 625 Squadron. He died 9 November 1944 at the age of 22 and is commemorated at the Reichswald Forest War Cemetery in Germany. He was the son of John D. and Ruth Wilmot of Winnipeg. ***Wilmot Island*** (63 N/12) in Sisipuk Lake was named after him in 1995.

Wilson, Gunner **Alexander** of Sperling (H 60064). Royal Canadian Artillery. He died 13 August 1944 and is commemorated at Beny-sur-Mer Canadian War Cemetery in Calvados, France. ***Wilson Lake*** (53 L/11), west of Gods Lake was named after him in 1962.

Wilson, Private **Bruce T.** of St. James (H 52034). Royal Canadian Army Service Corps. He died 17 April 1945 at the age of 25 and is commemorated at the Adegem Canadian War Cemetery in Belgium. He was the son of Charles H. and Ruby A. Wilson of Winnipeg. His niece recalls (2 December 1994):

Bruce Thomas Wilson was born on March 11, 1920 in Portage la Prairie – actually on a farm south of Portage. The family moved to St. James and he attained his education there. His special interests were sports and reading. Bruce enlisted in 1940 at the Fort Osborne Barracks.

Wilson Hill (64 G/14), east of Big Sand Lake was named after him in 1994.

Wilson, Lieutenant **Claude M.** of Winnipeg (339247). 29th Squadron, RFC/RAF, Distinguished Flying Cross.

Bold in attack, this officer never hesitates to join in an engagement with the enemy, regardless of their numerical superiority. On 18 August [1918], with four other machines, he attacked a large hostile formation. Five enemy machines were destroyed, Lt. Wilson accounting for one. In all, he had four machines and one balloon to his credit (*London Gazette*, 3 December 1918).

After serving in an artillery regiment, Wilson transferred to the Royal Flying Corps (later the Royal Air Force) in July, 1917. An S.E.5a pilot, he was posted to 29 Squadron on 4 May 1918. After scoring eight victories, he was killed in action when his aircraft was shot down by a Fokker D.VII (www.theaerodrome.com/aces/canada/wilson.html). He died 14 October 1918 at the age of 20 and is commemorated at Dadizeele New British Cemetery in Belgium. He was the son of Charles H. and Margaret Wilson of Vancouver. This photograph was taken by another RAF pilot and close friend Thomas J. Cook of Winnipeg who became a casualty of the Second World War (see entry). ***Wilson Island*** (52 L/6) in George Lake was named after Lieutenant Wilson in 1994.

Wilson, Pilot Officer **David Leslie** T. (a.k.a. Wesley) of Winnipeg (J 13633). No. 31 Operational Training Unit, RCAF. He died 31 January 1943 at the age of 21 and is commemorated at Brookside Cemetery in Winnipeg. He was the son of George and Jessie Wilson (née Harrison) of Winnipeg and was the brother of Sapper Douglas G. Wilson (next entry). ***Wesley Wilson Bay*** (53 N/3) in White Goose Lake was named after him in 1995.

Wilson, Sapper **Douglas Gordon** of St. Vital (H 36517). Royal Canadian Engineers. He died 8 December 1944 at the age of 34 and is commemorated at Brussels Town Cemetery in Belgium. He was the son of George and Jessie Wilson (née Harrison) and was survived by his wife Gertrude V. Wilson of St. Vital and their two children. He was the brother of Pilot Officer Wesley Wilson (previous entry). In a letter to Sapper Wilson's widow, another brother, Gunner Ted Wilson wrote:

Dear Vi and Lora: Received Lora's letter a few days ago and was very sorry to hear about Gord. It's hard to realize I won't be seeing him again. War is a terrible thing alright, much more than some people realize. It's when it's someone close to you that gets it. It makes you think. We have had some casualties lately ourselves. Sometimes I wonder how I manage to escape, with so many of the fellows getting it. Just fate I guess. It's sure hard to see your old friends getting killed in front of you. Often I wonder how I keep going but you just do somehow. Hoping the war may end soon and bring an end to this cold, mud and shells. I think it would be better to be out of it. However, it doesn't do to think that way. There is always something else to be done and more ... Germans to chase back. I hope you don't take it too hard Vi. I suppose we all have to die sooner or later and I guess Gord wouldn't know what hit him if he was in an accident. I sure feel sorry for you though. Out here we get kind of hardened to these things but we don't forget.

About my leave, I don't think we'll be getting it for a while as there are quite a few fellows ahead of me and they are going very slowly, only a few at a time. It sure would be swell to be back though. How are things going back there? Cold I'll bet. It is muddy and cold here. It would be better if it froze up. Dad had gone to the coast, but [I] don't know how he made out. Hope he hasn't made a mistake. Had a letter from Charley. He seems to be doing alright in his new job. How is Bobby and Gwen [her children] these days? Also your mother and Dad. Received a bunch of papers (St. Vital) and a letter from Gord just before Christmas. He said he'd received your parcel and would meet me in Berlin. Well I guess I'll close now. Hope to hear from you soon. All the best and keep the old chin up. Cheerio. As ever, Ted (n.d.).

Among his personal effects returned to his widow was a Christmas card drawn by his son. Prior to his enlistment, he had been employed by the Bank of Montreal. ***Wilson Esker*** (53 N/3), north of White Goose Lake was named after him in 1995.

Wilson, Flight Sergeant **Douglas K.** of Winnipeg (R 91753). No. 5 Bombing and Gunnery School, RCAF. He died 8 February 1944 at the age of 27 and is commemorated at Brookside Cemetery in Winnipeg. He was the son of John J. and Marie M. Wilson of Vancouver and was survived by his wife Molly Wilson of Winnipeg. ***Douglas Wilson Lake*** (64 C/13), south of McMillan Lake was named after him in 1995.

Wilson, Private **Duncan C.** of Winnipeg (H 19840). Queen's Own Cameron Highlanders. He died 19 August 1942 at the age of 36 and is commemorated at Dieppe Canadian War Cemetery in Seine-Maritime, France. He was the son of Steven J. and Margaret J. Wilson (née Halliday) and was survived by his wife of one year Annie "Nan" G. Wilson (née Thompson) of Glasgow, Scotland. His brother recalls (2 May 1996):

He was born at Hargrave, Manitoba in 1906. [He] joined the Queen's Own Cameron Highlanders in September, 1939 and was with the battalion advance party sent to England in early 1940. [He was] killed during the reconnaissance in force on the city of Dieppe.

Duncan Wilson Lake (64 F/16), east of Kustra Lake was named after him in 1995.

Wilson, Lieutenant **George T.** of Winnipeg. 12th Manitoba Dragoons. He died 6 April 1945 at the age of 24 and is commemorated at the Holten Canadian War Cemetery in Holland. He was the son of Horace J. and Minnie M. Wilson (née Tristram) and was survived by his wife Sheila M. Wilson. ***George Wilson Lake*** (64 O/11), north of Corbett Lake was named after him in 1995.

Wilson, Flying Officer **Harold E.** of Birtle (J 86677). No. 630 Squadron. He died 27 July 1944 at the age of 22 and is commemorated at Des Carmes-Dechaux Communal Cemetery in France. He was the cousin of Flight Sergeant James Wilson (see entry). ***Harold Wilson Lake*** (63 I/8), south of Logan Lake was named after him in 1995.

Wilson, Pilot Officer **Herbert Clarke** of Winnipeg (J 86417). No. 420 Squadron. He died 20 April 1944 at the age of 24 and is commemorated at Grandcourt War Cemetery in Seine-Maritime, France. He was the son of Henry H. and Mary Wilson. His brother recalls (16 July 1999) that he:

... was born in Elm Creek, Manitoba on the 17th day of April, 1920. He attended school in Elm Creek and later moved to Winnipeg where he completed his studies at Gordon Bell High School in 1937. After leaving school, Clarke's work schedule allowed little time for sports, however, he did manage to play some tennis which he enjoyed very much. He was employed by the Federal Grain Company until enlisting in the RCAF in January, 1942. He had made two previous attempts to join the RCAF starting in the spring of 1940, but was rejected for medical reasons. After completing an Air Bombers course in November, 1942, he went overseas in January, 1943. After joining Bomber Command, he had partially completed a tour of "ops" before being shot down.

Wilson Rapids (64 H/6) in the Churchill River was named after him in 1995.

Wilson, Flight Sergeant **James Averd** of Birtle (R 106028). No. 23 Operational Training Unit, RCAF. He died 29 January 1943 at the age of 20 and is commemorated at All Saints Churchyard in Honington, Suffolk, England. He was the son of Thomas A. and Sarah J. Wilson of Birtle, Manitoba and was the cousin of Flying Officer Harold Wilson (see entry).

Wilson attended public school in Birtle, obtaining twelfth grade standing after enlistment. He was a keen sportsman, played junior hockey in forward position and was active in scouting work. His late grandfather, E. J. Wilson, a pioneer of Birtle, was for fifty-two years the editor of the *Birtle Eye Witness* (Hill 1944).

Wilson Narrows (64 I/2) in Allan Lake was named after him in 1995.

Wilson, Sergeant **James M.** of Shoal Lake (R 59976). No. 19 Operational Training Unit, RCAF. He died 9 January 1942 at the age of 22 and is commemorated at Kinloss Abbey Burial Ground in Moray, Scotland. He was the son of James A. and Jane A. Wilson of Haney, British Columbia. His nephew writes (27 November 1987):

He was born in Neepawa, Manitoba in 1920 and took his schooling in Neepawa and Shoal Lake. He joined the Canadian Armed Forces in 1940 and trained in Trenton. He served in England and Scotland.

At the time of his enlistment, he was employed as a traveller for an elevator company. ***Wilson Bay*** (64 J/11) in Clifton Lake was named after him in 1989.

Wilson, Warrant Officer 1 **John H.** of Boissevain (H 19976). Queen's Own Cameron Highlanders. He died 17 August 1944 at the age of 31 and is commemorated at Bretteville-sur-Laize Canadian War Cemetery in Calvados, France. He was the son of Ernest R. and Nora Wilson. ***John Wilson Lake*** (64 I/4), west of Ashley Lake was named after him in 1995.

Wilson, Private **Kenneth E.** of Winnipeg (G 1760). Essex Scottish Regiment. He died 1 November 1944 at the age of 19 and is commemorated at Schoonselhof Cemetery in Antwerp, Belgium. He was the son of Herbert M. and Nettie M. Wilson of Sussex, New Brunswick. ***Kenneth Wilson Bay*** (54 E/11) in Bradshaw Lake was named after him in 1995.

Wilson, Pilot Officer **Norman A.** of Winnipeg (J 89886). No. 424 Squadron. He died 25 May 1944 at the age of 22 and is commemorated at the Runnymede Memorial in Surrey, England. He was the son of Elmer A. and Stella E. Wilson (née Hoffman) of Winnipeg and was survived by his wife Evelyn P. Wilson of Winnipeg. ***Norman Wilson Esker*** (53 L/6), east of Joint Lake was named after him in 1995.

Wilson, Private **Norman E.** of Rathwell (H 46059). Lake Superior Regiment. He died 21 August 1944 at the age of 28 and is commemorated at Bretteville-sur-Laize Canadian War Cemetery in Calvados, France. He was survived by his mother Margaret Ferris of Erwood, Saskatchewan and by his grandparents Mr. and Mrs. John A. Wilson of Rathwell, Manitoba. ***Norman Wilson Lake*** (53 M/7), northeast of Schwatka Lake was named after him in 1995.

Wilson, Pilot Officer **Robert J.** of Rapid City (J 18828). No. 424 Squadron. He died 29 July 1943 at the age of 24 and is commemorated at Enfidaville War Cemetery in Tunisia. He was seventh of the eight children of John and Mary E. Wilson of Rapid City, Manitoba. His sister recalls (21 October 2001):

> Bob trained at Edmonton, Virden and Dauphin receiving his Wings at Saskatoon in November of 1942. He went overseas in July, 1943 and was posted to North Africa. He had just turned 24 when he was killed. Wellington aircraft No. X304 exploded on take-off, crashed and burned at 424 Squadron airfield near Kairouan. The explosion was believed to be sabotage. Bob was not with his own crew when he was killed. The crew he was with were on their last mission before going on leave. Bob was with them as an Observer.
>
> It was a great blow when we received the telegram. Our parents received notification of his promotion to Pilot Officer shortly after it arrived. It was upsetting for all of us, just as it was when we later received letters he had written just before his death. My parents were asked what they wished to have inscribed on his headstone and they requested: "At the going down of the sun, and in the morning, we will remember them." How very appropriate; one never forgets.

Wilson Channel (54 D/7), between Ferris Bay and Stephens Lake was named after him in 1982.

Wilson, Leading Seaman **Ronald A.** of Griswold (V 10251). HMCS *Stormont*. He died 21 August 1944 at the age of 22 and is commemorated at the Halifax Memorial. He was the son of Charles A. and Ethel E. Wilson of Regina and was survived by his wife Edith I. Wilson of Griswold, Manitoba. ***Wilson Peninsula*** (64 O/16) on Baralzon Lake was named after him in 1995.

Wilson, Gunner **Stewart E.** of Dand (H 59953). Royal Canadian Artillery. He died 6 November 1943 at the age of 23 and is commemorated at the Moro River Canadian War Cemetery in Italy. He was the son of Peter and Maggie Wilson of Dand, Manitoba. ***Stewart Wilson Lake*** (64 A/4), east of Rock Lake was named after him in 1995.

Wilson, Private **William J.** of Winnipeg (H 6476). Winnipeg Grenadiers. He died 24 December 1941 and is commemorated at the Sai Wan Memorial in Hong Kong. He was the son of Mr. and Mrs. W. A. Wilson of Winnipeg. A British escapee described the fall of Hong Kong:

> … when Hong Kong finally surrendered Christmas Day, the Japanese had penetrated to the heart of the city and were within a few hundred yards of battle headquarters itself – a vast bombproof, shell-proof dugout housing the nerve centre of the defences. The Japanese bombed the British line for days and suffered heavy losses from point-blank machine-gun fire of British Tommies below the hill overlooking the Happy Valley race course. The stout defence was unable to hold the final charge of overwhelming, fresh Japanese forces.
>
> The British, Canadian and Indian garrison of some 10,000 suffered extremely heavy losses. Hong Kong's air force of six old planes was put out of action the first day and the invaders' dive bombers afterwards wrought havoc unopposed. In the final hour of surrender, flames and smoke shot skyward as the defenders blew up ammunition dumps. The Japanese had their victory, but it cost them sorely in lives and badly needed ammunition. Along toward the end, the electric and water systems were knocked out on the island, forcing the defenders to rely upon candles and oil lamps for light, ponds and wells of brackish water to quench their thirst.
>
> At least a division and a half of Japanese troops – perhaps 22,500 men – streamed onto the island before it fell, but the outnumbered defenders, Canadian, British and Indian troops, seldom saw more than 10 invaders at a time, such were the well-executed and converging battle tactics of the invaders. Describing the invasion, the survivor said the Japanese landed from transports and advanced behind heavy artillery-fire protection for their final assault. They split up into groups of no more than 10 men, each group armed with machine guns, trench mortars and hand grenades. Slowly they fanned out and surrounded their objectives. Then, following a fierce mortar shelling with a hand grenade charge, the Japanese suddenly [converged] upon the main Hong Kong defence points from all directions.
>
> The weary defenders, their ranks depleted by casualties, laid down their arms at 3 PM Christmas Day, but isolated fighting continued throughout the island and Japanese bombers kept the air humming until darkness. The Briton said the Japanese apparently had been aided by fifth columnists. He said the British command reported that what few prisoners they captured possessed detailed maps showing roads, hills and British positions. Some had maps showing the location and plans of Hong Kong's air raid shelters and tunnels. Civilian casualties were reported light (*The Winnipeg Tribune* 12 January 1942).

William Wilson Lake (54 E/13), northwest of Comeau Lake was named after Private Wilson in 1995.

Wilton, Flight Lieutenant **Walter T.** of Wawanesa (J 20218). No. 408 Squadron. He died 29 December 1943 at the age of 24 and is commemorated at the Reichswald Forest War Cemetery in Germany. He was the fifth of the eight children of Leonard G. and Euphemia W. Wilton (née Armstrong) of Wawanesa, Manitoba. His nephew recalls (26 November 2001):

> Walter was ... born September 16, 1919 at Glenboro, Manitoba. His family and he lived nine and one-half miles south of town until 1927 when they moved to the Wilton farm west of Glenboro. He attended Clifton Bank School, Stockton, Chesley and Wawanesa. In 1937, they moved to the Chesley district. Walter signed up in 1941 with B Squadron of the 12th Manitoba Dragoons, went to Shilo and then on to the RCAF where he became a Lieutenant. His 408 Goose Squadron (For Freedom) [aircraft] was shot down over Lingen on Ems, Germany and he died during that night raid on Berlin. He was remembered in his community as a great hockey player. His sister, Beth Graham visited his gravesite in 1987. His mother also wanted to go but was fearful of flying.
>
> In his book *A Thousand Shall Fall*, Judge Murray Peden of Winnipeg (QC and DFC) refers to his friend Walter Wilton as "Watt." They served on the same squadron overseas.
>
> There is a tombstone marker to Walter's memory just 2 1/2 miles from Lingen on Ems where his remains were exhumed and reburied in the Reichswald Forest at Kleve, Germany, just inside the German border from Holland. I was able to secure a photo of it by way of Robert Ferguson, a Legion member from Neepawa. Since his participation in

the 1991 Legion Pilgrimage of Remembrance, Robert has endeavoured, along with Dutch friend Henke Welting of the Netherlands, to locate as many of Manitoba's fatal war casualties as possible, place a flag on their grave, have a photograph taken and then forward it to the next-of-kin if they can be located.

Wilton Lake (64 P/6), southeast of Nejanilini Lake was named after Flight Lieutenant Wilton in 1974.

Wilwand, Sergeant **George A.** of Winnipeg (H 19837). Queen's Own Cameron Highlanders. He died 14 August 1944 at the age of 27 and is commemorated at Bretteville-sur-Laize Canadian War Cemetery in Calvados, France. He was the son of Robert R. and Olive Wilwand of Winnipeg and was survived by his wife Jennie Wilwand of Winnipeg. ***Wilwand Lake*** (64 H/15), east of Etawney Lake was named after him in 1995.

Winder, Pilot Officer **John S.** of Onanole (J 93659). No. 100 Squadron. He died 17 June 1944 at the age of 22 and is commemorated at Uden War Cemetery in Holland. He was the son of Gledhill and Bessie Winder of Onanole, Manitoba. ***Winder Lake*** (64 P/16), northeast of Nejanilini Lake was named after him in 1974.

Winder, Flying Officer **Robert G.** of Winnipeg (J 9925). No. 7 Squadron. He died 21 October 1942 at the age of 21 and is commemorated at the Runnymede Memorial in Surrey, England. He was the son of Henry and Mary E. Winder of Norwood. A local newspaper article printed shortly thereafter read in part:

Pilot Officer Robert Gledhill Winder, son of Henry Winder, 275 Kenny Street, Norwood, celebrated his 21st birthday Sunday, but no one knows just where, for he has been missing after air operations overseas since October, according to information received by his parents October 21. Born in Norwood, Pilot Officer Winder received his early education at Tache School, Norwood Collegiate and St. John's College. He was in his second year of civil engineering at the University of Manitoba when he enlisted May 3, 1941, in the air force. He trained at Brandon, Regina and Mossbank, Saskatchewan from where he graduated December 20, 1941. After taking a pilot's course at Rivers, he was commissioned as a Pilot Officer. He went overseas last January (n.d.).

Robert Winder Lake (64 O/12), north of Shannon Lake was named after him in 1984.

Windham, Flight Lieutenant **William T.** of Cypress River (76519). Royal Air Force Volunteer Reserve. Dave Everett of Penn, England recalls the last day of the SS *Anselm* on which Flight Lieutenant Windham was being transported:

Our troopship SS *Anselm* left Glasgow escorted by the destroyer *Challenger*. I remember scanning the bulletin board six days later: "For the attention of all servicemen," it said. "Pyjamas can be worn now that we are out of the danger area." A matelot with a stiff beard behind me growled: "That must have been written by a U-boat commander. Is there a safe place anywhere in the Atlantic?"

My pal Andy and I were both in the boxing team at our last station and to keep ourselves in trim we were up at 5 AM trotting around the deck. Saturday morning, July 5, was no exception. We had just completed one circuit when the torpedo struck. From then on it was a nightmare. The alarm sounded. By instinct, we headed for the lifeboat station. I witnessed chaos and panic beyond anything I could imagine. Despair and hopelessness was written on everybody's face.

I heard screams and howls from guys trapped down below. I watched guys fighting with each other, seemingly for no reason at all. The destroyer *Challenger* had nosed in towards the back of the ship, catching servicemen dropping from the stern.

Padre Pugh, the first padre at the RAF Bridgnorth station, was haggling with a couple of erks (Aircraftman) to lower him down so that he could bring solace to the doomed erks trapped below. His last words were "My love of God is greater than my fear of death."

The ship went down within 20 minutes. The reports of casualties ranged from 250 to over 400. Someone, somewhere made a cock-up with their sums.

Years later I read that Padre Hugh had been awarded the George Cross posthumously for his bravery. I recently met another survivor who had converted to Catholicism having witnessed this RC priest sacrificing his life. The irony was that it was a mistake. Padre Pugh was C of E, but he shared a cabin with a Catholic priest. In the pandemonium, each had donned the wrong tunic.

The Reverend Herbert Cecil Pugh (1898-1941) was awarded the George Cross posthumously in April, 1947. The official citation says he was last seen "kneeling with the men in prayer as the ship sank" (http://www.blackcountry.com/millennium/1900/1925-1949/1941.html). Flight Lieutenant Windham died 5 July 1941 at the age of 43 and is commemorated at the Runnymede Memorial in Surrey, England. He was the son of Reginald and Martha E. Windham. ***Windham Lake*** (53 L/1), southeast of Rochon Lake was named after him in 1995.

Wing, Gunner **Oscar W.** of Winnipeg (H 12085). Royal Canadian Artillery. He died 4 February 1944 at the age of 24 and is commemorated at the Moro River Canadian War Cemetery in Italy. He was the son of John P. and Evelyn Wing and was survived by his wife Margaret M. Wing of Victoria, British Columbia and their daughter. ***Wing Island*** (64 N/11) in Jonasson Lake was named after him in 1995.

Winnberg, Rifleman **Carl** of Great Falls (H 100219). Royal Winnipeg Rifles. He died 29 May 1943 at the age of 24 and is commemorated at Brookwood Military Cemetery in Surrey, England. He was the son of Carl and Louise Winnberg of Great Falls, Manitoba. ***Winnberg River*** (64 J/12), which flows northeast into the Fergus River was named after him in 1972.

Winter, Corporal **Edward M.** of Winnipeg (R 80494). Royal Canadian Air Force. He died 17 October 1946 at the age of 24 and is commemorated at Elmwood Cemetery in Winnipeg. He was the son of William E. and Jessie Winter of Winnipeg. ***Winter Island*** (63 N/13) in Bonald Lake was named after him in 1995.

Winters, Lance Corporal **Arthur E.** of Winnipeg (H 8826). Royal Canadian Engineers. He died 1 October 1944 at the age of 35 and is commemorated at Bergen-op-Zoom Canadian War Cemetery in Holland. ***Winters Bay*** (64 K/9) in Cantlon Lake was named after him in 1995.

Wintonick, Corporal **William B.** of Winnipeg (R 58840). No. 135 Squadron. He died 19 July 1942 at the age of 22 and is commemorated at Elmwood Cemetery in Winnipeg. He was the son of Peter and Paulie Wintonick of Winnipeg. ***Wintonick Lake*** (64 O/16), southwest of Baralzon Lake was named after him in 1975.

Wintoniw, Rifleman **Michael** of Zhoda (H 41884). Royal Winnipeg Rifles. He died 6 June 1944 at the age of 26 and is commemorated at Beny-sur-Mer Canadian War Cemetery in Calvados, France. He was the son of Nykola and Nellie Wintoniw of Zhoda, Manitoba. ***Wintoniw Lake*** (64 N/3), northeast of Lac Brochet was named after him in 1972.

Wise, Lieutenant **Richard A.** of Winnipeg. Queen's Own Cameron Highlanders, Mentioned in Dispatches. He died 19 August 1942 and is commemorated at Dieppe Canadian War Cemetery in Seine-Maritime, France. ***Wise Lake*** (54 L/3), southwest of Churchill was named after him in 1948.

Wishart, Rifleman **Henry Murray** of Russell (H 41217). Royal Winnipeg Rifles. He died 6 June 1944 at the age of 31 and is commemorated at Beny-sur-Mer Canadian War Cemetery in Calvados, France. He was the son of Andrew M. and Beatrice Wishart of Russell, Manitoba. ***Wishart Lake*** (64 H/13), northeast of Southern Indian Lake was named after him in 1963.

Wither, Staff Sergeant **David A.** of Winnipeg (H 40077). Veterans Guard of Canada, British Empire Medal. He died 11 November 1943 at the age of 47 and is commemorated at Elmwood Cemetery in Winnipeg. This World War I veteran was the son of Euphemia Wither of Winnipeg and was survived by his wife Margaret C. Wither of Winnipeg. She writes (12 April 1995):

> He was born in Ardrossan, [North] Ayrshire, Scotland [and] came to Winnipeg with his parents and family in 1904. He attended Rosswell and Elmwood schools. He enlisted at the outbreak of war with 8 Battalion and served all through the war with that battalion. At the end of the war, he stayed in France driving Colonel K. C. Bedson who was disposing of war equipment. That is about all I can tell you of his war service. He never talked about it. He returned to Winnipeg in 1919. Upon his return, he worked on various construction jobs in Canada and the United States until the outbreak of the Second World War.

Wither Lake (64 I/15), east of Shethanei Lake was named after him in 1957.

Withers, Flying Officer **J. A. William** of Winnipeg (J 10182). No. 487 Squadron. He died 6 December 1942 at the age of 21 and is commemorated at Bergen-op-Zoom War Cemetery in Holland. He was the son of Mr. and Mrs. R. A. Withers of Winnipeg and was survived by his wife of ten months June Withers (née Wilson) of Toronto. His obituary read in part:

> The young officer received his education at Lord Roberts and Daniel McIntyre schools and attended St. John's College. He was associated with the Your Tobacco Shop and spent two years in the employ of the Canadian News Company. During this time, he was connected with the Anglican Young People's Association of All Saints Church. Arriving in England in March [1942], a month after marriage, he was promoted to Flying Officer in November, 1942 (*Winnipeg Free Press* December 1942).

Withers Island (63 N/5) in Kipahigan Lake was named after him in 1995.

Withers, Sergeant **Reginald P.** of Winnipeg (H 41111). Royal Winnipeg Rifles. He died 12 May 1941 at the age of 37 and is commemorated at Truro Cemetery in Nova Scotia. He was survived by his mother Charlotte Withers of Reading, Berkshire, England. ***Withers Lake*** (52 M/14), northeast of Hutch Lake was named after him in 1979.

Witt, Pilot Officer **Ernest M.** of Winnipeg (J 17710). No. 405 Squadron. He died 14 July 1943 at the age of 20 and is commemorated at Jonkerbos War Cemetery in Holland. ***Witt Lake*** (64 P/1), northeast of Meades Lake was named after him in 1995.

Wityck, Flight Sergeant **Peter** of Brandon (R 80002). No. 405 Squadron. He died 5 January 1942 at the age of 20 and is commemorated at St. Catherine Churchyard in Barmby-on-the-Moor, Yorkshire, England. He was the son of Peter and Jennie Wityck of Brandon. ***Wityck Lake*** (64 P/5), south of Nejanilini Lake was named after him in 1974.

Wiwsianski, Pilot Officer **Michael** of Hilbre (J 90949). No. 432 Squadron. He died 23 May 1944 at the age of 20 and is commemorated at Le Mans West Cemetery in Sarthe, France. He was the son of John and Tienie Wish (sp.) of Mulvihill. According to a newspaper account:

> A three-year quest for the grave of a Manitoba airman, who was reported missing after an overseas bombing raid in 1944, finally came to an end the other day for Mr. and Mrs. John Wish of Mulvihill, Manitoba. Until a few days ago the last word they had of their son Michael, a Pilot Officer air gunner, was the official air ministry telegram telling them he had not returned from a mission over France on the night of May 23, 1944. Ever since then, the parents have sought answers to the questions asked by those whose loved ones have been declared missing in action: Where is his grave? Is it being looked after?
>
> All these questions were finally answered recently when the parents of Michael Wish received a touching letter from a French woman who has been tending the grave of their son faithfully for more than three years. The letter, written in French, is proof beyond words that the ordinary French people have never forgotten the sacrifices made by the Canadian airmen who helped them win back their freedom.
>
> "For three years I have unceasingly searched to locate the person who has the numbers (identification) from the Halifax plane which crashed at Moncé-en-Belin the 23 May, 1944," the letter reads. "I will be straightforward in my letter and will let you know the actual facts and happenings. How many times my thoughts are on this very spot where this crash happened and I am at a loss for words to convey my homage to all these brave boys and above all your dear son. [W]e were in our shelter, my daughter, my son and myself whilst a heavy bombardment was in progress at Mans (a small town several kilometres from here) … we heard continuous detonations in the distance. It was this one particular Halifax which had apparently to make a crash landing and took on fire. The rear gunner had apparently attempted to parachute out from the bomber, unfortunately, luck was against him, who fell face against a tree and killed him instantly … a German truck came and took away the remains of the bodies and took them to Mans Cemetery. Large crowds surrounded the truck and covered the remains with flowers. I have always (ever since) commemorated this area in the pines where these heroes crashed. I have placed a cross and a white marble stone (plaque) with inscribed remembrance. Each week I place flowers, and although flowers are not available in winter, I make my weekly visit. It would be a great pleasure if you could possibly send me a small photograph of your dear son. My heart bleeds when I think of all the families of these brave boys. My most ardent desire was to contact the eight families so as to let them know there would be a mother over here that does not forget them. It will be a satisfaction that you will learn that each commemoration day for our Dead that all of these heroes get similar honours."
>
> The letter was accompanied by a snapshot of the writer placing flowers at the site of the crash and another photo showing her 17 year-old son, in the uniform of the French air force, standing at attention on the spot. The letter was signed Yve Fortier, Moncé-en-Belin, (Sarthe), France. Mans, where the bombardment took place, is about 120 miles from Paris. In the aircraft's crew were six Canadians, one Australian and one Englishman (*Winnipeg Free Press* 1947).

Thirty years later his parents received the following letter from the Moncé-en-Belin Town Council:

> Dear Mr. and Mrs. Wish: It is my very great pleasure to inform you that the town council have decided to pay homage to the courage and sacrifice of your son who was killed in the region of Moncé-en-Belin during the

last war, by naming one of the streets in our village after him. I should be very grateful if you could let me know if this decision meets with your approval, The Chairman (7 July 1978).

His sister adds (20 November 2001):

When I said goodbye to my brother at the Hilbre train station, I had a strange feeling that I would not see him again. Madam Fortier sent my Mother and Dad a lovely, small wooden box with ashes from the bomber's wreck site. I buried it with my Mother when she passed away, as Mother and Dad never got over Mike's death.

St. Michael Street in Moncé-en-Belin, France was named after him in 1978 and ***Wiwsianski Lake*** (64 P/8), southwest of Caribou Lake was named after him in 1974.

Wojnarsky, Private **John** of Elphinstone (H 41668). Winnipeg Grenadiers. He died a prisoner of war 7 January 1942 at the age of 21 and is commemorated at the Sai Wan Memorial in Hong Kong. He was the son of Mike F. and Pauline Wojnarsky of Elphinstone, Manitoba. The cause of death was indicated as "Died of wounds." ***Wojnarsky Lake*** (64 J/8), south of Tadoule Lake was named after him in 1975.

Wolfaert, Corporal **Prosper** of Winnipeg (H 36764). Royal Canadian Army Service Corps. He died 7 May 1945 at the age of 59 and is commemorated at Belgian Sacred Heart Church Cemetery in St. Boniface. He was survived by his wife of 31 years Matilda Wolfaert of St. Boniface and their daughter, Irma. She writes (23 November 2001):

Prosper Wolfaert was born in Oostwinkel, Belgium on October 19, 1885. He joined the Belgian Army prior to the First World War and served Belgium in that conflict with the 2nd Regiment de Carabiniers and the Coy des Transports IBA. Prosper was gassed in the trenches at the front. At the end of the war, he continued to serve his country until he left for Canada on April 1, 1925. Arriving in Winnipeg, he worked at St. Boniface Hospital until Canada joined the Second World War. Prosper enlisted in the army of his new, adopted country Canada on November 8, 1940.

He was discharged for medical reasons on June 6, 1944. Succumbing to injuries at Deer Lodge Hospital on May 7, 1945, Prosper Wolfaert was buried on May 11, 1945 in the Military Section of the Belgian Sacred Heart Roman Catholic Church.

I have many memories of my father, starting with the fact that I was almost three years old before he returned from the front after World War I. He was a kind and gentle man whose life was governed by his love of God, his country and his family. He so loved his new home that when World War II broke out, he re-enlisted in the Canadian Army. Because of his age, his birth certificate had to be changed, making it look that he was still young enough to serve his adopted country. Dad's plans for retirement included life on his small farm on the outskirts of Winnipeg which is now part of Winnipeg. Instead, he was admitted to Deer Lodge Hospital. When it looked certain that the war would come to an end, one of dad's last words were: "now that the war is almost over, my country no longer needs me, so I can now die in peace."

Wolfaert Lake (53 M/11), northeast of Ransom Lake was named after him in 1996.

Wolfe, Gunner **Esfeld** of Winnipeg (H 52102). Royal Canadian Artillery. He died 30 November 1943 at the age of 44 and is commemorated at Brookside Cemetery in Winnipeg. He was survived by his wife Lora O. Wolfe of St. James. ***Wolfe Island*** (64 P/5) in Nejanilini Lake was named after him in 1995.

Wolfe, Corporal **Jacob H.** of Morden (H 41572). Lincoln and Welland Regiment. He died 8 March 1945 and is commemorated at the Groesbeek Canadian War Cemetery in Holland. ***Wolfe Lake*** (64 N/4), northwest of Lac Brochet was named after him in 1972.

Wolinsky, Private **Lone** of Winnipeg (H 20612). Hastings and Prince Edward Regiment. He died 10 January 1944 at the age of 25 and is commemorated at the Moro River Canadian War Cemetery in Italy. He was the son of Sam and Rose Wolinsky of Winnipeg. ***Wolinsky Lake*** (64 J/3), northeast of Big Sand Lake was named after him in 1975.

Wolk, Private **Walter** of The Pas (H 3954). Royal Montreal Regiment. He died 16 September 1942 at the age of 19 and is commemorated at Brookwood Military Cemetery in Surrey, England. His sister-in-law recalls (19 April 1995):

Walter was born October 11th, 1922 at home in The Pas. Our only memories of Walter after all these years are that he was a member of the Boy Scouts and enjoyed the field trips they engaged in. Later in his teens, he loved to go to work at the local newspaper and learning about what he hoped would be his future job – printing. Later, after he joined the army, he wrote us from England; he had found his real vocation and planned to make the army his lifetime career. Poor Walter got his wish but not exactly as he had planned.

He was survived by his mother Victoria Wolk of The Pas. His brother Mike was a CN Telegrapher stationed at Saskatoon at the time but happened to be in The Pas when Walter died. He was visiting the local telegraph office where he had trained when the wire arrived and he took it, not knowing it was for his mother. The local newspaper reported that:

Young Walter has joined the legion of those who have given their lives for the cause of Democracy. He wouldn't appreciate an editorial, being as he termed himself "a newspaperman myself" for Walter was only 19 at the time of his death, and heroics weren't his line. He was wounded severely when his motorcycle crashed somewhere in England and he died later of these wounds.

He started working with the *Northern Mail* when he was fourteen and was so quick to learn, so eager to do a service, so ready-witted that he became the favourite of the backshop where he ran a press larger than himself. He took a lot of teasing in the backshop – "You'll never get your name in the social" they'd say, but he always told them "Someday I'll do something big and then I'll be on the front page of this paper."

Well, Walter made the front page on Thursday, just as thousands of young men across Canada do who are remembered for their great sacrifice. To these many is owed so much that nothing can be said to those that survive them but "Their task well done, their peace well won" (*Northern Mail* 18 September 1942).

Wolk Lake (64 N/12), southeast of Kasba Lake was named after him in 1961.

Wolochatiuk, Private **John T.** of Ethelbert (H 616426). Royal Canadian Ordnance Corps. He died 10 January 1945 at the age of 33 and is commemorated at the Ukrainian Catholic Cemetery in Ethelbert, Manitoba. He was the son of Tony and Mary Wolochatiuk of Ethelbert and was survived by his wife Vera Wolochatiuk of Ethelbert. ***Wolochatiuk Lake*** (64 P/1), southwest of Caribou Lake was named after him in 1974.

Woloski, Gunner **William** of Winnipeg (H 60257). Royal Canadian Artillery. He died 24 September 1944 at the age of 21 and is commemorated at Gradara War Cemetery in Italy. He was the son of Nicholas and Catherine Woloski of Winnipeg. ***Woloski Lake*** (63 N/4), southwest of Kississing Lake was named after him in 1982.

Wolowiec, Flight Sergeant **Joseph M.** of Ashern (R 167285). No. 1661 Conversion Unit, RCAF. He died 17 May 1944 at the age of 21 and is commemorated at Brookwood Military Cemetery in Surrey, England. Wolowiec Lake (64 C/3), northwest of McKnight Lake was named after him in 1995.

Wood, Private **Alfred W.** of Miami (H 17515). Loyal Edmonton Regiment. He died 1 June 1944 at the age of 24 and is commemorated at the Cassino War Cemetery in Italy. He was the son of William and Violet M. Wood of Miami, Manitoba. ***Wood Rapids*** (64 I/10) on the South Knife River was named after him in 1995.

Wood, Warrant Officer 2 **Arthur L.** of Bradwardine (R 140857). No. 644 Squadron. He died 27 May 1944 at the age of 22 and is commemorated at All Saints Churchyard in Frindsbury, Kent, England. He was the son of John and Jessie M. Wood (née Dowland) of Bradwardine, Manitoba. His twin brother writes (10 August 1987):

> Arthur was named after mother's brother Arthur Dowland, killed in France during the First World War. Arthur joined the RCAF in January, 1942. Receiving his pilot's license, [he] was posted overseas in April, 1943. He continued his training on Oxfords, Whitleys and Halifaxes. [He was] posted to 644 Squadron April 1, 1944. This is of special interest to me because I also served overseas as a pilot with RAF Squadron 175. I am a life member of the Canadian Fighter Pilots Association.

He adds (21 November 2001):

> Art was flying a Halifax – towing a Hamilton glider which was fully loaded, testing for D-Day Operations. The engine failed on take-off and crashed into a forest. Art as well as Pilot Officer T. M. Stewart and Sergeant N. F. Wolf were killed.
>
> We were identical twins and were always the best of friends. We graduated from high school together and had many happy times. Art enjoyed all sports, was good natured, had a real sense of humour and made many good friends.

Wood Hill (64 K/16), south of Stevens Lake was named after him in 1989.

Wood, Pilot Officer **Duncan A.** of Norwood Grove (J 18772). No. 425 Squadron. He died 7 August 1943 and is commemorated at the Malta Memorial. This memorial commemorates those who lost their lives while serving with the Commonwealth Air Forces flying from bases in Austria, Italy, Sicily, islands of the Adriatic and Mediterranean, Malta, Tunisia, Algeria, Morocco, West Africa, Yugoslavia and Gibraltar, and who have no known grave. ***Duncan Wood Lake*** (63 O/8), west of Paint Lake was named after Pilot Officer Wood in 1995.

Wood, Private **George V.** of Winnipeg (H 19288). Queen's Own Cameron Highlanders. He died 1 August 1944 from wounds received at Caen. He was 24 of age and is commemorated at Brookwood Military Cemetery in Surrey, England. He was the only son of George H. and Isobella H. Wood of Winnipeg and was survived by two sisters, Lily and Isobel. His sister adds (6 November 2001) that: "George was in Dieppe as a Piper and stretcher bearer. He went overseas at age 19." ***Wood Esker*** (53 L/1), southwest of Rochon Lake was named after him in 1995.

Wood, Flight Sergeant **Keith R.** of Cypress River (R 91595). No. 51 Squadron. He died 26 June 1943 at the age of 21 and is commemorated at the Groesbeek Canadian War Cemetery in Holland. He was the only son of Reverend and Mrs. W. R. Wood of Stony Mountain. His father composed his epitaph:

> For, back within those nights of battle dread
> Amidst the blackness of that evil time,
> There opened for them a quiet door
> And love received them to a world of Peace.

Wood Creek (64 P/6), which flows southeast into Lewis Creek was named after Flight Sergeant Wood in 1995.

Wood, Pilot Officer **Richard** of Winnipeg (J 9131). No. 13 Operational Training Unit, RCAF. He died 15 December 1941 at the age of 29 and is commemorated at Elmwood Cemetery in Winnipeg. He was the son of Richard and Mary Wood of St. Vital and was survived by his wife Patricia Wood of Norwood. ***Richard Wood Rapids*** (64 A/11) in the Rasp River was named after him in 1995.

Wood, Lieutenant **Thomas P.** of Winnipeg. Calgary Highlanders. He died 2 December 1944 at the age of 29 and is commemorated at the Groesbeek Canadian War Cemetery in Holland. He was the son of Thomas F. and Isabella A. Wood of Winnipeg and was survived by his wife Edith M. Wood of Winnipeg. ***Wood Peninsula*** (64 H/2) on Fidler Lake was named after him in 1986.

Wood, Private **Wilfred** of Lac du Bonnet (H 8396). Loyal Edmonton Regiment. He died 27 December 1943 and is commemorated at the Moro River Canadian War Cemetery in Italy. He was the son of George T. and Violet M. Wood of Lac du Bonnet, Manitoba. ***Wood Point*** (54 D/6) on Stephens Lake was named after him in 1982.

Wood, Flight Lieutenant William J. of Winnipeg. No. 102 Squadron, Distinguished Flying Cross.

> Pilot Officer Wood has consistently displayed the utmost courage and determination. Early in 1943, when making an attack on an enemy submarine, his aircraft was hit by anti-aircraft fire and forced to alight on the sea. More recently, Pilot Officer Wood has attacked a number of important targets in occupied territory with excellent results, obtaining many valuable photographs (DFC Citation 1945).

He disappeared in an RCAF Dakota 19 January 1946 and is commemorated at St. James Cemetery in Winnipeg. ***William Wood Creek*** (64 I/9), which flows northeast towards North Knife River was named after him in 1978.

Woodcock, Flight Sergeant **Gerald Harvey** of Minnedosa (R 140867). No. 78 Squadron. He died 30 July 1943 at the age of 24 and is commemorated at Hamburg Cemetery in Germany. He was the son of John and Pearl Edith Woodcock of Sault Ste. Marie, Ontario and was the brother of Rifleman Kenneth Woodcock (next entry). His cousin writes (9 October 2001):

> He was posted to No. 78 Squadron, Royal Air Force in June, 1943. On 29 July 1943, Harvey, along with his crew mates, took off in their Halifax bomber JB798 to participate in a bombing raid over Hamburg, Germany. 777 aircraft took part in the operation. Harvey's aircraft was shot down 30 July 1943 southwest of Lubeck at Bad Oldesloe, Germany. All the crew were killed.

Woodcock Point (54 M/14) on Crave Lake was named after him in 1984.

Woodcock, Rifleman **Kenneth J.** of Bethany (H 41307). Royal Winnipeg Rifles. He died 30 March 1945 at the age of 24 and is commemorated at the Groesbeek Canadian War Cemetery in Holland. He was the son of John and Pearl Edith Woodcock of Scandinavia, Manitoba and was the brother of Flight Sergeant Gerald Woodcock (previous entry). His cousin recalls (9 October 2001):

Kenneth joined the Royal Winnipeg Rifles 25 June 1940. The Rifles were part of the 7th Brigade of the 3rd Division on the 2nd Corps in the 1st Canadian Army. The 2nd Corps was assigned the task of driving the Germans out of eastern Holland. To reach the Dutch border, they had to fight their way through the German city of Emmerich. The fighting practically destroyed the city. By nightfall 30 March 1945, the way was cleared for the Liberation of Holland. On 1 April, the Rifles moved forward crossing the border; Kenneth was killed in action 30 March.

Woodcock Lake (64 F/2), northwest of Barrington Lake was named after him in 1981.

Woodfield, Pilot Officer **Donald E.** of Winnipeg (J 12452). No. 45 Squadron. He died 28 May 1943 at the age of 20 and is commemorated at Fossvogur Cemetery in Reykjavik, Iceland. He was the son of Harry and Winnifred F. Woodfield of Winnipeg. ***Woodfield Lake*** (64 G/6), southwest of McPherson Lake was named after him in 1994.

Woods, Lance Sergeant **Albert T.** of Winnipeg (H 6012). Winnipeg Grenadiers. He died 21 December 1941 and is commemorated at the Sai Wan Memorial in Hong Kong. He was survived by his wife Jennie Woods (née Banks) of Winnipeg. ***Albert Woods Lake*** (64 N/2), northeast of Whitmore Lake was named after him in 1995.

Woods, Trooper **Lloyd A.** of Winnipeg (H 8567). South Alberta Tank Regiment. He died 9 September 1944 and is commemorated at the Adegem Canadian War Cemetery in Belgium. ***Woods Point*** (64 I/12) on Pott Lake was named after him in 1989.

Woods, Ordinary Signalman **Norman G.** of Winnipeg (V 9607). HMCS *Otter*. The *Otter* was destroyed by an accidental explosion and fire off Halifax. Two officers and 17 men were lost. Ordinary Signalman Woods died 26 March 1941 at the age of 20 and is commemorated at Brookside Cemetery in Winnipeg. He was survived by his mother Rose Woods of Winnipeg. ***Woods Island*** (64 G/15) in Trout Lake was named after him in 1995.

Woodward, Private **Cyril S.** of St. Vital (H 6137). Winnipeg Grenadiers. He died a prisoner of war 9 June 1944 at the age of 22 and is commemorated at the Yokohama War Cemetery in Japan. The official cause of death was listed as "infiltration of the right lung." He was the son of Sydney F. and Ada E. Woodward of Winnipeg. ***Woodward Island*** (52 L/4) in the Winnipeg River was named after him in 1973.

Woodward, Flight Lieutenant **John A.** of Winnipeg (J 9115). No. 432 Squadron. He died 27 September 1944 at the age of 24 and is commemorated at Brookwood Military Cemetery in Surrey, England. He was the son of Wilfrid and Anna O. Woodward and was survived by his wife Section Officer Margaret B. Woodward (née Pound) of Winnipeg. His wife received notification of the circumstances of his death:

Flight Lieutenant Woodward was very seriously injured in the attack with severe shrapnel wounds on the upper and lower side of his body. Despite these wounds, he flew the damaged plane back to make an emergency landing at Woodridge, Surrey, England. By this action, all other members of the crew returned safe and uninjured. He succumbed to his injuries shortly after landing (n.d.).

He had been employed by the Royal Bank prior to enlistment. ***Woodward Bay*** (64 P/2) in Spruce Lake was named after him in 1996.

Woodward, Private **Kivil C.** of Lavenham (H 60173). Royal Canadian Regiment. He died 18 September 1944 at the age of 23 and is commemorated at Coriano Ridge War Cemetery in Italy. He was the son of Charles and Edith Woodward, and was survived by six brothers and four sisters. His brother recalls (28 November 2001):

Kivil was determined to join the forces. When he first tried to join he was told he was underweight, but eventually the Army accepted him. He loved children. As an example, when his sister sent him a parcel containing chocolate bars, he wrote her saying that he had given them to the hungry children he had seen in Italy. Kivil also loved his country. He told his sister: "Canada is my country." That was his reason for joining the service. At the time of his passing, he had four brothers and one brother-in-law serving in the Canadian Armed Forces.

Woodward Lake (64 O/6), east of Calder Lake was named after him in 1989.

Wooffindin, Flight Sergeant **Walter** of Brandon (R 152968). Royal Canadian Air Force, Military Medal. He died 1 December 1945 at the age of 52 and is commemorated at Brandon Cemetery. He was the son of Henry and Mary Wooffindin and was survived by his wife Anna B. Wooffindin (née Ewen) of Brandon and their four children. ***Wooffindin Lake*** (64 P/5), south of Nejanilini Lake was named after him in 1974.

Woolgar, Flight Sergeant **James H. B.** of Winnipeg (R 59555). No. 61 Squadron. He died 10 September 1942 at the age of 21 and is commemorated at Rheinberg War Cemetery in Germany. He was the son of Norman H. and Mary E. Woolgar of Winnipeg and the brother of Flying Officer Frank Woolgar (next entry). ***Woolgar Island*** (64 N/3) in Thachuk Lake was named after him in 1995.

Woolgar, Flying Officer **William Frank** of Winnipeg (J 26712). No. 1667 Heavy Conversion Unit, RCAF. He died 6 September 1944 at the age of 20 and is commemorated at Stonefall Cemetery in Yorkshire, England. He was the son of Norman H. and Mary E. Woolgar of Winnipeg and the brother of Flight Sergeant James Woolgar (previous entry). ***Woolgar Lake*** (64 J/11), west of Tadoule Lake was named after him in 1975.

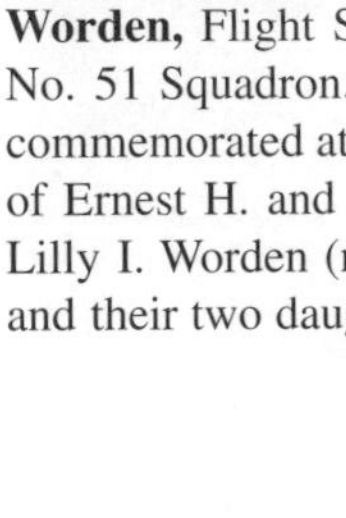

Woolverton, Flying Officer **Alan W.** of Winnipeg (J 23297). No. 428 Squadron. He died 20 February 1944 at the age of 23 and is commemorated at Enkhuizen General Cemetery in Holland. He was the son of John A. and Alice Woolverton of London, Ontario. ***Woolverton Lake*** (53 M/12), south of Split Lake was named after him in 1985.

Worden, Flight Sergeant **Arthur C.** of Crystal City (R 113195). No. 51 Squadron. He died 26 May 1943 at the age of 32 and is commemorated at Uden War Cemetery in Holland. He was the son of Ernest H. and Mable F. Worden and was survived by his wife Lilly I. Worden (née Plastow) of Rocky Mountain House, Alberta and their two daughters. She writes (31 March 1998):

[He was] born at Crystal City, Manitoba July 19, 1910. He lived with his parents, two brothers and three sisters on a farm [and] received his education at Crystal City. In 1933, he moved west to Alberta, taking up residence at Clive, Alberta where he had a grain grinding business for a few years, then he decided to take up farming. In 1935, he met Lilly Plastow of Tees, Alberta. They were married on December 28, 1937 [and] had two daughters, Frances and Lorna. In 1941, he enlisted in the RCAF [and] was sent overseas in 1942 as an air gunner.

Worden Lake (53 K/4), west of Red Sucker Lake was named after him in 1995.

Work, Leading Aircraftman **Cyril G.** of Winnipeg (R 59974). No. 124 Squadron. This native of the Orkney Islands in Scotland died 7 January 1943 at the age of 23 and is commemorated at St. John's Norway Cemetery in Toronto. He was the son of Thomas A. G. and Grace Work of Toronto. ***Work Lake*** (53 D/12), southwest of Shallow Lake was named after him in 1979.

Woronchuk, Rifleman **Eugene J.** of Brandon (B 142310). Royal Winnipeg Rifles. He died 6 June 1944 at the age of 28 and is commemorated at Beny-sur-Mer Canadian War Cemetery in Calvados, France. He was the son of Michael and Pauline Woronchuk of Brandon. ***Woronchuk Lake*** (63 I/9), west of Opiminegoka Lake was named after him in 1995.

Worthington, Pilot Officer **Robert F.** of Winnipeg (J 17985). No. 156 Squadron. He died 25 June 1943 at the age of 25 and is commemorated at the Runnymede Memorial in Surrey, England. His sister-in-law writes:

He was born in 1918 and graduated from Gordon Bell High School. He played basketball and baseball and was a member on the YMCA. Employed as a livestock buyer with Canada Packers, he enlisted in the RCAF in 1941 and after his training graduated as a Navigator, joining No. 156 Squadron.

His mother received a letter from Air Marshal Robert Leckie:

Dear Mrs. Worthington: I have learned with deep regret that your son, Pilot Officer Robert Franklin Worthington, is now for official purposes presumed to have died on Active Service Overseas on June 25, 1943. I wish to offer you and the members of your family my sincere and heartfelt sympathy. It is most lamentable that a promising career should be thus terminated and I would like you to know that his loss is greatly deplored by all those with whom your son was serving (8 February 1944).

Worthington Lake (64 F/2), south of Wells Lake was named after him in 1994.

Wotton, Lance Corporal **George** of Brandon (H 42302). Canadian Scottish Regiment. He died 28 March 1945 at the age of 27 and is commemorated at the Groesbeek Canadian War Cemetery in Holland. He was the son of Ernest G. and Florence N. Wotton of Brandon. According to his brother, Ralph Wotton (16 November 2001):

Having been born on a farm near Glenboro, Manitoba, George left school at an early age to help his father with the farm work. Some of his spare time was spent snaring, trapping or shooting rabbits and other wild game for their pelts, including numerous gophers, for which he received one cent for each tail. He also enjoyed twisting the dial on the old battery operated radio in search of cowboy and hillbilly music from distant American stations. When his parents moved to Brandon, George worked on local area farms for little pay and then later for Canadian National Railway at Maryfield, Saskatchewan. He was generous with what little money he had, helping his parents, such as at Christmas by purchasing a turkey or gifts and likely helped in other ways. Being his "little brother," I benefited from his generosity by receiving Christmas gifts such as a toy train, Meccano set etc., which I knew my parents could not afford. Prior to his enlistment, George was very active in his church, maintaining his faith in God while on active duty overseas, as evidenced by his letters to his parents.

Wotton Island (64 F/1) in Barrington Lake was named after him in 1995.

Wotton, Private **Lyall W.** of Flin Flon (H 1030). Argyle and Sutherland Highlanders. He died 12 August 1944 at the age of 21 and is commemorated at Uckfield Cemetery in Sussex, England. He was the son of Frank H. and Ella M. Wotton of Birch River and was survived by his wife Iris V. Wotton of New Town, Uckfield, Sussex. She recalls (5 May 1998):

Lyall was a very caring, honest and loving person. He was born in Foxwarren, Manitoba and attended school there until the age of 13. He then moved with his family to McKinley, seven miles from Birch River and continued his schooling there. He had many interests in sport, including hockey and baseball. Before joining the army, he was employed by the Hudson's Bay Company in Flin Flon. He was serving in Normandy where he was fatally wounded and died in a Basingstoke hospital here in England.

Wotton Lake (63 K/16), north of Reed Lake was named after him in 1973.

Wotton, Private **Thomas B.** of Winnipeg (H 800136). Princess Patricia's Canadian Light Infantry. He died 25 April 1951 at the age of 21 and is commemorated at the United Nations Cemetery in Pusan, South Korea. He was the youngest son of Reverend and Mrs. J. F. Wotton of Cardale, Manitoba. ***Wotton Bay*** (53 L/11) in Munro Lake was named after this Korean War casualty in 1998.

Woytowich, Private **Frank** of Howden (H 65230). Winnipeg Grenadiers. He died 25 December 1941 and is commemorated at the Sai Wan War Cemetery in Hong Kong. He was survived by his father John, brother Paul and four sisters. He:

... joined the Winnipeg Grenadiers in 1941 and trained at Winnipeg, Shilo and Vancouver. He went overseas to Hong Kong and was reported killed in action there. Before he enlisted, he was farming at Howden, Manitoba, where he attended the local schools (Hill 1944).

Woytowich Lake (64 N/4), north of Lac Brochet was named after him in 1972.

Wozniak, Gunner **Peter** of Winnipeg (H 10164). Royal Canadian Artillery. He died 1 May 1945 at the age of 22 and is commemorated at the Holten Canadian War Cemetery in Holland. He was the youngest of the four children of Ignacius and Tillie Wozniak of Winnipeg. His nephew writes (21 November 2001):

I never knew my uncle, but after looking through all his collections of albums, I found him to be a gentle and sensitive man who loved both sports and poetry. I have a picture of him on a horse at age 10 and it saddens me to think he gave his life for his country only ten years later.

Wozniak Lake (64 I/13), east of Shethanei Lake was named after him in 1974.

Wren, Major **John G.** of Winnipeg. Royal Canadian Artillery. He died 14 August 1944 at the age of 37 and is commemorated at Beny-sur-Mer Canadian War Cemetery in Calvados, France. He was the son of John and Margaret Wren of Winnipeg and was survived by his wife Mary C. Wren of Winnipeg. ***Wren Lake*** (64 N/12), southeast of Kasba Lake was named after him in 1972.

Wright, Pilot Officer **Andrew Roy** of Flin Flon (J 88789). No. 75 Squadron. He died 21 November 1944 at the age of 21 and is commemorated at the Runnymede Memorial in Surrey, England. His sister writes (11 November 1996):

> He was born in The Pas, Manitoba February 19th, 1922. It's fitting that Athapapuskow Lake was chosen to name a bay in his honour. As a young man just prior to the war, he lived in Flin Flon and spent time boating on Athapap. Roy enlisted in the Air Force in 1942. He chose a gunnery course and took his training in Mont Joli, Quebec and Chisholm, Alberta. His flight log book shows his operational flights started July 9, 1943.

She adds (3 November 2001):

> He was an easygoing, friendly boy [who] got along well with everyone, young and old. He spent his boyhood like most small town boys enjoying all outdoor activities. These included hiking and fishing and the neighbourhood ball games. The winter activities were usually hockey and a little bit of trapping to earn extra spending money. Money wasn't very plentiful during the depression. Prior to joining the air force, he worked for a short while in Flin Flon for Hudson Bay Mining and Smelting. While there, he joined the air force in 1942.

Wright Bay (63 K/12) in Athapapuskow Lake was named after him in 1984.

Wright, Pilot Officer **Archibald J. S.** of Bowsman River (J 86212). No. 158 Squadron. He died 3 June 1944 at the age of 25 and is commemorated at Evreux Communal Cemetery in Eure, France. According to his sister (6 June 1996):

> Since Archie was my only brother and I have no sisters (both of my parents have passed away sometime ago) going back all these years and now being able to learn what did happen to my brother on that night of 3-06-1944 has brought him closer somehow. He completed his Grade 12 in Swan River [and] prior to going into Business College in Winnipeg, he had been helping our father [with the] bookkeeping in his office in Bowsman. Father was the manager of [the] Caverly Lumber Company. He was on his last mission (shot down over France) before he was due to come home for a period of leave. Archie was a very outgoing and happy-go-lucky fellow, having a great many friends. He enjoyed music and dancing [and] was very active in sports. [He] played goalie on [the] local hockey team [and] second base in baseball. He and his friends went on many hunting trips in northern Manitoba. [He] also enjoyed fishing and boating.

Wright Point (64 O/9) on Croll Lake was named after him in 1995.

Wright, Trooper **Charles W. D.** of Griswold (H 26668). Fort Garry Horse. He died 11 June 1944 at the age of 23 and is commemorated at Bretteville-sur-Laize Canadian War Cemetery in Calvados, France. He was the son of Charles W. and Nellie M. Wright of Brandon. ***Wright Creek*** (63 O/6), which flows north into Wimapedi River was named after him in 1995.

Wright, Flight Sergeant **Edward J.** of Winnipeg (R 287664). No. 428 Squadron. He died 30 April 1945 at the age of 16 and is commemorated at Blacon Cemetery in Cheshire, England. His age was confirmed with his parents shortly after his death; it is suspected that he was the youngest airman to lose his life in the Second World War. He was the son of James A. and Alfreda M. Wright of Brighton, Sussex, England. In 1999, a memorial service was held near Sandon, Staffordshire where the fatal crash occurred. Flight Sergeant Wright's sister was in attendance.

> Hundreds of people turned out to pay their respects to a crew of airmen who were killed when their plane smashed to the ground near Stone during World War II. Six Canadians and one British man were killed in the tragedy which happened … when the Lancaster bomber they were flying spiralled out of control and crashed in a field between Sandon and Burston. Now, more than half a century later, villagers have unveiled a permanent memorial to the crew in a special dedication ceremony.
>
> Relatives of the crewmen were traced and invited to Saturday's ceremony which included a fly-past – by a Lancaster bomber and a Spitfire – and the sounding of the last post. Wreaths were laid by family members of the airmen who had travelled from as far afield as Scotland and Canada to attend the ceremony. All six Canadians are buried at the Commonwealth War Graves Cemetery near Chester while the British airman is buried in Scotland.
>
> The plane was on a training flight from Teeside when it crashed. Eye-witnesses reported the bomber going from side to side before coming down in a spiral and the tail section splitting off on impact with the ground. The memorial is a culmination of a chain of events which was sparked by Don Mitchell of Sandon. Twenty-two years ago, Mr. Mitchell moved into the house which previously belonged to village GP, Doctor Henry Bocking – one of the first people to arrive at the scene of the accident. Last year Mr. Mitchell discovered a portion of an aircraft cockpit in the loft and realised it must have come from the crashed bomber. He researched the crash and handed his dossier to Robert Selby, chairman of Sandon and District Royal British Legion whose members decided to erect a memorial stone and try to trace the airmen's relatives.
>
> Three relatives of the airmen attended the service, two from Canada and one from Scotland. Mrs. Patricia Flowers travelled from Ontario to attend the ceremony for her brother Edward Wright who was just 16 when he died in the crash. Mrs. Flowers, who was 10 at the time, said her brother had been a Flight Sergeant and had been with the air force for 18 months when he died. She said: "I feel very honoured to have been invited to come here and pay tribute to Edward and his colleagues who died" (Atkins 1999).

Upon her return, Mrs. Flowers said (28 December 1999):

> The Sandon and District Royal British Legion and the villagers erected the monument close to the road, just outside the field where the main part of the plane crashed. It was a very emotional time and a memory I will forever cherish, to think that after 54 years these good people had not forgotten the sacrifice that these young men made so that we might have peace. The tail of the plane where my brother was, broke away and landed in another part of the field. My brother who was only 16 at the time somehow managed to get out of the tail, but unfortunately his parachute did not open. He was found in a sitting position with his parachute still strapped to his back. We lived in Brighton, England from 1946 – 1951 when my father, who had been with the RCMP for 35 years, retired in Winnipeg and returned with his family to England where he was from.

She adds (26 November 2001):

> My brother Teddy was a very adventurous man, not your typical 15 year-old when he joined the RCAF a few days after his birthday. He thought joining the war effort was a great way to serve a cause and to see the world. He told the recruiting officer that he was 18 years of age. He was believable because of his experiences up to this point in his life. He had already joined the Army and after that the Merchant Navy. My father, a

high ranking official in the RCMP, was able to find out his whereabouts both times and had him released because he was under age. When it came to joining the RCAF, he was determined to stay in and said if necessary, he would use a false name to join up. I fondly remember him when he was home on leave, giving me and my twin brother dimes so he could practice his judo moves on us. Another vivid memory was when my Mother took me with her to see him when he was passing through at the train station on his way overseas. In part of a letter he wrote my father 23 October 1944 from England, he writes: "I'm in the billet now with a lovely fire blazing and it's pissing down outside, so I'm quite comfortable. We had a bit of an accident yesterday and I got a few cuts on my head. So I'm really a hard looking guy right now. We have made three emergency landings since I've been here, two on our own drome and one on another about 15 miles away. Two were flapless and one was a belly landing. I haven't bailed out yet, but I'm looking forward to it."

Edward Wright Lake (53 L/12), northeast of Windy Lake was named after him in 1995.

Wright, Company Quarter Master Sergeant **Eric D.** of Winnipeg (H 19453). Queen's Own Cameron Highlanders. He died 2 September 1946 at the age of 50 and is commemorated at Brookside Cemetery in Winnipeg. He was survived by his wife Sadie Wright of Winnipeg. ***Wright Peninsula*** (63 N/7) on Guthrie Lake was named after him in 1995.

Wright, Flight Sergeant **Fredrick D.** of Winnipeg (R 162279). No. 2 Construction Maintenance Unit, RCAF. He died 25 June 1945 at the age of 54 and is commemorated at Brookside Cemetery in Winnipeg. He was the son of John W. and Elizabeth J. Wright and was survived by his wife Jennie B. Wright of Winnipeg. ***Wright Narrows*** (53 L/6) in Stewart Anderson Lake was named after him in 1995.

Wright, Lieutenant **George B. "Sam"** of Winnipeg (O 79980). HMCS *St. Croix*. The *St. Croix* was torpedoed and sunk by U-305 south of Iceland while escorting Convoy ON.202. Five officers and 76 men were rescued by HMS *Itchen*, but only one of these survived the loss of the *Itchen* two days later. See **VanSickle,** Ordinary Seaman **Harold A.** for additional information. Lieutenant Wright died 20 September 1943 at the age of 33 and is commemorated at the Halifax Memorial. He was the son of George and Emma L. Wright of Winnipeg. His niece recalls (17 November 1996):

Sometime after obtaining his studies at the University of Manitoba, possibly attaining his B.A. degree, he was employed in the fur trading department of the Hudson's Bay Company, Winnipeg. He served with the Bay for several years in northern posts, one of which was Norway House. At the time of his death, he was the Torpedo Officer of the *St. Croix*, a Town Class Canadian destroyer.

Sam had a great sense of humour and loved the outdoors. He also appreciated the leather and beadwork skills of the Indians he traded furs with. He gifted a member of my family with a beaded fringed leather jacket and long cuffed mittens.

Wright Lake (64 I/10), northeast of North Knife Lake was named after him in 1974.

Wright, Sergeant **James D.** of Greenway (H 16782). Princess Patricia's Canadian Light Infantry. He died 15 June 1945 and is commemorated at the Holten Canadian War Cemetery in Holland. His action at the Hitler Line in 1944 was reported in a newspaper account:

For hours and even days, nobody knew the full story of the Princess Patricia's Canadian Light Infantry that May 23 when they assaulted the Hitler Line. They only knew that men had fallen until the ground seemed littered with them, that others went on until they reached their objective. One after another of the officers fell from the ranks of the company that started out behind the other two. Finally, Sergeant Leonard Davies of Vancouver found himself in command of two platoons under fire from a great variety of weapons. But he ran from man to man, rallying, encouraging and leading them to the objective.

When finally dusk and darkness came and a fresh advance was made on their flank, the Pats who could, withdrew, but men kept straggling back for hours after Patrols went out to seek out all the wounded and the stranded, but they didn't come back because the Hitler Line was still alive with snipers and guns. Privates like Ian Sangster, Roblin, Manitoba found themselves capable leaders when the crisis came. It was Sangster who took command of a small group of Pats, took them as far forward as they could go, deployed them, ordering a withdrawal after eight hours of fire and counter-attack. Corporal J. D. Wright, Rosebank operated the colonel's wireless set for eight hours, often under extreme risk. When his set was shot away he went back for another (*The Winnipeg Tribune* 28 June 1944).

James Wright Lake (64 A/15), northeast of Christie Lake was named after him in 1995.

Wright, Pilot Officer **James R.** of Brandon (J 17943). No. 156 Squadron. He died 17 June 1943 at the age of 30 and is commemorated at Rheinberg War Cemetery in Germany. He was the son of Robert H. and Annie L. Wright of Vancouver. ***Wright Hill*** (63 N/1), east of Craik Lake was named after him in 1995.

Wright, Private **John B.** of Fisherton (H 46161). Lake Superior Regiment. He died 13 November 1944 at the age of 27 and is commemorated at Schoonselhof Cemetery in Antwerp, Belgium. He was the son of James A. and Mary C. Wright of Fisherton, Manitoba. ***Wright Esker*** (64 I/13), north of Shethanei Lake was named after him in 1995.

Wright, Trooper **John Ross** of Gilbert Plains (H 63957). Fort Garry Horse. He died 11 June 1944 at the age of 21 and is commemorated at Beny-sur-Mer Canadian War Cemetery in Calvados, France. He was the son of Ernest E. and Florence M. Wright of St. Norbert. His brother recalls (28 March 1995):

He went to school in Carnduff [Saskatchewan] for a short time. Our parents moved to Gilbert Plains and Ross then went to a small country school near Dutton Siding. The school has long since gone and the name [is] now forgotten. Ross was not active in sports except some baseball and joined the army shortly after leaving school.

Ross Wright Bay (54 D/6) in Stephens Lake was named after him in 1995.

Wright, Private **John T.** of Winnipeg (H 16932). Princess Patricia's Canadian Light Infantry. He died 25 February 1942 at the age of 21 and is commemorated at Brookside Cemetery in Winnipeg. He was the son of Mr. and Mrs. John A. Wright of Winnipeg. ***John Wright Lake*** (64 G/5), west of Hurst Lake was named after him in 1996.

Wright, Private **Roland F.** of Winnipeg (H 6299). Winnipeg Grenadiers. He died 19 December 1941 at the age of 23 and is commemorated at the Sai Wan Memorial in Hong Kong. He was the son of John E. and Maud E. Wright. ***Wright Rapids*** (64 B/8) on the unnamed river which drains Pakwaw Lake was named after him in 1995.

Wright, Gunner **William D.** of Wellwood (H 800196). Royal Canadian Artillery. He died 21 November 1950 at the age of 20 and is commemorated at Riverside Cemetery in Neepawa, Manitoba. He was the son of W. J. and Leatha B. Wright of Neepawa.

At 10:35 hours, a train carrying troops of the 2nd Regiment, Royal Canadian Horse Artillery met another train, headed from Vancouver to Montreal in a head on collision just east of Canoe River, BC. The engines and leading cars of both trains were derailed, but there were no passenger casualties on the civilian train. The leading cars of the military train were thrown down an embankment and demolished. Survivors pitched in at once to rescue their comrades, while Dr. P. J. E. Kimmett of Edson, Alberta and a civilian nurse volunteered their services. It was not until hours later that a specially organized train carrying much needed medical supplies, two doctors and eight nurses arrived. The injured were returned to Edmonton, Alberta and the uninjured to Wainwright, Alberta. Recovery of bodies was made extremely difficult; an oil fire rendered many of them unidentifiable. The final toll of dead was 17, including four soldiers whose bodies were never recovered. The remains of the other 13 were flown to the homes of their next-of-kin by RCAF aircraft or sent by train in the case of those who lived nearby (Korea Veterans Association of Canada 1999).

William Wright Island (53 N/13) in the Fox River was named after this Korean War casualty in 1998.

Wright, Pilot Officer **William J. L.** of Kenton (J 88779). No. 429 Squadron. He died 1 August 1944 at the age of 27 and is commemorated at St. Martin-au-Bosc Communal Cemetery in Seine-Maritime, France. He was the son of William and Agnes Wright and was survived by his wife Evelyn Wright of Langley Prairie, British Columbia. ***William Wright Lake*** (64 P/14), east of Baralzon Lake was named after him in 1995.

Wylie, Corporal **Albert A.** of Winnipeg (H 35). Lord Strathcona's Horse. He died 28 January 1944 at the age of 30 and is commemorated at the Moro River Canadian War Cemetery in Italy. He was the son of Albert E. and Daisy L. Wylie of Winnipeg. ***Wylie Lake*** (52 L/11), south of Black Lake was named after him in 1982.

Wylie, Private **Lloyd K.** of Winnipeg (K 800117). Princess Patricia's Canadian Light Infantry. He died 7 March 1951 and is commemorated at the United Nations Cemetery in Pusan, South Korea. ***Wylie Island*** (53 E/15) in Island Lake was named after this Korean War casualty in 1998.

Wynne, Lance Corporal **Charles** of Fort Garry (H 17422). Princess Patricia's Canadian Light Infantry. He died 20 September 1944 at the age of 25 and is commemorated at Coriano Ridge War Cemetery in Italy. He was the son of Charles and Martha Wynne and was survived by his wife Dorothy I. Wynne of Fort Garry and their two sons. His wife recalls (15 November 2001):

Charlie was born in Bissett, Manitoba and was the father of two sons, Charles and Harvey. We enjoyed our short time together in Winnipeg. He was very proud to have his two sons. Charlie's duty in the army was as an instructor teaching basic training to new recruits at the University of Manitoba. The student dormitories on campus were converted into barracks for soldiers during World War II. Every two months a group of new recruits would come to the university for their basic training, then on to their advanced training.

In the beginning of 1944, Charlie's two brothers, John and Richard, were already in the war in Europe. Charlie wanted to do his part overseas. He took a voluntary demotion from Sergeant Major to Private in order to join his original unit, the PPCLI, uniting with his brother John in Italy. John was wounded on September 17, 1944 and sent to a hospital in Italy. Three days later, on September 20, 1944, Charlie and nearly his entire platoon were killed. It took two weeks before I received the telegram informing me that my husband was killed. Our two young sons, Charles Leslie and Harvey Douglas were only two and one when I received the sad news. I have fond memories of how he kissed and hugged the boys before he went overseas. He asked that I take good care of our sons while he was away. He was a very loving husband and father. I am very proud that a lake in Manitoba has been named for him.

His sister adds (15 November 2001):

As a younger sister in a family of eight children, I remember my brother Charlie taking care of us "little kids." He teased and played with us and gave us treats that were rare in the 1930s. When he went to work underground in the mine, he brought us all "new" winter snowsuits with his first paycheque. The last time he was home before going overseas, he said "I'll be back." I refused to believe he wouldn't "be back" until my other brothers came home without him.

Wynne Lake (64 N/2), northeast of Lac Brochet was named after Lance Corporal Wynne in 1972.

Wyton, Flying Officer **Arnold E.** of Newdale (J 21470). No. 90 Squadron. He died 9 October 1943 at the age of 21 and is commemorated at Hamburg Cemetery in Germany. He was the son of Sidney and Elsie W. M. Wyton of Newdale, Manitoba. ***Wyton Lake*** (63 N/7), northeast of Takipy Lake was named after him in 1988.

The Stormont, Dundas and Glengarry Highlanders of Canada enter Leeuwarden, Holland, 16 April 1945.
Courtesy of the National Archives of Canada (PA-131564).

X Y Z

Yakymiw, Private **Joseph** of Zbaraz (H 200184). Queen's Own Cameron Highlanders. He died 22 July 1944 and is commemorated at Bretteville-sur-Laize Canadian War Cemetery in Calvados, France. He was the son of Peter and Tinny Yakymiw of Zbaraz, Manitoba. ***Yakymiw Lake*** (63 K/16), west of Wekusko Lake was named after him in 1973.

Yankoski, Flight Sergeant **Anthony** of Russell (R 80041). No. 22 Operational Training Unit, RCAF. He died 25 June 1942 at the age of 21 and is commemorated at the Runnymede Memorial in Surrey, England. His brothers recall (12 November 2001):

> Mother was widowed in 1935 and left with seven boys to raise. Tony, the eldest, was the bread winner, selling magazines, driving a cream truck, driving a gravel truck, stooking at harvest time – you name it. We all had to pitch in. But the war changed all of that. From the family of seven boys, six joined the forces. Lawrence was the youngest and he had to keep the home fires burning.
>
> Tony took his training at Paulson, Rivers and Moose Jaw and was posted to "Y" Depot in Halifax in December, 1941. He was granted leave to spend Christmas with Mother and the rest of the family, but on Boxing Day he travelled by bus to Winnipeg and from there via troop train to Halifax to report at "Y" Depot. He went overseas in January, 1942 and in February the family received a letter postmarked Stratford-upon-Avon. The aerodrome was at Wellesbourne Operational Training Unit and consisted of mostly Canadian air crew. From here, he took part in the 1000-plane raids using Wellington bombers on June 25, 1942. Six months later, Mother received The Telegram: "Presumed killed in action."
>
> In 1972, Orpha and I toured Britain, spent a day at the Runnymede Memorial and took a photograph of Tony's name. This memorial was dedicated to all the Commonwealth airmen, over 22,000 of them, who have no known graves. "Lest We Forget."

Yankoski Lake (64 P/16), north of Caribou Lake was named after him in 1974.

Yaremkewich, Private **Peter** of Fisher Branch (H 501210). 12th Manitoba Dragoons. He died 1 October 1943 at the age of 25 and is commemorated at St. Nicholas Cemetery in Fisher Branch. He was the son of Paul and Maria Yaremkewich and was survived by his brother William Yaremkewich of Fisher Branch. Commemorative Certificates for Private Yaremkewich and seven fellow Manitoba Dragoons were issued c/o Herbert Nicholson, MM who explains:

> In 1946, the 12th Manitoba Dragoons returned from Europe, and with money from our Canteen Fund furnished two wards in the Children's Hospital, with a promise that as long as our Association lasts, we would continue to support the Children's Hospital Fund. Since 1946, we have contributed $1000.00 every year with donations received from the members. Also, we had a Plaque placed on the Hospital's 2nd floor, with names of our fallen comrades on one side and on the other side, the names of the departed comrades who have since passed away. This was done with the idea that one day the Regiment will again be together.
>
> Now this brings me to my request, that the Association's approximately 350 members, would after all your efforts to find next-of-kin, would like to become family and have the Name Certificate placed on the wall in the Children's Hospital in trust that if a next-of-kin comes forward the Certificate would be handed over to them (16 December 1998).

Yaremkewich Lake (64 K/14), east of Lac Brochet was named after him in 1972.

Yaremko, Corporal **Nestor** of Winnipeg (H 87333). Royal Canadian Army Service Corps. He died 26 March 1945 and is commemorated at Bergen-op-Zoom Canadian War Cemetery in Holland. ***Yaremko Lake*** (64 O/12), south of Nueltin Lake was named after him in 1995.

Yaroway, Private **Peter** of Fork River (F 42161). Lanark and Renfrew Scottish Regiment. He died 24 March 1945 at the age of 29 and is commemorated at Caserta War Cemetery in Italy. He was one of the 13 children of Nick and Pearl Yaroway (née Nysnyk) and was survived by his wife Mary Yaroway (née Gushka) and their three children. His nephew writes (3 December 2001):

> Peter Yaroway was born in April, 1914 in the Zelena District. His parents immigrated to Canada from western Ukraine. They met, married and made their home in the Zelena School District in the Rural Municipality of Mossey River. Peter grew up on the farm with his brothers and sisters. He received his education in Zelena School. After he completed his schooling, Peter continued to help his parents with the farm work and he worked as a farm labourer. He was very hard working and patient.
>
> Like the rest of his family, Peter was a kind, quiet and caring person. He was well liked by everyone who knew him. As a young man, Peter met Mary Gushka. They fell in love and married. Peter and Mary had three children, Maurice, Laverne and Shirley. Farming was the only life Peter knew. In 1939, he purchased one quarter of land, NE 4-30-20W. Life on the farm was very difficult. Peter sold the farm in 1941 and moved his family to Winnipeg. He hoped to make life easier for his family, however, his dreams of greener pastures came to an end. Peter was called to serve his country in World War II.
>
> Sadly, on March 9, 1942, Peter left his wife and young children to join the Royal Winnipeg Rifles. He trained as a gunner in Fort William, Camp Shilo and Halifax. He was transferred to the 28th 1 Lt. A/A Regiment. Peter left for overseas from Vancouver on January 26, 1943 for the front lines in the UK. Peter served as a gunner and on August 27, 1943 he was awarded the Canadian Volunteer Service Medal and Clasp for his bravery and excellent services.
>
> While fighting the enemy in the front lines, Peter was wounded several times. Each time, he spent his recovery time in the Canadian General Hospital. After each recovery, he returned to the battlefields and continued in the combat.
>
> On December 5, 1944, Peter was transferred to the Lanark and Renfrew Scottish Regiment. Again he was wounded. After his recovery, he returned to serve bravely in the fields of fire until March 24, 1945 when he was killed in action in Sicily at the young age of 29. The fear, pain and suffering was over. Peter's dreams of returning to his wonderful family and his beautiful homeland were shattered and never to come true. He gave up his life for the love of his country so that his family as well as the people of Canada could live in peace and enjoy the many freedoms. Peter's mother, Pearl Yaroway, received the memorial cross. She cherished it with pride and wore it around her neck for as long as she lived. The loss of her son brought her deep sorrow as well as fond, loving memories.
>
> Peter Yaroway, I would like to thank you for your remarkable service. Your dreams were destroyed just several weeks before VE-Day. Your family suffered much pain, sadness and disappointment. Nevertheless, you are remembered as a courageous, brave and honourable father, husband, son, brother, uncle and friend. I wish I could have known you. May you live in peace.

Yaroway Lake (64 H/10), southwest of Etawney Lake, was named after him in 1978.

Yarush, Flying Officer **Fred** of Grandview (J 24789). No. 420 Squadron. He died 21 November 1944 at the age of 26 and is commemorated at Stonefall Cemetery in Yorkshire, England. He was the son of John and Tekla Yarush of Grandview and was survived by his fiancée Leda. ***Yarush Lake*** (63 K/4), north of Rocky Lake was named after him in 1983.

Yelland, Pilot Officer **Horace G.** of Winnipeg (41892). No. 144 Squadron, RAF. He died 1 December 1939 at the age of 25 and is commemorated at Leuchars Cemetery in Fife, Scotland. He was the son of Lewis and Gertrude E. Yelland of Winnipeg. He had been a student at the University of Manitoba prior to enlisting with the RAF in December, 1939 (Allison 1978). ***Yelland Lake*** (54 F/3), northeast of Dewar Lake was named after him in 1995.

Yeo, Sergeant **John L.** of Winnipeg (R 59345). No. 16 Operational Training Unit, RCAF. He died 11 November 1941 at the age of 18 and is commemorated at Upper Heyford Cemetery in Oxfordshire, England. He was the son of Lenus E. and Maude C. Yeo of Winnipeg. His brother-in-law writes (26 January 1995):

> John ... was born December 31st 1922 in Winnipeg. [He] lived all of his early life on Harbison Avenue in Elmwood and attended Lord Selkirk School till Grade 11.

Yeo Lake (63 H/1), northeast of Weaver Lake was named after him in 1974.

Yeoman, Lance Corporal **William R.** of Winnipeg (H 66212). Royal Canadian Ordnance Corps. He died 6 February 1944 at the age of 28 and is commemorated at Brookwood Military Cemetery in Surrey, England. He was the only son of George and Mary Yeoman and was survived by his wife Noela I. Yeoman of Lorette and their baby daughter Louise. His sister recalls (22 October 2001):

> Our parents emigrated from England in 1911, settling in McIntosh, Ontario in 1912 or 1913. Dad was employed by the CNR as a pumpman. They later built and operated a general store and Post Office. William (Bill) and his twin sister Mary were born in Vivian, Manitoba because of the availability of a midwife there. He and his siblings grew and played together as children do in remote areas, winter sliding down hills, snowshoeing, summers swimming, fishing – first of all with a limb of a tree, a piece of string and bacon fat for bait, catching minnows. As we grew older we'd row a big old flat-bottomed boat, one would row, one would bail (as it leaked badly) and two would troll fish. When we were older and strong enough, we helped with the chores.
>
> In about the year 1927 or 28, the store was sold and the family moved to Winnipeg as the "kids" had to get some semblance of an education. Bill met and married his wife Noela in about 1938 or 39. Their baby daughter Louise was about a year old when he went overseas.
>
> He succumbed to injuries he received when he was crushed between two trucks while on manoeuvres during a blackout, living only a few days following the accident. It seems ironic that our father who married mom (he a widower) when he was about 50 and she 25, had lost an only son in the war of 1914 – 1918 and an only son in the war of 1939 – 1945.

Yeoman Lake (64 O/9), west of Nejanilini Lake was named after him in 1975.

Yonkers, Warrant Officer 1 **Zenon** of Winnipeg (R 91899). No. 78 Squadron. He died 14 July 1943 at the age of 20 and is commemorated at the Runnymede Memorial in Surrey, England. He was the son of Dr. Henry L. and Anna H. Yonkers of Winnipeg. ***Yonkers Lake*** (64 I/14), east of Shethanei Lake was named after him in 1974.

York, Private **Leslie S.** of Birtle (F 85624). Queen's Own Cameron Highlanders. He died 22 July 1944 at the age of 31 and is commemorated at Beny-sur-Mer Canadian War Cemetery in Calvados, France. He was the son of Sesson and Ella York of Birdtail, Manitoba and was survived by his wife Edith and their three children. Born in Birdtail in 1913, he enlisted in Nova Scotia in August, 1940 and trained at Valcartier, Quebec. He went overseas the following year and received further training in Scotland. ***York Bay*** (64 P/2) in McCann Lake was named after him in 1996.

Young, Trooper **Alexander C.** of Winnipeg (H 1479). Governor General's Horse Guards. He died 26 September 1944 at the age of 21 and is commemorated at Cesena War Cemetery in Italy. He was the son of Alexander C. and Tina M. Young of Grand Marais. ***Alexander Young Lake*** (53 K/6), east of Sharpe Lake was named after him in 1995.

Young, Flight Sergeant **Edwin A.** of Winnipeg (R 91847). No. 6 Operational Training Unit, RCAF. He died 31 May 1942 at the age of 27 and is commemorated at Spangereid Churchyard in Norway. ***Edwin Young Bay*** (53 E/15) in Island Lake was named after him in 1995.

Young, Flying Officer **Henry Kenneth** of Winnipeg (J 27272). No. 426 Squadron. He died 16 March 1944 at the age of 29 and is commemorated at Durnbach War Cemetery in Bavaria, Germany. He was the son of Ray W. and Katie A. Young of Winnipeg and was survived by his wife Bernice R. Young (née Beardsley) of Winnipeg. His sister recalls (4 May 1998):

> Henry Kenneth Young was born in June, 1914 in the City of Winnipeg. The family moved to Kelfield, Saskatchewan when Ken was four years old. He enjoyed the freedom of farm life, although he and his buddies had several miles to go to school. As I recall, they all rode horseback. Ken and his horse "Bess" were also responsible for rounding up the cows in the pasture and bringing them back to the barn in the evening.
>
> We moved back to Winnipeg when Ken was 10 years old. 80 Lenore Street was our new address – just across the avenue from Laura Secord School. We could reach the school from our house as the bell was ringing. Ken had a long trek when he attended high school at Kelvin Collegiate across the Assiniboine River. When the river was frozen during the winter it made a splendid short cut, eliminating the necessity of going all the way to the Maryland Bridge.
>
> Most of our sports were either played on the corner lots or the school grounds during the spring and summer. In the winter we had a rink on a corner lot two blocks from our house where we skated and the boys played hockey. It sported the usual pot-bellied stove in the green shack. Ken also belonged to a city lacrosse team, but I believe his favourite activity was diving. While we were holidaying one summer at Victoria Beach, he made a beautiful swan dive off the top deck of a pleasure ship that was tied up at the large pier. Of course it was on a dare that had to be satisfied.
>
> At times, he did try to curb his adventurous nature. He belonged to St. Matthew's Church Young People's group where he enjoyed acting in the various productions they put on during the winter. I remember seeing him perform in *The Bishop's Candlesticks*. He always seemed to enjoy life to the fullest.
>
> It was tough getting a job during the depression years. His first job was with the Salisbury House because he knew how to cook. It was on the same street as the T. Eaton Company where he visited the employment office frequently until they hired him in the men's furnishings.
>
> Ken married Bernice Beardsley on the 25th of October, 1941. My husband and I moved to Toronto shortly after the wedding so I saw very little of my brother before he went overseas. We still maintained a close relationship with Bernice after I returned to Winnipeg during the war. We also retained that friendship after my husband returned to civilian life and Bernice married Bert Sankey. That friendship continued after we were both transferred to Edmonton. We lost contact with them when we retired to Victoria in 1976.

Young Bay (64 O/9) in Procinsky Lake was named after him in 1995.

Young, Lieutenant **Hugh J.** of Winnipeg. Winnipeg Grenadiers. He died 21 December 1941 and is commemorated at the Sai Wan War Cemetery in Hong Kong. ***Young Peninsula*** (63 N/10) on Highrock Lake was named after him in 1995.

Young, Private **James** of Winnipeg (H 7055). Queen's Own Cameron Highlanders. He died 23 July 1944 at the age of 21 and is commemorated at Beny-sur-Mer Canadian War Cemetery in Calvados, France. He was the son of William and Florence Young and was survived by his wife Lena Young of Cambusland, Scotland. ***James Young Island*** (63 P/9) in Cauchon Lake was named after him in 1995.

Young, Flight Sergeant **James O.** of Winnipeg (R 134821). No. 429 Squadron. He died 23 April 1944 and is commemorated at the Reichswald Forest War Cemetery in Germany. ***Young Island*** (53 K/4) in Red Sucker Lake was named after him in 1995.

Young, Gunner **John F. "Jack"** of Minnedosa (H 103708). Royal Canadian Artillery. He died 23 August 1944 at the age of 22 and is commemorated at Assisi War Cemetery in Italy. He was the son of David F. and Alice Young of Crawford Park. His sister writes (20 March 1995):

My brother ... was born September 16, 1922 at Strathclair, Manitoba and moved at an early age with his parents to the Crawford Park district. He grew up on the family farm and attended elementary school at Clear Creek School No. 2147. He joined the Canadian Army in 1942 and completed basic training at Brandon. He went overseas with the 4th Anti-Tank Regiment and fought in the Italian Campaign.

She adds (3 December 2001):

Jack ... had every intention of becoming a farmer. He took great pride in his five-horse hitch. We had no car and the horse or a bicycle provided our means of transportation. A bicycle trip to Dauphin, more than 40 miles away, was a challenge mastered by Jack and his pals who also found that riding on the sloping roof of the local curling rink provided Sunday entertainment. In winter time, the outdoor rink provided Jack with a chance to engage in his favourite sport – hockey.

Young Hill (63 N/12), south of Sisipuk Lake was named after him in 1995.

Young, Captain **Norman A. T.** of Fort Garry. Queen's Own Cameron Highlanders. He died 19 August 1942 at the age of 41 and is commemorated at Dieppe Canadian War Cemetery in Seine-Maritime, France. He was the son of Thomas and Ellen T. Young and was survived by his wife Mary Grace Young (née Moody) of Winnipeg and their four children.

He was brought up by his father's sister and brother, Anna and Robert Young, who moved [from Montreal] to Winnipeg in 1907. He attended Winnipeg Schools and graduated from the University of Manitoba in 1923 with a gold medal in history, a lieutenancy in the officers' training corps and a Rhodes Scholarship which took him to Balliol College, Oxford where he spent two years. In 1925, he was appointed to the education branch of the British Colonial Service, on the original staff of Achimota College in British West Africa – an experiment in the education of African boys which was originated by a Canadian, Sir Gordon Guggisberg, then governor of the Gold Coast. In the same year he married Grace Moody of Winnipeg. He returned to Canada in January, 1929 and lectured in history at the University of Manitoba.

During the spring and summer, he worked out plans for the establishment of the school. For the next ten years all his experience, training and gifts were poured into the development of Ravenscourt:

- The school aims to send out boys with vigorous, flexible minds rather than with heads full of miscellaneous information: to teach not merely a curriculum, but an attitude towards life.
- Ravenscourt teams have developed a tradition of clean sportsmanship and of playing hard till the last whistle goes. Our chief concern is that every boy should leave the school possessed of the art of playing hard, of losing without resentment, and of winning without conceit.
- Bricks and mortar may be needed as incidentals, but the chief materials for the structure will be the qualities of mind and spirit which each of us possess.

In the autumn of 1937, he took up his commission with the Queen's Own Cameron Highlanders of Canada. The regiment was mobilized for active service on the day Britain declared war, September 3, 1939. He went overseas as an intelligence officer of the 6th Infantry Brigade, Second Canadian Division, with the rank of captain in November, 1940.

On August 19, 1942, he commanded "B" Company of the Camerons in the "reconnaissance in force" on Dieppe harbour. The Camerons went in at Pourville and Captain Young was killed in an assault on an enemy position inland along the river Scie. He is buried at Hautville-sur-mer where on August 19, 1945, the citizens of a shattered city consecrated a memorial in gratitude to the Canadians who died at Dieppe, the men who had changed the spirit of France from darkness to hope (Mackay 1945).

Young Rapids (64 I/8) in the South Knife River was named after him in 1995.

Young, Bombardier **Robert W.** of Winnipeg (H 12090). Royal Canadian Artillery. He died 30 September 1944 and is commemorated at Bergen-op-Zoom Canadian War Cemetery in Holland. ***Young Creek*** (64 B/3), which flows west into Rat Lake was named after him in 1995.

Young, Flying Officer **Roy A.** of Waskada (J 37531). No. 514 Squadron. He died 6 March 1945 at the age of 34 on a mission to Salzbergen, Germany and is commemorated at the Reichswald Forest War Cemetery in Germany. He was the son of Seymour and Iva Pearl Young and was survived by his wife Beatrice E. Young of Goodlands and their son. He writes (19 November 2001):

My understanding of my father was that he was an avid sportsman. He loved hunting and apparently played baseball. My wife and I went to the cemetery in Germany in 1995. I didn't personally know my father, but it was a very emotional experience. Although my father was older, the age of most of the soldiers in the cemetery was very young. What a terrible waste of the youth of our country.

Roy Young Bay (63 P/5) in Wintering Lake was named after him in 1995.

Young, Lance Sergeant **William H.** of Winnipeg (H 12174). Royal Canadian Artillery. He died 17 July 1941 and is commemorated at Brookwood Military Cemetery in Surrey, England. ***Young Esker*** (64 I/10), southwest of Lovat Lake was named after him in 1995.

Younger, Flight Sergeant **Robert L. R.** of Winnipeg (P 5509). No. 19 Operational Training Unit, RCAF. He died 12 September 1941 at the age of 22 and is commemorated at the Runnymede Memorial in Surrey, England. ***Younger Lake*** (64 O/15), east of Nueltin Lake was named after him in 1975.

Younie, Pilot Officer **William A.** of MacGregor (J 89867). No. 158 Squadron. He died 3 June 1944 at the age of 28 and is commemorated at Ecquetot Communal Cemetery in Eure, France. He was the son of William and Jessie Younie and was survived by his wife of five months Vera E. Younie of Caeron, Glamorgan, Wales. Pilot Officer Younie's Halifax was shot down over Ecquetot while returning from a bombing raid. Two of the crew survived, but were taken prisoner. A local newspaper reported:

> She and Mr. Younie, a Canadian, had been married for only five months, but had barely spent a month together, when his B3 Halifax bomber was shot down in June, 1944, killing five of the seven-strong crew while returning to their No. 158 Squadron base at Drifield, Yorkshire after raiding Trappes, near Paris. "It was a terrible blow to me and I have never really forgotten it. I can remember exactly where I was when they gave me the telegram saying that he was missing," Mrs. Williams said. "It all came back to me as I stood there looking at the grave, though I had been back once a long time ago. But I do not think I will go again now; it would be too much for me emotionally" (n.d.).

Mrs. Younie remarried in 1952 and their son took a particular interest in his mother's first husband. The following appeared in a local Welsh newspaper:

> An Ogwr man will fly to France in the summer to see the grave of his mother's first husband, shot down during a World War II bombing mission. Civic momentoes will be exchanged when 31 year-old Councillor Nigel Williams, of Bryn Terrace, Cefn Cribwr, goes to the town of Ecquetot in Normandy in August. With him he will take his parents Mr. And Mrs. Myrddin Williams of Tuberville Street, Moesteg and his six year-old son Ian. He will present to the mayor of the French town a model he has made of the Halifax Mark 3B bomber in which bomb-aimer William Alexander Younie, a Canadian, died on June 3, 1944. His mother, Mrs. Vera Williams, now aged 70, had then been married only a short time.
>
> "I feel somehow that Mr. Younie was a relative of mine, someone I knew, and at the same time I want my son to appreciate something of the events and the losses suffered by people during the war." A civilian worker at RAF St. Athan, Mr. Williams has been in touch with the Mayor of Ecquetot who has written back "a very cordial letter." "I think these contacts are important, and the French people seem to have a deep consciousness of World War II and what they and others who fought in it went through," said Mr. Williams. He added: "By a direct contact like this we might help foster good relations between the two countries and I will finally have seen Mr. Younie's last resting place" (n.d.).

Pilot Officer Younie's widow and other family members were invited to Ecquetot on the occasion of the 50th anniversary of the event. Arrangements were subsequently made for the formal "twinning" of Ecquetot and Cefn Cribwr, Wales and since that time residents and school groups from both villages have visited one another. ***Younie Lake*** (64 P/6), east of Nejanilini Lake was named after Pilot Officer Younie in 1974.

Yowney, Flying Officer **Myron** of Sherridon (J 22621). No. 61 Squadron. He died 20 February 1944 at the age of 26 and is commemorated at Rheinberg War Cemetery in Germany. He was survived by his mother Anne Yowney of Toronto. ***Yowney Lake*** (64 O/7), northeast of Sandhill Lake was named after him in 1995.

Yudell, Warrant Officer 2 **Isador Nicholas** of Morden (R 91968). No. 104 Squadron. He died 6 January, 1943 at the age of 22 and is commemorated at the Malta Memorial. He was survived by his uncle Milton Rabinovitch of Morden, Manitoba. ***Yudell Lake*** (64 I/12), south of Shethanei Lake was named after him in 1974.

Yuffe, Private **Hymie** of Winnipeg (H 8101). Royal Canadian Regiment. He died 9 December 1943 at the age of 20 and is commemorated at the Moro River Canadian War Cemetery in Italy. He was the son of Aaron and Fanny Yuffe of Winnipeg. ***Yuffe Lake*** (52 L/6), east of Lac du Bonnet was named after him in 1973.

Yuill, Sergeant **Kenneth F.** of Winnipeg (R 106035). No. 22 Operational Flying Unit. He died 6 July 1942 at the age of 30 and is commemorated at Hereford Cemetery in England. He was the son of James and Agnes Yuill of Winnipeg. ***Yuill Lake*** (64 H/15), east of Etawney Lake was named after him in 1995.

Yunsko, Pilot Officer **Walter** of Winnipeg (J 95475). No. 424 Squadron. He died 1 November 1944 at the age of 20 and is commemorated at Nederweert War Cemetery in Holland. ***Yunsko Lake*** (63 J/13), east of Wekusko Lake was named after him in 1972.

Yurkiw, Private **Joseph** of Dauphin (B 162172). Royal Regiment of Canada. He died 13 April 1945 at the age of 21 and is commemorated at the Holten Canadian War Cemetery in Holland. He was the son of Andrew and Tinnie Yurkiw of Dauphin, Manitoba. ***Yurkiw Lake*** (53 M/12), south of Split Lake was named after him in 1985.

Zadorozny, Pilot Officer **Stanley E.** of Sanford (J 95483). No. 432 Squadron. He died 18 December 1944 at the age of 21 and is commemorated at Choloy War Cemetery, Meurthe-et-Moselle, France. He was survived by his step-parents Mr. and Mrs. George Jessen of Sanford, Manitoba. His step-brother recalls (January 1994):

> We attended the ceremony when he received his wings as an air gunner at Macdonald, Manitoba. He expressed his sorrow that he had not applied himself a little more at the training, because if my memory is correct, he just missed getting a Pilot Officer's commission at graduation. I seem to remember 15 commissions were passed out and he was 17th in the class. Before going overseas, he took commando training at Lachine, Quebec. He rode the train from Lachine to Sanford to be with the family less than 24 hours. He completed a tour and wanted to go on one more trip. He was flying in a very fast aircraft commonly known as a "Pathfinder" that flew in ahead of the bombers to mark the targets. The last trip was to Duisberg, Germany and they were shot down. We were notified a few days before Christmas that he was missing in action. We felt he would be found alive as in school he always seemed to be very lucky. This was not to be, as his body was found and he was reported killed in action. Unknown to him, he had received his Pilot Officer's commission.
>
> In closing about Stanley, I would like to say a few words about Stanley's dog, Wimpy, which he had before joining the RCAF. There was nothing special about this dog except that it was a big, beautiful animal and was a one man dog. He would not play with anyone except Stanley. He was almost as tall as Stanley and the two always played very rough. When Stanley went overseas and didn't return, the dog would not eat and in a few weeks was dead.

Zadorozny Lake (64 J/13), southeast of Egenolf Lake was named after Pilot Officer Zadorozny in 1975.

Zadworny, Rifleman **Edward** of Pine Ridge (H 41233). Royal Winnipeg Rifles. He died 5 July 1944 at the age of 22 and is commemorated at Beny-sur-Mer Canadian War Cemetery in Calvados, France. He was the son of Joseph and Eva Zadworny of Winnipeg. ***Zadworny Lake*** (64 I/16), northeast of North Knife Lake was named after him in 1974.

Zaste, Corporal **Philias** of Ste. Rose du Lac (H 17822). Les Fusiliers Mont-Royal Regiment. He died 3 March 1945 at the age of 25 and is commemorated at the Groesbeek Canadian War Cemetery in Holland. He was one of the ten children of Alfred and Monique Zaste of Ste. Rose du Lac. His niece writes (9 December 1996):

> Philias was born and grew up near Ste. Amelie in the Ste. Rose area. Philias stayed and helped on the family farm for a time, but he also worked for other farmers in the Ste. Rose district. He received his education in the Waterhen and Ste. Rose areas. Among many of his pastimes besides hunting, fishing and trapping, Philias enjoyed sharing his gift of music. He enjoyed playing the accordion. Coming from a musical background, of which many of his family members enjoyed playing music – his father and two brothers, Philip and George, played the violin, his brother John plays the guitar and brother Auguste plays the harmonica. Philias and his twin brother Lance Corporal William Zaste were called to serve their country in the Second World War. Philias is fondly remembered by all family and friends who knew him.

Zaste Island (63 I/9) in Andronyk Lake was named after him in 1995.

Zaste, Lance Corporal **Willard** of Barrows (H 9355). Calgary Highlanders. He died 23 October 1944 at the age of 23 and is commemorated at Bergen-op-Zoom Canadian War Cemetery in Holland. He was the son of Elzear and Victoria Zaste of Barrows, Manitoba. ***Zaste Lake*** (62 N/15), southeast of Swan River was named after him in 1973.

Zastre, Lance Corporal **Antoine J. L.** of Guynemer (H 200097). Queen's Own Cameron Highlanders. He died 8 August 1944 at the age of 25 and is commemorated at Bretteville-sur-Laize Canadian War Cemetery in Calvados, France. He was the son of George and Josephine Zastre of Guynemer, Manitoba. ***Zastre Island*** (64 P/2) in Spruce Lake was named after him in 1995.

Zastre, Rifleman **Philip** of Ste. Rose du Lac (H 41456). Royal Winnipeg Rifles. He died 6 June 1944 at the age of 23 and is commemorated at Beny-sur-Mer Canadian War Cemetery in Calvados, France. He was the son of Alfred and Justine Zastre (née Lafreniere) of Headingley, Manitoba. ***Zastre Lake*** (64 I/4), west of North Knife Lake was named after him in 1974.

Zayets, Sergeant **Peter** of Winnipeg (R 124095). No. 1666 Heavy Conversion Unit, RCAF. He died 29 February 1944 at the age of 23 and is commemorated at Stonefall Cemetery in Yorkshire, England. He was the son of Alexander and Maria Zayets of Winnipeg and the brother of Sergeant Stephen Zayets (next entry). ***Zayets Lake*** (64 I/14), northeast of Shethanei Lake was named after him in 1974.

Zayets, Sergeant **Stephen** of Winnipeg (R 56703). No. 428 Squadron. He died 14 July 1943 at the age of 25 and is commemorated at Florennes Communal Cemetery in Namur, Belgium. He was the son of Alexander and Maria Zayets of Winnipeg and the brother of Sergeant Peter Zayets (previous entry). ***Zayets Creek*** (63 H/2), which flows northwest into the Mukutawa River was named after him in 1974.

Zbytnuik, Pilot Officer **Tony** of Portage la Prairie (J 86889). No. 428 Squadron. He died 18 April 1944 at the age of 23 and is commemorated at the Runnymede Memorial in Surrey, England. He was the son of Mike and Tilly Zbytnuik and was survived by his wife Stephie Zbytnuik and their son. She recalls (10 July 1987):

> Tony Zbytnuik was born on May 7, 1920 at Roblin, Manitoba in the Shell River Municipality. When he was a young child, the family moved to Norquay, Saskatchewan where he completed his elementary and high school education. He enlisted in the RCAF at Regina.
>
> He was stationed at St. Thomas, Ontario, Brandon, Manitoba and Mossbank, Saskatchewan and graduated as a bombardier at Portage la Prairie in April, 1943 – we also got married that month. His son was born in January, 1944.
>
> I remarried in 1952; my second husband Frank Luzny died in 1952, but my son carries his father's name (Zbytnuik) and when I showed him the article that was in the *Free Press*, he was very interested and asked me to find all the details. He thought it would be very nice to have a lake, river or whatever named after his father.

Twelve Halifaxes from this squadron were on a mine-laying operation at Kiel Bay. They were dropping 24 1500-pound mines from an altitude of 15,000 feet. Pilot Officer Zbytnuik and his entire crew were reported missing (Allison and Hayward 1991). ***Zbytnuik Lake*** near Ile-à-la Crosse, Saskatchewan was named after him in 1958.

Zdan, Pilot Officer **Benjamin H.** of Somerset (J 20606). No. 111 Operational Training Unit, RCAF. He died 19 March 1943 at the age of 21 and is commemorated at Nassau War Cemetery in the Bahamas. Born in Glenella, Manitoba in 1916, he was the eighth of the 10 children of Henry and Mary Zdan. Benjamin joined the Royal Canadian Air Force in 1937 as an Aircraft Technician. When war broke out he remustered to Air Crew, graduating as a pilot. He received his wings at the Brandon Flying Training School. Upon graduation, Benny married Betty Tedford of McCreary, Manitoba. He was transferred to Prince Edward Island for navigational training. Three months later he was transferred to a Royal Air Force Aircraft Transfer Squadron. Benny and another RCAF pilot crashed in a B25 Mitchell Bomber in Nassau, Bahamas in 1942. ***Zdan Island*** (63 I/7) in Lawford Lake was named after him in 1995.

Zdan, Flying Officer **Russell T.** of Somerset (J 24802). No. 428 Squadron. He died 23 September 1943 at the age of 21 and is commemorated at Rheinberg War Cemetery in Germany. He was the son of Peter and Millie Zdan of Somerset. His brother recalls (26 November 2001):

> Russell was born in Glenella, Manitoba May 18th, 1922 and attended school in Glenella and Riverton, Manitoba as well as St. Boniface College in Winnipeg. Russ was an avid sportsman and played intermediate baseball and hockey with teams in Riverton and Somerset. F/O Zdan, joined the RCAF in 1941 at Brandon Manning Depot and received instruction at Regina and Macdonald before going overseas in 1942.

Zdan Lake (63 N/2), east of Kississing Lake was named after him in 1972.

Zeavin, Flight Sergeant **Max** of Winnipeg (R 111112). No. 426 Squadron. He died 9 March 1943 at the age of 24 and is commemorated at the Runnymede Memorial in Surrey, England. He was the son of David S. and Esther Zeavin. ***Zeavin Lake*** (63 J/16), east of Setting Lake was named after him in 1972.

Zedan, Private **Michael** (H 41718). Winnipeg Grenadiers. He died a prisoner of war 5 December 1943 and is commemorated at the Yokohama War Cemetery in Japan. Corporal Edwin Smith returned from the Asian theatre in 1945 and described some of his experiences:

> Corporal Smith said he wished to express his gratitude for the aid given the prisoners by the Red Cross. He recalled the gift of 10 yen – about $10 – which each Grenadier had received from the Red Cross at Christmas, 1942. Urgently needed food was purchased with the money, he said.
>
> Salt was not supplied at the camp, remarked Corporal Smith, but the prisoners extracted small quantities from ocean water. Private Jack Goodey, 25, who was accompanied by his fiancée Mervyne Weeks of 824 Mulvey Avenue said he had served as the camp shoemaker. He had never practised the trade, but had picked up a few points by watching his father, an orthopaedic shoe expert who was recently employed at Deer Lodge military hospital. He did not have real leather to work with – just some ersatz material which wore out very fast (Anon. n.d.).

Zedan Lake (64 I/5), south of Shethanei Lake was named after Private Zedan in 1974.

Zeglinski, Private **Philip** of Vidir (H 102269). Princess Patricia's Canadian Light Infantry. He died 27 May 1944 and is commemorated at the Cassino Memorial in Italy. ***Zeglinski Lake*** (64 P/9), north of Caribou Lake was named after him in 1974.

Zoratti, Flying Officer **Victor** of Winnipeg (J 35036). No. 1666 Heavy Conversion Unit, RCAF. He died 11 July 1944 at the age of 30 and is commemorated at Stonefall Cemetery in Yorkshire, England. He was the son of Anthony and Caroline Zoratti and was survived by his wife Isabella R. Zoratti of Winnipeg. ***Zoratti Lake*** (63 N/1), southeast of Sherridon was named after him in 1970.

Zubek, Gunner **William R.** of Stonewall (H 67167). Royal Canadian Artillery. He died 18 December 1943 at the age of 22 and is commemorated at the Moro River Canadian War Cemetery in Italy. His sister recalls (11 January 1996):

> He was born in Komarno February 6th, 1921 and lived at home on the farm with family. He was always called Bill, not William or Ray. He did not have much time to develop many hobbies as he had to work the farm, being the only boy at home at that time. He enjoyed sleigh riding, baseball and the local dances. He enlisted in the RCA in November, 1941 and took his training at Fort Garry. He went overseas [in] April of 1942. He was with the Canadians in the Sicilian Campaign and had gone through many engagements in Italy. He was with some local boys from Stonewall when he was wounded and died. He wrote his last letter to family [on] December 8, 1943, but it was never mailed. It was found in his pocket and forwarded on to us.

Zubek Lake (52 E/14), southeast of Brereton Lake was named after him in 1974.

Zubriski, Sapper **Frank** of Shorncliffe (H 1950). Royal Canadian Engineers. He died 10 July 1943 at the age of 21 and is commemorated at Shorncliffe Cemetery in Manitoba. He was the son of William and Stella Zubriski of Riverton, Manitoba. ***Zubriski Lake*** (64 O/5), north of Egenolf Lake was named after him in 1975.

Zytaruk, Private **Metro** of Winnipeg (H 8817). Cape Breton Highlanders. He died 29 September 1944 at the age of 21 and is commemorated at Cesena War Cemetery in Italy. He was the son of George and Kate Zytaruk of Fort Garry. ***Zytaruk Lake*** (52 L/3), northeast of Brereton Lake was named after him in 1973.

View looking east along 'Nan White' Beach, showing personnel of the 9th Canadian Infantry Brigade landing on D-Day.
Courtesy of the National Archives of Canada (PA-137013).

References Cited

Allison, L.
1978 *Canadians in the Royal Air Force*. Solitaire Press, Duncan, British Columbia.

Allison, L. and H. Hayward
1991 *They Shall Grow Not Old: A Book of Remembrance*. Commonwealth Air Training Plan Museum Inc. Leech Printing Ltd., Brandon.

Altstedter, N.
1997 The Father He Never Knew. *Winnipeg Free Press*. March 6 Issue.

Amaron, D.
1944 Men Kept Word to Leader – But he didn't know it. *Canadian Press*. April 14.

Atkins, R.
1999 Fly-past Pays Tribute to Wartime Bomber Crash Dead. *The Sentinel*. August 30 Issue.

Barton, M.
1987 A Few Lines from the New Man in the Family. *Winnipeg Free Press*. November 10 Issue.

Bend, B.
1982 Remembering Those who Died. *The Stonewall Argus*. November 10 Issue.

Bernier, Father A.
1999 Lt. Jules-Armand Comeault. Free translation from the original. *The Journal*. November 9 Issue.

Bishop, A.
1995 *Our Bravest and Our Best: The Story of Canada's Victoria Cross Winners*. McGraw-Hill Ryerson Ltd., Toronto.

Bohuslawsky, M.
1994 Helplessness on the Homefront. *Ottawa Citizen*. May 31 Issue.

Brioux, M.
1998 Lasting Honour or Lasting Horror: The Hong Kong Veterans Compensation. Conference of Defence Associations Institute First Annual Graduate Student Symposium 13-14 November.

Buzzell, N.
1997 *The Register of the Victoria Cross*. This England, Cheltenham.

Cheadle, B.
1996 Watch Brings Airman to Life. *Winnipeg Free Press*. December 11 Issue.

Clemens, M.
2000 Locals Witness War Monument Unveiling in France. *The Clipper Weekly*. November 6 Issue.

Cook, J. A. M.
1943 Ex-Reginan over Pilsen. *Regina Leader-Post*. May 17 Issue.

Creighton, Rear-Admiral Sir Kenelm
1956 *Convoy Commodore*. Kimber, London.

Cunnings, T. A. J.
1986 *The Saga of Doctor Thor: Paul H. T. Thorlakson C.C. M.D.: A Biography*. University of Manitoba, Winnipeg.

Dexter, G.
1944 Canadians in the Bomber Command: The Riders of the Sky. *Winnipeg Free Press*. June 3 Issue.

Elton, M.
1994 Thomas Leonard Brandson 1915 – 1944. *The Icelandic Canadian*. Fall Issue 24.

English, W.
1990 Battle of Britain. *Winnipeg Free Press* (n.d.).

Farmer, M. E.
1978 Stonewall – Turning a Century: 1878 – 1978. Interlake Publishing, Stonewall.

Fell, D.
1989 Personal letter to G. A. Gallagher of Port Severn, Ontario.

Ford, G. H. (ed.)
1948 *The Making of a Secret Agent: The Pickersgill Letters*. Ryerson Press, Toronto. Reprinted and revised in 1978.

Galloway, S.
1979 Brave Yesterdays, Forgotten Canadians. *Legion Magazine*. March Issue.

Garland, A.
1975 Notes on the Geographical Names of Manitoba. Unpublished Manuscript on file with the Geographical Names Board of Canada, Manitoba Conservation, Winnipeg.

Goranson, F.
1997 Honouring a Life: Island Named after Local Soldier. *The Argus*. November 10 Issue.

Great West Life Bulletin
1941 Pilot Officer Huntley D. Brander. 32(10):258.

Halliday, H. A.
1970 Manitobans in Action 30 Years Ago. *The Winnipeg Free Press*. April 18 Issue.

Hay, B.
1979 Last Flight to the Stars. *Fragment*. War Amputees of Canada. Winter Issue.

Hayes, G.
1986 *The Lincs: A History of the Lincoln and Welland Regiment at War*. Maple Leaf Route, Alma, Ontario.

Headnotes and Footnotes
1988 *Winnipeg Foundation Announces Generous, Unexpected Bequest to the Faculty of Law for Scholarships and Bursaries*. The Manitoba Bar Newsletter 19 (11):1.

Hill, B. K.
1944 *The Price for Freedom*. The Garden City Press, Toronto.

Hornbeck, H. L.
1979 In Memory of Allister McLeod and Others from Balmoral. *The Stonewall Argus and Teulon Times*. August 29 Issue.

Hretchka, P.
1995 Remembrance Day Poppy has Meaning. *The Western Producer*. November 9 Issue.

Hunter, T. M.
1982 *Canada at Dieppe*. Balmuir, Ottawa.

Iverach, J. A.
1992 *Chronicles of a Nervous Navigator*. Published by the author. Winnipeg.

Jones, F.
1993 Mystery Stirs up Wartime Memories. *The Toronto Star*. October 9 Issue.

Korea Veterans Association of Canada
1999 *Canoe River, BC Tragedy, 21 November 1950, 2nd Royal Canadian Horse Artillery*. Memorial Service, 49th Anniversary, Korean War, Winnipeg.

Kubara, S.
1998 Key to Woman's Genealogy may be in Manitoba. *Winnipeg Sun*. August 25 Issue.

Leah, V.
1990 Buzz Horne's Name Adorns Lake. *Free Press Weekly*. August 12 Issue.

Leah, V.
1992 Dieppe. *Winnipeg Free Press*. August.

Mackay, A.
1945 *These We Honour*. Ravenscourt School, Winnipeg. Reprinted in 1979.

Mann, A.
2000 Play it Again, Al: Memoirs of Al Mann, Jazz Clarinettist. Published by the author, Kelowna.

Marchildon, P.
1993 *Ace: Canadian Pitching Sensation and Wartime Hero* (with Brian Kendall). Viking, Toronto.

Mardon, H. L.
2001 The Passing Parade. *Prime Times News*. April 1 Issue.

Martin, N.
2001 Vets Bask in Gratitude of Visiting Dutch Teens. *The Winnipeg Free Press*. July 7 Issue.

Mills, W.
1967 Something to Remember. *Ottawa Citizen*. November 10 Issue.

Morin, C. J.
1997 Morin Island. Association des MORIN d'Amérique.

Moyle, H.
1989 The Hampden File. Air Britain (Historians) Limited, Kent, England.

Neufeld, P. L.
1987 Commemorating the Supreme Sacrifice. *Seaports and the Shipping World*. January Issue.

Neufeld, P. L.
1989 The Legacy of Three Navy Sailors from a Prairie Town. *Seaports and the Shipping World*. November Issue.

Newman, R.
1989 Northern Island Honors Pilot. *The Interlake Spectator*. October 24 Issue.

Oder, A. R.
1975 *Hello Soldier*. North Star Press, Winnipeg.

Peden, M.
1988 *A Thousand Shall Fall: The True Story of a Canadian Bomber Pilot in World War Two*. Stoddart Publishing Company Limited, Toronto.

Pittman, C.
n.d. Notes and Interviews Concerning World War II and Korean Casualties of the Minnedosa and Neepawa Area. Unpublished Manuscript on File with the Manitoba Geographical Names Program, Winnipeg.

Purdy, C.
1996 Burmese Jungle Offers Clue to Site of Second World War Plane Crash. *The Winnipeg Sun*. November 21 Issue.

Reid, Ken
2001 *Memoirs of Stalag IV B*. Published by the author.

Rempel, Gerhard
n.d. Battle of Caen: The Stalingrad of the Hitler Youth.

Richey, P. H. M.
1990 Fighter Pilot: A Personal Record of the Campaign in France, 1939-1940. Leo Cooper, London.

Robinson, D.
1996 *Trident*. Maritime Command, Halifax.

Royal Canadian Air Force
1949 *The RCAF Overseas*. Oxford University Press, Toronto.

Schull, J.
1987 *Far Distant Ships: An Official Account of Canadian Naval Operations in World War II*. Stoddart, Don Mills, Ontario.

Shuttleworth, D. H.
1982 *Ten Decades to a Century*. Dyna Printing, Rexdale, Ontario.

Sinclair, G. Jr.
2001 Looking for Ghosts in Clouds. *Winnipeg Free Press*. March 26 Issue.

Stacey, C. P.
1955 *Six Years of War: The Army in Canada, Britain and the Pacific*. Queen's Printer, Ottawa.

Telpner, G.
1979a Tod Family Made its Mark on Second War History. *Winnipeg Tribune*. February 26 Issue.

1979b Lake was Named for Flyer Killed Day after War Ended. *Winnipeg Tribune*. March 21 Issue.

Tennant, J.
1999 Names Honour War Dead. *Calgary Sun*. January 22 Issue.

Vance, J. F.
2000 A Gallant Company: The Men Of The Great Escape. Pacifica Military History, Pacifica, California.

Webb, E.
1995 Island Dedicated to Stonewall Veteran. *The Argus*. November 6 Issue.

Williston, E.
1993 *Rainbows at Noon*. Quintessential Press, Gibsons, British Columbia.

Williston, F.
1996 *Through Footless Halls of Air: The Stories of a Few of the Many who Failed to Return*. General Store Publishing House, Burnstown.

Williston, F.
2000 Allen Laird Edy. *Elmwood Herald*. November Issue.

Wood, D.
1991 Forgotten Battalions. *The Globe and Mail*. December 7 Issue.